PREVIEW

DISCOVER
the multidimensional and integrative text that has become a favorite of students and instructors alike

José B. Ashford, Craig LeCroy, and Kathy Lortie's groundbreaking text offers students a balanced and engaging introduction to the rapidly changing content of human behavior in the social environment. This time-tested text succeeds by helping students connect foundation knowledge with practice concerns. Enhanced by the use of study tables and concept maps at the end of each discussion of dimensions of development, **Human Behavior in the Social Environment: A Multidimensional Perspective** explores biopsychosocial development across the lifespan using a multidimensional integrative approach that links practice, theory, treatment, and services to the study of developmental concerns.

The Third Edition of this respected text maintains the authors' proven framework and approach while adding timely references and new discussions of key developments in human behavior and the biopsychosocial sciences. Now available around the globe in several different languages, **Human Behavior in the Social Environment** continues to win praise for being a text that is:

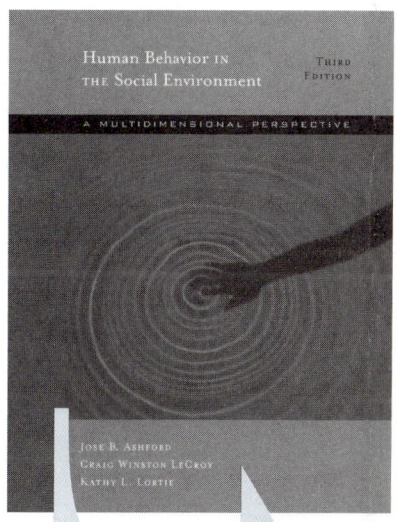

Comprehensive
A key strength of this text is the breadth of topics covered. In addition, the authors link theory, research, and practice in a way that allows students to understand their inter-relatedness. I anticipate using the text in the future because it provides a nice overview of human behavior at different life stages within the context of a multidimensional assessment.
Jan Ivery, Georgia State University

Applied
The enduring strength of this text . . . is its ability to link theory and research with social work practice.
Mary Rawlings, Azusa Pacific University

Accurate
I offered my students a bounty of 10 points on their **Human Behavior in the Social Environment** exam for finding errors, problems, lack of clarity, need for additional information, etc. in their text. No one has collected on the reward. Students and faculty like the book.
Steve Marson, University of North Carolina, Pembroke

The text is also **ENRICHED** with resources that will help you make the most of your time and your course. Your special Preview begins on the next page.

COMPREHENSIVE

The Third Edition features well over 200 new references dating from 2000 or later. You'll find a wealth of new content, including:

- **Timely discussions** in Chapter 4, "The Social Dimension for Assessing Social Functioning," on automatic forms of racism and discrimination, new developments in multiculturalism, and queer theory.

- **New coverage** in the human development chapters that includes infant health and systems for classifying infant mental health and development disorders, linguistics, grief and loss in children, transgender issues, suicide and self harming (cutting), schools and disabilities in middle childhood, bullying, and much more.

- **Updated discussions** of topics related to evolutionary approaches to human behavior in Chapters 2 ("The Biophysical Dimension for Assessing Social Functioning") and 7 ("Early Childhood"), such as new evolutionary theories of color, the nurture assumption, and the limitations of evolutionary psychology.

- A **new section** in Chapter 3, "The Psychological Dimension for Assessing Social Functioning," that reviews theories of self and new theories of memory and information processing.

PREVIEW

▸ Throughout the text, the authors address **policy issues** that are a function of human behavior assumptions and their consequences. Student activity sheets contained in the revised **Instructor's Manual** also feature these policy issues prominently (see page 8 of this Preview for details).

▸ Coverage of **life course theory**, which cites the latest research, highlights the effects of socio-historical contexts on life course variability and content on delinquency and other issues affecting communities of color.

The authors provide **broad and balanced coverage of micro, mezzo, and macro** (systems) content. Furthermore, the text lays a solid foundation in the biological, psychological, and social sciences, thus helping students apply concepts to direct practice.

PREVIEW

APPLIED

Personal narratives offer first-hand accounts of real-life experiences related to diversity issues, including racism, poverty, sexual orientation, and ageism. Through these different voices, students gain real-world flavors of the material discussed.

 Applying the Framework boxes conclude each lifespan chapter and immerse students in vivid, real-life case studies related to the developmental stage discussed, thus bringing theory to life. In addition to a developmental history, these realistic cases include biophysical, psychological, and social considerations, further integrating the holistic, multidimensional nature of the text.

PREVIEW

THE PSYCHOLOGICAL DIMENSION

conflict motivated by emotions that originate in social processes.

Emotions are experienced individually, but some emotions have deep roots in collective processes that are under increased scrutiny by sociologists. The American Sociological Association currently has a special section of its organizational structure that focuses on research topics involving emotions viewed from a sociological perspective. This research body recognizes that emotions cannot be understood strictly by studying biological and psychological processes.

ents' emotional states. From the theories discussed, we can distinguish between the experience of emotions and the expression of emotions. We experience our emotions within the central nervous system and its attendant cognitive structures, but we express these emotions through the somatic and autonomic response systems.

Clinical social workers also distinguish between mood and affect. **Mood** can be defined as a prevailing and enduring emotional state. **Affect** refers to a person's instant emotional state. In assessing affect, social workers focus on determining the presence or absence of specific types of emotional states. For instance, **lability** refers to the rapid shift from one emotion to another within a very brief period of time. If these shifts are extreme, some clinicians label them as representing a form of emotional "incontinence" (Ludwig, 1986). Social workers must learn the characteristics of normal and abnormal presentations of emotion. They must also have an understanding of how people learn to use their emotions ar played by notions of self and identity ior and emotions is a central area of For this reason, we will devote some to examining developments in psycho concerns.

Implications for Practice

Without emotions, individuals cannot develop meaningful responses to their environment. Social workers need to develop practical ways to describe changes in their cli-

Social Cognition and Regulation

How do we acquire social knowle ference between social and no Does social-knowledge acquisiti acquisition of other forms of know tions have helped psychologists c social cognition. Theorists in the topics such as whether we employ in acquiring knowledge about th ploy in acquiring knowledge ab debates have led to some general **social cognition** is widely conside about people. It includes "thinki about self and other individuals, tions between people, about soci and institutions" (Flavell, 1985, p attention is being devoted to und of the self-system in all areas of The *self-system* refers here to all the and other elements that are associa sense of self.

◀ *Implications for Practice* sections highlight critical issues for social workers and link foundation knowledge to assessment, prevention, intervention, and policy issues.

Understanding a person's mood and affect is an important clinical skill. What emotion is the person in this photograph displaying?

FOCUS ON NARRATIVE

TELL US WHAT LESBIAN FAMILIES ARE LIKE

Though I have been married, and my daughter has two fathers and other adults who adore her, for the most part, I've been parenting her on my own. I divorced her biological father when she was a year old, and it was after we were divorced that her stepfather really engaged as a parent. Now Heather is 16 and off to college next year. I am savoring our time together—inwardly leaning forward, listening as she composes her past, present, and future. Ribbons of conversation connect our lives apart and together. We talk about her days, her friends, politics—what she makes of our fragile and sacred world and how she sees herself in it. When we're home, we work separately together at our keyboards in our home office, take walks, watch foreign films, do chores, love our dogs and Pablo—the cat she named after Neruda, the Chilean poet. She works with seventh graders, creating cohesion and delight in a group of forty, and sometimes she's a little girl and I rub her back as she falls asleep, as I have done all her life. These exchanges, as common as the breeze today, will soon be echoes in my thoughts as I wonder how she is doing in her fledgling young-adult life. In a few months we will be fitting our conversation into telephones, e-mails, and occasional visits.

Heather was 9, I was 42 when I realized I was gay. I had been married to her stepfather for six years when I went on a backpacking trip and fell in love for the first time—with a woman. It suddenly became clear why my heart had never been in my relationships with men. My husband thought it was a phase. It wasn't. After the holidays, we sat down with Heather and told her, assuring her that we would both always be there for her. She was amazing—in an hour and a half, she ...trum of human emotions, ...rs to pride. The next day, ...b school at the university ...us to everyone. At the ...ol program director called ...id, "Heather, I don't think ...the other children about ...lied, "Miss Thomas, these ...t their parents haven't ex-...osexuality by now, they ...hy shouldn't I?" ...and Heather and I moved ...ad another teaching po-...ring, Heather's mom and ...prooted from her friends ...y lab school in Rhode Is-

land, and landed in Arizona—in the desert in a school system rated forty-eighth in the nation. She hated it. She became the tortured, smart, fat kid who used big words that nobody understood. The precociousness that had earned her plaudits in her lab school became evidence of otherness that ensured her ostracism. For two years, she was angry, depressed, and friendless, and petrified of further abuses should her peers learn that her mother was a lesbian. On her behalf, I joined her in the closet around her friends and teachers.

Meanwhile, I was going through late-blooming adolescence, discovering my sexuality and experiencing all the accompanying highs and lows. Having been really close, Heather and I were completely out of sync. Then, in an odd twist of nature, we simultaneously entered hormonal hell—menopause and early adolescence. Though I'd been a clinical social worker for two decades, we suffered a long while before I realized that this was more than a rocky family transition. In both of us, hormonal upheaval had induced clinical depression. It was a rough ride for a couple of years.

Now Heather's 16 and has survived Arizona's anemic attempts at gifted education. She's growing more independent by the day—driving, making her own life choices, working, managing her own money, applying to colleges, researching scholarships. I am exhaling in a way that only single heads of household understand. Parenting alone, particularly in the absence of family supports, is impossible. Yet millions of us are doing it. Growing up with divorced parents with a lesbian mom has its challenges, yet millions of kids are emerging from gay households healthy and whole, ready to do their parts in our world.

Lesbian families, like interfaith, interracial, single-parent, and stepfamilies before us, are often an invisible family form, beyond the mainstream imagination. When we do become visible, it is usually through dark lenses that portray us as godless deviants warping the development of our innocent children. Whereas other family forms are slowly emerging from stale air of social stigma, we're still breathing it. However, as poet Percy Shelley says in "Ode to a Skylark,"

If winter comes, can spring be far behind?

—BY MARGARET WALLER

The text's applied strengths are extended through:

- Special research assignments using **InfoTrac® College Edition** that allow for the inclusion of many topics that you may want to have your students investigate beyond what is covered in the text. A four-month subscription to **InfoTrac College Edition** is included with every new copy of the text.

- New cases, found on the **Book Companion Website**, that offer students increased opportunities for looking at the complexities of the multi-causal and reciprocal aspects of the biopsychosocial systems influencing human behavior.

- Strong connections between content covered in the text with newly developed activities and exercises found in the revised **Instructor's Manual**.

See pages 7 and 8 of this Preview for details on these resources.

▲ *Focus On* sections reflect current CSWE guidelines by examining different voices and perspectives, focusing in this edition on multiculturalism and narrative. A new *Focus On* section examines the experiences encountered by lesbian mothers in raising children.

PREVIEW

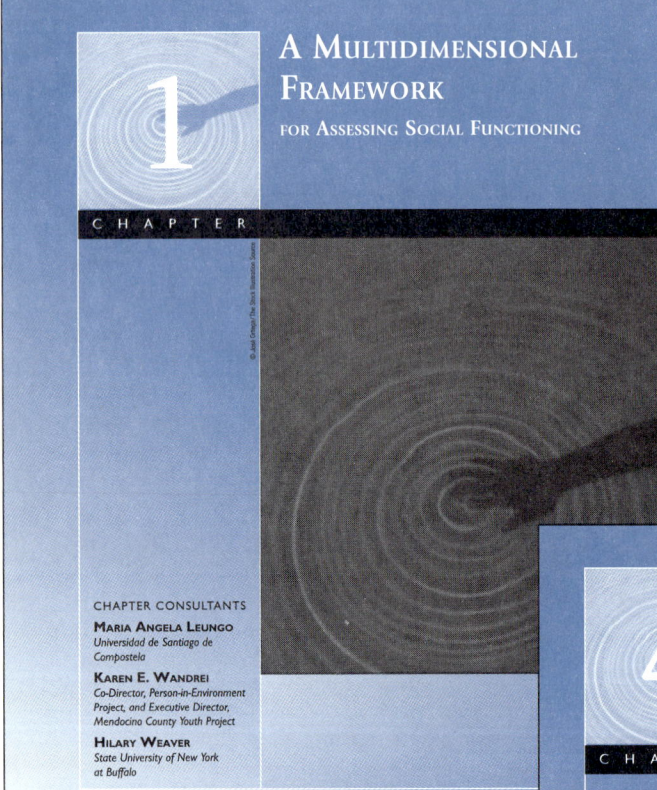

ACCURATE

◀ Chapter 1, "A Multidimensional Framework for Assessing Social Functioning," is modified to include additional content on role theory and other classical social theory by C. Wright Mills and others—providing a stronger theoretical foundation for understanding the role of social functioning assessment in human behavior.

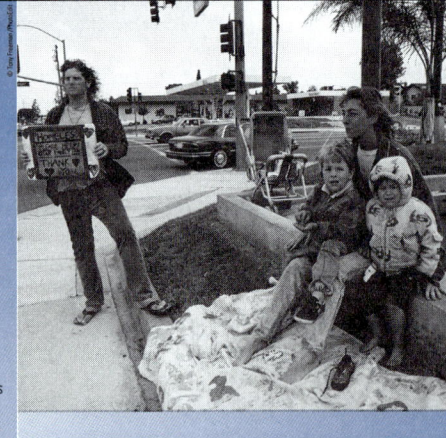

To ensure the accuracy and timeliness of the ▶ text, expert consultants in social work and other related areas carefully reviewed each chapter. This thorough review procedure ensures that relevant research by social workers receives proper coverage and that specific substantive areas have been covered—including the most up-to-date developments in their particular areas of research.

CHAPTER CONSULTANTS

Ronald Pitner
Washington University at St. Louis

Jane Holschuh
Humboldt State University

Rita Takahashi
San Francisco State University

Margaret Waller
Arizona State University

RESOURCES

ENRICHED

The Brooks/Cole Curriculum Connector
http://socialwork.wadsworth.com/connector

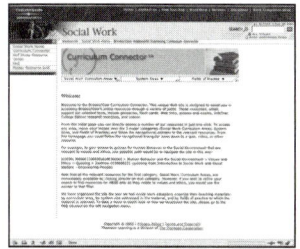

Let our innovative and convenient **Curriculum Connector** help you find and make the most of a rich selection of free, high-quality online resources. This exclusive new website is designed to help you take full advantage of Brooks/Cole's diverse online resources, which include:

Chapter Outlines • Crossword Puzzles • Flash Cards • Glossaries • **InfoTrac® College Edition** Research Exercises • Microsoft® PowerPoint® Presentations • Quizzes and Exams (self-scoring) • Videos • Web Links

From the **Curriculum Connector** home page you have quick and easy access to these resources with just a click. You can search by three major categories: *Social Work Curriculum Areas, System Sizes* (micro/mezzo or macro), and *Fields of Practice*. You then simply follow the navigational pointers to the relevant resources. From the home page, you can follow the navigational icons to a quiz, video, or other teaching or learning tool.

Using Brooks/Cole's Online Resources Effectively: A Primer for Instructors
0-495-00110-4

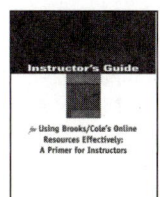

This brief booklet gives you the information you need to incorporate powerful technology into your teaching. The information and resources are useful for electronic assignments in a traditionally taught course, implementing an electronic course, or for a course conducted fully online. Features include an outline of competency components for a successful online instructor, examples of instructional assignments utilizing various **Curriculum Connector** resources, and guiding principles for teaching online.

Becoming a Successful Online Learner: A Primer for Students
0-495-00112-0;
packaged FREE with the text, use ISBN 0-495-05853-X

This guide includes exercises and tips based on the **Curriculum Connector** and its resources, making it an ideal companion as students learn to practice and apply what they study in the course.

The Social Work Resource Center
http://socialwork.wadsworth.com

Book Companion Website
http://socialwork.wadsworth.com/ashford3/

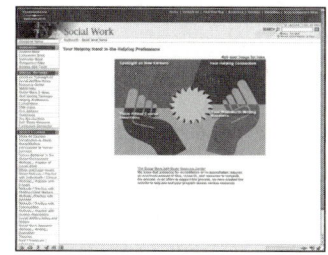

When you adopt **Human Behavior in the Social Environment: A Multidimensional Perspective, Third Edition**, you and your students have access to a rich array of teaching and learning resources that you won't find anywhere else. These outstanding websites feature everything from online quizzing to the latest social work news to journal and association links. It's the ideal way to make teaching and learning an interactive and exciting experience.

The text-specific **Book Companion Website** features a **continuous case study that focuses on the Perez family**, complete with numerous related exercises that allow students to investigate concepts within each lifespan stage. These cases offer students increased opportunities for looking at the complexities of the multi-causal and reciprocal aspects of the biopsychosocial systems influencing human behavior. Online quizzes help students prepare for tests. Adopting instructors may access password-protected Microsoft® PowerPoint® slides.

The **Social Work Resource Center** features: Brooks/Cole Self-Study Resource Center • Career Connection • Curriculum Connector • Social Welfare Policy Resource Center • Social Work E-News • Social Work Web Links • and much more!

RESOURCES

ENRICHED

Course preparation, management, and assessment

Instructor's Manual with Test Bank
0-534-64278-0

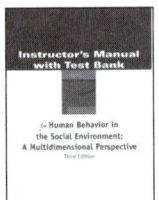

Featuring resources such as suggested class discussions and projects, this extensively revised **Instructor's Manual** can streamline and maximize the effectiveness of your course preparation. Numerous activity sheets, including new ones relating the Raul Sanchez case from Chapters 2 through 4 of the book, help to further illustrate concepts. The **Test Bank** offers many essay and multiple-choice questions.

WebTutor™ ToolBox on WebCT® and Blackboard®
Packaged with the text: WebCT: 0-495-05600-6
Blackboard: 0-495-05599-9

Preloaded with content and available free via access code when packaged with this text, **WebTutor™ ToolBox** pairs all the content of this text's rich **Book Companion Website** with all the sophisticated course management functionality of a WebCT or Blackboard product. You can assign materials (including online quizzes) and have the results flow automatically to your grade book. **ToolBox** is ready to use as soon as you log on—or, you can customize its preloaded content by uploading images and other resources, adding web links, or creating your own practice materials.

ExamView® Computerized Testing
Cross-platform CD-ROM: 0-534-64280-2

Create, deliver, and customize tests and study guides (both print and online) in minutes with this easy-to-use assessment and tutorial system. The **ExamView® Quick Test Wizard** guides you step by step through the process of creating and printing a test—you can even see the test you are creating on the screen exactly as it will look when printed. The **Online Test Wizard** allows you first to format a test for Internet delivery over local area network (LAN) or stand-alone computer, then to control who takes the test, when it may be completed, and what information (results, responses, answers, etc.) is provided to students.

Presentation tools

Brooks/Cole Annual "Clips for Coursework" Video for the Helping Professions
2005 Version: 0-534-53347-7

This exclusive video is available to you when you adopt any Wadsworth Helping Professions text! The video contains ten segments that explore social welfare strategies through interview and documentary footage that portrays experienced helping professionals in action. The central purpose is to expose students to counseling and social work issues and scenarios, first-person testimony of helping professionals, and experts in the field.

2006 Version: 0-534-53382-5

Research and investigation

InfoTrac® College Edition with InfoMarks®

When you adopt this text, you and your students will gain anytime, anywhere access to reliable resources with **InfoTrac College Edition**, the online library! This fully searchable database offers more than 20 years' worth of full-text articles (not abstracts) from almost 5,000 diverse sources—including top academic journals, newsletters, and up-to-the-minute periodicals such as *American Sociologist, Public Welfare, Social Theory and Practice, Social Work, Newsweek, Time, Science,* and *USA Today.*

Special research assignments using **InfoTrac College Edition** are found throughout the text, encouraging students to investigate further.

As part of **InfoTrac College Edition, InfoMarks®** allows you to use a simple "copy and paste" technique to create instant and continually updated online readers, content services, bibliographies, electronic "reserve" readings, and current topic sites. To take a quick tour of **InfoTrac College Edition**, visit http://www.infotrac-college.com/ and select the "User Demo." *(Journals subject to change. Certain restrictions may apply. For additional information, please consult your local Thomson representative.)*

HUMAN BEHAVIOR
IN THE SOCIAL ENVIRONMENT
A MULTIDIMENSIONAL PERSPECTIVE

THIRD EDITION

JOSÉ B. ASHFORD
Arizona State University

CRAIG WINSTON LECROY
Arizona State University

KATHY L. LORTIE
Tucson Unified School District

Australia • Brazil • Canada • Mexico • Singapore • Spain
United Kingdom • United States

Human Behavior in the Social Environment: A Multidimensional Perspective, Third Edition
José B. Ashford, Craig Winston LeCroy, Kathy L. Lortie

Executive Editor: *Lisa I. Gebo*
Assistant Editor: *Alma Dea Michelena*
Editorial Assistant: *Sheila Walsh*
Technology Project Manager: *Barry Connolly*
Marketing Manager: *Caroline Concilla*
Marketing Assistant: *Rebecca Weisman*
Marketing Communications Manager: *Tami Strang*
Project Manager, Editorial Production: *Mary Noel*
Creative Director: *Rob Hugel*
Art Director: *Vernon Boes*
Print Buyer: *Rebecca Cross*

Permissions Editor: *Joohee Lee*
Production Service: *Gretchen Otto, G&S Book Services*
Text Designer: *Lisa Henry*
Photo Researcher: *Annette Coolidge*
Copy Editor: *Angela Buckley*
Cover Designer: *Bill Stanton*
Cover Image: *Yukimasa Hirota/Photonica*
Cover Printer: *Phoenix Color Corp*
Compositor: *G&S Book Services*
Printer: *Courier Corporation/Westford*

© 2006 Thomson Brooks/Cole, a part of The Thomson Corporation. Thomson, the Star logo, and Brooks/Cole are trademarks used herein under license.

ALL RIGHTS RESERVED. No part of this work covered by the copyright hereon may be reproduced or used in any form or by any means—graphic, electronic, or mechanical, including photocopying, recording, taping, web distribution, information storage and retrieval systems, or in any other manner—without the written permission of the publisher.

Printed in the United States of America
1 2 3 4 5 6 7 09 08 07 06 05

ExamView® and ExamView Pro® are registered trademarks of FSCreations, Inc. Windows is a registered trademark of the Microsoft Corporation used herein under license. Macintosh and Power Macintosh are registered trademarks of Apple Computer, Inc. Used herein under license.

© 2006 Thomson Learning, Inc. All Rights Reserved. Thomson Learning WebTutor™ is a trademark of Thomson Learning, Inc.

Library of Congress Control Number: 053464772

Student Edition: ISBN 0-534-64276-4

Thomson Higher Education
10 Davis Drive
Belmont, CA 94002-3098
USA

For more information about our products, contact us at:
Thomson Learning Academic Resource Center
1-800-423-0563

For permission to use material from this text or product, submit a request online at
http://www.thomsonrights.com.
Any additional questions about permissions can be submitted by e-mail to **thomsonrights@thomson.com**.

BRIEF CONTENTS

1 **A Multidimensional Framework** for Assessing Social Functioning   1

2 **The Biophysical Dimension** for Assessing Social Functioning   41

3 **The Psychological Dimension** for Assessing Social Functioning   75

4 **The Social Dimension** for Assessing Social Functioning   114

5 **Pregnancy, Birth, and the Newborn**   167

6 **Infancy**   212

7 **Early Childhood**   270

8 **Middle Childhood**   328

9 **Adolescence**   386

10 **Young Adulthood**   452

11 **Middle Adulthood**   507

12 **Late Adulthood**   568

CONTENTS

PREFACE XV

1 A MULTIDIMENSIONAL FRAMEWORK FOR ASSESSING SOCIAL FUNCTIONING 1

The Limits of One-Dimensional Approaches 2

Why Do Social Workers Study Human Behavior and the Social Environment? 6
- Why Cultural Factors Matter 7
- What Is the Social Environment? 10
- Cultural Competence, Globalization, and Our Diverse Society 11
- Dimensions of Human Behavior and the Social Environment 13

Multidimensional Framework 14
- The Biopsychosocial Interaction 14
- Case and Situation Conceptualizations 16
- Reflections on the Spiritual Dimension by Margaret Waller 17

Applying the Multidimensional Framework 17
- Biophysical Hypotheses 18
- Psychological Hypotheses 19
- Social Hypotheses 20
- Selecting Interventions Based on Hypotheses 21

Models for Assessing Social Functioning 23
- The Person-in-Environment System (PIE) 25
- Models of Stress and Coping 27

Life-Span versus Life-Course Perspectives on Human Development 29
- Life-Span Perspective 30
- Life-Course Perspective 33
- Focus on Narrative: High School and College Transitional Experiences 34
- Prevention and Human Development 36

2 THE BIOPHYSICAL DIMENSION FOR ASSESSING SOCIAL FUNCTIONING 41

Biological Theories 44
- Evolutionary Theory and Developments in Evolutionary Psychology 44
- What Is Sociobiology? 46

Biophysical Growth and Development 47
- Genetics and Human Behavior 48
- Single-Gene Disorders 50
- Multifactorial Disorders 52
- Chromosome Disorders 53

■ *Implications for Practice* 54
- Genetic and Environmental Effects on Human Behavior 55

Biochemical Systems, the Brain, and Behavior 57
- Anatomy of the Brain 57
- Autonomic Nervous System 58

Biochemical Processes in the Nervous System 58
- Growth and Development of Neurons 62

■ *Implications for Practice* 64
- Focus on Narrative: Surviving the Residual Effects of Traumatic Brain Injury 65

*Biophysical Strengths: Physical
    Resilience and Allostasis* 66
  Cancer 67
  Cardiovascular System Problems 68
  Respiratory System Problems 69
  Endocrine System Problems 70
■ Implications for Practice 71

3 THE PSYCHOLOGICAL DIMENSION FOR ASSESSING SOCIAL FUNCTIONING 75

Psychological Theories 76
  Psychodynamic Theory 76
  Erikson's Psychosocial Theory 78
  Watson's and Skinner's Learning Theories 79
  Bandura's Social Learning Theory 80

*Cognitive Development and
    Information Processing* 81
  Piaget's Structural Approach to Cognition 81
  Information Processing 83
  Information-Processing
      Functions and Memory 89
  Implicit Memory:
      Remembering without Awareness 90

Communication 93
  Nonverbal Communication 94
  Spoken and Written Language 94
■ Implications for Practice 95

Attitudes and Emotions 95
  The Nature and Function of Attitudes 96
  Theories of Attitudes and Their Change 97
  Theories of Emotions 98
■ Implications for Practice 101

Social Cognition and Regulation 101
■ Implications for Practice 103
  Self and Identity 103
  The Self and Its Components 104
  Identities and Their Salience 106
  Focus on Narrative: Being Japanese 108
  Are Self and Identity Processes Universal? 109
■ Implications for Practice 110

*Psychological Strengths and
    Hazards* 110

4 THE SOCIAL DIMENSION FOR ASSESSING SOCIAL FUNCTIONING 114

Social Theory 115
  Ecological Systems Theory 115
  Modern Functionalism 118
  Conflict Theories 119
  Postmodernism and Theories of Society 120

Families and Groups 121
  Defining the Family 122
  Focus on Narrative: From Straight to Gay 123
  The Family Life Cycle 124
  Focus on Narrative:
      A Stepfamily's Life 126
  The Changing Family 127
  Focus on Narrative: Tell Us What
      Lesbian Families Are Like 128
  The Family of Our Times 129
  Groups as Social Subsystems 130
  Belonging to a Group 131
  Treatment and Task Groups 132
  Understanding How Groups Function 132
  Roles and Norms 132
  Communication Patterns 133
  Status and Power 134
  Cohesiveness 134
  Effect of Gender on Groups 134
  Decision Making in Groups 135

Support Groups and Communities 136
  Self-Help and Mutual-Aid Groups 136
  Characteristics of Self-Help
      or Mutual-Aid Groups 137
  Functions of Self-Help Groups 137
  Natural Helpers 139
  Communities 139
  Place as Community 139
  Identificational and Interest-
      Oriented Communities 141

Organizations and Social Institutions 142
  What Is a Formal Organization? 143
  What Is a Bureaucracy? 143
  Weber's Typology of Rational Action 143
  Scientific Management Traditions
      in Human Organizations 144
  Formal and Informal Relations
      in Organizations 144
  Social Institutions 146

Multicultural and Gender Considerations 147
Racial and Ethnic Considerations 148
Consequences of Intolerance to Difference 150
Prejudice and Discrimination 151
Race and Everyday Social Relations 153
Forms of Racism and Privilege 154
Ethnicity and Its Social Consequences 156
Core versus Surface Features of Ethnicity 156
Gender and Sexism 157
Sexual Status and Forms of Oppression 159
Sex-Role Stereotypes 159
Homophobia 160
Sexual Orientation 161

Social Strengths and Hazards 161

5 Pregnancy, Birth, and the Newborn 167

DEVELOPMENTAL THEMES 169
Abortion 171

BIOPHYSICAL DIMENSION 172

Biophysical Growth and Development 172
Physical Development of the Fetus 173
The Birth Process 174
Prepared Childbirth 175
Medications for Labor and Delivery 175
Characteristics of a Normal Newborn 176
Newborn Evaluations 176

Biophysical Strengths and Hazards 177
Complications of Pregnancy 177
Environmental Effects on Prenatal Development 178
Focus on Multiculturalism:
 Pica during Pregnancy 179
Prenatal Testing 183
Birth Defects and Ethical Dilemmas 184
Complications of Birth 185
Cesarean Section 185
Neonatal Complications: The High-Risk Infant 186

■ *Implications for Practice:*
   The Premature Infant 188

PSYCHOLOGICAL DIMENSION 191

Cognitive Development and Information Processing 191

Communication 192

Attitudes and Emotions 192

Social Cognition and Regulation 193
Newborn States 194
Newborn Reflexes 194
The Brazelton Neonatal Assessment Scale 194

■ *Implications for Practice:*
   Using the BNAS 196

Psychological Strengths and Hazards 196
The Baby's Experience of Birth 197

■ *Implications for Practice:*
   The Birth Experience and Development 197

The NICU Experience 197

■ *Implications for Practice:*
   Changes in NICU Practices 198

Multiple-Gestation Births 198

SOCIAL DIMENSION 200

Families, Groups, Communities, and Support Systems 200
Prenatal Intervention Programs:
 Every Birth a Healthy One 200
Postpartum Early-Intervention Programs 200
Adolescent Mothers 201

Multicultural and Gender Considerations 201
Infant Mortality:
 The African American–White Disparity 202
Circumcision 202
Focus on Multiculturalism: Cultural Differences of Newborns 203

Social Strengths and Hazards 203
Drug-Exposed Infants 204

■ *Implications for Practice:*
   Long-Term Effects of Prenatal Drug Use 204

Fetal Alcohol Syndrome 204

■ *Implications for Practice:*
   Preventing FAS 205

Domestic Violence 205

■ *Summary* 206

■ *Applying the Framework:*
   The Family of a Premature Infant 208

6 INFANCY 212

DEVELOPMENTAL THEMES 214

BIOPHYSICAL DIMENSION 215

Biophysical Growth and Development 215

■ **Implications for Practice:**
  Recognizing Developmental Delay 217
  Early Intervention for Developmental Delay 218

Biophysical Strengths and Hazards 218
  Illness 219
  Sudden Infant Death Syndrome 220

PSYCHOLOGICAL DIMENSION 222

Cognitive Development and Information Processing 222
  Piaget's Sensorimotor Stage 222
  Information Processing 223
  IQ Testing in Infancy 226

■ **Implications for Practice:**
  Should Babies Learn to Read? 226

Communication 226
  Crying and Cooing 226
  Babbling 227
  Holophrastic Speech 227
  Telegraphic Speech 228

■ **Implications for Practice:**
  Recognizing Speech Problems 228
  Adult Communication Patterns with Infants 228

Attitudes and Emotions 229
  Infant Temperament 230

■ **Implications for Practice:**
  Goodness of Fit 232
  Attachment 232
  The Parents' Behaviors 233
  The Infant's Behaviors 234
  Other Attachment Ideas 234
  Risk Factors Associated
    with Attachment Failure 234

■ **Implications for Practice:**
  Assessing Attachment Problems 235
  Focus On Multiculturalism:
    Cultural Considerations in Examining African
    American Attachment Patterns 236

Social Cognition and Regulation 237
  Regulation 238

■ **Implications for Practice:**
  The Terrible Twos 239

Psychological Strengths and Hazards 239
  Failure to Form an Attachment 239
  Separation after Attachment 240

■ **Implications for Practice:**
  Fostering Secure Attachment 240
  Failure to Thrive 241

■ **Implications for Practice:**
  Treating Failure to Thrive 242
  Infant Mental Health 242

■ **Implications for Practice:**
  *Assessment and Interventions
  of Infant Mental Health* 243

SOCIAL DIMENSION 246

Families and Groups 246
  Family Influences 246
  Fathers and Babies 246
  Grandparents and Babies 247
  Siblings and Babies 248
  Babies and Their Peers 248
  Playing with Baby 248
  Adoption 248
  Open Adoption 249
  Transracial Adoption 249
  Native American Adoption 250
  Birth Fathers 250

■ **Implications for Practice:**
  *Making Difficult Decisions in
  Adoption Practices* 251
  How Adoptive Families Fare 251

Communities and Support Systems 252
  Day Care 252

■ **Implications for Practice:**
  The Realities of Day Care 252
  Quality of Child Care 253

Multicultural and Gender Considerations 253
  Developmental Assessment
    of Minority Infants 254
  Focus on Multiculturalism:
    Understanding Different Cultural Beliefs 254
  Gender Issues 255

Social Strengths and Hazards 255
- Focus on Multiculturalism: Rural Unemployment and Effects on Families 256
- Environmental Context and Child Development 256

■ **Implications for Practice: Assessing the Home Environment** 257
- Infant Abuse 258
- Foster Care 259
- Lead Poisoning 260
- Parents with Mental Illness 260
- Parents with a History of Developmental Delay 261
- Teen Parents: Children Having Children 261

■ **Implications for Practice: The Importance of Social Support** 262
- Developmental Guidelines for Assessment in Infancy 262

■ **Applying the Framework: Failure to Thrive** 266

7 EARLY CHILDHOOD 270

DEVELOPMENTAL THEMES 272

BIOPHYSICAL DIMENSION 273

Biophysical Growth and Development 273
- Gross Motor Skills 273
- Fine Motor Skills 273

Biophysical Strengths and Hazards 274
- Asthma 274

PSYCHOLOGICAL DIMENSION 276

Cognitive Development and Information Processing 276
- Piaget's Preoperational Stage 277
- Information Processing 277
- Developmental Waves 278

Communication 279
- Communication Disorders 280

Attitudes and Emotions 281
- Fears 282
- Grief and Loss 283
- Aggression 285

■ **Implications for Practice: Curbing Aggression** 286
- Altruism and Empathy 287

■ **Implications for Practice: Helping Children Develop Empathy** 288

Social Cognition and Regulation 288
- Sociability of Preschoolers 290
- Regulation 291

Psychological Strengths and Hazards 292
- Diagnostic and Assessment Issues 292
- Elimination 293
- Anxiety Disorders 293
- Attention-Deficit/Hyperactivity Disorder (ADHD) 294
- Childhood Depression 294
- Autism 295

SOCIAL DIMENSION 298

Families and Groups 298
- Family Influences 299
- Parenting Styles 299
- Nontraditional Families 302
- Mother's Role 302
- Father's Role 302
- Children of Prisoners 303
- Siblings 303
- Peer Relationships 305

Communities and Support Systems 306
- Preschoolers' Play 306
- Preschool Environment 307
- Kindergarten 307
- Project Head Start 308
- Full-Service Schools 310
- Effects of TV on Preschool Children 310

Multicultural and Gender Considerations 311
- Cross-Culturally Adopted Children 312
- Gender-Role and Sexual-Identity Development 312
- The Effects of Sex Stereotyping 313

Social Strengths and Hazards 313
- Family-Group Decision Making: A Strengths Model 314
- Poverty and Development 314
- Child Abuse 315
- Factors That Contribute to Child Abuse 316
- Incidence of Child Abuse 316
- Reporting Child Abuse 317
- Investigation of Child Maltreatment 318
- The Effects of Child Abuse and Neglect 319
- Developmental Guidelines for Assessment in Early Childhood 319
- Focus on Narrative: A Child Called "It" 319

■ **Applying the Framework: Developmental Delay in a 4-Year-Old** 324

8 MIDDLE CHILDHOOD 328

DEVELOPMENTAL THEMES 330

BIOPHYSICAL DIMENSION 331

Biophysical Growth and Development 331
Motor Development 331
Physical Development 332

Biophysical Strengths and Hazards 332
Movement Skills 332
Poverty and Nutrition 333

PSYCHOLOGICAL DIMENSION 334

Cognitive Development
 and Information Processing 334
Intelligence and Intelligence Tests 335
Intelligence Tests: Good or Bad? 336
Information Processing 337
The Significance of Emotional Intelligence 337
Assessing Childhood Competency
 to Testify 338

Communication 339

■ *Implications for Practice:*
 Self-Instructional Training 340
Developmental Aspects of Sign Language 341
Speech Disorders in Children 342
Bilingual Children 342
Ebonics, Culture, and Language Abilities 344
Focus on Multiculturalism:
 Refugee Children—A New Life 344

Attitudes and Emotions 346
Emotional Competence 346

Social Cognition and Regulation 346
Social Role-Taking 346
Interpersonal Awareness 347
Interpersonal Awareness
 and Interpersonal Relationships 347

Psychological Strengths and Hazards 348
Self-Concept in Middle Childhood 348
Internalizing and Externalizing
 Problems of Childhood 350
Hyperactivity, or Attention-Deficit/
 Hyperactivity Disorder 350
ADHD and Medication 352

SOCIAL DIMENSION 357

Families and Groups 357
Normal Family Processes 357
Parental Discipline 357

■ *Implications for Practice:*
 Models of Parent Training 358
Groups 361
Group Formation 361
The Power of Peers 362
Teaching Isolated Children Social Skills
 for Friendship Making 363

■ *Implications for Practice:*
 Cross-Cultural Drug
 Abuse Prevention 364

Communities and Support Systems 365
Culture and Cooperation 365
School Influences 365
School Fears 365
Designing More Effective Schools 366
Teacher Expectations 366
Self-Expectations and School Performance 367
Disadvantaged Children
 and the Public School System 367

■ *Implications for Practice:*
 Enhancing School-Community
 Relationships 368
Schools and U.S. Public Law 94-142 369

Multicultural and Gender Considerations 370
Sex Roles in Middle Childhood 370
Focus on Multiculturalism:
 Heritage-Based Rites of Passage
 for African American Youth 371

Social Strengths and Hazards 373
Neighborhoods and Communities 373
Stopping the Bullying Epidemic 373
Focus on Multiculturalism:
 Primary Prevention for
 Traumatized Khmer Children 374
Marital Conflict and Divorce 374

■ *Implications for Practice:*
 Smoothing the Aftermath
 of a Divorce 377

Developmental Guidelines for Assessment
 in Middle Childhood 377

■ *Applying the Framework:*
 Attention-Deficit/Hyperactivity
 Disorder 381

9 ADOLESCENCE 386

DEVELOPMENTAL THEMES 388

BIOPHYSICAL DIMENSION 389

Biophysical Growth and Development 389
- The Pubertal Process 389
- Focus on Multiculturalism:
  The Apache Ceremony of the
  Changing Woman 390
- Hormonal Changes in Adolescence 390
- ■ Implications for Practice:
  Physical Changes and
  Psychological Consequences 391

Biophysical Strengths and Hazards 392
- Adolescent Brain Development 392
- Common Health Hazards in Adolescence 392

PSYCHOLOGICAL DIMENSION 395

Cognitive Development and Information Processing 395

Communication 396
- Adolescent Communication and Confidentiality 397

Attitudes and Emotions 397
- Adolescent Self-Esteem 398
- Self-Image and Adolescents in Foster Care 398
- ■ Implications for Practice:
  Enhancing Adolescents'
  Self-Concepts 399
- Focus on Multiculturalism:
  Do African American Adolescents
  Have Low Self-Esteem? 400

Social Cognition and Regulation 400
- Focus on Multiculturalism: Identity
  and Native American Youth 401
- Youth of Color and Adolescent Identity 401
- Focus on Narrative: An Open Letter to the World 402
- ■ Implications for Practice:
  Identity and Independence 402
- Social Cognitive Monitoring 403
- Regulation 403
- Critique of Kohlberg's Moral
  Development Theory 404
- ■ Implications for Practice:
  Adolescent Moral Development 405
- Moral Development: Three Theoretical
  Perspectives 406
- Egocentrism 407

Psychological Strengths and Hazards 407
- Internalizing and Externalizing Disorders 408
- Focus on Multiculturalism:
  Identifying Risk Factors for Suicide
  Attempts among Navajo Adolescents 409
- Conduct Disorder 409
- Delinquency 411
- ■ Implications for Practice:
  Approaches to Treating
  Delinquent Youth 412
- Self-Harm and Cutting 413
- Focus on Narrative: One Girl's
  Account of Cutting 413

SOCIAL DIMENSION 417

Families and Groups 417
- Family Influences: Development of Autonomy 417
- Parent-Adolescent Conflict 417
- Parent-Adolescent Attachment 418
- Focus on Narrative: An Adolescent's
  Perspective on Divorce 418
- ■ Implications for Practice:
  The Power of Authoritative
  Parenting 419
- Peers and Adolescent Development 419
- Peer Pressure and Conformity 420
- Friendships 420
- ■ Implications for Practice:
  Social Skills Training 420
- Adolescent Peer Groups 421
- Cliques and Crowds 422
- Gangs 422

Communities and Support Systems 423
- School Influences 423
- High School Dropouts 425
- ■ Implications for Practice:
  Recommendations for a Smoother
  Family Relocation 425
- Runaway Youths 426
- Focus on Narrative: Homeless Youth 427

Multicultural and Gender Considerations 427
- Peer Relationships and Adolescents of Color 427
- The Adolescent Immigrant 427

Gender Roles   428
The Voice of Adolescent Girls   428
Body Image and Adolescent Depression for Girls   430
Focus on Narrative:
  The Difficulty of Being a Girl in Today's Society   430

■ *Implications for Practice:*
  A Prevention Program for Adolescent Girls   430

The War against Boys   431
Adolescent Heterosexuality   431
Focus on Narrative:
  Adolescents' Views on Sex   432
AIDS Prevention and Adolescent Males   433
Gay, Lesbian, Bisexual, and Questioning Youth   433
Can Changing a Child's Sex Change His Sexual Orientation?   435

■ *Implications for Practice:*
  Guidelines for Adolescents Who Want to Consider Coming Out   435

Focus on Narrative:
  Being Gay in High School   436
Harassment   436

Social Strengths and Hazards   436
Building ASSETS for Youth: A Strength and Community-Based Approach   436
Adolescent Risk Behaviors   437
Youth Employment   438
Adolescent Pregnancy and Childbirth   439

■ *Implications for Practice:*
  Reducing Adolescent Pregnancy   441

Sex Education and Adolescent Development   441
Alcohol and Other Drug Use   442

■ *Implications for Practice:*
  Substance Use Prevention   443

Developmental Guidelines for Assessment in Adolescence   443

■ *Applying the Framework:*
  A Depressed Adolescent   448

10 YOUNG ADULTHOOD   452

DEVELOPMENTAL THEMES   454

Emerging Adulthood   454
Theories of Adulthood   454

BIOPHYSICAL DIMENSION   456

Biophysical Growth and Development   456
Reproductive System during Early Adulthood   456
Effect of Hormones on Women   456

Biophysical Strengths and Hazards   458
Cancer   458
Health Disparities and Minority Men   458

PSYCHOLOGICAL DIMENSION   459

Cognitive Development and Information Processing   459
Formal Operational Thought   459
Development of Postformal Thought   460
Wisdom and Cognitive Development   460

Communication   461
Styles of Communication   462

■ *Implications for Practice:*
  Communication Skills for Men and Women   462

Nonverbal Communication   463
Communicating with the Deaf   463

Attitudes and Emotions   464
Love   464
Isolation and Loneliness   465

■ *Implications for Practice:*
  Coping with Loneliness   466

Social Cognition and Regulation   466
Intimacy and Independence   466
Moral Development and Gender   467

Psychological Strengths and Hazards   467
Serious Mental Illness   468

■ *Implications for Practice:*
  Assessment of Clients with Mental Illness   469

Depression and Young Adulthood   469
Depression and Women   470

SOCIAL DIMENSION   472

Families and Groups   472
Marriage   472
Selecting a Partner   473
Focus on Multiculturalism:
  Marriage and Mental Retardation   474
Adjustment to Marriage   474
Marital Expectations and Myths   474
Satisfaction and Conflict in Marriage   475

Empowering African American Families   476
Diversity in Companionship   477
Remaining or Becoming Single   477
Gay Relationships   477
Homophobia   479
Internalized Homophobia   479
Transition to Parenthood   479

■ *Implications for Practice:*
   Preparing for the Transition
   to Parenthood   *480*

Gay and Lesbian Parents   480
Voluntary Childlessness   481
Infertility   481

■ *Implications for Practice:*
   The Infertile Couple   *481*

Miscarriage   482

Communities and Support Systems   483

Work Life   483
Women and Work   483
Peer Relationships and Forming Mentorships   484
Volunteerism and Social Services   484

Multicultural and Gender Considerations   485

Blending Religions   486
Gender Roles   486
Focus on Multiculturalism:
   When Will Women and Men Be Equal?   487

Social Strengths and Hazards   487

Welfare Reform   488
Families and Children with Disabilities   488
Divorce   489
When Lesbian and Gay Couples Break Up   491
Sexual Harassment   491
Sexually Transmitted Diseases   492
AIDS and Prevention   492
AIDS and Medication   493
Focus on Narrative:
   Spiritual Growth in Women with AIDS   494
Rape and Sexual Assault   495

■ *Implications for Practice:*
   Rape Trauma Syndrome   *495*

Focus on Multiculturalism:
   The Global War against Women   496
Domestic Violence in the Family   497
Social Workers in Managed-Care Systems   498
Alcohol, Tobacco, and Other Drugs   498
Alcohol Use among College Students   500
Developmental Guidelines for Assessment
   in Young Adulthood   500

■ *Applying the Framework:*
   Schizophrenia   *504*

11 MIDDLE ADULTHOOD   507

DEVELOPMENTAL THEMES   509

BIOPHYSICAL DIMENSION   510

Biophysical Growth and Development   510

Personality Type and Disease   510
Menopause   511
Ethnicity and Menopause   513
Estrogen Replacement Therapy   514
Sexuality in Middle Adulthood   515

Biophysical Strengths and Hazards   516

Becoming Physically Fit in Midlife   516
Cancer   516
Prostate Cancer   517
Focus on Narrative:
   An African American Woman's
   Experience with Breast Cancer   518
Focus on Narrative: Cancer Affects Us All   519
A Family-Systems Look at Couples and Illness   519

■ *Implications for Practice:*
   Psychological Interventions
   for the Seriously Ill   *520*

Women and Health Care: A Short History   521
Midlife and the Widening Midsection   521
Effects of Brain Injury on the Family   522

PSYCHOLOGICAL DIMENSION   525

Cognitive Development and Information Processing   525

Adult Development   525
Effect of Professional Obsolescence   525

Communication   526

The Forgiveness Process   527
Execution and Therapeutic Revenge   527
The Illiterate Adult   528
Non-English-Speaking Adults   528
The Hard-of-Hearing Adult   529

■ *Implications for Practice:*
   Clients with Hearing Loss   *529*

Legal Implications: Title V   530

Attitudes and Emotions   530

Well-Being and Anxiety   530
Midlife as a Crisis   531

Social Cognition and Regulation   531

Psychological Strengths and Hazards 532
    Developing Optimism and Happiness 532
    Alcohol and Drug Addiction 533
    Women and Drugs 534
    Focus on Narrative:
        Goodbye, Johnnie Walker 535

■ *Implications for Practice:*
    Addiction and AA's Twelve-
    Step Program 535
    Codependency 536

■ *Implications for Practice:*
    When to Seek Professional Help 537
    False Memory Syndrome 538

SOCIAL DIMENSION 541

Families and Groups 541
    Blended Families or Stepfamilies 541
    Marriage and Intimate Relationships at Midlife 542
    Marital Satisfaction among African Americans 543
    Extramarital Affairs 543
    Parent/Adult-Child Relationships 544
    Middle-Aged Parents and Their
        Adolescent Children 544
    Middle-Aged Parents and Their Adult Children 545
    Middle-Aged Adults and Their Aging Parents 546
    Families of Adults with Mental Retardation 547

■ *Implications for Practice:*
    Adjusting to the Role of Caregiver 547
    Grandparenthood 548
    Grandparents Raising Their Grandchildren 548

Communities and Support Systems 549
    Career Development and Job Satisfaction 550
    Work as a Way of Life 550
    The Spirituality of Work 550
    Career Changes at Midlife 551

Multicultural and Gender Considerations 551
    Focus on Narrative:
        A Bicultural Life—Living in Two Worlds 552
    Gender Concerns 552
    The Men's Movement 553

■ *Implications for Practice:*
    Men in Therapy 555
    Gender, Work, and the Family 556

Social Strengths and Hazards 556
    Joblessness 557
    Homelessness 557
    Predictors and Prevention for Inner-City
        Homeless Individuals 559
    Adapting to Midlife 559

Developmental Guidelines
    for Middle Adulthood 559

■ *Applying the Framework:*
    Alcoholism in Middle Age 563

12 LATE ADULTHOOD
by Kathryn Bett Adams 568

DEVELOPMENTAL THEMES 570

Focus on Narrative:
    Life Is So Good 573

BIOPHYSICAL DIMENSION 575

Biophysical Growth and Development 575
    Health Care and Medications 577
    Sexuality 578
    Physiological Changes and Sexual Activity 578

■ *Implications for Practice:*
    Sexuality in Late Adulthood 579

Biophysical Strengths and Hazards 579
    Chronic Health Problems 579
    Focus on Multiculturalism:
        Health Disparities for Older Members
        of Minority Groups 580
    Death and Dying 581
    Advance Directives for Health Care 582
    Focus on Multiculturalism:
        Death as a Natural Process 582

■ *Implications for Practice:*
    End-of-Life Care 583

PSYCHOLOGICAL DIMENSION 585

*Cognitive Development
    and Information Processing* 585

Communication 588

Attitudes and Emotions 588
    Loss, Grief, and Mourning 588
    Loneliness 590

Social Cognition and Regulation 590
    Age and Self-Concept 590

■ *Implications for Practice:*
    Reminiscence Groups in Long-
    Term Care 591

    Psychological Strengths and Hazards 591
    Wisdom 592

Spirituality and Religious Beliefs   592
Cognitive Impairment: Alzheimer's Disease
    and Other Dementias   592
Focus on Multiculturalism:
    Alzheimer's Disease in African Americans   594
Mental Illness in Late Life   595
Depression   596

■ *Implications for Practice:*
   Helping Depressed Older People   596

Suicide   598
Alcohol and Other Drug Use in Late Adulthood   598

SOCIAL DIMENSION   602

Families and Groups   602

Families   603
Focus on Narrative:
    Maryland Sisters Still Side by Side   603
Couples   604
Gay Male and Lesbian Elders   605
Widowhood   605
Parent-Child Relationships   606
Grandparenthood   607

Communities and Support Systems   608

Friendships, Neighbors, and Support Networks   608
Focus on Narrative:
    The Church Ladies   609

Retirement, Work, and Volunteering   609
Housing Options   611
The Continuum of Care   611

Multicultural and Gender Considerations   612

Older Racial or Ethnic Minorities   612
Gender Issues   614

Social Strengths and Hazards   614

Social Support for Older Adults   614
Elder Abuse and Neglect   615
Developmental Guidelines for Assessment
    in Late Adulthood   616

■ *Applying the Framework:*
   Depression in an Older Woman   619

Epilogue: The Journey of Life   625

GLOSSARY   627
REFERENCES   635
PHOTO CREDITS   675
NAME INDEX   677
SUBJECT INDEX   687

PREFACE

We have been extremely gratified by the positive reception of the two previous editions of our integrative approach to examining the rapidly changing content of human behavior and the social environment. Our second edition was translated into several languages, including Chinese. At the same time, we have been sensitive to the feedback of professors and students about how to remain as comprehensive as possible in coverage of content while presenting this complex material as simply and clearly as possible. Indeed, a major goal of this revision was to address recent developments in the study of human behavior and to update the references and in the biopsychosocial sciences.

We have updated the third edition to include increased coverage of such topics as globalization and diversity, why culture and the social environment matter, theories of self and identity, role theory, the new institutionalism, biopsychosocial strengths, research contributions by social workers, developmental pathways, theoretical developments surrounding research on racism and discrimination, queer theory, new developments associated with the Diagnostic Classification of Mental Health and the Developmental Disorders of Infancy and Childhood, an entirely new chapter on development in late life. We have also added concept maps to aid students in understanding the key concepts covered in each of the developmental chapters and study tables to aid students in studying for examinations. Each chapter has received a substantive review by at least two social work scholars. In addition, the instructor's manual and other course ancillaries have been modified to demonstrate how to change the focus of instruction so that the book can be used effectively at both the undergraduate and graduate levels.

We are really excited about many of these changes in the third edition. While many textbooks in psychology have capitalized on the use of subject area experts for reviewing chapters for accuracy and relevance, this will be the first textbook in social work on Human Behavior to employ this review procedure in addition to obtaining the traditional confirmatory reviews of the book. This new procedural approach to obtaining reviews played a major role in the completion of the third edition. It was included to ensure that (1) relevant research by social workers receives proper coverage in a textbook that is geared to the training of social work professionals; and (2) specific substantive areas have been covered, including the most up-to-date developments in a particular area of research.

Each chapter continues to have separate sections focusing on biological, psychological, and social dimensions of human behavior, enabling instructors to assign part of a chapter instead of a whole chapter per week. Other major formatting changes in this edition are intended to help instructors in identifying or focusing on specific areas that they will stress in the individual design of their classes. We are attempting to provide instructors with a comprehensive but flexible format that will allow them to select the areas they wish to emphasize in each class. But, the overall goal remains to help students learn how to use an integrated and multidimensional approach to implementing a biopsychosocial formulation in assessing cases and social situations. To this end, the introductory chapter has been modified to include additional material on role theory and classical social theories by C. Wright Mills and others that provides a stronger theoretical foundation for understanding the role of social functioning assessment in human behavior than was the case in the last edition.

While we are still committed in this edition to writing a comprehensive textbook on the subject, we have learned from many professors and students that they believe that the key ingredient in any instructional process remains the instructor. For this reason, we have worked exceptionally hard in this edition to do a better job of connecting content covered in the text with newly developed activities and exercises in our revised instructor's manual. Each chapter now contains special research assignments using Infotrac® College Edition that allow for the inclusion of many topics that instructors want students to investigate beyond those covered in the current textbook.

In addition, some professors requested that we provide an increased number of cases in the instructor's manual that did not have predetermined answers so that they could do a better job of challenging their students to think critically about cases. To this end, we have made a number of significant and exciting changes. In the instructor's manual, we have introduced a specific activity sheet that helps guide an instructor's review of the Raul Sanchez case for use with Chapters 2, 3, 4, and 5. We also have created a comprehensive case (the Perez Family) with detailed posted exercises on the Book Companion Website to help the professor work with students in looking at the same case across each stage of the life span.

In addition, we provide assignments associated with the comprehensive case that help the professor modify aspects of the case (the family's ethnicity or other variables) so that students can consider how their assessments would change given an important variation in the characteristics of the person or situation. The manual also includes a number of more specialized cases that lack specific answers, which professors can use to enhance their graduate students' skill in assessing social functioning within the multidimensional biopsychosocial framework of the book.

In summary, the third edition has countless major and minor updates, well over 200 new references dated 2000 or later, new and improved illustrations, and fresh exercises in the instructor's manual and on the Book Companion Website. Here are highlights of some of the major updates:

- The text devotes increased attention to the voices of individuals to help clarify concepts.
- The PIE system—and how it takes into account notions of strengths—is discussed more fully; specific activity sheets in the workbook have been developed to help students apply this system to cases across the span of life.
- Information on using hypotheses in assessing cases now appears early in Chapter 1, as does information about case and situation formulations.
- Chapter 1 also includes a new discussion of how life-span and life-course perspectives influence understandings of delinquency.
- Policy issues that are a function of human behavior assumptions and their consequences are included throughout the text and are also emphasized in student activity sheets in the revised instructor's manual.
- Additional material on evolutionary approaches to human behavior is presented, including new evolutionary theories of color and the limitations of evolutionary psychology.
- The role played by glial cells in the nervous system has been clarified.
- The presentation of psychological theories has been reorganized.
- Sections on emotional regulation, language development, and developments in behavioral genetics, such as the nature vs. nurture debate, are more fully developed.
- The discussion of emotional competence in middle childhood has been expanded.
- Information on hormone replacement therapy research has been updated.
- Major updates on late life have been provided.

The third edition also includes many new sections on such subjects as

- Theories of self and identity
- Memory processes and new information processing models
- Automatic forms of racism and discrimination
- Native American Persons with Two-Spirits in Native American traditions
- Transgender issues
- The experiences of lesbian mothers raising children
- Psychosocial transitions to parenthood
- The effects of day care on child development outcomes
- Issues surrounding child-care quality
- Infant mental health and systems for classifying infant mental health and developmental disorders (DC:0-3)

Other important topics include:

- ADHD and medication issues
- The role of bullying in middle childhood
- Adolescent brain development
- Adolescents and issues of confidentiality
- Self-harm and cutting

- Health disparities and minority men
- Depression in young adulthood
- Fear and anxiety issues in middle life
- The role of optimism and happiness in later years

As in the other editions, the most challenging task we faced in revising this textbook was in selecting what scientific findings to include. To this end we obtained excellent help from a number of invaluable colleagues in the field. Our outside reviewers have made excellent contributions to this process from the very inception of this project. Without their advice and counsel, our first two editions would not have been as well received by our students and colleagues.

Given the many suggestions provided by our colleagues, we were not able to address all of their recommendations at this time. Some will need to be addressed in future revisions because they require further thought and research. Social work educators are amazingly helpful to textbook authors. They send comments and have their students send comments about concerns and areas requiring further clarification. We are extremely thankful for this level of cooperation and interest in our textbook.

In our first two editions, we did a good job including research developed in the general health, social and behavior sciences. However, we wanted to do a much better job in this edition of identifying extant research from our own profession. For this reason, we identified social work and other subject matter consultants to assist us with this important task. We hope that this added level of review is well received by our colleagues and students. With the many changes in format and content in this edition, we have done a better job in trying to realize our initial vision of doing something very different in educating social workers about the Human Behavior and the Social Environment curriculum.

While our first edition pioneered a new generation of HBSE textbooks, we still have much to learn from students and professors about linking our integrative and multidimensional perspective of human behavior to practice concerns. However, we believe that we did a much better job in this third edition in realizing this important educational challenge. The new cases contained on the book's companion website and in our instructor's manual offer students increased opportunities for looking at the complexities of the multicausal and reciprocal aspects of the biopsychosocial system's influence on human behavior.

Acknowledgments

We have been very fortunate to have Lisa Gebo as our editor. She has challenged us to look substantively at many aspects of the Human Behavior and the Social Environment curriculum area. In doing so, she has helped us address many of the most salient pedagogical concerns. In addition, she has been very supportive in motivating us to complete this stimulating but very exhausting process. Without her constant encouragement, we would not have finished this edition in a timely fashion. The rest of the acquisition staff also worked tirelessly on this project: Alma Dea Michelena, assistant editor, and Sheila Walsh, editorial assistant

In addition, we could not have completed this edition without the invaluable assistance of the subject matter consultants, who read one or more chapters, and the reviewers of the overall integrity of the entire book. For the third edition, we thank the following reviewers, especially those who have continued with the project since the first edition: Beverly Black, Wayne State University; Elizabeth Danto, Hunter College-CUNY; Stephene Diepstra, Calvin College; Jan Ivery, Georgia State University; Ameda A. Manetta, Winthrop University; Stephen Marson, University of North Carolina at Pembroke; Mary Rawlings, Azusa Pacific University; and James L. Wolk, Georgia State University.

Numerous students and colleagues also provided support. In particular we want to extend special thanks to Margie Waller for her independent contributions to the textbook on spirituality and blended families. She has provided invaluable critiques of each of our editions and offered detailed consultation on the strengths perspective and other models and/or neglected voices in this curriculum area. We are also very grateful for all the work and creative energy provided to the project by Jennifer Brougham. Jennifer was responsible for pushing us to investigate alternative methods for using cases to improve on assessment and knowledge integration issues. For this edition, she took prime responsibility for helping with the revision of our instructor's manual.

We are also thankful for all the assistance that we have had from former students, practitioners from the field, and students taking the course. The diligent research of Allyson Labrue, Nancy Alpert, Ike Shipman, and Melissa Fairfield require special mention. In addition, we want to thank all those who enriched the process by providing special voices on many topical concerns, especially Debbie Hunt, Dan and Sarah Brosmer, and Kieko Hamada.

We are also grateful for the excellent illustrations provided by Rachel Flores from her trip across the country. She is a tireless advocate for migrant workers who captured in many of her photographs why the needs of immigrants and farmworkers cannot continue to be ignored.

Finally, we want to thank our families for their continued patience and help in living our own life course adventures to their fullest.

JOSÉ B. ASHFORD is a Professor of Human Behavior and the Social Environment in the Arizona State University School of Social Work and affiliate faculty of Justice Studies and Social Inquiry. Professor Ashford is the associate editor of the *Journal of Sociology and Social Welfare* and serves on a number of other editorial boards including *Social Work, Journal of Social Work Education*, and *Research on Social Work Practice*. His coedited book (with Bruce D. Sales and William H. Reid), *Treating Adult and Juvenile Offenders with Special Needs*, received honorable mention from the Manfred S. Guttmacher (2002) Awards Committee of the American Academy of Psychiatry and Law and the American Psychiatry Association for the outstanding contribution to the forensic psychiatry literature. He is the recipient of numerous research, training, and evaluation grants (as principal investigator or evaluator): the Mentally Ill Offender Crime Reduction Grant (California Board of Corrections); Family Drug Court Engagement and Retention in Drug Treatment Pilot (NIDA); Native Pathways (CSAP); Salt-River Pima-Maricopa Indian Community's Circles of Care Project (CMHS); clinical training grant for SEBD children and adolescents (NIMH); and the Red Road Substance Abuse and HIV-AIDS prevention program (CSAP). He is also a research and program evaluation consultant for Mercer Human Resource Consulting in their Behavioral Health and Clinical Solutions group. Professor Ashford is a widely sought-after expert witness on mitigating factors in capital murder cases. He has published widely in areas of forensic and correctional mental health, juvenile justice, offender risk and needs assessment, procedural justice, and conflict and its management.

To my wife, Nancy, for being a constant inspiration and support.

J.B.A.

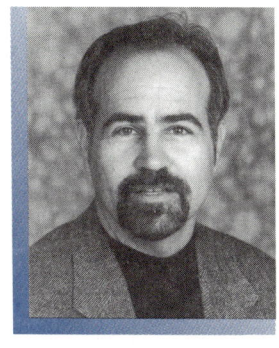

CRAIG WINSTON LECROY is a professor in the School of Social Work at Arizona State University. He has been a visiting professor at the University of Canterbury, New Zealand, the Zellerbach Visiting Professor at the University of California–Berkeley, and is currently a senior Fulbright specialist. His other books include *The Call to Social Work; Case Studies in Child, Adolescent, and Family Treatment; Case Studies in Social Work Practice; Empowering Adolescent Girls; Social Skills Training for Children and Adolescents*; and *Handbook of Child and Adolescent Treatment Manuals*. He is the recipient of numerous grants including (as principal investigator or coprincipal investigator): interventions for risk reduction and avoidance in youth (NIH), evaluation of Healthy Families (a child abuse prevention program), a mental health training grant for improving service delivery to severely emotionally disturbed children and adolescents (NIMH), and Youth Plus: Positive Socialization for Youth (CSAP). Professor LeCroy has published widely in the areas of children's mental health, social skills training, prevention, risk and needs assessment with juvenile offenders, and adolescent treatment.

To my son, Skyler A. Milligan LeCroy, who has taught me much about human behavior and development; I love watching you grow!

C.W.L.

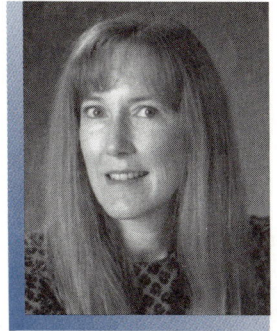

KATHY L. LORTIE is a school social worker with the Tucson Unified School District. She was previously a pediatric social worker at University Medical Center, University of Arizona, Health Sciences Center. She coteaches Social Work in Health Care, a graduate course at Arizona State University. A certified childbirth educator, she has taught classes on childbirth, parenting, and infant care and has worked as a labor assistant. She is also the author of *Special Delivery: A Labor Guide for Expectant Parents*. Her current interests include child abuse prevention, infant mental health, school social work, and coping with chronic illness in adolescence.

To my babies, Sarah, Susan, David, my first child, Shawn, and to Michael: thanks for giving me the family I always wanted.

K.L.L.

A Multidimensional Framework
for Assessing Social Functioning

CHAPTER 1

CHAPTER CONSULTANTS

Maria Angela Leungo
Universidad de Santiago de Compostela

Karen E. Wandrei
Co-Director, Person-in-Environment Project, and Executive Director, Mendocino County Youth Project

Hilary Weaver
State University of New York at Buffalo

CHAPTER ONE

The Limits of One-Dimensional Approaches

CASE A   EL CENTRO*

AN AGENCY in east Los Angeles has the primary function of teaching Latinos how to read and write in English. El Centro targets people from the ages of 18 to 65. This agency is supported by national, state, and local funding and is governed by a five-person board appointed by the mayor of Los Angeles. The board determines all the policies for the organization. One of its members serves as the agency's director. None of the board members is from the Latino community. The agency has four language teachers and six bilingual Mexican American assistants, who are under the supervision of the language teachers. The assistants are hired by the director and do outreach work in the community to encourage Mexican Americans and other Latinos who speak little or no English to enroll in language classes.

Teachers at El Centro attribute agency problems to the board, but they concur with administrators that the agency is not reaching as many members of the community as it should. One of the teachers told outside social-work consultants that, to be effective, the agency needs at least five more teachers. Agency teachers also express concerns about the lack of up-to-date instructional materials, and they have sharply criticized the board's belief that English-teaching methods should be the same as they were 25 years ago. In addition, some teachers believe that the underutilization of the agency's instructional services is caused in part by the values of east Los Angeles Mexican Americans, who the teachers think do not recognize the importance of learning English. (Many people are able to find jobs without having achieved competency in English.)

Administrators of the board believe that, in general, the agency is doing a good job. The program appears to be cost-effective and is meeting the board's goal of saving taxpayers' money. Board members attribute the community's lack of interest in the program to factions in the agency. They believe that some of the teachers are trying to stir up their assistants. The administrators want to handle this by firing the teachers who they believe are responsible for the problems. However, they don't want to fire any of the Mexican American assistants, because doing so could further weaken the program's ability to reach members of the Mexican American community. The director of the program told an outside consultant that "Mexicans are not really bad, but they are somewhat lazy and must be taught to change their ways." He doubts that they would ever be able to run things by themselves. He assumes that if he changes the employees in his program, the agency will start doing a better job of "selling" the program in the Mexican American community.

The teaching assistants from the Mexican American community believe that both the board and the teachers are at fault for the program's inability to enroll sufficient numbers of students. They do not believe that the board is willing to spend the kind of money needed to pay for classes with adequate student-teacher ratios. They agree with the teachers that the program needs newer teaching materials. Several assistants who plan to leave the agency also pointed out that many of the teachers "really don't like us and accept us as Mexicans." One assistant told a consultant that "they want to make us like them." Another assistant said, "We often feel that we are being used by everyone. Why don't they give us the money, and we will do it all; it's our money too" (adapted from Ziegler, 1994).

Which statement offers the best understanding of El Centro's situation? Explain your choice.

A. This agency's board is suffering the consequences of what some organizational theorists have termed *bureaupathic behavior*; this behavior begins with a need for people in authority to control those in subordinate positions. Moreover, the director has a bureaucratic personality and harbors biases toward Mexican Americans that are affecting his relationships with staff.

---

*The cases in this book are loosely based on several actual cases; names and other identifying details included in the cases in this book are fictitious.

B. The teachers in the agency are displacing their anger and frustration onto their assistants because of feelings of powerlessness. They also resent their dependence on their assistants in recruiting students for the program.
C. El Centro has teachers and administrators who have learned stereotypes about Mexicans that influence their behavior toward students and employees, and these stereotypes are causing much of the conflict.
D. The social institutions in this agency are not functioning well. In these institutions, people learn structured ways of relating to one another. Each group's norms are in conflict with the others', triggering anger, frustration, and evidence of breakdown in institutional or socially structured patterns of relating.
E. El Centro has not adopted a system of service delivery that recognizes the strengths of its target populations.

CASE B JEAN DAVIS

JEAN DAVIS is a 19-year-old woman who is experiencing difficulties in college. She moved out of the dorm because she thought other students were out to ruin her life. Her former roommate said that Jean would stay up all night reading the Bible and laughing inappropriately. Jean claims that other students in the dorm were jealous of her because of her special powers. She will not tell anyone what these powers are; when asked, she just smiles strangely. Her mother recently learned that Jean stopped attending classes. Whenever the mother talks to her, Jean tells her that she needs to prepare because the end is near. Jean told the social worker that God speaks to her all the time, telling her that she needs to be prepared. But Jean says that she cannot tell anyone what she is preparing for. Her mother is frightened because this is not like the Jean she previously knew. She is concerned because Jean is not eating and is disturbing her neighbors, who have complained about hearing Jean pace the floor of her apartment throughout the night.

Which statement offers the best understanding of Jean's situation? Explain your choice.

A. Jean is suffering from schizophrenia.
B. Jean has developed an extreme fear of others and is seeking refuge in her spiritual beliefs.
C. Jean has learned to adapt to the stresses of college and young adulthood by withdrawing from others.
D. The lack of support in Jean's school environment has caused her to seek refuge in fantasy and other escapist activities.
E. Jean is acting irresponsibly so that she can avoid the stressful expectations in her everyday life.

CASE C JEFF JOHNSON

JEFF JOHNSON is a 27-year-old man who was arrested for two counts of sexually inappropriate behavior. He was accused of having sex with two boys from his scouting troop. Jeff previously had been arrested and convicted for sex with minors, but he was placed on probation, on the condition that he obtain treatment. Jeff has virtually no relationships with people his own age. He lives with his parents and is currently employed as a truck driver for a company that collects old newspapers. His probation officer eventually learned that Jeff keeps this low-paying job primarily because it takes him near an area with underprivileged children, whom he has often paid for sexual favors.

When Jeff was 12 years old, he became involved in a sexual relationship with an older man. He was in this sexual relationship for approximately five years. He also recalled being fondled in a closet by an older boy at his school when he was around 8 years old and being ambivalent about the experience. Jeff reports no relationships with a female or male over 16 years of age since he stopped seeing the older man. He prefers having sex with young boys and provides vivid descriptions of what stimulates him about them physically.

Which statement offers the best understanding of Jeff's situation? Explain your choice.

A. Jeff is suffering from a mental disorder called *paraphilia of the pedophilia type*.
B. Jeff's inappropriate sexual orientation is due to his immature personality.
C. Jeff learned his interest in molesting children from his own experience of molestation.
D. Jeff's social situation does not provide him with effective social outlets.
E. Jeff's behavior is morally "disgusting" or bad.

CASE D TIM LAD

TIM LAD is a 7-year-old boy who was referred by the school counselor for running away from school and for constantly fighting with other students. Tim lives with his brother, sister, and mother in a poor section of a small southwestern town. Tim's father, who was an alcoholic and had a history of trouble with the law, deserted the family when Tim was 2½ years old. Tim is very impulsive and has difficulties controlling his behavior. His teachers say that he often misinterprets the actions of others. For instance, he bumped into a boy the other day in class, and the boy told him to be careful. Tim responded, "No one tells me what to do," and proceeded to attack the other youth. Tim also has difficulties with reading and sitting still in class. Tim's mother works long hours in a restaurant and says she is exhausted when she gets home. She reports that she is not sure she can control Tim any longer. Ms. Lad reported that Tim has always had a bad temper but is generally sorry for whatever he does wrong. When the social worker met with Tim, he was very cooperative and friendly throughout the interview.

Which statement offers the best understanding of Tim's situation? Explain your choice.

A. Tim has attention-deficit/hyperactivity disorder and a possible conduct disorder.
B. Tim is acting out his need for love.
C. Tim has learned that the only way to get what he desires is to act on impulse. He has not learned to reflect on his actions.
D. Tim is acting out because he is in a school system without adequate special-education resources. His school situation needs to provide him with a substitute father figure.
E. Tim is a bad child who needs to learn discipline and responsibility.

In selecting appropriate statements to describe each of the preceding cases, some of you may have believed that all the descriptions applied. Others may have thought that none applied. In fact, all the descriptions may apply to some degree; they were based on established approaches for assessing human behavior. Each of these theories has roots in biological, psychological, and social theory, and each includes concepts social workers can use in assessing individual and social issues.

The presenting problems and social issues encountered by social-work practitioners can be extremely complex. Any single theory almost certainly will be incapable of accounting for the whole range of forces influencing a person's behavior in the social environment (Lyons, Wodarski, & Feit, 1998). Various approaches to assessing human behavior have guided the activities of social-work professionals. These approaches include medical, psychoanalytic, social-learning, social-group, community, and organizational models, as well as moral models and the strengths perspective. They direct the way practitioners define problems and seek solutions.

Did you notice a pattern in the descriptions of the cases that opened this chapter? All the "A" statements are similar; all the "B" statements are similar; and so on.

"A" Statements and Limitations

The A descriptions represent the *medical approach*, which is directed toward treatment of identified diseases and disorders. The medical approach implies that health is the absence of a disorder or disease. Diagnosis of a problem is based on criteria such as the ones that define disorders in the *Diagnostic and*

Statistical Manual of the American Psychiatric Association*, Fourth Edition (DSM-IV-TR). Although the first case does not have a DSM-IV-TR diagnosis, the A statement relies on a disease metaphor in structuring its description of the organizational difficulties expressed.

The major drawback of the medical approach is its focus on prevention or treatment of a disorder or disease; problems of living are essentially ignored. Thus the danger ensues that a problem of living may be treated as a disease or a medical condition. **Problems of living** are normative aspects of everyday life. No one can avoid normal life troubles, such as the loss of a job, the death of a family member, or interpersonal conflicts. For example, normal anxiety over a divorce could be treated with medication designed for anxiety disorders, in spite of the absence of an actual anxiety disorder. The medical approach is also basically person centered or illness centered; it ignores many personal troubles that are fundamentally a result of variables in a person's external environment.

"B" Statements and Limitations

B statements represent the *psychodynamic approach*, which is based on the work of Sigmund Freud and includes the theoretical modifications in the analytical tradition, such as ego psychology. Assessment focuses on symptoms and identifying the causes of the symptoms. Such causes could be traumatic life events or experiences; for example, depression could be attributed to loss of a loved one or to anger turned inward. Intervention is concerned with eliminating symptomatic behavior.

The danger of this approach is that it may increase the number of pathological labels assigned to clients based on questionable assumptions about theoretical **etiology** (that is, the study of the origins and causes of psychological problems). This approach focuses on identifying causes of symptoms rather than on describing the presence of clusters of signs and symptoms associated with an established system of disease classification, as do the medically based A responses.

"C" Statements and Limitations

The C statements represent the *learning approach*. This approach assumes that people learn adaptive and maladaptive functioning. Intervention is based on a client learning new behavior by manipulating the antecedent and consequential environmental conditions that maintain adaptive and maladaptive forms of behavior.

The learning approach focuses only on behavior. It does not take into account affective (emotional) dimensions of the human experience, and it ignores the role emotions can play in motivating behavior. It also overlooks the contributions of genetics and other biological determinants of human behavior that place individuals, families, and groups at risk for developing a number of negative life outcomes.

"D" Statements and Limitations

D statements represent *social, group, community, institutional*, and *organizational approaches*. These approaches focus on how the structure and function of social relationships contribute to problems in human behavior. That is, these approaches assess how conflicts in the normative environment contribute to problem behaviors. In addition, they focus on how relations with other people influence individual, family, group, and societal behavior. The structural aspects of behavior are seen as key determinants of many forms of social action.

The problem with these approaches is that explanations for behavior are limited to factors—roles, norms, or institutions—extrinsic to the person. An individual's intrinsic factors often are held constant and are not assumed to play a pivotal role in variations in observed behavior. Interventions based on these approaches focus on changing external factors. For instance, social approaches often exclude from consideration the contributions of an individual's biological and psychological systems. This exclusion raises an important question: Can neurological impairments or other internal processes influence how people react to situations?

"E" Statements and Limitations

E responses represent the **strengths perspective** and normatively based perspectives. The strengths perspective emerged as an alternative to the problem-solving approaches to human-service interventions. This perspective introduces a different way of relating with and assessing clients. The professional does not act as an expert with clients in this approach. The focus is less on ends and more on cooperative means. The practitioner's goal in the assessment process is to identify and appreciate the life experiences, wisdom, and resources (the strengths) of an individual or community.

The E responses also include statements from what is termed *moral* or *utopian* views of human behavior. Here the focus is on moral expectations or ideals, as defined by a utopian viewpoint. For example, theorists can evaluate behavior based on values or ideals that they presume are right or wrong.

How do we determine what is a strength or an ideal behavior? There is little agreement about what is considered moral, ideal, or normal behavior. Is the concept that childhood is a time for play rather than responsibility a fact, or an ideal? Do individuals have inherent needs for growth and self-actualization, or do these values reflect Romantic conceptions of the self and its development? Cross-culturally speaking, is female circumcision a way to protect a woman's position in society, or is it a form of oppression?

Because the strengths perspective does not advocate considering the helper as expert, strengths-based interventions are a function neither of best practices nor of definitions of strengths defined in terms of specific factual criteria (Peterson & Seligman, 2004). To put it more simply, in this approach, judgments about behavior are not based on knowledge or facts.

If all people and situations were alike, applications of grand theories or models of assessment would be sufficient to guide social-work activities in conceptualizing cases and situations. However, in social work, we know that all individuals and their situations have unique characteristics that contribute to various types of diversity. Diversification involves any process that influences variations observed in people and environments. People come from different ethnic backgrounds; have different likes and dislikes; convey various attitudes and prejudices; are different colors, shapes, and sizes; have different predispositions and vulnerabilities; and come with distinct developmental histories. Indeed, diversification in people and their environments makes the world interesting (Dalton, Elias, & Wandersman, 2001).

This book takes issue with accepting any one particular approach to human behavior, whether it is person centered or environment centered. A key theme in this book is that human behavior cannot be understood by isolating the internal variables of people from the external variables in their environments. For this reason, the subject matter of human behavior and the social environment is examined here using an *integrative multidimensional approach*. One-dimensional approaches are discussed in the book because they provide an invaluable context for understanding the subject matter at various levels of analysis. Today, however, none of these approaches is considered scientifically viable if taken alone (Barlow & Durand, 2005; Garcia Coll, Bearer, & Lerner, 2004). We now recognize that no form of influence—biological, psychological, or social—ever takes place in isolation (Garcia Coll et al., 2004). Instead, human behavior is better viewed as part of a system or feedback loop involving multiple causal processes (Barlow & Durand, 2005). This system can have independent inputs at many different points, but as each input is integrated within the whole, it cannot be considered independent (Barlow & Durand, 2005). For this reason, practitioners must learn how to weave together scientific findings from the behavioral, cognitive, genetic, health, and social sciences in assessing social functioning and other concerns. To this end, we introduce a multidimensional framework that focuses on the integration of theory and scientific findings from the biological, psychological, and social dimensions of human behavior and the social environment.

Why Do Social Workers Study Human Behavior and the Social Environment?

What most influences our behavior? Is it our biological makeup, our psychological characteristics, or our social setting? As you will learn in this book, human behavior takes place in a diverse array of geophysical, psychological, and social contexts. In these contexts, people confront biological, psychological, and social demands that require effective human responses. The ability to respond effectively to these demands on individuals, families, groups, communities, and organizations is known as **adaptation**.

Understanding the process of adaptation is vital to practice in any human-service profession. In the field of social work, Human Behavior and the Social Environment (HBSE) is the curriculum area that provides the foundation of knowledge needed for a basic understanding of human adaptation.

Social work, unlike many other human-service professions, sees *social adaptation* as one of its primary areas of expertise. In social life, people adapt to many occurrences and situations. "Personal relationships, changes in work schedules and living habits, and major happenings such as war, a poor economy, or a natural disaster are some of the events that require good coping skills from almost everyone, no matter how healthy or disabled" (Duffy & Wong, 1996, p. 94). Adaptation to such factors can be enhanced by expanding or improving the environment or by increasing a person's behavioral competence in adapting to environmental demands (Dalton, Elias, & Wandersman, 2001).

The capacity of humans to adapt and thrive in changing environments is related to their capacity for "developmental flexibility" (Mahoney, 1991, 2000). Because human development is an important sociocultural process, adaptation is not limited to genetic or biological considerations. Beliefs, skills, values, and social expectations also must adapt to the conditions of rapidly changing environments. These adaptations are possible because of the flexibility of our social institutions and our cultural heritage. As humans, our developmental capacity for adaptation is heavily connected to cultural practices and traditions (Kornblum, 2003; Rogoff, 2003). "Culture here refers to the entirety of psychological, social, material, and symbolic (knowledge based) resources that humans have developed over millennia and that are transmitted across generations" (Staudinger & Bluck, 2001, p. 25). A central theme in this book is that cultural and social processes matter in accounting for changes in behavior, people, institutions, and societies.

Why Cultural Factors Matter

It would hardly be fish who discovered the existence of water.

—Clyde Kluckhohn

All of us tend to take for granted the way people in our community do things. When we travel to distant places, our assumptions about our own social life and its cultural practices may be challenged. For instance, the segregation of children by age outside of school is very uncommon in many parts of the world. Children in Mayan communities of Central America spend less than 10% of their time outside of school with other same-age children. They are much more likely to spend time with siblings and other young relatives who are not in their age group (Angelillo, Rogoff, & Morelli, 2002). In contrast, it is much more common for children in Canada and the United States to spend most of their free time with peers in organized activities such as soccer, ballet, chess clubs, and street games.

However, social scientists are noting some major changes in the relationships between parents and our current generation of children and youth. The University of Michigan's Institute for Social Research reports that between 1991 and 1998, the average child from 3 to 12 years of age spent 31 hours per week with his or her mother, up from 25 hours a week in 1980, and 25 hours a week with the father, up from 23 hours. (These numbers reflect waking hours only.) The researchers attribute these changes to what they have termed the "quiet revolution" in how parents are raising their children: Many middle-class parents have contributed to raising one of the most supervised generations in human history. These parents currently are committed to "producing happy and successful children. Parents become co-CEOs in the manufacture of junior achievers" (Brooks, 2004, p. 140). They allow children minimal opportunity to participate in unsupervised activities that can promote their development during critical periods for acquiring the capacities for success and well-being—the very things their parents desire for them. This change has not necessarily been observed among poor or working-class parents in the United States.

Although many societies, like the United States, engage in the ordering of life according to years following birth, some societies do not even track chronological age. For instance, some Mayan tribal groups do not rely on age as a marker of a child's identity. When adults meet a child for the first time, instead of asking his or her name, as many European Americans would, they ask, "Who are your mother and father?" Because identity in this culture is defined by relationships and place in the community, Mayans are more likely to attempt to describe a child in terms of other people in their family, and not in terms of the child's individual characteristics, including age. This view of children is also common among other indigenous groups, including some Native American and Canadian First Nations people, and immigrants from Central and South America to the United States.

In general, U.S. society currently places significant emphasis on issues of age, and many people take for granted that we have always used time-since-birth as a marker of human development. Yet in the United States, before the end of the 1800s, people tended to place little emphasis on age. Most people were born at home, and there were very few social institutions that organized their lives around the concept of chronological age. Barbara Rogoff (2003) wrote, "It was not until the 20th century that Americans commonly referred to ages and began to celebrate birthdays regularly" (p. 155). Like the Santa Claus tradition in America, many of the practices and customs associated with celebrations of birthdays are of relatively recent origin. The ditty "Happy Birthday to You" was not widely adopted until around 1930, when it was in a hit from a Broadway play (Rogoff, 2003).

Birthday celebrations are not the only social practices we take for granted. As we master our culture, we often do not notice how it shapes many aspects of our lives. For example, why does it shock Americans that French citizens are alarmed by any discussions of decentralization (the empowerment of local, regional, or state government) in their analyses of governmental practices? Don't France and the United States share similar democratic traditions? Clearly, many Americans fail to see that we do not. The French have a long history of appealing to absolutism and centralization of government, and these political structures are supported by social institutions that differ from those of Australia, Canada, England, and the United States (Nadeau & Barlow, 2003). Similarly, the French strongly emphasize cultural assimilation, which raises issues that many Americans have problems understanding, including France's 2003 ban disallowing Muslim girls to wear head scarves to school, in keeping with their religious and cultural traditions.

Nadeau and Barlow (2003), in their recent book *Sixty Million Frenchmen Can't Be Wrong* describe how perplexed the French are by our focus in the United States on local-community self-governance, affirmative action, and private charity. The word *état* ("the state," or "government") triggers distinctly different reactions in France than in the United States. Nadeau and Barlow observed that the term *state* is to the French as *the Constitution* is to most Americans. The French assign high value to civil servants or governmental employees, because the state has been the primary source of stability in times of war, political instability, and other disruptive social forces. In addition, the state is associated with the actual unification of France, and this association contributes to corresponding assumptions about what some believe it means to be French and about how the French should implement notions of equality.

Before the end of the eighteenth century, most of the population of what we now know as France did not speak French. In many areas, local cultures prevailed and people spoke the regional languages of Breton, Occitan, Catalan, Basque, Alsatian, Flemish, and Provençal. This diversity contributed to divisive factions that some believed threatened the potential for achieving a democracy. Many political theorists believed that overcoming the monarchy required a strong state that would create a national identity (Forbes & Kelly, 1995; Nadeau & Barlow, 2003). To this end, the state began to run the economy and other key social institutions, as well as to define the culture and language (Forbes & Kelly, 1995; Nadeau & Barlow, 2003). Many people often ignore this important historical and cultural context, which explains French assimilation and the related fear of regionalism or local-community rule. Whereas the state is central to life in France, in America the government generally is seen more as a backup institution for guaranteeing individual freedoms. Clearly, *freedom* can have a different meaning and a different value in different cultural contexts (a hotly debated issue during the 2004 elections in the United States).

Values are a major component of any culture. Rokeach (1973) identified 36 values that people everywhere share to differing degrees. To suggest that Americans value freedom does not mean that the French do not value it. As Ferrante (2003, p. 72) wrote, "Societies are distinguished from one another not on the basis of which values are present in one society and absent in another, but rather according to which values are most cherished and dominant." Americans value the state, but they generally do not cherish it as the French do. Social workers and social scientists need to learn these differences in working with people from various cultures and societies.

In human discourse, we often expect that others share our assumptions about social life. We typically do not know when we are making these assumptions. When others question or challenge our own community's ways of doing things, it can trigger feelings of discomfort, especially when we have not thoroughly examined our own cultural practices. For instance, many parents and social workers assume that it is appropriate to withhold food or snacks as a form of discipline or punishment. However, in Kenyan society, for a mother to withhold any form of food would be unthinkable or even akin to child abuse, given the problems with food scarcity in Kenya. But Kenyan mothers, unlike European American mothers, would have no difficulty using physical discipline with their children. The meaning of each of these disciplinary practices cannot be understood

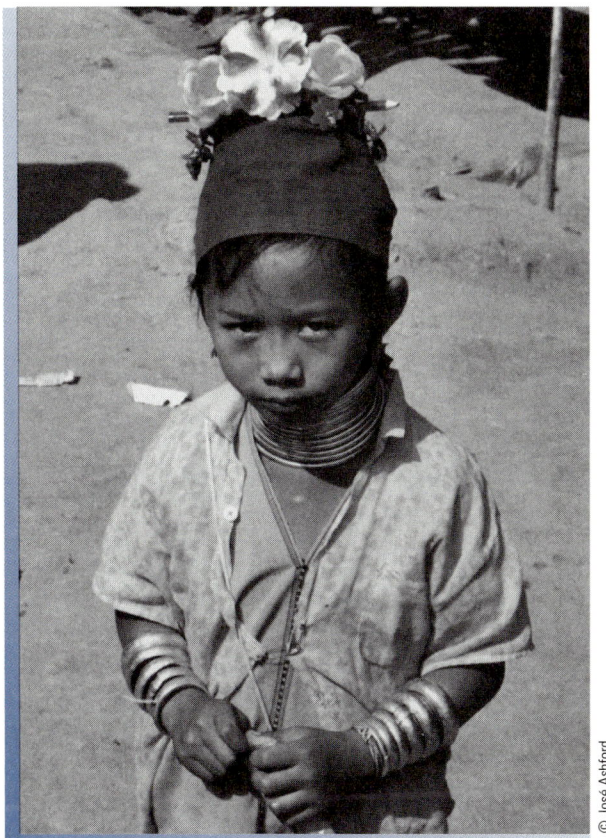

The Karen woman's neck illustrates a desirable trait sought by women in her community. The young girl is learning to shape her neck with the metal rings.

strictly from an outsider's perspective. When outsiders apply their meanings to a situation, they are likely to judge the practices of the other community in terms of their own values. Indeed, if a Kenyan judges American childrearing practices strictly on the basis of their own value system, then the Kenyan is clearly likely to see the behavior of American parents as inappropriate.

Does the cultural relativity of values mean that we should condone all practices of other cultures? As social-work professionals, our aim should be to adopt a perspective that allows us to understand rather than to condone or discredit the behavior or thinking of others. With this understanding, we are in a better position to engage in true dialogue on many issues. For instance, many African American artists who are involved in hip-hop culture believe that the media and the middle-class African American establishment do not understand their form of artistic expression (George, 1998). The 2003 documentary film *Tupac: Resurrection* provides a historical context for the development of Tupac Shakur's concepts of "thug life" and "gangster rap." This contextual information is essential to understanding the significance of his music. However, many outsiders have deemed this form of music inappropriate without understanding its full context and its meaning to the artists and to members of their community.

"To impose a value judgment from one's own community on the cultural practices of another— without understanding how those practices make sense in that community—is ethnocentric" (Rogoff, 2003, p. 15). *Ethnocentrism* is a major challenge for social workers in our increasingly global society. It refers to the tendency to judge or consider the practices of others as immoral, inappropriate, or inferior, based on the values and standard of one's own community.

For example, some women of the Karen, a hill-tribe of Northern Thailand and Laos, wear metal rings that create the appearance of a greatly elongated neck. This traditional practice causes a permanent modification in the body. If these women were to attempt to live without the tubing around their necks, they could die. This elongation of the neck is considered beautiful among the Karen. However, many members of other tribes, and children from Thailand, are frightened by the Karen women. Some people call them "the giraffe women." The origin of this practice is not clear, although some believe it developed to protect the women from tiger attacks when the men left the villages in hunting parties. (Tigers take their prey by the neck and drag them into the jungle.)

To avoid ethnocentrism does not mean that we should condone the continuation of this tribal custom, the degrading of women in hip-hop music, or any other form of cultural practice. Instead, our aim should be to understand the meaning or the significance of the practice from the point of view of cultural insiders. However, to do this is not always easy.

Many Americans do not attempt to understand, for instance, why some Koreans and people from Laos and other Asian countries eat dogs. This type of practice is easily judged if one does not try to understand its context. Whereas Americans are dismayed by societies in which dogs are eaten, communities of nonaffluence judge Americans for the amount of resources that they "waste" on dogs and cats while people around them are starving (Ferrante, 2003). These judgmental intercultural responses are a major challenge facing our global community. And we must not overlook the fact that our sciences and professional practices, although designed to help us understand these cultural differences, also contain many unexamined assumptions (Lerner, 2002). The social and cultural embeddedness of any form of science is an issue that cannot be ignored (Vandermassen, 2005).

Social work, as a profession, assumes that behavior cannot be understood without taking into account the role of the social and cultural environment. For many years, however, psychologists assumed that human behavior could be understood independent of its social context. Early models of psychology assumed that human behavior was determined by universal biological mechanisms that dictated human growth and developmental processes (Lerner, 2002). Indeed, many early psychologists argued that personality was governed by a person's genes and that parents were important not for how they treated their children, but for the genes that they gave them.

It is true that children are born with specific temperaments, but we cannot ignore the fact that the way children are treated in their environment influences how temperament is expressed (Bronfenbrenner & Ceci, 1994; Dweck, 1999; Lerner, 2002). Rothbart and Putnam (2002, pp. 19–20) defined *temperament* as "constitutionally based individual differences in reactivity and self regulation, influenced over time by heredity and experience." (*Reactivity*, in their view, refers to the excitability, responsiveness, or arousal level of the physical and behavioral systems to immediate stimulus events or internal changes.) Like Thomas and Chess (1977), Rothbart and Putnam emphasized in their definition of temperament that the behavioral style of emotionality, attention, and activity levels are closely linked to experiences that influence self-regulation of these biologically based tendencies. (Self-regulation includes inhibitory aspects of fear and other systems of self-regulation that are heavily dependent upon a person's social environment and cultural meaning systems.) We now have compelling evidence that emotional or temperamental tendencies are influenced by the beliefs and goals people hold based on experiences in their social environment (Dweck, 1999).

What Is the Social Environment?

What are the characteristics of the social environment? How does it differ from other environments that influence behavior? Geographers are scientists who have a substantive interest in understanding the associations or connections between people and their **habitat**, or physical environment. Early geographers who subscribed to environmental determinism looked at associations between habitats and human activities as simple cause-and-effect relations. They assumed that the differences observed in cultural activities from the deserts of Arabia to the British Isles were due to the different environments causing different types of human adaptations. However, nondeterminist positions eventually developed in the field and assumed that "the physical environment offers people a variety of possibilities from which to select ways of using their habitat" (Nelson, Gabler, & Vining, 1995, p. 10). This new approach came to be known as **possibilism** (Nelson, Gabler, & Vining, 1995).

Scientists not only recognized that the physical environment can place limits on behavior, but that this is also true of the social environment. The sociologist Shils (1985, p. 805) wrote:

> Human actions are limited or determined by environment. Human beings become what they are at any given moment not by their own free decisions, taken rationally and in full knowledge of the conditions, but under the pressure of circumstances which delimit their

range of choice and which also fix their objectives and the standards by which they make choices.

Shils suggested that people's choices are never entirely free. Their decisions are determined to some extent by environment, including the social environment. The **social environment** refers here to all the expectations, motives, and incentives that place limits on behavior and that are constructed by other people who live in a person's social world (Kornblum, 2002; 2003). Social workers are most concerned about understanding the social environment (the people, families, groups, organizations, and communities) within which a person's biography unfolds. This is why the Council on Social Work Education has established the explicit expectation that students of social work understand how a person's behavior is influenced by membership in different-sized social systems (dyads, families, small groups, communities, and organizations). "Certainly each individual has unique choices to make in life, but the social world into which the person was born—Native American reservation, an urban ghetto, a comfortable suburb, or an immigrant enclave in a strange city—determines to varying degrees what those choices will be" (Kornblum, 2003, p. 5). The field of social work has historically assumed that social problems cannot be understood by limiting analysis to the inner life of particular individuals and their relationships to family or close friends. Consider the spate of school shootings during the late 1990s.

In October 1997, in Pearl, Mississippi, Luke Woodham killed his mother and then went to school and killed three students and wounded seven. In that same year, Michael Carneal killed three students at a high school prayer meeting in West Paducah, Kentucky. In March 1998, Mitchell Johnson and Andrew Golden killed four students and a teacher in Jonesboro, Arkansas. This tragedy was followed by a shooting in Edinboro, Pennsylvania, at an eighth-grade graduation dance, where a 14-year-old boy named Andrew Wurst shot and killed a teacher and wounded another teacher and two students. On May 21, 1998, Kip Kinkel walked into a school cafeteria in Springfield, Oregon, and shot 24 students, two of whom died.

James Garbarino (1999), an expert on human development in areas of violence and trauma, considers the year between 1997 and 1998 a turning point in our country's experience and understanding of kids who murder. All the acts we just listed were committed by white youths from the suburbs or small rural towns. The public is now recognizing that violence is not limited to urban areas with high concentrations of minority youths.

What about the Hispanic youth who opens fire on a street full of children with an automatic weapon, or the African American kid who shoots two boys who made fun of his shoes, or the Asian American kids who open fire on a store where other kids from school are hanging out? We rarely see demands by the media and other social institutions to make sense of these acts of violence. "Is it easier for the media and the general public to forget or demonize the low-income minority kids who kill?" (Garbarino, 1999, p. 3).

Since the publication of Garbarino's book *Lost Boys: Why Our Sons Turn Violent and How We Can Save Them*, there have been additional school shootings in Colorado, Minnesota, and Georgia. The most noteworthy of these events is probably the Columbine High School shootings in the town of Littleton, Colorado, in which 14 people were killed, including the two perpetrators. The two assailants in this tragedy were members of a group of outcasts known in the school as "the Trenchcoat Mafia." Although this group is considered by some theorists to be a youth gang, its upper-middle-class members have escaped being branded with many of the negative labels commonly assigned to members of urban gangs.

The differences in the ways various groups in society respond to events involving violent human behavior illustrate that social workers cannot underestimate the role played by social-environmental factors in understanding social and behavioral issues. Events of this nature are not isolated errors in socialization processes or the result of individuals being intrinsically bad. The perpetrators are part of an environment that influences their behavior, as well as how we react to it.

Cultural Competence, Globalization, and Our Diverse Society

Health authorities in the United States estimate that in just 30 years, 40% of Americans will belong to ethnic and cultural groups that are predominantly of non-European origin (President's New Freedom Commission, 2003). People from these groups often must access social and health services that are not culturally or linguistically appropriate for them.

The U.S. Department of Health and Human Services (HHS) Office of Minority Health (OMH) is committed to ensuring that all people entering our health-care system receive equitable treatment (1999). This governmental agency has developed national healthcare standards for Culturally, Linguistically Appropriate Services (CLAS standards) to help health-care professionals eliminate disparities in health care that can be attributed to culturally and linguistically inappropriate services.

The authors of the CLAS standards quoted Michael Katz about the significance of culture in describing the key concepts guiding its document. Katz wrote:

> Culture defines how health care information is received, how rights and protections are exercised, what is considered to be a health problem, how symptoms and concerns about the problem are expressed, who should provide treatment for the problem, and what type of treatment should be given. In sum, because health care is a cultural construct, arising from beliefs about the nature of disease and the human body, cultural issues are actually central in the delivery of health services treatment and preventive interventions. By understanding, valuing, and incorporating the cultural differences of America's diverse population and examining one's own health-related values and beliefs, health care organizations, practitioners, and others can support a health care system that responds appropriately to, and directly serve the unique needs of populations whose cultures may be different from the prevailing culture" (personal communication, November 1998).

Katz's view is consistent with calls from other professional organizations, including the National Association of Social Workers and the Council of Social Work Education, for increased cultural competence. The National Association of Social Workers' (NASW) code of ethics requires that social workers "understand culture and its function in human behavior and society, recognizing the strengths that exist in all cultures" (NASW, 1996, Section 1.05, p. 9).

The notion of **cultural competency** has been promoted for many years as a solution to the barriers to care and help encountered by ethnic, racial, and foreign-born groups in many of our service systems. It implies that professionals need to be able to work effectively within the contexts of the cultural beliefs, behaviors, and needs presented by diverse consumers and their communities, including individuals from groups that are marginalized because of religious beliefs, physical disabilities, social class, or sexual orientation. In order to do so, one must accept the challenge that culture is a major contributor to working effectively with people and their communities.

The United States has witnessed dramatic social changes since the early 1900s. In 1900, one in eight Americans was not white. Between 1900 and 1950, minorities represented 13% of the total population. The 2000 census indicated that 30% of the population—more than double that of the first half of the century—was composed of ethnic minorities. In the state of California, ethnic minorities constitute the majority of the population (Zane, Nagayama-Hall, Sue, Young, & Nunez, 2004). And in 1998, the number of African Americans, Latinos, American Indians, and Asian Americans nationwide was estimated at 74.9 million. If this population constituted an independent country, it would have more people than Great Britain, France, Italy, or Spain (Pollard & O'Hare, 1999). These are major changes in the ethnic makeup of our society.

The changes in the country's population are impacting all facets of American life, including its health and welfare institutions. As Anderson and Taylor wrote, "Understanding diversity is critical to understanding society because the fundamental patterns of social change and social structure are increasingly patterned by diverse group experiences" (2003, p. 11). Global communications also influence how people conceptualize their sense of who they are and their patterns of relating with one another (Castells, 2002).

Today, no society can be understood without examining the influences of the global economy, global communications, the information age, and other aspects of the globalization process (Castells, 2002). Some of the changes introduced by globalization are welcomed. But clearly, some terrorists involved with the 9/11 tragedy were motivated by threats to their established social order posed by freedoms enjoyed by women in the West—in dress, in sexual behavior, and in other areas that they observed in movies (Chau, 2004; Kornblum, 2003). Similarly, there are individuals in the United States who are threatened by the exporting of industrial production, the decline of rural communities, the "McDonaldization" of social life, and other changes induced by different aspects of globalization (Chau, 2004; Ritzer, 2004). These changes are all part of a new social context that is influencing our understanding of human change and behavior processes. Social workers need to develop effectiveness with the new person-in-environment contexts that are being produced by the rapid social changes of globalization and its attendant diversification of our society (Appleby, 2001). The interconnectivity of the world is increasing in various life domains and has corresponding implications for many behavioral practices.

Dimensions of Human Behavior and the Social Environment

What are appropriate measures for assessing human behavior? Are there different measures for assessing the social environment (Friedman & Wach, 1999)? Social-work practitioners must be clear about how they will systematically assess, measure, or describe the characteristics of their clients and their various life troubles in our changing social context. Any assessments practitioners make will depend on their perspective. As Anderson and Carter (1990) have noted, any viewpoint is relative to one's own perceptions and to the system being described, as well as to its environment. Social-work professionals seek a perspective of human behavior that is consistent with the principles of their professional code of ethics, their commitments to respecting individual uniqueness, the strengths and empowerment perspectives, ecological theory, and principles from General System Theory.

Many terms can be used to classify or define individuals and their environments. The sciences have systems for classifying and measuring areas of interest. Likewise, social-work professionals are expected to use empirically validated classifications of behavior that transcend the biases associated with "common sense" and other forms of "conventional wisdom." These scientific classifications are needed to make important distinctions about client functioning. If practitioners lack categories or classifications for making such distinctions, they are unlikely to understand their clients' needs and concerns. Although social work has not established a unified system of human-behavior classification, it has advocated the use of a biopsychosocial approach to understanding human behavior and the social environment.

The framework we use in this textbook subscribes to this approach. It is conceived of as a perspective and not as a theory. This perspective offers practitioners a way to consider various points of view and integrate them in their assessments of human behavior as it occurs at individual, family, group, organizational, community, and societal levels. The biopsychosocial approach is based on principles from systems thinking that assume that "[e]ach person is composed of molecules, cells and organs; each person is also a member of a family, community, culture, nation and world" (Eisendrath, 1988, p. 36). The fundamental assumptions underlying this framework are as follows:

- There are three basic dimensions for assessing human behavior and the social environment: biophysical, psychological, and social.
- These three dimensions are conceptualized as a system of biopsychosocial functioning.
- This system involves multiple systems that are organized in a hierarchy of levels from the smallest (cellular) to the largest (social).
- This ascending hierarchy of systems is in a constant state of interaction with other living systems and with other nonliving components of the system's physical environment.

We assume that the multiple systems in this framework are needed to guide practitioners in understanding human behavior. They incorporate units of analysis for assessing the interaction of person-in-environment transactions. "The interactive process takes place at various levels from micro to macro at the same time, and at all these levels it can be analyzed theoretically and empirically using two perspectives: current and developmental" (Magnusson & Torestad, 1992, p. 91). Whereas the **current perspective** involves assessing how biological, psychological, and social systems influence current states of affairs, the **developmental perspective** focuses on how these systems interact in leading up to the current state of affairs. These dimensions provide perspectives on human behavior that form the bases for various kinds of intervention strategies. They also allow social workers to maintain their commitment to taking into account strengths and competencies in person-environment transactions when designing intervention strategies. Practitioners all too often focus on presenting problems and fail to zero in on areas of strength that can facilitate change in a person's situation (Saleebey, 1992b; Saleebey, 2001).

This book introduces social-work students to a multidimensional framework for integrating knowledge and theory from the biological, psychological, and social perspectives on human behavior. We stress the need for social workers to take into account the interactions of these dimensions in assessing people and situations in their social environment.

Multidimensional Framework

The **biophysical dimension** of the multidimensional framework consists of the biochemical systems, cell systems, organ systems, and physiological systems (Nurcombe & Gallagher, 1986; Nurcombe, 2000). This dimension, which is arranged hierarchically, helps in the assessment of an individual's physical growth and development and is described in Chapter 2. The functioning of this system refers to the balanced exchange of energy among its biophysical components. This dimension relies on biological theory and seeks to identify and explain the relationship between biological and physiological mechanisms that influence human behavior. Any change in this dimension will have corresponding changes in the other dimensions inside and outside this system. Humans are limited by their biological heritage and their health status, and social workers need to understand these potential limits on human behavior (Saleebey, 2001).

Regardless of your innate qualities, physical factors affecting your health status, such as extreme sleep deprivation, can place limits on your performance. For this reason, it is important in any assessment to identify physical strengths (factors that can enhance physical performance) and physical hazards (factors that can impede physical performance) that may affect an individual's behavior in a specific situation or circumstance. The biophysical dimension helps us look at the person as a physical organism or as a biological entity. Structural mechanisms and undefined impulses are the physiological foundations for the roles people play. In some role contexts, the physical foundations are more essential to behavioral outcomes than others (Gerth & Mills, 1953).

The **psychological dimension** represents the systems that contribute to the organization or integration of the individual's mental processes. This dimension involves several functions designed to help the person satisfy his or her needs. These psychological functions involve the systems of information processing and cognitive development, communication, attitudes and regulation of emotions, self-concept and identity, social cognition and self-regulation, and psychological strengths and hazards. These psychological systems are described in detail in Chapter 3.

The **social dimension** refers to the systems of social relationships that a person interacts with individually or in a group (Nurcombe & Gallagher, 1986; Nurcombe, 2000). This dimension is described in Chapter 4. The social groups and relationships included in this system are families, communities, and other support systems; gay and lesbian relationships; cultural groups and ethnic groups; and social institutions such as churches, political parties, schools, health-care providers, and welfare services.

This dimension contains categories that help practitioners locate the conduct of individuals in various social institutions and other relevant social systems. Also stressed in the social dimension are issues involving a person's social positions in racial, ethnic, gender, sexual-orientation, and other groups. Conceptual models are needed to guide how we study the human development of people of color and the consequences of color in their social lives (Garcia Coll et al., 1996). In the categories included in this dimension, we stress both social position and social-stratification constructs. By focusing on these concepts, we can place issues of social class, culture, ethnicity, and sexual orientation at the core of our assessment process, rather than at the periphery (Garcia Coll et al., 1996; Johnson et al., 2003). In addition, we can examine how these positional, institutional, and social-system variables serve as strengths or as hazards (risks) to social functioning.

An emerging paradigm in the developmental sciences recognizes a need for integrating the sociological, psychological, and biobehavioral approaches to understanding developmental concerns (The Carolina Consortium on Human Development). In this paradigm, patterns of adaptation represent interactions across levels within and without the person. Exhibit 1.1 illustrates a multilevel concept of human development that subscribes to this approach.

This book adopts the assumptions stressed in this new synthesis by emphasizing that development cannot be understood without taking into account biopsychosocial interactions across multiple levels.

The Biopsychosocial Interaction

Individuals and their environments represent multiple systems that extend from the biochemical to the psychosocial realm (Nurcombe & Gallagher, 1986; Puri, Laking, & Treasaden, 1996). The biological realm of an individual extends from the molecular to the molar, or structural, level; the psychological realm extends from the emotional to the behavioral. The social realm of an individual includes the family and other groups, the neighborhood, the cultural set-

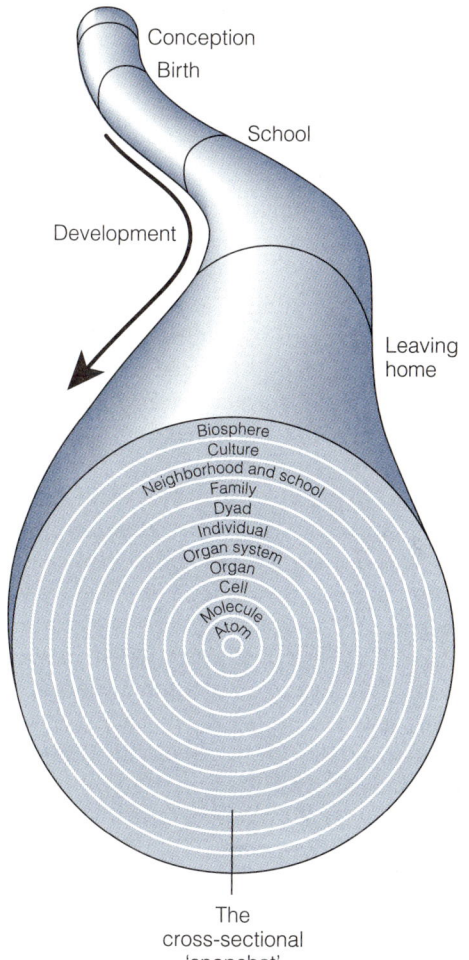

EXHIBIT 1.1 Multilevel concept of human development

ting, and the context of society. Such multiple sources of influence can be described as a person within a body, within a family, within a state, within a country, within the world, within the solar system, within the galaxy, and within the universe. This approach is sometimes referred to as "developmental contextualism" (Lerner, 2002).

A person refers to who he or she is individually (genetic makeup, past learning, role combinations, role history, and so forth) and socially or environmentally (the social forces and people in the person's environment). Behavior is the result of interactions between the person and the environment. No single factor can be solely responsible for causing a behavioral response. Multiple factors, within a complex system, interact to produce specific behaviors. When we think of the biopsychosocial interaction, we recognize that certain biological problems, cognitive processes, and/or environments can increase the likelihood that a particular behavioral response will develop. A person's biological makeup can limit his or her capacity to respond to the environment in certain ways.

Biology is not destiny, however. We must also consider psychological and social or environmental variables in accounting for human behavior. For example, attention-deficit/hyperactivity disorder (ADHD) in children can be genetically influenced. However, some children who possess this genetic component will not develop ADHD, indicating that biological factors alone do not account for the disorder. A child with a small tendency toward hyperactivity could be influenced by a parent in such a way as to reinforce and promote more hyperactive behavior. Conversely, a child exposed to high amounts of lead—through lead-based paint, for instance—might develop symptoms of ADHD, yet the symptoms can be moderated by appropriate environmental responses.

The influence of environment on ADHD illustrates an important developmental concept—**human plasticity**. Human physical and psychosocial structures are subject to changes introduced by variations in the environment. For example, it has been demonstrated in a seminal study that the setting has a definite influence on personality and on social and intellectual functioning, independent of a person's genetic makeup (Brim and Kagan, 1980).

Social workers must understand that adequate explanations of human behavior need to be multidimensional. Historically, social work seems either to have emphasized the total picture through a systems or holistic mode, or to have focused on specific components with highly specific theories that often do not take into account important contextual factors. Unfortunately, neither approach is adequate. Systems explanations are useful for understanding the total picture of the client but are not specific enough to be helpful in planning prevention and intervention. Social workers must consider the broad picture in assessing a client and then move to an understanding of some of the factors that could be influencing the client's behavior. We suggest examining independent factors and formulating hypotheses within a framework of broader systems issues. Moving from individual factors to social and environmental factors will help you think about human behavior from a multidimensional perspective.

Case and Situation Conceptualizations

Case or situation conceptualizations in social-work assessments provide a description of what a client and his or her situation are like, as well as an explanation of why the client and the situation are the way they are (Berman, 1997; Eells, 1997). They offer hypotheses about the effects of biological, psychological, and social factors on behavior as it occurs at individual, group, organizational, community, and societal levels. In some contexts, case or situation conceptualizations are referred to as "case formulations" (Eells, 1997; Porzelius, 2002). Like any other type of formulation, they offer a systematic way of coming to an explanation or understanding of a problematic situation.

Based on the findings from the hypotheses generated in case formulations, practitioners of social work design plans of prevention and intervention for individuals, families, groups, communities, organizations, and societies. Case or situation formulations vary in terms of the concepts or theories used. There is no one concept for guiding the development of cases in social work or any other human-service profession. There are no universal theories that must be used in conceptualizing people, behaviors, problems, and situations (Peterson, 1992; Porzelius, 2002). Yet "[a]ll assessment is guided by some conception that tells investigators where to look, even if it is silent about what they will find" (Peterson, 1992, p. 128).

Research has documented that practitioners commonly apply preferred theoretical orientations in developing case formulations (Beutler & Harwood, 1995). Not very long ago, case or situation formulations in social work were guided by grand theories of change and development typically named after their originators: Freud, Erikson, Mead, Merton, Parsons, Perlman, Rank, Richmond, and so on. They were considered grand theories because each provided a powerful framework that guided all the questions asked by practitioners in gathering information needed to understand issues involving human behavior (Renninger & Amsel, 1997). However, "competing theories have existed side by side, and integration of theories has seldom or never taken place" (Magnusson & Torestad, 1992, p. 89).

One of the fundamental threats to the integration of theories in conceptualizing human behavior is the practice of seeking its determinants either in external social conditions or in people's internal dispositions (Bronfenbrenner, 1996; The Carolina Consortium on Human Development, 1996; Magnusson & Cairns, 1996; Magnusson & Torestad, 1992). A key theme in this book is that human behavior cannot be understood by artificially separating the biological, psychological, and social systems. Assessments must take all three into account.

In using this approach to conceptualizing cases, whether they involve an individual or some larger social system, we recommend two procedures. First, establish hypotheses for each dimension of the multidimensional framework. This procedure clarifies in a concise fashion the main concerns in the case situation. Second, provide a detailed case analysis including evidence that backs up the statements contained in the initial hypotheses. The analysis should include a comprehensive study of strengths (strong points, positive features, successes, coping strategies, skills, factors that can augment change efforts) and weaknesses (concerns, issues, problems, symptoms, intervention barriers, and so forth) based on the questions systematically covered in the multidimensional framework (Berman, 1997).

In developing a case conceptualization, you will use information from many different sources, such as client interviews, collateral interviews with family members or significant others, rapid-assessment instruments, psychological tests, behavioral observations, key informants, community planning documents, and local oral and written histories. In organizing and evaluating this information, and in trying to identify factors that have caused and maintained a person's concerns, it is important to apply more than one construct (Porzelius, 2002). For example, although a person might present with depression after a specific argument with her boss, broader conflicts might be important targets for change in designing an appropriate plan of intervention. What combination of factors could be contributing to the individual's depression? Are physical factors, such as mood changes caused by menopause or the onset of another type of physical illness, contributing to her problem? Does she have communication problems with her husband? Is she experiencing broader role conflicts about work, identity, career, and other life choices? (Porzelius, 2002) If these factors are overlooked, the intervention can ignore important targets for change that are maintaining the client's problem. For this reason, practitioners must have a broad command of concepts to guide their assessments, including information about a person's spirituality.

Reflections on the Spiritual Dimension by Margaret Waller

The most beautiful thing we can experience is the mysterious. It is the source of all true art and all science. He to whom this emotion is a stranger, who can no longer pause to wonder and stand rapt in awe, is as good as dead: his eyes are closed.

—Albert Einstein

What do we mean by *spirituality*? Why is it important for social workers to understand the spiritual dimension of experience along with the biological, psychological, and social dimensions?

Spirituality is the domain of human existence that pertains to the essence of every human being and to awareness of something greater than ourselves. Our relationship to the divine, however we define it, enables us to make sense of our lives and provides us with a sense of stability, guidance, purpose, power, and direction (Bullis, 1996; Schuster & Ashburn, 1992).

Whereas *spirituality* refers to subjective experiences of relationship to a universal power, *religion* refers to formal, institutionalized systems of belief including dogmas, creeds, denominational identity, and related rituals (Bullis, 1996; Zastrow & Kirst-Ashman, 1990). Most religions maintain that human beings experience a process of spiritual development over time (Swinburne, 1986) and describe the stages of that development in a similar way. Theologian Caroline Myss (1996) has highlighted the parallels between these stages in Hindu, Judaic, and Christian spiritual development. Some human-development theorists (Erikson, 1988; Fowler, 1981; Goldman, 1968) have adopted this developmental view of spirituality and described stages of spiritual development that parallel stages of development in the biological, psychological, and social domains.

Linguistically, there is a close connection between spirituality and human development. The words *spirit*, *inspire*, and *inspiration* come from the Latin word *spiritus*, meaning "wind" or "breath." So *spirit* means "something that inspires or gives life." The word *psychology* comes from the Greek word *psyche*, meaning "spirit" or "soul." Taken literally, the word *psychology* means "the study of the spirit or soul." The root of the English word *health* is the Greek word *holos*, which means "something that is whole or complete." These linguistic connections reflect a belief, common to many cultures and religions, that spirituality, human development, and healing are inextricably intertwined.

Given the central role of spirituality in all cultures, the spiritual domain will have an effect on what takes place between social worker and client (Green, 1995), whether or not spirituality is openly discussed (Canda, 1989). If client and social worker come from different spiritual orientations, language and behavior may have different meanings. Therefore, understanding the client's spiritual beliefs is essential to culturally competent practice (Green, 1995). For all of these reasons, an examination of the spiritual domain completes the biopsychosocial understanding of human functioning (Schuster & Ashburn, 1992).

Beckett and Johnson (1995) have suggested several possible explanations for the recent increase in interest in spirituality within the social-work profession, including recognition of the success of twelve-step programs, which acknowledge the existence of a higher power; systems theories, which emphasize a holistic approach to understanding individuals; increased interaction with Eastern cultures, within which spirituality is an integral part of existence; and research results indicating the importance of spirituality to particular populations. Bullis (1996) has described ways to incorporate the spiritual domain in assessment and intervention and has presented strategies for collaborating with spiritual healers.

In her classic work *Common Human Needs*, first published in 1945, social-work theorist Charlotte Towle asserted that spiritual needs "must be seen as distinct needs and they must also be seen in relation to other human needs" (Towle, 1945, p. 8). The social-work profession, long estranged from its spiritual roots, is now beginning to come full circle and reawaken to the importance of the spiritual domain of human experience.

Applying the Multidimensional Framework

To understand a person's total functioning, the social worker makes an assessment of all aspects of the person's life and experience. It is helpful to take a hypotheses approach to each primary dimension and its underlying functions. Hypotheses from the biophysical, psychological, and social dimensions are posed in order to examine possible etiology and explanations of the client's functioning. Social workers can use a hypotheses approach to help guide questioning and data gathering during the assessment phase. The identification of potential causal factors should include consideration of precipitants/activating situations to the problem, predisposing and/or risk factors for the problem, and factors that are maintaining the problem.

The following outline suggests specific areas of questioning to consider for each hypothesis in making an evaluation of a client.

1. Biophysical hypotheses
   a. Biophysical growth and development
   b. Biophysical strengths and hazards
2. Psychological hypotheses
   a. Cognitive development and information processing
   b. Communication
   c. Attitudes and emotions
   d. Self and identity
   e. Social cognition and regulation
   f. Psychological strengths and hazards
3. Social hypotheses
   a. Families and groups
   b. Communities and support systems
   c. Organizations and social institutions
   d. Multicultural and gender considerations
   e. Social strengths and hazards

We expand on this outline by presenting a brief overview of how this framework can be applied in gathering data in an assessment. But first, we provide examples of some potential assessment considerations to use in making your evaluation. This is not a conclusive list of assessment questions; other information can and should be considered. Each of the developmental chapters in this book goes into further detail and provides other considerations for you to use. When reading the case study at the end of each developmental chapter, keep these suggested considerations in mind. Also, think of additional questions you would want to ask or obtain answers to when evaluating the client's problem in each case study, including the case of the Perez family, located online at http://info.wadsworth.com/ashford.

Biophysical Hypotheses

Physical or biological hypotheses refer to assumptions about the client's functioning as a result of a biological catalyst. Examples include influences from the autonomic nervous system or the neuroendocrine system, physical dependence on a drug, or a biological reaction to an environmental event. The social worker should seek to understand the client's general physical condition. Assess information about the client's medical history, including any diseases, neurological impairments, or physical impairments; current physical condition; any medications being taken; and any nonprescribed drugs. A person's psychological or social-functioning problems can be affected by any of these physical factors. Any physical problem that interferes with or impairs sleep, energy, or appetite will have consequences for the psychological and social systems. That is, a client's problem may be related to or a direct result of the following biological determinants.

Biophysical Growth and Development

Prenatal Growth and Development. Assessment considerations include mother's nutritional status during pregnancy; mother's health status; father's health status; length of gestation; prenatal substance abuse by mother; pregnancy complications; family genetic history; genetic abnormalities; chromosomal abnormalities; and physical birth defects (cleft palate, heart defects).

Client's History of Attaining Developmental Milestones. Assessment considerations include when client took first steps; said first word; fed self; dressed self; achieved toilet training; had first menses or first nocturnal emission; and developed secondary sex characteristics.

Client's General Health Status. Assessment considerations include stability of weight; regularity of menstrual periods; regularity of sleep-wake cycle; level of physical activity and level of nutrition; presence of biochemical imbalances; presence of physically handicapping conditions; use of substances such as tobacco, alcohol, and drugs; assessment of client's general appearance (does client look his or her stated age?); and client's ability to perform activities of daily living (ADLs).

Biophysical Strengths

High energy levels, good sleep patterns, and overall physical vitality can be important elements to capitalize on in designing effective interventions. Good genetic history is an important asset for a variety of developmental and health outcomes. Good physical appearance, history free from physical disabilities, and other physical characteristics are also important resources. Early physical maturation can be another example of a physical resource that can be capitalized on in designing appropriate intervention strategies.

Biophysical Hazards

Assessment considerations include family history of heart disease; respiratory problems; cancer; diabetes; health status of close relatives; causes of death of close relatives and their age at death; client's current and past health status; and presence of symptoms related to a major illness. Porzelius (2002, p. 8) wrote, "People who are unattractive, disfigured, in a wheelchair, or overweight are often exposed to serious discrimination and prejudice, which could contribute to psychological problems. Sometimes, in a misguided attempt to deny any personal prejudice, therapists may simply ignore an undesirable characteristic, such as overweight." By ignoring physical characteristics, the practitioner may miss important information about how the person is responded to by others, a factor that could be a significant target of potential change.

Psychological Hypotheses

The social worker must consider many relevant psychological hypotheses when making an assessment in this dimension. Psychological data can be gathered through a variety of means. Most relevant to the social worker is the individual or family interview. In addition to the traditional psychosocial interview, social workers are making use of semi-structured interviews, as well as psychological tests, behavioral observations, personality tests, and rapid-assessment instruments.

A client's problem may be either related to or a direct result of the following psychological determinants.

Cognitive Development and Information Processing

Client's Attention Span, Memory, Concentration, and Capacity for Abstract Thought. Assessment considerations include ability to focus attention; ability to complete tasks appropriate to age; and capacity for memory.

Client's Reality Base. Assessment considerations include client's cognitive functioning; client's ability to discern reality; and content of client's thoughts and perceptions.

Client's Learning Abilities and Performance. Assessment considerations include school performance; problem-solving abilities; and capacity for insight and reflection.

Client's Language Ability and Vocabulary. Assessment considerations include bilingual expectations; use of language; and general verbal and nonverbal abilities in self-expression.

Client's Self-Perception. Assessment considerations include negative and positive perceptions of self; view of self with others; comparison of self with expectations of others; and perception of what others think about the person.

Client's Emotional Responses. Assessment considerations include full range of emotions evident and excessive emotions such as anger, sadness, and frustration.

Client's Self-Statements. Assessment considerations include content of self-talk; amount of irrational ideas present; and relationship between self-talk and problem behavior (for example, fear and hopelessness).

Social Cognition and Regulation

Client's Social Knowledge about Others. Assessment considerations include client's understanding of social interactions; client's view of friendship; and client's expectations of others.

Client's Capacity for Empathy. Assessment considerations include client's capacity for perspective taking; client's sense of morality; and client's interpersonal understanding of others.

Client's Capacity for Impulse Control. Assessment considerations include stability in jobs, relationships, play activities, and other interpersonal relationships.

Client's Capacity for Emotional Regulation. Assessment considerations include assessment of affect and mood changes; whether the affect is appropriate to the situation; and the duration and intensity of moods.

Client's Social Skills. Assessment considerations include appropriateness of client's social interactions; client's knowledge of social skills; and client's ability to communicate effectively.

Client's Social Problem-Solving Skills. Assessment considerations include client's ability to generate solutions to problems; client's ability to think of consequences; and client's means-ends thinking (cognition of steps needed to solve problems).

Client's Maladaptive Behavior Patterns. Assessment considerations include client's behavioral responses to problem situations; client's patterns of behavior that lead to difficulties for self, others, or society; and client's desired behavior changes and patterns.

Client's Coping Skills. Assessment of how clients have handled stress; poor social conditions; threats; and environmental, biological, or other concerns.

Psychological Strengths

Strengths may include an easy temperament, a good regulation of emotions, a high intelligence quotient, good emotional intelligence, an extroverted personality, a sense of mastery, a belief in changeable social traits, and other psychological qualities. Also included are a positive history of experience with parents, authority figures, and significant others. In addition, if a client has had experiences of being valued by others, subjected to positive discipline in critical life stages, and other positive life experiences, these would be considered psychological strengths.

Psychological Hazards

Client's Experience of Past Life Events. Assessment considerations include client's description of significant events in childhood; experience with parents and other adult figures (especially whether any physical or sexual abuse occurred); experience with emotional abuse; experience with peers; psychosocial living environment; history of mental disorders; and history of use of antidepressants or antipsychotic medications.

Client's Experience with Recent Life Events. Assessment considerations include client's description of significant life events in recent years; recent experiences with adult and peer figures (especially involving events such as divorce or parents' divorce, or death of a loved one); present use of antidepressants or antipsychotics; and use of other prescription drugs.

Social Hypotheses

The social worker's assessment extends beyond the biological and psychological dimensions to include the social dimension. Social factors include the family, community, and other social support systems; access to resources; and the impinging social environment. What are the client's social relationships? And what is the environmental context of the client's social relationships? For example, does the client live in poverty? Does the client face racism on a daily basis? The social worker must assess how the client is viewed by society, by the social systems he or she interacts with, and by the individuals directly involved with the client on a daily basis, such as friends and family.

A client's problem may be related to or a direct result of the following sociological or environmental determinants.

Families and Groups

Family's Boundaries, Role Systems, and Subsystems. Assessment considerations include open or closed family system; family structure (for example, enmeshed or disengaged); and how the family defines itself.

Family's Patterns of Communication. Assessment considerations include content and process of interaction; patterns of conflict; and verbal and nonverbal expressions of affect.

Family's Roles. Assessment considerations include role assignments within the family; satisfaction with roles; expectations and definitions of roles; allocation of power; and role strain and support.

Groups the Client Interacts With. Assessment considerations include patterns of interaction in peer and work groups; influence of group norms and other group dynamics; and behavior of the individual in the group.

Communities and Support Systems

Communities the Client Is a Member Of. Assessment considerations include the degree of attachment the client has toward the place they live; ethnic communities and the significance of ethnic location for the client's identity; the unique values adopted by the person's community; the supports and strengths identified within the person's community; and whether the community is inhibiting or promoting development.

Support Systems Available to the Client. Assessment considerations include social supports (family, friends, extended family, social-support groups and self-help groups); institutional supports (child support, welfare, health benefits); access to resources (day care, recreational facilities, police protection); barriers to support systems; and need for new resources and support systems.

Institutional Contributions to Client's Problem. Assessment considerations include whether the structural aspects of the person's environment are constraining or promoting certain behavior choices; whether the institutions are in conflict; and whether the institutions fit with existing social conditions.

Organizational Contributions. Assessments should include informal norms; formal organization rules; lines of communication; span of control; and styles of leadership.

Multicultural and Gender Hypotheses

Assessment considerations include ethnic or gender identity; degree of acculturation; sexual orientation; language barriers; amount of interaction within and outside the ethnic group; and expectations influenced by cultural, gender, or sexual-orientation considerations. Regarding cultural, gender, or sexual-orientation considerations, we recommend taking into account the positional variables identified by Garcia Coll and her colleagues for assessing people of color (1996). (We believe that the model can be extended to other positional variables, including social class, sexual orientation, and disabilities.) Their conceptual model focuses the assessment on the unique ecological or social environmental circumstances faced by persons of color. **Positional variables** are considered the attributes of a person that societies use in processes of stratification (race, social class, ethnicity, and gender) (Johnson et al., 2003). "These positional factors represent social addresses that influence or create alternative developmental pathways" (Garcia Coll et al., 1996, p. 1895).

Practitioners need to understand how these factors affect human behavior. In most instances, they do not directly influence outcomes. These positional variables are mediated through the pervasive social processes of racism, prejudice, discrimination, and oppression (Johnson et al., 2003). We examine each of these variables in more detail in Chapter 4. The model developed by Garcia Coll and her colleagues (1996) demonstrates how the positional variable of race operates through the creation of segregated contexts that have a pervasive influence on the development and behavior of children of color (see Exhibit 1.2). Segregation in this model is considered a multifaceted concept. It combines residential, economic, social, and psychological dimensions that are influenced by processes of segregation. Because segregation leads to nonshared experiences and distinct conditions that children of color face daily, these processes impact directly what Garcia Coll and her colleagues have termed **inhibiting and promoting environments**. Examples of these environments include schools, neighborhoods, and other central social institutions. Children of color develop in these environments, which directly influence their personal and family development.

Social Strengths

The person's life experiences, language, cultural traditions, cultural continuity, family supports, and other resources must be identified. Resources from friends, neighbors, and other informal supports are key strengths that can augment intervention plans.

Social Hazards

Assessment considerations include high rates of unemployment; divorce; poverty; discrimination; inadequate social institutions; and impoverished neighborhoods.

Selecting Interventions Based on Hypotheses

When you select a hypothesis as a way of explaining a person's behavior, it should help you select an appropriate intervention. For example, if your assessment suggests that the best hypothesis is based on the client's biochemical makeup or brain chemistry, then an intervention that changes physiology should

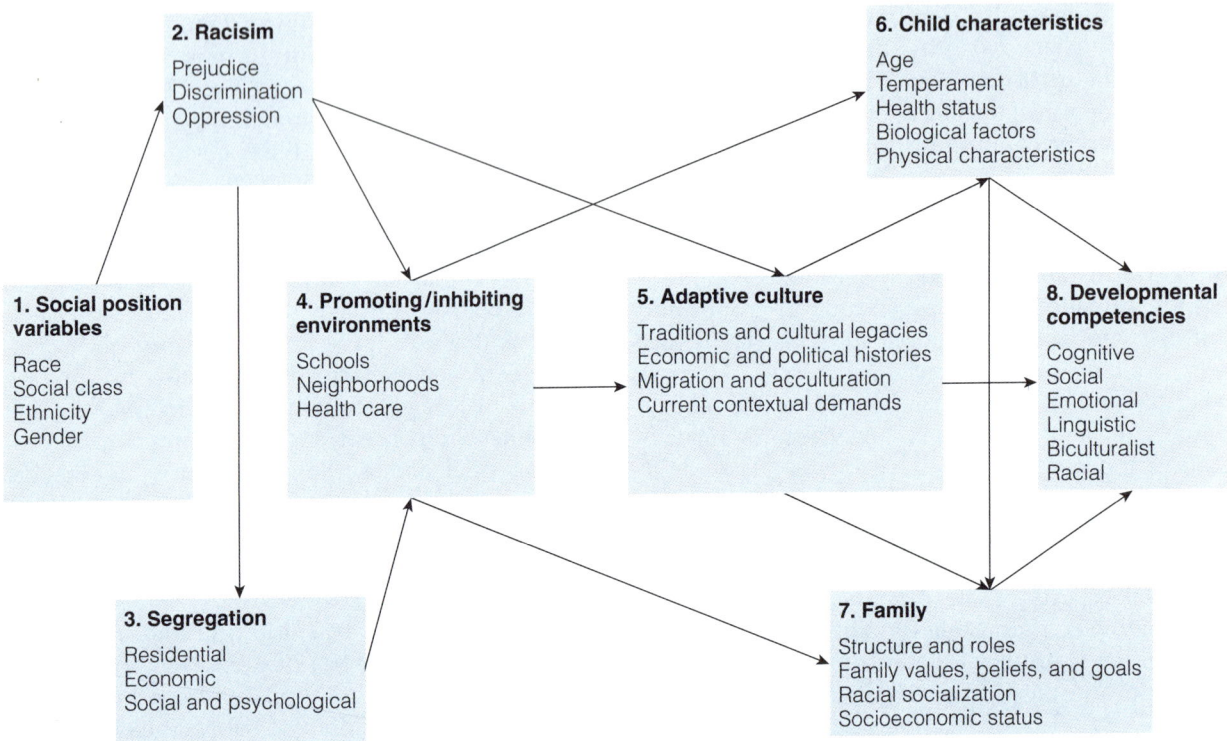

EXHIBIT 1.2 Integrative model for study of developmental competencies in minority children

SOURCE: From C. Garcia Coll et al., "An integrative model for the study of developmental competencies in minority children," in *Child development*, 67: 1891–1914. Copyright © 1996 Society for Research in Child Development.

be considered. If a client is diagnosed as having a schizophrenic disorder caused by biological factors, then he or she should be referred for psychotropic drug treatment (of course, the client might also need psychosocial treatment).

If you develop a hypothesis that a person's difficulty is caused by inappropriate social learning, then the intervention will focus on providing the client with a new learning experience. For example, if the person has developed a serious phobic disorder of open spaces (*agoraphobia*), and you believe it is related to negative learning experiences, then the intervention will attempt to provide new, positive learning experiences, such as contact desensitization, the goal of which is to induce a state of relaxation and then expose the client gradually to the feared stimulus.

If you develop a hypothesis that the person's problems are related to the environment, then the intervention should focus on environmental changes. For example, you may be working with a child with extreme withdrawal behavior and discover that the child is suffering from serious physical abuse. The determinant of the child's problem is primarily environmental. Here, the intervention is to change the child's environment. You may make arrangements for the child welfare authority to remove the child from his or her home environment. By giving the child a new environment—placement in a foster home, for example—you control the child's environment and provide new experiences to meet the child's needs for safety and proper development.

Helping clients obtain new resources is another way of instituting change. Often clients simply need information and other resources. For example, a client may need help in obtaining housing or material resources such as food. The intervention consists either of providing the information or resources or making a referral so the client can access them.

In summary, hypotheses help you think about the various determinants of human behavior. We encourage you to think about human behavior in terms of different hypotheses. In this way, you will become better skilled in assessment. And the better you are in assessment, the more effective you will be in providing services. Social workers, as professionals, typically are responsible for assessing issues involving social functioning in the implementation of most multidimensional assessment processes.

Models for Assessing Social Functioning

Werner Boehm (1958) made a major contribution to social work's knowledge base by clarifying the profession's focus. Before the late 1950s, social work's approach to understanding people, problems, and behavior had not been clearly distinguished from other human-service professions. Boehm (1958, p. 14) wrote that the complexity of humans' "functioning and the increase of scientific specialization have made it necessary for each profession to take one aspect . . . as the primary focus of its activities." In Boehm's view, the physician focuses on enhancing a client's physical functioning, and the social worker should focus on enhancing the client's social functioning.

Social functioning is a technical term that supports the social-work profession's focus on person-in-environment transactions. It refers to the client's ability to accomplish the tasks necessary for daily living (such as obtaining food, shelter, and transportation) and to fulfill his or her major social roles, as defined by the client's community or subculture (Williams, Karls, & Wandrei, 1989; Karls & Wandrei, 1994). Social functioning "involves addressing common human needs that must be adequately met to enable individuals to achieve a reasonable degree of fulfillment and to function as productive and contributing members of society" (Hepworth & Larsen, 1993, p. 5).

Boehm's social-functioning framework (1959, p. 31) led to the formulation of five major educational objectives for social workers in the curriculum area of Human Behavior and the Social Environment:

1. Understanding biological endowment (genes, dispositions, and so forth) as the source of the potential for human functioning
2. Understanding environmental forces that may enhance or endanger the potential for social functioning
3. Understanding interaction of endowment and environmental forces as enhancing or endangering the potential for social functioning
4. Understanding the person's response to change and stress

Werner Boehm, the developer of the social-functioning framework.

5. Understanding assessment of the potential for social functioning

The concept of social functioning developed by Boehm had roots in social-interaction theory and role theory. These theories assume that through the performance of social roles, people achieve a sense of self-worth and belonging. When people fail to locate themselves correctly in their social environment, this violates others' expectations. "Failure and disappointment with oneself and the reactions of others to oneself are critical in locating oneself within the 'normative' ecology (i.e., to answering the question 'How well am I doing?')" (Levine & Perkins, 1997, p. 206). Concluding that he or she is not doing well forces a person to make appropriate adaptations (Levine & Perkins, 1997). The **social-functioning perspective** directs social workers to focus on factors relevant to the performance of roles expected of individuals by virtue of their participation in various social groups. In this perspective, the point of connection between people and environments is the **social role**. The social role is the unit of analysis that links individuals with various social systems. In assessing human-behavior concerns, this emphasis on role behavior allows for a shift in focus from the individual to the interaction of an individual with various social systems.

The concept of "role" is key to any definition of social functioning, because it is central to any approach to defining a person and social environments. The concept of "person" comes from the Latin *persona*, which is defined as "mask." *Person* refers here to an individual who is playing roles. In this definition of personhood, the person is formed by the particular combination of social roles incorporated within her or his self-definition and behavior patterns. Through the playing of roles, the other levels of the biopsychosocial system are impacted, as is the person's self-definition—the organization of the biophysical and psychological functions cannot be understood without reference to the roles a person plays. Clearly, the expression of emotions, perceptions, and other psychological and physical processes is mediated through the roles that individuals learn and enact. Gerth and Mills (1953, p. 20) described this process thus:

> In order for inner feelings to become emotions, these feelings must be linked with socially recognizable gestures. And the person must become aware of them related to his [or her] self. The same physical environment and same physiology . . . may be present, but in one case these conditions may lead to fear and flight, and in another to rage and attack. The difference between the two experiences and behaviors cannot be adequately explained physically or organically. The social definition of the occasion, the meaning it comes to have for certain types of persons, provides the clue to which emotion and which conduct will arise.

Indeed, these meanings arise from the roles the person plays in the situation. Psychological functions and personality are formed by the particular combination of social roles that the person incorporates from the social environment (Gerth & Mills, 1953). By enacting various roles, the person incorporates

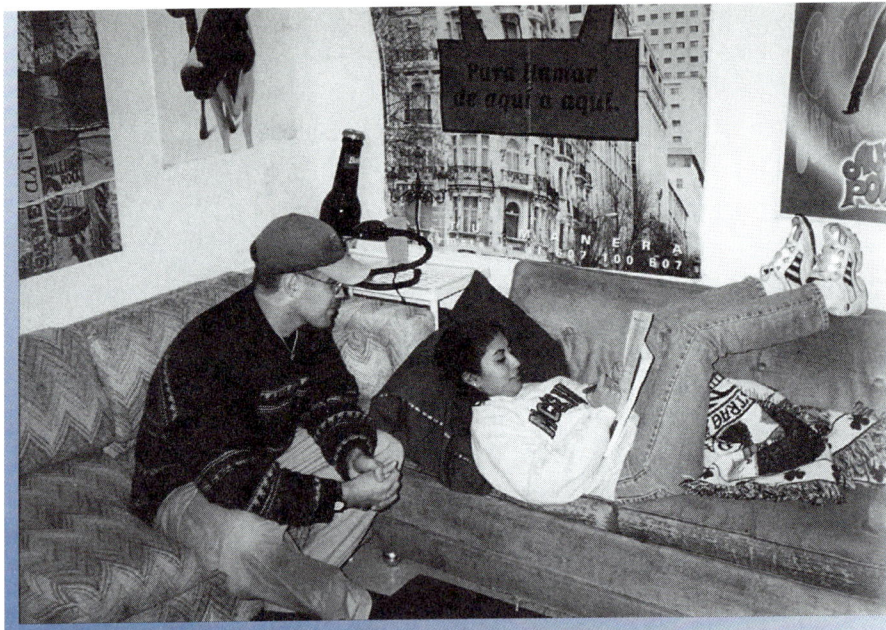

This college student's life in a dorm illustrates how she is part of two distinct cultures with different perspectives—the dominant society's system, and her own Latin cultural background.

certain objectives, purposes, motivations, and values that direct his or her conduct.

The concept of *role* is also the central unit upon which some theorists have defined institutions. Gerth and Mills (1953) defined an *institution* as "the organization of roles." They assumed that by choosing the social role as the central concept, we can reconstruct the inner experience of the person and the institutions that make up her or his social environment. With the role as our unit of analysis, we not only can look at how roles are organized, but we can also look at the functions served by the institutions. Each of our institutions emerged in response to specific human needs and functions. The way these institutions link with one another in serving functions allows us to look at what Gerth and Mills defined as "the broader social structure," or "society." These additional role-based concepts (institutions and social structures) have been adopted by social workers to understand the interactions of people and their environments. Also, the concept of *role* is very useful to social workers because it allows them to link a person's individual biography with the broader social context. **Biography** refers here to the changes in roles as they are taken up and discarded in the passage from one age group to the next over the course of an individual's life.

Role theory has a number of propositions that are central to the implementation of the social functioning perspective:

- People spend much of their lives participating as members of groups and organizations.
- Within these groups, people occupy distinct positions (fullback, advertising executive, police sergeant, and the like).
- Each of these positions entails a role, which is a set of functions performed by the person for the group. A person's role is defined by expectations (held by other group members) that specify how he or she should perform.
- Groups often formalize these expectations as norms, which are rules specifying how a person should behave, what rewards will result for performance, and what punishments will result for nonperformance.
- Individuals usually carry out their roles and perform in accordance with the prevailing norms. In other words, people are primarily conformists; they try to meet the expectations held by others.
- Group members check each individual's performance to determine whether it conforms to the group's norms. If an individual meets the role expectations held by others, then he or she will receive rewards in some form (acceptance, approval, money, and so on). If he or she fails to perform as expected, however, then group members may embarrass, punish, or even expel that individual from the group. The anticipation that others will apply sanctions ensures performance as expected (Michener, DeLamater, & Myers, 2004).

The next section describes a model developed by social workers for examining the person in his or her environment. This model considers social roles to be an important factor in assessing person-environment transactions.

The Person-in-Environment System (PIE)

The **person-in-environment (PIE) system** was designed to assess problems in social functioning. It provides social workers with a common classification system for communicating about client problems (Williams, Karls, & Wandrei, 1989). This system uses four factors to describe client problems:

- Factor I: Social-role problems
- Factor II: Environmental problems
- Factor III: Mental disorders
- Factor IV: Physical disorders

All four factors are considered necessary for describing a client's problems. The first two factors address the components in a social-functioning assessment handled primarily by the social-work practitioner. Factor III addresses mental disorders, and Factor IV includes any medical conditions that might affect social functioning. This system sets up explicit categories for identifying problems in social-role functioning and for establishing a list of environmental systems and problem areas. The system also "seeks to balance problems and strengths; it delineates problems pertinent to both the person and the environment and qualifies them according to duration, severity, and the client's ability to solve or cope with them" (Karls & Wandrei, 1994, p. 3).

This framework uses the established categories and codes defined in the manual for describing client problems. Like the DSM-IV-TR, this system operationally defines the categories, terms, and codes used in classifying client problems. Use of this system might increase social workers' reliability in defining social-functioning concerns. Without reliable definitions of social-functioning problems, we cannot accurately assess whether problems are increasing or decreasing. We also lack a shared system for communicating about problems. The PIE system has undergone some field testing, but not to the extent of the DSM-IV-TR (Karls & Wandrei, 1994). With the benefit of a universal definition of social functioning, researchers will have an easier task trying to assess the prevalence rates of problems in social functioning typically found in the practice of social work.

The following example illustrates how a complete case would look when the PIE system is applied (based on Williams, Karls, & Wandrei, 1989). This case involves a 68-year-old woman who was admitted to the hospital with fever and confusion. Neighbors reported that the confusion had been increasing over the last few weeks. The patient was diagnosed with a urinary-tract infection and was treated with intravenous antibiotics. However, when the medical problem was resolved, the confusion and disorientation were not. Because of this situation, the hospital staff determined that it would not be safe for the woman to return to her apartment alone. But the woman had no savings and only a limited income from Social

Security, so she was unable to afford in-home care. The woman's son wanted to help out, but because of his lifestyle as a musician and single father, he was unable to care for her in his home. The patient was adamant about returning to her own apartment. The social worker obtained a psychiatric evaluation of the woman, which determined that she was suffering from dementia and was unable to make her own decisions. On discharge from the hospital, the social worker and the son, against the patient's wishes, placed the woman in an assisted-living home that was willing to accept the Social Security payments in exchange for care. During the next two weeks, the woman, who had always been proud of her independence and strength, became increasingly despondent over her living arrangements.

Factor I
Social-role category: other/nonfamilial (tenant), and medical patient
Social-role problem: status/status change
Severity: 4, high
Duration: 5, two weeks or less
Coping skills: 4, inadequate

Factor II
Environmental system: economic/basic needs
Environmental problem: shelter and care (unable to care for self in own apartment)
Severity: 4, high
Duration: 5, two weeks or less

Factor III
Dementia

Factor IV
Urinary-tract infection, resolved

Most clients referred to social workers for assistance are having difficulties in their social functioning. The worker who applies the PIE system is expected to establish the type of role problem, its severity, and its duration in Factor I: Social Functioning Problems. There are four categories of role problems to select from: (1) family roles; (2) other interpersonal roles; (3) occupational roles; and (4) special life situation roles. Each of these categories has explicit definitions and includes subcategories that help in defining the role problem. For instance, *other interpersonal roles* are defined as "social roles that are also played out in interpersonal relationships between individuals, but these persons are not members of the same family" (Karls & Wandrei, 1994, p. 25). The five subcategories that exist for this role category are: (1) lover role; (2) friend role; (3) neighbor role; (4) member role; and (5) other interpersonal role.

After designating the role relationship, the practitioner is expected to identify the type of interaction problem affecting it. There are nine types of interaction problems to select from: (1) power type; (2) ambivalence type; (3) responsibility type; (4) dependency type; (5) loss type; (6) isolation type; (7) victimization type; (8) mixed type; (9) other type. These types are designed to help the social-work practitioner describe the nature of the strain, disruption, or break in the role relationship. For instance, "a Spousal Role Problem in which the client is complaining of loneliness and confusion related to death of a spouse is described as loss type," according to Karls & Wandrei (1994, p. 27). This type of interaction problem, as Karls and Wandrei explained, "is significantly different from a Spousal Role Problem in which the client is complaining about a spouse's physical and psychological abuse, which would be described as power type" (1994, p. 27).

For Factor II, the worker identifies the physical or social environmental systems affecting the client and the type of problem, its severity, and duration. This factor tries to capture the physical and social context in which the person lives, and it identifies targets for change in the person's external environment. The PIE system includes six environment areas: (1) economic/basic needs system; (2) educational/training system; (3) judicial/legal system; (4) health, safety, and social-service system; (5) voluntary association system; and (6) affectional support system. Each of these categories also contains specific definitions and subcategories to help define environmental problems.

A key benefit anticipated from this system, besides research, is a shared approach for communicating and defining client problems that results in improved treatment effectiveness. Other applied models exist for examining person-environment interactions. These other models focus on preventing normal stressors and other life events from turning into negative life outcomes. They are consistent with the PIE framework.

The task force responsible for developing the PIE system made a concerted effort to include recognition of a client's strengths to cope with their problems. Karls and Wandrei wrote (1994, p. 14):

> The idea is a simple one: Every person has the potential to adapt to stress and solve the problems of living that occur. Indeed, most of social work intervention is

aimed at mobilizing and enhancing personal strengths and resources to solve both interpersonal and environmental problems. Client strength, also referred to as coping ability, is generally interpreted as the client's use of knowledge, experience, and psychological and physical strength to master stressful situations.

Because we lack agreed-upon measures for assessing coping abilities, social-work practitioners must have solid grounding in assessing how people cope with stressors. They are expected in the PIE system to make a judgment about the client's coping abilities. This skill is also a key element in many other assessment frameworks.

Models of Stress and Coping

Stress is a major concept that plays a fundamental role in understanding many forms of human adaptation. Monat and Lazarus (1977, p. 3) have pointed out that stress represents "any event in which environmental demands, internal demands, or both tax or exceed the adaptive resources of an individual, social system, or tissue system." However, the word *stress* has been defined and used in different ways, depending on the aims of theorists (Weiten, 2000).

This complex concept was first studied by Hans Selye (1936; 1956; 1982), a Canadian scientist who spent his entire career researching the body's physical responses to stress. His model of those responses is known as the **general adaptation syndrome (GAS)**. Professor Selye identified three stages associated with this syndrome: the alarm stage, the resistance stage, and the exhaustion stage. In the alarm stage, the sympathetic nervous system is activated, which increases the heart rate, respiration, and other physiological processes needed to combat the challenges to the body's adaptive processes. This response has also been characterized as the *fight-or-flight response* (Weiten, 2000). The second stage, the resistance phase, involves the body trying to resist the stress when it persists over a period of time. During this phase, the individual appears to be doing fine, but his or her bodily defenses are actually beginning to erode (Duffy & Wong, 1996). In the final stage, exhaustion is reached. Exhaustion occurs because the body's resources for combating stress are limited. After exhaustion is reached, arousal decreases, and so does one's capacity for resistance, which results in disease as an adaptation to the biological threat or challenge (Weiten, 2000). (See Exhibit 1.3.)

Other theorists have focused primarily on psychological and emotional responses to stress. When

EXHIBIT 1.3 Stress responses

Stress responses vary according to the following conditions:
1. Physiological reactions, such as ulcers, asthma, and high blood pressure
2. Psychological reactions, such as avoidance of a stressful event in the future
3. Serious mental conditions, such as learned helplessness, anxiety disorders, and dissociative disorders

under stress, people typically confront two problems. "One is to manage the internal stress, anxiety, tension, depression, anger, restlessness, difficulty in concentrating, sleeplessness, and fatigue and the associated thought content, self doubt, and self blame" (Levine & Perkins, 1997, pp. 215–16). This first problem requires what has been termed a form of **emotion-focused coping** (Folkman & Lazarus, 1980). The second problem involves what a person should do in response to the stress or stressor. This kind of response is generally termed **problem-focused coping**. Problem-focused coping strategies seek to deal directly with the source of the stress, whereas emotion-focused coping seeks to reduce one's emotional response to the stress. People use both of these types of coping, to varying degrees, in stressful situations (Heller, Price, Reinharz, Riger, & Wandersman, 1984).

As social workers, we are interested in understanding all forms of stress that place people at risk for developing poor adaptations, poor health, and other negative life outcomes. These forms of stress include factors in the physical and social environments, such as poverty, social class, sexism, racism, and unemployment, that are known human stressors. These factors are often highly correlated with a person's position or location in the social structure. In addition, factors such as high population density, air pollution, heat, noise, and toxic chemicals are recognized by environmental psychologists as major contributors to stress (Heller et al., 1984; Wapner et al., 1997). (See Exhibit 1.4.)

Barbara Dohrenwend (1978) has developed a model of stress that takes into account both person and environment. She assumed that what determines how people respond to stress are **moderating factors** such as one's personal characteristics and one's social resources. "A moderating factor is considered to be operative when, if in its presence, the relationship of stress to illness (mental or physical) is weaker than

EXHIBIT 1.4 Sources of stress

There are three sources of stress in the environment:
1. A person's position in the social structure
2. Characteristics of the physical environment
3. Life changes

---

in its absence" (Duffy & Wong, 1996, p. 99). In the Dohrenwend model, having sufficient psychological and situational mediators is what reduces a person's vulnerability to stress and risk of developing health impairments (Dohrenwend, 1998).

Crisis theory is compatible with the model of stress developed by Barbara Dohrenwend. In crisis theory, differences in outcome from stressors is a function of the environmental supports and psychological mediators available to a person. Exhibit 1.5 shows an illustration of Dohrenwend's (1978) model of how psychosocial stress induces psychopathology and clarifies for readers the potential role psychological and situational mediators can play in this process.

Crisis theory originated with the work of Eric Lindemann (1944). He is known for his follow-up study of the relatives of victims of a tragic nightclub fire in Boston at the Coconut Grove Dance Hall in 1941. Lindemann learned from his study of the survivors' grief responses that the survivors had to change by detaching in some manner from their relationships with the deceased and forming new attachments. Those who did not adapt developed some form of disabling mental disorder. **Crisis** refers in this context to "any rapid change or encounter that provides an individual with a 'no exit' challenge, no choice but to alter his or her conduct in some manner" (Levine & Perkins, 1997, p. 207).

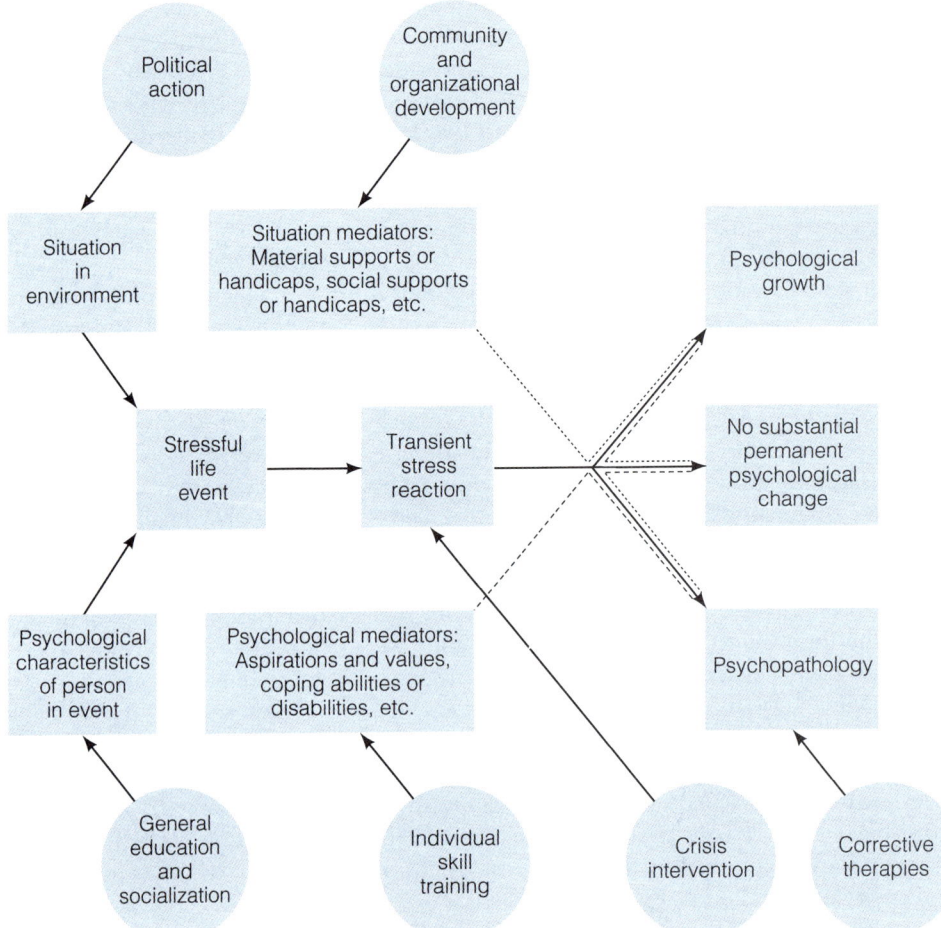

EXHIBIT 1.5 Stress and psychopathology

Model of the process through which psychosocial stress induces psychopathology and some conceptions of how to counteract this process

SOURCE: From B. S. Dohrenwend (1978), "Social stress and community psychology," *American Journal of Community Psychology*, 6, 2. Copyright 1978 Plenum Publishing Corporation. Reprinted by permission of Springer Verlag.

Gerald Caplan, Lindemann's colleague at Harvard School of Public Health, recognized that other situations, not just loss events involving extreme stress, place people at risk for developing serious mental disorders. From his research, he concluded that normative life changes also are capable of producing symptoms of psychopathology. His definition of **crisis** includes any significant change in a person's life situation. Such a change becomes a crisis when internal adjustment or external adaptation is beyond the person's capacity. Caplan's research inspired a growing field of inquiry presently known as *life events research*. As a result of this body of research, we now know that change associated with nonextreme events in life also contributes to stress and can place people at risk for developing severe mental disturbances (Dohrenwend, 1998; Gotlib & Wheaton, 1997).

The word *crisis* comes from a Greek root word meaning "to decide." In some contexts, it refers to a point in a disease or disorder process that is "decisive" for recovery or death (Levine & Perkins, 1997). In a more general sense, it refers to a critical turning point (just prior to the need for a decision) in a process in which a decisive change for better or worse is approaching. To some extent, this is the meaning adopted by Erik Erikson in his theory of psychosocial crisis. For Erikson, a crisis is considered a challenge or turning point at which there are opportunities for individuals to choose between polarities associated with key developmental tasks, such as trust or mistrust (Newman & Newman, 1999).

In crisis theory, winning the lottery is viewed as a challenge to a person's previous state of adaptation. Accepting a new job or becoming the boss also involve changes, which require new adaptations that tax personal and social resources. To understand these challenges, social workers are expected to have a theoretical and an empirical understanding of crisis theory and of life changes resulting from normal developmental processes.

Life-Span versus Life-Course Perspectives on Human Development

The curriculum in social-work education historically has looked to the developmental sciences for knowledge of change processes in people and their environments (Austrian, 2002; Hutchison & Charlesworth, 1998). Development as an area of science focuses on the causes and consequences of biopsychosocial changes (Davies, 2004). These changes contribute to positive and negative outcomes in human behavior, as well as positive and negative patterns of life. Traditionally, psychologists have focused in their research on understanding changes in behavior across a person's life span, with a particular focus on clarifying the contributions of age to understanding biopsychosocial changes.

Sociologists' research and theory construction, by contrast, has focused on understanding the contributions of social changes to the age-differentiated life course (Clausen, 1986; Dannefer, 1984). Sociologists are much more interested in studying changes in patterns of life or in social-environmental pathways. Phyllis Moen (2003) wrote, "A life-course approach investigates people's life paths as they play out in historical context as well as in the situational circumstances and chance events shaping them" (p. 13).

Social workers need to place in proper perspective what each of these academic traditions will bring to our understanding of changes in people and environments. That people change across life is not a particularly contentious issue. However, precisely how and why people change was the topic of many a debate in the twentieth century (Garcia Coll et al., 2004; Dixon & Lerner, 1999). Life-span development is a major theme in this book.

Most research and writing in the life-span tradition adheres to one of two styles. The first is the study of behaviors, dispositions, skills, and traits over a substantial period of the life span. For example, Terrie Moffitt and her colleagues have studied the traits of emotionality, constraint, and intelligence over time in birth cohorts in New Zealand and in the United States (Hagan, 1995). Their research specifically tracks the role of the continuity of individual differences in explaining deviant behaviors (see Moffitt et al., 1996). The second style of research in life-span studies focuses on clarifying how specific psychological functions, traits, and skills in one stage of development compare with other stages (Lyons, Wodarski, & Feit, 1998). That is, the life-span perspective is also known for providing a description of age-related biological, psychological, and behavioral changes from birth to death (Hutchison & Charlesworth, 1998). For instance, life-span theorists are interested in discerning what development is like in midlife and how it differs from other stages of development.

Life-Span Perspective

A dominant controversy in life-span research is whether traits or behavioral propensities are continuous or discontinuous. This controversy raises an important question about change. How hard is it for people to change? Some theories and theorists assume that once a person's self or personality is formed, change is very difficult (Mahoney, 1991; 2000). For example, Freud assumed that the bulk of personality is formed by age 7 and minimal changes in personality occur after this age. From this perspective, once personality patterns are formed they can be continuously modified, but the basic personality structure remains the same—because of processes of **cumulative continuity** or **self-selection**. "Cumulative continuity refers to the way in which behavior at one point in life influences opportunities and behavior later in life" (Benson, 2002, p. 14). For instance, early failure in school can generate stereotypes and other expectations that facilitate future failure in school. **Self-selection**, on the other hand, refers to a person's tendency to select contexts and experiences that are consistent with personality traits. The process of continuous change is not limited to personality. It is also applicable to many other traits, propensities, or dispositional characteristics addressed by developmental theorists.

One of the theoretical propositions advanced by life-span theory is that change occurs across the entire span of life. In some contexts, this is referred to as *plasticity*, or "the human capacity for change" (Mahoney, 1991; Lerner, 2002). However, some earlier theories of development subscribed to a **funnel theory**. In this hypothesis, it is assumed that possibilities for change contract over time (Mahoney, 1991). Exhibit 1.6 provides a graphic depiction of this thesis. The funnel theory assumes that people have a declining capacity for change as they age. This assumption supports biological models that limit development to the first half of life and processes of aging and decline to the second half (Mahoney, 1991). Although early concepts of development supported this thesis, recent research based on the life-span tradition has disproved this assumption. We now know that development is not the passive unfolding of prewired maturational programs or mechanistic reactions to environmental stimuli (Staudinger & Bluck, 2001). People are in constant transactions with their environments. They actively select contexts, change contexts, and are changed by contexts that vary from time period to time period (Staudinger & Bluck, 2001).

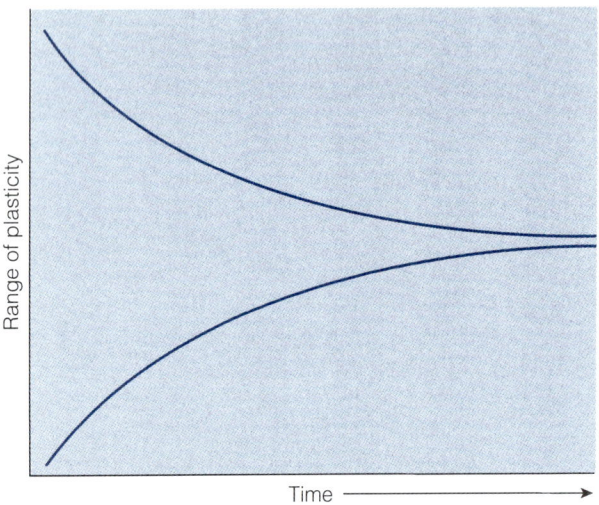

EXHIBIT 1.6 Funnel theory

SOURCE: From *Human change process* by Michael J. Mahoney. Copyright © 1991 by Basic Books, Inc. Reprinted by permission of Basic Books, a member of Perseus Books, L.L.C.

Delinquency is a major problem that social workers confront in many different arenas. For this reason, it offers an excellent context for demonstrating how researchers are implementing life-span concepts. What does the life-span perspective offer practitioners in trying to understand the social phenomena of juvenile delinquency and crime? Is delinquency caused by a specific trait or propensity to crime that remains constant over time? Is there a critical period for the development of this propensity? Once this propensity is developed, how likely is the person to change? Note that each of these questions, if answered in the affirmative, is consistent with what is known in the literature as a *general theory of crime and delinquency* (Lahey & Waldman, 2003). In this theory, it is assumed that the behavior of delinquents is sufficiently homogeneous to be explained by a single or common set of causal factors (Ashford, Sales, & Reid, 2001a). An excellent example of this viewpoint is Gottfredson and Hirschi's (1990) *A General Theory of Crime*. Their theory has identified poor self-control as the key factor associated with all forms of crime.

If delinquency is determined by poor self-control, then preventive interventions must address personal and social factors that place individuals at risk of developing poor self-control. Research on the

EXHIBIT 1.7 Arrest rates per 1,000 by age
SOURCES: From M. L. Benson, *Crime and life course*, p. 71. © 2002 Roxbury Publishing Company. Reprinted with permission.

subject has identified differences in early parenting experiences, as well as neuropsychological processes, that are associated with the development of poor self-restraint (Benson, 2002; Moffitt, 2003; Simons, Simons, & Wallace, 2004). If these factors are not modified before age 10, then a propensity for crime is established that remains relatively stable across the life span (Benson, 2002). This theory has a very pessimistic outlook on the potential effectiveness of treatment interventions after age 10. Clearly, in this viewpoint, variations in types of offender patterns are attributed to variations in the criminal propensity of the offender. According to this approach, treatment must target the individual's capacity for self-control, and this type of intervention would hold increased promise for success prior to age 10.

In the field of developmental criminology, however, this viewpoint is not seen as truly developmental (Benson, 2002). Other developmental approaches assume that the causes of delinquency and crime can change over the life course of the offender. These approaches are consistent with life-span assumptions of human development. As in life-span theory, developmental criminologists do not assume that the causes of crime are universal. These developmental theories assume that offenders are too heterogeneous to be explained by a common set of causes. According to this viewpoint, offenders should be categorized into distinct types or classes in order to identify distinct causal processes (Ashford et al., 2001b).

Terrie Moffitt's theory of crime and delinquency has identified two types of offenders: **life-course persistent** and **adolescent-limited**. "According to Moffitt, these two types of offenders follow distinctly different trajectories in crime and antisocial behavior over the life course, and their differing trajectories are caused by fundamentally different factors" (Benson, 2002, p. 82). Moffitt's (1996) research demonstrates that the age of onset of crime and conduct problems for life-course persistent offenders begins earlier in life than the onset for the adolescent-limited type. Moffit found that the life-course-persistent offender differs substantially from offenders with an onset of crime and deviance in adolescence. Moffitt (2003) identified neurodevelopmental and family risk correlates for the early-onset type. The participants in the second type, adolescent-limited, are likely to desist from crime as they age out of adolescence. Moffitt has hypothesized that each of these types is caused by different factors. Adolescent-limited crime tends to be caused more by peer processes than is life-course-persistent crime. Patterson, Reid, and Dishion (1992) have identified similar types, *early starters* and *late starters*, but attribute different causal processes to understanding them: family processes. Unlike Gottfredson and Hirschi (1990), most developmental criminologists assume that there are different crime pathways or trajectories caused by different causal processes.

Developmental theories of crime also attempt to explain important societal-age crime patterns. When we compare rates of crime across age groups, we learn that adolescents and young adults are at the greatest risk of involvement in crime. "The calculation of

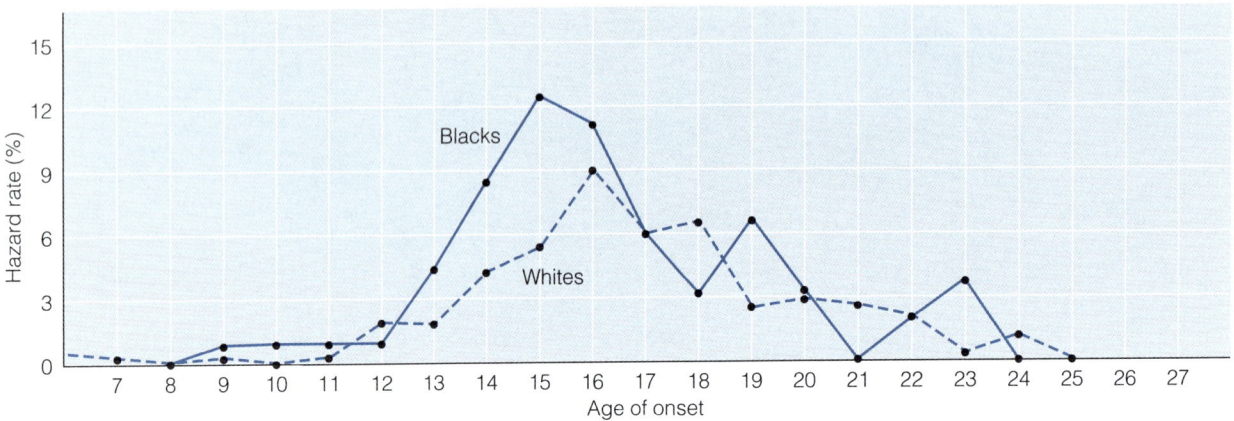

EXHIBIT 1.8 Hazard rate for onset of serious offending

SOURCE: From K. A. Dodge, "Developmental psychology," in M. H. Ebert et al., *Current diagnosis & treatment in psychiatry*, pp. 1–17. © 2000 McGraw-Hill Companies, Inc. Reprinted with permission

age-adjusted arrest rates clearly shows that arrests occur much more frequently during the late teenage years than at any other time in the life course" (Benson, 2002, p. 71). Why is this true? This question is the type of substantive problem that life-span theory helps practitioners focus on, and its answer has important policy and practice implications. Exhibit 1.7 shows the age-adjusted rates for 1999. These results demonstrate that youth between 15 and 20 years of age are much more likely to be arrested for crimes than are adults between 35 and 40. What is the significance of this empirical fact? Does it mean that we should institute policies that prevent young offenders from engaging in crime by ensuring that they are imprisoned until they grow out of the risky age group? What are the problems with this type of thinking? How would developmental theories of delinquency help?

The data reported in Exhibit 1.7 is cross-sectional information on crime rates. This information is important, but it tells us very little about individual types of offenders and their individual potential for change. In order to address the issue of individual change, we need longitudinal data, as well as data that helps identify different types of offenders. Exhibit 1.8 presents information on the age of onset of serious involvement in crime over time. This information provides different information of relevance to understanding types of offenders. We currently know that a small percentage of offenders commit the majority of crimes. In addition, a small percentage follow a life-course-persistent pattern. For this reason, some theorists would argue that we clearly do not want to subject individuals who are likely to grow out of crime to long periods of incarceration, and that the group that we need to target for such interventions would be the individuals who fit a life-course-persistent profile.

In this brief discussion, we have attempted to show how information about age and development can guide societal responses to delinquency. Clearly, different theories will provide different approaches to understanding many age-related considerations.

Exhibit 1.9 depicts the developmental trajectories of aggressive behavior for three 10-year-old children. These trajectories illustrate the types of traits that are studied by scholars from the life-span tradition. Child A has maintained a high rate of aggression over time. Child B's trajectory shows a constant rate of aggression over time. And child C's trajectory shows a pattern of accelerated growth of aggressive behaviors. In order to interpret these trajectories, the practitioner needs to not only consider the current intensity or level of the child's aggressive behavior, but also the developmental trajectory of aggressive behavior and its relation with age norms for that type of behavior. Developmental research provides this type of information. Intra-individual changes are best understood when we defer to longitudinal data. Life-span developmental theory provides excellent information about changes in specific traits over time and about the norms appropriate for evaluating these changes. Life-span information also helps us in trying to isolate whether the changes observed in traits, skills, functions, and so forth are caused by the *age* of the

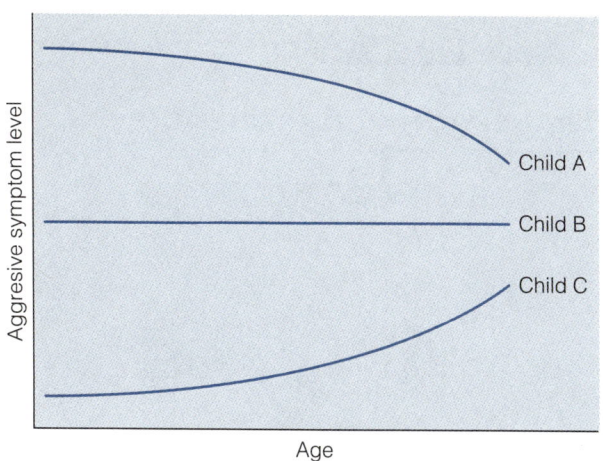

EXHIBIT 1.9 Developmental trajectories for aggressive behavior
SOURCE: From K. A. Dodge, "Developmental psychology," in M. H. Ebert et al., *Current diagnosis and treatment in psychiatry*. p. 4. © 2000 McGraw-Hill Companies, Inc.

individual, the *cohort group*, or specific *contextual factors* in the person's immediate environment.

Life-Course Perspective

The life-course perspective originated in sociology and has some similarities with the life-span perspective. In some contexts the terms are used interchangeably, but in order to clarify differences, we will treat them as separate. The life course is considered both a concept and a distinct theoretical perspective (Bronfenbrenner, 1996; 1999; Clausen, 1986). The **life course** is defined as age-differentiated life patterns embedded in social institutions that are subject to historical changes (Elder, 1991; 1996). This approach focuses on understanding changes in patterns of life, rather than on understanding changes in personality, traits, or behavior. The life-course perspective uses the concept of *trajectory* to understand the **environmental paths** followed by people in key social domains of life: work, marriage, crime, and parenthood (Elder, 1996). What is the common pathway—the sequence of events or transitions—to having children? Does this pathway vary with socioeconomic status? Does the current pathway differ from known pathways at the turn of the eighteenth century?

Life-course theorists are also interested in understanding the causes of other life destinations or outcomes (Gotlib & Wheaton, 1997; Paternoster & Brame, 1997; Robins & Rutter, 1990). They want to describe and explain life destinations in terms of trajectories and transitions. A **trajectory** is defined by Wheaton and Gotlib (1997, p. 2) as "the stable component of a direction toward a life destination . . . characterized by a given probability of occurrence." *Trajectory* refers in this context to a specific path or line of development followed by a person to a specific life outcome, regardless of whether the outcome is positive or negative. What is the pathway to homelessness? Do marker events for this life destination differ from those for graduating from college? Do role paths or trajectories to graduate school in social work differ from role paths to medicine?

In the life-course perspective, it is assumed that role transitions are embedded in trajectories and that both the transitions and the trajectories can be analyzed at either micro or macro levels. They are also conceptualized in many writings as a series of linked states (Elder, 1996). A change from one of these states to another constitutes what is technically termed in the life-course literature as a *transition*. **Transitions** are defined as short-term state changes that are marked by life events. Each life trajectory is marked by an ordered sequence of life events, roles, and transitions that are embedded within a specific life trajectory such as work, crime, or marriage (Elder, 1991; Paternoster & Brame, 1997). Some life-course theorists prefer focusing on the sequence of roles in a particular life domain, rather than on changes in life events. However, the goal for both of these approaches is to identify the ordered sequence of role and event changes in a person's life.

The Focus section on page 34 presents narratives that describe school transitions to illustrate the use of different methods for obtaining knowledge about life transitions. Personal narratives are an important source of knowledge. For instance, *Reflections: Narratives of Professional Helping*, a journal published by California State University, Long Beach, examines narratives of special interest to members of the social-work profession.

Transitions are clearly an inevitable part of any person's life. "Until death stops it all, human lives are always in transition" (McAdams, Joselson, & Lieblich, 2001, xv). Although it is cliché to say that the only thing that will ever remain the same in life is change, we often proceed as if our lives were simple, not complex and fleeting, as they really are. We subscribe to what has been termed the **myth of**

FOCUS ON NARRATIVE

HIGH SCHOOL AND COLLEGE TRANSITIONAL EXPERIENCES

Starting High School: Sarah's Apprehensions

I was nervous and excited to go to high school. I was coming from a small grade school where I knew everyone and going to a high school with 600 students where I only knew a few people. I was also moving to the bottom of the pecking order. I was going to be a lowly freshman instead of a great big eighth grader. I would have to work my way up in the ranks once again.

While still in eighth grade, my classmates and I discussed what we worried about most. The two main things were having no one to sit with or where to sit at lunch, and arriving late for class or going to the wrong classroom. On my first day of class, I confronted many of these issues. During the first homeroom, besides learning everyone's name, we quickly looked at our schedules to see who had lunch together. People with the same lunch would plan where to meet so they could sit together and not have to worry about eating alone. The plan worked, and when we entered the huge cafeteria the first day, we all felt secure and calm. Luckily, the school had put plastic table mats on certain tables that were reserved only for freshmen. They left these on for the first two weeks, and it gave us a sense of security. It was also helpful because we also did not need to worry about whether we were sitting at a seniors' table.

My first day of classes ran smoothly. I found all of my classrooms easily and was not late for any of them. Of course, I had highlighted what path I would take to get to each classroom on the map that we had received from the school. I knew what direction to go in and what staircase I would take. Although I was okay, some of my friends weren't as lucky. I was in English class after lunch the second day and the teacher was assigning seats. Everyone was standing at the back of the room waiting for their seat assignment. Everyone's name was called except my friend's. She was standing alone in the back of the room. The teacher asked for her name and it was not on the list. Then the teacher asked for her schedule. By now, everyone in class was staring at her, and she was turning different shades of red. It turned out she had English the next period and was supposed to be in History. My teacher gave her a late pass and she left. She never made the same mistake again.

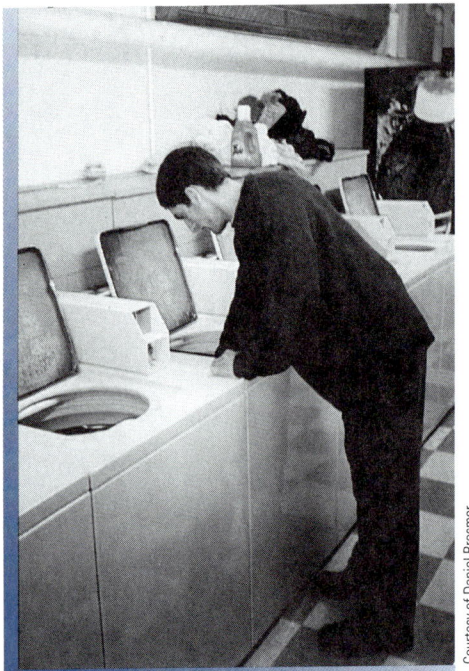

Students experience transitions when they change from the home environment to the college environment.

Courtesy of Daniel Brosmer

—SARAH BROSMER

Handling College's Freedoms

A teenager's transition into college life can be very exciting, yet very stressful and confusing at the same time. After living at home for 18 years with the security provided by my parents, I was thrown into a whole new world with as little as a few weeks' time for making an adjustment. Time flew by so fast that I had to try very hard to get a firm grasp on my personal situation before everything passed me by.

In preparing for my first fall semester, I was really concerned about my future roommates. I was going to live in one room with three other guys. I considered this a double-edged sword. However, the positives proved to outweigh the anticipated negatives. Rather than the four of us constantly getting on each other's nerves, we got to know each other very quickly and were constantly together. This, of course, did not come without patience and the kinds of generosity that all roommates must put forth if they are to get along. When one roommate is playing the guitar, the second is talking on the phone, and the third is watching television, sacrifice is definitely needed.

Meeting new friends was the best thing about my first year at college. My friend Paul has a very zany personality, just as I do, so when we first met that fall, I thought that he was absolutely hilarious. We distinctly remember our first two months as friends because every time we saw each other, we simply laughed ourselves silly. Also, after having a girlfriend for most of my senior year, it was nice not having a "significant other" during my freshman year. I could go out and meet as many people as I could, and I made several female friends that I know I'll be close to for a long time. One of my roommates started dating a girl the first week of school, and when they broke up with each other after a couple of weeks, he hardly knew anyone. He spent all of his time with her, and probably missed getting to know many people.

Another change that naturally evolved pertained to my relationship with my parents. My mother was pretty open-minded about the "whole college thing." She actually expected me to start drinking, even though I did not. When I came home for breaks and the following summer, my parents automatically gave me more responsibility, as the word "curfew" was never even mentioned. When one of my friends discovered the same thing, her response was, "What happened to my old parents?" Because of the family atmosphere of my dorm and the friends that I met, I felt very comfortable being an eleven-hour drive away from home. I called home every Sunday night to keep in touch with the home front, and I often e-mailed my father to update him on little things, but I honestly never really missed my parents this past year. Although it sounds sort of insensitive, I think that it shows that I grew up as an individual. At college, I enjoyed the freedom that I received, and I believe that I used it in a responsible manner. It really made me more mature and more ready to handle the life ahead of me.

—DANIEL BROSMER

---

arrival. Mahoney (2000, pp. 2–3) wrote, "This is the myth that someday after hard work and survived crises, life will be what we always wanted. We will have our 'self' and our 'life' together, living in the relationships for which we have longed, in the house of our dreams, in the job (and at the salary) we have wanted and so on." However, every inevitable transition involves meaning making in the lives of people. Life-course theorists who work with narratives attempt to understand how people make meaning out of these life transitions. In their viewpoint, people make meaning out of their lives through the use of storytelling—"the construction and the sharing of stories of the self" (McAdams et al., 2001, p. xv). The stories people tell help them position themselves in their social and cultural worlds. One key element of these stories is their location within the social clock prescribed by their culture and its age-grading institutions.

The connection or relationships between the age and the timing of events or role transitions is a key principle of life-course theory. The timing of the event in relation to a person's chronological age can have significant implications for the consequence of the event (Lerner, Perkins, & Jacobson, 1993). For instance, Elder found in his research that younger children were more seriously impacted by the adversities of the Great Depression than were older children. Similarly, when and for how long a child is subjected to abuse have important implications. For this reason, a central concern in the life-course perspective is assessing the timing of a specific event and trying to determine its influence on a person's life trajectory. Some transitions under circumstances of adversity can lead to major turns in the direction of a person's life.

Considerable research in the life-course tradition has been devoted to studying individuals under conditions of maximum adversity, such as the Holocaust (Levav, 1998), natural or human disasters (Giel, 1998), and childhood victimization (Widom, 1998). Research using this perspective recognizes that the life course, as an institution of socialization, can be influenced by major processes of social change, including wars, economic depressions, natural disasters, and other macro-oriented events, such as 9/11

(Heinz, 1996). Elder's (1974) seminal work on the effects of the Great Depression on life patterns is an excellent example. (See also Clausen's 1986 and 1993 research on children of the Great Depression.) What sets these researchers apart from other developmentalists is their interest in how developmental changes are influenced by period or by history effects. Other examples of history effects include growing up during the Civil Rights Movement; for Native American children, growing up after or prior to Wounded Knee; and changes in U.S. society pre- and post-9/11. In the life-course perspective, issues of time and timing often shift from focusing on the characteristics of the person to features of the environment, including the historical period (Bronfenbrenner, 1999; Friedman & Wach, 1999; Shanahan & Elder, 2002). It is important for social workers to take into account various historical events in examining many aspects about human development.

Robert Sampson and John Laub (1990, 1993, 1997) are developmental criminologists who have developed an age-graded theory of informal social control for explaining crime and delinquency. Their theory is predicated on the fundamental assumption that delinquency and crime are natural occurrences. If people are not prevented from following their natural inclinations, then they are at risk for engaging in antisocial or criminal behavior (Benson, 2002). In Sampson and Laub's view, there are different environmental pathways of informal social control that vary across a person's span of life. In childhood, the key components of this environmental pathway are the family, school, and peer groups. In these groups, children are exposed to informal controls of their behavior that determine whether they will engage in crime. As in other delinquency research, the family is consistently documented in this approach as an important contributor to delinquency (Simons, Simons, & Wallace, 2004). Children whose parents do not monitor them are at increased risk for delinquency. However, these environmental pathways change in young adulthood. In this phase of development, work, marriage, and the military are the key domains associated with crime prevention and informal social control. That is, if a person is being controlled by work or marriage, then she or he is less likely to engage in crime. In fact, Sampson and Laub found that marriage and work were key determinants of whether a youth with high propensities toward crime experienced a turning point in his or her crime trajectory (Sampson & Laub, 1993; Simons, Simons, & Wallace, 2004).

In essence, the life-course perspective from sociology offers a different view of the role of time and age in human change from that of life-span models of psychology. It focuses much more on the contributions of the context or the environment on observed changes in behavior. Biographical time (the life span) in the life-course perspective is conceived as a socially constructed pathway of role transitions. Researchers who use this approach are interested in explaining how the biographical timing of events is influenced by social institutions and by historical changes (Weymann & Heinz, 1996). Thus, a benefit of the life-course perspective is that it allows for an examination of the multiple dimensions of time—biographical time, social time, and historical time—in understanding human behavior (Weymann & Heinz, 1996).

In early life-span developmental theory, social structure was often taken for granted or treated as a given (Hagestad, 1991; Heinz, 1991b). Dannefer (1984) and other sociologists have challenged this approach. They adopt approaches to development that assume that social policy and other sources of social change can influence institutions of training, employment, kinship, and socialization that have implications for the life course (Laub & Sampson, 1993). This focus on policy assumes, of course, that the timing of change in the life course can be subject to the influences of social processes. In other words, developmental change in this theoretical approach is not limited to modifications in the organism's physical structure. Social changes can influence developmental patterns whether they are due to social policy, macro events, or other environmental circumstances. Immigration policy, for example, has significant implications for the life course of many people.

By focusing on understanding developmental changes, social workers are better equipped to engage in prevention. The science of prevention is becoming a key component of practice in social work. Many social workers are involved in primary, secondary, and tertiary prevention.

Prevention and Human Development

A good way to think about prevention is in terms of end states to be prevented: delinquency, divorce, HIV, and so on. **Primary prevention** seeks to stop a problem or situation from occurring in the first place. The aim is to focus on populations that have not developed problems or to focus on groups of people at risk for developing an identified end state—for example, children of divorced parents or alcoholics, individuals growing up in poverty, survivors of a recent loss, and so on. **Secondary prevention** is designed to intervene as early as possible in a problem situation, before it becomes severe or persistent. **Tertiary prevention** involves reducing the complications or negative consequences of a problem situation by preventing handicaps or impairments that are its known consequences.

In the practice of social work, practitioners need knowledge of factors that place individuals at risk for developing negative life destinations. They also must be cognizant of what internal and external factors serve as turning points. A **turning point** is defined as "a change in direction in the life course, with respect to a previously established trajectory, that has the long-term impact of altering the probability of a life destination" (Wheaton & Gotlib, 1997, p. 5). A turning point is a useful concept to social workers because it "implies alternative pathways that have real and important differences in life chances attached to them—whether or not the alternative pathway seemed to differ only slightly from each other at the time of the point of choice" (Wheaton & Gotlib, 1997, pp. 3–4).

In sum, the developmental sciences recognize that some of the changes in people's behavior and lives are ordered forms of change. These predictable changes that are tied to a person's age are termed **normative age-graded influences**. Other changes with degrees of predictability can be caused by what is often termed **normative history-graded influences**. These changes involve social factors or mechanisms of influence that operate during a particular historical era or period of time. They are also termed in the literature **cohort effects** or *period effects*. A *cohort* consists of individuals who have birth years in the same generation. A *generation* refers here to a time period of approximately 20 years. Some of the generations that have been studied by developmental scientists include the GI Generation, which consists of people born from 1901 to 1924; the Silent Generation, born from 1925 to 1945; the Baby Boomer Generation, from 1946 to 1960; Generation X, from 1961 to 1981; and the Millennium Generation, from 1982 to 2003.

However, many changes observed in people and their environments are caused by non-normative events. **Non-normative events** encompass all our chance encounters—things that do not happen to everyone and that do not follow any predictable timetable (Lemme, 1995; 2001). We lack knowledge of the sequencing of these events and their causes relative to issues of time and place. They also cannot be time-based on assessments of either a person's age or cohort years. For this reason, any assessment in social work must try to develop hypotheses about the causes of observed changes. Are these changes caused by something to do with the person's age, the person's cohort group, or the immediate context or social situation? The goal of each of the developmental chapters in this book is to provide you with foundation information for making professional judgments about the developmental dimensions of a person's problems, behavior, and social situations. In doing so, you need to rule out the contributions of age, cohort, and contextual factors to observed changes in people and in situations.

OVERVIEW

In the first part of this book we describe theoretical and conceptual themes that influence development within the biophysical, psychological, and social dimensions of human behavior. In the second part of the book, on life-span development, each life stage is introduced with a review of developmental themes. These sections reflect Erik Erikson's view that each stage contains certain life tasks that need to be achieved for optimal development. Each developmental chapter then discusses in-depth factors that affect behavior in the biophysical, psychological, and social dimensions. Each of the dimensions in this framework provides a distinct outlook on problems in social functioning; each also suggests different strategies for intervention that must be synthesized for an appropriate response to a client's problem. For example, a client suffering from a severe psychosis needs interventions directed at multiple levels. Biological concepts from neurobiology suggest psychopharmacological interventions to address the psychotic systems, psychological concepts to deal with the client's expectancies regarding his or her condition, and social concepts to address the supportiveness of the individual's environment. These various strategies are needed because of the complexity of the problem situations encountered in the practice of social work. Social workers do not have the luxury of limiting their description of problems to a single dimension. Using a single dimension to assess social functioning ignores the total person; it also implies the existence of a unified theory of human behavior. Because there is no unified theory of social functioning, practitioners must not adhere to a single explanation of that functioning.

Our multidimensional framework cannot be considered comprehensive. Other dimensions can be used to assess social-functioning concerns. However, we will review only those dimensions that have received the profession's sanction and are supported by established scientific disciplines. This does not mean that you should ignore other dimensions in your evaluations of client functioning. In fact, careful evaluation of information from these specified dimensions will sensitize you to additional issues relevant to assessing social-functioning concerns.

A person is more than the sum of his or her parts. Each dimension of human behavior is in constant interaction with other dimensions.

SUMMARY

Social workers need a multidimensional framework for integrating the knowledge and theories from biological, psychological, and social perspectives on human development. No single theory or approach to intervention can account for the whole range of forces influencing social functioning. A multidimensional framework includes the following assumptions: (1) There are three dimensions for assessing human behavior—biophysical, psychological, and social; (2) these dimensions constitute a system of biopsychosocial functioning; (3) systems are organized in a hierarchy of levels from smallest to largest; and (4) each system is in constant interaction with other systems.

Social functioning is the primary focus of a social worker's orientation to human development. Social functioning takes a person-in-environment perspective, which suggests that common human needs must be met for individuals to function effectively in society. How individuals perform their roles in order to participate in society represents the interaction of the individual with the environment. The social-functioning framework is similar to social-competence models. In the social-competence model, the focus is on helping people achieve their potential and on understanding the normal stresses and demands that affect them in their interactions with the environment. (A useful way of looking at this is to examine the tasks that confront people in adapting to their environmental situation.) In addition, how people respond to these tasks can be better understood by studying their coping abilities. The PIE system was specifically designed by social workers to assess problems in social functioning and includes assessments of coping.

System explanations are useful in alerting us to the multidimensional nature of human behavior. When combined with a hypotheses approach, a multidimensional perspective allows us to systematically evaluate the effects that different dimensions and their complexity have on client functioning. This perspective also ensures that practitioners focus their attention on the client's whole situation, including his or her personal and environmental hazards and strengths. The multidimensional framework includes the following components.

1. Biophysical dimension
    a. Biophysical growth and development
    b. Biophysical strengths
    c. Biophysical hazards
2. Psychological dimension
    a. Cognitive development and information processing
    b. Communication
    c. Attitudes and emotions
    d. Self and identity
    e. Social cognition and regulation
    f. Psychological strengths
    g. Psychological hazards
3. Social dimension
    a. Families and groups
    b. Communities and social supports
    c. Organizations and social institutions
    d. Multicultural and gender considerations
    e. Social strengths and hazards

CONCEPT MAP

Key Terms

- adaptation
- adolescent-limited delinquency
- biography
- biophysical dimension
- cohort (period) effects
- crisis
- crisis theory
- cultural competency
- cumulative continuity
- current perspective
- developmental perspective
- emotion-focused coping
- environmental paths
- etiology
- funnel theory
- general adaptation syndrome (GAS)
- habitat
- human plasticity
- inhibiting and promoting environments
- life course
- life-course persistent
- moderating factors
- myth of arrival
- non-normative events
- normative age-graded influences
- normative history-graded influences
- person-in-environment (PIE) system
- positional variables
- possibilism
- primary prevention
- problem-focused coping
- problems of living
- psychological dimension
- secondary prevention
- self-selection
- signs
- social dimension
- social environment
- social functioning
- social-functioning perspective
- social role
- spirituality
- strengths perspective
- stress
- tertiary prevention
- trajectory
- transitions
- turning point

Online Resources

Websites

Go to http://info.wadsworth.com/ashford to find specific links to these web pages.

National Center for Cultural Competence

The Georgetown Center for Child and Human Development has developed a resource with conceptual models and tools for increasing cultural competence in service delivery.

The John D. and Catherine T. MacArthur Research Network on Socioeconomic Status and Health

This site provides research and reports on coping strategies.

Bronfenbrenner Life Course Center

This site contains information about research projects on the life course at the Bronfenbrenner Life Course Center. This center is located in Cornell University's College of Human Ecology.

Slave Narratives

This is an excellent resource provided by the University of Kansas for studying the history of American slavery through narratives.

Hazards and Human Adaptations

This site, which provides information on natural hazards, is housed at the Natural Hazards Center (at the University of Colorado at Boulder), which is a national clearinghouse on natural hazards and human adjustment to hazards and disasters.

Environment and Community Psychology

This site links you to other sites that deal with ways that psychological processes interact with natural and man-made environments.

InfoTrac College Edition Keywords

For interesting materials related to what you have just read, please go to the InfoTrac College Edition website and search using the following keywords:

- life course
- social functioning
- stress
- social competence
- life paths
- generations

Book-Specific Resources

Book-specific resources, which can be found at http://info.wadsworth.com/ashford, include the following:

- case studies
- quizzes to test your knowledge
- PowerPoint presentations

CHAPTER 2

THE BIOPHYSICAL DIMENSION
FOR ASSESSING SOCIAL FUNCTIONING

CHAPTER CONSULTANTS

JILL LITTRELL
Georgia State University

JOHN A. MORRIS
University of South Carolina Medical School

41

WHAT BIOLOGICAL PROCESSES affect human growth and development? Exactly how do these processes affect aspects of an individual's behavior? What information helps social workers understand how biology affects behavior? Since the inception of social work as a profession, biological knowledge has been recognized as a fundamental foundation for effective practice (Schwitalla, 1930). The basics of human biology must be integrated in social-work professionals' knowledge (Ginsberg, Nackerud, & Larrison, 2004). Yet the knowledge base of social workers in clinical and other areas of practice has been almost unaffected by the veritable explosion of knowledge in the biological sciences (Saleebey, 1985; 2001). Social workers tend to be better versed in the psychological and social facets of the profession's biopsychosocial framework (Johnson et al., 1990). Nonetheless, as Saleebey wrote, social workers "will be called upon to deliver assessments of people that reflect the complexities of these elements of the human condition—body, mind, soul, environment" (2001, p. 92).

Many functions performed by social workers require biological knowledge (Ginsberg, Nackerud, & Larrison, 2004; Johnson, 1999). These functions include screening, referral, coordinating services with medical and psychiatric caregivers, case monitoring and advocacy, and psychotherapy (Johnson et al., 1990). It follows that, without relevant biological knowledge, practitioners can make bad referrals or engage in inappropriate screening and other caregiving activities. Most reviews of the social-work curriculum during the 1980s revealed minimal evidence that the profession was translating biological knowledge into assessment, intervention, prevention, and education strategies (Saleebey, 1985). This problem was particularly acute in the area of clinical practice (Cohen, 1988; Gerhart & Brooks, 1993; Libassi, 1990; Littrell & Ashford, 1994). As a result, the Council on Social Work Education (CSWE) took specific actions aimed at increasing the social-work student's knowledge of adverse effects of psychotropic medication on patients (Ashford & Littrell, 1998; Johnson, 1999; Libassi, 1990). Of course, there are other reasons social workers need to understand brain-behavior relationships and their biochemical substrates (Lyons, Wodarski, & Feit, 1998; Salzman, 2001). As Allen-Meares and DeRoos (1997, p. 380) pointed out, social workers in the twenty-first century will be far more likely to confront issues in the health and mental-health fields that involve matters of biochemistry, neuroscience, and biotechnology than they were in the recent past (Roobeek, 1995). "Whether our concern is mental illness or the attachment between mother and newborn, we must understand as best as we can how body, mind, and environment interact" (Saleebey, 2001, p. 19). Integration of this knowledge allows social workers to respond to the important calls for changes in services by the Institute of Medicine, described in *Crossing the Quality Chasm: A New Health System for the 21st Century* (2002), and the President's Freedom Commission's report *Achieving the Promise: Transforming Mental Health Care in America* (2003).

The case of Raul Salazar includes a number of elements that require some biological knowledge to place them in proper perspective. This case history will be used in the next three chapters to illustrate the independent contributions of each of the dimensions in our multidimensional framework. For more activities and assignments that examine the biophysical, psychological, and social dimensions of the Salazar case, go to http://info.wadsworth.com/ashford.

CASE RAUL SALAZAR

RAUL SALAZAR has just started the fourth grade. He was referred to the school's multidisciplinary team because of reports of difficulties in school and concerns about his home situation. Teachers are questioning whether he has a learning disability. They are also asking the team to determine whether he is an appropriate candidate for medications. He often does not follow instructions well. However, his current teacher is "surprised by his vocabulary." It is "much better than many of the other Puerto Rican kids in his class." Nonetheless, his performance in school has steadily deteriorated. He especially has problems with reading and mathematics and on occasion comes to school with dirty clothing and falls asleep in class.

Raul's performance was better when he was attending a smaller, parochial school. There, his work in the first grade was average, but his records indicate that the teachers at the other school considered him to be a very anxious child. The teachers also reported that Raul constantly moved in his seat and had problems with writing but did well in other fine-motor tasks.

Raul's father works for the City of New York as a painter, and his mother is a teaching assistant. She completed two years of college but had to discontinue her education when she became pregnant with her oldest son. Raul has two other siblings. There is a three-year difference in age between Raul and his older brother, and a twelve-month difference between Raul and his younger sister.

Raul's mother's family moved to the mainland when she was 8 years old. Her father was a teacher, and her parents were not pleased when she "had to marry" Raul's father. Mr. Salazar's family came from a poor rural area on the island. His own father had a history of alcoholism and left the family when Mr. Salazar was very young.

Mrs. Salazar reported to the social worker that she had serious problems with her nerves throughout her life and that they became worse whenever she was pregnant. Otherwise, she felt her pregnancy with Raul had been normal. However, school staff learned that there had been some fear that she might lose Raul during the pregnancy, and as a result she was prescribed bed rest during the last trimester.

Mrs. Salazar did not have any problems with her first pregnancy, but her third child, Maria, was born prematurely. This premature birth really hit the family hard, Mrs. Salazar said, because Maria required so much care when she finally came home. She reported that this was possibly the most stressful period in her life.

Unfortunately, Mr. Salazar was released from his job shortly after Maria's birth. When Maria was about 4 months old, Mrs. Salazar's doctor considered placing her on medication after she had a seizure. However, testing did not reveal any evidence of the presence of a seizure disorder.

Mrs. Salazar reported a history of fainting and said she had other seizure-like experiences when she was a teenager. In addition to problems with her nerves, she says, she has been very sickly throughout her life. She also told the social worker that "she was always the weakest one in her family."

When Raul was about 18 months old, Mrs. Salazar's closest brother was killed in a car accident. She reports not being able to get out of bed for weeks following the news of his death. Raul's medical records indicate that at approximately this time he started banging his head in order to fall asleep. This habit continued until he was about 6 years old. He also developed some other habits that persist to this date. He still bites his fingernails (and he bit his toenails when he was younger). Raul's history also reveals that he was extremely frightened of the dark as a child and has an extreme startle response, for which his brother and father often tease him.

Raul's father is a strict disciplinarian. He told workers that he often loses his temper and yells at the children, but he says that he has never physically abused them. He reported to the social worker that he cannot tolerate the kids being noisy. When he comes home from his new job, his wife is often in bed, and things are a mess. Mr. Salazar is under lots of pressure at work. His supervisor does not like Puerto Ricans and gives him all the worst job assignments. The Salazars no longer live near other family members, because they moved for Mr. Salazar to get his city job. Mrs. Salazar started working as a teaching assistant, but Mr. Salazar believes that this job is not necessary because the kids need her at home. He is hoping to apply for a transfer to a position with higher pay. Mr. Salazar told the social worker that the family is willing to pay for any services that will help his son do well in school.

We hope that Raul Salazar's case has stimulated your interest in trying to figure out what factors are contributing to his difficulties in school and in other areas of social functioning. If you were performing a multidimensional assessment of this case, you would need to begin by generating biological hypotheses.

~~~~~~

This chapter reviews the biophysical dimension, which is included in our multidimensional framework for assessing social functioning. It looks at aspects of cell systems, genes, and organ systems involved in human growth and development. This chapter also examines neurons and the brain, and their development. Understanding these biological factors allows a social worker to formulate essential questions about Raul's case history:

Does Raul have any problems that are genetically based?

What role, if any, does inheritance play in this case history?

Did any areas in his history pose threats to his neuronal or brain development, either prenatally or during his postnatal life? If so, what are they, and how do they explain why he is experiencing certain kinds of problems?

Could critical periods in the development of Raul's brain have been affected by risk factors in his environment? If so, what are they?

This chapter also covers several theories concerning the biological aspects of development. We begin our examination of biological theory with a review of concepts and principles from the theory of evolution and evolutionary psychology.

Biological Theories

Evolutionary Theory and Developments in Evolutionary Psychology

Evolution is a theory that has played a significant role in creating a biological basis for understanding human behavior. Although the theory of evolution is often credited to Charles Darwin (1859), Alfred Wallace independently developed the same idea, which Richard Dawkins (1976) summarized as another way of expressing the notion that those elements that are the most stable will continue to exist (Petri & Govern, 2004). This theory helps us understand processes of survival and the mechanisms and factors that have contributed to the development of humans as a species. Evolution tries to identify how much the species has changed over time and to explain why these changes have occurred. A key concept in this field of study is *variation*.

Variations are differences between individual organisms that affect their functioning. Some variations in organisms are caused by outside conditions involving the physical and social environment—for example, weather, soil richness, availability of nutritious food, effective social supports, presence of predators, and other external factors. The variations or differences in organisms produced by these factors are considered acquired developmental characteristics.

There is an entire area of psychology that focuses on individual differences; it is concerned with explaining variations observed in behavior patterns caused by evolutionary processes. However, the abuse of individual-differences research in areas of race and gender contributed to the demise of evolutionary thinking in many sectors of scientific psychology and the other social and behavioral sciences. It is an area of science that introduced substantial misogyny and racism in popular and professional modes of thought (Vandermassen, 2005).

David Buss (1999) has refocused attention on the role of evolutionary processes in psychology. He is advocating a new theoretical paradigm for psychology known as *evolutionary psychology* (Buss, 1999). This paradigm assumes that evolution caused by natural selection, as described below, is the only known causal process that can account for the complex organic mechanisms associated with adaptation (Buss, 1999).

Buss pointed out that, "as Symons (1987) phrased it, 'we're all Darwinians' in the sense that all (or nearly all) psychologists believe that evolution is responsible for who we are today. If another causal process exists that is capable of producing complex psychological and physiological mechanisms, it has not been made generally known to the scientific community" (1995, p. 2). One such disproved theory for explaining variations in psychological and physiological mechanisms is *Lamarckism* (Buss, 1999). Jean-Baptiste Lamarck, an early evolutionary theorist, believed that acquired traits could be passed from generation to generation. In other words, as an explanation for why a particular tribe of people eats a certain plant, Lamarck's theory might hold that they learn to eat it because it is abundant and tastes good—and that the knowledge to eat this food would then be inherited by offspring of the tribe.

Lamarck's thesis was challenged by Charles Darwin in his 1859 book *The Origin of Species*. Because of Darwin's work, we now know that acquired developmental characteristics cannot be inherited. Instead, Darwin established the principle of natural selection as the key mechanism underlying variations observed in species. This mechanism selects traits that are useful to the survival of the species. According to natural selection, a tribe would eat a certain plant not only because it is plentiful and tastes good but also because the tribe possesses an enzyme that allows them to digest that plant and use it as food. This digestive ability would be inherited, and people who possess this enzyme would be able to utilize a plentiful food supply and therefore have a greater chance of survival than would those who do not possess the enzyme.

An interesting area of biological variation with a long history of theoretical controversy and speculation deals with issues surrounding variations in skin color. This area has been fertile ground for theorists interested in evolution. An important article on this subject, published in *Scientific American*, revisited this issue (Jablonski & Chaplin, 2002). Until quite recently, most theorists assumed that nature selected for variations in skin color to prevent cancer. New discoveries have called this early evolutionary explanation into question. The cancer explanation grew out of a number of early scientific observations about the potential functional significance of skin color. Most indigenous individuals with darker skin pigmentation tended to live near the equator, and people with lighter skin color lived near the poles. In trying to explain this nonrandom pattern of the distribution of skin colors, theorists observed a link between the evolution of skin pigmentation and hairlessness in observations of chimpanzees. Chimpanzees' skin is light in color, but is covered by hair over most of their body. However, the pink areas of their skin become freckled or dark in these areas as they are exposed to sun with age (Jablonski & Chaplin, 2002). The areas that grow dark are protected with *melanocytes*—cells that are capable of synthesizing the dark brown pigment *melanin* in response to exposure to UV radiation. Because chimpanzees and humans are believed to share a common ancestor, these observations led to other significant inferences about skin color.

Scientists had found in other areas of research that people with the disease xeroderm pigmentosum, a condition in which melancocytes are destroyed by exposure to the sun, developed higher-than-normal rates of skin caner. This fact led some theorists to conclude that to prevent sun cancer, evolutionary processes must have favored individuals with biological traits that compensated for the protection previously provided by hair. But this theory was viable only if an evolutionary explanation could be found for the development of hairlessness in humans.

Peter Wheeler came up with a potential explanation for the development of hairlessness over the body (Jablonski & Chaplin, 2002). He hypothesized that the longer legs of Turkana Boy, a famous skeleton with longer legs than Lucy and other fossils with links to Homo sapiens, allowed humans to walk much greater distances than did earlier hominids. But they needed mechanisms for cooling the body down from the energy being exerted by this new capacity. In addition, they needed something to protect their brains from overheating. According to the principles of natural selection, then, individuals with more sweat glands on the surface of the body, and with less hair covering the body, enjoyed greater chances of survival and reproduction, ensuring the prevalence of increased self-cooling abilities.

Once our ancestors lost their body hair, they needed something to help protect their skin from the damaging effects of sunlight. Thus, darker skin, especially among those who lived near the equator, was selected for. This theory dominated most evolutionary explanations of skin-color variations, despite facts that were not supported by the theory: (1) the indigenous Inuit people of Alaska and northern Canada did not fit predicted skin-color patterns; and (2) most skin cancers develop after reproductive life phases and therefore would be less likely to influence selection because of the late onset of the problem.

In 1991, researchers found that light-skinned individuals who were exposed to simulated sunlight developed abnormally low levels of the B-vitamin folate. When blood serum was also exposed to similar conditions in experiments, the blood lost as much as 50% of folate content within one hour. Folate or vitamin-B deficiencies are associated with neural-tube and other types of birth defects. In addition, vitamin B is essential for the synthesis of DNA in dividing cells, and in boosting sperm counts. These observations led scientists to hypothesize "that dark skin evolved to protect the body's folate stores from destruction" (Jablonski & Chaplin, 2002, p. 75).

As this example illustrates, evolutionary theorists focus their inquiries on identifying the general adaptive functions served by physical, behavioral, or cultural mechanisms. Functional explanations are gaining prominence because they offer an alternative to approaches that assume that most problems in behavior and society are due to developmental or psychosocial processes that have deviated from rational principles. Instead, evolutionary approaches attempt to explain processes that are viewed as essential to "sustaining immediate individual survival as a member of a cohesive group that continually contends with challenges to general survival in the wider material and social world" (Weinreich, 2003, p. 3). In other words, social and personal problems are not viewed in evolutionary theories as deviations from rationality, but as behavior that has origins in fundamental psychological or social processes that serve survival functions (Weinreich, 2003).

The principle of natural selection offers a general explanation of how humans changed from lower to higher forms. Yet natural selection does not offer an explicit description of the specific mechanisms involved in the process of inheritance. This mechanism was not known until Gregor Mendel's work on genetics was rediscovered (Vale, 1980). It was not until we understood genes that we had more explicit explanations for variations in organisms. For example, people in a tribe choose a particular plant as food because tribe members possess a gene that produces the enzyme that allows them to digest the plant. They would pass that gene to their offspring, giving them a survival advantage over another group of individuals who did not possess the gene and could not utilize this plentiful food source. "In physical evolution, those characteristics that enable the individual to survive and pass on its genetic code are ones that will eventually occur more frequently in the population" (Michener, DeLamater, & Myers, 2004, p. 16).

Darwin's theory was not easily accepted. Before Darwinism, humans were perceived as being special creatures distinguished from animals on the basis of their intelligence. This fundamental notion was turned upside down when Darwin linked the development of humans to the development of animals. This linkage involved the connection of animals to intelligence and, by logical extension, of humans to instincts (Vale, 1980). Thus Darwin's contribution increased our understanding of human development yet also challenged cherished conceptualizations of human nature and of creationism.

Like Darwin, current evolutionary psychologists are challenging cherished notions about behavioral topics such as mate selection, parental investment, and language development. Evolutionary psychologists are attempting to describe and understand the specific adaptive problems that a behavioral pattern was selected by nature to solve. For example, evolutionary psychologists contend that observed visual-spatial differences between males and females are associated with specific adaptive functions. In their opinion, women have better spatial-location memory than males primarily because of their responsibility for gathering food in early modes of social organization. Men perform better on visual tasks that involve mental rotation of images, map reading, and maze learning, which are better adapted to the hunting responsibilities of earlier societies (Weiten, 2000, 2002). In other words, evolutionary psychologists attend to the evolutionary significance of observed behavioral variations in humans. They believe that all our current psychological functions can be described and explained in terms of their adaptive function. Researchers in this field have applied this approach to domains in psychology as diverse as reasoning, social exchange, language, aggression, jealousy, sex, status (Buss, 1995), and morality (Petrinovich, 1995). "Evolutionary theory is a theory of the interplay between evolved mechanisms and the social and physical environments they were designed to deal with" (Buss & Kenrick-Jones, 1998, p. 988). In the field of social psychology, the same principles hold (Kenrick, Ackerman, & Ledlow, 2003). Social behavior cannot occur without the existence of mechanisms that can receive social input that produces overt social behavior. Understanding these mechanisms helps in the understanding of basic social functioning, including the biological bases for these psychological mechanisms.

What Is Sociobiology?

The discipline of sociobiology involves studying the biological contributions to the social aspects of behavior observed in animals. In 1975, E. O. Wilson published *Sociobiology*, a book that primarily focused on understanding animal behavior but that also offered some controversial speculations about the contributions of biological processes to the social aspects of human behavior. Wilson summarized his book in a frequently quoted dictum: "Genes hold the culture on a leash." Wilson and other sociobiologists believe that important similarities exist between human and animal behavior. Did you ever wonder why animals, including insects, display courtship rituals before mating? Lower animals also commit "crimes" similar to those committed by humans. Mallard ducks commit rape; chimpanzees form groups that conduct warlike raids on neighboring tribes; and ant colonies have a social hierarchy that includes slaves. Lower animals also commit acts of altruism not unlike those of people. Bees will die to save the beehive, and a bird often will warn of an oncoming predator even though the warning most likely will result in the bird's death. Wilson's work was significantly influenced by the principle of genetic altruism. William D. Hamilton, an entomologist, put forth this principle in 1964 (Maxwell, 1991), which is referred to elsewhere in the literature as the "selfish gene." "The key point is that altruism is not 'really' performed for the good of others; it is performed for the good of the gene that selfishly 'wants' to be included in future generations" (Maxwell, 1991, p. 6). According to this reasoning, when a mother runs back into a burning house to save her two sons, sociobiologists believe she is compelled at a biological level. This self-sacrificing, altruistic behavior is simply a gene's way of working to ensure continued existence.

Wilson's sociobiology was initially seen as a new form of social Darwinism. **Social Darwinism** refers to the social-theoretical movement that ascribed the domination of one group over another to the selection by nature of the fittest group, a process commonly referred to as "survival of the fittest." Many researchers approached social Darwinism with grave suspicion (Vandermassen, 2005). Yet, this idea stimulated them to explore a number of issues involving the relationship between genes and culture. It eventually led to the collaboration of Lumsden and Wilson (1981) in developing a theory of gene-culture coevolution. This theory addressed a number of interesting problems, such as why very distant cultures have many characteristics in common and, more generally, how cultures originated. The emphasis was on trying to understand the genetic bases for many cross-cultural universals observed in human behavior.

Ideas stimulated by this theory have been some of the most controversial issues of the nature-versus-nurture debate. Some argue that the theory is too simplistic, that genes do not plan and scheme on their own accord. Instead, it could be argued that people learn new ways to behave in response to situations, and they teach their offspring these learned behaviors. Also, if selfish genes do exist, social norms would be likely to conquer them. Other theories, such as behaviorism, contend that people act certain ways based on what they have learned from the environment. The ideas of coevolution bring the nature-nurture controversy into perspective. People are more than genes. Genes have the power to influence behavior but do not directly control it. Genetic evolution occurs because a form of behavior is selected for its adaptive function. In the end, behavior is a combination of genes, culture, and environment, although their proportional influence remains a topic of debate.

The field of biology has many theories like sociobiology and evolution that provide an understanding of mechanisms that play an important role in social and other forms of human functioning (Ginsberg, Nackerud, & Larrison, 2004). For this reason, we start our examination of biological foundations with a brief discussion of basic growth and development concepts.

Biophysical Growth and Development

The growth and development of the biophysical person play a central role in the study of human behavior, and social workers are expected to understand how changes occur in biophysical processes. **Growth** is the technical term that refers to the addition of new biophysical components, such as new cells, or an increase in body size (Wilson, 2003). **Hyperplasia** refers to the type of growth observed in the fetal and early phases of development, which involves an increase in the number of cells (Schuster & Ashburn, 1992). It is eventually replaced by **hypertrophic growth**, or growth involving an increase in the size of cells. Most of our growth after adolescence involves hypertrophic growth.

Development refers in the biophysical dimension to the changes and refinement or improvement of body components. Most adherents of a maturational view of human development assume that any species will follow a typical path of development that is limited by genetic processes. The process by which people inherit general pathways that constrain their growth and developmental processes is referred to as **canalization**. Some aspects of human development seem to be canalized, or genetically determined, and regardless of environmental conditions, these predetermined pathways limit the degree of variation observed in a species. For instance, most normal human infants will learn to walk. This ability is genetically determined, and only a severely deprived environment would alter the development of walking in a normal infant.

In a biological sense, development can be studied from a hierarchical perspective. The biophysical dimension in our framework is part of the larger biopsychosocial system. This larger system represents the person in the social environment and is organized in a hierarchy from the smallest (biological) to the largest (social). Biological systems can also be organized from the smallest to the largest, beginning at the cellular level and progressing to tissues, organs, and organ systems. The study of physical development can follow this progression.

Cells are the smallest unit of living matter known to scientists. Most cells are too small to be seen without the aid of a microscope. They are all made up of a cell body (soma) that contains a watery liquid known as the **cytoplasm** (Exhibit 2.1). The cell is bounded by the **cell membrane**. "Inside the soma, various tiny structures, called *organelles*, are found: the nucleus, nucleolus, endoplasmic reticulum, Golgi complex, and microsomes, mitochondria and ribosomes" (Wilson, 2003, pp. 27–28). When cells are grouped together, they form tissues, which have varying characteristics according to their function. Examples include connective tissue, muscular tissue,

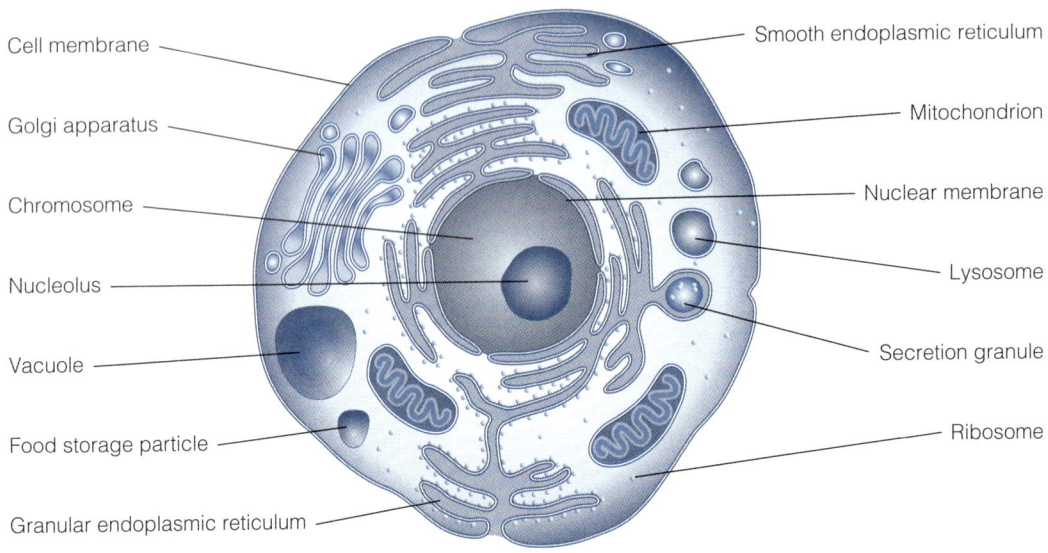

EXHIBIT 2.1 The parts of a cell
The cell body, or soma, is bounded by a cell membrane and contains numerous structures, including the nucleus, ribosomes, and mitochondria.
SOURCE: Wilson (2003): p. 28.

nervous tissue, and epithelial tissue (the outer surface of the skin) (Wilson, 2003). Tissues combine to form organs. Organs serve specific functions in the body's system but do not work independently of one another. They combine to form systems that serve various functions in maintaining life forms. Each of our organs is assumed to experience optimal growth periods. If in an optimal growth spurt the organism is subjected to adverse conditions, then there is a danger of serious impairment; that is, body tissue is most sensitive to permanent damage in these periods of rapid growth (Kalat, 2004).

A key structure within any cell is the **nucleus**, which is one of the places in the cell that contains its genetic information, in the form of nucleic acids (DNA). Nucleic acids are considered a specialized form of phosphoric acids that are very abundant in the nuclei of all cells. The information in these cells consists of coded strings of nucleic acid that is located in the chromosomes. A human cell typically contains twenty-three pairs of chromosomes. The only exceptions are the ova and sperm cells; these cells contain twenty-three unpaired chromosomes. There are approximately 200,000 genes encoded in the twenty-three pairs of chromosomes in each human cell. "The sum total of these genes is called the genome, and the same genome is found in every cell in an individual's body" (Wilson, 2003, p. 28).

We will begin our discussion of how biophysical growth and development can affect human behavior by looking at the genetic transmission of coded information in the cell nucleus and its implications for understanding diversity. This is followed by a description of a special form of cells known as *neurons* and how they change during brain development. We also explore in this discussion specific biochemical processes in the nervous system.

Genetics and Human Behavior

Social workers must possess basic knowledge of cellular growth, because they encounter many people with dysfunctions or defects in cellular processes (Ginsberg, Nackerud, & Larrison, 2004). These breakdowns in natural growth processes can occur in formative or growth phases of development, or after the organism has reached maturation. Such defects can play a significant role in many aspects of a person's behavior. Inadequate growth can place the person at risk for behavioral dysfunctions and for disease. For this reason, we will provide a brief overview of cellular growth processes from a genetic perspective. We chose a genetic perspective primarily because it represents one of nature's key control mechanisms for directing the kinds and amounts of cells needed for effective adaptation.

THE BIOPHYSICAL DIMENSION   49

EXHIBIT 2.2 Characteristics of chromosomes
The top portion of the figure shows chromosomes during mitosis. The bottom portion shows matched and sorted chromosomes.

Genetic information is contained within each cell of the human body. This information is located on chromosomes—threadlike structures found in the nucleus of the cell (see Exhibit 2.2). These threadlike structures are *nucleic acids*. The nucleic acids are specialized phosphoric acids of two fundamental types: deoxyribonucleic acid (DNA) and ribonucleic acid (RNA). Specific traits, such as hair color, eye color, and height, are coded in genes by means of these acids. DNA is located primarily in the nucleus of the cell, and RNA is located generally in the ribosomes. **Ribosomes** are the very small structures located in cells that are responsible for the production of the protein for cells. Each body cell contains forty-six chromosomes of our genetic information, and this information reflects our distinct genome.

Other tiny cellular structures that contains genetic information are the **mitochondria**. The mitochondria are responsible for producing the energy source for our cells. "For all cells, this energy source is *adenosine triphosphate*, or ATP. ATP is the body's fuel that is used by cells in most of the metabolic reactions that keep us alive" (Wilson, 2003). These metabolic reactions cannot occur without the necessary fuel and oxygen that the mitochondria require to function properly (Kalat, 2004). Behavioral geneticists are developing interests in the mitochondria because the mitochondria also contain DNA that has been associated with a number of disorders: migraine headaches, movement disorders, mental depression, and neurodegenerative disorders that produce seizures, blindness, deafness, and severe headaches (Kato, 2001; Wilson, 2003). Scientists attribute these conditions to mutations observed in the mitochondrial DNA. This type of DNA problem is inherited only from the mother. Other forms of DNA that can lead to various disorders are inherited from both parents.

Mitosis is the cellular process in which a body cell reproduces itself by dividing and producing two new daughter cells, each with forty-six chromosomes. When cells reproduce themselves, they do so at varying rates. For instance, blood cells reproduce as rapidly as every ten hours (Kalat, 2004), whereas muscle cells can wait several years before reproducing, and nerve cells do not reproduce at all once a full complement has been established. It is through these processes of cell division that growth and development occur.

The cell division that creates the reproductive, or sex, cells is called **meiosis**. The sperm and egg cells (also known as *gametes*) formed in this process have only half the parent cell's genetic material, or twenty-three chromosomes. At conception, the mother and father each provide twenty-three chromosomes through each gamete. The offspring then develops from a single cell formed by the union of these two gametes—a sperm and an egg. The single cell formed from this union contains forty-six chromosomes, or twenty-three pairs of chromosomes. Of these pairs, twenty-two pairs are autosomes. **Autosomes** are any chromosomes other than sex chromosomes. The pair of sex chromosomes consists of two X chromosomes in females, and one X and one Y chromosome in males (so named because of their shape). Each of these autosome and sex chromosome pairs consists of many genes, which represent the basic units of inheritance.

If the human species has evolved through variations caused by genetic inheritance, how have these variations occurred? One source of variation observed in humans involves problems in cell division. In this variation, one parent contributes "something other than exactly one copy of each chromosome" (Kalat, 1995, p. 462). Any process that affects this copying of chromosomes from each of the parents contributes to major variation in an organism's characteristics. **Chromosome disorders** occur when an alteration takes place either in the structure or the number of chromosomes. They are defined as any malformation of chromosomal pairs at the time of conception and include Down syndrome, fragile X syndrome, cystic fibrosis, muscular dystrophy, metabolic disorders, and sickle-cell disease.

As we have discussed, in the process of fertilization, male and female gametes should unite twenty-three single chromosomes from each parent and produce a single cell containing forty-six chromosomes. However, errors can occur in which the offspring has more or fewer than the normal forty-six chromosomes. Problems with chromosomes that affect growth and development are discussed in the section on chromosome disorders.

Problems that affect development also can occur with the genes located on the chromosomes. When two parents unite in a reproductive effort, there are approximately 1 million genes available for forming a new progeny (Beck, Rawlins, & Williams, 1988). This potential for the recombination of genes is why offspring have a new combination of genes that differs from their parents'. *Recombination* is a major source of the variations observed in offspring. "For example, a mother with curly blonde hair and a father with straight black hair could have a child with curly black hair or straight blonde hair" (Kalat, 2004, p. 11). Variations in organisms also can be caused by changes in a gene. This process is referred to as **mutation**. Mutations are random and rare events that can distort key characteristics in an organism's growth and development. Kalat (2004) wrote that random changes are rarely helpful. Most mutations produce recessive genes, and these genes will not be expressed unless both mates possess the same harmful gene.

We will explore various types of genetic disorders and their causal mechanisms in the following sections of this chapter. This discussion is intended to sensitize you to the types of disorders commonly encountered in direct practice. Basic knowledge of these disorders is needed to counsel family members and make appropriate referrals for genetic counseling.

The three fundamental types of genetic disorders are single-gene, multifactorial, and chromosomal. **Single-gene disorders** are inherited dysfunctions or defects that result from dominant, recessive, or X chromosome–linked genes.

Single-Gene Disorders

Dominant Single-Gene Disorders

Huntington's chorea is a disorder involving a dominant autosomal gene. This disorder has a 50-50 chance of occurrence in an offspring of a person carrying the gene. Huntington's chorea strikes about 1 person in 10,000 in the United States (Kalat, 2004). Because the gene for Huntington's chorea is dominant, we will refer to that gene as H and the recessive, or non-Huntington's, gene as h. An affected individual will have a genotype of Hh and a phenotype of having the disease. A **dominant gene** is a gene that produces a strong effect whenever it is present, and a **recessive gene** demonstrates its effects only when it occurs with another recessive gene. Whereas the **genotype** refers to the person's actual genetic structure (e.g., Hh), the **phenotype** is defined as the observed expression of the genotype. When the individual affected with Huntington's chorea reproduces, the chance of that child inheriting the dominant, or H, gene is 50%. Each parent contributes a gene to the offspring. The affected person with the genotype of Hh might contribute the dominant H or the recessive h gene. When the parent with this allele contributes a recessive h rather than the dominant H, the child will have an hh pair and avoid the disorder. However, when the parent with the Hh allele contributes the dominant H, then the offspring will have Huntington's chorea. This disorder is serious; it is characterized by progressive chorea (purposeless motions) and the eventual development of dementia (mental deterioration). Motor symptoms generally appear first. The disorder usually begins with arm jerks, followed by the appearance of facial twitches, and eventually tremors begin and spread to other parts of the body. This disorder is of particular concern because it often does not manifest until the fourth decade of life, so that the affected individual likely will already have had children before discovering that he or she has the disease. And some of these children may also have the disease.

Some dominant genes that are present with a recessive gene do not entirely control the inherited characteristic. This condition is called *incomplete dominance*. For instance, the dominant gene for red blood cells that are round does not totally mask the effects of a recessive gene for sickle-cell disease. Individuals with sickle-cell disease have sickle-shaped blood cells that tend to clump together. This clumping causes severe pain for the individual. These sickle-shaped cells also distribute less oxygen through the circulatory system than do normal cells (Sigelman & Shaffer, 1991). Sickle-cell disease occurs most often in African Americans in the U.S. and does not have a cure (Rauch, 1988). Some individuals who are carriers of this disease can have many round cells but are likely also to have some sickle cells. These sickle cells do not have an effect on the person's functioning except in stressful circumstances. In stressful situations, people with this condition of incomplete dominance may experience some symptoms of the disease.

People working with members of the African American community often encounter sickle-cell disease. One out of every twelve African Americans carries the gene for this condition, and 8–10% of this population have the disease (Rauch, 1988; Robins, Dev, & Limaye, 2001). This condition also occurs in people of Mediterranean extraction, from Greece, Italy, and Turkey, and has been found in persons from malarial regions of the world such as Indochina and China. A prominent feature of this disease is anemia. A person with sickle-cell disease has a life expectancy that is significantly compromised, but many adults with this condition have lived well into their 70s. Social workers involved with people affected by this condition seek to reduce the stresses that place the affected individuals at risk for serious health complications.

Recessive Single-Gene Disorders

Most single-gene disorders affect some aspect of the body's structure and are often serious and life threatening (Rauch, 1988). Single-gene disorders are not limited to those caused by dominant genes. Autosomal recessive genes also contribute to genetic disorders. We all carry abnormal recessive genes. These genes will cause no ill effects unless we mate with a person who is also carrying an abnormal gene. If two people carry the same abnormal gene, the chance is 1 in 4 that their offspring will inherit two of these recessive genes (Abuelo, 1983). For example, one in twenty African Americans and one in thirty whites carry the recessive gene for cystic fibrosis on chromosome 7. If two people with this recessive gene marry and have a child, each parent has a genotype of Cc—one dominant gene that does not cause the disease, and one recessive gene that does. Because the dominant gene overpowers the recessive gene, the parents do not have this disease. However, when these parents have a baby, there is a 25% chance that the child will have a genotype of two dominant genes CC and will not have the disorder; a 50% chance that the child will have the genotype Cc and, like the parents, not have the disease; but a 25% chance that the baby will inherit two recessive genes cc and have cystic fibrosis.

Cystic fibrosis (CF) is a serious disease of the exocrine glands that causes secretion of excessively thick body fluids. The disease occurs in 1 out of 1,600 to 1 out of 3,600 live births. The affected individual has difficulties with lung function and digestion, among other problems. In years past, many children died of cystic fibrosis, but with improved medical care, children with this disease are living into adulthood. The average life span in 1993 was 29.4 years. For a person born in 1998, the median expected life span is 40 years (Cystic Fibrosis Foundation, 2005). As adults, individuals with CF are still quite ill and often are limited in their ability to function. These individuals may require the services of a social worker, especially in coping with chronic illness and reduced life expectancy as a young adult.

The risk of both parents carrying a recessive abnormal gene is increased for people who are related by blood. First cousins are at a substantially higher risk of having a child with birth defects because they have one-eighth of their genes in common (Abuelo, 1983). For example, the risk in the general population of having an offspring with mental retardation is approximately 3–4%, whereas the risk of mental retardation for the offspring of cousins is approximately 6–8% (Abuelo, 1983). (Please note that this is a population statistic for individuals whose genotype is unknown. The risk for people related by blood of each having a recessive gene is higher, but for any two individuals, related or not, where both are known to have a recessive gene, the risk of the offspring having the disorder is 25%.)

The prevalence of abnormal recessive genes is often higher in certain ethnic groups. For instance, Ashkenazi (Eastern European) Jews have a 1 in 30 chance of being a carrier of the recessive disorder **Tay-Sachs disease**, a neurodegenerative disorder characterized by progressive mental and physical retardation. Most children with this disease die between 2 and 4 years of age. The chances of occurrence of this disorder are 1 in 300 in the general population (Abuelo, 1983).

Whenever social workers encounter a rare genetic disorder, they should take a genetic history and explore whether the parents are related. In isolated rural areas and on islands, the gene pool is reduced, which results in individuals running the risk of sharing a common ancestor without knowing it. Careful questioning is needed to discern any indication of potential consanguinity. Also, it should be noted that the risk for abnormalities in offspring from an incestuous relationship rises as much as 30%, whether it involves father and daughter or brother and sister (Abuelo, 1983). Thus, social workers should rule out the possibility of incest whenever there is a history for a rare recessive disorder and a teenage mother is involved.

X Chromosome–Linked Disorders

The third form of single-gene disorders involves any condition that is associated with X chromosome–linked genes. That is, these disorders are influenced by a single gene that is probably located on the X chromosome. Y chromosomes are shorter than X chromosomes and, as a result, have fewer genes. The genes on the X chromosome then have no corresponding allele on the Y chromosome that could possibly overpower the effects of a harmful gene on the X chromosome. For instance, red-green color blindness occurs most often in males. This scenario is most probable if a male has a recessive gene for color blindness on his X chromosome, because it cannot be overpowered by a matching dominant gene on the Y chromosome. Thus, males are more likely to have red-green color blindness because they lack a gene for this trait on the Y chromosome. Females can have this condition only if they have recessive genes for color blindness on both of their X chromosomes (Sigelman & Shaffer, 1991).

Hemophilia is a condition caused by a defective gene on the X chromosome that creates a problem with blood coagulation. This condition is often referred to as the "bleeder's disease." Hemophilia also occurs mostly in males, who have no corresponding gene on the Y chromosome to overcome the effects of this X chromosome–linked gene. Duchenne muscular dystrophy is another form of X-linked genetic disorder. However, "[n]ot all types of muscular dystrophy are X-linked recessive; some are autosomal dominant or autosomal recessive. In other cases, there is no family history of muscular dystrophy; these so-called sporadic cases are thought to be due to a change in a gene (mutation)" (Rauch, 1988, p. 62).

Lesch-Nyhan syndrome is another disorder that involves a gene on the X chromosome. It is characterized by mental retardation, spasticity, and self-mutilation (Abuelo, 1983). Children with this condition often bite their fingers and lips and have abnormal physical development. This genetic disorder creates an inborn error in the metabolism of purine. Infants with this condition appear normal at birth. In fact, the first sign of difficulty emerges when a primary caregiver discovers orange sand in the infant's diapers. This sand is crystals of uric acid that result from the infant's inability to metabolize purine (Abuelo, 1983). Children with this condition often stand out in terms of their aggressiveness. Fragile X syndrome is another disorder linked to the X chromosome. However, it is considered a chromosome disorder and therefore will be discussed in that section.

Multifactorial Disorders

This second major group of genetics disorders is called **multifactorial disorders** and is characterized by the interaction of multiple genes and environmental factors. The mechanisms underlying these disorders are poorly understood, and it is difficult to isolate the effects of environmental factors on multifactorial conditions. The environment can play a significant role in the presentation of multifactorial disorders. For instance, if the environment prevents the person from reaching a given threshold necessary for the appearance of a condition, then the person will not develop the characteristics of a particular genetic aberration. Increasing evidence indicates that people who develop certain multifactorial disorders have relatives with the condition. However, such a genetic liability does not mean that a person will develop the disorder (Rauch, 1988). An excellent example of this principle is seen in cancer. Many individuals with relatives who have had cancer do not develop the condition.

A group of disorders known to be associated with multifactorial inheritance is neural-tube defects. These disorders involve conditions in which a child has an open defect in the brain or spinal cord. Included in this group are anencephaly, encephalocele, and spina bifida. (Neural-tube defects are described in more detail in Chapter 5.) These serious conditions are usually accompanied by severe mental retardation and sometimes result in death (Abuelo, 1983). In the United States, the risk for neural-tube defects is 1 in 500. The condition with the best prognosis among neural-tube defects is spina bifida. In fact, percentages of persons with this condition who have developed severe mental retardation have decreased in recent years. Surgical advancements have greatly improved the prognosis for persons with this condition. Although some cases of anencephaly and other neural defects may have a genetic basis, others may have solely environmental causes, such as lack of folic acid in the mother's diet during pregnancy.

In effect, multifactorial disorders have a genetic component, but this component is dependent on the environment for its presentation. For instance, some fetuses may be at greater risk than others for developing structural abnormalities in utero as the result of a minimal exposure to alcohol. Thus, the interaction of many variables are involved in the causation of multifactorial disorders, and one or more of these variables will be genetic. Careful assessment is needed, because it is difficult to isolate the genetic component(s) of many forms of multifactorial conditions.

Chromosome Disorders

Chromosome disorders represent the last major class of genetic disorders. These disorders are caused by a variety of problems in cell division; of which *nondisjunction* is the most common problem.

Meiotic errors, during the process of forming gametes, can occur in the formation of either the sperm or the egg and are not hereditary. Remember that during meiosis the pairs of chromosomes must separate to form sex cells with only twenty-three chromosomes each. During this process, a piece of a chromosome may break off and attach to another chromosome. This is called *translocation*, or *deletion*. The remaining chromosome fragment, which lacks genetic material, causes defects that are contingent on what genetic information was deleted from the chromosome.

Chromosome disorders are often a result of too many or too few chromosomes—for example, forty-five or forty-seven chromosomes rather than the normal forty-six. Failure of paired chromosomes to separate during meiosis is called **nondisjunction**. Nondisjunction can cause three chromosomes in one cell (trisomy) or only one chromosome in a cell (monosomy). These types of abnormalities underlie many identified chromosomal disorders.

Down syndrome, or trisomy 21, was the first chromosome abnormality identified by scientists (Foster, Hunsberger, & Anderson, 1989). About 95% of Down syndrome cases result from an extra number-21 chromosome. At conception, the newly formed cell has three number-21 chromosomes because chromosome 21 did not separate during meiosis. Thus the offspring received one number-21 chromosome from one parent and two number-21 chromosomes from the other. Risk for this problem is highly associated with advancing maternal age. After age 35, the risk increases and remains about the same up to about age 40. At 40, the risk increases dramatically. The association between age and increased risk for Down syndrome is thought to be that all of a woman's eggs actually are created when she herself is still a fetus in utero; thus, her eggs are as old as she is, and as the eggs age, they become less viable. Another factor may be the aging of the body's system in general. That is, the body fails, as a result of age, to recognize and spontaneously abort chromosomal abnormalities. Another explanation often given in the literature is that the eggs are exposed to environmental threats for longer periods of time and accordingly are more likely to encounter errors in the meiotic process.

Down syndrome is not the only type of disorder resulting from an additional chromosome. There are two other syndromes, with a lower frequency of occurrence, associated with extra chromosomes: trisomy 18 (trisomy D) and trisomy 13 (trisomy E). Trisomy 18 is the second most common autosomal disorder, with an incidence of 1 in 3,000 live births. It is characterized by multiple deformities and severe mental retardation. This disorder is more prevalent in females, and survival is generally for no more than three months. Trisomy 13 occurs in approximately 1 in 5,000 births and is present on rare occasions on chromosome 14 or 15. This disorder is associated with many types of central nervous system abnormalities. Newborns with this syndrome rarely live beyond six months.

The last major type of chromosomal disorder that we will discuss in this overview involves the X chromosome. The **fragile X syndrome** is a form of serious mental retardation that is identified in karyotype studies (microscopic study of the chromosomes) by a constriction at the end of the long arm of the X chromosome. In some circumstances, the portion below this constriction is broken, which is why the disorder is labeled fragile X syndrome. Although the exact incidence of this condition is unknown, fragile X is believed to be second only to Down syndrome as a genetic contributor to mental retardation. This syndrome, which occurs in males, is characterized by nonspecific mental retardation, large testes, speech defects, and large, protuberant ears (Foster, Hunsberger, & Anderson, 1989). Exhibit 2.3 provides an illustration of the clinical features of fragile X syndrome.

Many gender-linked defects in chromosomes are undetected until early adolescence because some of these disorders are identified only by an individual's failure to develop secondary sex characteristics. Klinefelter's and Turner's syndromes are distinct examples. In **Klinefelter's syndrome**, the most common of the sex-chromosome disorders, the child is born with an extra X chromosome (XXY). Males with this condition have gynecomastia, or female-like breasts; mild mental retardation; underdeveloped testes; and attendant personality difficulties involving body-image problems. It is the most common condition associated with male infertility.

Turner's syndrome is the chromosomal disorder resulting from only one X chromosome, and it occurs in 1 out of 3,000 live female births. Females with this condition have an XO genotype and a number of physical stigmata that correlate with a lack of secondary sexual characteristics (Lemeshow, 1982). Women with this condition are short in stature, have a webbed neck, and often have congenital heart problems and kidney difficulties. However, mental retardation is not necessarily a characteristic, and, when present, it is generally mild. Doctors have begun treating these women with estrogen during adolescence to enhance their development of secondary sex characteristics. Most women with Turner's syndrome will achieve an adult height of 5 feet. Genetic counseling is needed when a mother has a child with this condition, to identify future risk for additional children and to clarify any misconception about the etiology of a syndrome (Foster, Hunsberger, & Anderson, 1989).

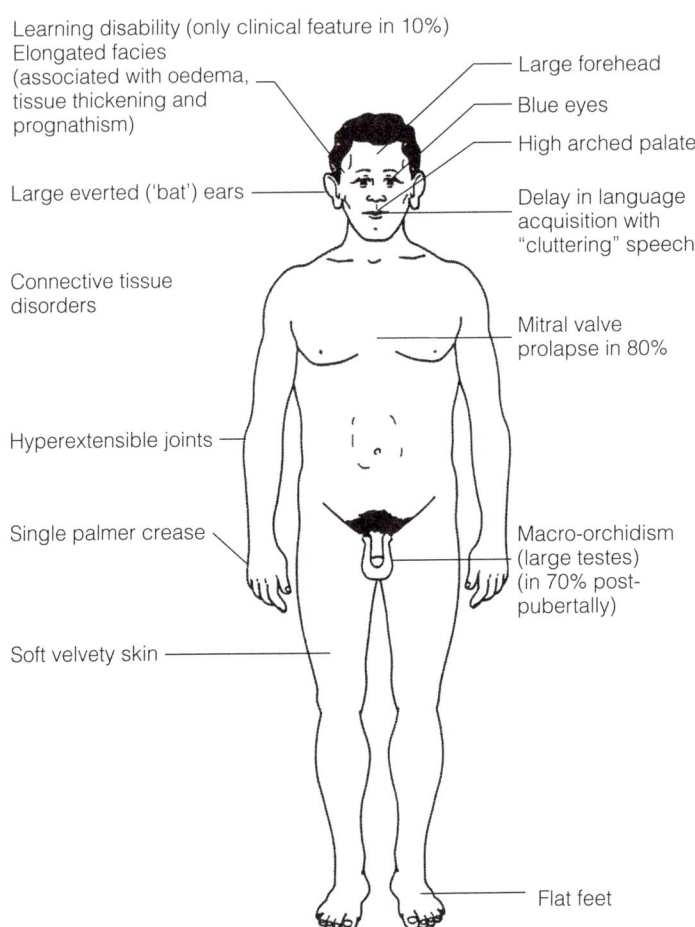

EXHIBIT 2.3 Clinical features of fragile X syndrome

Source: Reprinted from *Textbook of psychiatry*, by B. K. Puri et al., p. 326. © 1996, with permission from Elsevier.

Implications for Practice

Social workers often deal with clients who have irrational beliefs about the causes of disabilities observed in their children. Parents may unnecessarily blame each other for the child's problem or blame themselves for behaviors that have no bearing on the true cause of the child's problem. Social workers must understand the different types of genetic disorders in order to make effective referrals and dispel clients' misconceptions. Many parents operate on a number of false assumptions that are easily addressed by exposing them to relevant educational materials. Parent education is among social workers' many important responsibilities, because families have been destroyed by misinformation about developmental and physical disabilities.

Social workers are also operating more and more in autonomous capacities (Lebassi, 1990). In these situations, social workers end up determining whether clients are referred for genetic counseling. Genetic counseling is an essential service that helps family members identify the risk of occurrence of a given genetic disorder and make plans about having children. Genetic counseling also provides information and advice about options available to a couple, given each partner's family history. When parents have a disabled child, some of the stress associated with deciding to have additional children can be minimized if they learn that their child has a disorder with a low probability of reoccurrence. Often, parents are in a state of shock when they are given the initial diagnosis. Thus, the genetic counselor or social worker can play a major role in clarifying information that has been unintentionally distorted by uninformed friends or family members.

Social workers also need to focus on genetic issues in their assessments to help clarify the etiology of many of the problems encountered in practice. If social workers do not consider family genetic history in their investigations, they may fail to identify patterns that can provide essential clues to the causes of various behavioral and developmental disturbances. Although many conditions with a genetic basis often follow similar patterns among family members, this information may be overlooked unless the social worker obtains family background information. The contributions of genetics to behavior raise a number of interesting theoretical and practical issues. What individual differences (including abnormalities) are due to genetics, or to interactions between genetic and environmental factors? With the benefit of research involving twins, we are in a better position to answer questions about the contributions of genetics to behavior, because such studies control for the influence of comparable genetic backgrounds. ∎

Genetic and Environmental Effects on Human Behavior

Jim Springer and Jim Lewis are identical twins, separated just six weeks after they were born. Reunited thirty-nine years later in a study of twins conducted at the University of Minnesota, they discovered that they had married and divorced women named Linda, married second wives named Betty, and named their first sons James Allan and James Alan, respectively. They both drove the same model blue Chevrolet, often vacationed at the same small beach in St. Petersburg, Florida, and owned dogs named Toy (Begley, 1988, p. 80).

Are the striking similarities between these two brothers the result of similar environmental influences, pure coincidence, or the fact that they share the same genes? And what accounts for their differences? To what extent does one's genetic makeup influence behavior, and to what extent is the environment a factor? This issue is commonly referred to as nature versus nurture.

There are two major methods for studying whether family resemblance is a result of shared heredity or shared environment. The first method is twin study, in which researchers examine whether identical twins raised in the same environment are more similar to each other on particular attributes than are fraternal twins raised in the same environment. If heredity is an important prerequisite for the occurrence of a trait, identical twins, because they share the same genotype, should be more alike than fraternal twins (Plomin, 1990).

The other common family study is adoption study, which focuses on siblings who are adopted and reared apart from each other. An example would be our identical twins who were adopted into different homes at birth and raised in different environments. The degree to which these twins are alike reveals the effect of heredity; the degree to which they are like

The two male twins share a genetic history.

members of the family in which they were raised reveals the effect of environment.

Family researchers suggest that about 50% of the differences between people on IQ scores are the results of genetics (Plomin, 1990). Personality characteristics, such as extroversion and neuroticism, show heritability of about 40%. Various forms of psychopathology, such as schizophrenia, also show evidence of genetic transmission—about 30%. Genes also seem to influence behaviors such as delinquent and criminal activity.

Recent research by Robert Plomin (1994) indicated a significant genetic influence in human social development for attributes including empathy, attachment, and social competence. In fact, Plomin predicted that in the not too distant future, researchers will no longer have to rely on twin and adoption studies but will be able to pinpoint specific genes that directly affect genetic variability among individuals. Recently, scientists have found a link between a particular gene and the personality trait of novelty seeking. People with a gene for novelty seeking score higher on traits such as impulsiveness, excitability, quick temper, and extravagance (Ritter, 1996).

According to recent research, therefore, one-third to one-half of all behavioral characteristics can be attributed to genetic inheritance. This means, however, that most differences in human behavior are a result of the environment. How, then, does the environment shape behavior?

Previously, researchers believed that shared environment contributed to similarities among family members. **Shared environment** refers to the physical environment of the home, the family's socio-economic status, parenting style, and so on. Research now seems to indicate that shared environment has almost no influence on differences in behavior among siblings (Tellegen et al., 1988). Thus, when family members behave similarly, this resemblance is due to genetics.

Family members are different because of their non-shared environment—those aspects of the environment that they do not share. Examples of non-shared environmental influences include parental response to a child's gender, birth order, and temperament. In other words, parents respond differently to an easygoing firstborn female than they do to an intense, demanding younger son. Another source of non-shared environmental influence is the interaction among siblings. An older sibling with the responsibility for caring for younger siblings may develop more assertive, responsible behaviors; a younger sibling may learn to be more passive and cooperative. Other examples of non-shared environment include outside influences particular to each family member, such as interactions with teachers and peers.

According to this research, you are similar to your siblings because you share similar genes. You are different from your siblings because you experience different environmental influences through your interactions with parents, siblings, peers, and others.

To what extent, then, do genetics and environment interact in determining human behavior? A current popular belief is that genes influence behavior by determining the type of environment that people choose. People seek out environments that match their genetically determined preferences (Bouchard et al., 1990; Scarr & McCartney, 1983). As children grow older, they are less influenced by their parents and freer to choose their own environmental influences. Research shows that siblings become less alike the longer they live together (Plomin & Daniels, 1987). Athletic, outgoing children may choose to play team sports, whereas more introverted children may choose to read or play computer games by themselves. Because of genetic preferences, these two types of children experience very different environments.

Research by Scarr and McCartney (1983) indicated that the non-shared environmental influences that children experience may also result from the fact that their different genetic makeup causes them to elicit different reactions from others. Parents may respond more positively to an alert, smiling baby than to a fussy, demanding one. An extroverted child may have more positive interactions with peers than an introverted child. It would appear, then, that a child's genetic makeup determines, to some extent, that child's non-shared environmental influences.

Research by Thomas Bouchard and his colleagues (1990) seems to indicate that twins reared apart are similar because their genetic makeup causes them to choose similar environments. This research states that, although it does appear that most psychological variance is the result of learning through experience, the experiences are self-selected. We choose our environment based on our genetic preferences. According to this theory, the twins in our story are alike not because of coincidence or because they ended up in similar homes, but because they have the same genes, which caused them to choose similar environments and experiences and to elicit similar responses from the people in their environments. Therefore, it is less appropriate to talk of nature *versus* nurture than to study "nature via nurture" (Bouchard et al., 1990).

Biochemical Systems, the Brain, and Behavior

After exploring biophysical growth and development at the cellular level, we will now turn to biochemical processes in the nervous system that can have a significant effect on behavior. We will first focus on the brain, because it is the key organ in our nervous system. In addition, we will review the characteristics of our autonomic nervous system and the structure and function of nerve cells and processes involved in their development. This should provide you with the necessary foundation for understanding biochemical subsystems that contribute to the functioning of key psychological processes.

Anatomy of the Brain

It is difficult to understand brain functions without some fundamental knowledge of neuroanatomy, the study of structure and function of the nervous system. The brain's cerebral cortex (its convoluted outer layer) is divided into two hemispheres, and each of these hemispheres is divided into four lobes. These four lobes were named after bones in the human skull: frontal, parietal, occipital, and temporal (see Exhibit 2.4). The **frontal lobe** is the portion of the brain that participates in body movements, thinking, feelings, imagining, and making decisions. It is the lobe that includes the largest portion of the brain. It also plays a critical role in social inhibitions and emotional expressiveness (Kalat, 1998). People who

EXHIBIT 2.5 Broca's area and Wernicke's area
SOURCE: Goldstein (1994).

develop impairments in this area of brain functioning may exhibit marked changes in personality and in planning abilities. The left side of the frontal lobe also contains an area known as Broca's area, which plays an important role in speech production (see Exhibit 2.5).

The **parietal lobe** is primarily involved in the process of integrating sensory information. This lobe is located next to the motor components of the frontal lobe. When this area is damaged, it generally causes difficulty with interpreting sensory information. For instance, the affected individual may not be able to identify objects by touch and may have a poor sense of coordination. The **occipital lobe** is located below the parietal lobe and is involved in the receiving and sending of visual information.

Last, the **temporal lobe** is involved in emotions and human motivation. "Damage to the temporal lobes can lead to unprovoked laughter, joy, anxiety or violent behavior" (Kalat, 1995). The left side of the temporal lobe contains an area referred to as Wernicke's area, which has been identified as being important for language comprehension (see Exhibit 2.5).

The brain has three major divisions besides the four lobes: the forebrain, midbrain, and hindbrain (see Exhibit 2.6). The forebrain, or cerebrum, is the largest portion of the human brain. This area of the brain includes important structures such as the pituitary gland, which regulates certain hormones; the basal ganglia, which control certain aspects of movement; and the limbic system, which regulates behaviors including eating, drinking, sexual activity, anxiety, and aggression (Kalat, 1998). The midbrain is the portion of the brain that includes parts of the brain

EXHIBIT 2.4 The parts of the brain
SOURCE: Heller (1996).

EXHIBIT 2.6

Structures and areas in the human brain

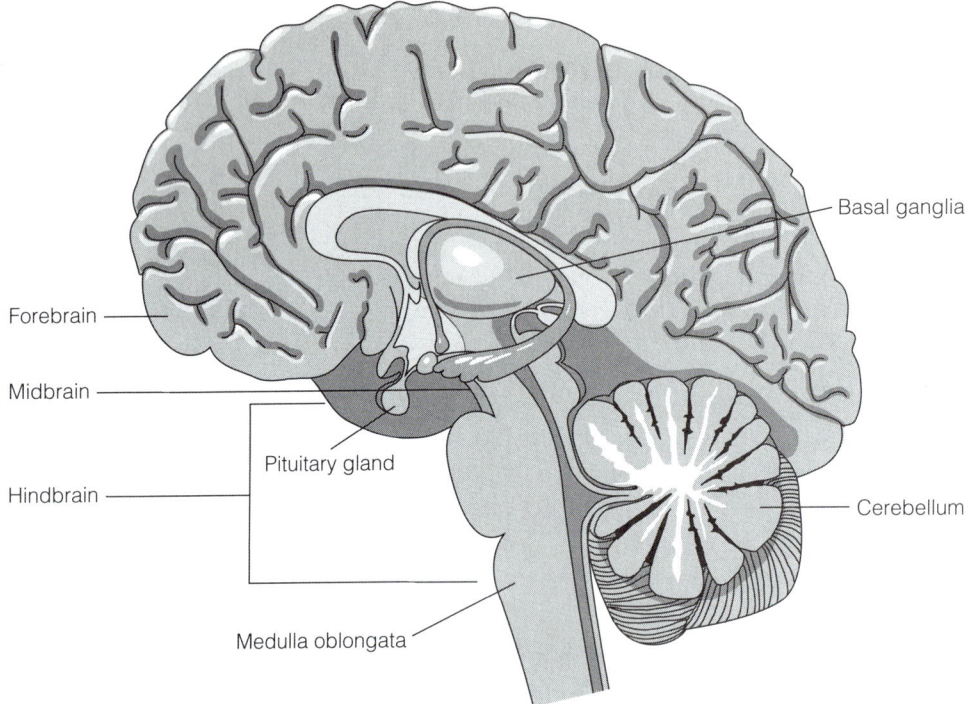

stem (the portion of the brain above the spinal cord). The midbrain also includes the reticular system, which monitors the state of the body through connections with the motor and sensory tracks. The third and final division of the brain is the hindbrain, which includes the medulla oblongata and the cerebellum. The medulla is considered a portion of the spinal cord and is involved in controlling heart rate, vomiting, salivation, and other vital reflexes (Andreasen, 1984; Kalat, 1998). The cerebellum is the portion of the brain concerned with a person's sense of balance.

Autonomic Nervous System

Our nervous system is divided into the central nervous system and the peripheral nervous system. The peripheral nervous system also has two divisions: the somatic nervous system and the autonomic nervous system. The somatic nervous system controls our skeletal muscles, or striated muscles. This system allows us to move skeletal structures in a voluntary fashion. The autonomic nervous system involves, however, the sympathetic and the parasympathetic nervous systems (see Exhibit 2.7). The autonomic nervous system controls glands, internal organs, smooth muscles, the stomach, and intestines. This system plays a significant role in the human stress response. It also contributes to many of the symptoms and signs observed in people with anxiety disorders. Under stress, the **sympathetic nervous system** prepares the body to participate in the fight-or-flight response. This system speeds up the heart rate, increases the blood supply to the organs and skeletal muscles, and prepares the body to respond to a perceived threat (DiMatteo, 1991).

The **parasympathetic nervous system** serves the opposite function—it counteracts the stimulatory effects of the sympathetic system (DiMatteo, 1991). The parasympathetic system of nerves plays the important role of conserving energy. This nervous system is called *parasympathetic* because it consists of nerves located next to the sympathetic nerve pathways. "We can identify the nervous system anywhere in the body because of the presence of nervous tissue, which consists of two different types of cells, *neurons* and *glia*" (Wilson, 2003, p. 27). In the next section, we focus on trying to understand these different cell functions.

Biochemical Processes in the Nervous System

We currently know that the brain consists of various groupings of neurochemical systems (Andreasen & Black, 1991). These systems vary depending on the

EXHIBIT 2.7 Autonomic nervous system

Sympathetic		Parasympathetic
Pupils dilated, dry; far vision	**Eyes**	Pupils constricted, moist; near vision
Dry	**Mouth**	Salivating
Goose bumps	**Skin**	No goose bumps
Sweaty	**Palms**	Dry
Passages dilated	**Lungs**	Passages constricted
Increased rate	**Heart**	Decreased rate
Supply maximum to muscles	**Blood**	Supply maximum to internal organs
Increased activity	**Adrenal glands**	Decreased activity
Inhibited	**Digestion**	Stimulated

SOURCE: Goldstein (1994).

ing organisms are the nucleic acids. The two kinds of nucleic acids important in the study of development are deoxyribonucleic acid (DNA) and ribonucleic acid (RNA). These nucleic acids are important in the transmission of genetic information and in the synthesis of proteins (Steiner & Pomerantz, 1981, p. 3). In this section, we will explore the influence of biochemical processes by examining the biochemical aspects of our nervous system.

Although proteins are involved in all processes of growth and development, social workers need to understand their functions in the central and peripheral nervous systems (see Exhibit 2.8). The **central nervous system** (CNS) consists of the neural cells and their attendant chemical processes within the brain

function they perform in the nervous system. Social-work practitioners cannot directly assess these biochemical systems and are not expected to do so. However, they should understand how these systems operate and how they relate to various forms of human behavior.

The structural organization of any true living system has the cell as its basic unit of organization. This fundamental unit consists of three kinds of molecules: proteins, lipids, and nucleic acids. **Proteins** are the fundamental substances involved in the building of cells, muscles, skin, and internal organs. In fact, the term *protein* is derived from the Greek word *proteious*, meaning "of first rank" (Page, 1981). A protein is defined as any organic compound that has a large combination of amino acids. Scientists have identified more than 100 amino acids, 20 of which are the building blocks for forming proteins. Eight of the amino acids must be obtained from dietary sources: isoleucine, leucine, lysine, methionine, phenylalanine, threonine, tryptophan, and valine. These eight amino acids are referred to as *essential amino acids*. Any dietary deficiency in these amino acids can contribute to the problems involving delayed growth and development, emotional disturbance, and various physical conditions, all of which can be observed in social work. Protein molecules also include a class of biochemical catalysts called *enzymes*. Enzymes facilitate chemical reactions in cells and aid proteins in achieving their structural and transport functions in the cell processes of human organisms (Steiner & Pomerantz, 1981). The other key molecules in liv-

EXHIBIT 2.8 Central and peripheral nervous systems
SOURCE: Goldstein (1994).

EXHIBIT 2.9

Neuron and neurotransmitter

SOURCE: Goldstein (1994).

or the spinal cord. The **peripheral nervous system** (PNS), in contrast, involves all the neural cells and cell processes that lie outside the brain and the spinal cord (Hoyenga & Hoyenga, 1988). Our entire nervous system consists of thousands of nerve cells, and each nerve cell receives information from about one thousand other nerve cells (Hoyenga & Hoyenga, 1988).

There are two kinds of cells in our nervous system: glia and neurons. **Glia** cells make up the bulk of our brain. It is estimated that there are 10 times as many glia cells as neurons (Wilson, 2003). They are also smaller than neurons. There are various kinds of glia in our nervous system: astrocytes, microglia, radial glia, and more common type of glia—Schwann cells and oligodendrocytes. Glia are often referred to as "supporting cells" (Kalat, 1998), but we are gaining information about their actual functions. We now know that they play a number of important roles in the running of the nervous system, including (a) providing nourishment for neurons; (b) removing waste products and dead neurons; (c) forming scar tissue in the nervous system; (d) directing development of the nervous system in embryos; (e) providing insulation for axons; (f) contributing to the blood-brain barrier; (g) communicating information to neurons; and (h) serving as the brain's immune system (Pfrieger & Barres, 1997; Wilson, 2003). We also know that they are not as plentiful in the brains of nonhuman species (Kalat, 1995).

The **astrocytes** help to synchronize the activities in the axons of neurons. They also remove waste material when neurons die and are responsible for making sure that neurons get the glucose, water, amino acids, and oxygen that they need (Kalat, 2004). Microglia are very tiny and function as *macrophages* that gobble up dead neurons and also remove waste, including viruses, fungi and other microorganisms (Kalat, 2004; Wilson, 2003). The radial glia are responsible for making sure that neurons arrive at their correct destination in the body. "In the central nervous system, the glial cells forming the myelin sheaths are called oligodendrocytes; whereas in the peripheral nervous system, they are called Schwann cells" (Kalat, 2004, p. 35).

Neurons are generally what people refer to when they speak of nerve cells (see Exhibit 2.9). Neurons are the cells involved in conveying information from one cell to another. Some of these cells are long and have branched extensions that diverge from their bodies. The single long extensions are called **axons**, and the short extensions are called **dendrites** (Lickey & Gordon, 1983). Axons are long fibers that carry the impulses from the cell body of a neuron to other cells. Dendrites perform the opposite function. They are the branched fibers on a cell body that relay messages to the cell body of the neuron. Neurons are the only cells in the human body that are separate from one another (Maxmen & Ward, 1995). Because neurons are separate, they need to communicate across the open spaces between individual neurons and between neurons and other cells. The space between any two neurons or a neuron and another cell is called the **synaptic cleft** (see Exhibit 2.10).

How are messages transmitted across this synaptic cleft from one cell to another? At the tip of the axon is a small, bulblike swelling called the *axon terminal* (Lickey & Gordon, 1983, p. 18). An axon terminal is generally found near a dendrite of another cell body. The axon terminal of the neuron sending the message is referred to as the *presynaptic terminal*, and the receiving portion of the neuron is referred

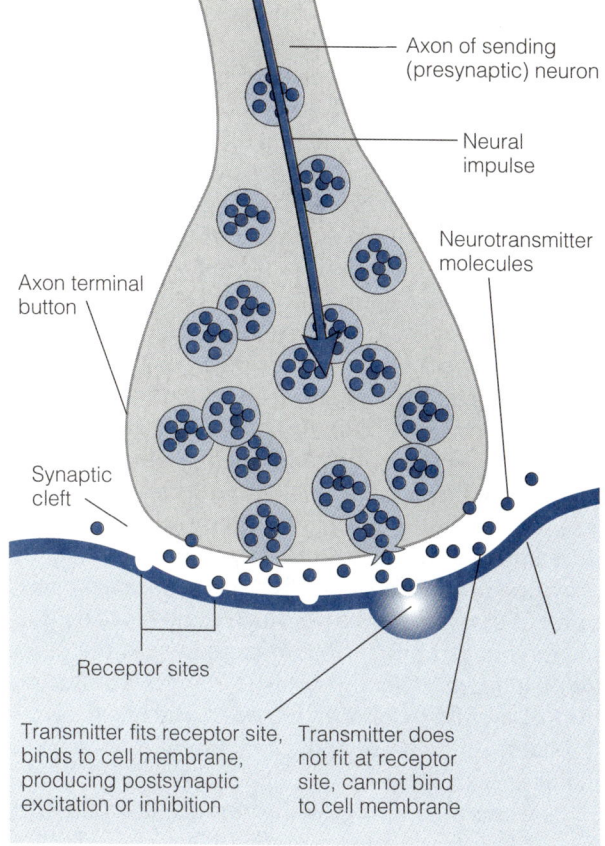

EXHIBIT 2.10 Synapse
SOURCE: Weiten (1995).

amino acids—acids containing an amine group (NH-2) such as glutamate, GABA (gamma-aminobutric acid is the most abundant inhibitory neurotransmitter), and others.

peptides—chains of amino acids such as endorphins (opiate transmitters that inhibit pain messages), substance P (used by pain receptors to signal tissue damage and pain), neuropeptide Y (found in the hypothalamus that stimulates intake of carbohydrates), and others. (A protein is also a chain of amino acids; the term *peptide* is generally used for short chains, *protein* for long chains.)

acetylcholine—is a neurotransmitter that is similar to an amino acid but is based on a different chemical composition from an amino acid.

monoamines—non-acidic neurotransmitters containing an amine group (NH-2) formed by a metabolic change of certain amino acids: serotonin (indoleamines), dopamine, norepinephrine, and epinephrine (catecholamines).

purines—adenosine and several of its derivatives, ATP (adenosine triphosphate, the principal fuel for cells), and others.

gases—nitric oxide and possibly others (see Kalat, 1998; p. 56).

to as the *postsynaptic membrane*. Conveying information from the transmitting cell to the receiving cell across the synaptic cleft requires mechanisms, known as synapses, for communicating the impulse or the message. There are different types of synapses, some chemical and others electrical (Grebb, Reus, & Freimer, 1988). Chemical synapses involve the signaling of information from one cell to another by means of chemical substances. Different cells in the nervous system release different kinds of chemical substances to transmit the information across the synaptic cleft. In our discussion, we will focus on the actions of one type of chemical substance, the neurotransmitters, because they play a central role in current treatments of mental disorders.

Neurotransmitters are chemicals that are synthesized inside the neuron. "Each neuron synthesizes its neurotransmitters from materials in the blood" (Kalat, 1998; p. 55). Dozens of chemicals function as neurotransmitters. Some of their names include the following:

These neurotransmitters are released from the axon's end or presynaptic terminal, where they diffuse across the synaptic cleft and bind onto receptors on the membranes (or edges) of adjacent cells (the postsynaptic terminal) (Maxmen & Ward, 1995; Kalat, 2004). Neurons actually act like a wet sponge. When they fire, they contract to release neurotransmitters; when not firing, they expand and reabsorb the neurotransmitters (Maxmen & Ward, 1995).

Receptors, located on postsynaptic membranes, are the special protein molecules to which neurotransmitters will attach, in a lock-and-key relationship. When a neurotransmitter is released from one nerve cell, diffuses across the cleft, and attaches to a receptor site on another cell, that process is called *binding*. This binding process activates chemical changes in the receiving neuron. Sometimes the chemical change encourages the production of a nerve impulse, and other times it discourages nerve impulses. When the chemical process encourages the production of a nerve impulse, this is called *synaptic excitation*; when the chemical process in the membrane discourages an impulse, it is called *synaptic inhibition*.

In sum, a transmitting neuron releases a chemical substance known as a *neurotransmitter* from the presynaptic terminal. This chemical crosses the space between the cells and binds onto the postsynaptic membrane of the receiving cell. The chemical then either encourages the receiving cell to fire a nerve impulse or discourages the cell from firing an impulse.

Growth and Development of Neurons

Neurons develop very rapidly before we are born; 250,000 neurons are added each minute during many phases of prenatal development. When a child is born, it has a full complement of neurons. Nature provides us with perhaps twice as many neurons as we need (Sheibel, 1997). A newborn infant's nerve cells appear much like a mass of unconnected electrical wires. Imagine having the job of trying to connect all these neurons! Fortunately, no one is individually responsible for this monumental task, but we do know that a connection is made among these nerve cells every time the infant is touched, held, or has some other form of experience with primary caregivers. In other words, the nurture part of the nature-versus-nurture expression plays an important role in how our brains are wired and organized. In fact, most of the development of the brain following birth involves the wiring and rewiring of different neuronal systems. "Our genes set up an enormous number of neurons, connections, and potential connections, and then experience determines how many and which ones will survive" (Kalat, 1995; p. 151).

A conservative estimate is that the newborn's brain consists of about 100 billion nerve cells in need of being connected (Nash, 1997). The infant's brain at this point has been described as being like "the Pentium chips in a computer before the factory preloads the software. They are pure and almost infinite potential, unprogrammed circuits that might one day compose rap songs and do calculus, erupt in fury and melt in ecstasy" (Begley, 1996; p. 54). The "programming" of these "chips" is provided by the infant's experiences. In fact, we know that the growth and development of brains suffer serious consequences if children are deprived of stimulating environments during the first three years of life. "Early stimulation with toys in an enriched environment dramatically alters brain structure, resulting in greater branching of nerve cells, and increased number of supporting glia. Stimulated lab animals developed 25% more synapses per nerve cell and 80% more blood vessels to nourish each cell" (*Los Angeles Times*, 1996). Thus, experience plays a major role in the formation of the synapses and connections between neurons that are characteristic of the major neuronal systems that make up the human brain. This includes the systems responsible for enabling us to learn a second language, play an instrument, and learn mathematics. In fact, we now know that there are critical periods for a number of human functions to develop during the early years of a child's life: emotional control, ages 0–2; vocabulary, ages 0–3; social attachment, ages 0–2; math/logic, ages 1–4; music, ages 3–10; and second language, ages 0–10 (Begley, 1996; Rutter & Rutter, 1993).

Unlike most other human organs, the brain has three major growth spurts (Rutter & Rutter, 1993), the first of which occurs during the last trimester of the prenatal phase of development. If the fetus has inadequate intake of protein and calories during this last trimester, the number of brain cells can be reduced by as much as 40% (Kalat, 1998). Exhibit 2.11 provides an illustration of five stages of brain development that indicates how much growth occurs during the final trimester, in comparison with the other two trimesters. This figure also provides an illustration of a child's brain at age one, which represents the status of the brain at the conclusion of its second major growth spurt.

The second major growth spurt occurs in the first year of an infant's development. In fact, about half of the brain's entire postnatal growth is achieved by the end of the first year. By as early as six months, the infant's brain has reached half of its final mature weight. Most of the growth during this spurt is caused by the formation of synapses and the myelination of axons. The human brain weighs about 350 to 400 grams at birth. At the completion of the first year of postnatal life, the brain weighs about 1,000 grams, which is very close to the adult brain weight of approximately 1,200 to 1,400 grams (Kalat, 1998). Exhibit 2.12 reviews average brain weights at different ages of development.

The final brain spurt in brain growth, which occurs just prior to puberty, involves increased growth of gray matter in the frontal-lobe areas of the brain (Bower, 2004; Ortiz, 2004). (**Gray matter** refers to the areas of the nervous system with a high density of cell bodies and dendrites, but few myelinated axons.) Following this spurt, the brain begins purging itself of unused neurons and myelinating the neurons that are used most often. As in the growth spurts, experience plays a central role in how the brain is wired. Given the data on brain maturation in adolescence, foes of the death penalty challenged the legitimacy of executing juveniles because of their lack of brain maturity (Bower, 2004; Ortiz, 2004).

EXHIBIT 2.11

Five stages of brain development

SOURCE: Kalat (1998).

Assessments of variations in brain weight at various stages of development stimulate a number of questions about brain growth and developmental processes. For example, how does the brain continue to grow if it does not produce any new neurons after birth? Do changes in brain weight correspond to other noteworthy psychological or behavioral changes? For instance, do the onsets of object permanence, concrete operations, and formal operations (cognitive developmental structures identified by Piaget, see Chapters 3, 6, 7, 8) correspond with any observable changes in the brain's neuronal structures? We have learned over the years that students are better equipped to answer many of these questions, as well as frame new ones, once they have developed a general understanding of the four stages involved in the development of neurons: proliferation, migration, differentiation, and myelination.

EXHIBIT 2.12 Brain weights at different ages of development

Age	Brain weight (grams)
20 weeks gestation	100
Birth	400
18 months	800
3 years	1,100
Adult	1,300–1,400

The **proliferation** stage involves all the processes involved in the production of new cells. We have devoted an entire chapter to the prenatal phase of development, which covers many proliferation processes. For this reason, in this chapter we will not address all the threats in the environment that can harm genetic and other biological mechanisms involved in the proliferation of neurons in the brain or other components of the nervous system. This does not mean that proliferation is not an important stage of neuronal development. In fact, a sizable proportion of social work's involvement in areas of prevention should be devoted to eliminating the occurrence of conditions in a person's environment that can destroy or impede the formation of needed neurons.

Neurons created in the proliferation process divide to make new cells. "Some of these new cells remain where they are, continuing to divide and redivide. Others become primitive neurons and glia that migrate (move) toward their eventual destination in the brain" (Kalat, 1995, p. 147). Some of these neurons use fibers from the glia and axons of other nerve cells to migrate to the brain's outer layers. "By studying normal neuron migration and factors that can disrupt it, scientists may find ways of preventing or treating epilepsy and many other developmental brain disorders" (Society for Neuroscience, 1995, p. 1). The migration of some neurons covers great distances. This is especially true of the neurons that form the outer layers of the cortex. Researchers are trying to understand how these neurons "know" which destinations to migrate to in the brain. Scientists do recognize that they migrate from the inside out, or from the center of the brain outward, but they do not completely understand factors that drive this process. It is clear, though, that genetic mutations, drugs such as cocaine and alcohol, and radiation can interfere with processes of neuronal migration (Society for Neuroscience, 1995). "For instance, many people who received radiation in the womb during the World War II atomic explosions at Hiroshima and Nagasaki, Japan, had incomplete neuron migration leading to brain abnormalities" (Society for Neuroscience, 1995, p. 2).

After neurons migrate to their destinations in the brain, they begin to differentiate. In the **differentiation** phase, they start forming axons and dendrites. In general, the axon grows before the dendrite, but some axons grow while the neuron is still migrating (Kalat, 1998). The last stage in the developmental process involves **myelination**. This is the stage in which axons are insulated by sheaths of myelin. These sheaths are composed mainly of fat that serves as an insulator. The insulation provided by the myelin sheaths lets signals travel through axons about 100 times faster than through an unmyelinated axon. This is important because the better myelinated the axons are in your brain, the more likely your brain is capable of working at a fast rate. That is, myelin speeds up the circuits in your brain and thus makes certain activities easier for you to learn or perform.

We now know that different regions of the brain become myelinated at different stages of an individual's development. For instance, Wernicke' area, which deals with language comprehension, becomes fully myelinated about six months before Broca's area even starts to demonstrate evidence of myelination. This finding fits with the commonsense notion that one would need to comprehend a language before being able to produce that language. (Recall that Broca's area deals with processes involving language production. This component of language acquisition logically should follow the formation of processes involving language-comprehension abilities [Markezich, 1996].)

When you are reading the following chapters on development, try to note when the brain is undergoing increased processes of myelination, because this process can help mark other forms of developmental changes in behavior or cognition. That is, myelination processes form the bases for many cognitive and other mental abilities observed in humans across the life course (Sowell, et al. 2003).

Implications for Practice

Social workers play a critical role in service-delivery systems for traumatized youth, for people with serious mental disabilities, and for people suffering from various types of brain injuries. In each of these areas, knowledge of the brain and how it is compromised by environmental threats is essential to designing corrective and preventive interventions. Bruce

Perry and his associates estimate that the number of children exposed to a traumatic event in the United States is well above 4 million. Included in this conservative estimate are children who are exposed to physical or sexual abuse, who live in the fallout zone of domestic or community violence, who are a party to a serious car accident, and so on (Perry et al., 1995). Perry and his associates have concluded that such traumatic situations can dramatically influence the brain during periods of vulnerability, when brain systems are organizing. This research on brain development is contributing to reforms in public policy that recognize that children are not as resilient as we once thought (Perry et al., 1995). Extreme traumatic experiences can contribute to lifelong traits of personal disturbance. Children will not necessarily get over bad or toxic social environments that they are exposed to early in life (Garbarino, 1995).

Knowledge of the brain and its development is also critical for the design of appropriate forms of early intervention. If practitioners can develop interventions that reduce the intensity and severity of a child's response to trauma, then there is less danger that he or she will develop a negative use-dependent response. That is, the more a child is in a fear state, the greater the probability becomes that he or she will begin to develop a hyperarousal or dissociative response that will be transferred across situations and time (Perry et al., 1995).

Understanding the brain and how it develops also has implications for the design of programs intended to prevent child abuse and neglect, such as Healthy Families America. Our society needs more of these programs that target risk for abuse and neglect during critical periods of brain growth and development. In addition, research on the use-dependent features of brain organization points to the significance of providing support services for new mothers at risk for developing serious mental disorders. Depressed mothers are not available for their children; this fact can affect their responses to normal threats in their environment. This is especially true during windows of opportunity for the development of social attachment, emotional regulation, and so forth.

In sum, practitioners in direct and indirect services are obtaining more information about the role of biological factors in forming many traits and life destinations that social work is committed to eliminating. The profession is unlikely to realize this objective if it does not consider the biological threats to brain development.

The next Focus section is a narrative written by a brain-injured social-work student. Her brain injury introduces special challenges in her work, and she describes in this narrative her personal ways of coping with her disability.

FOCUS ON NARRATIVE

SURVIVING THE RESIDUAL EFFECTS OF TRAUMATIC BRAIN INJURY

My injury happened when I was a young teenager. I was in a car accident that damaged my brain stem and temporal lobe. As a result of the accident, I was in a coma for two months and incurred residual brain damage that changed my life and is still present. An injury of this type can cause alteration of consciousness, seizures, memory loss, and disorientation to purpose, time, and place. My traumatic brain injury has caused me to have problems with my ability to stay awake. My short-term memory and recall are also affected by my injury. My specific problems are *retrieval failure* and *anterograde amnesia*. *Retrieval failure* refers to an inability to bring up or retrieve information that I have stored in my memory. *Anterograde amnesia* refers to my inability to lay down new memories because the process that moves information from my short-term memory to long-term memory is damaged.

My brain disability affected my ability to complete an internship during the second year of my MSW program. The internship was at a mobile crisis agency. I will describe a specific incident that illustrates how my brain injury has influenced my school experiences and continues to affect my day-to-day activities.

We were sent out on a suicide call, and the client was sharing some of his suicidal ideations when we arrived. The client told me and other members of my team that he planned to kill himself. During this important component of the visit, I started to become drowsy and my eyes began to close. I struggled to become alert, but that did not happen right away and I started having what I call one of my "sleep attacks." When the call was finished, we went back to the agency. Nothing was immediately said about what happened on the call. But when I went to the agency for the next shift, my liaison and field instructor were there and we had a small meeting to discuss what

(continues)

FOCUS ON NARRATIVE (continued)

happened on this crisis visit. Basically, my internship ended because of that incident.

As a disabled person, I try to hide the more obvious aspects of my disability. For example, when a sleep attack begins and I am in class or at an internship, I get up and walk around to try to stay awake. Hopefully, nobody will notice. I take medication to prevent the attacks, but they can still happen. Sometimes I can return home so I can lie down for a short time when I feel an attack coming on, but I cannot stop them from happening.

Besides sleep attacks, I have to cope with my memory-loss problems. This additional problem affects my interactions with coworkers and classmates. But I have learned different ways to cope with this problem. I have learned over the years how to cover up my memory deficit. For instance, I usually agree with people or try to go along with whatever is happening, so that I will not draw attention to my memory problems. I also try to learn the protocol of a job as quickly as possible so no one will recognize that I am less aware of what is going on than they are. These tactics have worked in some circumstances, although if I am in a high-stress situation, people often will recognize that something is wrong with me because I am not as effective at hiding my problem. I also can go into what my doctors have termed my "fight or flight" mode. When this occurs, I can space out from what just happened. This problem has occurred when I am working with clients. What I generally do is ask them to tell me again what happened to them, and that will begin laying down the memory once again and also strengthen my rapport with the client. Unlike others, I have to go over and over things in order for me to remember some of the information. It takes a lot of energy.

The Disability Resources Center at the university and Vocational Rehabilitation Services have been able to help me obtain note-takers, have extra time to take tests, and take tests in the testing center. These accommodations have made attending the university more successful for me. But I am encountering different difficulties in making a transition from school to the work environment. Whereas the university was supportive, employers have not been as supportive. I feel that I need to find a work setting that will fit best with the residual effects of my traumatic brain injury. As you can see, this is important for me, but I am finding the experience very challenging. Unfortunately, many people do not appreciate how difficult it is to negotiate relationships with other people when you often cannot recall what happened with them during previous meetings. My solution to this problem has been to find ways to get them to repeat things without having them notice my memory problem. I can remember some things, but it takes lots of repetition to lay down a memory of what I will need to know or do in future encounters. I also have developed other ways of trying to reinforce my memories. In preparing for a test or doing a job task, it takes me much longer to learn the key steps. As long as there is not too much variation from the protocol, I can do the task without calling attention to my disability.

—By Debbie Hunt

Biophysical Strengths: Physical Resilience and Allostasis

Many biological factors contribute to humans' resiliency at various phases of their development. Biological resilience involves a variety of protective processes that enable a person to adapt to stress and other challenges to good health. **Physical resilience** refers to a person's resistance to physical injury or harm. It increases the rate at which a person heals and is predictive of how likely a person is to bounce back from injury. Newer research is identifying a group of biological markers that can indicate the human biological system's capacity for responding effectively to changes, including adverse ones. The concept of **allostasis** in biology and biomedicine refers to the capacity for achieving stability through change (McEwen & Wingfield, 2003). This concept focuses on the internal physiological mechanisms that require adaptations to changes in the internal biological system that place the system at increased risks for disease and other negative health outcomes. "Through allostasis, the autonomic nervous system, the hypothalamic-pituitary-adrenal (HPA) axis, and the cardiovascular, metabolic, and immune system protect the body by responding to internal and external stress" (Ryff, Singer, Wing, & Love, 2001, p. 159).

With knowledge of allostasis, researchers in the social and behavioral sciences have begun to study **allostatic load**—the price paid by the body to maintain its systems. Allostatic load "is a measure of the wear and tear that results from chronic overactivity or underactivity of the level stabilizing allostatic systems" (Ryff et al. 2001, p. 160). We now know that people with low allostatic loads have better health outcomes than those with high allostatic loads. This measure has also helped to confirm that social relationships play an important role in physical- and mental-health outcomes (Ryff et al., 2001) and in establishing basic immunity from disease (Coe & Lubach, 2001). Clearly, diet, physical and social environments, social relationships, and psychological factors strongly affect our key biological systems. For this reason, it is important to recognize that the influence of these factors varies at different stages of development and that their relationship to allostatic systems can cause health implications to vary. Social workers need to understand how people can maintain allostatic balance at various phases of their development.

Biophysical Hazards

We currently know that any deficits or dysfunctions in physiological structures will have some bearing on a person's social functioning. The social worker's duty is to assess how these physiological impairments influence the person's capacity to meet life tasks. Before appropriate support services can be identified, the social-work professional must have a general understanding of the person's disease, impairment, or disability. This generalized understanding is not possible without a basic understanding of key human biological systems.

This understanding of biological systems is markedly improved whenever the social worker has a basic understanding of disease and health terminology. In fact, many social workers, in addition to health social workers, are expected to review the client's health status and history when doing background studies. This common expectation requires an understanding of human biosystems and health-related concepts. This section provides a brief, rather than a comprehensive, overview of biologically related concepts encountered in multiple-practice contexts. Further discussion of these topics is systematically provided in subsequent chapters on developmental content, under the heading "Biophysical Hazards." Our multi-dimensional framework seeks to make you aware of the need for a developmental perspective on such hazards. This knowledge enables assessment in direct practice, as well as planning in preventive programming. This section cannot cover all the relevant biosystems, and that task is also beyond the scope of this book. Instead, we hope to sensitize you to the various types of medical and physical information you will need in your practice.

Cancer

Any living organism can develop cancer. Cancer is a serious disease that involves improper—purposeless—cell growth. As we have discussed, our cells grow by the orderly process of cell division known as **mitosis**. Mitosis involves one cell dividing into two cells, two cells becoming four, and so forth. The process of

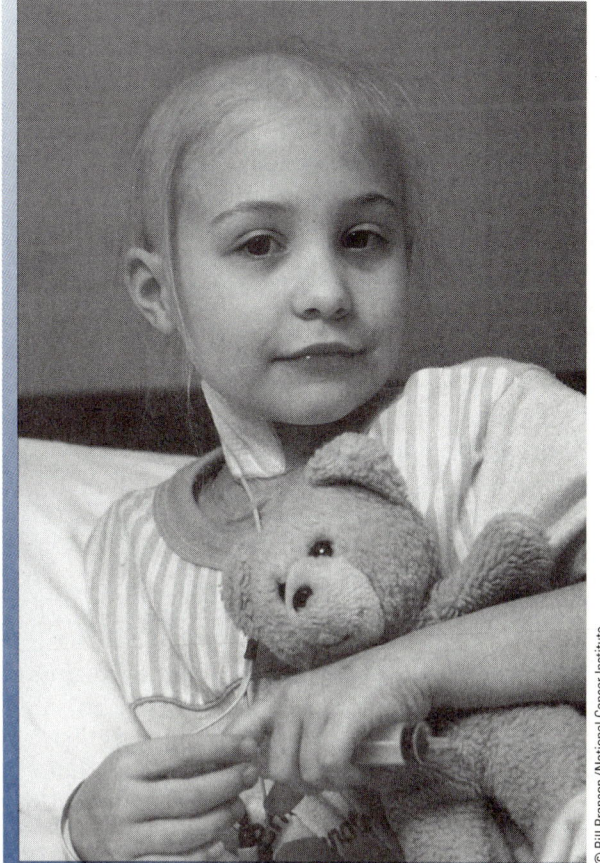

Cancer is a disease with many psychosocial aspects. For example, adjustment to hair loss is difficult both for people with cancer and for those around them.

cell division is normally controlled by other natural processes. Any process that interferes with these controls can lead to rampant cell growth. This cell growth can lead to the buildup of a mass of purposeless tissue referred to as a **tumor**. Self-contained tumors are called **benign tumors**; tumors that are spreading, or are not self-contained, are generally referred to as **malignant tumors**. The spread of these cells to other areas of the body is known as **metastasis**. When cancer metastasizes, the cells begin to grow in other organs and the disease is much more difficult to cure.

Though progress has been made in the diagnosis and treatment of cancer, this disease remains a leading cause of death, surpassed only by heart disease.

Cardiovascular System Problems

The heart is a hollow "muscular pump" that provides the energy needed to force a person's blood through the body. It is one of the few human organs that works constantly. This necessity for continuous work makes the heart vulnerable to a wide variety of injuries and abnormalities (Meyers, 1972). The heart is divided into four chambers: two atria and two ventricles (see Exhibit 2.13). The wall that runs down the center of the heart is called the **septum**. There are two chambers on each side of the septum. The top chambers are atria, and the bottom chambers are ventricles. The structures that control the flow of blood through these chambers are valves. Blood gets into the heart by means of veins. The arteries carry blood from the heart to the rest of the body.

The heart is about the size of a human fist. It is enclosed in a thin sac called the **pericardium**, which covers the middle muscular layer of the heart. This important muscle is known as the myocardium. The function of the heart and its valves may be impaired in a variety of ways. For example, the heart or any of its components may be malformed at birth, a condition known as a **congenital heart disease**. (Numerous factors may contribute to a congenital heart condition. Many of these factors will be discussed in our presentation of prenatal development.) Also, the heart can be exposed to infections or other factors that damage or injure its muscle (a condition called **myocarditis**) or its valves (**endocarditis**) (Meyers, 1972). There is also a technical term used when the sac surrounding the entire heart is diseased: *pericarditis*.

The most common lesion in valvular heart disease involves a condition known as *mitral valve insufficiency*.

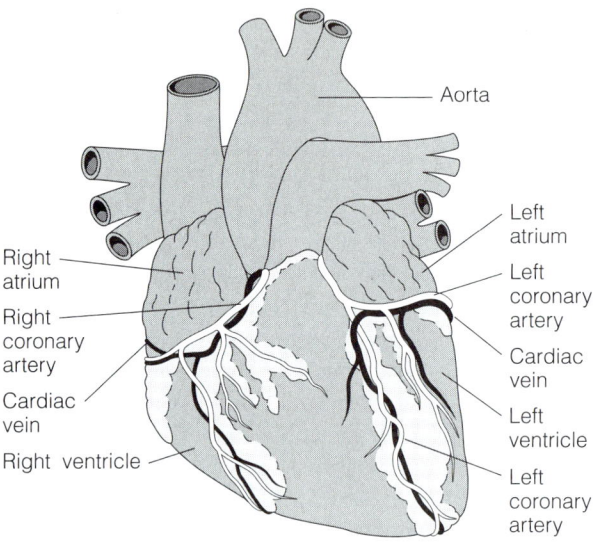

EXHIBIT 2.13 Cardiovascular system
SOURCE: Brannon & Feist (1997).

In this condition, the valve fails to prevent the regurgitation of processed blood. *Mitral stenosis* is another valvular disease, involving the hardening or narrowing of the mitral valve, which is located between the left atrium and left ventricle. Social workers in mental health may encounter people with severe anxiety symptoms that result from a condition known as **mitral valve prolapse**. This valvular disease involves the protrusion of one or both cusps of the mitral valve back into the left atrium. This protrusion can contribute to a backflow of blood. Common symptoms are chest pain, palpitations, fatigue, or dyspnea (shortness of breath and labored respiration). This is one of the conditions that a mental health worker should be aware of in performing differential assessments. The worker may need to make a referral to have this condition ruled out by a physician, because it is often confused with anxiety disorders and other forms of psychological distress.

The force of the blood moving through the heart may also injure any component of the cardiovascular system: heart, arteries, veins, or capillaries. This force of the blood moving through the body is known as **blood pressure**. Normal blood pressure is expressed in two numbers, the systolic pressure and the diastolic pressure. The **systolic pressure** involves a measure of the heart when it is contracting and pumping blood out of the heart and through the body. This is the highest number, or measure of the blood's force through the heart. Normal blood pressure in a young adult is about 120 mm Hg (hydrargyrum, a measurement using mercury) systolic and 70 to 90 mm Hg diastolic (DiMatteo, 1991, p. 25). **Diastolic pressure** is the measure of the blood's flow during the relaxation, or diastole, of the heart. When a person's systolic pressure is above 140, or if the diastolic pressure is above 90, the person is considered to have hypertension, or high blood pressure. *Essential hypertension* refers to having a chronically elevated blood pressure over a long period of time.

Angina pectoris is a coronary condition involving pain and a tightness in the chest. This condition results when the heart muscle does not receive sufficient oxygen. When insufficient oxygen is directed to the heart's muscle, resulting in the death of part of the heart's tissue, this is referred to as a **myocardial infarction**, or heart attack. A number of processes can contribute to the blockage of arteries and to a myocardial infarction. For example, arteriosclerosis, a condition contributing to decreased blood supply, commonly contributes to heart attacks. This condition is often associated with aging and may be referred to as *hardening of the arteries*. Atherosclerosis, a form of arteriosclerosis, involves the buildup of plaque on the walls of the arteries. Plaque is produced by a fatty substance known as *cholesterol*; it clogs up the arteries and impedes appropriate blood flow.

The heart beats at a rate of 60 to 80 times per minute. A measurement of 100 beats or more per minute following normal activities is an indicator of potential difficulties. An elevated heartbeat can indicate structural or functional impairment, or the influence of some type of psychoactive substance. The heart rate, or pulse, must change to respond to the body's demands for oxygen. The heart generally beats faster when a person is involved in a strenuous activity. However, it also beats faster when a person is angry, anxious, or otherwise emotionally excited. During pregnancy, the heart works harder because it is also handling the needs of the fetus. This is one of the major reasons some women experience secondary heart complications during pregnancy.

The blood flowing through the heart and cardiovascular system consists of several formed elements—red cells (erythrocytes), white cells (leukocytes), and platelets (thrombocytes)—in a liquid medium known as *plasma*. The number of red blood cells ranges from about 4.5 to 5.5 million per cubic milliliter of blood (Meyers, 1972). If a person has a red blood count of below 4 million or a blood hemoglobin count (protein compound in the blood) below 12 grams, he or she is considered to have anemia. Anemia is a condition that involves inadequate red-blood-cell production. Red blood cells are responsible for carrying oxygen from the lungs to various tissues in the body. Anemia then may result in less oxygen being available to the body and can cause fatigue and dizziness.

White blood cells number about 5,000 to 10,000 per cubic milliliter and protect the body against infections and other foreign substances. The platelet number is approximately 200,000 to 400,000 per milliliter. Platelets play a critical role in blood clotting. Platelet problems can result in difficulties with excess bleeding.

Respiratory System Problems

The respiratory system handles the inhalation of oxygen and the exhalation of carbon dioxide. This system consists of the lungs, diaphragm, major air pathway (trachea or windpipe), and other air pathways (Meyers, 1972). (See Exhibit 2.14.) The chief organs involved in the respiration process are the lungs. The lungs are two pyramid-shaped structures that lie in the chest cavity. They consist of spongy tissue that is divided into numerous small air sacs called *alveoli*.

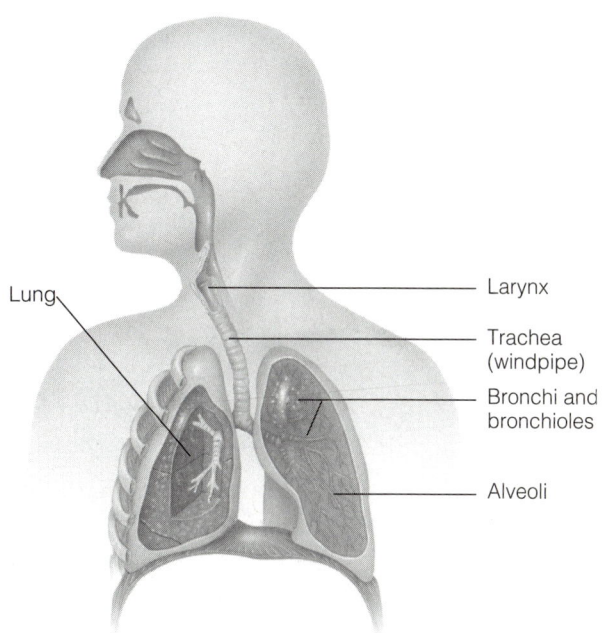

EXHIBIT 2.14 Respiratory system
SOURCE: Ingraham & Ingraham (1995).

These air sacs have in their walls a network of tiny blood vessels called *capillaries*. The capillaries cover the alveoli and take the oxygen from the air into the bloodstream.

Bronchial asthma is a condition of the lungs characterized by intermittent attacks of shortness of breath. The cause is often an allergic response associated with the constriction of the *bronchioles*, tubes that carry air from the trachea to the air sacs, or alveoli. During an asthma attack, the bronchial muscle constricts and thick, sticky mucus is produced. This mucus further obstructs air pathways. Air intake may be normal, but only partial expiration is achieved. In severe attacks, mucus can plug or block the bronchi.

Acute bronchitis is a disorder involving a bacterial infection of the bronchi, whereas chronic bronchitis is a progressive inflammatory disease that is caused by exposure to irritants (Wilson, 1987). Chronic bronchitis may develop in middle age, often in people with a history of chronic smoking. This disorder contributes to extreme difficulty in breathing, or dyspnea. The condition is aggravated by damp and cold. If the alveolar walls are ruptured because of chronic bronchitis, the person will develop emphysema or chronic obstructive pulmonary disease. This condition destroys the walls between the alveoli and decreases the surface within the lung that can be used to exchange gases (DiMatteo, 1991, p. 29).

Endocrine System Problems

The endocrine system is made up of ductless glands controlled by the autonomic nervous system. The system consists of the pituitary, thyroid, and adrenal glands; the sex glands (or gonads); the pancreas; and other glands (Meyers, 1972). (See Exhibit 2.15.) These glands release chemical substances called *hormones* into the bloodstream. The stimuli that cause the release of these hormones are controlled by the nervous system, which is linked to the endocrine system by means of the pituitary gland and its connections with the hypothalamus (DiMatteo, 1991).

DiMatteo (1991) has summarized this process in relation to stress. When the sympathetic nervous system becomes aroused in response to an emergency, the hypothalamus chemically stimulates the pituitary to release ACTH (adrenocorticotropic hormone) into the blood. ACTH stimulates other hormones in response to stress. The adrenal glands, located on top of the kidneys, are stimulated to produce epinephrine

EXHIBIT 2.15
Endocrine system
SOURCE: Goldstein (1994).

Pituitary
The "master gland"; produces hormones that influence secretions of the thyroid, pancreas, adrenals, and gonads; also secretes growth hormones

Thyroid
Produces hormones that regulate metabolic rate

Adrenal glands
Control salt and carbohydrate metabolism; secrete hormones active in arousal and sleep

Pancreas
Produces insulin and glucogen to control sugar metabolism

Gonads
Ovaries (females) and testes (males) produce hormones involved in development of secondary sex characteristics and reproduction

and norepinephrine (adrenaline and noradrenaline), which speed up the heart and respiration and increase the liver's output of sugar to the muscles. Cortisol is also released by the adrenal glands during perceived emergencies, to help control swelling should injury occur (p. 36). The role the pituitary plays in stress responses is just one example of the importance of endocrine glands in human emotions and behavior.

The pituitary gland consists of three lobes and is located just below the hypothalamus. The posterior pituitary collects *vasoprine*, an antidiuretic hormone, and *oxytocin*. Vasoprine is involved in the regulation of water reabsorption by the kidneys, and oxytocin with contraction of involuntary muscles in the uterus (Green, Beatty, & Arkin, 1984). The thyroid gland is located at the front of the neck and secretes the hormone *thyroxin*. This hormone is essential for normal body growth and development. Hyperthyroidism is a condition that results from overactivity of the thyroid gland. The gland in this condition is generally enlarged. Clinically, hyperthyroidism is characterized by nervousness, tremor, constant hunger, heat intolerance, hyperactivity, and insomnia.

The pancreas is another important ductless gland and is located below the stomach. It secretes substances such as digestive enzymes, insulin, and glucagon. Problems with insulin production and utilization lead to the disease *diabetes mellitus*. In this condition, insufficient production or inadequate use of insulin results in body cells being unable to absorb glucose (sugar) from the blood for metabolism. As a result, glucose builds up in the blood and causes high blood sugar and the problems associated with diabetes mellitus. This disease occurs in two forms: Type I, or juvenile-onset diabetes (insulin dependent), and Type II, or adult-onset, diabetes. Type I diabetes is caused by failure of the pancreas to produce sufficient insulin. People with this type of diabetes must have daily insulin injections to replace what the body fails to produce. In adult-onset diabetes, the body has decreased ability to utilize the insulin produced, so the pancreas must produce more insulin to compensate. Blood sugar also builds up, causing problems. Diabetes, especially juvenile-onset, can lead to many complications, including blindness, renal failure, and infections in the lower extremities that could result in amputations. People with diabetes must pay careful attention to diet and weight and must carefully regulate their blood-sugar levels. Regulation of blood sugar often requires finger sticks to check the blood. Social workers may be involved in helping clients with diabetes mellitus adjust to the lifestyle changes necessary to maintain good health.

The other hormones produced by the endocrine system also play vital roles in human functioning. For example, researchers are exploring the role played by hormones in sexual and aggressive behavior.

Abnormalities in systemic processes can be major contributors to emotional disturbances and should not be ignored by social-work practitioners in assessing dysfunctions in the affective domain.

Implications for Practice

Health status is significantly related to a person's sense of well-being. As a result, practitioners must be knowledgeable about conditions that threaten key health functions. They also must understand the effects of various conditions on a person's sense of self, behavior, and expectations. Diseases or biological defects in organ systems can significantly change people's perceptions of themselves and their relationships to others. For instance, people who have had a heart attack may (1) develop new approaches to handling stress; (2) change their lifestyle; (3) eliminate previous coping behaviors that contributed to the heart attack; and (4) change diet and exercise practices. They also may develop new maladaptive responses to fears that

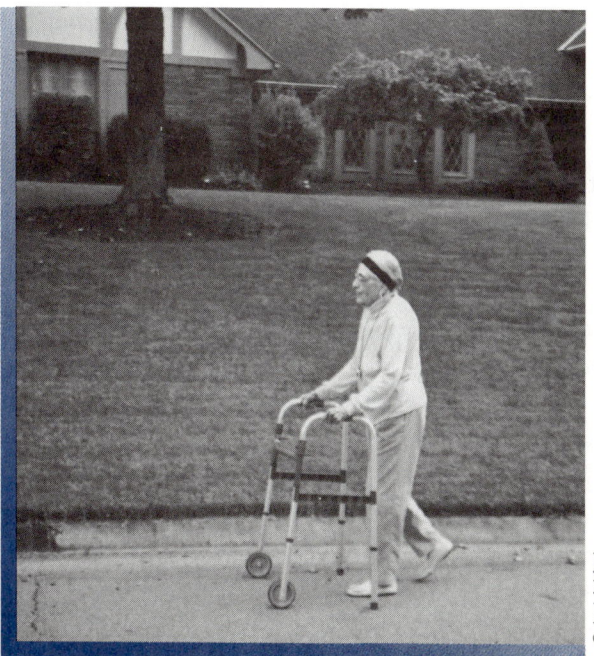

Falling is a major physical hazard that requires seniors to make a number of adjustments.

have no realistic basis in their recovery process. Thus, it is essential for the social worker to appreciate these conditions in addition to developing a basic understanding of the organ systems affected by common disease processes. With such information, social workers are better equipped to engage in effective education, prevention, and treatment.

In health social work, practitioners also need to have a basic understanding of illness behavior. *Illness behavior* refers to how people respond to their subjective realization that they have an illness. Illness behavior can vary directly with the biological systems involved in the client's illness. Some clients have better adaptive coping skills for dealing with physical disorders and distress than other clients do. And, although some people do not handle physical illnesses well, these people may have excellent skills for handling mental disorders. The social worker must understand how basic biological systems function and how these systems affect human behavior processes in order to improve client responses to physical and mental disturbances.

Overview

Social workers who ignore the biophysical dimension will compromise the quality of both their theory and their practice in their efforts to understand human behavior (Saleebey, 1992a). As Saleebey has argued, "the profession of social work has given only superficial attention to taking into account the body's urges, promptings and energies" (1992a, p. 112). We have attempted to compensate for this limitation by examining key biophysical systems that play a fundamental role in understanding human behavior. We assume that the body-mind-environment connection requires the integration of each of the biological subsystems examined in this chapter.

Individual variations in biological systems must be identified in social-work assessments. Social workers must not hold biological variables constant in their practical assessments, and practitioners must be as diligent about assessing biological dimensions as they are about assessing social and psychological dimensions. If social workers do not take into account these biological variations, they run the risk of subscribing to abstract conceptions of client concerns and run the additional risk of ignoring vital biological sensations or needs that make up the fundamental characteristics of the human experience.

Summary

Biophysical Growth and Development

Any understanding of human growth and development must take into account key biophysical systems. Human growth includes all the processes that contribute to the addition of new components of a person's physical structure, including biophysical components like cells that result in increased size of a person's body. Growth differs from development, which refers to all the processes that contribute to the improvement or change in body components.

Cells represent the smallest unit of living physical matter. Basic cellular functions are under the control of DNA and RNA, the nucleic acids that determine our hereditary characteristics. A gene is a small portion of the DNA molecule and provides the blueprint for the other nucleic acids that control the fundamental properties of human organisms.

Chromosomes are located in the nucleus of every cell and contain sets of genes from each of the parents. The mother and father each provide twenty-three chromosomes to the zygote, or fertilized egg. These chromosomes contain many genes that influence our inherited characteristics.

Social workers must understand the fundamental processes that influence variations in inherited characteristics in order to help clients understand inherited physical and developmental processes. The fundamental kinds of inherited disorders encountered by social-work practitioners include single-gene disorders (dominant, autosomal recessive, sex-linked recessive), multifactorial disorders, chromosomal disorders (Down syndrome, Trisomy 18 and 13), and sex-chromosomal disorders. Cell-division problems occur in both meiotic and mitotic processes. Translocation and nondisjunction are the most common problems in cell division. Each of these problems influences biophysical growth and development.

Biochemical processes, especially those in the central and peripheral nervous systems, influence many aspects of human behavior. The central nervous system (CNS) consists of the nerve cells (neurons) and their attendant chemical processes within the brain and spinal cord. The peripheral nervous system involves all the nerve cells and cell processes that lie outside the brain and spinal cord. The nervous system consists of thousands of nerve cells, and each nerve cell receives information from about one thousand other nerve cells through biochemical substances called neurotransmitters. The growth and development of neurons have optimum periods for the establishment of specific functions. Many human traits are influenced by factors in the environment that determined how key neuronal systems were programmed.

Biophysical Strengths and Hazards

Biological resilience involves a variety of protective biophysical systems and processes. The biophysical system has markers that can measure a biological system's capacity for responding to effective changes. **Allostasis** refers to the capacity to achieve stability through change.

Impairments in any organ or physiological system have significant implications for social functioning. Cardiovascular-system problems are a major concern at various stages of the life cycle. There are many ways to measure the cardiovascular organ system's functioning. Blood pressure represents the force of blood moving through the body, and it is expressed in two numbers: systolic pressure and diastolic pressure. Social workers should know the ranges of normal blood pressure at various stages of development and in various social situations. The heart rate, which is typically 60 to 80 beats per minute, changes in response to the body's demands for oxygen and is measured as a pulse. Abnormalities in the heart, respiratory, and endocrine systems can contribute to many forms of emotional disturbance.

Social workers need a basic understanding of the range of physical conditions that contribute to emotional and behavioral disturbances in each of the key organ systems outside the nervous system.

CONCEPT MAP

Key Terms

- allostasis
- allostatic load
- amino acids
- angina pectoris
- autosomes
- axons
- canalization
- central nervous system
- chromosome disorders
- cystic fibrosis
- dendrites
- development
- diastolic pressure
- differentiation
- dominant gene
- Down syndrome
- endocarditis
- fragile X syndrome
- frontal lobe
- genotype
- glia
- gray matter
- growth
- hemophilia
- Huntington's chorea
- hyperplasia
- hypertrophic growth
- Klinefelter's syndrome
- Lesch-Nyhan syndrome
- malignant tumors
- meiosis
- mitosis
- mitral valve prolapse
- monoamines
- multifactorial disorders
- mutation
- myelination
- myocardial infarction
- myocarditis
- neurons
- neurotransmitters
- occipital lobe
- parasympathetic nervous system
- parietal lobe
- peptides
- pericardium
- peripheral nervous system
- phenotype
- proliferation
- proteins
- purines
- recessive gene
- shared environment
- single-gene disorders
- sympathetic nervous system
- synaptic cleft
- systolic pressure
- Tay-Sachs disease
- temporal lobe
- tumor
- Turner's syndrome
- variations

Online Resources

Websites

Go to http://info.wadsworth.com/ashford to find specific links to these web pages.

Assessment activities on the Thomson website for examining the Raul Salazar case

Brain Networks

The Central Nervous System and Brain Disorders Network and the Alliance of the National Foundation of Brain Research have links on this site.

Neurotransmitters

This is a resource for searching on neurotransmitter issues.

Brain Development

This site presents a curriculum for the promotion of balanced care relevant to brain development.

Diabetes among Native Americans

This site provides data on diabetes as a growing problem for Native Americans.

InfoTrac College Edition Keywords

For interesting materials related to what you have just read, please go to the InfoTrac College Edition website and search using the following keywords:

- nature and nurture
- mental retardation
- gene therapy
- behavior genetics

Book-Specific Resources

Book-specific resources, which can be found at http://info.wadsworth.com/ashford, include the following:

- case studies
- quizzes to test your knowledge
- PowerPoint presentations

CHAPTER 3

THE PSYCHOLOGICAL DIMENSION
FOR ASSESSING SOCIAL FUNCTIONING

CHAPTER CONSULTANTS

ANDRE IVANOFF
Columbia University

PAULA NURIUS
University of Washington

BRUCE THYER
Florida State University

WHAT DO WE MEAN by the term *psychological*? Although we may have an intuitive understanding of psychological processes, it can be difficult to define our psychological characteristics and functioning. Although the discipline of psychology is relatively new, questions and concerns about the mind's operations have interested humans since the inception of our history (Viney & King, 2002). Our ancestors explored dreams, memory, ideas, perception, and other key mental functions. They also were curious about what we would refer to today as *personality*, or individual differences.

Psychologists with an interest in personality are guided by questions such as, what factors account for patterns in character and behavior? How is each of us unique? Can we differentiate ourselves from others around us? Further questions address the psychological aspect of human behavior: What role do intuition and subjective experience play in understanding the mind or cognition? What determines the formation of our individual personalities? What are common human needs and emotions? How do people learn and forget information? What motivates people to behave as they do? How is information represented and stored in our minds?

This chapter addresses the psychological dimension of psychosocial functioning. The psychological system serves the purpose of mobilizing our biological and social resources to attain goals (Anderson & Carter, 1984; 1990). Anderson and Carter (1990) have pointed out that the function of goal attainment is what differentiates the psychological system from the other major systems of psychosocial functioning. The psychological system also plays critical roles in helping to avoid danger and in organizing and motivating human thought, emotion, and behavior.

Psychological Theories

The psychological dimension includes many subsystems with key concepts social workers can use in assessing psychological contributions to problems of social functioning. Each of these subsystems includes concepts that are useful in assessing psychological contributions to human behavior. For instance, what psychological systems are useful in assessing Raul Salazar's case, introduced in the last chapter? Is Raul experiencing any difficulties in his emotions, attitudes, or perceptual abilities? Does he have problems with concentration or attention? (And what is the difference between concentration and attention?) Are Raul's reported activity levels a function of problems with behavior or emotions? Are his behavioral problems learned?

Answers to these questions involve systematically gathering data about key psychological functions covered in this chapter. Knowledge of these functions is also useful in distinguishing the psychological system from the social and biological systems in our multidimensional framework. We will begin this chapter with a look at several classic theories of psychological explanations of human behavior.

Psychodynamic Theory

Sigmund Freud, a physician and neurologist, developed the first major theory of personality during the late nineteenth century. He became interested in patients with mental problems and encouraged his clients to explore their childhood experiences. Freud believed that early experiences were possibly the most important factor in the formation of adult personality and psychopathology. His contributions to psychology are perhaps unmatched in terms of their overall influence (Schultz & Schultz, 1999; Viney & King, 2002). His concepts and views of human nature are incorporated in popular culture, most areas of social science, literature, and the humanities. He clarified for practitioners how we can study the unconscious by observing its clinical manifestations.

All human behavior, according to Freud, is driven by a special kind of energy referred to as the libido. The **libido** is in constant search of pleasure. This "libido theory" is considered the cornerstone of contemporary psychoanalysis (St. Clair, 2004). "With this theory, all human behavior could be related to the driving force of the sexual instinct and the counterforces that kept it in check" (Gaylin, 1986, p. 47). The libido is associated with instinctual drives such as hunger, elimination, and sex, which are biologically determined. These drives must be released to reduce tension, and this release is experienced as pleasure. These drives operate according to the pleasure principle, which insists on immediate gratification of urges. Even an infant's behavior is motivated by these unconscious, pleasure-seeking urges (St. Clair, 2004). The id, one of the three components of personality, is the instinctive component and operates from the basis of the pleasure principle. The **id** is often referred to as the storehouse of psychic energy. This psychic energy is limited to **primary-process thinking**, which is based on irrational, illogical, and fantasy-oriented notions; it is disconnected from reality.

EXHIBIT 3.1 Freud's stages of psychosocial development

Stage	Sexual focus	Key tasks	Fixations
Oral (0–1)	Mouth	Weaning from breast or bottle	Obsessive eating, talking, smoking, drinking
Anal (1–3)	Anus	Toilet training	Obstinacy, compulsiveness, possessiveness
Phallic (3–6)	Genitals	Oedipal crisis, identification with adult role models	Homosexuality, narcissism, arrogance, adult role models, flamboyance
Latency (6–12)	None	Focus on social relationships	
Genital (puberty)	Genitals (intercourse)	Development of intimate relationships	

The **ego** saves us from being victims of our own pleasure. It is the executive branch of one's personality and makes rational decisions. It is able to postpone pleasure until an appropriate time. The ego operates within the context of the reality principle by bringing individual pleasure within the boundaries of reality. The ego must create balance between the other two personality components, the id and the superego. In attempting to create a balance, the ego is sensitive to the desires for immediate gratification and also acknowledges social realities such as norms, rules, and customs that influence behavior. The ego is responsible for mediating between the id and the superego. Mastery of this task leads to mature and adaptive behavior. Such adaptive behavior is referred to as **secondary-process thinking**, which is based on realistic and rational approaches to problem solving. The ego desires to avoid any negative social consequences and thus helps the person conform to society's rules by serving as the executor and mediator of the conflicts between id and superego. The ego is an abstract concept that is often defined by its functions. These functions represent the way a person adapts to his or her environment (Goldstein, 1984; St. Clair, 2004).

The **superego** is the moral guidance that helps balance the drives associated with the id. It represents the social standards derived from society and the family; as children grow up, they are exposed to moral standards for behavior. The id and the superego are not too friendly with each other, because they are oriented toward different goals—one toward pleasure, and the other toward moral standards. The ego mediates between these two components, taking into account instinctual impulses and moral values. Freud assumed that the superego emerges from the ego at about 3–5 years of age.

For Freud, the superego emerged from the ego through identification with intimate authority figures or from the selective reactions of an individual's environment to certain behaviors (Andrews & Bonta, 1998). In many of his writings, he considered the process of identification to be the most important determinant of moral conduct. Freud also believed that the superego consists of two elements: the conscience and the ego-ideal. The **conscience** involves internalized mental representations of conduct that are subject to punishment, whereas the **ego-ideal** is considered the mental representation of conduct that is positively valued by the environment (Andrews & Bonta, 1994; 1998).

From a Freudian perspective, how does personality develop? Psychoanalytic theory is based on a stage theory of development. We move through various stages, and how well we master those stages forms the basis of our personality. As children mature, their sexual energy (urge for physical pleasure) is invested in biologically predetermined areas of the body. Each stage in Freud's psychosexual development represents a different area of sexual focus that influences the adult personality. Infants are dominated by an oral focus, early childhood moves through an anal and phallic focus, middle childhood is represented by a latency period, and the psychosexual stages end at puberty, when the focus is on the genitals.

Personality depends on how each of these stages is handled. Children may experience excessive gratification or excessive frustration while in one of the stages. When this happens, fixation occurs, whereby the child cannot move on to the next stage of development. Fixation can be apparent during the adult years. For example, many people are familiar with the label "anal." A person is referred to as anal because his or her fixation is exhibited by compulsiveness. Exhibit 3.1 presents Freud's stages of psychosexual development.

According to Freud, early-childhood development is critical in the development of personality. In fact, personality is laid down by the age of 5 or 6 as the child completes the primary psychosexual stages. The last two phases of development are latency and genital. During the latency stage, a child's sexual energy subsides (Austrian, 2002). During the genital stage in adolescence, the conflicts of early childhood are revived. If they have been mastered appropriately, then the child moves into normal heterosexual relationships. This foundation of one's personality is reexperienced in adulthood, and adult conflicts are related to early crises that occurred in childhood.

Many theorists did not like Freud's notion that personality development is confined to the early years. Most notable among them was Erik Erikson (1902–1994), who believed that personality evolves across the lifespan. His work, as well as Freud's, is criticized for its emphasis on heterosexual relationships (Austrian, 2002).

Anna Freud (1895–1982) is known for her work on defense mechanisms and how defensive reactions determine our behavior. Because of the focus in her work on the adaptations of the ego to the demands of the environment, she is seen by some as the first proponent of the modern-day field of **ego psychology**, or self theory (Durand & Barlow, 2005). These approaches focus on understanding how the self copes with the demands of the environment. In ego psychology, ego functioning is determined by assessing a person's impulse control, frustration tolerance, and affect regulation. Data on these functions provides mental-health professionals with information about the quality of ego functioning and about the defenses a person utilizes to cope with stressful circumstances (Stoudemire, 1994; St. Clair, 2004).

Erikson's Psychosocial Theory

Erik Erikson developed a psychosocial approach to human development. Before immigrating to the United States in 1933, Erikson worked with Sigmund Freud. But Erikson's work includes several key departures from Freud's thinking. In Erikson's view, Freud placed far too much emphasis on the role of biological and sexual forces in human development, resulting in Freud's neglect of development after adolescence. Erikson, in contrast, was interested in explaining development from birth through death.

Erikson assumed that people follow a sequence of stages of development from birth through death. These developmental stages include tasks that result from both biological forces and age-related social or cultural expectations. The biological forces follow an inborn plan that governs when and how aspects of the biological system arise. This plan is technically referred to as the **epigenetic principle**. It refers to the biological blueprint that dictates how the organism grows and reaches maturity. This plan guiding the biological forces combines with the changes in the social expectations of a society to structure the person's adaptation to his or her environment.

Erikson has identified eight psychosocial stages of human development, as shown in Exhibit 3.2. Each of these stages is marked by differential tasks. "They are patterned sequences of stages encompassing appropriate physical, emotional, and cognitive tasks that the individuals must master in the struggle to adjust to the demands of the social environment" (Okun, 1984, p. 16). This patterned sequence of changes is not considered complete in adulthood; it continues across the lifespan. A fundamental issue underlying this sequence of changes is how individuals define their sense of identity.

For Erikson, each of the eight stages of development should be viewed as a psychosocial crisis or conflict. "Whether the conflict of a particular stage is successfully resolved or not, the individual is pushed by both biological maturation and social demands into the next stage" (Sigelman & Shaffer, 1995, p. 269). These conflicts involve bipolar tasks, such as trust versus mistrust. With the successful resolution of each of these conflicts, the person acquires new ego strengths. For instance, during the first stage of development, a person develops a healthy balance between trust and mistrust. For our survival, we cannot be too trusting or distrusting but need an appropriate balance between these opposite qualities.

In many of our discussions of developmental themes, we refer to Erikson's psychosocial tasks, which have influenced theory and research on human development. His approach has appealed to social workers because of its sensitivity to the effect of social and cultural variables on processes of human development. But the age-grading associated with many of his identified stages is not without controversy. Many individuals do not adhere to the age-grading implied in his stages of psychosocial development. Furthermore, his stages reflect a historical bias toward heterosexuality, marriage, dual-parent families, and other social formations that differ from many of our current realities.

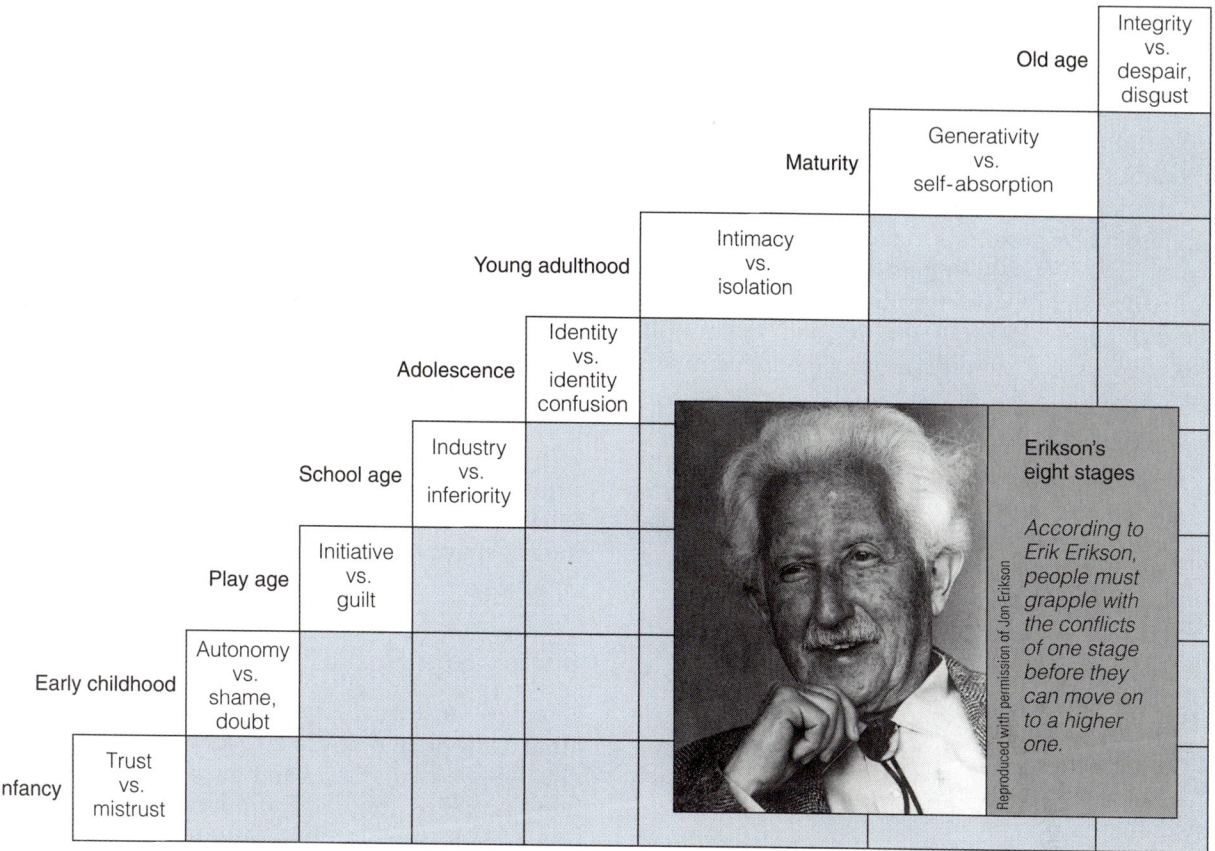

EXHIBIT 3.2 Erikson's eight psychosocial stages
SOURCE: Adapted from "Reflections on Dr. Borg's life cycle," by E. H. Erikson, in "Adulthood," *Daedalus*, 105(2), Spring 1976, p. 43. Copyright © 1976 American Academy of Arts and Sciences. Adapted with permission.

Watson's and Skinner's Learning Theories

John B. Watson brought behaviorism into the forefront of psychology in 1913 when he asserted that psychology must abandon its focus on subjective "mentalistic" concepts and instead focus exclusively on behavior. Watson is recognized as the father of behaviorism, a learning theory that is based on observable behavior. Watson was extreme in his position that at birth a person is a tabula rasa—a blank slate. A well-known statement of his represents his thinking:

> Give me a dozen healthy infants, well formed, and my own specified world to bring them up in and I'll guarantee to take any one at random and train him to become any type of specialist I might select—doctor, lawyer, artist, merchant, chief, and yes, even beggar-man and thief, regardless of his talents, penchants, tendencies, abilities, vocations, and race of his ancestors (1925, p. 82).

Clearly, Watson believed that development depends on learning: given the proper experiences, learning will proceed. This theory is quite different from those of Freud and Piaget, which assume that changes in behavior take place as children move through different stages. Furthermore, behaviorists reject notions such as the id, ego, and superego because these mental functions cannot be observed and studied. Instead, they focus on studying observable stimuli and observable responses to stimuli.

Watson demonstrated the importance of learning in an experiment designed to prove that children's fears are learned and not inborn. A child named Albert participated in an experiment whereby he learned to fear cute little white rats. The procedure was simple: Albert was presented with a stimulus, the cute white rat, and at the same time was exposed to a second stimulus, a loud, frightening sound. Through repeated presentations of the rat and the sound, Albert learned to associate the white rat with the frightening noise. Soon, just presenting Albert with a white rat led to a fearful reaction. Thus, Watson demonstrated that fears can be learned through experience.

This style of learning is referred to as **classical conditioning**—learning that occurs when a neutral stimulus acquires the capacity to elicit a response that was originally elicited by another stimulus. Classical conditioning is a widely accepted explanation for the acquisition of certain emotional responses, such as fear and anxiety. You can easily see how a phobia or fear could be developed in this manner. For example, if you got into a serious automobile accident, you could develop a fear of driving. The previously neutral stimulus of driving a car is now associated with your frightening accident. So when you recover from the accident and get into the driver's seat again, you may not be able to drive the car without a heightened sense of fear and panic.

B. F. Skinner built on Watson's learning theory (1953) by advancing the study of **operant conditioning**, a form of learning that occurs when responses are controlled by their consequences. Skinner observed that behavior is repeated when followed by positive consequences and that it is not repeated when followed by neutral or negative consequences. When consequences such as rewards and punishments are made contingent on behavior, they can have a powerful influence on behavior.

Two critical concepts in operant conditioning are *reinforcement* and *punishment*. **Reinforcement** refers to anything that follows a behavior and increases the likelihood of that behavior. **Punishment** is anything that follows a behavior and decreases the likelihood of that behavior. These concepts are really quite simple, and part of the attraction of operant conditioning is that it is a straightforward theory about behavior.

Two other operant learning processes contribute to how behavior is acquired. **Negative reinforcement** occurs when a behavior increases because it is followed by the withdrawal of an unpleasant stimulus. **Extinction** occurs when a conditioned response that was previously reinforced stops producing positive consequences.

Consider the following example: A child whines and nags his mother for a cookie, until she eventually relents and gives him one. In this example, the child's whining is strengthened through positive reinforcement; the whining was followed by a positive consequence, the cookie. However, the mother's behavior is influenced by negative reinforcement. The child's whining, an aversive event, is terminated by the mother giving in and rewarding him with the cookie. The mother's giving-in behavior is an example of negative reinforcement because this response is strengthened by the termination of the aversive event.

From a developmental point of view, Skinner's theory of operant conditioning provides an understanding of how learning takes place. Our behavior can be influenced—over the life course—by the positive and negative consequences we experience. Many theorists, although in agreement with Skinner about the influence of the environment on behavior, have argued that our beliefs or thought processes also can influence how we learn. Watson would be surprised to learn that many modern-day behaviorists have acknowledged a role for cognition in understanding behavior, because he felt that psychologists should study behavior, not mental factors that cannot be observed.

Bandura's Social Learning Theory

Foremost among the new cognitive behaviorists, more appropriately referred to as *social learning theorists*, is Albert Bandura. Bandura attempts to understand people as conscious, thinking beings who can have an influence on their environment. Unlike Skinner, who believed learning is passive, Bandura believes that people can process information to actively influence how the environment controls them.

Bandura's cognitive emphasis in learning becomes obvious when we examine his perspective on how observation can lead to learning. Observational learning occurs when people observe role models and learn new behavior as a result of those observations. In this context, learning occurs without any reinforcement for imitating what is being observed. In essence, observational learning is a kind of indirect learning. The learning process is considered cognitive because people must pay attention to the role models and process this information in their memory.

According to **social-learning theory**, models are critical in the development of personality because of the principle of observational learning. Bandura assumed that learning can occur by observing others, without direct involvement in the learning experience. Social-learning theory is an approach that combines learning principles with cognitive processes, plus the effects of observational learning, to explain behavior. How do children learn to develop aggressive tendencies? Bandura thinks it has a lot to do with the kind of social role models children are exposed to. In perhaps his most famous research experiment, Bandura demonstrated the dramatic influence of observational learning. He and his colleagues (Bandura, Ross, & Ross, 1963) exposed one group of children to a film that showed children displaying aggressive behaviors and exposed another group of children to a neutral film. Following the films, children were taken to a playroom and allowed to interact freely. Children who had seen the aggressive film and had been exposed to aggressive models engaged in more aggressive behavior than did children who had been exposed to the neutral film. This study became a classic because it demonstrated the negative influence that media can have on children's behavior.

An important aspect of Bandura's approach to social-learning theory is the notion of self-efficacy (Bandura, 1997). **Self-efficacy** refers to a person's belief about his or her ability to perform behaviors that lead to expected outcomes. When people have a strong belief in their ability to perform certain behaviors, their confidence is high. This confidence means they are likely to persist in their endeavors. When people have low self-efficacy, they are not very confident, and so are likely to give up easily. Thus, the decision to engage in a situation, as well as the intensity of the effort expended in the situation, is determined by a person's self-efficacy.

From a human-development perspective, self-efficacy is helpful in understanding how individuals adjust and adapt to new situations and roles. A strong sense of self-efficacy can help a person engage in new situations and persist. For example, if a person, say, a single woman, moves to a new city and does not know anyone, a strong sense of self-efficacy might help her adjust to the move. If she is confident in her ability to meet new people (has a strong sense of self-efficacy), she is more likely to pursue situations that give her the opportunity to do so. Furthermore, her self-efficacy could help her persist in finding new friends—not an easy task, which may take repeated attempts.

Cognitive Development and Information Processing

Cognitive psychologists investigate processes involving human sensation, perception, and cognition. **Sensation** refers to the processes by which the organism detects internal and external stimulation at its various receptor sites. **Perception**, in contrast, refers to the interpretation of this sensory input. It involves the use of signals and symbols to understand and differentiate among sensations. **Cognition** is the process of obtaining, organizing, and using sensory and perceptual information from the environment, from past experience, and from other mental activities, such as plans and strategies (Kietzman, Spring, & Zubin, 1985). Cognitive psychologists examine each of these cognitive processes. Prominent among the classic cognitive psychologists is Jean Piaget, whose concepts about cognition have been widely applied and tested in various areas of cognitive science and continue to influence many areas of social-work practice.

Piaget's Structural Approach to Cognition

Jean Piaget was formally trained as a biologist, and his biological perspective influenced his eventual work in cognitive psychology. He published his first scholarly work at age 10, on an albino sparrow that he observed in a park (Cohen, 1983). An important benefit of this accomplishment was his introduction to Paul Godet, a zoologist and a curator of the Museum of Natural History in Neuchâtel, Switzerland. After Godet saw Piaget's one-page article, he invited him to go on walks in the countryside, where Godet showed Piaget how to make observations. By age 16, Piaget was given the job of curator of mollusks at the local museum of natural history. He continued research in this area and completed his doctoral thesis on the habits and habitat of Valais mollusks (Cohen, 1983).

Piaget's interest turned to psychology, and he collaborated with Alfred Binet on the development of intelligence tests. In conducting these tests with children, Piaget was intrigued by how they reasoned about their wrong answers. Rather than study how to measure intelligence, he became interested in how children use their intelligence. He developed his theories of cognition by closely observing his own children.

Piaget built his career on studying the relationship between how we develop and how we learn. He believed that we mature into logic rather than learn it. It was because of this important distinction that American psychologists ignored some of his early works. According to many behaviorists, logic and other knowledge skills are products of learning. Many behaviorists consider the mind at birth to be a blank slate that is written on by experience. But Piaget assumed that there are inborn, invariant processes in humans that play a fundamental role in understanding reality. These processes are *adaptation* and *organization*.

The concepts of adaptation and organization are critical components of Piaget's theory of cognitive development. People use cognitive structures—schemata (singular *schema*)—in the process of adapting to and organizing their world. A **schema** is a unit of information that an individual possesses; **adaptation** deals with the individual's relation to the external world and the ability to change or adapt to that world. The process of adaptation involves the twin processes of **assimilation** and **accommodation**. According to Piaget, what we perceive in the external world does not always fit our internal schemata, or what we know. So we can assimilate new information into our existing schemata or thought structures and thereby change what we perceive (assimilation). Or we can accommodate our thought patterns to what we perceive—in other words, change what we think (accommodation).

Organization is the other invariant feature of human cognition. "Organization is the tendency for all members of a species to systematize their processes into coherent systems, physical or psychological" (Ginsburg, 1985, p. 180). It is the way we make sense out of what we perceive. To understand this concept, it is often helpful to keep in mind Piaget's biological perspective on the role of heredity in human development. In Piaget's view, individuals are endowed with physical structures that are species-specific. In other words, each species has distinctive physical structures, and, as humans, we inherit several key physical structures that are specific to our species. Thus, through heredity, everybody possesses the same basic nervous systems, perceptual structures, and other similar attributes (Ginsburg, 1985).

The concept of organization suggests that the specific heredity of humans guarantees that they have in common a universal potential for acquiring a specific type of cognitive development. The expression of this potential requires an adequate environment. For instance, humans have the inherited potential for abstract thought, but they will not develop this psychological function without an environment that stimulates the need for the development of abstract adaptations.

As children develop, they begin to explore their environment with increased curiosity.

This tendency toward organization is what Piaget's theory of cognitive development seeks to explain. He provided a stage description of the developmental variations in the systems or structures of thought observed in humans. In his approach to cognition, he proposed that individuals go through a series of mental stages:

the sensorimotor period (from birth to about age 2)
the preoperations period (ages 2 to 7)
the concrete operations period (ages 7 to 11)
the formal operational period (ages 11 and above)

These stages illustrate why we observe variations in knowledge between children and young adults. These variations are not due merely to children lacking facts, experience, or information; children think differently because of the mental structures that define their stage of development. The role played by mental structures in his theory of cognitive development led to Piaget being termed a *structuralist*.

Piaget's structural approach has significantly affected how clinicians work with children. In the past, minimal attention had been given to a systematic approach for working with children from a cognitive-developmental perspective. Today, cognitive development is gaining recognition as a critical consideration in choosing appropriate interventions for children.

Although adults recognize that children lack the capacity to understand many events in their lives,

Piaget's work provides an invaluable basis for explaining observations that are often taken for granted. For instance, throughout history the limitations in the abilities of children have been recognized. But these developmental abilities are often ignored in actual interventions. An excellent example of the dangers associated with ignoring cognitive-developmental abilities is addressed in the work of Berrick and Gilbert (1991) on the child sexual-abuse-prevention movement.

Berrick and Gilbert argue that prevention services were created to respond to the perceived epidemic of sexual abuse without regard for potential consequences and age appropriateness. In fact, the first child sexual-abuse-prevention program relied heavily on principles from rape-prevention programming developed for adults (Ashford, 1994). In these adult programs, the concept of empowerment was a key organizing principle. This principle, coupled with the now well-recognized "good and bad touches" continuum, were incorporated into the early child sexual-abuse-prevention programs. Berrick and Gilbert's assessment of these prevention strategies indicates that efforts to sensitize preschool children to be assertive in their responses to good and bad touches is developmentally inappropriate. The researchers offer a different approach to this problem—one that takes children's developmental needs into account. Many of these needs involve cognitive considerations requiring actual prevention efforts by adults. Their suggestions are consistent with many of Piaget's propositions.

It is now becoming widely known among clinical professionals that they should use a cognitive developmental approach when planning interventions for children. In addition, social workers are often asked to counsel children about very complex emotional or traumatic events. In fact, this was a key role played by social workers following the bombing of the federal building in Oklahoma City in 1995 and post 9/11. Members of the media asked mental-health specialists, including social workers, to provide consultation to parents about how they should explain this horrible event to their children. Piaget's theoretical approach offers some general guidelines for this type of practice task. It cautions practitioners to be sensitive to children's cognitive abilities. In his theoretical approach, it is assumed that the preoperational child cannot understand the notions of cause and effect commonly understood by adults. In fact, one of the fundamental aims of many of Piaget's experiments was to understand how children develop these fundamental notions of causality. These developmental differences in understanding the causes of events must be taken into account in trying to explain complex issues (such as why people would kill children with a bomb) to children.

At what age is it reasonable to assume that children can self-monitor their behavior? Do preschool children have understandings of death, divorce, war, and other events similar to those of adolescents and adults? The answers to many of these questions will be covered in the developmental chapters of this book, and propositions from Piaget's cognitive theory of development are useful in answering these questions.

Though Piaget's work provides valuable insight into cognitive development, more recent research has shown that we cannot make accurate assessments of key cognitive functions without understanding the information-processing system. This system and its subsystems play a fundamental role in most of our cognitive activities. Today, social workers cannot rely on just one theory of cognition to address the multifaceted problems they encounter in their practice situations. For this reason, we explore key psychological functions and components of the psychological system in the remaining portions of the chapter and begin this process with a discussion of information processing.

Information Processing

For social workers to assess the mental functioning of their clients, they must have a basic understanding of human information processing. The goal of most human information-processing approaches is to understand how stimuli generated internally or externally enter the perceptual awareness of individuals and result in some kind of response. **Information processing** examines the uptake, selection, coding, and storage of information (Weinman, 1987). This perspective assumes that a sequence of stages takes place between the initial stimulus and the subsequent response. These stages follow procedures analogous to those followed by the computer, as shown in Exhibit 3.3.

Although computer metaphors have been widely used in describing how the brain works, it is important to note that new developments in neuroscience indicate a need to modify earlier images for expressing the information-processing functions (Berlin,

EXHIBIT 3.3
Computer as an analogy to information processing
SOURCE: Weiten (1995).

2002). Most early models using computer imagery assumed the existence of a central processing unit with single storage locations in the brain. Newer connectionists and parallel-distributed processing (PDP) models assume that knowledge and information are not stored; instead, the brain stores the strengths of connections between units that allow patterns of information to be repeated. "These models assume that information processing takes place through interactions of large numbers of simple processing elements called units, each sending excitatory and inhibitory signals to other units" (McClelland, Rumelhart, & Hinton, 1986, p.10). For instance, cognitive scientists are differentiating between mental images that represent an analog form of the physical appearance of an object and representations in the brain that store propositional knowledge about the semantic relations among object, features, and events: *perception-based knowledge* and *meaning-based knowledge*. The scientists assume in PDP models that these forms of representation are distributed in associative networks in various locations in the brain. The representations are seen as different patterns of activation across a number of simple processing units (Klihlstrom, Beer & Klein, 2003).

PDP models have three fundamental principles:

1. The representation of information is distributed and not local.
2. Memory and knowledge for specific things are not stored explicitly. They are stored in the connections between units.
3. Learning can occur with gradual changes in the strength of connections through experience.

These principles currently guide studies of key cognitive functions, including memory, perception, and learning. However, many clinical methods still view memory and knowledge acquisition according to earlier metaphors (Berlin, 2002). These models assume explanations involving serial and sequential mental processes, such as attention, encoding, short-term memory, and consolidation (Corrigan & Penn, 2001). However, linear models are being replaced by models of the mind as a *parallel processor* that is capable of organizing multiple, simultaneous memory processes that are distributed in various locations in connected networks (Corrigan & Penn, 2001). Unfortunately, with the exception of a few clinical theorists, mental-health practice has not kept pace with all of the scientific discoveries in this area (Berlin, 2002; Teasdale & Barnard, 1993).

Nonetheless, each stage of information processing contains many classically recognized substages and concepts that are widely used by researchers and practitioners. Breaking down cognition and other processes into conceptual elements can enhance research in those areas. For instance, practitioners and researchers ask questions such as, what are the information-processing deficits in people with schizophrenia? (Corrigan & Penn, 2001; Green, 1998). Deficits or problems in any stage of information processing will contribute to impairments in cognitive functioning. For this reason, we will briefly review several key functions in the information-processing subsystem, regardless of how theorists assume that they are represented in the brain: consciousness and orientation; perception; attention; learning; memory; comprehension; and reasoning and judgment.

Consciousness and Orientation

Consciousness is considered the most fundamental element of human cognition, and it is defined as awareness of internal or external stimuli. This includes awareness of self, others, and various aspects of the physical environment (Ludwig, 1986). Healthy individuals experience a wide zone of awareness in their day-to-day activities, from alertness to sleep. Although consciousness can be described in many ways, it is difficult to operationalize—that is, to define consciousness in identifiable or measurable terms.

One approach, other than the sleep-wake cycle, for dealing with the definitional problems associated with consciousness is to examine levels of consciousness along a continuum from coma to full alertness. Coma represents a mental state in which verbal, motor, or other responses cannot be elicited even with noxious stimuli. Alertness, in contrast, refers to the ability to respond to any emotionally meaningful, noxious, or novel stimulus (Ludwig, 1986; Kalat, 2004).

Social workers can test a client's level of consciousness by evaluating the individual's response to various types of stimuli. Have you ever called out the name of a person who is seriously intoxicated? Your efforts to arouse awareness may elicit a response, but immediately afterward, the person will drift back into a state of unawareness of his or her surroundings. People in deep sleep can also experience difficulties in being made aware of their surroundings. These states of low alertness, which affect a person's potential for many kinds of cognitive processes, are called **disoriented states**. In a disoriented state, a person loses specific levels of awareness: awareness of time, place, and person.

Disorientation can indicate an organically based mental disorder. Generally, if a person's sensory registers are clouded or restricted, then problems in orientation will likely result. Social workers employed in nursing facilities and in situations in which they encounter people suffering from serious mental disorders often see orientation difficulties. Orientation, therefore, is a form of consciousness that social workers assess in determining the status of a client's mental processes by asking clients questions about the time, hour, day, date, month, year, place, city, and so forth.

Perception

Our knowledge of our physical and social realities rests on the functioning of our senses. Can we have pure knowledge of these sensory experiences? This puzzle has intrigued philosophers and scientists throughout human history. What are the differences between sensations and perceptions? As previously discussed in this chapter, *sensation* refers to the process in which receptors detect information that is transmitted to the brain. We currently know that infants detect light, sound, and other stimuli at birth, but they do not understand what this information means. *Perception* is the interpretation of this sensory input (see Exhibit 3.4). There are very few things people do that do not involve perception. As a result, a number of theories about perception have developed in the field of psychology. We will briefly discuss two of these theories: enrichment theory and differentiation theory.

Enrichment theory is often associated with the work of Jean Piaget. In Piaget's view, the information received by our sensory receptors is formless. For this reason, Piaget assumed that we must enrich this fragmented information to make sense of it. Exhibit 3.5 illustrates this point. At first glance you will probably see a young woman looking back over her shoulder. However, you might also see an older woman with her chin placed on her chest (the young woman's ear becomes the older woman's eye). People who are led to expect to see a young woman or an older woman generally end up seeing what they expect (Weiten, 2003). Our cognitive expectations enrich this visual sense experience; that is, our perceptions help us construct interpretations of our reality. In social work, many individuals we encounter in practice situations have faulty perceptions that are rooted in negative life experiences. For instance, many children of abuse often misperceive the actions of other children. They will perceive hostile intentions from

EXHIBIT 3.4
Distinction between sensation and perception
SOURCE: Weiten (1995).

Sensation

Sensory organs absorb energy from physical stimuli in the environment.

Sensory receptors detect stimulus energies and convert them into neural impulses, which are sent to the brain.

Perception

The brain organizes this input and translates it into something meaningful.

EXHIBIT 3.5
Exercise in perception
SOURCE: Based on Boring (1930).

A famous reversible figure

Unambiguous drawings of the young and old woman

The Psychological Dimension

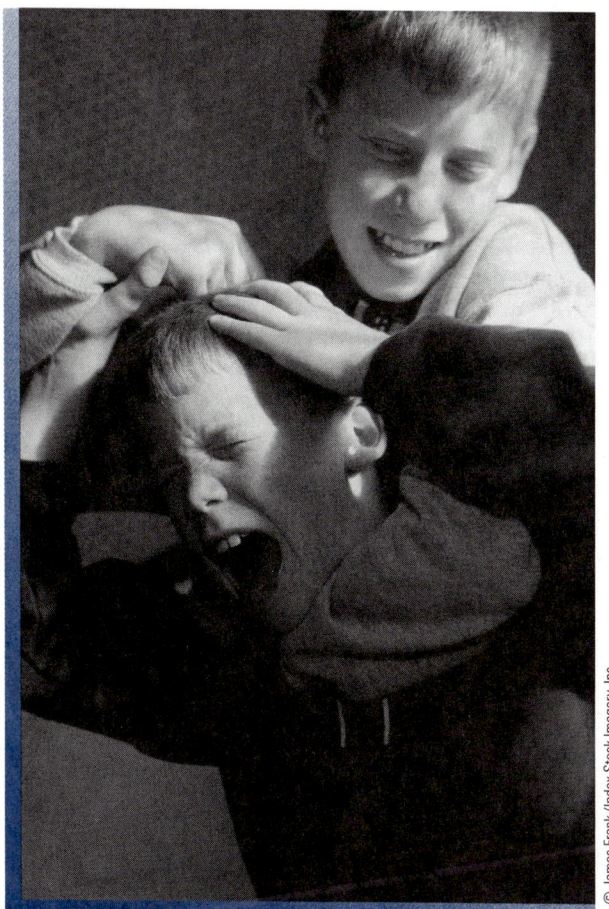

Aggressive children have been found to perceive events in such a way that they overattribute the actions of others as hostile.

neutral acts such as someone accidentally bumping into them.

In contrast, **differentiation theory** contends that all the information we need is contained in the sensations themselves. Our task is to differentiate the various aspects in the stimulations that were there all along.

These two theories hold different understandings of how we make sense of reality. Many factors can influence human perceptions. In fact, the same situation will trigger different perceptual responses among different individuals. As social workers, we must understand how individuals perceive objects and persons. Social psychology devotes substantial attention to trying to discern the factors that influence our perceptions of other human beings in our environment. Other areas of psychology focus on perceptual difficulties in dealing with physical objects in reality.

Attention

Attention is a fundamental cognitive function that plays an important role in memory. Although clients can demonstrate levels of alertness in their functioning, this does not mean that they are attentive. **Attention** differs from alertness in that "it pertains to the ability to focus on a specific stimulus without distraction by irrelevant stimuli" (Ludwig, 1986, p. 17). Attention is often evaluated in clinical practice by having clients perform what is known as *serial 7s*. Serial 7s give an indication of the client's ability to attend. The client is asked, on interview, to subtract 7s in a repeated fashion from 100. To accomplish this task, the client must focus on the remainder while performing the serial subtractions. Some workers prefer to have clients spell words such as *world* backward to test attentional abilities. Another test is to ask a client to recite the months of the year backward.

Clinical scientists have identified other aspects of attention with significance in human behavior assessment—vigilance and concentration. **Vigilance** differs from attention in that an individual must be able to sustain outward attention over a prolonged period of time. In dangerous or unpredictable situations, this is a very important cognitive function. Individuals must be able to scan the environment with a high degree of vigilance to guard against potentially harmful events. Individuals experiencing anxiety disorders often engage in this process in circumstances in which it serves no function. **Hypervigilance** refers to an excessive focus on outward factors in the environment. For example, people suffering from posttraumatic stress disorder are hypervigilant about scanning their environment for danger (Nurcombe, Gwirtsman, & Ebert, 2000).

Concentration is another cognitive function that involves attentional abilities. It refers to a person's ability to sustain inner mental operations without disruption (Ludwig, 1986; Nurcombe et al., 2000). Social workers must distinguish the type of deficit in a client's attentional processes when describing the problem for other professionals.

Learning

The issue of how people learn new information has fascinated humans at least since the time of Aristotle. In fact, Aristotle is noted for having instituted a special tradition in philosophy that continues to have influence on the field of learning psychology—**associationism**. Association is probably one of the oldest and most influential constructs in the field of psychology (Bourne, Ekstrand, & Dominowski, 1971). It involves the formation of mental associations that are registered or stored in the mind (Richardson, 1988). These associations are the result of three fundamental factors: continuity, similarity, and repetition.

Continuity refers to associations formed in the mind because two events occur together in time or space. For instance, if a person connects the sensory experience of furriness with a cat, this can lead to the lasting association between furriness and the concept *cat*. Other associations occur in memory because of the principle of **similarity**. This principle refers to associations being formed because events or ideas that occur close together have features that are similar. Associationists also believe that ideas are likely to become associated when they occur together often. This process is referred to as **repetition**.

Some associationists have made a distinction between sensory association and stimulus-response association. Sensory association assumes that there is a direct connection between the experience of an event and the sensation—called an idea, or image—of that event in the brain. This viewpoint suggests that the connection in the brain is what contributes to ideas being associated with one another. This form of associationism was eventually replaced by stimulus-response associationism. It was believed that stimulus-response associations were easier to study. In a stimulus-response approach, learning involves the development of chains of stimulus-response associations, or connections, in the mind.

Interest in studying processes of association led researchers to discover another major factor contributing to the learning process—reinforcement. Classical conditioning and instrumental, or operant, conditioning are two fundamental models of learning that employ a slightly different definition of *reinforcement*. In **classical conditioning**, reinforcement involves the strengthening of an association between a stimulus and a response through the presentation of a second stimulus. For example, a dog can learn to flex its paw in response to a bell (first stimulus) that is associated with a second stimulus (a shock). In **operant conditioning, reinforcement** refers to the acquisition of new responses because of their effect on the environment. For instance, if a response solves a problem for a child, the child will repeat that response if provided with a similar situation, because of the associated result.

Other factors besides reinforcement contribute to learning in humans. A close relative of operant conditioning is learning through observation, or social learning. In this approach, individuals learn by observing events that they do not directly experience. Bandura (1997) is one of the most noteworthy contributors to this learning theory. He has identified four fundamental components of observational learning: attentional, retentional, motor-reproduction, and motivational processes. These processes explain how people can learn information without experiencing firsthand the consequences of, or reinforcement for, their behavior. (See the discussion of Bandura's social learning theory earlier in this chapter.)

Memory

In addition to the various reinforcement theories of learning, some cognitive approaches include information-processing theories. In the information-processing model, memory is considered the most critical component of the learning process. Clinical professionals have devised specific ways to describe the various components of our memory processes. These descriptions help practitioners identify areas of impairment in people's memory functions that affect their capacity to learn new information. We have already reviewed this approach for understanding memory in our discussion of information processing. We will now discuss some specific concepts used in the mental-status evaluation to assess human memory functions.

The first distinction made in clinical assessment is between immediate memory and short-term memory. **Immediate memory** refers to information that is retained for up to 10 seconds, and we can test for immediate memory by having a person perform the task of *digit span*. A digit span is administered by having a person repeat a list of numbers given forward and backward. An unimpaired individual should be able to repeat five to six digits forward and up to four or five digits backward. Intermediate memory can also be tested by asking the person to repeat three pieces of information. Andreasen and Black (1991) offer the following example—the color green, the name Mr. Williams, and the address 1915 High Street. The objective is to assess whether the client can recall this information immediately after being told it by the practitioner.

In the information-processing approach, memory involves four stages: registration, rehearsal, retention, and recall. Ludwig (1986) refers to these four stages as the "Four Rs." Registration cannot occur without receptor elements being intact; we register or receive information through our senses (sensory registration). Injuries in the brain caused by a stroke or by a physical trauma can affect portions of the brain that play a major role in the registration of information. Short-term memory loss generally is caused by an impairment in some areas involving registration, rehearsal, or consolidation of information (Ludwig, 1986), whereas long-term memory loss is generally caused by a problem in recall or in the retrieval of the needed information. When assessing memory, social workers often warn clients that they will ask them within five minutes to recall the specific information they were given. After five minutes of pursuing other topics in the interview, the client will be asked to recall it.

Short-term memory has definite limits. It can maintain unrehearsed information for about 20 to 30 seconds, or, with rehearsal, between 5 and 10 minutes. *Rehearsal*, a critical strategy for retaining information, refers to the process of repeating by verbalization, imagery, or thought the information received from stimuli. When individuals cannot rehearse unfamiliar information, it is easily lost from their short-term memory.

Short-term memory is also limited in the number of items it can hold. George Miller (1956) wrote a famous paper on this topic called "The Magical Number Seven, Plus or Minus Two: Some Limits on Our Capacity for Processing Information." As a result of Miller's research, we now have a better understanding about short-term memory capacity. When information is added to short-term memory, some of the older information will have to be displaced. For instance, if you are reciting a telephone number to yourself provided by the operator and stop to ask yourself where you placed your pencil, the additional information about where you placed the pencil will displace some of the information already in your short-term memory. In fact, Miller discovered that if you are memorizing 10 items, the ninth or tenth item will knock out earlier items in your memory.

Information-Processing Functions and Memory

Let's look at the stages involved in the process of memory by considering the example of remembering a telephone number told to us by an operator. The first stage of information processing is referred to as *sensory registry*. At this stage, the phonetic sounds on the phone provided by the operator stimulate the listener's acoustic nerve. This information is then transmitted to the cortical area of the brain that deals with auditory information. Initially, this phonetic information is not necessarily categorized as a number or as any other signal or symbol value. The assignment of symbolic value does not occur until the second stage of processing. A sizable proportion of auditory sensations that we receive are not processed beyond the stage of sensory registration. Individuals must attend to the specifics of the sound in order to progress to the subsequent stages (Kietzman, Spring, & Zubin, 1985).

The next stage in information processing involves perception and is often referred to as *pattern recognition*. The attachment of meanings or symbols to the auditory sounds indicates that pattern recognition has taken place. In our case, when the sounds of the operator are recognized as numbers, pattern recognition has occurred. Language and other factors associated with experience are located in long-term memory and play a significant role in this process. The pattern-recognition stage is followed by the short-term-memory stage. Any deficits in these three processes can influence how information is stored in long-term memory.

The digits of the phone number fill up short-term memory. Many people hold the number in short-term memory by saying or thinking (rehearsing) the number until they have entered it. Remembering the phone number long enough to enter it is only a short-term-memory issue. Committing the number to long-term memory will require other memory functions, such as association or learning through repetition.

Think of short-term, or working, memory as containing seven slots or drawers. Each drawer can handle only a single item of information (Howard, 1983). This means that we cannot add additional information to these drawers without displacing the information already contained in them. Some recent theorists further subdivide short-term memory into phonological, visual, spatial, conceptual, echoic, and central-executive components (Harris, 2004). These divisions clarify just how complex our memory processes are.

Long-term memory refers to the retention of information for days, to months, to years. Most individuals easily remember events from their past. In assessing long-term memory, social workers may ask clients to recall the last five presidents. Social workers can also ask about personally relevant information that was obtained before the interview. For example, they can ask about significant childhood experiences that they learned about from the client's relatives.

Long-term memory has been divided into a number of different segments (episodic, semantic, procedural, and other forms of information processing), but these are surely incomplete. For instance, the distinction between semantic memory (context-free knowledge about some specific aspect of the world) and episodic memory (autobiographical memory of events experienced by the self) does not seem to hold for topographical forms of information (Harris, 2004; Kihlstrom, Beer, & Klein, 2003). Other theorists have noted marked differences in what is termed *person memory* (Newman, 2001). Each of these forms of memory can be associated with fundamentally different networks in the brain.

Long-term memory has an unlimited capacity for storing information. There are many views on the length of time that memory can be stored in our brains. One view is that long-term memory, unlike other types of memory, is permanent. Evidence of its permanence is often illustrated in cases of "flashbulb memories," memories involving vivid and detailed recollections. Examples include persons remembering explicit details about where they were and how they felt when they learned of the bombing of Pearl Harbor, the assassinations of President Kennedy and Martin Luther King Jr., and the explosion of the Challenger spacecraft. Additional evidence of the permanency of memory is often found in cases involving exceptional forms of recall triggered by hypnosis. Penfield and Perot (1963) provided additional evidence in some of their early brain research. They found that they could trigger long-lost memories in experiments in which subjects had portions of their brains electrically stimulated.

In spite of various forms of evidence, many scientists are not certain that long-term memory is permanent (Weiten, 1995; 2000). Some scientists use the analogy of a barrel to illustrate how memories are lost. The permanency view holds that memory is stored as if we were placing small stones in a barrel. In this view, all the stones remain. When people forget information, it is because they cannot retrieve or pull out the desired stones contained in the barrel; the problem has to do with how the information is organized in memory. This organizational problem makes it

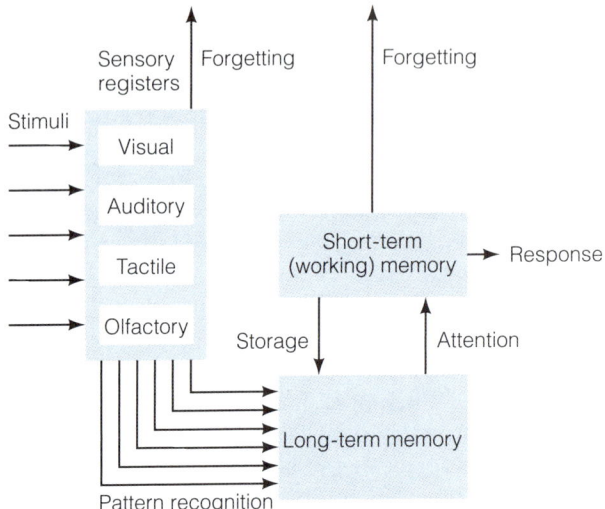

EXHIBIT 3.6 Diagram of short-term and long-term memory

SOURCE: From *Cognitive psychology: Memory, language and thought*, by D. V. Howard, p. 18. Copyright © 1983. Reprinted by permission of Pearson Education, Upper Saddle River, NJ.

difficult to locate the bit of information. The contrasting view assumes that some memories can vanish because the barrel is leaky and allows some of the stones to fall out of the storage area (Weiten, 1995; 2000).

Exhibit 3.6 provides an illustration of the key memory systems in our psychological system: sensory registers; short-term, or working, memory; and long-term memory. In particular, note that we register many forms of information in our sensory registers, but because our attention can focus on only a few items at a time, much of this information is not committed to long-term memory.

Implicit Memory: Remembering without Awareness

Memory generally refers to awareness of events from our past. When we say we remember what we did this past weekend, we are saying that we know that the weekend was an explicit event that we experienced in the past and that we are currently thinking about that event. What we are thinking about right now reading this text can stay in our mind for a few seconds before we forget what we were thinking about. Psychologists, philosophers, and neuroscientists have questioned where this information goes when we are not thinking about it. When you remember a past event that you had not been thinking about, this kind of memory or re-awareness of the experience is referred to as **explicit memory** (Weiten, 2000).

Researchers have also identified another form of memory that involves changes in behavior or performance of a task because one has previously experienced an event. This other form of memory has been termed **implicit memory**. Jacoby and Witherspoon (1982) documented the existence of implicit memory in a study of amnesiacs. They gave a series of tests to amnesiacs and normals that showed that performance on earlier tasks influenced performance on subsequent tasks. Subjects with amnesia were more likely to spell correctly a word for which they had a previous experience, even though they could not recall the word itself. In this study, subjects were asked the following general-knowledge question: "Name an instrument that employs a reed." The next test involved asking the amnesiac to spell *reed*. Jacoby and Witherspoon (1982) found that amnesiacs who had previously been asked about musical instruments that use reeds were more likely to spell *reed* correctly. They concluded that the prior experience primed the amnesiacs to perform better on the spelling test. These results have triggered research into the identification of factors that affect priming.

What is distinct about implicit memory is that it is characterized by a lack of conscious awareness in the act of recollection. That is, when the information is being encoded, the person has no awareness that they are encoding it. This type of memory is a form of learning that is not affected by traditional variables, such as attention, in information-processing models of memory. Instead, we have a better understanding of this form of memory using associative network models of memory (Berlin, 2002; Kihlstrom, Beer, & Klein, 2003).

Practitioners also make distinctions between recent and remote memory in their evaluations of clients. **Recent memory** refers to retention of information individuals need to perform their daily functions. It is usually tested by asking a person about events occurring within the last 24 hours. Individuals should be able to recall, for example, what they did on the day before the interview, how they got to the interview, what they had for breakfast, and other immediate happenings in their daily life. **Remote memory** refers to information occurring several weeks or months in the past.

In assessing memory functions, social workers should consider recall of both auditory and visual information. At points, the social worker will need to capitalize on visual memory when auditory capacity is impaired. For instance, some individuals lose the capacity to remember verbal information but can remember how to read. In other words, if reading is preserved, then this capacity can be used to help the person remember specific information. Visual memory is usually tested by having a person reproduce a simple design. The clinician will draw it and ask the client to reproduce it.

The assessment of memory functions has always played an important role in evaluating psychological functioning. Social workers will probably experience increased demands for their expertise in handling memory impairments, because as our population ages they may have increased contact with people suffering from various kinds of dementia. To assess the functioning of these individuals, they will need to determine the extent to which memory has deteriorated.

Comprehension

Practitioners confront many problems caused by deficits in comprehension. For instance, social workers often encounter clients experiencing difficulties in the comprehension and expression of language, which is closely associated with memory impairment. Nurcombe and Gallagher (1986) point out some of the key areas in which comprehension and expression overlap. They both depend on the following:

1. Amount of information in long-term memory (storage)
2. Amount of information that can be retrieved from long-term memory (retrieval)
3. Arrangement of information in long-term memory (organization)
4. Capacity to apply to problems the schemata, structures, scripts, or maps in long-term memory (p. 46)

Although comprehension and expression are intimately related, practitioners doing clinical assessments often differentiate them. Deficits in human comprehension are represented in various forms of disorders commonly encountered in social-work practice. For example, clients suffering from brain damage caused by stroke, Alzheimer's disease, or trauma experience *aphasia*, which is a disorder that involves deficiencies in the comprehension or expression of language. There are two fundamental types of aphasia: sensory and motor. *Sensory aphasia* refers to language deficits that are caused by problems in the receptive mechanisms of the brain; *motor aphasia* refers to an inability to express one's thoughts through language. This is why motor aphasia is also referred to as an expressive form of aphasia. Motor aphasia is often caused by some form of neurological impairment.

Reasoning and Judgment

People can understand stimuli in their environment; however, this does not mean that they will interpret this information effectively. Our mental functions also involve a number of other cognitive abilities. For example, problem solving and abstract reasoning differ in many ways from the cognitive functions previously discussed in this chapter. Scientists make important distinctions between thinking and other cognitive functions such as remembering and comprehending. Although they define these functions differently, thinking cannot occur without them. In the field of cognitive psychology, thinking is often divided into three areas: problem solving, reasoning, and conceptual thinking.

We will begin this description of human thought processes by discussing problem solving. Social workers are interested in understanding why people cannot solve their life problems. To begin to understand this concern, first we need to define what we mean by the term *problem*. A problem is assumed to exist under the following conditions: "First, there is some initial state in which the person begins. Second, there is some goal state that is different from the initial state and which the person wishes to achieve. Third, the actions that are necessary to convert the initial state into the goal state are not immediately obvious" (Howard, 1983, p. 407). If any of these conditions are not present, then the situation is not considered a problem. We often desire to move from an initial state to another state, but the solution is obvious, in which case any initiated behavior would not be considered a problem-solving activity.

Much of our everyday life involves a need to change our state of being. Cognitive scientists are interested in understanding why people fail to arrive at adequate solutions to these problems. One common factor is *rigidity*. We currently know that people often use a solution from their past that worked well in other situations to solve problems, even though there might be a better way of solving the new problem. This represents a special form of rigidity referred to as a *response set*, so called because the person continues to use a response that worked well in other situations (Howard, 1983).

EXHIBIT 3.7 Solution to Duncker's problem

Rigidity in problem solving can be of concern. All too often, humans use only one perspective in perceiving a problem. This represents a form of perceptual rigidity called a **perceptual set**. This type of set occurs whenever people perceive objects as having only their most common or recent functional significance. Duncker (1945) is known for describing a famous problem in psychology that illustrates this point. He asked subjects to figure out how to mount a candle on a plywood board so that it could act as a lamp. They were asked to solve this problem with a group of common items placed on a table, including candles, a box of matches, string, and some tacks. To solve this problem, the subjects needed to change their perspective about the objects on the table. The solution is illustrated in Exhibit 3.7.

People often have difficulties solving Duncker's problem because they fail to see the matchbox as having a function other than holding the matches. It is interesting that when this experiment is repeated with the matches outside the box, subjects generally solve the problem more easily. The barrier to solving this problem is known as *functional fixedness*. We cannot solve many problems in living without finding novel uses for known objects.

Another key barrier to problem solving is the use of irrelevant information, a fact that has been clearly illustrated in a number of psychological experiments.

See if you can solve the following problem (Weiten, 1995): 15% of the people in Topeka have unlisted telephone numbers. You select 200 names at random from the Topeka phone book. How many of these people can be expected to have unlisted phone numbers? (p. 281)

The correct answer to this problem is "none," because you will not find anyone with an unlisted phone number in the phone book. If you had trouble answering this problem correctly, it was probably because you committed a common error in the human reasoning process. You focused on irrelevant information in the problem statement. The numerical information in this problem is not relevant to its solution.

Also, whether we can solve a problem depends on how it is mentally represented: verbally, visually, mathematically, or spatially. Some problems cannot be solved unless we can properly represent them in our minds. This point is often illustrated by the "Buddhist monk problem": At sunrise, a Buddhist monk sets out to climb a tall mountain. He follows a narrow path that winds around the mountain and up to a temple. He stops frequently to rest and climbs at varying speeds, arriving around sunset. After staying a few days, he begins his return journey. As before, he starts at sunrise, rests often, walks at varying speeds, and arrives around sunset. Prove that there must be a spot along the path that the monk will pass on both trips at precisely the same time of day.

Research has demonstrated that subjects who represent this problem verbally or mathematically have tremendous difficulties arriving at the correct solution. However, it is easy to solve this problem by using graphic representation. See Exhibit 3.8 for the solution.

Humans use a number of problem-solving strategies, one of the most noted being **trial and error**. This approach involves the sequential application of possible solutions to a problem. These solutions are tested and then eliminated when they do not work. Other approaches include means-ends analysis, changing the representation of the problem, searching for analogies, and many others. In clinical practice, it is difficult to assess these mental functions, so practitioners often examine specific types of problem-solving abilities. In particular, it is common for clinicians to ask their clients mathematically oriented problems involving the need for the client to complete a series of numbers. These problems are often referred to as *series-completion problems* (A, 3, B, 6, C, ?). To complete these series correctly, clients must have the ability

EXHIBIT 3.8 Solution to the "Buddhist monk problem"
SOURCE: Weiten (1995).

to sort relevant from irrelevant information and adopt a strategy to solve the problem. They also must detect a pattern in the sequence. In fact, **problem solving** is defined as the "ability to sort out relevant from irrelevant information and to adopt a strategy or plan for completing the task" (Ludwig, 1986, p. 21).

Abstract thinking is another cognitive function that is difficult to assess. **Abstraction** involves the ability to recognize the meaning of symbols. For this reason, it is often tested by asking clients about similarities and differences among objects. This is also why psychiatrists often ask their clients to interpret commonly known proverbs. For example, they may ask clients if they have ever heard the saying "People in glass houses shouldn't throw stones." These simple questions can help the clinician determine whether the client can handle abstract tasks. Without the ability to abstract or problem solve, a person will have severe impairments in judgment. Clinicians often test this function by asking clients to solve a simple life problem like "What would you do if someone jumped in front of you in line at the movies?" People with serious impairments in abstract thought processes will have difficulty solving this problem.

Communication

Communication is considered one of the most important elements in human affairs. It involves oral and written language, nonverbal gestures, and other forms of exchanging information. Throughout this book, we will examine various aspects of linguistic and nonlinguistic forms of communication. In particular, social workers need to have an understanding of speech and language acquisition. These two aspects of communication play a pivotal role in understanding human behavior. We will assume in this discussion that when we communicate with language, it involves two basic activities: speaking and listening, which both provide important clues about a person's psychological makeup and implications for his or her ability to interact with others.

We cannot have any form of culture or civilization without some form of speech and language. Brown observed that language "is nothing less than an inventory of all the ideas, interests, and occupations that take up the attention of the community" (Brown, 1958, p. 156). Although this is a figurative description of the term, it does not provide a clear definition. Before providing a definition of *language*, we should point out that *language* and *speech* are not synonymous (DeVito, 1970). People can fail to develop speech but possess a system of symbols and rules that function as a language. As Ferdinand de Saussure (1959) pointed out, language is a social thing shared by an entire community, whereas speech is considered an individual product. (Saussure [1857–1913] was a famous linguist who significantly influenced many theoretical approaches to the study of language and was one of the major contributors to the field of modern linguistics.)

Nonverbal Communication

As mentioned, speaking and listening are not the only way in which individuals communicate. We also communicate nonverbally and by writing. *Nonverbal communication* includes the facial expressions, gestures, and other actions that send a message to a receiver. These forms of communication have many characteristics in common with language systems. However, unlike verbal communication, nonverbal communication has multiple channels for the transmission of messages. That is, information can be transmitted through gestures, facial expressions, eye movements, and other channels, whereas verbal communication is limited to one fundamental channel of communication (Weiten & Lloyd, 1997). In effect, human communication consists of four basic components: (1) the source, (2) the message, (3) the channel used to send the message, and (4) the receiver. In addition to these fundamental elements, communication theorists have added *feedback* as another major consideration. Clinical social workers are particularly interested in the role of feedback in understanding human communication.

Spoken and Written Language

Spoken language and written language are the two key elements in the human-communication process of interest to social workers. To understand them, researchers have developed several subfields in the language sciences: phonology, semantics, syntactics, and pragmatics. **Phonology** examines the system of sound in languages. Every language is made up of two basic units: phonemes and morphemes. The basic identifiable sound in the language system is known as a **phoneme**. We currently know that the simplest language has about fifteen phonemes, and the most complex about eighty-five. English has forty-five phonemes; each letter of the alphabet has a related phoneme, and some letters have more than one—for example, the letter *i* in "pipe" differs from the *i* in "pit." Every word in the English language can be broken down into sound patterns, or phonemes. The smallest unit of meaning in any language system is called a **morpheme**. An example of a morpheme is *-ing*. There are approximately 50,000 morphemes in the English language.

Semantics is the area in language studies that deals with meaning. It is concerned with understanding how signs and symbols signify actual referents. Because speech and language serve the important function of communicating meaning, semantics is of interest to most social-work professionals, who are often asked to "decode" client communications. In doing so, they must understand the role of symbols and signs within the individual's language system, culture, class position, and nationality. A **symbol** stands for things or ideas but does not necessarily have a direct relationship with them. A symbol does not relate directly to the object it is describing. In fact, the attribution of a symbol in a language is often arbitrary. DeVito illustrated this point clearly: "[T]he word small is actually larger than the word big, and the symbol green—on this paper—is just as black as the symbols black and white" (1970, p. 7).

Signs differ from symbols in that they do bear a valid relationship with the thing for which they stand (DeVito, 1970). When we say a person has a fever, some linguists assume that there is a real rather than an arbitrary relationship between a sickness and the sign—fever. Although this viewpoint is controversial, it clarifies an important distinction that linguists often make between signs and symbols.

In the study of language, **syntax** focuses on the rules that govern the way words are combined to form sentences. We learn these rules quickly. With the exception of a few salutations and clichés, most of the sentences expressed by a person are made for the first time. Would any speaker of the English language accept the following string of words as fitting the rules of the English language? "Time break heard about and." Even very young children intuitively know that this phrase is not legitimate communication. Linguists assume that children recognize that this phrase violates the fundamental rules of their language system. However, many linguists predict that children would show little hesitation in accepting a word string such as "All mimsy were the borogoves, and the mome raths outgrabe" (from Lewis Carroll's nonsense poem "Jabberwocky"); although the words are strange, it would be considered a legitimate utterance because it conforms to English-language rules (Vetter, 1969).

Grammar is the element of language that provides its coherent features and makes language a predictable process. The role of grammar in language studies has had a long and extensive history. In fact, grammar was considered a fundamental component of early Greek philosophy (Carroll, 2004). Most early linguists set out to uncover the units in each language system. However, the views of Noam Chomsky on transformational generative grammar (TGG) have revolutionized the field. TGG captures an element about language that is distinctive to human communication processes—generativity. When linguists state that human language is generative, they mean that humans can use a limited number of symbols in infinite ways. Although chimps can use symbols to communicate, very few studies have uncovered evidence of a generative grammar in their communication competence. Chimps have been taught to use symbols, but their messages often lack spontaneity.

The complexity of language acquisition has triggered significant investigation into a variety of issues. One topic that is gaining in popularity is the study of *bilingualism*. A bilingual individual is someone who can speak two languages that differ in sounds, vocabulary, and syntax (Carroll, 2004). Although Americans have seen bilingualism as an unusual occurrence, it is a more pervasive characteristic in the world community than many Americans realize. Many educated individuals from other countries speak more than one language. For instance, many people in Holland speak Dutch, English, and German. Moreover, English is becoming a second language in many parts of the world. The demand for bilingual skills in New York, Chicago, Los Angeles, Miami, Phoenix, San Francisco, and other major cities is increasing. The social worker should understand how having two systems of grammar influences basic psychological functions (Carrol, 2004).

Pragmatics, the final major area in the language sciences, is the study of the rules that specify how language is used across social contexts. All human speakers must master what can and cannot be said to people in a social context. Grammar relates words to words, whereas pragmatics involves the study of the relationship between words and behavior in the social environment. What is polite or appropriate language behavior in relating to one's boss? Many clients avoid contact with individuals who communicate with them in a fashion suggesting a lack of respect. Issues of respect and politeness vary among language systems and different eras. This area of linguistics crosses into social concerns often examined by sociolinguists and anthropologists.

Implications for Practice

Social workers must reflect constantly on the content of messages conveyed by the language and words used in all aspects of direct and indirect practice (Schriver, 2004). What should we call the place for providing services to people with mental disorders? If we want to target a program for new mothers to prevent child abuse and neglect, what should we call this program? Some names contain meanings that can alienate the very people who need the services most.

What is the best way to tell parents about their child's future? Why do foreign born individuals often regress to their first language system following a stroke? What is the best way to enhance language acquisition in bicultural environments? The answers to these questions require knowledge of human communication processes, including aspects of speech and language development. Throughout this book, we will examine key developmental milestones that involve these basic communication functions. ■

Attitudes and Emotions

So far, we have looked at factors that play a critical role in cognitive development. Now we will look at parts of the psychological system that play a role in motivating behavior. We will explore the role of attitudes and emotions in human behavior. Attitudes and emotions have been subjected to substantial empirical and theoretical scrutiny by researchers in both social work and psychology. Students of human motivation are interested in solving many motivational puzzles: Why do some people have greater propensities toward altruism? What motivates individuals to be achievement oriented? Why do some people prefer antisocial over pro-social activities? We will begin this discussion of motivational subsystems by examining the role of attitudes in human behavior.

The Nature and Function of Attitudes

What are attitudes? How do we form them? What purpose do they serve in our day-to-day activities? An **attitude** is defined as "a learned evaluative response, directed at specific objects, which is relatively enduring and influences and motivates our behavior toward these objects" (Lippa, 1994, p. 214). Gordon Allport (1935) considered attitudes "the keystone in the edifice of American social psychology" (p. 708). Social psychology is a branch of psychology that links the behavior, attitudes, and emotions of the individual to the broader social context of which the individual is a part. Language is one way of making this connection between the individual and society, and attitude is a common element of everyday language. All of us have at some time heard or made comments about other people's positive or negative attitudes.

Some social psychologists attempt to distinguish attitudes from other mental structures, such as values and beliefs. **Values** are considered abstract goals that do not have specific objects or reference points (Deaux, Dane, & Wrightsman, 1993; Michener, DeLamater, & Myers, 2004). Examples of values include abstract judgments about topics such as beauty, freedom, and health. These values can contribute to the development of attitudes and other belief systems. We also use values to evaluate information in making many of our decisions. In fact, attitudes play a mediating role in turning our values into action (Deaux, Dane, & Wrightsman, 1993).

We need to be able to distinguish beliefs from attitudes. Beliefs include information about objects. But what distinguishes a belief from an attitude? Technically speaking, **beliefs** are observations about the qualities of objects (Michener, DeLamater, & Myers, 2004). For instance, we can have information or beliefs about the harmful consequences of smoking. Are these beliefs the same thing as an attitude? As this example points out, it is difficult to make distinctions between attitudes and other mental structures. We may hold beliefs about smoking, but those beliefs may not determine whether or not we smoke.

It is assumed in social psychology that attitudes are more likely to influence behavior than are general beliefs. Fishbein and Ajzen (1975) directly addressed this issue in their theory of reasoned action. They set out to determine what factors, in addition to attitudes, influence our behavior. In their approach, they made an interesting distinction between attitudes and subjective norms. They suggested that attitudes refer to our evaluative feelings; for instance, negative internal feelings you may have about smoking reflect your attitude about this activity. **Subjective norms** would be your beliefs about what important people or significant others think about smoking (Lippa, 1994; Myers, 2001). You may learn scientific information about smoking and its negative consequences, but this does not mean that you will develop a negative attitude. In Fishbein and Ajzen's (1975) theory, attitudes and subjective norms combine to influence our behavioral intention.

Behavioral intention refers to our subjective estimate of how likely we are to engage in a specific behavior. For instance, what is the likelihood that you will smoke in the next month? Fishbein and Ajzen's (1975) theory predicts that, in many circumstances, people's internal attitudes will better predict their behavioral intention than will their subjective norms. This theory allows for a comparison of internal and external influences on our behavior: Our attitudes represent the internal influences on our behavior, and our subjective norms represent the social or external influences.

Fishbein and Ajzen's theory is useful in understanding intentional behaviors: Do you intend to have a baby? Do you intend to increase your study time? These behavioral questions are influenced by some combination of your attitudes, subjective norms, and perceived behavioral control. But, in examining these factors, you should also consider the consequences of the behavior you are trying to predict, and you should personally evaluate these consequences. For instance, two people might agree on the consequences of increased studying—improved grades and less time with friends—but each may evaluate these outcomes differently (Exhibit 3.9).

From research on Fishbein and Ajzen's (1975) theory, we know that attitudes are most likely to pre-

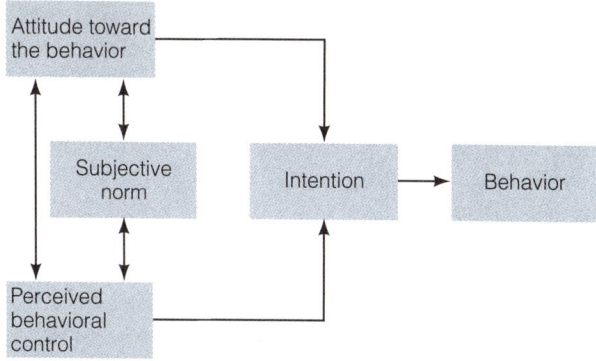

EXHIBIT 3.9 Relationship between attitudes and intentional behavior

SOURCE: From "Attitudes, traits, and actions," by I. Ajzen (1987), *Advances in Experimental Social Psychology, 20*, 1–63. Copyright © 1987 Academic Press, Inc. Reprinted with permission.

dict smoking among adults. Subjective norms, however, are more likely to predict the smoking behavior of adolescents, and adolescents are more likely to be influenced by the subjective norms of their peers. Information of this nature is useful to social-work professionals who assist in the development of preventive interventions. With the benefit of theories on attitudes, social workers are better equipped to develop effective programs intended to change client attitudes.

Attitudes differ from emotions in several important ways. Unlike attitudes, emotions do not have to be directed at a specific target or object. Furthermore, attitudes tend to be enduring. If you are opposed to racism today, you probably will be tomorrow. Attitudes also predispose a person to respond to an object in a favorable or unfavorable way (Michener, DeLamater, & Myers, 2004). Emotions, however, can come and go in a matter of seconds. Although you are angry with your best friend today, this does not mean that you will be angry with him or her tomorrow. Attitudes differ in many respects from emotional responses.

However, there is a feeling, or affective, component, to attitudes that we cannot ignore. Feld and Radin (1982) cite definitions of **attitude** that emphasize this point. Fishbein and Ajzen's (1975) theory includes a definition of *attitude* that stresses emotional reactions. In their theory, attitudes are considered emotional responses to objects, in the form of favorable or unfavorable feelings. People have favorable feelings toward many objects in their environment. In fact, this is what many scientists attempt to capture in their research.

Regardless of how we define *attitude*, social workers must be able to modify or change attitudes. Whereas social psychologists debate the best definition of attitude, social workers need validated theories to guide their efforts. In *Social Psychology for Social Work and the Mental Health Professions*, Feld and Radin (1982) have identified theories in social psychology that social workers may find helpful in achieving their practice objectives (for example, cognitive-dissonance theory and self-perception theory). Social workers need to develop a strong competency in understanding attitude formation and change. For this reason, we provide systematic coverage of factors in human development that contribute to the formation of attitudes. These attitudes are assumed to play a fundamental role in human motivation and development.

Theories of Attitudes and Their Change

In social work, we assume that changing the attitudes of our clients will influence their behavior. This means we believe that we can predict behaviors from attitudes and that attitudes influence behavior. Although many studies have uncovered a relationship between attitudes and behavior, this relationship is not consistent. Yet at an intuitive level, people expect consistency between attitudes and behavior. This assumption has contributed to the development of an entire group of theories on attitudes known as *consistency theories*.

Consistency theories in social psychology refer to the idea that people strive to maintain consistency in their views of themselves and of their environment, and in their relations with others (Lindgren, 1969). People are motivated to keep their attitudes and behaviors consistent (Deaux et al., 1993; Michener, DeLamater, & Myers, 2004). This desire for consistency implies that if people have attitudes inconsistent with their behaviors, they feel uncomfortable. Discomfort will motivate them to reestablish some form of balance or consistency between their attitudes and behavior.

Leon Festinger (1957) is known for proposing another important consistency theory, known as *cognitive-dissonance theory*. "Cognitive dissonance" describes the feelings of anxiety that arise when a person is aware of two cognitions, or a cognition and a behavior, that are inconsistent. In Festinger's theory, whenever an attitude and a behavior are inconsistent, this inconsistency generates dissonance. Festinger assumed that this distress motivates individuals to reconcile the inconsistencies in their cognitions or between cognition and behavior. However, Festinger found that subjects did not always experience dissonance as a result of these conflicts. In his view, they experience a sense of dissonance only if the thoughts or attitudes are relevant to each another.

Festinger's theory initially focused on inconsistencies in cognitions and predicted that dissonance would motivate a person to change one of his or her cognitions. In his early research, he discovered that change in behavior could trigger changes in attitudes. In fact, his theory predicts that people will change their attitudes to be consistent with performed behaviors. In his now-famous forced-compliance experiments, this finding occurred on a regular basis. He subjected individuals to dull tasks and paid them to lie to other students about how interesting they found the tasks to be. The individuals who participated in the dull tasks were then given a questionnaire to determine their private attitudes about the tasks. Some individuals had been paid $1 and others $20 to engage in these tasks. The individuals who were paid $1 experienced greater dissonance (Cooper, 2004). Dissonance theory suggests that they became more motivated to believe that the tasks were really interesting because the justification for their actions—a measly dollar—was insufficient. Early dissonance theory triggered substantial controversy, because the results of research from this theory often challenged fundamental principles of reinforcement theories (Cooper, 2004).

Self-perception theory, another theory about attitude changes, was developed by D. J. Bem (1967). It seeks to explain the same types of behavior addressed by cognitive-dissonance theory; however, it offers a different explanation for why a person might change an attitude after performing a behavior (Feld & Radin, 1982). Self-perception theory suggests that, when we are not sure of our attitudes about a certain topic, we infer them from our behaviors and from the context within which those behaviors occur. Using this theory, Bem set out to offer an alternative explanation of what occurred in Festinger's experiment. In Bem's view, the subjects defined the tasks as interesting not because of dissonance but because they had merely inferred their attitude from their actual behavior. "That is, one dollar is not enough money to induce someone to lie, so subjects in that condition looked back at their behavior and decided they must have enjoyed the experiment because they had said they enjoyed it; no inconsistency, no discomfort, no dissonance" (Deaux et al., 1993, p. 170). According to Bem, the individuals in the experiment were essentially asking themselves, "What must my attitude be if I am willing to behave in this fashion?"

Bem's theory has led to important findings widely used to obtain the cooperation of clients. His theory has also led to the discovery of what is known as the "foot-in-the-door effect," or the tendency for individuals who have complied with a small request first to agree to a larger request later. Researchers thought that this phenomenon occurred because of individuals' changes in self-perception. Bem's theory predicts that "if individuals observe themselves doing something out of free choice, the behaviors are attributed to their disposition, not to external forces, and the conclusion reached is that 'I am that sort of a person'" (Feld & Radin, 1982, p. 175). Some theorists also predict that people who comply with small requests are likely to conclude, "I am the type of individual who agrees to socially desirable requests." Thus, there are competing theories of why changes in behavior can result in changes in attitudes.

Theories of Emotions

What are emotions? How can we explain our emotions and their role in human behavior? Are emotions caused by internal and bodily changes, or by some form of cognitive appraisal? The answers to these questions are quite controversial. In this section, we will provide a brief overview of some of the different theoretical perspectives in psychology on human emotions.

In early history, the word *emotion* meant "to move or agitate in a physical sense" (Petri, 1986; Petri & Govern, 2004). It later came to mean "an agitated or aroused mental state." Although there is no commonly accepted definition of the term, there are a number of widely debated theories or models of human emotions.

In his 1872 book *The Expression of Emotions in Man and Animals*, Charles Darwin was the first theorist in modern times to assume that both emotions and their expression are innate. The bulk of his writings on the topic focused on the manner in which emotions are expressed. Today, there is still controversy as to whether there are universal ways to channel the expression of our emotions.

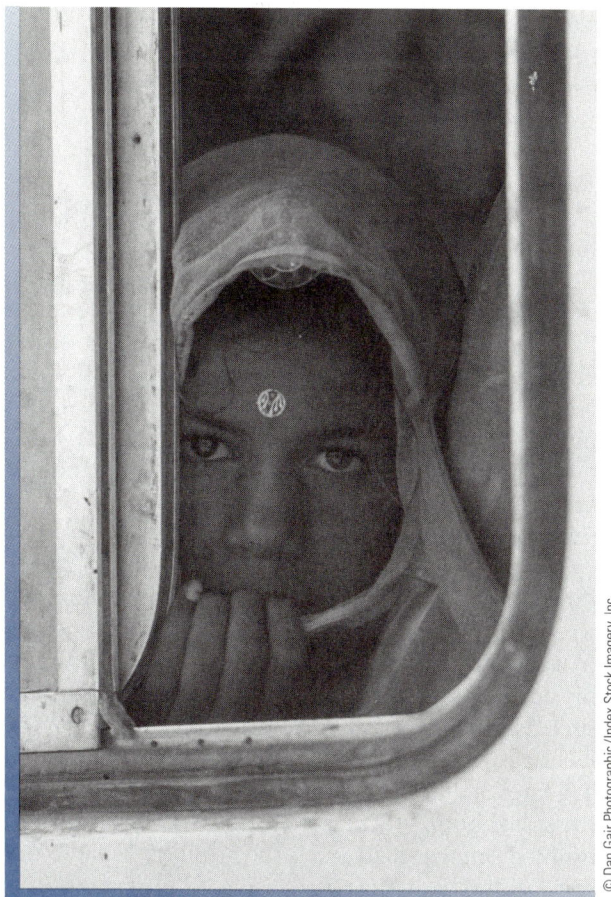

Fear plays an essential role in human functioning. This child appears to be frightened by something in the environment.

Although humans have expressed concerns about the control of emotions since ancient times, Ross Buck proclaimed in 1988 that "psychology has rediscovered emotions." As we pointed out earlier, psychology shifted during the 1950s and 1960s to investigating cognitive functioning. Emotions were relegated to a second-class position in the psychological sciences. Shame, guilt, and anger were studied, but much of the research in this area was motivated by clinical or neuropsychological interests. Much of the controversy in this area of study dates back to the writings of William James (1884).

William James and Carl Lange arrived at a similar conclusion about emotions that challenged traditional assumptions. They identified the following order for describing emotions: perception to bodily change to emotion (Hilgard, 1987). This theory turned common sense upside down. "Everyday logic suggests that when you stumble onto a rattlesnake in the woods the conscious experience of fear leads to visceral arousal (the fight-or-flight responses)" (Weiten, 1992, p. 363). This means that the order of events is: perception to emotion to bodily expression (Hilgard, 1987). Independent of each other, James and Lange arrived at views that contradicted this assumption. James placed greater stress on perception of change in striate muscles, and Lange emphasized changes in heart rate and blood pressure. Their approach to emotions is referred to as the "James-Lange theory of emotions," and it emphasizes the role of physiological determinants in emotions' expression.

Stanley Schachter is noted for developing a two-factor theory that includes physiological explanations in looking at the experience of emotion. In his theory, the experience of emotion requires the two factors of (1) autonomic arousal and (2) cognitive interpretation of the visceral or autonomic arousal. According to Schacter's approach, a person will experience physiological arousal and then search his or her environment for an explanation. If you are in a threatening situation, your explanation of your arousal will probably fit the situation. Schachter's model was the first to stress the important role played by cognitive appraisal in experiencing emotions, but it stressed the need for both factors to be present.

Zajonc (1980) has argued for the primacy of affect in experiencing emotions. He (1984) based his theory on observations of animals and contended that emotion is a universal phenomenon in the animal kingdom, but the cognitive processes and systems observed in humans are not transferable to animals. "Indeed," Zajonc noted, "a rabbit would rarely have time to assess all the attributes of a snake in order to decide whether to fear it; the rabbit feels fear and reacts. Such reactions may also occur in people" (Petri & Govern, 2004, p. 389). That is, people probably acquired the same emotional mechanisms before the development of cognitive systems. Thus, Zajonc assumed that the emotions of humans have much in common with the emotions of animals. Another argument that he provided in support of the primacy of affect is that we cannot avoid emotions. If logic occurs before emotions, then logic should affect our emotional responses to stimuli. Yet this is not always what occurs. Overall, Zajonc has argued that emotions are innate reactions that are part of our evolutionary makeup (Petri & Govern, 2004).

Evolutionary theories of emotion are once again regaining popularity in psychological research. The theorists in this area include Silvan Tomkins, Carroll

EXHIBIT 3.10 Summary of emotions according to different theorists

Silvan Tomkins	Robert Plutchik	Carroll Izard
Fear	Fear	Fear
Anger	Anger	Anger
Enjoyment	Joy	Joy
Disgust	Disgust	Disgust
Interest	Anticipation	Interest
Surprise	Surprise	Surprise
Contempt	Sadness	Contempt
Shame	Acceptance	Shame
Distress	Sadness	

SOURCE: Based on Mandler (1984).

Izard, and Robert Plutchik, who set out to identify the fundamental human emotions. These emotions are considered to be innate and to have evolved before cognition did. Tomkins, Izard, and Plutchik assumed that people exhibit between 8 and 10 primary emotions. A summary of these emotions is presented in Exhibit 3.10. Note the similarities between the elements in their lists. These theorists did not assume that our emotions are limited to these primary emotions. Plutchik has pointed out that, from our primary emotions, we can develop many secondary blends of emotions.

Shame and the Sociology of Emotions

Sociologists have devoted increased attention in recent years to the study of the role of shame and other emotions in social interaction, called the **sociology of emotions**. This is particularly true of sociologists with an interest in social-psychological concerns. Shame is one of the emotions alluded to in early sociological writings of Simmel, Cooley, Marx, and Goffman. However, their writings seem to take for granted how shame is defined (Scheff, 1999).

For instance, George Simmel (1904), in writing about fashion, pointed out that fashion has roots in shame: "People want variation and change," he argued, "but they also anticipate shame if they stray from the behavior and appearance of others. Fashion is the solution to this problem, since one can change along with others, avoiding being isolated, and therefore shame" (Scheff, 1999, p. 4). As Scheff (1999) pointed out, Simmel assigned an important role to conformity of thought and behavior to expectations considered fashionable by a group. When people deviate from these group expectations, they are vulnerable, in Simmel's opinion, to shame. But Simmel never really defined *shame* in his writings about fashion.

Charles Horton Cooley (1922), known for his conception of the "looking-glass self," also included shame in his writings, but, like Simmel, he never provided an explicit definition of this concept. For Cooley, pride and shame are important social emotions that rely heavily on self-monitoring processes. Cooley (1922, p. 184) pointed out that self-monitoring involves three steps: "the imagination of our appearance to the other person, the imagination of his judgment of that appearance, and some sort of self-feeling, such as pride or mortification."

Scheff (1999) has attempted to define *shame* through the lens of the sociological imagination. He wrote: "By shame I mean a large family of emotions that includes many cognates and variants, most notably embarrassment, humiliation, and related feelings such as shyness that involve reactions to rejection or feelings of failure or inadequacy. What unites all these cognates is that they involve the feeling of a threat to the social bond" (Scheff, 1999, p. 14). Scheff further pointed out that if shame is the result of threat to the social bond, it should be considered the most social of the basic emotions.

An important piece of research on shame is included in the book *The Hidden Injuries of Class*, by Sennett and Cobb (1972). These field researchers performed a participant-observation study, in Boston communities, schools, clubs, and bars, of white working-class males of Italian and Jewish backgrounds. They found that these men felt that their class and occupational position were the reasons why others did not accord them respect. The subjects experienced this lack of respect in many contexts, including interactions with teachers, bosses, and even their own children. Sennett extended his examination to broader structural issues in another one of his books, *Respect: In a World of Inequality* (Sennett, 2003).

Structural contributions to negative emotions should not be overlooked by social workers. Factors such as class, race, and gender are the source of many forms of emotion behind current social problems. For instance, issues of respect triggered by dominant-group rejection play a major role in gang formation in many communities (Sennett, 2003). Respect also plays a pivotal role in many other forms of social conflict motivated by emotions that originate in social processes.

Emotions are experienced individually, but some emotions have deep roots in collective processes that are under increased scrutiny by sociologists. The American Sociological Association currently has a special section of its organizational structure that focuses on research topics involving emotions viewed from a sociological perspective. This research body recognizes that emotions cannot be understood strictly by studying biological and psychological processes.

Implications for Practice

Without emotions, individuals cannot develop meaningful responses to their environment. Social workers need to develop practical ways to describe changes in their clients' emotional states. From the theories discussed, we can distinguish between the experience of emotions and the expression of emotions. We experience our emotions within the central nervous system and its attendant cognitive structures, but we express these emotions through the somatic and autonomic response systems.

Clinical social workers also distinguish between mood and affect. **Mood** can be defined as a prevailing and enduring emotional state. **Affect** refers to a person's instant emotional state. In assessing affect, social workers focus on determining the presence or absence of specific types of emotional states. For instance, **lability** refers to the rapid shift from one emotion to another within a very brief period of time. If these shifts are extreme, some clinicians label them as representing a form of emotional "incontinence" (Ludwig, 1986). Social workers must learn the characteristics of normal and abnormal presentations of emotion. They must also have an understanding of how people learn to use their emotions and behavior. The role played by notions of self and identity in regulating behavior and emotions is a central area of social-work practice. For this reason, we will devote some additional attention to examining developments in psychology involving these concerns.

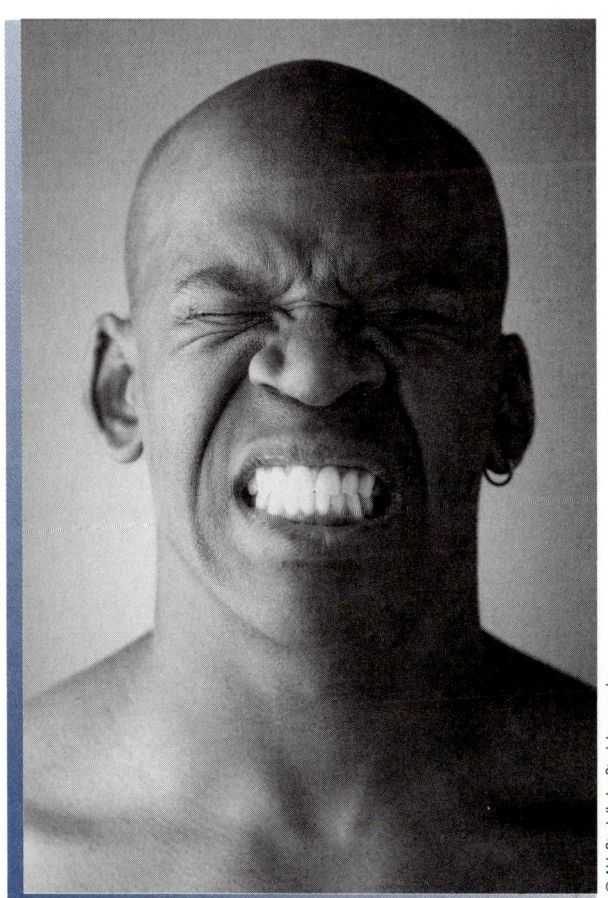

Understanding a person's mood and affect is an important clinical skill. What emotion is the person in this photograph displaying?

Social Cognition and Regulation

How do we acquire social knowledge? Is there a difference between social and nonsocial cognition? Does social-knowledge acquisition differ from the acquisition of other forms of knowledge? These questions have helped psychologists clarify the nature of social cognition. Theorists in the field have explored topics such as whether we employ different processes in acquiring knowledge about things than we employ in acquiring knowledge about people. These debates have led to some general conclusions. Now **social cognition** is widely considered to be cognition about people. It includes "thinking and knowledge about self and other individuals, about social relations between people, about social customs, groups, and institutions" (Flavell, 1985, p. 159). Substantial attention is being devoted to understanding the role of the self-system in all areas of human cognition. The *self-system* refers here to all the feelings, thoughts, and other elements that are associated with a person's sense of self.

In the mid-1970s, it was rare to encounter theorists with identified interests in social cognition. Social cognition is considered a newly discovered convergence of two distinct disciplines: social psychology and cognitive psychology. Developments in each of these disciplines have created major shifts in traditional approaches to scientific inquiry in social psychology (Howard & Renfrow, 2003). However, the way that scientists use the concept of social cognition often is influenced by their discipline. As a result, the definitions of social cognition in the literature vary considerably (Corrigan & Penn, 2001; Newman, 2001). For instance, the sociologists Howard and Hollander (1997) have emphasized that social cognition goes beyond intra-information processing to examine how cognitions mirror the norms and values of societal structures. Brothers's (1990) definition is linked to behavior. He defined social cognition as "The mental operations underlying social interactions, which include the human ability to perceive the intentions and dispositions of others" (1990, p. 28).

Social psychologists have identified many deficits in their approach to studying human behavior, including judgment processes. Most of their early research focused on understanding the effects of situational and individual differences on various forms of social behavior. As disenchantment with stimulus-response models increased, social psychologists started to realize that this approach to research was not clarifying the fundamental psychological processes that underlie social behavior. To rectify this problem, they turned to cognitive theory (Wyer & Srull, 1984; Newman, 2001).

Many of the concepts introduced in this chapter that examine cognitive functions are now being employed in psychology to address a number of social processes. These same processes are examined in sociology and other fields of inquiry. We have included social cognition in our psychological dimension primarily because we employed a psychological orientation to studying these social processes. The fundamental aim of social cognition, as a field of inquiry, is to understand the interdependence between cognition and social behavior (Ostrom, 1984; Howard & Renfrow, 2003). Isen and Hastorf (1982) referred to this field as "cognitive social psychology" instead of "social cognition." This area of study in psychology focuses on individual-level explanations of social behavior. Anthropology and sociology also examine various aspects of social behavior but rely primarily on group-level explanations (Lippa, 1994). Social psychologists with a sociological perspective place less emphasis on the individual cognitive processes and focus more on collective cognitive structures (Howard & Renfrow, 2003).

In this book, we explore various factors in social development that influence individuals and their sense of self, their ability to control their behavior, and their sense of social competence. Because social cognition is a useful framework for examining each of these concerns, we cover topics from that field in each chapter.

Researchers in the field of social cognition have recognized that a significant component of social behavior is motivated by our innate need to control various aspects of our environment. Robert White (1959) referred to this as a form of competence motivation. *Competence* is the capacity to interact effectively with one's environment. In essence, the goal of this motive is to bring about a sense of efficacy for the individual. This assumption is also acknowledged by social workers in models of interaction that take into account principles of social cognition (Brower & Nurius, 1993).

The need for a sense of control has received further scrutiny by Richard deCharms. In his view, the primary motive at the root of most social behavior is the need to be effective in producing changes in our environment. He referred to this as a need to achieve a sense of personal causation.

As deCharms noted, we typically describe motivation in relation to the goals toward which a behavior leads: When hungry, we seek food; when thirsty, we seek water; and so on. Though we speak of the hunger motive, personal causation is the force requiring that we be able to respond in ways that will get us food. Thus, deCharms saw personal causation as the underlying principle of most motivated behaviors (Petri, 1986; Petri & Govern, 2004).

Regulation of behavior, emotions, and cognition is an important area of research developing in the field of social cognition. By employing principles of social cognition, it is possible to link processes of social regulation with individual cognitive processes. This linkage allows for the identification of external and internal factors contributing to the regulation of our emotions and behavior. "Self regulatory competencies and strategies are person variables of special relevance for the clinician because they include the diverse executive functions that make it possible—or difficult—for individuals to pursue their goals and to self regulate their own behavior, as in goal-directed delay of gratification and other forms of self-control" (Mischel, 2004, p. 191).

Regulation is an important human behavior function and will receive substantial attention in our developmental chapters. We now know that humans learn considerable information from others that helps in regulating various aspects of their behavior. The focus in social-cognition research is on understanding how people acquire this information from other individuals.

Implications for Practice

Brower and Nurius (1993) have written on the utility of social cognition in what they have termed a "cognitive-ecological model for direct practice." In their view, social cognition and social transactions serve as "the backdrop for understanding our clients' presenting problems and for developing change strategies that will positively build upon these normative processes" (p. 3). They have claimed that social cognition plays an important mediating role between people and their environments, and they have contended that if we integrate our knowledge of the self-system with information-processing knowledge and knowledge of human problem solving, we can deal more efficiently with clients' concerns.

By using this cognitive approach, we can better evaluate the effect of immediate and distant factors on specific forms of human behavior. Ecological and broader social influences are important, but the concepts of social cognition enable us to isolate key personal factors that play unique roles in an individual's behavioral choices. That is, social cognition is an approach that allows us to bring together important person-and-environment factors. It places tremendous emphasis on self-constructs and recognizes the highly interdependent relationship between self and society. Unlike personality constructs, the self-system in social-cognitive approaches does not artificially isolate people from key social realities. Moreover, concepts and principles in the social-cognitive approach are highly useful in achieving social work's commitment to making person-and-environment interactions central in its approach to understanding human behavior. Social-cognitive methods allow us to understand individual processes underlying our tendency to make selective appraisals of situations based on our personally constructed schemata and life images.

Berlin (2002) has also extended knowledge of social cognition to the development of an integrated cognitive perspective for social-work practice. Her 2002 book *Clinical Social Work Practice: A Cognitive-Integrative Perspective* assists social workers in understanding the role of oppressive environments and negative interpersonal relationships in shaping personal meaning. She considers these personal meanings primary targets for social-work interventions. In her opinion, practitioners cannot understand how to change the minds of clients without understanding how their clients process negative sources of social or interpersonal information. ∎

Self and Identity

"Who am I?" This question confronts everyone at various points in life. "Each of us has unique answers to this question, answers that reflect our self-schema or self concept, the organized structure of cognitions or thoughts we have about ourselves" (Michener, DeLamater, & Myers, 2004, p. 79). Erik Erikson (1968) asserted that forming a viable sense of identity for participation in society is a key task of adolescence. His writings also explored how a sense of identity remains a constant challenge throughout a person's life (Weinreich, 2003). An excellent exercise for yourself is to write your own answer to the question "Who am I?" using the twenty-items test (see Exhibit 3.11). In this exercise, you will create a product that can provide useful information for helping you differentiate between the concept of self and the concept of identity. Are there differences between these concepts? If so, what are these differences?

There are also a number of other issues that you will need to examine in analyzing your responses to this exercise. What is your self? How did it arise? How does the self that you describe guide your plans and behavior? How does it serve as both a source and an object of your actions? Is the acquisition of your sense of self different from your sense of identity? The answers to each of these questions are quite complex, and this is why we are once again witnessing a burgeoning body of research and writing on issues of self and identity in the social and behavioral sciences (Michener, DeLamater, & Myers, 2004; Leary & Tangney, 2003). Owens (2003) wrote that self and identity are probably two of the most popular concepts in the field of social psychology.

Any examination of self or identity constructs rests on a set of implicit assumptions about what it means to be a person (Foddy & Kashima, 2002). However, not everyone assumes that the concept of self equates with the concept of person (Leary & Tangney, 2003), and not everyone currently agrees on

EXHIBIT 3.11 Self-concept exercise

To measure a person's self-concept symbolic interactionists often use a twenty statements test (also known as the "Who Am I?" test), developed by Manford Kuhn. We would like you to complete this test.

Take a piece of lined paper and number from 1 to 20. On each of the numbered lines, we want you to write a different answer to the question "Who Am I". You should answer the question as if you were giving the answers to yourself, not someone else. You should also write your answers quickly. The order in which they occur does not matter. You do not have to worry about the "logic" or "importance" of your responses.

1.
2.
3.
4.
5.
6.
7.
8.
9.
10.
11.
12.
13.
14.
15.
16.
17.
18.
19.
20.

the definition of the self that is being examined by researchers. Here lies a central problem in the use of self theory. As you recall, the person is an important element in any social-work assessment of person-and-environment transactions. However, the science surrounding the examination of this concept fell out of favor in psychology during the thirty years that behaviorism dominated this field of study (Mischel and Morf, 2003). In behaviorism, all mental concepts such as ego and self were considered suspect. Mischel and Morf (2003) wrote that the clinical-personality area acted as the sole guardian of the self-construct when behaviorism was the reigning paradigm in psychology. To some extent, the self-construct fell out of favor in the science of psychology because there was no specific location for the self in a person's brain or body. In addition, scientists were troubled by its continued use in clinical areas because they could not directly observe or measure the self. Many writers termed the concept a "phantom" or a "ghost" that presumably resided somewhere in the person or the machine (body). Nonetheless, self theory regained prominence in psychology during its cognitive revolution (Ashmore & Jussim, 1997). In particular, information-processing models began to identify issues that helped move the field to metaphors involving neural networking, which in turn are starting to facilitate the development of newer models and methods for studying the self (Berlin, 2002; Kihlstrom, Beer, & Klein, 2003). We now recognize that information about the self is not stored in any discrete location in the brain. Instead, like many other forms of memory processes, it involves more than one central processing unit, or parallel processing units, and these units are linked or connected by a number of different systems in the brain. The key empirical issue, however, involves determining the key units within this self-system that is represented in the brain (Mischel & Morf, 2003).

The Self and Its Components

What is the self? Is there a universally accepted definition of this construct? Social and behavioral scientists currently use terms including self-perception, self-awareness, self-motivation, self-efficacy, self-monitoring, self-control, self-mutilation, self-regulation, self-image, self-schema, self-beliefs, ideal self, self-affirmation, and self-defeating behavior. Clearly, *self* does not mean the same thing in each of these uses (Leary & Tangney, 2003). This list of uses illustrates that the self is not a unitary concept, but a complex system of different constructs that require various forms of investigation and probably have different networks that are involved (Ashmore & Jussim, 1997; Schaffer, 1996). For this reason, we will begin our discussion of the self by focusing on the different assumptions and dimensions that various theorists address in their conceptual examinations of self and identity.

William James (1890) introduced notions of the "I" and the "me" to capture two important distinctions in conceptualizing the self as a psychological construct. In his definition of the self, the individual actor is viewed as both the source and the object of human behavior. "The active aspect of the self is labeled the *I*, and the object of the self-action is labeled the *me*" (Michener, DeLamater, & Myers, 2004, p. 31). In other words, the self can be both the driving force behind the behavior and the object of the judgments being made by the self. This merger of the knower with the known raises a number of serious issues about the role of introspective or reflexive processes in self-knowledge (Devos & Banaji, 2003). Is introspection or reflection the only means for self-awareness? What role is played by the unconscious, the emotions, and motivational considerations in self-awareness processes? Most early interactional theories ignored many of these concerns, because they assumed that the self was strictly a product of reflexive psychosocial processes. This is an important assumption that we need to devote some additional attention to understanding, because reflexive behavior continues to play a central role in many theories of the self.

As an example, if a student in social work has to complete a field contract by Tuesday, she might engage in the reflexive process of self-control by making the following decision: "I will not go to a movie with my boyfriend on Sunday but will instead work on my contract." She might also engage in a number of other self-relevant processes: "If I get this done by Sunday, then I will be able to go out with him after my Monday-night class." In this instance, she is using her self as both a motivator and as a regulator of her behavior. However, she can also shift from the active aspects of her self to a more passive aspect: "My teachers have always told me that I do not perform well when I have to work under tight deadlines." In this circumstance, she is reflecting on her capacity to achieve her aims given her time constraints.

In each of the prior circumstances, Susan is shifting from a subject that is initiating her activities to an object that is being judged. Her self is both a source of her behavior and the object of her judgments or reflections. This capacity for self-reflection is considered a key component of the self and is also recognized as an important factor that differentiates humans from animals (Leary & Tangey, 2003; Michener, DeLamater, & Myers, 2004).

Self-reflection contributes to knowledge or awareness of the *me* identified by James (1890) and George Herbert Mead (1934). This awareness is not present at a person's birth. Most sociologists and theorists from the symbolic-interaction tradition assume that the self emerges through the process of social experience, interactions with others, and other forms of social activity (Sandstrom, Martin, & Fine, 2003). This theoretical orientation assumes that the self is essentially a social product and that this capacity for reflecting on one's self develops and changes over time in accordance with changes in an individual's social experiences. Mead enhanced our understanding of this close connection between social experience and the self in a now-famous aphorism: "The self and society are two sides of the same coin."

George Herbert Mead's best-known book, *Mind, Self and Society* (1934), resulted from the lecture notes for a course on social psychology he taught at the University of Chicago. In this book, Mead highlighted how, through language, humans evolved a way to free themselves from many of the constraints on other animals by developing the ability to create a social world apart from the demands of nature (Sandstrom, Martin, & Fine, 2003). Mead also concluded that the symbolic nature of human behavior and communication is what distinguishes humans from animals. "Unlike animals that respond to one another through instinctive gestures, such as growls, hisses, nips, or chirps, people communicate through exchanging symbols" (Sandstrom, Martin, & Fine, 2003, p. 6).

Mead also concluded that a highly developed brain was not sufficient to make a mind. The emergence of a person's mind requires involvement in a society or interactions with others. He assumed that a mind emerges in an infant because the infant needs to adjust and adapt to a social world of organized forms of symbolic action. This social world is made up of rules, roles, relationships, and institutions (Sandstronm, Martin & Fine, 2003), and in order for the infant to participate in it, she or he must acquire a sense of self through "taking the role of the other." Cooley (1908) was the first to note the close tie between role taking and language skills. "One of the earliest signs of role-taking skills is the correct use of the pronouns you and I. To master the use of these pronouns requires the role of the self and of the other simultaneously" (Michener, DeLamater, & Myers, 2004, p. 83).

Cooley also coined the term *looking-glass self*. He considered parents and immediate family members the most important looking glasses for children in their early stages of development. These individuals reflect views and images of the self that infants use in constructing who they are. However, children's images will change as the social relationships they develop change and reflect different views of themselves. These interactional assumptions focus primarily on the knowledge-acquisition components of the self that are a product of processes of social interaction. They illustrate how the *me* develops and changes in processes of interaction. This notion that the self is an interpersonal self-construction system is still accepted in current theoretical writings on the subject (Mischel & Morf, 2003).

Based on Cooley's notion of the looking-glass self (1902), a person's self-conception is viewed as a reflected or mirror image of the self based on awareness of the self accumulated through interactions with others in a social environment. Awareness of these self-images unfolds gradually during the course of the first two years of development (Lewis & Brooks-Gunn, 1979). This form of awareness is measured by examining whether the child has the ability to visually recognize who he or she is in a mirror. Lewis and Brooks-Gunn (1979) applied a spot of rouge on the nose of children in their seminal empirical investigation of this subject. The results showed that when children could recognize that the mirror image was their image by reaching for the spot on their noses, we could assume that they were demonstrating self-awareness. In their studies, no children under the age of 1 touched their noses. Most demonstrated this awareness around 21 months, but some were capable of demonstrating awareness around 15 months. This form of self-awareness is also associated with the ability of children to define themselves in terms of social categories, such as age, sex, and size (Shaffer, 1996).

Lewis and Brooks-Gunn (1979) also noted that infants have a primitive sense of separateness that does not emerge until around 3 months and a sense of continuity that is not seen until around 9 months. These aspects of the self are considered to be more consistent with active than with reflective aspects of the self. Infants learn about the active or agenic (agency) aspects of the self by learning that their own behavior can affect the behavior of other people and objects in their environment. But it is assumed that the foundation of the *me* components of the self are laid when individuals can monitor and reflect on their own behavior and actions.

William James (1890) is also noted for having identified what he referred to as the "empirical self." He wrote that the empirical self consisted of the material self, social self, and spiritual self. Scholars who are committed to notions of unity have often questioned this notion of multiple selves. What connects these different manifestations of the self? There must be some process that integrates these various components. McAdams (1997) wrote that this is exactly what many theorists have ignored. In his opinion, the self is a process of what he has termed "selfing." Selfing refers to the process by which the *I* of James will seek to fashion a unified and purposeful *me*. He wrote, "The I is not a thing. Nor is it a part, a piece, a component, or even a facet of the self. The I is rather the process of being a self—a process we give the label selfing" (1997, p. 56).

Schaffer (1996) wrote that Lewis (1990) was also troubled by the multiplicity of selves and the issue of unity and built on William James's *I* and *me* by establishing what he termed the *existential* and *categorical* selves. The existential form of self is what he was referring to as the primitive form of self that emerges around 3 months, and the me is consistent with more categorical notions of the self. The existential component addresses the fundamental sense of being distinct from all else and of possessing a sense of continuity across time (Schaffer, 1996). This existential aspect of the self is consistent with what many other writers refer to as identity (Rosenberg, 1997). One of the key aspects of identity is the notion of continuity. In the next section, we will examine the roles of identity and continuity in personal and social behavior.

Identities and Their Salience

A person's sense of identity has strong roots in processes that foster a sense of difference from others, as well as the management of this difference (Woodward, 2002). By interacting with others, people participate in appraisal or valuation of the meanings they attach to themselves and others. Clearly, identity helps people make sense of their experiences. When a person defines him- or herself as a member of a group, the characteristics of this group provide standards that the person uses for future thoughts and actions. The person also can use roles or institutions in defining identity (Owens, 2003). All of these socially based experiences are sources for its formation (Michener, DeLamater, & Myers, 2004).

If a person's self is involved in conflicting or incompatible experiences, how is identity or sense of sameness determined? For centuries, this issue of sameness has motivated philosophers in examining the concept of identity. What is it that remains the same about a person's experiences? Is it the body? Does the body really remain the same? If a person's identity is determined by participation in a group, how can others be considered identical with that person when they are not the same as the person in many other respects? The Spanish language uses different words to address variant forms of sameness. *Igual* refers to a general qualitative form of identity or sameness, and *mismo* refers to a more numerical identity or sameness (Weinreich, 2003). That is, *mismo* assumes that the object or person will be the same today as it was yesterday, and *igual* refers to sameness in terms of general characteristics that are part of some general identified category. The English language does not make this distinction.

For many theorists, identity marks the ways that we are the same as others in a group, geographical area, gender, race, or institution. However, it is also what prevents me from being considered identical to anyone else (Maalouf, 2000). Identity clarifies how I am different from others. I can be considered different from others because I belong to groups with specific attributes that differ from the participants in other groups. However, this notion of identity differs from other notions of identity, such as the conceptualization of identity as *unity of consciousness*.

In unity-of-consciousness notions of identity, a person's biographical self provides a sense of coherence or continuity in his or her presentations of self to others. Each of us brings a relatively stable and enduring sense of identity to social situations, which are influenced by prior interpretations of ourselves, and our future aspirations (Weinreich, 2003).

The focus on continuity in differentiating the self from identity is not, however, without controversy (Owens, 2003). Exponents of the postmodern turn in human history contend that the self is so saturated with multiple values resulting from globalization and its attendant technological advances that it is difficult for individuals to maintain a stable sense of identity (Gergen, 1991). How can a person maintain an integrated or unified identity by adopting the perspective of members of one's community when the community is so diverse and in a state of rapid social change (Gergen, 1991, Rosenberg, 1997)? Do people in this context need a flexible identity to function effectively (Zurcher, 1977)?

In medieval Western Europe, the self was not problematic and did not focus on notions of individuation or choice (Holland, 1997). A person's sense of self was determined by the social role that she or he occupied. This role was embedded in the group or community (Smith, 2002). As a consequence, this was a period when the self was more collectivist than individualistic in nature. However, from the fifteenth century to the twentieth century, the self-concept began to emphasize notions of individualism and choice. Individual agency and causal influence gained special prominence during the Enlightenment period. This type of self-construct dominated conceptions of self until the emergence of what some scholars have referred to as a Romantic conception, which prevailed during the late eighteenth and the nineteenth centuries (Danziger, 1997; Baumeister, 1997). The Romantic self was in some sense a response to the Enlightenment conception of self and its overemphasis on rationality. The Romantic era introduced notions of uniqueness, creativity, and the human potential for growth in its conceptualization of the self (Smith, 2002). During the twentieth century, we saw oscillations between the purely rational conceptualizations of the early Enlightenment period and more romantic nations that were associated with the human potential movements. Notions of rationality and unity of self started to unravel, however, in the early 1960s. Now researchers believe that emergent cultural conditions will lead to the development of a new self-concept that is consistent with the characteristics of our current information age and its network-oriented societies (Castells, 2002).

Many writers are describing the lives of people who negotiate these postmodern conditions, which are characterized by conflicting cultural roles and values. "Take the case of a Serbian man and a Muslim woman who met 20 years ago in a café in Sarajevo, fell in love and got married. They can never perceive their identity the same way as does a couple that is entirely Serbian or entirely Muslim; their

FOCUS ON NARRATIVE

BEING JAPANESE

I had an opportunity to study in the United States for four years. Without this experience, I don't think I would have learned as much about what it means to be Japanese. I am surprised by how much I learned about my home county and myself from this experience.

One of my first confrontations with my identity occurred when I took a course on oppression and diversity. On the first day of class, my professor asked all of the students to introduce themselves. During this exercise, most students shared their name, where they were from, and what they were doing prior to starting graduate school. However, we were also asked by our professor to talk about our ethnicity and our religious background. I had no difficulty talking about most of the items mentioned by the professor, but I had never thought before about sharing my ethnicity or religion with others to tell people who I was. From this experience, I learned that ethnicity and religion would help in explaining to others who I was in the United States, but I was puzzled because I did not think it really said anything personally about who I am.

In Japan, I would never think of saying that I was Japanese. In Japan, it would not be necessary to share this type of information because 95% of the people in Japan are Japanese. We also do not make distinctions in Japan about religion in establishing our identity, because we generally share the same religion. So, this exercise was an interesting introduction to American culture.

However, I continued to be challenged in terms of the differences between my culture and the American culture. This was shocking for me because I had watched so many programs on television from America. Because I believed that I understood what was going on in these programs, I thought that I would not have any real problems making the transition. I don't know if other students from Japan have had this experience. I did not find the experience easy. I had to work very hard to improve my English so that I could understand what others were saying. But the challenge never seemed to end. I consciously tried to hang out with American students so that I would learn faster, but I started getting angry with myself because I was not making as much progress as I wanted. This transition was much more difficult than I ever anticipated.

While driving to school one day, I turned on a tape of Japanese pop music that my brother sent me. Although I was so relaxed, it hit me all of a sudden how easy it was for me to understand every word they were saying. I was surprised, because I was listening for the first time, in a long time, without having to concentrate. When I realized this, I started crying and could not stop.

I had tried not having contact with other Japanese students so that I could improve my English, but the personal effort and cost was something that I had not given much thought about until this experience with the tape. From television, I was so struck by life in America that I wanted in some way to be American. But, in trying to do so, I found that life in America challenged me to reexamine my own identity.

One of my ESL teachers had suggested that I consider taking an American name. He told me that if I adopted an American name I would find that my shy character would also change to fit with the American name that I chose. My friends identified a number of potential names for me. However, I found the entire experience very uncomfortable. I felt that if I did this, then in some way, I would be denying or rejecting my identity. By taking an American name, I would be saying that being Japanese is in some way wrong. But at the same time I realized that my name was in some way contributing to some of my difficulties in making an adjustment to American culture. I found that many Americans could not say my name. So, all in all, I was confused, but I decided to not take the teacher's suggestion.

I have returned to Japan and I have given this some thought. I believe that my difficulties with the language and culture made it difficult for me to become an American. However, I am not sure why I made being an American such an important issue. At the end of the day, I now realize that the only thing that I should be worried about is being myself and not an American or a Japanese. In addition, I learned that there is more to being a member of a culture than just the language, but language is also an important contributor to one's identity.

—BY KEIKO HAMADA

view of religion and mother country will never again be what it was before" (Maalouf, 2000, p. 11). This new social context is introducing interesting issues about the salience of various identities in a person's life. Researchers are examining other excellent examples that involve the complex forms of cultural allegiances emerging in many communities (Horenczyk & Munayer, 2003).

For instance, how would a Palestinian Christian Arab living as a citizen of Israel manage his or her ethnic identity? How does a Mormon Native American living on a reservation in the United States, manage their identity while living in southern Arizona near the Mexican border, where Spanish was formerly the primary language? Issues of this nature are becoming more commonplace in our new global society. People have multiple allegiances to various groups, and it is hard to predict whether religion, language, or ethnicity will be bases for establishing a sense of identity (Maalouf, 2000). These individuals are participating in lifestyles and worldviews represented by each of these groups. Many broader social processes are contributing to the development of different types of identity, some instances to enable people to cope with the contradictions brought about by the multiple allegiances they experience in their day-to-day lives (Castells, 2002).

Are Self and Identity Processes Universal?

Anthropologists have for many years stressed the important role that culture plays in how people think, act, and behave. Yet most of our theories and assumptions about the meaning and importance of the self and identity are strictly relevant to Western European and American audiences (Matsumoto, 2000). Richard Nisbet, a prominent American psychologist, had been a long-term universalist when it came to human thought processes. He had long believed that the process of reasoning was separate from what people reasoned (Nisbet, 2003)—he assumed that human inference processes were universal. For instance, he thought that cognitive processes employed by a rural African American, a Navajo sheepherder, a dot-com entrepreneur, and a Korean farmer were the same. However, he has modified this position in his book *The Geography of Thought: How Asians and Westerners Think Differently . . . and Why* (2003).

Anthropologists are also performing studies that call into question our longstanding beliefs about

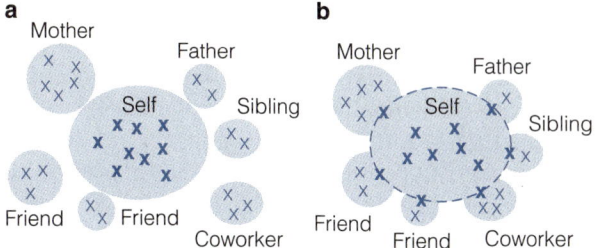

EXHIBIT 3.12 Conceptual representation of the self
(a) Independent construal of self; (b) interdependent construal of self.
SOURCE: "Culture and self: implications for cognition, emotion, and motivation," by H. Markus and S. Kitayama (1991). *Psychological Review*, 98: 224. Copyright © 1991 American Psychological Association. Reprinted by permission of the authors.

the evolution of self-concepts outlined by many Western historians. They have identified what they have termed **independent** and **interdependent** conceptualizations of the self. The independent self-schemas are most commonly seen in individuals who have been socialized to be unique, to express themselves, to realize and actualize the inner self, and to promote personal goals. In the researchers' view, these are specific tasks that the culture selected over the course of its history to encourage the development of "the independence of each separate self" (Matsumoto, 2000, p. 56). Markus and Kitayama (1991) created a graphic illustration of this and other concepts of the self (see Exhibit 3.12). In their illustration, there is no overlap between the self and the others in the person's social environment for the independent construal of the self. In addition, the most relevant aspects of the self are associated with the attributes indicated in this graphic by the bold X's. Nisbet (2003) has attributed this specific focus on attributes to geographic and social conditions in early Greece, where this approach to the self originated. The Greeks developed a strong interest in categorization, and this facilitated the types of advancements noted in Western science. However, East Asians are much more sensitive to attending to objects in their broader contexts rather than to reducing objects to their most basic attributes (Nisbet, 2003). In Nisbet's opinion, this has contributed to different approaches to thought and also to different conceptions of the self.

In many non-Western cultures, minimal value is placed on separateness of identity. East Asians are noted for devoting much more attention to valuing and maintaining interdependence among individuals. "Individuals in these cultures are socialized to adjust themselves to an attendant relationship or a group to which they belong, to read one another's minds, to be sympathetic, to occupy and play their assigned roles, and to engage in appropriate actions" (Matsumoto, 2000, p. 57). Markus and Kitayama also provide an illustration of what they termed "interdependent construal of self" (see Exhibit 3.12b).

Because this concept of self is more flexible and contingent, will East Asians be better suited to the demands of a postmodern environment? Because of the lack of research on the subject in the West, we cannot answer this question. Western scholars are using concepts that still serve as barriers to many of these previously unexamined contributions of culture to understanding self and identity. Nonetheless, researchers in the West are beginning to accept the fact that the environment does influence conceptions of self and that different conceptions do have consequences for cognition, motivation, and emotions (Matsumoto, 2000; Nisbet, 2003). For instance, we now know that cultural differences in self-concepts determine whether a person's own behavior or the behavior of others will influence her or his future behavior (Iyengar & Brockner, 2001).

Implications for Practice

The turning points in a person's life trajectory, which we discussed in Chapter 1, can be moments of crisis that alter self-images and identity. "These moments typically arise when a person is rapidly propelled from one status to another, either willing or unwillingly" (Sandstrom, Martin, & Fine, 2003, p. 85). For example, when a person is diagnosed with HIV/AIDS or some other serious disease, this represents an important new status—a status that can shatter cherished beliefs, self-images, and even one's identity. However, the biological change in and of itself does not lead automatically to a person becoming an individual with HIV/AIDS. The identification with the new roles associated with this status change requires new processes of socialization and of identity transformation (Sandstrom, 1990, 1996). Individuals with these diagnoses have to renegotiate many different senses of self and identity with implications for intimacy and sexual relations. Social workers help to facilitate how people adapt to these important self- and identity-relevant tasks.

Notions of self and identity are not challenged only when people experience turning points in their life trajectories. These ideas also influence how people appraise various life experiences, including disturbances of self and identity in personality disorders (Westen & Heim, 2003). Social workers have had a longstanding commitment to working with people who are experiencing interpersonal difficulties caused by distorted self-concepts arising from experiences in environments of violence, maltreatment, and neglect. Social workers are also involved with identity politics and their consequences for emerging conceptions of identity.

Psychological Strengths and Hazards

The psychological system facilitates our processing of information from our internal and external world and helps us communicate and respond to the demands of everyday lives. It includes processes and functions that are vulnerable to many kinds of hazards occurring at the biophysical, psychological, and social levels of functioning. However, the majority of these processes help us cope with the demands of our environment. Humans have strengths involving attitudes, arousal levels, and cognitive-processing styles that contribute to many of their positive social-functioning outcomes. In our developmental chapters, we will review information about each of these processes and their contributions to understanding social functioning.

Psychological hazards include events, experiences, abilities, skill deficits, cognitive impairments, emotional impairments, and behavioral impairments that compromise the mental processes and functions employed by individuals to control the biopsychosocial system.

Individuals are exposed to many experiences that constitute risks to their mental functioning. A risk occurs whenever there is a lack of harmony in the person's psychological system. Individuals are also at risk when there is a lack of opportunity to develop mental and motor processes that enable them to meet the demands of their life circumstances.

A crisis presents a problem in living that requires more than habitual coping (Nurcombe & Gallagher, 1986; Nurcombe, 2000). Whenever an individual cannot cope with problems, he or she is at risk for many kinds of psychological harm. This harm has many different forms of presentation, including learning disabilities, mood disturbances, abstract-reasoning deficits, and perceptual disturbances.

Overview

This chapter provided a description of key developments in the cognitive and psychological sciences that help us understand individual-level explanations of human behavior. We reviewed concepts from major theoretical perspectives that assist us in understanding the cognitive and individual psychological bases for human behavior. These factors play a critical mediating role between our biological and social systems. They involve many functions that people need in order to engage in planned behavior intended to resolve their life problems. Each of the subsystems in our psychological system also provides internal motivation for many of our activities. The psychological system consists of several key functions employed by humans in directing their behavior to achieve desired ends. These individual processes differ significantly from the social processes that will be described in the next chapter.

CONCEPT MAP

Summary

The objective of the psychological system is goal attainment. This system consists of many functions associated with our mental processes. These processes are needed to help people achieve their desired goals.

Cognitive Development and Information Processing

Cognitive development is an approach to assessing cognitive functions. Piaget's structural approach is useful for social workers. It explains how cognition is organized or structured at various phases of life. Different mental structures direct cognitive processes for individuals at different stages of development.

The information-processing subsystem of the psychological system includes seven major functions: (1) consciousness and orientation, (2) perception, (3) attention, (4) learning, (5) memory, (6) comprehension, and (7) reasoning and judgment. Information processing is not only a major function in the psychological system but also an established approach in psychology for studying human cognitive processes. Information processing resembles a computer and explains the uptake, selection, coding, and storage of information.

Consciousness involves the processes that allow us to be aware of internal and external stimuli. *Orientation* is a form of consciousness assessed by clinical professionals in evaluating the status of a person's mental functioning. *Perception* refers to the interpretation of information detected by our senses. *Attention* is the component of the information-processing system that pertains to the ability to focus on a specific stimulus without distraction by irrelevant stimuli. *Vigilance* involves the ability to sustain outward attention over a prolonged period of time. *Concentration* refers to a person's ability to sustain inner mental operations without disruption.

Memory is considered a key component of the learning process in our information-processing system. It consists of four stages: registration, rehearsal, retention, and recall. There are definite limits on our capacity for processing information. Our short-term, or working, memory can hold only a limited number of items (seven, plus or minus two). Unlike short-term memory, long-term memory has unlimited capacity to store information. Key processes, besides memory, assessed by social workers include problem solving, abstract reasoning, and judgment.

Communication

Communication involves oral and written language, nonverbal gestures, and other forms of exchanging information. Language is a social product, but speech is an individual product. Human communication consists of four basic components: the source, the message, the channel used to send the message, and the receiver.

Attitudes and Emotions

Attitudes and emotions play a fundamental role in motivating behavior. *Attitude* refers to our evaluative feelings and other evaluative responses directed at specific norms. There are different theories of what influences changes in attitudes: consistency theories and self-perception theories. *Emotion* is difficult to define, but there are several noteworthy theoretical conceptualizations of emotions: the James-Lange theory, Schacter's two-factor theory, and evolutionary theories. Without emotions, individuals cannot develop meaningful responses to their environment.

Social Cognition and Regulation

Social cognition refers to knowledge about people. Social and cognitive psychologists assume that acquisition of social knowledge differs from acquisition of other forms of knowledge. The norms learned from social-cognitive processes constrain and regulate our behavior in social situations.

Psychological Strengths and Hazards

Psychological hazards include anything that compromises mental functioning. A risk to mental functioning occurs when there is disharmony in the psychological system or a lack of opportunity to develop mental and motor processes needed to cope with life's demands. When people have a crisis and cannot cope with these demands, they are at increased risk of psychological harm.

Key Terms

- abstraction
- accommodation
- adaptation
- affect
- assimilation
- association
- attitude
- behavioral intention
- beliefs
- classical conditioning
- cognition
- concentration
- conscience
- consciousness
- continuity
- differentiation theory
- disoriented states
- ego
- ego-ideal
- ego psychology (self theory)
- enrichment theory
- epigenetic principle
- explicit memory
- extinction
- grammar
- hypervigilance
- id
- immediate memory
- implicit memory
- information processing
- lability
- libido
- long-term memory
- mood
- morpheme
- negative reinforcement
- operant conditioning
- organization
- PDP models
- perception
- perceptual set
- phoneme
- phonology
- pragmatics
- primary-process thinking
- problem solving
- punishment
- recent memory
- reinforcement
- remote memory
- repetition
- schema
- secondary-process thinking
- self-efficacy
- semantics
- sensation
- short-term memory
- signs
- similarity
- social cognition
- social-learning theory
- sociology of emotions
- subjective norms
- superego
- symbol
- syntax
- trial and error
- values
- vigilance

Online Resources

Websites

Go to http://info.wadsworth.com/ashford to find specific links to these web pages.

Raul Salazar assessment activities for graduate and undergraduate students located on the Thomson website.

Current Research in Social Cognition

Peer-reviewed electronic journal dealing with the whole of social cognition

Psyche: An Interdisciplinary Journal of Research on Consciousness

Psyche is a refereed electronic journal dedicated to supporting the interdisciplinary exploration of the nature of consciousness and its relation to the brain.

Emotions and Emotional Intelligence

Offers a new theory to get rid of unwanted feelings.

InfoTrac College Edition Keywords

For interesting materials related to what you have just read, please go to the InfoTrac College Edition website and search using the following keywords:

Jean Piaget	empathy
repressed memories	social perception
problem solving	

CHAPTER 4

The Social Dimension
for Assessing Social Functioning

CHAPTER CONSULTANTS

Ronald Pitner
Washington University at St. Louis

Jane Holschuh
Humboldt State University

Rita Takahashi
San Francisco State University

Margaret Waller
Arizona State University

The aim of this chapter is to define and describe how social systems guide the multidimensional framework. A whole host of debates occur in the social sciences about the merits of micro versus macro approaches to social analysis. This kind of dualism, along with the dualisms of agency versus structure and individual versus society, is avoided in this chapter by using systems principles to describe the characteristics of social life.

For purposes of clarity, we treat the social systems and categories included in our framework as if they were independent of one another. However, you should keep in mind the following principles:

- Any analysis of a social system must take into account the interactions of that system with other systems.
- All social systems and structures are highly interrelated and have many points of intersection that are critical to understanding processes of social domination and other forms of social inequality.
- Social structures are sources of both support and oppression.
- Any analysis of social, cultural, and individual experience cannot ignore key multicultural foundations.

The preceding chapter covered the role of psychological systems in human development. However, these psychological processes do not occur in a vacuum. All forms of goal-directed activities involving humans take place in an established environment. If we are going to understand how the environment influences behavior, we need a framework that allows us to compare elements in one social context with those in another. To this end, our multidimensional framework provides a description of ways to conceptualize the key systems making up the social system. It also identifies variables and concepts that are useful for looking at different levels of social organization.

Revisit the case of Raul Salazar (in Chapter 2). What structural factors are contributing to his problems? Are any social institutions influencing how the school responds to Raul and his family? Is there something about Raul's social location that is influencing teacher assessments of his functioning? What social systems are playing a role in his problems? Is there evidence of cultural conflicts in this case? What influence do social-system variables have on the etiology of his condition? The social dimension described in this chapter should help structure your assessment of Raul Salazar's case. We begin this description of the

Carol Germain was a noted social-work theorist who developed the ecological perspective for the practice of social work and furthered the understanding of human behavior in multiple environments.

social dimension by defining the social system and its utility in studying human development.

Our approach to human behavior in social work deals not only with developmental events but also with the context in which these events take place. The term *context* in the social-work literature is often used interchangeably with *space, setting, situation, territory, locus, milieu,* and *environment*. In this book, we define many forms of contexts in terms of systems principles. We subscribe to this approach because we assume that social workers must adhere to a people-in-systems view of human behavior, as illustrated in the principles derived from ecological systems theory.

Social Theory

Ecological Systems Theory

Ecology is the study of the interrelationships of organisms with one another and with the environment (Hanson, 1962). **Ecological systems theory**

(Germain, 1991) recognizes that human beings, like all other living beings, can be understood only in the context of the systems in which they live. Critical to the ecological perspective is its holistic view of people. The ecological perspective functions as a metaphor that provides an understanding about the reciprocal transactions that take place between people and the social environment in which they function. A central principle of all forms of systems theory is **holism**. Holism refers to the idea that the whole is more than the sum of its parts (Richardson, 2000). Therefore, people and environments are part of a holistic system in which each shapes the other (Germain, 1991).

The scientific opposite of holism is **reductionism**. "Reductionism assumes that the whole is the sum of its parts, and attempts to understand problems by focusing on smaller and smaller units" (Oltmanns & Emery, 2004, p. 37). The central principle of reductionism is that ultimate explanations can be found when issues are reduced to their smallest possible components. This form of thinking is pervasive in science and in everyday thinking about human behavior. For example, when scientists find that brain chemistry in people with depression differs from that of individuals without depression, they often assume that this means that the brain caused the depression. However, the change in brain chemistry may be caused by adverse life experiences. Explanations that reduce the understanding of behavioral concerns to molecular variables are no better than approaches that reduce them to molar, or larger, system variables. For this reason, we have adopted in this book an *integrated multidimensional approach* that is based on principles from systems theory. This approach assumes that each level of a system offers a different analysis of people, behaviors, and problems.

Following are some of the basic ideas of the ecological systems perspective (Germain, 1991; Hearn, 1979):

- Social-work practice is based on a dual focus. This focus includes the person and situation, and the system and its environment.
- Social-work practice occurs at the interface between the human system and its environment, and the ways each influences the other.
- Social-work practice is best conducted when the transactions promote growth and development of the organism while simultaneously being ameliorative to the environment, thus making it a better place for all systems that depend upon the environment for sustenance.

In examining any social context, the social system plays an important role. A **system** represents any set of elements that affect or influence one another. We cannot solve the problem of any system without taking into account all the factors that influence the system and its components (Bronfenbrenner, 1999; Churchman, 1978). A social system is a system in which the components are people. These people participate in a number of social systems that influence their development—family, school, work setting, neighborhood, community, nation, and so forth. For this reason, we need to develop knowledge of the key dimensions of social systems, their interrelations, and their environment.

Brim (1975) and Bronfenbrenner (1977) identified four categories, or levels, of systems that are useful to social workers: microsystems, mesosystems, exosystems, and macrosystems. **Microsystems** involve face-to-face or direct contact among system participants. As social workers, we are interested in categories that enable us to classify behavior that takes place in these systems. This type of analysis is limited, however, if it neglects the relations between the microsystem of primary attention and other key microsystems. If we understand how multiple microsystems are interconnected, we can have a more informed understanding of the behavior in a particular context. **Mesosystems** are the category systems theorists use to address this level of analysis. Mesosystems are the network of personal settings in which we spend our social lives. Each of our clients lives in a similar but different mesosystem. It is critical to have an understanding of the network of personal settings affecting a particular microsystem under investigation.

Individuals are members of a number of different microsystems. What happens to them in any one microsystem can influence their behavior in other settings. For example, if you are working with an adolescent, you should not ignore the fact that events in his or her peer group can influence the degree of conflict observed in his or her school or family setting. The makeup of the mesosystem must be taken into account in analyzing any identified microsystem issue.

Exosystems in Bronfenbrenner's scheme are the larger institutions of society that influence our personal systems. These include institutions such as government agencies, which, although we may not directly work in them, have profound effects on our lives. Exosystems are considered any of the systems in which an individual is not directly involved. For instance, parents' work settings can affect their children's lives in many ways, yet the children have no direct involvement in these work settings. An exosystem level of analysis stresses the need to take into account clients' broader social environment by examining the influence of significant social institutions.

Last, **macrosystems** are the larger subcultural and cultural contexts in which microsystems, mesosystems, and exosystems are located. Macrosystems have the most pervasive level of influence on social activities. **Culture** is defined as a system of meanings and values shared by a population and transmitted to future generations (Sigelman & Shaffer, 1995). It includes all the key artifacts developed during the history of a population—all its material and nonmaterial (symbolic) products. Every sociocultural group has its own history, but in recent years scholars of race, class, and gender studies have pointed out, through the voices metaphor, that many of histories have been silenced. The voices metaphor comes from the efforts of scholars to break the silence that has surrounded the experiences of many groups in our society. These scholars focus on ignored aspects of diversity of our society by "listening to the voices" of representatives of the silenced groups (Andersen & Collins, 1998; 2004). The goal of much of current multicultural scholarship is to help people think about the experiences of previously silenced groups (Andersen & Collins, 2004; Dominelli, 2002; Sakamoto & Pitner, forthcoming). The material and symbolic aspects of culture influence all facets of our behavior, and they are given significant attention in the analysis of social systems by most practice frameworks in social work.

Bronfenbrenner used these four systems to describe the environmental contexts of human development. (See Exhibit 4.1.) These same systems have been adopted by social-work scholars to conceptualize the environmental component of our professional focus on person-and-environment transactions. Before the emergence of ecological-systems thinking in social work, there were many simplistic views of the environment in the profession. These views frustrated most practitioners' efforts to achieve any objectives involving "environmental modification" (Grinnell, Kyte, & Bostwick, 1981). Grinnell and colleagues pointed out that these early concepts of environment represented "(1) social structures (for example, social class system, ethnicity); (2) social conditions (for instance, unemployment, discrimination); (3) social systems (for example, economic, health, and educational networks); and (4) specific neighborhood or community resources (for instance, schools, churches, day-care centers, job training programs)" (1981, p. 153). Many

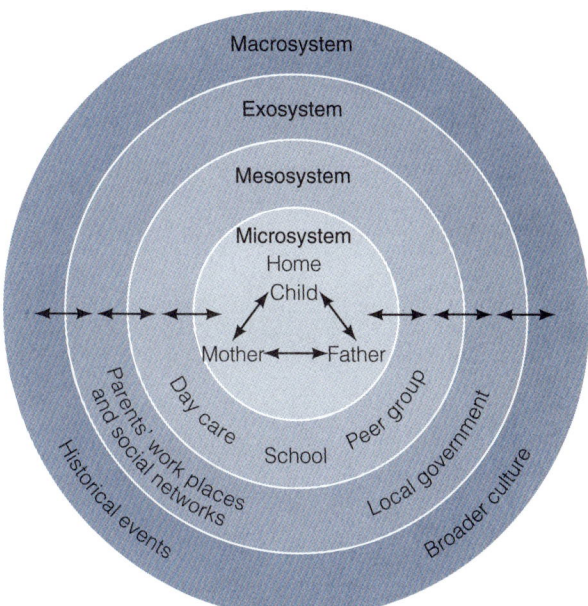

EXHIBIT 4.1 Bronfenbrenner's ecological model
Source: From *Developmental science*, edited by R. B. Cairns et al. © 1996 Cambridge University Press. Used with permission.

other dimensions and classifications have been used in social work to categorize the environment. However, ecological-systems thinking, unlike the other approaches, enhanced our ability to look at the environment in a way that allowed for its modification. This perspective redirected attention to the transactions between people and environment, rather than focusing on either the person or the environment.

Principles from systems theory direct social workers to identify relevant systems, their subsystems, and the suprasystems of which they are a part (Anderson & Carter, 1990). Social workers often achieve these ends by drawing an ecomap. Hartman and Laird (1983) are known in social work for having originally developed this tool for use by social workers in the field of child welfare. **Ecomapping** highlights the points of connection between systems that influence a person's life, and it facilitates the identification of points of conflict and points of support. Exhibit 4.2 presents a case example to illustrate the application of an ecomap to a social-work situation.

Ecological systems theory has not been the only conceptual approach to understanding social systems. *Functionalism* is another major theoretical tradition that developed in the social sciences for studying social systems and that has been adopted by social workers.

EXHIBIT 4.2

Ecomap

SOURCE: From *Clinical assessment for social workers: Quantitative and qualitative methods,* by Cathleen Jordan and Cynthia Franklin, p. 23. Copyright © 2003 Lyceum Books, Inc. Reprinted with permission.

Modern Functionalism

Talcott Parsons and Robert Merton are two of the major contributors to functionalist thought in American sociology. Their work was significantly influenced by the early sociologists and the first functional anthropologists—Malinowski and Radcliffe-Brown. Talcott Parsons is considered "the most dominant theorist of his time" (Turner, 1991, p. 51) and is known for having established a general theory of social systems. Before developing this dominant analytical approach to the social system, he viewed social life as a matter of agency. **Agency** is a technical term in sociology that includes the idea that goal-oriented people act in intentional ways (Waters, 1994). Any theory of social behavior that examines the process of acting in relation to a set of meanings or intentions is referred to as a **theory of agency**.

Parsons considered action systems to be formed by a series of alternative courses of action called **pattern variables**. These variables prescribe the limited choices available to individuals in social situations.

In Parsons's schema, individuals can choose only one of the options in a pattern variable. For example, a person confronting another person in a situation can choose only one option from each pattern variable to judge the other person: (1) in terms of his or her performance (achievement); or (2) in terms of his or her qualities (ascription). For instance, some societies reward a person based on who his or her family is rather than on what the individual has accomplished. Because these societal choices influence the social arrangements in the society, they were widely used to classify differences in social structures among societies.

Parsons modified his approach to studying the structure of social systems to give them a stronger functional focus, which led him to emphasize the importance of social systems. This change in his theory became known as **structural functionalism**. In this phase of his theoretical writings, Parsons identified four functional imperatives that are essential to the survival of any social system. These four system requisites are referred to as the **AGIL scheme**:

adaptation
goal attainment
integration
latent pattern maintenance

Any social system must meet these requisites if it is to survive. These requisites also help us understand the role played by key social systems in a society. To illustrate this point, we will use the **AGIL scheme** to provide a conceptual description of the needs of any social system (Waters, 1994). These needs are represented as follows:

Social System Need → Fulfilled by
1. Adaptation → The economy—money
2. Goal attainment → The political system—power
3. Integration → The social system—social controls, norms, and legal rules
4. Pattern maintenance → Socialization—family, schools

This classification scheme helps us make sense of the major social institutions in our society. Functional principles help us study our social institutions, and social institutions represent the final step in the process in which cultural values are translated into customary behavior. A social institution is technically defined as an "integrated set of social norms organized around the preservation of a basic society value" (Leslie, Larson, & Gorman, 1973, p. 109). Parsons and his followers identified five basic institutions: family, religion, education, economy, and government. (See the extended discussion of social institutions on page 146). Each of these institutions plays a critical role in the social system's survival. A common assignment for social-work students is to examine the social welfare system using principles from Parsons's institutional conceptualizations.

Robert Merton also looked at the functions of social structures, but he extended his study of social systems to include dysfunctions. For instance, he would analyze a system such as poverty in terms of its dysfunctions but would also seek to uncover any of its alternative functions. According to Merton, we need to examine the manifest and latent functions of any social institution.

For example, Herbert Gans, a noted sociologist, set out to discover why poverty exists. To the surprise of some, he uncovered fifteen functions that were served by poverty, including the provision of job opportunities for individuals who serve the needs of the poor. Some functionalists assume, therefore, that balanced approaches to understanding problems cannot be arrived at merely by looking at their functions. Instead they argue that questions should also be asked about the manifest and latent functions, as well as the dysfunctions of any social system (Ferrante, 1995). These concepts provide social workers with a conceptual approach for thinking about the influence of social systems on behavior by defining the key units of a social system. Because social systems theory assumes that stability is essential in understanding behavior, another group of social theorists developed an alternative lens for understanding social behavior that focused on notions of conflict.

Conflict Theories

Conflict theories focus on issues involving conflict, coercion, and the role of power in social relations. The best-known conflict theorist was Karl Marx—without a doubt the most influential thinker from this group of early-nineteenth-century social theorists. His theory assumes that all of human history represents a struggle over material or monetary resources involving conflicts between the classes, and it places significant emphasis on understanding the material structures of production. For Marx, the relations of production were the fundamental organizing principles of human society. To illustrate this point, we need to review his key assumptions and theory of structural contradiction.

Marx considered production to be a fundamental quality of human nature. He contended in his materialist view of history that the first act of human history was to produce the necessary materials for survival. To achieve this end, humans entered into social relationships that are "independent of their will." "These are the relationships which surround the production process and which will vary according to the particular historical stage of development of the system of production—technically referred to as the *mode of production*. These relations of production are the foundation of society, its economic base" (Waters, 1994, p. 101). In Marx's view, this economic base is the fundamental determinant of the structure and development of social life. The social organization of production (referred to as the *economic substructure*) plays the determining role not only in the productive processes but also in the formation of a society's superstructure. The *superstructure* in Marxian theory includes all the idealist structures in society, such as religion, law, and philosophy (Timasheff, 1967). In his view, the characteristics of these superstructures are determined by the economic base of the society.

For Marx, social change occurs as a result of the contradictions between the material forces of production and the relations of production. He defined the forces of production as all the factors required in the production process—raw materials, technology, and so forth. The relations of production refer to the social organization of the production process, especially the relations surrounding ownership of the means of production.

Waters (1994) contended that that this conflict between the material forces of production and the social relations is the key form of structural contradiction within societies that Marx assumed contributes to changes in social relations.

Other conflict theorists have identified forms of conflict between groups that contribute to harmony and change in social systems, including interest-group conflicts, value conflicts, and conflicts in authority relations. Denisoff and Wahrman (1979) provided an overview of some of the basic assumptions in more modern conflict approaches:

1. Interests are basic elements of social life.
2. Social life involves coercion.
3. Social life involves groups with different interests.
4. Social life generates opposition, exclusion, and hostility.
5. Social life generates conflict.
6. Social differences involve power.
7. Social systems are not united or harmonious.
8. Social systems tend to change.

This summary of assumptions indicates that stability is not of primary concern. In addition, it illustrates that an important issue in conflict is who is benefiting from a particular form of social arrangement. This perspective invites social workers to ask questions such as, whose interests are involved and who will benefit or suffer from the existing social conditions? For social workers, this perspective is most helpful in studying issues of social inequality. Conflict theorists do not assume that inequality exists because it is functional for a society as a whole. Instead, they assume that these inequalities result from some group's ability to achieve power over another.

While conflict theories focus on understanding the contributions of conflict to understanding social change, cultural theorists have identified changes in ideology that help social workers in understanding the postmodern conditions of social life.

Postmodernism and Theories of Society

Many scholars define *postmodernism* by contrasting it with modernism. Postmodernism is considered a new phase of history that follows the period known as *modernism*. Brown (1994) argued that many scholars assume that there were two great events in human history: the appearance of horticulture and the emergence of "modern societies." We are now on the verge of a third major event, which involves the appearance of a "yet unnamed 'post modern' social and cultural formation" (Brown, 1994, p. 13).

Modern societies are characterized by industrial economies, territorial states, mass culture, and scientific rationality (Smart, 1993). Other theorists differentiate modern societies from other social formations by focusing on the relationship between modernism and the spirit of Enlightenment, or what is known as the Age of Reason. In this historical period, tradition and religious dogmas as the grounds for truth and knowledge were replaced. Modernity promotes instead the pursuit of innovation, novelty, and dynamism through the process of instrumental rationality (Kellner, 1990). This highly rational, changeable, and instrumental way of life associated with modernism did not emerge in human history until after feudalism, or the Middle Ages, around 1600.

The postmodern age, by contrast, is a "time of troubles" marked by the collapse of rationalism and the ethos of the Enlightenment (Kellner, 1990). It is considered a period in which social engineering and other forms of scientific thought are looked upon with great suspicion. Most postmodernists are critical of views that support the notion that social work can solve the problems of social life with the aid of principles of science. In their view, this is an arrogant belief that is doomed to failure.

One of the major formulators of the postmodernist perspective is Jean-François Lyotard. Lyotard (1984) wrote *The Postmodern Condition*, wherein he stated that "the status of knowledge is altered as societies enter what is known as the postindustrial age and culture enters what is known as the postmodern age" (p. 3). In the modern age, science was elevated to a position of high status because it replaced the fictions and myths of tradition with facts derived from the scientific method. For Lyotard, the idea of postmodernity represents a fundamental change in the ways in which we relate to science and knowledge. In the postmodern period, we relate to science as another language game of mythical narrative. The goals and values of Western culture are no longer considered universal, and they are not considered to be the primary points of reference for any form of social organization or knowledge. In the views of many postmodernists, the decentering of Western knowledge and values is reflected in many of the controversies of our times. We will encounter many of these controversies in trying to define key social system concepts. In the next sections, we confront the dilemmas posed by postmodernism in attempts to define family, community, and other key social concepts.

Families and Groups

The family is increasingly being recognized as a social system—a whole composed of interrelated parts, each of which affects and is affected by the others, and each of which contributes to the functioning of the whole. This systems perspective helps us recognize that understanding a family is not as simple as understanding the mother-and-child relationship. Indeed, the family is influenced by many factors: the father and his relationship with the mother and child, the grandparents and their relationships with the parents and the child, and the environmental context—the kind of support the family receives from friends, church groups, and the neighborhood. The important point about understanding families as systems is to recognize how different interactions within and outside the family system affect the family.

Garbarino and Abramowitz (1992a, p. 16) have discussed an ecological approach to human development that emphasizes the interaction between the individual and environment. This approach views the process of development as the expansion of the child's conception of the world and ability to act on that world. An individual organism and the environment engage in reciprocal interaction: Each

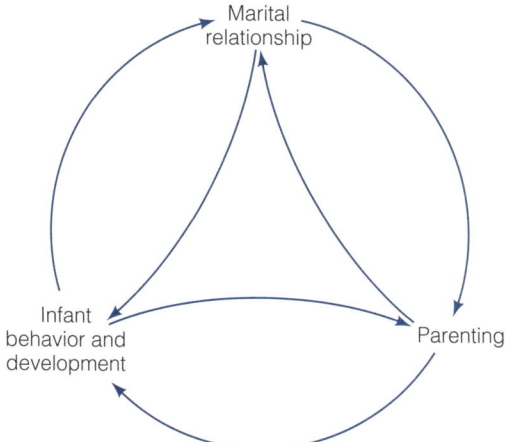

EXHIBIT 4.3 Diagram of the family as a social system
SOURCE: From "Early human experience," by J. Belsky (1981), *Developmental Psychology 17*, 3–23. Copyright © 1981 American Psychological Association. Reprinted with permission.

influences the other in an ever-changing interplay of biology and society, with intelligence and emotion as the mediators and identity and competence as the outcomes.

Belsky (1981) described the family as a social system, wherein the family is bigger than the sum of its parts. Parents can influence the child, who can influence each parent and thus the marital relationship (see Exhibit 4.3). Consider the following example. An infant is interacting with its mother and is involved in a process of reciprocal interaction (reciprocal because the infant can influence the mother and the mother can influence the infant). If the mother responds to the infant's smile with a corresponding smile and high-pitched talk, the infant is likely to reciprocate with laughter. When the father walks into the room, the mother-infant dyad is transformed into a family system (Belsky, 1981). The family system can be affected by any pair in the family. For example, mothers are less likely to play with their infants when the fathers join the dyad. In addition, the marital relationship affects the relationship between the parent and child, and, in turn, each parent's relationship with the child affects the quality of the marriage.

Family practitioners and clinical social workers use a systems perspective to help them understand the social context of a family problem. When a family is seen for a child's problem, the assumption is that the child's problem cannot be understood separate from the family system. The problem is related to how the person is treated in the family system, so the solution to the problem involves changing all members of the family system, not just the "problem" child.

No family system can be completely understood without also considering external factors and influences. Thus, to the already complex family system we must add influences such as the extended family, the school system, the neighborhood, the church or religious affiliation, the friends, the work environment, public policy, and so forth.

Defining the Family

What exactly is a family? How you answer this question can have important implications for how you practice social work. Indeed, how we as a society define *family* has important implications for the benefits and rights that family members receive. For example, if gay and lesbian couples are not considered to be families, this affects certain legal situations. In the United States, married couples have approximately 1,400 legal rights as a result of their marital status. Typically these are composed of about 400 state benefits and more than 1,000 federal benefits (Ontario Consultants on Religious Tolerance website). Imagine, for example, if a husband and wife did not have the right to visit each other in the hospital, make medical decisions in crises, share health insurance, and so on. These rights are not extended to nontraditional families. However, the definition of family is evolving, just as it has evolved in the past. Societal norms related to marriage and family has changed and will continue to change (Starbuck, 2002). In some states, before the Civil War, African American slaves were not permitted to marry, and it was illegal for interracial couples to marry (Ontario Consultants on Religious Tolerance website).

Currently, controversy surrounds gay and lesbian couples who want to marry and enjoy the same rights and responsibilities that straight couples do. Many individuals and groups argue that legitimizing gay and lesbian marriage and families would ruin the institutions of marriage and family — as though change were dangerous, rather than inevitable in all living systems.

Schriver (2004) has used the term *familiness* to broaden the traditional concept of family. He stated that "this concept reminds us as individuals and as members of particular families to think always about possible alternative structures and sets of functions that constitute family for others" (1995, p. 220).

Sociologists who attempt to answer the question "What is a family?" stress three functions: getting married, having children, and developing kinship ties. Reiss (1980, p. 29) summarized a global perspective regarding the family as "a small kinship-structured group with the key function of nurturant socialization." Duvall's (1971, p. 5) definition of the family is "a unit of interacting persons related by ties of marriage, birth, or adoption, whose central purpose is to create and maintain a common culture which promotes the physical, mental, emotional, and social development of each of its members." A less traditional definition of the family was offered by Hartman and Laird (1983, p. 576), who stated that a family is created when "two or more people construct an intimate environment that they define as a family, an environment in which they generally will share a living space, commitment, and a variety of the roles and functions usually considered part of family life." In this view, a family is a composition of people who decide to act as a family. This definition takes into account diverse forms of the family that might include gay or lesbian couples, single-parent families, elderly people not related by blood but living together as a family group, and other extended family groupings. Although the family is clearly changing, it remains a strong thread that ties together society as it functions to help provide socialization and companionship for diverse groups of people.

Adrian Nicole LeBlanc (2003), a journalist, has written an excellent book that many social workers enjoy because it captures the realities encountered by families living in poverty. It also provides an excellent vantage point for looking at the limitations of many of our middle-class and traditional notions of family. *Random Family: Love, Drugs, Trouble, and Coming of Age in the Bronx* follows the lives of several individuals who illustrate how they make family where they can find it. Some of the teenagers in this book are exposed to numerous separations, violence, and other events and experiences associated with the life of children who grow up in poverty (Evans, 2004). These environmental circumstances contribute to a qualitatively different sense of family. However, life in the inner city is not the only context where the family is undergoing significant changes.

The following Focus section provides personal narratives of family transitions, including coming out to one's children, as well as stepfamily issues.

FOCUS ON NARRATIVE

FROM STRAIGHT TO GAY

It's a sunny August afternoon in the mountains near Flagstaff, Arizona. Robin and Tracy have rented a log cabin and invited a group of friends to celebrate Robin's 40th birthday. I'm sitting on the porch with my laptop, working on this piece about being a single lesbian mother. Tracy asks what I'm writing, and next thing I know, all of us are sitting on the porch, talking for hours about our experiences as lesbian mothers and partners of mothers. Although lesbian families are as varied as heterosexual families, our group of friends has in common the experience of transitioning from heterosexual to lesbian families, or, for those of us without kids, from being single to being a stepparent. Three themes emerge from our stories: coming out to our children, reshaping our families to include our partners, and becoming stepparents.

TRACY: It was really hard for Robin. She moved in when my kids, David and Trisha, were 12 and 16. They had to deal with my coming out and with a new adult in the house. Sometimes she was in the middle, like, "Why can't they (the kids) turn the TV off?" "Why can't they turn the lights off?" "Why do they talk back to you?"

The parent has to educate her partner about the family norms. The partner sees a different view of what's going on between the mother and the kids. And it's frustrating to be the partner and not have authority with the kids. David was so angry. It was so hard because Robin would see how much he was hurting me.

ROBIN: It took me till the last three to four years before I could even be in the same room with David—because he was so mean to her.

TRACY: I've always had an easier time with my daughter, Trisha. Now she has a fiancé, and she just told him, "Well, my brother's gay and my mom's gay, so you have to deal with it." Trisha tells me, "What difference does it make? Everybody's gay any more." I just could not even imagine not having my two children in my life. I just got to meet his (her fiancé's) family last summer and we found out we have horses in common and we got along just fine.

Sylvia and I have six boys. I was married twice and widowed twice. My kids were 11 to 23 when their father died of pancreatic cancer. He was the best father. But there was always some dissatisfied part of me that could not get satisfied. Then, where I was working, I met some gay women and we would go off for weekends. Pretty soon I realized I was gay, but I couldn't stand the thought of disrupting my kids' lives. What I didn't know until after my husband died was that he was gay also. After he died, I sat my kids down in two groups—the younger group and the older group. I told them that their father had been gay and that I had recently realized that I was gay, as well. Out of all of them, Tim, the 11-year-old, was the only one who had a hard time—his father died and came out at the same time, and then his mother came out. At the time, he was going to a conservative church with his friends and so when he found out I was gay, he was sure I was going to hell. Until he was fifteen he would never let his friends come in the house.

But then I met Sylvia—she's in Atlanta, and I'm in Phoenix for the next year till I finish school. Right away Sylvia started sending Tim notes about this and that. Then I wanted to send her a CD of photos and Tim showed me how. And then my other son has been struggling with alcohol and Susan's a recovering alcoholic, and she helped me understand some of the things he was going through.

DE: My children were 19 and 24 when Georgie and I got together five years ago.

GEORGIE: I thought the kids would be gone.

DE: My stepdaughter, Heather, is 29 now. She decided she couldn't be part of my life as a lesbian. When she got married, she said that if Georgie was going to come to the wedding, I shouldn't go. She wanted it at the swank golf club where Georgie works, but she didn't want Georgie there. I finally did go, but I was way in the back, far from the head table. When she got pregnant, I wasn't invited to the baby shower. I raised her from the age of two. Now I have a grandchild who is going to be two whom I've never seen. Heather has sort of adopted my younger sister, and she's the one who does the mother things, like arranging all the occasions that I'm not invited to.

(continues)

FOCUS ON NARRATIVE (continued)

But then, at another family wedding, my nephew's partner, who's very flamboyant, saw me and Georgie walk in and said, "The lesbians are here!" And this was a tiptop Texas wedding with hundreds of people and everything just so.

My son, Chris, is completely different from my stepdaughter. He's 24 now, living in Tucson. A few months ago, Chris, in front of his five roommates—and the other seven or so who wander in and out—said, "This is my mom, and this is my other mom." Right there in the kitchen with all his friends around.

As we sipped cool drinks and exchanged stories on that refreshing autumn afternoon in the mountains, I realized that our difficulties were not limited to gay families. These challenges—new loves and divided loyalties, old hierarchies and new management, the exhilaration and resentment related to changing roles, relief and discomfort, ambivalence and hope—are the challenges typical to any blended family. Even the added stress of living in a hostile social climate that invalidates and pathologizes your family was typical for stepfamilies until recently. Realizing this parallel, I am heartened. U.S. society *has* become less hostile to stepfamilies. We're waiting.

—MARGARET ANN WALLER, PH.D.

The Family Life Cycle

One way of understanding family life is to consider the family life cycle—a sequence of developmental stages that families typically move through. Carter and McGoldrick (1988) have described a six-stage model of family development. An overview of the model is presented in Exhibit 4.4.

As couples move through the family life cycle, they have different sources of satisfaction and frustration. Some researchers have attempted to examine the effect of the life-cycle stage on various behaviors and attitudes. For example, how does the stage of the family life cycle affect marital satisfaction? In general, researchers (Belsky, 1990; Rollins & Feldman, 1970) have found a U-shaped relationship between life-cycle stage and marital satisfaction. Marital satisfaction starts high, with the newly married couple, and decreases to its lowest point at the stage where families have school-aged children. The next stage, families with teenage children, begins the upward incline to the final stage, the aging family, where satisfaction reaches a level similar to that of the newly married couple. Exhibit 4.5 presents the U-shaped relationship across the family-life-cycle stages.

Although the family-life-cycle perspective helps us understand how traditional families change over time, it also presents common patterns of the typical family. However, families today are not easily described using typical norms. Therefore, transitions from one stage to the next may depend on the unique aspects of the family and the family's previous experience. Indeed, changes in the "typical" family, such as divorce, working mothers, delayed childbirth, and blended families, add sets of tasks and challenges that may differ from those of the traditional family.

A stepfamily is created when one or both partners bring a child, or children, from a previous relationship into the family. The term *blended family* is often used to refer to a stepfamily. However, *stepfamily* is the preferred term in some professional circles, for simple reasons: children in stepfamilies are often part-time members of more than one family and have more than one mother and/or father. By definition, these families are not blended. Trying to blend a family often forces children to divide their loyalties, creating unneeded conflict (Stepfamily Association of America, 2003).

Families are generally defined by the parent-child relationship, and the term *stepfamily* is consistent with the definition of a family. Activists hope that through education, the negative connotation associated with the prefix *step-* will help society accept stepfamilies as true families.

It is difficult to determine how many children live in stepfamilies. The U.S. Census Bureau counts children only in their primary residences. The Stepfamily Association of America (2003) estimates that 23% of American children spend time in a stepfamily. The number rises to about 30% when cohabiting couples are included. Additionally, it is estimated that half of all Americans will spend some time in a stepfamily during their lifetimes.

EXHIBIT 4.4 Family life cycle

Stage of the Family Life Cycle	Key Developmental Task	Changes in Family Status Required to Proceed Developmentally
1. Between families: the unattached young adult	Accepting parent/offspring separation	Differentiation of self in relation to family of origin Development of intimate peer relations Establishment of self in work
2. The joining of families through marriage: the newly married couple	Commitment to new system	Formation of marital system Realignment of relationships with extended families and friends to include spouse
3. The family with young children	Accepting new members into the system	Adjusting marital system to make space for children Taking on parenting roles Realignment of relationships with extended family to include parenting and grandparenting roles
4. The family with adolescents	Increasing flexibility of family boundaries to include children's independence and grandparents' frailties	Shifting of parent-child relationships to permit adolescent to move in and out of system Refocus on midlife marital and career issues Beginning shift toward concerns for older generation
5. Launching children and moving on	Accepting a multitude of exits from and entries into the family system	Renegotiation of marital system as dyad Development of adult-to-adult relationships between grown children and their parents Realignment of relationships to include in-laws and grandchildren
6. The family in later life	Accepting the shifting of generational roles	Maintaining own functioning, couple functioning, or both, and interests in face of physiological decline; exploration of new familial and social-role options Support for a more central role for middle generations Making room in the system for the wisdom and experience of the elderly; supporting the older generation without overfunctioning for them Dealing with loss of spouse, siblings, and other peers and preparation for own death; life review and integration

SOURCE: Adapted from *The changing family lifecycle*, by B. Carter and M. McGoldrick, p. 15. Copyright © 1988 Allyn & Bacon. Adapted with permission.

EXHIBIT 4.5 U-shaped relationship of marital satisfaction across the family life cycle

SOURCE: From "Marital satisfaction over the family life cycle," by B. C. Rollins & H. Feldman (1970), *Journal of Marriage and the Family, 32,* 20–28. Copyright © 1970 National Council on Family Relations, 3989 Central Ave. NE, Suite 550, Minneapolis, MN 55421. Reprinted with permission.

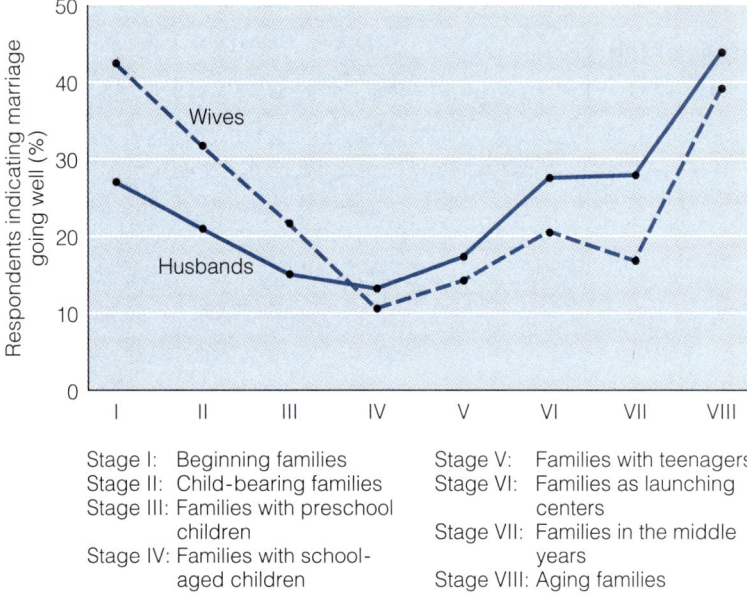

Stage I: Beginning families
Stage II: Child-bearing families
Stage III: Families with preschool children
Stage IV: Families with school-aged children
Stage V: Families with teenagers
Stage VI: Families as launching centers
Stage VII: Families in the middle years
Stage VIII: Aging families

FOCUS ON NARRATIVE

A Stepfamily's Life

Story 1

I loved my stepchildren before I met them. How could I not? They were Bruce's children. After spending the summer with them during their annual visit, my love felt deeper because they were both so much like their father. They were nice to me, and I had a fabulous time that summer before marrying their father, getting to know them. When it was time for them to leave, I sobbed like a baby at the airport and for days after.

When Bruce and I got married, I was thrilled to be their stepmother. I couldn't believe my luck at meeting a man who was a good father, with kids who liked me! But things changed after we got married: the kids weren't nice, or even respectful, to me. It seemed like they were deliberately trying to create conflict between their father and me. I hated how my husband catered to their every whim—to the point of serving them. When I suggested we have dinner together each evening, Bruce said the kids simply wouldn't like it. I told my husband they didn't have to like it, but that he could make them do it. I was angry and hurt, and my husband was unaware—entirely focused on doing anything his children wanted, even if it was unhealthy or extravagant. I was miserable and confused.

We went to Disneyland that summer. When I got hungry around noon our first day there, I suggested to my husband we get lunch. Bruce asked his oldest son whether he wanted to eat yet. When the 10-year-old replied that he wasn't hungry, Bruce told me to get a snack while he took the boys on another ride. I was furious, but my husband wouldn't budge. The boys watched my tantrum with a smile. Just as I was finishing my snack, about ten minutes later, my stepson was suddenly famished. We went to lunch. This is the incident that got us into therapy.

In therapy, my husband and I learned our problems were common to stepfamilies in formation. We learned that the boys' behavior toward me was, ultimately, the responsibility of my husband. The boys were reacting normally to their father's marriage, wanting assurance he still loved them. We learned that creating a healthy stepfamily takes a great deal of work and commitment. I don't think we would still be married had we not gotten help with our marriage and education about stepfamilies.

It's been more than ten years now since I became a stepmother. It has simultaneously been the most difficult, rewarding, and thankless job I have ever had. My stepchildren are nearly grown, both in college. I don't love my stepchildren in the same way their biological parents love them, but I do love them as a parent—a stepparent. The love I feel for my stepchildren is so great it cannot be put into words. I would not be the person I am today without my husband or without my stepchildren, and I am grateful. (P.S. They love me, too!)

Story 2

As I grew older, I knew if I got married, it would probably be to someone who had children. When I married a man with two young boys, I was sure his previous marriage was simply a mismatch. My husband was so wonderful, I didn't believe it could have been anything else.

As a new stepmother, I planned to include the boys' biological mother in everything. After all, how could I create a home for them if I didn't include the person who was most important to them? She was not hostile, but she was cold, even impolite. She would write thank-you notes to my husband for personal gifts from me. I made excuses for her because I was confident I would win her over. I knew we were going to be one big, happy family.

Then, my younger stepson had a serious problem in school while he was with my husband and me. She blamed me for this problem, shouted at my husband over the phone, and told me she was going to do everything in her power to make sure her children never saw me again because I was "dangerous." I was devastated, and I didn't understand. It was hard enough trying to find help for my stepson without her accusations.

My stepson got the help he needed, and today he is okay. His problem was not my fault, or anyone else's. We communicate with the boys' biological mother through a facilitator only, and it has helped tremendously. I have managed to recover from the hurt and pain.

Sometimes I think about how naive I was, imagining we'd all be a happy family, and I feel stupid. I'm no longer naive, but I still consider the bio-mom of my stepchildren a member of my family. We're just not talking right now.

The thing I want people to know about stepparents is that, whether anyone likes it or not, we are in a parenting role. We are parents, not biological parents, but parents nonetheless.

—Anonymous author

The Changing Family

As we have seen, the family is a complex system. It is not static, however, and as a developing system, the family reflects a changing world. As we noted earlier, even the definition of family is changing to accommodate rapid shifts in our society. Therefore, understanding the family includes staying informed about these trends, including the following (Sigelman & Shaffer, 1995):

- More adults are living as singles today than in the past.

It is increasingly recognized that *family* does not mean two heterosexual parents and child—families represent great diversity, as this lesbian family demonstrates.

- Many young adults are delaying marriage while they pursue educational and career goals.
- After marriage, couples are having fewer children.
- An increasing number of couples are deciding to remain childless.
- Most women, including those who have children, work outside the home.
- Up to 50% of young people are expected to divorce sometime in their marriage.
- Up to 50% of children born in the 1980s will spend some time in a single-parent family.
- Because more couples are divorcing, more adults, about 75%, are remarrying.
- Adults today are spending more of their later years as couples or as single adults without children in the home, primarily because people live longer than they used to.

The following Focus section provides a narrative of family life after divorce and the effects of the mother's transition from being straight to being lesbian. Lev's (2004a) *Complete Lesbian and Gay Parenting Guide* provides excellent additional content on the subject.

FOCUS ON NARRATIVE

TELL US WHAT LESBIAN FAMILIES ARE LIKE

Though I have been married, and my daughter has two fathers and other adults who adore her, for the most part, I've been parenting her on my own. I divorced her biological father when she was a year old, and it was after we were divorced that her stepfather really engaged as a parent. Now Heather is 16 and off to college next year. I am savoring our time together—inwardly leaning forward, listening as she composes her past, present, and future. Ribbons of conversation connect our lives apart and together. We talk about her days, her friends, politics—what she makes of our fragile and sacred world and how she sees herself in it. When we're home, we work separately together at our keyboards in our home office, take walks, watch foreign films, do chores, love our dogs and Pablo—the cat she named after Neruda, the Chilean poet. She works with seventh graders, creating cohesion and delight in a group of forty, and sometimes she's a little girl and I rub her back as she falls asleep, as I have done all her life. These exchanges, as common as the breeze today, will soon be echoes in my thoughts as I wonder how she is doing in her fledgling young-adult life. In a few months we will be fitting our conversation into telephones, e-mails, and occasional visits.

Heather was 9, I was 42 when I realized I was gay. I had been married to her stepfather for six years when I went on a backpacking trip and fell in love for the first time—with a woman. It suddenly became clear why my heart had never been in my relationships with men. My husband thought it was a phase. It wasn't. After the holidays, we sat down with Heather and told her, assuring her that we would both always be there for her. She was amazing—in an hour and a half, she went through the whole spectrum of human emotions, from curiosity to shock to tears to pride. The next day, she went off to school—a lab school at the university where I taught—and outed us to everyone. At the end of the day, the after school program director called Heather into her office and said, "Heather, I don't think you should be explaining to the other children about homosexuality." Heather replied, "Miss Thomas, these children are nine years old. If their parents haven't explained to them about homosexuality by now, they probably aren't going to, so why shouldn't I?"

That spring, we divorced, and Heather and I moved 2,000 miles away, where I had another teaching position. In one tumultuous spring, Heather's mom and stepdad divorced, she was uprooted from her friends and a cutting-edge university lab school in Rhode Island, and landed in Arizona—in the desert in a school system rated forty-eighth in the nation. She hated it. She became the tortured, smart, fat kid who used big words that nobody understood. The precociousness that had earned her plaudits in her lab school became evidence of otherness that ensured her ostracism. For two years, she was angry, depressed, and friendless, and petrified of further abuses should her peers learn that her mother was a lesbian. On her behalf, I joined her in the closet around her friends and teachers.

Meanwhile, I was going through late-blooming adolescence, discovering my sexuality and experiencing all the accompanying highs and lows. Having been really close, Heather and I were completely out of sync. Then, in an odd twist of nature, we simultaneously entered hormonal hell—menopause and early adolescence. Though I'd been a clinical social worker for two decades, we suffered a long while before I realized that this was more than a rocky family transition. In both of us, hormonal upheaval had induced clinical depression. It was a rough ride for a couple of years.

Now Heather's 16 and has survived Arizona's anemic attempts at gifted education. She's growing more independent by the day—driving, making her own life choices, working, managing her own money, applying to colleges, researching scholarships. I am exhaling in a way that only single heads of household understand. Parenting alone, particularly in the absence of family supports, is impossible. Yet millions of us are doing it. Growing up with divorced parents with a lesbian mom has its challenges, yet millions of kids are emerging from gay households healthy and whole, ready to do their parts in our world.

Lesbian families, like interfaith, interracial, single-parent, and stepfamilies before us, are often an invisible family form, beyond the mainstream imagination. When we do become visible, it is usually through dark lenses that portray us as godless deviants warping the development of our innocent children. Whereas other family forms are slowly emerging from stale air of social stigma, we're still breathing it. However, as poet Percy Shelley says in "Ode to a Skylark,"

If winter comes, can spring be far behind?

—By Margaret Waller

The Family of Our Times

Tommy needs to eat at 6:00 because of a school function at 7:00. His sister, Martha, must be picked up from her field-hockey game, but their mother, Sarah, has an office function and can't get home until after 8:00—thus, no dinner and no transportation. Sarah asks her husband, Rick, to come to the rescue, but he has to work late to prepare for a flight to Dallas the next morning. It is also Sarah's mother's birthday the next day, but Sarah is not prepared. Urgent messages await on the answering machine, one from a longtime friend of Rick's, in town for a day and wanting to drop by, and another from a close friend of Sarah's, in tears because of her floundering marriage (Gergen, 1991, p. 29).

This description of the modern family portrays what Gergen has referred to as the "saturated family." Unlike family life a century ago, new technologies have infiltrated our lives and become necessities, with the effect that the individual's experience of the cultural and social world has expanded and become more complex. In this electronic age, which has brought new forms of communication—fax machines, copy machines, Internet connections, electronic mail—there is a new reality concerning our abilities to interact. At the social level, we confront a multiplicity of relationships. One result of all this, Gergen points out, is that it is increasingly difficult for people to discover what they believe in. This experience of the world and the self is referred to as "social saturation" (Gergen, 1991). We are simply bombarded with new causes, different inner voices, and mixed opinions, and it is increasingly difficult to get a sense of the "right way."

The preceding example of typical family life is characterized by what Gergen refers to as a "slapstick style of turmoil now so pervasive that it seems unremarkable" (Gergen, 1991, p. 29). Do families have consensual goals that provide direction in their lives? Gergen believes that the technologies of social saturation make this very difficult. "The ordinary, daily confluence of multiple lives within one household makes for a sense of fragmentation, as if the members of the family were being scattered by the centrifugal force of postmodern life" (Gergen, 1991, p. 29). This predicament leads to the inability to define "family." In fact, Gergen refers to the **floating family**, which is a formless array of familial relationships that are in a continuous state of flux. Such a lack of boundaries leads to a blurring of ideals, whereby there is no sense about what it means to be a "good" family. Because there is no shared sense of reality, the family often becomes the site of multiple confrontations and conflicts. Furthermore, the floating family must adapt to a loss of power structure. Traditional notions of hierarchy and authority structure are becoming increasingly less relevant.

Such changes have led to more intense discussions about what a family really is and how to function within a family. Gergen believes that in this new world "the postmodern family can provide a kind of emotional sustenance that seems uniquely suited to the needs of people in a saturated world" (p. 34). The home is not just a place where one can "be oneself," but it is a place where people can "be their many selves." So, although the family is undergoing

EXHIBIT 4.6 Sampling of definitions of *group*

Central Feature	Definition
Communication	"We mean by a group a number of persons who communicate with one another, often over a span of time, and who are few enough so that each person is able to communicate with all the others, not at second hand, through other people, but face-to-face" (Homans, 1950, p. 1).
Influence	"Two or more persons who are interacting with one another in such a manner that each person influences and is influenced by each other person" (Shaw, 1981, p. 454).
Interaction	"A group is a social system involving regular interaction among members and a common group identity. This means that groups have a sense of "weness" that enables members to identify themselves as belonging to a distinct entity" (Johnson, 1995, p. 125).
Interdependence	"A group is a collection of individuals who have relations to one another that make them interdependent to some significant degree" (Cartwright & Zander, 1968, p. 46).
Interrelations	"A group is an aggregation of two or more people who are to some degree in dynamic interrelation with one another" (McGrath, 1984, p. 8).
Psychological significance	"Descriptively speaking, a psychological group is defined as one that is psychologically significant for the members, to which they relate themselves subjectively for social comparison and the acquisition of norms and values, . . . that they privately accept membership in, and which influences their attitudes and behavior" (Turner, 1987, pp. 1-2).
Shared identity	"A group exists when two or more people define themselves as members of it and when its existence is recognized by at least one other" (Brown, 1988, pp. 2-3).
Structure	"A group is a social unit which consists of a number of individuals who stand in (more or less) definite status and role relationships to one another and which possesses a set of values or norms of its own regulating the behavior of individual members, at least in matters of consequences to the group" (Sherif & Sherif, 1956, p. 144).

many new adaptations, it remains an adaptive social system.

Groups as Social Subsystems

How many groups do you belong to? To answer this question, you need to think about what makes up a group. When you are together with your friends, is this a group? What about the members of the Human Behavior and Social Environment class you are presently taking—is that a group? Are all the college students from your hometown a group?

A group can de defined as "two or more persons who are interacting with one another in such a manner that each person influences and is influenced by each other person" (Shaw, 1981, p. 8). Brown (1991, p. 3) defines a group as "a small, face-to-face collection of persons who interact to accomplish some purpose." Therefore, although you have a lot in common with all the college students from your hometown, they do not constitute a group in Brown's definition, because the people don't depend on one another to accomplish shared goals.

A definition of what constitutes a group depends on the focus of the theorist. Forsyth (1999; 2005) has provided an overview of the range of definitions contained in the literature (see Exhibit 4.6). Some of these definitions of groups highlight different variables, such as influence, identity, and structure. However, they often ignore other important characteristics, such as group size. Shaw's definition of *group* defines the barest requirements of a group but leaves unanswered other questions about groups (Forsyth, 1999; 2005).

Groups are often classified as either formed or natural. **Formed groups** are created through an outside influence or intervention and are convened for a particular purpose; **natural groups** are created by naturally occurring events, interpersonal attraction, or the mutual needs of the individuals involved (Toseland & Rivas, 1995; 2001).

Belonging to a Group

People belong to particular groups for a variety of reasons. Why would you want to be a member of a particular group? Do you seek membership in groups because they provide you with a sense of security, intimacy, or identity? To what extent are groups a fundamental "bridge" between you and society at large (Forsyth, 2005)? Clearly, there are a variety of reasons why people belong to groups. Schein (1980) suggests that these reasons revolve around five essential goals we want to accomplish in groups:

1. To fulfill our need for affiliation
2. To increase our sense of identity and our self-esteem
3. To obtain a source for social comparisons between ourselves and others
4. To obtain a greater sense of security and power
5. To accomplish a particular task or set of tasks

Social psychologists interested in identifying basic human needs have long identified the fundamental need for people to belong to groups. The way people fulfill this need must be assessed by social-work professionals, because the fulfillment or frustration of this and other social needs will lead to inclinations that explain why people turn to others in either positive or negative ways (Staub, 2004). Some other social needs include the needs to understand, to be effective, to find the world benevolent, and to maintain self-esteem (Stevens & Fiske, 1995; Staub, 2004). "The fulfillment of basic needs also fosters effective functioning, well-being, and continued growth or optimal human functioning" (Staub, 2004, p. 52).

People can identify with and belong to a variety of small groups, such as family, peer or friendship groups, ethnic groups, civil rights groups, and formal organizations. Membership in these groups is a major source of self-validation and standing (Hogg, 2003; Ashford & Faith, 2004). Tyler (1989) has contended that people value membership in social groups because group identifications are psychologically rewarding. The groups to which we belong tell us about out status or our place in society. This is why self-esteem is so closely associated with how a person evaluates the groups to which he or she belongs. It is assumed in social-identity theory that people are motivated to overvalue their own groups and that doing so enhances their self-esteem. Maintaining a positive sense of identity is a major social need recognized by many theorists (Erikson, 1959; Hogg, 2003; Staub, 2004).

According to social-identity theory (Tajfel, 1978, 1982; Tajfel & Turner, 1986), identity in interpersonal interactions can depend completely on an individual's membership in a social group (social identity). This differs from circumstances involving a person's identity being determined by personal characteristics or traits (Hogg, 2003; Stephan & Stephan, 1996). "A major premise of Tajfel's social-identity theory is that social identity creates and maintains attitudinal and behavioral discriminations favoring the ingroup" (Stephan & Stephan, 1996, p. 91). That is, Tajfel assumes that people are motivated to overvalue their own group and by doing so increase their own self-esteem. This overvaluation includes (1) making positive comparisons between groups that individuals are members of and relevant out-groups and (2) seeing important differences in one's own group but assuming similarity or homogeneity in out-group members (Blaine, 2000; Stephan & Stephan, 1996).

Overvaluation of one's groups contributes to many forms of intergroup conflict (Hogg, 2003), including actions by members of groups to exclude others from desired activities and resources. Social rejection is a form of social conflict that takes on many different faces and varies from context to context. Some theorists assume that this and other forms of social conflict are inevitable aspects of human existence but that intergroup conflict can be managed so that it results in constructive rather than destructive outcomes (Boardman & Horowitz, 1994).

We need groups to function effectively in society. All of us have special needs for affiliation and want to enhance our self-esteem. Groups also help us achieve important goals, such as developing an increased sense of security and power (Staub, 2004). As Johnson and Johnson (1989) have pointed out:

> From the moment we are born to the moment we die, relationships are the core of our existence. We are conceived within relationships, are born into relationships, live our lives within relationships. We are dependent on other people for the realization of life itself, for survival during one of the longest gestation periods in the animal kingdom, for food and cognitive development, for guidance in learning essential competencies required to survive in our world, and for fun, excitement, comfort, love, personal confirmation, and fulfillment. Our relationships with others form the context for all other aspects of our lives (p. 107).

Interdependence in our social relationships is significantly influenced by the social groups to which we belong. For this reason, we must make distinctions among groups to understand their contributions to human behavior.

Treatment and Task Groups

In social work, an important classification of groups is whether they are treatment oriented or task oriented (Toseland & Rivas, 1995; 2001). In general, the two types of groups serve different purposes. In **treatment groups**, the purpose is to meet members' socioemotional needs. Different types of treatment groups include groups for support, education, therapy, growth, and socialization. In **task groups**, the primary purpose is to complete the work for which the group was convened (Toseland & Rivas, 2001). The task group is not specifically linked to the needs of the members of the group. Using selected characteristics, Toseland and Rivas provided a comparison of treatment groups and task groups, as shown in Exhibit 4.7.

Although we have presented a distinction between two types of groups, treatment and task, many different group purposes exist within these two types of groups (Toseland & Rivas, 1995, p. 20):

- Rehabilitation: Restoring members to their former level of functioning
- Habilitation: Helping members grow and develop
- Correction: Helping members who are having problems with social laws or mores
- Socialization: Helping members learn how to get along with others and do what is socially acceptable
- Prevention: Helping members develop and function at an optimum level and helping them to prepare for events that are likely to occur
- Social action: Helping members change their environment
- Problem solving: Helping members resolve complex issues and concerns
- Developing social values: Helping members develop a humanistic approach to living

Understanding How Groups Function

Groups can have a powerful influence on human behavior. What factors can account for this influence? To answer this question, we must understand group dynamics, or group process. These factors can influence the behavior of both the individual in the group and the group as a whole. In social work we direct our attention to the helpful influences of group dynamics. However, we must recognize that group dynamics also can unleash harmful forces (Galinsky & Schopler, 1977). The group dynamics that help explain these forces include norms that guide the behavior of group members; roles that members play in groups; communication patterns, which influence the manner in which people interact; power and status, which affect the influence members have on one another; and cohesiveness, which determines how much sharing takes place in the group.

Roles and Norms

Norms are expectations and beliefs regarding appropriate behavior in a group. When you are with your group of friends, there are certain informal, unwritten laws about what constitutes appropriate behavior. For example, name-calling may or may not be appropriate depending on the norms of your particular group. In some groups, this is a sign of affection or is expected behavior; however, in other groups, this would be considered inappropriate and rude behavior. How you decide whether to engage in behaviors such as name-calling will depend on the norms of your group. Rosenblatt (1962) notes that the influence of norms on behavior will depend on the extent to which they are considered binding. In general, however, group norms exert a powerful influence on the behavior of individuals. As Toseland and Rivas (1995, p. 81) pointed out, "[S]oon it becomes clear that sanctions and social disapproval result from some behaviors and that praise and social approval result from other behaviors." The development of group norms can be helpful to the individuals and to the group itself. Norms provide a predictable group environment and add stability and security for members. Through the development of group norms, groups can develop procedures for coordinated action to reach goals (Toseland & Rivas, 2001). Alternatively, norms can develop destructive patterns of behavior that are harmful to others or unethical.

A **role** is a pattern of behavior that a person acts out in a group. It is a shared expectation about the functions of the individuals in the group. For example, there are role expectations about your status as a student, a mother, a spouse, and your many other roles in society. In groups, individuals also act according to certain roles, which can be important contributors to the group's effectiveness. "Roles are

EXHIBIT 4.7 Tasks and Socioemotional Roles in Groups

Task Roles

Role	Description
Information seeker:	Emphasizes "getting the facts" by calling for background information
Opinion seeker:	Asks for more qualitative types of data, such as attitudes, values, and feelings
Elaborator:	Gives additional information—such as rephrasing, implications—about points made by others
Coordinator:	Shows the relevance of each idea and its relationship to the overall problem
Orienter:	Refocuses discussion on the topic whenever necessary
Evaluator-critic:	Appraises the quality of the group's efforts in terms of logic, practicality, or method
Energizer:	Stimulates the group to continue when discussion lags

Socioemotional Roles

Role	Description
Encourager:	Rewards others through agreement, warmth, and praise
Harmonizer:	Mediates conflicts among group members
Compromiser:	Shifts his or her own position on an issue in order to reduce conflict in the group
Gatekeeper or expediter:	Smooths communication by setting up procedures and ensuring equal participation
Standard setter:	Expresses or calls for discussion of standards for evaluating the quality of the group process
Group observer and commentator:	Informally points out the positive and negative aspects of the group's dynamics and calls for change if necessary
Follower:	Accepts the ideas offered by others and serves as an audience for the group

SOURCE: Adapted from "Functional roles of group members," by K. D. Benne & P. Sheats, (1948) *Journal of Social Issues, 4*(2), 41–49. Copyright © The Society for the Psychological Study of Social Issues. Used with permission.

important for groups because they allow for division of labor and appropriate use of power" (Toseland & Rivas, 1995, p. 82). By accepting a particular role, individuals agree to behave in a certain manner.

Roles, like norms, can vary from being explicit to vague and informal. Bales (1958) has identified two categories of roles: task-related roles and socioemotional roles. *Task-related roles* require actions that move the group toward the completion of its goals. *Socioemotional roles* require actions that keep the interactions in the group positive, friendly, and supportive. Exhibit 4.7 shows seven different task-related roles and seven different socioemotional roles that are used in groups.

Communication Patterns

Communication patterns reflect the nature of how the members in the group communicate—in both verbal and nonverbal ways. A communication process is always occurring in the group, because people communicate whenever they are together in a group. Communicating in a group has a number of functions (Kiesler, 1978):

- Understanding people and finding out where they stand in relation to other people
- Persuading others
- Gaining or maintaining power
- Defending oneself
- Provoking a reaction in others
- Making an impression on others
- Gaining or maintaining relationships
- Presenting a unified image to the group

Communication patterns vary within a group and may be either centralized, meaning the leader is usually the central figure, or decentralized, meaning members share equally in communication and the pattern of interactions is more group centered. What kind of communication pattern is best for groups? Research by McGrath (1984) found that, when problems are simple, centralized groups are efficient in resolving them. Centralization tends to "increase social interaction, group morale, and members' commitment to group goals" (Toseland & Rivas, 1995, p. 74). However, when problems are more complex, a decentralized pattern of communication is more effective. Group members have greater satisfaction in more decentralized groups.

Status and Power

How do some group members obtain more status and power than other members? **Status** refers to the ranking of each group member's position in the group relative to the other members. **Power** refers to the potential ability of a member to influence the group's decision or the behavior of other individuals in the group. Although status and power often go hand in hand, this is not necessarily the case. A person's status is based on two different factors. First, what is the person's prestige or position outside the group? Is the person recognized as a leader in the community? Second, what kinds of roles does the person assume when he or she becomes a member of a group? Is the person a coordinator and a standard setter, influencing how the group achieves its goals? Because status is defined relative to other group members, a person's status is influenced by how others in the group perceive him or her.

"Power" is a difficult concept to define, but French and Raven (1959), in a classic analysis, identified five sources of power in groups:

1. Reward power: Based on the person's ability to reward others as a means for obtaining power
2. Coercive power: Based on the person's ability to apply sanctions such as punishments and threats toward others
3. Expert power: Based on the person's ability to demonstrate superior skills and abilities as a means of influencing others
4. Referent power: Based on the person's personal characteristics, such as likeability and respect, that give him or her influence over others
5. Legitimate power: Based on the person's perceived legitimate right to make demands of other people

Cohesiveness

A **cohesive group** is one in which individual members have strong bonds with one another and to the group itself. Group cohesion is the dynamic that compels individuals to remain part of the group (Festinger, 1950). Therefore, cohesive group members are often emotionally close, are loyal to one another and to the group, and have a strong sense of camaraderie.

Fundamentally, the factors that make a group cohesive are those that promote positive, caring relationships among the members—for example, when group members are similar in attitudes, or have great liking and respect for one another—and that are successful in achieving goals (Ridgeway, 1983). When members are attracted to a group, there is a greater likelihood of developing group cohesion. Attraction to the group is influenced by people's desire for affiliation, the group's access to resources and incentives, the expectations group members have about the outcomes that can be achieved in the group, and the relative comparison to other groups (Cartwright, 1968).

Group workers believe that an important skill for a group leader is the ability to influence group cohesion (Rose, 1989). This skill is important because a cohesive group has a number of benefits (Cartwright, 1968; Dion, Miller, & Magnan, 1970; Evans & Dion, 1991; Rose, 1989; Yalom, 1985):

- Members are more likely to stay in the group
- Members are more likely to persevere in attempts to accomplish group goals
- Attendance is higher
- Members accept more responsibility for group functioning
- Members are more satisfied
- Members are less likely to feel psychological distress
- Members are more likely to have increased self-esteem and self-confidence

Effect of Gender on Groups

How does gender influence small-group interactions? Not surprisingly, the small group is similar to society in general. Therefore, status and power differentials in the larger society are reflected in the small group. As a result, gender roles can play an important function in how individuals and groups behave. Kanter (1977) has written that when men and women are in mixed-gender groups, there exists tension that places many women at a disadvantage. In essence, because men and women do not have equal power and status in society, there is little reason to believe that equal power status would exist in the small mixed-gender group.

Indeed, research on mixed-gender groups has found that, in line with traditional gender-role expectations, men are more likely to assume task-oriented roles, and women are more likely to assume socioemotional roles (Eagly & Wood, 1991; Wood, 1987). Wood (1987) further discovered that when groups confront problems that require a task orientation, all-male groups do better, but when problems are based on complex social interactions, all-female groups do better.

Decision Making in Groups

Whatever the composition of the group, its members often have to confront group decision making, and social psychologists have developed interesting theories about this topic. In a classic study, Stoner (1961) asked individuals and groups to make decisions about scenarios involving conditions of uncertainty, such as the following: An electrical engineer has a small family to support. He makes an adequate income and has good job security. After attending a conference, he is offered a job at a small new company with an uncertain future. However, if he takes the job, he can participate in a share of the ownership.

Stoner compared how individuals and groups resolved such dilemmas and found that, overall, groups made riskier decisions than individuals did. This observation became known as *risky shift*.

Additional research found that the shift can occur in either direction. A group may start out mildly opposed to an idea, but, after discussion, the sentiment against the idea can become stronger. In contrast, a group may start out favorably inclined toward an idea, but, after discussion, this sentiment can grow stronger. This shift toward the more extreme position is referred to as *group polarization*. Group polarization results when discussion strengthens a group's perspective and then shifts it toward a more extreme position in the same direction.

Another important group phenomenon is groupthink. **Groupthink** occurs when a cohesive group emphasizes consensus at the expense of critical thinking when attempting to problem solve. The concept of groupthink is based on the keen observations of Irving Janis (1972; 1982), who described groupthink in an effort to explain how President John Kennedy and his advisers could so mistakenly decide to invade Cuba at the Bay of Pigs in 1961. Janis was amazed at how botched the invasion was. "How could bright men like John F. Kennedy and his advisers be taken in by such a stupid, patchwork plan as the one presented to them by the CIA representatives?" (1973, p. 16).

Based on this question, Janis developed his model of groupthink, which is described in Exhibit 4.8.

EXHIBIT 4.8 Janis's Model of Groupthink

Antecedent Conditions
High cohesiveness
Insulation from the group
Lack of methodological procedures for search and appraisal
Directive leadership
High stress and a low degree of hope for finding a better solution than the one favored by the leader or other influential groups

Concurrence-Seeking Tendency
Symptoms of Groupthink
Illusion of invulnerability
Collective rationalization
Belief in inherent morality of the group
Stereotypes of out-groups
Direct pressure on dissenters
Self-censorship
Illusion of unanimity
Self-appointed mind guards

Symptoms of Defective Decision Making
Incomplete survey of alternatives
Incomplete survey of objectives
Failure to examine risks of preferred choice
Poor information search
Selective bias in processing information at hand
Failure to reappraise alternatives
Failure to work out contingency plans

SOURCE: From *Decision making: A psychological analysis of conflict, choice, and commitment*, by Irving L. Janis and Leon Mann. Copyright © 1977 The Free Press. Reprinted with permission of the Free Press, a division of Simon & Schuster.

When groupthink sets in, members of the group fail to use their own critical judgment. Because the group is cohesive, members develop group norms against dissent, and the pressure to conform becomes great. Also, the group's viewpoint is protected by "mind guards," who withhold information from the group if it contradicts the group's perspective.

If the group's view is challenged from the outside, then an in-group and an out-group are created. The in-group includes everyone who agrees with the group perspective, and the out-group is everyone who is not part of the in-group. Via the perception of the out-group as different from the in-group, the out-group can easily become the enemy, and an "us-versus-them" mentality develops. An additional symptom of groupthink is a biased approach to examining information and facts. Everything is seen from the viewpoint of supporting the group perspective.

The groupthink theory suggests that the way individuals in groups process information may not be the best approach to problem solving. Janis reports that groupthink was an underlying problem in President Roosevelt's lack of preparation for Pearl Harbor, President Johnson's continued involvement in the Vietnam War, and President Nixon's cover-up of the Watergate scandal. However, as Weiten and Lloyd (1997) noted, groupthink is likely to be observed in everyday life as groups struggle with the many decisions they have to make.

What would be the likely causes of groupthink? Janis noted three critical factors: first, the isolation of the group; second, the influence of directive leadership; and third, the use of unsystematic procedures for generating and evaluating decisions. Additional factors include the stress present in the situation, the particular characteristics of certain leaders, and the level of cohesiveness in the group. Although research has found that groupthink is not inevitable, it can occur and can lead to profoundly negative consequences (Weiten & Lloyd, 1997).

Research like Janis's has led to the implementation of new procedures in approaches to group decision making. For example, the Institute for Cultural Affairs, a nonprofit organization designed to empower people to facilitate change, has developed a method called the Technology of Participation (Spencer, 1989). This process teaches people a specific method for focused conversation via four steps for groups to follow: be objective, reflective, interpretive, and decisional. Then group members use five steps of the Technology of Participation in decision making: (1) set the context; (2) brainstorm data and ideas; (3) order the data; (4) name the categories; and (5) evaluate the work and its implications.

Support Groups and Communities

Children and families do not develop in isolation. They grow and develop in interaction with many other systems, such as school systems, neighborhood systems, and extended family systems. These systems can offer a needed source of social support. Caplan (1974, p. 4) defines **social support systems** as "continuing social aggregates that provide individuals with opportunities for feedback about themselves and for validations for their expectations about others, which may offset deficiencies in these communications within the larger community context."

Germain (1991) classified support systems into five different types: formal organizations, formed groups, self-help groups, social networks, and natural helpers. For our discussion, we are concerned primarily with informal support systems, which include self-help groups, social networks, and natural helpers. Understanding social support is important in social work, because the notion of social support expresses the person-in-environment perspective and is critical to making a social-work assessment (Germain, 1991). Silverman (1987a) notes that social support groups are important for people who are undergoing transitions in certain roles, which can be a critical time for change. Social support groups help people develop appropriate expectations and learn appropriate role behaviors for obtaining a new integration into society.

Self-Help and Mutual-Aid Groups

Social support is offered through self-help or mutual-aid groups. These groups seek to offer mutual aid through the exchange that occurs when people share a common problem. Such exchanges may have strong biological and social roots. People are often drawn to small groups, and this may be because of the evolutionary benefit of being in such groups; groups provide emotional and physical security. As Dubos (1978) points out, evolution took place in the context of small groups, which provided security from predators. In a similar sense, small groups provide protection in contemporary life, where we "experience urbanized mass society as stressful, despite its attractions and advantages. We protect ourselves by maintaining noninvolvement through depersonalized, detached interactions with those outside our own 'band'" (Germain, 1991, p. 77).

In **self-help groups**, people join together to help one another cope more effectively with shared problems. These groups are often a part of voluntary organizations in which members control the resources and policy decisions. In this sense, they are self-help organizations. Silverman (1987a) uses the term *mu-*

Self-help groups provide a format in which people can help one another to cope effectively with shared problems.

tual help to describe these organizations, noting that the help goes two ways.

Mutual-aid groups can be classified into two basic types: social-change groups and personal-coping groups (Germain, 1991). Social-change groups may be involved in changing public laws or attitudes; examples are groups that support gay and lesbian issues, and groups for parents with disabled children. These groups are often involved in awareness campaigns and efforts to ensure that group members receive the kind of services and treatment that they are entitled to. Personal-coping groups focus on getting help for individual members that will influence their behavior or personal growth. The best example is Alcoholics Anonymous, the oldest self-help organization of its kind. Both of these types of groups are examples of mutual-help organizations because the "members retain control of resources and are actively involved in helping programs built on their own experience" (Silverman, 1987a, p. 171).

Characteristics of Self-Help or Mutual-Aid Groups

What makes a self-help group different from other types of groups? One of the fundamental differences is that, in self-help organizations, the members control the resources and policies — that is, the groups are self-governing and self-regulating (Silverman, 1987a). However, the nature of the organizations' structures varies considerably. For example, some very informal organizations have little or no organizational structure, and the members that participate control the organization. Other groups emulate voluntary organizations, using parliamentary procedures, establishment of committees, and election of officers (Silverman, 1987a). For example, La Leche League is a service organization for mothers who breast-feed, and local offices follow national leaders for directives in running the local chapters. Typically, such groups use dues from affiliated chapters that support the national office. Other self-help groups are less formally organized and use a consensus model in managing the activities of the group.

Functions of Self-Help Groups

Silverman (1987a, p. 173) identified three primary functions in a mutual self-help organization: "(1) Receive information on how to cope, (2) obtain material help when necessary, (3) feel cared about and supported." Self-help groups are fundamentally based on the idea that people with like experiences can offer the best information regarding these three functions. Silverman described the functions this way: The helper and the beneficiary become peers, if only in the sense that they share a common problem. As they discover that what seemed unusual is common to others in a similar situation, they no longer feel alone with their problems. Their emotions and experiences are legitimated, and a framework is provided for coping with the situation. They receive specific guidance on how to implement change, thus expanding their repertoire of appropriate coping strategies.

Each self-help group or organization has its own approach to aiding its members. Alcoholics Anonymous is the best-known self-help organization, and

EXHIBIT 4.9 Some Support Groups and Anonymous Organizations

Adult Children of Alcoholics	OURS (for adoptive parents)
Adult Children of Sex Addicts	Overeaters Anonymous
Adults Recovering from Incest (women's group)	Parents Anonymous
Alcoholics Anonymous	Pills Anonymous
Al-Anon	PMS Peer Support group
Child Abusers Anonymous	RESOLVE: Infertility Education Support
Chronic Pain Outreach	Sex Addicts Anonymous
Cocaine Anonymous	Sex and Love Addicts Anonymous
Coc-Anon	Sexaholics Anonymous
Concerned United Birth Parents	Co-Sexaholics Anonymous
Eating Disorders	Shoplifters Anonymous
Emotions Anonymous	Smokers Anonymous
Families Anonymous	Spenders Anonymous
For Accountability in Religion	S-Anon
Gamblers Anonymous	Survivors of Incest Anonymous
Men for Sobriety	Twelve Steps for Christian Living group
Depressive and Manic-Depressive Association	Women for Sobriety
Narcotics Anonymous	Women with Multiple Addictions

its basic structure and philosophy are used as a model for similar self-help groups for addictive behavior and other personal problems. Examples of such groups include Overeaters Anonymous and Incest Survivors Anonymous.

The relationship between self-help groups and professional organizations has not always been cooperative. Indeed, self-help groups may be reluctant to associate with professionals, fearing their autonomy may be compromised. Furthermore, many people who use self-help groups may have had poor experiences with formal helping systems. Many professionals have attempted to intervene with self-help groups in an effort to impose their professional knowledge. As a result, there is often tension between professionals and self-help organizations. However, some research (Toseland & Hacker, 1982) has found strong connections between self-help groups and professionals. Social workers increasingly recognize that self-help groups can be an important resource that is often more flexible and responsive than formal service systems (Toseland & Rivas, 2001).

The number of self-help organizations has grown so rapidly that many people now refer to "self-help" as a movement. Exhibit 4.9 presents only a sample of self-help groups that were available in one community. Germain (1991, p. 74) has noted that "the rapid expansion of self-help reflects the readiness (always present, but until recently not acknowledged or recognized) of people in all segments of society to solve their own problems, in concert with others like themselves." Libraries, grocery stores, and community organizations list information about self-help groups. Computer access through the Internet has greatly increased people's ability to find others with like problems and join self-help groups electronically (Finn, 1995). There are many computer-based self-help groups, such as those for sexual abuse survivors and for recovered substance abusers (Finn, 1996).

Why has the self-help movement gained such popularity? Part of the answer to this question lies in the evolutionary benefit achieved by such groups. The growth may also be due to the expanding professionalism and depersonalization of care being offered (Gartner & Riessman, 1977). Perhaps the rapid changes taking place in society are limiting the opportunities for people to obtain needed social support. The growth also parallels the consumer movement, which advocates greater personal involvement in one's care and less reliance on outside professionals. Silverman (1987a) concluded that the growth in self-help reflects the fact that people want a different form of help that is simply not available in the existing service system. People often seek help that can be made available to them only through association with others who share similar experiences.

Natural Helpers

Closely related to self-help organizations are **natural helpers**—"central figures in a social network or in a neighborhood who have gained recognition for their unique wisdom, resourcefulness, and caring qualities" (Germain, 1991, p. 81). Pancoast, Parker, and Froland (1983) described mutual-help groups as natural helping networks, and Collins and Pancoast (1976) described neighborhoods where natural helpers are a critical resource, providing social support to families at risk for child abuse and neglect.

Developing and using natural helpers may be critical in efforts to assist people who are isolated and without access to traditional support services. For example, Patterson, Brennan, Germain, and Memmot (1988) found that natural helping in rural communities is characterized by reciprocity—helpers provide for friends and are in turn cared for by them. Germain (1991) quoted a natural helper's description of her role:

> He was abusive and very, very abusive of their son. When the divorce was finally completed, it made her very sad because it all started because of alcohol. She really still liked the guy, but she was determined this was it. As a result she was badly in need of friends. And that's where I thought I helped her—more for listening than anything else because I couldn't do anything else (p. 82).

Interest in natural-helping networks has grown as part of the larger interest in prevention, self-help, and community building at the local level (Pancoast & Collins, 1987). Informal helping is now a legitimate part of the continuum of helping strategies (Whittaker & Garbarino, 1983). The growth of this type of intervention has led to the development of a new role for the social worker. The social worker is expected to be not an expert but instead a partner with the natural helpers. As Pancoast and Collins (1987) put it, "it is important for social workers to be careful not to usurp the position of the natural helper or to take on a customary professional position of leadership and direction" (p. 180).

Communities

Communities are key contexts for social-work interventions (Fellin, 1995). As Heller and his colleagues (1984) pointed out, community is considered one of the most important environmental contexts for understanding human behavior and issues of personal and social well-being. Although we have known since Hippocrates that personal well-being is determined by contexts, the role of factors external to the individual are being newly appreciated by members of the scientific community in understanding human behavior (Gallagher, 1993). This is especially true of conceptions of community.

The concept of community means different things to different theorists. As Paul Hoggett (1997) has explained, nowhere is the idea of community more dominant than in areas of contemporary public policy. "We hear of care in the community, community policing, community architecture, community development, community mental health, and, to add a very contemporary twist to our vocabulary, we now even hear of punishment in the community" (Hoggett, 1997, p. 3). In fact, many jobs held by social workers have the term *community* attached to the job description. Yet there is no agreed-on theory or conceptualization of "community." Some theorists focus on community as a place, whereas others focus on community as representing relationships. Still others focus on it as a source of identification, and others as a resource (Moffitt, 1996). We begin this discussion of community with the traditional focus on place or location.

Place as Community

Place has been a longstanding problem for many inhabitants of the North American continent, where non–First Nations people have a history of migratory spasms (Pindell, 1995). These spasms include flight from the Old World to the New, followed by flight from ways of life in the newly formed cities to the frontier, followed by migrations from farms back to the cities, and then from cities to the suburbs (Pindell, 1995). These shifts have produced a number of unforeseen consequences that are evident in many aspects of life in American society. As Pindell (1995) pointed out, our migratory restlessness "shows in locales with few physical edifices that last beyond a generation or two, as if all we know are beginnings, and so we frenetically tear down and pave over every last generation's best effort. It shows in the cities that the middle class has abandoned to the rich and the poor. It shows in the fallen suburban ideal where we lived an isolated existence remote from the settings of human discourse" (p. xiii).

Technological advances, such as the Internet, video culture, and other technological developments, are transforming the importance of place in people's lives. "Certainly in many urban areas the idea of community in its traditional sense, as something referring to as a place or neighborhood with which one feels some sense of identification, may well be waning" (Hoggett, 1997, p. 3). Some of the present-day threats to traditional notions of community were brought about by the development of the car. This invention allowed people to live in places other than where they worked, socialized, and shopped for basic necessities. Indeed, the suburbs do not provide the sense of identity, belonging, or significance that people require to provide them with direction in their lives. In other words, Lynd's (1929–37) model of community, in which people conducted virtually all their interactions and with whose location they strongly identified, used to exist in many areas of American society but no longer does.

In premodern forms of social organization, community was considered the geographical location in which people carried out the majority of their activities. People in these traditional communities knew how to behave based on their positions within the community. Their behavior was predictable primarily because people in these communal societies shared a system of beliefs and values that tied them together. What ties people together if they lack shared beliefs and values? Is there a different sense of community in modern, urban ways of life?

In most early European societies, communities were tied together by shared religious beliefs and a feudal system of social relationships. In France, these shared beliefs and values were destroyed when the authority of the church and aristocracy were challenged by the Jacobins, who played a major role in the French Revolution. In fact, a goal of the Jacobins was to replace traditional society, and its corruption and superstition, with a new order of solidarity or community based on principles of science and reason (Denisoff & Wahrman, 1979). This social movement contributed to the development of an individualistic libertarian community. "Solidarity in such communities is brought about because each individual within it realizes that community will safeguard the right of each individual to exercise his/her individual autonomy short of violating the autonomy of others" (Lowery, 1993, p. 43).

Following the French Revolution, many social thinkers questioned whether notions of community or solidarity were possible in France. "If people refused to take on unquestioningly the traditional moral standards of their ancestors, how would they behave?" (Denisoff & Wahrman, 1979, p. 14). Would the shift from rural-local communities to cities as a place to live mean that community would disappear? Debates on topics of this nature brought about the development of sociology as a science. Auguste Comte (1798–1857), who is often thought of as the father of sociology, did not believe that industrialization and the other social changes following the French Revolution would lead to the destruction of societies. However, he agreed with many of the conservative thinkers of his time that the primary problem facing society was the breakdown of the traditional shared system of beliefs and values that tied people together (Denisoff & Wahrman, 1979). In its place, he called for a humanist religion led by priest-sociologists who worked at producing order and progress.

Emile Durkheim (1858–1917) supported Comte's view that industrialization would not necessarily destroy solidarity or community, but he believed that societies needed a new basis for social bonding that could replace the beliefs and values provided by the Catholic Church. Durkheim assumed that what would hold people together in industrialized societies would no longer be the similarities of its members. "What Durkheim called the mechanical solidarity of the past (based on similarity) had to be replaced, if society were to hold together, by some kind of new bond between people" (Denisoff & Wahrman, 1979, p. 18). In his view, this new bond would be based on the characteristics of the emerging division of labor. *Division of labor* refers here to people performing distinct jobs that other people depend on for their survival. These relationships also involve contractual arrangements entered into by free individuals. This view of community has been questioned in the sociological literature, because it defines *community* in a way that is not too different from what many sociologists have termed a *society* (Moffitt, 1996). Indeed, it raises fundamental questions about whether there are qualitative differences between communal and other kinds of interpersonal connections that are characteristic of modern and postmodern societies.

Rousseau (1991) considered the controversy between contractual and communal theories of association a key element in understanding fundamental differences in views about what brings people into unity with one another. Contractual theorists focus on understanding the various kinds of agreements, negotiations, and other processes that characterize relationships in societies with high divisions of labor. This includes premarital agreements, labor contracts, and so forth (Rousseau, 1991). These relationships meet interests agreed on by individuals, but the people in these associations are not bonded in terms of deeper sentiments or in terms of the broader senses of identification traditionally attributed to many place communities. In other words, place communities involve mutual obligations among members involving a sense of commitment and identity not commonly observed in associations that are strictly contractual in nature. In fact, a number of social critics (for example, Etzioni, 1993; Bellah et al., 1996) are committed to a **communitarian agenda** which is designed to place responsibilities to others in balance with claims for individual rights.

Many people continue to search for places that will provide them with a better sense of community. They are seeking the benefits once found in traditional communal ways of life in the places where they desire to live. This is clearly evident in the growing trend in urban design toward what is termed *new urbanism*, or *neotraditionalism*. This movement seeks to recreate in urban settings places that offer opportunities for increased interaction among residents. Examples of these designed communities include Seaside and Celebrity in Florida. These planned communities offer individuals a greater opportunity to achieve what psychologists have termed a **sense of community**. A sense of community involves the feeling an individual has for his or her relationship to the place or community of which he or she is a part. It can also include the sense of what it means to belong to a particular collective or location. A sense of community typically includes the following elements:

1. Membership means that people experience feelings of belonging in their community.
2. Influence signifies that people feel they can make a difference in their communities.
3. Integration, or fulfillment of needs, suggests that members of the community believe that their needs will be met by resources available in the community.
4. Emotional connection implies that community members have and will share history, time, places, and experiences (Duffy & Wong, 1996, p. 18).

For many modern urban dwellers, neighborhoods have served as the bases for this sense of community. In fact, neighboring is a concept identified by Unger and Wandersman (1985) that is closely related to sense of community. **Neighboring** refers to an individual's "emotional, cognitive and social attachment to a neighborhood that makes him or her more likely to participate in neighborhood organizations" (Duffy & Wong, 1996, p. 18). Many adolescents in urban settings consider the "barrio" or "hood" the location that fulfills their sense of identity. Of course, inner-city neighborhoods often are identified with conflict, rather than with community. Despite the many strengths such neighborhoods exhibit in building community, the effects of poverty and other social problems can place some neighborhoods in conflict with surrounding areas, and internal conflict can be generated where the social challenges outweigh people's ability to find community solutions.

Identificational and Interest-Oriented Communities

Because the Balkans lacked any fundamental sense of identity derived from the communist way of life that survived the fall of the Soviet Union, people in this region looked to their ethnic groups for a sense of identity beyond that which was afforded by the secular communities within which they had been living. As this conflict illustrates, forms of community that fulfill a person's sense of identity are not limited to a geographical location. *Community* also refers to the perceived relationships associated with groups that define a person's social location within the broader society.

In England, for instance, social class is a category that provides a sense of community for its members. Social class is also important in the United States, but it has provided less of a symbolic identification for its class members (Gilbert, 2003). Other kinds of identificational communities include racial and ethnic-group communities (the African American community, Latino community, Mexican American community, Jewish community, and so on), gay and lesbian communities, religious denominational communities, and professional communities. The sense of belonging and value provided by these groups is what creates bonds between its members.

Castells (2002) has contended that any social construction of identity will take place in a context of power relationships. He has identified three types of identity structures: (1) legitimizing identity, a form of identity constructed by the dominant institutions of a society, which rationalizes the existing sources of its structural domination; (2) resistance identity, which is generally associated with people in contexts that are devalued or stigmatized by dominant factors, thus contributing to resistance to the domination; and (3) project identity, which occurs when individuals use available cultural and social resources to transform or build a new identity.

Indeed, a person's identificational community often becomes a major resource for resistance and struggle against other opposition groups. This notion of community as a resource for opposition fits with another major conceptualization of community (besides Castell's [2002] notion of resistance identity) that defines it in terms of communicational networks. In this approach, one focuses on a person's informal social networks. "Informal social networks refer to a person's relations with relatives, friends, neighbors, co-workers, and acquaintances" (Heller et al., 1984, p. 133). These relationships have important implications for a person's social and personal well-being. According to Moffitt (1996, p. 217), they offer "a new kind of life-sustaining and identificational mix." However, they are determined primarily by processes of affinity rather than proximity. In other words, a network definition of *community* consists of a web of functional activities and communicative interactions that are linked together in many ways other than via place. These linkages trigger different kinds of communal loyalties from those of traditional local communities, but the two can be equally satisfying.

However, research by Robert Putnam (2000), author of the well-received book *Bowling Alone*, in-

This African American community listens to a Kwanzaa storyteller.

dicates that membership in associations and many traditional types of informal networks is significantly declining. Although participation in community groups had increased during the 1960s, current data shows marked declines in the participation in bowling leagues, service societies, and other civic-oriented associations (Putnam, 2000). This decreased engagement in traditional associations and increased participation in cyber associations marks a major change in social networks. This aspect of the cyber revolution is triggering major debates about life in our information age (Castells, 2002).

Informal networks are not the only contexts in which needs are met in modern societies. People also depend on relationships with formal organizations and other societal institutions that mediate their needs and obligations. The differences between informal and formal relationships are examined in the next section.

Organizations and Social Institutions

Organizations are a special context in which humans live. Social workers and other social scientists assume that organizations can be studied apart from the people who constitute them, because organizations continue even after their members die, quit, or retire (Ferrante, 1995). Much of our life takes place within these impersonal structures. Most of us begin life in a hospital; attend school in a formal organizational setting; eventually work in a bank, factory, office, or corporation; have contacts with members of governmental agencies; and depend on multinational organizations for meeting many of our other needs.

Formal organizations differ significantly from situations in which people have most of their needs met by primary groups. For instance, it was rare in many parts of traditional China for members of a rural village to come in contact with a governmental official or non–primary group member (Giddens, 1989). They lived for the most part in small-group settings without the influence of formal organizations.

What Is a Formal Organization?

A **formal organization** is any large social group that is designed to achieve specific objectives rationally. Organizations have carefully designed structures that coordinate the activities of their members with the goal of achieving the greatest possible efficiency. The relationships among the members of a formal organization are based on each person's position or location in the organization. The duties and rights associated with position are attached to the office itself and not to the individuals. For most formal organizations, we can draw a chart that reflects the relationships of the various positions in this social system without making any reference at all to the actual individuals working in the organization.

Without a doubt, our way of life in a postindustrial society is still highly dependent on the existence of formal organizations. Although fewer and fewer individuals work in large factories, most individuals have some form of affiliation with a formal organization, such as a governmental agency, multi-national corporation, telecommunication organization, or educational system. In fact, formal organizations appear very natural to most individuals who were born and raised in an industrial society. During their lives, they have had very few opportunities to escape the influence of these designed social systems, which employ highly impersonal structures to achieve their specified aims.

In the preindustrial era, families and neighbors provided for most of an individual's needs. Primary groups were responsible for providing the food, instructing the children, and managing leisure-time activities. Today, most of our needs are met by people whom we have never met. In this type of social context, there is a need for extremely effective coordination of actions and resources. The most common structure used for achieving this objective is a bureaucracy.

What Is a Bureaucracy?

When organizations are large and complex, they often adopt what is known as a *bureaucratic structure*. Most modern organizations have bureaucratic qualities. The word *bureaucracy* was first coined in 1745 by Monsieur de Gournay. "He added to the word 'bureau,' meaning both an office and a writing table, a term derived from the Greek verb 'to rule.' 'Bureaucracy' is thus the rule of officials" (Giddens, 1989, p. 277). As Giddens points out, the term has been used in disparaging ways since its inception. De Gournay questioned the emerging power of governmental officials and even alluded to them as having an illness that he called *bureaumania*. Today, *bureaucracy* still carries negative connotations, and these connotations are not limited to governmental organizations. *Bureaucracy* conjures many images of excessive red tape, inefficiency, and alienation of its participants. Yet Max Weber, the most influential writer on the topic, defined **bureaucracy** as representing, in theory, a "rational organization" (Ferrante, 1995).

Weber's Typology of Rational Action

For Weber, rationalization was the major trend of the modern world. He identified four fundamental types of social action:

- Instrumental rationality: Involves action that is rational in relation to a goal. The individual selects the best means available to achieve an intended goal. It is also referred to as *goal-rational action*.
- Value-rational action: Involves action that is considered rational in relation to a value. The individual acts in terms of what is right—for instance, acts in relation to a commitment to a higher-order value such as beauty, justice, or God.
- Affective action: Action that is determined by feelings, passions, psychological needs, or other emotional concerns.

- Traditional action: Any action dictated by custom; that is, it is performed because that is the way it has always been performed. (From *Modern sociological theory*, by M. Waters. Copyright © 1994 Sage Publications Ltd. Reprinted with permission.)

Weber used these hypothetical types as ideals against which to evaluate any kind of intentional action. In his view, instrumentally rational actions were, in the modern world, replacing actions guided by traditions, emotions, and other nonrational processes. He was interested in the transformation in Western societies from power structures based on claims of tradition to structures based on claims of reason. Weber extended this view of rational actions to his theory of bureaucracy and his widely known theory of authority relations.

For Weber, the bureaucracy is considered an ideal type. An **ideal type** refers to an abstract description derived from real cases that were analyzed to determine their essential features. A real agency will not necessarily conform in all respects to this type.

In Weber's view, a bureaucracy is an ideal type that has the following features:

- Its activities are governed by rules
- It has a specific sphere of competence
- It is organized hierarchically
- Its members are specifically trained for their occupations
- Its officers do not own the means of production
- They do not own their jobs, but can be dismissed from them
- Its actions are recorded in files (Waters, 1994, p. 224).

For Weber, an organization with features that resemble these is likely to be efficient at coordinating the activities of its members and in achieving specific objectives.

Scientific Management Traditions in Human Organizations

Shafritz and Whitbeck (1978) pointed out that any theory must be evaluated in the context of its time. This is also true of organizational theory. Early management theory, in this sense, originated before workers began to enjoy even limited rights. Times were harsh, and workers were seen merely as interchangeable parts in a highly impersonal "industrial machine." "Consequently, the first theories of organizations were concerned with the anatomy or structure of formal organizations. This is the hallmark of classical organization theory—a concern for organization structure that is premised upon the assumed rational behavior of its human parts" (Shafritz & Whitbeck, 1978, p. 1).

Within this context, the first notions of organizational principles were developed. It is often customary to begin discussion of the origins of management theory with the early writings of Adam Smith. In his famous work *An Inquiry into the Nature and Causes of the Wealth of Nations* (1776), in a chapter entitled "Of the Division of Labor" Smith examined the optimum functioning of a factory. This chapter clarified how increased specialization of labor contributed to the enhanced productivity of a pin factory. In Smith's view, the factory represented the "most appropriate means of mass production." This view was shared by Frederick Winslow Taylor, who believed that factory workers could be even more productive if their jobs were scientifically designed. Taylor is considered by most authorities as the founder of scientific management.

For Taylor, there was "one best way" of accomplishing a job task, and the goal of the scientific manager was to ensure that the best way is followed by the employees of the organization. Taylor is noted for instituting time-and-motion studies and piece-rate wages. In 1954, Peter Drucker observed that scientific management "may well be the most powerful as well as the most lasting contribution America has made to Western thought since the Federalist Papers" (see Shafritz & Whitbeck, 1978, p. ix). In one sense, the major focus in the writings of Taylor was on issues of technology.

Management, as a separate discipline, emerged in the United States after World War I and was heavily influenced by scientific management principles. In fact, this approach is often referred to as *Taylorism*. In 1937, Luther Gulick introduced the famous mnemonic POSDCORB, which defined the elements required to manage an organization: planning, organizing, staffing, directing, coordination, reporting, and budgeting. These elements are still examined today by modern organizational theorists.

Formal and Informal Relations in Organizations

Weber's approach to understanding organizations focused primarily on issues of formalization and structure. The more an agency is bureaucratized in its organization, the more formal its relationships are. In fact, Weber had very little to say about the role of informal relations in the operations of modern organizations. We now know that informal relationships and networks exist in most formal organizations. People in organizations know one another in many ways besides their official positions. They develop informal procedures for handling problems, negotiating their way through the hierarchy, and achieving assigned tasks. The Hawthorne studies at the Western Electric Company in 1932 documented these processes. In fact, the results of this research led to a specific approach in organizational studies known as the **human relations school**. This tradition in organizational studies focuses on understanding the influences of informal networks on all forms of organized activities.

The human relations school was in many senses a reaction to the overemphasis on structural rationality in the writings of Weber and members of the scientific-management school (Netting, Kettner, & McMurtry, 2003). Chester Barnard (1938) proposed the first real theory on human relations that challenged the other classical approaches. He pointed out the important role of cooperation and other social processes in organizations. He is noted mostly for introducing researchers to the study of "natural groups within the organization, upward communication, authority from below rather than from above, and leaders who functioned as a cohesive force" (Perrow, 1978, p. 315). His focus on cooperative processes was well timed; he wrote during the Great Depression (Perrow, 1978), when there was significant labor unrest and conflict between labor and management.

The human relations school ushered in a wealth of research on the traits of effective leaders in organizations. Also, social psychologists in this tradition studied task groups to determine the effect of social factors on human efficiency. However, this school has not been without its critics. Netting and colleagues (2003) argued that several studies have shown that informal organizational structures might not be as prevalent in organizations as many human relations writers suggest. Furthermore, democratic leadership may have less to do with productivity than with other factors in human motivation, such as economic benefits. Nonetheless, this school has introduced many concepts in organizational research that encourage more humane treatment of organization members. In fact, it directs us to look at the assumptions about human nature included in any theory of organizations.

Douglas McGregor's work (1960) is an excellent example of theory resulting from the shift from analysis of structure to analysis of participants' behavior in organizations. His work focused on understanding the factors that motivate employees. He identified two distinct approaches to leadership or management in organizations: Theory X and Theory Y. Theory X approaches to management assume that managers must adopt coercion in their style of leadership, because coercion is necessary to obtain good work performance by employees. McGregor (1960) argued that the theories of Taylor and Weber were highly supportive of this type of management style. He assumed that workers need to be controlled by the structure of the organization because: "(a) people have an inherent dislike for work; (b) they must be coerced in order to work; (c) the average worker prefers to be told what to do; and (d) monetary reward is the worker's primary motivator" (Netting et al., 1993, p. 133). Theory Y approaches assume that, in trying to motivate workers, management needs to take into account many of the higher-order needs identified by Maslow. Theory Y's assumptions are as follows:

1. Work is as natural an activity as rest or play, thus people do not necessarily have to be forced to do it.
2. Workers will commit to organizational goals if they are able to meet their own needs in so doing.
3. Workers will accept responsibility for meeting goals that are congruent with their needs.
4. Organizational tasks should be structured to allow workers to exercise creativity and imagination in fulfilling these responsibilities (Netting et al., 1993, p. 133).

Theory Y approaches are sensitive to individual workers' needs but ignore the motivational needs of people. To this end, William Ouchi (1981) developed an approach that he terms *Theory Z*. "Theory Z had its roots not in traditional Western assumptions about humans, but in assumptions about humans based on Japanese culture and reflected in many Japanese organizations and approaches to management" (Schriver, 1995, p. 421). Ouchi contrasted these approaches to management in Japan with approaches in the United States. (See Exhibit 4.10.)

Social workers need knowledge not only of theories of organizations but also of management. But views of management cannot be limited to U.S. viewpoints. The United Nations estimates that there are

EXHIBIT 4.10 Japanese and U.S. management approaches

Japanese Organization	U.S. Organization
Lifetime employment	Short-term employment
Slow evaluation and promotion	Rapid evaluation and promotion
Non-specialized career path	Specialized career paths
Implicit control mechanisms	Explicit control mechanisms
Collective decision making	Individual decision making
Collective responsibility	Individual responsibility
Holistic concern	Segmented concern

SOURCE: From W. G. Ouchi, *Theory Z: How American business can meet the Japanese challenge*, p. 58, copyright © 1981 Addison-Wesley Publishing Company, Inc. Reprinted by permission of Addison-Wesley Publishing Company, Inc.

approximately 35,000 multinational corporations worldwide. A disproportionate number of their headquarters are in the United States, Japan, and Western Europe. Corporations in Japan and Western Europe may subscribe to distinctly different approaches to management and views of human nature, a fact that social workers cannot ignore. Multinational corporations are a special type of organization with characteristics that can contribute to many social problems encountered by social-work professionals. When students are asked about how their lives are affected by our increased global contexts, we often learn of the effect that multinational corporations are having on them and their families. That is, they can point out how their lives have changed because of some connection with a corporation that has significant international ties.

Social Institutions

Every society requires the formation of institutions in order to survive. Giddens (1989) considered these institutions to be the cement that holds together all forms of social life. They constitute the basic social arrangements within which people live most of their daily lives.

In social work, we rarely assess individuals without taking into account their behavior in larger social contexts, including key social institutions. In particular, we are interested in understanding the primary institutional arrangements that contribute to the health and welfare of our clients. Most societies have large social institutions that encompass and cut across many segments of their members' social lives. The institutions of economy, kinship, education, law, polity, and religion are observed in most industrial or postindustrial societies. These institutions contribute to the stability of statuses, roles, and norms observed in the behavior of people in these communities. This relationship of structure to human behavior is what social scientists grapple with when they examine human behavior in terms of its structural or institutional properties.

William Graham Sumner (1906), in his classic work *Folkways*, examined how social institutions are formed in nonindustrial societies. He contended that the first task of life is to survive, stating, "Need was the first experience and it was followed by some blundering effort to satisfy it" (Sumner, 1906, pp. 17–18). In Sumner's view, the yardstick for measuring the success of these blundering efforts is pleasure and pain. Pleasure and pain underlie all our trial-and-error methods of testing solutions to our survival needs. Our early ancestors tried to profit from the successful experiences of other group members. The most expedient ways of achieving survival ends were generally adopted by the group, and these ways turned into what are known as *customs*. In effect, successful ways of doing things become institutionalized in any society. In Sumner's view, this is how folkways arise in natural group processes.

This concept of folkways is a key foundation underlying most of Sumner's theoretical observations (Cotterrell, 1984). For Sumner, **folkways** represent group ways of solving problems and of doing things. These ways are handed down through tradition, imitation, and authority. They "provide for all the needs of life: They specify the best way to make a fire, to cook meat, to greet one's neighbor, and to raise one's children" (Cotterrell, 1984, p. 20). Folkways are sanctioned in many premodern societies by fear of ancestors. That is, the ghosts of ancestors will seek vengeance if members of the community deviate from the ancient ways of doing things. This implies that folkways are transformed at some point in societal evolution from representing merely utilitarian ends to having a position of right or truth. When folkways start to be viewed in terms of right and wrong ways of doing things, they are elevated to what Sumner termed **mores**.

Folkways and mores prescribe the rules that govern the behavior of people in primary-group relations. These rules exist prior to a person's birth and structure how life is to be lived. As societies change over time, traditional rules are gradually replaced by formal law. Formal law has proven to be the type of system capable of maintaining moral order in a complex society that has a high division of labor. In this system, "All citizens are, in theory, formally equal under the law. Law is also autonomous from other social institutions" (Horwitz, 1990, p. 2). That is, the law functions to maintain a culture and set of norms that are distinct from the rules of religion, political systems, and economic interests. This view differs from the views of law espoused earlier by Sumner.

In Sumner's view, the law needs to be rooted in the mores of society, an assumption that has been challenged by other legal scholars. Many aspects of law are in opposition to people's customs and mores. Civil-rights law in the United States is an excellent example: The customs and mores of southern society were in violation of modern case law that made segregation illegal.

Clearly, there are many different ways for viewing social institutions such as the law. Scott (2001) has written about three general pillars upon which most institutions rest: *regulative*, *normative*, and *cultural-cognitive*. Some theorists see institutions strictly as resting on their regulatory pillars. These theorists are concerned primarily with addressing rules and enforcement systems that maintain social institutions. In their opinion, the continuity of institutions is dependent upon the ingredients of force, fear, and expedience (Scott, 2001). A second group of theorists views institutions as being determined primarily by what Scott has termed the *normative pillar*. This approach relies less on formal regulatory systems than on prescriptive notions of social obligation. That is, institutions are preserved and changed based on both values and norms. "Normative systems are typically viewed as imposing constraints on social behavior, and so they do. But, at the same time, they empower and enable social action" (Scott, 2001, p. 55). The third and last group of theorists is generally made up of anthropologists who focus on the centrality of cultural-cognitive elements associated with institutions. For them, taken-for-granted cultural-cognitive frames guide and maintain social institutions, and compliance occurs in many circumstances because other types of behavior are considered inconceivable. Individuals view their routines as the only way of doing things (Scott, 2001).

Institutions have assisted sociologists in assessing organizations, social change, and many areas of social life since the inception of this scientific discipline. Some sociologists are revitalizing interest in promoting institutional analysis in the field of sociology, because these scholars believe that many theorists have overemphasized rational-choice approaches to the study of social policy, social change, and economics (Scott, 2001). This relatively recent movement in sociology and economics is being termed the *new institutionalism* (Brinton & Nee, 1998). Institutions are also an important component of social work. Many programs contain special classes on social-welfare institutions, which are witnessing dramatic changes in our information/network society. The consequences of these changes for social life are an area of substantial controversy in many areas of policy and practice.

Multicultural and Gender Considerations

One of the most interesting aspects of the human species is its diversity. Yet this diversity contributes to significant intergroup conflict and social inequality (Adams et al., 2000). Every society has some way of making distinctions among its members. But some of these distinctions are used for purposes of discrimination and of stigmatization. **Discrimination** is the application of prejudice or bias to a person based on particular characteristics, such as physical or cultural traits. In the United States, physical and cultural differences influence the life chances and experiences of many women and people of color. As a consequence, race, ethnicity, gender, sexual orientation, and able-bodiedness are key variables in assessing social and interpersonal relations.

Stigmatization between in-groups and out-groups is also quite common. "Modern American usage of the words 'stigma' and 'stigmatization' refers to an invisible sign of disapproval which permits insiders to draw a line around 'outsiders' in order to demarcate the limits of inclusion in any group" (Falk, 2001, p. 17). This marking of outsiders enables in-groups to maintain solidarity and loyalty by using outsiders as examples. "The European Jews were 'outsiders' in Christian Europe for two thousand years and were the perpetual example to which Christian clergy pointed when seeking to insure loyalty of their followers" (Falk, 2001, p. 17). Race and ethnicity are often involved in processes of stigmatization, as are being old, being gay, being overweight, or being an immigrant, or belonging to other social categories that point to differences between insiders and outsiders (Sandstrom, Martin, & Fine, 2003). It is important for social workers to understand the processes by which race and ethnicity are used to oppress and stigmatize others in society (Appleby, 2001a). With this knowledge, they are in a better position to help with processes of destigmatization (Sandstrom, Martin, & Fine, 2003).

Racial and Ethnic Considerations

The United States is witnessing many demographic and cultural changes. "People of color constitute the fastest growing population in the United States" (Comas-Diaz & Greene, 1994, p. 3). If current trends in immigration and birth rates continue, the Hispanic/Latino population will increase by an estimated 21%, the Asian-American population by about 22%, and the African American population by approximately 12%, whereas projections for growth rates in the white population are for an increase of about 2%. By the year 2056, it is projected that typical residents of the United States will trace their ancestry to Africa, Arab nations, Asia, Latin America, or the Pacific Islands (Takaki, 1993). These trends in birthrate projections and immigration patterns suggest the arrival of increased cultural pluralism within the United States.

The United States has been pluralistic since its inception. Yet this fact is often overlooked in discussions about multiculturalism. Many early ethnic groups immigrating to this country maintained their original group identities but incorporated customs and practices from other cultures into these identities to adapt to their new environment. In fact, this process is referred to in the West Indies and in Spanish and French settlements in the Americas as **creolization** (Ancelet, Edwards, & Pitre, 1991). Ancelet and colleagues have pointed out that "migration, whether voluntary or not, caused a break in ancestral patterns. While individual cultures did preserve some of their old ways in the New World, the frontier environment also provided the opportunity for them to create new ways based on the old" (1991, p. xiv). These new ways contribute to many of the rich traditions observed in Cuba, Haiti, Puerto Rico, Mexico, Louisiana, New Mexico, and Texas that include a blending of many different cultural influences.

Throughout American history, groups have interacted and intermarried with neighbors of different

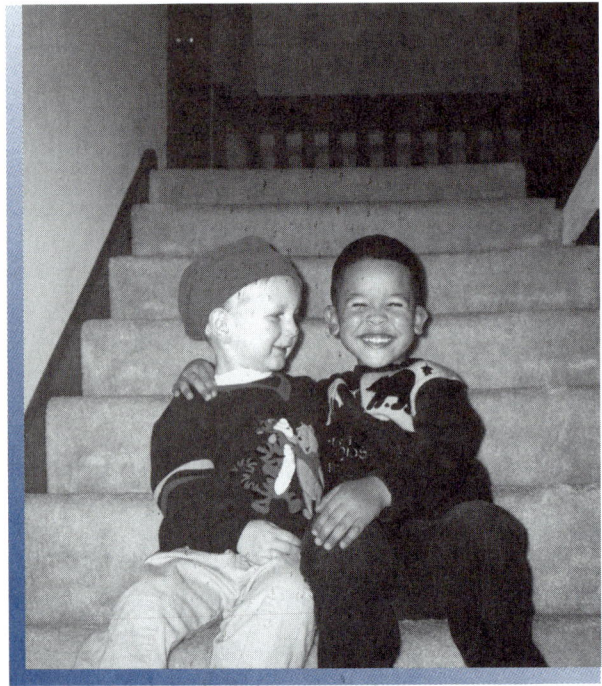

Our society is becoming increasingly multicultural.

cultures and races. This blending produced some interesting cultural variations that make up our current ethnic landscape. Cajuns are a distinct ethnic group in this country that we will use to illustrate the process of creolization. When the Cajuns, originally from France, were exiled in 1755 from the region of Canada known as Acadia, some migrated to the French settlements in Louisiana. In Louisiana, they encountered new groups of Native Americans with traditions and customs different from those they were accustomed to in Canada. They also encountered people born in Louisiana who were direct descendants of French-born individuals (Creoles). Some of the Acadian immigrants attempted to join the French plantation society. Others isolated themselves from this group and intermarried and interacted with Native Americans, African Americans, and many different immigrants to this region, including German Alsatians, Spaniards, Anglo Americans, the Irish, and the Scots. This blending of cultures and races produced a new cultural group with its own distinctive identity.

Today, many individuals in Louisiana identify with the Cajun ethnic group but can trace their ancestry to other groups outside of Canada. "This is why one finds people who call themselves Cajuns yet who have last names like Hoffpauir and Schexnayder, Ortego and Romero, Johnson and Reed, and McGee and Melancon" (Ancelet, Edwards, & Pitre, 1991, p. xv). The Acadians had significant interaction with Africans born in the region, who influenced their music, dancing, and cooking practices. Cajuns are members of an ethnic group that many modern French-speaking Canadians and Europeans find difficult to understand. In fact, their culture has minimal points of commonality with those of other, more dominant French regions of the world. In particular, European and Canadian French "are surprised at the Cajun's love of fried chicken and iced tea, forgetting this is also the American South; at their love of hamburgers and Coke, forgetting this is the United States; at their love of cayenne and cold beer, forgetting this is the northern tip of the West Indies" (Ancelet, Edwards, & Pitre, 1991, pp. xvii–xviii).

In efforts to define America, historians have tended to ignore the experiences of Cajuns and other groups who don't support the Anglo-conformity ideology that underlies our espoused national identity (McLemore, 1991). This identity, although false, has supported the assumption that an American is a white person of European origin who has abandoned language ties and adopted a distinctive American culture. Ronald Takaki's (1993) book *A Different Mirror: A History of Multicultural America* points out that the histories of Asian Americans, African Americans, and other people of color are not included in existing constructions of the American identity. He begins the book by describing a personal incident experienced by many Americans who are nonwhite and of non-European origins. He was riding in a taxi to a conference on multiculturalism in Norfolk, Virginia, when the taxi driver asked him how long he had been in this country. For Takaki, this situation illustrates the narrow view shared by many Americans about its history and its people. Takaki's family had lived in this country for well over 100 years, yet this driver adhered to a very narrow but commonsense definition of the American identity as "white" and primarily European in ancestry.

The changing racial and ethnic makeup of the country is threatening the identity of many Americans. As Takaki (1993) stated, the country has been racially diverse since its inception, but evidence of increased diversity is triggering fearful responses in many sectors of our society. Some long for "a more cohesive culture and more homogeneous America" (Takaki, 1993, p. 3). However, this view ignores the significant diversity in our country's past that was systematically purged from most major accounts of its history. Because of this oversight, many universities are introducing curricula to assist students in forming a more accurate view of their country's history (Schoem et al., 1993). This approach to history has not been without controversy. In fact, the demands for increased multiculturalism in education are starting to retest the legitimacy of valued notions of tolerance previously considered the hallmark of most Western liberal societies (Horton, 1993b), a dynamic clearly seen in students' objections and protests regarding multicultural courses that have been required on many college campuses.

Most modern liberal societies celebrate diversity and other forms of difference. In fact, this country considers tolerance of difference an important element underlying its reason for existence. Yet "it has become an increasingly urgent issue of theory and practice as to how tolerant liberalism is, or can be, of cultural and religious groups which do not themselves subscribe universally or without qualification to what have been taken to be the basic values of liberalism" (Horton, 1993, p. 1). These values include liberty, equality, rights, neutrality, and autonomy. That is, all modern liberal societies are experiencing immigration patterns that involve cultures with distinct value traditions that are in opposition to the values of modern liberal thought. Does this mean that there are limits to what are considered acceptable or tolerable forms of cultural diversity in these societies?

Steven Lukes (1991) points out that liberalism was born out of religious conflict, and toleration was central to the development of liberalism. At the heart of this toleration is the notion that one will not interfere with other groups' cultural beliefs and behaviors. Does this view also apply to Jewish, Buddhist, and Islamic traditions? Muslims in France and England have asserted that Muslim girls ought to be educated in a context that prepares them for roles in Muslim society rather than in the values of secular liberalism. Muslims were also in violent disagreement with the kinds of free speech that permitted the vilification of their culture's most sacred beliefs with the publication of *The Satanic Verses*, by Salman Rushdie. These kinds of situations in our liberal societies lead to issues of tolerance being reexamined. Current multicultural scholars are noticing that much of the acclaimed tolerance is not being extended to non-Christians or non-whites.

As Gundara (1993) explained, if we assume that the imposition of a single culture or value system in a country such as Trinidad is improper, then these same principles should apply to American, British, and other European countries. Liberal critics have vigorously attacked countries that advocate a single-value orientation in Africa, Latin America, and Asia because of their totalitarian implications. Yet many new writings are emerging in our own society that promote intolerance toward ethnic, religious, and linguistic variations. In fact, a number of politicians are arguing that English should be made the official language of the United States. What is the implication of this from a multicultural perspective and principles of liberal egalitarianism?

Multiculturalism is a relatively recent phenomenon within many areas of political and social theory. Multiple cultures, or pluralism, have been present for quite some time, but up until about twenty years ago, we did not have debates involving appropriate political theory for taking into account issues of multiple cultures within many of our civil societies (Kelly, 2002). Brian Barry's (2001) book *Culture and Equality* is one of the first attacks in leftist political discourse on the potential incompatibilities between having a commitment to cultural protections and having a commitment to egalitarianism. Barry claimed that "the multiculturalist preoccupation with culture is a distraction from the real sources of unequal treatment and injustice" (Kelly, 2002, p. 13). In his book, he contended that many laws and practices should be liberalized for all rather than for a specific group. For Barry, the issue to consider is the public interest, not that of making accommodations for specific groups. For example, should exceptions for marijuana use be made for Rastafarians who use it as part of ritual and worship, in order to respect their cultural differences? In Barry's view, the answer is no, because if no public interest can be documented for prohibiting the use, then all should be afforded equal treatment regarding this concern (Kelly, 2002).

Although Barry considered multiculturism flawed as a theory, other theorists have seen his argument as equally flawed in many other respects (Chambers, 2002; Shapiro, 2002; Kukathas, 2002). Although political theorists debate the merits of multiculturalism, many immigrants believe that both conservatives and liberals are failing to recognize many of their group claims, which they believe the philosophy of political liberalism is not capable of responding to in a just fashion. These immigrants, First Nations people, and others who share identities and cultural practices that differ from those of the majority believe that liberalism and other political ideologies place significant barriers in their way to receiving equal treatment and opportunities in many societies.

Consequences of Intolerance to Difference

The *Intelligence Report*, a publication of the Southern Poverty Law Center, chronicles the recent increases in violence toward immigrants in our society. The center reports that hostility toward immigrants is at its highest level in seventy years, a figure supported by the findings of Jack McDevitt, associate director of the Center for Applied Research at Northeastern University and an expert on hate crimes. He has stated that attitudes toward immigrants in recent years are "frighteningly similar to those of the mid-1920s when the United States passed restrictive laws to halt massive immigration from southern Europe" (Southern Poverty Law Center, 1994, p. 3). Examples of hate crimes the Southern Poverty Law Center is tracking include the following:

- A 19-year-old Vietnamese American pre-med student in Coral Springs, Florida, was beaten to death by a mob of white youths who called him "chink" and "Vietcong."
- A Hispanic man in Alpine, California, was beaten with baseball bats by six white men at a camp for homeless migrant workers. The assailants later reportedly bragged about "kicking Mexican ass."
- A Hispanic immigrant activist in Davis, California, was assaulted twice in April 1993 by white men who wrote "wetback" on her body.
- An Indian immigrant in New York City was beaten and burned with a cigarette by three teenagers who reportedly told him they did not like Indians.
- Two lesbian organizers were killed in Medford, Oregon, in a crime of hatred.

Official government statistics are not completely accurate, but 8,832 hate crimes were reported in the United States in 2002 (FBI, 2002). Hate crimes are often underreported, for many different reasons. The American Psychological Association (FBI, 2002) has observed that in these crimes, people are typically attacked for some aspect of their identity. The Center for Gay and Lesbian rights has noted that since 1991 the number of hate crimes based on sexual orienta-

The Social Dimension

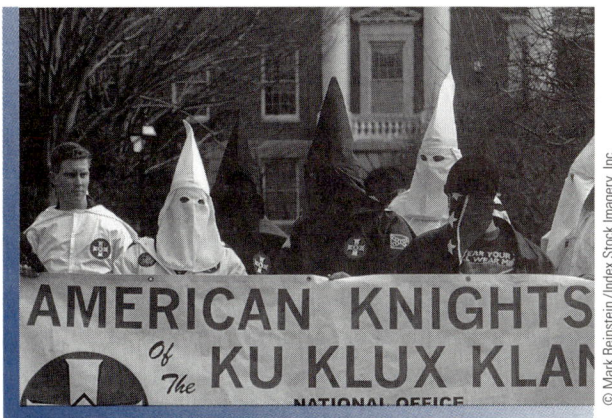

Intolerance is mounting among white racist groups who perceive the advances of many racial and ethnic groups as a threat to their own interests.

tion has more than tripled. Sexual-orientation hate crimes rank third after race and religion (Center for Lesbian and Gay Rights, 2004). Hispanic visibility is increasing in every sector of American life (National Council of La Raza, 2004), including hate crimes. The number of attacks against Hispanics and others because of nationality has also dramatically increased.

The shameful intolerance of ethnic differences is a frightening but all-too-prevalent characteristic of our times. Understanding intolerance is, therefore, a significant issue that social workers in all areas of practice need to address. Baldwin and Hecht (1995) have adopted what they refer to as a "layering metaphor" for describing how intolerances develop. In their view, layering is a useful metaphor for illustrating that alternative ways of experiencing the world "are continually juxtaposed and played off of each other and/or blended together" (Hecht, 1993, p. 76). For instance, "the perception of a certain group begins at a young age, when people around the individual speak of group members in terms of their distinctiveness from the person's own group. Images and messages from parents, media, friends, textbooks, and teachers, as well as personal experiences with members of the 'other' group layer upon each other and interplay with one another to form the person's own, often inconsistent view of the 'others'" (Baldwin & Hecht, 1995, pp. 61–62). By examining these layers, we can get a better perception of what is happening at different levels of a person's experience. Each level of experience provides another clue to the puzzle of how prejudicial and hateful attitudes develop.

Prejudice and Discrimination

Although there has been much progress in human affairs during this century, it has been marked by horrible episodes of prejudice (Lippa, 1994). This century has seen the mass murder of Armenians by Turks; the Nazis' "final solution" in Europe for Jewish and other "non-Aryan" peoples; the "ethnic cleansing" by Serbs in Bosnia; the mass lynching of African Americans in the first half of this century in the United States; and vicious attacks in New York at the Stonewall Bar, which triggered the gay-rights movement. **Prejudice** is a generalized negative attitude directed toward another person's membership in a socially defined group. Like most attitudes, it occurs at the cognitive (beliefs), behavioral (overt action), and affective (emotional) levels. It can include negative emotional responses to a group of people resulting from intolerant, unfair, or unfavorable attitudes toward the targeted group (Deaux, Dane, & Wrightsman, 1993). It also can involve discriminatory actions or practices.

The cognitive component of prejudice involves the beliefs we hold about a target group. A structured set of beliefs about any identifiable social group is referred to as a **stereotype**. Stereotypes can be either positive or negative. A negative stereotype is highly interchangeable with what is known as prejudice. That is, stereotypes represent an important foundation on which prejudices are built.

Basow (1992) has used a familiar story to demonstrate the pervasiveness of stereotypes in modern life: A boy and his father were involved in a serious automobile accident. The father was killed instantly; the son was severely injured. An ambulance rushed him to the nearest hospital, and a prominent surgeon was called in to perform the operation. On entering the operating room, however, the surgeon exclaimed: "I can't operate on this boy. He's my son." How can this be (p. 2)?

If you came up with the answer of a stepfather, adopted father, or some other similar response, then you are not unlike most Americans. Most Americans see surgery as a predominantly male field. As a result, you would have ignored the fact that the surgeon probably was the boy's mother. Stereotypes of this nature are highly prevalent in our society and can contribute to various types of discrimination. Stereotypes can be directed at any group: Hispanics, short people, physically disabled people, gay men and lesbians, and fundamentalist Christians. When individuals act on their prejudicial stereotypes, this leads to what is known as individual, or attitudinal, discrimination. Individual discrimination involves overt acts that treat members of a target group in an unfair manner. Generally, the bases for these discriminatory treatments have roots in negative stereotypes.

Some forms of discrimination in society are legal. In addition, many individuals justify discriminatory practices on what they consider moral grounds. For instance, in many societies, "senior citizens" are allowed to pay cheaper rates for using public facilities: movies, buses, public parks, and museums. Publishers of some professional journals also engage in differential treatment of customers when they provide different subscription rates for people from different income categories. Are these practices unlawful or without moral justification? Although these forms of differential treatment are considered lawful, they are always open to moral challenge. This raises the important question of whether there are circumstances when it is legitimate to make differentiations in treatment of people in terms of race, sex, class, or age. What distinguishes differentiation from discrimination?

Most world religions do not think it is discriminatory to bar women from holding positions of leadership in their hierarchy. Yet many members of these same communities assume that these practices are without moral justification and are discriminatory. How do we determine whether this form of differential treatment is to be considered discriminatory? In most modern industrial societies, disputes involving issues of discrimination are handled by legal institutions. However, this is a relatively recent historical phenomenon. Notions of unlawful discrimination took a long time to develop in Western legal systems. Banton (1994) has written that the first recorded use of the term *discrimination* was in a speech by President Andrew Johnson in 1866, in discussing debates surrounding the denial of the benefits of full citizenship to African Americans. Robert MacIver (1948), however, is known for educating the public "to distinguish between discrimination as a form of behavior and prejudice as an attitude" (Banton, 1994, pp. 6–8).

Most early considerations of discrimination in the United States involved issues of race; *discrimination* was not used in a more general sense to include other groups until around 1958. In that year, the International Labour Office (ILO) defined *discrimination* as "any distinction, exclusion or preference made on the basis of race, colour, sex, religion, political opinion, national extraction or social origin" (Banton, 1994, p. 7). In recent years, discrimination law has been extended to many other areas. However, the issue of discrimination in law focuses primarily on protecting people from unfair treatment in public life.

Discrimination law does not apply to private life or private decisions. "In Great Britain and the United States the main protected fields are those of the administration of justice, employment, education, housing, and the provision of goods, facilities and services" (Banton, 1994, p. 8). For instance, people may limit invitations to parties on the grounds of race or gender. As you might imagine, the legitimacy of such actions is a major societal concern. Still, there is substantial controversy about what constitutes the private and public spheres of life. Should the law protect individuals from unfair treatment by private clubs or other organizations? Should the law of discrimination apply to treatment in voluntary organizations such as churches? For instance, should the law address actions within churches regarding issues of equality for women? Churches and other religious institutions are organizations that presently do not fall under the legal protections of antidiscrimination law. But this does not mean that these institutions do not violate moral definitions of discrimination shared by many members of a society.

In social work, we encounter many forms of discrimination that contribute to a diverse array of social disadvantage and other forms of inequality. For this reason, it is important that the social worker have a fundamental understanding of race, ethnicity, sex roles, and other areas in which people can be subjected to unfair social practices. Our goal as social-work professionals is to engage in activities that will reverse structural contributions to harmful discriminatory practices in voluntary social organizations and in public social institutions.

Institutional discrimination is a special type of discrimination derived from structural arrangements in the society. It refers to inequalities rooted in the normal operations of society and its social institutions (Feagin & Feagin, 1978). This form of discrimination has little to do with attitudes or prejudices. Even when we eliminate prejudice in a society, the inequalities between groups often remain because they are rooted in the everyday operations of existing social institutions. That is, discrimination can continue in a society even though its members are not intent on discriminating. For instance, a Mexican American family can be denied access to housing that would lead to better schools not because of intentional bigotry by realtors but because their previous restriction to low-paying jobs inhibits their ability to purchase a home with access to superior schools. Institutional discrimination has much more subtle characteristics than the more visible forms of attitudinal, or individual, discrimination. For example, in social-service agencies, institutional racism may be present when supervisors assign low-income clients of color to MSW students and middle-income whites to senior staff, a particularly problematic practice because low-income clients of color have higher dropout rates and may benefit more from an experienced social worker.

Race and Everyday Social Relations

What are the differences between race and ethnicity? **Race** is a social term used to refer to groups that are defined according to their physical characteristics. It is important to recognize that the characteristics used to define a racial group are socially defined; the word *race* is a fundamentally meaningless biological concept. Although humans can be traced back well over a million years, today's racial differences are quite recent in origin (Robertson, 1977). "Whatever the seeming diversity of races in the modern world, all contemporary human beings trace their origin to ancestral populations that lived in east Africa about 200,000 years ago" (Green, 1995, p. 11).

People attach meanings to physical differences that are either real or imagined. "From a sociological point of view, then, a race is a large number of people who, for social or geographical reasons, have interbred over a long period of time; as a result, they have developed visible physical characteristics and regard themselves and are regarded by others as a biological unit" (Robertson, 1977, p. 262). However, it is not easy to classify humans into different races. In fact, determining race by blood sample would be impossible because human population groups are not distinct; rather, they form a continuum. This is why physical anthropologists prefer using terms such as *population* or *gene pool* to explain physical differences, rather than using terms such as *race* (Green, 1995). For these scientists, "The genetic diversity within populations that share certain visible physical traits is as great as those between groups" (Giddens, 1989, p. 246). Accordingly, many scientists argue that race is not a useful concept and should no longer be used (Giddens, 1989).

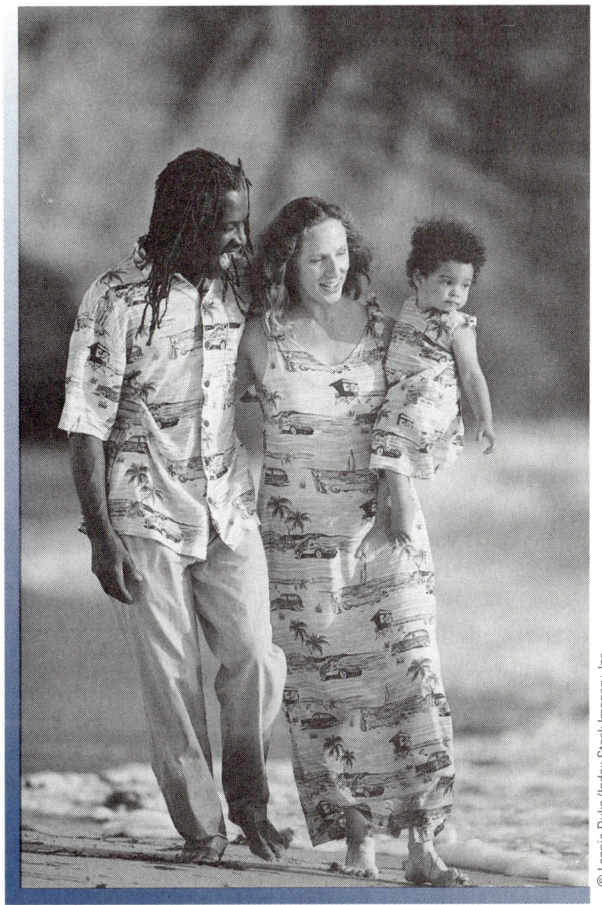

Multiracial families are on the rise.

The Anglo ideology of assimilation has always emphasized that immigrants should conform to the dominant culture and leave behind their ethnicity. "Full assimilation, in this view, is achieved when the descendants of the immigrants blend into the majority group and are no longer distinguishable from it" (McLemore, 1991, p. 106). But this ideology has not applied to people of Indian, Asian, and African decent. People of color cannot blend into the societal matrix as do white ethnics. As Rushdie (1982) has pointed out, there are two different worlds in Anglo societies, and which one you inherit depends on the color of your skin.

Until recently, in Germany, individuals were entitled to citizenship, regardless of their country of origin, if they could prove that they were of German ancestry. That is, the criterion for German citizenship was biological. This law made life difficult for people who had lived their entire lives in Germany but who did not look German or who lacked German biological ancestry (Ferrante, 1995). Turks, Arabs, and East Indians were subjected to serious discrimination in Germany because of this emphasis on biology. Even though some African Germans can demonstrate German ancestry, they are still discriminated against because they do not fit the German biological stereotype. Biracial individuals also have a confusing identity in the United States.

Although, by convention, people are assigned to one of three racial categories—Caucasoid, Mongoloid, or Negroid—many people do not easily fit into one of these groups. Yet although these classifications are difficult to implement, people continue to apply them. In South Africa, the classification of races was still a major societal enterprise in the late 1980s. The following quotation illustrates the difficulties this society encountered in trying to classify people racially. A woman classified as "Colored" reports:

> Under South-African law, I am officially considered Colored. But so is my light-skinned sister with brown hair and my brother who has kinky hair and skin even blacker than mine. The state determines what color you are. At 16, you have to fill out some forms, attach a photograph and send them to a state authority where your race will be decided. Differences in color are noted by official subdivisions. For example, I am a Cape Colored whereas my sister is called Indian Colored. Of course, many people categorized as Colored are of mixed Black and White ancestry. In fact, if you can prove having had a white grandparent or parent and are yourself very light skinned, you can even make an application to be reclassified from Colored to White (Chapkis, 1986, p. 69).

Sociologists are interested in negative classification schemes that include beliefs about the abilities or traits of a racial group. They are also interested in studying any actions a society takes to use racial classifications to subordinate members of a group on the basis of color or other biological characteristics. These societal classifications change over time and are products of many social, historical, and political forces. In the United States, shifting relations of power have influenced our racial classifications. In 1860, the three classifications for the census were whites, blacks, and mulattoes; in 1890, five additions were added (quadroon, octoroon, Chinese, Japanese, and Indian); in 1990, five different groups were listed (white; black or African American; Asian or Pacific Islander; American Indian, Eskimo or Aleut; and the ethnicity Hispanic). Each of these changes is indicative of key sociohistorical contingencies.

Forms of Racism and Privilege

Racism is technically defined as a system of power and privilege that can be manifested in attitudes, actions, and/or institutional structures based on people's color characteristics (Andersen & Collins, 2004). Today, it is less socially acceptable to show blatant forms of racism than it once was. However, racism has remained in other more symbolic or subtle ways, which in the social-psychology literature are called *modern racism*. Modern racists convey their negativity toward others by opposing issues that promise equality for the races. They do not blatantly attack people on racial grounds, but they defend practices that maintain social privilege. For instance, they may oppose equal-opportunity hiring by arguing against the use of quotas, rather than by directly attacking individuals on presumed notions of inferiority (Deaux et al., 1993). Clearly, welfare reform is a hotly contested area in American politics that allows many modern racists to advocate traditional values that also happen to disadvantage many African Americans (Neubeck & Cazenave, 2001).

Many modern racists are motivated by beliefs that African Americans are being unreasonable in many of their demands and expressions of anger, because they believe that discrimination is no longer a problem (Fiske, 1998). Many of these racists have been influenced by societal changes that have made it no longer normatively acceptable to express racial prejudice. These normative changes make their own racism aversive. As a consequence, they avoid acting in overtly discriminatory ways (Dovidio, Gaertner, Nier, Kawakami, & Hodson, 2004). But this does not mean that they do not discriminate in indirect or unintentional ways. This form of racism has been termed **aversive racism** because of the duality of attitudes and the ambivalent feelings possessed by racists.

"Because aversive racists consciously recognize and endorse egalitarian values and because they truly aspire to be good and just people, they will not discriminate in situations in which discrimination would be obvious to others and to themselves" (Dovidio et al. 2004, p. 145). They are more likely to engage in discrimination in nonobvious situations. In these situations, they can maintain their perception of being nonprejudicial, but the consequences of their behavior are still harmful to the members of the racial group subjected to their discriminatory behavior. The aversive-racism framework has helped theorists understand how respondents can endorse egalitarian attitudes but simultaneously, in selected circumstances, engage in highly harmful and discriminatory forms of behavior (Dovidio et al., 2004).

Aversive racism illustrates that there are some aspects of racism that are automatic and unconscious. Automatic categorizations and associations are the products of experiences that are now considered the cause of bias toward people from other racial and ethnic groups (Fiske, 1998; 2004). These processes are recognized as a by-product of normal processes of cognitive categorization. "Research traditionally stressed reportable (conscious), explicit stereotyping and prejudice, but cognitive (stereotypic) and affective (prejudiced) associates can be overlearned and operate outside of conscious awareness" (Fiske, 1998, p. 364).

The systemic features of racism are a key part of social structures that social workers must understand. "In a racist system, well-meaning white people benefit from racism even if they have no intentions of acting or thinking like 'racists'" (Andersen & Collins, 1995, p. 60). That is, they might not question the built-in system of privilege for whites in our social system. Peggy McIntosh (1995) has pointed out in her groundbreaking essay "White Privilege and Male Privilege" that systems of privilege become invisible to the people who most benefit from them. In her view, people are carefully socialized not to recognize these privileges.

After experiencing significant frustration with men who did not recognize male privilege, Peggy McIntosh set out to understand her own privileges as a white female. She wanted to know what advantages she had as a white person in our society. Through this exercise, she realized that her own difficulties in facing privilege as a white person were similar to the difficulties faced by men in experiencing their privilege. She wrote, "Only rarely will a man go beyond acknowledging that women are disadvantaged to acknowledging that men have unearned advantage" (McIntosh, 1995, p. 77). In her view, many layers of denial prevent white women and men from examining their unearned advantages. McIntosh (1995) identified these special circumstances and conditions as part of her day-to-day privileges as a white woman:

1. I can, if I wish, arrange to be in the company of people of my race most of the time.
2. I can avoid spending time with people whom I was trained to mistrust and who have learned to mistrust my kind or me.
3. If I should need to move, I can be pretty sure of renting or purchasing housing in an area that I can afford and in which I would want to live.
4. I can be reasonably sure that my neighbors in such a location will be neutral or pleasant to me.
5. I can go shopping alone most of the time, fairly well assured that I will not be followed or harassed by store detectives.
6. I can turn on the television or open to the front page of the paper and see people of my race widely and positively represented.
7. When I am told about our national heritage or about "civilization," I am shown that people of my color made it what it is.
8. I can be sure that my children will be given curricular materials that testify to the existence of their race.
9. If I want to, I can be pretty sure of finding a publisher for this piece on white privilege.
10. I can be fairly sure of having my voice heard in a group in which I am the only member of my race.
11. I can be casual about whether or not to listen to another woman's voice in a group in which she is the only member of her race.
12. I can go into a book shop and count on finding the writing of my race represented, into a supermarket and find the staple foods that fit with my cultural traditions, into a hairdresser's shop and find someone who can deal with my hair.
13. Whether I use checks, credit cards, or cash, I can count on my skin color not to work against the appearance that I am financially reliable.
14. I could arrange to protect our young children most of the time from people who might not like them.
15. I did not have to educate our children to be aware of systemic racism for their own daily physical protection.
16. I can be pretty sure that my children's teachers and employers will tolerate them if they fit school and workplace norms; my chief worries about them do not concern others' attitudes toward their race.
17. I can talk with my mouth full and not have people put this down to my color.
18. I can swear, or dress in secondhand clothes, or not answer letters, without having people attribute these choices to the bad morals, the poverty, or the illiteracy of my race.
19. I can speak in public to a powerful male group without putting my race on trial.
20. I can do well in a challenging situation without being called a credit to my race (pp. 79–81).

Although race is not a fact of nature, it continues to structure many aspects of social reality. Moreover, many Americans consider it to be an unchanging part of the natural world sanctioned by God (Green, 1999). These views sanction negativity toward the mixing of races and the ascription of rank along selected racial lines. As social workers, we cannot ignore the fact that race influences social relations at all levels of social life. Also, people's experience with race will depend on their location in social space. That is, it will also vary with their social class, gender, age, sexuality, and other markers of social location (Andersen & Collins, 2004).

Ethnicity and Its Social Consequences

Ethnicity, like race, focuses on differences in people. But it is not always easy to identify true ethnic differences: "When we try to determine what differences mean, the idea of ethnicity becomes complex and frequently troublesome" (Green, 1995, p. 16). There are many definitions of *ethnicity* in the social sciences, and each definition captures a different layer of an ethnic group's experiences. Some definitions stress distinctive values underlying the behavior of group members, whereas others focus more on the association of ethnicity with social class, political processes, or other forms of social experience. Although these approaches to difference may be useful in many forms of social analysis, they often lead to the formation of needless stereotypes. For this reason, we subscribe to a more process or transactional definition of ethnicity developed for social-service professionals by James Green.

Green (1999) has contended that we should study ethnicity in terms of boundaries, control, and meaning construction. "Ethnicity has less to do with distinct and enduring groups than it does with the perceptions of boundaries, with how contrasts are manipulated, managed, denied, asserted, and proclaimed. With ethnicity, we are dealing, first, with meanings that define separateness, and, second, with the enforcement of meanings and separateness through power" (Green, 1995, p. 19). In other words, we need to understand how individuals assert their sense of ethnicity and how others treat this ethnicity in various social contexts. In particular, we need to understand how dominant-group individuals use ethnic differences to isolate or exclude individuals from inclusion in the most valued segments of social life.

Core versus Surface Features of Ethnicity

Many surface aspects of ethnicity are used to identify various ethnic groups in our society. These include "clothing preferences, speech patterns, behavioral styles, physical characteristics, housing locations and types, living arrangements and decor, food items, and family and community rituals and celebrations" (Green, 1995, p. 19). These manifestations of ethnicity are used to distinguish outsiders from insiders. As Green (1999) has informed us, these aspects are what many Americans think of when making references to ethnic differences. But they should not be confused with what is truly ethnic about ethnicity. Pinderhughes has provided one of the more descriptive definitions of ethnicity that includes these core elements: "Ethnicity refers to connectedness based on these commonalities that have evolved as a result of shared identity and history based on religion, nationality, and so on" (1994, p. 265).

Nash (1989) has also tried to differentiate between surface and core elements of ethnicity. Core

This adopted child from China is keeping connected with the traditions and dress of her ancestors.

elements are the real grounds on which all forms of boundary maintenance rest. They represent the central psychic and social foundations that underlie human identification with group relationships. Nash has broken down these core elements into three fundamental components: kinship, commensality, and a common cult. He provided a definition of each of these components in his book *The Cauldron of Ethnicity in the Modern World*. He stated:

> The most common ethnic boundary markers, in the ethnographic record, and the most pervasive, in any system of ethnic differentiation, are kinship, that is the presumed biological and descent unity of the group implying a stuff or substance continuity each group member has and outsiders do not; commensality, the propensity of eating together indicating a kind of equality, peership, and the promise of further kinship links stemming from the intimate acts of dining together, only one step removed from the intimacy of bedding together, and a common cult, implicating a value system beyond time and empirical circumstance . . . (1989, pp. 10–11).

The previous description of the core elements of ethnicity indicate the levels at which sentiments surrounding ethnic identity occur. They describe the dimensions that define people's sense of connection to their social context. Obviously, these senses of bonding will vary with a person's position in the social structure and his or her life experiences. These fundamental elements of ethnicity can play a major role in the way clients respond to social-work interventions.

Pinderhughes (1994) wrote that "culture determines what clients see as a problem, how they express it (that is, whether symptoms are somatic, behavioral, or affective; what specific symptoms clients manifest), who they seek out for help, what they regard as helpful and the intervention strategies they prefer" (pp. 293–94). To respond to each of these levels, the social worker must be exposed to the life experiences of many different ethnic groups and to multiple representatives from these groups. This is critical, because there is as significant a diversity within ethnic groups as there is between ethnic groups.

In this book, we assume that culture influences many aspects of behavior. For this reason, we will systematically review documented variations in human development involving cultural variables. We will not, however, provide a laundry list of key historical events or characteristics of ethnic-group members. We believe that clients will define and manage their ethnic boundaries and identities as situations demand, ethnic boundaries being how an individual defines his or her own sense of ethnicity. The relevance of historical events is contingent on individuals' current boundary-maintenance need; that is, time and other historical factors will be used differentially by clients in setting their ethnic boundaries. Some clients will seek a sense of revival of ethnic ties; others will struggle with their significance in current situations and contexts. Thus, our aim as social workers is to assess the factors contributing to ways in which contrasts are asserted by individuals with ethnic differences and how dominant-group members respond to these differences.

Gender and Sexism

Can women perform on an equal basis with men as firefighters or police officers? Why or why not? Many women are currently employed in these and other professions, including the military, previously dominated by men. The current debate about the role of women in the military reflects a larger debate about sex roles in our society. To place these debates in context, it might be useful to review recent history about the roles of women in our society.

As recently as the nineteenth century, women were denied the right to vote, to be a member of a jury, to have sole custody of their children, and to attend most institutions of higher education. Many of these practices were justified by false beliefs about differences between males and females. In fact, a major area of research in the social sciences focuses on the existence or nonexistence of sex differences between males and females. Social scientists use the word **sex** to refer to the biological status of being female or male. These scientists research the structural and other biophysical characteristics that distinguish females from males. **Gender**, in contrast, refers to the social definitions of male and female. It represents a socially constructed concept and not a fact of nature with specific biological imperatives.

In assessing human behavior, social workers need to have a good understanding of the consequences of gender roles and beliefs. Gender issues incorporate all the factors that structure the relationships between women and men, including all the social processes that dictate how women are to behave in social life. In work and other social contexts, the relations of women are structured differently from those of men. The specific structures that establish how they should behave are also a part of each of the other major social institutions in their lives. Sandra Lipsitz Bem (1993) has termed this process **gender polarization**, which refers to "the organizing of social life around the male-female distinction" (Bem, 1993, p. 192). In fact, in a gender-polarized society, every aspect of a person's life is connected to his or her sex in some way. This includes "modes of dress, social roles, and even ways of expressing emotion and experiencing sexual desire" (Bem, 1993, p. 192).

Gender differences, like racial and cultural differences, can be used to distort many aspects of social life. "Anthropologists, for example, use the term exotic bias to refer to the investigators' tendency to focus only on those aspects of a group or society that differ from their own group or society" (Deaux et al., 1993, p. 350). This type of bias is often found in situations in which actual differences are noted in women. For instance, many studies have shown that the average male is more aggressive than the average female. But our biases can influence how we interpret the findings from these studies. Exhibit 4.11 presents a graph of male and female distributions of aggressiveness. As you can see, many of the females in these studies have aggressiveness scores that are higher than those of the males. Also, these distributions indicate that many of the women and men have similar aggressiveness scores. The information on averages can be used to distort the realities of many of the women and men in these studies by supporting the bias toward an assertion of fundamental difference between males and females.

Hooyman (1994) has identified three conceptual frameworks in social work for examining women's content: women's issues, nonsexist perspectives, and feminist perspectives. The women's-issues approach has also been referred to as "add the women and stir," and it is probably the most dominant approach to education in social work. In this approach, separate attention is devoted to understanding the distinct issues that pertain to women. This approach is typically criticized because in many circumstances it perpetuates the treatment of women as "others." This means that they are treated as a special population in knowledge discourse rather than as a pivotal group representing 51% of the world population (Hooyman, 1994). As a group with special consideration, they are judged in relation to male criteria, and this perpetuates the structural features of many of their problems.

The second approach is the nonsexist, or equal-rights, model. This approach does focus on structural factors within systems that maintain sexist practices,

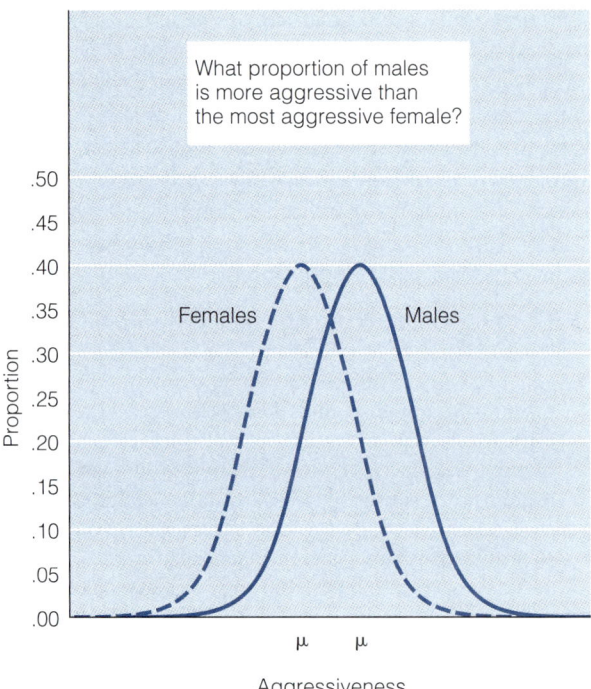

EXHIBIT 4.11 Overlapping distributions on aggressiveness for males and females
SOURCE: Deaux, Dane, & Wrightsman (1993).

and it assumes that "the range of problems experienced by women are rooted in and influenced by societal expectations for women's behavior and in societal restrictions of life possibilities" (Hooyman, 1994, p. 321). In such a view, problems should not be assessed in terms of culturally prescribed sex-role behaviors. This view has important implications for practice because it indicates that behaviors by women that do not conform to traditional role expectations should not be considered deviant. For instance, women who choose not to care for their aging parents and instead leave the task to their brothers should not be viewed as deviant or pathological.

The feminist model, in contrast, rejects many traditional notions about gender and starts from the assumption that current knowledge of human behavior is for the most part sexist. Social reality as we know it is shaped by the male perspective known as **androcentricity** (man as norm) (Hooyman, 1994). Essentialist thinking about gender is challenged in this approach. In essentialist approaches, gender is often considered absolute, or fixed in nature as a biological fact. The feminist perspective rejects the binary conceptualizations of males and females and sees gender as one "strain" among others in our layered experiences. This point of view "opens up the possibility of diversity among men and women in specific historical, social, and cultural constructs" (Hooyman, 1994, p. 325). It also allows analysis and action to focus on the experiences of women without neglecting the other "isms"—like racism and ageism—that threaten the well-being of humanity. In fact, feminism sees its fundamental aim as that of ending domination and resisting all forms of oppression (Van Den Bergh & Cooper, 1987).

Feminism is more than an analytical approach; it is also an ideology that involves a "call for transforming the world from competitive, hierarchical, and authoritarian relationships to a world based on gender and racial equality" (Van Den Bergh & Cooper, 1987, p. 611), and it has a long history in Western society. In fact, gender stratification is more deeply rooted in human history than are class distinctions and many other social categories of current oppression. Like class, gender stratification has varied over the ages, as has feminist ideology (Calvert & Calvert, 1992).

Sexual Status and Forms of Oppression

The ideology of sexism takes on many forms, but regardless of its form, sexism supports a system of oppressive gender relations for women. "Like racism, sexism is a system of beliefs and behaviors by which a group is oppressed, controlled, and exploited because of presumed gender differences" (Andersen & Collins, 1995, p. 67). For this reason, we need to approach issues of gender difference with extreme caution. Sexism pervades all aspects of our cultural symbols and ways of doing things. In fact, our language itself has supported the dominance of males in human relations. Until the 1960s, few questioned the use of terms such as *mankind* when referring to humans or humanity. We also used the pronoun *he* when speaking of a person whose sex was unspecified, because the English language does not have a pronoun representing "he or she." Sexist language is being challenged, but its existence reflects the extent to which sexism is deeply rooted in our cultural traditions.

Sex-Role Stereotypes

What are sex-role stereotypes? Sex-role stereotypes involve beliefs about men and women that describe not how men and women actually differ but how societal members believe they differ (Rothblum & Franks, 1983). Baumgartner and Papageorgious (1982) asked a group of elementary and high school students how their lives would be different if they were a member of the opposite sex. These students' responses reflect many of the stereotypes within our society. In particular, it is interesting to note that boys perceived that the change would result in more negative consequences. This is a sample of some of their responses:

- "I would start to look for a husband as soon as I got into high school."
- "I would play girl games and not have many things to do during the day."
- "I'd use a lot of makeup and look good and beautiful . . . I['d] have to shave my whole body."
- "I'd have to know how to handle drunk guys and rapists."
- "I would not be able to help my dad fix the car and truck and his two motorcycles" (pp. 2–9).

Girls, however, imagined more activity and less restrictiveness in their lives if they were a member of the opposite sex:

- "I would have to stay calm and cool whenever something happened."
- "I could sleep later in the mornings since it would not take [me] very long to get ready for school."
- "My father would be closer because I'd be the son he always wanted."
- "I would not have to worry about being raped."
- "People would take my decisions and beliefs more seriously" (pp. 5–13).

Baumgartner-Papageorgious (1982) found similar beliefs among college students. This study points out how much of our lives are organized around male-female distinctions. In fact, the quotations from respondents in these studies indicate that there is even a gender-belief system that influences how people make decisions (Ferrante, 1995).

The pressure to conform to established sex-role stereotypes can contribute to many psychological problems: depression, sexual dysfunction, obesity, and other clinical concerns (Rothblum & Franks, 1983). Women confront many dilemmas in the face of sex-role stereotypes. Their strategies for coping with these dilemmas are important for social-work practitioners to understand. A number of other consequences should be taken into account, as well.

Gender influences self-esteem, psychological well-being, and physical health. In addition, it structures how and with whom we establish friendships and introduces many barriers in the social relationships between males and females. It also has important consequences for family relationships and forms of labor-force participation. Throughout our discussion of human development, we will treat gender as a social category that affects each of these areas of social behavior. Also, we will try to provide a diverse sample of experiences that women encounter in their development. Without this knowledge, social workers cannot engage in activities designed to remove the key structural barriers that affect the liberty and life chances of women in our society.

Homophobia

Gender oppression is also closely linked with the other system of oppression involving gender: sexual orientation. **Homophobia** refers to the fear and hatred of sex with a same-sex partner. In our society, power and privilege are structured in terms of sexual orientation, and our system has institutionalized heterosexual forms of gender identity. In fact, a heterosexual gender identity has been considered the yardstick for determining normality and has contributed to the isolation and oppression of gays, lesbians, and bisexuals (Lev, 2004b).

As feminists point out, women and men are not monolithic groups; they have significant within-group diversity. Many Native American communities have a different viewpoint about gender and sex roles. Some members of tribal communities are considered *two spirits*. "The term two spirit is derived from the Algonquian *niz manitoag* and refers to a human being with both masculine and feminine qualities that are simultaneously manifested in a variety of ways" (Vernon, 2001, p. 22). Many of these two-spirit men encounter various forms of oppression in their communities. As a consequence, they often attempt to escape the oppression on the reservation by moving to an urban area. When they arrive, they often feel sexually liberated and engage in very high-risk sexual behaviors. In addition, many of them encounter problems obtaining work. The lack of employment is a central factor that leads them to engage in street prostitution and other high-risk methods of survival (Ashford, Gonzalez-Santin, & Perry, 2004). Many of these men having sex with men (MSM) assume that they have two spirits and do not consider themselves to be gay. Transgender males also engage in many forms of risky behavior, including having sex with other males (MSM), but do not assume that they have a gay sexual orientation (Kammerer, Mason, Connors, & Durkee, 2001).

Katz (2005) has examined the historical development of the concept of heterosexuality. **Heterosexuality** refers to individuals who have an attraction to or engage in sexual activities with those of the "opposite biological sex" (Steele, 2005). Katz's paper "The Invention of Heterosexuality" examined how the concept of heterosexuality is only one particular historical way of categorizing the social relations of the sexes. He wrote, "The heterosexual belief, with its metaphysical claim to eternity, has a particular, pivotal place in the social universe of the late nineteenth and twentieth centuries that it did not inhabit earlier" (Katz, 2005, p. 50). The conception of heterosexuality introduced the pleasure principle or eroticism into sexual relationships. Prior to this, sexual relations adhered to a procreative imperative. In fact, Kraft-Ebing's influential book *Psychopathia Sexualis* (1933) introduced readers in the United States to the notion that "hetero-sexual" refers to an erotic feeling for the different sex and "homo-sexual" to the erotic feeling for the same sex. His writings helped introduce a shift in standards of normality for sexuality from procreation to the standard of pleasure. During the same period, gender standards also shifted from Victorian notions of the "true woman" and "true man" to newer standards that served to eroticize heterosexual and homosexual relationships (Katz, 2005; Seidman, 2005).

The writings of Katz (2005) and others who have focused on understanding essentialist categories of heterosexuality as dominant social norms are considered in sociological and other behavioral science literatures as "queer theory" (Epstein, 2005). The late 1980s marked the adoption, in various circles, of the word queer, as a new characterization of "lesbian and gay politics and, indeed, as a potential replacement for the very terms lesbian and gay" (Epstein, 2005, p. 69). Queer theorists have looked closely at the genealogy of the homosexual and heterosexual divide and have shown how the terms have meant different things in different social contexts. By demonstrating that the terms are social constructs, they have introduced a more fully "co-sexual form" of politics that puts men and women on equal footing in areas involving sexuality or sexual orientation.

Sexual Orientation

Sexual orientation is a critical life-span issue that has multiple dimensions and layers of experience that constitute an integral part of the human experience (Newman, 1994). For this reason, we will examine this topic using a life-span perspective. From this perspective, equal time should be allotted to the issue of sexual orientation as will be given to other gender issues, such as gender identity and gender roles. But biases in our research institutions have contributed to some regretful deficiencies in this area of our knowledge base, making this task difficult.

Longres (1995, 2000) has stated that gays and lesbians are not socialized into roles, values, and positions in society the way that heterosexuals are. As a consequence, gay males often have more in common with heterosexual males before they "come out." After coming out, gay males can learn the customs and ways of the gay community. The stigma associated with their sexual orientation also structures how they relate with gay and nongay persons in heterosexual (straight) interactions. How they negotiate this marginalization by the dominant society at various phases of life becomes an important knowledge issue for social-work professionals. Queer theory is offering gays and lesbians a specific form of critique that is confronting their marginalization by dominant social norms.

In sum, issues of diversity are highly complex and require close scrutiny by members of the social-work community. You will be exposed to many studies in this book that suggest fundamental differences between males and females, between racial and ethnic groups, between heterosexual and gay and lesbian people, and between able-bodied people and people with disabilities. You must always approach the interpretation of the findings from these studies with extreme caution. Some researchers have a bias toward finding differences that perpetuate many forms of insensitivity or oppression. Thus, we advise that you take a critical stance in evaluating the social consequences of any findings suggesting behavioral tendencies that are attributable to any form of human difference. This is not to imply that there are not important physical, psychological, and social differences. Instead, our aim here is to sensitize you to the fact that you are responsible for making distinctions between real and false differences supported by compelling and unbiased evidence.

Social Strengths and Hazards

Our relationships are recognized as key contributors to our health and personal well-being (Ryff & Singer, 2001). Sociologists now recognize that these contacts are also a key component of what is termed social capital. **Social capital** is a theory that social networks or social relationships have value, much like the value that is associated with notions of physical capital and human capital. **Physical capital** is defined as the materials required to be productive (the buildings, tools, and so forth), and **human capital** refers to the education and personal skills needed to be productive in situations of competitive employment. Social capital is also a factor that contributes to a person's overall productivity in society. Social contacts are a strength that a person possesses and that have an influence on their access to resources associated with their capacity for being productive.

People learn many social skills from their contacts. These skills and associations provide many forms of support that enhance a person's social functioning. A person's social environment can facilitate achievement of life goals and support the realization of many personal objectives that enhance quality of life (Rapp, 1998). Indeed, these contacts serve as facilitating environments for many positive social outcomes. However, many social and cultural conditions in our lives place us at risk for forms of harm. These include conditions of poverty, inequality, injustice, dependency, relative deprivation, segregation, powerlessness, underrepresentation, postindustrialism, and postmodernism.

Our economy has become more global in scope and is experiencing a major social transformation. Unemployment is rising in many industrial sectors of our economy, and technology is eliminating many positions in manufacturing and service sectors. These economic pressures reduce available resources for sustaining our welfare systems. In fact, debate about the viability of welfare systems and of the welfare state is increasing in American society. Crime, substance abuse, domestic violence, homelessness, poverty, and urban decline are also increasing at exponential rates in some sectors of our society. Rivers and other sources of drinking water are diminishing, and pollution of our waterways and air are threatening the well-being of individuals and communities.

Grandparents transmit the wisdom of their generation to their grandchildren by teaching them stories, songs, customs, and beliefs. This wisdom is an important strength that social workers cannot overlook.

as "the impoverishing of the child's world so that the child lacks the basic social and psychological necessities of life." Children need many things to grow up happy and competent—for example, the basic necessities of food, water, and shelter; affection and love; proper medical care; proper educational stimulation; and positive social interactions. Without these things, children may end up "at risk" for impaired development (Garbarino & Abramowitz, 1992a). Adults are also at risk for impaired development or other deficiencies if they are deprived of needed resources.

Other quality-of-life concerns are gaining the attention of more and more people in major metropolitan areas. Natural resources are being depleted, and food shortages are increasing in sectors of our society and the world at large. Immigration is increasing, and public tolerance of difference is decreasing. Racial and ethnic tensions are mounting, and peaceful relations between the straight sector and gay and lesbians is in jeopardy in many communities. These conditions differ from the conditions encountered by other birth cohorts in our society's history and will contribute to distinct variations in life-span development.

The physical environment of poverty has numerous consequences for social and personal development that cannot be ignored in assessing potential hazards (Evans, 2004). We know that lower-income children are exposed to greater levels of violence, family disruption, and family separation than are children of middle-income families. Many studies also have documented that social resources vary depending on the quality of a person's neighborhood (Evans, 2004; Levanthal & Brooks-Gunn, 2000).

One way of understanding how critical such factors can be to the well-being of a child is to examine them in the light of sociocultural risk. Garbarino and Abramowitz (1992a, p. 35) defined *sociocultural risk*

Two significant sources of sociocultural risk include social impoverishment and cultural impoverishment. *Social impoverishment* is the lack of critical social resources in a child's life, and *cultural impoverishment* refers to values that undermine the child's healthy development. "Both of these forms of impoverishment find their most significant expression in the day-to-day content and structure of formal and informal support systems in a family's environment" (Garbarino & Abramowitz, 1992, p. 65).

Impoverishment of this nature is the result of unavailable, dysfunctional, eroded, or destroyed support systems. When institutional and community forces prevent supportive relationships from becoming established and being maintained, children and families are placed at increasing risk (Davies, 2004). This risk transcends the material resources and, in fact, is particularly destructive when accompanied by social deprivation. The combination of social deprivation and poverty produces devastating consequences (Garbarino & Abramowitz, 1992).

Sociocultural risk for children depends on the extent to which parents' functions are supported (Garbarino & Abramowitz, 1992). If parents are supported, encouraged, and helped by others who have a significant investment in the child's long-term future, sociocultural risk is significantly reduced. Community efforts to create healthy living environments

These children live in impoverished conditions that reflect many physical, social, and cultural shortcomings.

for children need to examine the support that the community provides for parents and children. Reducing sociocultural risk is part and parcel of community development.

For example, community efforts to reduce child abuse need to examine the available support that can be offered to offset the sociocultural risks families face in their daily existence. Pregnancy complications can be reduced when support systems are made available to women (Nuckolls, Cassel, & Kaplan, 1972). Via support through home visitors, development can be enhanced for infants at high risk due to poverty, maternal depression, and caretaking inadequacy (Lyons-Ruth et al., 1990). Turner and Avison (1985) found that maternal adaptation to the parental role is distinguished, in part, by social support. In essence, women who do not obtain the needed level of social support have difficulty providing the most positive and healthy environment for their children. Social support enhances parental functioning by providing feedback about children and parenting, norms for nonabusive child-rearing, and increased opportunities for reducing stress and problem solving.

Overview

This chapter presented a way of conceptualizing the key systems that make up our social system, which integrates and regulates how we relate to one another. The social system also involves all the processes and structures that contribute to various forms of social organization. In discussing these elements that make up the social system, we presented traditional and nontraditional concepts from the social-work and social-science literature. We also examined structures in social relationships that contribute to various forms of oppression and social support, and we described how these social structures are interrelated, as well as where they intersect. This form of knowledge is essential in trying to individualize the experiences of clients. Social workers need to understand the consequences of race, class, and gender on each aspect of human behavior.

In the next section of the book, we begin applying each of the dimensions in our framework to the many phases and events associated with the process of human development.

Summary

The social system serves the function of integrating people into a life shared with others. Its key components are people in interaction with one another. The various contexts in our lives can be analyzed as separate systems, and there are four levels of subsystems: microsystems, mesosystems, exosystems, and macrosystems. These systems can be used to examine the environmental contexts of human development.

Principles from systems thinking help us identify relevant systems, subsystems, and the suprasystem of which problems, people, and behaviors are a part. This approach is aided by drawing an ecomap. An ecomap highlights the points of connection between systems influencing a person's life and allows for the identification of points of conflict and points of support in a person's life space.

Structural functionalism, conflict theory, and postmodern theory are other social theories that focus on differential aspects of social systems. **Structural functionalism** links key social structures with manifest and latent functions that help maintain social structural arrangements in our society. Conflict theories assume that conflict is natural and focuses on understanding issues involving conflict, coercion, and the role of power in social relations. Postmodern theory examines broader changes in the culture of society and examines their implications for observed changes in the basic organization of society under postmodern conditions.

The family is a key system within the larger social system. By treating the family as a system, the social worker can better understand the social context of family difficulties. The family is a system that is considered bigger than the sum of its parts. There are traditional and nontraditional definitions of the family. A useful definition that takes into account the conditions of our times is as follows: A **family** is a composition of people who decide to act like a family. Families, like individuals, experience a sequence of developmental stages. Carter and McGoldrick have described a six-stage model of family development that is useful in understanding how families change over time.

Examining family structure and function helps us understand how families work. **Family structure** refers to the manner in which each family organizes itself into interactional patterns. The key subsystems in a family are the couple subsystem, parental subsystem, sibling subsystem, and parent-child subsystem. Families function best when the subsystems maintain their own unique roles, identities, and boundaries. Family systems involve a number of key processes, such as homeostasis, information, and feedback, and communication plays a major role in family relations. Families are functional to the extent that they have good problem-solving, negotiation, and decision-making skills.

Another key context for understanding human behavior is the group. Groups are any small face-to-face collections of people who interact to accomplish some purpose. Groups are often classified as (1) formed or natural and (2) treatment groups or task groups. Understanding how groups function requires knowledge of group dynamics and processes, including knowledge of norms, roles, communication patterns, power and status relationships, and cohesiveness. Most groups must resolve the issue of how they will make decisions.

Support systems are a special type of social context. They represent continuing social aggregates that provide individuals with opportunities for feedback about themselves and for validation of their expectations about others. There are five different types of support systems: formal organizations, formed groups, self-help groups, social networks, and natural helpers. Self-help groups are a major social trend. Closely related to self-help groups are natural helpers. Natural helpers are considered central figures in a social network or in a neighborhood who have gained recognition for their unique wisdom, resourcefulness, and caring qualities.

Organizations and institutions are other types of contexts within which humans live. A formal organization is any large social group that is designed to achieve specific objectives rationally. Some formal organizations develop bureaucratic structures. All forms of organization meet critical goals necessary for the survival of a society.

Another key social context that influences our lives is our social institutions. These include the institutions of economy, kinship, education, law, polity, and religion. They contribute to the stability of status, roles, norms, and power in our relationships. Our location in social space is significantly influenced by our social institutions. There are many terms employed by social scientists to describe variations in a person's location in social space: social distance, social integration, social marginality, and hierarchy.

We live in a multicultural world, which means that social workers must have knowledge of factors contributing to tolerance and intolerance in social relationships. *Prejudice* refers to a generalized negative attitude directed toward another individual's membership in a socially defined group. Discrimination involves overt acts that treat members of a target group in an unfair manner. Race is a social and not a biological concept, and it can be used to make distinctions that have unfair consequences. Ethnicity also focuses on differences in people, but it is not as easy to identify ethnic differences as it is to identify racial and sex differences. Ethnicity, gender, and sexual orientation should be examined in terms of acquired meaning. These meanings have little to do with distinct differences that can characterize each of these social categories.

Many social conditions, such as poverty, inequality, and postindustrialism, place people at risk for forms of harm. Major transformations in society continue to take place, affecting the status of social conditions. Examining sociocultural risk is one way of identifying and understanding conditions such as poverty and inequality. Sociocultural risk occurs when a child's world is so impoverished that the child lacks basic social and psychological necessities, and it includes two aspects: social impoverishment and cultural impoverishment. Community efforts can be designed to increase support and reduce the risks families face.

CONCEPT MAP

Key Terms

- agency
- AGIL scheme
- androcentricity
- aversive racism
- bureaucracy
- cohesive group
- communication patterns
- communitarian agenda
- creolization
- culture
- discrimination
- ecomapping
- exosystems
- family
- family structure
- floating family
- folkways
- formal organization
- formed groups
- gender
- gender polarization
- groupthink
- heterosexuality
- holism
- homophobia
- human capital
- human relations school
- ideal type
- institutional discrimination
- macrosystems
- mesosystems
- microsystems
- mores
- natural groups
- natural helpers
- neighboring
- norms
- pattern variables
- physical capital
- power
- prejudice
- race
- racism
- reductionism
- role
- self-help groups
- sense of community
- sex
- social capital
- social support systems
- status
- stereotype
- structural functionalism
- system
- task groups
- theory of agency
- treatment groups

Online Resources

Websites

Go to http://info.wadsworth.com/ashford to find specific links to these web pages.

The Thomson website has assessment activities for applying the social dimension to the Raul Salazar case.

Race, Racism, and the Law

This website has law reviews that examine race, racism, and racial distinctions in the law.

American-Arab Anti Discrimination Committee

This is a website tailored to the needs of the American Arab community.

Southern Poverty Law Center

This organization promotes strategies for tolerance and provides other free resources.

The National Gay and Lesbian Task Force

This website features an excellent resource library online.

International Center for Research on Women

This site promotes social and economic development with the full participation of women.

InfoTrac College Edition Keywords

For interesting materials related to what you have just read, please go to the InfoTrac College Edition website and search using the following keywords:

- intergroup relations
- group identification
- sexism
- hate crimes

CHAPTER 5

Pregnancy, Birth, and the Newborn

CHAPTER CONSULTANTS

Kristine (Chris) Sifert
University of Michigan

Kathleen Rounds
University of North Carolina

DEVELOPMENTAL THEMES	
	Accepting the reality of the pregnancy. Adjusting to the role of parenthood. Work and parenting. Abortion.
BIOPHYSICAL DIMENSION	
Biophysical Growth and Development	Physical development of the fetus: germinal period (rapid cell division); embryonic period (internal organs develop); fetal period (growth and weight gain); birth. Prepared childbirth. Medications for labor. The normal newborn. Newborn evaluations: Apgar score.
Biophysical Strengths and Hazards	Complications of pregnancy: hyperemesis gravidarum, vaginal bleeding, placenta previa, toxemia, preeclampsia, gestational diabetes, polyhydramnios, IUGR. Environmental effects on prenatal development: maternal age; multiple gestations; maternal nutrition, illness, alcohol use, and stress. Prenatal testing. Complications of birth: anoxia, meconium aspiration, malpresentation, prolonged labor. Cesarean births. Neonatal complications: prematurity, birth defects and developmental disorders. Strengths: mothers with good health.
PSYCHOLOGICAL DIMENSION	
Cognitive Development and Information Processing	Fetal responses to pain, light, touch, taste.
Communication	Fetal response to sound: habituation to sound. Fetal learning: newborn response to maternal voice.
Attitudes and Emotions	Effect of mother's emotional state on fetus. Parental interactions with fetus and newborn emotional health.
Social Cognition and Regulation	Newborn states, newborn reflexes. The Brazelton Neonatal Assessment Scale.
Psychological Strengths and Hazards	Newborn attachment: question of a "sensitive period." The birth experience: LeBoyer "gentle" birth. The neonatal intensive care unit. Multiple-gestation births.
SOCIAL DIMENSION	
Families, Groups, Communities, and Support Systems	Prenatal intervention programs, postpartum early-intervention programs. Adolescent mothers.
Multicultural and Gender Considerations	Infant mortality: the black-white disparity. Cultural differences among newborns. Circumcision.
Social Strengths and Hazards	Poverty's effect on prenatal development. Drug-exposed infants, fetal alcohol syndrome, domestic violence.

DEVELOPMENTAL THEMES

It has been said that pregnancy is an act of faith until the birth of the baby, when nine months of waiting culminate in a new life. Upon seeing their infant for the first time, new mothers have been heard to exclaim, "Oh my God, it really is a baby!" Whether planned or unplanned, confirmation of pregnancy is often a shock. The first task for the expectant parents is to accept that the pregnancy is real and involves the growth of a real fetus.

Reva Rubin, who has researched the developmental tasks of pregnancy, described two questions women ask throughout **gestation** (the length of pregnancy): "Now?" and "Who, me?" (Rubin, 1970). If the pregnancy is unplanned, the woman may have to decide whether to terminate it or continue it. Even if the pregnancy is expected, the woman may still wonder whether it is such a good idea at this time. She may have thoughts such as, "Wait, am I really ready for this?" Even the most wanted pregnancy is often the source of considerable anxiety. The woman may worry about the birth process and wonder, "How is this baby going to get out, and how much will it hurt?" A young, single woman may ignore the reality of the pregnancy for months, refusing to admit even to herself that she is expecting. Many of these issues are further compounded when the mother is an adolescent.

Social workers must learn how to assess parents' level of preparation for this important role change. Gorski (1999) has identified five subject areas to examine when meeting with expectant parents: (1) attachments and commitments; (2) how they are mentally representing the fetal infant; (3) past history of social and professional support; (4) history of loss; (5) sense of security.

Pregnancy causes many changes. Expectant parents need to reconsider and renegotiate relationships with each other, other children, family of origin, and their careers (Murray, McKinney, & Gorrie, 2002). "The history and current nature of the relationships between expectant parents and their own parents become central for expectant parents and for helping professionals to understand the sources of support and conflict that will likely influence the interactive relationship with the fetus and newborn" (Gorski, 1999, p. 14).

Once pregnancy has been confirmed, many mothers have ambivalent or conflicting feelings about being pregnant. The meaning of pregnancy, even when desired, is often influenced by the changes that the parents must make in their lives. During the first few weeks and months, the woman's primary focus is on herself and not necessarily the fetus (Murray, McKinney, & Gorrie, 2002). The mother turns inward and becomes self-centered. She becomes preoccupied with her own thoughts and feelings. Physical changes, such as nausea and fatigue, make the pregnancy clearer in her mind than the reality of the fetus, which seems much more distant of an experience. During this phase, hormone changes influence her mood and her affect. "Her mood can change quickly from contentment to irritation or from optimistic planning to an overwhelming need for sleep" (Murray, McKinney, & Gorrie, 2002, p. 163). Clearly, the partner can be confused by many of these changes.

As the pregnancy progresses and the woman feels the fetus move, hears the heartbeat, and perhaps sees the fetus via ultrasound, she usually becomes reconciled to the reality of the pregnancy. At this point, she may begin to integrate the notion of the baby being part of her. The focus is less on being pregnant and more on having a baby, and the baby begins to become a real and separate person. Now the mother begins to plan for the birth. She fantasizes about her baby, dreams about her baby, and plans for her baby. She may begin to think of her own childhood and her relationship to her family. Pregnancy can reactivate unresolved developmental conflicts for a woman (Schuster & Ashburn, 1992; Gorski, 1999) and lead to the task of resolving identity confusions and assuming the role of mother. She may analyze her own identity, her relationship to her mother, and her relationship to her partner. She may worry about balancing career and family and about being a good mother without losing her own identity (Lederman, 1996; Gorski, 1999).

Research indicates that ultrasound results augment mothers' responses to the perception of fetal movement and other activity states. Mothers start using this information to personify the fetus. But these stimuli and personifications are also mediated by the parent's self-concept, self-esteem, mood, hopes, dreams, and fears (Gorski, 1999). Grief work is also involved. Women often experience a sense of sadness when they realize that they need to give up certain aspects of their previous sense of self (Murray, McKinney, & Gorrie, 2002). The practitioner needs to develop a relationship with the parent that will allow for the discussion of some of her concerns about role losses.

Pregnancy is as much of an adjustment for the father as it is for the mother (Tulman & Fawcett, 2003). He also has many worries about his ability to parent, to provide for a family, and to live up to his wife's expectations. The pregnancy is even less real for him, and his task often is to assimilate the fact that the fetus is real and is his without the benefit of the biological processes associated with pregnancy. The same can be said of a lesbian coparent. Feeling fetal movement, hearing the heartbeat, attending childbirth-preparation classes, and being present at the birth all help to include the father or other parent in the pregnancy and birth process. "Some men are emotionally invested and comfortable as full partners and wish to explore every aspect of pregnancy, childbirth, and parenting. Others are more task oriented and view themselves as managers" (Murray, McKinney, & Gorrie, 2002).

One example of a cultural practice that has served to establish the man as the father of the baby is *couvade*. In certain indigenous communities, the father is expected to behave as if he, like the mother, must avoid certain foods and engage in restraint in performing some physical activities. Also, a common feature of couvade is that while his wife is delivering the infant, the father goes to bed and may even complain of labor pains (Mason & Elwood, 1995). This custom symbolically establishes the man as the father of the baby and gives him legal rights as the parent. In modern societies, up to 65% of men report symptoms of pregnancy during their partner's gestation (May & Perrin, 1985), including nausea, fatigue, back pain, and even abdominal pain. Though many different reasons have been suggested for this phenomenon—an expression of underlying biological changes in the male, envy of the pregnant woman, somatic anxiety—its prevalence is not entirely understood. Could the modern version of couvade be the result of the male identifying strongly with his mate and thereby symbolically assuming responsibility for his role as father of their child? Could these symptoms help make the pregnancy more real for him? Some research suggests that couvade brings the father into a "paternal state" and that this might reduce the risk of the father abusing the child (Mason & Elwood, 1995). Although there are no definitive answers about this syndrome, research indicates that men have psychological, emotional, and physical needs related to fatherhood that should be addressed.

Through the nine months of pregnancy, then, the couple faces the tasks involved in becoming a mother and a father. When the baby is born, both must give up the fantasy baby each has dreamed of for nine months and accept the very real baby that has been born. Clearly, the transition to pregnancy requires new adaptations in roles for the mother and her partner. The postdelivery process also includes an additional set of adaptations that are heavily determined by the health status of the mother and the availability of appropriate supports. Poor immigrant mothers are especially vulnerable to not having access to good support and parenting services (Takanishi, 2004). Indeed, "children are born in varying socio-cultural and economic circumstances that affect their opportunities in life, with important consequences for their well-being both as children and as adults" (Takanishi, 2004, p. 62).

In addition to role changes, mothers confront many postpartum physical changes, including, "discomfort from an episiotomy or Caesarean section incision, uterine cramps, breast-engorgement or infection, nipple irritation, poor appetite, fatigue, anemia, thyroid disorders, hot flashes, increased sweating, dizziness, acne, sleep disturbances, carpal tunnel syndrome, hand numbness, or tingling, excessive vaginal bleeding . . . and sexual concerns" (Tulman & Fawcett, 2003, p. 74). Women also expect to lose weight after the pregnancy. They typically lose between 19 and 24 pounds in the first few weeks. From 12 to 13 of these pounds are accounted for by the fetus, the placenta, amniotic fluid, blood loss, water loss, and other factors. Most women gain more than recommended amounts during pregnancy. For this reason, it takes a year on average for them to gradually lose the weight in a healthy manner. In addition, they must adapt to a number of psychological and social changes in adjusting to the new member of the family (Tulman & Fawcett, 2003).

Mothers also confront the key issue of work. Today, the dual-earner family is the most common form of two-parent families with children (Starbuck, 2002). Dual-earner families have increased dramatically since the 1960s, but the increase is even more dramatic for women with children under 3 years of age (Altucher & Williams, 2003; Winkler, 1998). In the past, husbands' careers were primary and took precedence over the careers of women, but falling real earnings for men, combined with rising labor-force participation for women, have had an impact on decision making among couples. Data from the

Current Population Survey indicated that 23% of women earned more than men, and this change is affecting many household decisions, including whether to have a baby (Winkler, 1998). "The question of who works, who takes care of the children and how whoever this is will manage to fulfill these tasks, is still contested and in flux as shifting cultural expectations come into conflict" (Altucher & Williams, 2003, p. 49). In addition, research is now showing that delayed childbearing is leading to many women deciding to forgo having children because of career and work demands. As of 2000, the percentage of childless women reached 19 percent, up from 15 percent in 1992 (Altucher & Williams, 2003).

The Cornell Couples and Careers Study has examined the work and leisure of dual-earner parents with children under age 6 (Clarkberg & Merola, 2003). The results showed that childless women under the age of 40 work about 9.7 hours per workday, a rate that does not differ statistically from males who are nonparent husbands. Males, on average, work at their jobs 10 hours a day, whether or not they have children. However, women, once children enter the relationship, average approximately 7.5 work hours a day (Clarkberg & Merola, 2003). The Cornell study also looked at housework and found that in the launching stage—that is, when a family has children—men do about 1.5 to 2 hours of housework per day. Women, on the other hand, averaged about 3 hours a day of housework on a workday. Clearly, the decision to have children dramatically affected the lives of the professionals in the Cornell study, but having children meant that in the areas of child care and housework, the females shouldered more responsibility than did the males.

Many women can choose to abort a pregnancy because of conflicts with work expectations or for other reasons. For a woman of any age, it is a difficult decision.

Abortion

For a woman of any age, the abortion decision is often one of the most difficult and distressing choices she will make in her life. Abortion is a complicated and controversial issue with strong arguments both for and against. Some pro-life advocates believe that termination of a pregnancy at any point for any reason is murder and is morally wrong. Pro-choice advocates believe that a woman has the right to control her own reproductive process and determine her own fate.

The abortion question has a long history. In 1973, the Supreme Court decided in *Roe v. Wade* that states could not deny a woman her right to have an abortion. Since that time, however, several other laws and rulings have eroded that right. As early as 1976, the Hyde amendment stopped Medicaid funding for abortions, which made it more difficult for poor women to obtain abortions. Before that time, 33% of abortions were paid for by federal funds. In 1989, a more conservative Supreme Court ruled on *Webster v. Reproductive Health Services*, allowing states once again to limit abortions. The Webster ruling allowed states to ban abortions in public hospitals and clinics and prohibit public employees from assisting in abortions. Since then, the Supreme Court has accepted even more cases, with the result that abortion is still legal but less available, especially to young, poor women. For instance, more than thirty states require girls under 18 to notify or get permission from their parents to obtain an abortion—in some states, permission is required even from a noncustodial parent. And employees of federally funded family-planning clinics cannot discuss abortion with clients; only the doctor can mention abortion as an alternative or even offer abortion counseling (Guernsey, 1993). And fewer and fewer doctors are available to perform abortions. Some simply are untrained in the procedure, whereas others become discouraged by the violence associated with abortion protests. However, as of this writing, many women still have a choice.

How does a woman make such a difficult decision? She needs to explore honestly how she personally feels about abortion. She needs help in exploring alternatives such as putting the baby up for adoption, raising the child herself, or allowing a family member to raise the child. She needs to think through what each choice means for her now and in the future.

A social worker can play an important role in helping a woman make the abortion decision. But this is one instance in which it is vital to be able to separate personal from professional values. The most important consideration is that the woman needs to make the decision herself; no one can make it for her. In this situation, a social worker's role is a supportive one. In a Swedish study, more than one-third of the women contemplating abortion felt that their social-support system was inadequate, a finding that illustrates their need for social-work intervention (Hamark, Uddenberg, & Forssman, 1995). Though many women feel some guilt and depression after an abortion, most women have less regret and fewer emotional problems when the choice has not been forced on them by other people (Reeder, Mastroianni, & Martin, 1983). In fact, fewer than 10% of women experience psychological problems after an abortion (Lembau, 1988; Olson, 1980). Women who do have a high incidence of emotional problems following abortion were more ambivalent before the procedure, felt coerced, or already had symptoms of personality problems (Schuster & Ashburn, 1992).

Women who have been denied an abortion may have more problems with the child born as a result of that denial. One study in Czechoslovakia (Matejcek, Dytrych, & Schuller, 1979) found that, at the age of 9, children born to women denied an abortion had more hospitalizations, poorer school grades, poorer relationships with peers, and more irritable dispositions than other children.

A woman who is encouraged to take some time and carefully analyze her options before coming to a decision will be better able to live with that decision. Counseling before and after the abortion can help a woman deal with her feelings about her choice. The goal is to help a woman make a decision that—whether she feels good or bad about it at the time—she ultimately believes is the right one. The decision to have a child contributes to choices that begin the important biophysical process of pregnancy.

Even after a parent decides to have a child, many factors can contribute to the ending of a pregnancy. Technically, the ending of a pregnancy before the fetus is viable is considered an abortion. "Lay people often use the term *miscarriage* to denote an abortion that has occurred spontaneously" (Murray, McKinney, & Gorrie, 2002). However, the accepted medical definition of abortion is "either a spontaneous or induced ending of pregnancy." In the next section, we introduce the growth and developmental processes associated with pregnancy and the birth process, which will be covered in our biophysical level of analysis.

STUDY TABLE: Developmental themes in pregnancy, birth, and the newborn

Developmental Themes	During pregnancy, the couple goes through several stages in preparation for the baby's birth. At first, the couple must accept the reality of the pregnancy. As pregnancy progresses, the woman integrates the fetus as part of herself. She turns inward and begins to resolve her own identity crisis. Toward the end of pregnancy, the woman begins to prepare for the birth and to see the fetus as a separate being. At birth, the couple must reconcile the real baby with their fantasy baby.

BIOPHYSICAL DIMENSION

Biophysical Growth and Development

What will eventually become a baby begins as a single cell. About midway through her menstrual cycle, a woman produces a mature ovum, or egg, in a fluid-filled sac on one of her ovaries. At ovulation, the sac bursts and the mature ovum is swept into the fallopian tube to begin the journey to the uterus.

When the ovum enters the fallopian tube, it continues along toward the lower one-third of the tube. Sperm deposited in the vagina during intercourse swim up through the cervix, into the uterus, and then into the fallopian tube, where one sperm fertilizes the ovum.

The fertilized ovum is known as a *zygote*. After a brief rest of twenty-four to thirty-six hours, the zygote begins the process of regular cell division. It then takes three days for the zygote to travel down the fallopian tube and into the uterus. By then, it has developed into a fluid-filled sphere of about 150 cells. The inner layer of cells develops into the embryo, and the outer layer of cells forms the *chorionic villi*—fingerlike tendrils that give the zygote a shaggy appearance. These chorionic villi burrow into the uterine lining (implant) and provide early nutrients. This process of implantation of the zygote, known as the *germinal period*, takes about two weeks. After implan-

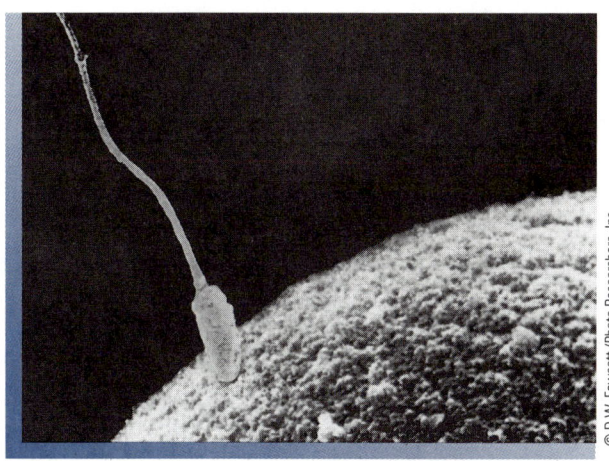
Sperm and egg: A magnified image of the process of conception.

tation, the zygote, now known as an *embryo*, begins to secrete human chorionic gonadotrophin (HCG) to maintain the pregnancy. HCG can be detected in the mother's blood six to eight days after conception, and presence of this substance is the basis for early pregnancy testing. An at-home early-pregnancy test can detect HCG in the mother's urine as soon as one day after the missed menstrual cycle. The next few weeks after conception, from two to eight weeks, is the embryonic period.

Physical Development of the Fetus

no one, not even the rain, has such small hands
— e. e. cummings

After eight weeks, the embryo begins to look quite human; it is 90% formed, with most of the basic structures, including a face, arms, legs, feet, and hands. From this point on, the embryo is referred to as a *fetus*, and this period is called the *period of the fetus*. Between eight and twelve weeks, the chorionic villi develop into a functioning placenta attached to the mother's uterus, and the fetus is connected to the placenta by the umbilical cord. For the remainder of the pregnancy, the placenta acts as the fetus's lungs, digestive tract, kidneys, and liver. Oxygen and nutrients from the mother pass through this semipermeable membrane to the fetus, and carbon dioxide and other wastes pass from the fetus to the mother. It was once thought that the placenta acted as a barrier and protected the fetus from any harmful substances ingested by the mother. Now, however, we know that what the mother eats, drinks, sniffs, or inhales is passed on to the developing baby (Murray, McKinney, & Gorrie, 2002). The effects of these substances on the fetus will be discussed in a later section.

The fetus floats in amniotic fluid inside the *amniotic sac*, or bag of waters. This fluid regulates the temperature, cushions the fetus from injury, and allows freedom of movement. After twelve weeks, the fetus begins to move in this fluid, drink it, and urinate into it. By this time, also, it is possible to determine the sex of the fetus.

By twenty weeks, the mother can feel the first fetal movements, commonly described as "butterflies" fluttering in her lower abdomen. Often this is the time when the expectant parents first hear the fetal heartbeat during a prenatal visit. The fetus is covered with fine, downy hair called *lanugo*. Some babies are born with a substantial amount of this hair on their bodies, although many babies lose most of this body hair before birth (Berger, 2005).

By twenty-four weeks, the fetus resembles a tiny baby. This baby appears to be rather red and wrinkled, though, because it has not put on much fat. At this time, the fetus is covered with a substance called vernix, which looks a lot like shortening and protects the skin from prolonged exposure to the amniotic fluid. Babies at term are sometimes born with some of this vernix still covering their skin. A fetus at twenty-four weeks makes breathing motions, hiccoughs (sometimes felt by the mother), responds to sound, and sleeps and wakes in noticeable cycles. With the advanced technology now available in high-level neonatal intensive care units (NICU), babies born at twenty-four weeks have a chance for survival (Murray, McKinney, & Gorrie, 2002).

Traditionally, if born at twenty-eight weeks, the fetus has a good chance of survival. Now the fetus opens and closes its eyes and may even suck its thumb. A fetus usually assumes the head-down position in the uterus at this time, because the head is the heaviest part of the body.

During the last two months of pregnancy, the fetus stores fat and gains weight. The fetal lungs undergo important development, and each week the fetus remains in the uterus increases its chances of survival. Although today a premature baby has greater chances of survival at earlier and earlier stages of pregnancy, problems related to low birth weight and prematurity remain.

The fetus is full term and ready for life outside the uterine environment between thirty-eight and forty-one weeks. How is the "due date" determined? If pregnancy is defined as beginning at the time of concep-

EXHIBIT 5.1

Birth process

SOURCE: Adapted from *Before We are Born: Basic embryology and Birth Defects*, Third Edition, by K. L. Moore, copyright © 1989, with permission from Elsevier.

tion, then birth occurs after 266 days, or thirty-eight weeks. The mother's due date, however, is usually calculated according to Nagele's rule. To determine a woman's due date, count back three months from the first day of her last menstrual period and add seven days. According to this procedure, pregnancy begins on the first day of the last menstrual period and lasts 280 days, or forty weeks. In most clinical situations, pregnancy is calculated in this way, so, for our discussion of prenatal development, pregnancy is based on menstrual dates and lasts forty weeks.

The Birth Process

Doesn't it seem that in popular-media depictions of birth, labor begins with the woman doubling over in sudden, intense pain? This is followed by a frantic rush to get to the hospital in time for the birth. Although some cab drivers have delivered babies, in reality most women find that labor begins more slowly, allowing ample time to make it to the hospital.

Labor is divided into three stages (see Exhibit 5.1). During the first stage, the cervix opens up, or dilates, to ten centimeters to allow the passage of the baby's head. The average length of the first stage of labor is twelve to fourteen hours. In early labor, the contractions can be up to twenty minutes apart and usually last less than one minute. Most women are pretty comfortable in the early part of labor and are excited about having the baby at last, though a little anxious over the process. As labor progresses, toward the end of the first stage, the contractions may come one right after another and last up to two minutes. During this phase, a laboring woman needs a lot of support and encouragement. And if she has not gone to the hospital or birthing center yet, now is the time to rush or hope the cab driver knows what he or she is doing.

When the cervix has fully dilated to ten centimeters, the second stage of labor begins. During this stage, the baby is born. A woman can now actively participate in the birth process by pushing the baby down the birth canal. This process can take from ten minutes to more than three hours, depending on how many previous births the woman has had and how much medication she has been given.

During the third stage of labor, the placenta is delivered, which usually takes from five to thirty minutes. At this time, the mother and her partner or support person are busy marveling over the baby. Sometimes a fourth stage of labor is included; this is the recovery time, one to two hours after birth. During this time, the mother is watched for excessive bleeding or other recovery problems. This is usually the time for the new family to get to know one another. In the next section, we will review the child birthing process and the preparations for delivery. Child preparation practices vary from country to country and from generation to generation.

Prepared Childbirth

Having a baby involves some degree of pain, which is caused by cervical dilation and the sensation of the baby's head pushing through the pelvis. Through the years, different methods have been used to help ease this pain.

Many of the early drugs given to relieve the pain of childbirth rendered most women unconscious during delivery. Because the mother was not awake and could not help push the baby out, the baby was usually delivered with a high degree of medical intervention. The mother's partner would wait in the fathers' waiting room. After birth, the baby was kept in the hospital nursery and brought to the mother only at scheduled feeding times. Understandably, women began to want more control over and participation in their birth experiences. Also, such a heavy reliance on drugs for pain relief during birth had major side effects for the baby. In response, other methods of pain relief, without drugs, were developed.

The most popular method of prepared childbirth was developed by a French obstetrician, Fernand Lamaze. In the Lamaze method, the father or other support person stays with the mother through her labor to provide help and encouragement. The mother and her support person attend classes where they learn about the birth process and specific relaxation techniques. Knowledge and relaxation help reduce fear and thereby reduce pain. The woman is taught to replace the normal responses to pain of fear and tension with more useful and distracting responses, such as patterned breathing and relaxation.

More recently, studies have shown that women who walk and move around during labor have shorter labors, experience less discomfort, and need less medication than women who lie down (Balaskas, 1992). Studies have also shown that the presence of a supportive female birth attendant, or doula, during labor results in less medication, less medical intervention, fewer birth complications, and a shorter labor (Klaus, Kennel, & Klaus, 1993).

Over the years, hospitals have attempted to make birth more family centered. Many hospitals have spe-

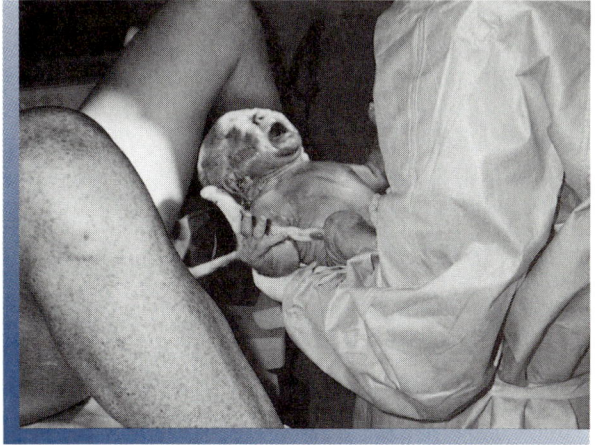

At birth, babies leave the comfort of the uterine environment and must immediately adapt to the outside environment.

cial birthing rooms, which resemble a regular bedroom. The mother is allowed to have any number of attendants present for the birth; even siblings may be included. After the birth, the baby is handed to the mother, and she can keep the baby in the room with her and feed it on demand. Birthing centers, outside the hospital setting, allow for homelike birth with the possibility of medical intervention if necessary. Some women choose to have their babies at home, but in case of last-minute complications, most obstetricians prefer to deliver babies in a hospital or a birthing center. Nonetheless, there is a marked increase in the use of midwives in some areas of the United States. In 1975, midwives attended to about 1% of births, 5.5% in 1994, and 9% in 1998. Yet, 80% of the world's babies are born with midwives, who often provide much better prenatal care than is achieved in the United States (Ladyman, 2005; Walsh, 2005).

Medications for Labor and Delivery

Development of prepared-childbirth methods has allowed women to be awake and active participants in the birth process. Being rendered totally unconscious with drugs is now usually only an option during an emergency cesarean section. However, prepared childbirth does not eliminate the pain of labor. Today, "natural" childbirth does not necessarily mean unmedicated childbirth.

The most commonly used medications in labor today are narcotics and regional anesthesias. Narcotics, such as Demerol, are given before the end of the first stage of labor so that most of the drug will pass out of the baby's system before birth. If the baby is born with the narcotic in its system, it may experience difficulty breathing or sucking. Because the narcotic is sometimes given with a tranquilizer, the baby also may be sleepy at birth, in contrast to unmedicated babies, who are more alert.

Regional anesthesias include the epidural. In the epidural, an anesthetic is injected into the mother's lower spine. Though little of this drug reaches the baby, its long-term effects on the baby are still unknown. Some studies show mild effects on early newborn behavior (Sepkoski, 1992), whereas others have found little or no effect. Over the years, some studies have indicated that there are effects on the birth process itself. For instance, the epidural may increase the length of labor and the need for medical intervention, including the use of forceps (a pair of instruments that resemble salad tongs used to guide the baby out of the birth canal when the mother is not able to push the baby out) and the possibility of a **cesarean section** (birth through an incision in the mother's abdomen) (Thorpe & Breedlove, 1996; Cohen, Yeast, & Hu, 1994). However, studies reviewed by Thorpe & Breedlove (1996) suggested that the epidural is the most safe and effective method of pain relief for women in labor, with associated benefits such as relaxing women and helping labor progress (see also Erickson, 1996).

Although most women who are prepared for childbirth use less medication than those who are not, the use of medication in labor in many hospitals remains quite high. In fact, in some hospitals the rate of epidural use approaches 85–90%. All obstetric medications given to the mother cross the placenta and alter the baby's environment in the uterus (Balaskas, 1992). Conclusive evidence of the long-term effects of these drugs is not yet available. Thus, use of medications during birth may still be an important factor to consider in making an assessment.

Characteristics of a Normal Newborn

How does a newborn infant look? Bill Cosby described the experience of seeing his new baby for the first time and telling his wife, "Congratulations, dear. You have just given birth to a . . . lizard." Although most newborns bear little resemblance to reptiles, they are not exactly the "Gerber baby."

Normal newborns at term weigh between 5.5 pounds (2,500 grams) and 9.5 pounds (4,300 grams). The head of a vaginally delivered newborn

A striking comparison of the baby at birth and at 4 weeks. The newborn's head is elongated, and the baby's face shows the pressures that occurred during the birth process.

is often elongated or cone-shaped. This molding of the head results from the fact that the bones in a newborn's head are not fused together. These bones shift during birth, allowing the head to change shape to fit through the birth canal. (Infants delivered by cesarean section always have round heads.) Passage through the birth canal also can cause facial bruising and swelling. Many newborns have a bluish color to their skin until they begin breathing. After birth, the newborn's skin may be red, wrinkled, and scaling. But to the new parents, their newborn is usually a beautiful sight (Berger, 2005).

Newborn Evaluations

One of the first questions asked by new parents at delivery is, "Is my baby okay?" One objective measure of newborn health is the **Apgar score** (see Exhibit 5.2). In 1953, Virginia Apgar developed a scale that looks at the infant's adaptation to life outside the womb. A newborn is given an Apgar score at 1 minute and 5 minutes after birth. At these times, the physician evaluates the baby on skin color, heart rate, response to stimulation, muscle tone, and breathing effort. In each area, the physician gives the baby a score of 0, 1, or 2. Normal newborns usually lose a point or two for skin color, because the hands and feet remain somewhat blue for a time after birth. (There is an old joke that only fellow obstetricians' babies receive a

EXHIBIT 5.2 The Apgar score

Sign	Score		
	0	1	2
Heart rate	No heartbeat	Fewer than 100 beats per minute	100 to 140 beats per minute
Breathing	No breathing	Irregular shallow breathing	Strong breathing and crying
Reflex	No response	Weak reflexive response	Strong reflexive response (sneezing, coughing, grimacing)
Muscle tone	Limp	Weak flexion of arms and legs	Strong flexion of arms and legs
Color	Blue body	Body pink, blue extremities	Body and extremities pink

SOURCE: Zigler & Stevenson (1993).

perfect score of 10.) A score of 7–10 is considered good. A score of 5–7 is poor, and the baby may need some medical intervention. A score of 0–4 is very poor; the baby very likely requires resuscitation and has increased risk of mortality. A score of 0–4 at 5 minutes is significantly associated with increased risk of mortality and neurological defects.

Biophysical Strengths and Hazards

Birth is as safe as life gets.
—Harriette Hartigan

As discussed in Chapter 2, when a social worker is gathering developmental data about a client for a psychosocial history, it may be helpful to obtain prenatal information about the client, including any problems or complications that occurred during the pregnancy or birth. These complications may have an effect on the individual's postnatal development. For instance, some early research (Colletti, 1979) suggested that children with learning disabilities had a significantly higher incidence of pregnancy and birth complications than did normal children. Other, more recent, evidence suggests a link between attention deficit disorder and pregnancy, birth, and neonatal complications (Sprich-Buckminster, 1993). In the next sections, we will discuss some of the possible complications of pregnancy and birth.

Complications of Pregnancy

Many women experience nausea, or morning sickness, during early pregnancy. This nausea and occasional vomiting usually clear up by the fourth month of gestation. If a woman vomits several times a day for a long period of time, however, she runs the risk of nutritional problems and dehydration. This frequent vomiting during pregnancy is called **hyperemesis gravidarum**. Some women have vomiting so severe that they require hospitalization.

A complication that can have serious consequences is **vaginal bleeding**. In early pregnancy, this bleeding can be the result of spontaneous abortion. Seventy-five percent of spontaneous abortions occur in the first twelve weeks of pregnancy. Not all incidences of first-trimester bleeding end in loss of the pregnancy, though. Sometimes the bleeding abates and the pregnancy is carried to term. But, because many spontaneous abortions are the result of fetal abnormalities, it may be helpful to note instances of early-pregnancy bleeding.

Vaginal bleeding in later pregnancy may indicate placental problems. This bleeding is usually the result of a placenta located low in the uterus and covering the cervix (**placenta previa**) or a placenta that begins to separate from the wall of the uterus (*abruptio placentae*). Significant bleeding in late pregnancy due to these conditions can be very serious and threaten the survival of the mother and the baby.

Toxemia and eclampsia also can be serious complications of pregnancy. Toxemia of pregnancy refers to an abnormal condition of pregnancy involving the toxic substance of proteinuria (protein in the urine). Early stages of toxemia are referred to as **preeclampsia**. In preeclampsia, the pregnant woman exhibits elevated blood pressure, swelling (especially of the hands and face), weight gain, and protein in her urine. These symptoms are not always easily noticed by the mother and are often caught at a prenatal visit. This is one reason that regular, consistent prenatal visits are so important to pregnancy outcome. If these early signs are not detected and treated, the condition can advance to eclampsia and serious complications, including maternal death, fetal death, and fetal brain damage.

Diabetes is one of the most common metabolic abnormalities of pregnancy. **Gestational diabetes**, defined as carbohydrate intolerance with onset or first recognition during pregnancy, makes up 80% of cases of diabetes in pregnancy. A woman diagnosed with diabetes before pregnancy is at an increased risk of both maternal and fetal complications and may require intensive medical management before, during, and after her pregnancy. A woman who develops gestational diabetes must monitor her blood glucose levels, controlling them through diet and possibly insulin injections. Women experiencing gestational diabetes should be routinely monitored by a physician postpartum, because up to 62% of these women develop diabetes after pregnancy (Pasui & McFarland, 1997).

Sometimes the pregnant woman has too much amniotic fluid, or **polyhydramnios**. This excess fluid can signal problems with the baby. Remember, the baby drinks the fluid. If for some reason the baby cannot drink it, it builds up in the uterus, causing the mother to exhibit an overly large abdomen.

A good example of a complication of pregnancy that can be caused by factors in the maternal environment is **intrauterine growth retardation (IUGR)**. This condition occurs when the fetal weight falls below the 10th percentile for gestational age. Many factors can affect the quality of the maternal uterine environment and result in this growth slowdown, including the mother's nutrition, weight gain, age, number and spacing of previous pregnancies, health status, level of environmental stress, and ingestion of substances such as cigarettes, alcohol, and drugs. In many instances, this growth reduction is in some way caused by intrauterine deprivation. Because of this deprivation, IUGR increases the risk of fetal death and the risk of problems for the infant after birth.

Environmental Effects on Prenatal Development

The child is born into a family environment that will shape and influence his or her lifelong development. Even before birth, however, human development occurs in an "environment" that exerts significant influence on the growing fetus. The fetal environment exists inside the mother's uterus, and this environment can be influenced by numerous factors, such as the mother's health, her diet, her ingestion of substances such as alcohol and drugs, and her emotional state and level of stress. In this section we will discuss maternal health factors and practices that can adversely affect prenatal development.

Maternal Age

Problems in pregnancy attributable to maternal age arise in mothers under 18 and over 35. Older mothers have an increased risk for illness and for pregnancy complications. Specifically, the incidence of chromosomal abnormalities such as Down syndrome goes up significantly for older women. The risk of having an infant born with Down syndrome is 1:1,600 for a 21-year-old woman, whereas the risk is 1:83 for a woman at age 41.

Teenage mothers also can have problems with pregnancy, including increased risk of infant death, pregnancy complications, and infant mental retardation. One contributing problem for teenage mothers may be that they are less likely to obtain prenatal care than are older women (Eberstadt, 1991). For either end of the age spectrum, good medical management of the pregnancy through prenatal visits increases the likelihood of a successful outcome. Some outcomes, however, may not be what we expect.

One researcher (Geronimus, 1991, 1992) has discovered some interesting information about low-socioeconomic-status teens. This researcher found that economically disadvantaged women who give birth as teens have healthier babies than do comparable older women. In particular, in regard to birth outcomes for low-SES African American sisters, those who gave birth as teenagers had healthier babies and more family support than did the sisters who gave birth in their 20s. One suggested explanation for this outcome is that low-SES women are healthier as teenagers. As they enter their 20s, the health of these women declines as a result of poor living conditions and unsafe health habits.

At the other end of the age spectrum, more women in their thirties are giving birth. Multiple-gestation births are more common in this age group generally, and because fertility levels for women over 30 are lower, fertility interventions are used. These also may lead to multiple-gestation births. As the following section discusses, these births carry special risks.

Multiple Gestations

A pregnancy involving more than one fetus increases the risk of complications of pregnancy, especially for IUGR and premature labor. Whereas the average gestational age for single fetuses is thirty-nine weeks, for twins it is thirty-five weeks, triplets thirty-three, and quadruplets twenty-nine. Multiple gestations are twice as likely to have birth defects (Feinbloom, 1993). These and other complicating factors often result in multiple-gestation infants spending more time in the hospital after birth than do "singleton" infants (Wilcox et al., 1996).

Assisted reproductive technology (ART), such as in vitro fertilization, has been a contributing factor to the increase in multiple-gestation births. In fact, research estimates that ART-associated conception has contributed to an increase of approximately 38% of triplet and higher-order gestation births since the 1970s (Wilcox et al., 1996). Because of the increased risk of multiple gestation, women and couples interested in ART should receive information and counseling regarding the procedure.

Women who have several closely spaced pregnancies also experience increased problems with fetal health.

Maternal Nutrition

A pregnant woman needs an extra 300 calories a day of high-quality food for good nutrition. Physicians used to advise pregnant women to limit their weight gain to fifteen to eighteen pounds. Physicians now advise their patients to "eat to appetite" and to gain twenty-five to thirty pounds. Poor nutrition can result in IUGR and low birth weight. Lack of certain vitamins and minerals can cause problems; for example, lack of folic acid has been linked to neural-tube defects. Severe malnutrition increases the likelihood of congenital defects and fetal death. A good diet adequate in protein is most important during the last three months of pregnancy, when the baby is gaining weight and developing brain cells.

To help ensure adequate nutrition for low-income women during pregnancy, the government developed the Supplemental Food Program for Women, Infants and Children (referred to as *WIC*). This program provides vouchers to pregnant women and new mothers with children to age 5 for high-protein, iron-fortified food. The program also provides nutritional education and counseling.

> ### FOCUS ON MULTICULTURALISM
>
> #### PICA DURING PREGNANCY
>
> A nutritional problem for women in some communities is pica, the ingestion of nonfood substances such as paint chips, starch, dirt, clay, and ice. Sometimes the pregnant woman may ingest enough of these substances to interfere with her appetite for normal food. As a result, she may experience nutritional problems that can affect fetal growth and development. Though pica can be a craving for a particular substance, it also can be a cultural phenomenon. In some ethnic communities, women ingest nonfood substances with the belief that these substances will relieve the symptoms of pregnancy or benefit the fetus.
>
> A study at a prenatal clinic in Washington, D.C., found that 8.1% of the African American patients engaged in a form of pica called pagophagia—the ingestion of ice or freezer frost. These women ate up to two cups of ice a day and as a result showed a tendency toward anemia. This study suggested that these urban women ate ice chips to help alleviate stress. In fact, the authors found that pica was higher among women who had a poor social-support network (Edwards et al., 1994b). And, interestingly, the women who ate ice chips used fewer illegal drugs.

Maternal Illness

Several illnesses can cause serious problems with a pregnancy or for the fetus at birth. In particular, several nonbacterial infections, referred to as the TORCH complex, can cause multiple complications, including blindness, deafness, brain damage, miscarriage, fetal death, and mental retardation. These infections include toxoplasmosis, an infection caused by a parasite found in raw meat and cat feces; rubella, or German measles, a virus that can result in serious defects if contracted during the first three months of pregnancy; cytomegalovirus, a viral infection; and active herpes, a sexually transmitted virus.

Sexually transmitted diseases, such as syphilis, gonorrhea, and HIV, can have a profound effect on the fetus. Syphilis can be passed to the fetus through the placenta, and fetal infection with syphilis can result in miscarriage or eye, ear, bone, or brain damage. A woman with gonorrhea can pass the infection to her newborn during birth, resulting in blindness in the infant. As a safeguard, most hospitals treat a newborn's eyes with erythromycin ointment or silver nitrate. About 50% of mothers infected with HIV transmit the virus to their babies. In infected babies, the disease progresses rapidly and kills 95% of infected children by the age of 3.

The Centers for Disease Control (1997) state that perinatal transmission accounts for almost all new HIV infections in children. However, progress has been made in reducing the incidence of mother-to-child transmission. From 1984 through 1992, the number of perinatally infected children with AIDS was on a steady increase, but a decline of 43% was seen between 1992 and 1996. What has caused this dramatic decline? HIV counseling, testing of mothers, and the increased use of AZT during pregnancy are factors that are thought to have made an important contribution to the reduced rate of transmission. What can be done to continue this trend? The CDC recommends that state and local outreach to pregnant women be intensified to further reduce the mother-to-child transmission rate. To assist with this task, the Ryan White CARE Act provides resources for care and services to HIV-infected individuals and also requires states to examine their perinatal HIV-prevention programs.

Diabetic mothers have increased risk of pregnancy and birth complications. Uncontrolled diabetes can result in miscarriage, fetal death, and birth defects. Also, babies born to diabetic mothers tend to be large, with an increased risk of birth injury because of their size. For this reason, infants of diabetic mothers are often delivered early, resulting in problems associated with prematurity.

Another problem that can have serious effects on pregnancy outcome is not a maternal illness but is related to a maternal characteristic—the mother's blood type. This problem is known as **Rh incompatibility**. This problem arises when a mother with Rh-negative blood has a partner with Rh-positive blood, bringing about the possibility that their fetus will have Rh-positive blood. During pregnancy, the blood of the mother and fetus can sometimes mix through small tears in the placenta. If an Rh-negative mother is exposed to fetal blood that is Rh positive, the mother forms antibodies against the fetal blood. During a first pregnancy this is usually not a problem. But in subsequent pregnancies, Rh-negative mothers who have been sensitized to Rh-positive blood will have these antibodies in their system. If these antibodies enter the fetal blood supply, they destroy fetal red blood cells, resulting in fetal anemia and possible death. A fetus that survives to birth is at risk for mental retardation. For this reason, Rh-negative mothers are given Rhogam, a drug that counteracts the Rh antibodies, within 72 hours of a delivery or miscarriage to prevent sensitization. A fetus with this Rh problem can sometimes be saved by a blood transfusion.

Maternal Drug Use

Substances that cause birth defects are known as **teratogens**. The serious effects of drugs acting as teratogens can be illustrated with the story of thalidomide, a mild tranquilizer sold over the counter in the early 1960s for symptoms of morning sickness. The drug had been tested on pregnant laboratory rats and deemed safe for use by pregnant women. Although thalidomide was widely used in West Germany and Britain, the FDA never approved its use in the United States, "pending further study." Unfortunately, thousands of women who used the drug in early pregnancy gave birth to babies with birth defects. The most striking defect was short or missing limbs, so that hands and feet were attached to the torso. This story illustrates that the effects of a substance on a developing fetus cannot always be accurately assessed in the laboratory. A pregnant woman is now advised not to take any over-the-counter medications without consulting her physician. Exhibit 5.3 lists several other drugs that have been identified as teratogens.

Though the long-term effects of illegal substances on development are still uncertain, mothers addicted to street drugs, such as cocaine, heroin, and barbiturates, can give birth to addicted infants. These infants suffer the withdrawal problems associated with these drugs, including seizures, vomiting, agitation, tremors, and sleep disturbances. In addition, illicit drug use can increase the incidence of miscarriage, fetal death, hemorrhage, and low birth weight. Because of the dangers associated with drug usage during pregnancy, a number of controversial policies are generating significant debate in many policy circles.

Mandatory Drug Testing of Pregnant Women

Laura arrived at the hospital emergency room in early labor. On questioning, Laura admitted that she had received no prenatal care. When the nurses requested a urine sample, Laura left. Three days later Laura returned, hemorrhaging, and an emergency cesarean section was performed. Because of the lack of prenatal care, Laura was screened for drug use, and her lab

EXHIBIT 5.3 Drugs that may affect prenatal development

Alcohol	Prenatal/postnatal growth retardation; developmental delays; facial anomalies; microcephaly (small head); heart defects; hyperactivity; behavioral problems; mental retardation
Amphetamines	Premature birth; stillbirth; neonatal irritability; poor feeding in newborn
Antibiotics	
Streptomycin	Hearing loss
Tetracycline	Premature birth; stained teeth; short arms or legs; webbed hands; inhibited bone growth
Aspirin	Bleeding problems in mother or infant
Dilantin (seizure medicine)	Head and facial abnormalities; heart defects; cleft palate; mental retardation
Barbiturates	Fetal addiction with subsequent withdrawal symptoms, including seizures, vomiting, agitation; also can cause neurological problems
Hallucinogens (LSD, mescaline)	Possible chromosomal damage; miscarriage; possible behavioral abnormalities
Lithium	Heart defects; lethargic newborn
Cocaine	Low birth weight; seizures; microcephaly; SIDS; premature birth; IUGR; miscarriage
Heroin (methadone)	Toxemia; IUGR; miscarriage; premature birth; low birth weight; stillbirth; SIDS; neonatal addiction with withdrawal symptoms, including restlessness, vomiting, tremors
Hormones	
DES	Reproductive-system anomalies; cancer of reproductive system
Estrogens	Feminization of males
Androgens	Masculinization of females
Tranquilizers (valium)	In first trimester, can cause cleft palate, respiratory distress, poor muscle tone, lethargy in newborn
Tobacco	IUGR; premature birth; stillbirth; low birth weight; miscarriage; SIDS; possible hyperactivity; possible learning problems
Vitamin A	Cleft palate; heart defects
Accutane (acne medicine)	Microcephaly; blindness; heart defects; miscarriage; fetal death
Caffeine	Low birth weight; IUGR; premature birth
Antihistamines	Anomalies; fetal death
Corticosteroids	Anomalies; cleft palate; IUGR

results were positive for methamphetamines. Laura's baby was born lethargic, with low muscle tone and an irregular heartbeat. He was immediately transferred to the neonatal intensive care unit for further evaluation. The hospital notified Child Protective Services.

The effects of drug use in pregnancy take their toll on innocent infants, so many people favor laws that allow a pregnant woman to be tested and treated for substance use without her consent. These people believe that if the pregnant woman does not comply with treatment, she should be jailed. Although there can be little dispute over protecting unborn children from maternal drug abuse, how effective are mandatory testing and threatening a mother with possible jail as preventive measures? Jannke (1994) has questioned the ethics, legality, and effectiveness of these punitive laws.

First of all, is it ethical to test a woman without her consent? Such practices may undermine the relationship of health-care providers with drug-using families. Such families often mistrust medical workers and fear these workers are trying to take their children away. Testing a woman without her consent, with the intent of jailing her, only further reinforces this fear and may lead these women to become more distrustful and ultimately to avoid contact with health providers (Jannke, 1994).

As to the question of legality, it should be noted that many of the women who would be tested for drugs or jailed are African American. Although a study conducted in Florida found little difference in rates of abuse between private insurance patients and those on public assistance, or between white and black clients, providers are less likely to suspect white, middle-class women with health insurance of drug abuse. In fact, a booklet produced by the U.S. Department of Health and Human Services states, "Reports indicate that a pregnant woman's race, ethnicity, and socioeconomic status have an overwhelming impact on whether or not she is screened" (Mitchell, 1993, p. 48). So, poor, ethnic-minority women may be singled out by these laws.

How effective are these laws? Women who use drugs during pregnancy often know the risks to the fetus but are unable to stop the abuse because of the nature of addiction. Threat of prosecution only makes women avoid prenatal care. In fact, as described above, the mother may avoid reporting to the hospital when she is in labor, hoping that a delay will give her some time and reduce the possibility of a positive drug screen.

Is jail the answer? Drugs are readily available in jail, so imprisoning the mother may not protect the fetus at all. Also, adequate medical care for high-risk pregnant women is not provided in most jails. Few prisons provide education for expectant mothers on childbirth and parenting (Jannke, 1994).

What about treatment? Often, even when the mother agrees to drug treatment, the treatment options are inadequate or not available. In fact, only 11% of pregnant addicts get into treatment (Cronin, Ludtke, & Willwerth, 1991). Many treatment programs have a long waiting list, many do not take pregnant women, and those that do often do not allow the woman to keep her other children with her during treatment. For an addicted mother, residential treatment, when available, can mean up to a year's separation from her family. Sometimes her children are placed in foster care. If the woman's partner is also abusing drugs, treatment for him is even more difficult to find. Programs that consider the needs of whole families are rare. Even in communities that do not prosecute and jail pregnant substance abusers, the women often experience neglect from the health care and service delivery systems.

A report entitled "Pregnant, Substance-Using Women," written in 1993 by a panel for the U.S. Department of Health and Human Services, stated, "The Panel does not support the criminal prosecution of pregnant, substance-using women. Furthermore, there is no evidence that punitive approaches work" (Mitchell, 1993, p. 2). This report recommended that individuals who work with addicted mothers should provide counseling and education, drug treatment, and assistance in general living skills.

Maternal Alcohol Abuse

Though the media have given much attention to "crack babies," the leading known preventable cause of irreversible mental retardation in the Western world is a common legal drug: alcohol (Abel & Sokol, 1987). In the past, doctors recognized that some infants were born with an unidentified syndrome of facial abnormalities and behavioral problems. Having no other term to describe this particular set of abnormalities, physicians would enter "FLK" in the infant's chart. These initials did not specify a particular medical diagnosis, but reflected the doctors' bewilderment at the nature of the disorder; FLK stands for "funny-looking kid." Today, this set of abnormalities has been associated with infants born to alcoholic mothers. Mothers who drink heavily during pregnancy may give birth to newborns with the particular set of birth defects now recognized as fetal alcohol syndrome (FAS).

FAS birth defects have lasting consequences. As previously stated, alcohol abuse in pregnancy is the leading known preventable cause of mental retardation. The physical signs include facial abnormalities such as a small head, small eyes or short eye openings, a poorly developed philtrum (that part of the face between the nose and upper lip), a thin upper lip, a short nose, and a flattened midfacial area (Warren, 1985) (see Exhibit 5.4). Children with FAS have problems with learning, attention, memory, and problem solving, along with lack of coordination, impulsiveness, and speech and hearing impairment. Adolescents and adults with FAS exhibit impulsiveness, lack of inhibitions, poor judgment, and a lack of understanding of socially appropriate sexual behavior (Mattson & Riley, 1998). These behavioral characteristics make it difficult for these individuals to hold a job or establish successful peer relationships.

Less severe birth defects that may be related to alcohol use are termed *fetal alcohol effects* (FAE). The

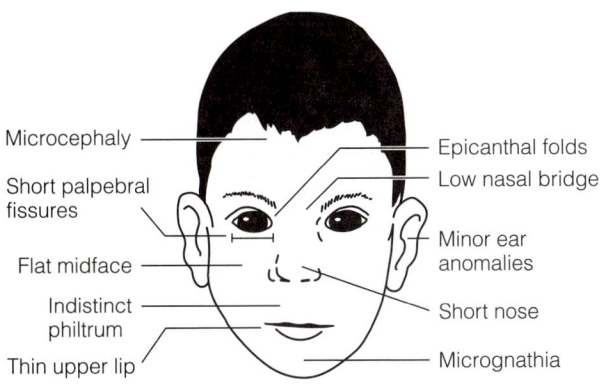

EXHIBIT 5.4 Facial characteristics of fetal alcohol syndrome

characteristics of FAE include low birth weight, irritability, and hyperactivity in the newborn, and short attention span and learning disabilities in the child (Little & Ervin, 1984). Having an abnormality that can be attributed to alcohol use is termed an *alcohol-related birth defect* (ARBD).

Maternal Smoking

Inhaling cigarette smoke increases the level of carbon monoxide in the blood, and in a pregnant woman, this in turn decreases oxygen to the fetus. Smoking increases the risk of prematurity, infant death, miscarriage, and other complications of pregnancy and birth. Women who smoke during pregnancy risk retarding the growth and development of their fetus, often resulting in low-birth-weight infants (Jedrychowski & Flak, 1996). Smoking also has been suspected of causing a higher risk of sudden infant death syndrome (SIDS). Other research suggests that maternal smoking decreases in-utero fetal responsiveness to external stimuli (Azar, 1997a). A growing number of studies now are showing that the effects of smoking during pregnancy may be long-term. Children of smokers are smaller and show problems with cognitive development and educational achievement; Drews, Murphy, Yeargin-Allsopp, and Decofle (1996) have suggested that smoking during pregnancy increases the risk of mental retardation by 50% compared with nonsmoking mothers. Infants of smokers show differences in responsiveness by 1 week of age. Through the preschool years, these children scored lower on verbal tests than did children of nonsmokers (Newman & Buka, 1991).

Maternal Stress

In the *New England Journal of Medicine*, Davidson (1992) stated that we need to assess the role of stress in pregnancy as a contributing factor to premature and low-birth-weight infants. Other studies have shown a significant relationship between IUGR and stress (Goldenberg, 1991). In what exact ways does maternal stress contribute to complications of pregnancy?

A mother's physical response to stress could result in reduced blood flow to the uterus. This reduced blood flow, in turn, could decrease the amount of oxygen and nutrients to the fetus. Fetuses of women under stress exhibit different in-utero movement and heart-rate patterns than fetuses of less stressed women (Azar, 1997a).

More important, however, are the effects that stress can have on the mother's coping responses. Pregnant women may cope with environmental stress by engaging in poor health behaviors such as smoking, drinking, and using drugs—activities that have all been shown to increase the risk of premature birth and low birth weight (Brooks-Gunn, McCormick, & Heagarty, 1988).

Prenatal Testing

Several prenatal tests developed in recent years allow genetic screening during pregnancy. It is now possible to determine before birth the sex of the fetus and whether the fetus has a specific genetic anomaly. The ability to obtain information about the sex and health of the fetus before birth brings up several legal and ethical issues.

Ultrasound is now used almost routinely in prenatal care. During an ultrasound, or sonogram, high-frequency sound waves are passed through the mother's abdomen to form a picture of the developing pregnancy. The procedure is used often during pregnancy, in particular to determine the gestational age of the fetus, the location of the placenta, whether there are multiple pregnancies, and to assess the growth and development of the fetus. Ultrasound can identify anomalies of the fetus and other pregnancy complications.

Another noninvasive procedure is **alpha-fetoprotein blood screening**. This procedure is used to detect **neural-tube defects**. Neural-tube defects are any of the group of congenital conditions involving defects or malformations in the skull or spinal cord, such as spina bifida, an opening in the spinal column. Alpha-fetoprotein (AFP) can leak out of this opening and be absorbed into the mother's bloodstream. Alpha-fetoprotein blood screening is done at sixteen weeks' gestation and detects the presence of AFP in the mother's blood.

A much more invasive procedure is **amniocentesis**. During this procedure, a needle is inserted through the mother's abdomen into the amniotic sac to collect a sample of amniotic fluid. This fluid contains fetal skin cells, which can be grown in a culture for genetic screening. The skin cells are used for a karyotype—a genetic picture of the fetal chromosomes. This procedure can detect chromosomal abnormalities such as Down syndrome and trisomy 13. Amniocentesis can also determine the sex of the fetus.

Amniocentesis is usually performed at fifteen to sixteen weeks' gestation. Growing the cells for genetic testing takes another three weeks. This means that by the time the mother receives the test results, she could be almost halfway through her pregnancy. She may have already felt the baby move. The decision to terminate the pregnancy for genetic reasons is a difficult one at this point, because termination requires a second-trimester abortion. By the time the mother has the abortion, the baby may almost be viable, or able to live outside the womb. Another problem with amniocentesis is the slight risk of spontaneous abortion brought on by the procedure.

In contrast, a **chorionic villus sample (CVS)** can be performed at eight weeks' gestation. In this procedure, the physician inserts a catheter into the uterus through the cervix and obtains a piece of the chorionic villi—the developing placenta. These cells contain the same genetic material as the fetus. Because these cells are growing rapidly, chromosomal test results are available within a couple of days. The decision to terminate the pregnancy can be made early in the first trimester. CVS is thought to have a slightly higher risk of spontaneous abortion than amniocentesis. CVS and amniocentesis are valuable resources for identifying potential birth defects, but these tests pose a number of important ethical and policy dilemmas.

Birth Defects and Ethical Dilemmas

Many parents who find out they are carrying a fetus with a major birth defect choose to have an abortion. This elective abortion of defective fetuses brings up many questions that social workers need to address.

Does this practice of elective abortion mean that living with a disabling condition is now unacceptable? How do these practices reflect our society's attitude toward people with disabilities? For example, there has been a recent increase in "wrongful life" and "wrongful birth" lawsuits allowed by courts. These suits are filed by parents who claim that the physician failed to recommend prenatal testing that would have detected a genetic abnormality. As a result, the parents want to hold the physician responsible for the birth of a child with disability and require the physician to pay damages. Do these actions endorse the notion that defective fetuses should be aborted and that life with a disability is not worth living (Lamb, 1994)?

Street and Soldan (1998) have discussed the many psychosocial issues faced by parents undergoing genetic testing. They found that Rolland's psychosocial typology of chronic illness could also be applied to genetic conditions, because both involve the feature of uncertainty about outcome. Parents faced with the issue of whether to abort a fetus might think about these five factors regarding genetic conditions in making their decision: onset, course, outcome, incapacitation, and uncertainty. *Onset* refers to whether the condition is sudden or gradual. Huntington's disease is an example of a condition that is gradual but increases in severity. *Course* refers to whether a condition stays consistent, changes, or worsens over time. *Outcome*: How will the condition affect the life span of the child? The degree of *incapacitation* is also a factor: What degree of impairment will the child have? Finally, *uncertainty* refers to the unpredictability of the condition, or how much is known or not known about the nature of the condition and the rate of changes that might occur. A social worker might consider these factors when working with parents who have had or are considering genetic testing.

To what extent should prenatal testing be used to determine which characteristics are desirable? In some parts of the world, where male infants are preferred, prenatal testing is used for sex selection. If prenatal sex selection becomes acceptable in the United States, what other undesirable characteristics may be weeded out? A poll of New England couples showed that 11% would abort a fetus predisposed to obesity. How many couples would choose to abort a fetus destined for short stature or low IQ (Lamb, 1994)?

Another question that needs to be addressed concerns who receives prenatal testing. The tests are expensive and may not be available to lower-class families. Will this result in more disabled individuals among the lower classes?

Activists and ethicists urge us to carefully consider these questions concerning the use of prenatal tests before coming to the decision of who does and who does not live. Although prenatal testing procedures can identify serious birth defects, they cannot predict many types of birth complications that have equally serious consequences.

Complications of Birth

Birth complications have been linked with everything from schizophrenia (Verdoux, 1993) and violent crime (Raine, Brennan, & Mednick, 1994) to sleep disorders (Coren & Searleman, 1985) and left-handedness (Van Strien, Bouma, & Bakker, 1987). Other studies have failed to establish conclusively a connection between difficulties of birth and later problems. As we have already stated, some evidence exists, however, that suggests a link between learning disabilities and attention deficit disorder and pregnancy and birth complications. Further research may yet turn up relationships between abnormal development and problems during the birth process, so complications of birth may be an important factor to consider in making an assessment.

One birth complication that has an effect on development is **anoxia**, or insufficient oxygen to the fetus during delivery. Oxygen loss to the fetus can be caused by such problems as maternal blood loss, maternal overmedication, or umbilical cord compression. Lack of oxygen to the fetus during labor can cause fetal distress, which can be detected by an electronic fetal monitor that records the baby's heart rate during labor and birth. When the baby is in distress, the heart rate drops or fluctuates. Lack of oxygen can cause brain damage or, in some instances, death. One consequence of anoxia is cerebral palsy—a condition that can result in movement and speech problems. Even mild reduction in oxygen to the fetus during delivery has been shown to produce problems with early development.

Meconium aspiration can cause problems for the newborn baby. Meconium is the waste material in the baby's bowels at birth. It is black and tarry. If problems occur during delivery, the baby may have a bowel movement into the amniotic fluid during labor. If the baby inhales or aspirates amniotic fluid containing meconium, the baby can have respiratory problems at birth.

Another problem of birth is **malpresentation**. In 95% of deliveries, the fetus is in a head-down, or vertex, position, with the result that the head is the first part of the baby to be born. In 5% of births, however, some other part of the fetus presents for delivery. In a breech presentation, the feet or buttocks of the infant are the first part through the birth canal. Breech presentations carry a higher risk of injury and death for the baby. For this reason, many physicians deliver breech babies by cesarean section. Another presentation that requires a cesarean birth is transverse lie. Here the infant is across the mother's abdomen with a shoulder or arm presenting into the pelvis.

A **prolonged labor** is one lasting more than twenty-four hours for a first-time mother or more than twelve hours for a woman who has previously given birth. Long labors can leave a woman exhausted and dehydrated. The baby faces a risk of intracranial hemorrhage (bleeding in the brain) from prolonged pressure to the head during the long labor. A baby with severe intracranial bleeding can be stillborn or suffer from mental retardation or cerebral palsy.

Recent research shows that labor takes longer for overweight and obese women (NICHD, 2004). "The median labor for overweight women was 7.5 hours, for obese women 7.9 hours, and for normal weight women, 6.2 hours" (NICHD, 2004, p. 2.) Researchers are recommending that pregnant women who are overweight or obese should speak to their treating physician about an appropriate diet and exercise program. Their weight status increases chances for the mother developing gestational diabetes, pregnancy-associated hypertension, and preeclampsia (NICHD, 2004). In addition, overweight women are at increased risk for having a c-section.

Cesarean Section

Jane and Gary expected that their first child's birth would be an uncomplicated vaginal delivery. Gary had actively participated with Jane in childbirth classes. As a graduation present, she had given him a dark blue T-shirt with "Coach" printed on the front. Jane's labor was long and slow. She spent most of her labor in bed, with an epidural for pain relief. She never dilated beyond six centimeters. After eighteen hours of labor, the baby was delivered by cesarean section. Now, six weeks after the birth of a beautiful baby girl, Jane is tired and weepy. In addition, she feels guilty about her sadness because she thinks she should be happy just to have a normal, healthy baby.

In the past, some of the complications of birth could result in fetal death or injury. Today, however, many babies are saved through birth by cesarean section. Though a c-section can be a life-saving solution to a birth complication, the procedure itself carries increased risks for the mother and the baby. A cesarean birth increases the mother's risk of pain, trauma, and surgical complications and has two to four times the risk of maternal mortality as a vaginal birth (Mutryn, 1993).

In addition, some studies have shown that women who give birth by cesarean suffer from depression more than do women who give birth vaginally (Edwards, Porter, & Stein, 1993; Gottlieb & Barrett, 1986). Depression is a common consequence of major surgery (Mutryn, 1993), and a c-section is major surgery. A woman who gives birth by cesarean not only must recover from surgery but also must care for a newborn infant. This experience may leave her feeling tired and drained, and her fatigue and depression may interfere with mother-infant interactions.

Many fathers or support persons now attend cesarean births. It has been said that a c-section is the only circumstance in modern medicine under which an individual watches a loved one undergo major surgery. The support person may be a bit overwhelmed.

C-section births have increased over the past 30 years from around 5% to as much as 35%. This means that, in some hospitals, more than one-third of all babies are delivered surgically. Mutryn (1993) has claimed that, in recent years, because of the increased incidence of surgical births, cesarean delivery has been trivialized. Even childbirth educators describe a cesarean as "just another way to have a baby." This attitude may overlook the fact that surgery is one of life's most frightening experiences. As a surgical procedure, c-sections involve some risks for mothers and possibly for infants. More general neonatal health risks are discussed in the following sections.

Neonatal Complications: The High-Risk Infant

One of the major risk factors for the newborn infant is low birth weight. A low-birth-weight infant is one born weighing less than 2,500 grams, or 5½ pounds. A low birth weight can be the result of **prematurity** (being born before the 38th week of gestation) or intrauterine growth retardation (having some sort of prenatal deprivation that retards growth). In the past, all babies born weighing less than 5½ pounds were considered premature. However, a baby born before 38 weeks to a diabetic mother can weigh 5½ pounds but still be premature and encounter problems associated with early birth. A baby born at 40 weeks weighing less than 5½ pounds is mature but will encounter the problems associated with retarded fetal growth and development.

Intrauterine Growth Retardation (IUGR)

Growth retardation can occur at any point in the pregnancy. A fetus is considered growth retarded or small for gestational age (SGA) if its weight is less than the 10th percentile of the normal weight of an infant at that particular stage of gestational development. A premature baby whose weight is normal for gestational age has low birth weight because of being born too early; but a small-for-gestational-age baby is low birth weight because of abnormal growth. There is evidence that these babies are at risk for perinatal asphyxia, often requiring resuscitation after delivery (Nieto et al., 1998). As we have already seen, this abnormal prenatal growth can be caused by factors such as maternal illness, poor nutrition, and drug and alcohol abuse.

The problem for growth-retarded infants is not just that they are born small; they are small because some sort of prenatal deprivation affected their growth and development. In terms of long-term developmental problems, these children exhibit increased abnormal brain-wave patterns and an increased risk of learning disabilities (Reeder, Mastroianni, & Martin, 1983). In terms of long-term growth improvement, the outcome for growth-retarded infants is good. With appropriate medical care, most of these infants catch up in their growth during the first three months of life and tend to follow normal growth curves by 1 year of age (Vandenbosche & Kirchner, 1998).

Prematurity

Seven percent of births occur before the end of the thirty-seventh week of pregnancy and are classified as premature. Though premature babies may be growing and developing at a normal rate, they face the problems associated with low birth weight as the result of being born too early, such as respiratory difficulties, feeding problems, and jaundice. The lower the birth weight and the earlier the gestational age, the more likely it is that these problems will occur.

Problems Associated with Premature Birth

During the last month of pregnancy, the fetal lungs mature in preparation for birth. A baby born before the lungs are fully mature can suffer from respiratory distress syndrome (RDS). The baby may need supplemental oxygen, which needs to be carefully monitored, because it has been discovered that high oxygen levels can cause blindness (retinopathy of prematurity).

A baby with RDS may need a ventilator to assist with breathing. A baby on a ventilator has a breathing tube placed down his airway, or trachea. If the baby requires this breathing tube for a long period, scarring and narrowing of the airway may occur. If the narrowing becomes severe enough to prevent normal air intake, then to breathe on his own after being removed from the ventilator, the baby will require a tracheostomy. In this procedure, a small opening is made in the baby's throat and a small tube is placed in this opening so that the baby breathes through this tube instead of through the nose or mouth. Taking home a baby with a tracheostomy can be a scary experience for new parents. A baby with a tracheostomy cannot make a sound, so the parents cannot hear their baby cry. Long-term placement of a tracheostomy may interfere with development of speech.

After being removed from a ventilator, a premature baby can experience a respiratory problem called **bronchopulmonary dysplasia (BPD)**. BPD is diagnosed when a baby continues to require oxygen after reaching 36 gestational weeks. BPD develops as a result of lung injury, most often caused by mechanical forces, such as a ventilator (Bank et al., 1999). In other words, premature infants who require a ventilator can sustain lung damage that results in the long-term need for oxygen to ensure adequate respiration. BPD is the leading cause of lung disease in infants in the United States and the third leading cause of lung disease in children (Singer & Yamashita, 1997). There may even be long-term consequences for in-

The birth of a premature infant can be difficult for new parents who are separated from the baby.

fants with BPD. Singer and Yamashita (1997) found BPD in infants to be a significant predictor of poor motor coordination at 3 years of age. Current respiratory therapies are assisting infants with BPD to have better outcomes.

Another breathing problem of premature infants that can cause distress to new parents is apnea, or periods when the baby stops breathing. Apnea is common among premature babies after periods of exertion, such as following a feeding. Babies experiencing apnea may need to be on a monitor to signal when breathing has stopped, so the baby can then be stimulated to resume respiration.

The reflexes of a premature infant are often weak or lacking. In particular, the sucking reflex is not well established until thirty-four weeks' gestation. A baby born before thirty-four weeks, then, may have feeding problems and be unable to nurse or take a bottle. These babies must be fed through a tube passed through their noses, down their throats, and into their stomachs (gavage feeding). The baby then has to learn to suck in order to feed from a bottle or the breast.

Preterm infants have more problems with jaundice than do full-term infants. Before birth, the fetus has extra red blood cells circulating in the blood. After birth, when the baby begins to breathe, these extra red blood cells are not necessary and are broken down in the baby's body. As these cells break down, they produce a byproduct known as bilirubin. In a normal newborn, this bilirubin is broken down by the liver and excreted. A preterm infant's immature liver cannot effectively break down the excess bilirubin, so the substance builds up in the baby's system. Because bilirubin is orange-colored, this buildup results in a yellowish-orange tint to the baby's skin, called jaundice (also known as hyperbilirubinemia). High levels of bilirubin deposited in the infant's brain can lead to a form of brain damage that can result in mental retardation. Babies with jaundice, or hyperbilirubinemia, are usually placed under lights because the light helps break down the bilirubin. A baby under these *bili lights* must wear a mask to protect the eyes.

Developmentally, premature babies need to be assessed according to their expected due date instead of their actual birth date. Therefore, babies born two months early will have the capabilities of newborns when they are two months old. With good care, many of the problems of premature infants discussed up to this point resolve in the first few years after birth, allowing the children to develop normally. But the smaller and more immature the infant, the greater the risk of long-range problems. With the high technology now available in neonatal intensive care units (NICU), smaller and smaller babies are surviving. With good care, 67% of infants born weighing between 750 and 999 grams (1 lb. 10 oz. to 2 lb. 3 oz.) live. What is even more amazing, up to 44% of babies weighing between 500 and 740 grams (1 lb. 2 oz. to 1 lb. 10 oz.) can be saved. What are the long-term developmental consequences of being born so small?

These very small babies run a high risk of central nervous system bleeding or infection, which can result in permanent disabilities such as mental retardation, seizure disorder, and cerebral palsy (Jason & van de Meer, 1989). Sometimes parents and practitioners face the very difficult decision of whether to use high-technology procedures and knowledge to save a very small infant who may later have severe handicaps, or to let the baby die.

Implications for Practice:
The Premature Infant

A premature birth can be a difficult adjustment for new parents. Depending on gestational age and weight, the baby may spend several weeks or months in an isolette, an enclosed infant bed that helps regulate temperature and guard against infection. New parents may feel intimidated by the high-technological and medical atmosphere of the NICU. They may hesitate to interact with a small, fragile infant hooked up to an intravenous line, a feeding tube, and a ventilator. When the parents do interact with the baby, they may find the experience frustrating. It may be hard to attract and keep the baby's attention. Yet too much stimulation can cause the baby to withdraw. Parents need help in learning to read their baby's cues and in learning to know when to interact and when to back off. The combination of an immature nervous system and a lengthy stay in an overstimulating hospital environment may make the baby irritable and difficult to parent (Jason & van de Meer, 1989).

In addition, many premature infants are born to young, poor, uneducated, single mothers. In fact, low-birth-weight births "are often associated with poverty and its cofactors (for example, low maternal education, high unemployment, and teenage motherhood), which are themselves associated with decreases in child well-being" (Fongruey & Brooks-Gunn, 1994). For these infants, it is hard to separate the effects of deficits in the home environment from those of problems caused by prematurity.

Research by Bradley and colleagues (1994) has underscored the importance of the home environment in the development of low-birth-weight children. Overall, the researchers found that low-birth-weight children born into poverty function poorly in all areas of development (Bradley et al., 1994). However, they also found that babies who did well had stimulating toys and materials available, responsive parents who understood and accepted the baby's behavior, and space for play and exploration. The low-birth-weight infant, then, may benefit from a home where parents are sensitive and attentive and provide a rich array of objects and people for the child to interact with (Bradley et al., 1987). ■

Birth Defects and Developmental Disorders

In spite of all of the possible things that can go wrong in the prenatal period and during the birth process, most infants are born normal and healthy. About 3 babies out of 100, however, have some kind of anomaly or malformation at birth. Many of these congenital disorders or anomalies can affect development.

Congenital heart defects include hearts with openings between the chambers and hearts that are malformed. Sometimes heart disease is associated with other genetic anomalies, such as Down syndrome. If the heart defect is severe, it can interfere with growth and development. The baby may need corrective surgery at some point.

Neural-tube defects occur in 1 out of 500 births. A common neural-tube defect is spina bifida, a condition in which one or more vertebrae do not close over the spinal cord, leaving the cord uncovered in a portion of the spinal column. When the cord bulges

Children with Down syndrome, one of the more common chromosomal abnormalities.

through the opening, this increases the risk of fetal death and paralysis.

Several congenital conditions can affect an infant's brain. *Hydrocephalus* is a condition in which there is excess fluid in the baby's head. Because of the pressure of this increased fluid, hydrocephalus can result in mental retardation, paralysis, lack of coordination, and seizures. A shunt can be placed in the head to drain off the excess fluid. Infants with *microcephaly* have a much smaller than normal head. Because of a small brain, these infants can be mentally retarded. In *anencephaly*, the baby lacks all or part of its brain, and the life expectancy of these infants is very short. The question has arisen regarding the ethics of using these infants as donors for organ transplants. Should an infant with no brain who will die in a matter of days or weeks be sacrificed to save the life of another child?

Several chromosomal abnormalities can affect development. The most common is Down syndrome, or trisomy 21, which results from an extra chromosome. Infants born with this disorder are at higher risk of heart defects and increased infant mortality. Babies with Down syndrome also have some degree of mental retardation, but the degree of retardation varies with each child. Early-intervention programs can help these children reach their full potential. Many learn to read, hold jobs, and live in group housing. Babies born with other problems involving extra chromosomes, such as trisomy 13 and trisomy 18, usually do not live beyond six to twelve months.

Metabolic problems include phenylketonuria (PKU). A baby with this condition cannot metabolize a substance known as phenylalanine, found in protein. This substance builds up and can cause mental retardation. For this reason, babies are tested for PKU at birth. Children with this condition must eat a restricted diet and avoid foods containing phenylalanine.

Babies who acquire brain damage from lack of oxygen or intracranial bleeding, either before or during birth, can develop **cerebral palsy**. The major problems with this condition are paralysis, muscle weakness, and lack of coordination. Some children with cerebral palsy also have mental retardation. Many of them, 70–80%, have some combination of speech and hearing problems, visual problems, learning problems, and seizures.

When the Baby Isn't Perfect

The birth of an infant with a disability can initiate a time of grief and loss for new parents. These parents have lost the perfect fantasy baby they dreamed of throughout the pregnancy and must now adjust to the reality of a less-than-perfect infant.

Parents of a child with a disability often go through an initial phase of grief, shock, and denial. Though faced with indisputable medical evidence of their child's condition, many parents attempt to minimize the seriousness of the disability (Jackson, 1985). One mother remembers thinking as the nurse checked her wristband before handing the baby over at discharge, "Please God, let her tell me I have the wrong baby."

As the parents develop a sense of awareness of the problem, they are often overcome by a sense of guilt and failure. They may feel they are being punished for past indiscretions or for wanting the baby to be of a particular sex instead of just a healthy baby. They may agonize over what they could have done to cause the disability. They may feel that they are biological failures for not being able to make a baby "right" (Jackson, 1985).

The sorrow and grief that accompany the birth of a child with a disability are chronic and pervasive (Kowalski, 1985). Parents of a child with a disability are faced with their loss every day. Each new crisis renews the feelings of intense sadness and guilt.

Such a situation increases stress for the family at a time when the family is also faced with added financial burdens. Families can feel lonely and isolated, cut off from former friends and acquaintances. The divorce rate in families with children with mental retardation is three times the national average (Kowalski, 1985). Investigators have found that families with children with developmental disabilities experience problems with adjustment, poor health, and family relations (Schilling, Gilchrist, & Schinke, 1984).

Research indicates that families with children with developmental disabilities need personal coping skills and an adequate social-support network. Personal coping skills include problem-solving abilities, relaxation techniques, and self-praise. Adequate social support includes physical assistance, information, and emotional support. Supportive social networks are associated with increased personal well-being for the parents and enhanced development for the child (Dunst, Trivette, & Cross, 1986).

STUDY TABLE: Biophysical dimension in pregnancy, birth, and the newborn

Biophysical Growth and Development	Conception occurs with the union of sperm and egg in the fallopian tube. From conception to implantation (about two weeks), the fertilized egg is known as a *zygote*. From two to eight weeks, it is an embryo. During the period of the embryo, most major organs and features are formed. At eight weeks, the embryo becomes a fetus. From this time until birth, the fetus grows and puts on weight. The birth process is divided into three stages. The first stage lasts 12–14 hours and ends with the cervix (opening to the womb) fully dilated (opened) and the woman ready to push the baby down the birth canal. The second stage is the actual birth and can last from minutes to three hours. The third stage is the delivery of the placenta, or afterbirth. Many births involve some form of pain-relieving medication, but long-term effects of these medications are still unknown. A normal newborn weighs between 5½ and 9½ pounds. Full-term pregnancy lasts 38–41 weeks. The Apgar score is an objective exam of the newborn's adjustment to life.
Biophysical Strengths and Hazards	Expectant mothers who are thin, in good health, and aware of potential biological risks in the family are less likely to experience complications. Parents with good health practices make easier transitions to the changes, such as in eating and sleep, needed to support health during pregnancy. The mother's biophysical structure determines how she transitions through each phase of the pregnancy process. Planning involves consideration of risks and benefits associated with the biological timing of the pregnancy. What are the benefits of having a baby at a particular time period? In early phases of adulthood, women tend to be more fertile and have more physical resources to handle the stress associated with the pregnancy process. Complications of pregnancy may affect child development. These complications may include persistent vomiting, vaginal bleeding, toxemia or preeclampsia, and intrauterine growth retardation (IUGR). Several environmental factors may affect pregnancy outcome, including maternal age (mothers under 18 or over 35), multiple births, poor nutrition, illness, drug use, alcohol use, cigarette use, and stress. Alcohol use during pregnancy may cause the child to suffer from fetal alcohol syndrome (FAS), the leading known preventable cause of mental retardation in the Western world. Several tests screen for fetal problems, including ultrasound, alpha-fetoprotein blood screening, amniocentesis, and chorionic villus sample (CVS). Birth complications also may affect later development. Such complications include anoxia, meconium aspiration, malpresentation, and a prolonged labor. Birth complications can necessitate birth by cesarean section (birth through an abdominal incision). A major risk factor for newborns is low birth weight, either from intrauterine growth retardation (prenatal deprivation) or prematurity (birth before 38 weeks). Premature babies may face problems with breathing, feeding, and jaundice. Birth defects that may affect development include heart defects, neural-tube defects, chromosomal abnormalities, phenylketonuria, and cerebral palsy.

CONCEPT MAP

PSYCHOLOGICAL DIMENSION

Cognitive Development and Information Processing

True or False?

- Psychosocial development is a continuous process from about the twelfth week of intrauterine life through the preschool years.
- There is a high correlation between intrauterine fetal activity and a newborn's level of activity.
- Babies of stressed mothers have higher levels of fetal activity and exhibit more problems after birth than babies of nonstressed mothers.
- Mothers with a fetus who becomes very active at bedtime should place a flashlight under the covers and turn it on.
- A fetus prefers Mozart to the Rolling Stones.
- Fetuses of all cultures really like the music of Boy George.
- A newborn responds to its mother's voice.

Surprisingly enough, recent research indicates that all the preceding statements are true. And yes, researchers have found that individual fetuses, not yet born into any culture, really do prefer the music of Boy George (St. James, 1987). It was once thought that before birth the fetus could not experience sensation, emotion, learning, personality, or thought. New ways of studying fetal behavior, however, have revolutionized understanding of the prenatal period. Advancements in ultrasound, intrauterine photography, and measurement of fetal movement and heart rate, as well as the survival of infants at earlier and earlier stages of development in neonatal intensive care nurseries, have provided valuable insight into prenatal behavior. Information is gained through ultrasound; by recording changes in fetal movement, heart rate, and breathing motions; and by noting changes in swallowing and sucking behaviors in response to stimulation. Noting the responses of infants as early as twenty-four weeks' gestation in an NICU has provided information on the behavior of the fetus during the last sixteen weeks of intrauterine development.

Because of this new information, psychosocial development is considered to be a continuous process from the twelfth week of intrauterine life through the preschool years. And enough research now exists to allow us to look at the unborn child's various responses and capabilities.

There is much evidence that a fetus responds to various types of stimulation. For instance, the fetus has been observed to react to invasive obstetrical procedures. During amniocentesis, doctors have noted the fetus to respond by drawing away from the needle, decreasing breathing motions, and exhibiting an erratic heartbeat. Also, during intrauterine blood transfusions, doctors have noted signs of fetal distress, including vigorous body and breathing movements and increased fetal cortisol and B-endorphin levels, an apparent sign of hormonal stress response to needle invasion (Giannakoulopoulos et al., 1994).

The fetus also responds to light. Shining a bright light on a pregnant woman's abdomen causes an increase in fetal heart rate. In fact, it is now believed that the fetus may see light through the abdomen as a rosy glow. Many women report that the fetus becomes more active at bedtime; this increase in activity could be due to the darkness in the womb when the woman turns out the light and goes to bed. Placing a flashlight under the covers could serve as a nightlight for the fetus (Schuster & Ashburn, 1992).

The fetus seems to respond to touch. By the seventeenth week of gestation, almost all parts of the fetal body will react to being stroked by a hair. Many fetuses will kick back at a spot on a pregnant woman's abdomen when it is pressed.

In addition, babies in the womb show a preference for certain tastes. Fetuses will increase their swallowing of amniotic fluid when drops of a sweet-tasting substance are introduced into the womb, and they will stop swallowing when a bitter substance is introduced (Chamberlain, 1994b).

Communication

Much anecdotal evidence suggests that a fetus responds to sound. When a pregnant woman laughs or coughs, fetal movement increases. Many women report that the fetus is startled by noises such as a door slamming. Women at loud concerts or viewing violent movies report increased fetal activity. Researchers have found that fetuses seem to become more active in response to loud rock music, whereas classical music has an apparently calming effect (St. James, 1987). Research has shown that at twenty-six weeks' gestation, a fetus will respond to a sound vibration. After several repeats of the sound stimulus, the fetus will stop responding. This failure to respond after repeated stimulation is evidence of the ability of the fetus to habituate—a form of learning (Chamberlain, 1994a).

Fetal learning ability is also evidenced by the fact that a newborn responds to the mother's voice over another woman's and to music heard in the womb. Newborns also prefer to hear their native language (Mehler, cited in Chamberlain, 1994a). The fetus hears these familiar sounds, learns to distinguish them from others, and prefers them after birth. In fact, studies by DeCasper and Fifer (1980) found that newborns who had heard, in utero, their mothers read *The Cat in the Hat* twice a day, preferred that story over *The King, the Mice and the Cheese*, which they had not heard.

Attitudes and Emotions

The mother's emotional state also seems to affect the fetus. Some evidence suggests that depressed or highly anxious women give birth to children with lower birth weights, higher levels of crying, and more neurological problems (Creno, 1994). Excessive crying and inconsolability of newborns has been linked to the mother's score on a depression scale during pregnancy (Zuckerman, cited in Chamberlain, 1994a).

Chamberlain (1994b) reported that "current research reveals prenatal pain, preferences, interests, learning, memory, aggressive behavior, fear, crying, smiling and affection.... Observation from conception to birth reveals a continuum of prenatal and postnatal behavior in which sensory, motor, emotional and cognitive features are constantly intertwined" (p. 19).

A small but growing number of parents and mental-health professionals now believe that a child's emotional health begins at conception. These parents and professionals believe that meditation and communication with the fetus increase bonding and result in the child's better emotional well-being (Creno, 1994). Whether or not these beliefs hold up under close examination, they can be used in work with expectant parents.

The practitioner can encourage the parents to talk, play music, read, and sing to their unborn child. Parents who see that the baby will kick back at a spot pressed on the mother's abdomen can experience the fetus as a real, interactive being. These activities can help the parents relate to the baby and may increase their level of attachment to their child. Some researchers believe that this early attachment may help prevent later child abuse.

Researchers have also come up with some ingenious ways to determine what very young infants prefer. Here's how DeCasper and his associates found out that babies prefer sounds heard in the womb. In one of their studies, these researchers had pregnant women read a passage from *The Cat in the Hat* twice a day during the last six weeks of pregnancy. When the baby was born, the researchers set up an experiment using a pacifier hooked up to a tape recorder. By sucking more quickly or slowly, the baby could control what was heard through a set of earphones. Some of the babies heard *The Cat in the Hat* when they sucked fast and heard *The King, the Mice, and the Cheese* when they sucked slowly. For some babies, this was reversed so that they heard *The Cat in the Hat* when they sucked slowly. The researchers found that the babies would change their rate of sucking to hear the familiar story. This was true even when a woman other than the baby's mother read the story. In similar studies, newborns would vary the rate of sucking to hear their mother's voice, their native language, and certain types of music.

Researchers have also devised a method using sucking to determine what an infant likes to look at. In these studies, an infant sucks on an artificial nipple hooked up to a slide projector. Whenever the infant sucks, a new picture is projected. So, if the infant wants to look at a particular picture, he or she quickly learns to stop sucking. The researchers can gauge an infant's interest in a picture from the length of time the infant pauses in sucking to look at it.

Social Cognition and Regulation

At birth, a newborn infant is sensitive and responsive. During the first hour after delivery, the baby is usually in a state of quiet alertness and spends most of this time quietly listening and looking around with eyes wide open. A newborn can focus on objects about eight to twelve inches away—the distance from a mother's arms, cradling the infant against her, to her face. In fact, studies have shown that newborns prefer looking at contrasting, complex patterns with curves—especially faces. Newborns will orient toward a sound, and they prefer high-pitched sounds, such as a female voice. They recognize their mother's voice and prefer it to that of another woman. Newborns can discriminate tastes and prefer sweet over salty, acidic, or bitter. A 6-day-old baby knows its mother's smell and can distinguish her breast pad from another woman's.

Infants interact with their environment and begin learning from birth, and perhaps even earlier, as we have discussed. Research shows that a fetus is capable of basic types of learning. Infant preferences such as those mentioned above (mother's voice and specific foods) may develop in utero (Azar, 1997b). Although researchers do not suggest that parents should begin teaching their babies prenatally, they do point out the importance of prenatal care for the baby's physical and cognitive development.

Newborn infants can imitate facial expressions such as sticking out the tongue. They also move in response to speech in a sort of rhythmic dance. In studies, 1-day-old infants were trained to turn their heads to the right upon hearing a bell, for a reward of sugar water. They learned to discriminate the bell from a buzzer and not to turn at the sound of the buzzer. They were then trained to turn for the buzzer and not the bell (Klaus & Klaus, 1985).

Newborn States

A newborn infant spends most of its time in one of six states. Ten percent of each 24 hours is spent in the quiet alert state, listening and looking around. This time provides a good opportunity for making eye contact and interacting with an infant. The infant also may be in an active alert state—moving, looking around, and making small sounds. This state occurs when the infant begins to get hungry or fussy. When really hungry or uncomfortable, the infant enters the crying state—not at all hard to recognize. After feeding and before falling asleep, the infant is in the drowsiness state—relaxed and moving a little with eyes half-closed and unfocused. Then the newborn has two periods of sleep, which alternate every 30 minutes. In *quiet sleep*, the baby is relaxed, moves little, and breathes regularly. During *active sleep*, the baby's eyes move under the eyelids and may even flutter open; the baby moves around, making faces and breathing rapidly. This state of sleep is also referred to as rapid eye movement (REM) and is comparable to adult REM sleep, in which dreaming occurs, although it is not known whether infants dream.

An infant spends most of its time in sleep states, though sometimes it does not seem that way to tired new parents. Infants also use sleep to control their environment. When overstressed or overstimulated, they cope by going to sleep.

Newborn Reflexes

Babies at birth are equipped with many reflexes and survival skills. When placed face down, they will turn their head to the side or will turn away from something obstructing their breathing. If a scarf is placed over their face, infants will swipe at it with their hands and arms in an effort to remove the scarf. If you touch the side of a baby's face, the baby will turn toward the touch and open its mouth, displaying the rooting reflex. By touching the appropriate side of an infant's face, a breast-feeding mother can get the baby to turn toward her breast and open its mouth in preparation for feeding. Infants also have sucking and swallowing reflexes.

When pricked on the foot, babies will withdraw the limb to avoid the prick. When placed in an upright position with feet touching a hard surface, infants will place one foot in front of the other in a walking pattern. The crawling reflex is similar: When placed on their stomach, infants will push against something placed next to their feet. Babies also have a palmar grasp reflex and so will grasp hold of a finger or an object placed against their palm. When pulled to a sitting position, babies will open their eyes. This is a good way to wake a sleepy baby for a feeding. When startled, babies exhibit the *Moro reflex*—arching their back, throwing out their arms, and grasping with their fingers. When stroked on the bottom of the foot, babies exhibit the *Babinski reflex*, fanning out their toes. The tonic neck reflex, or fencing reflex, occurs in the following way. To help prevent the baby's head from falling, babies' neck muscles are linked to the babies' arms. So, when babies turn their head to the side, as happens when they lie on their back, they extend the arm and leg on that side while flexing the arm and leg on the opposite side. If you look closely at babies in this position, you will see that one hand is now directly in their line of sight. In fact, one of the first moving objects babies study closely is their hand. So regardless of the evolutionary significance of this reflex, by turning the head to the side and extending the arm, a baby has something interesting to look at.

The Brazelton Neonatal Assessment Scale

The **Brazelton Neonatal Assessment Scale (BNAS)** can be used with infants up to 1 month of age to assess such items as the newborn's muscle tone and reflexes, as well as response to and control of stimulation (see Exhibit 5.5). For instance, the practitioner pulls the baby to a sitting position and notes whether she holds her head steady or lets it fall back; or the practitioner holds the baby upright on a table to elicit the walking reflex. In another test, the practitioner rings a bell to see whether the baby will turn toward the sound. Then the practitioner rings the bell to see how long it takes the baby to habituate and stop turning toward the bell. In all, the baby is evaluated on thirty-seven behavioral items and eighteen neurological reflexes.

The exam is especially helpful in looking at how babies use different responses and states of consciousness to control their reactions to environmental stimulation. A baby who has had too much stimulation may respond by averting his or her gaze,

EXHIBIT 5.5 Brazelton Neonatal Assessment Scale

Items Assessed	Examples	Scoring
Neurological Items		
Elicited reflexes and movements	Plantar grasp Hand grasp Ankle clonus Babinski Standing Automatic walking Crawling Tonic neck reflex Moro Rooting Sucking Passive movements of both legs and both arms	These neurological items are rated on a three-point scale for low, medium, and high intensity of response; asymmetry and absence are also noted.
Behavioral Items		
Specific behaviors observed or elicited	Focusing and following an object Reaction to an auditory stimulus Reaction to persons Reaction to a voice Reaction to a person's face and voice	These behavioral items are rated on a nine-point scale. The midpoint of the scale denotes the expected behavior of a 3-day-old normal baby.
General behaviors observed	Degree of alertness Motor maturity Cuddliness Consolability with intervention Peak of excitement Irritability Amount of startles Self-quieting activity Hand-to-mouth facility Number of smiles	

falling asleep, or crying. The practitioner can help the parents understand their infant by pointing out the baby's needs and preferences in interactions. The practitioner can frame the baby's response in a positive light: "Look at how she is telling you she has had enough; that's amazing." The parents can learn to look for signs that the baby is stressed or that the baby is ready for more interaction, and they can learn to vary the level of stimulation to make the interaction pleasant for both parents and baby.

Implications for Practice: Using the BNAS

Several studies have highlighted the benefits of using the Brazelton Neonatal Assessment Scale with new parents. After participating in the BNAS, mothers of high-risk infants show more responsiveness to their babies (Widmayer & Field, 1980). Other studies have shown that use of the assessment increases the parents' confidence in their caregiving abilities, increases the effectiveness of parent-child interactions, and increases the parents' understanding of their newborn's behavior (Myers, 1982). Fathers who participate in the assessment have shown more involvement in the care of their babies and more confidence in their parenting skills (Myers, 1982). Some studies tentatively conclude that use of the BNAS increases later cognitive development in infants (Tedder, 1991).

The assessment is inexpensive, and parents seem to enjoy participating. Some hospitals use the BNAS as part of their discharge teaching for new parents. Use of the assessment is a good way to introduce new parents to the individuality of their baby and to help them appreciate their newborn as a unique human being with strengths and resources.

Psychological Strengths and Hazards

In the past, hospital routine separated mother and infant at birth. During the hospital stay, they were reunited every four hours for a feeding. Then, in 1976, pediatricians John Kennel and Marshall Klaus published a study indicating that mothers who received extra contact with their infants beginning immediately after birth exhibited better mothering skills than did mothers who received the routine hospital mother-infant contact. These pediatricians concluded that human mothers experienced a **sensitive period** just after birth for bonding with their infants in the same way that other species, such as goats, cows, and sheep, do.

Over the years, many articles have been published on the importance of early mother-infant contact. These findings have been important in changing hospital birthing practices to allow more contact between mothers and babies. In most hospitals now, healthy, full-term infants are handed to their mothers at birth for skin-to-skin contact. Face-to-face contact and breast-feeding are encouraged immediately after delivery. Many clinicians involve new parents in newborn examinations such as the BNAS in an effort to enhance parent-child interactions by introducing the parents to their baby's characteristics. Nurses in the NICU are trained to encourage interactions with premature and sick infants and their families. Some believe that early bonding can reduce child abuse and neglect.

These ideas of early contact helped change the way women give birth, but have these ideas set up unrealistic expectations for new families? What implications does this bonding issue have for the woman who has an emergency C-section and is not conscious immediately after birth? Or for the woman who lives in a remote area of an Indian reservation and has no transportation to go to the NICU for regular visits with her infant? Or for the woman who adopts a much-wanted infant when the baby is several months old?

Some practitioners now believe that the importance of early bonding should not be overemphasized to the exclusion of other social and emotional factors that can affect the mother-infant relationship (Eyer, 1994). For example, some accepted bonding practices may be in conflict with childbearing practices and rituals of certain cultures (Symanski, 1992). In some cultures, other female family members assume the major care of the newborn while the new mother recovers from giving birth. In some Native American and Hispanic cultures, women do not attempt breast-feeding for the first two to three days postpartum, until their mature breast milk "comes in." And, for cultural reasons, some mothers may not engage in extended eye contact with their newborns.

Research has failed to show that early contact has any long-term benefits for forming attachments (Goldberg, 1983; Grusec & Lytton, 1988). In fact, many researchers now believe that forming an attachment is an ongoing process and that the immediate postpartum period is not the only opportunity for establishing lifelong ties. Mothers of premature infants or adopted babies can and do love and care for their infants. And although evidence exists that early interventions such as introducing the baby to the mother by doing the BNAS improves subsequent mother-infant interactions, this immediate postpartum period does not represent the only opportunity to enhance family relationships. Finally, early bonding is not the magical answer to child abuse and neglect. Bonding should not be overemphasized at the cost of dealing with the complex social and emotional problems of the family, such as poverty and social isolation (Eyer, 1994, p. 90).

The Baby's Experience of Birth

The use of medications has made labor and delivery less painful for the mother, but to what extent have obstetrical interventions made the process more painful for the baby? Potentially painful procedures for the infant include internal fetal monitoring, in which an electrode is placed under the baby's scalp, and fetal-blood scalp sampling, in which blood is taken from the baby's head during delivery. Babies born by forceps delivery often have forceps marks on their faces for several hours after birth. Babies delivered vaginally often have elongated heads and facial bruising and swelling caused by the birth process. Is being squeezed through a small opening into a bright, cold world traumatic for the baby? What effect, if any, does birth trauma have on later development?

In 1929, Otto Rank described birth as a traumatic event that affected an individual's ability to cope with stress later in life. In particular, he believed that a long, complicated labor led to an anxious and neurotic adult. In 1975, Frederick LeBoyer, a French obstetrician, wrote a book called *Birth without Violence*, in which he advocated reducing the trauma of birth. At that time, infants were routinely delivered in brightly lit, cold operating rooms. After birth, the baby was struck to stimulate breathing and often was separated from the mother for several hours. LeBoyer suggested that the newborn receive gentle handling for the first fifteen to thirty minutes of life. In the LeBoyer method, the infant is born in a quiet, warm, dimly lit setting. The physician places the newborn on the mother's abdomen and waits until the cord stops pulsing before cutting it. Shortly after birth, the baby is given a warm bath to simulate the amniotic fluid of the uterine environment.

The benefits of a gentle birth, however, are questionable. It is difficult to regulate the temperature of the bath, and it is hard for the physician and nurses to see in a dimly lit room. In addition, there is no evidence that these gentle techniques result in a happier, more well-adjusted child. One study looked at 385 neonates at a hospital in Quebec and found no evidence that gentle birth techniques or other perinatal circumstances, such as use of medication or delivery by c-section, had any effect on infant temperament in the first year of life (Maziade, 1987).

Despite the controversy over the benefits of gentle birth, many hospitals and physicians have adopted some of these techniques for routine births. As was previously described, in many hospitals, babies are born in homelike birthing rooms. Physicians no longer strike the infant to start its breathing, and, immediately after delivery, the baby is placed on the mother's abdomen. The mother can ask for a delay in administering silver nitrate or erythromycin drops to the baby's eyes to facilitate eye contact in the minutes following birth. The baby is often weighed and examined in a warm bed with the mother and father watching. Hospital procedures now encourage early contact between the new parents and the baby. But most hospitals do not give the baby a bath until several hours after birth.

Implications for Practice: The Birth Experience and Development

The birth process may be beneficial to the baby. The contractions of labor help clear the lungs of mucus; babies who are born by cesarean section have more respiratory difficulties than do babies born vaginally. One study suggests that the increase in catecholamines—presumably caused by the stress of birth—enhances the neonate's chance of survival (Lagercrantz, 1986). However, some therapists believe that prenatal trauma and birth trauma have a profound effect on psychological development. Some research has suggested that a relationship exists between near-death experiences at birth and later suicide, and between barbiturate and opiate use in labor and later drug addiction (Jacobson, 1987; Roedding, 1991). Although these notions are controversial, you may still find it helpful to note the method of delivery and occurrence of any birth trauma when making an assessment. ■

The NICU Experience

What are the long-term developmental consequences of spending the first three months of life in an NICU? Do the stresses of painful procedures, separation from parents, and overstimulation have an effect on later personality development? At this point, there are no clear answers to these questions.

Some studies have shown that infants who spent time in special-care nurseries were at higher risk for child abuse (Lynch, Roberts, & Gordon, 1976). This increase in risk was attributed to the fact that the infant and parents were separated and did not form an attachment. Although Klaus and Kennel (1976) emphasized the importance of early contact for bonding in the postpartum period, other studies have failed to establish the existence of this "sensitive period." However, numerous studies have shown the importance of touch for the premature infant (Harrison,

Leeper, & Yoon, 1991; Harrison & Woods, 1991). Parental touch results in increased weight gain, a better-developed nervous system, and more rapid development. Other studies have indicated that the high levels of stress and stimulation in the NICU affect the infant's blood oxygen level and contribute to chronic lung disease. The increased level of stimulation to the premature infant brain may also affect early brain development (Als et al., 1994).

Implications for Practice: Changes in NICU Practices

NICUs now allow more parent-infant interaction. NICU staff are encouraged to promote parental involvement in the baby's care. An innovative concept in the care of premature infants is Kangaroo Care. Instead of spending most of the time in an isolette, the baby lies in skin-to-skin contact with the mother or father's chest while receiving NICU care. Proponents of Kangaroo Care claim that this procedure improves the baby's temperature regulation, heart rate, breathing patterns, weight gain and growth, behavioral states, emotional states, and interactions with parents (Ludington-Hoe & Golant, 1993).

A concept for reducing the high levels of stress and stimulation in preterm infant care is individualized developmental care (Als et al., 1994). In this approach, nurses are specially trained to recognize signs of stress (changes in skin color, pauses in breathing, finger splaying, arching, averting gaze) in premature babies and to help the infant with self-calming techniques. For instance, babies are placed in a flexed position for sleep to promote restfulness, and they are comforted before and after taxing or painful procedures. Babies are allowed to sleep, wake, and feed on their own individual schedules. The neonatal unit is kept relatively dark and quiet. Special equipment, such as a hammock, a soft nipple on a terrycloth strip, and terrycloth bunting, is also used to help soothe the infant. Researchers found that these measures resulted in calmer infants with better medical and developmental outcomes than did routine care.

Multiple-Gestation Births

The experience of having a baby is thrilling yet challenging. Parents may feel excited yet wonder if they will be able to live up to the tasks of parenting. Parents have these feelings when they come home from the hospital with one baby; imagine what it would be like to come home with two, three, or more babies. With multiple-gestation births on the rise, this situation is becoming a reality for more and more families.

Follow-up work with families having multiple births indicates that parents often experience more stress and depression than do families with singleton infants (Wilcox et al., 1996). Leonard (1998) has suggested that as many as 25% of parents, particularly mothers, experience depression or anxiety disorders, including panic attacks and obsessive-compulsive disorder. Such disorders obviously affect the parent; however, they also affect the infants. Studies show that infants of depressed mothers have increased heart rates, decreased muscle tone, and more sleeping and eating disturbances than infants of nondepressed mothers (Leonard, 1998).

A social worker can assist families of multiple-gestation infants by providing a nonjudgmental environment for parents to talk about their experiences. In some situations, the social worker may need to discuss seeking mental-health services that may include appropriate medications (Leonard, 1998).

STUDY TABLE: Psychological dimension in pregnancy, birth, and the newborn

Cognitive Development and Information Processing	Research indicates that the fetus responds to stimulation. The fetus can see, hear, taste, and respond to touch.
Communication	Newborns recognize their mother's voice, indicating fetal learning in utero.
Attitudes and Emotions	A woman's emotional state affects the fetus. Some professionals now believe that a child's emotional health begins at conception and that prenatal experiences affect emotional development.
Social Cognition and Regulation	Newborns interact with and respond to their environment. They recognize their mother's voice and her smell. They imitate facial expressions, and they can learn. Newborns experience several states, ranging from quiet alertness to fussiness to

	sleep. Babies also are equipped with reflexes and survival skills. The Brazelton Neonatal Assessment Scale measures a baby's responses to stimuli and ability to regulate those responses.
Psychological Strengths and Hazards	In the past, many experts believed that there was a sensitive period for mother-infant bonding in the first few hours after birth. This belief led to changes in hospital practices. However, many people now feel that the first few hours after birth are not so critical and that bonding is an ongoing process. Gentle birthing procedures were developed by LeBoyer to make the birth process less traumatizing for the baby, but the benefits of gentle birth are questionable. The long-term effects of spending the first weeks or months of life in a neonatal intensive care unit are still unknown, but many NICUs now encourage parent-infant interaction and developmental care procedures.

CONCEPT MAP

SOCIAL DIMENSION

Families, Groups, Communities, and Support Systems

Each child is born into a family environment. What effect does that environment have on development? What is necessary for optimal development? Research by Bradley (1987) indicated that stimulation and support are the most important requirements in the home. New babies need parents who respond to them and talk to them. They need a structured, safe home with stimulating play and interesting toys. And new babies especially need a small group of adults who are warm and nurturing and eager to meet the infants' needs. (The next chapter will explore infants and families in more detail.)

Prenatal Intervention Programs: Every Birth a Healthy One

Adequate prenatal care is vital in ensuring the best pregnancy outcome. Yet in many poor communities, access to health care is still a problem (Brooks-Gunn, McCormick, & Heagarty, 1988). Barriers to health care in poor neighborhoods include the large number of pregnant adolescents, the high number of non-English-speaking clients, and the prevalence of inadequate literacy skills. In addition, cultural ideas about health-care practices may be hard to overcome, so that even when health care is available, pregnant women may not understand the need for early and regular prenatal care.

How, then, do we encourage pregnant women to seek care? One answer is to set up programs that use indigenous layworkers to recruit pregnant women into prenatal care. The idea behind such programs is that community members can have more influence on the health practices of their neighbors than can a health-care professional. An example of this type of prenatal outreach program is Woman to Woman, in Tucson, Arizona. This program uses trained lay health-care workers in disadvantaged neighborhoods to locate and educate expectant mothers. These layworkers, or *promotoras*, are volunteers who receive 40 hours of training. Following the formal training period, the promotoras attend regular group meetings for ongoing training, case review, and support. Outreach workers recruit clients in the community by distributing flyers, putting up posters, and setting up booths at health fairs and other neighborhood events. After a woman is enrolled in the program, other workers visit her in her home to offer emotional support; help her get to medical and agency appointments, prenatal education, and information; help her make contact with community resources; and help her obtain services and information on problem-solving skills. Ideally, outreach workers in these programs can overcome some of the barriers to prenatal care in poor communities and help get better care for their neighbors.

Postpartum Early-Intervention Programs

Many new families may be facing less-than-ideal conditions, and few programs exist to help them. After an uncomplicated vaginal birth, if the mother isn't bleeding and the baby is stable, both are discharged from the hospital to home after a forty-eight-hour stay, whether or not they actually have a home. These new families can be dealing with problems such as homelessness, domestic violence, stress, poverty, and unemployment. A two-day hospital stay does not allow much time to deal with these problems, and unfortunately, taking a baby home to such an environment increases the risk of abuse and neglect (Belsky, Gilstrap, & Rovine, 1984).

Some researchers believe that early-intervention programs that include home visitation can greatly benefit new families at risk for abuse and neglect. Evidence suggests that these programs improve poor children's cognitive development and school performance (Ramey & Ramey, 1998b) and reduce the incidence of delinquent behavior and conduct disorder (Fongruey & Brooks-Gunn, 1994; Zigler, Taussig, & Black, 1992). Seitz and colleagues (1985) found that, ten years after conducting a comprehensive early-intervention program using home visitation, lasting positive outcomes could be observed in parental socioeconomic status, children's behavior and social adjustment, and parent-child relationship in comparison with a control group.

An example of a program that includes home visitation is Healthy Families Arizona (LeCroy, Ashford, Krysik, & Milligan, 1996). Healthy Start/Healthy Families began as a three-year demonstration project in Hawaii in 1985, with the primary goal of supporting the family's optimal functioning. Results from the Hawaii program showed that, out of the 241 intervention families, none had reports of child abuse or neglect.

The Arizona program screens families at the time of an infant's birth for risk factors that can cause high stress levels. Families at risk for abuse and neglect are then visited weekly by paraprofessional workers. The workers attempt to reduce each family's stress level by providing support, assisting parents to identify needs and solve problems, and coordinating with community services appropriate to the family's needs. Practical assistance is provided for obtaining food, housing, diapers, utilities, child care, and transportation.

The workers also seek to strengthen family functioning. They provide information and activities designed to improve the parent-child relationship and enhance parents' understanding of child development and appropriate discipline techniques. The worker encourages parents to provide the child with adequate nurturance and stimulation and helps parents find appropriate toys and other play materials.

The family support worker assists parents in developing social supports, managing stress and anger, and developing skills to avoid and resolve crises. The worker maintains contact with the family until the target child is 5 years old and ready to attend school. Other interventions address specific target groups with high-risk characteristics, such as adolescent mothers.

Adolescent Mothers

My inner strengths are like when I make a goal, I always complete it. It's just something that I am real good at. And when I got pregnant, I—I wasn't thinking of myself anymore, I just was thinking of my daughter. And I did not want to be—I knew I was a statistic already, but I did not want to be one of the ones that was looked down on. I wanted to be one that you could look towards. You know it's already done, then let's see where we go on from there. Let's not just look towards the bad.

—V., an adolescent mother

In American society, adolescent pregnancies typically have been seen as social tragedies and the product of a spiraling intergenerational cycle. Adolescents have been described as emotionally unstable with poor decision-making skills and school failures, as well as being considered burdens on the country's resources due to their financial dependency. Research has focused on the problems of adolescent mothers but has not dealt as much with their strengths and resilience.

Who are the adolescents who are able to successfully adjust to their roles as mothers? What characteristics help them succeed as both students and mothers? Interviews with "successful" adolescent mothers have identified major areas of strength and resilience. These teens were found to have insight or a healthy realism about their situations and were able to recognize their weaknesses without giving up. They were proactive, taking charge of their lives and using the resources available to them in the community. Relationships also played a large role in the teens' success. Specifically noted were strong relationships with parents, families, teachers, peers, and the baby's father.

These findings clearly are not meant to encourage pregnancy in adolescent girls, but they do provide an interesting framework that could be included in parenting and intervention programs. Perhaps the outcomes for many teen mothers could be improved if they learned to focus on their strengths rather than on the reasons they are destined to fail.

Multicultural and Gender Considerations

Up to this point, we have looked thoroughly at the biological birth of the infant. But many cultures include another aspect of birth—the social birth of the child as a new member of the community. In fact, many cultural and ethnic groups have specific rites or ceremonies that welcome the child into the group. For instance, in many cultures, during a special ceremony, someone other than the parents receives the child into the society and expresses the desire to help raise him or her. In some cultures, godparents accept responsibility for the child. During a baptismal ceremony, an entire church congregation welcomes the child and vows to oversee the teaching and nurturing of the infant. In some cultures, circumcision is used as a birth ceremony. Removal of the foreskin of the penis is a symbolic act that establishes the child as a member of a particular culture or religion. Other cultures may have naming ceremonies to welcome the child into the community. In some Native American naming ceremonies, the new infant is held up to the rising sun, as described in the following passage by Byrd Baylor (1977/1978):

And high on a mesa edge in Arizona they were holding a baby toward the sun. They were speaking the child's new name so the sun would hear and know that child. It had to be sunrise. And it had to be that first sudden moment. That's when all the power of life is in the sky. (p. 8)

Infant Mortality: The African American–White Disparity

Although medical advances have reduced the overall infant mortality rate in the United States, the current rate is still higher than that in many other developed nations. This variation is due in part to the powerful racial disparities that exist in U.S. infant mortality rates. In 1996, the infant mortality rate for white infants was 6.1 per 1,000, whereas the rate for African American infants was more than twice as high, at 14.1 per 1,000 (National Center for Health Statistics, 1998). What factors are causing this alarming disparity?

For white infants, the leading cause of death is congenital anomalies, whereas for African American infants, it is low birth weight. Although many consider poverty and lack of prenatal care to be contributing factors for low birth weight, after controlling for sociodemographic factors, the proportion of low-birth-weight babies is still twice as high for African Americans as for whites (Eberstadt, 1991).

Interestingly, several studies have found that the Hispanic infant mortality rate is as low as or, in some instances, lower than Caucasian infant mortality, even though Hispanics tend to have a lower socioeconomic status, have less education, and encounter language and cultural barriers that make them three times less likely to receive prenatal care than non-Hispanics (Council on Scientific Affairs, 1991; Furino & Munoz, 1991; Rogers, 1989; Warner, 1991). So, even though some Hispanic women have to deal with poverty and lack of prenatal care, their infant mortality rate is significantly lower than that of African American women. Why?

It has been suggested that Hispanic women have favorable birth-weight distributions in part because of their low rates of smoking and drinking and their strong familial, cultural, and social ties (Rogers, 1989). In other words, Hispanic women have a strong social-support network, which seems to mediate the effects of poverty and lack of prenatal care (Mason, 1991). If socioeconomic factors and lack of prenatal care fail to account for the infant mortality disparity, what, then, is the cause?

More than 90% of the excess risk of low birth weight among African American infants is related to the mothers' increased risk for high blood pressure, placental problems, or premature labor (Davidson, 1992). These factors can all be seen as related to maternal health and behavioral practices that can be affected by stress. African American women are often segregated into black neighborhoods, lack social support, and experience increased problems owing to their ethnicity. All these factors increase the pregnant woman's level of environmental stress, and this increased stress can lead to poor health habits, such as abusing substances and failing to obtain adequate health care. These poor health habits, in turn, affect pregnancy outcome.

To reduce the infant mortality of African American infants, the United States may need to focus more on social problems than medical ones. This implies taking measures to increase the social support and decrease the environmental stress in an African American woman's life.

Circumcision

Circumcision of newborn males is a controversial issue. For years, removing the foreskin of the penis shortly after birth was standard procedure in the United States. Circumcision was done for religious reasons, for hygienic purposes, and because many parents wanted their baby boy to resemble his father—and most of the other men in the United States. Other countries, though, had much lower circumcision rates. In 1975, the American Academy of Pediatrics (AAP) decided to no longer endorse circumcision of newborns. Their policy stated that there was no proven medical rationale for newborn circumcision.

Many began to argue against routine circumcision. Critics brought up the possible hazards of strapping a newborn baby boy down and removing a part of his anatomy without using anesthesia. These critics also pointed out the possible complications of circumcision, including infection and bleeding. Some insurance plans began to refuse to pay for routine circumcision at birth. And the rate of circumcision of newborns began to decline.

In 1989, because of research that showed potential medical benefits, such as lower risk of urinary-tract infections, sexually transmitted diseases, and inflammation and infection of the penis, the AAP acknowledged the medical benefits of circumcision.

> ## FOCUS ON MULTICULTURALISM
>
> ### CULTURAL DIFFERENCES OF NEWBORNS
>
> How much of the cultural difference in temperament is learned, and how much is inherited? Daniel Freedman tested infants from different cultures on their "defense reaction," measured by the following:
>
> - The babies' reaction to a cloth pressed over their noses
> - How quickly the babies stopped crying when picked up
> - How long it took the babies to adapt to a light shone in their eyes
> - How they reacted to a sudden loss of support of the head and neck
>
> In response to the cloth pressed over their noses, the white and African American babies fought the cloth by turning away and swiping at the cloth with their hands. In contrast, Chinese and Navajo babies did not try to remove the cloth, but lay on their backs and breathed through their mouths. Also, crying Chinese and Navajo babies quieted immediately upon being picked up, whereas white babies cried for longer periods. Puerto Rican babies were also easier to console and were less likely to be startled in response to stress than white and African American babies were. In response to the light shone in their eyes, white babies took longer to adapt than Chinese babies. In response to having head and neck support withdrawn, white babies became agitated and began crying, whereas Navajo babies remained calm and unconcerned.
>
> Freedman concluded that what we consider cultural conditioning may in fact have a biological basis. Take, for example, the use of the cradleboard by Navajo mothers. Navajo babies are generally introduced to the cradleboard in the first month of life, but it is not forced on them—if the baby starts to fuss, he is released. However, most Navajo babies accept the cradleboard and do not begin protesting until after they are 6 months old, and most give up the cradleboard by the time they are 1 year old. In contrast, a study by Chisholm of Caucasian infants raised on cradleboards found that these babies fussed and protested more than the Navajo infants. All the Caucasian babies were completely off the board before they were 6 months old. Although we have assumed that Asian and Native American mothers conditioned their children to be quiet and compliant, these children may actually have just been born that way.
>
> Adapted from Freedman & DeBoer (1979)

Then, in 1999, the AAP again revised its policy on newborn circumcision. The academy's statement indicated that, despite the potential benefits of circumcision, findings were not sufficient to recommend routine circumcision in newborns.

Physicians used to believe that newborns did not feel pain and that, even if they did, anesthesia carried too much risk for them. However, babies do feel pain, and the procedure is painful. The academy now recommends that some form of pain relief, such as topical or local anesthetic, be used. Additionally, circumcision is appropriate only for infants who are healthy and in stable condition (American Academy of Pediatrics, 1999).

In cases in which circumcision is not essential to the child's well-being, parents should be given adequate information about the potential risks and benefits of the procedure to enable them to make an informed decision (American Academy of Pediatrics, 1999).

Social Strengths and Hazards

In this chapter, we have focused mainly on the biological risk factors that can affect prenatal and perinatal development: gestational age, prenatal environment, genetic anomalies, and so on. Throughout the discussion, though, you may have noticed a strong undercurrent of associated risk—the social factors that can have a negative effect on developmental outcomes. Social risk factors include unemployment, lack of maternal education, parental mental illness, a large family, an absent father, an adverse neighborhood, economic recession, and inadequate healthcare systems (Fongruey & Brooks-Gunn, 1994). Many of these risk factors have a common denominator: poverty.

Children born into poverty have an increased risk of health and developmental problems (Kleigman, 1992). Poverty is a factor in lack of prenatal care, low birth weight, prematurity, and poor maternal health habits. In particular, low income is strongly associated with child maltreatment (Jones & McCurdy, 1992), and children who are abused and neglected have a higher risk of developmental problems (Goldson, 1991). Of course, this does not mean that poor families love their children any less than affluent families do. The high levels of environmental stress associated with poverty can inhibit good parenting and prevent parents from providing a stimulating and nurturing environment (Bradley et al., 1994). In later chapters, we will continue to explore the effects of poverty on development.

Drug-Exposed Infants

Newborns who were exposed in utero to drugs have a very low sensory threshold because of their fragile and disorganized nervous systems. These infants have trouble actively engaging in their environments. They very rarely reach and maintain a quiet and alert state. In response to stimulation, these infants spend a lot of time either sleeping or crying uncontrollably. Interactions with them can be difficult, because they are easily overwhelmed by the sight of a human face (Griffith, 1988).

The mother of the drug-exposed infant is or has recently been a drug user. Drug-addicted women often come from dysfunctional homes and, as a result, may have very low self-esteem and an exaggerated need for affection. Such women may have become pregnant to have someone—the baby—who will love them unconditionally (Griffith, 1988).

So what happens when such a mother tries to interact with this baby? The mother approaches the baby expecting love and acceptance or at least a smile, and the baby, upon seeing a human face, begins to cry uncontrollably. The mother now feels rejected and inadequate, and the baby is at risk for abuse and neglect. The mother may stop trying to interact with the infant and let him sleep all the time, or she may become angry when her attempts to soothe him fail to stop his constant crying.

Implications for Practice: Long-Term Effects of Prenatal Drug Use

Little research has been done to verify the long-term effects of cocaine and other illegal substances on infants. Griffith (1992) described the major risk factors for drug-exposed infants as being related to the fact that women who are chronic substance abusers receive inadequate prenatal care and have poor prenatal nutrition. After birth, the major risk to the infant is having parents who continue to abuse drugs. Chronic drug abuse also is associated with an increased incidence of child abuse and neglect. Drug-abusing parents may fail to provide the child with adequate nutrition, appropriate medical care, or a stimulating learning environment.

Children who are removed from the home do not necessarily fare any better. These children may be shifted among foster homes for the first several years of life and may be at increased risk for failure to thrive and attachment problems.

Mothers of drug-exposed infants can be taught how to interact with their babies. Swaddling, use of pacifiers, vertical rocking, and control of intensity of stimulation can help these babies reach a quiet, alert state (Griffith, 1988). Although the effects of prenatal drug exposure are still unclear, some research (Griffith, 1992; Newman & Buka, 1991) suggests that, with early recognition, early intervention, and the benefits of a stable home environment, drug-exposed children can achieve normal development. ■

Fetal Alcohol Syndrome

Children with **fetal alcohol syndrome (FAS)** are at high risk for physical and sexual abuse, abandonment, and neglect. These children are hard to care for, even for nonalcoholic parents. FAS babies may be hyperactive and irritable, and they may need to be fed hourly. An alcoholic home is often characterized by few economic resources and little emotional support, and a study of FAS children revealed that by the age of 6, 64% of them were no longer living with their biological mother. In this study, many of the mothers of FAS children had died from alcohol-related problems, and many FAS children were in the foster-care system, where they experienced multiple-home situations (Streissguth, LaDue, & Randels, 1988). Although early intervention can help with development, no amount of social services can reverse the devastating effects of prenatal alcohol abuse on children.

Implications for Practice: Preventing FAS

Prevention of fetal alcohol syndrome involves teaching pregnant women about nutrition and the harmful effects of drinking during pregnancy. Practitioners should screen for alcohol problems at the first prenatal visit and work with women through support groups and classes to promote healthy pregnancy outcomes.

A manual from the U.S. Department of Health and Human Services stated, "The birth of a child with FAS can be a pivotal point in a family's decision to seek alcoholism treatment" (Streissguth, LaDue, & Randels, 1988, p. 46). The authors noted that extensive support services are needed for these families, to help them deal with the tasks of overcoming alcoholism and parenting a child with a disability. Exhibit 5.6 provides an overview of the type of prenatal information to collect in making assessments.

In the next section, we examine the influence of domestic violence on the mother and the fetus. Domestic violence is a major risk factor in the environment of many families encountered by social-work professionals. Domestic violence is as serious a threat to the health and welfare of the fetus as other potentially toxic conditions.

Domestic Violence

Teri arrived in the hospital in premature labor brought on by cocaine use. Teri is 33 weeks pregnant and has had no prenatal care. After further questioning by the social worker, Teri disclosed that, although she has been abusing cocaine during the pregnancy, her contractions started shortly after her husband shoved her against the refrigerator. She claims that he often becomes violent after drinking and sometimes pushes or shoves her. Teri and her husband live in the desert in a pop-up trailer with no heat, no running water, and no indoor toilet. They have no car. Teri's husband makes it to his $6-an-hour job during the week and often helps at night with the kids. But after work on Fridays, he starts drinking and, by the end of the weekend, usually ends up pushing Teri around some. Teri copes by using cocaine.

Domestic violence is a risk factor for a pregnant woman and her fetus. For many women, battering starts or becomes worse during pregnancy. Studies indicate that up to one in four women are physically abused at some point during pregnancy. This abuse

---

EXHIBIT 5.6 Prenatal information to obtain in making an assessment

Gestation
Duration of pregnancy—was baby full-term or premature?

History of maternal substance abuse

Medications taken by mother during pregnancy

Mother's nutritional status

Maternal illness during pregnancy

Maternal exposure to radiation, toxic wastes

Other maternal factors during pregnancy: fever, accidents, diabetes, toxemia, threatened abortion (vaginal bleeding), previous stillbirths

Birth
Presentation of infant—was baby breech or normal?

Type of delivery—cesarean or vaginal?

Birth weight

Multiple or single birth

Complications—prolonged labor, fetal anoxia (fetal distress)

Newborn
Problems with newborn—hyperbilirubinemia (jaundice), hypoglycemia (low blood sugar), cerebral hemorrhage, infections

Duration of hospitalization (more than forty-eight hours, or less)

SOURCE: Adapted from "Etiological Factors Contributing to Deviant Development," by D. Willis and E. Holden, in J. Johnson and J. Goldman (Eds.), *Development assessment in clinical child psychology*, p. 39. Copyright © 1990. All rights reserved. Adapted by permission of Allyn & Bacon.

---

increases the risk of miscarriage, preterm labor, and low birth weight (Bullock & McFarlane, 1989; Newberger et al., 1992). Because of social isolation, battered women have less access to prenatal care (Chambliss, 1994). In addition, because of the increased stress experienced in a violent relationship, battered women have a high incidence of poor health habits, such as cigarette use and drug and alcohol abuse, all of which can have adverse effects on a developing fetus (Newberger et al., 1992).

Women do not usually volunteer information about abuse; they need to be asked. During the interview, the woman should be separated from her male partner (McFarlane et al., 1992; Newberger et al., 1992). A woman is more likely to disclose abuse to another woman offering sympathy, help, and support. With a hesitant client, the interviewer should use open-ended questions such as, "When I see injuries like yours, often it is because someone has done it on purpose. I'm wondering if that's what happened to you."

The home situation also needs to be assessed. What is the level of violence? Are there any weapons in the home? Is the woman afraid of her partner? Is she afraid for her children? What previous experiences has she had with the police and courts?

The woman needs to develop a safety plan. Whom can she call? Where can she go? Can she put some money away? Does she have copies of identification for herself and her children (for example, birth certificates, Social Security cards, legal documents)? The battered woman needs information about shelters and emergency housing, as well as referrals to legal and medical care and to counseling and support groups. Most of all, a battered woman needs to be reassured that no one deserves to be hurt by someone she loves.

SUMMARY

In this chapter, we examined prenatal and perinatal factors that can affect lifelong development of an individual. Complications of pregnancy and birth, hazards in the prenatal environment, maternal habits, prematurity, genetic abnormalities, and social influences are all risk factors for developmental problems. An adequate assessment of prenatal and perinatal risk factors may sometimes provide a clue to possible contributions to an individual's problem (see Exhibit 5.6).

Prevention is crucial. Early prenatal care, identification and treatment of substance abuse, parent education, promotion of good health practices, and adequate social support can go a long way in optimizing development.

For high-risk infants and families, early-intervention programs that are "intensive, comprehensive, well integrated into other community services and flexible in responding to a family's unique needs produce the most consistent and impressive outcomes" (Daro, 1991).

Given all the hazards and complications, and all that can possibly go wrong, the birth of a healthy infant truly is a miracle.

STUDY TABLE: Social dimension in pregnancy, growth, and the newborn

Families, Groups, Communities, and Support Systems	Every child is born into a family environment that influences the child's development. For optimal development, babies need adequate stimulation and loving, caring adults. Preparation for childbirth should include preparing a safe home with opportunities for stimulating play and toys to interact with. Prenatal intervention programs attempt to get women into prenatal care. Indigenous workers can be helpful in recruiting women into prenatal care. Home-visitation programs often work with women on prenatal care and provide support and guidance after the baby is born. Outcome studies have shown some promising effects.
Multicultural and Gender Considerations	Many societies and cultures have rituals that welcome the baby as a new member. Although the overall mortality rate for African Americans in the United States is decreasing, it remains quite high. This high rate is attributed to risk factors that are influenced by environmental stress. The solution to this problem may need to include social as well as medical considerations. Even though the circumcision rate is falling, the majority of male infants in this country are circumcised at birth. But many people now question the practice of performing the procedure without anesthesia.

Social Strengths and Hazards

Mothers with good support systems are less likely to have birth complications. Prevention programs in low-income areas are a real plus for preventing prenatal difficulties. Drug-exposed infants are disorganized and may have a low sensory threshold. They are difficult to care for and may be at risk of abuse and neglect. Early intervention may benefit these babies. Infants with fetal alcohol syndrome are also at increased risk for abuse and neglect. Parents who continue to abuse drugs and alcohol after the baby's birth may not provide an adequate environment for development. Poverty is also a risk factor for infant development.

CONCEPT MAP

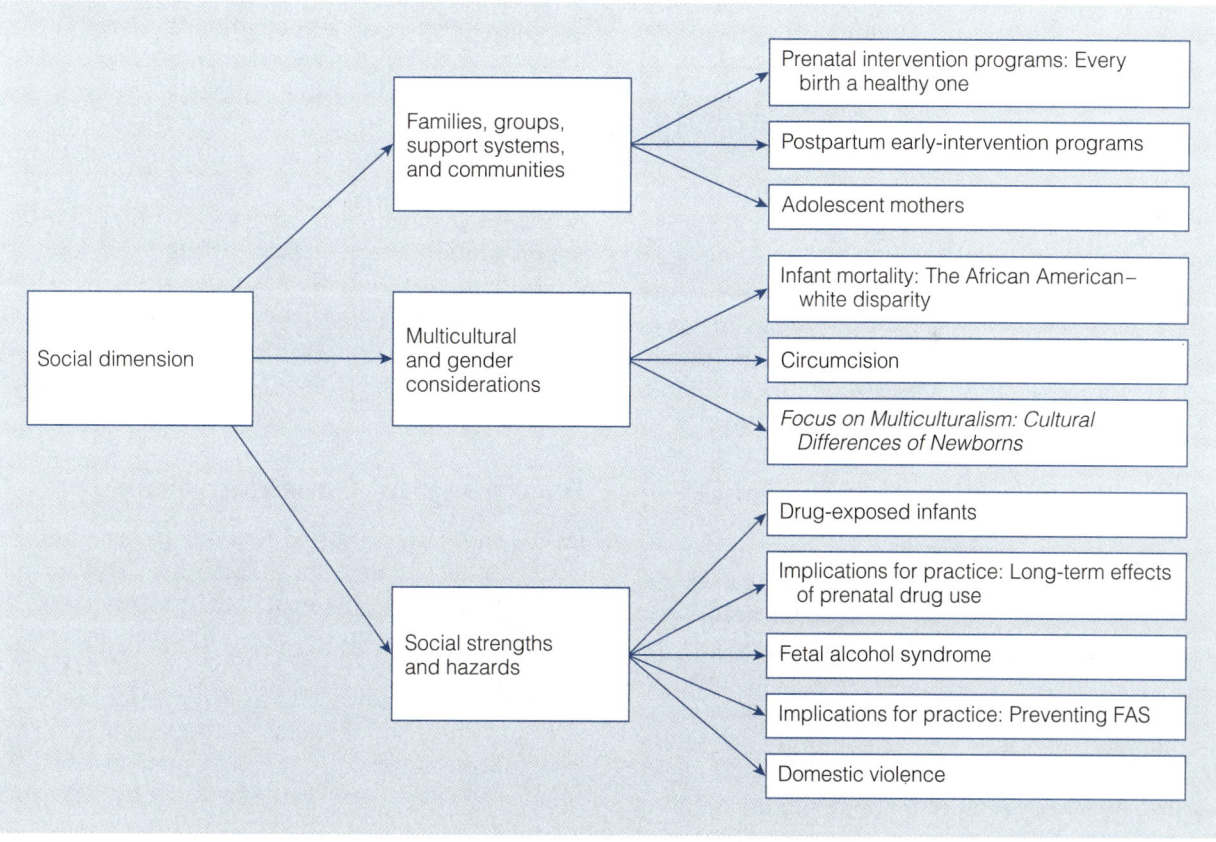

APPLYING THE FRAMEWORK

THE FAMILY OF A PREMATURE INFANT*

Jessica and Travis asked to see the hospital social worker to discuss their concerns about their 2-week-old infant, who was in the hospital NICU. The baby had been born nine weeks premature. The couple was displaying some fear and apprehension in interacting with their baby during his stay in the NICU. They were apprehensive about their ability to parent their infant. They were worried about how they would ever be able to care for the baby on their own at home. They also were concerned about future developmental problems for their child.

Developmental History

Travis and Jessica had been attempting to have a baby for several years. Two previous pregnancies had ended in miscarriage. Fifteen months after her last miscarriage, Jessica became pregnant for the third time. She did not use alcohol or drugs during the pregnancy, but she did continue to smoke. After learning she was pregnant, though, she had managed to cut down to four or five cigarettes per day. Preterm labor began for Jessica in week twenty-six of her pregnancy, and she was placed on bed rest and medications at home to stop her labor. Several weeks later her cervix started to dilate, and she was hospitalized in the high-risk obstetrics unit for the duration of the pregnancy. Eric was born at thirty-one weeks' gestation and weighed 1,134 grams (2 lb. 8 oz.). The Apgar scores were 6 at one minute and 7 at five minutes. Immediately after birth, Eric began to experience respiratory distress. After a brief viewing by his parents, he was transferred to the neonatal intensive care unit.

Biophysical Considerations

On admission to NICU, Eric was placed under an oxygen hood. He required cardiac and respiratory monitoring. Because he was too small to maintain his body temperature, he was placed in an incubator. He required intravenous lines for maintaining fluids and administering medications. Eric's very low birth weight and gestational age placed him at potential risk for continued respiratory difficulty, anemia, infection, intraventricular hemorrhage, jaundice, and retinopathy of prematurity.

Fortunately, Eric's condition improved quickly. His lungs were mature enough for his need for supplemental oxygen to end when he was removed from the oxygen hood three days after birth. He then developed jaundice (hyperbilirubinemia), which was successfully treated with phototherapy (being placed under lights). Because he was born before his sucking reflex was well established, he required oral gavage feedings. Eight days after birth, he was transferred to the area of the NICU for "growing preemies," where he would remain until he had developed coordination to nipple- or breast-feed and had gained enough weight for discharge home.

Psychological Considerations

Jessica and Travis reported that, on entering the NICU for the first time, they found themselves totally unprepared for the sight of their baby. Alongside the machines and other technology, he appeared weak and vulnerable. Travis described his thoughts on that day: "We had lost control of the situation and felt completely intimidated. There were machines everywhere, and he just looked so small." Travis and Jessica began to worry about possible complications for their baby. As do many families faced with high-risk perinatal situations, Jessica and Travis became focused on possible medical outcomes instead of on their new baby.

Worry and uncertainty over their child's fate began to interfere with parental attachment and bonding. Jessica and Travis found it difficult to bond with a baby they feared might die or be se-

---

*The cases in this book are loosely based on several actual cases. Names and other identifying details included in the cases in this book are fictitious.

verely handicapped. Jessica described her bonding process with Eric as a roller-coaster ride. "I loved him, but it felt like a risk."

Jessica felt she did not know her infant—that she had lost control of the baby to the NICU staff. She felt inadequate and incompetent in her ability to care for her very ill child. Jessica remembered those early moments following Eric's birth. "He was taken away so quickly, and we had no idea where they were taking him. I looked at Travis and started crying. It wasn't what we expected." Just minutes after finally becoming a new mother, Jessica had relinquished her role of primary caregiver to the nurses and medical staff. This feeling was further reinforced when Jessica attempted to hold her baby. He slept most of the time, and when he was awake he was irritable. When Jessica held him, he would cry, put up his hands, and turn away from her. Jessica felt that the baby was rejecting her.

Social Considerations

Family Situation

Jessica and Travis were in their mid-20s and had been married for six years. Travis worked as a manager in a supermarket. Jessica worked as a medical transcriber in a hospital. They recently had purchased their first home. Jessica had planned to take three months off from work to care for her new baby, but because she was on bed rest for five weeks before the birth and had been visiting her baby in NICU daily since his birth, Jessica already had used up half of her maternity leave. She was afraid of losing her job, but she did not see how she could return to work full-time with such a small baby to care for. Yet the couple did not believe they could make their mortgage payments on just Travis's salary. They had little savings. There was a possibility that Jessica could work part-time and perhaps do some transcription at home.

Jessica's parents lived in town, and she reported having a warm and close relationship with them. Her mother had expressed a desire to help with the baby's care, but because of back problems, her participation would be limited. But her mother stated she might be able to come and watch the baby while Jessica worked at home.

Groups, Communities, and Social-Support Systems

Travis and Jessica attended a Methodist church in their neighborhood. Many church friends and neighbors had offered support and prepared meals for them throughout the past six weeks. Jessica's friends from work had also helped out by throwing a baby shower a few days after the baby's birth and providing her with needed baby items.

The community in which the couple lived provided an early-intervention program for low-birth-weight babies. The program offered weekly in-home visits, as well as regular developmental follow-up in a clinic.

Summary and Impressions

The assessment showed that this family had the following problems:

1. Low-birth-weight infant because of prematurity
2. Medical complications of hyperbilirubinemia and respiratory distress with need for supplemental oxygen
3. Problems with parent-infant interactions
4. Unknown long-term prognosis for the infant
5. Family financial problems

Looking at the couple's strengths and resources showed that they had a stable home life with an adequate environment for a low-birth-weight baby. They had family and friends who were supportive and caring. The parents were interested in and willing to be involved in learning to care for and interact with their infant. The hospital staff was very supportive of the new parents and willing to be involved in enhancing positive parent-infant interactions. The community provided an early-intervention program for parents of low-birth-weight infants.

After meeting with the social worker, Jessica spent time every day with Eric, initially just observing others caring for him. His primary nurse explained his capacity for interaction, "time out" signals, proper handling, and positioning. The nurse showed Jessica how to swaddle the baby and hold him quietly for a feeding. She taught Jessica to wait until the baby began to look around searchingly before trying to make eye contact and

(continues)

APPLYING THE FRAMEWORK

(continued)

talk to him. The nurse explained that when Eric held up his hand and spread his fingers, he was signaling that he was tired and needed some time alone. Given information and support from the nurses and from the social worker, Jessica was able to interact positively with her infant.

As time went by, both parents learned about and participated in Eric's care. Their involvement helped establish and enhance their bond to the baby. They kept a calendar of events and took photos of Eric's days in the NICU—the transition from incubator to open crib, first tub bath, first attempts at feeding. Thus they were able to share their tiny son's struggles and accomplishments with friends and family.

After five weeks in the hospital, Eric weighed 1,843 grams (4 lb. 1 oz.), was breast-feeding well, and was ready to go home. Jessica and Travis were ready to accept the responsibility for him at home, but the excitement of discharge was still tempered with apprehension about the transition. The long-term effects of the baby's prematurity were still unknown. And though they were now independent in their caring for Eric, they still felt "dependent on the NICU staff for backup." They admitted to still feeling a bit incompetent and unsure of their ability to adequately care for their small son. Travis recalls that "leaving the hospital was almost as stressful as being there, but we were glad to be taking our baby home. Finally!"

Cathy Jaworski, R.N., provided information for this case.

Key Terms

- alpha-fetoprotein blood screening
- amniocentesis
- anoxia
- Apgar score
- Brazelton Neonatal Assessment Scale (BNAS)
- bronchopulmonary dysplasia (BPD)
- cerebral palsy
- cesarean section
- chorionic villus sample (CVS)
- fetal alcohol syndrome (FAS)
- gestation
- gestational diabetes
- hyperemesis gravidarum
- intrauterine growth retardation (IUGR)
- malpresentation
- meconium aspiration
- neural-tube defects
- placenta previa
- polyhydramnios
- preeclampsia
- prematurity
- prolonged labor
- Rh incompatibility
- sensitive period
- teratogens
- toxemia
- ultrasound
- vaginal bleeding

Online Resources

Websites

Go to http://info.wadsworth.com/ashford to find specific links to these web pages.

La Leche League International

Provides information and encouragement to women who want to breast-feed. Site contains educational and self-help information and links to other pregnancy, birth, and health websites.

Centers for Disease Control (CDC)

The CDC's goal is to promote health and good quality of life through the control and prevention of disease, injury, and disability. This site contains a broad range of health and disease information, but it also has specific links to data and statistics related to pregnancy and birth.

Childbirth.org

Provides educational and self-help information regarding pregnancy, birth, and women's health in general.

Planned Parenthood

The official website of Planned Parenthood Federation of America. Provides information regarding family planning, birth control, and reproductive health.

American College of Obstetricians and Gynecologists

Provides educational and self-help information for health-care professionals, women, and teens regarding general health, pregnancy, birth, and birth control.

InfoTrac College Edition Keywords

For interesting materials related to what you have just read, please go to the InfoTrac College Edition website and search using the following keywords:

prenatal care
genetic screening
teen pregnancy
fetal alcohol syndrome
domestic violence

Book-Specific Resources

Book-specific resources, which can be found at http://info.wadsworth.com/ashford, include the following:

Case studies
Quizzes to test your knowledge
PowerPoint Presentations

CHAPTER 6

INFANCY

CHAPTER CONSULTANTS

AURORA JACKSON
University of California at Los Angeles

BETH AUERBACH-DIXON
University of Arizona Health Sciences Center

DEVELOPMENTAL THEMES	
	Child-care practices: history, caregiving environment. Stage: trust versus mistrust. Formation of attachments, acquisition of knowledge, development of a sense of self.
BIOPHYSICAL DIMENSION	
Biophysical Growth and Development	Physical growth. Brain development. Normal development: rapid growth and normal motor development. Developmental delay: early intervention.
Biophysical Strengths and Hazards	Accidents, childhood illness and disease, immunizations, colic, SIDS. Strengths: full term and good temperament.
PSYCHOLOGICAL DIMENSION	
Cognitive Development and Information Processing	Piaget's sensorimotor stage. Information-processing techniques and ideas. IQ testing in infancy. Teaching infants.
Communication	Infants' acquisition of language. Crying and cooing. Babbling. Holophrastic speech. Telegraphic speech. Recognizing speech problems. Adults' infant-directed speech.
Attitudes and Emotions	Development of emotions. Stranger anxiety, separation anxiety; differences in infant temperament and goodness of fit; different attachment patterns. Parents' behaviors. Infant's behaviors. Strange Situation Procedure. Attachment risks and problems.
Social Cognition and Regulation	Development of a sense of self. Learning to say no. Understanding standards of right and wrong. Terrible twos.
Psychological Strengths and Hazards	Separation and loss. Disorders of attachment. Fostering a secure attachment. Failure to thrive. Infant mental health.
SOCIAL DIMENSION	
Families and Groups	Interactions between infants and their families, mothers, fathers, grandparents, siblings, and peers. Playing with baby. Adoption. Open adoption. Transracial adoption. Native American adoption. Birth father and adoption. Adoptive families.
Communities and Support Systems	Day care. Quality of child care.
Multicultural and Gender Considerations	Issues involving developmental assessment of minority infants. Cultural considerations in assessment. Gender differences and sex stereotyping.
Social Strengths and Hazards	Impoverished environment. Poverty. Environmental context. Lead poisoning. Parents with mental illness. Parents with a history of developmental delay. Teen parents. Importance of social support.

DEVELOPMENTAL THEMES

Before modern times, the major developmental task of infancy was simply to survive it. In premodern Europe, 40% of all children died before they were 5 years old. And babies who did survive were not exactly treated like cherished little bundles of joy. Many families, hesitant to invest in someone with such a high probability of dying, sent their babies to be raised by wet nurses (women hired to breast-feed babies) for the first two years of life—until the babies had survived infancy. This practice continued in France until around World War I (Mercer, 1998). With improved nutrition and control of infection and childhood disease, the infant mortality rate improved dramatically. This important social change had an impact on child-care practices in many developed countries (Mercer, 1998). Over the years, there has been an accompanying increase in interest in babies and their development. Ideas of infant development changed during the 20th century, from the early belief that babies were "blobs" that could not see, hear, think, or feel to the more recent belief that babies are highly sensitive creatures whose experiences in early infancy affect personality and other characteristics for the rest of life. The first three years of life are now regarded as a special time of growth and development. We now know that the experiences of infants in the early years of development influence intellectual, emotional, and social development.

Changes in attitudes and lifestyles in developed countries, in addition to reductions in infant mortality, have affected viewpoints about infant development. In the United States, major interest in infant development emerged in the early 1960s, when people began to recognize that "poor development in early life had multiple and expensive consequences, including the need for special education and, potentially, a lifetime on welfare or in prison" (Mercer, 1998, p. 3). Programs such as Head Start were developed to address problems of early life that placed children at a distinct disadvantage in making effective transitions to school. The success of this early-intervention program suggested to researchers and policy advocates that even earlier interventions were probably needed.

A number of important social changes in the second half of the 20th century have affected current child-care practices. Many of these changes are closely tied to employment considerations, including both parents working, parents having to go back to work sooner after their babies are born, increased numbers of unmarried women, and increased numbers of teenaged mothers. Clearly, these changes have increased the role played by day care in the lives of infants. From 1942 to 1945, the Lanham Act provided government support for child care, to enable mothers to participate in the workforce as part of the war effort. However, these funds were withdrawn approximately six months after the war's end. Day care did not increase again until the 1970s (Mercer, 1998; Davies, 2004). In the 1980s and 1990s, economic pressures influenced demands for changes in the age at which day-care placement began. This trend has been institutionalized and has been playing a major role in the lives of mothers of poverty since the passage of welfare-reform legislation signed by President Clinton in 1996. In addition, grandmothers are a major form of residential and child support under present mandates for unmarried mothers to live at home or in an adult-supervised setting (Gordon, Chase-Lansdale, & Brooks-Gunn, 2004).

Another major change has been increased substance abuse by mothers during the prenatal and postnatal phases of development. An epidemic of cocaine and crack use began in the 1980s. Most women who use cocaine also use other substances, such as marijuana, alcohol, and tobacco (Brown, Bakeman, Coles, Platzman, & Lynch, 2004). The teratogenic effects of these substances are certainly important, but researchers now realize that we cannot ignore the postnatal caregiving environment of children with prenatal cocaine exposure (Brown et al., 2004).

The caregiving environment is a central theme in the study of infant development (Davies, 2004), and research recognizes the important role of the caregiving environment in the early years of a child's life (Jackson, 2003b). A substantial body of research is developing on the effects of day care during infancy. The seminal study by Brooks-Gunn and colleagues (2002) showed that there is a link between the mother's employment in the first year of life and cognitive-developmental outcomes.

According to Erikson, infancy is the stage of trust. Infants are born totally dependent on their caregivers. They must receive appropriate and consistent care in order to develop a sense of security. Infants whose needs are met consistently in a warm and nurturing manner learn that the world is a safe place and that people are dependable. They learn trust. This trust allows babies to develop positive emotional bonds or social attachments to their caregivers (Davies, 2004). Babies who are neglected, rejected, and inconsistently cared for learn to be suspicious and fearful of the world around them. These babies develop mistrust, which can prevent or delay cognitive development and hinder movement into other stages (Murray, McKinney, & Gorrie, 2002). A baby also must develop a sense of self, form an attachment to caregivers, and acquire knowledge (Davies, 2004; Kagan, 1984b; Shaffer, 1996). These tasks will be explored in depth in this chapter as we consider the physical, cognitive, emotional, and social development of a child from birth to age 2.

Attachment between infant and a primary caregiver is crucial for healthy development.

STUDY TABLE: Developmental themes of infancy

Developmental Themes	According to Erikson, infancy is the psychosocial stage of trust vs. mistrust. During infancy, babies learn to trust, they develop a sense of self, they form an attachment to a caregiver, and they acquire knowledge about the world and how it works. In premodern times, infant survival rates were low, which affected child-care practices and interest in babies. As nutrition and medicine improved, interest in babies increased.

BIOPHYSICAL DIMENSION

Biophysical Growth and Development

At birth, the newborn weighs a little more than seven pounds (less than a gallon of milk) and is about twenty inches long (Berger, 2005). Here's how to have some fun with a 2-year-old: Measure her and predict her future size. At the age of 2, a child has already grown to half her adult height. During the first two years, she quadrupled her birth weight and now weighs between 27 and 30 pounds. As you can see, the first two years of life are a time of rapid growth and development. Several processes occur to take the child from being a sedentary infant to a busy, active toddler.

At birth, an infant's bones are soft and pliable. During infancy the bones harden, or ossify, to allow the child to stand and walk. The infant's skull comprises several bones that are not fused together, to allow molding of the head for a vaginal birth.

Fontanelles, or soft spots, mark the spots where the skull bones do not join. By the age of 2, these soft spots fill in and harden. Many cultures have developed traditions about the fontanelles. For examples, mothers are taught in traditional Mexican communities about the condition known as *caida de mollera*. This condition involves fallen fontanelles and is associated with dehydration and other life-threatening physical symptoms. Mexican folk traditions also have introduced proscriptions against touching the spots, to protect the infant before they harden. Many U.S. doctors and midwives also examine the fontanelles in assessing the hydration of infants.

No aspect is more critical to the biophysical development of humans than the rapid growth of the brain, which is considered one of the most complex structures in the universe (Berger, 2005; Thompson, 2000). An infant's brain grows to more than half its adult size by the end of the first year. "By age 2, the brain is about 75 percent of adult weight, while the body is only about 20 percent" (Berger, 2005, p. 125). It grows so rapidly that, between the seventh month of gestation and the age of 1, the brain gains 1.7 grams per day (Shaffer, 1993). Diet during this period of rapid brain growth is crucial. It takes a substantial amount of high-quality protein to sustain this rate of growth. Inadequate nutrition in infancy can have a detrimental effect on brain development (Kalat, 2004).

Most of the infant's brain neurons are created before birth. At birth, the human infant's brain has billions of neurons (Kalat, 2004). Of these neurons, 70% make up the cortex (the brain's outer layer, also known as the neocortex). This portion of the brain mediates a sizable proportion of our thoughts, feelings, and other sensations, and it includes the auditory, visual, and frontal cortexes. The frontal cortex plays a pivotal role in assisting humans in planning, self-control, self-regulation, and other executive functions. Besides humans, mammals are the only other class of animals that has a cortex (Berger, 2005; Kalat, 2004). Experience plays an important role in how the brain grows during this period (Davies, 2004).

During the first two years of an infant's life, major spurts of growth and refinement take place in the cortex. During this period, the number of dendrites in the brain's cortex increases fivefold. This process is called **transient exuberance**. It is estimated that as many as 15,000 new connections via dendrites are established for each neuron in the twenty-four-month period after birth (Thompson, 2000). "This exuberant proliferation enables neurons to become

EXHIBIT 6.1 Age norms for motor development

Skill	Age (in months) at which:	
	50% of Infants Have Mastered Skill	90% of Infants Have Mastered Skill
Lifts head 90° while lying on stomach	2.2	3.2
Rolls over	2.8	4.7
Sits propped up	2.9	4.2
Sits without support	5.5	7.8
Stands holding on	5.8	10.0
Walks holding on	9.2	12.7
Stands alone momentarily	9.8	13.0
Stands well alone	11.5	13.9
Walks well	12.1	14.3
Walks up steps	17.0	22.0
Kicks ball forward	20.0	24.0

SOURCE: Adapted from "The Denver Development Screening Test," by W. K. Frankenberg and J. B. Dodds (1967), *Journal of Pediatrics*, 71, 181–191. Copyright © 1967 C. V. Mosby Company. Used with permission.

connected to, and communicate with, a greatly expanding number of other neurons within the brain" (Berger, 2005, p. 127).

Another concept of brain development is myelinization, which begins in the prenatal period and continues after birth. In **myelinization**, a substance called myelin forms around neurons and acts as insulation, allowing faster and more efficient transmission of nerve impulses. Myelinization occurs from the brain downward and from the spinal cord out to the extremities. Motor development follows the growth of this myelin sheath, downward and outward. Therefore, a baby's development is referred to as **cephalocaudal** (from the head to the feet) and **proximodistal** (from the spine to the extremities). For example, first the baby gains control of her head and neck and can lift her head up. Then she gains control of her trunk and can roll over. Likewise, a baby can grasp an object in her palm before she can pick up an object with thumb and forefinger.

Motor development follows this sequence: hold up head, roll over, sit, roll from back or stomach to sit, crawl or creep, move from sit to crawl and back again, pull to stand, stand alone, cruise (walk holding on to furniture), walk. Exhibit 6.1 lists typical ages for attaining motor development in infancy.

Although age norms for motor development vary culturally, infants the world over obtain these motor milestones in the same sequence. This is evidence of a maturational theory of development—that developmental achievements are genetically programmed to occur in a particular sequence as the baby grows.

Many maturational theories of infant brain development assume that there is a general progression of the maturation from posterior to anterior regions, "with the primary sensory areas being functional from around the time of birth, and the frontal lobes and prefrontal cortex argued to be the last parts of cortex to develop" (Johnson & Karmiloff-Smith, 2004, p. 124). Based on recent brain-imaging results for adults, neuroscientists have observed that many of our assumptions about particular functions being considered localized within a specific region of the brain might be false (Johnson, 2001; Friston & Price, 2001; Johnson & Karmiloff-Smith, 2004). Instead, they contend that many functions are probably determined by patterns of connectivity of a specific region with other regions, as well as by their current states of activity (Johnson & Karmiloff-Smith, 2004). In infancy research, they have identified some observed biases in how inputs and outputs are processed. In addition, they have noticed processes of selectivity that contribute to various types of functions observed in different areas of the brain. They believe that an area can have a general type of response to stimuli but over time will become selective and specialized in responding to a specific class of stimuli.

The sleep-wake states provide useful information for assessing the integrity of the newborn infant's nervous system. Wolff (1966) made an intensive observation of infants and differentiated between **active sleep** (periods with eye movement) and **quiet sleep** (periods with no eye movements) (Thoman, 2001). His research contributed to scientists' recognition of the importance of states in infant human behavior. A number of early electrophysiological studies identified the specific sleep characteristics associated with various forms of atypical brain development. For example, children with a diagnosis of autism showed a delay in the development of sleep patterns, and unstable sleep patterns also have been observed in premature infants and infants with developmental disorders. Researchers now know that the physical states of infants are highly complex systems related to many future developmental outcomes. Some studies have predicted that recordings of sleep during the first two days after birth have predicted six-month Bayley mental and motor scores. Research on physiological states such as sleep hold significant promise for unraveling the contributions of temperament and other factors useful for assessing aspects of human development processes (Thoman, 2001).

Implications for Practice: Recognizing Developmental Delay

How can you tell whether a baby is developmentally delayed? This is where knowledge of developmental norms becomes important. To make an accurate assessment of developmental problems, you have to be able to contrast a child's current level of functioning with what is expected of typical children his age (Johnson & Goldman, 1990). Basically, infants may need developmental assessment if they fail to demonstrate a skill at an age when 90% of babies can perform that skill (refer to Exhibit 6.1).

However, recently there has been an increased incidence of delay in babies learning to roll over and gain head and neck control. This delay is the result of a trend to place babies on their back or side to sleep instead of on their stomachs, as was the old norm. Parents used to be encouraged to place babies on their stomachs in case they spat up while asleep. However, studies have suggested that babies who sleep on their stomachs run a higher risk of dying from SIDS (American Academy of Pediatrics, 1992; American Academy of Pediatrics, 1996). (See Sudden Infant Death Syndrome, page 220.) Now pediatricians recommend that parents put babies to sleep on their backs, and a decrease in SIDS deaths has been observed. However, because infants spend less time on their stomachs, they do not strengthen the arms, head, neck, and trunk by rolling over or pushing themselves up. Early-intervention programs now recommend that parents allow a baby to have some "tummy time," or special time to play on his stomach, while awake. Tummy time may also prevent the formation of flat spots on the back of the baby's skull, which may result from sleeping on the back.

The National Center for Infants, Toddlers, and Families has promoted a new system for classifying mental-health and developmental disorders for infants from 0 to 3 years of age. The Zero to Three Diagnostic Classification Task Force (1994) focused on ways of assessing infants that promoted treatment of the very young in the context of the family. Social-work practitioners are now developing substantial expertise in this burgeoning field, known as infant mental health. This field promotes healthy social and emotional development for children from birth through 3 years of age. **Infant mental health** was defined by the Zero to Three Task Force (1994) as "the developing capacity of the child from birth to age 3" to accomplish the following: "(1) experience, regulate, and express emotions; (2) form close and secure interpersonal relationships; (3) explore the environment and learn all in the context of the family, community and cultural expectations for young children" (National Center for Infant Mental Health, 2004). This new field requires a strong understanding of developmental considerations, including the achievement of key physical milestones.

Early Intervention for Developmental Delay

Margaret's first baby was born with a severe neural-tube defect. The baby had a *meningocele*, or an opening in the back of her head. Unfortunately, the problem was not detected prenatally, and after a long and difficult labor, the baby was delivered with forceps. The baby suffered brain damage. Margaret's doctor told her that the baby would be severely mentally retarded and would never learn to walk, talk, or feed herself. He suggested placing the baby in an institution, but Margaret took her daughter home. The community in which Margaret lived provided an early-intervention program for infants with disabilities, and the baby started a formal program at the age of 3 months. Margaret spent hours each day doing exercises and activities with her infant. And, although the child would never be completely normal, at the age of 6 Margaret's daughter could not only walk, talk, and feed herself, but also, every day after school, she went outside and roller-skated around the block.

Until the 1970s, parents were encouraged to institutionalize babies with mental retardation. But information began to accumulate on the abilities of very young babies. Researchers learned that infants could process information from birth; newborns could see, hear, and understand (Berger, 2005). Programs were developed to begin interventions for infants with disabilities. In 1986, the federal law known as PL 99-457 (Part H), Services for Infants and Toddlers with Handicapping Conditions, was enacted to provide special services to children born with disabilities.

Most communities now provide infant-stimulation or early-intervention programs for infants with disabilities and their families. In most cases, the parents are involved as the infant's teachers. The parents are taught exercises and activities to perform with the child at home to enhance the child's development.

For instance, babies with Down syndrome have weak muscles and poor muscle tone, which lead to delayed motor development. At an age when typical babies are lifting their heads, grabbing at interesting objects, and learning from these interactions, Down syndrome babies, who because of weak neck muscles cannot lift their heads, receive less stimulation and interaction. By exercising the baby's neck, parents can help strengthen the muscles so the baby can lift its head. Helping babies with mental retardation lift their heads, reach for objects, move around, and interact with the environment enriches their experiences and enhances their cognitive and physical development.

What about other disabling conditions? Infants with visual impairments are delayed in their ability to reach for objects, crawl, and walk. Blind infants will not begin to crawl until their second year (Zigler & Stevenson, 1993). Parents of blind infants can be taught to use auditory and other forms of sensory stimulation to enhance their infants' development. Hearing-impaired infants often appear to develop normally for the first few months. These babies begin to vocalize and babble at the same age that unimpaired infants do. However, after 9 months these infants show problems in learning language. The language deficit affects acquisition of other cognitive skills, and parents who do not know that their baby is deaf may think the child has some mental retardation. Early detection of and intervention for a hearing impairment can enhance the child's development.

Biophysical Strengths and Hazards

To new parents, babies often may seem like accidents just waiting to happen. Infants climb on chairs that topple over, fall down stairs, eat poisonous plants, choke on small objects, and fall headfirst into buckets of water. Infants require constant attention to protect them from injury. Parents need to babyproof the house carefully and anticipate possible hazards to their child. Parents should remember that not all homes are babyproofed, which means that when visiting other people's homes, they should be alert to possible hazards, such as swimming pools, medication bottles within the baby's reach, and exposed electrical outlets. Exhibit 6.2 lists some considerations for preventing accidents and injury.

EXHIBIT 6.2 Preventing accidents and injury in infancy

Hazard	Prevention
Falls	Don't leave infant unrestrained on any surface. Even very small infants can move and fall off a bed or couch. Don't place a baby in an infant seat on a table. The baby may wiggle the seat off and fall. Avoid use of infant walkers.
Poisoning	Lock up all hazardous materials, including cleaning supplies and medications. Use childproof caps on medications. Keep poisonous plants out of reach. Keep number of poison control near phone.
Choking	Keep small objects out of reach. Don't tie anything around baby's neck, including the pacifier. Cut food into small pieces. Avoid hard foods such as nuts, hard candy. Parents and caregivers should learn the Heimlich maneuver.
Suffocation	Don't prop the bottle to feed. Keep plastic bags out of reach. Remove doors of old refrigerators. Don't shake baby powder onto baby (put in your hand and apply). Avoid use of pillows, soft toys, and several blankets in crib. Use approved crib. Watch for drapery or blinds cords near crib and within baby's reach throughout the house.
Drowning	Never leave baby unattended in bathtub. Keep toilet seat down. Be careful of all containers of water. Babies can drown in only a few inches of water in a bucket. Use pool safety gates. Never leave baby unattended near pool or any water. Parents and caregivers should take a CPR class.
Burns	Lower temperature of water heater to 120°–130°. Check temperature of bathwater with elbow. Push pot handles toward back of stove. Use nonflammable clothing. Install smoke detectors. Don't heat bottles in microwave.
Auto accidents	Always buckle child into approved car seat. Never place a baby in the front seat of a vehicle that has air bags.

SOURCE: Reprinted from *Family-Centered Nursing Care of Children*, by R. Foster, M. Hunsberger, and J. Anderson. Copyright © 1989, with permission from Elsevier.

Illness

Although babies are born with some natural immunity to rubella, measles, mumps, polio, and diphtheria, this immunity does not last past the age of 3 to 6 months. In addition, babies are susceptible to chicken pox, tetanus, whooping cough (pertussis), and strep infections during this time (Foster, Hunsberger, & Anderson, 1989). As stated at the beginning of this chapter, in the past many children did not survive infancy because of these diseases. In fact, pertussis is still a major problem in the United States; pertussis vaccine is the only vaccine that has not reached immunization levels of 90% (Teitelbaum & Edmunds, 1999). Immunization is an important issue for both parents and children; Exhibit 6.3 lists the immunization schedule for childhood.

Babies are also very susceptible to upper respiratory infections (colds). Exposure to tobacco smoke can increase the risk of respiratory problems for infants, placing them at higher risk for bronchitis and

EXHIBIT 6.3 Immunization schedule for infants

Age	Immunization
Birth	Hepatitis B (Hep-B)
1–4 months	Hep-B
2 months	Diphtheria, tetanus, pertussis (DTP), polio (OPV), hemophilus influenza (Hib) (for meningitis), rotavirus (RV)
4 months	DTP, OPV, Hib, RV
6 months	DTP, Hib, RV
6–18 months	OPV, Hep-B
12–15 months	Hib, measles, mumps, and rubella (MMR)
12–18 months	Varicella (chicken pox)
15–18 months	DTP
4–6 years	DTP, OPV, MMR
11–12 years	Tetanus, diphtheria

SOURCE: Based on recommendations by the Advisory Committee on Immunization Practices, the American Academy of Pediatrics, and the American Academy of Family Physicians, 1999.

pneumonia. Respiratory syncytial virus (RSV) is the most common respiratory pathogen in infants and children. RSV infection causes respiratory distress in infants and results in increased risk of hospitalization for them, especially those who are premature, during the winter months.

Meningitis, a bacterial infection of the lining of the brain, is especially hazardous to infants. This illness can result in a 1–5% death rate or in neurological complications, including learning disabilities. Babies with meningitis are irritable, run a fever, have a high-pitched cry, and often have bulging fontanelles.

Colic can develop between 2 and 6 weeks of age. **Colic** refers to patterns of sudden and unexplained outbursts of inconsolable crying. The outbursts typically occur at about the same time each day and spontaneously resolve. At other times the infant cries normally. Colic has been attributed to food allergies, to an immature digestive system or immature nervous system, and to a nervous caregiver. To the relief of parents, babies outgrow this condition by about 3 months of age.

Sudden Infant Death Syndrome

At 4:00 in the morning, Dana woke sweating. Something was wrong. She had put her 2-month-old baby to bed at 7:00 the previous evening, and he was still asleep. He had never slept longer than six hours before. In fact, lately he had been sleeping poorly because he had a cold and had been waking often with a stuffy nose. Dana went to check on the baby and found him lying on his stomach, wedged up at the top corner of his crib. The sheet was crumpled, his blankets were kicked off, and there was a little blood on the mattress. Dana put her hand on the baby's back and discovered he was not breathing. Dana's screams woke her husband, John, and he called the paramedics. Unfortunately, efforts to resuscitate the baby failed, and he was pronounced dead at the hospital.

Sudden infant death syndrome (SIDS) refers to the unexpected death of an infant, for which no physical cause can be found. SIDS is the most common cause of death in the first year of life (Krugman et al., 1994). SIDS occurs in approximately 1 in 400 babies and results in 7,000 deaths each year. Most SIDS deaths involve babies who are between 2 and 4 months old (NICHD, 2004b). In addition, African American babies are two times more likely to die of SIDS than are white babies (NICHD, 2004). Although investigators still do not know what causes SIDS, several risk factors have been identified. SIDS occurs more often in male infants, low-birth-weight infants, premature infants, babies with low Apgar scores, babies with a sibling who previously died of SIDS, and babies who sleep on their stomachs (Martinez, 1996). Several maternal factors also increase the risk of SIDS, including young age, multiple births, smoking, prenatal drug abuse, low socioeconomic status, no prenatal care, and closely spaced pregnancies (Martinez, 1996).

Several theories on what causes SIDS have been proposed, but none of these theories is conclusive. Autopsies show that SIDS babies often have changes in the airway, and many had a viral infection. The majority of babies had blood-stained frothy secretions in their mouths and left this substance in the bed, and the bed showed signs of a struggle (Berry, 1993). These clues—changes in the airway, an infection, and signs of a struggle—suggest that something may be wrong in the babies' lungs (Martinez, 1996). Other evidence supports this conclusion. Premature babies have more respiratory problems and a higher risk of SIDS. Breathing secondhand smoke can contribute to respiratory problems, and babies of mothers who smoke have a definite increase in risk of SIDS.

What about putting babies to sleep on their stomachs? As mentioned previously, babies have been put to bed this way for many years. In 1992, the American Academy of Pediatrics began recommending that babies be put to sleep on their sides or backs, rather than on their stomachs. Since the release of the academy's recommendations, the number of SIDS deaths in the United States has decreased 15–20% (American Academy of Pediatrics, 1996). In countries where this position has been discouraged for many years, the death rate from SIDS has been reduced by 50% (Willinger, Hoffman, & Hartford, 1994). In 1996, revisions to the academy's original recommendations were made. These included comments that the supine position (sleeping on the back) confers the lowest risk, as opposed to the side position, and that soft sleeping surfaces and gas-trapping objects in the crib should be avoided. Note that the current recommendations are for healthy infants only. Infants with respiratory or digestive problems should be put to bed as recommended by their pediatricians (American Academy of Pediatrics, 1996). "Tummy time" is recommended during periods when the infant is awake and supervised to assist in motor development and to help avoid the formation of flat spots on the back of his or her skull, which may result from sleeping in a supine position. However, the National Institute of Child Health and Human Development initiated the Back to Sleep Campaign in October of 2002. This campaign recognizes that babies are safest when they sleep on their backs.

Other evidence suggests that babies who fall into deep sleep may be at higher risk of SIDS. As an example, babies who sleep alone can go into deep sleep, but infants who sleep with their caregiver adjust their sleep patterns to synchronize with the caregiver's. So, as the caregiver drifts in and out of deep and light sleep, the infant's sleep patterns follow. In fact, rates of SIDS are lower in countries where infants routinely sleep with their mothers (Stipp, 1995). However, a lack of scientific evidence in support of these observations has prevented the AAP from recommending bed sharing for SIDS prevention (American Academy of Pediatrics, 1997).

As yet, no one knows what causes babies to die unexpectedly, but parents who lose an infant this way often blame themselves and try to determine what they did wrong, and their grief is almost unimaginable. Parents coping with the loss of an infant to SIDS need much support. Although finding a cause for SIDS may help prevent future deaths, at present no particular cause has been identified. The Back to Sleep campaign holds significant promise for preventing many SIDS deaths.

STUDY TABLE: Biophysical dimension in infancy

Biophysical Growth and Development	At birth the newborn weighs a little more than seven pounds. By age 3, a child has grown to half her adult size. This is a period of rapid growth and development. At birth, the bones are soft and pliable. The infant's skull is not fused together, and this allows for movement of the infant through the mother's birth canal. Fontanelles are the soft spots on the skull where the bones are not joined. By age 2, the spots should harden. Caida de mollera is a Mexican folk illness involving fontanelles. Mothers are trained to identify when the fontanelles have a sunken appearance. The brain goes through rapid growth during the first two years. The brain also grows to half its adult size by age 1 and is 75 percent of its adult weight by age 2. Diet is very important during this period of rapid brain growth. The majority of brain neurons (billions of them) are created before birth. Of these neurons, 70 percent make up the neocortex. Experience plays an important role in brain growth during this period. The number of the brain's dendrites increases fivefold. This process of transient exuberance allows neurons to become connected. Myelinziation also begins in the prenatal period, but increases during the first year after birth. This form of brain growth occurs in a downward and outward direction. Motor development also follows this cephalocaudal sequence of growth. Many theories of brain development assume a general progression of maturation from posterior to anterior regions. Primary sensory functions are functional at birth. The prefrontal cortex is the last area to develop. New research questions notions about the localization of key brain functions. Instead, it is now assumed that brain functions are determined by patterns of connectivity in our neuronal systems. The newborn's sleep-wake cycle provides useful information in assessing the integrity of the infant's nervous system. A delay in the development of sleep patterns and unstable sleep patterns are associated with premature infants and with some developmental disorders.
Biophysical Strengths and Hazards	For an infant who is full term, appropriate size for gestational age and an appropriate temperament are key biophysical strengths. Because infants climb and explore, the normal household can hold physical hazards for the developing infant. Childhood illnesses such as rubella, measles, and mumps are other important hazards. Sleep patterns also place infants at risk for SIDS. Parents should be encouraged to have their child sleep on their back.

CONCEPT MAP

PSYCHOLOGICAL DIMENSION

Cognitive Development and Information Processing

Suddenly a piece of space stands out. It's a pillar, thin and taut. It stands motionless and sings out a bright melody. Now, from close by, different notes drift in. There is nearby another pillar of space. It, too, sings—but in harmony with the first. The two melodies mingle in a tight duet, one melody loud, the other quiet. . . . Then from somewhere else, sounds a different note. A shooting star, it flashes past and quickly disappears.

—Daniel Stern

In this passage from *Diary of a Baby*, Daniel Stern describes a 6-week-old infant turning his head and seeing first one crib bar and then another. Try to imagine what the shooting star could be. (It is the baby's hand passing through his line of vision.)

People have long been intrigued with trying to determine what babies think about, what they perceive, and how they process information. In the past, theories of infant development were based on the "clinical infant"—a construct developed by the therapist working with adult clients trying to remember early experience. Theories of infant development from developmental psychology are based on the *observed* infant. Today, researchers realize that infants hold important keys about understanding mind, brain, and evolution (Meltzof, 2004), and they are setting up experiments to observe babies to determine their responses and capabilities (Stern, 1985). Although Jean Piaget was well regarded for his ability to observe human development, in the field of infant cognition, Piagetian theory no longer reigns (Meltzoff, 2004). We are seeing an explosion of new findings in this field that are revealing the presences of richer innate states that are possessed by infants than were presumed by Piaget. Still, Piaget's classic writings on cognition provide useful insights into infant sensory and motor capabilities.

Piaget's Sensorimotor Stage

Piaget developed his theories of cognitive development by closely observing first his own children and then others. He classified the time from birth to age 2 as the **sensorimotor stage**. During this stage, the infant goes from having mostly random reflex actions to displaying goal-directed behavior. For example, instead of just watching a hand shoot past her eyes, she learns to use that hand to push a chair over to the kitchen counter so she can climb up and get cookies. **Goal-directed behavior**, then, means putting together a series of actions to achieve a desired result. The infant in this stage also develops **object permanence**—the ability to hold an image of an object or person in the mind. According to Piaget, very young infants forget an object as soon as they can no longer see it. For instance, if you show a 4-month-old infant a toy and then place that toy under a cloth, the baby will not lift the cloth to find the toy, even if the baby saw you put it there. But 2-year-olds remember that those cookies are on the counter even though they can't see them, and they may thoughtfully solve the problem of how to get to them.

Piaget's sensorimotor stage is divided into six substages:

1. Reflex activity (birth to 1 month): Piaget believed that the reflexes present at birth are the basic building blocks for intelligent behavior. Touch the baby on the cheek, and the baby will turn toward the touch with open mouth. Place a nipple in the baby's mouth, and the baby will suck. Place an object in the baby's palm, and the baby will grasp it. Ring a bell, and the baby will look for it. These actions are not intentional but are the result of inborn reflexes. The baby quickly begins to learn about the environment through these random reflex actions.
2. Primary circular reactions (1 to 4 months): During this stage, the baby learns that certain reflex actions bring about pleasurable results. The baby then begins to repeat those actions. For instance, babies learn that sucking to eat reduces hunger and gives comfort. If a baby accidentally places his hand in his mouth, he will suck on it and find this sucking comforting. He will then repeat placing the hand in the mouth for comfort. Through accidental reflex activity, the baby acquires new patterns of behavior. The baby is focused on its body (primary) and on repeated actions (circular). Piaget believed that babies in this stage could repeat actions only they themselves initiated and could not imitate actions of others.
3. Secondary circular reactions (4 to 8 months): Now babies' focus shifts from their own body to objects in the world (secondary). They learn to control not just their body but other things as well and will repeat random actions for their results. For instance, if a baby is lying in a crib looking at a mobile and the baby kicks its feet and the mobile moves (and the baby finds this movement interesting), the baby will kick its feet again to see whether the mobile will move. Babies at this stage will re-create actions to see interesting results.
4. Coordination of secondary schemes (8 to 12 months): In this stage, the baby learns to take several random activities and put them together to achieve a goal. This is known as **intentional means-end behavior**. Now the baby can begin to solve problems. The baby also begins to develop object permanence. If you hide a toy under a cloth, a 9-month-old baby will lift the cloth to find the toy. But if you then hide the toy under a different cloth, the baby will continue to search for the toy under the original one. Even if you show the baby you are hiding the toy in a new place, the baby will still look in the original hiding place. Another characteristic of this stage is that babies are able to imitate actions performed by others. If you show babies how to clap, they can repeat the action after watching you, but they cannot initiate the action on their own.
5. Tertiary circular reactions (12 to 18 months): Babies at this age are little explorers. They no longer rely on random activity but can now think up activities on their own. If you show babies at this age that you are hiding a toy under one cloth and then show them that you are hiding it under a second cloth, they will be able to find the toy. But if you put the toy under a box and then place the box under a cloth, then tip the toy out of the box and leave it under the cloth and return the box to its original location, the babies will search for the toy under the box. They will not look under the cloth, even though they can see the bulge the toy makes in the fabric. Babies at this stage are said to be unable to understand invisible displacements.
6. Beginning of representational thought (18 to 24 months): Here babies make a transition from being action oriented to being symbol oriented. Babies now have full object permanence and can hold an image of an object or person in their minds and solve problems. So, they will search for a toy even if they didn't see you hide it. They will look for cookies in the cookie jar on the counter because they remember that is where the cookies are kept, even though they didn't see you place them there. Now babies can repeat actions without having to watch someone else, so they can clap for themselves when they are pleased with their accomplishment.

Information Processing

New research is finding that babies may be more competent than Piaget ever imagined (Davies, 2004). Innovative techniques make it possible to observe infants much more closely than Piaget did. These techniques look at how babies actually process the information they receive through sensory stimulation.

One way of observing babies is by studying their attention patterns. Infants display **obligatory**

attention; that is, they will look intently at or fixate on something interesting and not be distracted from it (Stern, 1990). Researchers can determine how babies process information by measuring how long it takes a baby to stop paying attention to the same stimulus (**habituation**) and how long it takes the baby to become interested in a new stimulus (**dishabituation**). Babies will look longer at something they find interesting. After becoming familiar or bored with that stimulus, they stop looking at it, or habituate; then they will pay attention to a new stimulus, or dishabituate.

Researchers have discovered that babies not only pay attention to stimuli they have never seen before, but they also pay more attention to events they have some control over, such as watching a mobile they can shake by kicking, and to events they did not expect to happen. Using this information, researchers have discovered some amazing capabilities of young infants.

Cohen and Strauss (1979) found that 30-week-old infants were able to categorize (place objects into groups) on the basis of similarities. They habituated one group of infants to a single individual (Sally) by showing them a picture of a female face until they became bored with it and looked away. They habituated another group of infants to a series of individuals (Sally, Mary, Barbara, and Joan). These infants paid less attention to each subsequent picture of a new female face. Then each group was shown a picture of a new face (Elizabeth). The infants who had seen only Sally dishabituated to Elizabeth and looked intently at that picture. The infants who had seen the series of faces (Sally, Mary, Barbara, and Joan) were not interested in another female face and remained habituated—they would not look at the new face. Although the individual stimulus was new, these infants had formed a category for the series of female faces and were then habituated to the category. Research has shown that infants as young as 6 or 7 months display **categorization** (Bjorklund & Bjorklund, 1992). Categorization is the process of placing new experiences into older categories for classifying experiences.

Some research suggests that very small babies can transfer information gained from one sense to another sense. This process is referred to as **cross-modal transfer**. An example would be exploring an unseen object with your hands and then trying to recognize a picture of that object. Piaget argued that babies learn this capability gradually through repeated as-

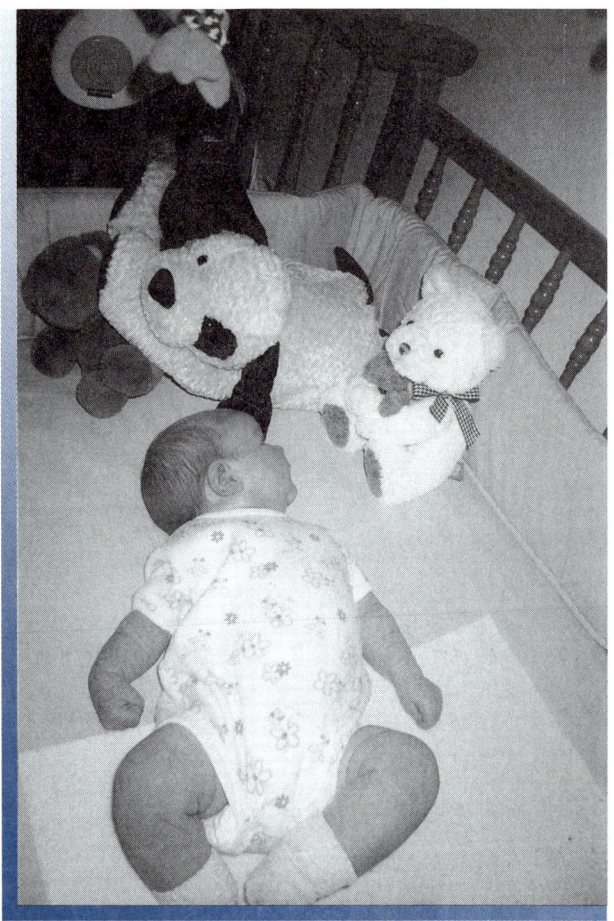

Crib toys are excellent devices for getting a baby to focus attention on objects in the external environment.

sociated actions, such as watching their hands grasp objects. But current research suggests that this ability may be present in very young infants.

In one study (Meltzoff & Borton, 1979), 3-week-old infants were blindfolded and given a pacifier with an unusual nipple shape to suck (see Exhibit 6.4). The nipple was then removed and placed next to another unusually shaped nipple. When the blindfold was removed, the babies would look longest at the nipple they had sucked. These babies were able to detect the shape of the nipple in their mouths and then, based on that information, determine the visual appearance of the nipple. But wait, didn't we just state that babies who become familiar with an object, or habituate, prefer to look at an object they have never seen before? If this is true, then it would be expected that an infant shown two nipples would prefer to

EXHIBIT 6.4 Pacifiers used to test cross-modal transfer

SOURCE: "Intermodal matching by human neonates," by A. Meltzoff and R. Borton, *Nature, 282*, 403–404. Copyright © 1979 Macmillan Magazines Limited. Reprinted with permission from *Nature*.

look at the one they had not sucked. Yet in this study, the infants looked at the nipples they *had* sucked. This apparent contradiction may be explained by the fact that the babies in the Meltzoff and Borton study were only 3 weeks of age. Some researchers argue that very young infants may take longer to habituate to a new stimulus and therefore would look at the same nipple they had sucked. As babies become older, they habituate more quickly, and their ability for cross-modal transfer becomes more developed (Rose, Feldman, Futterweit, & Jankowski, 1998).

Rose and colleagues (1998) found support for an interesting hypothesis regarding cross-modal transfer in infants and children. They found that cross-modal performance was better when tactile exploration was done with the left hand. Why would the left hand be better? First, sensory input from one side of the body goes primarily to the opposite hemisphere of the brain. Second, the right cerebral hemisphere, which is primarily processing the information taken in using the left hand, has a special ability for tactile processing. Taken together, these two factors produce the so-called left-hand advantage in cross-modal transfer. So, if a baby touches an object hidden in a box with the left hand, she will be able to identify it by sight more easily than if she touches it with her right hand.

Other research has found that infants have better memories than had been believed. Rovee-Collier and colleagues (1980) placed 2.5-month-old infants in a crib and attached a mobile to a leg or an arm with a ribbon. The babies learned to shake the mobile by moving that arm or leg. Two weeks later, when placed back in the crib with the same mobile, the babies tried to shake the mobile by moving the appropriate limb, even though the ribbon was not attached.

Indeed, studies seem to show that babies have an innate sense of how the world works. For example, in experiments conducted by Spelke (1994), babies attended more to unexpected physical actions, such as a ball seeming to roll through a solid barrier or a ball hanging in midair. Spelke found that babies also can recognize the position of a moving ball when it leaves their view and then look to where they expect the ball to be when it comes back into sight. Another researcher, Wynn (1992), discovered that babies seem to have a sense of addition and subtraction. In these experiments, researchers would show a 5-month-old baby a doll and then place the doll behind a screen. Then they would show the baby another doll and place that one behind the screen. They would then remove the screen to reveal either two or three dolls. The babies would look longer at the unexpected result of three dolls instead of two.

Sophisticated technology has also contributed to knowledge of information processing. Haith and Canfield (1991) had babies lie in a black box and look at a TV screen. The babies would see a sequence of colorful objects appear in different positions while the researcher watched the babies' eye movements with an infrared camera hooked up to a computer. After seeing a particular sequence five times, the babies would begin to predict where the next object would appear and look to that position. With practice, babies as young as 3 months could remember a four-step series. Two weeks later, when they were placed in the box, they still remembered that series.

This new research indicates that object permanence may occur much earlier than Piaget hypothesized; babies show surprise when objects disappear behind a screen or behave in unexpected ways (Baillargeon, 1987; Spelke, 1985). And babies may be able to imitate others earlier than Piaget believed possible (Meltzoff & Moore, 1977, 1983).

What does all this mean? Spelke (1994) suggested that, in addition to being born with basic reflexes, newborns have an innate core of knowledge of the world and how it works that begins to emerge very early in life. As more sophisticated methods for observing infants are developed, more knowledge about their information-processing capacities will become available. In addition, we are starting to improve extant methods for testing IQ in infants.

IQ Testing in Infancy

Do the capabilities of young infants have any predictive value for later cognitive performance? In general, scores of mental development in the first months of life do not predict later IQ. Prediction of later IQ becomes much more reliable after the baby is 2 years old and no longer an infant. Predicting future functioning in infants is most accurate for those who score significantly below average (Honzik, 1976). In other words, a baby who walks at 9 months may not be brighter than one who walks at 13 months, but a baby who does not walk until 22 months may have cognitive delays.

To date, the Bayley Scale of Infant Development (BSID) is one of the best measures of infant development available (Culbertson & Gyurke, 1990). As already stated, this measure does not predict later cognitive ability if the scores are average to above average. However, the measure is predictive of cognitive problems if the scores are significantly below average. Tests such as the BSID, then, are valuable in identifying developmental problems. The BSID tests cognitive and motor skills of infants aged 2 months to 30 months. The infant is assessed on scales that cover memory, perceptual abilities, problem-solving skills, object permanence, verbal skills, gross and fine motor skills, and personal-social skills. Test administration requires special equipment and a trained clinician.

Interestingly, recent research suggests that measures of information processing in infancy may be more predictive of future learning problems than are tests such as the BSID. For instance, infants who fixate on visual stimuli briefly and habituate quickly have been found to do better on cognitive scores at ages 2 and 4 (Bornstein & Sigman, 1986) and also at age 12 (Sigman, 1991). Additional researchers have provided support for the speculations that speed, reaction time, and memory in infancy are predictors of later childhood IQ (Dougherty & Haith, 1997; Rose & Feldman, 1997). So, bright babies may be able to process visual information more quickly; that is, they learn more about the stimulus and retain the information in a briefer period of time than less bright babies do.

Some evidence indicates that the ability to demonstrate cross-modal transfer and object permanence predicts later IQ (Rose et al., 1998; Rose, 1991). In fact, Rose (1992) found that 6-year-old children at risk for learning disabilities had demonstrated low scores on processing visual information at 7 months of age and on performing cross-modal transfers at 1 year. Further research may make it possible to use information-processing measures to identify children at risk for later learning problems.

Implications for Practice:
Should Babies Learn to Read?

If babies are so brilliant, should parents devote time and energy to teaching young children to read or perform math problems? Should parents place note cards that name items around the house to encourage language development?

Parents who attempt structured teaching of young babies may become invested in the success of their endeavors. Such attempts at early enrichment may turn into stressful parent-child interactions. Babies involved for long periods in a structured teaching session may miss out on opportunities for free play and exploration. Most young babies do not need to know how to read or add—they have better things to do. In addition, no evidence suggests that enrichment programs create superbabies (Zigler & Stevenson, 1993). Parents should be encouraged to provide an interesting environment for the child to explore; to provide stimulating play materials; and to talk to, play with, and enjoy their baby.

Communication

Although newborn babies cannot speak words, they can communicate and are born ready to respond to the human voice. Babies will move in synchrony to human speech in a kind of dance that is slow and rhythmic (Condon, 1975). Neonates prefer human speech to noise; they prefer their own language to others; they prefer baby talk to adult speech; they prefer a female voice to a male voice; and they prefer their mother's voice to another woman's. By the end of infancy, the baby begins to learn to speak a language. Anyone who has tried to learn a new language as an adult knows how hard this can be. But a baby does it quite well and in a consistent and predictable fashion. Babies all over the world and throughout time have developed speech in the same sequence.

Crying and Cooing

The newborn communicates primarily by crying. At first crying is unintentional, simply a response to discomfort or need. But as the caregiver responds to the infant's cries, the baby learns to cry for specific reasons. New parents often ask, "Why does the baby

EXHIBIT 6.5 Developmental milestones for speech and language

Age (in months)	Milestone
2–3	Coos
3–6	Babbles
9–17	Says "mama" and "dada"
12–15	Uses two to three words besides "mama" and "dada"
15–18	Uses many words and can point to body parts
20–24	Uses two- to three-word sentences
24	Refers to self by own name

SOURCE: Adapted from "Etiological factors contributing to deviant development," by D. Willis and E. Holden, in J. Johnson and J. Goldman (Eds.), *Development assessment in clinical child psychology*, p. 5. Copyright © 1990. All rights reserved. Adapted by permission of Allyn & Bacon.

cry?" Babies cry when they are hungry, tired, cold, wet, hot, scared, lonely, in pain, bored—whatever. Most caregivers learn to distinguish between cries, such as the loud, piercing cry of pain or the fussy, whiny sound of tiredness or boredom.

By the end of the first month (3 to 5 weeks), babies begin to coo or make vowel sounds such as "Aaaaah" or "Oooooh" (see Exhibit 6.5). At around 3 or 4 months, the baby throws in some consonants such as "b" or "k."

Babbling

Between 3 and 6 months, the baby puts vowel and consonant sounds together, repeats them over and over, and begins **babbling**. Common early babbling sounds include "mamama," "papapa," and "dadada." It is probably no coincidence that in many languages the common names by which infants to refer to their mother and father are mama, dada, and papa.

Babies all over the world begin making these repetitive sounds at this age. Babbling seems to be a maturational process, because even deaf babies who have never heard language will begin to babble by 6 months; however, with no auditory reinforcement, they stop babbling by 8 months. (But if the hearing impairment is caught early and the parents communicate with the baby through sign language, the baby will repeat some signs over and over and "sign babble.")

Why do infants babble? Babbling may be a form of practice to develop the throat, lips, and tongue for producing sounds (Zigler & Stevenson, 1993). Or it may be a way for infants to begin to relate socially with family members and to learn the basic social skills of communication (Bjorklund & Bjorklund, 1992). For the first six months, infants vocalize at the same time as someone talking to them. By 7 or 8 months of age, though, the baby begins to take turns in vocalizing. Now the baby will listen while someone else is speaking and then respond with babbling. By 8 months, the infant takes on the accent of the native language, matches the speaker's tone of voice, and ends phrases with upward or downward inflection (Bjorklund & Bjorklund, 1992). The baby is learning the basics of communication.

The infant then begins to make sounds that refer to specific objects, people, or actions. For instance, the baby may make an "rrrrr" sound when seeing a truck or say "mmmmm" when seeing food. Babies also accompany their speech with gestures such as pointing to get their message across. A popular form of this type of communication is the scream-and-point method. Babbling increases until the age of 9 to 12 months, when babies say their first word.

Infants with hearing loss also use vocal prelinguistic communication. Some research suggests that infants with and without hearing loss use the same amount of vocal and gesticular communication (Spencer, 1993).

Holophrastic Speech

Babies begin to say their first words by 9 to 12 months. At this point, their receptive language is better than their expressive language; in other words, they understand more words than they can say. By the time babies speak their first word, they can understand almost 100 words (Benedict, 1979). The baby begins to add new words slowly, one at a time, until she has a vocabulary of 10 words (Shaffer, 1993). Then the baby has a vocabulary spurt, or naming explosion, when new words are added rapidly (Zigler & Stevenson, 1993). By 20 months, a baby has a vocabulary of about 50 words; by 24 months, about 180 (Shaffer, 1993).

During the early-speech phase, the baby uses one word to express the meaning of a whole sentence, which is referred to as **holophrastic speech**. For instance, a baby may point to a pitcher, whine, and say, "Juice," meaning, "I would like some juice to drink." When you pour a cup and hand it to him, he may smile and happily say, "Juice," meaning, "Oh, good, some juice to drink at last." When the cup tips and spills juice on his shirt, he may grab the shirt, cry, and say, "Juice," meaning, "I've spilled juice all over me and now I'm wet and uncomfortable and I want a clean shirt." Babies at this age also use one word in a fashion referred to as **overextension**. This means that the word becomes generalized to include a larger category. For instance, babies often use the word *dog* to refer to any furry animal, but this overextension does not mean that the baby can't tell the difference between a dog and a cow. The baby often can accurately point out animals in a book before being able to name them. (Remember, babies know more words than they can say; but when your usable vocabulary consists of four words, and you know the large mooing animal is not Mommy, Daddy, or ball, then *dog* is your best guess.) Often the adult will then provide the proper name of the animal for the baby: "That's a cow. A cow goes moo. Can you say cow?" By mislabeling the animal, the baby has gained more knowledge and an increased vocabulary. So the baby now points to the cow and says . . . "Dog." It may take a few tries to get it right.

What are the first words babies learn? Babies learn words that refer to things that interest them or are important to them — often people or objects such as caregivers (Mommy, Daddy), toys (bear, doll), food (milk, cookie), and animals (dog, kitty). They also like things that move or make noise (airplane, truck) or that can be acted on (ball).

Telegraphic Speech

Between 18 and 24 months, babies begin to put words together to form simple phrases or sentences. Because these sentences are abbreviated, like the message in a telegram, they are referred to as **telegraphic speech**. When you have to pay for each word you use, as you do when sending a telegram, then you want to use only words that are absolutely necessary to convey your message. So, in telegraphic speech, babies use nouns, verbs, and adjectives. They omit auxiliary verbs, prepositions, articles, and pronouns. For example, 18-month-old Sarah had never said more than one word at a time. One day she was sitting quietly at her mother's feet looking at a lamp. After a few minutes, she climbed into her mother's lap and said, "Mommy, lamp, hot, burn, ouch." With a few words she had communicated the message that if you touched a hot light bulb you would burn yourself, and it would hurt.

This period of development is an exciting time. Parents begin to get a glimpse of what is going on in their child's mind. But what is going on in an infant's mind? Again, infants use words that are important to them: words that convey action (throw ball), possession (my truck), recurrence (more juice), nonexistence (all gone), location (doggie out), and naming and labeling (cow).

Implications for Practice: Recognizing Speech Problems

Although infants develop speech in a predictable sequence, the amount of speech individual children evidence at age 2 can vary greatly. Some 2-year-olds speak in simple two-word phrases, whereas others speak in longer sentences. Both are normal. But, as we mentioned earlier, it is important to recognize delays in speech, especially in the case of hearing-impaired children. If the hearing loss is caught early, children can learn sign language in the same progression as they would have learned spoken language. Hearing loss is often undetected because the infant begins to babble on schedule. Parents should instead note how the infant responds to loud noises. A baby who does not startle when hearing a loud noise, or does not look to find the source of a noise, may have hearing problems.

As we have seen, to develop speech, infants need to hear spoken language. But even some infants without hearing impairments can have problems with adequate verbal stimulation. Parents who lack developmental information may assume that a 7-month-old infant doesn't understand speech and thus may fail to interact verbally with the baby. This can be a particular problem with teenage parents. Adolescent parents need to be encouraged to speak to the baby, even if the essence of the speech is silly nonsense. ■

Adult Communication Patterns with Infants

Have you ever heard an adult say something like, "How's my little schnookums?" What happens to mature, sophisticated adults when they see a baby? All of a sudden they begin speaking in a singsong, high-pitched voice, using short phrases, asking lots of questions, using many repetitions, and adding exaggerated emphasis to certain words.

"How's Daddy's little schnookums? What do you see? Is that a doggie? Yes? Where's the doggie? Hello, doggie. Nice doggie."

This kind of speech directed toward infants occurs in other cultures and is initiated by both sexes and people in various age groups, from elderly gentlemen to 4-year-olds. Some parents attempt to avoid talking to their baby using this infant-directed speech, or baby talk, fearing that their baby will end up talking this way. But new research suggests that failure to use baby talk may be a mistake. Babies love to listen to this type of speech and actually seem to learn language better when addressed in this fashion.

Anne Fernald (1987), the leading researcher in infant-directed speech, has suggested that babies prefer baby talk. She trained babies to turn their heads to hear different types of speech, and these babies turned to hear infant-directed speech more than they did to hear regular adult speech. In an effort to explain why babies prefer baby talk, Fernald is studying the musical qualities of infant-directed speech. The sounds in baby talk cover two octaves, with a sing-song quality that may help modulate infants' emotions. Also, this type of speech may help teach babies language, because it engages the babies' attention. Remember, babies prefer high-pitched sounds to low-pitched ones. (Babies are able to respond to vocally expressed emotion before they can respond to facial expressions of emotion.) In addition, certain sounds in baby talk have different meanings, such as high-pitched sounds stressing the importance of a particular word.

In another study by Fernald (1991), when an adult who used either baby talk or adult talk asked babies under 18 months to look at a picture of an object, the babies would recognize the name of the object only when the adult emphasized that word using baby talk (Adler, 1990). According to Fernald, then, baby talk is important for normal infant development. In fact, instead of just being silly chatter, it may be music to their ears (Adler, 1990).

Attitudes and Emotions

In the past, research concentrated on cognitive development, with emotion being seen as the outcome of cognitive activity. The baby would engage in activities and learn that some were pleasant, some were sad, and some were scary (Bremmer, 1988). Recent research, however, indicates that emotions have a strong biological component. If this is true, then babies do not learn to be afraid of unfamiliar situations; they enter a developmental stage in which they begin to exhibit fear of strange people and places.

Research by Izard (1982) and associates suggests that babies all over the world develop emotions at the same ages in a predictable sequence. Izard videotaped infants' expressions during various situations, such as being separated from and reunited with their mothers, being approached by a stranger, hearing a balloon pop nearby, tasting lemon rind, and receiving scheduled inoculations. He then had independent observers classify the infants' expressions. This type of research has found that at birth babies display interest, distress, disgust, and happiness. Between age 2.5 months and 6 months, infants display other primary emotions: anger, sadness, surprise, and fear.

Fear is one of the emotions that develops during the first year of life. At 5 to 6 months, babies begin to show **stranger anxiety**. Before this age, if given time to warm up, babies will smile at anyone. At 8 months, though, babies will cry and turn away from an unfamiliar face. Between 8 and 10 months, babies begin to display **separation anxiety**; babies now cry at being left by the primary caregiver. This fear begins to diminish at about 13 months, when the baby has acquired object permanence and can remember the mother when she is away and anticipate her return. At this time, the baby also may have a **transitional object**— a blanket, toy, or teddy bear to use for comfort in the caregiver's absence. During the second year of life, babies add complex or secondary emotions of embarrassment, shame, guilt, and pride. These emotions may require that the child have a sense of self and knowledge of appropriate conduct; in other words, the baby would realize that "Baby has done something wrong." By 18–24 months, babies are fairly accomplished in the emotional area and can display a wide range of emotions and even fake certain emotions, such as sadness, in order to manipulate others (Shaffer, 1993).

Research suggests that emotional expression in infancy is predictive of later childhood emotional characteristics. Shy babies grow up to be shy children. Huebner (cited in Trotter, 1987) had babies look at a human face, a mannequin face, and an inanimate object with scrambled facial features. Five years later, the babies who had looked longest at the human face were the most sociable, whereas those who had looked the least time at the human face were shy and withdrawn.

Many researchers have wondered whether babies can read facial expressions. Research on younger infants is inconclusive, but there is clear evidence that by 8 to 10 months of age, babies are affected by the moods of others (Shaffer, 1993). Termine (1988) found that babies of sad mothers exhibited a similar expression and showed less exploratory and play behavior than did babies of happy mothers. When confronted with strange situations, babies at this age look to the mother for emotional cues. For instance, if the baby sees a new toy that looks like a pink bunny noisily beating a drum, the baby will look to see how the mother feels about this object. If the mother smiles, the baby may approach the toy. By 12 months, babies will even look to strangers for cues on how to react. Looking to others for emotional information is known as *social referencing*. In a study by Klinnert and colleagues (1986), 12-month-old babies would play with an unfamiliar toy if a nearby stranger smiled at them but would not approach the toy if the stranger showed fear. Older babies, then, take cues from others as to which situations are safe or not.

Jerome Kagan studies human infant development, and Stephen Suomi conducts developmental studies of monkeys. These researchers have found that extremely inhibited children and uptight monkeys often behave in similar ways when faced with novel situations. They found that these species have similar physiological reactions, as well. Kagan believes that the limbic system—particularly the amygdala and hypothalamus—in these children and monkeys is activated more easily and that this overactivation is inherited. Kagan found that timid children show a pattern of excessive physiological responses to mildly stressful situations that do not occur in more easygoing children. Under stress, these children have dilated pupils, a more rapid heartbeat, and elevated blood cortisol. Suomi's uptight monkeys, when stressed during infancy by brief separations from their mothers, showed the same rise in blood cortisol and increase in heart rate. The researchers found that neither the monkeys nor the children tend to outgrow these abnormal physiological responses to stress.

Suomi and Kagan agree that this extreme timidity seems to have a genetic foundation. The monkeys were reared together in nurseries and in peer groups, so parenting was not influencing their individual reactions to stress. Research by Robert Plomin and David Rowe has indicated that identical twins tend to exhibit the same reaction to strangers, supporting the notion that humans possess a biological predisposition to extreme shyness (Adler, 1989, 1990; Asher, 1987). About 20% of monkeys and 15% of children seem to be genetically predisposed to timidity. However, being born shy does not doom a child or monkey to lifelong social difficulties.

Suomi found that monkeys can be helped to overcome their stress responses through changes in how they are reared (Adler, 1989, 1990; Asher, 1987). Environmental influences such as having a nurturing mother can offset the genetic tendency toward shyness. Surrounding a monkey with friendly, outgoing peers and a nurturing foster mother or grandmother helps the monkey learn coping strategies. When stressed, this monkey can seek out a nurturing friend or mother figure. This activity prevents the normal high-stress physical response. Growing up with a nurturing mother figure often helps these monkeys respond better than their peers and become leaders in their group.

Kagan's studies of human children provide evidence that, although timid toddlers tend to stay shy, these children can overcome this tendency with help from their parents (Adler, 1989, 1990; Asher, 1987). Social workers can help parents of very shy children recognize the problem early, protect the child from too much stress, and help the child learn coping skills. Parents can help the child by inviting other children to the home to play with the child and by teaching the child how to cope with the physical response brought on by stressful situations.

The work of Suomi and Kagan has helped to clarify how heredity and environment interact to influence behavior and development. Some children may be born shy, but a supportive and nurturing environment can help them to later develop social success.

Infant Temperament

Though all babies seem to possess primary emotions at birth, those emotions vary in how they are exhibited among individual newborns. Some babies are easily comforted and sleep and eat on a regular schedule. Some babies are more difficult to comfort and have very unpredictable daily patterns. The characteristic pattern in which an infant responds to and interacts with the environment is referred to as **temperament**. Some consider temperament to be the basis of later personality development. And for the most part, temperament is thought to be biologically determined (Thomas & Chess, 1989).

EXHIBIT 6.6 Dimensions of temperament

Activity level: Active babies are in motion most of the time, even while sleeping. Quiet babies can be placed almost anywhere, as they will not move much.

Rhythmicity: Some babies are very regular in the times they eat, sleep, and have bowel movements. Others are very irregular and unpredictable.

Approach or withdrawal: When presented with a new toy, some babies respond positively by smiling, vocalizing, and reaching for it. Other babies cry, turn away, or push the toy away.

Adaptability: Some babies adapt to changes in routine easily and quickly. They may be shy with a new sitter at first but accept the sitter after a brief time. Some babies become very upset at even slight changes. They may cry for days even if their familiar sitter only changes hairstyle.

Threshold of responsiveness: Some babies sleep through loud noises and cry briefly when they fall down. Others wake easily in response to sounds and cry long and loud when even slightly hurt.

Intensity of reaction: Some babies cry softly and giggle gently. Others scream and kick and laugh out loud.

Quality of mood: Some babies are pleasant and contented most of the time. Others are fussy and irritable.

Distractibility: Some babies can be easily distracted from something they want. If you offer them a toy, they will stop trying to turn on the TV. Other babies are intent on figuring out how the TV works no matter what you do.

Persistence and attention span: Some babies are very persistent in their activities. If they are looking at a book, they need to turn every page before they will let you put on their shoes. Other babies turn a few pages of the book and move on to something else. Some children are temperamentally "difficult," displaying negative moods and sleep, eating, and elimination irregularities. These children are less adaptable, more vulnerable to adversity, and more likely to produce and elicit adverse responses.

In an extensive study of temperament, Alexander Thomas and Stella Chess conducted the New York Longitudinal Survey in the mid-1970s. They looked at 133 individuals from infancy through adulthood and identified nine dimensions of temperament, including activity level, rhythmicity, approach or withdrawal, adaptability, threshold of responsiveness, intensity of reaction, quality of mood, distractibility, and persistence and attention span . (See Exhibit 6.6.)

Based on the data obtained from their work, Thomas and Chess (1977) determined that the combination of these nine dimensions described three types of children: the easy child, the slow-to-warm-up child, and the difficult child. Approximately 40% of the children in their sample fit the description of the **easy child**. This baby is characterized by regular, positive responses to new stimuli, high adaptability to change, and mild or moderately intense mood, which is usually positive. In other words, this infant is apt to easily accept new toys, foods, individuals, and settings. This baby has predictable eating and sleeping schedules and is usually happy and pleasant.

Of the children studied, 15% were classified as slow to warm up. As babies, these children exhibit a more sedate and less exuberant orientation to the world. They have more negative responses and are slower to adapt to new situations. Like the easy child, the **slow-to-warm-up child** usually has predictable eating and sleeping schedules. Although these infants are wary of new experiences, such as visiting a new house, they are able to adjust over time, if not hurried or pushed during the transition.

In contrast to the other types, the **difficult child** has unpredictable daily habits. As babies, they wake up at a different time every day and do not establish a regular napping schedule. Their appetite also varies from day to day. These infants exhibit negative responses to new stimuli, adapt slowly or not at all, and usually express an intense, negative mood. These babies protest loudly when introduced to new toys, foods, people, or situations; throw temper tantrums when agitated or frustrated; and squeal loudly when excited. Of the children in the sample, 10% fit this description.

Since the work of Thomas and Chess, much research has been conducted to examine the validity

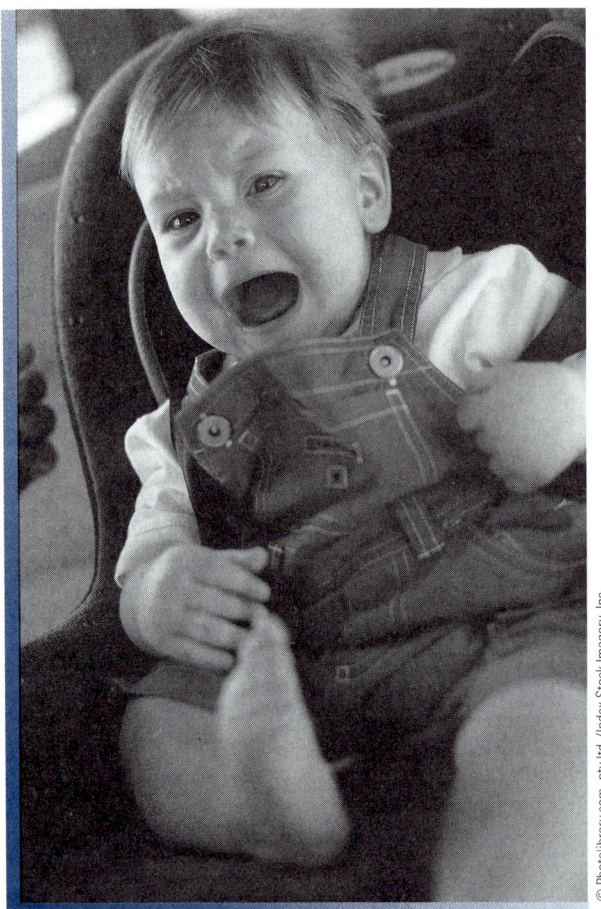

Some children are temperamentally "difficult," displaying negative moods and irregularities in sleep, eating, and elimination. These children are less adaptable, more vulnerable to adversity, and more likely to produce and elicit adverse responses.

of inborn temperament. Studies of twins have found temperament to be biologically determined to some extent (Emde et al., 1992). Our review of studies by Kagan found that shy babies grow up to be shy children, and difficult babies grow up to be difficult adults. In Thomas and Chess's study, 70% of the difficult infants entered psychiatric treatment later in life, but only 18% of the easy infants did so.

Implications for Practice: Goodness of Fit

Although research has found that one's personality seems to be partially genetically determined, the environment shapes the balance of personality development. One way that environment can affect personality development is through **goodness of fit**. Goodness of fit refers to how well the demands of the environment match the child's behavioral style. An active, intense baby with outgoing, high-energy parents who encourage loud play and exploration will have a better fit than will such a baby born to quiet, introspective parents who expect the baby to sit and look at books.

Research indicates that the family environment can play a role in the child's later development. Maziade and colleagues (1990) discovered that all 38 of the children in their study, who were identified at age 7 as having a difficult temperament and a poorly functioning family with little behavioral control, were diagnosed as having a clinical disorder in preadolescence or adolescence. A slow-to-warm-up baby may experience stress if the parents are highly sociable and always on the go. An easy child with a more difficult sibling may be ignored while the parents concentrate their energy on their other child.

Parents can be helped to understand their babies' different temperament styles and to alter the environment to fit that style and enhance the child's development. Researcher Alicia F. Lieberman (1993), author of *The Emotional Life of the Toddler*, focuses on all three temperament types described by Thomas and Chess, as well as an additional type, which she calls the active child. Lieberman makes recommendations as to how best to interact with each type of child. Parents of difficult children should not take the children's behavior personally, should keep a sense of humor about the children's behavior, should be patiently available to the children, should have clear guidelines for behavior, and should develop a support system that allows the parents time away from the children. Parents of active children should structure the house and yard to allow for robust play. Parents of slow-to-warm-up children should take special measures in introducing their children to new situations. Parents should essentially stay near the children until their mood has changed from caution to enjoyment, then step back. Lieberman reminds parents that easy children can be taken advantage of. They may not demand attention or complain, even when they should, and may therefore be ignored in the hectic pace of everyday life. ∎

Attachment*

Anyone who has had the privilege of a friendship with a small child may have noticed changes in how the child interacts with you as he grows. Before 3

---

*Ellen Blessington, MSW, contributed to this section.

EXHIBIT 6.7 Bowlby's phases of attachment

	Age	Behaviors
Phase 1	Birth–2 or 3 mos.	Displays indiscriminate smiling, cooing, clinging toward anyone.
Phase 2	2–3 mos. to 6–7 mos.	Begins selective interactions. Develops a true social smile directed at preferred caregivers. Compares a stranger's face with caregiver's.
Phase 3	6–7 mos. to 1 year	Clearly attached to primary caregiver. Cries when caregiver leaves. Crawls after caregiver. Wary of strangers and strange situations.
Phase 4	Second year of life	Has full object permanence. More secure in knowledge that caregiver exists when not in sight. More sociable with other people.

months, the baby will come to you, smile, and make eye contact. Around 4 months, the baby may frown at seeing your face, look to the mother's face, and then back at you. It may take a few minutes of coaxing to get the baby to come to you. By 8 months, the baby may whine and turn away to hug the mother when you approach. You may have to resort to bribing with a toy or treat to get the baby to come to you. But the baby may still refuse, obviously preferring her mother now. Because of these actions, you may begin to feel the child no longer likes you. Then one day you go to visit your active toddler friend and you are greeted with a big grin. The child takes your hand, waves goodbye to Mom, and wants to go home with you (see Exhibit 6.7).

This scenario illustrates the process of **attachment**, or forming a strong emotional tie to a caregiver. Researchers have long been interested in what motivates a baby to form this close bond with a caregiver and to prefer that caregiver to other people. Early theories held that attachment was the result of need satisfaction. In other words, a baby loves his mother because she feeds and takes care of him. But classic research by Harlow on infant rhesus monkeys failed to support this idea. These monkeys were separated from their mothers at birth and raised in a cage with an inanimate surrogate mother made of either wire or cloth. Some monkeys were fed by the wire surrogates and some by the cloth ones. But when the infant monkeys needed someone to cling to, they preferred the cloth mother even when they had been fed by the wire mother. These monkeys showed no preference for the wire surrogate who had fed them.

Today, attachment theory is most closely identified with psychiatrist John Bowlby (1958). According to his theory, attachment has a biological, evolutionary basis. A baby forms a close, intimate relationship with a caregiver to ensure its survival. In an evolutionary sense, when a predator threatens, someone needs to protect the vulnerable young. And infants need a particular caregiver to remember to pick them up when everyone else is running away.

This theory suggests that parents and infants may be biologically programmed to form an attachment. The caregiver and the infant each exhibit specific behaviors that facilitate the process of forming a bond.

The Parents' Behaviors

Parents of an infant engage in several activities meant to engage the baby's attention. They position their faces directly within the infant's visual field, about 22.5 cm from the baby's face (Papousek & Papousek, 1992). This is a very interesting phenomenon considering that a newborn can focus on objects no more than 30 cm away. Parents seem to know instinctively how far the baby can see. Parents also attempt to get the infant's attention through a series of facial expressions known as the "greeting response." In this response, parents tilt their head back, open their mouth halfway, and raise their eyebrows (Papousek & Papousek, 1987). In addition, parents use baby talk when addressing the infant. Research suggests that these behaviors are not conscious but intuitive in nature (Papousek & Papousek, 1992). Parents just seem to know what babies like.

The Infant's Behaviors

The biggest contribution the infant makes in the attachment process is having "the look." Babies are cute. Adults just cannot seem to resist the rounded facial features and "babyishness" of infants. Adults are also drawn to babies' responsiveness. Parents like to feel recognized and needed, and newborns seem equipped to meet that need. Babies show a particular fondness for a human face and respond to adults with smiles and vocalizations. As we have already seen, babies recognize their mother's voice at birth. Newborns also respond by imitating facial expressions.

The infant's reflexes—in particular grasping, sucking, rooting, and turning—serve as responses to parental caregiving and also reinforce parental interaction, making the parents feel needed. In addition, infants quickly learn who is caring for them and make responses that reinforce that care. For instance, within three days of birth, a newborn will respond to being placed in the feeding position by moving in the direction of the mother, turning toward the breast, and opening the mouth (Call, 1964).

Other Attachment Ideas

According to Mary Ainsworth and her colleagues (1978), the infant uses the primary caregiver as a secure base, leaving him or her to explore the environment, then returning for comfort and security. Using this idea, Ainsworth developed a method of measuring attachment by observing an infant's response to various events occurring in a strange situation. This laboratory assessment procedure, known as the Strange Situation Procedure, involves eight structured episodes occurring during about twenty-five minutes:

Episode 1: Mother and baby are introduced to a playroom.
Episode 2: Mother and baby are left alone to explore the contents of the playroom.
Episode 3: An unfamiliar woman joins them.
Episode 4: The mother leaves the room and the stranger attempts to play with the baby.
Episode 5: The mother returns.
Episode 6: The child is left completely alone.
Episode 7: The strange woman returns.
Episode 8: The mother returns.

Analysis of the responses of infants in the strange situation led to a classification of attachment patterns. Ainsworth identified three levels of attachment:

1. Secure attachment: These infants use their mothers as a secure base from which to explore the playroom. They are aware of the mother's presence and keep checking to make sure she is available if needed. When their mothers leave them, these infants cry or protest. When the mothers return, these infants seek them out for comfort and physical contact.
2. Anxious attachment: These infants are clingy and reluctant to explore the playroom even with their mother present. When their mothers leave, these infants become extremely upset and cry for long periods of time. When their mothers return, these infants seek physical contact but also hit their mothers or pull away. They are not easily soothed by their mothers. According to Ainsworth, these infants do not trust their mothers to meet their security needs.
3. Avoidant attachment: These infants demonstrate a marked indifference toward their mothers. They do not use their mothers as secure bases but actually act as if their mothers are not present. They do not seek eye contact or attention from their mothers. They are not distressed when their mothers leave and show indifference upon their return.

Of middle-class infants, 65% display secure-attachment behaviors. What factors influence the attachment process? How do 35% of infants end up not securely attached?

Risk Factors Associated with Attachment Failure

Factors involving the baby, the mother, and the home can interfere with attachment. First of all, characteristics of babies can affect the mother-infant relationship. For instance, premature babies may be at risk for attachment problems; these babies are not as "cute" as full-term infants and also are less responsive. Preterm infants can be less engaged with their mothers and receive less enjoyment in mother-involved play activities (Field, 1983). In addition, preterm infants often spend an extended period of time in the neonatal intensive care unit, making contact with the mother difficult (Niven, Wisniewski, & AlRoomi, 1993). However, this may be only a temporary interruption for the mother and infant, with attachment possible once the mother takes the baby home. In fact, a recent research study failed to show a difference in attachment patterns between extremely premature and full-term infants (Wintgens et al., 1998). Other infant-related factors that can affect attachment include drug exposure (Lester, 1992) and difficult temperament.

A parent-related problem that affects the attachment relationship can occur with adolescent mothers. These mothers on average engage in less verbal exchange with their children and have trouble interpreting and responding to their cues (Crockenberg, 1981; Field, 1981; Hann et al., 1990). Another problem arises with depressed mothers, who may have more problems bonding with their babies. A depressed mother is wrapped up in her own feelings and may not be responsive to an infant. She may be so busy concentrating on her own pain that she misses the baby's social cues. The baby then tends to match the mother's mood even with other nondepressed adults. Research shows that the way a mother expresses her depression can influence the attachment pattern of the infant (Rosenblum, Mazet, & Benony, 1997). Depressed mothers who express themselves as stressed and anxious tend to have infants who develop insecure-ambivalent attachment. These babies appear anxious and restless when separated from the mother but show mixed behaviors when reunited with her. Infants often develop insecure-avoidant attachment when the mother expresses her depression by appearing disinterested and withdrawn. Babies with insecure-avoidant attachment seem independent when separated from the mother and avoid contact when reunited. Other parental factors that may affect attachment include alcoholism, childhood abuse and neglect, and an unplanned pregnancy.

Factors in the home also can affect attachment. A mother with lots of small children may not have time to respond to a new infant. The marital relationship has an effect on the primary caregiver's interactions with an infant. When spouses or partners are supportive, mothers are more responsive and affectionate toward their babies (Crnic, 1984). And a mother's level of social support is critical, especially when she is parenting an irritable infant. A secure attachment is more likely when a mother has an adequate social-support network (Crockenberg, 1981). High levels of environmental stress also influence mother-baby interactions (Booth et al., 1987). Mothers dealing with poverty, domestic violence, and their own personal trauma may not have enough emotional energy to engage an infant.

A new category of attachment failure has been suggested by Main and Solomon (1986, 1990): disorganized/disoriented attachment. Children in this category exhibit unclear, inconclusive, or contradictory attachment patterns. This category can include children who are hard to classify and do not fit into one of Ainsworth's three patterns. Children with this pattern often come from families with the problems just mentioned.

Implications for Practice: Assessing Attachment Problems

Bowlby believed that a warm, intimate, and continuous relationship with the mother was vital for a child's later personality development. Recent research suggests that the quality of a child's attachment with a primary caregiver is an excellent predictor of later functioning (Cicchetti & Wagner, 1990). Securely attached children exhibit a healthy mix of self-reliance and the ability to ask for help from others (Stroufe, Fox, & Pancake, 1983). Children with secure attachments relate better to their peers than do those with insecure attachments (Lieberman, 1977; Matas, Arend, & Stroufe, 1978). A strong parent-child bond also seems to result in better self-knowledge (Pipp, Easterbrooks, & Harmon, 1992) and in better school performance (Jacobsen, Edelstein, & Hoffman, 1994).

If attachment is so important to development, what are the signs to look for in assessing children that would point to attachment problems? Children with attachment problems are believed to exhibit the following behaviors in interactions: They do not show a preference for a particular adult; they may seek affection and attention from anyone and run up to and hug total strangers. They will wander away from their caregiver—the caregiver frequently loses the child in crowds and in public places. The child may be reckless and accident-prone, and excessively clingy or aggressive toward the caregiver. The type of behaviors that Zeanah and Emde (1994) believe are suggestive of an attachment difficulty in young children are listed in Exhibit 6.8.

EXHIBIT 6.8 Assessing attachment problems in young children

Behaviors	Signs of Attachment Disorders
Showing affection	Lack of warm and affectionate interchanges across a range of interactions; promiscuous affection with relatively unfamiliar adults
Comfort seeking	Lack of comfort seeking when hurt, frightened, or ill; comfort-seeking in odd or ambivalent manner
Reliance for help	Excessive dependence, or inability to seek and use supportive presence of attachment figure when needed
Cooperation	Lack of compliance with caregiver requests and demands by the child as a striking feature of caregiver-child interactions, or compulsive compliance
Exploratory behavior	Failure to check back with caregiver in unfamiliar settings, or exploration limited by child's unwillingness to leave caregiver
Controlling behavior	Oversolicitous and inappropriate caregiving behavior, or excessively bossy and punitive controlling of caregiver by the child
Reunion responses	Failure to reestablish interaction after separations, including ignoring/avoiding behaviors, intense anger, or lack of affection

SOURCE: From "Disorder of attachment" by C. Zeanah, O. Mammen, and A. Lieberman, in C. Zeanah Jr. (Ed.), *Handbook of infant mental health*, p. 346. Copyright © 1993 The Guilford Press. Reprinted with permission.

FOCUS ON MULTICULTURALISM

CULTURAL CONSIDERATIONS IN EXAMINING AFRICAN AMERICAN ATTACHMENT PATTERNS

Practitioners should be aware that the cross-cultural validity of identified attachment behaviors has been called into question. As stated by attachment researcher Jacquelyne Faye Jackson (1993), "[b]oth execution of the 'strange situation' procedure and unequivocal classification of infant attachments have been technically difficult in cultures outside the USA (Sagi et al., 1985; Takahashi, 1986), and no transcultural distribution of types has been found (Van Ijzendoorn & Kroonenberg, 1988)" (p. 91).

Jackson (1993) presented a compelling argument that the African American practice of sharing child-care responsibilities among relatives results in a negative misinterpretation of African American infant-attachment patterns. Jackson explained that, as a consequence of discrimination, African American mothers have, historically and currently, needed to work outside the home. As a result of this economic reality, African American culture has developed a distinct, adaptive cultural pattern to ensure that children receive the nurturance and care they require.

This cultural pattern includes the exposure of the child to a multitude of extended-family caregivers. Jackson (1993) noted research (Young, 1970) indicat-

Cultural considerations are important when assessing attachment in African American families.

ing that, because of a cultural context that encourages the acceptance and development of caring interactions with a number of different caregivers across a variety of settings, African American children develop an independent and outgoing orientation. Hence, she asserts that when African American children are assessed using the Strange Situation, they may mistakenly be viewed as not being securely attached because of their greater confidence in examining novel environments and their high level of trust as to the comings and goings of caregivers in general.

Jackson (1993) therefore maintained that it is not surprising that a relatively high proportion of African American children appear to be insecurely attached when assessed according to the standards for majority children. In support of her contention, she cited the work of Hansen (1980), who also questioned whether the African American children he had examined when employing the Strange Situation had experienced the degree of stress necessary to elicit attachment behaviors. The children he studied actively explored the playroom, did not demonstrate noteworthy distress at times of separation, and were not specifically solicitous of maternal attention at times of reunion. Furthermore, these children had an overall genial demeanor during the procedure. Thus, it can be argued that these children did not experience the Strange Situation in the same fashion as do majority children, both in terms of their expression of distress and their reunion behaviors. Moreover, given the infants' observed pleasant attitudes toward their mothers, it is also questionable whether these infants could be seen as fitting Ainsworth's typology for resistant or avoidant infants.

Because she believed that the Strange Situation is inadequate in assessing African American infant-attachment patterns, Jackson (1993) conducted an exploratory study that employed a laboratory assessment procedure developed by Kotelchuck (1976). Kotelchuck's playroom strategy includes two attachment figures, in contrast to the Strange Situation, which includes only one. Jackson found that African American infants use both their mothers and secondary attachment figures as secure bases from which to explore the environment. She also found that the majority of the African American infants she studied were simply not upset by being left in a playroom for a brief time period with an amicable stranger. As a result of her exploratory study, Jackson believed that, although Kotelchuck's procedure is an improvement in assessing African American infant attachment by the inclusion of multiple caregivers, it is not sufficiently stressful to activate distress reactions in African American children. Hence, she concluded that culturally relevant assessment instruments need to be developed and that researchers should be cautious in arriving at negative conclusions regarding African American infant-attachment patterns.

Courtesy of Ellen Blessington

Social Cognition and Regulation

At what age does a baby know that she is a baby? Lewis conducted experiments to test babies' awareness of self (Lewis & Brooks-Gunn, 1979). He put a spot of rouge on the baby's nose and had the mother sit with her infant in her lap in front of a mirror. If the babies recognized themselves in the mirror, they touched their own nose. Babies under 1 year looked in the mirror but did not touch their nose. Some babies at 15 months would touch their nose; but by 18 months, 75% of the babies recognized themselves in the mirror and touched their nose. Further research by Lewis has suggested that most babies have a sense of self by 18 months.

Margaret Mahler felt that developing a sense of self as separate from others was a major developmental process with a significant effect on personality development. In Mahler's view, the infant grows from being a newborn with no sense of self as separate from her caretaker to being an autonomous, independent individual. She termed this process **separation-individuation**. During the first month of life, infants are in the normal autistic phase, unaware of self, other people, or the world. At 1 to 5 months, the babies are in the normal symbiotic phase, aware that someone is caring for them but unaware of that person as separate from themselves. At 5 to 9 months, in the differentiation phase, babies begin to get a sense of self and non-self. At this age, babies will sit in their mother's lap and explore the mother's face visually and tactually. As babies begin to crawl and then walk between 9 and 14 months, they enter the practicing phase. Now they can move away from the mother, but they need to check back often for emotional refueling (a look, a smile, a hug). The rapprochement phase occurs between 14 and 24 months. Babies know they

EXHIBIT 6.9 Developmental milestones for social behaviors

Age (in months)	Milestone
0–2	Smiles in response to a voice or touch
3–5	Smiles spontaneously
	Reaches for familiar people
9–11	Plays pat-a-cake and peek-a-boo
	Becomes upset when separated from caregiver
20–23	Plays near but not with other children
28–31	Is aware of differences between sexes
32–35	Can identify own sex
	Can separate easily from caregiver

SOURCE: Adapted from "Etiological factors contributing to deviant development," by D. Willis and E. Holden, in J. Johnson and J. Goldman (Eds.), *Development assessment in clinical child psychology*, p. 5. Copyright © 1990. All rights reserved. Adapted by permission of Allyn & Bacon.

are separate from the mother but still need to check back regularly. The consolidation phase occurs between the age of 2 and 3. Now babies can separate from the mother without becoming too upset.

Remember that Mahler's theories of separation-individuation are based on the clinical infant, the adult recalling the past in psychotherapy. In experiments involving information processing, Daniel Stern (1985) has done extensive research on the observed infant. On the basis of data from these experiments, Stern concluded that infants have a sense of self from birth, that babies are always able to differentiate self from others. How? As we discussed in the Information Processing section of this chapter, babies are able at birth to accurately discriminate sensory input. Even newborns seem to have an innate core of knowledge about the world. They can tell when they are sucking their own or someone else's fingers. They can tell when they are moving their own arm or having it raised by someone to play "How big is baby?" And they can tell when they are causing actions or when someone else is.

In any case, by the end of infancy, children have a well-established sense of self as separate and independent. This notion of self is important for later development. For instance, as you may remember, a baby must have a sense of self before being able to express more complex emotions, such as guilt and shame. More important, a sense of self is a necessary foundation for social development. "The acquisition of the self by the end of the second year not only facilitates the acquisition of social knowledge, but underlies social competence, peer relations, gender identity, and empathy" (Brooks-Gunn & Lewis, 1984, p. 234). Some important milestones in social development are listed in Exhibit 6.9.

Regulation

Somewhere around the age of 2, the baby learns to say "No!" This is a statement of independence and autonomy. The baby now has a sense of self and what that self wants and does not want. The ability to know right from wrong, good from bad, and want from not want begins to develop after the age of 18 months. Regulation can begin when the infant has adequate language skills, a sense of self, more complex emotions of guilt and shame, and a sense of autonomy (Lyons-Ruth & Zeanah, 1993). Even babies who have been "easy" up to this point may not be as compliant now. They are more difficult to distract. They can formulate certain goals and realize whether or not they have obtained them (Lyons-Ruth & Zeanah, 1993). And, in terms of moral development, they have internalized certain standards and become upset when those standards are not met. Where did they get these standards and ideas of right and wrong, good and bad?

These standards and ideas are based on the previous responses of others. Remember, babies engage in **social referencing**; that is, they look to an adult for guidance in how to respond in new situations. Babies learn through experience that, when they throw things on the floor and break them, Mother becomes upset. They learn that when they pour their juice on the floor, Father becomes upset. So now when babies break or spill something, they become upset. At this age, babies often will reach out for an object and then look to their mother to see if she is going to stop them.

Babies at this age also are unsure of many standards, and they test parents to determine which actions are acceptable and which are not—usually more than once. "Will Mother get mad at me if I eat the food in this bowl on the floor? She lets the cat eat it. But Mother yelled at me last time I ate it. Why? Let's see what happens this time."

Through repeated experimentation, babies learn to be reasonably obedient in the presence of parents. But they do not possess the ability to obey when parents are not watching until about 36 months (Lyons-Ruth & Zeanah, 1993). To the 2-year-old, it's okay to eat cat food unless Mom catches you. In this context, the reason to be good is to avoid displeasure from Mom.

Implications for Practice:
The Terrible Twos

During the second half of the second year of life, babies can become much more difficult. They begin to develop a sense of autonomy and independence. They want to do things for themselves, they want to do it now, and they want to do it their way. *No* becomes their favorite word. Even when asked whether they want ice cream, children may reply "No" and then cry when the parents don't provide the ice cream. Some parents become locked in power struggles with their children, sometimes erupting into food battles. Parents may try to force the child to eat, only to discover that some children would rather starve than eat when coerced. And some parents allow the toddler to run the house. They hesitate to provide any structure for the baby, failing to set limits or establish regular routines. Even though toddlers struggle to obtain it, they are often afraid of their growing independence. Parents should be encouraged to set limits and provide structure and routine for the child but to allow independence when appropriate and avoid power struggles. ∎

Psychological Strengths and Hazards

What exactly are the effects on psychological development of losing a caregiver at a young age or even of failing to establish a bond with a primary caregiver at all? Loss of a primary caregiver has often been referred to as maternal deprivation, which can occur through separation from the caregiver, failure of the caregiver to interact with the infant, or neglect or abuse of the baby. If the loss occurs before 6 months of age, it can interfere with the baby's forming an attachment to a caregiver. If the loss occurs after 6 months, it can disrupt an existing attachment (Bremmer, 1988).

Failure to Form an Attachment

What happens to babies who fail to form an attachment? Research on this issue has to rely on separations that occur naturally, and it usually involves babies who have been institutionalized. A classic study was conducted by Spitz (1945) on children in orphanages in the United States and Germany. These babies received adequate medical attention, food, and physical care, but they received little social interaction. Most of their time was spent in cribs with a sheet over the rails. The death rate for children under 2 in these institutions was high; many died from childhood diseases such as measles. The babies were emotionally apathetic and retarded in physical, mental, and social growth.

What about institutions that offer more stimulation? Tizard and Rees (1974) looked at good British orphanages that had a high caregiver-to-baby ratio and lots of interaction. These institutions provided stimulating toys and materials but had a high staff turnover. Some babies experienced 50–80 caregivers before preschool age. These children were normal in intellectual development but had problems socially and emotionally. At the age of 8, many were restless, disobedient, and unpopular with their peers and constantly sought attention. Tizard found that the longer the babies were in the institution, the more trouble they had with peer relations.

Infants who move from one foster home to another can have attachment problems. What happens when these children grow up? Bowlby (1980) looked at adolescents who had spent their infancy and childhood in institutions or foster care, often with repeated moves. These adolescents, who were not loved consistently as babies, were unable to love as teens. They displayed a lack of empathy and affection for others. Many children who fail to form attachments as infants grow up to exhibit disturbed behavior such as delinquency, disregard for life, and lack of empathy. These are the children who kill animals—the ones who would stomp a cat to death (Trout, 1995).

So, early deprivation of a consistent caregiver can affect cognitive, emotional, and social development. But can these effects of early deprivation be reversed with good care at a later age? Quite by accident, Skeels (1936) had an opportunity to explore this question. Two infant girls aged 13 and 16 months from neglectful families were admitted to an overcrowded orphanage in Iowa. Because they appeared retarded and functioned at the age of 6 or 7 months, they were placed in a home for women with retardation. Six months later these girls were alert, lively, and functioning normally. Why? They had become the "darlings" of the women in the home and received a great deal of stimulation and interaction. Skeels followed these girls' development and found that they remained normal. He then conducted a study comparing children in the orphanage with children placed in the home for women with retardation (Skodak & Skeels, 1945, 1949). Even as adults, the children who had been placed with the attentive women functioned better than did those who had been in the orphanage.

Suomi and Harlow (1972) raised infant rhesus monkeys in social isolation for six months. These isolated monkeys displayed a lack of social skills. For "therapy" these monkeys were placed with a 3-month-old monkey for two hours a day, three days a week. Young monkeys were used as "therapists" because they would not know that the behavior of the isolated monkeys was abnormal and would not be as aggressive toward them as older monkeys would have been. Because the young monkeys learned social skills from the regular monkey colony in which they spent most of their time, they taught the isolated monkeys how to interact. After six months of this type of therapy, the isolated monkeys learned social skills similar to those of normal monkeys.

So it appears that the effects of early deprivation can be reversed to some extent. But what happens to infants who form an attachment to a caregiver and then lose that caregiver?

Separation after Attachment

Babies who are separated from their primary caregiver show immediate effects (Rutter, 1981). At first, they display acute distress by crying and complaining loudly. This is known as the protest phase. Then babies go into the despair phase, showing general misery and apathy. When the caregiver fails to return after a period of time, the baby becomes unconcerned and relatively peaceful once again. This is the detachment phase. The amount of distress a baby displays depends on the circumstances. For example, there is a difference between going to Grandma's for a week and being admitted to the hospital for surgery. In the hospital, the baby may be separated from the whole family and experience scary and painful procedures. Children who are in another family situation—especially if with a sibling or other family member—adapt more easily (Bremmer, 1988).

How does loss of a caregiver affect the child after these immediate responses? Recent studies have corroborated what Anna Freud suggested, "that separation is always traumatic in one way or another, but that it is particularly so for the young child" (Gerard & Dukette, 1954). The most profound responses occur if the separation takes place when the child is between 6 and 28 months (Trout, 1995). These responses include a drop in developmental quotient (the child scores lower on standard developmental tests), low frustration tolerance, eating disturbances, depression, social withdrawal, inconsolability when left alone, and repeated efforts to make the lost object reappear (opening cabinet doors, waiting by doors). In particular, a sudden loss can be overwhelming for a small child and have long-lasting effects (Trout, 1995).

So which is worse, to have loved and lost (separation from a primary caregiver) or to have never loved at all (failure to form an attachment)? Rutter (1981) looked at children from homes broken by divorce and children from homes where the mother had died. For children, the effects of these two circumstances (death and divorce) can result in similar short-term and long-term consequences (Kastenbaum, 1977). Rutter found that children from broken homes displayed higher rates of delinquent behavior than did children from intact homes. But what was causing the behavior problems—the breakup, or difficulties in the home that led to the breakup? Rutter found that there was more delinquency in children from homes with family problems that caused the breakup than in children from stable homes where the mother had died. So it may not have been the loss of the caregiver that caused the behavior problems, but difficulties in the broken homes. In general, there appear to be more problems for children who fail to form an attachment than for those who lose their primary caregiver (Bremmer, 1988).

Implications for Practice: Fostering Secure Attachment

Labeling early loss or separation as maternal deprivation implies that the mother is solely responsible for her infant's well-being. However, there are actually few effects from the lack of attachment to a biological mother (Bremmer, 1988). What is important is the quality of stimulation the child receives and some sense of continuity. A baby needs care that is consistent and continuous (Zigler & Stevenson, 1993). Consistent care means that one caregiver is predictable and reliable over time so that the baby can form a bond with that person. The mother is not the only person qualified for this role. Fathers, grandmothers, adoptive parents, aunts, and friends all can serve as primary caregivers. In fact, babies can form attachments to more than one person. A baby who receives nurturing care from a few people can form several attachments (Bremmer, 1988).

But this care needs to be consistent during infancy. Separations from the caregiver should be well planned, because babies tolerate separations better if they are prepared for the separation in advance. Trout (1995) has suggested that even a very young infant be given information about a pending separation over and over. The child should be told that he may feel afraid, lonely, and sad. Children in foster care should receive regular visits with parents unless the parents are dangerous or there is no possibility of a reunion. Babies separated from caregivers do better if they are placed in a familylike environment. In fact, spending some time away from the caregiver—at Grandma's or a friend's home—may help children deal with later, more difficult separations (Stacey et al., 1970).

In general, recovery from early separation and loss depends on the child, the circumstances of the loss, and what occurs after the loss. With good, loving care, children may be able to overcome the effects of early deprivation. Although it was once believed that trauma and deprivation in infancy would scar a person for life, research shows that infants are extremely resilient. With an adequate environment, appropriate intervention, and care provided in an enduring fashion, children may recover from early loss and deprivation (Emde, 1987). ■

Failure to Thrive

By definition, **failure to thrive** occurs when a child's weight falls below the 5th percentile for his age. Many failure-to-thrive babies begin life at normal weight but then decrease their rate of weight gain significantly. Some babies may be constitutionally small and naturally fall into this weight range. But for these babies, their height and weight, in relation to other infants, drop simultaneously. For failure-to-thrive babies, weight drops before their relative height or head circumference begins to decline (Frank, Silva, & Needlman, 1993).

Cases of failure to thrive are usually divided into two classifications—organic and nonorganic. In *organic failure to thrive*, there is an underlying medical condition such as congenital heart disease, cystic fibrosis, or renal disease that causes the growth decline. In *nonorganic failure to thrive*, no medical cause can be found. Cases of nonorganic failure to thrive usually have been attributed to emotional deprivation. Selma Fraiberg (1980) stated that nonorganic failure to thrive "is almost universally associated with the impairment of the mother's capacity to nourish, both in the material and in the psychological sense of the word" (p. 104). In this instance, then, failure to thrive can be considered to have a psychological cause: maternal deprivation. And, in fact, many mothers of failure-to-thrive infants are found to have been deprived in some way in their own childhood. Many of these mothers report an unhappy childhood and a difficult relationship with their own mothers. These factors may interfere with a woman's ability to emotionally respond to her infant and adequately meet his needs. Some believe that this emotional deprivation causes a decrease in the amount of growth hormone produced in the infant's pituitary gland, resulting in slow growth. Emotional tension also may increase the likelihood of the infant having vomiting and diarrhea or loss of appetite (Schuster & Ashburn, 1992).

However, Dr. Deborah Frank and colleagues (1993) stated that emotional disturbance in itself does not cause slow growth. According to Frank, although emotional stress may be a contributing factor, failure to thrive is a problem of inadequate caloric intake. And it is not helpful to label the condition organic or nonorganic. Babies with heart or lung disease may have a medical cause for slow growth, but they also may have developed a feeding problem. And babies with nonorganic failure to thrive may have a genetically determined temperament that makes them difficult to feed. Failure to thrive, then, would not be solely the result of maternal deprivation but of an interaction between biologic and environmental factors.

Failure to thrive can happen in families in which parents obviously care about their children. Some babies are very difficult to feed—for instance, babies with cerebral palsy. An example would be the feeding scene from the movie *My Left Foot*, where a harried mom, in a very stressful family situation with a nondemanding child with cerebral palsy, spoons a couple of bites of mush into her child's mouth and then goes off to do a mountain of chores.

Another failure-to-thrive situation occurs among premature babies. Of infants who fail to thrive, 20–40% started out with low birth weight (Zigler & Stevenson, 1993). Low-birth-weight, premature babies can be difficult to feed. Premature babies also can be irritable and hard to care for. Similarly, some babies have chronic ear infections or sore throats, and these babies often may not feel well enough to eat. Because they have inadequate nutrition, they are more prone to be sick, and because they are sick, they are less likely to eat.

Family situations also can contribute to failure to thrive. Families with high levels of stress may have a chaotic lifestyle and may fail to establish regular mealtimes. Family members may be too preoccupied with problems of living to notice that the child is not eating. They may feed the child in front of the TV, which can be very distracting. Some parents may be too controlling and get into "food battles" with their toddler. In this situation, the child gains power by not eating. Some weight-conscious parents may think that fat is bad and switch the baby to low-fat milk. Some mothers may be struggling with their own eating disorder, such as anorexia nervosa or bulimia, and may fail to understand the caloric needs of small children. Some families are dealing with depression, substance abuse, or domestic violence. Parents with developmental delay may have trouble understanding nutritional requirements for babies. And of course, another contributing factor may be poverty. The Supplemental Food Program for Women, Infants and Children (WIC) provides only enough formula to meet 75% of an infant's daily needs. Some families may run out of money for food before the next TANF (Temporary Aid to Needy Families) check, packet of food stamps, or paycheck comes. These parents may dilute formula to make it last longer. Poverty also contributes to overcrowding, disorganization, and increased distractions in the home, all of which can interfere with feeding an infant (Frank, Silva, & Needlman, 1993).

Implications for Practice: Treating Failure to Thrive

Infancy is a time of rapid growth, and good nutrition during this time is vital for optimal development. Nutritional deficits during infancy can have long-lasting effects, including growth deficits, decreased resistance to infection, later personality problems, learning disorders, poor academic performance, and mental retardation. But blaming the mother for her infant's slow growth only makes her defensive and resistant to help. Ephross (1982) stated that failure to thrive is not the result of maternal emotional deprivation but is a problem of family dysfunction with multiple causes. Failure-to-thrive families are not "bad" families but people with problems who need help.

These families may need counseling to deal with depression, substance abuse, grief and loss issues, and environmental stress. Parents may need help in establishing techniques to deal with a difficult, hard-to-feed infant. Many parents need help in improving parent-child interactions, especially in creating positive, rewarding feeding experiences free from coercion, food battles, and the distraction of television. Information on infant developmental norms and the nutritional needs of babies can benefit many new parents. Because of their risk for developmental delay, failure-to-thrive infants often are eligible for early-intervention services. Infants with severe failure to thrive may require hospitalization, but many families require intensive outpatient and in-home treatment for many months from a team of professionals including a pediatrician, a nutritionist, and a social worker (Frank et al., 1993).

Infant Mental Health

On hearing the term *infant mental health*, many people laugh and ask how you do therapy with a baby. Does he lie in a crib and free-associate? Actually, in the last 20 years there has been a significant increase in the knowledge of the emotional, social, and cognitive functioning of infants. Along with this knowledge has come an interest in working with the problems of infancy. Infants are vulnerable creatures subject to abuse and neglect. They may withdraw from interactions and even seem to suffer from depression. They also can develop problems with feeding, sleeping, and behavioral regulation (Emde, 1987). But as we have seen, they are very resilient and can respond to appropriate intervention.

Problems in the infant-parent relationship can occur as the result of many different factors, including previous pregnancy loss, postpartum depression, medical/developmental problems of the infant, drug use by parents, abuse of the infant, prolonged separations, family stress, mental illness of a parent, or a parent with a longstanding attachment disorder of his or her own.

Out of concern about the psychological problems of infancy has come the multidisciplinary specialty of infant mental health. This specialty is concerned with the factors that affect the psychological health of infants and with development of methods to assess and treat these small clients (Lieberman, 1985). The traditional knowledge base and intervention skills of social workers are especially suited for work in this field (Bonkowski & Yanos, 1992). The Education of the Handicapped Act Amendments of 1986 require that states provide family-based services for at-risk children from birth to age 3. This requirement opens opportunities for social workers to become actively involved in providing services to infants and their families.

Implications for Practice: Assessment and Interventions of Infant Mental Health

The University of Southern Maine has developed a tool to assess and enhance the emotional well-being of children from birth to 5 years. This brief assessment instrument is called AIMS, which is an acronym for the following areas:

Attachment—The emotional tie between a primary caregiver and an infant

Interaction—A communicative exchange of information between caregiver and child

Mastery—The child's development of increasingly complex physical, cognitive, linguistic, emotional, and social abilities

Social support—A network of people, resources, and influences available to families that enhances healthy attachment, interaction, and mastery of developmental skills

The AIMS tool looks at children ages 2 weeks; 2, 4, 6, 9, 12, and 18 months; and 2, 3, 4, and 5 years of age. At each age level, the tool offers guidelines for psychosocial practice, including interview questions and points of observation to use in assessing each of the AIMS areas of emotional development. The tool also suggests brief interventions to help strengthen each area of emotional development. The following interventions are suggested to help strengthen attachment of children aged 0–5 years:

1. Show admiration for the baby/child (appearance, personality, health, behavior) in the presence of the parent.
2. Point out parent's ability to "hear" child's cries/requests and to respond appropriately.
3. Discuss the role of the other parent in caregiving.
4. Discuss upcoming stages of infant/child development.
5. Comment on how proud the parent must be to see the baby/child doing so well.

For more information, contact Project AIMS Human Services Development Institute, University of Southern Maine, 96 Falmouth St., Portland, Maine, 04103, (207) 780-4430.

Other specific interventions include the following:

- Speaking for the baby—expressing what you interpret the baby is trying to say to the parent, such as, "I would like to eat now"
- Watch, wait, and wonder—having the parent observe the infant and wonder what the infant is thinking or feeling or is trying to communicate
- Developmental play—guiding the parent in age-appropriate play activities with child
- Nurturing the dyad—encouraging the parent to engage in nurturing activities with infant (rocking, cuddling, massage)

STUDY TABLE: Psychological dimension in infancy

Cognitive Development and Information Processing	Infants are in the sensorimotor stage of development. This stage is divided into six substages: reflex activity, primary circular reactions, secondary circular reactions, coordination of secondary schemes, tertiary circular reactions, and representational thought. The infant in this stage develops object permanence. Information-processing research is demonstrating that infants are more competent than Piaget ever imagined. Their attention is influenced by their interest, and as a consequence they demonstrate what is termed "obligatory attention." Attention processes are studied by observing the habituation and dishabituation to stimuli. Infants as young as 6 or 7 months display preliminary capacity for categorization. Very small babies can transfer information gained from one sense to another sense, which is termed "cross-modal transfer."
Communication	Infants are born ready to respond to the human voice. They move in synchrony to human speech. Newborns prefer human speech to noise, and they prefer the higher-pitched voices of females. By the end of infancy, the baby begins learning to speak. Prior to this phase, they communicate by crying. By the end of 5 months, babies begin to coo. Between 3 and 6 months they babble by putting vowel and consonant sounds together. Babbling is a form of practice for using the throat, lips, and tongue to produce sounds. A baby's first words are

(continues)

STUDY TABLE: Psychological dimension in infancy (continued)

	said between 9 and 12 months. Early speech uses one word to express a whole sentence, which is known as "holophrastic speech." Overextension is another characteristic of the speech of babies—overextending the meanings of words to fit a specific situation. This differs from telegraphic speech, in which they forget auxiliary verbs, which begins between 18 and 24 months.
Attitudes and Emotions	Recent research shows that emotions have a strong biological component. Some emotions appear in babies with greater frequency in specific stages of development. Between ages 2.5 and 6 months, the infant displays anger, sadness, surprise, and fear. Fear is an emotion that develops during the first year of life. Stranger anxiety begins between 5 and 6 months and diminishes at about 13 months. At this point, a baby may develop a transitional object. Emotional expression in infancy is predictive of later childhood emotional characteristics. Infants are influenced by the emotions of others when they are around 8 to 10 months. When infants look to others for emotional information, around 12 months, this is known as "social referencing." The characteristic pattern in which an infant responds to and interacts with the environment is referred to as "temperament." Many theorists believe that temperament is biologically based. Alexander Thomas and Stella Chess identified the key dimensions of temperament: activity level, rhythmicity, approach or withdrawal, adaptability, and threshold of responsiveness. It is important to determine the degree of fit between the infant's temperament and the primary caregiver. Development of attachment to the caretaker is a primary task of infancy. The parents and the infant's behavior influence attachment. Attachment failure can be caused by the mother's mood (depressed). How the mother expresses the depression also influences the nature of the attachment.
Social Cognition and Regulation	Babies under 1 lack awareness of themselves. Most babies develop a sense of self at around 18 months. Separation individuation is the process, identified by Margaret Mahler, in which the infant shifts from no sense of self as separate from the caretaker to being autonomous or independent. In her theory, some sense of self and nonself begins between 5 and 9 months (the differentiation phase). Between 9 and 14 months, infants enter the practicing phase, which is associated with exploration of their environment. The rapprochement phase occurs between 14 and 24 months. During this phase, the baby realizes that he or she is separate from the primary caregiver but checks back for emotional refueling. The consolidation phase occurs between the age of 2 and 3. Somewhere around age 2 the baby learns how to say no. This phase of development cannot occur without some sense of self.
Psychological Strengths and Hazards	A strong parent-infant bond can have important and lasting effects on a child's development. Separation after attachment can place infants at risk for emotional and other disturbances. Loss of a parent can have serious consequences for infants. A key complication during infancy is failure to thrive. This technically occurs when a child's weight falls below the fifth percentile for his or her age. Cases of failure to thrive are divided into two classifications—organic and nonorganic. Infant mental health is a burgeoning field that focuses on the psychological problems of infancy. From birth to age 3, infants need to be able to (1) experience, regulate, and express emotions; (2) form close and secure interpersonal relationships; (3) explore the environment and learn in the context of the family, the community, and the cultural expectations of young children.

CONCEPT MAP

SOCIAL DIMENSION

Families and Groups

A baby is no longer seen as a passive creature controlled by her basic instincts but is viewed as an active participant in the family environment (Emde, 1987). Treatment of an infant cannot be separated from treatment of the family. Interventions with infants require a systems approach, because problems with a baby do not reside in the baby but in the interactions between the baby and a caregiver or the baby and the family. So, in working with infants, you do not concentrate on the baby alone or the parent alone but on the parent-child relationship and on relationships among other family members (Jennings, Wisner, & Conley, 1991).

Many researchers now feel that an infant needs to be viewed less as an individual and more as a social product. Sameroff (1993) described a transactional model of infant development: "the development of the child is seen as a product of a continuous dynamic interaction between the child and the experience provided by his or her family and social context" (p. 6).

Family Influences

Factors in the family that can affect development include parental personality and temperament, parental mental illness, major family transitions such as death and divorce, and periods of parental unresponsiveness, such as those that occur with depression (Crnic & Harris, 1990). Intergenerational patterns also often affect the family environment. Parenting styles are passed on from parents to children, who then use the same style with their own children (Lyons-Ruth & Zeanah, 1993). Parents who abuse their children often were abused as children themselves.

Interactions in the family seem to occur in a circular pattern. Parents who are satisfied with the marriage may interact positively with the baby and have a responsive infant. Stress in the relationship can preoccupy the parents and affect the quality of their interaction with the infant. Marital problems, then, can negatively affect the baby's development. Ironically, one of the major sources of stress in the relationship can be the babies themselves. A demanding infant can increase the family stress level, which can then interfere with the parents' interactions, which in turn can affect the baby's responses.

Belsky (1981) described these interactions as **circular influences**. He stated that "what transpires between husband and wife might affect a parent's caregiving attitudes and/or behavior, which in turn could influence the infant's functioning, which, coming full circle, might affect the marital relationship." And Clarke-Stewart (1978) looked at this circular influence another way: The mother's stimulating involvement with the infant enhances the infant's development. This responsive infant increases the father's participation in parenting. The father's interest in the infant further increases the mother's involvement with the baby.

Other family relationships also can play an important role in determining the quality of the family environment. In general, a mother's relationships affect how she cares for the infant, and this care affects the infant's development (Crockenberg, Lyons-Ruth, & Dickstein, 1993). The more support the caregiver receives, the better care the infant receives. As we have seen, social support is especially important for caregivers of handicapped or premature infants, and for caregivers with problems such as depression. Caregivers deal with stress better—whether it is from the infant or other factors of life—if there is adequate support (Crnic & Harris, 1990). Jackson's (1998) research on the role of social support found this to be especially true of low-income, single black mothers.

If we consider that the mother is usually the caregiver, where does she receive most of this support? A study by Levitt (1986) asked mothers of 13-month-old infants to identify individuals who supplied support for them. The top two people on the list were family members—the father of the baby and the maternal grandmother. These two family members, then, can indirectly affect the infant's development by supplying support for the mother, but what direct influence might they also have on the infant?

Fathers and Babies

On the birth of his first son, one of the authors of this book asked, "When do I get to throw him in the air?" Studies have found that this is a usual male response to interacting with an infant. In general, fathers spend less time with the baby than mothers do.

When they do spend time with the baby, that time usually involves playing more than caregiving. Mothers actually play more with babies, but that is because they spend more time overall with the infant. And the quality of the play that fathers engage in with the infant differs from that of mothers. Mothers involve the infant in verbal interactions, whereas fathers are more physical and rough with their babies. They tend to move the infant's limbs and bounce and lift the infant in the air (Yogman, 1982).

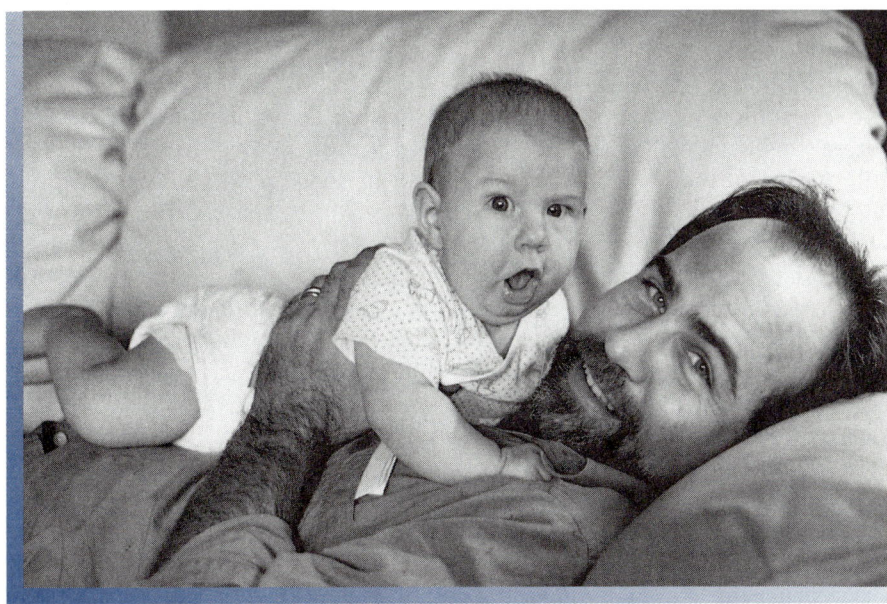

Fathers are an important source of sensory, affective, and social stimulation for infants.

Belsky, Gilstrap, and Rovine (1984) found that fathers also spent more time reading and watching TV with infants, whereas mothers spent more time nurturing and caring for them. This does not mean, however, that fathers cannot be nurturing and sensitive caretakers. Fathers who do spend more time with babies and engage in caretaking activities can be sensitive to an infant's cues (Lamb, 1982). What happens when the father is the primary caregiver? The father is just as competent in giving care as the mother is (Parke & O'Leary, 1976), but the father still plays in a more physical way with the infant (Field, 1978).

Fathers, then, can be competent primary caregivers. Babies can form an attachment with fathers much the same as they do with their mothers (Lamb, 1982). The more fathers interact with infants, the greater effect they can have on development.

But what about a father who is not married to and not cohabitating with the mother of his baby? What sort of role will he have in raising his baby? Research has shown that roughly 90% of these fathers spend some time with their babies during the first 15 months of life, but contact tends to decrease over time (Vosler & Robertson, 1998). Single mothers, especially adolescent ones, often return to live with their parents. Sometimes, if there is not a strong relationship between the baby's father and the mother's family, the maternal grandmother can act as a barrier to the father's interaction with the baby (Vosler & Robertson, 1998). Additional factors, such as poverty, maternal depression, and minimal parental education also can contribute to father noninvolvement in nonmarital coparenting situations (Vosler & Robertson, 1998).

Here's an interesting question: Can fathers experience postpartum depression? While it is not termed as such, some research supports the notion, specifically for inexperienced fathers. Ferketich and Mercer (1995) found that inexperienced fathers evidence significantly more depression than experienced fathers do, largely because of the changes in identity and lifestyle that first-time parents experience.

Grandparents and Babies

Next to the baby's father, the maternal grandmother is the main source of support for most mothers. For single mothers, the maternal grandmother is often the first source of support. In the case of teenage mothers, the grandmother can even step in as the infant's primary caregiver.

Three out of five children see their grandparents at least once per week (Tinsley & Parke, 1987). Studies have found that infants who have frequent contact with their grandparents interact with grandparents in the same manner they do with their parents (Crockenberg, Lyons-Ruth, & Dickstein, 1993), and babies whose grandparents interact with them show higher developmental scores (Tinsley & Parke, 1987), much as they do when they have highly responsive parents. When the mother is struggling with difficulties that interfere with her ability to care for a baby, the grandmother can mediate the effect of these maternal problems on the infant. When the mother is young, single, mentally ill, addicted to drugs, or unable to care for the infant, the grandmother can provide consistent and nurturing care for the baby.

In addition, with so many mothers returning to work after the birth of their babies, grandmothers often are assuming child-care responsibilities (Lewis, 1987). This is especially true for lower-SES families. In some cases, because of parents' substance abuse, poverty, hopelessness, and disability from AIDS, grandparents serve as primary caregivers and raise the children. Oyserman, Radin, and Benn (1993) have suggested that grandfathers can fill the role of absent fathers for children of single mothers. In fact, the American Association for Retired Persons (AARP) now publishes a newsletter for grandparents raising grandchildren; it also provides a grandparent information center.

Siblings and Babies

Often the mother of an infant with an older sibling, when asked the age of her baby, will reply with something like, "He's 18 months, but he thinks he's 4." Infants with an older sibling may spend a large portion of their time in his or her company, which certainly can influence development. Infants tend to imitate their older siblings. If the interactions with the sibling are positive, the baby can learn sharing and cooperation (Dunn, 1991). However, 25% of all interactions between 18-month-olds and their siblings involve conflict and aggression. Dunn and Munn (1986) found that the level of aggression of an older sibling correlated with the level of aggression of the younger child six months later.

Crockenberg, Lyons-Ruth, and Dickstein (1993) stated that because infants imitate older siblings, it is important to understand how siblings influence infant development. More research is needed in this area. Can a sibling help provide comfort and support when parents are emotionally or physically unavailable? Can an aggressive sibling teach the baby to be more aggressive in interactions with others?

Babies and Their Peers

Young babies often interact by curiously poking each other in the eyes. Actually, babies really do interact with one another—at least to some extent. In the first year, babies look, smile, touch, and vocalize with one another (Mueller & Vandell, 1979). In the second year, toys become more important in interactions. Of course, many of these interactions involve babies taking toys away from each other. But babies also can play some simple games together (Mueller & Lucas, 1975). Babies will play contingency games, in which one will perform an action and the other will respond to it; say, one baby will throw a doll up in the air and the other will scream. At 20 months, babies begin to interact more fully with one another. They begin to take turns in an activity and may be able to roll a ball back and forth without running to retrieve the ball before it reaches the other baby.

Playing with Baby

Every baby is unique, and each may enjoy a different amount of stimulation through play. For new parents, as well as parents of special-needs babies, it can be difficult to know when and how much a baby wants to play. Following are a few guidelines that parents can keep in mind (adapted from Griffith, D., 1992):

1. Never "force" a baby to play when she is distressed or disinterested. Look for signs such as distress due to overstimulation, baby averting her eyes, yawning, sneezing, skin-color changes, rapid breathing, and crying. Stopping play at the first signs of distress can help a baby regain control, which aids in the development of self-regulation skills.
2. Calm baby immediately if she reaches a frantic state of crying. Swaddle the baby to help her relax and control body movements. Providing a pacifier for sucking can help a baby soothe herself.
3. Play with the baby at times when she is calm and alert. Avoid overstimulation by presenting only one toy at a time, keeping the toys relatively simple (for example, rattles, balls).
4. Increase intensity of play (duration, frequency, new objects) as the baby becomes more comfortable.
5. Unswaddle baby during play and at times when he is awake and calm. This allows him the freedom to explore and provides him with opportunities to develop motor control.

Adoption

California couple, financially secure, with much love and affection to offer, wishes to adopt white newborn to age 1. Suburban home, lots of pets. Can provide a secure and rewarding life for your baby.

Newspapers are full of such ads placed by couples looking for a baby to adopt. Many ads specify white newborns, but with the number of young girls who choose abortion or single parenting, the search for a white infant can be long and frustrating.

Adoptions can be arranged through an agency or a private source. Most states have agencies in the state welfare department or department of children's services that handle adoptions. Children also can be adopted through private agencies that are regulated by the state. However, the wait for an infant through an agency may take years, so some couples seek other adoption options.

In some states, private adoptions can be arranged through a physician or a lawyer. Adoptions can even be started through ads placed in a newspaper and then processed privately by a lawyer. However, more problems are connected with these private adoptions. Parents pursuing this type of adoption may receive less background information on the birth parents than they would through an agency, and birth mothers receive less counseling. The financial costs to the adopting couple can be high. And private adoptions may involve more legal problems than agency adoptions (Costin, Bell, & Downs, 1991).

Because the supply of white infants is so limited, some parents choose to adopt older children, special-needs children, or foreign infants. One-half of children adopted are over 2 years old. Special-needs children include those who have disabilities, and the state may provide a subsidy to adopting parents to help cover medical expenses. International adoptions constitute 10% of adoptions (Schuster & Ashburn, 1992).

Open Adoption

In years past, parents who adopted a child as an infant often debated whether or not to tell him or her about the adoption. Many children grew up not knowing they were adopted, and the birth mother's identity was kept secret from those who did know. Parents are now encouraged to be honest with the child from the beginning. In 1975, laws changed to allow adults who had been adopted to obtain information about their birth parents if those parents did not object. This change in attitude toward adoption information has led to open adoptions.

In **open adoption**, the birth mother and sometimes the birth father participate in choosing a family for their baby. That family may choose to attend childbirth preparation with the birth mother and be present at the baby's birth. The birth mother may stay in contact with the family as the child grows, exchanging letters and photographs. Sometimes visits are arranged between the birth mother and the child. In some cases these visits are arranged through the adoption agency and are limited to once or twice a year, whereas in other cases the birth mother may serve as the child's babysitter (Foster, Hunsberger, & Anderson, 1989).

Open adoptions can lead to problems, though. What about families with adopted children from different birth parents? What if one birth mother stays in contact and the other does not? What if the birth mother ceases contact with the child at a later time? In addition, adoptive parents may agree to any conditions of the birth mother in order to have a baby. How does this affect their parenting abilities (Costin, Bell, & Downs, 1991)? Also, the birth mother may change her mind after the baby is born, leaving a couple—who may have waited through the pregnancy, furnished a nursery, and attended the birth—without a child. But when both sets of parents agree on the conditions of the open adoption, this arrangement can be satisfactory to all involved.

Transracial Adoption

Adoption of children of a race different from that of the adopting family—**transracial adoption**—is highly controversial. The majority of couples looking to adopt a child are white, but many of the children available for adoption are not. This means that, without transracial adoption, many white couples remain childless while minority children wait in foster care for permanent homes twice as long as white children (Smith, 1995). But the National Association of Black Social Workers (NABSW) is opposed to transracial adoptions. They believe that African American children raised in a white home will lose connection with their race and culture—that the children will grow up not fitting into either culture.

The Multiethnic Placement Act of 1994 prohibits adoption decisions based solely on race, color, or national origin. This law was developed in order to reduce the amount of time minority children wait to be adopted. (This law does not affect the Indian Child Welfare Act, discussed in the next section.) The National Association of Social Workers (NASW) still states that efforts should be made to place a child in the home of parents who are of similar racial and ethnic background. The NABSW now recommends that transracial adoptions be considered only as a last resort.

Prospective foster and adoptive parents need to become familiar with and understand racial and cross-cultural issues before adopting a child of different race. Efforts need to be made to increase the number of prospective foster and adoptive parents from all races and cultures (Smith, 1995).

Native American Adoption

Another controversy surrounds the adoption of Native-American children. In the 1950s and 1960s, 25–35% of all Native American children were removed from their families. Many of these children were taken from parents who were poor and lived in homes with no indoor plumbing. After adoption, these children were often raised in circumstances that deprived them of their culture and heritage. Many believed that this practice threatened the future of Native American tribes (Doyle, 1995).

In 1978, Congress passed the Indian Child Welfare Act, giving tribes control over adoption of Native American children. Adoptions involving Native American children require not only a release from the birth parents but also a release from the tribe. Even when the parents agree to the adoption by a non-Indian family, the tribe can veto the process and place the child with a Native American family. Critics claim that children have been removed from adoptive parents and returned to a tribe even when the birth parents did not live on a reservation and had no tribal affiliation. Tribes argue, however, that to preserve heritage, Native American children need to be raised by Native American families.

Birth Fathers

The rights of birth fathers is another area of concern. The well-publicized case of Baby Jessica illustrates this problem. Jan and Roberta DeBoer adopted a 1-week-old baby girl after the baby's birth mother agreed to

Many families choose to adopt. This family has adopted two children of mixed race.

the adoption and signed the release. However, the birth mother lied about the identity of the baby's father, claiming the father was her present boyfriend. She changed her mind about the adoption after several weeks and told the real father of the baby—her ex-boyfriend, Dan Schmidt—of the child. He then petitioned for custody of the baby on the grounds that he had not signed a release for the adoption as the father of the infant. The DeBoers challenged the petition in court for two years. Finally, the Supreme Court refused to hear the case, upholding a lower-court decision giving custody of the baby to the birth parents, who had in the meantime married and given birth to another child. As the nation watched on television, Jessica, then 2 years old, was removed, crying, from the arms of her adopted mother and turned over to her birth parents.

In 1972, the Supreme Court ruled that unwed fathers could not be denied custody of their children unless they were proved unfit as parents. But how long a time period should an unwed father have to assert his parental rights? Some states allow six months, which is a long time for a baby to wait for a home. Some agencies will not consider an adoption unless the birth mother names the father of the baby so his release may be obtained. But some birth mothers will not do so, sometimes out of fear, or simply because they do not want him to be involved (Foster,

Hunsberger, & Anderson, 1989). Many men do not learn of the birth of a child until the child has been placed in an adoptive home. At that point, should the baby be removed from a home he may have lived in for several months and be turned over to the birth father? Or, if the man is not an unfit parent, should the birth mother be allowed to decide the fate of his child without his consent?

In 1983, the Supreme Court ruled that men could not claim rights to a child unless they had established a relationship with the child. How can a man establish a relationship, though, if the birth mother keeps the pregnancy and birth a secret from him? In response to this problem, New York and other states have established a putative-father registry for unwed fathers. An unmarried man must register so that he can be notified of any adoption proceedings involving a potential offspring.

Implications for Practice: Making Difficult Decisions in Adoption Practices

Adoption brings up the question of what takes precedence: the best interests of the child, or the rights of the birth parents, ethnic group, or tribe? Children have been removed from homes they have lived in for months because of issues of paternal rights, same-race placement, and tribal affiliation. Some claim that children's rights should be considered first and that the children should remain in homes where they have come to consider the adoptive parents their family. But the issue is very complicated. For instance, many were appalled that baby Jessica was removed from the only home she had ever known and given to total strangers who just happened to be her parents. But her birth father had petitioned for parental rights when she was only 3 weeks old. The DeBoers fought a long battle that lasted two years, but some believe that the best decision for the child would have been to surrender the baby in the beginning instead of keeping her until she was attached to her adoptive family.

Social workers need to consider these issues carefully. What are the rights of birth fathers? Should children be raised in same-race homes? How long should children wait in foster care for same-race families? Should tribes have the right to protect cultural heritage?

Another issue concerns children placed in foster care because of abuse or neglect. These children may wait for years for parental rights to be terminated so that they are released for adoption. Many believe that these children should be permanently removed from their parents and placed for adoption without delay. Others favor family-preservation efforts with the ultimate goal of reuniting children with their birth families. They believe that poor people are penalized by having their children taken away. Many birth mothers are poor and single, whereas couples wishing to adopt are financially secure and married. And sometimes children love their parents even though those parents are inadequate. ■

How Adoptive Families Fare

About 25% of adopted children, compared with 15% of nonadopted children, require clinical intervention for severe behavioral problems." Researchers, however, have found that research shows "adopted children and their adoptive families do quite well (see DeAngelis, 1995a.

David Brodzinsky at Rutgers University has been studying adoption for more than 20 years, and he reports that approximately 75–80% of adopted children are well within the normal psychological range. Adopted children are most often referred for clinical treatment for problems such as acting out or aggression starting at age 5 to 7 years, when they are just beginning to understand that they've lost their birth family and gained an adoptive family. Brodzinsky found that coping styles affected their experiences; children in adoptive families that had a problem-focused, assistance-seeking style of coping fared much better than did those with an avoidant style of coping. He also found that adopted children have neither more nor fewer serious problems than do nonadopted children when their parents divorce—it affects both groups "in a serious way."

Anu Sharma and her colleagues at the Search Institute in Minneapolis conducted a study of 181 adopted adolescents and found that most of the teens were functioning within the normal mental-health range and that the teens described themselves as attached to their parents. It also has been found that openly adopted children, who maintain contact with their birth mothers, are not confused about their parents' identity, as some people had feared. Harold Grotevant at the University of Minnesota and Ruth McRoy at the University of Texas at Austin found that the children view their adoptive mother as their mother and view the birth mother as an aunt or friend.

Adoptive parents grow closer to each other by sharing the adoption experience. Cornell University researcher Jeffrey Haugaard has found this to be especially true in cases in which the child has problematic behavior, because the parents must cooperate to deal with this behavior. Haugaard also found that older adoptees form stronger attachments to their adopted fathers than to their adopted mothers; he speculated that this may be because they feel abandoned by their birth mother. Ellen Pinderhughes at Vanderbilt University has developed a family-systems model to research situations such as those in which birth mothers' maternal rights have been terminated owing to abuse or neglect (Brodzinsky & Pinderhughes, 2002).

Communities and Support Systems

Day Care

In Chapter 11, we discuss the fact that, in general, maternal employment may have a positive effect on children's development. But what about infants less than a year old whose mothers work full-time outside the home? Does maternal employment in the first year interfere with attachment? Do babies who grow up in day care suffer any ill effects? Many researchers have tried to answer these questions (see, for example, Jackson, 2003).

Belsky and Rovine (1988) looked at attachment in infants with working mothers. Their research suggested that babies whose mothers worked more than 20 hours a week were at risk of forming insecure attachments. However, Clarke-Stewart (1989) argued that such studies run into problems because they use the Strange Situation procedure to assess attachment. Children in day care may be more used to strangers and may not exhibit apprehension in a stranger's presence. When assessed using the Strange Situation procedure, then, these children would not be wary and would therefore not receive a secure attachment rating. In fact, other studies (Chase-Landsdale & Owen, 1987) have found no difference in attachment for children in day care. In relation to day care affecting attachment, Belsky and Rovine (1988) concluded that it is too hard to say what the effects are because it depends "on the child, the family, and the particular day care arrangements." In fact, some professionals are beginning to think that day care gives children a secure caregiver with whom to form an attachment when the home lacks a secure, reliable caregiver (Brown et al., 2004). However, recent research by Brooks-Gunn and colleagues (2002) showed negative outcomes between maternal employment during the first year of life and children's cognitive development at age 3. These results were based on data obtained on 900 European American children from the National Institute of Child Health and Human Development Study of Early Child Care.

Implications for Practice: The Realities of Day Care

Although it is interesting to discuss the effects of day care on child development, many mothers do not have much choice about whether or not they return to work after the birth of a baby. Financially, many women need to work to pay the bills and buy necessities. Some women return to work within weeks of giving birth. Some studies have suggested that good day care can increase the cognitive and social functioning of disadvantaged children (Broberg et al., 1997; Brock, 1980; Devaney, Ellwood, & Love, 1997). One study examining the cognitive effects of the federal Head Start program found that children who attended Head Start showed more cognitive improvement than either children who did not attend preschool or children who attended a preschool program other than Head Start (Devaney, Ellwood, & Love, 1997). However, many jobs available to low-income women do not pay enough for them to afford good day care, and there are not enough federally subsidized day-care centers for low-income women (Specht & Craig, 1987). Without federally subsidized care, these women must rely on other arrangements that may not be as beneficial to the baby's development. Indeed, many mothers employed in low-wage jobs are not very comfortable about their main child-care arrangements, especially when their preschool child is a boy (Jackson & Huang, 1998).

Economists recognized that the cost of child-care affects the labor-market decisions of mothers with young children (Blau & Hagy, 1998). In 1997, 58% of married couples with children under 6 years of age and 69% of single-mother families with children under the age of 6 were employed (Gabe, Lyke, & Spar, 2001). Some of the latest available data shows that poor families devoted 18% of their family income to paid child care, whereas nonpoor families devoted about 7% of their income (U.S. Census Bureau, 1995). The lack of affordable child care is often a key impediment to having poor families leave welfare (Gabe et al., 2001). The cost of quality child care also reduces the incentives and returns for working families who are not poor and make more money.

Kahn and Kamerman (1987) wrote that the fourth-largest expenditure for families with children after housing and other essentials is for child care. Financing and providing child care are not free of traditional dilemmas of providing welfare services in mixed economies (Perry, Ashford, & Gonzalez-Santin, 2003). In other words, "child care currently operates within a mixed economy of welfare provision that combines public transfers, market transactions, corporate welfare benefits, and private family and community arrangements" (Myers, 1990, p. 559). The Dependent Care Tax Credit (DCTC) is another piece of federal legislation that is designed for families with tax liabilities. It offers parents a tax credit to offset part of their costs for child care.

Research in the past 20 years has demonstrated that quality early child care and early-childhood education are among society's best hopes for optimizing the long-term outcomes for low-income children and children living in poverty (National Center for Early Development and Learning, 1997). Outcomes that have correlated with program quality include cooperative play, sociability, creativity, ability to solve social conflicts, self-control, language, and cognitive development (Frede, 1995; Love, Schochet, & Meckstrom, 1996; NCEDL, 1997). Quality of child care means different things to different people. Some authorities define quality strictly in structural terms: group size, child-staff rations, physical space, teacher qualifications, staff training, wages, and safety (Perry, Ashford, & Gonzalez-Santin, 2003). Indeed, proper stimulation and nutrition in the earliest months and years of life play a pivotal role in influencing future development (National Governors' Association & National Association of State Budget Officers, 1998; Perry, Ashford, & Gonzalez-Santin, 2003). ■

Quality of Child Care

More than half of the children living in the United States are in the care of someone other than their mother for significant periods of time. What type of child care best supports a child's healthy psychological development? Until now the answer wasn't clear, but a study of child care conducted by the National Institute of Child Health and Human Development (NICHD) provides some revealing data.

In 1990, a team of NICHD researchers recruited 1,364 infants from two-parent and single-parent families across the United States representing a range of socioeconomic and sociocultural backgrounds (Azar, 1995). The study included a random sample of infants, of whom approximately 60% had mothers who worked or attended school full-time, 20% had mothers who worked or attended school part-time, and 20% had mothers who stayed at home full-time. The infants' parents chose a variety of child-care situations, including care provided by the fathers and grandparents of the child, provided in a home setting, and in a day-care center.

Researchers found that children are most likely to receive higher-quality care when there are fewer children being cared for and the child-to-adult ratios are low (Azar, 1995). The study also revealed that less authoritarian beliefs about child-rearing on the part of caregivers, as well as the provision of stimulating physical facilities, were likely to result in higher-quality caregiving. According to the research, the highest quality of caregiving was provided by fathers and grandparents as well as in-home caregivers, whereas the lowest quality of caregiving was provided by child-care centers. However, regardless of care type, an adult-child ratio of 1 to 1 was the best predictor of high-quality caregiving. Anna Fels's *Necessary Dreams: Ambition in Women's Changing Lives* (2005) and Judith Werner's *Perfect Madness: Motherhood in the Age of Anxiety* (2005) are popular books that examine many of the frustrations and obstacles encountered by women in trying to balance work and family with the availability of poor child care services in this country.

Multicultural and Gender Considerations

When feeding their infants, mothers in Yorkshire, England, tell them something about the spoonful of food "going to Auntie Mary's in Bradford." Mothers in Newfoundland tell small children that if they don't eat the crusts of their bread, the Crust Man will steal the children away. Many American mothers fly spoonfuls of food like airplanes into their children's mouths. In other cultures, such as among the Malay, as soon as children learn to walk they are expected to feed themselves when they get hungry with no encouraging comments from the mother (Dettwyler, 1989). These various feeding practices illustrate the fact that parents in different cultures bring different beliefs, attitudes, and practices to the raising of their children. Even in the United States, the child-raising practices and beliefs of ethnic groups can be quite different from those of the majority culture.

Minority infants are more likely to live in homes with younger mothers, single mothers, and large extended families (Coll & Myer, 1993; Maccoby, 1998). Minority families face problems including socioeconomic disadvantage, inadequate access to health care, residential segregation, substandard housing, and unemployment. Coll and Myer (1993) have emphasized the importance of ethnic and minority status in working with families:

If we recognize that these minority and ethnic families experience different cultural expectations, family constellations and access to economic and social resources, in addition to being subjected to prejudice, racism, classism, sexism, and segregation, we would expect that their world view and their infants' developmental outcome would be profoundly affected by these life experiences. (p. 60)

Developmental Assessment of Minority Infants

Of particular concern is the developmental assessment of minority infants, because the norms established for developmental-assessment instruments are based on the majority of children in this country, who are Anglo. Compared with these norms, some minority children may appear abnormal. In particular, African infants appear developmentally advanced, whereas Native American and Asian infants may be a bit reserved on standard measures. You may remember from the last chapter that there is some evidence these characteristics may be genetic, but infant-care practices among cultures also vary and may contribute to this difference. African infants are handled vigorously by their mothers from birth. Their mothers place them in an upright position for most of the day and encourage early sitting, standing, and walking (Cintas, 1988). Native American and Asian infants, in contrast, are more protected by their parents.

Cintas (1988) has cautioned that practitioners should be sensitive to developmental differences associated with culture:

> [Practitioners] working among a heterogeneous population such as that in the United States need to be cognizant that cultural variations in developmental patterns do exist. Further, since infant care practices appear to have some influence on neuromotor performance, North American therapists and families can perhaps benefit from knowledge of parent care methods in other cultures. (p. 17)

FOCUS ON MULTICULTURALISM

UNDERSTANDING DIFFERENT CULTURAL BELIEFS

Understanding different cultural beliefs is important when working with minority families with infants. Coll and Myer (1993) discussed the clinical implications of working with families from minority cultures. First, the family with different attitudes and beliefs may not feel that a "problem"—whether biological, psychological, or social—exists. For instance, in some cultures, having a baby as a teen is a way to gain status and respect in the community. Dealing with the "problems" of teenage motherhood in this community, then, could be difficult in those circumstances. In fact, Burton (1990) found that in one African American community with a high level of male unemployment, teenage childbearing was encouraged; because the maternal grandmother would be caring for the infant, she (as the mother of the teenager) would be young enough to take care of and enjoy the baby. Families have different ideas as to the origin of a problem, as well (Coll & Meyer, 1993). Some families may see a developmental problem as an act of God, as a punishment for past sins, or as a test of faith. Some may turn to faith healers or religious leaders for a cure. Families also differ in their expectations of treatment. Play therapy to facilitate parent-infant interactions may be inappropriate for cultures that do not see the mother's role as including playing with her children. In those cultures, grandparents, siblings, and other children are expected to interact with infants. Asian mothers often take on the role of teacher of their infants (Coll & Meyer, 1993).

Coll and Meyer (1993) suggest a series of cultural-assessment questions that can help provide an idea of how a family views a problem—what the problem is, how it originated, and what the family expects in terms of treatment:

1. What do you think caused your child's problem?
2. Why do you think it started when it did?
3. What do you think the problem does to your child? How does it work?
4. How severe is your child's problem? Do you expect it will have a short- or long-term course?
5. What kind of treatment do you think your child should receive?
6. What are the most important results that you hope your child will receive from treatment?
7. What are the main challenges the problem has caused for you and your child?
8. What do you fear most about your child's problem?

Gender Issues

Some mothers joke that the first time you hand a baby boy a truck, he will push it on the floor and say, "Rrrrrrr," or some other appropriate truck noise, whereas a baby girl will try to feed it her bottle. Just how different are baby boys and girls, and how much of that difference is learned from their parents?

Although children do not label themselves as boys or girls until they are 2.5 to 3 years old, they display gender differences in behavior from birth (Coll & Meyer, 1993; Maccoby, 1998). As summarized in Bjorklund and Bjorklund (1992), boys are more aggressive and more active, take more chances, are more demanding of parental attention, and get into more mischief as toddlers. Girls are more nurturing and more compliant at this age.

In the second year of life, infants begin to show toy preferences. By 18 to 22 months, boys play more with trucks and cars, and girls play with dolls and soft toys (Smith & Daglish, 1977). But to what extent do parents and others encourage children to play with these sex-associated toys?

Babies actually are treated differently from birth. Parents are more rough and active with baby boys and more verbally interactive with baby girls. Studies by Fagot (1978, 1991) show that fathers give fewer positive responses to boys who play with cross-sex toys, and mothers give more verbal instructions to girls. Parents encourage girls to participate in dancing, playing dress-up, and playing with dolls, whereas they encourage boys to play with blocks, trucks, and push-and-pull toys. Interestingly, children of parents who encourage sex-associated toy play can accurately label themselves as boy or girl sooner than other children (Fagot, 1989, 1992).

Even parents who want to be non-gender-specific in interactions with their infants may unconsciously alter their responses. For instance, consider a 14-month-old girl who brings a truck to show to her mother. Her mother wants to encourage her daughter to play with typically male toys, so she says, "What have you got there, a truck? That's good, honey." Then the baby approaches her mother with a doll and mother says, "What a pretty baby. Is she your baby? Is she hungry? Are you her mommy? Maybe you should feed her. Go get her bottle and give her some milk. You be the mommy and feed your baby." Which toy do you think the little girl has been rewarded for playing with? Given such interactions with parents and others, children may refuse to play with cross-sex toys by the age of 18 to 24 months (Shaffer, 1993).

Coll and Meyer (1993) have offered this conclusion about the literature on gender and infants:

> Gender differences in behavior from birth have been documented in a variety of cultures.... But more important than actual sex differences in behavior may be the caregivers' interpretations of an infant's behavior, development, and needs as a function of the infant's gender. (p. 59)

Social Strengths and Hazards

As we discussed in the last chapter, poverty can have a detrimental effect on development. Infants in poor families are more likely to have inadequate nutrition and also are more likely to have increased blood lead levels. Poor infants have more health problems and more injuries, and when abused or neglected they are more likely to be removed from their homes. Duncan and Brooks-Gunn (2000) have pointed out that income appears to matter most for children's development in early childhood:

> Low income affects children in a number of ways, including parental mental health, and neighborhood of residence. For example, studies have found that parents' economic stress and hardship are environmental factors that are associated with increased depressive symptoms, less nurturant parenting and, thereby, less optimal child outcomes. (Jackson, 2003b)

Infants living in poverty are more likely to have an impoverished environment with irregular daily routines, overcrowding, little attention for the baby, and lack of parental responsiveness (Halpern, 1993). Poverty adds to the caregiver's stress and can contribute to depression, making it difficult to care for an infant (Sachs, Pietrukowicz, & Hall, 1997; Jackson, 2003b). The effects of prenatal poverty may have resulted in a premature birth or a baby with complications. This infant may need extra care and parental responsiveness, but the energy of the mother must go to dealing with the problems of living and not to the infant. Halpern states that "a fussy, disorganized, low-birthweight infant is likely to overtax the limited physical and emotional resources of an already overstressed mother" (p. 75). The mother may then avoid interacting with the infant.

FOCUS ON MULTICULTURALISM

RURAL UNEMPLOYMENT AND EFFECTS ON FAMILIES

The Globe-Miami area of southern Gila County, Arizona, has a population of 9,422 residents (U.S. Census, 2000). Observing this small community, of which 385 members are Hispanic, offers a unique opportunity to witness aspects of cultural variability that are not always so readily apparent in larger populations. The reduction in workforce at the area's largest employer, an open-pit copper mine, provides a recent illustration of particular components of cultural variability within a rural mining community. In January of 2002, 64% of the 250 mine employees who lost their jobs at this mine were Hispanic males, between the ages of 45 and 57. The effects of premature loss of income on these men and their families have not been formally researched.

Fox and Bartholomae (2000) reported that familial stress is related to the deleterious effects of insufficient economics on all aspects of family relationships. Parenting practices are negatively impacted because parental support is reduced. Many adults in midlife serve the function of supporting younger couples with infants, but this is not possible when their middle-aged parents are struggling with unanticipated unemployment in a small town.

Economic stress can be a culprit in contributing to increased levels of depression and antisocial behaviors in children. Family economics are also the single strongest indicator of a child's sense of health. Marital satisfaction also may be compromised, contributing to hostility on the part of the husband and a reduction in warmth and supportiveness toward his spouse (Fox and Bartholomae, 2000). However, these and other correlates of economic strain have been generalized in the literature and were not specific to Hispanic families. Observations appear to support the relevance of these findings and is directly relevant to the Hispanic experience. Divorce petitions and notices of bankruptcies filed by people with Hispanic last names, printed in the local paper, have increased substantially during the last two years.

Many Hispanic families in the Globe-Miami area who were affected by the copper mine's reduction of its work force exhibit depression and high levels of anxiety. Copper mining is the last viable industry in this area. There are no employment opportunities within the community that offer comparable wages and benefit packages. Many Hispanic families assist in supporting their parents financially, in addition to raising and supporting their own children. It is not feasible to relocate, as the intergenerational connections and responsibilities are strong. Hence, the charge specific to social workers representing rural minorities, whose cultural identity and economic well-being often are enmeshed with industries in decline, is to identify ways to provide incentives to achieve higher levels of education and to recognize alternative opportunities within their communities of origin (Davenport & Davenport, 1995).

By Melinda Fairfield

Homeless infants are at highest risk. Having no home makes it very difficult to meet the needs of an infant. How does a homeless caregiver prepare bottles, store infant food, wash clothes, provide a safe environment to explore, and find toys? Because of poverty, then, a difficult-to-care-for infant may be born to an overstressed mother with few resources. The infant adds to the mother's stress, and the baby is at increased risk of abuse and neglect.

The Focus section above looks at the consequences for Latino families of a mine closing in a southwestern town. Circumstances such as these pose increased risks for infants.

Environmental Context and Child Development

So far, in considering factors that can affect development, we have looked at the characteristics of the child and then of the family. A third important variable in optimal development is the type of environment the child experiences—in other words, the child's home. The quality of the home environment affects the health and development of an individual, and a poor environment may result in poor development. Halpern (1993) discussed aspects of the infant's environment that contribute to good developmental outcomes, including the cognitive, socioemotional, and physical environment of the home.

Cognitively, infants develop well if they receive rich and varied verbal interaction from their caregivers. The caregivers should place an emphasis on learning and provide a variety of stimulation for the baby. In the socioemotional realm, infants need parents who are responsive, warm, and nurturing. Harsh punishment can have negative effects for the baby. The physical environment should be safe and well organized. The baby should have adequate areas to explore. Appropriate and stimulating toys and play materials should be available for the infant to investigate and manipulate. Early intervention was mentioned previously in the chapter as a means of assisting infants who have developmental delay or mental retardation. But early-intervention programs also can help infants who are at risk because of socioeconomic factors. Research shows that at-risk infants involved in early intervention between 0 and 3 years of age exhibit improved cognitive development and social competence (Ramey & Ramey, 1998a). And these benefits seem to be long-lasting. Positive effects of preschool-age and continued intervention can be maintained through age 12 (Campbell & Ramey, 1994).

Taking these factors into consideration, what is an impoverished environment? This would be a home that is overcrowded, noisy, and disorganized. The baby would have no set routine or predictability. Multiple caregivers would come and go. Siblings as young as 9 years old would be responsible for watching the baby (Sachs, Pietrukowicz, & Hall, 1997). Someone might calm the baby by handing the child a bottle filled with cola. The baby might be confined to a small area with few toys or interesting objects to manipulate. The baby could receive little or no verbal interaction or warmth from caregivers. Caregivers might fail to respond to or meet the baby's needs.

Unfortunately, the negative effects of the infant's environment can have long-term consequences. In one longitudinal study, Shaw et al. (1997) found that environmental and family problems, as well as infant temperament and parenting factors, contribute to internalizing problems seen in the child at age 5.

As we have discussed, infants and children living in poverty are exposed to an array of problems that put them at risk for biological, psychological, and social difficulties. Poor nutrition, lack of health insurance, and poor or inconsistent caregiving are some risk factors that children in poverty consistently face. Federally funded programs have been instituted that specifically target risk factors such as these.

The Supplemental Food Program for Women, Infants, and Children (WIC) was mentioned in Chapter 5 as a source of supplemental nutrition for low-income pregnant women and their children up to 5 years of age. This program has proven to be highly successful in its goal of providing nutrition for low-income infants, with statistics showing close to 100% coverage of eligible babies. Unfortunately, only 57% of eligible children between 1 and 4 years old are enrolled.

Medicaid was created in 1965 to provide health insurance for single mothers, infants, and children. Medicaid eligibility for children varies from state to state and is based on the family's income. However, eligibility was expanded in the 1980s to extend coverage to more low-income children. Although efforts to provide low-income children with health insurance have increased, many children from working-class homes are uninsured because their parents make too much money to qualify for Medicaid but too little to afford private insurance.

Finally, there is the project Head Start (see also Chapter 7), which was created in 1965 to improve the cognitive, intellectual, and social development of preschool-age children living in poverty. Head Start has grown to be the nation's primary federally funded child-development preschool program. In the 1990s, Early Head Start was created, which is a program that specifically targets children from birth to 3 years of age. Its goal is to enhance infant and toddler development by working closely with parents and families (Lally & Keith, 1997).

Programs such as WIC, Medicaid, and Head Start cannot eliminate the existence of poverty, but they can help in counteracting many of its negative effects.

Implications for Practice: Assessing the Home Environment

Quality of the home environment should be considered when making an assessment. Researchers have developed various methods for measuring the quality of a

EXHIBIT 6.10 Sample items from the home inventory (infant-toddler version)

Emotional and Verbal Responsiveness of Parents
Parent responds to the child's vocalizations with verbal response.

Parent caresses or kisses child at least once during visit.

Acceptance of Child
Parent does not shout at child during visit.

Parent does not interfere with child's actions or restrict child's movements more than three times during visit.

Organization of the Physical and Temporal Environment
When parent is away, care is provided by one of three regular substitutes.

Someone takes child to grocery store at least once a week.

Provision of Appropriate Play Materials
Child has some muscle-activity toys or equipment.

Parent provides toys or some interesting activities for child during visit.

Parental Involvement with Child
Parent consciously encourages developmental advance.

Parent structures child's play periods.

Opportunities for Variety in Daily Stimulation
Father provides some caretaking every day.

Family visits or receives visits from relatives once a month.

SOURCE: Adapted from *Pediatric Nursing*, 14(2), 1988, p. 98. Reprinted with permission of the publisher, Jannetti Publications, Inc., East Holly Avenue Box 56, Pitman, NJ 08071-0056; Phone (609) 256-2300.

child's home. The most widely used measurement is the Home Observation for Measurement of the Environment (HOME) Inventory (Caldwell & Bradley, 1984). This instrument is designed to measure the quality and quantity of stimulation and support available to the child in the home. It consists of 45 items separated into six subscales: parental responsiveness, acceptance of child, organization of environment, play materials, parental involvement with child, and variety of stimulation (see Exhibit 6.10). Assessment of the environment consists of observation of the home and a semistructured interview conducted in the child's home with a primary caregiver (Bradley & Brisby, 1990).

Infant Abuse

One-third of the child victims of abuse are less than 1 year old. Factors that put children at risk for abuse and neglect during the first year of life include poverty, minimal maternal education, maternal depression, presence of other young children in the home, and the mother's separation from her own mother before age 14 (Kotch et al., 1995). A common injury to babies at this age is head trauma. Infants who are difficult to soothe and who cry uncontrollably are at particular risk of this type of injury (Mrazek, 1993). Head trauma may occur from someone hitting the baby's head against a hard object, but a head injury also can occur if someone shakes the infant. This form of abuse is known as **shaken infant syndrome**. Some parents who would never dream of hitting a baby's head against a wall will pick a crying infant up and, out of sheer frustration, shake the baby. Difficult and demanding infants may be at a higher risk for this type of abuse. The frustrated parent shakes the infant to stop him or her from crying. Unfortunately, it works; the baby suffers a head injury, and possibly a concussion, and becomes quiet. The next time the infant cries, the parent is more likely to shake the infant again. But shaking an infant can cause severe injury. Babies have weak neck muscles and cannot control their heads well. When shaken, the head moves back and forth rapidly, and the brain hits the skull. There is usually no external evidence of injury, such as bruising, but there is usually bleeding of the brain and retinal hemorrhage. Many shaken infants suffer permanent neurological damage, seizure disorders, blindness, and deafness. Visible symptoms of a shaken baby include lethargy, crying, vomiting, loss of appetite, and seizures. Among infants with these injuries, 25% die.

Parents at risk of physically harming their infants need help. They need information on ways to deal with a crying infant. They need to understand that the baby's responses are not intentional; the baby is not out to get them. They need help in learning to control and modify their infant's responses, and they may need to adjust the level of stimulation the baby receives. They need to understand differences in temperament—that a difficult, demanding baby cannot help being that way. They may need help in dealing with stress in their lives and in finding adequate resources and social support. These parents need to know that, when they are at the end of their rope and on the verge of lashing out at the infant, they should put the baby in the crib, close the door, and take a break. They can call someone else to come over and deal with the baby for a while. They especially need to know to never shake a baby and that they should consider obtaining treatment for depression.

Another form of infant abuse is **Munchausen's syndrome by proxy**. In this form of abuse, the caregiver (usually the mother) induces symptoms of illness in her child. The mother may administer syrup of ipecac to the baby to induce vomiting or may place drops of blood in the infant's urine. Of particular concern are babies who seem to be suffering from apnea (episodes where breathing stops). This apnea may be a result of efforts by the mother to fabricate by smothering the infant and then seeking help to resuscitate her or him. This form of abuse places infants at high risk of death. Infants who are intentionally suffocated by the caregiver are sometimes dismissed as a SIDS death. Normally, a complete autopsy and death investigation must be conducted to determine a diagnosis of SIDS. Unfortunately, SIDS death and death from suffocation cannot be distinguished by autopsy (American Academy of Pediatrics, 1993). In fact, one study estimated that close to 5% of SIDS deaths were caused by abuse (American Academy of Pediatrics, 1994). Situational and familial factors play an important role in helping distinguish abuse from SIDS, such as history of apnea in the presence of one caregiver, death at an age greater than 6 months, and unexplained deaths of one or more siblings (American Academy of Pediatrics, 1994). An example of child abuse mistaken as SIDS is the case of Marie Noe, who in 1999, confessed to suffocating eight of her babies between the years 1949 to 1968 (McCoy, 1999). At the time, each infant's death was attributed to "crib death," a term used before the concept of "SIDS" was established.

Other evidence of abuse of infants includes bruising, skull fractures, broken bones, and burns. Exhibit 6.11 discusses ways to differentiate between accidental and inflicted injuries.

Foster Care

Infants who are abused or neglected may be removed from their parents and placed in foster care. In many cases, the aim is to return the child to the parents

EXHIBIT 6.11 Accidental versus inflicted injuries (child aubse) what to look for

Accidental Injury

The story of how the injury occurred is clear and consistent.

The resulting symptoms occur immediately after the accident.

The caregivers seek treatment for the infant immediately after the injury occurs.

The accident is witnessed by another person.

Someone knows the answer to "What happened?" and "How did it happen?"

A major injury that is an accident is the result of a major event. For example:

- Major injuries occur outside the house.
- Falls are not a major cause of death or injury.
- Falls that cause injury are from a significant height (more than 10 feet).
- The child is old enough to be active and climbing.

Inflicted Injury

No one knows how the injury occurred and/or the story changes.

The symptoms occur up to days after the alleged injury.

The caregivers may delay seeking treatment for the symptoms.

No one saw the accident, or it occurred while only one person was present.

The story is "the same old story"; that is, the baby fell off the couch or bed. (Police refer to "the killer couch.")

A major inflicted injury is described as being caused by a minor event, such as the following:

- A fall from a height of 2–3 feet.
- A sibling dropped the child.
- Several minor injuries occurred to explain the major injury.
- The child is nonmobile—that is, the child is not yet active and climbing.

when the abusive or neglectful situation changes. Some children, though, remain in foster care for a long time, waiting to return home or to be placed for adoption. And some children move from one foster home to another. This lack of permanence and continuity of care can have detrimental effects on an infant. There is evidence that abuse, neglect, and late age of adoption placement increase emotional and/or behavioral problems in children (Dumaret, Duyme, & Tomkiewicz, 1997), which can influence the success of foster-care placement. Dumaret, Duyme, and Tomkiewicz have suggested that foster and adoptive families should be made aware of a child's history so they can be more sensitive to the child's needs.

Fahlberg (1991) offered the following guidelines for children placed in foster care. The child's previous caregivers should participate in the placement decision. The caregivers should be included in a separation interview to help determine what type of placement would be best for the child. Caregivers should continue visiting the child in foster care; visitation allows the attachment relationship to continue and allows the caregivers to practice positive interactions with the child. Davis, Landsverk, Newton, and Ganger (1996) found that parents who visited their children as recommended by the courts had high rates of reunification, although compliance with visitation was not a predictor of which children remained in their parent's home after 12 months. Whenever possible, siblings should be placed in the same foster home.

Lead Poisoning

In older buildings, constructed before 1950, walls were painted with paint that contained up to 50% lead. As the buildings aged, the paint began to peel off the walls. In poor areas, many neglected, run-down dwellings have problems with peeling lead-based paint. It is estimated that more than a million children under the age of 6 live in these buildings ("Ongoing efforts," 1999). Infants will put anything in their mouths, including paint chips. Eating this paint causes lead to build up in their systems. Children with high lead levels in their blood may have problems with learning and with delayed growth and hearing loss. One out of six children in the United States has toxic blood lead levels that can affect intellectual functioning. The percentage of poor children with high lead levels is nine times higher than that of more affluent children. The lead levels of African American children are on average six times higher than those of Caucasian children (Bellinger & Needleman, 1985).

Unfortunately, the lead does not even have to be directly ingested. Even in homes where the paint is not peeling off the walls, household dust can contain lead. In fact, the Community Lead Education and Reduction Corps has found that household dust, ingested unintentionally through normal hand-to-mouth contact, is the primary source of lead exposure for children ("Ongoing efforts," 1999). Studies have shown that daily exposure to even low levels of lead in the environment can result in inattention, hyperactivity, and irritability (Marlowe, 1985). Although older housing is the main source of lead exposure, lead in the environment also is produced through industrial emissions and from the exhaust of leaded gasoline. Drinking water also can contain lead.

Social workers need to be aware of programs to remove lead-based paint from older dwellings. But that is only part of the problem. Because lead is present in the environment from other sources, many children are at risk of lead poisoning. And researchers are finding that even low lead levels can affect learning. For this reason, it is now being recommended that all children with learning disabilities or behavior problems be screened for lead exposure. Early identification and treatment reduce the risk of permanent damage, and an inexpensive blood test can identify lead exposure (Marlowe, 1985). An affected child should then be removed from the source of the exposure. If the lead level is high, medications can help remove lead from the body. Recommendations for reducing the potential for lead exposure include using of air-filtration (HEPA) devices; washing walls, floors, and trim with lead-specific detergent; and monitoring children's hand-to-mouth activity and hygiene.

Parents with Mental Illness

Children whose parents have a mental illness are more at risk of developing mental illness themselves (Seifer & Dickstein, 1993). Some of this risk is genetic, but some risk comes from the parents' behavior. The risk is particularly high if the parent has bipolar disorder or schizophrenia, is addicted to alcohol or drugs, or is depressed. These types of mental illness can interfere with parent-infant interactions.

For example, a depressed mother may fail to make eye contact when feeding the infant, may be less inclined to play with the infant, and may be less responsive to the infant. To a depressed mother, the infant may seem demanding and troublesome. Because the mother is more likely to be negative in her interactions with the baby, the baby then reflects the mother's mood and is more negative in interactions with both the mother and with other adults. As a toddler, the child of a depressed mother seems more negative and impulsive, engages in more conflict with the mother, and may exhibit an insecure attachment (Seifer & Dickstein, 1993).

Maternal depression is of particular concern because some women seem to suffer from a form of depression after giving birth. A large percentage of women experience some low feelings after having a baby; these feelings are usually attributed to changing hormones or fatigue. This postpartum depression clears up in a few days or weeks. But some women may display clinical signs of depression that last for months. Women who have postpartum depression have been shown to be less attuned to their infants and are less affirming of the infant's experience (Murray et al., 1996). The affective interaction of a depressed mother also can influence the infant's attachment. There is some question as to whether this type of postpartum depression is different from other forms of depression (Seifer & Dickstein, 1993). In fact, the DSM-IV classifies postpartum depression as "Major Depressive Episode with Postpartum Onset" if the depression occurs within four weeks of delivery. Women who experience postpartum depression should not pass the depression off as "baby blues" but should be encouraged to seek treatment.

Parents with a History of Developmental Delay

Jill took her 1-month-old daughter to the ER. The baby was having seizures and was admitted to the Pediatric Intensive Care Unit. Jill was a 20-year-old developmentally delayed (DD) mother. She lived with her daughter and the baby's father, who was also DD. Jill had proven to her DD case worker that she could manage her own finances, so her case was closed. However, after the birth of the baby, she had trouble making ends meet each month. She had been evicted three times in the past year for failing to pay the rent. By the end of each month, she had run out of WIC vouchers and money for food and milk. Jill's mother usually helped out with food for the baby. Jill explained to the social worker that at the end of this month, her mother was out of town and she had had no money to buy food or milk for the past week. As a result, the baby had not eaten or had milk to drink for the last two days.

Several problems can arise for infants of parents with a history of developmental delay. Many mothers with mental retardation have low self-esteem (Bromwich, 1985). They may not be emotionally available to the infant, and they may lack skills in reading and responding to the baby's cues. They may lack judgment about what is safe handling of an infant and may be rough with the baby. They may lack the ability to be flexible and adapt their responses to the changing needs of a growing child (Bromwich, 1985). They may be unable to budget and plan finances adequately or access resources in a crisis.

In-home help and parenting programs can benefit many parents who are developmentally delayed. Having another adult in the home can make a critical difference (Bromwich, 1985). Some parents with mental retardation live with their own parents, who provide support and help with child care.

Several issues need to be considered in this situation. Federal and state laws have assured equality to people with disabilities, including the right to have children (Bromwich, 1985). But what is in the best interests of the baby? Should a baby who is not growing be removed from the home? What if the baby is attached to the parents? What happens as the unimpaired child grows up with parents with mental retardation? Perhaps more programs need to be developed that address the needs of children living with such parents and that can help those parents provide adequate care for their children. Bromwich (1985) suggested that, as we protect the rights of parents with a history of developmental delay to have children, we must also protect the rights of those children "to be exposed to social and educational experiences that will foster their healthy growth and allow them to develop their own capabilities to the fullest" (p. 12).

Teen Parents: Children Having Children

Nancy, a hospital social worker, was surprised to receive a request from the nurses on the postpartum unit for a social-work visit to an 11-year-old new mother. She thought there must be some mistake. But on entering the room, she found a young girl holding a beautiful baby boy and watching *Barney and Friends* on TV.

Teen parents come with their own set of risks and problems. Adolescent parents are more likely to be

Teen parents and their infants may need additional support. Often, teen parents do not understand developmental milestones and offer limited cognitive stimulation to the baby.

living in poverty. In addition, they themselves are at risk of developmental problems that can interfere with their ability to interact with an infant. As we shall see in the chapter on adolescence, teens are in the developmental stage of identity formation. As illustrated in the preceding example, some teen mothers are still just children themselves and may have problems with establishing an identity while trying to care for an infant.

Compared to adults, teen parents are more prone to depression (Osofsky, Hann, & Peebles, 1993). In addition, as parents they are less verbally interactive with the infant and less responsive and so do not offer the baby enough cognitive stimulation. Many teens lack knowledge of developmental milestones. For instance, some adolescents may have unrealistically high developmental expectations for the baby, whereas some may fail to recognize developmental problems. In general, compared to adults, adolescents perceive their infants as more difficult and engage in more punitive child-raising practices. With toddlers, teens are less sensitive, more intrusive, and more negative in interactions. Infants of adolescent parents may have more problems with attachment (Osofsky, Hann, & Peebles, 1993).

Osofsky, Hann, and Peebles (1993) have discussed factors that help teens succeed as parents of an infant. These factors include having support, being able to complete their education, and receiving help to cope with depression, increase their self-esteem, and understand their infant's temperament.

Teen birth rates fell to 13% between 1991 and 1995, but the 1996 birth rate (54.7 live births/1,000 teen females) was higher than the rate in 1980 (American Academy of Pediatrics, 1999). However, the trend between 1990 and 2000 represents an overall rate of decline in teen births, from 116.9 per 1,000 to 83.6 per 1,000 teen mothers between 15 and 19 years of age (Wind, 2004). Social workers should consider teen mothers to be a population that continues to need support and intervention.

Implications for Practice: The Importance of Social Support

Infants need a safe and stimulating environment and nurturing, responsive caregivers. Several difficulties may interfere with a caregiver's ability to provide an adequate environment or to interact with an infant. As we have seen, these problems include poverty, drug and alcohol addiction, mental illness, marital difficulties, adolescent parenthood, and developmental delay. In all these situations, we have stressed the importance of social support. Mothers interact more positively with their infants if fathers are supportive and help with child care. Single teen mothers do better with the help of involved grandparents. Parents of handicapped infants and of difficult infants fare better when they have friends who call to ask how the parents are coping or who offer to sit for the child to give the parents a break.

New parents need the help of other people—family, friends, neighbors, churches, agencies, and community programs. You may hear this African proverb often in your career, but it describes social support so well: "It takes a whole village to raise a child." ∎

Developmental Guidelines for Assessment in Infancy

Exhibit 6.12 presents the developmental guidelines for infancy. These guidelines help social workers understand development when making assessments.

EXHIBIT 6.12 Developmental considerations in assessment in infancy

Routine Observations
Perceptual abilities
Reflexes
Weight gain and growth (height)
Sleep patterns
Patterns of crying, cooing, and body language
Feeding patterns
Rhythms and capacity for self-regulation
Temperament
Fit between infant temperament and parenting style
Attachment and strategies for maintaining relationships
Parents' nurturing capabilities
Parental supports
Child-care resources

Strengths and Landmarks of Development
Good health
Well-developed senses
Shows preferences
Recognizes primary caregivers
Demonstrates responsiveness to caregivers
Play develops within attachment relationships
Ability to entertain self for brief periods of time by 6 months
Flexible attention
Reaches physical milestones for fine motor, crawling, and grasping
Regular sleep, wakefulness, feeding, and elimination

Developmental Issues (Not Problems)
Some difficulties warming up
Sleep irregularities
Infant is perceived as fussy
Limited interest in eating
Object permanence
Limited vocalizations
How infant sleeps (on stomach)
Teen parents
Poor parental preparation for the infant
Preparation of siblings for arrival of infant

Developmental Observations Requiring Attention
Lack of physical growth (failure to thrive)
Insecure attachment
Colicky
Overarousal or underarousal in the infant
Parent depressed or has other mental illness
Lack of supports and good child care
Serious health problems in the child
Serious parental health-care concerns
Insecure attachment
Separation after attachment
Infant neglect or abuse
Poor fit between infant temperament and parenting styles

STUDY TABLE: Social dimension in infancy

Families, Groups, Communities, and Support Systems	All interventions with infants require assessments of the interaction of the infant with the family. Mother-father relations influence infant development. The transactions in these relations create circular influences on infant development. Most of the social support for mothers probably will come from the father or partner. Fathers and partners have been neglected in the study of infants. However, fathers spend less time with the baby than do mothers. The quality of the relationships also differs. There is some debate in the literature about whether fathers can experience postpartum depression. Inexperienced versus experienced fathers differ in terms of their depression. Grandparents also play an important role, because three out of five children see their grandparents at least once per week. Babies also benefit from relationships with older siblings and relationships

(continues)

STUDY TABLE: Social dimension in infancy (*continued*)

	with peers. Adoption leads to the formation of families. Some families do not tell the child that they are adopted during their formative years. Open adoption is when the birth mother and sometimes the birth father participate in choosing a family for the baby. Transracial adoption is highly controversial. The Multiethnic Placement Act prohibits adoption decisions based on race, color, or national origin. Another controversy surrounds the adoption of Native American children. The issue of daycare is also hotly debated, and research has examined the effects of daycare on childhood development. Newer studies suggest that the quality of early child care and early-childhood education represents one of society's best hopes for optimizing the long-term outcomes for low-income children and children in poverty. The lack of quality child care is an impediment to having poor mothers leave welfare.
Multicultural and Gender Considerations	Minority infants are more likely to live in homes with younger mothers, single mothers, and large extended families. Cultural assessment questions that can be used in assessment include (1) What do you think caused your child's problem? (2) Why do you think it started when it did? (3) What do you think the problem does to your child? How does it work? (4) How severe is your child's problem? Do you expect it will have a short or long term course? (5) What kind of treatment do you think your child should receive? (6) What are the most important results that you hope to have your child receive from treatment? (7) What are the main things that the problem has caused for you and your child? (8) What do you fear most about your child's problem? Families that you are working with may not assume that the child has a problem. These differences have been documented across cultures. Male and female infants behave differently at birth, and they are treated differently. By the second year of life, infants begin to show toy preferences.
Social Strengths and Hazards	Neighborhood is an important contributor to the developmental outcomes of children. A good neighborhood is a key factor to promoting positive developmental outcomes. It improves access to quality child care and other family life choices. The home environment can affect development. Infants need verbal interaction; a variety of stimulation; warm, responsive caregivers; a safe, well-organized home and freedom to explore it; and appropriate and stimulating toys. Poverty can have a detrimental effect on development. Infants born in poverty to overstressed caregivers are at increased risk of abuse and neglect. Forms of infant abuse include shaken infant syndrome and Munchausen's syndrome by proxy. Lead poisoning from eating paint chips or absorbing environmental lead can cause learning problems and delayed growth and development. Children born to parents with mental illness, parents with a history of developmental delay, and teenage parents may be at increased risk for developmental problems. Early intervention and social support can mediate problems in these families.

CONCEPT MAP

APPLYING THE FRAMEWORK
Failure to Thrive

Roberto was referred to the Growth and Nutrition Clinic by his pediatrician. The social worker in the clinic completed the initial psychosocial assessment. The baby is a 15-month-old Hispanic male who weighs 19 pounds 2 ounces. His rate of growth has been dropping since he was 2 months old and is now well below the 5th percentile for his age. Roberto's parents both have a history of developmental delay. His pediatrician is concerned about Roberto's lack of growth and his parents' ability to care for him adequately. For this reason, he has referred the case to Child Protective Services (CPS) for failure to thrive.

Developmental History

This was the first pregnancy for Roberto's mother, Angelica. She carried the baby to term and had a normal vaginal delivery. Roberto weighed 5 pounds 12 ounces at birth, with Apgar scores of 8 and 9. Angelica denies any drug or alcohol abuse during the pregnancy. She reports that she experienced persistent vomiting throughout the first half of the pregnancy. Until her sixth month of gestation, she was almost unable to hold down any food or drink, and she was hospitalized three times for dehydration. She states that she and her husband, Raul, very much wanted a baby. Although she was very happy to be pregnant, she was so sick that she was glad when it was over.

At 15 months, Roberto is only now beginning to pull to stand. His mother is not sure whether he says any words other than "mama" and "dada."

Biophysical Considerations

Since he was 2 months old, Roberto has suffered from almost constant ear infections. Roberto was bottle-fed, and his mother reports that he was a very slow eater, sometimes taking more than an hour to finish a bottle. Often he would take only a couple of ounces at a feeding. Roberto is especially hard to feed when he is ill. Then he has a very poor appetite. The doctor believes that Roberto's failure to gain weight makes him more susceptible to illness.

Psychological Considerations

Cognitive Development

Roberto's development seems delayed; he does not walk alone yet. His mother reports that he did not sit alone until he was 9 months old. Roberto appears to be thin and sickly and quite wobbly on his feet even when holding on to something.

Communication

Roberto says no words other than an occasional "mama" or "dada." He does startle to loud noises. He sometimes appears to comprehend basic requests but often ignores them. He communicates mostly by pointing and grunting.

Attitudes and Emotions

Roberto's mother reports that as a baby he was loud and intense. He was very unpredictable in daily habits. He never has liked cuddling very much and has always been difficult to calm. On observation, when Roberto looks to his mother, she looks past him. When asked to hold the baby in her lap, she faces him away from her. He squirms to get down and screams until she lets him go. He plays well with his father. They make eye contact and smile at each other. His father talks to him, shows him interesting objects, wrestles on the floor with him, and changes his diaper when needed.

Social Cognition and Regulation

Roberto makes few social overtures to his mother or to the social worker during the interview. He ignores all requests from anyone. He seems interested only in exploring the room, and he can be distracted only by physical play with his father. According to his parents, Roberto is very hard to feed. He often refuses to eat. Roberto will sit in his high chair only for a few minutes before wanting to get down. His parents have been so worried about his lack of weight gain lately that they now spend longer than an hour trying to force the baby to eat. Mealtimes have become a nightmare for everyone. When Roberto does eat, he refuses to eat from his own plate but takes food from his mother's. In other areas, the baby seems to have no set routine. He has no regular bedtime or bedtime routine. His parents allow him to stay up until he falls asleep on the living-room floor.

Social Considerations

Family

Roberto's parents are married and live in a one-room apartment in a poor section of town. They are both Mexican American. Roberto's father is from Mexico and does not speak English. On standardized tests, both parents exhibit developmental delay. Roberto's father works as a food server in a Mexican restaurant, and his mother stays at home to care for the baby. Though she has poor reading skills, Angelica graduated from high school. Raul completed the sixth grade in Mexico. Angelica's mother and sister live in town, but all of Raul's family live in Mexico. Angelica thinks her baby is doing well. She says he is just not that interested in eating, but she feeds him when she can. Angelica says that as a child, she didn't have much of an appetite either, but that was good because her family did not have much to eat. She doesn't understand why everyone is so worried about her son's weight.

On observation, Angelica is a small, thin woman who looks sad most of the time. She does not brighten even when her baby comes up to her. Even when he smiles at her, Angelica avoids eye contact with her son.

Although they are developmentally delayed, Angelica and Raul have been doing well on their own. They maintain an apartment, hold a job, and pay the bills. Though they live in a poor neighborhood, the apartment is clean; the baby has few toys to play with. Also, they have no transportation and rely on public transportation, which is somewhat lacking in their town. This lack of reliable transportation makes getting to appointments a long ordeal. Lunchtime is often spent in waiting rooms or on the bus.

Social Support

Angelica has a close relationship with her mother and sister. They babysit for her sometimes and come over to help out. Angelica and Raul attend parenting classes through the Department of Developmental Disabilities. They have an in-home parent aide who visits them once a week. They really don't have any friends, and although they are religious, they do not attend church on a regular basis. The local Child Protective Services has a day-care program. CPS will pay for the child to attend a day-care center full-time where he can experience a set routine, can receive up to three meals a day, and can observe other children eating and enjoying mealtimes.

Multicultural Considerations

When Roberto has been sick with ear infections, his parents have often used folk remedies. They say he doesn't like to take his antibiotics; in fact, he tries to spit out the medication. So Raul's grandmother suggested they feed the baby sweetened manzanita tea. He likes it and will drink it, and his parents think it helps with his fevers.

When asked what she thinks is wrong with the baby, Angelica replies emphatically that she had "nervios" during pregnancy. When asked to elaborate, Angelica explains that Raul lost his job when she was five months pregnant, and they had no money until Raul found his present job three months later. Angelica was under a lot of stress during this time and worried constantly about how they would support a baby. She is sure this is why Roberto is so irritable and hard to feed.

Because they are unable to get him to eat enough, the parents often light candles and recite prayers asking that they will get to keep their baby and not lose him to CPS. They pray that he will soon eat well, grow, and walk on his own, so that everyone will think they are good parents and they can keep their son.

Raul is the higher-functioning parent, but he does not speak English. Because no one at the clinic speaks Spanish, communication with Raul

(continues)

APPLYING THE FRAMEWORK

(continued)

is through a volunteer interpreter. The interpreter often seems to be changing what was originally intended in the messages to Raul. The staff suspects that the interpreter is giving his own advice to the parents. On one occasion, a staff member with some understanding of the language thought she heard the interpreter tell Raul not to worry, that he just needed to make sure the baby drank *la leche* (milk). It is often difficult to tell whether the parents understand instructions about their baby.

Summary and Impressions

Roberto seems to have the following problems:

1. Failure to thrive
2. Possible developmental delay, possibly due to inadequate food intake
3. Chronic ear infections, which may contribute to lack of appetite
4. Difficult temperament
5. Behavioral problems with feeding

Additional problems:

1. Parents with a history of developmental delay
2. Poverty
3. Possible poor environment
4. Lack of routine and order in care
5. Possible poor mother-infant interactions
6. Possible maternal depression

The parents have many strengths and resources. They are able to maintain an apartment on their own. Angelica and Raul obviously love and care for the infant. Though Angelica in particular may have some problems in interactions with the baby, she is very concerned about his health and development. The parents have kept all their appointments at the clinic. They cooperate well with the parent-training program and with the parent aide. The baby seems to be especially attached to his father.

Both parents are highly motivated to do whatever is necessary to keep their baby. They can follow simple written instructions regarding care and feeding of their child. They are keeping clear and accurate food logs about what Roberto eats each day. They are willing to work at establishing a schedule for the baby—to feed him six times a day and to establish a regular bedtime routine. They are also considering the day-care program for Roberto. The baby has been referred for developmental assessment. Several members of the clinic staff have signed up for an accelerated Spanish course.

Key Terms

active sleep
attachment
babbling
categorization
cephalocaudal
circular influences
colic
cross-modal transfer
difficult child
dishabituation
easy child
failure to thrive
goal-directed behavior
goodness of fit
habituation
holophrastic speech
intentional means-end behavior
Munchausen's syndrome by proxy
myelinization
object permanence
obligatory attention
open adoption
overextension
proximodistal
quiet sleep
sensorimotor stage
separation anxiety
separation-individuation
shaken infant syndrome
slow-to-warm-up child
social referencing
stranger anxiety
telegraphic speech
temperament
transient exuberance
transitional object
transracial adoption

Online Resources

Websites

Go to http://info.wadsworth.com/ashford to find specific links to these web pages.

Thomson website

The activities and case materials associated with the Perez family are found on the Thomson website. This case examines different issues across the span of life of a single family and includes considerations related to infancy.

American Academy of Pediatrics (AAP)

Provides information for health-care professionals and the public regarding AAP recommendations related to pediatric issues, such as vaccination and sleeping-position guidelines. Also provides educational and self-help information for parents.

Head Start: Administration for Children and Families—U.S. Department of Health and Human Services

Information for providers, parents, volunteers, and community organizations regarding Head Start programs, specific services offered, and site locations.

Children's Bureau: Administration for Children and Families—U.S. Department of Health and Human Services

The Administration for Children and Families funds state, tribal, and community child-welfare programs, such as child protective services, family preservation, and foster care. This site provides information regarding this agency's programs, as well as information and statistics related to child-welfare issues.

National Institute of Child Health and Human Development—National Institutes of Health

Focus of the NICHD is on research and epidemiology related to child and human development. Highlights of this site include relevant research publications, federal health-program updates, and information regarding research studies, including information about participation in NICHD studies.

Lead Programs: Office of Pollution Prevention and Toxics—Environmental Protection Agency

Provides policy information and links to other relevant sites that address the issue of lead poisoning.

Zero to Three website

This website provides information to parents and professionals about infants, toddlers, and families.

InfoTrac College Edition Keywords

For interesting materials related to what you have just read, please go to the InfoTrac College Edition website and search using the following key words:

sudden infant death syndrome
day care
children temperament
lead poisoning
transracial adoption
fatherhood

Book-Specific Resources

Book-specific resources, which can be found at http://info.wadsworth.com/ashford, include the following:

Case studies

Quizzes to test your knowledge

PowerPoint Presentations

Early Childhood

CHAPTER 7

CHAPTER CONSULTANTS

Kim Jaffee
Syracuse University

Diane Jacobs
Tulane University

DEVELOPMENTAL THEMES	
	Stage: autonomy versus doubt. Development of greater autonomy, physical ability, and language skills; mastery of basic self-help skills; increased social skills. Play is critical for healthy development.
BIOPHYSICAL DIMENSION	
Biophysical Growth and Development	Physical development. Gross motor skills. Fine motor skills.
Biophysical Strengths and Hazards	Nutrition. Oral rehydration therapy. Physical activity. Prevention and treatment of asthma.
PSYCHOLOGICAL DIMENSION	
Cognitive Development and Information Processing	Imaginative thought. Piaget's preoperational stage. Information processing. Infantile amnesia; memory. Developmental waves.
Communication	Language as innate. Language development by age. Mastering morphological rules; syntax; semantic skills; conversation. Communication disorders.
Attitudes and Emotions	Emotional regulation. Emotion coaching. Fears. Posttraumatic stress disorder. Grief and loss. Aggression. Altruism and empathy.
Social Cognition and Regulation	Self-concept. Self-esteem. Sociability of preschoolers. Social-skills training for preschoolers. Regulation.
Psychological Strengths and Hazards	Growth in psychological functioning, flexibility. Disorders of childhood. Diagnosis and assessment issues. Elimination problems: enuresis, encopresis. ADHD. Anxiety disorders. Depression. Autism.
SOCIAL DIMENSION	
Families and Groups	Family influences. Parenting styles. Nature versus nurture. Nontraditional families. Mother's role. Father's role. Children of prisoners. Sibling relationships. Peer relationships.
Communities and Support Systems	Play. Preschool environment. Kindergarten. Head Start. Full-service schools. Effects of TV.
Multicultural and Gender Considerations	Development of racial identity. Cross-cultural adoption. Development of gender role and sexual identity. Sex stereotyping.
Social Strengths and Hazards	Social capital, family-group decision making, poverty, child abuse.

DEVELOPMENTAL THEMES

When Skyler's parents ask him a question, his response is a predictable "No, no, no!" "Skyler, you like ice cream?" "No, no, no!" He continues to shake his head. Skyler grabs his father by the finger, pulls him into the family room, and demands that he put in a *Sesame Street* video. His father reluctantly complies. Afterward, Skyler is ready for refueling—obtaining some emotional closeness before moving on to his next activity.

Early childhood often represents a struggle for independence and self-mastery. Children expend a lot of energy striving for inner control. They push for independence, yet at the same time feelings of dependence overwhelm them. A critical task at this age is achieving a balance between these two forces. Perhaps one of the most amusing phases of development is the toddler/preschool years. The "terrible twos" are a result of this desire to establish autonomy. Even when offered something desirable, the toddler, like the child in the paragraph above, exclaims "No!" The "No!" demonstrates the strength of the toddler's desire to be in control, and it also confirms her ability to make her own decisions. Erikson referred to this toddler (2–3 years) stage as "autonomy versus doubt." Children who successfully master this stage develop a sense of self-control and adequacy. Children at this age are fast becoming more independent, trying out all kinds of activities and learning many self-care skills that facilitate their autonomy. Children who do not realize a sense of independence and self-control at this age are likely to have feelings of self-doubt and shame about themselves.

During the toddler/preschool years, from ages 2 to 5, children are transformed from infants and toddlers into little boys and girls. Exhibit 7.1 presents a striking comparison between 1-year-old and 4-year-old children. Physical and cognitive changes continue to unfold, but perhaps the most profound changes during this period occur in children's social and emotional growth and language acquisition. Preschoolers are honing the skills they will need in preparation for formal education in the middle-childhood years.

Children in this stage increasingly demonstrate greater autonomy, physical ability, and language skills in their activities and relationships. They revel in their sense of accomplishment and mastery in the areas of basic self-help skills such as toiletry, dressing, and hygiene and in recreational skills such as running, jumping, and bike riding. This mastery also extends to verbal skills used in expressing thoughts, singing, playing pretend games, and playing social games.

Older preschool children, ages 3–5, face the psychosocial crisis Erikson referred to as "initiative versus guilt." Children at this period ideally initiate motor, cognitive, fantasy, imaginative, and language activities, and they achieve some proficiency and mastery in these areas. Perfection is not a goal; however, feeling that their efforts will be encouraged and praised is crucial to children developing a healthy sense of initiative. Children who feel that they can take on and participate in a task with the expectation that they will achieve some degree of mastery will be more ready to meet the challenges involved in learning at school.

The primary tasks of early childhood, between the ages of 2 and 5 years, include developing better-coordinated gross motor skills, acquiring social skills to enhance relationships, and achieving immense growth in cognitive abilities and expressive language skills, all of which are fostered during play. Play is crucial to physical, cognitive, and emotional growth for preschool children. Learning and relationship skills are acquired through daily, active play. By the end of the preschool period, most children will have developed the necessary attention, coordination, and social skills to transition successfully to middle childhood, when school and peers will become the primary focus of children's days.

EXHIBIT 7.1 Comparison of 1- and 4-year-old children

One-year-old children	Four-year-old children
Goal is to master mobility	Mobility is used for exploration and independence
Imitates sounds	Masters spoken language, communicates thoughts
Manipulates physical world to learn	Uses mental symbols
Sense of self begins but connected to parents	Pursues relationships separate from parent

STUDY TABLE: Developmental themes in early childhood

Developmental Themes	Development of independence, self-mastery, and inner control. Toddler stage (2–3 yrs.): autonomy versus doubt. Preschool stage (3–5 yrs.): initiative versus guilt.

BIOPHYSICAL DIMENSION

Biophysical Growth and Development

Physical development refers to two processes. Physical development encompasses the growth of the entire human body and the ability to perform motor skills. The average preschool child grows 2.5 inches and gains five to seven pounds a year. Girls remain only slightly smaller and lighter than boys, a pattern that lasts through most of childhood until puberty. During early childhood, both boys and girls slim down and their body-fat percentages decline slowly. Girls tend to have more body fat than boys overall, and boys tend to have more muscle tissue than girls, even at this young age. As their body fat decreases and trunks lengthen, preschoolers lose their babyish look, although their heads are still relatively large compared with their bodies. By the time children turn 3 years old, they have doubled in height and are four times heavier than they were at birth.

Gross Motor Skills

Early childhood is an exciting time of physical growth and motor development. At this age, children run, jump, climb, and tumble repeatedly for the sheer joy derived from challenging their bodies. They are stimulated and delighted by their accomplishments. The typical 3-year-old child can ride a tricycle, walk up and down stairs, throw a ball overhand, and catch a ball that is bounced. Many can even turn a forward roll and gallop. Catching a ball thrown through the air will still be a relatively difficult feat, but some children begin to practice with large balls. By age 4, children refine their coordination of large muscle groups and can jump higher and farther, run faster, throw a ball with more speed and precision, and hit a ball off a tee. They can hop on one foot and descend stairs with one foot on each stair. Five-year-olds can hit a ball pitched to them, jump rope, and roller-skate (Lee & Graves, 2000). Girls tend to develop both gross and fine motor skills slightly before boys do. Just as infants love "peekaboo," preschoolers never tire of "chase" and "hide and seek," games that allow them to shriek and run at high speeds with someone in hot pursuit.

Fine Motor Skills

Fine motor coordination during early childhood progresses rapidly, as well. However, children in this age group can be frustrated by the limitations in their precision and dexterity. Some projects are difficult for preschoolers because they can cognitively conceive the goal but cannot achieve the intended result because of fine motor limitations. For example, a child might want to make a beautiful necklace but struggles to loop tiny beads on a string. That same child might want to build a tower as tall as his or her brother's, only to watch it wobble and topple. Do you think preschools should encourage 3-year-olds to engage in an organized-sports program? Applying a multidimensional perspective to understand behavior would suggest this is not a great idea because 3-year-olds are just beginning to learn basic motor skills (Santrock, 2003).

The average 3-year-old likes to build tall towers and enjoys solving large-piece puzzles and manipulating figures in cars and playhouses. Three-year-olds also strive to conquer zippers, snaps, and scissors. Four-year-olds enjoy building complicated towers and buildings and begin to understand basic structural and design requirements to accomplish the task. Four-year-olds can manage buttons and draw stick figures. Five-year-olds can print capital letters, simple letters, and numbers. Preschoolers learn to master scissors, paints, pencils, and crayons quite readily. They enjoy the tactile and creative expression afforded by these media.

Preschoolers can be more adept at operating video players than are their parents. With the proliferation of CD and DVD players in home computers, many children also learn to successfully and fearlessly

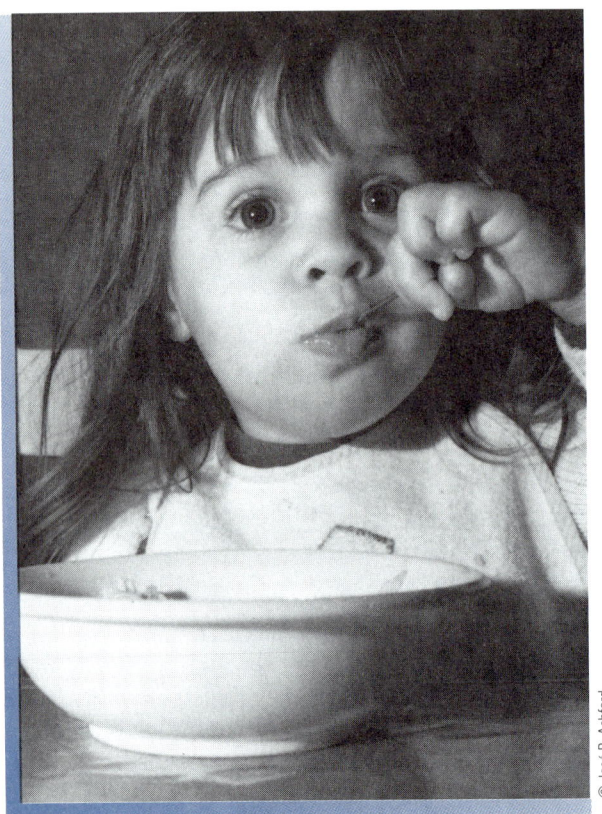

The ability to eat independently—a major milestone of early childhood—is a task that challenges the fine motor skills of the child and the patience of her parents.

navigate educational and recreational software games. For this age group, computer-based programs that are interactive and "speak" to the child, without requiring any reading, are preferred sources of play and learning. Although children in this age group typically do not formally read, they can recognize letter patterns and logo designs as meaningful symbols in much the same way as they will later recognize letters and words.

Biophysical Strengths and Hazards

Perhaps the greatest biophysical strength in early childhood is being healthy and using the developing fine and gross motor skills. Good nutrition is important because what children eat impacts their skeletal growth, body shape, and ability to fight diseases. This is why the federal government provides money for school lunches—to offer nutritional meals that can benefit a child's growth and development. Knowledge of proper nutrition and health care can save millions of children from death in developing countries, where it is estimated that every week, a quarter of a million children will die worldwide because of infection and undernutrition. The leading cause of death, dehydration and malnutrition as a result of diarrhea, is completely treatable. **Oral rehydration therapy** is a treatment that prevents dehydration when a child experiences diarrhea, by providing sufficient fluid intake for the child (Gray & Payne, 2001).

Physical activity plays a fundamental role in children's health. A quick observation at the local park will reveal preschool children in their element. You can observe them walking toward the slide with their heads up and arms swinging, a confident and purposeful stroll. You can also hear this confidence in their voices. "Mom, look at me, look at me!" they shout as they perform various activities. By age 5 they become even more adventurous and proud of their abilities. Preschool children are at a special point in development where they thrive on activity—at the age of 3, the activity level is higher than at any other age in the human life span. Helping children obtain the energy (through nutrition) they need and get the exercise they crave will maximize their developmental strengths during this period.

The most significant biophysical hazards of early childhood include the fatal disorders of birth defects, cancer, and heart disease. Fortunately, the number of deaths in developed countries recently has been reduced as a result of improvements in health care and treatment (Bender, 2002). Prevention strategies to reduce the fatality rates for children under age 5 include adequate birth spacing, prenatal care, breastfeeding, immunizations, and special feedings before, during, and after serious illnesses.

Asthma

An estimated 3 million children under the age of 18 suffer from asthma, the leading chronic illness among children (National Institute of Environmental Health Sciences, 2004). Asthma is the leading cause of school absenteeism and the number-one reason for pediatric emergency room visits (Perzanowski, Perzanowski, Raymond & Platts-Mills, 2001). It is estimated that there are about 5,000 asthma-related deaths in the United States each year (Welch, 2000). With recent advances in the knowledge and treatment of asthma, asthmatic children are no longer restricted in activity and can anticipate leading normal lives. Learning to manage asthma can prevent serious medical and psychological complications.

What is asthma, and how do we recognize an asthma attack? **Asthma** is a respiratory illness that makes breathing difficult because of narrowing of the bronchial tubes. The lung tissues swell, the muscle surrounding the bronchial tubes goes into spasms, and mucus accumulates within the air passages. Asthmatic children can be recognized typically by the wheezing sound or cough produced when the air is squeezed out through the narrowed tubes. They also experience congestion or tightness in the chest, difficulty exhaling, and rapid breathing.

Although most incidences of asthma in early childhood are triggered by viral illnesses, allergens—such as dust mites, mold, and pollen—cold air, tobacco smoke, and smoke from a wood-burning fire can trigger or exacerbate episodes. Also, children in cockroach-infested homes are more likely to suffer from asthma and need more emergency room visits or hospitalizations.

Asthma is also considered to be hereditary, although the complex genetics of the disease are not fully understood (Welch, 2000). Risk factors associated with development of asthma in young children include maternal smoking during pregnancy, exposure of the child to secondhand smoke, and low birth weight (Farber & Boyette, 2001). Researchers also believe that infants who are exposed to allergens in utero and during early infancy may be more likely to develop allergies, wheezing, and childhood asthma. Treatment includes use of bronchodilators in young children to relax the muscles around the bronchial tubes and anti-inflammatory drugs to treat the swelling of the lung tissues. Reducing the exposure to allergens, even before birth, is recommended, especially for children who have a family history of asthma (Welch, 2000). A first (or serious) asthma attack can be a life-threatening event and cannot be managed without the care of a physician.

A particular concern for social workers is the failure to provide necessary medical treatment to children who suffer from asthma, especially poor inner-city children. Research points to the importance of the home environment in understanding and treating asthma. Home treatment of asthma typically includes protecting against dust mites and cockroaches by replacing bed and pillow covers with allergen-proof zip-up covers; installing air filters; vacuuming regularly with Hepa filters; and exterminating cockroaches (see Farber & Boyette, 2001). Social workers often have played a key role in the case management of asthmatics by teaching families how to treat the illness, conducting home visits, and teaching children how to properly use inhalants when needed (National Institute of Environmental Health Sciences, 2004).

STUDY TABLE: Biophysical dimension in early childhood

Biophysical Growth and Development	Average child grows 2.5 inches, gains 5–7 pounds. Girls smaller than boys, more body fat; boys more muscle tissue. By 3 years, children have doubled height and are four times heavier than at birth. Great physical growth and development that is stimulated by children's accomplishments. Children can ride tricycles, throw a ball, catch a bounced ball. The highest activity level of any age group exhibited by 3-year-olds. Daily physical exercise that uses large muscles is important. Development of fine motor skills, yet dexterity is limited, which can be frustrating. Mastering snaps, zippers, and scissors is important. At age 5, children can print letters but typically do not formally read.
Biophysical Strengths and Hazards	Maintaining health and developing fine and gross motor skills are strengths at this age. In developing countries, malnutrition and dehydration have led to millions of child deaths that could have been prevented with oral-rehydration therapy. The fatal diseases of early childhood include birth defects, cancer, and heart disease. Reductions of fatalities have occurred with birth spacing, prenatal care, breast-feeding, immunizations, and proper nutrition after illness. Asthma is the leading chronic illness among children (3 million). Asthma is a respiratory illness that makes breathing difficult because of narrowing of bronchial

(continues)

STUDY TABLE: Biophysical dimension in early childhood (continued)

tubes. Asthma occurs because of viral illnesses, allergens (dust mites, pollen), and heredity. Treatment is typically medical with a bronchodilator, but increasingly this approach is combined with home visiting. Social workers often visit the home to reduce allergens in the environment and teach families proper medical care.

CONCEPT MAP

PSYCHOLOGICAL DIMENSION

Cognitive Development and Information Processing

Early childhood is a time of fanciful, creative, and imaginative thought. Children can think about themselves and others in new and important ways. Imaginative thought leads the way for the development of humor, empathy, and altruism. Consider these examples of both the strengths and limitations of preschoolers' minds (Marti, 2003, p. 257):

- Nicholas, a 3-year-old boy, asks his mother why his blood does not come out from his mouth when he opens it.
- Nora, a 5-year-old girl, tells her sister that the box of candies is empty because she does not want her to find them.
- Joe, a 3-year-old boy, calls elevators "flying wardrobes."
- Carlos, a 3-year-old boy, says that thunders have big mouths because they make a lot of noise.

The fascinating mind of the preschooler has been studied by many researchers, notably Piaget and, more recently, scholars in the information-processing field. This chapter will address what we know about the cognitive functioning of the child in early childhood.

Three-year-old children can use abstraction and symbols in increasingly complicated ways. They can classify objects according to one feature, such as color or shape, and recognize that cats and dogs fit into different categories. At about age 4, children can begin to categorize objects along two dimensions and understand that both cats and dogs fall into the larger category of animals. Numbers symbolize more than just words for the preschool child, who learns to understand the meaning and function of numbers and to use them in everyday tasks. For example, a child may count three books to read at naptime or ask for five more pitches before dinner.

Preschoolers can understand objects as ideas that exist mentally when the object is not physically present. Until children reach the age of about 5, they have little concept of time, past or future. They have difficulty imagining something they have never experienced before. Without a concept of time, they cannot think logically about cause and effect. However, around age 5, a sense of time and logical thinking begin to take shape. Five-year-olds begin to imagine likely outcomes of their behavior. In addition, they have more experience on which to base these logical consequences.

Piaget's Preoperational Stage

Piaget's work laid important foundations for our understanding of what children know (Piaget, 1967). Piaget labeled the early childhood years, roughly from the age of 2 to about 7, the "preoperational stage" of cognitive development. Children in the preoperational stage cannot perform certain mental tasks that older children can handle. For example, they cannot understand the meaning of properties such as weight, volume, size, or height without a physical representation of the concept.

During the preschool years, mental reasoning, stable concepts, egocentrism, and magical beliefs emerge in children's thoughts as they make the transition from a simple use of symbols to more sophisticated use. Piaget described two substages of **pre-operational thought**: symbolic function and intuitive thought. The ability to think symbolically is called *symbolic function*. Children between the ages of 2 and 4 typically possess abilities characteristic of the symbolic-function substage. This means that they can now represent objects mentally that are not present in their immediate environment. At this stage, children can draw scribbles that represent an object or person (Marti, 2003), play pretend games alone and with other children, and talk about people and things not present. They can begin to imagine whole scenarios about other people and themselves and incorporate these ideas into their play and language. For instance, children in the symbolic-function stage can play "house" or "school," taking the roles of mother, father, student, or teacher. Because they can now conceive of and share increasingly complex thoughts and ideas, their social interactions move to a deeper level of involvement and satisfaction.

Egocentrism is another characteristic feature of the symbolic function substage, according to Piaget's theory. Egocentric children cannot distinguish between their own perspective and another person's. For example, preschool children playing hide and seek will think that if they cannot see you, you cannot see them. They cannot understand that you have a vantage point different from theirs. Another familiar example is that of a preschooler nodding his head on the phone without speaking, not realizing that the person on the other end cannot see him.

Piaget's second substage of the preoperational stage, intuitive thought, develops between the ages of 4 and 7. Children in this substage employ primitive reasoning but not formal logic. During this substage, children typically ask a lot of questions, want to know the "how" and "why" of everything, and are sure of what they know but not certain of how they came to know it. Some developmentalists question if thinking emerges in the exact manner described by Piaget. Small variations in the procedure of an experiment have led to different conclusions, such as instructing a child to attend to relevant aspects of the experiment and finding greater cognitive ability as a result of the instructions. Additional critiques of Piaget's work have focused on the applicability of his work to racial and ethnic groups and low-income children. A lot of contemporary researchers are now using an information-processing model to study how cognitive abilities mature and explore the broader applicability of these ideas. The information-processing method identifies the various components of the task the child is performing. Researchers have found that, when tasks are made simpler and more interesting, children tend to show greater cognitive maturity than revealed by the studies of Piaget (Hawkins et al., 1984).

Information Processing

The research in the field of **information processing** focuses on how children come to know something, rather than on what they know when. Examples of information processes include developmental changes in attention and memory. During early childhood, children make great strides in both abilities.

As you will remember, infants' attention spans tend to be relatively short and wandering. Preschoolers, in contrast, develop the capacity to attend for longer and longer periods of time if they are motivated by the activity. For example, children at this age are interested in books that tell a story, especially about a favorite topic, can watch about a half-hour of a show such as *Teletubbies* or *Blue's Clues*, and can play simple board games. By the time they begin school at age 6, children can attend for increasingly long periods of time. This increased attention span is necessary for the child to benefit from formal education.

One of the limits in attention demonstrated by preschool children is an inability to attend to the relevant aspects of a task. This deficit imposes limits on children's problem-solving abilities, because children attend to the more exciting aspects instead, such as bright colors, lights, movement, and novelty. The process of learning to attend to relevant aspects is referred to as children's "acquiring cognitive control of their attention." When this change occurs, preschool children act less impulsively and engage in more reflective thought (Gelman, 2003).

A second important process in children's cognitive development involves retention of information over time. The process of information storage and retrieval depends heavily on how children understand and represent information (Gelman, 2003). As we have mentioned, infants as young as 7 months old are capable of conscious memory.

However, most children have little or no memory for specific events before the age of 3. This phenomenon is known as **infantile amnesia**. This lack of conscious memory means very young children cannot recall their suffering. They will not remember getting their immunizations, taking a tumble off of a bed, or having a diaper rash. According to many experts, this is why in cultures across the world, painful procedures are preformed in infancy. As children develop a sense of self that allows them to represent autobiographical material, the resolution of infantile amnesia emerges.

Stein (1995) has found that, when a particular event is relevant and meaningful to a child, children as young as 3 can recount the memory with as much description and complexity as a 14-year-old. Stein's work generally relies on children's memories of salient events that made them feel happy, sad, or scared. Stein concluded that emotionally charged events can be stored accurately even by young preschool children. At age 3, children can begin to embellish their stories, and these additional details help put their memory in context. Still, as children grow older they are socialized to remember things, and memories take on a different kind of importance. Recounting stories is a way of communicating with others. Therefore, to understand children's eyewitness testimony we need to consider children's basic memory abilities and their reasons for recalling events. In fact, before the advent of recorded public information, people used memory as a public record. When one person sold a piece of land to another, they would gather a group of small boys from the area to observe the exchange of money for land. Then they would beat the boys so they would not forget the transaction, as they grew older.

Memory processes involve both the storage and retrieval of information. Howe (1995) has found that, for children from 1 year old to 11 years old, problems in storage were three times greater than retrieval failure rates. The average 3-year-old child can repeat two digits in succession; the average 7-year-old can repeat five digits. Preschoolers' memories fade faster than those of older children and adults. Researchers believe that either young children's memories are not completely stored or their ability to organize autobiographical events is not sufficient to guarantee storage. In their book *The Social Work Interview*, Kadushin & Kadushin (1997) noted that interviewing children, especially when conducting assessments, requires an understanding of their encoding and retrieval skills.

Developmental Waves

Do children develop in a series of stages or steps? This question has been nagging developmental psychologists for decades. A growing number of researchers now believe development doesn't occur in this step-lock fashion so much as in **developmental waves**. Because of the great variability in children's development, traditional theories are being challenged by a new model that suggests that "overlapping waves," as opposed to steps, better account for how children learn and use strategies (Siegler, 1998). This theory of developmental waves represents the natural ebb and flow of the continuity and transitions in children's thinking. Siegler (1998) has advocated a shift from emphasizing how children think at different ages to examining how many and what kinds of strategies children use at any age. In addition, information about how children change the use of strategies can be gleaned from this focus.

Siegler's theoretical suppositions are supported by findings from his research: Children learn a new strategy slowly, and they frequently revert to using the old strategy as they are learning the new; they tend to use older, more time-consuming strategies for difficult tasks; and they choose a correct strategy more often when approved by their partner while working in pairs. Also, children tend to use three or more strategies to solve problems such as telling time and as many as seven strategies when faced with moral-reasoning problems. Numerous studies support the notion that children always use more than one strategy to solve all kinds of problems. Although this work has introduced new ways of thinking about how development advances, it does not discount the previous work put forth by stage or level theorists. These theoretical viewpoints may complement each other to broaden our understanding of children's cognitive development.

Communication

Most of what we know about how language develops comes from observing children learning to speak. As children develop, they learn the "rules" of speech—not "The cookie I want" but rather "I want the cookie." For a long time, the presumption was that the child's mind was a blank slate on to which the rules of language were written (Pinker, 2002). Experts now believe that structural facets of language, the ground rules, must be innate. A well-known perspective offered by the linguist Noam Chomsky is that individual languages are variations on a single pattern, which is referred to a *universal grammar*. Why do we believe this? Observations show that all children have an appreciation of language. Infants show a clear preference for speechlike sounds over all others. In this sense, children are programmed to learn language. Consider that all children the world over, learn language in basically the same manner, starting with labels, such as "me," and advancing to subject-verb structures, such as "me want." Next comes subject-verb emphatics: "me want now." Cross-cultural studies show that children all begin to babble in a systematic way. Some aspects of language still baffle us: children always learn to say *no* before *yes*.

Preschool children's comprehension precedes their speech. They can understand much of what is said around them and to them before they can verbally express their ideas on the subject. The process of acquiring language skills proceeds in a relatively uniform way for most children, although the time frame may vary. Language acquisition during the preschool years is quite remarkable when we think of children advancing from putting one and two words together to, in just a few months' time, forming complex sentences and questions incorporating the correct morphology, syntax, semantics, and pragmatics of conversation.

What kinds of speech can we expect from preschool children? Three-year-old children have a vocabulary of about 900 words. Exhibit 7.2 shows the rapid development of language across age by first words, increased vocabulary, and use of sentences. By age 6, their vocabulary will have increased to between 8,000 and 14,000 words. They will have learned an average of 7–8 words a day since they were 1 year old (Byrne, 1998). At about age 3, children also can converse about people, objects, and places not present. Once children have matured cognitively to achieve mental representation of things not physically present, they can think about them and talk about them.

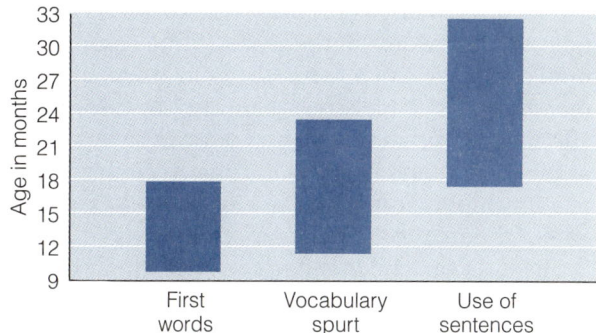

EXHIBIT 7.2 Progression of language development
SOURCE: Based on Bloom (1998).

Once children put two words together consistently, they begin to use morphological rules. We hear children at this age use plurals, possessives, and verb tenses—including the present-progressive tense (*-ing* endings). Children also attempt to make language conform to more logical rules than the language itself may possess. For example, they will overuse the rules, a practice referred to as *overregularization*. Examples include saying "mouses" for "mice" and "he goed" instead of "he went," which children may have said correctly earlier. These mistakes and overuse problems imply that children "know" the rules, yet their perception and understanding of the world is limited by their developmental level (Santrock, 2003). Knowledge of morphological rules has been demonstrated by asking preschool and first-grade children to read fictional words, recall the correct word, and apply the correct ending. Because the words were fictional, the children were forced to rely on rules and not memory. Preschool children could complete this task, as could first graders. During early childhood, children also learn to use articles such as *a* to refer to something initially and *the* for later references to the same noun.

Children learn to apply the rules of syntax as their language skills progress. They first learn to add "wh" words, such as *where* and *what*, to the beginnings of sentences to form questions. Later, they learn to invert the subject and verb. Early-preschool children will ask, "What we are going to do now?" and "Where my ball is?" As they approach the elementary school years, children speak in more complex ways, such as combining ideas in one sentence (Santrock, 2003).

Children's semantic skills improve readily as well. Children at this age learn the meaning of relationship words, such as big/little, fast/slow, I/you, and use them accurately in sentences. However, they do not use these words in the sense of true comparison until about age 4 or 5, when they can articulate comments such as "I am bigger than you." To carry on an effective conversation, children must know to use "I" as the speaker and "you" as the object. This semantic relationship appears to be one of the first ones that young children come to know.

In addition, children become increasingly skilled at the pragmatics of conversation during early childhood. For example, preschool children speak differently to younger children than they do to adults. Gelman (2003) found that 4-year-olds spoke in short sentences to toddlers and elaborated, using more polite diction, when speaking to adults. Also, children at a very young age can recognize that their requests are more likely to be met if they speak patiently and politely. Savvy 3-year-olds quickly rephrase "I wanna go now!" to "Please, can we go now?" We even see preschoolers correcting their own ambiguous messages when they are not understood. They also will let a speaker know when a message has not been clear enough for them to respond. Clarifying ambiguous messages is a skill that develops more fully in middle childhood.

Language development also appears to be encouraged by the frequency and type of responses verbalized to children by adult speakers. Parents who ask their children lots of questions and initiate frequent verbal interaction tend to promote syntactical rule learning and longer utterances in their preschool children. These children tend to recognize more letters and numbers by age 5–6 and score higher on second-grade reading proficiency tests compared with children of parents who are less conversant (Mayes & Cohen, 2003).

In addition, children exposed to adults who speak in slightly more complex and longer sentences, and who both expand and recast the child's telegraphic statements into new grammatical forms, acquire syntactical principles faster than other children do (Budwig, 2003; Hoff-Ginsberg, 1986). We can glean from these findings that, although children do not learn language simply by imitating adults, environmental exposure to slightly more advanced language provides an opportunity for language expansion in young children.

Research shows that preschoolers who are bilingual may learn to read faster than those who are monolingual (Bialystok, 1997). Although preschoolers usually know the alphabet and can spell their names, they often are unable to read without the use of pictures. In a study by Bialystok (1997), 4- and 5-year-olds were shown pictures of objects along with the words that named the objects and were then asked to name each word after the corresponding picture card was removed. Bialystok found that the bilingual children scored twice as high as the monolingual children, illustrating the fact that the bilingual children understood the meaning of the written word independent of the object's picture. Bialystok concluded that children who know more than one language may learn to read faster because they have figured out the rules for two different language systems.

As children get older, they begin to integrate language and thought more effectively. Consider one of the author's sons, who wanted to stay up late and watch a special TV show on the brain. Unlike a 4-year old, who would say, "I need to watch that show," he said, "I have to do a science report, and maybe I'll do it on the brain." Unlike a 4-year-old, this 7-year-old can consider what other people value. Most important, for preschool children, language begins to serve a wide range of functions: reasoning, solving problems, making friends, and playing games of imagination (Mayes & Cohen, 2003). In preschool children, communication is an instrument of thought. Toddlers, in contrast, use language as a road map to what they see and do. Language for the preschooler not only represents a means of expressing needs, but it also becomes a social reinforcement. Language allows children to share and interact with others in ways not previously available to them. Language opens up a whole new world of secrets, jokes, cooperative play, and positive reinforcement. Furthermore, language skills facilitate independence, allowing children to respond to and initiate verbal requests.

The peer group is already a powerful socializing agent. Never mind that parents are mortified when their child screams at the top of his lungs to a departing friend, "Bye-bye, Butthead!" The other child roars with delight at the compliment and returns the salutation. Such is the social language of the preschool child.

Communication Disorders

Language develops rapidly during the preschool years. For the most part, children learn language in an orderly, sequential fashion. Developmental delays can occur, however. Communication disorders we are likely to see in preschoolers include expressive language disorder, phonological disorder, and stuttering.

Expressive language disorder can be either developmental or acquired. The acquired type generally follows some known neurological insult, whereas the developmental type does not. The identifying features of this disorder, which will vary according to age of the child and severity of the disorder, include limited speech and vocabulary, shortened sentences, difficulty learning new words, misuse of words, limited and simple grammar, and slowed language acquisition. Language comprehension is usually normal (American Psychiatric Association, 2000).

Developmental expressive language disorder is usually evident by the time a child is 3 and occurs in 3–5% of children. About half of these children outgrow the problem, whereas the remainder suffer long-term complications. Fewer children also exhibit mixed expressive-receptive language disorder, in which they experience difficulty understanding language, as well (American Psychiatric Association, 2000).

Phonological disorder affects at least 2.5% of preschoolers and is more prevalent in males. The defining characteristics include difficulty articulating speech sounds, especially those learned later in the developmental sequence (such as *l, r, s, z, th,* and *ch*), and making errors in the order of sounds in syllables or words, such as "aks" for "ask." Most children with mild cases recover by the early elementary years without intervention (American Psychiatric Association, 2000).

Attitudes and Emotions

An early-childhood play scene might include the following interaction: Recess starts with a swift run to the basketball hoop. James shows Sam how to dribble and do a layup. Sam takes the ball and heads for the basket but misses. Gary, sitting on the sidelines, asks tenuously, "Can I play?" After a head nod from James, he runs out into the court and trips. Tom, the class bully, comes over quickly to laugh and make fun of Gary.

What do attitudes and emotions have to do with development? For one, they can have a great impact on the nature of our social interactions. One child may become angry when his goal-directed behavior is thwarted. In our example, Sam was intent on learning the layup and could become angry at efforts that slowed his progress. Gary's interactions were entirely different, because his attitude was cautious and he displayed a lack of confidence in his abilities. Tom displayed an irritable attitude, easily provoked when others are perceived to be "in his way." Attitudes and emotions are central to children in early childhood, as they are still learning about how their emotions impact others and the importance of emotional regulation.

Preschoolers often need a lot of support for developing emotional regulation (Denham et al., 2002). This support can help children learn the most effective ways to manage their increasingly complex emotions. Adults can assist children in using cognitive coping strategies: "Visualize yourself giving your presentation to the class," a parent might advise. Adults also are quite focused on helping children learn emotional language to help them understand and regulate their emotions. Finally, many parents will spend time with their children problem solving around emotional situations and either teaching a form of behavioral coping strategies or suggesting an environmental strategy, such as agreeing not to have two friends over at the same time since there is usually a problem.

One of the major developments in understanding children's attitudes and emotions has emerged from research referred to as "emotion coaching":

> "I want Zebra! I want Zebra!" she moaned again. Then she started to cry... By now I was getting "do something" looks from the passengers, the airline attendants, from my wife seated across the aisle... I felt bad. Then it dawned on me: I couldn't get Zebra right now, but I could offer her the next best thing—a father's comfort... "You wish you had Zebra now," I said to her. "Yeah," she said sadly. "You're tired now, and smelling Zebra and cuddling with him would feel real good. I wish we had Zebra here so you could hold him"... "Yeah," she said with a sigh. "I'm so sorry," I said, watching the tension leave her face. She rested her head against the back of her safety seat. She continued to complain softly a few more times, but she was growing calmer. Within a few minutes, she was asleep... Finding out that I understood how she felt seemed to make her feel better... it was a memorable testament to the power of empathy. (Gottman, 1997, pp. 69–70)

This exchange between a father and his daughter represents "emotion coaching." Emotion coaching is a process by which a parent or caregiver assists a child in recognizing his emotions and then uses the experience as a way for the child to learn about himself and to problem solve. Gottman (1998) has described emotion coaching as consisting of five steps:

1. Become aware of the child's emotion;
2. Recognize the emotion as an opportunity for intimacy and teaching;
3. Listen empathetically, validating the child's feelings;

4. Help the child find words to label the emotion he is having;
5. Set limits while exploring strategies to solve the problem at hand.

Gottman has found that children whose parents used emotion-coaching techniques were better able to regulate their own emotions, soothe themselves when they were upset, better focus attention, and respond well in difficult situations (for example, in conflicts with other children). Gottman believes that negative emotions are important for children to experience and that they can provide rich opportunities for teaching and relationship building between a child and parent. Social workers can draw from Gottman's model when working with families, as a way of assisting parents to understand their child's emotions and to help him or her develop adaptive coping skills.

Fears

Preschool children enjoy wonderfully exciting imaginations and fantasy lives. Firstborn children often invent an imaginary friend at this age to serve many purposes. An imaginary friend can try out negative, risky, and even miraculous behaviors and feelings, provide companionship, and foster creativity. Children's imaginary friends should be respected and, for the most part, allowed to be just that—the child's own imaginary friend.

A preschool child's emerging cognitive abilities and imagination also promote empathy and humor. However, the down side of these new cognitive abilities is the onset of new fears. Fears become issues for preschool children, as do nightmares and **night terrors**. Fears of the dark, monsters, loud noises, and strange places crop up in imagination in ways that were not possible before the child was capable of symbolism and abstraction. Most children try to squelch these fears and strong emotions while awake, holding in their reactions so others will not be displeased. As a result, these fears often surface at night when the child's conscious guard is down, especially during REM dream sleep. The dreams may be terrifying to the preschool child because they may portray aggressive feelings and actions the child has been trying to control in response to fears while awake.

Several steps can be taken to help children learn to handle negative feelings and fearful thoughts adaptively. Children benefit from discussions to prepare and reassure them about their fears and strong emotional responses. We also can teach children to talk about their feelings. Preschool children may not be able to act on these suggestions but will benefit from the discussion and may themselves generate some healthy coping strategies through the process (Denham et al., 2002).

Increasingly, social workers must consider how disasters impact children's development. Recent events such as Hurricane Andrew, the Oklahoma City bombing, and the September 11 terror attacks provide ample evidence. It can be difficult for adults to comprehend and process disasters such as these. For children, it can be even more frightening and confusing.

Children who are directly impacted by a disaster, such as a child who had a firsthand experience or experienced a personal or material loss, can be the hardest hit and the most likely to experience long-term emotional problems following a disaster. These children might begin to show symptoms of **posttraumatic stress disorder**, a psychological disorder that involves the child feeling as though she is re-experiencing or reliving the trauma, sometimes months or years after it occurred (APA, 2002). Parents might notice behavior changes in these children, including difficulty sleeping or nightmares, increased aggression, increased "clinging," crying or sadness, appetite changes, social withdrawal, obsessive play, hyperactivity, and increased physical complaints, such as stomachaches and headaches.

When children experience a disaster or feel threatened by events, such as war, their emotional reactions can be complex. The following are some common emotional reactions children can experience (American Academy of Pediatrics, 2002; National Association of School Psychologists, 2002; Sleek, 1998):

- Fear: Children may fear for their safety and the safety of those they care about. They may have fantasies about the tragedy or imagine additional disasters occurring, sometimes acting these out in their play or artwork.
- Loss of control: Like most adults, children can feel overwhelmed and confused because of the loss of control they may experience during or following a disaster. Parents may notice that children will look to keep any control they can, refusing to cooperate or clinging to parents for safety.
- Anger: Anger is a common reaction, and it is most often directed at those to whom the child feels the closest, such as parents, teachers, and peers.
- Loss of stability: Children can feel unsettled and anxious because of disruptions in their usual routines.

EXHIBIT 7.3 Responding to children's emotional needs during times of crisis: Tips for parents and caregivers

Take care of yourself first.	Children need to feel safe and secure. Children will likely be more affected by a parent or caregiver's emotional state than by their words. Discuss your concerns with another trusted adult.
Watch for unusual behavior that might suggest your child is having difficulty coping.	Watch for symptoms such as depressed or irritable moods, sleep disturbances (increased sleeping, trouble falling asleep, nightmares, nighttime waking), changes in appetite, social withdrawal, obsessive play (repeatedly acting out a traumatic event to the point of interfering with normal activities), and unusual hyperactivity.
Talk with your child about the event.	Silence can suggest to a child that the event is too horrible to speak of.
Ask your child what she has already heard about the events and what she understands.	Listen for misinformation, misconceptions, and underlying fears or concerns.
Explain, simply and directly, the events that occurred.	Older children may benefit from more detailed information than younger children. Take cues from your own child as to how much information to share.
Limit television viewing of events.	This is particularly important regarding younger children. When older children watch television coverage of the event, try to watch with them and discuss what you watch, encouraging them to share their feelings.
Encourage questions from your child and answer questions directly.	Children can better cope with a crisis if they understand it.
Don't force the issue with your child.	Extend multiple invitations to your child to have discussions about the event and provide increased physical and emotional presence as you wait for your child to accept an invitation.

SOURCE: Adapted from APA (2002).

- Isolation: Children may feel particularly isolated if they have family members in military service. They may not have friends who relate to their situation, which can feel lonely and sometimes trigger jealousy toward children whose families are not affected.
- Confusion: Children can feel confused by the uncertainty and unpredictability of certain disasters, particularly terrorist attacks and war. Also, children may feel confused about the differences between a violent disaster that takes place in real life and the violence that they see on television or in movies.

How can social workers help children to cope with these complex emotions in the aftermath of a disaster? First, be alert for behavioral changes in children, as these changes often can be reflective of emotional and psychological problems. When dealing with parents, it is important that they do not feel as though they need to handle everything that's happening with their child. Just like children, parents feel stressed when crisis occurs, and they need to remember that there are services and professionals in their community who are available to provide additional support and assistance to their children, as well as to the parents themselves. Exhibit 7.3 outlines suggestions by the American Academy of Pediatrics on how parents and other caregivers can respond to children's emotional needs during times of crisis.

Grief and Loss

When disasters or crises occur, children can, unfortunately, be faced with death and loss. Conceptualizing death can be complex for a child and dependent on their emotional and cognitive development. As discussed earlier in this chapter, children in the early-childhood years are in the preoperational stage of cognitive development. Because children in this stage of cognitive development cannot conceptualize properties, such as weight, size, or volume, without seeing them represented physically, it goes without saying that children of this age would have difficulty understanding the concept of death. As children get older, and they develop cognitively, they become capable of understanding more complex concepts, such as death. For example, a 5-year-old child might see death as a temporary or reversible state, whereas a child who is 12 would likely realize that death is permanent. How can parents talk with their young children about death? Exhibit 7.4 provides suggestions for parents in talking to their children of all ages.

EXHIBIT 7.4 Child development and grief

Approx. Age/Stage	Grief Symptoms/Reaction	Helpful Approaches
0–2 years Piaget's sensorimotor stage (goal directed behavior, object permanence) Erikson's trust vs. mistrust stage	Don't understand what death is. Sense feelings of adults. Depend on non-verbal communication. Won't remember the deceased person. General distress, sleeplessness, shock, despair, protest. Nervousness, uncontrollable rages, frequent sickness, accident prone, antisocial behavior, rebellious behavior, hyperactivity, nightmares, depression, compulsive behavior, memories fading in and out, excessive anger, excessive dependency on remaining parent, recurring dreams, wish-filling, denial, disguised anger.	Need physical care, affection, and reassurance. Need a consistent nurturing figure to take the place of a mother. Include in funeral rituals.
2–5 years Piaget's preoperational thought (egocentrism, animism) Erikson's autonomy vs. doubt and initiate vs. guilt	Confusion, agitation at night, frightening dreams, regression. Child often understands that a profound event has occurred. May seem unaffected. Repeated questioning. Child's understanding of "death" is limited. May know the word "dead" but have little understanding of its meaning. View death as being temporary or reversible. Question cause of death. May feel the loss of someone loved as a punishment. Have difficulty handling abstracts, such as "heaven." Feel sadness, which is short-lived. Regress. Increased aggression. Idealize the lost person. Give up attachment to the loved one, attach to substitute people (teachers, neighbors, etc.). Escape into play, at times, to relieve themselves of the reality of the loss; seem not to be reacting to the loss or indifferent. May not remember the deceased person. Fear is that no one will take care of them. May fear losing the other parent and, thus, cling desperately to them.	Simple, honest words and phrases. Reassurance. Secure, loving environment. Drawing, reading books, playing together. Include in funeral rituals. Need reassurance, love, care, honesty, daily routine, and structure.
5–8 years Piaget's preoperational thought (egocentrism, animism) Erikson's industry vs. inferiority stage	Begin to conceive finality of death. Fear own death and others dying. Feel anger and guilt (blame self for death). Have difficulty expressing feelings in words. Express feelings through behavior (compulsive caregiving and good behavior or aggressiveness as a defense against feeling helpless). Ask concrete questions. Identify with the deceased person as a means of hanging on to him or her. Have difficulty with abstractions such as heaven. Want to understand about death in a concrete way but thinks "it won't happen to them." Denial, anger, sorrow, general distress, disoriented, confused. May behave as if nothing has happened. Desire to conform with peers. May ask questions repeatedly. May need physical activity on a regular basis.	Simple, honest words and phrases. Answer questions honestly and simply. Look for confused thinking. Offer physical outlets. Reassurance about the future. Drawings, reading books, playing together. Include in funeral rituals.
8–12 years Piaget's concrete operational thought (reversibility, conservation, logic) Erikson's industry vs. inferiority stage	Shock, denial, anxiety, distress. Facade of coping. Finality of death understood, phobic behavior, morbid curiosity, peer conformity. May need physical activity on a regular basis. Recognize irreversible nature of death. May be troubled about own death. May experience denial (try not to think about it, don't want to talk about it). Fear of future is high. Hide feelings. May feel anger, repress sadness, be depressed. May have physical complaints. Religious beliefs questioned. Ask logical, concrete questions like "What happens to the body?" and "How did they know he was dead?"	Answer questions directly and honestly. Reassurance about future. Create tie to talk about feelings. Offer physical outlets. Reading. Include in funeral plans and rituals.
Adolescence Piaget's formal operational thought (abstract thought, hypothetical-deductive reasoning, assimilation, accommodation) Erikson's identity vs. identity confusion stage	Recognize irreversible nature of death. May be troubled about own death. May experience denial (try not to think about it, don't want to talk about it). Fear of future is high. Hide feelings. May feel anger, repress sadness, be depressed. May have physical complaints. Religious beliefs questioned. Shock, anxiety, distress, denial, anger, depression, withdrawal, aggression. May react similar to adult but have less coping mechanisms. May feel young and vulnerable; may need to talk.	Allow and encourage expression of feelings. Encourage peer support. Groups are helpful. Appropriate reading. Invoke other supportive adults. Maintain consistent environment. Include in funeral plans and rituals. Encourage involvement in family.

SOURCE: Adapted from *Children's developmental stages and reactions to grief* (The Hospice Foundation of Florida Suncoast) and "Helping children cope with the death of a parent," by L. Costa & D. Holliday (1994), *Elementary School Guidance and Counseling, 23*, 3, 206–212.

Aggression

Our connotations of aggression are usually negative and call up various images of violence. But how do we define aggression when we think of this concept in developmental terms? What forms might aggression take as children mature? What are the meanings of aggressive acts? And do these forms and meanings change over time with development?

To grow, develop, and survive, we must be equipped with a biological drive for aggression. There are more than 200 definitions of **aggression**, although most definitions include two elements: (1) the behavior is intended to harm another person, and (2) the victim perceives that he or she has been hurt (Underwood, 2002). Researchers have divided aggression into two subtypes: reactive and proactive aggression. **Reactive aggression** is angry and includes retaliation; **proactive aggression** is aggressive behavior to achieve specific goals. It is well accepted that boys engage in higher rates of physical fighting than girls do. However, recently it has been recognized that this finding ignores more subtle forms of hurtful behaviors that are often used among girls (Underwood, 2003). For example, girls may engage in a more indirect form of aggression where a person is not attacked physically but through some form of social manipulation.

In general, if you were to observe a preschool classroom you'd see fairly high rates of anger and physical aggression. Preschool aggressive acts diminish after age 4 as children learn better negotiating skills. They also learn to resolve differences verbally in tandem with the increased expectations of parents and teachers preparing children for elementary school (Underwood, 2002). Olweus (1980) found that highly active, impulsive boys tended to be the most aggressive. Mothers of these boys were found to be more tolerant of their aggression, but when they could no longer ignore the behavior, they reacted with physical punishment to get their sons in line. Parents who fail to monitor and supervise their children effectively are frequently the parents of deviant adolescents, as discussed in Chapter 9.

Children express aggression and problems sharing in many ways. Most preschool children have not developed social skills to control their aggressive behavior.

What can research tell us about preschool children's aggressive behaviors? Research findings (Coie & Dodge, 1998; Hartup & Abecassis, 2002; Underwood, 2002) of normal preschool aggressive behavior are summarized as follows:

- The total amount of aggression tends to peak at about age 4, and then it decreases. Temper tantrums with no recognizable antecedent tend to decrease during the preschool period and are almost nonexistent after age 4.
- At about age 3, preschoolers increase their retaliatory aggression in response to frustration or attack.
- Young preschoolers, age 2–3, tend to behave aggressively after parents have set limits. Older children tend to act aggressively in response to peer conflict.
- Young preschoolers tend to kick and hit to get something they want, such as a toy. Their aggression is primarily proactive in nature. Older preschoolers tend to use verbal aggression in the form of teasing, name calling, and tattling. They still argue over objects, but their aggressive acts become more hostile, designed to hurt another.
- During the early school years, individual differences in aggression appear to be related to

family factors such as socioeconomic status and parenting and to how children process social information.

Although aggression is a necessary drive that is hardwired into the brain, research suggests that a child's future propensity for aggressive behavior may be influenced by what happens during gestation in the womb. When factors such as poor maternal health habits, such as smoking or substance abuse, and exposure to hazardous substances, including lead and toxic fumes, are found during pregnancy, there is an impact on the neurological development in areas of the fetal brain that control temperament and self-control (Sleek, 1998b). As children exposed to such substances during pregnancy get older, studies show, they are more prone to be aggressive (Sleek, 1998). This seems to suggest that interventions that include working with mothers to improve their prenatal health will assist in prevention of future aggressive behavior in some children.

What happens to aggressive preschoolers? Research has shown us that aggression in preschoolers tends to be associated with aggression in middle childhood (Olweus, 1977) and even adolescence (Rigby, 2002). Although stability in aggression usually has been considered a male attribute, recent research has documented stability of aggressive tendencies among females, as well (Underwood, 2003). It is also important to look at the families with aggressive children.

Patterson and colleagues (1989) researched parent-child interactions in families with at least one aggressive child and found these home environments to be characterized as coercive. The researchers described coercive interactions as ways of making someone stop irritating another and included crying, whining, complaining, yelling, and hitting. Negative reinforcement, the removal of a noxious behavior, was also used to control family members. Parents may be negatively reinforced when they "give in" to the demands made by their child because it removes a noxious behavior. Yet children in this example are positively reinforced because they succeeded in getting what they wanted from their parent. Social reinforcement, affection, and approval were rarely articulated in these families as a means of achieving and rewarding desired behavior. Children are also exposed to numerous incidences of violence in society via the television, sports, and superheroes. We will consider the effects of these social systems in a later section.

How can we alleviate the propensity for aggressive acts among preschoolers in our society? Assertive aggression often takes the form of separating from parents, achieving independence, and striving to master new skills, all of which are necessary if a child is to survive in the world. **Hostile aggression**, however, is often intended to hurt or coerce, physically or verbally, another child into doing what the aggressor wants. This kind of aggression is not favorably regarded, yet, for children, the meaning of the act must be understood before we can help them achieve their goals any other way.

There is always an underlying message when children use aggression of any kind. Say, for example, we see a preschooler wrestle another child to the ground to retrieve a toy. The meaning of the behavior may be to say to the other child, "See what I can do," or "I'll show you who I am," or "I'll do what I feel like doing." The child may be making a plea for attention from the other child or adults. All in all, preschoolers' aggressive behaviors are ways of defining themselves and asserting their independence.

Even when preschoolers cannot verbalize their rationale, we can model other, more appropriate and effective ways of asserting ourselves. These include asking the children about their feelings and needs, acknowledging their feelings, and redirecting their energies toward more helpful ways of expressing negative feelings. Children should be encouraged to assert themselves in ways that help define them as unique individuals and to establish their autonomy by setting personal limits in order to maximize their own growth and development, not to exploit or take advantage of others.

Implications for Practice: Curbing Aggression

With the increase in school shootings in recent years, added emphasis has been placed on watching for signs of aggression in children, starting as early as preschool. The hope is that aggressive acts in later years can be avoided if aggression is curbed early in a child's life. Exhibit 7.5 lists numerous warning signs for aggression and violent behavior in toddlers, preschool-age children, and school-age children.

Several strategies for decreasing hostile aggressive acts have been researched. We will describe each of these procedures briefly. Remember, the goal is not to deny or negate the preschool child's very real emotional experience.

Rather, the goal is to help the child find adaptive ways of expressing and asserting needs and interacting with others.

- Ignoring or the Incompatible-response technique (Forehand & Long, 2002): This technique promotes prosocial behaviors and reduces aggressive acts by simultaneously ignoring all but dangerous, aggressive interchanges and positively reinforcing acts incompatible with aggression. This method has been shown to reduce verbal and physical aggression while promoting helpfulness. Another advantage lies in the avoidance of punishment and attention paid to aggressive acts. Therefore, children are not reinforced for attention-seeking aggressive acts, and aggression in the form of punishment is not modeled to the children.
- Time-out procedure (Forehand & Long, 2002): This technique allows adults to attend to and prevent harmful acts of aggression in nonpunitive ways by removing the child from the activity and providing a safe place for the child to regain control of behavior. The adult does not unwittingly provide reinforcement for attention-seeking behavior, because attention is withdrawn until appropriate behavior can be maintained.
- Modeling and coaching strategies (Rose & LeCroy, 2005): This method relies on adults and other children to serve as models and teachers of nonaggressive conflict-resolution strategies. Children are more likely to use these alternative strategies if they see someone else obtain success using these methods. This technique has proved effective with chronically aggressive children who have poor problem-solving skills.
- Creating nonaggressive environments (Forehand & Long, 2002; Smith & Connolly, 1980): This method relies on the ingenuity of adults to create play spaces that minimize conflict and the need for physical contact. Large play spaces allow children to play vigorously without physically contacting each other. Play environments that have enough equipment for all the children also prevent conflict. Also, when aggressive toys are provided, children tend to get into more fights. Keeping aggressive toys out of the play areas of young children can prevent aggressive behavior in the form of play and real fights.

Altruism and Empathy

For young children, **altruism**—helpful behaviors that arise out of a concern for the welfare of others—begins with sharing. Learning to share becomes much of the focus of social interactions during a child's first

EXHIBIT 7.5 Warning signs for violence and aggression in children

Toddler and Preschool-Aged Child

Has multiple temper tantrums in a day, each lasting more than 15 minutes; child is not easily calmed by parent or caregiver

Has frequent aggressive outbursts, often with no reason or cause

Behaves impulsively and fearlessly

Frequently refuses to follow directions and listen to adults

Appears not to be attached to parents

Spends a significant amount of time watching violent television shows

Engages in play that has violent themes

Acts cruelly toward other children or animals

School-Aged Child

Often disrupts classroom activities in school

Gets into frequent fights at school

Reacts to disappointment, criticism, or teasing with intense anger, blame, or revenge

Watches violent television shows and/or plays violent video games

Has few friends at school; is often rejected by other children because of his or her behavior; makes friends with other children known to be aggressive or unruly

Does not listen to adults

Does not exhibit sensitivity to the feelings of others

Acts cruelly toward pets or other animals

SOURCE: Adapted from APA (1996).

years. Eisenberg (1982) has studied children's sharing behavior extensively. She concludes that by age 3, children generally share because sharing promotes fun in play. By age 4, children show more empathic sharing as they develop an ability to recognize and understand the feelings of others. In addition, through parental encouragement, 4-year-olds have internalized the belief that they have an obligation to share. This does not mean they always act on this knowledge, however. Sharing is a difficult concept to grasp, one that takes many years to develop. Still, children at this age do not share in an altruistic sense. Rather, they are usually motivated to share as a means of getting their way.

How do children learn to share and develop a sense of altruism? For the most part, peers provide the primary influence in this arena, above and beyond adult direction to share and give. Peers accomplish this by providing opportunities and subsequent reinforcement through their responses to the give-and-take of social play (Grusec, Davidov, & Lundell, 2002). When a child happily hands over the treasured race car, there is no more powerful reinforcer than the friend's exuberant smile. Additionally, research shows that children who observe others sharing are more likely to share (Grusec et al., 2002).

Each of us has an innate capacity for **empathy**, the ability to understand the feelings and attitudes of others. Children are predisposed to empathize with the emotions of others from a very young age. Even infants demonstrate this capacity to detect and model the feelings of another when they use social referencing. Children need adult encouragement to develop their natural capacity for empathy, however. Modeling can be an important tool for adults to use, including demonstration of empathetic responding, helping the child identify her own emotions, and pointing out the consequences of the child's actions for others.

Preschool children cannot cognitively understand another person's feelings. Yet they are equipped with the emotional ability to sense another's feelings, recognize them independently of their own, and match them with their own experiences. To match another's feelings, first a child needs to be able to identify the feeling. Preschoolers feel the basic emotions of happiness, sadness, and anger intensely and can empathize quite readily with these feelings in others. The terms *empathy* and *sympathy* are sometimes used interchangeably; however, they refer to two different aspects of emotional responding. Whereas empathy requires an understanding of another person's feelings, sympathy involves feeling sorrow or concern for another person (Eisenberg, Wentzel, & Harris, 1998).

Altruism has been found to be a highly stable attribute, similar to its counterpart, aggression (Underwood, 2002). Children who act prosocially in one setting are likely to do so in others. When sex differences are found, girls tend to be more helpful and empathic, but sex-difference findings in general tend to be controversial (Grusec et al., 2002). One factor found to contribute to children's altruistic behavior was opportunities to provide compassionate, helpful care to younger siblings (Radke-Yarrow, Zahn-Waxler, & Chapman, 1983).

The most systematic study of cultural differences in prosocial behavior was based on observations of children from six different countries (Whiting & Whiting, 1975). This study found that children from Kenya, Mexico, and the Philippines showed more nurturing behavior, such as offering help, than did those from Okinawa, India, or the United States. The factor that accounted for most of the differences in prosocial behavior was the assignment of chores to children—in particular, the care of infants. These findings reveal how different aspects of the socioeconomic organization of a culture can limit or expand its children's opportunities to develop prosocial behaviors (Grusec et al., 2002). The conditions in which women's overall workload to the family are greatest led to women delegating more responsibility to their children and hence providing more opportunities to practice prosocial behaviors. Also, Western societies often place a higher value on competition and individual achievement. As a result, children from industrialized societies often score lower on measures of altruism compared with children from cultures in which the group is valued over the individual (Whiting & Whiting, 1975).

Implications for Practice:
Helping Children Develop Empathy

How do we, as adults, encourage the development of empathy in children? First, we need to help children understand a range of emotions and learn to identify and label them accurately. To accomplish this task, we can honestly express our own emotions and provide children with word labels for their own future experiences. Praising prosocial behavior and talking to children about their feelings increases their emotional and cognitive understanding. When children do something that pleases us, we should be quick to let them know our feelings. We also can let children know that their concern for us makes us feel better. Sometimes children will laugh, not because seeing someone feeling bad strikes them as funny, but because they do not understand more complex emotions like frustration and embarrassment. They have usually felt this way at one time, too, but cannot identify or label the emotion when they see it in another person.

Social Cognition and Regulation

Preschoolers' self-concepts are determined largely by their physical characteristics and physical abilities. They learn to classify themselves and others first according to age, then gender, and then by what they can actively do, such as play baseball or climb a tree, and sometimes by what they physically possess. Their self-evaluations tend to be unrealistically positive because of their inability to distinguish between the real self and the desired self (Bosma & Gerlsma, 2003). This method of classifying themselves is referred to as **single representations**. We hear 3- to 5-year-olds refer to themselves as little or big boys and girls, depending on how independent they feel at the moment. And although they are also likely to know that they are either boys or girls, they may still believe these are transitory properties they could change if they wanted to (Kohlberg, 1969). By school age, children recognize gender as a fixed feature of identity and have some ideas of culturally sanctioned roles that parallel one's sexual identity. (Gender development will be more fully addressed in a later section.)

During the preschool years, children become able to make increasingly fine distinctions between physical attributes. Preschool children can make basic distinctions between their private selves and public selves, but not until middle childhood do they consistently attribute *psychological* characteristics to themselves or to others. They can, however, understand that others do not know everything they think or feel. Preschool children have been shown to fake an emotion to manipulate another person, demonstrating their belief that only they have access to some personal information (Bretherton & Munholland, 1999). They recognize that their own private talk, which accompanies many problem-solving tasks, is not the same as speaking to another person. Four- and 5-year-olds, especially, know that thinking goes on in their heads; others cannot "see" what they are thinking, and inanimate objects do not think (Bosma & Gerlsma, 2003).

A discussion about children's self-concept would be amiss without addressing the debate that has raged over the utility of promoting self-esteem versus competency. In fact, some developmental psychologists would argue that self-esteem is not the important ingredient in children's success (Damon, 1995; Seligman, 1995) and that false praise actually can do some harm (Dweck, 2000; Seligman, 1995). Critics of the self-esteem movement offer several points in contention of praising kids indiscriminately for any effort put forth (Dweck, 2000; Seligman, 1995).

First, they argue, data legitimately show positive self-esteem to be highly correlated with academic achievement; positive social skills; and resistance to drug involvement, early sex, gangs, and delinquency. However, they strongly assert that proponents of self-esteem as a "vaccine" to protect against social ills misinterpret the data to infer causality. Instead, the reverse conclusion is just as likely but cannot be inferred from existing data, either. That conclusion states that self-esteem increases as a function of increased competency and mastery, better skills for dealing with problems, and an improved ability to evaluate oneself accurately.

Their second argument pertains to the practice of dispensing praise liberally and with no real basis. This practice can actually produce the opposite effect, causing children to distrust both adults' opinions and their own judgment. Furthermore, as a result of unwarranted praise, children do not learn to assess their strengths and weaknesses accurately.

In his book *The Optimistic Child*, Seligman (1996) pointed out that "failure, in itself, is not catastrophic." Rather, it is the child's interpretation of the failure that can lead to problems such as depression (p. 14). The child's explanatory style, or the way she thinks about causes, can strongly influence how she thinks about the good and bad events that happen to her. Seligman argued that a child who has an optimistic explanatory style is better equipped to deal with the ups and downs of life. Seligman conceptualized explanatory style using three dimensions: permanence, pervasiveness, and personalization:

- Permanence—sometimes versus always: When bad events happen, a pessimistic child believes they are permanent. An example of a pessimistic statement regarding a negative event might be "I never do well on spelling tests." An optimistic child would explain a negative event as something temporary with the potential to change, saying, "I didn't do well on the spelling test today." Also, an optimistic child would explain a good event as having a permanent cause, such as, "I received good grades because I work hard," as opposed to a temporary cause, "My grades were good because Mom made me study."
- Pervasiveness—specific versus global: When causes are seen as pervasive, they are projected onto many aspects of life, not just a single episode. A global, or pessimistic, statement might be "Everyone hates me," whereas a specific, optimistic statement might be: "Mary doesn't like me." Regarding good events, optimistic statements are global ("I'm a smart person"), and pessimistic statements are specific to a situation ("I do well at reading").

- Personal—internal versus external: Personalization involves deciding who caused something to happen or, simply, who is to blame. Children can blame themselves (internal) or other people or situations (external). Children who continually blame themselves when bad things happen tend to have lower self-esteem. However, this does not imply that the way to feel good is to blame others; children must hold themselves accountable for their wrongdoings and faults. The key is for children to use behavioral, rather than general, self-blame. Behavioral self-blame is optimistic in nature (temporary and specific)—for example, "I was punished because I disobeyed the rules." General self-blame is pessimistic (permanent and pervasive): "I was punished because I'm a bad kid."

Seligman (1995) concluded that, instead of helping children "feel good," parents, teachers, and social workers should assist children in "doing well," which involves developing the "ability to think and to cope with the basic challenges of life" (p. 32). Like Gottman (1997), Seligman felt that negative emotions and experiences are important to a child's emotional growth. Seligman would likely argue strongly against the recent trend in some schools to eliminate failing grades. In being prevented from failing, they are also missing the opportunity to experience normal and natural emotions, such as sadness, anxiety, and anger. From this perspective, by protecting children from failure, we make it more difficult for them to develop the skills of mastery, and this results, ironically, in lowered self-esteem.

Sociability of Preschoolers

As children age, they naturally come into contact with a larger social audience that includes other adults, teachers, peers, siblings, and older children. Children aged 2 and 3 still stay physically close to adults and seek physical affection. Older preschoolers tend to seek the attention and approval of their peers through antics and playful gestures (Hartup & Abecassis, 2002).

Researchers have examined the question of sociability among preschoolers from several angles. Baumrind (1971) has focused attention on features of parent-child relationships that promote sociability. She has found that warm, supportive parents who set reasonable standards and expectations for their children's social interactions tend to raise well-adjusted, socially competent children. However, permissive parents who do not set or enforce social rules tend to raise children who are more rebellious, aggressive, and uncooperative.

Observational studies (Shea, 1981) have examined the social behavior of 3- and 4-year-old children attending preschool. Over the course of the observational period, children began to interact more with one another than with the teacher and became more playful and outgoing as opposed to forceful and aggressive. Results concluded that children's social skills were enhanced by their participation in preschool. Some children who lack social skills tend to miss more school for unknown reasons. (Hymel et al., 1996). Social-skills training becomes essential for these children, so they, too, can reap the benefits of the preschool social environment.

Longitudinal studies have produced data suggesting that sociability is a highly stable trait. By the age of 2, children's social behaviors are fairly predictable. The social behaviors assessed include reactions to play sessions, initiation of social interactions, and time spent interacting with other children. Measures of children's sociability at age 2 predicted sociability at age 3.5 in preschool (Cillessen et al., 2000; Rubin, Bukowski, & Parker, 1998). These findings are particularly salient when one considers the long-term effects on unsociable children. Later on, in middle childhood and adolescence, peer rejection becomes a forceful determinant correlate of behavioral and emotional difficulties (see Rubin et al., 1998).

To develop sociability skills in children, we must first consider exactly what skills we would like to improve. Asher and Dodge (1986) defined these skills as initiating play activities; communicating effectively; cooperating; giving help, affection, and approval to their peers; and resolving conflicts. The development of effective social skills is exceedingly important; because poor peer relationships are often the result of poor social skills. Poor peer relations, especially rejection by peers, have been linked steadily with increases in delinquency, psychopathology, and low self-esteem.

Several therapeutic approaches have been designed to remedy social-skills problems in children. These approaches include reinforcement, modeling, and cognitive strategies. Reinforcement and modeling strategies may be necessary at first to make immediate gains and motivate children to pursue more complicated strategies, such as problem solving and role play, that are associated with long-term gains.

To implement positive-reinforcement strategies, two essential elements must be present. First, positive reinforcement in the form of verbal praise, attention, and even tangible rewards can be used to shape socially appropriate responses. For example, every time a child shares, praise can be bestowed. This works best if the praise is awarded consistently to every child who demonstrates desirable social behavior according to a group reinforcement plan (Landy, Osofsky, & Landy, 2002). In this way, unsociable children can see others rewarded for positive behavior, as well. While positive social behavior is being rewarded, less desirable behaviors such as solitary play and aggressive behaviors are ignored as much as possible, so as not to reinforce them inadvertently.

Second, the environment often requires slight manipulation to provide and instigate social contact that can then be reinforced. We can structure a play setting relatively easily by introducing social games, such as tag and duck-duck-goose, that draw in the less sociable children. In addition, children deficient in social skills can be given a valuable commodity such as treats to give out to playmates. This strategy creates a social interaction in which everyone will want to interact with the unsociable child.

Modeling techniques also have been shown to help socially shy or withdrawn children enter the play group with less fear. The best models are people who are like the unsociable children in appearing initially hesitant to engage others socially. When the models' positive social behaviors (and the natural benefits of those behaviors) are pointed out to the group, undersocialized children more often imitate the positive behaviors (Landy et al., 2002). Not only did the shy children engage in positive social behaviors such as smiling, helping, and initiating contact, but so did the other children in the room. The benefits were reciprocal, in that all the children responded in socially positive ways to one another (Cooke & Apolloni, 1976).

More complex social-skills-training approaches, such as teaching cognitive strategies, require more activity on the part of the unsocialized child. The child actively participates in thinking about and practicing scenarios to develop helpful tools for problem solving. In coaching, the therapist both demonstrates and provides the rationale for particular socially desirable behaviors. The child then practices the behavior with the therapist and, even better, in live settings where interaction and cooperation are encouraged.

Role-playing techniques represent another cognitive-therapy strategy. In this case, children discuss hypothetical problems and generate potential solutions for them. Shure & Digeronimo (1996) developed a 10-week program aimed at preschoolers. The children used puppets to act out problem scenarios and helpful solutions. Then the preschoolers were guided in discussing the feelings of all the characters involved in the problem situation. Gains were made not only in the puppet exchanges, which became less aggressive, but also in the kinds of solutions worked out by the students themselves in the classroom.

Regulation

Young preschool children rely on physical means of expressing their emotions, both positive and negative. When preschoolers are happy, they are happy with their whole bodies, from smiling faces down to dancing feet. When they feel angry or frustrated, they strike out physically, as well. They throw tantrums, hit, kick, throw objects, and even bite. These behaviors allow them to assert their autonomy in the only way they know.

As preschoolers develop better language skills, and as their adult role models set reasonable limits and model social cooperation as well as acceptable ways of expressing negative emotions, children begin to incorporate these skills into their repertoire of self-assertive techniques. They are displaying the first signs of self-control when they use words and not physical aggression to communicate their feelings (Spitz, 1966). However, the preschooler's first choice of words rarely would win a peace prize. They use fighting words—words chosen to arouse a reaction in another child, not to mediate the problem. Not surprisingly, for young preschoolers, much of the vocabulary of the day revolves around body parts and bodily functions. Preschoolers often begin to use "bathroom talk," use swear words, and say, "I hate you" (American Academy of Child Psychiatry, 2000). The emotion conveyed at that moment, not the content of the remark, is what is important. The content may be dealt with another time, when the child is calm enough to hear what adults say. We can tell children that those words hurt others' feelings, but they can't cooperate when their emotional energy is high.

Children who learn to use words instead of physical aggression will eventually learn to use more socially sanctioned verbal approaches, as well (American Academy of Child Psychiatry, 2000). The process of internalizing self-control takes time over the course of early and middle childhood (Marti, 2003).

Children whose parents acknowledge their feelings and teach them to use alternate behaviors and means of expressing their feelings also learn cooperation and internalize self-control. Children who are taught to obey and comply regardless of how they feel do not learn to internalize cooperation skills. They may strike out, engaging in less mature behaviors when the threat of punishment is not there.

Psychological Strengths and Hazards

Early childhood represents enormous growth in the psychological functioning of the child. In fact, children's brains become nine-tenths of their adult size during this time period. The child truly comes into his or her own, through the development of a clear sense of "I," as an individual person. Genetics and experience work together to mold each child's preferences and personality. Some children are timid, some are keen observers, some are socially skilled, and others are more adept physically. One of the critical principles of our evolutionary nature is that diversity brings strength. Each child begins to bring this strength into reality during early childhood. Although much of this chapter has emphasized the presence of individual differences in children, it is critical for social workers to appreciate the value of children's individuality. Successful work with the early child needs to recognize and help develop each child's special strength—whether it is running, computer games, or drawing. Too often, the pressure is to get children to conform to general expectations rather than help each individual child expand his or her interests and skills.

The philosopher Rousseau described the nature of early childhood: "Is it nothing to skip, to play, to run about all day long?" The busy, adventurous, and exploring child shows us his or her flexibility and teaches us how to abandon fear in the pursuit of fun and continued development. Yet for some children, development can be thwarted as psychological hazards take hold.

Many disorders of childhood affect behaviors in very specific domains, such as eating, sleeping, eliminating, speaking, paying attention, and learning. Mood disorders, including anxiety and depression, and even the beginnings of antisocial conduct can be seen in children as they attempt to cope with normal developmental issues as well as situational and traumatic stressors. These disorders are considered developmental in that they represent an aberration in the normal course of development.

The disorders of childhood generally fall into one of three categories: developmental delays, developmental disorders, and developmental psychopathology. Developmental delays represent a slowed rate of skill acquisition, or normal behaviors such as bedwetting that occur at an inappropriate age. Delays can occur in almost any area of functioning; however, most children catch up before any real damage is done. Delays in critical areas, such as speech, tend to be more readily recognized and produce more profound negative effects for the child.

Developmental disorders occur in the areas of eating, sleeping, speech, eliminating, and attending (DeGangi, 2000). These disorders are characterized by a disruption in the performance of these skills. As such, they tend to cause problems for those caring for the children as well as for the children themselves. Children with developmental disorders are more likely to be referred for treatment than are children who show delays in the acquisition of normal behaviors, unless the delays are extreme. Examples of developmental disorders include enuresis, encopresis, stuttering, attention deficit disorder, and night terrors.

Developmental psychopathology results when a child's healthy adaptation is impeded by an inability to rally resources and cope with stressors. Although the child's response may, in fact, be a reasonable response to an identifiable stressor, the child's functioning becomes impaired by an inability to cope with and recover from trauma. Instead of one behavioral domain being affected, multiple areas of the child's life are compromised, including peer and family relationships, school performance, activities, and developmental goals. In this sense, developmental psychopathology is pervasive. Examples of developmental psychopathology include mood disorders such as anxiety and depression. Although these disorders have counterparts in adult psychopathology, the etiology, course of the disorder, and prognosis are different for children (see Campbell, Cummings, and Davies, 2002).

Diagnostic and Assessment Issues

Age is a critical factor in determining whether a particular behavior falls within an expected and normal developmental range. Children develop and change rapidly compared with adults, making a diagnosis of problem behavior difficult for parents and professionals. This difficulty is compounded by the fact that many normally developing children experience occasional transitory problems to which they quickly adjust.

Children are dependent on adults not only to recognize the existence of a problem but also to seek help for them. Parents who have grown accustomed to a child's usual pattern of behavior, and those who do not have the opportunity to observe their child in the company of age mates, may not possess the requisite understanding of normal developmental behavior patterns to ascertain whether their child needs help. Furthermore, treatment of childhood disorders frequently involves the cooperation and participation of parents and family members, only some of whom are capable and willing.

In the following sections we will examine childhood disorders involving elimination, speech, attention, anxiety, and depression.

Elimination

Problems in toilet training can arise from unreasonable parental expectations, because children must be physically, emotionally, and cognitively mature enough to master the task. In our culture, children are generally daytime toilet-trained by the time they enter the preschool years and nighttime trained about one year later. Girls' ability and motivation generally precede that of boys, and a wide normal range exists among children.

Enuresis is defined as a lack of bladder control after age 5 (American Psychiatric Association, 2000). *Primary enuresis* refers to bladder control that was never achieved by age 5, and *secondary enuresis* refers to a loss of ability after first achieving control. Approximately 5–7 million children have nocturnal enuresis, boys three times more often than girls (Thiedke, 2003). At 5 years old, 15–25% wet the bed, but by 12 years old, 8% of boys and 4% of girls are still bed wetters. During the normal course of the disorder, about 5–10% of affected children spontaneously recover each year. Nocturnal enuresis was once thought to be a psychological condition. It now appears that psychological problems are the result of enuresis, not the cause (Thiedke, 2003). Bed-wetting is not likely to be an act of rebellion, as many people believe. It is believed that enuresis is a heritable disorder, as 75% of enuretic children have an immediate family member who once had the disorder (Geroski & Rodgers, 1998). The most effective treatment for enuresis is the bed-wetting alarm (Thiedke, 2003).

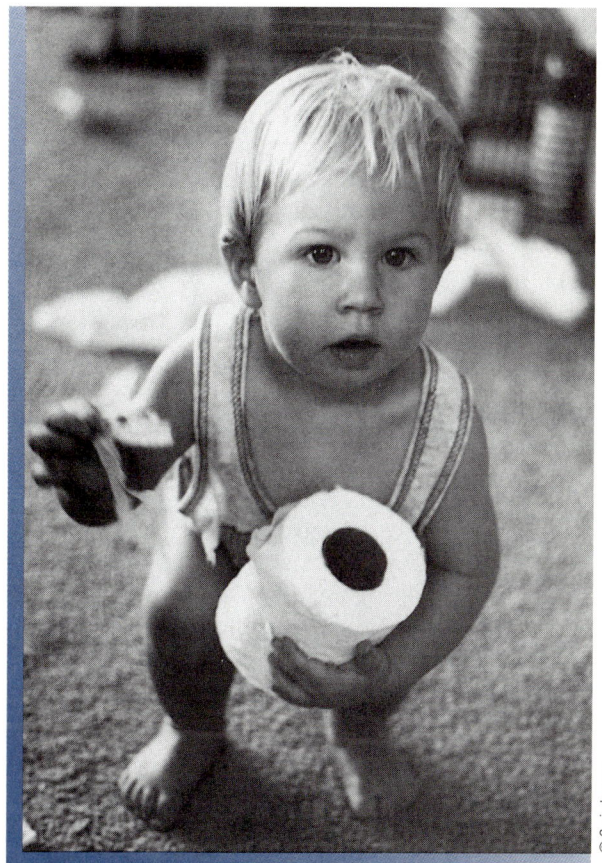

A child's mastery of toilet training requires coordination of biophysical, psychological, and social domains of development.

Encopresis is defined as a lack of bowel control after a normal age and is distinguished as either primary or secondary. Encopresis is not diagnosed before age 4. The disorder is more common in boys than in girls and occurs in about 1–3% of the population (Christophersen & Mortweet, 2001). About one out of four encopretic children are also enuretic. Factors associated with encopresis include inconsistent toilet training, painful bowel movements, and psychosocial stressors, such as entering school or the birth of a new sibling. Encopresis rarely becomes chronic, and well-developed behavior-management strategies have been used in its treatment (Christophersen & Mortweet, 2001).

Anxiety Disorders

Separation anxiety disorder, characterized by severe anxiety about leaving home or separating from the child's primary attachment figures, is not uncommon, occurring in about 4% of the population (American

Psychiatric Association, 2000). Children typically fear harm will come to them or their family if separated, and they go to great lengths to prevent separations. Children develop somatic complaints, refuse to attend school, and behave in clingy, demanding ways with parents to ensure their closeness. These children also experience sadness, loss of interest in activities, withdrawal, and difficulty concentrating on school or play. In the course of normal development, separation anxiety peaks at about 1 year and gradually lessens with age. Separation anxiety is most frequently seen in very tight-knit families and following some sort of trauma for the child. In the general population, separation anxiety is more prevalent in females than males; however, gender rates are about equal in clinical samples (American Psychiatric Association, 2000).

Avoidant disorder, commonly called a fear of strangers and strange or new situations, can be socially debilitating to a child. This response is normal between the ages of 8 months and 2–3 years, but in some cases it may continue into childhood. A child may severely limit involvement in social and academic settings to avoid this fear. As a result, the child may feel lonely and depressed and lose self-confidence, causing further avoidant behavior (American Academy of Child and Adolescent Psychiatry, 2000).

Overanxious disorder, or generalized anxiety disorder, is distinguished from separation anxiety in that the child's fears have no specific focus. In the case of overanxious disorder, children anticipate something going wrong in almost any situation and worry about the possibility. Children with these unfocused worries doubt themselves and their abilities. Worries often center on school and sports performance, and children frequently redo tasks in an attempt to make sure they are good enough. Children living in homes where love and acceptance are granted for good behavior tend to be approval-seeking and perfectionistic (American Psychiatric Association, 2000). A vicious cycle unfolds when children's performance is handicapped by worries and anxiety, which, in turn, cause them to fail, which produces even more anxiety.

Attention-Deficit/Hyperactivity Disorder (ADHD)

Attention-deficit/hyperactivity disorder (ADHD) is characterized by persistent inattention and/or hyperactivity (American Psychiatric Association, 2000) and is the most common behavioral disorder of childhood (Herrerias et al., 2001). Although many children meet the diagnostic criteria for this disorder, it is often difficult to diagnose in children younger than 5 years because of the behavior variation normally seen at this age (American Psychiatric Association, 2000). Additionally, until children begin kindergarten or elementary school, they do not typically have many demands on their attention, which makes an attention disorder difficult to recognize. Yet many children as young as 4 or 5 years old are diagnosed with ADHD and prescribed Ritalin or other pharmaceutical medication (Hancock, 1996). This phenomenon spurs the question: Do these children have actual attention and hyperactivity problems, or have adults simply lost patience with active children? Proponents for the use of medication in controlling ADHD believe that some children cannot sit still without the help of psychopharmaceuticals such as Ritalin. Opponents, however, argue that using medication is simply an easier solution to the problem because it takes less time than developing a behavior-management plan. With roughly 1.3 million of America's 5- to 14-year-olds taking medications for ADHD (Herrerias et al., 2001), it appears that this debate will continue. However, research studies are showing that a combination of medication and behavior management is the most effective treatment (Jensen, 2001). It is being increasingly recognized the ADHD coexists or has "comorbidity" with many other behavior problems, such as oppositional defiant disorder, conduct disorder, anxiety disorder and depressive disorder (Herrerias et al., 2001). Concern has also been raised about whether children with ADHD and treated with stimulant medication are more likely to develop substance abuse in adolescence and adulthood. A recent longitudinal study (Barkely, 2003) found that at a 13-year follow-up, participants who received medication for ADHD were not more likely to have substance-abuse problems than were a comparison group of children.

Childhood Depression

Only 40 years ago, most professionals doubted the existence of depressive disorders in children because they believed children lacked the cognitive structure to experience such problems. Depression in children does occur but is frequently unrecognized. It affects 2% of prepubertal children and increases substantially in adolescence (Son & Kirchner, 2000). Symptoms can range from simple sadness to a major depression or bipolar disorder. The symptom pattern can differ from that exhibited by adults. Children tend to display more than one symptom and can act clingy, disobedient, irritable, sad, and hopeless; refuse to attend school; and show a decreased interest in usual activities. Children are rarely suicidal, although this possibility increases in adolescence. Children who experience depression tend to have mood disorders as adults (Rice, Harold, & Thapar, 2002). Prevalence rates for prepubertal males and females are about equal, but by the time girls reach adolescence and adulthood, they are more than twice as likely as males to report depression (American Psychiatric Association, 2000). Depressive episodes often result from a severe psychosocial stressor in a child's life, such as the loss of a loved one, separation, or other trauma.

Autism

Kevin's parents thought he was a little odd as a baby. He was rather fussy. When they fed him and tried to stroke his back, he would stop eating and fuss until they stopped the stroking. When they picked him up for play, he would often avert his gaze or look past them. As a toddler, he liked to play by himself. He would sit for long periods of time just watching a patch of sun on the floor or dropping blocks over and over. His language development seemed especially slow, but he was their first baby and they had no expectations regarding language acquisition. The pediatrician told them Kevin would learn to speak soon. When he went to preschool at the age of 3, however, the teacher called the parents in for a conference because Kevin would not play or interact with any of the children in the class. He spent most of his mornings sitting and rocking, and he rarely spoke to anyone. In fact, the only thing the teachers had heard him say was "water" when he needed a drink.

Childhood **autism** is a pervasive developmental disorder with profound implications for the child's ability to function (American Psychiatric Association, 2000). Children with autism suffer psychological, cognitive, and social deficits that impair their functional capacities in nearly every realm of their lives.

Although the disorder is typically present at birth, autism is often not diagnosed until the child is about 3 years old, when language deficits can be distinguished from speech delays. It is these speech and language delays that distinguish autism from Asperger's Disorder, a pervasive developmental disorder in children that shares many of autism's diagnostic criteria but does not involve language delays (American Psychiatric Association, 2000).

Language deficits are prominent in autistic children. More than half do not speak at all, whereas others whine, scream, or demonstrate **echolalia**, repeating songs and phrases from others' conversations. These verbalizations are distinct from social communication because they are rarely intended as a means of interacting with or communicating information to another person. More often, verbal expression is used as a means of self-stimulation or for getting a simple need met. The severity of language deficits has been found to be the best predictor of the child's overall prognosis. Children who have developed recognizable speech by the age of 5 fare the best in terms of leading independent lives.

Mental retardation appears to be a stable feature of autistic disorder, with more than 70% of children testing at an IQ level below 70. Boys are three to four times more likely to develop autism than are girls.

Significant social deficits and poor relationship skills also characterize autism. These children typically react to others not as people but as objects in their environment. They do not relate physically, seek comfort, communicate, or otherwise interact unless they need something they cannot manage themselves (National Research Council, 2001). They prefer the company of inanimate objects, and when with other people, autistic children frequently do not respond to their own names, make eye contact, smile, initiate communication, or respond when spoken to. More often, autistic children will not acknowledge the presence of another human being.

We see autistic children play in rigid, unimaginative ways. They do not use make-believe or imitative play. Furthermore, they do not engage in social play, instead preferring to occupy themselves alone. They also engage in nonfunctional routines and rituals (APA, 2000). These children demand sameness and predictability in their environments and daily routines. They also exhibit distorted body movements. Autistic children can be seen flapping their arms, hands, and fingers; banging their heads; and twisting their bodies in unnatural ways.

Researchers continue to work toward understanding the genetics of autism, with the hope that breakthroughs in this area will contribute to improved diagnosis and more effective treatments in the future (McIntosh, 1998). Twin and sibling studies have revealed that autism is a highly heritable disorder, present because of genetic abnormalities in the DNA

(Veenstra-Vanderweele & Cook, 2003). However, it is likely that autism involves multiple genes and chromosomal regions, so that its study and characterization are complex (McIntosh, 1998; Veenstra-Vanderweele & Cook, 2003).

Parenting an autistic child can be extremely difficult, frustrating, and sad. When a child does not respond or relate, the quality of parental and sibling interactions and stimulation can taper off. Treatment efforts result in slow, minimal gains. Behavioral-therapy techniques have documented empirical support. These techniques include token-economy strategies, modeling, social-skills training, and language and speech training. Treatment is often an individually based program, in which each child's developmental profile is considered and treatment components are designed accordingly. One factor that may make a difference in the success of treatment is early diagnosis, as this would provide opportunities for earlier therapeutic intervention. As previously stated, most autistic children are not diagnosed before the age of 3. However, newer screening methods have been developed. The Autism Diagnostic Observational Schedule and the Modified Checklist for Autism in Toddlers are two such methods that show promise in diagnosing autism, or the need for additional follow-up, as early as 18 months (Azar, 1998; MacReady, 2002).

STUDY TABLE: Psychological dimension in early childhood

Cognitive Development and Information Processing	Imaginative thought begins in early childhood. Children can categorize objects in two dimensions (at 4 years old). The meaning and function of numbers is understood. At age 5, time and logical thinking begin. Children (2–7) are in Piaget's operational stage of development, which has two substages: symbolic function, and intuitive thought. They are egocentric, being unable to distinguish between their perspective and another person's. Children at this stage begin primitive reasoning but not formal logic. In their information processing, children begin to acquire cognitive control of their attention. Children younger than 3 have little or no memory for specific events. After 3, children can begin to recount memories and develop processes for the storage and retrieval of information. Early developmentalists assumed children developed in stages, today, changes are believed to occur more as "developmental waves." A more complex understanding of information processing has emerged from research.
Communication	Language development was previously believed to be imprinted on a blank slate. It is now recognized that language is more innate. Children use a universal grammar demonstrated by the subject-verb structures that emerge ("me want"). A 3-year-old has a vocabulary of 900 words; by age 6, the vocabulary is 8,000–14,000 words. Morphological rules and syntax develop as children use plurals and possessives, ask questions, and so forth. At ages 4–5, semantic skills develop—comparisons such as big/little can be made, and children understand "I" as the speaker and "you" as the object. Talking with children can promote their language development. Children who develop bilingual skills perform better on measures of language than monolingual children. Language begins to take on more social functions as the child gets older. Communication disorders such as expressive language disorder, phonological disorder, and stuttering can begin to emerge.
Attitudes and Emotions	As children begin more social interactions, the impact of attitudes and emotions becomes more central. Emotional coaching is recommended for children as they learn about themselves and how to problem solve in the face of difficult emotions. Emotion coaching consists of a five-step process: awareness, using

emotions to teach, validating the child's feelings, helping the child label the emotion, and setting limits and problem solving. Fears and phobias, especially fear of the dark, begin to develop in early childhood. Social events such as September 11 can evoke fears in children. Post-traumatic stress disorder can emerge when children experience trauma. When experiencing a traumatic event children may feel fear, loss of control, anger, loss of stability, isolation, and confusion. Grief and loss are difficult for young children to comprehend. In preschool there is a lot of social aggression (peaks at age 4), which is defined as intending to harm another person and the victim perceiving that he or she has been hurt. Aggression is divided into two subtypes: reactive and proactive. Although aggression is considered a normal drive, higher levels are related to family and social factors as well as poor maternal health habits. Aggression demonstrates stable qualities for both boys and girls as children develop. Aggressive children often come from homes characterized as coercive. Warning signs for aggression have been identified, and strategies for reducing aggression include ignoring, time-out, modeling and coaching, and creating nonaggressive environments. Altruism and empathy begin to take hold in early childhood. At age 4, children show empathic sharing primarily in the context of peer interactions; however, children cannot cognitively understand another person's feelings. Modeling can enhance empathic responding in children. Prosocial behaviors have been found to differ according to cultural background. Children's altruistic behavior is influenced by opportunities to provide compassion. In particular, the Western values of competition and individual achievement can lower altruistic behavior.

Social Cognition and Regulation	Preschoolers' self-concepts are based on their physical characteristics and physical abilities. Their self-evaluations are positive because they cannot distinguish between the real and desired self. In the past, much effort has been focused on increasing children's self-esteem. Critics believe that indiscriminately praising kids can be harmful. Instead, critics recommend an optimistic explanatory style that uses three dimensions: permanence (sometimes versus always), pervasiveness (specific versus global), and personalization (internal versus external). The overall strategy is not to help children "feel better" but to help them "do better," which includes thinking and coping with life's challenges. In preschool, children need to develop their social skills, and preschool provides an environment that facilitates children's sociability. Sociability is a highly stable trait. When difficulties in children's social behavior exist, social-skills training can be helpful. Sociability skills such as communicating effectively, cooperating, and giving help are taught through reinforcement, environmental modification, modeling, role playing, and problem solving. As children develop, they gain more regulation over their emotions and actions. Tantrums stop, and verbal control begins to take hold. Instead of physical aggression they learn to use words.
Psychological Strengths and Hazards	Growth in psychological functioning. Brains become nine-tenths of their adult size. The development of a clear sense of "I" begins. Many children's individual strengths emerge. The disorders or hazards that emerge are usually developmental delays (bed wetting), developmental disorders (ADHD), or developmental psychopathology (pervasive mood disorders). Age and development must be considered in any psychosocial assessment. More common childhood disorders include elimination problems, anxiety disorders, ADHD, childhood depression, and autism.

CONCEPT MAP

SOCIAL DIMENSION

Families and Groups

By the time a child reaches the period of early childhood, the family has undergone numerous changes. These changes are noted in the marital relationship, parent-child relationships, work, and family systems dynamics. The couple has become a family, and that family may continue growing again with the birth of another child. The developing child plays an active role in promoting healthy change in the family structure and dynamics while adjusting to the changes.

For the preschooler, parents and family remain the primary socializers and sources of companionship and comfort. However, as children progress through the preschool years, they relate to and rely on a larger circle of adults and peers because their needs no longer center so much on physical care. Preschoolers are growing, exploring, investigating, and refining motor, social, and emotional skills at an exhilarating and enthusiastic pace. They also discover new sources of anger, frustration, jealousy, and elation as they interact within a wider social environment.

Parenting roles and tasks shift from those involving physical care to setting limits, encouraging increasing amounts of independence in self-care and play skills, and using language and reason as methods of social control. Throughout all these very profound changes in the preschooler's social environment, the family continues to provide the basis for support, attachment, and exploration.

Family Influences

As we mentioned briefly, parenting roles begin to shift as children traverse the preschool years. Children still need their parents as the primary sources of attention, care, love, encouragement, and security. Children living in homes where their changing needs are met can attend to their developmental tasks unencumbered with worries or fears for their safety and for that of their family members. Parents who are too preoccupied with their own identity issues, ambitions, or survival will struggle with child-rearing tasks that seem extremely demanding because they compete for energy with their other pressing needs.

Parents of preschoolers begin to change their focus from physical care to encouraging self-care, greater independence, and compliance with rules of social systems such as the family, peer group, preschool, and society. Effective parents allow their children to try out new activities and develop some self-sufficiency, and they set reasonable limits with their children. Parents who are too rigid or demanding impose unrealistic expectations on their children, causing them to feel as if they cannot measure up and to feel guilty for failing to accomplish something on their own.

According to Erikson's theory, the psychosocial crisis facing children during the preschool years is one of initiative versus guilt. The parent of a preschooler, much like the parent of the adolescent, must help the child discover personal and social abilities and limits while enjoying their accomplishments and sense of self-reliance. In this way, measured against the back-

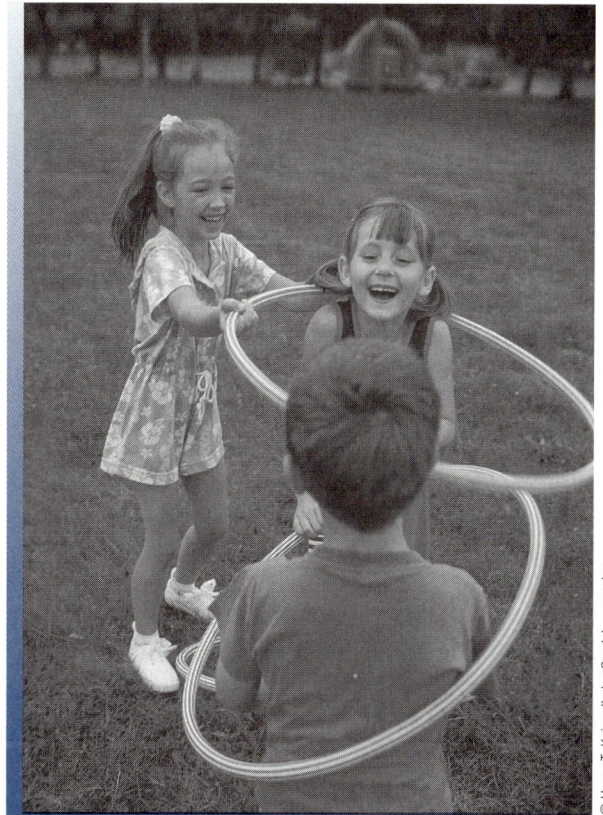

Play increases social contacts, conversation, and social skills.

drop of peers and society, children continue to learn about themselves.

Parenting Styles

Some of the most influential research on parenting has come from Diana Baumrind, who believes that the best parenting results when parents are neither too punitive nor too aloof but focused on developing clear rules within the context of warm and affectionate parenting. She has investigated parenting styles over several decades (1971, 1991), and her research has described three styles of parenting and their consequent effects on children: authoritarian, authoritative, and laissez-faire (permissive). Maccoby and Martin (1993) have further differentiated the permissive parenting style to include two distinct types, neglectful and indulgent. *Parental warmth* refers to the acceptance and approval shown to children across a number of different occasions. These parents offer their children encouragement and praise and are generous with affection. Hostile parents, on the other hand, tend to criticize, reject, or ignore their children

EXHIBIT 7.6 Effects of parenting styles on children

Parenting Style	Characteristics	Effects on Children
Authoritarian	Restrictive, punitive style; sets firm limits and encourages effort; few verbal exchanges allowed.	Average social, cognitive competencies; fearful, unhappy, vulnerable to stress.
Authoritative	Warm, nurturing, accepting; encourages independence, but with limits; verbal exchanges using negotiating, compromise, and reason also encouraged; responsive to needs of child.	High social, cognitive competencies; cope well with stress; curious, self-controlled, cooperative with adults, energetic, friendly, self-reliant.
Permissive Indulgent	Very involved in child's life; few demands placed on child; lax control; allows freedom of expression, encourages creativity, confidence.	Low self-control; difficulty focusing own behavior; expect to get their own way; poor social, cognitive competencies; not popular with others.
Permissive Indifferent	Very uninvolved with child; few demands placed on child; lax control; allows freedom of expression and impulses.	Low self-control; poor social, cognitive competencies; rebellious, impulsive, aggressive.

and their bids for attention. Parents tend to be characterized as either warm and approving or hostile and rejecting, and these styles tend to be mutually exclusive.

The construct of parental control taps into the number of demands, restrictions, and limits that parents place on their children. Permissive parents encourage their children to explore and make independent decisions. Restrictive parents impose more demands and enforce more rules on their children, controlling their actions and decisions. Parents tend to become more permissive as children age and develop the experience and ability to make healthy decisions for themselves. All children need guidance and monitoring, which can be flexible and change according to their developmental needs.

What effects do we see on children reared within the context of these distinct parenting models? Parents need to adapt their style of relating and interacting, as well as discipline, to their child's developmental level. As children enter the preschool years, parents can begin to rely on verbal exchanges, reasoning, moral sanctions, and giving and withholding of special privileges. Exhibit 7.6 highlights the features associated with each parenting style and the behavioral effects on children. Discipline strategies that invoke logical and immediate consequences tend to be the most effective for preschool children, because they are beginning to understand cause and effect. Such strategies also help children develop the ability to think logically about actions and to make choices based on likely outcomes. Furthermore, the use of logical consequences helps avoid power struggles between parents in imposing discipline (Dreikurs, 1993). Logical consequences just happen, because of their very nature, and the child begins to learn about problem solving in the real world.

Mothers and fathers often approach discipline differently (Russell & Saebel, 1997). For example, when toddlers explore you are more likely to hear a mom say, "Come down from there!" as she focuses on protection. Yet the father may like to encourage these behaviors and say, "Climb up higher!" Sleep problems in children can also show gender differences, as mothers want to comfort the child and fathers are more likely to encourage letting the child fuss. Mothers tend to verbalize more, whereas fathers give more commands (Leaper, Anderson, & Sanders, 1998; Sears & Sears, 1995). Differences also emerge when researchers examine the interaction between parents and sons and daughters. Both parents provide sons with more task-oriented, directive, and approval-based instructions than daughters (Yelland, 1998). Girls, on the other hand, are taught to be more cautious and cooperative and are provided feedback about their performance more than are boys. The subtle but clear messages to boys and girls from both parents convey stereotypical gender-role expectations. More aggressive behavior is tolerated, if not encouraged, in boys, whereas girls are taught cooperation and empathy through parental play and teaching (Yelland, 1998).

Many researchers have documented the positive effects on children raised by parents who are warm and affectionate and who set consistent, reasonable rules for their children, as opposed to those who behave in a punitive or aloof manner (Baumrind, 1971). Of course, most of this research has been conducted on middle-class white families. These findings may neglect the fact that not all children are raised to participate and succeed in the same environment.

A major issue in recent years in the discussion of parenting is the "nature versus nurture" debate. As mentioned in Chapter 2, extensive studies have been conducted to try to determine whether genetics or the environment has a larger impact on human behavior. In her 1998 book *The Nurture Assumption: Why Children Turn Out the Way They Do*, Judith Rich Harris stirred up more controversy in this area, and Steven Pinker (2002) continued to fuel the fire with his book *The Blank Slate: Modern Denial of Human Nature*.

Most of the current thinking about the strong influence of human nature emerges from research referred to as **behavioral genetics**. As a fundamental principle, behavioral genetics asserts that all human behavioral traits are heritable. A *behavioral trait* refers to any stable property of a person, including an underlying talent or temperament. Most people are surprised to learn about the types of properties that can be linked to genetics. Culture influences what language you speak, what religion you worship in, and what political party you belong to. Yet surprisingly, traits such as how proficient you are with language, how religious you are, and how liberal or conservative you are reflect heritable personality traits (Pinker, 2002). Research on identical twins who were separated at birth and reared apart has revealed a lot of information about the relative importance of genes and environment. (These twins share all of their genes and none of their environment, so any correlation between the two individuals is an effect of their genes.) Twin research has led to the conclusion that about half of variation in intelligence and personality is heritable, and it has shown that much of what we thought was an effect of families or parenting may instead be an expression of genes. Thus, if a researcher measures a trait in parents and in their children, then reaches a conclusion about the effects of parenting, they may unknowingly be recording the effects of the shared genes (e.g., aggressive parents are likely to have aggressive children).

Harris's book attracted a lot of media attention for her claim that most of the conventional wisdom about childrearing is dead wrong. According to Harris, parents have been led to believe that the entire fate of their children is in their hands. Her conclusion, based on a wealth of research studies, is that growing up in a particular family has little or no effect on one's intellect and personality. But if genes account for only half of the variation among individuals, where are the other influences? Harris argued that a child's personality and behavior are more strongly influenced by peers and interactions with peers than they are by parents and what happens in the home. Harris's **group socialization theory** states that peer and community influences have the most impact on a child's identity, with the influence of parenting coming into play mainly when a child is in the home. Once the child is away from the home, whether at school or elsewhere, the influence of peers takes precedence.

Harris does credit parents with having some ability to positively affect their child's development, by providing a strong genetic makeup and by choosing to raise their child in a good community with good schools. Although most parents would like their children to grow up in safe and socially stimulating neighborhoods, this is certainly not realistic for the population of this country who live in poverty. Does this fact suggest that a child's personality is indirectly influenced the income and social status? Not necessarily. Although Harris's theories are strong and may challenge conventional beliefs about parenting and child development, they are criticized as not being fully substantiated by research (Efran & Green, 1999). The debate over "nature versus nurture" is clearly not over, but it does seem that Harris has opened a new door that will likely be investigated by future researchers.

Research studies of lower-income and lower-educational-status families suggest that these parents tend to be more authoritarian in their child-raising practices; they expect more obedience from their children, engage in less verbal exchange, and exhibit less warmth (Maccoby, 1980). But does this make lower-income parents less desirable or effective parents? There are several reasons why lower-SES parents may be more authoritarian with their children (Shaffer, 2002). They may be facing more stress, which makes it harder for them to be warm and caring. They may be preparing their children for the types of jobs the parents themselves hold, in which obedience and respect are positive attributes. The children themselves may be more difficult to parent. Many lower-income mothers are young and may not have received adequate prenatal care. As a result, these mothers may have delivered premature, low-birth-weight, or drug- or alcohol-exposed babies. As we have discussed, such babies are more difficult to care for. Also, lower-SES parents may feel that authoritarian parenting is necessary to protect their children from environments full of risks that increase the likelihood of delinquency, school dropout, early pregnancy, and substance use.

Children from risky environments may not be permitted the luxury of experimentation without dire consequences that children from more affluent environments are afforded. Some researchers have found that low-income, inner-city parents who are strict and set stringent rules for their children, yet also provide high levels of warmth, assist their children in resisting the negative influences in their school and neighborhood environments that lead to low achievement and delinquency (McLoyd, 1998). Unfortunately for children growing up in families facing multiple stressors, such as poverty and inadequate housing, parenting is not the only factor that determines a child's outcome. Results from The New Chance Observational Study suggest that making changes in parenting style alone does not significantly impact outcomes for children (Sleek, 1998). As a result, children from lower-SES families may play by and adopt a different set of values according to the roles, goals, and relationships they aspire to. These ecological constraints are not always incorporated into the interpretations of findings on the most effective parenting style for children. We must remember that as the cultural context changes, so do expectations of behavior and beliefs. For example, Slaughter-Defoe (1995), in reviewing her previous research regarding parenting by African American women living in a low-income area of Chicago, found that these women used mothers' discussion groups and extended family for support and as protective factors for their children. Ethnocentric biases prohibit us from understanding which parenting styles promote competent children in differing cultures and subcultures (Laosa, 1981). But regardless of the parental style, or the reasons for that particular style, parental warmth and approval remain important ingredients in the parent-child relationship.

Nontraditional Families

In today's society, there are many different types of "nontraditional" families. For example, many children are now being raised in families with same-sex parents. These families are sometimes criticized by those who feel that gay or lesbian parents cannot raise a well-adjusted child. However, studies reveal that children raised by gay or lesbian parents show no psychological or adjustment differences from children raised in "traditional" families (Chan, Raboy, & Patterson, 1998; Drucker, 2001). However, some critical differences do emerge, such as receiving less support from extended family members and experiencing greater stress. Lack of support and intolerance from the general public are often significant sources of stress (Drucker, 2001). The research states that the bottom line is that it is not the parent's sexual orientation that influences the child's adjustment, but rather the quality of the parent-child relationship and the relationship between the two parents that impact the child (Russell, Mize, & Bissaker, 2002).

Mother's Role

Although preschool children need their mothers less for physical care than they did as infants, the need for emotional support and encouragement is just as great as ever (Russell et al., 2002). Still, much of a mother's time with her preschooler revolves around child-care duties (seven times more than fathers), whereas fathers tend to spend much less time in direct care and more time playing (Russell & Saebel, 1997).

What kinds of things do preschoolers learn from their mothers? Studies reveal that mothers tend to introduce soothing activities to their preschoolers, such as reading, drawing, and music. In this way, children learn how to soothe and comfort themselves. Children also learn a great deal about feelings and relationships from their mothers. During play, mothers tend to be more verbal and visual with their preschoolers than fathers. This interaction style during play may contribute to the child's understanding of relationships and coping strategies.

In addition, preschoolers are attuned to learning about the meaning of their gender and begin to identify with the same-sex parent, all the while learning how to relate to the opposite-sex parent. Preschoolers observe that males and females act differently. Research has supported the idea that males and females rely on different strategic approaches to solve problems (Denham et al., 2002). Males tend to focus on only one relevant aspect of the problem and base their decision on that aspect alone. Females, on the other hand, tend to gather lots of information and attend to the context of the situation before determining a solution. In this way, children learn about diversity and alternative approaches to events in their lives.

Father's Role

The relationship between preschoolers and their father broadens the children's perspective on the world. For the most part, even today, preschool boys and girls are raised in almost exclusively female environments. They spend most of their time with mothers and with babysitters and teachers, who are usually female. The child's father may be the only male figure with whom contact is regular.

As we discussed in the last chapter, fathers play differently with their children than mothers do. Remember, father play has been described as more provocative and vigorous, and less conventional and verbal than mother play. These differences were found to be especially true of play with preschoolers, and with sons more so than with daughters. Fathers who play physically and roughly with their children tend to raise children with increased social competencies (Parke et al., 1988). This physical play is important to children because how they learn to cope with the exhilaration, challenge, and unpredictability of their fathers' physical play prepares them for later life experiences.

By watching and interacting with their fathers, children also learn that there are numerous ways to complete a task. The father may not do things exactly the way the child's mother does, and the child is shown another way to solve a problem. Of course, family structures and parenting styles vary. Mothers and fathers may assume complementary but nonstandard roles that work just as well for their children and family.

Around age 4 or 5, both boys and girls find their relationship with their fathers especially appealing and important, and they seek him out as a playmate more often than they seek their mother (Lamb, 1981). Adult males help young boys define their own developing masculinity by encouraging and supporting their accomplishments. Boys model themselves after their fathers at this age. Girls also seek out fatherly attention and time. The father's role helps girls define their feminine side. Also, preschool girls may tend to be resentful and jealous of their mother's special relationship with their father. Involved fathers help preschool children understand more about themselves and the larger world.

Children of Prisoners

Although both mothers and fathers play important roles in the child's development, some children must cope with a missing parent because of incarceration. There are approximately 2 million people incarcerated in the United States. Eighty percent of these individuals are parents, leaving 1.5 million children in this country with at least one parent in prison (DeAngelis, 2001; Bilchik, Seymour, & Kreisher, 2001). Children of prisoners often live in homes with poverty and substance abuse or violence before parental arrests occur (Bilchik, Seymour, & Kreisher, 2001). After a parent is arrested, many children then find themselves placed in a new living situation. Some children can be placed with a grandparent, but more than one-quarter will be placed in foster care or in informal arrangements with extended family or friends (Bilchik, Seymour, & Kreisher, 2001). Researchers have begun to examine the effects that having a parent in prison can have on children.

Children with parents in prison are more likely to develop emotional and behavioral difficulties, such as withdrawal, aggression, anxiety, and depression (DeAngelis, 2001; Bilchik, Seymour, & Kreisher, 2001). These children are also at high risk for second-generation incarceration; statistics indicate that children with parents in prison are six times more likely to become criminally involved and enter the criminal-justice system themselves, as compared to their peers (Bilchik et al., 2001).

How can these children be helped? In 2001, the American Psychiatric Association formed a task force to explore issues related to children of prisoners, such as identifying the best interventions and prevention strategies for children in out-of-home care and looking into public-policy issues that might result in increased funding of research and treatment (DeAngelis, 2001). Some programs targeting this group of children already exist in this country. One program, run out of California's Center for the Children of Incarcerated Parents, provides children with therapy, skill-building, and social activities, and another California program targets attachment building between incarcerated mothers and their babies and young children. Although there is still work to be done in this area, programs such as these around the country may hold promise for ameliorating the effects of having a parent in prison.

Siblings

Most children grow up in a family enriched and complicated by the presence of siblings. In the United States and Britain, this figure is estimated to be about 80%. The birth of a sibling often occurs when the first or previous child enters the preschool years. The exact influence of one sibling over another depends on many factors, including birth order, birth spacing, number of siblings, and gender.

Sibling rivalry tends to begin early. Frequently, an older child has to make adjustments and concessions, willingly or not, as soon as the next baby arrives. Even before the birth of a sibling, during pregnancy mothers can be incapacitated and unable to perform all of their usual child-care responsibilities. For most children, the period of adjustment to a new sibling is relatively short. As the youngest becomes capable of responding to an older child, positive interactions soon begin to dispel the initial reaction of anger and resentment. The children also develop a relationship of their own, not contingent on the parents' involvement.

Siblings offer challenges to the development of interpersonal relationships.

What do we know about sibling relationships? They appear to have three primary characteristics (Dunn, 2002). First, sibling relationships are noted for their emotions, which are powerful and expressed without inhibitions. When you compare parent-child relationships with sibling relationships, you find that children demonstrate more affection, compliance, and positive social responses to parents than to their brothers and sisters. Children will direct more negative behaviors, such as teasing, hitting, and yelling, at their siblings than at parents. Fighting and rivalry among siblings provides a safe opportunity to practice resolving conflicts and, in fact, may toughen up children, making them less vulnerable to the pain and hurt that can be a part of peer relationships.

In spite of the strong emotions, a second characteristic of sibling relationships is the intimacy between siblings. They spend more time interacting with each other than with parents, and they know each other extremely well. Yet this intimacy also is the means for conflict. Teasing depends on knowing the person well enough to "push their buttons" and be able to predict the reaction. Teasing by siblings is observed early in the second year of life and increases rapidly over the next several months (Dunn, 2002).

Third, a characteristic of sibling relationships is the great diversity in differences that they represent. The extremes are well known—intense affection, cooperation and support contrasted with hostility, aggression and even dislike. The intriguing but unanswered question is why are some siblings so supportive and others so hostile?

Although sibling rivalry may come and go between brothers and sisters, there are those siblings who seem as though they will never get along. Researchers hypothesize that, in these cases, there may be a "clash" in temperament between the two children that prevents them from developing a quality relationship (Dunn, 2002; Brody, 1998). The concept is similar to "goodness of fit," as discussed in Chapter 6, where the temperament of the baby is very different from the personality and lifestyle of the parents. With siblings who have very dissimilar temperaments, conflict can arise simply because each child's emotions, behaviors, and coping mechanisms are different. However, just because two siblings have very different temperaments does not mean that they will never have a quality relationship. Other factors, such as the parent-child relationship, parental management of sibling conflict, and a positive and prosocial family environment, can ameliorate the conflict between siblings (Brody, 1998).

Even with this range of difference, for the most part, when children live together as siblings, they contribute to each other's development in unique ways. They serve as teachers and models of both prosocial and negative behavior, communication partners, playmates, and rivals. Even children as young as preschoolers provide valuable and attentive emotional support to younger siblings, especially when they have been shown basic care skills and can identify the baby's source of distress (Stewart, 1983). Siblings also can be an important source of support to children faced with stressful experiences. For example, studies (Jenkins, 1992) found that children growing up in conflicted homes have fewer problems when there is a good sibling relationship.

Siblings also benefit from assuming the role of teacher or learner. Firstborn children with younger siblings, compared with only children, have been shown to excel in academic achievement, an attribute believed to stem in part from playing the role of tutor to younger siblings. Younger siblings benefit from instruction in social skills, negotiation, and academic basics such as ABCs and 123s by playing games like "school." Children who do not have siblings display solid social adjustment gained through social interactions with peers and extended family.

Peer Relationships

During the early-childhood period of development, children continue to rely heavily on their parents for social and emotional support, care, and companionship. However, the security fostered by healthy family relationships provides children with the stability necessary to initiate play and friendships confidently with peers (Hymel, Vaillancourt, McDougall, & Renshaw, 2002). By about 4 years old the majority of children (75%) will be involved in mutual friendships (Hartup & Abecassis, 2002). Friendship networks will remain fairly small, averaging 1.7 for boys and .9 for girls and increasing to 3–5 during middle childhood. Throughout this period of development, peers play an increasingly important role in the child's life.

Just how important are peer relationships in early childhood? We see peers providing a different learning environment from that of the family. Compared with the nonegalitarian family atmosphere, peer relationships tend to be of equal status. Preschoolers need other peers close in age to compare skills and their own abilities, learn social skills and information, and try out ways of interacting in a safe environment. Through this comparison, children find out more about themselves and others (Shaffer & Cavanaugh, 2001). Peer relationships have been associated with normal social development, whereas peer isolation and rejection have been linked to a host of behavioral problems in children, including delinquency and poor mental adjustment (Hymel et al., 2002). Peer rejection has been shown to predict more deleterious effects than peer isolation.

In a classic study epitomizing the importance of peer relations, Anna Freud (Freud & Dann, 1951) studied six children found in a concentration camp after World War II. The children all had lost their parents and had reared themselves with very little consistent contact from adults. They were one another's constant companions and refused to tolerate separation. They shared easily and were more concerned for the others than for themselves. After thirty-five years, the children all had grown to lead successful lives, with no evidence of psychosis or criminality. The companionship, nurturance, and skills they learned from one another supplanted those received from adults in their early years.

How would we characterize preschool children's peer groups? Preschoolers typically play with children of the same sex, a pattern that develops as early as ages 1–2 and continues through middle childhood. This observation should not come as a surprise to us, given that children are socialized by parents who may think boys should play with boys and girls with girls. Furthermore, because gender-role development and stereotypical behaviors and interests peak during these years, we would expect children to play with others who share their interests.

What kinds of influence do preschool friends exert on each other? Even preschoolers distinguish preferred playmates from acquaintances. They share more readily, are less hostile, and make more personal sacrifices for the benefit of a friend (Hartup & Abecassis, 2002). They also reinforce sex-appropriate behavior and extinguish behavior that does not conform. Preschoolers have also been observed to imitate and mimic a friend to instigate a positive social encounter and influence the other child.

In addition, several factors were found to contribute to the popularity of preschoolers with their peers. Research has found that popular children are more sociable, helpful, and cooperative than less popular children. They also display better leadership and perspective-taking and problem-solving skills. Finally, they are perceived to have some assets, such as being athletic, attractive, and stylish (Hymel et al., 2002). Children born without some of these innate characteristics may benefit from developing compensatory social skills to achieve positive status within their peer group.

Communities and Support Systems

Preschoolers' Play

As we have stated in previous sections, play is the primary medium for learning among preschool children. Play, for all ages, is a pleasurable activity, rewarding in its own right for the positive feelings engendered. In addition, frustrations, tensions, conflict, and anxiety can be explored through play experiences. Play increases children's peer affiliations, social contacts, conversation abilities, and social skills. Piaget (1967) observed that children's cognitive skills are exercised and promoted during play. Vygotsky (1962) emphasized the importance of imaginative play for preschoolers. Berlyne (1960) described how play fulfills a child's need for exploration, curiosity, surprise, and novelty. Pellegrini (2002) has discussed the value of rough-and-tumble play, especially for young boys. These opportunities provide children with information about themselves and their world.

Mildred Parten (1932) observed and categorized preschool children's play according to the amount of social interaction. Her findings are described in Exhibit 7.7. Parten concluded that 3-year-olds engaged in more solitary and parallel play, whereas 5-year-olds more frequently played associatively and cooperatively. Barnes (1971) replicated Parten's study to find that play styles of children had changed over the decades. He found that children spent less time play-

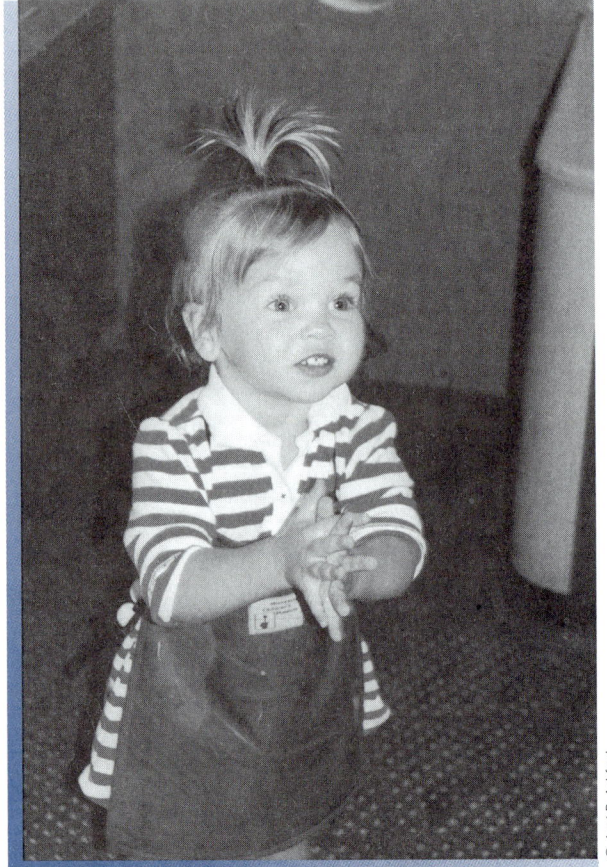

This child is showing pride over a recent accomplishment, which can help build an optimistic outlook.

EXHIBIT 7.7 Preschool children's play styles

Play Type	Child's Behavior
Unoccupied play	Unengaged with other children or activities, not goal directed, least frequent type of play.
Solitary play	Child plays alone, engaged in task but not with other children, typical of 2- to 3-year-olds.
Onlooker play	Child watches other children play and talks, asks questions, and participates verbally but does not engage in the play directly. Interested, but not involved.
Parallel play	Child plays with toys like those others are using, but does not play with other child. More common among younger children than older ones.
Associative play	Children play actively together. The interaction is more important than the task or organization of the play. Social skills such as turn-taking, follow-the-leader are objects of the play.
Cooperative play	Children play an organized activity with a lot of social interaction. Social games, formal activities arranged by a teacher, competitive games fall into this category. Not as frequent among preschoolers.

EXHIBIT 7.8 Development of children's play

Play Category	Activity Description
Sensorimotor play	Typical of infancy, to explore sensorimotor abilities.
Practice play	A means of practicing new skills, developing motor coordination, mental mastery. A skill or behavior is repeated until the skill is mastered. Important for sports and other games. Common throughout life and accounts for about one-third of preschoolers' play time (Rubin, Fein, & Vandenberg, 1983).
Pretense/symbolic play	Sociodramatic play when children use the physical environment as symbolic of something else, pretend play, try out fantasy, and role-play. Begins between 9 and 30 months of age and peaks at about ages 4–5.
Social play	Social interaction with peers, rough-and-tumble play, running, chasing, wrestling, and jumping are examples.
Constructive play	Combines sensorimotor and symbolic play, games that are created by the children, or projects developed by the children themselves. Organized games with rules are more common in elementary school–aged children.

ing associatively or cooperatively than the children in the 1930s, perhaps due to the effects of TV and technological toys that require a single operator and less imagination.

Current research now looks at play as a function of both social interaction and cognitive ability. Preschoolers primarily engage in pretense or symbolic play, constructive play, and rough-and-tumble play. These current representations of children's play are described in Exhibit 7.8.

Preschool Environment

Today, many preschoolers will attend preschool or day care for three to five years. The emphases of preschool programs vary greatly; some focus primarily on cognitive, academic development and others focusing almost exclusively on social and emotional development. However, for a child to appreciate a preschool setting fully, the curriculum should closely match the child's developmental goals.

Overall, preschool children tend to perform well in school when they have learned some self-control and self-discipline. These skills allow them to work with others, delay gratification, and handle the frustration inherent in problem solving that accompanies school tasks. The family environment, and parents in particular, can create situations in which the child experiences frustration and mastery, as well as learns to accept no for an answer. Children will learn internal self-control by first learning to accept external control of their behavior imposed by parents. As a side effect that is beneficial to the child-teacher relationship, children learn to respect and cooperate with adults and those in authority but not to fear them. These skills smooth children's transition to formal educational settings.

Kindergarten

The concept of kindergarten was first developed by Freidrich Froebel in the 1840s. He conceived of kindergarten as a "garden for children," where they would be carefully nurtured, like plants. However, over the course of shifting trends in social and educational practices, some kindergartens have become too focused and concerned with success and achievement as opposed to nurturing the developing child. This approach also worries some developmental experts, who fear that too much pressure is placed on children to succeed and achieve at the expense of real learning.

One issue that has received a lot of attention is what to do when children aren't ready for kindergarten. Schools have traditionally sought one of two solutions, delayed entry into school, or retaining the child for an extra year. Conflicting research suggests that neither practice offers an ideal way to assist children who are not ready to succeed in kindergarten (Holloway, 2003). Coley (2002) has argued that to reduce inequalities in students' success in school the differences that exist among children must be

EXHIBIT 7.9 Summary of promising practices to involve families in the transition to kindergarten

Transition Practices	Core Partners
Contact with preschool families	School personnel (teachers, principals)
Contact with preschool children	Parents and children
Kindergarten visits	Preschool and Head Start personnel
Home learning activities	Community groups
Informational meetings	
Partner with local PTAs	
Information dissemination	
Home visits	
Parent support groups	
Maintain informal contact with preschool "graduates"	
Facilitate early registration	
Staff ECE and kindergarten with bilingual teacher aides as needed	

SOURCE: Bohan-Baker & Little (2002).

addressed before they start school. His approach is based on identifying children who are at risk for school failure and providing preschool experiences that ensure they have the opportunity to develop readiness skills. He has cautioned policymakers not to target students on the basis of a single criterion, such as income. The National Association for the Education of Young Children (2002) has suggested it is not productive to adjust children to meet specific expectations of a kindergarten program but that schools should respond to the diverse range of abilities within any group of children. One alternative suggested is the opportunity for children to engage in full-day kindergarten as a way to improve their skills and reduce chances of being retained in kindergarten (Miller, 2002).

Whatever the model taken for children to enter kindergarten research has confirmed the importance of a good transition to school for all children (Bohan-Baker & Little, 2002). In a review of research studies, family involvement has been determined to be a critical aspect of the successful transition to kindergarten. The ecological context of the school can provide important ingredients to facilitate parent involvement in the transition, such as attitudes of the teachers toward parent involvement, attitudes of supervisors, and development of a school and program transition team. Exhibit 7.9 provides a summary of the promising practices to involve families in the transition to kindergarten. Although preschool and kindergarten are among the resources available to assist in preparing children for formal education, parents play the largest and most critical role in preparing their children for school.

Project Head Start

Project Head Start was spearheaded in 1965 as part of Lyndon Johnson's Great Society initiative. The overall goal was to break the cycle of poverty by providing a preschool experience for children from economically disadvantaged families at risk for school failure. Several research studies (Chow, Jaffee, & Snowden, 2003; Kim, Hong, & Rowe, 2000) have documented that various outcomes for children (e.g., school performance, mastery, educational aspiration) are impacted by the experience of economic hardship. According to this research, parents in these families feel helpless to control events in their lives and, as a result, are detached from their environment and are unresponsive to their children's needs. They fail to teach their children ways of mastering their environment, and the children in essence inherit the attitude of helplessness. When the children cannot fulfill their own expectations to perform well in school, they become detached, as well, and feel helpless to succeed.

Their natural curiosity and motivation are thwarted from the beginning.

To counteract this phenomenon, the program was first offered to 4- and 5-year-olds during the summer preceding their kindergarten year. Now the program is available for an entire year prior to enrollment in kindergarten. In some areas of the country the Early Head Start program directs its interventions toward infants and toddlers in an effort to enhance development through the creation of partnerships with parents (Lalley & Keith, 1997). Head Start shares many features of other early intervention programs (Richmond, Stipek, & Zigler, 1979), yet it makes unique contributions in the areas of parent participation, health, and nutrition. The specific curriculum for each Head Start program is determined by the individual program, with about 2,000 programs existing in slightly different forms. However, all Head Start programs are committed to improving the quality of life for the children and family participants. Efforts are under way to reduce the funding of Head Start, and such reductions are likely to have serious implications for the readiness of low-income preschoolers to enter kindergarten.

What have we learned over the past 30 years of administering Head Start and other early-intervention programs? First, we have refined our evaluation skills. We have learned that specific goals must be outlined for any project to ensure a proper evaluation of the program's intended effects. Initially, the effects of Head Start were evaluated only in terms of increases in children's IQ scores. But this situation represents only one small factor in determining school success. Effects on the health and motivation of the children and on the parent component were not examined, although they clearly influence school achievement, as well (Zigler & Trickett, 1978). As a result, the evaluation failed to measure change in the most prominent areas of the program and caused undue disenchantment with the program. An ex-

Head Start programs promote education and partnership with parents, and they improve the quality of life for poor children.

ample of this dissatisfaction stemmed from the Westinghouse Learning Corporation's (1969) evaluation, which showed that, even after a full year of Head Start, children's IQ scores were initially increased only to decrease a short while later in elementary school. Head Start proponents have had to battle for funding and acceptance ever since. Fortunately, more comprehensive, better-designed follow-up evaluations of Head Start have shown that children who participated in this program were more likely to succeed at school and less likely to be placed in remedial-education programs (Consortium for Longitudinal Studies, 1983). Additionally, research studies have found certain specific factors that, when included in early-education/intervention programs, make a difference in positive child outcomes (Ramey, 1999):

- Two or more years of enrollment in preschool are better than one.
- More hours per day and more days per year provide greater benefits to children and often better meet the needs of families.
- Involvement of parents is critical for the child's success.
- Program effectiveness is greatly influenced by the quality and training of its teaching staff.
- Low-resource and special-needs families benefit from comprehensive support services.

- Program quality improves when there are low staff-to-child ratios.

Although Project Head Start has served about 7.5 million children during the first fifteen years of operation, this number represents only about 20% of those eligible (Schuster & Ashburn, 1992). The program is still underfunded and cannot provide enrollment for all eligible children. Federal and local monies fund the program, which is provided free to all eligible children.

Full-Service Schools

A handful of what are called "full-service" schools exist in the United States. A full-service school is one that brings together education, health, and social-service agencies under one roof. In her book *Full-Service Schools*, Dryfoos (1994) explained the need to bring community agencies, such as health care, child care, parent education, case management, and welfare, into the school. Doing this, she argued, would be responsive to the needs of the community and provide accessibility to those who need the services the most. Proponents of full-service schools believe that these schools can improve education, improve access to services, and serve as a center for neighborhood revitalization (Dryfoos, 1994).

Effects of TV on Preschool Children

Television has been noted as an important socializing agent and influence on children's behavior. American children spend more time watching television than they do with their parents or in school, an average of twenty hours per week (Nielsen Media Research, 1998). Recent studies have found that 43% of children less than 2 years old watch television every day and that 68% of children under 2 years old spend two hours a day using screen media (Rideout, Vandewater, & Wartella, 2003). The television has become a convenient babysitter. Parents often use television to hold children's attention so they can accomplish household chores. Many parents find that in today's fast-paced world, they have less time to interact with their children. Bronfrenbrenner (1986) commented that TV becomes a negative influence not because of what is provided but instead because of what is prevented. He suggested that the presence of TV decreases the amount of time families spend actively participating in mutual activities requiring discourse, argument, and reciprocity, which promote children's learning (such as playing games, going on outings, and talking). The American Academy of Pediatrics (AAP) also agreed with the argument that TV decreases family time. In a press release, the AAP stated that, especially for babies and toddlers, direct interaction with parents and caregivers is needed to assist in healthy brain growth and psychological and social skills (American Academy of Pediatrics, 1999). A new study published in *Pediatrics* (Christakis, Zimmerman, DiGiuseppe, & McCarty, 2004) found that early television exposure in children ages 1–3 is associated with attention problems at age 7. The study found that each hour of TV watched per day at ages 1–3 increases the risk of attention problems by almost 10 percent at age 7. More research is needed to carefully investigate and validate these critical findings, especially because it may be that children at risk for attention difficulties are more likely to watch TV, rather than that TV leads to attention difficulties.

Television has also been criticized for negatively influencing children's lives—for example, by promoting increased passivity, because television is not an interactive method of learning. Another criticism is that television perpetuates unrealistic views and expectations incompatible with real life, such as fairy-tale endings. A third criticism is that television promotes aggressive behavior and flaunts gratuitous sex. Finally, television casts women, older people, and ethnic minorities in stereotypical roles, often unfavorably as victims, villains, criminals, and/or incompetents (Brody, 1987). In addition, Condry (1989) found that ethnic minorities tended to be underrepresented on TV compared with whites.

A more recent concern is that TV can have an addictive influence over people (Kubey & Csikszentmihalyi, 2004). Unhealthy dependence is characterized by specific criteria, such as spending time using the substance, using it more often than intended, making repeated unsuccessful efforts to reduce use, giving up important social and family obligations to use it, and experiencing some sense of withdrawal when one stops using it. Kubey and Csikszentmihalyi (2004) believe that these criteria can easily apply to some people who are bent on watching a lot of TV. Nationwide surveys have found that many individuals will admit that they spend too much time watching TV. Why is it that TV watching can have such an influence? It may act a lot like the effects of some drugs. Brain research shows that when you watch TV, you enter a relaxed state. As a result, people are likely to become conditioned to associate watching TV with rest and reduced tension. Have you ever felt a headache coming on and self-prescribed some TV watching to relax? In these ways, TV viewing can slowly increase to a point where individuals actually crave more TV watching, similar to drug addictions. But there is also another factor that may come into play, the "orienting response." This is our instinctive visual and auditory reaction to any sudden or novel stimulus. Babies can be easily observed to pay rapt attention to the TV, and adults often "just can't turn away" from it even when they are in conversation with someone. All of this may be due to the orienting response. Whether TV can be classified as an "addiction" will likely be debated for a long while; however, when TV watching starts to interfere with important aspects of life, it is a dependence that needs careful attention.

Nonetheless, television has no doubt also brought advantages to children's lives, including educational programs that expose them to information, knowledge, and alternative lifestyles and points of view to which they would not normally have access. But the images and themes of entertainment television often erode these advantages.

Originally, educational television shows such as *Sesame Street* were developed and marketed to reach underprivileged children. The goal was to prepare children for school by helping them learn letters, numbers, colors, counting, classifying, and simple problem solving. Evaluations of *Sesame Street* confirmed the intentions of the show. Children who watched *Sesame Street* often made cognitive gains that lasted into the early elementary years. This finding was especially strong for 3-year-olds compared with 5-year-olds who already had some of the skills taught on the show (Bogatz & Ball, 1972). The only criticism logged against *Sesame Street* is that children from advantaged homes tend to watch the show more than do the underprivileged children for whom it was originally intended.

How children are affected by television viewing is determined, to a large extent, by what they are watching. In addition, parents can discuss the themes, staging, cultural biases, and peddling of consumerism depicted on television with their children. Open, nonjudgmental discussions can teach children to be informed viewers and not just consumers of television hype.

Bandura (1965) was one of the first researchers to study the effects on children of watching television violence. In his experiment, one group of children watched a violent television show, and one group did not. He found that children who had been exposed to the violence on television were later more likely to hit a doll repeatedly than were those who had not been.

In another study, Steuer, Applefield, and Smith (1971) observed preschool children playing outdoors at nursery school and paired these children according to how much aggressive behavior, such as hitting and kicking, they displayed. One child in each pair was shown a violent television program every day for two weeks. The other child was shown a television show free of aggressive and violent acts. The researchers found that those children shown the violent show, despite their previous level of aggressive behavior, became more aggressive in their play.

From these studies, we can conclude that television violence promotes increased levels of aggressive behavior in the play of preschool children. Research has demonstrated that this effect was strongest for children who engaged in more aggressive behaviors before viewing violence on television. Children who were not rated as aggressive to start with were hardly affected by the television violence. So, although violent television may contribute to aggressive acts in children, it is only one of many factors.

Multicultural and Gender Considerations

The preschool years are important for developing a positive and unique sense of self (Marti, 2003). Preschool children begin to recognize ethnic physical characteristics in themselves and in others. One of the early classic studies on racial awareness was conducted by Clark and Clark in 1939. The researchers asked three 5-year-old African American children to identify themselves from a series of drawings that included various animals, a clown, a white boy, and an African American boy. They discovered that by age 4, children would begin to identify the African American boy, and by age 5 their identification with the African American boy was well developed.

Young preschoolers may not understand ethnicity as a fixed personal attribute until they have developed the concept of conservation, which occurs close to age 5. Preschoolers do not understand that these features may have a social significance beyond what is visible to the eye. Just as children cannot cognitively understand the meaning of sexuality, they cannot understand the social meaning of membership in one culture or another. As soon as they identify with one ethnic group, children learn who they are in comparison with others. They learn to evaluate themselves along the dimensions of appearance, ability, group membership, and hopes for the future (Gelman, 2003).

What preschool children come to know about their own heritage is determined largely by their parents and extended families. They have not often branched out into the larger community unprotected by caregivers. Children who feel valued in their own right learn to respect themselves and others. In addition, parents who teach their children the truth about racial inequality and discrimination may be preparing them to deal squarely with problem situations when they are encountered.

Cross-Culturally Adopted Children

As we mentioned, children learn about their heritage and ethnicity largely through their parents and extended families. But what about a child who has been adopted into a culture that is different from his or her birth culture? What factors are involved in the development of this child's ethnic identity?

Although very young children cannot cognitively understand the process of adoption, they are able to recognize that there are physical differences between themselves and their parents (Friedlander, 1999). Especially for internationally adopted children, there may be no opportunity to see or interact with people who share their culture of origin, and this can make ethnic identity formation more difficult. Unable to identify with either their birth culture or their adoptive culture, these children can find themselves confused about where they belong. This is especially true for adopted children of color who often realize that they are different because of comments and questions from teachers and friends.

How can social workers assist families who want their cross-culturally adopted child to develop a positive sense of identity? Generally, it is the new culture into which the child will assimilate. Research indicates ways in which parents can assist their child in developing a healthy ethnic identity (Friedlander, 1999). Social workers can assist the parents in including the following into their parenting practices and family environment:

- A nurturing home environment
- Acknowledgment of the physical differences between themselves and their child, with emphasis on emotional, psychological, and social similarities
- Exposure of the child to affirmative role models from their country of origin

Although no distinct guidelines exist for raising a child in a culture different from her culture of origin, studies find that transracially and internationally adopted children do not differ in their self-esteem or adjustment compared to children adopted into same-race families, especially when the child is adopted at a young age. It does appear, however, that the child's environment, family, and community play an important role in successful adjustment and ethnic-identity formation.

Gender-Role and Sexual-Identity Development

Gender-role development and sexual-identity development are separate yet intrinsically linked processes. What factors contribute to gender- and sexual-identity development? As we discussed in the last chapter, babies show gender differences from birth, and certainly social and cultural expectations permeate childrearing from a very early age. Parents, families, teachers, peers, and physical and cognitive development all contribute to a child's sexual-identity formation.

By the preschool years, boys will play with boys and girls with girls (Hartup & Abecassis, 2002). This represents the beginning of gender-role identity, in that boys and girls tend to play differently during the preschool years. Preschool boys and girls already have strong notions of sex-typed play (Golombok & Hines, 2002). They can identify whether boys or girls cook, play with cars, fight, climb trees, and kiss. Gender-specific toy preferences are also evident at this young age, and parents encourage sex-typed play in young children, as well. This is especially true of fathers, who may tolerate tomboyish activities for girls but tend to express more concern about cross-sex activities for boys (Maccoby, 1998). Also, boys adopt sex-typed behavior and toys earlier than girls do.

At this time, children also strengthen their identification with the same-sex parent. They will dress like them and engage in sex-stereotypic behaviors. They are busy exploring what it means to be a boy or girl in their world. By age 3, children have a fundamental sense of gender identity. They can correctly answer the question "Are you a boy or girl?" By age 4, children develop gender stability and realize that gender does not change over time. However, they still believe that children can change gender by changing their behavior—if a boy wears a dress he can become a girl.

Sex play becomes more common in this age group and is usually nothing more than a healthy curiosity about their bodies. Children at this age are fascinated with everyone's body and bodily functions. Modesty and privacy are not concepts that have any meaning to them; curiosity wins out. Masturbatory play is also common during this period. The preschool years are an excellent time to introduce the notion of "private" and "public" selves. In addition, these concepts become useful in talking about safety and in preventing sexual abuse of children.

Although many gender-role qualities are learned, two characteristics appear to be genetically transposed: aggression and nurturance. Boys tend to be more aggressive than girls and engage in more aggressive play, from rough-and-tumble sports to "fights" with guns and superheroes (Maccoby, 1998; Maccoby & Jacklin, 1974). Girls display more nurturance than boys and play more games oriented to relationship themes. These qualities do not describe every boy or girl, but, as we have stated before, they do tend to remain fairly constant over the course of development for most children.

The Effects of Sex Stereotyping

Tyrone's mother was determined to raise her children in a non-gender-specific way. In particular, she wanted her son to develop characteristics of warmth and nurturance, free from the constraints of sex stereotyping, so she discouraged aggressive play and aggressive toys. Tyrone spent most of his time at home with his mother and sister, playing quietly. He often joined his sister in playing with her dolls and stuffed animals. Tyrone's mother did not become worried about him until he began wearing a dress-up skirt and pretending his name was Tara. Then she took him to a therapist, who told her to forget the dolls, throw out the skirt, and buy him a cowboy outfit.

Many people argue that parents should not raise gender-neutral children, because gender differences have real meaning and value in our society and to the children themselves. Children may need to identify as one sex or the other, not only in a physical sense as they learn about their bodies, but also from a role standpoint as they learn about who they are in the larger society.

But what exactly are children learning about their sex roles in this society? By early childhood, children have been found to attribute greater competency to boys than to girls. In one study, 3- to 5-year-old children, when asked who was smart, pointed to the baby that was labeled the "boy" (Haugh, Hoffman, & Cowan, 1980). And parents tolerate a girl acting like a boy more readily than they do a boy acting like a girl. In fact, a common societal notion is that girls spend their developmental years trying not to be babies, but boys spend these years trying not to be girls. Even children's literature makes being a boy more interesting than being a girl. In traditional literature, boys have adventures, whereas girls get rescued and clean up after dwarfs. This same representation of gender roles is also seen in television cartoon characters. Male cartoon characters outnumber female characters almost four to one, and, as in children's literature, the male characters are usually portrayed as powerful, strong, and smart, while the female characters are often portrayed as "damsels in distress" (American Psychological Association, 1997).

Many people believe that these attitudes have contributed to inequality of women in our society, and they support teaching children to be androgynous. **Androgyny** refers to a combination of feminine and masculine attributes in the same individual. Advocates for androgyny argue that many girls and women have suffered from a loss of opportunity because of traditional sex stereotypes. Classic research by Bem (1974) suggested that well-adjusted people possess qualities that are both masculine (assertiveness, competitiveness) and feminine (cooperation, nurturance).

However, preschool children have been found to be very rigid in their sex-type behaviors and attitudes (Maccoby, 1998). Maybe this rigidity is necessary for the child to develop a gender identity. After this identity has been well established, children can then alter their ideas about sex roles and characteristics. In fact, Hall and Halberstadt (1980) found that 27–32% of 8- to 11-year-olds could be classified as androgynous.

Perhaps the real problem is not in gender-role differences but in the cultural value assigned to those roles and sex-type characteristics.

Social Strengths and Hazards

Many people—educators, policy makers, families, and the public at large—agree that families of young children need support and that we as a society value providing that support. It is this essence that each of us plays a part in every child's life that emerges clearly in early childhood. This is why Hilary Clinton's reflection on the now famous African proverb "It takes a village to raise a child" became so well known. It was an important reminder that children can thrive when families are thriving and when society supports them. Social strengths are reflected in social programs and policies that embrace the ideas of creating a caring community. In order to build such communities, we need to enhance our collective connectedness.

Such connectedness is often referred to as **social capital**, which is the network of norms, obligations, expectations, and trust that can occur among people who share common values. Early-childhood policies and programs cannot be properly supported without such connectedness—in other words, not having this social capital is a major impediment. Sociologist theorists such as Amatai Etzioni and Robert Bellah have been outspoken in their criticism of society's focus on individualism. They have pointed out the need, instead, for communities with common values that can counteract individualism.

Family-Group Decision Making: A Strengths Model

In many ways, the rise of family-group decision making or family-group conferencing is an apt example of social capital and a strengths based approach to the serious social problem of child abuse and neglect. In recent years there has been an ongoing focus on involving the family in the processes of child protection. A model that originated in New Zealand, based on Maori culture (Connolly & McKenzie, 1999), emerged from legislation that formalized the principles of family decision making in child-protection work. This model of child-welfare practice was spurred by several developments in the field, such as increasing numbers of children living in out-of-home care, and living in such care for longer periods; children experiencing multiple out-of-home placements; the large representation of minority families; and concerns about providing ethnically sensitive services. In essence, family-group decision making is a new approach to working with families involved with the child-welfare system. The process involves bringing family members (including extended family) and professionals together for a "conference" to make a decision about the care of a child who has become part of the child-welfare system. The social worker identifies families appropriate for family-group decision making and brings professionals and families together in a one-day conference that begins with information sharing. This is followed by the family meeting, in which families typically meet in private and the focus is on a plan to ensure the child is cared for and protected from further harm. The family then reconvenes with the child-welfare workers, and they agree on the terms of the final plan. The family-group decision making model is family centered and strengths oriented, culturally based and community based. It places an emphasis on the family because they have the most information about themselves to make well-informed decisions. The model explicitly encourages families to connect with each other and their communities in solving their problems. While new models of community support are receiving a lot of attention, a critical hazard for children in industrialized societies is the experience of poverty.

Poverty and Development

As discussed in the previous chapter, poverty and social class affect children's lives even before they are born. In 2000, it was estimated that 17% of the children in the United States were living in families with incomes below the federal poverty threshold (Annie Casey Foundation, 2004). The poverty threshold for a family of two adults and two children was $17,463. The United States child poverty rate is among the highest in the developed world.

How does poverty affect the preschool child's development? Years of research have examined this question and documented the negative child outcomes associated with living in poverty (see Brooks-Gunn & Duncan, 1997, for a review). These negative effects are most pronounced during the first five years of life. In general, studies find negative effects in three primary areas (poor physical health, lower intellectual attainment, and poor school performance) and report the increased presence of social, emotional, and behavioral problems. It is noteworthy that the children living in the most extreme poverty have the worst outcomes (Guo, 1998). In spite of these negative effects, many impoverished children show **resiliency** to the conditions they have experienced and they become positively adjusted. What makes these children and families so resilient is a critical question addressed by much research.

Additionally, research has shown that teachers perceive low-income children differently than higher-income children and often have lower achievement expectations, provide less positive attention, and give less positive reinforcement to them (McLoyd, 1998). Thus, it may often be the case that low-income children receive less cognitive stimulation not only in the home but also in school. Preschool children's fundamental questions center on their developing sense of mastery and worth. Through their behavior they ask, "Can I make a difference in my world?" and "Am I valued and loved for myself?" Children growing up in poverty depend heavily on their parents' ability to attend to their children's needs despite their own pressing worries. This is a formidable task, not easily met by any class of parents.

Child Abuse

Child abuse, or the maltreatment of children, implies a range of conditions that violate social norms regarding the care, security, and safety of minors. Although state laws regulating the treatment of children vary, each state defines child maltreatment to include one or more of the following: physical abuse, sexual abuse, physical neglect, educational neglect, and psychological abuse (Maluccio, Tracy, & Pine, 2002).

Physical abuse involves injuries such as broken bones, serious and minor burns, head injuries, and bruises. In addition, there may be physical contact, such as slapping, punching, and striking a child with a belt or a paddle, that do not always result in a visible injury.

Sexual abuse typically refers to various forms of touching, penetration, and exploitation. *Molestation* is the term used to describe inappropriate touching—which may or may not involve genital contact—of minors. *Exploitation* refers to involving a child in sexual activities such as prostitution or pornography. *Penetration* includes oral, anal, or genital contact and can involve the use of body parts (fingers, penis) or objects.

Child neglect can include less explicit forms of abuse because it refers to both active and passive behaviors from adults. Physical neglect includes abandonment, delay or refusal of health care, inadequate supervision, and inadequate provision of basic care such as food, housing, clothing, and personal hygiene. If these areas of neglect are to be avoided, then parents need continual support, resources, and initia-

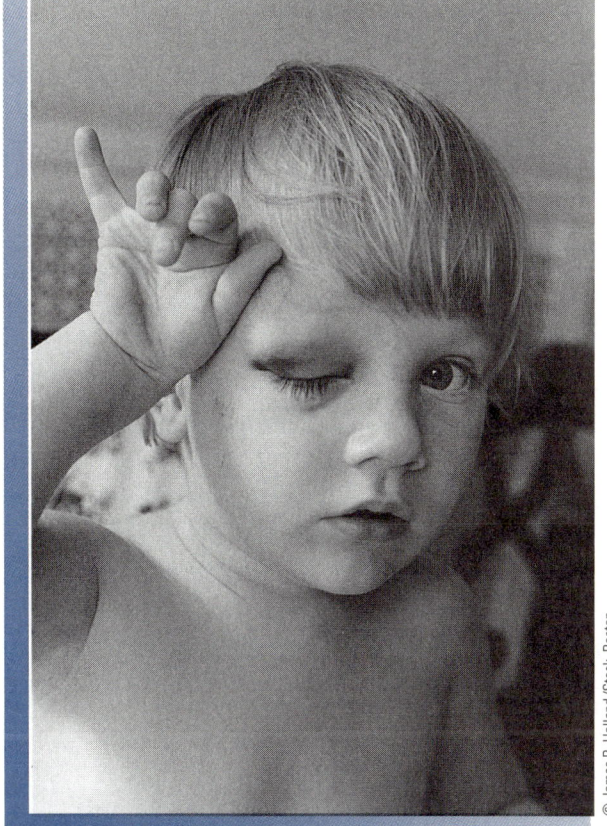

Child abuse is a serious problem in the United States—with far-reaching consequences.

tive in caring for their children. Often, child neglect is the result of severe lack of resources.

Educational neglect includes not enrolling a child in an educational program, allowing frequent absences from school, and refusing to respond to special educational needs. At times, parental values surrounding the role of formal schooling and the problems of handicapping conditions may come into conflict with the mandates of education laws and the values of special-education providers. These potential conflicts cloud the issues of educational neglect, thereby creating difficulty in substantiating negligence in some cases.

Psychological abuse refers to physical restraint, repeated threats, exploitation, rejection, and degradation. Although its definition is less concrete, descriptions of psychological abuse suggest that verbal messages should be regulated with regard to their effect on children's well being. For example, negative labels and name-calling are forms of degradation.

People often think of child maltreatment as abusive behavior from a parent. In fact, children can be mistreated by any adult who is responsible for their general well being and supervision. Thus, the adults potentially involved in child maltreatment may include parents, members of extended family, teachers, child-care providers, clergy, and so on.

Factors That Contribute to Child Abuse

Many factors that contribute to child maltreatment have been identified, including family stress, child and family characteristics, interaction style, parental problems, and values regarding violence. (Exhibit 7.10 presents a framework for organizing the factors that have been found to contribute to child abuse and neglect.) The most consistent factor is that parents who abuse or neglect their children often were abused or neglected in their own childhoods. Another major factor in child maltreatment is substance abuse. The use of crack, cocaine, or methamphetamines can seriously affect one's ability to care for children. Alcohol abuse also contributes to the risk of child abuse, especially when combined with other drug abuse. Children who are perceived as different, such as handicapped children and children with difficult temperaments, are at increased risk for abuse. Marital conflict, domestic violence, employment and financial stress, and social isolation all exacerbate negative interactions within a family that can increase the risk of child maltreatment (Child Abuse and Neglect Clearinghouse, 2004). A history of animal abuse has been related to child abuse. Many studies have established a strong relationship among poverty, social isolation, and child abuse or neglect (See Pecora, Whittaker, Maluccio, & Barth, 2000). In addition, unemployment, lack of housing, daily stress, and community violence contribute to increased risk. Specifically, researchers have found that families who live in communities with little social support or lack of community identity have higher incidences of child abuse and neglect, as well as juvenile delinquency, drug trafficking, and violent crime (Cicchetti, Lynch, & Manly, 1997). But, as we have pointed out in previous chapters, the presence of these factors does not automatically mean that family caregivers will abuse their children. Factors that contribute to child abuse in one family many not result in child abuse and neglect in another family. Although it is noted that child abuse is related to living in poverty, it must be remembered that most people living in poverty do not harm their children.

EXHIBIT 7.10 Risk factors associated with child abuse and neglect

Parent or Caregiver Factors
Personality and psychological well-being
History of child abuse
Substance abuse
Attitudes and knowledge
Age

Family Factors
Family structure
Marital conflict and domestic violence
Stress
Parent-child interaction

Child Factors
Age
Disabilities

Environmental Factors
Poverty
Unemployment
Social isolation
Lack of social support
Violent communities

SOURCE: Adapted from National Clearinghouse on Child Abuse and Neglect (2004).

Incidence of Child Abuse

With the help of television and newspaper reporting, widespread awareness of child abuse and neglect has been achieved in recent years. It is not uncommon to learn of someone's personal experiences as a victim via a television talk show. As a result of this increased reporting, there appears to have been an increase in the awareness of child abuse and neglect as a serious social problem.

According to the most recent statistics from the National Child Abuse and Neglect Data System, more than 3 million reports were made to Child Protection agencies in the year 2000, with two-thirds of

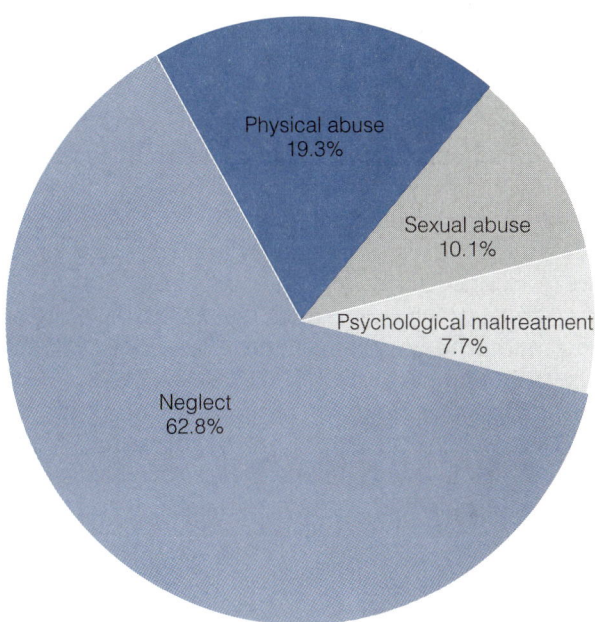

EXHIBIT 7.11 Types of child abuse and neglect
SOURCE: Based on National Clearinghouse on Child Abuse and Neglect (2004).

those cases being "screened in" for investigation for potential child abuse or neglect. The true number of children abused or neglected is not known, but it was estimated that in the year 2000 almost 1 million children were victims of maltreatment (National Clearinghouse on Child Abuse and Neglect, 2004). More specifically, for every 1,000 children in the population in that year, approximately 12 were victims of maltreatment (1,200 child deaths were recorded). From 1990 to the present, the rate has varied from a high of 15.3 per 1,000 to a low of 11.8.

Exhibit 7.11 shows the distribution of the types of child maltreatment. We also know that slightly more girls (52%) than boys (48%) are victims of child maltreatment and that more girls than boys are sexually abused. Also, it is well established that the youngest and more vulnerable children, those under age 3, have the highest rate of abuse. In terms of child-maltreatment perpetrators, 78% of children were abused by a parent. Approximately 60% of perpetrators were women, and 42% of these women were younger than 30 years old.

Reports of child maltreatment include people from all educational, economic, and ethnic backgrounds. However, poor people and minorities are more likely to be reported (Pecora, Whittaker, & Maluccio, 1992).

Reporting Child Abuse

Diane, a social worker in a clinic, sees a new client, a mother referred with a 14-month-old child diagnosed with failure to thrive. The doctors have been unable to find any medical reason for the child's slow weight gain, although he is well below the third percentile for his age. His head, however, is unusually large, and he is showing signs of developmental delay. Diane's task is to do a psychosocial assessment to see if there are any social reasons for the child's failure to thrive and to offer interventions. Diane quickly establishes a good rapport with the mother, and the mother begins to discuss her home life at length and in great detail. During the course of the interview, the mother divulges the following information:

- She has an older son, age 3, who was and still is failing to thrive with no medical reason.
- She has a daughter, age 4, who repeatedly runs away from home. In fact, the child needs constant supervision because she runs away whenever she gets the chance—for instance, if someone leaves the door unbolted. The police have been called several times to help find the child, and they have reported the family to Child Protective Services (CPS) three times. Lately, the mother has resorted to tying the child to a chair or to her person to keep her from running away.
- She has a son, age 6, who has just been held back in kindergarten because of problems in school. He is very aggressive and has problems interacting with other children; he often hits or kicks them.
- Her husband is an alcoholic who has been arrested twice for domestic violence and once for child abuse when he struck the mother while she was holding their 4-month-old child, injuring the infant. However, he is able to keep steady employment and earns a good income. He has agreed to go to counseling sessions with his wife.
- There is no open CPS case presently. The mother is obviously stressed and has little social support. She pays no notice to the child's attempts to gain her attention during the interview.

What is the social worker's legal obligation regarding contacting CPS in this case involving a severely malnourished child? In other words, should you call

CPS to report this mother who has just confided this information to you, knowing that the child may be suffering from the social situation?

Deciding whether to report child maltreatment may be one of the most challenging situations that a person can face. Concerns about false reporting and the potentially negative or stigmatizing outcome for the children and families involved may create a predicament for the person making the decision.

Social workers, however, are mandated reporters. This means that they are legally obligated to report even a suspicion of child abuse or neglect to CPS. As a result, many cases that are reported involve suspected or mild abuse or neglect. CPS then investigates and determines whether the report is substantiated and if intervention is necessary. Remember, reports involving 3 million children are made each year. Of these reports, only one-third are substantiated. Of the cases that are substantiated, 40% receive no services, as the result of limited time, money, and resources. Very few cases, less than 20%, involve any court action. Most families are encouraged to seek voluntary treatment (Maluccio, 2002). So, in the preceding case involving a stressed mother who is seeking help for her child, what do you do? You are required to report the case if you suspect abuse or neglect, yet CPS may be unable to offer much help to the family, and a report may only undermine your therapeutic relationship with the mother. But remember, the rights of client-professional confidentiality (except attorney-client) are usually waived in child abuse and neglect reporting. And there is a penalty for failure to report. Mental-health professionals face such dilemmas regularly when working with families.

Investigation of Child Maltreatment

Child abuse is often difficult to substantiate. Confirming the history of child maltreatment requires comprehensive, time-consuming assessments, but child protection workers often must make immediate decisions with limited data. The child's safety must be ensured, but the rights of the parents and children involved must also be protected (Maluccio, Tracy, & Pine, 2002).

Workers making child placement decisions often are faced with competing values—keeping the family together versus protecting the child (Pecora, Whittaker, & Maluccio, 1992). Often the worker has a poor history, little information, and limited time in which to come to a decision about whether to remove the child from the home.

People's mobility also contributes to the difficulty in substantiating abuse that has supposedly occurred over a long period of time, owing to a lack of continuity between different agencies' efforts. Mobility also may contribute to the delay of interventions and to a lack of effectiveness in helping families.

Child protection organizations use an assessment system that addresses the nature and severity of child maltreatment and the further risk to child safety. The collected information is used to determine what services are needed and what services are available, as well as the intervention's chances of producing a successful outcome (Pecora, Whittaker, & Maluccio, 1992).

In conducting the initial assessment/investigation, the primary issues to consider include the following (Child Abuse and Neglect Clearinghouse, 2004):

Is the child safe? If not, what measures are necessary to ensure the child's safety?
Did the child suffer maltreatment, or is he or she threatened by harm as defined by the state reporting law?
Is maltreatment likely to occur in the future? If so, what is the level of risk of maltreatment?
Are there emergency needs in the family that must be met?
Are continuing agency services necessary to protect the child and reduce the risk of maltreatment occurring in the future?

Collecting this information is a time-consuming task. Thorough interviews of adults and children involved in child maltreatment require extensive time and skill. Often, the adults involved are not willing to divulge information concerning individual and familial history, the nature and extent of stress present in the family, negative feelings toward the child, and the possibility of irresponsible behavior on their part. Parents may be reluctant to discuss their situation fully for fear that the only outcome is losing their child.

Interviewing children to confirm abuse is very difficult because of several developmental concerns, including language, cognition, emotional growth, and attachment to significant adults. Before age 5, children's expressive language is still developing, so that a child may not have the expressive vocabulary and sentence structure to describe experiences with accuracy and detail. Also, very young children have difficulty distinguishing real events from imagined ones. Children who are awakened from a deep sleep during an abusive incident may have difficulty orienting to the time, place, and authenticity of abusive behavior.

Feelings of guilt about the abuse are common among victims. Children who have been convinced that they are somehow responsible for an adult's reactions may internalize the blame or assume responsibility for abusive conditions. Some children may believe that if they could just be "good," the abuse would stop. The loyalty and bond between children and the significant adults in their lives may also contribute to a child's feelings of guilt about disclosing abuse. Children may realize that disclosure of the abuse could break up the family and may worry about its well-being. For instance, if the father is the sexual-abuse perpetrator and goes to jail as a result of the disclosure, the family may lose its main source of income.

The Effects of Child Abuse and Neglect

Although it is difficult to pinpoint direct consequences of child abuse and neglect, there are effects that can be documented for some children. Infants who suffer head trauma or shaking can have long-lasting neurological deficits including blindness, deafness, mental retardation, and cerebral palsy. Children can also suffer psychological effects, including bed-wetting, tantrums, hyperactivity, low self-esteem, school problems, social withdrawal, oppositional behavior, compulsivity, and aggression (Child Abuse and Neglect Clearinghouse, 2004). Children who are physically abused exhibit more self-destructive behavior, such as suicide attempts and self-mutilation. Children who have been maltreated are also at risk of attachment problems that can affect interpersonal relationships throughout life.

Developmental Guidelines for Assessment in Early Childhood

Exhibit 7.12 presents the developmental guidelines for early childhood. These guidelines are meant to be helpful to social workers who need to understand development when making assessments.

FOCUS ON NARRATIVE

A CHILD CALLED "IT"

The *New York Times* bestseller *A Child Called "It"* is the story of a young boy severely abused by his alcoholic mother. He is not allowed to interact with the rest of the family. He sleeps in the basement. His mother refuses to feed him for days at a time. When she catches him stealing food to survive, she makes him throw it up and then eat it again. She pushes his face into a soiled diaper. She cuts him with a knife. Here is his account of the psychological effect of years of abuse:

> At the core of my soul, I hated myself more than anybody or anything. I came to believe that everything that happened to me or around me was my own fault because I had let it go on for so long. I wanted what others had but saw no way to get it, so I hated them for having it. I wanted to be strong, but inside I knew I was a wimp. I never had the courage to stand up to The Bitch, so I knew I deserved whatever happened to me. For years Mother had brainwashed me by having me shout aloud, "I hate myself! I hate myself!" Her efforts paid off. A few weeks before I started fifth grade, I hated myself so much that I wished I were dead.
>
> School no longer held the exciting appeal that it had years ago. I struggled to concentrate on my work while in class, but my bottled-up anger often flashed at the wrong times. One Friday afternoon in the winter of 1973, for no apparent reason, I stormed out of the classroom, screaming at everyone as I fled. I slammed the door so hard I thought the glass above the door would shatter. I ran to the bathroom, and with my tiny red fist I pounded the tiles until my strength drained away. Afterwards, I collapsed on the floor praying for a miracle. It never came.

From Pelzer (1995), p. 21

EXHIBIT 7.12 Developmental considerations in assessment in early childhood

Routine Observations
Gross and fine motor skills
Toileting
Speech
Use of mental symbols
Peer relationships and siblings
Play preferences
Nursery school
Limits, discipline, and daily routine
Dreams and night terrors, fears
Interest and skill development

Strengths and Landmarks of Development
Parallel play (2½), Collateral peer play (3), cooperative play (3–4)
Bedtime ritual (transitional objects early on)
Two and three word speed (2), creative use of speech (3–4)
Successful toilet training (2–3)
Accepts limits (2–3)
Development of special skills/talents, e.g., music, dance, manipulative skills
Self-talk to guide behavior
Some leadership capacity in groups (3–4)

Developmental Issues (Not Problems)
"Stuttering"
Occasional soiling or wetting
Messy play
Won't put things away
Stubbornness
Aggressive and possessive play
Refuses new foods
Immature behavior when ill or sick
Asserts independence and fusses
Occasional temper tantrums
Unreasonable fears (short-lived)

Developmental Observations Requiring Attention
Persistent soiling and wetting
Persistent eating problems
Disturbed sleep patterns
Nonspeaking (beyond 18 months)
Inappropriate play behavior
Excessive body rocking, finger sucking, and tics

STUDY TABLE: Social dimension in early childhood

Families, Groups, Communities, and Support Systems	Families move from addressing the physical care of children to setting limits and encouraging self-care, play skills, language development, and other methods of enhancing the child's self-control. Some parents can impose unrealistic expectations that can lead to feelings of guilt. The Erikson stage for preschool children is: initiative versus guilt. Baumrind recognized three styles of parenting: authoritarian, authoritative, and laissez-faire (permissive). Permissive parenting also includes two subtypes: neglectful and indulgent. Parents can be classified as warm or hostile. Parents need to adapt their parenting style to the child's developmental level. Parents begin to rely on discipline strategies based on logical and immediate consequences. Discipline styles of mothers (verbalizations) and fathers (commands) differ. Sons are encouraged to be more task oriented, girls more cooperative. Behavior genetics suggests that all traits are heritable. Twin studies have led to the conclusion that half of all variation in intelligence and personality is heritable. The effect of parenting may be due more to genetics than good parenting. According to Harris's work (*The Nurture Assumption*), a child's behavior may be influenced more by peers than by parents (group socialization theory). Low-income parents tend to use more authoritarian parenting for a variety of reasons. In addition to parenting, the cultural context can shape children's

behavior. Studies show that children raised by gay parents show no adjustment differences compared to children raised in "traditional" families. The parent-child relationship is the most important factor. Mothers are involved in primary child-care duties, and fathers spend more time playing with children. Mothers provide soothing activities and are more visual and verbal than fathers, who are more provocative and physical in their interactions. Preschoolers identify with the same-sex parent, but at age 4–5, children find fathers important and seek them out as playmates. Of incarcerated adults, 80% are parents, making children of prisoners a significant issue, especially because they represent children with identifiable risk factors (particularly for criminal activity). About 80% of children grow up with siblings, and adjustment to the new family member becomes an issue. Sibling relationships are characterized by strong emotions, intimacy, and diversity but provide the benefits of teaching and support. By age 4, 75% of children have developed friendships—typically with children of the same sex. Peer relationships are essential to development, and peer rejection is a strong predictor of a host of behavioral problems. Popular children are more sociable and cooperative, and they display better leadership and problem-solving skills.

Play is an important aspect of a child's healthy development. It is related to positive feelings, reduced tension and conflict, the exercise of cognitive skills, and the development of social skills. Play behavior has been categorized into five types: sensorimotor, practice, symbolic, social, and constructive. Preschool programs can vary; some emphasize academics, others emotional development. Skills in self-control facilitate a positive preschool experience. Kindergarten was designed to nurture the developing child, but children must be ready for the experience. When they aren't, schools may use delayed entry or retain children for an extra year. Alternatively, many experts argue that children who are at risk for school failure should be identified and provided preschool experiences that support their development of readiness skills. Family involvement has been shown to be vital in the successful transition to kindergarten, and promising practices exist to promote such involvement. Head Start is a government program designed to address poverty by providing a preschool experience for children, to help successful transition into kindergarten. Evaluations that examined Head Start found disappointing results when IQ was used as an outcome. However, other evaluations, using a broader range of outcomes, have documented the program's effects. Like Head Start, which provides for enhancing parent participation, health, and nutrition as well as school readiness, many communities are developing "full-service schools" that bring health care, parent education, and case management into the school. At an average of 20 hours per week, children spend more time watching TV than they do with parents or in school. TV is a major babysitter in American householders and is criticized not so much for what it provides but by what it prevents. Some research finds TV viewing is associated with attention problems in children and that TV may have an addictive influence over people. Because of the relaxed state TV can put people into, people may become conditioned to associate TV viewing with reduced tension. Also, TV has an "orienting response," which may explain why it is hard for people to stop watching. Advantages also exist for TV, such as exposure to information, knowledge, and learning. *Sesame Street* is a well-known example. Studies on the development of aggressive behavior have shown that TV can provide modeling of violent behaviors.

(continues)

STUDY TABLE: Social dimension in early childhood (*continued*)

Multicultural and Gender Considerations	Preschool children recognize ethnic characteristics in themselves and others. Ethnicity as a fixed attribute emerges at age 5; preschoolers do not understand that physical features have a social significance. When children do identify with an ethnic group, they will begin to make comparisons with others. Children adopted cross-culturally face special issues in the development of their identity. A healthy ethnic identity can be promoted through certain parenting practices. In preschool, gender-role identity begins. Sex-typed play is common. Children strengthen identification with the same-sex parent. By age 3, children have a sense of gender identity, and at age 4 there is gender stability. Two behaviors that appear to be genetically influenced are aggression in boys and nurturance in girls. The effects of sex stereotyping emerge in early childhood, and children this age are rigid in their sex-type behaviors. As a result, many people advocate teaching children to be androgynous.
Social Strengths and Hazards	Early childhood is a time when most people agree families need support in their efforts to nurture children. Social programs and policies are more likely to be embraced by the community for this developmental period. In this sense, there is some social capital to be harnessed in support of families. One example of a strengths-based model of family programs is family-group decision making, an alternative to traditional child welfare in which family members "conference" to make a decision about how they can care for a child who has become part of the child-welfare system. Poverty takes its toll on young children, and 17% of children live in families below the federal poverty threshold (2 adults, 2 children making less than $17,463). Research documents the many negative consequences for children who grow up in poverty (poor health, poor school performance, more social and behavioral problems). Teachers often have lower achievement expectations for low-income children. Child abuse is a serious social hazard for young children. Child neglect can include abandonment, inadequate supervision, or severe lack of resources. Psychological abuse is also a concern. Several factors contribute to child abuse and neglect, including family stress, child and family characteristics, parent problems, and violence in the home. Past abuse of parents and substance abuse are consistent factors for predicting child abuse. Environmental factors such as poverty, unemployment, and community violence are also crucial. Estimates are that about 1 million children are abused every year. Children under the age of 3 have the highest rate of abuse. Social workers are mandatory reporters and have legal and ethical obligations in reporting child abuse and should be aware of state laws that govern their actions. Child protection organizations use an assessment or classification system to investigate reports of child maltreatment. The consequences of child abuse and neglect can be serious. They include neurological deficits and psychological effects such as bedwetting, social withdrawal, and self destructive behavior. Considerations for assessment are outlined according to routine observations, strengths and landmarks of development, developmental issues, and developmental observations requiring attention.

CONCEPT MAP

APPLYING THE FRAMEWORK
DEVELOPMENTAL DELAY IN A 4-YEAR-OLD

Developmental History

Missy, a 4-year-old white girl, was referred to the Speech and Language Center by her pediatrician. Missy's mother, Mrs. Jones, stated that she was not concerned about Missy until her relatives started commenting about her speech. She reported they would say things like, "Well, she'll probably be talking in whole paragraphs once she gets going." Other than this small problem, Mrs. Jones stated that Missy had been "pretty much average, just like my first daughter" in development. She reports no pregnancy or birth complications that she can remember. She added that she has not found her daughter to be a problem and that they get along well and "understand each other just fine."

Biophysical Considerations

Missy is rather small for her age, appearing thin and tired. She has some trouble with gross motor coordination and cannot skip or throw a ball yet. Her fine motor coordination appears to be normal, although she is hesitant to initiate tasks and slow to complete them. At the preschool teachers' request, Mrs. Jones had Missy's hearing tested a year ago. The examination concluded that Missy's hearing was within normal limits.

Psychological Considerations

Information Processing

Missy exhibits difficulties with information-processing tasks. Specifically, she is inattentive at times, staring out into space rather than paying attention to the task at hand. She appears easily distracted during conversation, but she plays the same games for hours on end at home, according to her mother. Her memory is poor in testing; however, her mother says she can replay events over and over days after they happened. Mrs. Jones related that Missy attended preschool last year for a brief time, but she removed her because the school "wasn't right for her." When asked to elaborate about this, Mrs. Jones added that there was not enough structure in the school program, and Missy would just play imaginary games by herself all day. The teachers asked Mrs. Jones about hearing and speech difficulties. Mrs. Jones followed up with her pediatrician and had Missy's hearing tested.

The Wechsler Preschool and Primary Scale of Intelligence was administered to Missy, and she achieved a Full Scale IQ score of 92, placing her in the average range. Her Performance IQ score was 97 and her Verbal score was 80. Assessment of Missy's intellectual functioning revealed that her scores for expressive language development were below her overall intellectual functioning scores. Also, her scores on tests of her ability to understand language were in the normal range, significantly above her expressive language scores. Furthermore, her performance on the visual-motor tasks showed slight impairment.

Communication

Missy speaks when spoken to, hardly ever initiating communication. During the interview, her speech was slow and quiet. Her mother reports that she responds to questions at home but does not carry on lengthy conversations. Her mother added that Missy's older sister often completes sentences for her. Testing revealed Missy's vocabulary was limited for her age. In addition, she used the wrong tense in her responses to questions. Missy tended to hesitate when speaking, as if waiting for someone to help her. She nodded her head or gestured whenever possible.

Attitudes and Emotions

Missy's mother reports that Missy is a compliant child who usually does what she is told and does not argue or "sass back." Missy's demeanor is quiet, but she can become quite animated and insistent when playing with her dolls. Missy rarely cries or calls attention to herself in the family, Mrs. Jones recalls. To her, Missy looks content most of the time and is never demanding of attention. Her mother completed the Child Behavior Checklist (Achenbach & Edelbrock, 1983), and Missy's scores were in the normal range, with no elevations. However, her scores for internalizing behaviors were significantly higher than her externalizing behavior score.

When asked, Missy reports that she feels "fine." She states she rarely has upsets but admits to feeling sad much of the time, except when playing with her dolls. When asked if she cries very often, Missy says that she does not. She plays with her dolls or goes to the neighbor's house when she feels sad. When asked about her favorite activities, she listed playing with dolls and playing with the family dog alone outside in the backyard.

Missy agreed to draw a picture of herself for formal assessment. She did so hesitantly and slowly. Her picture was developmentally appropriate, although very small and in one corner.

Social Cognition and Regulation

Mrs. Jones reports that Missy has one friend she plays with in the neighborhood. Together, they play dolls. Usually Missy visits the friend's house and brings her dolls along. She is quite willing to share as long as her game is being played. Missy does not often play with her sister or her brother, but instead plays alongside them. Mrs. Jones noted that her oldest daughter spends a lot of time at her aunt's house next door. Mrs. Jones commented that Missy usually talks "baby talk" when playing dolls and her older sister complains about this when they do play together. Missy's older sister is often rude to Missy, too, according to her mother. She calls her names and teases her.

Missy relates that she likes her older sister but also likes it when she is away from home at her aunt's house, stating she doesn't have to "worry so much." Missy never argues with her sister. Neither Missy nor Missy's mother report any incidences of verbal or physical aggression instigated by Missy. Her friend does not seek out her company but will usually play when asked. Missy often tries to convince the friend to play dolls when the friend wants to play another game instead.

In terms of Missy's self-care skills, she generally has no difficulties. She feeds herself, brushes her teeth, and dresses herself but does not fasten her own buttons. She sometimes has difficulty choosing clothing to wear and will wait until her mother comes in her room to ask for help. Mrs. Jones states that Missy goes to bed easily but often lies in bed for over an hour before falling asleep. Missy denies nightmares or fears associated with sleep. She admits to worrying about her family and says she "sometimes just waits and listens." She says she likes to have her dog sleep in her room with her at night. Mrs. Jones reports that Missy is not a big eater but will usually nibble at whatever she is served. Missy states her appetite is adequate but that she doesn't feel like eating very often.

Social Considerations

Family Situation

Missy lives with her mother, father, older sister, and younger brother in a small house owned by her father's sister. Mrs. Jones reluctantly admitted that her marriage is not perfect. She stated that she and her husband argue frequently about money, his help in the family, and the children. She added that he blamed her for the children's problems because she "partied too much and did too many drugs in high school." Neither she nor her husband finished high school, and both are currently unemployed. Mrs. Jones reported that her husband does not spend much time with the children, even though he is home most of the day. He yells at them when they are too loud, but he has never struck the children. She described the home as usually quiet, without anybody talking to the others unless something is wrong. Mrs. Jones stated she has thought about leaving her husband but has nowhere else to go. Mrs. Jones added that she often feels trapped in the house; her husband will not let her go out without him very often, except to take the children to their appointments. Mrs. Jones conceded she spends little time recreating with her children because most of her time is spent performing household duties, child care, and taking her children to their appointments.

Missy stated she was closer to her mother but was afraid her father would be angry if he knew. In vague terms, Missy admitted to worrying about what will happen to her family. She says she likes to play at the neighbor's house and was happy

(continues)

APPLYING THE FRAMEWORK

(continued)

going to school. Missy states that she plays dolls most of the time and stays in her room when home. She is not allowed outside to play very often, even though she lives near a school.

Groups, Communities, and Support Systems

Missy's family interacts primarily with social welfare institutions. Her family receives assistance in the form of temporary aid for needy families and food stamps. Her mother goes with the children to the appointments because her father will not attend, nor will he baby-sit the children when she is out.

Multicultural and Gender Considerations

Missy lives in a fairly homogeneous neighborhood and rarely has contact with people of a different ethnic background. Her family does not participate in community events, and the preschool she had attended briefly was also primarily white.

As for her gender development, Missy plays with stereotypical girl toys when she has the opportunity. She identifies herself as a girl and drew long hair and a bow on herself in her figure drawing.

Summary and Impressions

Missy has several problems that became evident during the assessment.

1. Expressive Language Disorder — mild (American Psychiatric Association, 1994)
2. Poor peer relations and lack of social skills
3. Excessive worries interfering with sleep and appetite
4. Possible childhood depression
5. Inadequate self-system
6. Possible problems with coordination

Additional difficulties include the following:

7. Poor family communication
8. Inadequate social and peer opportunities
9. Marital conflict and possible abusive behavior directed toward her mother by her father
10. Inadequate gross motor play opportunities

Missy was cooperative with the social worker. However, her limited verbal skills, including poor vocabulary, inaccurate sentence structure and grammar, and reluctance to engage in conversation, made information gathering a difficult task. Some concern also exists about Mrs. Jones's ability to attend to Missy's physical and emotional needs. Furthermore, the Jones family does not appear capable of providing a sufficiently interactive and stimulating environment to promote healthy growth and remedy Missy's language delays.

On a positive note, Missy possesses adaptive skills in the sense that she can adjust her behavior to minimize the damage her environment imposes on her. She is quiet and does not make demands on a family already stressed by unemployment and marital conflict. In addition, she and her mother appear to have a close relationship compared with other family members. She also has a friend with whom she enjoys spending time and with whom her feelings are reciprocated to some degree. Last, she would most likely develop more friendships and improve her motor skills if given the opportunity.

Key Terms

aggression
altruism
androgyny
asthma
attention-deficit/ hyperactivity disorder (ADHD)
autism
avoidant disorder
behavioral genetics
child abuse
developmental waves
echolalia
egocentrism
empathy
encopresis
enuresis
expressive language disorder
group socialization theory
hostile aggression
infantile amnesia
information processing
night terrors
oral rehydration therapy
overanxious disorder
phonological disorder
physical development
posttraumatic stress disorder
preoperational thought
proactive aggression
reactive aggression

resiliency
separation anxiety disorder
single representations
social capital

Online Resources

Websites

Go to http://info.wadsworth.com/ashford to find specific links to these web pages.

National Institute of Mental Health

This is a searchable site that provides information on many psychological issues and disorders. Topics relevant to early childhood include ADD/ADHD, autism, and learning disorders.

American Psychological Association

Contains information relevant to mental-health professionals, the public, and students on broad and specific mental-health topics. This is a searchable site that includes press releases and literature pertaining to early-childhood development.

Prevent Child Abuse America

This site provides information and resources regarding child-abuse prevention. Includes information for reporting abuse, literature, statistics, and numerous links to other relevant sites.

Child Welfare League of America

This is the official website of CWLA, a nonprofit organization that advocates for policies and programs meant to protect children of all ages. The website describes the mission of the organization, relevant programs, professional conferences and trainings, and searchable literature.

InfoTrac College Edition Keywords

For interesting materials related to what you have just read, please go to the InfoTrac College Edition website and search using the following keywords:

childhood anxiety disorders   autism
self-esteem   parenting styles
social skills training   head start

Book-Specific Resources

Book-specific resources can be found at http://info.wadsworth.com/ashford and include the following:

Case studies
Quizzes to test your knowledge
PowerPoint presentations

CHAPTER 8
MIDDLE CHILDHOOD

CHAPTER CONSULTANTS

SANDRA ALTSHULER
Eastern Washington University

IKE SHIPMAN
Arizona State University

DEVELOPMENTAL THEMES

Child culture: games. Stage: industry versus inferiority. Development of physical and cognitive skills. Greater interaction with peers; increased capacity to learn from others.

BIOPHYSICAL DIMENSION

Biophysical Growth and Development

Slow, consistent growth until prepubertal years. Motor development: sports, sit-down games, concentration. Sex differences: boys develop more gross motor skills, girls more fine motor skills. Importance of exercise; decrease in physical activity.

Biophysical Strengths and Hazards

Development in cognitive and physical capacities. Movement skills assist with peer interactions and positive emotional health. Poverty and nutrition: cretinism; rickets.

PSYCHOLOGICAL DIMENSION

Cognitive Development and Information Processing

Concrete reasoning: conservation; mental reversal of operations. Intelligence and testing. Information processing. Emotional intelligence. Childhood competency to testify.

Communication

More correct and complex language, development of abstract connotations, reading and writing abilities refined. Developmental aspects of sign language. Speech disorders: stuttering. Bilingual children. Ebonics.

Attitudes and Emotions

Emotional competence. Social cognition and regulation. Social role-taking. Moral development moves from what's-in-it-for-me fairness to interpersonal conformity, cooperation, and reciprocity in interpersonal awareness; at later stages (ages 11–13) role-taking skill can be evident. Development of skills in friendship making.

Psychological Strengths and Hazards

Self-worth. Self-concepts become more individuated. Erikson's theory and industriousness. Externalizing and internalizing problems. Achenbach Child-Behavior Checklist. ADHD; medication.

SOCIAL DIMENSION

Families and Groups

Family strength. Normal family process. Parental discipline: power assertion, love withdrawal, induction. Parent-training models. Peer groups: group formation, power of peers in psychological development. Teaching skills for friendship making. Drug-abuse prevention.

Communities and Support Systems

Culture and cooperation. School influences. School phobia. Good schools. Impact of teacher expectations, self-expectations. Enhancing school-community relationships. Public Law 94-142.

Multicultural and Gender Considerations

Individual racial and gender identification develop and broaden the continued development of ethnic and gender roles. Rites of passage for African American youth; sex-role stereotypes.

Social Strengths and Hazards

Neighborhoods and communities. Violence. Bullying. Marital conflict and divorce.

DEVELOPMENTAL THEMES

A white 1970 Volkswagen Beetle passes by. "Slug bug," says the 7-year-old sitting next to me, and he punches me in the arm. Ten minutes later, an old VW bug with a sunroof goes by. "Double slug bug." I get two more punches.

"I pinch you, you can't pinch back, for I see a man in a white straw hat."

"Oh, wow! Check it out! Made you look! Made you look!"

"Roses are red, / violets are blue, / I'm going crazy / just like you."

Middle childhood is characterized by a child culture—a whole reality of rules, reciprocity, and fairness (Konner, 1991). "Slug bug" is a very popular game for children in middle childhood, and its appeal comes from a long tradition. The game "I pinch you, you can't pinch back, for I see a man in a white straw hat" was well known in the 1950s in England (Opie & Opie, 1987). "Made you look!" has been around for as long as we can remember. It is great fun for kids because they can trick you into doing something, and they love that. "Roses are red, violets are blue"—this line fills many pages of yearbooks and provides an opportunity for wonderful poetic expression.

All these examples of games probably sound familiar to you. Although its particular style may change, such play is universal for children in middle childhood. In middle childhood, games and play form a common children's culture—a culture that children can control and that belongs to no one but them (Konner, 1991). As children move from early childhood to middle childhood, their capacity to play such games unfolds. Their focus is on developing rules, ensuring fairness, and creating sanctions for rule breakers. Children at this age can be in charge of the rules—in fact, they can create their own new rules. Piaget learned a great deal from children's games, referring to them as "the most admirable social institutions." The philosopher Rousseau said that the work of children is play, and they learn and grow from it. Such play seems particularly critical in the middle-childhood years.

Middle childhood is the stage in life that begins at age 6 and ends at age 12, when adolescence begins. Children at this stage are ending their preschool years and beginning to learn new skills and competencies. This stage was often referred to by Erikson as one of industry (which means "to build") versus inferiority. Children in this stage develop competence in intellectual, social, and physical skills. Children who fail to gain this sense of competence may develop feelings of inferiority.

Many of the skills most important to children at this age are indicated by their daily pursuit of games, sports, reading, writing, and other school-related activities. This is a critical time for the development of coordination, physical strength, and flexibility. During this stage, children continue to make impressive cognitive gains in their intellectual functioning. As they move closer to adolescence, they develop some sophisticated logic and problem-solving abilities. The development of role-taking abilities becomes important as children's interactions with peers become more important. Successful adaptation to friendships and peer groups is a major developmental task for this age group. Much of this adaptation is played out in the school system, because this is where the child now spends half of his or her waking hours. Successful adaptation can be complicated by psychological problems associated with learning or communication, or by social problems such as peer difficulties or family disruption and divorce.

STUDY TABLE: Developmental themes in middle childhood

Developmental Themes	Middle childhood, ages 6–12, is characterized by a child culture that comprises rules, reciprocity, and fairness. Erikson described middle childhood as industry vs. inferiority. As children make the transition from early to middle childhood, their capacity to play games unfolds. Their focus is on developing rules, ensuring fairness, and creating sanctions for rule breaking. Successful adaptation to friendships and peer groups is a major developmental task for this age group.

BIOPHYSICAL DIMENSION

Biophysical Growth and Development

Throughout middle childhood, children experience a slow but consistent growth pattern. This slow growth is sandwiched between the rapid growth of early childhood and the growth spurt of the prepubertal years (10–13 years old for girls, 12–16 years old for boys). For instance, during the early- and middle-childhood years, children grow an average of two to three inches per year. The average 6-year-old child reaches almost four feet. Girls are generally shorter than boys at age 6, but by age 10, girls are slightly taller than boys. They continue to be taller through age 13. Girls weigh less than boys until age 11, when they have a growth spurt and end up weighing three pounds more than boys within the span of only one year. By age 14, boys exceed girls in weight and height, and they continue to do so throughout adulthood.

In middle childhood, fat tissue develops more quickly than muscle tissue, although through middle childhood there is actually a decrease in the growth of fatty tissue and an increase in muscle development. Girls retain the fat tissue longer, and boys develop muscle tissue more quickly. In physical appearance, then, girls are rounder, softer, and smoother than boys.

Motor Development

In middle childhood, development in both the large and small muscles facilitates changes in the child's coordination, agility, and smoothness. Whereas only one child in a thousand can hit a tennis ball over the net by age 4, by age 11 most children can learn to play tennis well (Santrock, 2003). Elementary-school children become fascinated with many sports activities, such as climbing, throwing and catching a ball, swimming, skateboarding, and skating. At this age, gross motor activity is emphasized. Often school-age children have difficulty controlling their impulses—they jump, run, bicycle, and climb everywhere. Such activity can sometimes lead to unrecognized fatigue that becomes exhibited in quarrelsome or crying behavior. By 7 and 8 years of age, children, although still very active, develop more interest in sit-down games, because they have an increased attention span and better cognitive abilities. By 8 and 10 years of age, children are involved in activities that require longer and more concentrated attention and effort, such as baseball, gymnastics, or soccer. As children get to the end of middle childhood, they become more interested in peer-related physical activities.

During middle childhood, boys' gross motor development exceeds that of girls. However, girls are

In middle childhood, children become more coordinated and have increased attention spans, abilities that promote the development of specialized skills.

better than boys at fine-motor skills. Boys' greater gross motor development may partially explain why they are more interested in physical activity than girls are (Pica, 2003).

A worn-out statement that child developmentalists like to use is this: Children are not miniature adults, although they become increasingly adultlike. Many of the child's physical elements are not completely developed. The child's optic nerve is not completely developed, and therefore the child cannot see as well as an adult. The child's bone growth and muscular development are far from complete. It is important to understand the child developmentally, because without such an understanding, we may expect certain behaviors at an age at which the child is not physically or intellectually prepared to perform them. The result is likely to be discouragement on the part of the child. **Readiness** is an important concept in understanding human development. For example, if we give a child special reading lessons at the age of 4, he or she can learn over the course of one or two years, whereas the average 6-year-old will learn to read in a matter of weeks.

Physical Development

Children's physical development has received increased attention in recent years, particularly because many children are not getting the exercise they need.

Although video games may help hand-eye coordination, there is nothing better to help a child develop than good old exercise. However, in America, older children are gaining weight and becoming increasingly sedentary. Physical activity is dropping off significantly during childhood and adolescence (Pica, 2003). For example, from the ages of 6 to 18, boys decrease their activity by at least 24% and girls by at least 36%.

Why is there such a marked decline in physical activity? Psychologists speculate that many children leave sports teams as athletics become more competitive, as academic demands take over, and as parents stop signing them up for sports classes and camps. Others cite children's fixation on video games and television. And many blame children's lack of knowledge about exercise's benefits and the failure of parents and physical-education (PE) teachers to instill in children a lifelong exercise ethic.

For example, if you observe a PE class, you may see most of the class standing around waiting for their turn while one or two children practice a skill. In one study, researchers found that elementary students spent only 8.5% of PE time in vigorous activities; middle-school students spent 16% in such activities. These percentages are both much lower than the 50% active time standard set by the National Office of Disease Prevention and Health Promotion. The old-fashioned notion of physical education where students work to "get in good physical shape" has been superseded by games and activities that may not accomplish the same goals.

Because kids do not recognize the health benefits as adults do, adults must be creative. For example, exercising with a friend, making up stories while running, or seeing who can spot the bluest cars while bicycling may entice couch-potato children into getting outdoors. Additionally, PE programs should help make children fitter as a primary goal, as well as teach them games of physical activity and the learning of self-discipline and goal setting. The bottom line is this: If you do not train them while they are young, they won't exercise when they are adults.

Biophysical Strengths and Hazards

Middle childhood is a period of major cognitive and physical development. A child who develops cognitively will begin to show advanced reasoning, increased vocabulary, and interest in reading. All these developments lay a pathway to positive growth. On the other hand, major advances in motor-skill development and physical activity can be hampered under extreme conditions of poor living.

Movement Skills

An important biophysical strength in middle childhood is the opportunity for children to develop their movement skills. Like other skills, movement skills need to be learned and practiced for the child to obtain maximum benefit, and developmental theory proposes "critical periods" when movement learning can have its greatest impact on various aspects of a child's development. For example, the refinement of fine motor skills can play an important role in biopsychosocial development, because a 7- to 10-year-old child is often asked to join in some type of physical play. With good motor skills, the child can maximize these opportunities. More broadly speaking, movement skills can influence the extent to which a child participates in culture. Having "movement competence" contributes to the positive emotional development of children.

Most children demonstrate a strong innate capability to grow in an orderly, healthy sequence. However, both the rate and pattern of growth can be altered by adversity. When the environment does not meet the child's fundamental needs, growth can be affected. Nutrition, amount of rest and sleep, opportunities to learn, amount of affection, extent of security—these and other factors can determine how fast and to what degree a child develops.

Poverty and Nutrition

If we take a worldwide perspective, it is easy to discover that children suffering from poverty and lack of food are unable to achieve healthy development. Also, conditions that exist during times of war, such as lack of food, constant fear, and loss of or separation from parents, can lead to permanent physical damage. Although human development is marked by great resilience, some environmental conditions will produce marked changes in growth. For instance, lack of iodine in community drinking water will lead to an increase in **cretinism**, a chronic disease characterized by physical deformity and dwarfism. And **rickets** is caused by a deficiency in vitamin D and produces permanent damage to the bones, resulting in a flat chest, a deformed pelvis, and/or a crooked back.

STUDY TABLE: Biophysical dimension in middle childhood

Biophysical Growth and Development	In middle childhood, boys and girls exhibit a slow but consistent growth pattern. Girls retain their fat tissue longer than boys do; boys develop muscle tissue more quickly. Continued development in the large and small muscles enhances the child's coordination, agility, and smoothness. Sports become popular as boys and girls enjoy climbing, throwing, swimming, and skating. Boys have greater motor development, and girls are better than boys at fine motor skills.
Biophysical Strengths and Hazards	Middle childhood is a time when children experience major development in both cognitive and physical capacities. Development shows advanced reasoning, increased vocabulary, and interest in reading. Movement skills contribute to a child's peer interactions and emotional development. Environmental conditions can affect the child's health and development. Poverty and a lack of food can be very damaging. Impoverished conditions can lead to problems such as cretinism and rickets. Physical activity drops off significantly during childhood and adolescence, causing overweight children.

CONCEPT MAP

PSYCHOLOGICAL DIMENSION

Cognitive Development and Information Processing

Middle childhood is an exciting period of study in terms of cognitive development. Piaget classified children in this age group as operating from concrete operational thought. He described the concrete operational stage as a series of operations or mental actions that are reversible. Such an operation is characterized by rules of logic. This stage is referred to as *concrete* because the child's thinking is limited to real objects. A child at this stage cannot use the logic of formal operations to compare the ideal with the actual or to think hypothetically. This stage is characterized by becoming less egocentric. As the chapter will explain, the child begins to decenter and demonstrates the operation of reversibility. Children at this stage also show conservation skills.

The best way to understand these concepts is through the mind of Piaget himself. Piaget was a frequent observer of children and he devised many ingenious experiments or tasks to test his ideas. His task of conservation is one of the most famous and is a hallmark of the concrete-operations stage.

Conservation has to do with the quantitative aspects of objects or things that do not change unless something has been added to or subtracted from the object (although other changes may lead to perceptual differences). Exhibit 8.1 shows tasks that can be used to measure conservation of number, mass,

EXHIBIT 8.1
Tests of conservation
SOURCE: Weiten (1995).

Typical tasks used to measure conservation	Typical age of mastery
Conservation of number Two equivalent rows of objects are shown to the child, who agrees that they have the same number of objects.	6–7
One row is lengthened, and the child is asked whether one row has more objects.	
Conservation of mass The child acknowledges that two clay balls have equal amounts of clay.	7–8
The experimenter changes the shape of one of the balls and asks the child whether they still contain equal amounts of clay.	
Conservation of length The child agrees that two sticks aligned with each other are the same length.	7–8
After moving one stick to the left or right, the experimenter asks the child whether the sticks are of equal length.	
Conservation of area Two identical sheets of cardboard have wooden blocks placed on them in identical positions; the child confirms that the same amount of space is left on each piece of cardboard.	8–9
The experimenter scatters the blocks on one piece of cardboard and again asks the child whether the two pieces have the same amount of unoccupied space.	

length, and area. Let's look at an example of conservation of mass. Suppose we give a child two equal balls of clay, then take one ball and roll it out into a long, narrow shape. The child is asked whether the snakelike object contains the same amount of clay as the original ball of clay. A child who is 5 or 6 will say that the long, narrow piece of clay contains more. However, a child of 7 or 8 is likely to reason that, although one ball of clay was rolled into a snakelike shape, it could be reformed into a ball and it would still contain the same amount of clay. This task also shows

Children under the age of 7 intuitively assume that a volume of liquid increases when it is poured from a short, wide container into a taller, thinner one.

that the child can use the operation of **reversibility**. Rather than focusing exclusively on the physical characteristics of the objects, the child is able to *coordinate* information about both shapes of the clay, demonstrating concrete operational thinking (thought processes governed by rules of logic).

Although Piaget's influence on and contribution to understanding cognitive development is unmistakable, there are some important new developments in the field. In particular, Piaget argued that children's cognitive development proceeded according to a predetermined sequence of stages. However, recent research has discovered that there is tremendous individual variation in the performance of children of the same age and supposedly the same stage. In addition, changing the instructions for the task—even slightly—can throw off the results considerably. Consequently, many of the researchers who continue in the Piagetian tradition now refer to "levels," which are considered less specific developmental milestones than "stages."

Intelligence and Intelligence Tests

Although we discuss and refer to intelligence often in our everyday world, the concept of intelligence is quite complex and difficult to measure. However, most people are familiar with Alfred Binet's concept of **mental age**, which is the age level at which the child scored on an intelligence test. Binet developed the first intelligence test in 1905. The Stanford-Binet is a well-known, widely used **intelligence quotient**, or IQ, test. Most of us think of the IQ test in terms of the following formula:

$$IQ = \frac{\text{mental age}}{\text{chronological age}} \times 100$$

IQ is calculated by comparing the child's mental age with his or her chronological age. Because IQ tests can have important implications in the planning of services for children, let's examine the two IQ tests commonly encountered in school reports or case records, the Stanford-Binet and the Weschsler.

Stanford-Binet

This test must be administered individually by a trained person. It is most often used with young children, although it is designed for individuals 2 to 18 years old. The Stanford-Binet is considered to be a verbal test of intelligence because it contains a large number of items that rely on verbal abilities. Exhibit 8.2 gives examples of representative tasks used in the test.

The Stanford-Binet comprises four areas: verbal reasoning, quantitative reasoning, abstract/visual

EXHIBIT 8.2 Sample tasks from the Stanford-Binet test

Age	Sample Tasks
2	Identify parts of the body on a large paper doll. Place a circle, square, and triangle in the appropriate three holes of a form board.
5	Complete a drawing of a man. Fold a paper triangle in a manner similar to that modeled by examiner.
8	Answer questions about a story that has been read by the examiner. Indicate how objects are similar and different.
12	Define a number of words. Repeat five digits backward.

reasoning, and short-term memory. The IQ is a composite score that is referred to as a measure of "adaptive ability." The Stanford-Binet has been administered to many people, and the results show that people's IQ scores form a normal distribution; most of the cases fall in the middle of the distribution. The Stanford-Binet has a mean of 100 and a standard deviation of 16. (*Mean* refers to the average score, and the *standard deviation* is a measure of how much the scores vary.) Reviewing some basic statistical concepts, one standard deviation from the mean constitutes 68% of the cases. The 68% is considered the average range, with scores ranging from 84 to 116.

Wechsler

Another popular test developed for use with children is the Wechsler Intelligence Scale for Children, third edition (WISC-III). This test differs from the Stanford-Binet in that it groups the test items into subsets that make up separate verbal and performance scales. The WISC-III is unique because it taps both verbal and performance abilities, producing three values: a verbal IQ, a performance IQ, and a full-scale IQ. The verbal scale samples the degree of knowledge about general information; the ability to master concepts, think abstractly, and concentrate; use of judgment; and memory. The performance measure samples visual-motor skills, planning ability, attention to detail, and other attributes. The various subtests of the WISC-III allow the examiner to determine particular areas of strength and weakness. In addition to this test, there is the Wechsler Preschool and Primary Scale of Intelligence–Revised (WPPSI-R), which has been developed for children between the ages of 4 and 6.5.

Kaufman Assessment Battery for Children (K-ABC)

The K-ABC battery of tests is a new method of assessment based on the **Das-Luria model of cognitive functioning** (Lichtenberger, Broadbooks, & Kaufman, 2000). The model is based on the notion that there are two modes of processing information: simultaneous processing and successive processing. Simultaneous processing is concerned with the immediate processing of related stimuli, whereas successive processing is concerned with the processing of stimuli that reflect a sequence, or ordering. From this perspective, intelligence is based on the ability to use both simultaneous and successive strategies effectively in goal-setting and planning behavior.

This test, like the WISC-III, comprises a number of subtests, each related to various abilities. Some of the subtests include the Mental Processing Composite Index, which assesses general intellectual functioning, and the Achievement Index, which assesses knowledge of facts, language concepts, and other school-related skills such as arithmetic, reading, and vocabulary. The developers of this test have provided extensive data in support of its reliability and validity.

The K-ABC may be of particular interest to social workers in the school, because one of the test's specific functions is to provide information to help plan teaching and remediation, especially with learning-disabled children. Central to the model is the ability to construct a cognitive map of a particular child so that his or her specific strengths and weaknesses can be identified. Instructional strategies are then based on the results of the cognitive mapping.

Intelligence Tests: Good or Bad?

Since their inception, intelligence tests have been controversial. Early concerns about IQ tests centered on their use to label and classify children. It was common to find children labeled "average" if they scored 105 on a Stanford-Binet, "mentally retarded" if they scored 65, and "genius" if they obtained a score of 150. Such labels should not come from the results of a single test. Indeed, additional information should be carefully gathered and assessed if a child is going to be classified. Unfortunately, many children are still being classified by the results of a single test and will receive a label from their classification that will stay with them for many years.

Another major issue concerning the use of intelligence tests is whether they can be considered culturally biased. Many of the tests rely heavily on verbal intelligence that reflects a middle-class bias. Adrian Dove dramatized this point when he developed the Chitling Test. Sample items from this test included defining such things as a "gas-head," a "blood," and "Bo-Diddley" and knowing how long to cook chitlings. His point was clear: The emphasis on verbal abilities in many IQ tests reflected an environment that was familiar to middle-class white children. Many of the IQ tests have attempted to improve their cultural fairness. For example, the Stanford-Binet, known for its emphasis on verbal abilities, is considered less accurate for children whose language development is different from or slower than that of the average middle-class child. The latest edition of the test has been designed to ameliorate this problem. The more recently developed Kaufman Assessment Battery for Children is being promoted as more culturally fair than existing intelligence tests (Lichtenberger et al., 2000).

Are intelligence tests good or bad? Often it is not the intelligence test that is problematic but the misuse of the test. We must remember that intelligence is a complex concept. It is not fixed, and it cannot be measured easily. If a child is despondent and unmotivated when tested, this could easily influence the results. If an IQ test is administered in English and that is not the person's native language, the results are not likely to be accurate. Also, intelligence tests are not easily linked to success, and therefore their use should be carefully scrutinized. Social workers must ensure that children receive fair and accurate assessments. Understanding the benefits and weaknesses of intelligence tests is a start in this direction.

Information Processing

Researchers are beginning to study how children process information about their social world. For instance, information processing may be linked to aggressive behavior. Consider the following scenario: Justin walks by Sean's desk and accidentally knocks a book off of his desk. Sean immediately jumps up and pushes Justin. The teacher runs over to break it up. The teacher is familiar with this scenario because Sean often gets into fights. Sean immediately responded to Justin as if Justin's actions were hostile, and this response led him to an aggressive reaction. Kenneth Dodge has studied boys like Sean because he believes they have skill deficits in their ability to detect social cues. In a series of studies (Kupersmidt & Dodge, 2004), children viewed videotaped vignettes that depict a social interaction in which one child provokes the other. Different scenes show different intentions—hostile, prosocial, and accidental—and children are asked to differentiate among the intentions. The findings show that children who are identified as being socially rejected do not perform as well as do children who are popular or average. Children who are deficient in **intention-cue detection** are likely to make errors and view acts that are prosocial or accidental as hostile.

How we process information can be critical to our mental health and well-being, so information processing has become a major approach to understanding the developing child. Three factors are fundamental to the information-processing approach: (1) how knowledge develops—its creation; (2) the processes and strategies that become part of the knowledge base or the processes used to retrieve information from the knowledge base; (3) the child's awareness of self as a knower able to use and evaluate strategies, also referred to as **metacognition**, which is knowledge about knowing. As we progress with the developing child, we will return to these early notions of information processing to examine the role of cognitive development.

Although cognitive development has been studied extensively with regard to traditional notions of IQ, we are learning that emotions and information processing, not IQ, may be the true measure of human intelligence.

The Significance of Emotional Intelligence

Do you believe that a scientist can see the future by watching 4-year-olds interact with a marshmallow? The researcher invites the children, one by one, into a plain room and begins a gentle torment. You can have this marshmallow now, he says. But if you wait while I run an errand, you can have two marshmallows when I get back. And then he leaves.

Some children grab for the treat as soon as the researcher walks out the door. Some last a few minutes before they give in. But others are determined to wait. They cover their eyes; they put their heads down; they sing to themselves; they try to play games or even fall asleep. When the researcher returns, he gives these children their hard-earned marshmallows. And then science waits for them to grow up.

By the time the children reach high school, something remarkable has happened. A survey of the children's parents and teachers has found that those who as 4-year-olds had the strength to hold out for the second marshmallow generally grew up to be better adjusted, more popular, adventurous, confident, and dependable teenagers (Shoda, Mischel, & Peake, 1990). The children who gave in to temptation early on were more likely to be lonely, easily frustrated, and stubborn. They buckled under stress and shied away from challenges. And when some of the students in the two groups took the SATs, the kids who had held out longer scored an average of 210 points higher. What does this mean?

It seems that the ability to delay gratification is a master skill, a triumph of the reasoning brain over the impulsive one. It is a sign, in short, of **emotional intelligence (EQ)** (Goleman, 1997; Gottman, 1998). And EQ does not show up on an IQ test. The phrase "emotional intelligence" begins to describe qualities such as understanding one's own feelings, empathy for the feelings of others, and regulating emotions in ways that enhance life. When it comes to predicting people's success, brain power as measured by IQ and standardized achievement tests may actually matter less than the qualities of mind once thought of as "character."

How do EQ and IQ complement each other? How does one's ability to handle stress, for instance, affect the ability to concentrate and put intelligence to use? Researchers are trying to answer these questions, but they generally agree that IQ counts for about 20%; the rest depends on "nurture" factors such as environment and experiences.

Perhaps the most visible emotional skills, the ones we recognize most readily, are "people skills," such as empathy, graciousness, and the ability to read a social situation. Researchers believe that about 90% of emotional communication is nonverbal.

Like other emotional skills, empathy is an innate quality that can be shaped by experience. Infants as young as 3 months old will exhibit empathy when they get upset at the sound of another baby crying. Even very young children learn by imitation; by watching how others act when they see someone in distress, these children acquire a repertoire of sensitive responses. However, if the feelings they begin to express are not recognized and reinforced by the adults around them, not only do they cease to express those feelings, but they also become less able to recognize them in themselves and others.

Nowhere is the discussion of emotional intelligence more pressing than in schools, where both the stakes and the opportunities seem greatest. Instead of constant crisis intervention, or declarations of war on drug abuse or teenage pregnancy or violence, preventative medicine should be the focus. Schools can implement an "emotional literacy" program, which teaches kids to learn to manage anger, frustration, and loneliness. Educators can point to many examples that support the importance of teaching the qualities that make up EQ. Students who are depressed or angry literally cannot learn. Children who have trouble being accepted by their classmates are two to eight times more likely to drop out than children who are accepted. An inability to distinguish feelings or handle frustration also has been linked to eating disorders in girls.

However, any campaign to refine emotional skills in children may end up teaching that there is a "right" emotional response for any given situation—for example, one should laugh at parades, cry at funerals, sit still in church. Emotional skills, like intellectual ones, are morally neutral. Just as a genius could use his or her intellect either to cure cancer or to engineer a deadly virus, someone with great empathetic insight could use it to inspire colleagues or exploit them. Without a moral compass to guide people in how to employ their gifts, emotional intelligence can be used for good or evil. The knack of delaying gratification that makes a child one marshmallow richer can help him or her become a good citizen or—just as easily—a brilliant criminal. In the next section, key issues in children's cognitive development (especially regarding their mastery of moral concepts and the ability to distinguish truth and falsehood) are explored.

Assessing Childhood Competency to Testify

Is a child in the period of middle childhood cognitively competent to testify as a witness? Children are sometimes needed as witnesses to acts of crime and negligence. They are also victims of abuse, crime, or neglect. To testify in these matters, they must be able to truthfully and accurately communicate their personal knowledge of relevant facts. The law presumes that children under 10 or 12 years of age, depending on the jurisdiction, are incompetent to testify (Stern, Stern, & Lamiell, 1999). The justification for this presumption is the child's developmental immaturity. Although this presumption is refutable in most jurisdictions, it requires a solid understanding of a child's individual development.

The validity and reliability of a child's testimony has been challenged on a number of grounds: memory, cognitive development, moral development, and suggestibility (Westcott, Davies, & Bull, 2002). The memory issues relate to children's capacity to communicate their recollections of an event in response to questions presented in court. Will children describe "true memory" of an event, or will their memory of an event be the product of suggestions from others with whom they have discussed the event? Will the child describe actual occurrences, or occurrences based on fantasy? As you recall, fantasy and language are schemata used by preoperational children to adapt to their environment. Ongoing research continues to examine children's capacity to recall events in a manner not limited by their development.

Cognitive development affects the child's conceptualization or comprehension of events. Can a child conceptualize complex acts and order these acts in time and space? Does the child understand the meaning of terms and behaviors of relevance to a legal inquiry? The answers to each of these questions are influenced by knowledge from cognitive development. Children acquire cognitive competencies at different ages. Miscommunication is often an impediment to obtaining reliable information from children. Developmentalists also note inconsistencies in children's cognitive capacities across situations and tasks encountered in middle childhood.

Will children's immaturity influence their likelihood of being truthful in their testimony? This issue of moral development is often raised as a critical issue. Some research finds that children are no more prone to lying than are adults (Stern et al., 1999). How development affects children's morality is in their ability to provide reasons or justifications for their behavior. Development also affects children's comprehension of terms such as *oath, truth,* and *court.* However, this type of comprehension has no bearing on their propensity to tell the truth. Data on suggestibility is less clear, although research has not found as many age differences as one might expect (Stern et al., 1999).

A primary fear is that children's testimony will be determined by their perceptions of adult expectations of how they should behave — that is, the type of testimony that the adult examiner is expecting of them. There is also a fear that children are more susceptible to leading questions. However, children appear to be no less affected by leading questions than adults are (see Stern et al., 1999).

Each of these issues presents different assessment objectives for practitioners. Melton and his colleagues (1987) have provided guidelines for evaluating children's competency to testify. Evaluators should assess the following areas of the child's development:

1. Understanding of the obligation to tell the truth
2. Reliability of memory
3. Ability to perceive reality accurately
4. Vulnerability to suggestion

These guidelines cannot be implemented without understanding the key cognitive developmental milestones for early and middle childhood.

Communication

Middle childhood is the period of linguistic refinement. In early childhood, the focus in language development is on things such as correcting the past tense of irregular verbs. Children's use of language becomes increasingly grammatically correct and more complex than simple yes-or-no questions or the general "why" questions. Language develops in deaf children much as it does in hearing children. (The section on Developmental Aspects of Sign Language, page 341, gives a description of how sign language develops.) As children develop, they become increasingly aware that words can have multiple meanings, and they understand the notion of abstract connotations. This ability to "go beyond the information" is referred to as **metalinguistic awareness** (Sigelman & Rider, 2002). As this ability develops, children begin to appreciate the humor in jokes, riddles, and puns. At about age 10, children can begin to understand and use metaphors such as "People who live in glass houses shouldn't throw stones."

Language development is central to healthy development in children. Language is the door to obtaining information from others. It allows you to make requests of other people and makes a wealth of information accessible. In fact, early language researchers believed that language was necessary for thought (Whorf, 1956). However, most child developmentalists now believe that thought is a prerequisite to language.

Piaget's research led him to the conclusion that many logical concepts are learned before the development of the language that corresponds to those concepts. For example, a child first learns the concept of bigger and then begins to use the language that describes the concept.

Recent research has found that difficulties in communication can result in the case of listeners who fail to detect **uninformative messages**, or messages that do not clarify the exact meaning being communicated (Beal & Belgrad, 1990). Children 6 to 7 years old will clarify an uninformative message they judge to be problematic. However, younger children, having at least some idea of what is meant by a statement, will overlook the problem in the message and assume that the speaker's intentions are clear. For example, "Bring me that toy" is an ambiguous statement when two toys are next to each other. A young child will hear the request and assume the speaker wants the closest toy, whereas 8- to 10-year-olds will question the ambiguity and ask for clarification.

We can teach children with communication difficulties better communication skills by having them learn to focus on the differences among the stimuli in their conversations (Pratt, McLaren, & Wickens, 1984). Also, we can teach children to be better listeners by having them evaluate what they hear and ask questions to clarify statements they don't understand.

Another important aspect of communication is the developmental theory of **verbal control** that came from the work of Russian psychologists Vygotsky and Luria (Luria, 1961; Vygotsky, 1962). They believed that speech develops through three successive stages: other-external, whereby the behavior of a child is controlled through the verbalizations of others; self-external, whereby the child's own overt verbalizations provide control over his or her behavior; and self-internal, whereby the child's behavior is controlled by his or her own covert self-verbalizations. This early work on the role of speech and behavior was groundbreaking, because it suggested the relationship between self-verbalizations and self-guidance. An important developmental aspect of speech and behavior also was discovered: Luria observed that as children got older, they were able to inhibit behavior not only by following adult instructions (other-external) but also in response to their own self-instructions (self-internal). If, as the Russian researchers suggested, internal speech can control overt behavior, then why not teach children who lack self-control to use their own speech to gain more control over their actions? This work laid the groundwork for the development of self-instructional training, a popular treatment approach for impulsive children who lack self-control.

Implications for Practice: Self-Instructional Training

Self-instructional training has become a major treatment modality for practitioners working with children who have difficulties with self-control. Researchers have developed a fairly specific sequence of training activities that include the following: (1) The therapist performs the task while asking questions aloud about the task, giving self-guiding instructions and making self-evaluations of the performance. (2) The child imitates the therapist's overt self-instructional sequence while doing the task. (3) The therapist repeats the task, this time using a whisper. (4) The child imitates the therapist's performance and self-instructions using a whisper. (5) The therapist models covert self-instructions while performing the task. (6) The child imitates the therapist's covert self-instructions and performance. Research has found that it is important to perform tasks in ways that are not perfect and then teach children how to cope with errors in their performance (Kendall, 2000).

One program (Camp et al., 1977) developed a "think-aloud" approach to working with aggressive, impulsive children. The approach incorporates the cognitive-behavioral techniques using self-instructions for solving problems. Children were taught to ask and answer four questions: (1) What is my problem? (2) What is my plan? (3) Am I using my plan? (4) How did I do? The practitioners used various cognitive problems and interpersonal problem-solving games requiring the children to control their impulses to teach the self-instructional skills. In a similar manner, Kendall and Treadwell (1996) developed the FEAR treatment protocol for children suffering from anxiety, whereby children guide themselves with these steps: (1) Feeling frightened? (2) Expecting bad things to happen? (3) Actions and attitudes that help; and (4) Rate and reward. Kazdin and Frame (1983) worked with an aggressive 11-year-old boy and taught him problem-solving steps that could be used in everyday situations. Their training focused on the following set of questions and statements:

What am I supposed to do?
I need to look at all my possibilities.
I have to focus in (concentrate).
I have to make a choice.
How well did I do?

Social workers interested in applying such techniques should keep in mind the following recommendations. First, self-statements should be developmentally appropriate—in effect, ones the child can understand and retain. The statements should be practiced until they are memorized, and practitioners need to keep them simple to avoid overburdening the child. Research has found that general self-statements ("I need to look at all my possibilities") are better than specific self-statements ("Just kick the ball, and don't get mad"). Last, keep the self-instructions geared to problems that represent difficulties in real life. ■

Developmental Aspects of Sign Language

Although we normally think of communication as exclusively verbal, this is not necessarily so. Many people communicate using sign language. Children who are born without the ability to hear and who therefore cannot communicate with an oral language often learn American Sign Language (ASL), an advanced system of communication that includes the use of both hands in various gestures, like the ones in Exhibit 8.3.

Children learn ASL just as they would an oral language. Children who are born to deaf parents begin to learn to communicate with signs at a very early age. Most deaf children will learn their first sign at around 9 months of age, which is three months before hearing children begin to use words (Bonvillian, Orlansky, & Novack, 1983). Like hearing children, deaf children begin to communicate by "babbling," but they do it in signs that they have observed their parents using. As the children develop, they begin to use the equivalent of one-word phrases—a single sign that communicates several messages. Interestingly, the kinds of signs that children first begin to use are essentially the same as the categories of words that speaking children first learn. Deaf children's ability to communicate continues to develop as they begin to combine signs similar to the telegraphic statements made by speaking children. Communication becomes increasingly refined as deaf children learn the complex rules inherent in communicating their thoughts and feelings.

ASL is a creative and advanced system of communication. Similar to oral language, signs combine to form declarative statements and ask questions. ASL users are fond of making plays on words (puns), just as oral communicators do. Research studies

EXHIBIT 8.3 Sign language
SOURCE: Ohio School for the Deaf.

suggest that children enrolled in "total communication" have greater advances in language development (Marschark, Lang, & Albertini, 2001). Total communication is using any combination of communication (such as sign language, voice, finger spelling, lip reading, amplification, writing, gesture, and visual imagery) to create the least restrictive learning environment for the deaf student. Also, many people believe it enhances the quality of interactions between deaf and hearing people. Recent developments with cochlear implants are also impacting language development among the deaf. As more implants are used with children, more research will be needed to understand the linguistic, cognitive, and social effects of cochlear implantation. However, even if children with implants begin to depend more on spoken language than on sign language, early exposure to language is essential for deaf children's cognitive development and literacy skills (Tomblin et al., 1999).

It is very common for children with hearing problems of any degree to also have difficulties with speech (although such challenges are not limited to these children). Many speech disorders have enormous effects on a children's lives.

Speech Disorders in Children

The development of a speech disorder can have a negative effect on a child's healthy development. It is not uncommon for children with speech disorders to have difficulties with intellectual and academic achievements, as well as emotional difficulties. Such children may be teased and as a result have low self-confidence. Family problems also can develop, especially if family members pressure the child.

There is a wide variation in the nature of speech disorders. Some are extremely mild and almost unnoticeable; others can be so serious that they affect day-to-day living. We don't know what causes the majority of speech disorders, but there can be a combination of physiological, psychological, or environmental circumstances. Speech disorders manifest themselves in a variety of forms, including articulatory problems, voice abnormalities, stuttering, or aphasia, the inability to speak. Speech disorders are more common among children who have hearing impairments, physical impairments (such as cerebral palsy), mental retardation, and emotional disturbances. Two of the more common speech disorders are stuttering and faulty articulation.

Stuttering refers to interruptions in communication produced by repetitions, hesitations, or other forms of "blockages" of sounds or words. Some children with more serious forms of stuttering also have overt indications of tension. Stuttering is four or five times more common in boys than in girls, and an estimated 5% of all children may suffer from a stuttering problem for various periods of time. Most cases

Not all communication is verbal; many children must communicate using sign language. These children learn American Sign Language (ASL), a system of communication based on hand gestures.

of stuttering begin early—by age 4 or 5—and usually clear up spontaneously, but professional speech therapists are sometimes needed.

Research from a biological perspective has found that the incidence of stuttering is higher when there is a family history of stuttering. Furthermore, research on the brain has demonstrated that the neural organization of stutterers differs from that of nonstutterers. However, other research supports environmental factors; for example, stuttering varies quite dramatically across cultures. Anthropologists have noted the relative absence of stuttering in cultures with permissive child-rearing practices. In contrast, industrial cultures that stress competition, pressure to speak at an early age, and standards of achievement have produced a higher incidence of stuttering. Most speech-disorder experts believe that the causes of stuttering, like many other individual characteristics, develop from an interaction between biological and environmental factors (see Cohen, 2001).

Bilingual Children

Language and communication are difficult skills for children to develop, and this development can be even more complicated when two languages being learned at the same time. **Bilingual** children (those who can speak more than one language) are often spoken to in one language at home and taught another language in school. Does being bilingual impede a child's language proficiency or negatively influence his or her intellectual development? In the past it was thought that bilingualism did have negative outcomes, such as lower test scores on linguistic-knowledge and intelligence tests when compared with monolingual peers. But today we realize that such conclusions were flawed. The studies that generated such conclusions were based on first- or second-generation immigrants from lower socioeconomic backgrounds who were not very proficient in English. Furthermore, the tests were given in English as opposed to the language the child was most proficient in. The results are obvious: poor students who didn't speak good English scored less well than middle-class English-speaking students when given a test in English (Shaffer, 2002).

People often think that exposing a child to multiple languages will cause confusion and linguistic problems. These fears are unfounded.

The policy implications were that schools began limiting the teaching of different languages until after age 10 in order to allow students to give full attention to learning English. As researchers began to look carefully at children who were successfully bilingual, clearer findings emerged. Children could learn to be bilingual at early ages. Before age 3, children develop good proficiency in two languages (although there is some mixing up of both languages). Well-designed research (where important variables are matched when making a comparison) has consistently found that there are advantages to bilingual education. Students learning to be bilingual show higher scores than monolingual peers on measures of IQ, Piagetian conservation tasks, and language use (Diaz, 1985), **metalinguistic awareness** (Bialystok, Shenfield, & Codd, 2000), and selective attention (Bialystok, 1999).

In spite of these studies and support for bilingual education from the government, public opinion is very negative toward bilingual education. An important policy result is that a large number of states are voting to make English the official language. The impact of this is to support efforts at teaching non-native English speakers only in English. The unfortunate result is that when non-English speakers are put into English-only immersion programs there can be negative academic effects (DeiCampo & DeiCampo, 2000).

An alternative with growing support is two-way bilingual education. This is when English-speaking children and children with limited proficiency in English are instructed one half of the day in their primary language and the other half in their second language. Research has found that programs where children with limited English proficiency are instructed primarily in their native language are not working well. These children do not appear to learn the English literacy skills they need to be successful (DeiCampo & DeiCampo, 2000). But with two-way bilingual education, students have shown proficiency in both their native language and in English (Cummins & Swain, 1986). Effective bilingual education can build success with students who have limited English proficiency, promote greater awareness of cultural diversity, and prepare everyone for future living in a multicultural world.

Ebonics, Culture, and Language Abilities

A child's language abilities can be influenced by cultural experiences. Disadvantaged children stereotypically have a restricted vocabulary and construct sentences that are less grammatically correct than middle-class children's. Although lower-class children score lower on tests of vocabulary and sentence structure, the issue of appropriate use of grammar is controversial. A distinction needs to be made between language performance and language competence (Ashburn et al., 1986). Grammatical "correctness" may be a relative or arbitrary issue. Children whose dialect differs from middle-class white children's may be using appropriate grammatical sentences that can express clear emotional and logical thoughts. Much of the attention involving dialect has revolved around Ebonics, referred to as Black English or Black English Vernacular.

Ebonics is considered to be a dialect of American English spoken in many African American communities. The unique characteristics of Ebonics that separate it from standard English include changes in pronunciation in certain patterns, distinctive slang, and the use of different tenses (Turner, Mille, & Montgomery, 2002). The origins of Ebonics are from the culture of enslaved Americans with mixed elements from West African languages. It is considered common for oppressed people like the African slaves in the U.S. to develop a different dialect from their oppressors. The notion is that this is a subtle form of rebellion against the oppressor, helps to differentiate the group, and can foster a sense of pride among the community.

When a child says, "Me and him ain't goin' to no movie," the child is speaking an imperfect sentence according to the American school system of the larger middle-class society. However, this construction is typical in African American dialects in which the verb "to be" incorporates a tense, referred to as *habitual* (Turner et al., 2002). The habitual tense expresses an action that occurs frequently or continually. Therefore, "He be playin'" in standard English is "He's still playing," "He's always playing," or "He's been playing." "He playin'" means "He is playing currently." Such nonstandard speech is perfectly reasonable when used among members of a culture. Children with this type of language are not necessarily deficient in the ability to learn to speak standard English; they are merely the product of their environment. An important issue in children's use of Ebonics is that people, like teachers, are likely to judge someone's pronunciation as wrong and arrive at unwarranted judgments about the person's intelligence or ability.

So how should a child from this culture speak? When the child is in his or her cultural environment, it is appropriate and adaptive for him or her to speak using nonstandard grammar. When attempting to be biculturally adaptive, the child will need to speak "correctly," especially if the child is seeking socioeconomic advancement.

A controversial question is, does nonstandard grammar lead to substandard language competence? According to the language-deficit theory, this language is deficient and inferior. This deficiency affects students' academic achievement and their intellectual development. Subsequently, students' opportunities for employment advancement are limited. These language deficiencies are the result of impoverished environmental circumstances. The language difference theory argues the opposite—that nonstandard grammar does not reflect deficient language development. As noted earlier, the dialect, or use of nonstandard grammar, represents a well-ordered and highly structured language that simply differs from standard English.

The following Focus section examines the various challenges refugee children must face to succeed in their new American homeland.

FOCUS ON MULTICULTURALISM

REFUGEE CHILDREN—A NEW LIFE

Imagine traveling, sometimes by bus or boat, but mostly on foot, hundreds of miles with your family. But this isn't just a hiking trip—you are fleeing your home, village, and country from "bad people" who want to hurt you and your family. You are 7 years old. You often get hungry and tired, but there isn't much food, and there is little time to stop and take rests. You are fleeing for your lives. How do you feel—what do you think—when you cross the border and must begin a whole new life?

Within the field of child welfare, refugee children have received relatively little attention. These are children who have made international migrations because of political oppression in their home countries. Approximately 100,000 refuges are admitted into the United States each year—almost 1.3 million since 1982. Many of these refugees are children. Refugee children may arrive with immediate or extended family members or as unaccompanied minors who are placed with relatives or in foster care. The majority of these refugees have been fleeing from Southeast Asia, the former Soviet Union, Eastern Europe, Cuba, and Haiti after political upheaval in their respective countries.

On resettlement, refugee children face additional hardships. In addition to language barriers, a variety of unique stressors are experienced. First, for children who are with their families, there are often intergenerational problems. Frequently, children adopt the customs of the new country much more quickly than their parents do, resulting in a role reversal whereby children become translators of language and cultural norms for their parents. This frequently leads to a lack of respect for elders, which is an extremely important value in many of the original cultures. Second, problems may develop with child discipline; some types of discipline used in the native culture may be considered child abuse in the Unites States. A third source of stress is strong expectations for achievement placed on children by their parents. Many older refugees have given up hope for their own achievement; however, they view their children's opportunity to live a better life as redeeming their own suffering.

Another common issue is post-traumatic stress disorder. A significant number of refugee children have witnessed death, torture, rape, and/or imprisonment of family members. Disease and starvation are also common. Many refugees leave their homeland in boats and are at sea for long periods without adequate food, water, shelter, or sanitation. Frequently, when they arrive in the United States, they undergo long stays in refugee camps that have poor housing and shortages of clothing and water. All these factors contribute to post-traumatic stress.

In addition to intergenerational conflicts and post-traumatic stress, refugee children experience difficulties with **acculturation** and cultural identity. In their homes they are expected to behave in accordance with the native culture, whereas in school, they are expected to behave as Americans. Thus, they must live a dual life for which they have no role models.

In recognition of some of the unique difficulties faced by refugee children, U.S. legislative policies have been developed and implemented to provide services to this population. From the post–World War II period to 1980, refugee assistance was provided on an ad hoc basis in response to crises in different parts of the world. The Refugee Act of 1980 and the Refugee Education Assistance Act of 1980 established for the first time a set of comprehensive, permanent, and systematic policies for refugee assistance. These policies guide the provision of cash assistance, medical assistance, and social services to refugees. Services specifically for refugee children include special education, English-language training, child welfare, and health care.

Even though these policies represent an improvement, additional policy advances for refugee children and their families should be sought. Social workers who work with refugees must continue to advocate increased humanitarian treatment of refugee children. Policies should develop a long-term outlook in recognition that the achievement of refugee economic stability is a very lengthy process. Supportive services for refugee children should be aimed at promoting long-term adaptation as opposed to short-term "crisis stabilization." School-based programs for refugee children must address the multiple stressors experienced by these populations—specifically, intergenerational conflict, post-traumatic stress, and acculturation. One way to do this is through support groups that encourage children to share their feelings and experiences and develop healthy coping strategies. Intervention programs must be tailored to each ethnic group. Clearly, Soviet and Haitian children, for example, have had vastly different experiences.

Like all children, refugee children represent an investment in our nation's future. Equitable and effective policies and programs that improve these children's chances for success in adulthood will strengthen the well-being of the nation as a whole.

Based on Potocky (1996).

Attitudes and Emotions

In middle childhood, emotional development becomes prominent, especially in the context of social interactions. Many parents seek advice because their child does not respect their authority and expresses "inappropriate emotions." Children in this age group often begin to be seen as more irritable, cranky, and easily provoked. They often strike out at those who are blocking their goals. Or, equally common, children become increasingly uncomfortable with their emotions when relating to age mates, becoming embarrassed or wanting to avoid rejection. Whatever the context for interaction, emotional regulation is a key task for the middle-age child.

Emotional Competence

There are three aspects to emotional competence: experiencing emotions, expressing emotions, and understanding emotions (Denham et al., 2002). In this framework, experiencing emotions refers to both the awareness and recognition of one's own emotions and the effective regulation of one's emotional expression. When a child is selected by a team to be the soccer goalie, how does she deal with this peer endorsement? Does she simply breathe deeply and concentrate on performance prior to each game? These are efforts at emotional regulation that may or may not work. An important aspect of emotional competence is recognizing that one is experiencing an emotion.

The second aspect of emotional competence is expressiveness. Emotionally competent children are able to express their emotions in a manner that is socially appropriate to the situation. First you have to be aware that an affective message is needed, and then you have to deliver a convincing affective message. Middle-school children often struggle with "being a good sport," which is in part delivering an appropriate affective message while being aware of your emotions. In a parenting context, children must learn how regulate their anger in the face of negative consequences for a rule infraction.

Lastly, understanding emotions is crucial to emotional competence. A child needs to learn how to read other people's emotions, to learn to ask, *What is the affective message that this person is sending me?* Without knowing, the child cannot respond appropriately. Children also begin to understand that people have different emotional styles.

Social Cognition and Regulation

One of the most important concepts in understanding human behavior comes from the field of social cognition. **Social cognition** refers to the level of awareness one has regarding other people's thoughts, feelings, and intentions. Social cognition has a tremendous effect on how children relate to other children and adults. As children mature and develop, their cognitive growth gives them a new understanding of themselves and other people. Perhaps most critical is the child's developing capacity concerning role-taking abilities, or perspective-taking skills.

Social Role-Taking

Social role-taking ability, or the reduction of egocentric thought, is viewed as a critical aspect of healthy social development. Based on the early work of Piaget (1929), this concept refers to children's inability to decenter the focus of their conceptual efforts. In other words, children without role-taking abilities just can't see things from another person's perspective. Young children cannot empathize with the feelings of other people; this social cognitive capacity develops as the child grows older.

How does a child develop role-taking abilities? This skill matures through exposure to role-taking opportunities that involve an exchange of differing perspectives. Role-taking is related to moral development, which depends on a person's ability to perceive and comprehend the differing perspectives of other people. Role-taking should be considered a parallel stage to moral development; it is a necessary but not sufficient condition for moral reasoning. The next chapter discusses in greater detail aspects of moral development. For now, let's see why an understanding of role-taking has important implications for understanding and working with children.

Role-taking ability begins to change around 12 years of age, when the ability to think about oneself and one's social relations becomes more advanced (Selman, 2003). As the child grows older, he or she can begin to infer others' feelings, thoughts, and intentions. Although cognitive abilities begin to expand during this developmental period, this period is still characterized by egocentrism, or the inability to assume another person's role or viewpoint.

Role-taking ability is closely related to the development of social skills in children. Role-taking is a prerequisite for the emergence of many social behaviors, such as cooperation and altruism (Chandler, Sokol, & Wainryb, 2000). Understandings about social cognition are increasingly being linked with the development of social skills. The connection is between the variety of social behaviors that are strengthened by a child's ability to take the role of another person. One researcher, Robert Selman, has expanded the concept of social role-taking to help explain how children's friendships and peer relationships develop.

Interpersonal Awareness

Robert Selman's work has focused on what he refers to as interpersonal awareness—how the child conceives his or her own interpersonal relationships, particularly friendship and peer group relationships. Can distinctive ways of reasoning about such relationships be ordered along a developmental continuum? Furthermore, do children who have social and emotional problems reason at a different level compared with better-functioning peers? These are the questions that Selman sought to answer in his research. Before we reveal the answers, let's look a little closer at his theory of interpersonal awareness.

As we learned from the classical work of Piaget, children's physical-cognitive development proceeds according to specific stages:

0—preoperational
1—transitional preoperational
2—consolidated concrete operational
3—transitional concrete/early formal operations
4—consolidated formal operations

In a similar manner, Selman (1980; 2003) has suggested that developmental levels can account for social perspective-taking abilities:

0—undifferentiated and egocentric perspective-taking skill
1—differentiated and subjective perspective taking
2—self-reflective and reciprocal perspective taking
3—third-person and mutual perspective taking
4—societal/symbolic perspective taking

At the first stage of perspective taking, children cannot differentiate between the physical and the psychological aspects of people. Beginning with level 1, children (ages 5–9) begin to differentiate the physical and psychological characteristics of individuals. For example, they can distinguish between intentional and unintentional behavior. By level 2 (ages 7–12), major advances occur, and children can take a self-reflective view. Children recognize that there can be a difference between the physical self and the psychological self. Level 3 is known as the mutual perspective-taking level (ages 10–15), because children can take a third-person perspective; that is, they can truly see things from different perspectives. Level 4 emerges after age 12, but it may not be present until adulthood. At this level, one can think abstractly about the various levels of understanding and can recognize that each level can have a different point of view. Although this material is theoretically complex, you will see in the following section how it can be useful in understanding and working with children.

Interpersonal Awareness and Interpersonal Relationships

Continuing with Selman's theory (1980; 1990), we can take interpersonal awareness and examine how the child conceives his or her own interpersonal relationships, particularly friendship and peer-group relations. As Exhibit 8.4 indicates, there are stages of friendship and peer-group formation that relate

EXHIBIT 8.4 Developmental stages across impersonal and interpersonal awareness

	Impersonal	Interpersonal	
Stage	Cognitive	Friendship	Peer Group
0	Intuitive preoperational	Momentary physical playmate	Physical connections
1	Transitional preoperational/concrete operational	One-way assistance	Unilateral relations
2	Consolidated concrete operational	Fair-weather cooperation	Bilateral partnerships
3	Transitional concrete/early formal operational	Intimate-mutual sharing	Homogeneous community
4	Consolidated formal operational	Autonomous interdependence	Pluralistic organization

SOURCE: Adapted from "Interpersonal awareness in children," by R. L. Selman, D. Jaquette, and D. Lavin (1977), *American Journal of Orthopsychiatry, 47,* 264–274; and from *The growth of interpersonal understanding,* by R. L. Selman, copyright © 1980 Academic Press. Adapted with permission.

EXHIBIT 8.5 Stages of friendship showing sample responses

Stage	Friendship	Sample Responses
0	Momentary physical playmate	Alan, age 4, said he trusted his friend, Eric. When asked why, he said, "If I give him my toy he won't break it . . . he isn't strong enough."
1	One-way assistance	"I trust a friend if he does what I tell him."
2	Fair-weather cooperation	"Trust means if you do something for him, he will do something for you."
3	Intimate-mutual sharing	Trust is "when they can get it off their chest if they talk with you; things that are going on in your life and in the other person's life."
4	Autonomous interdependence	"Trust means that you've got to grow—the more you hold on to, the less you have. You have to have confidence in yourself as a good friend; then you'll have trust in your relationship."

Source: Based on Selman, Jaquette, and Lavin (1977).

to the physical-cognitive stages of development. For example, in the transitional preoperational/concrete operational stage, the corresponding stages are one-way assistance in friendship and unilateral relations in the peer group.

Selman's research sought to answer this question: Can distinctive ways of reasoning about relationships be ordered along a developmental continuum? Based on his research, he identified the stages shown in Exhibit 8.4.

Let's look even more closely at how to apply his work. We can take one issue that is relevant to friendship—interpersonal trust—and see how the developmental stages of friendship apply (Selman, Jaquette, & Lavin, 1977). Exhibit 8.5 shows the stage, level of friendship, and sample responses that would indicate the stage the child is in.

As Exhibit 8.5 indicates, children reason differently about trust, depending on their level of interpersonal awareness. The researchers gathered these sample responses by presenting children with different dilemmas and then asking a series of questions, such as "What is trust?" and "Why is it important for friends to trust each other in order to stay friends?" With this kind of interviewing, they established the different stages of interpersonal awareness.

By studying the levels of interpersonal awareness of normal and emotionally disturbed children, Selman hopes he can develop a set of therapeutic and educational goals oriented to developing greater maturity of interpersonal awareness. Selman's research suggests that children who have experienced extremely inconsistent or disruptive interpersonal experiences, and who manifest severe difficulties in their interpersonal relations, do not develop through the domain of social reasoning as steadily as do children with more consistent, dependable, and mutual relations with friends or peers. A 15-year-old who defines a friend as "someone who does what I want him to do" is going to have difficulty establishing friendships with adolescents, who generally perceive friendship as cooperation and reciprocal affection (Selman, Jaquette, & Lavin, 1977). How can we help children develop better ways of reasoning about friendships and peer relations? The key is providing children with role-taking opportunities and encouraging them to think in ways that expand their social reasoning

Psychological Strengths and Hazards

One of the most important psychological strengths of middle childhood is the continuing development and refinement of self-esteem or self-worth. In early childhood, conceptions of self were limited primarily to physical qualities—motor skills, sex type, and age. In middle childhood, conceptions of the self expand to include things such as ideal self, ethnic awareness, and conscience development. In middle childhood the self is most often described in terms of traitlike characteristics, such as "smart" or "shy" (Bosma & Gerlsma, 2003). In addition to gaining an expanded self-concept, children at this age begin to have a more differentiated self-concept—a more individuated view of themselves—and their self-concept becomes increasingly stable.

Self-Concept in Middle Childhood

This differentiated view of oneself is a less global view than the one held previously. Children who earlier thought of themselves as "not talented" might now recognize that, although they are not very good at sports, they are better than most children at playing a musical instrument. Children's self-concepts also become more individuated, so that they begin to see themselves as different from others, as unique: "I am the fastest person in my school." Their self-concepts are developing into a more integrated sense of who they are. Self-concept will continue to change, but the early threads of the self are being sown as children continue to develop their more complete self.

Self-concept is complex and difficult to measure; however, Harter (1985) has developed a unique measure of self-concept called the Self-Perception Profile for Children (see Exhibit 8.6 for examples of sample items). Her measure is based on children's evaluations of five aspects of self-worth:

1. Scholastic competence: feeling smart, doing well in school.
2. Behavioral conduct: not getting into trouble.
3. Physical appearance: feeling good-looking.
4. Social acceptance: feeling liked, being perceived as popular.
5. Athletic competence: being good at sports.

This measure has received a lot of praise because, unlike other measures that ask about a child's perceptions regarding his or her abilities in a variety of areas, Harter's scale breaks up the notion of self-concept into different areas. Each area then measures a child's self-concept in that domain. Exhibit 8.6 shows the multidimensional nature of self-worth. Family, peers, and school provide a context for self-worth, and five aspects of self-worth revolve around the center, which is overall self-worth.

Research using this scale has led to some interesting findings (Harter, 1999), the most important of which is that children make distinctions about their competencies in different areas. Therefore, a child's self-esteem depends on the situation or circumstance. A measure of a child's overall self-concept could be misleading because it may depend on the area being assessed. A child may have positive self-esteem in the classroom but a poor self-concept on the playground, where sports games are played.

Also important is the finding that children's evaluations of themselves resemble the way other people perceive them. For example, a child whose self-rating was high on social competence was in fact found to have a lot of friends who considered her to be a good friend. In a similar manner, a child's self-evaluation of cognitive competence was related to how teachers evaluated the child's academic achievements. These research results provide continued support for the idea that how other people perceive us has a lot to do with who we are (Harter, 1999). In this case, the "looking glass" represents how others perceive a child's self-esteem, and, as the looking-glass theory would predict, it accurately reflects the child's own self-esteem.

These findings also lend support to Erik Erikson's notion that the psychosocial crisis that 6- to 12-year-olds confront is industry versus inferiority. At this age, children measure themselves against their peers to establish a sense of who they are. The focus is on personal and social competence, or, according to Harter's research, on cognitive and social competencies. Children work hard to develop their cognitive skills (writing, reading, and arithmetic), as well as their social skills (cooperation, fairness, and receiving approval from others). Erikson's theory predicts that children who develop these skills will successfully master a sense of "industriousness," and they will be able to move on to the next stage of development, the identity crisis of adolescence.

EXHIBIT 8.6 Sample items from the Self-Perception Profile for Children

Really True	Sort of True				Sort of True	Really True
☐	☐	Some kids find it hard to make friends.	BUT	For other kids it's pretty easy.	☐	☐
☐	☐	Some kids like school because they do well in class.	BUT	Other kids don't like school because they aren't doing very well.	☐	☐
☐	☐	Some kids feel they are better than others their age are at sports.	BUT	Other kids don't feel they can play as well.	☐	☐
☐	☐	Some kids think that maybe they are not very good people.	BUT	Other kids are pretty sure that they are a good person.	☐	☐

SOURCE: Reproduced with permission from S. Harter, *Self-perception profile for children* (University of Denver, 1985).

As children enter middle childhood, their self-concepts begin to change as the result of their increasing ability to understand how other people view them. The looking-glass theory helps explain how children's self-concepts begin to change in middle childhood; they have a much better ability to look into that glass and see how their behavior can elicit certain reactions from others. Children begin to control their own actions depending on what kind of social self they want to display.

Psychological hazards do become more pronounced as children reach middle childhood. Most childhood disorders can be classified into one of two categories: problems of undercontrol and problems of overcontrol. Undercontrol problems are often referred to as externalizing problems, and overcontrol problems are referred to as internalizing problems (Achenbach & Edelbrock, 1983). **Externalizing problems** consist of behaviors that reflect a tendency to "act out"—for example, aggressive behavior like fighting, acting defiantly, and hyperactivity. **Internalizing problems** consist of behaviors that reflect an "inner state," such as anxiety, loneliness, shyness, social withdrawal, and depression. Two of the most common problems of middle childhood are attention-deficit/hyperactivity disorder (ADHD), an externalizing problem, and depression, an internalizing problem.

Internalizing and Externalizing Problems of Childhood

The following section shows how to use the Child Behavior Checklist and the internalizing and externalizing model developed by Achenbach.

Empirical Assessment: The Achenbach Child-Behavior Checklist

An empirical approach to assessment gathers systematic ratings of children from significant others, parents, teachers, and/or practitioners. One well-known approach to empirical assessment is the Child Behavior Checklist developed by Thomas Achenbach. The Child Behavior Checklist is a standardized rating scale that is typically filled out by parents and teachers. It examines behavior across a number of domains or syndromes, such as depressed, obsessive-compulsive, socially withdrawn, and aggressive. The items include statements such as "Can't concentrate," "Can't pay attention for long," and "Disobedient at home." The parent circles 2 if the item is always true or often true; 1 if the item is somewhat true or sometimes true; and 0 if the item is not true.

The checklist is scored on the Child Behavior Profile (see Exhibit 8.7). Each of the syndromes of the profile (for example, anxious/depressed, aggressive behavior) were developed through extensive research (see Achenbach, McConaughy, & Howell, 1987). To score the profile, the 1s and 2s under the syndrome are summed to obtain a total score. This score is then charted on the profile. For example, on the profile for Jenny, there were several 1s and 2s under the withdrawn syndrome. When these scores are summed, Jenny receives a score of 8, which is entered as the total on the bottom of the profile and then charted. The Child Behavior Checklist is normed, which means one can compare scores against the scores obtained from a normal population of children. For example, Jenny's score of 8 on the social-withdrawal scale is around the 98th percentile (normal range is marked on the left of the profile, and the dotted line represents the upper boundary of normal). This means that a score of 8 on the social-withdrawal scale is higher than the scores obtained by 98% of the 4- to 18-year-old girls in the normative sample.

The behavior profile for Jenny led to the following observations: Jenny's mother completed the Child Behavior Checklist during her intake visit to the Child Guidance Clinic. Two of the scales from the Child Behavior Checklist suggest problems: socially withdrawn, anxious/depressed. The anxious/depressed scale showed scores on all the items. A score of 2 was listed on four items: lonely, worthless, sad, and worried. The social-withdrawal scale had scores on six items: rather be alone, won't talk, shy, sulks, sad, and withdrawn. These results suggest some serious problems for Jenny, especially in the areas of depression and social withdrawal. The practitioner would want to seek additional information (teacher reports, observations, clinical interviews) to corroborate these results before reaching any conclusions (Achenbach, 1991). Similar caution and thoroughness should be used in assessing for the most common disorder affecting school-age children today, attention-deficit/hyperactivity disorder. The case study in the next section illustrates an approach to diagnosing ADHD.

Hyperactivity, or Attention-Deficit/Hyperactivity Disorder

Carlos was referred to the outpatient mental-health clinic by his teacher, who required that Carlos get some help to control his behavior. Carlos, age 7,

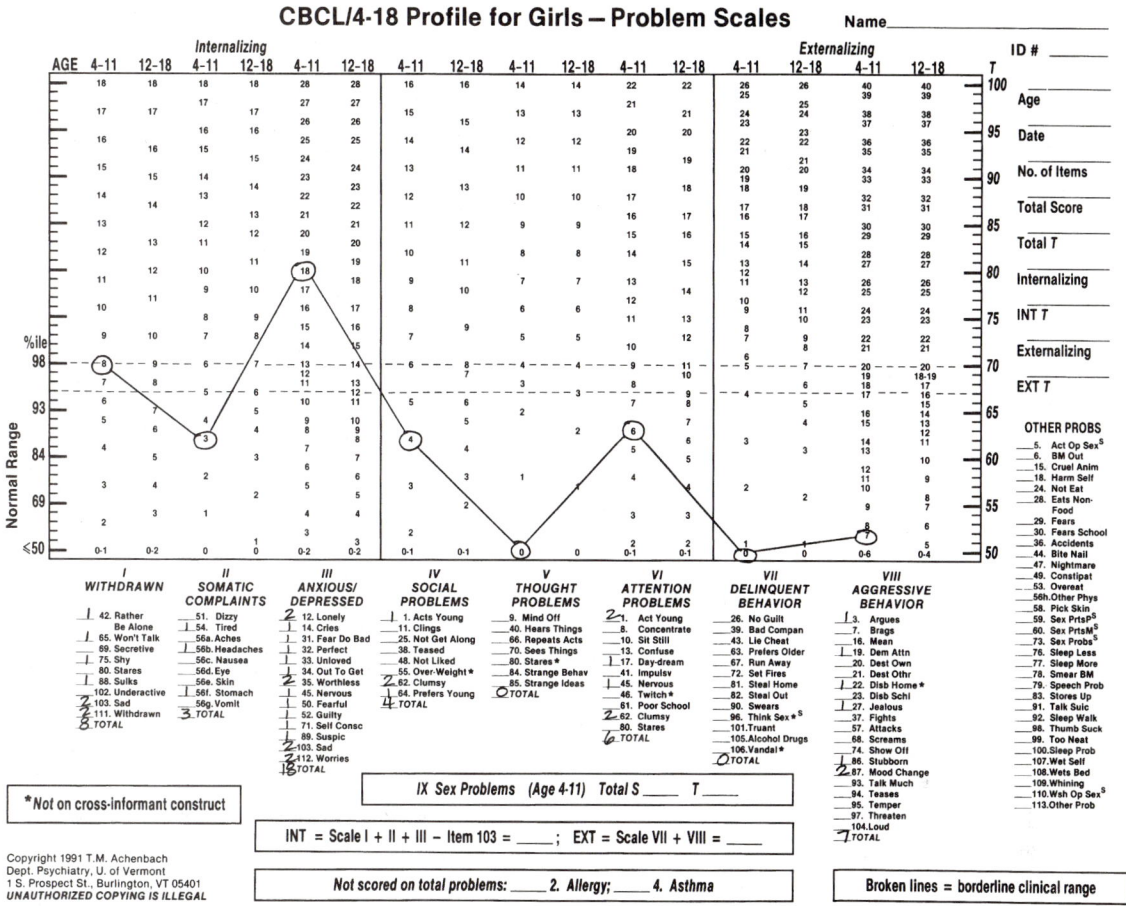

EXHIBIT 8.7 Revised Child Behavior Profile

SOURCE: From *Manual for the child behavior checklist/4-18 and 1991 profile*, by T. M. Achenbach. Copyright © 1991 T. M. Achenbach. Reproduced by permission.

demanded the attention of almost everyone around him and constantly disturbed the other children in the class. The teacher noted that Carlos could not sit still, concentrate on his work, or complete his tasks. He was always on the move. Even when sitting in his seat, Carlos fidgeted and moved about, this disturbed other students next to him. His mother reported that he was a motor mouth; was unable to stick to any one chore, task, or game; and was often found away from the house where he was not allowed to be. She described several examples of Carlos's poor judgment and problem-solving abilities.

Carlos, of course, is a typical 7-year-old boy who suffers from **attention-deficit/hyperactivity disorder (ADHD)**. Carlos has three important characteristics of the disorder: excess motor activity, impulsiveness, and inattention. ADHD is the most common neurobehavioral disorder of childhood (American Academy of Pediatrics, 2000). In fact, it is considered one of the most prevalent chronic health conditions affecting school-age children. It is a serious concern, as ADHD is associated with many psychosocial difficulties, such as poor school achievement, school difficulties, interpersonal difficulties with peers, family problems, and low self-worth (Barkley, 2000). Furthermore, ADHD present in childhood may continue into adolescence and later life. It is estimated that about 8–10% of children can be diagnosed as having ADHD and that, of those with the disorder, there are three ADHD boys for every one ADHD girl (American Academy of Pediatrics, 2000).

Although most researchers and clinicians who work with children like Carlos agree that there is a true syndrome or disorder in which you can classify such children, to do so in a reliable manner is problematic. Nylund (2002) has pointed out the many diagnostic problems that exist with ADHD. For example, the criterion "has difficulty sitting still or fidgets excessively" assumes that everyone will agree on what it means to fidget. But what is excessive fidgeting? Without any normative criteria (recorded observations of how much the average child fidgets), applying this criterion is difficult. Consider, for example, that in one study, teachers of 8-year-olds classified 43% as having short attention spans (Werry & Quay, 1971). Children at this age are often considered "bundles of energy," and a certain amount of hyperactivity occurs in children who would be considered "normal." Therefore, behavior problems in children must be considered within the context of developmental norms. A child with ADHD is developmentally abnormal; otherwise, many average children would be classified as hyperactive.

To assist in proper identification, checklists have been developed that can help in identifying children who are likely to suffer from ADHD. Usually parents or teachers are asked to fill out a checklist indicating which behaviors are characteristic of the child. A rating scale is then used in assessing ADHD in children. There are many types of rating scales available. A new and easy-to-use scale is the SWAN rating scale (Swanson, 2004) which is shown in Exhibit 8.8. Although rating scales are helpful in diagnosis, multiple sources of information are needed to confirm a diagnosis of ADHD. Smucker and Hedayat (2001) suggested the following questions be answered before a diagnosis of ADHD can be confirmed:

1. Do the child's symptoms fulfill DSM-IV criteria for the diagnosis of ADHD?
2. Does the child have normal vision and hearing?
3. Does the child's history suggest the presence of a comorbid psychiatric disorder?
4. Does the child have a learning disorder?
5. Has the child's development proceeded normally?
6. How has the family responded to the child's behavior?
7. Do the findings of the child's history or physical examination suggest the need for additional diagnostic testing?

Researchers are still unclear about the causes of hyperactivity. It used to be thought that hyperactivity was caused by some form of brain dysfunction; in fact, hyperactivity used to be referred to as "minimal brain dysfunction." Much research has been conducted to investigate the role of brain dysfunction in hyperactivity. Researchers believe that the most likely cause of ADHD is an imbalance in the brain's neurotransmitter chemicals. Research has found that the levels of glucose used by the areas of the brain that inhibit impulses and control attention show significant differences between individuals who have ADHD and those who do not. Glucose is a measure of the brain's activity level because it is the brain's main source of energy. Overall, the evidence suggests that there are genetic factors in ADHD (American Academy of Pediatrics, 2000).

ADHD and Medication

Many people are familiar with the pharmacological treatment of children with ADHD. A high percentage of children diagnosed with ADHD receive some form of medication (for example, Ritalin, Dexedrine, Cylert, or Benzedrine). The majority of children are helped by the medication, which increases the child's ability to sustain attention. The well-designed Multimodal Treatment Study of Children with ADHD compared four treatments: medication alone, behavioral treatment alone, combined medication and behavioral treatment, and community care (MTA Cooperative Group, 1999). The study found that the combination treatment did not improve core ADHD symptoms better than medication alone, but both treatments were better than community care. The fact that behavioral treatment was nearly equal in effectiveness to community care confirmed the utility of behavioral treatment for parents who prefer not to use psychotropic medications. Most professionals (e.g., the American Academy of Child and Adolescent Psychiatry) recommend a multimodal treatment plan. It is important to note that medications have little effect on the child's functioning in educational or social domains.

Although it is clear that medication helps ADHD children in the short term, the long-term benefit of medication has been questioned. In addition, many practitioners are concerned about the side effects of medication on children. Two common reactions to medication for hyperactivity are appetite reduction and sleep disturbance (Smucker & Hedayat, 2001). In spite of these problems, medication seems to make children less distractible. It also enhances the way classmates perceive the hyperactive child, which may produce important social benefits.

Most experts believe that medication should be supplemented by behavioral treatment. This hunch was confirmed by studies that have found that the combination of medication with cognitive-behavioral treatment produced the most benefit. Thus, it seems necessary to provide treatment beyond medication that will address academic performance, an

EXHIBIT 8.8 The New SWAN (Swanson) Scale

Name: _____ Gender: _____ Age: _____ Grade: _____

Completed by: _____ Class size: _____ Type of Classroom: _____

Ethnicity (circle one which best applies):   African-American   Asian   Caucasian   Hispanic   Other

Children differ in their abilities to focus attention, control activity, and inhibit impulses. For each item listed below, how does this child compare to other children of the same age? Please select the best rating based on your observations over the past month.

Compared to other children, how does this child do the following:	Far below avg.	Below avg.	Slightly below avg.	Avg.	Slightly above avg.	Above avg.	Far above avg.
1. Give close attention to detail and avoid careless mistakes	___	___	___	___	___	___	___
2. Sustain attention on tasks or play activities	___	___	___	___	___	___	___
3. Listen when spoken to directly	___	___	___	___	___	___	___
4. Follow through on instructions and finish school work or chores	___	___	___	___	___	___	___
5. Organize tasks and activities	___	___	___	___	___	___	___
6. Engage in tasks that require sustained mental effort	___	___	___	___	___	___	___
7. Keep track of things necessary for activities	___	___	___	___	___	___	___
8. Ignore extraneous stimuli	___	___	___	___	___	___	___
9. Remember daily activities	___	___	___	___	___	___	___
10. Sit still (control movement of hands and feet or control squirming)	___	___	___	___	___	___	___
11. Stay seated (when required by class rules or social conventions)	___	___	___	___	___	___	___
12. Modulate motor activity (inhibit inappropriate running or climbing)	___	___	___	___	___	___	___
13. Play quietly (keep noise level reasonable)	___	___	___	___	___	___	___
14. Settle down and rest (control constant activity)	___	___	___	___	___	___	___
15. Modulate verbal activity (control excess talking)	___	___	___	___	___	___	___
16. Reflect on questions (control blurting out answers)	___	___	___	___	___	___	___
17. Await turn (stand in line and take turns)	___	___	___	___	___	___	___
18. Enter into conversations and games without interrupting or intruding	___	___	___	___	___	___	___

ADHD-In	ADHD-H/Im
#1 ___	#10 ___
#2 ___	#11 ___
#3 ___	#12 ___
#4 ___	#13 ___
#5 ___	#14 ___
#6 ___	#15 ___
#7 ___	#16 ___
#8 ___	#17 ___
#9 ___	#18 ___
Total = ___	= ___
Average = ___	= ___

The 7-point response is scored +3 to −3 (far below avg. = 3, below avg. = 2, slightly below avg. = 1, average = 0, slightly above avg. = −1, above average = −2, and far above average = −3). Subscale scores on the SWAN are calculated by summing the scores on the items in the specific subset (e.g., inattention) and dividing by the number of items (e.g., 9) to express the summary score as the average rating-per-item.

SOURCE: Swanson (1995). © 1985 by J. M. Swanson, Child Development Center at UC Irvine. Reproduced by permission.

aspect of behavior not affected by medication. Chase and Clement (1985) found that having children set goals for reading assignments and give themselves points to exchange for reinforcers increased both the amount of work completed and its accuracy.

In many instances medication makes sense for children, but are we overmedicating children? Although the Food and Drug Administration (FDA) forbids the marketing of antidepressants, such as Prozac, for children, it is hard not to view candy-flavored pills as a move in that direction (Prozac comes in peppermint flavor). Even with the FDA's mandate, physicians have prescribed psychiatric medications to children for a number of "off-label" uses. For example, in 1996, doctors wrote 735,000 prescriptions for Prozac, Ritalin, and other psychiatric medications for children ages 6 to 18—an 80% increase in two years. Still, a recent report in the *Journal of the American Medical Association* claims that charges of overdiagnosis and overmedication of children with ADHD are exaggerated (Goldman et al., 1998).

Although some practitioners believe the trend means children are finally getting the treatment they need, others are concerned about inadequate research, the substitution of medications for behavioral treatments, and the fact that some psychotropic drugs do not seem to work on children. Physicians often lack crucial information on drugs' effects on children. They may not know the long-term effects on developing physiology or even the proper dosages to give. Further complicating these issues is that psychotropic medication for very young children has increased substantially in the last decade (Coyle, 2000). Opponents view the trend as an epidemic of inappropriate prescribing.

It is hard not to see an economic motivation behind all the prescriptions for children. The cost of a 100-tablet bottle of Ritalin, for example, begins at about $50, making it a far less expensive alternative than behavioral therapy and a far more attractive choice to insurers cutting costs. Further, many doctors are writing prescriptions without ordering psychological or educational tests.

A related problem is that once the FDA approves a drug to treat a particular condition, any physician may prescribe it to any patient, regardless of age. And the push to put children on these drugs comes from everyday people—parents and teachers. Some overly rambunctious children have been sent home with a note from the principal saying they may not return to school unless they have a Ritalin prescription. As mentioned in the previous section, teachers are given checklists of behavior that could be symptoms of ADHD, as though they can diagnose it. Effective treatment of ADHD is complicated, and we need to be open to both medical and behavioral treatment options.

STUDY TABLE: Psychological dimension in middle childhood

Cognitive Development and Information Processing	Children at this age operate from concrete operational thought; that is, thought processes are governed by rules of logic. This stage is characterized by becoming less egocentric. Children can show reversible thought and conservation skills. For example, they understand that certain transformations do not change the quantitative features of objects. Although Piaget's ideas have withstood the test of time, it is now recognized that cognitive changes do not proceed according to predetermined sequences of stages. As a result, levels is a better conceptual notion than *stages*. Information processing is also relevant to a child's social relationships. Research has found that skill deficits in how children process information may influence their behavioral interactions. Children's intelligence is often measured with an IQ test. IQ is measured by dividing mental age by chronological age and multiplying by 100. The Stanford-Binet is a widely used IQ test that includes four areas: verbal reasoning, quantitative reasoning, abstract/visual reasoning, and short-term memory. It has a mean of 100 and a standard deviation of 16. Other similar tests used with children include the Wechsler tests and the Kaufman Assessment Battery for children, based on the Das-Luria model of cognitive functioning. Concerns about the use of IQ tests include the labeling and clas-

sification of children, and cultural bias. Information processing evaluates (1) how knowledge develops; (2) the processes and strategies of the knowledge base and retrieval of that information; and (3) the child's metacognition. Emotional intelligence (EQ) describes qualities such as understanding one's own feelings, empathy for the feelings of others, and regulating emotions in ways that enhance life. The concept of EQ is becoming more important for educators, who notice the effect of negative emotions on students' abilities to learn.

Communication

Middle childhood is considered a period of linguistic refinement. As children develop their language skills, they become capable of metalinguistic awareness and appreciate humor in jokes, riddles, and puns. Children who are deaf learn language in much the same manner as hearing children. As communication becomes increasingly important for the social life of children, deficits in communication have social consequences. For example, speech disorders like stuttering can lead to academic as well as emotional difficulties.

Verbal control develops as children move from external control to covert self-verbalizations. Self-instructional training is a major treatment approach for children who have difficulties with self-control. Bilingual children can have both positive and negative outcomes, depending on how the two languages are used. A child's language abilities can be influenced by cultural experiences. Disadvantaged children have a restricted vocabulary and construct sentences that are less grammatically correct than those of middle-class students.

Attitudes and Emotions

Emotional development becomes prominent, especially in the context of social interactions. Middle-age children often are seen as more irritable, crankier, and more easily provoked. Emotional competence has three aspects: experiencing emotions, expressing emotions, and understanding emotions.

Social Cognition and Regulation

Social role taking is the reduction of egocentric thought, egocentric thoughts being children's inability to decenter the focus of their conceptual efforts. Role-taking ability—to see things from another person's perspective—changes around 12 years of age, when a child can think about himself or herself and social relations become more advanced. A child's interpersonal awareness can be ordered along a developmental continuum, and concepts such as friendship and peer groups can be viewed as a series of steps through which children progress. How children think and reason about such concepts can influence their adjustment. Children may benefit from training that helps facilitate this reasoning.

Psychological Strengths and Hazards

One of the most important strengths of middle childhood is the continuing development and refinement of self-esteem or self-worth. The differentiated view of oneself is a less global view than the one held previously and more individuated. The Self-Perception Profile for Children is a measure of self-concept that includes scholastic competence, behavioral conduct, physical appearance, social acceptance, and athletic competence. Childhood disorders can be divided into two categories: externalizing problems of overcontrol, and internalizing problems of undercontrol. ADHD, an externalizing disorder, is a common disorder (8-10% of children; three boys for every one girl) that affects a child's attention and activity levels. Medication alone is commonly used to treat this disorder, but a combination of medication and behavioral treatment is recommended. The most likely cause of ADHD is an imbalance in the brain's neurotransmitters.

CONCEPT MAP

Social Dimension

Families and Groups

Family strength is an important concept that has dramatically influenced social-work practice. Social workers are increasingly concerned about offering families opportunities to use their strengths. For too long, social workers did not recognize family strengths and instead were concerned only with a family's pathology. Today, family strength is emphasized, because we recognize that the family environment holds the key to unlocking a child's capacity to grow and develop in a healthy manner.

A child can grow up in many different family contexts—as one of ten other children with little or no individual parental attention; in a family with an alcoholic parent; as the target of a stepparent's physical and sexual abuse; or in poverty and with gang warfare and drug abuse as part of everyday life. In contrast, children also can grow up in large families whose members care deeply about one another and work together to provide for themselves; in families where alcoholism afflicts one of the parents but an abiding love exists between the parents; in situations where child abuse has devastated and torn apart families but they have worked to create a new context in which they can live peacefully together; and in situations where poverty and drug abuse are all around but where enough love exists to protect against negative influences. All children are caught in the complex web of family relationships that significantly shape their future.

Normal Family Processes

By the time children reach late childhood, they spend much less time with parents and more time with peers. Studies have found that parents spend less than half as much time with their children between the ages of 5 and 12 than they did before. However, the family continues to be an extremely important influence on the child. At this age, the family provides an important base for the child to continue growing and developing. Children need the safe, authoritative structure that parents can provide. Although children show less love and respect for their parents, they depend on them for unconditional love and as sources of information and authority. The role of discipline continues to be critical to good parenting.

Parental Discipline

Three major parental disciplinary strategies identified by Hoffman (1970) are **power-assertive discipline**, which includes physical punishment, threat of punishment, and physical attempts to control the child's behavior; **love withdrawal**, which involves withdrawing love when the child's behavior is viewed as inappropriate; and **induction**, which involves the use of explanation and rationality in attempting to influence the child's actions.

What effects do these different strategies of parental discipline have on children? Research studies have shown that parents who use power assertion (punishment) increase their children's aggressive tendencies. There are several possible explanations of why punishment would lead to aggressive behavior in children. As you learned earlier, parents who act aggressively toward their children provide a model of aggressive behavior for the child to imitate. Also, children involved in physical confrontations with their parents learn that this is how disputes are resolved—through fighting, arguing, and threats of punishment. Have you ever observed a child being physically punished by his or her parents? You may also have noticed the child is embarrassed and ashamed, and that the punishment demeans the child. Children with low self-worth may be more likely to respond with aggressive behavior in the absence of more appropriate social skills.

Parents who use love withdrawal do so by verbally discounting children, threatening to send the children away, and indicating to the children that they are not loved because of their actions. Love withdrawal also includes parental actions such as persistently ignoring the child, refusing to talk with the child (the silent treatment), and generally not interacting with the child. Of course, this behavior is unfair and often makes the child fearful. Research has found that this form of parenting can lead to excessive anxiety in children and inhibit needed expression of emotions (Hoffman, 1970).

Consider the difference between these two types of parental discipline strategies: "Chen, get in this house right now! If you don't do as I say, I'll take the paddle to your butt"; and "Chen, you need to come in and get ready for dinner. Your aunt is expecting us later tonight and we don't want to be late." How would a child feel in response to these two statements? The first response is likely to elicit anger and resentment, whereas the second response is more likely to elicit cooperation and understanding. The use of induction helps the child develop an understanding of why he or she should act in the requested manner. Other examples include telling a child, "Please don't climb on that wall, because it isn't strong enough to hold your weight" (appeal to prevent injury); "You can't watch TV tonight because you broke our rule about no more throwing temper tantrums" (appeal to fairness); "Don't chew food with your mouth open—that's not appropriate at the dinner table" (appeal to standards of conduct).

Induction is an important parental strategy because it helps children develop internal moral standards (Turiel, 2000). Children disciplined by induction methods gain experience in exercising self-control and learn to display more consideration and generosity toward others when compared with children who have been disciplined with power-assertion techniques (Turiel, 2000). Induction is really a strategy based on principles of moral development. Understanding a child's social, cognitive, and moral development supports successfully using such discipline strategies. An understanding of parental discipline styles is pivotal in helping parents learn effective parenting techniques.

Implications for Practice: Models of Parent Training

Many social workers are called on to do some form of parent training. They may run parent-training groups for parents of noncompliant children, work directly with foster parents, or conduct parent-training classes to help prepare pregnant adolescents to become better parents. Indeed, parent-training courses have been introduced everywhere—in schools, hospitals, community mental-health centers, and churches. Professionals approach parent training from many different perspectives, ranging from humanistic to psychoanalytic, and although there are some similarities, there are also some important differences. Let's examine four of the more popular approaches to parent training you will likely come across in your work: parent-effectiveness training (Gordon, 2000); parent-involvement training (reality therapy for parents, inspired by William Glasser); behavior modification (Forehand & Long, 1996; Barkely, 2000); and systematic training for effective parenting (Adlerian therapy for parents, originated by Dreikurs

and best represented by the work of Dinkmeyer et al., 1997). We will briefly examine some of the fundamental principles involved in each of these approaches (based on Brown, 1976; Jaffe, 1991; Smith, Perou, & Lesesne, 2002).

Parent-Effectiveness Training (P.E.T.)

This humanist approach to parenting emphasizes the need for respect between parent and child. Central to Gordon's ideas about parenting is his complete rejection of parental power. P.E.T. encourages parents to give up, forever, the use of power. He has argued two reasons for this. First, power is damaging to people and relationships, and second, it undermines P.E.T.'s no-lose method of resolving conflicts. Another interesting concept in P.E.T. is its conceptualization of children's behavior. P.E.T. holds that there is no such thing as children's misbehavior; children simply behave. All behavior is aimed at getting needs met.

The first strategy of P.E.T. is to encourage parents and children to enlarge the no-problem aspect of their relationships. This goal can be accomplished via approaches such as environmental modification—putting things where children can't reach them—or minding your own business, or relaxing and staying calm.

When this doesn't work, the parent turns to the critical techniques of P.E.T. The parent is taught to first ask the question "Who owns the problem?" If the child owns the problem, the parent learns to use active listening. For example, the child comes home and is upset because her homework was lost and so wasn't turned in to the teacher. The parent is taught to help the child understand, accept, and deal with her feelings: "You really look upset—it means a lot to you to get your homework turned in on time." Often a parent's inclination is to use other ineffective strategies, including getting mad at the child, attempting to reassure the child, or presenting rationalizations or solutions.

When the behavior is unacceptable to the parent, the parent owns the problem, and the first strategy is to use I-messages: "I really need some quiet time—could you please turn off the stereo?" Parents are taught to use this rather than the familiar you-message: "You always have to turn the stereo up too loud." These messages, according to P.E.T., only demean the child and can be damaging to the child's self-esteem.

When active listening and I-messages do not resolve the problem, the parent turns to the no-lose method of problem solving. The parent elicits the child's cooperation in problem solving and follows these six steps: (1) define the conflict; (2) use brainstorming with the child to generate solutions; (3) evaluate the solutions on the list; (4) see if there is a solution that satisfies both parties, and, if so; (5) decide how to implement it; and (6) evaluate the solution later to see if it worked.

Parent-Involvement Training (P.I.T.)

A large part of the P.I.T. program focuses on getting parents involved. The P.I.T. theory holds that no behavior change can take place without a helping relationship based on trust, warmth, and respect. You must believe in your child for any behavior or self-concept to change. P.I.T. uses direct strategies for getting kids involved, including teaching parents to stop what they are doing and attend to their children, especially if the children are upset. Other strategies involve specific instructions for things such as dinnertime conversations and games to play. The program is based on seven steps:

1. Establish and maintain involvement. Strongly recommended is conversation—talking about topics of mutual interest.
2. Help children see what their current behavior is and understand that it is something they have chosen. Although feelings are important, behavior is critical.
3. Suggest that children evaluate their behavior. Self-judgment is stressed by asking children whether what they are doing is helping them.
4. Help children plan increasingly responsible behavior. Help them set realistic goals and have successful experiences.
5. Get children to make a commitment to the plan. Contracts like this increase their motivation and involvement.
6. Accept no excuses; if children fail to meet the commitment, start again with step 3.
7. Don't use punishment. This can cause the children physical or mental pain and may lead to loneliness, isolation, or hostility. Instead, use praise for successes—it will encourage involvement.

Behavior Modification

The use of behavior modification in parent training involves teaching parents how to apply the principles of behavior to their children. The principles of behavior include concepts such as reinforcement, punishment, extinction, differential reinforcement of other behaviors, and stimulus control. Parent-training programs usually start out by teaching parents how to define the behavior they would like to see changed. After learning how to define behavior precisely, parents choose a home project to begin to put the principles to work. Parents must choose a behavior, define it, and develop a method of tracking and record-keeping. If parents are working on reducing the number of temper tantrums, they must define what a temper tantrum is and record this behavior. Often they chart the behavior for a week or more with graph paper in order to assess the extent of the problem and to have a comparison after introducing an intervention.

Parents are then taught ways to either increase or decrease behaviors. Most parents choose to implement a reinforcement program based either on praise (social reinforcement) or on a home-style token economy, where points are exchanged for tangible reinforcement (money, prizes, or special privileges). When working to decrease behaviors, parents are taught to use various forms of punishments. For example, a parent working on reducing bedtime crying may use extinction, which involves ignoring the behavior (because the parent's attention was what kept the child crying night after night). Two of the most widely used punishments are time-out and the withdrawal of privileges. Time-out is time without reinforcement, and the child must sit quietly in a chair in the corner of a room for 2–6 minutes. The strategy is to make the time-out boring and unrewarding to the child. Withdrawal of privileges is often used on older children in conjunction with token economies. When unacceptable behaviors continue, the child loses a predetermined privilege. For example, a parent trying to reduce sibling fights would withdraw the privilege of watching TV that night for any instance of fighting during the day.

Most behavior-modification programs work hard to teach parents the hidden value of using praise and reinforcement with their children. Parents are encouraged to increase the use of praise dramatically. They are taught to rewrite rules using positive language, to record and increase the number of times they use praise, to make and display cards to encourage praise (like "catch your child being good"), and to display charts proudly showing the progress that the child is making.

Systematic Training for Effective Parenting (STEP)

This approach to parent training rests on the belief that a misbehaving child is a discouraged child. The STEP program teaches parents that there are four goals to a child's misbehavior: attention, power, revenge, and inadequacy. STEP teaches parents to use techniques of encouragement and discipline. Encouragement strategies emphasize giving the child a lot of responsibility and avoiding overprotection and unnecessary service. Whereas most parents will serve the child by pouring the child's milk, STEP recommends letting the child pour his or her own milk. If the child spills it, wipe it up and let the child try it again. STEP strongly recommends that parents not be overprotective but allow children to learn from their own behavior. This is well demonstrated by the STEP approach to discipline.

Discipline involves the use of natural and logical consequences. Again, the idea is to get parents to allow children the opportunity to experience the effects of their choices and behavior—good and bad. Unlike behavior modification, in which parents reward and punish the child's behavior (which means the parents are responsible for the child's behavior), STEP says children should be allowed to make their own decisions. If their choice is good, they experience the benefits; if their choice is bad, they suffer the consequences. This encourages children's actions to become more responsible and adult oriented, guided by natural outcomes and not by parental interference.

The idea behind **natural consequences** is that they follow directly from the child's behavior in the absence of parental intervention. For example, children who arrive home late and miss dinner will have to prepare their own dinner. Children who leave the house without a coat will have to deal with being cold. Children who miss the bus are expected to walk to school. These are natural consequences because they follow directly from the behavior. When this is not possible because natural consequences are not available or would be dangerous, STEP teaches parents to use **logical consequences**. For example, if the parent cannot trust the child to play outside, the child must play inside; or if the child colors on the wall with a crayon, the crayons are taken away. Natural and logical consequences are considered preferable to rewards and punishments because they avoid power struggles and give children the opportunity to learn from real-life consequences.

Exhibit 8.9 presents a summary of the different models of parent education. All approaches to parent education stress that proper parenting is essential to the welfare of our society (Smith et al., 2002). What greater responsibility exists than to parent a child? Parenting is a demanding job that provides many benefits for children and society. Surprisingly, reviews of parent education (See Smith et al., 2002) have found we know a lot about child development and parenting but have a long way to go to understand what factors influence parents in ways that benefit child outcomes. Still, parent-education programs emphasize the fundamental principle of a strong parent-child relationship. Many of the programs focus on "behavior management," but this is done through positive, caring, and skillful interactions with the child. Although there is a clear mandate for parent education, and parent-education programs have much to offer, practitioners often find parent recruitment the biggest obstacle to helping parents.

EXHIBIT 8.9 Parent education models

Model Developer	Major Assumptions/Goals	Key Ideas
Parent-Effectiveness Training (Gordon)	Humanist approach. Parents should give up use of power.	Ask, "Who owns the problem?" to focus efforts. When child owns problem, use active listening. If parent owns the problem, use "I" messages. If these fail, use no-lose method of problem solving.
Parent Involvement Training (Glasser)	Helping relationship between child and parent is critical. Goal is to get parents more involved with their children.	Talk to your child about topics of mutual interest. Help child understand behavior is a choice. Help children use self-judgment and evaluation. Encourage responsibility, goal setting, and planning.
Parent Training (use of behavioral methods) (Forehand & Long; Barkley)	Changing children's behavior involves effective use of the principles of behavior (e.g., reinforcement).	Define behaviors to change. Track and monitor progress. Implement a behavioral plan (e.g., praise, token economy, time out). Be consistent in approach.
Systematic Training for Effective Parenting (STEP) (Dinkeyer et al.)	Adlerian approach. Need to understand the child's goals for misbehavior. Focus on developing child's responsibility for behaviors.	Four goals of misbehavior: attention, power, revenge, and inadequacy. Focus is giving child increased responsibility, avoiding overprotection, and using natural and logical consequences.

Groups

In middle childhood, children increasingly begin to prefer spending time with their peers. This shift is clearly illustrated by Exhibit 8.10, from a study by Ellis, Rogoff, and Cromer (1981). The figure reveals the dramatic increase of child companions from age 1 to age 8. This increase is accompanied by a similar decrease in the number of adult companions. Also interesting is the fact that these children actually spent less time with age-mates (children within one year of their age) than with children who were either younger or older.

What makes a peer group? Is it just a few children who are similar in age and who hang out together? Apparently not, because researchers have defined **peer groups** as groups of age-mates that are durable and involve interactions based on an established set of social relationships. Peer groups have shared values and goals. Often, children in cliques are identified by their similar social prejudices, speech, and/or clothing styles. Within the group, each individual will have a certain role or status. Although formal groups often elect individuals to certain roles, like team leader, similar roles emerge naturally in informal peer groups. Let's examine the ways that peer groups are formed, as well as the social interactions within peer groups and their possible influences on members' behavior.

Group Formation

As children increase the number of stable encounters they have with age-mates, they begin to form groups. These groups often start when the child enters school and has increased regular contact with peers. Peer groups are important throughout the life course, but their nature and function change. Preschool children describe friends in terms of reciprocity ("we play"): elementary-school children describe friends in terms of loyalty, trustworthiness, and time spent together; and preadolescents describe friends in terms of sympathy, self-disclosures, and intimacy (Hartup & Abecassis, 2002).

In early middle childhood, children are involved in informal groups that lack much structure. Few rules govern the behavior of the members, and there is a high turnover in membership. As a result, the influence of peer groups is limited until the child reaches late childhood. Beginning with the junior high school years, group formation becomes increasingly important and peer relationships take on a new significance. At this age, groups become more formalized and roles emerge more clearly, as do the social rules that govern the groups—for example, "We only allow girls from our soccer group." Children begin to feel a cohesiveness that binds them to the group's values.

The most famous study of group formation was done by Sherif and colleagues (1961), who conducted a fascinating experiment with boys in a camp setting. The children were divided arbitrarily into two groups, and many of the boys resented being separated from their friends. As the groups participated in separate activities, group members' cooperation and cohesiveness developed. Soon, each group had developed its own rules of conduct, leadership hierarchy, and status relationships. The children in each group now identified more closely with peers from their own group. The experiment continued by bringing the two groups together for an intergroup conflict phase. The children were exposed to win-lose competition and planned frustration to increase the tension between the groups. These activities increased the level of animosity harbored by the two groups. In the last phase of the experiment, the researchers explored ways to reduce the intergroup conflict. When Sherif

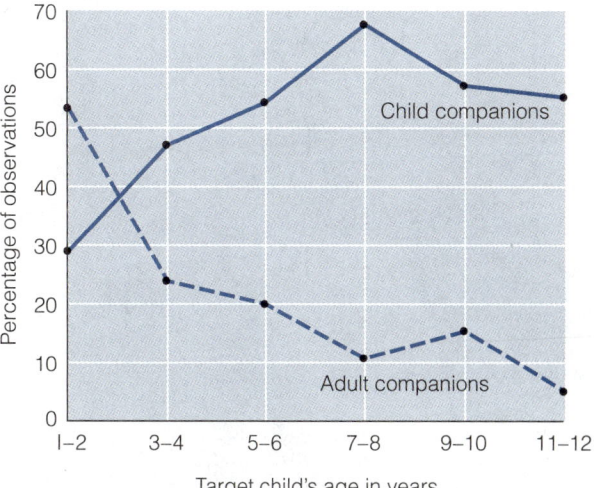

EXHIBIT 8.10 Developmental changes in children's companionship with children and adults

SOURCE: From "Age segregation in children's social interactions," by S. Ellis, B. Rogoff, and C. C. Cromer (1981) *Developmental Psychology*, 17, 399–407. Copyright © 1981 American Psychological Association. Reprinted with permission.

and colleagues sought to reduce the conflict, they brought the two groups together under noncompetitive conditions. However, this only heightened the conflict. When the two groups were brought together to work on a common goal that required cooperation (the researchers deliberately broke a water line so both groups would have to help), the boys were able to reduce the conflict.

This study has many important implications. First, the study illustrated the importance of cooperation and common goals in the formation of cohesive groups. It also showed that groups, independent of any previously shared interest, can develop bad feelings and learn to discriminate against an "out" group. The study found that competition and frustration could increase hostility between groups. Lastly, the study found that such hostility could be reduced when a common goal is introduced and groups are required to work together. Additional studies have supported the notion that cooperative activities can decrease negative social behaviors that sometimes emerge in groups (Richard et al., 2002).

The Power of Peers

Early research by Merrill Roff (1963) was groundbreaking in its discovery of the importance of peers for healthy psychological development. Roff conducted a number of follow-up studies that examined children who had poor peer relationships and found that years later, as adults, these people had more than the usual number of mental-health adjustments, had more problems adjusting to military service, and had more serious mental-health problems.

Peer groups are important throughout a child's development. In early middle childhood, they are informal and lack structure, but by late middle childhood, peer groups become more formalized, with distinct roles and social rules governing them.

These studies now confirm Roff's early hunches that difficulties in social adjustment are likely to lead to poor mental health. Research by Cowen and colleagues (1973) demonstrated the predictive power of not getting along with peers. His well-known study began by identifying first-grade children who were having poor peer relationships and were thought to be at increased risk for mental-health problems. To test his idea, he followed several first-grade classes until the children reached early adulthood. He found that the children identified to be at increased risk because of poor peer relationships were disproportionately represented as suffering from psychiatric problems as adults. Research has confirmed that peer acceptance and rejection are integral to group functioning in middle childhood (Smith & Hart, 2002).

Even more interesting for social workers was Cowen's finding that assessment of children's social competence by their peers is a more powerful predictor of later behavior problems than assessment by parents, teachers, or mental-health practitioners. Indeed, we now realize that peers are crucial to the healthy development of a child—perhaps second in importance only to the influence of parents. People have an innate desire for human companionship, and peer friendship is critical if we are to feel connected and socially involved with one another. The following letter is from an adult who was deprived of peer friendships while growing up (Hartup, 1979, p. 155):

> I am an only child, now 57 years old, and I want to tell you some things about my life. Not only was I an only child, but I grew up in the country where there were no nearby children to play with. My mother did not want children around. She used to say, "I don't want my kid to bother anybody and I don't want nobody's kids bothering me."
>
> From the first year of school I was teased and made fun of. For example, in about third or fourth grade I dreaded to get on the school bus to go to school because the other children on the bus called me "Mommy's baby." In about the second grade I heard a vulgar word. I asked what it meant, and they made fun of me. So I learned a lesson—don't ask questions. This can lead to a lot of confusion to hear talk one doesn't understand and not be able to learn what it means . . . I never went out with a girl while I was in school—in fact I hardly talked to them. In our school the boys and girls did not play together. Boys were sent to one part of the playground and girls to another. So, I didn't learn anything about girls. When we got into high school and the boys and girls started dating, I could only listen to their stories about their experiences.
>
> I could tell you a lot more, but the important thing is I have never married or had any children. I have not been successful in an occupation or vocation. I believe my troubles are not all due to being an only child . . . but I do believe you are right in recommending playmates for preschool children, and I will add playmates for the school-agers and not have them strictly supervised by adults. I believe I confirm the experiments with monkeys in being overly timid sometimes and overly aggressive sometimes. Parents of only children should make special efforts to provide playmates for [their children].

This letter supports various research studies that have documented the significance of good peer relationships. Reviews of the literature (Hartup, 1979; Hartup & Abecassis, 2002) have summarized the importance of friends and enemies on child development and made the following conclusions:

- Poor peer relations are associated with discomfort, anxiety, and a general unwillingness to engage the environment.
- Children master their aggressive impulses within the context of peer relations.
- Sexual socialization cannot take place in the absence of peer interaction.
- Peer relations are related to role-taking ability, empathy, and moral reasoning.
- Children who are rejected by their peers are at greater risk for delinquency, school dropout, and mental-health problems.

Friendships are critical because they provide opportunities for learning social skills and a beginning sense of group belonging. The recent emphasis on peer relationships has stimulated research and program development in two areas, social-skills training and social cognition.

Teaching Isolated Children Social Skills for Friendship Making

A well-known study that taught children social skills was conducted by Oden and Asher (1977). This study was designed to assess coaching as a method of training socially isolated children in social skills for gains in peer acceptance. Children (ages 9–10) were selected for this study on the basis of the results of a sociometric assessment that used a roster-and-rating questionnaire. Children rated each other

EXHIBIT 8.11

Interpersonal model of school adjustment

SOURCE: Reprinted with permission from G. W. Ladd et al., "Children's interpersonal skills and relationships in school settings: Adaptive significance and implication for school-based prevention and intervention programs," p. 296, in P. K. Smith and C. H. Hart (Eds.), *Blackwell handbook of childhood social development* © Blackwell.

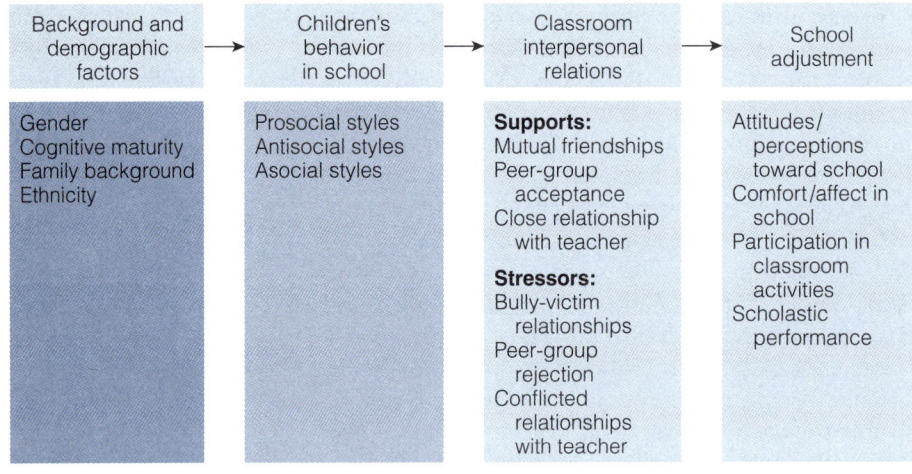

in answer to two questions administered separately during the same session: "How much do you like to play with this person at school?" and "How much do you like to work with this person at school?" The children used a rating scale consisting of five points from 1 ("I don't like to") to 5 ("I like to a lot"). Based on these results, children who were rated as less accepted became the participants in the study. These children were randomly assigned to one of three groups: coaching, peer pairing, or control. The coaching group included instructions from an adult in social skills for friendship making; playing games with peers to practice social skills; and a postplay review session with the coach. In the peer-pairing group, isolated children played the same games with the same peers but did not receive instruction or review. In the control group, isolated children were taken out of the classroom with the same peers but did not interact or receive verbal instruction or review. To measure the effectiveness of the intervention, the researchers used the sociometric measure previously described and a "best friends" peer-nomination inventory in which children were asked to name one, two, or three of their best friends in the classroom. The overall results of the research found that the coaching procedure was effective in increasing isolated children's peer acceptance. In particular, the coaching group showed significant increases on the play sociometric rating from pretest to posttest when compared with the peer-pairing and control group. This study points to the potential for enhancing isolated children's peer relationships through direct intervention.

The implications of understanding children's interpersonal relationships extend beyond just isolated children. Ladd, Buhs, and Troop (2002) have described how children's interpersonal skills are directly related to successful adaptation in school settings. Exhibit 8.11 presents their interpersonal model of school adjustment. The figure suggests a child's interpersonal relationships—friendships, peer acceptance, rejection, and conflict—relate directly to school adjustment. Such interpersonal skills have been overlooked in their significance for school adjustment.

Interpersonal relationships also can play a role in preventing the development of problems including drug abuse.

Implications for Practice: Cross-Cultural Drug Abuse Prevention

No matter what a child's ethnic background, the factors that lead to drug abuse are largely the same. This fact is important when one is designing and implementing drug-abuse prevention programs in "real world" America, because here we have many different ethnic groups living, working, and going to school together. After hundreds of years of the "melting pot," it is difficult to implement an intervention that focuses on one specific ethnic population.

"Life Skills Training" (Botvin, 2000) is a prevention program developed to determine the extent to which the same intervention will work with many different kinds of kids. This school-based drug-abuse prevention program has been shown to lower tobacco, marijuana, and alcohol use among white middle-class seventh graders as well as inner-city African American and Hispanic youths. In addition, Life Skills Training works equally as well with boys or girls. Because the program teaches skills to resist social pressures and fosters students' anti-drug attitudes and perceptions, it also lowers adolescents' intentions to use drugs in the future. Regular classroom instructors teach a range of social and personal skills that increase young people's ability effectively to handle the challenge of adolescent life and reduce the probability that they will use alcohol and drugs. The teachers are encouraged to make the program's role play realistic by changing some of the scenarios and using familiar language. The teachers who tailor the program to their class understand that the Life Skills Training curriculum's success depends on engaging the kids. ■

Communities and Support Systems

Culture and Cooperation

Cooperation is a fundamental concept in understanding peer interactions. Do children from different cultures respond to cooperation in different ways? Under certain circumstances—for example, when there is an element of competition—differences occur in the degrees of cooperation. Researchers have found that children from small Mexican villages are more cooperative than urban Mexican, Mexican American, African American, and white American children (Madsen & Shapira, 1970). Other, similar studies have found differences between urban and rural children (Richard et al., 2002). These results show that simple, agrarian cultures often foster cooperation in children, whereas more complex urban cultures reward competition more.

School Influences

School is a major socialization agent for our children. Children begin school by age 6 and spend five hours every weekday interacting with teachers and peers in ways that will affect their social and emotional development. When most of us think of schools, we think of the three Rs—reading, 'riting, and 'rithmetic. However, schools go far beyond academic basics. Children must learn to conform to the rules set forth in their school, respond to teacher demands, interact successfully with age-mates, and manage their day-to-day responsibilities. Schools often invite opportunities such as ganging up on peers, involvement in drugs, and new experiences with sex. Clearly, schools have a major responsibility in the proper socialization of children.

School Fears

Although many children look forward to going to school each morning, some hate leaving the comforts of home for the trials of school—a place where they might wear the wrong clothes or give the wrong answer in class. Some children even refuse to go to school, throwing tantrums or complaining of stomachaches, headaches, or nausea. These children suffer from what is commonly called school phobia, or school refusal. Broadly defined, **school phobia** is anxiety and fear related to being in school.

The development of school phobia in children is a serious concern among parents, teachers, and mental-health professionals. This disorder affects 5–10% of U.S. schoolchildren and can lead to serious problems with school absenteeism. Researchers have found that chronic absence puts students at risk for psychological problems later in life, such as alcohol abuse and criminal behavior, as well as underemployment and even marital difficulties (Kearney, 2001).

A closer look at what constitutes school phobia reveals several issues. Some children experience generalized anxiety about their abilities. Others have fears specific to a school-related activity, such as walking down the hallway between classes. A related issue, social phobia, involves worry over peer relations and public speaking.

Most social phobias, such as school phobia, begin around ages 11 or 12, a time when children tend to insult and pick on one another most viciously. Some children are extremely fearful of being humiliated or embarrassed. Peers' opinions tend to be crucial, so children obsess over how others judge them. Particularly at risk for developing peer-related phobias are children harassed for physical traits, such as obesity and skinniness, or physical disabilities. Intellectual ability also can incite taunting from peers; some children suffer for their braininess, and others get ridiculed for their academic slowness.

Overcoming the problem of social phobia requires a team effort involving teachers, parents, and school social workers. For example, teachers and school staff can encourage children to stay in class and urge them to check their anxiety by talking through it or using breathing exercises to calm rapid breathing. Calling parents from school should be the last resort. Parents, for their part, can more firmly set and enact rules about school attendance. Creating a regular morning routine prevents children from dwelling on anxiety and developing school-related aches and pains. Finally, therapy can be used to help children face their fears with the use of coping-skills training and other types of behavior-related therapy (See Kearney, 2001; Csoti, 2003).

Designing More Effective Schools

What does make for a good school? Most important to a school's effectiveness are its atmosphere and its quality as a social institution (MacIver et al., 1995). Effective schools and classrooms are likely to do the following:

1. Strongly emphasize academics (demand a lot from students, expect a lot, assign regular homework, set clear classroom objectives)
2. Focus on task-oriented behavior (reinforce good work, provide clear instructions, discourage wasting classroom time)
3. Manage discipline problems effectively (be clear about the rules, use consequences consistently, avoid physical or excessive punishment)

The Center for Research on Education, Diversity, and Excellence has developed a growing body of evidence indicating that effective implementation of five standards promotes positive learning outcomes for students (Doherty et al., 2002): (1) joint productive activity, (2) language and literacy development, (3) contextualization, that is, connecting school to students' lives, (4) challenging activities, and (5) instructional conversation. These standards have been found to reduce the achievement gap between mainstream and diverse learners, and they are universal in nature, allowing for application across all subjects. The center has created a research tool that schools can use to evaluate their progress on the standards.

Recent examination of several inner-city middle schools (Wulf, 1997) helps answer the question, what is a good school? There are no stock answers or single defining factors, such as mandated wardrobe or test scores or classroom size. But some universal truths have been identified. A good school is a community of parents, teachers, and students. A good school, like a good class, is run by someone with a vision, passion, and compassion. A good school has teachers who still enjoy the challenge, no matter what their age or experience. A good school prepares its students not just for the SATs or ACTs but also for the world beyond the school doors.

These conclusions come in the wake of a large change in United States education policy in the No Child Left Behind Act of 2001. This act requires schools to use scientifically based research to improve student achievement. Such research provides evidence on how and why a program or practice works, its effects on student achievement, and its success in various settings.

Particular attention has been paid to inner-city schools, where standards sometimes fall significantly below expectations. Lessons learned from improving curricula in these city schools encompass four ideas (Wulf, 1997). First, good after-school programs that engage the interests of both students and staff can extend and improve the regular school day's learning. Second, computers as a learning tool, in classrooms with teachers who are properly trained to integrate technology into curriculum, are vital for all children, not just those from families who can afford a home computer. Third, small classes work best for reading and math in the early primary grades because they allow increased personal interaction between students and teachers. Also, small classes tend to reduce paperwork, so teachers can spend more time planning lessons. And fourth, if we want to have high expectations for students, we have to have high expectations for teachers. Because teachers must be prepared for the challenge of today's classrooms, colleges are raising their standards, creating extended internships, and developing partnerships with public schools. Once on the job, teachers should have opportunities to continue their education.

Teacher Expectations

One of the most famous educational research studies documented the well-known influence of teacher expectations on student performance. Rosenthal and Jacobson (1968) gave a group of students an IQ test and convinced their teachers that this test could predict which students would develop rapidly in intellectual growth. Teachers were then given the names of students who were likely to show such bursts of intellectual growth. In fact, the teachers had been given the names of ordinary students who were chosen at random. When the researchers retested these children, the "brightest" students showed significantly greater gains in IQ and reading achievement than did other students in the class. The effect of the teacher expectations was dramatic: Their expectations became self-fulfilling prophecies.

Additional research (Madon, Jussim, & Eccles, 1997) supports the theory that teachers' beliefs in students' abilities influence their performance. But, contrary to assertions that the teacher who underestimates a student's potential seriously undermines the student's performance, the study found that underestimating student achievement hurts students' test scores only marginally—by 10 percentiles. However, teachers with high hopes can raise students' test scores as much as 30 percentiles. The researchers believe that the average teacher wants his or her students to succeed and will help out as much as possible. Low achievers respond well to prodding and prompting from teachers because most students want to do well; they just need encouragement.

The following section continues the discussion of students' self-perceptions with regard to learning.

Self-Expectations and School Performance

Although the influence of teacher expectations on school performance has long been considered significant, more recent concern has focused on students' self-expectations or motivation in learning. Carol Dweck has conducted extensive research on motivation and learning. Her work has examined how children develop feelings of helplessness in their learning and the how both mastery and performance goals influence achievement. Research by Dweck (1999) examined students who could be classified as either mastery oriented, likely to attribute their successes to ability and effort, or helplessness oriented, likely to attribute their failures to luck or the difficulty of the task—causes over which they have no personal control. Studies that have looked at the differences between these two types of students have found that mastery students are confident in their performances on various tasks, whereas helpless students see themselves not only as helpless but also as lacking confidence in their abilities. They think they will likely confront failure in the future. In one study, the helpless children gave up after a single failure, although they had both the ability and the motivation to perform on subsequent tasks. The study of learned helplessness also has implications for the psychological functioning of children.

Can emotional distress, such as depression and anxiety, color children's view of themselves and the world around them? Research by Pomerantz and Rudolph (2003) suggested that emotional distress can create distortions of how children see themselves and the world. Fourth through sixth graders were followed in a yearlong study that measured self-reported levels of depression and anxiety, along with an assessment of the children's views of themselves and the world. They found that distressed children tended to blame themselves for failures and view their successes as based on external factors, two hallmarks of **learned helplessness**.

Although many children experience learned helplessness, research has demonstrated that these children can be taught to attribute their failures to insufficient effort rather than to lack of ability. This affects their sense of self-efficacy, and they learn to persist in spite of a failure (Seligman, 1995).

Disadvantaged Children and the Public School System

The public school system is a middle-class institution, and as a result, it can have a negative effect on disadvantaged children. Seligman (1999) outlined three barriers that low-income and minority students face in the school system: low parental expectations for school performance, low teacher expectations for school performance, and lack of culturally relevant educational materials.

Academic expectations may be quite different when we compare middle-class parents with low-income and minority parents. Whereas middle-class parents value "getting ahead," parents of disadvantaged children often emphasize "staying out of trouble." These varying expectations are likely to influence the academic behavior of children, either to work hard to get ahead or work just enough to get by. Sometimes disadvantaged parents inadvertently influence school performance; they simply participate less in school activities, and as a result their children place less value on school. However, when parents of disadvantaged children do get involved and expect good school performance from their children, their children are likely to do well (Comer, 1993). Social workers should keep in mind that parental involvement and interest in the child's school performance can make a difference.

The "relevance" of school material also can be a barrier for low-income and minority children. Imagine reading only stories about well-to-do white children when you are an African American who lives in a low-income neighborhood. The stories might not be of much interest, because they lack any cultural relevance. One study that examined this issue found that Hispanic Americans (who spoke only English) scored far below Anglo classmates in reading proficiency. The reading material dealt mostly with middle-class interests and values and was not culturally relevant. However, these same Hispanic American students performed much better in comparison with white students on mathematical ability, the testing of which involves less culturally oriented material. In general, our schools need to do a better job of providing minority students with culturally relevant material.

Earlier we presented information about the importance of teacher expectations. If teachers hold negative expectations about low-income and minority children, they will build critical barriers to academic success. Unfortunately, it appears that teachers do have lower expectations for children from low-income families (Minuchin & Shapiro, 1983). A common practice in many schools is to advance students to the next grade regardless of their accomplishments. This action may represent teachers' negative expectations that these children are not going to do well anyway. Such "social promotions" may

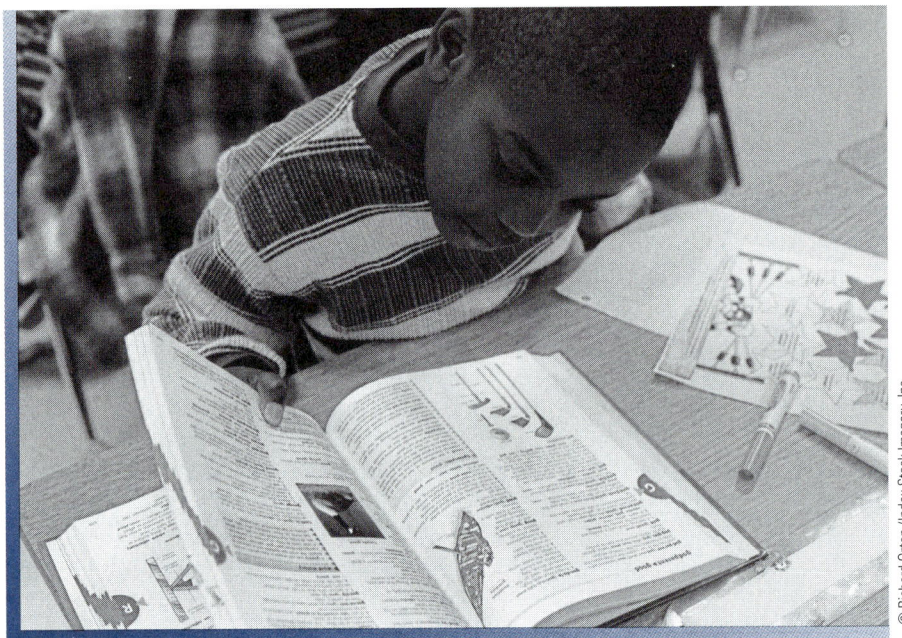

In the public school system, low-income African American students can face significant barriers, including low parental and teacher expectations regarding school performance and lack of culturally relevant educational materials.

perpetuate social inequality by depriving children of the opportunity to acquire necessary academic skills.

Implications for Practice: Enhancing School-Community Relationships

Social workers, in particular school social workers, often have the opportunity to influence the way in which school systems, teachers, and school officials interact with community members. One goal of a school social worker in a low-income community might be to minimize the barriers, like those just described, that low-income families and families of color confront. The social worker could act as a consultant to the school system and work with teachers to help them encourage better performance from minority students, work with families to help them get more involved in school activities and have more say regarding school materials, and work with school officials in an attempt to examine their school policies, such as "social promotions," to evaluate whether they truly benefit the children involved.

Often, the primary role of the school social worker is to enhance school-community relations. Constable (2002) has described some of the remedial tasks school social workers are likely to perform in addressing school-community relations:

- Identify children or target groups of children needing alternative educational planning or programs and support services
- Consult and collaborate with community representatives to identify the effects of interacting school/community/pupil characteristics and develop resources to meet needs of the child or target group
- Collaborate with community agencies in the development of alternative education programs and support services
- Clarify and interpret specific roles and responsibilities of the community in promoting school attendance
- Set objectives, monitor progress, and measure outcomes of service

School social workers often provide a vital link between the community and the school. Often the child and his or her family need specialized services from other agencies—for example, health services, counseling, and respite care. Students also are sometimes involved in other major socialization agencies, such as the juvenile-justice system or the child-welfare system. The school social worker must interact with community agencies in efforts to provide needed planning (Constable, 2002).

Schools and U.S. Public Law 94-142

One of the most significant changes to affect schools was the adoption and implementation of U.S. Public Law (PL) 94-142, the Education for All Handicapped Act. This law has been referred to as a "bill of rights for the handicapped" because it established the right to a free, appropriate public education for all "handicapped" children aged 3 through 21. This seminal law was amended and renamed the Individuals with Disabilities Education Act (PL 101-476) in 1990. Also, the term "handicap" was replaced throughout the act with the term "disability." The amended law strengthened the educational rights of disabled children and their parents and for the first time addressed transition services, which were defined as a coordinated set of services that promote students' movement from the school environment to postschool activities, such as postsecondary education, vocational training, supported employment, and independent living. The law specifically defines "related services" to include "social work services" and "rehabilitative counseling."

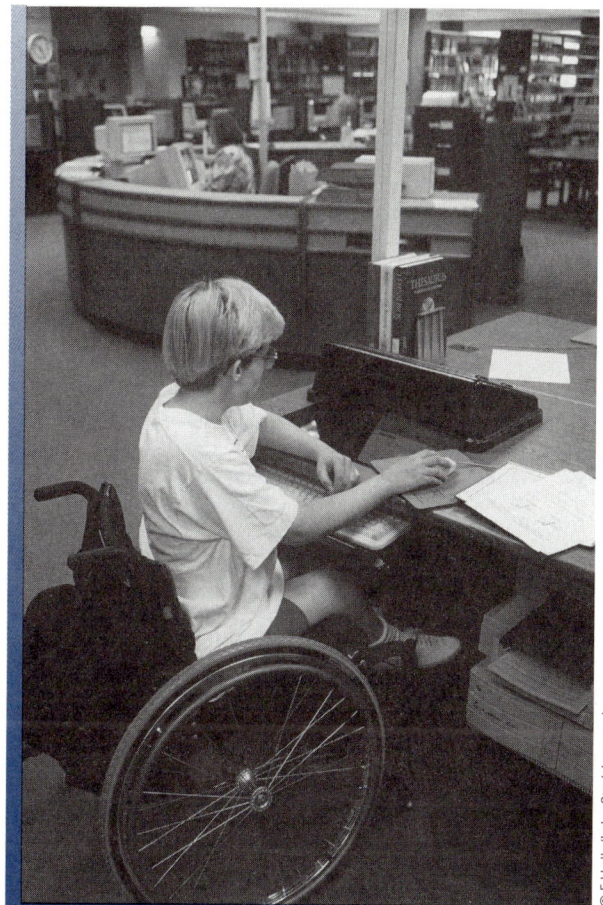

Public Law 94-142 and other developments in education have contributed to the mainstreaming of children with physical and developmental disabilities.

Children included under the provisions of this law are evaluated according to a multidisciplinary team that develops their objectives, and, together with special education and related services, provides each child with a written **Individualized Education Program (IEP)**. This law guarantees children the right to special education and related services, including any service that helps the child benefit from special education. Services that are recommended in the IEP must be provided to the child and his or her family at no cost. Of particular interest to social workers is the fact that seriously emotionally disturbed children fall under the category of "disabled."

This law has provided, in essence, a legal mandate for school social-work services. School social workers become involved in the development and coordination of the Individualized Education Program required for every student (Bishop, 2002). The multiple tasks required of the school social worker point to the importance of understanding the school environment and its influence on children's development. Indeed, it is essential to understand the school as a social organization. School social workers often must act as change agents within the school, working toward organizational change to meet the needs of the students they serve.

Multicultural and Gender Considerations

Imagine a child who turns on the TV Sunday morning and becomes engrossed in a TV series. He or she begins to identify with one of the characters on the show and imagines being them. However, the characters in this TV program are all white. Suddenly, one day the child is not really sure he or she can be like these people and begins to realize that many people will consider him or her an outsider. The child is Hispanic, unlike the characters in the TV program. The pervasive and subtle effects of racism are beginning to be felt in the child's everyday life.

By middle childhood, racial identity begins to be form. Children begin to think about who they are in terms of similar peer groups, their appearance, and their aspirations. How is the development of a child's self-concept affected in a society that imports negative meanings to being a minority? Do these children as a consequence develop feelings of self-doubt, inferiority, and low self-esteem?

Studies of Mexican American children show that ethnic awareness develops after gender and race awareness. Researchers (DeAngelis, 1994) have found that young preschool children have limited knowledge of their ethnic identity. But, as they get older, their understanding of their heritage grows broader and more complex. (In addition, bilingual Mexican American children were found to be more aware of their ethnic identity than those who spoke only English.) In fact, both ethnic and racial constancy are not attained until a few years after gender constancy. This finding contradicts the Piagetian view that once children reach a concrete operational stage where certain relationships are viewed as stable regardless of appearance, these mental operations should lead to general social constancy.

The developmental findings highlight the need for teachers and others who work with ethnic-minority children to attend to the youngsters' developmental stages—for example, by developing educational materials aimed at the level of understanding of each child.

Researchers also found that families who identify more with their ethnic roots are more likely to teach their children about their ethnic background and that children's ethnic identity is related to ethnically based behavior, such as cooperation and respect (Fishman, 2000).

During middle childhood, parents can no longer protect their children from the hostility caused by prejudice because of a child's color, appearance, attitudes, ethnic background, or neighborhood. However, parents and teachers can accentuate the child's strengths and abilities. Inner-city children can be remarkably self-reliant and independent. These children clearly grow up fast and develop functional characteristics to help them adapt to many of the hardships in life. Unfortunately, many teachers fail to recognize these abilities as strengths. Still, much progress has been made by parents, teachers, and others who recognize the strengths evident in all children. The benefits are clear: children's identity and self-esteem can be strengthened by providing them with a sense of belonging and reassurance about their differences (Fishman, 2000; Rapalje, Degelman, & Ashburn, 1986). Their differences need to be associated with positive attributes, not with societal projections that equate "different" with "bad" or "less worthy." The following section examines rites of passage that can help redirect young African American men.

Sex Roles in Middle Childhood

During middle childhood, girls and boys begin to learn about their differing roles and start to incorporate this information into their self-concept. Middle childhood is a significant time in the formation of **gender identity**—the developmental process by which culturally assigned values and behaviors are considered appropriate for members of that sex.

Egan and Perry (2001) have described gender identity in terms of five major components:

1. Membership knowledge (i.e., knowledge of membership in a gender category)
2. Gender typicality (i.e., the degree to which one feels one is a typical member of one's gender)

FOCUS ON MULTICULTURALISM

HERITAGE-BASED RITES OF PASSAGE FOR AFRICAN AMERICAN YOUTH

In south-central Los Angeles, a 6-year-old boy from a low-income family walks to school in plastic flip-flops because his family cannot afford to buy him sturdy shoes. A young African American man—who happens to be a member of a street gang—sees him on the street, picks him up, feeds him, gives him a pair of sneakers, and drops him off at school.

This real-life scenario is not what mainstream society would consider typical. The media portray young African American males as drug dealers and killers who do not want to learn to be responsible. The fact is that 90% of young African American men go to school and help their community. A national movement is helping young black men cope with the difficulties they face from stereotyping and other societal pressures. Rites of passage and mentoring programs are providing new services for African Americans.

Western societies have lost the traditions used to initiate boys into manhood. Initiation rites now consist of getting a driver's license, getting drunk, and having sex. Rites-of-passage programs use traditional practices from Africa and adapt them to the contemporary needs of young men in urban communities. The programs instill a values system and a sense of pride and self-worth in the young men that encourage them to succeed. They emphasize leadership, critical thinking, decision making, and problem solving.

These programs have an Afrocentric value system. They promote, for example, "Nguzo Saba"—unity, self-determination, collective work, responsibility, co-operative economics, purpose, creativity, and faith. Nguzo Saba is the cornerstone of the African American holiday Kwanzaa, in which communities give thanks for the past year and prepare for the new one.

Each member spends two years in the programs. On completion, a circle of elders returns as he graduates to the community in a formal ceremony. Each young man presents what he has learned from the program. The community is then asked to accept the young men as new members and support them in their roles. Teaching youth what is needed to make the transition into adulthood successfully is vital to create a sense of responsibility and pride in their heritage, and to encourage them to succeed.

Through initiation rites, the programs reinforce values such as self-respect, responsibility, and dedication to family, community, and one another. They meet several objectives: Youngsters develop a value orientation; adults gain a sense of empowerment and commitment through helping the children; and the sponsoring organizations improve the troubled status of young black males in the community.

Culture, the entertainment industry, social networks, and adults give young black men negative messages about their capabilities and coping skills. Therefore, some youths become totally discouraged by the school experience because of how teachers treat them and decide to opt out, finding it too difficult. African American boys also battle the attitude that if they succeed in school, they are "copping out" or "being white." The gifted ones are pressured to bury or underplay their talent to be accepted by their peers.

Stereotypes can create an "invisibility syndrome": African American males are often treated as if they do not exist or should be feared. The stereotypes represent a set of assumptions and expectations that create the lens through which African American males are seen. Children experience the stereotypes of how they are viewed by some teachers and police. The media give the impression that African American males do not want to make an honest living—that they just want to hang out on street corners selling drugs. As a result, youths are put on the defensive. It is not uncommon for police to hassle innocent young black men just because they *are* young black men, a controversial practice sometimes referred to as "racial profiling."

Rites-of-passage and mentoring programs have grown in the United States to assist young men in their fight against stereotypes. African American institutions, including churches, fraternities, social clubs, and schools, are implementing the programs. Teachers and community members identify the program's voluntary participants. They choose young men who demonstrate either negative or positive leadership among their peers. The goal is for the youths to form a network and re-channel some of the energies they might use to get into trouble into becoming a positive influence on others.

3. Gender contentedness (i.e., the degree to which one is happy with one's gender)
4. Felt pressure for gender conformity (i.e., the degree to which one feels pressure from parents, peers or oneself to conform to gender stereotypes
5. Intergroup bias (i.e., the extent to which one believes one's own sex is superior to the other)

Their research found that these components of gender identify in preadolescent children were independent and stable over a school year. Furthermore, gender typicality and gender contentedness were positively related to adjustment, whereas felt pressure and intergroup bias were negatively associated with adjustment.

With their increased ability to understand other people's expectations for them, children, especially boys, begin to show some changes in gender identity. The behavior and attitudes of boys become increasingly masculine in orientation. However, girls in middle childhood do not show a corresponding change toward femininity; in fact, they have a preference for masculine interests and activities (Richardson & Simpson, 1982). (Remember, this tendency began in the preschool years.) For example, in examining the Christmas wish lists of boys and girls, Richardson and Simpson (1982) found that most requests were sex-typed but that more girls than boys asked for "opposite sex" items. What can account for this tendency for girls to show interest in masculine-oriented behavior? Shaffer (2002) has suggested three possible reasons: (1) Girls are becoming increasingly aware that masculine behavior is more highly valued; (2) girls are permitted to engage in more cross-sex play than boys are; and (3) masculine games may simply be preferred because they are more action-oriented than playing with dolls and doll houses.

The development of **sex-role stereotypes** reflect how we categorize people according to our general impressions of what we consider "male" and "female." What do you consider to be the major differences between men and women? Do you believe that women are more submissive, more passive, less competitive, more home oriented, less adventurous, or less confident than men are? Do you believe that men are more aggressive, more objective, more active, more competitive, or more direct than women are? The ideas you have about such differences between men and women reflect the stereotypes you have learned. In previous chapters, we pointed out that sex differences exist from birth and are noticeable through the preschool years. However, disagreement exists about whether these differences result from biology or from socialization. What are the true differences between men and women?

A famous review of more than 1,500 studies by Maccoby and Jacklin (1974) attempted to set the record straight. The results are surprising, because most of us have grown up with many myths about gender differences that reinforce our sex-role stereotypes. The results found only four actual gender-related differences:

1. Females have greater verbal ability.
2. Males have better visual/spatial ability.
3. Males have better mathematical skills.
4. Males are more aggressive.

Our myths about gender differences are quite strong, but as only four differences can be accounted for, the following list describes some of the more common myths about gender differences that you should review and consider rejecting. If this is difficult for you, then you know firsthand how difficult it can be to change stereotypes.

- Boys are more active than girls.
- Girls are more suggestible than boys.
- Boys are more competitive than girls.
- Girls are more sensitive than boys.
- Boys are more dominant than girls.
- Girls are more social than boys.

One of the reasons it is hard for us to change our views about gender myths is that sex-role stereotyping begins at a very early age. Recall the study by Haugh, Hoffman, and Cowan (1980), in which 3- and 5-year-olds watched a film with two babies playing, one identified as male and one as female. When asked to point to the baby that was "smart," the children almost always chose whichever one had been labeled a boy.

We learn to develop such stereotypes at home and at school. Parents often have different expectations of boys than of girls. Not surprisingly, one study (Parsons, Adler, & Kaczala, 1982b) found that parents expect their sons to do better in math than their daughters. These attitudes also affected their children's own assessments of their math abilities and their beliefs about whether they can be successful in the future. In other words, children's beliefs about their own math abilities were better reflected by their parents' beliefs in their math potential than by their own past experiences in math. A child's academic self-concept is strongly influenced by his or her parents' stereotypical notions about that child's academic potential. Add this type of influence to findings showing that teachers praise a boy's ability when he is successful but praise a girl's neatness and effort when she is successful (Dweck, 1999), and you can see why we have a long way to go in changing sex-role stereotypes.

Social Strengths and Hazards

As middle children reach out and become increasingly independent, the neighborhood and community offer opportunities for growth and hazards for healthy development.

Neighborhoods and Communities

The experience of childhood takes place in a social context—in the neighborhood and community where the child lives. The neighborhood is perhaps most critical to the middle child in molding experiences and shaping adjustment to the social world. The neighborhood opens up an important arena for exploration and social interaction and contributes to the child's physical and social development (Garbarino et al., 1992). As the child moves beyond the boundaries of the front yard, he or she is affected by who is in the neighborhood and how safe the neighborhood is. Consider the multitude of neighborhood factors that contribute to the child's development—neighborhood safety, available health and social services, recreational activities, quality of the local schools, and the surrounding economic conditions.

The notion of "community" becomes increasingly important for the child's healthy development. The nature and types of social interactions available influence the quality of life for families. Consider the difference between the types of social interactions that occur in a housing project in Chicago and in an upper-income suburb in Chicago. As you can see, consideration of the social hazards alerts us to how the community affects the development of the child. Indeed, studies have shown that, when a community's economy is negatively affected, rates of domestic violence increase (Straus, Gelles, & Steinmetz, 1980).

One reality not widely recognized is that children are more prone to victimization than adults. Sadly, in cases of family violence, adults report that they inflict almost twice as much severe violence on a child in their household than against their adult partner (Finkelhor & Dziuba-Leatherman, 1994). This violence includes beating, kicking, and hitting with a fist or an object. Further, when we add to family violence the frequent occurrence of peer and sibling assaults against younger children, we see a picture in which children are victims of violence far too often. Families that live in high-risk neighborhoods and communities face a large number of stresses.

Another instance of children being victimized is the age-old and now widely criticized and researched act of bullying.

Stopping the Bullying Epidemic

The issue of bullying in this country's school systems has gained more attention in recent years, particularly in light of the increase in the prevalence of school shootings. New research is exploring the various factors involved in bullying, including characteristics of bullies and psychosocial factors present, to assist in the creation of more effective intervention programs.

Research done by the United States Secret Service and the U.S. Department of Education (2002) provides information about some of the characteristics of school shooters from a sample of 37 school shootings. The report indicates that before the shooting occurred, almost three-quarters of the shooters felt in some way bullied, threatened, or attacked by others, sometimes over long-term periods. Additional facts from this report indicate that the attackers were all boys, they did not threaten their targets before the shooting, and they exhibited some form of behavior that caused concern in others before the shooting (i.e., writing poems essays with troubling content). One of the more disturbing facts uncovered was that in 80 percent of the cases, at least one person knew that the shooter was planning an attack.

Bullying typically occurs most frequently between the sixth and eighth grades. In a study by Nansel et al. (2001), both bullies and the victims of bullying were found to have difficulty adjusting to their environments and experienced difficulty making friends. Depression and anxiety are found to be experienced more often than average by children who are considered victims of bullying or who both are bullied and bully others themselves (Swearer et al., 2001).

> ### FOCUS ON MULTICULTURALISM
>
> #### PRIMARY PREVENTION FOR TRAUMATIZED KHMER CHILDREN
>
> In an attempt to resettle Khmer refugee children in Tacoma, Washington, Duncan and Kang (cited in Williams & Berry, 1991) created a creative and culturally sensitive treatment program. These children lived through the Pol Pot atrocities in Cambodia and had been forced from their families when they arrived by themselves in Tacoma. They experienced trauma and loss that included the separation from families without the resolution of grief and loss. In addition, these children experienced serious acculturative stress. Posttraumatic symptoms emerged soon after their arrival and included sleep disturbances, nightmares involving family members, and disturbing visits by spirits, including those of parents and grandparents.
>
> The primary prevention program included three Theravada Buddhist ceremonies and rituals to honor the children's dead families. These included Ban Skol, a memorial for absent family members; Pratchun Ban, an annual family reunion of living and deceased relatives, and religious observances for absent family members that took place during the Khmer New Year's celebration. Also included was special consultation with Khmer Buddhist spiritual leaders. Last, the program included placements in ethnically similar foster homes.
>
> The Ban Skol ceremony, a joint effort between the foster parents and the social-service agency, was held at the child's foster home. A special meal was provided to the monks, family, guests, and agency staff. The child prepared a list of the family members and was instructed to burn it and to douse the ashes slowly with water. This symbolic cremation was prepared for those children who had witnessed dead bodies that were simply left to rot, and the refugee child was the primary focus of the ceremony. This ritual was intended to provide protective functions to the child. As Williams and Berry (1991, p. 637) pointed out, "through the process of the ceremony, the child was able to begin seeing the foster family, their friends, and the agency's caseworkers as sources of support."
>
> During the ceremony, many of the children were either withdrawn or overcome with feelings of loss and grief. This allowed the foster family and others to console the children and offer support. There were anecdotal reports after the ceremony of decreased sleep problems, fewer spirit visits, increased bonding with the foster family, and greater grief resolution.
>
> Adapted from Williams & Berry (1991).

The types of interventions or strategies that address bullying have been inadequate at solving the problem of bullying. Relying on adults to identify bullies is typically ineffective, because adults, including teachers, often prove unable to identify bullies and also overestimate their ability to identify them (Swearer & Doll, 2001). Group interventions have been used in some schools to address bullying. However, these programs can be problematic for the victims if bullies are included in the same group. The use of peer mediation can be successful as long as the students participating are in equal positions of power. Because bullying is a form of victimization, power equality may be difficult to achieve.

Researchers are now beginning to investigate the biopsychosocial factors involved in bullying in order to develop more effective interventions. One program, the Olweus Bullying Prevention Program, involves using the school as a community to work together to change the climate of the school and the social norms (Olweus, Limber, & Mihalic, 1999). In addition, the Bullying Prevention Campaign seeks to increase public awareness about bullying and develop prevention and reduction strategies (Crawford, 2002).

Marital Conflict and Divorce

Marital conflict and divorce constitute major impediments to the adjustment of children of all ages. Divorce rates of about 50% reflect increased societal acceptance of divorce. Nearly 1 million children will experience divorce each year. One out of four children lives in stepfamilies. Half of all children will live in single-parent families for some part of their childhood; recent statistics show that 23% of children under 18 live with their mothers only and 5% live with their fathers only (U.S. Bureau of the Census, 2002).

EXHIBIT 8.12 Stressors that occur with divorce

Life Changes	Consequent Effects on Children
Hostilities between parents	Sadness, anger, loyalty conflicts
Distraught custodial parent	Anxiety, put in roles of parent, co-parent to custodial parent
Loss of relationship with noncustodial parent	Self-blame, low self-esteem, depression
Parent dating	Competitive feelings with parent's new partner, fear of loss of parent's affection, curiosity (for older children) about parent's sexuality
Remarriage	Sharing parents, accepting parents' intimacy, forming relationships with stepparents and stepsiblings, accepting new parent as authority, resolving issues of loyalty to new stepparent and parent of same gender
Poverty, associated	Downward economic mobility, emotional stresses, changes in residence, loss of peer relationships and familiar school environment, change in consistent caregivers

SOURCE: Adapted from Kalter & Schreier (1994).

In this section, we will focus on the experience of divorce from the child's point of view. Although we tend to think of divorce as occurring at a fixed point in time, for the child and family, the reality of divorce looks and feels more like a succession of painful experiences (Heatherington & Kelly, 2002). In fact, children experience a series of stressors when their parents divorce. The stressors outlined by Kalter and Schreier (1994, p. 308), in order of significance, are described in Exhibit 8.12. In the presence of such extreme stressors, children's energy is diverted from their own needs to worries about security, safety, and survival for themselves and their loved ones.

Wallerstein and Blakeslee (2003) have described three stages of divorce, all of which affect children's ability to focus on their developmental tasks. The acute phase is characterized by parental fighting, conflict, anger, depression, and the actual separation, which often is not mutual. This phase represents a crisis and often lasts for more than a year, and it is particularly difficult for children because they witness arguments and must live amid household instability and parental neglect. Parents do not often consider the effects of their behavior on their children when they are embroiled in a heated, prolonged battle. During this phase, children usually bear the brunt of poor parenting, although the quality generally improves after a year.

The second phase described by Wallerstein and Blakeslee is the transitional phase, in which parents and children try to adjust to their new life in a restructured family. The transitional phase usually lasts several years before the family settles into new roles and routines. In the third phase, the stabilizing phase, the family has typically adapted to the shifts in roles and allegiances. An optimal level of functioning is regained, and the family has moved on to tackle new changes. Not every family experiences each of these stages, however. Individual family members will vary in the level of functioning they achieve postdivorce.

Divorce is especially taxing on children because it disrupts one of the core relationships in their lives and dissolves the family structure they depend on for secure development (Long & Forehand, 2002). More often than not, children of divorce face adjustment issues throughout the course of their lives. The stresses evoked by divorce are not limited by time and will resurface in different forms as children develop. Although research has cited marital conflict as contributing more to children's distress than the actual divorce (Amato, 1993), many factors have been identified as determinants of children's adjustment (Amato & Booth, 1996). These factors include the personality and temperament of the child, the quality of the parent-child relationship pre- and postdivorce, the stability of the custodial parent's household, financial security, and the postdivorce relationship between the ex-spouses (Wallerstein & Blakeslee, 2003).

For all children, regardless of age or gender, the loss of a parent engenders feelings of insecurity, loss of self-worth, loss of love and feeling lovable, anxiety, loneliness, anger, resentment, guilt, fear of abandonment, depression, and helplessness (Long & Forehand, 2002). Children also must face issues of relocation to new homes and schools; maternal employment; custodial parents who are themselves under stress, impatient, and overburdened; disorganization and unpredictability in daily events such as meals and bedtime; and difficulties in school performance and peer relationships. Unfortunately, just when children need their parents the most, parents' ability to attend to their children effectively is compromised (Amato, 1993; Wallerstein & Blakeslee, 2003).

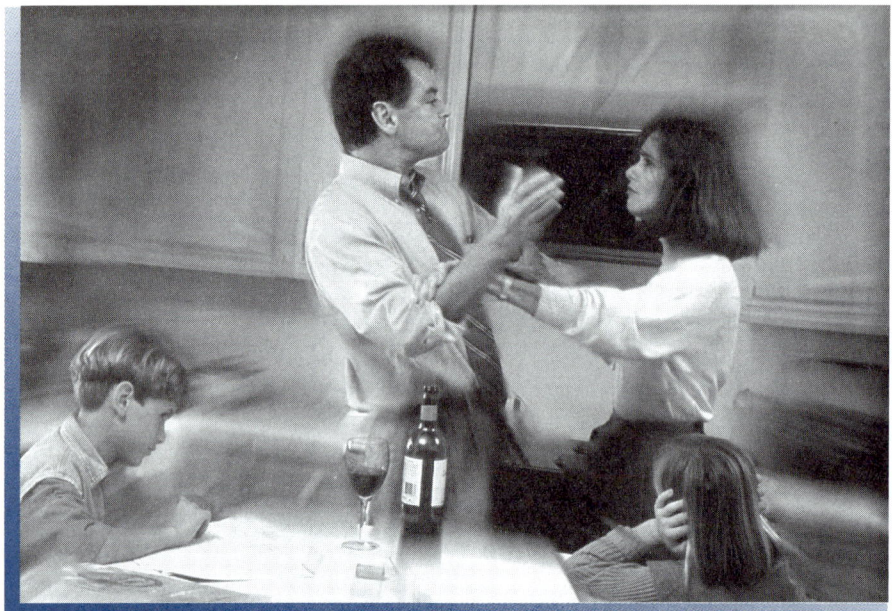

Marital conflict and divorce are major impediments to the adjustment of children.

So how do children fare when marital conflict and divorce become part of their life history? The age of the child at the time of divorce influences short- and long-term adjustment. Young children initially suffer more fear because they are more dependent on their parents and are more limited cognitively in their ability to understand the reasons for divorce; they tend to blame themselves. Because they are working on separation issues during the early-childhood years, fears of abandonment become heightened with the reality of divorce. Research by Wallerstein found that young children's adjustment tended to deteriorate during the year and a half following the divorce and continued to be poor even after five years. This was especially true for boys, who were more aggressive and disruptive at home and at school. Young children's development rests more completely on the quality of care in the home. Consequently, they suffer more than older children when the quality is diminished. Older children possess a larger coping repertoire with direct access to more resources than do younger children, which can buffer them from the initial hardships imposed by divorce.

However, young children tend to have better long-term prognoses for adjustment when assessed 10 years later. Interestingly, children who were young at the time of the divorce fantasized about their parents reuniting even a decade after the divorce. These children reported feelings of sadness over the loss of their family and worries about future relationships and commitments, especially with the opposite sex. Younger children reported feeling more hopeful about relationships than did their older siblings. Adolescent girls reported the most anxiety (Wallerstein & Blakeslee, 2003).

Differences in adjustment outcome for boys and girls also have been noted and depend, to a large extent, on the sex of the custodial parent. Overall, girls tend to fare better following divorce than do boys. Most girls tend to adapt faster and better to divorce, with the exception of those who mature early at puberty. These girls were found to be less compliant and more argumentative, and to have lowered self-esteem and more problems in heterosexual relationships than on-time and late-maturing girls (Heatherington, 1988). Boys who resided with mothers who never remarried tended to experience the hardest adjustment from preschool through adolescence. Generally, children living with custodial parents of the same sex demonstrated increased self-esteem, social competencies, independence, security, and maturity.

These findings may be attributed to the fact that most children reside in the custody of their mothers and are provided with role models and sources of support. Some people believe that sons need fathers more than daughters do. Girls may in fact find role models in their mothers and learn relationship skills from them that boys need to learn from fathers. These findings also may reflect the difficulty that many single mothers of teenage boys confront when disciplining and controlling their sons. The power structure embedded in many cultures within our society attributes more value and autonomy to males than to females. As a result, mothers may have little authority over their sons, and daughters may have fewer rebellious aspirations.

In a contrasting perspective, Heatherington and Kelly (2002, p. 7) have suggested that divorce's "negative long-term effects have been exaggerated to the point where we now have created a self-fulfilling prophecy." Their findings indicate that about 25% of children from divorced families have serious social and emotional programs, compared to 10% of children in a comparison sample of two-parent families. In a long-term follow-up twenty years later, she found the two groups were more similar than different.

Implications for Practice: Smoothing the Aftermath of a Divorce

Sigelman & Rider (2003) have identified five factors that can help smooth the path in the aftermath of a divorce:

1. Adequate financial support: Research studies confirm the notion that families do much better in adjusting to divorce when their finances are not seriously depleted. The challenge is helping single-parent households retain a reasonable amount of financial support. Social-policy experts have been encouraging states to pursue noncustodial parents who do not pay their child support. Unfortunately, only about half of noncustodial fathers pay child support.
2. Adequate parenting by the custodial parent: Because parents are under increased stress and pressure, their parenting usually becomes less effective. However, if parents can be supported in these stressful times and encouraged to continue a relationship based on warmth and consistent discipline, their children will be less likely to experience problems.
3. Emotional support from the noncustodial parent. One serious consequence of many divorces is the intense hostility and anger that the spouses feel and express. As a result, children feel insecure, are torn between the parents, and are more likely to experience behavior problems. Also, many children lose contact with their noncustodial parent. In fact, about one-third of the children lose contact with their fathers. Research suggests that regular contact with supportive fathers can help children, particularly sons, adjust to the divorce. When children have supportive relationships with both parents and there is an effort to reduce the conflict between parents, they are more likely to make a positive adjustment to a single-parent household.
4. Additional social support: Social support also plays an important role in helping both parents and children adjust to the negative effects of divorce. Parents who have close friends are less depressed, and children also benefit from close friendships. Children who participate in divorce groups have an opportunity to share their feelings and learn positive coping skills. Also, adolescents in single-parent homes commit fewer delinquent acts when a relative helps with the childrearing and supervision. Helping a family find social support can lessen the negative effects of divorce.
5. A minimum of additional stressors: The divorcing family may face many new changes—decreased income, moves to new neighborhoods, legal battles, and extended-family complications. Not surprisingly, the ability to cope successfully with divorce can be facilitated by reducing the amount of stress.

Many factors influence how a family reacts to a divorce. The five factors just described represent a beginning point for thinking about how to help families who must face this crisis. Sigelman & Rider (2003) have reminded us of how these factors demonstrate that the family is a social system within larger social systems. Adjustment to divorce must take into consideration how the mother, father, and children all influence one another, as well as the family's experience in its interactions with the surrounding world. ■

Developmental Guidelines for Assessment in Middle Childhood

Exhibit 8.13 presents the developmental guidelines for middle childhood. These guidelines are meant to be helpful to social workers, who need to understand developmental aspects when making assessments.

EXHIBIT 8.13 Development considerations in assessment for middle childhood

Routine Observations
Peer relationships and play behavior
Adaptation to school
Family relationships
Interests and skills
Physical development (prepubertal changes), interests, and abilities
TV/movie/computer viewing habits
Sleep and dreams
Daily routine
Independent self-care
Academic achievement and classroom behavior
Reading/literacy skills
Reasoning abilities

Strengths and Landmarks of Development
Enjoys reading (by third grade)
Comfortable away from home/with peers
Development of moral thinking
Good at catching a ball (5–7)
Can solve simple puzzles (5–7)
Friendship development with same sex (8–10)
Participates in a peer group (9–11)
Physically active
Developing preferences for friends and activities (5–7)
Sexuality awareness

Developmental Issues (Not Problems)
Oversensitive to criticism
Prefers play to school and home responsibilities
Short-term fears develop
Noncompliance with parental requests
Doesn't always share
Teacher-child conflicts
Poor table manners
Excessive aggressive behavior
Talking back
Moodiness
Temper outbursts
Secretiveness

Developmental Observations Requiring Attention
Persistent fearfulness
Lying
School failure
Language and speech problems
Victimized by bullies
Inappropriate sexual behavior
Overdependence
Running away
Fire setting
Persistent thumb sucking
Strange, bizarre, or withdrawn behavior
Lack of communication
Cruelty to animals/pets
Lack of friends
Disturbed sleep patterns, enuresis
Persistently emotional over small things

STUDY TABLE: Social dimension in middle childhood

Families, Groups, Communities, and Support Systems	By the time a child reaches late childhood, he or she is spending much less time with parents and more time with peers. Still, the family provides a safe, authoritative structure that children need. Discipline continues to be critical for good parenting. Three major parental disciplinary strategies are power-assertive discipline, love withdrawal, and induction. Parent training is recommended by social workers for families that are having problems. Four approaches to parent training include parent-effectiveness training, parent-involvement training, behavior modification, and systematic training for effective parenting. Children begin to have an increasing preference for spending time with their peers. They begin to

form peer groups, which are often referred to as "cliques." The process of group formation can have important implications for peer cooperation and respect, and peer conflict and/or discrimination. Children who are rejected by their peers are at risk for adjustment problems. The importance of friendships and positive peer relationships has been uncovered by several studies. Friendships may provide for unique learning of critical social skills. Children who are rejected by their peers can be taught the social skills needed for friendship making.

Schools are a major socializing agent. A good school is a community of parents, teachers, and students. Attributes such as good after-school programs, computers in all classrooms, smaller class sizes, high expectations for students as well as teachers, and opportunities for teachers to continue their education will contribute to excellent schools. Effective schools can be differentiated from less effective schools on the basis of strong academics, focus on task-oriented behavior, and effective management of discipline problems. A percentage of children (as much as 10%) experience school phobia, an anxiety and fear related to being in school. Teacher expectations and a child's self-expectations can influence school performance. Three barriers that low-income and minority students face: low parental expectations, low teacher expectations, and a lack of culturally relevant material. The No Child Left Behind policy was designed to measure the effectiveness of schools. Schools have not made many accommodations for disadvantaged students. School social workers sometimes must act as advocates in school-community relationships. U.S. Public Law 94-142, the "bill of rights for the handicapped," or people with disabilities, is a case in point.

Multicultural and Gender Considerations	By middle childhood, racial identity is beginning to form. Families who identify with their ethnic roots are likely to teach their children about their ethnic background. Children's ethnic identity is related to ethnically based behavior, such as cooperation and respect. The effects of racism can influence a child's sense of identity. Rites of passage and mentoring programs are helping young African American men cope with the difficulties they face from stereotyping and other societal pressures. Through initiation rites, the programs reinforce values such as self-respect, responsibility, and dedication to family, community, and one another. Sex-typed behavior begins at this age. Children also begin to develop sex-role stereotypes. Although many stereotypes exist about differences between the sexes, one review study found only four gender differences: females have greater verbal ability, males have better visual/spatial ability, males have better mathematical skills, and males are more aggressive.
Social Strengths and Hazards	Neighborhoods and communities provide a social context for the child's development. Both bullies and victims of bullying are found to have difficulty adjusting to their environments and making friends. Bullying occurs most frequently between the sixth and eighth grades. As in early childhood, in middle childhood divorce is a significant social hazard. Divorce rates of 50% reflect increased social acceptance of divorce. Three stages of divorce are the acute phase, denoting a crisis; the transitional phase, describing adjustment; and the stabilizing phase, describing adaptation. Age of the child influences short- and long-term adjustment to divorce. Gender also plays a role, as girls tend to fare better following a divorce than do boys. Five factors help the adjustment to divorce: financial support, adequate parenting by the custodial parent, emotional support from the noncustodial parent, additional social support, and a minimum of stressors.

CONCEPT MAP

APPLYING THE FRAMEWORK
ATTENTION-DEFICIT/HYPERACTIVITY DISORDER

Developmental History

Tommy is a 7-year-old African American child who was referred to the Child Guidance Clinic by his teacher. Tommy's mother, Ms. Paul, reports that Tommy's birth was not planned and that Tommy's father was not pleased about her pregnancy. She was upset that Tommy's father did not want the child and concerned about what would happen. Ms. Paul reported that she was in labor for a very long time and that she was given Demerol during the birth process. Complications in childbirth were mostly a result of her failure to dilate properly.

Ms. Paul noted that Tommy developed "normally" and began walking and talking at developmentally appropriate times. She noted that at about age 5 Tommy became much more difficult to manage. She began getting complaints about his behavior at school.

Biophysical Considerations

At about age 5, Tommy developed problems with his eye muscles. He received optometric treatment for about a year. Ms. Paul reports that she had a very difficult time getting him to do his required eye exercises. Tommy stopped receiving treatment last year when Ms. Paul changed jobs and lost her health insurance.

Psychological Considerations

Cognitive Development and Information Processing

Tommy has difficulties with information processing. In particular, his attention span is exceedingly short. This has led to his diagnosis of attention-deficit/hyperactivity disorder (ADHD). Teacher reports indicate that constant supervision is required to keep Tommy from talking to the other children. Also, his teachers state that he "cannot sit still" and that he "cannot concentrate." Tommy's school performance has gotten much worse over the last year. His teacher reports that he is at least one full school year behind. Achievement tests suggest this is true but that his poor performance may be caused by his impulsiveness.

The parent interview supported similar conclusions. Ms. Paul has difficulty managing Tommy because he is "all over the place." She also indicated that he lacks judgment. He will apparently do things that disturb other children and not be aware he is offending them. She says that he does not come in from play when he is supposed to and that she cannot get him to take responsibility around the house. Ms. Paul completed a Child Behavior Checklist, and Tommy received an "often true" or "sometimes true" rating in nine of the eleven items that assess hyperactivity. The items included the following: can't concentrate, can't pay attention long, can't sit still, confused, daydreams, destroys his own things, impulsive or acts without thinking, poor school work, and prefers playing with younger children. Tommy scored well above the clinical cutoff score for hyperactivity.

Tommy was referred for a psychological evaluation, and the psychologist noted that Tommy could not maintain his attention, although he did stay in his seat. During an IQ task, Tommy gave up very quickly, making the assessment difficult. He also had difficulty maintaining his focus in conversations with the psychologist.

The Wechsler Intelligence Scale for Children–III (WISC-III) indicated that Tommy's overall intelligence is in the average range (FSIQ = 98), with similar verbal (VIQ = 101) and performance ability (PIQ = 99). Tommy's achievement scores show he is slightly below average for his age.

Communication

Ms. Paul reports that Tommy can communicate appropriately for his age. She complains that at times Tommy can become a "motor mouth" and will not stop talking after repeated requests for

(*continues*)

APPLYING THE FRAMEWORK

(continued)

him to do so. Although Tommy has difficulty getting along with peers, he does appear to be able to communicate with them in an age-appropriate manner.

In the clinical child interview, Tommy spoke clearly and loudly to the social worker. Although his language appeared normal, Tommy had difficulty completing his thoughts when responding to questions.

Attitudes and Emotions

Ms. Paul describes Tommy as an unhappy child who has many social problems and gets angry easily. She says that Tommy does have difficulty "controlling his emotions." Ms. Paul reports that Tommy had numerous temper tantrums when he was younger and that he has problems with his anger. As an example, she described a recent incident when Tommy got angry and began throwing his toys against the wall. Ms. Paul noted that it took her at least twenty minutes to get Tommy under control. Ms. Paul reports that Tommy does not easily admit to feelings of sadness; however, he does get into crying spells that last for a long time. She reports no specific fears, saying that at times he appears "fearless." Ms. Paul believes that Tommy is very upset over his father's leaving the family, although he never wants to talk about it. She feels that much of Tommy's current difficulties stem from her divorce.

In the interview with Tommy, he denied feeling lonely or being sad about anything in his life. When asked if he was sad that his parents were no longer together, he said, "They just want to go off and be by themselves." He agreed that sometimes his anger gets him into trouble. "I can really get mad," he said with some pride. Tommy reported that he did have difficulty in school and that he was "bad at school most of the time." He also did not see himself as able to please his mother at home: "I don't do what she wants me to do." When asked about games and sports, Tommy said, "I am sometimes the best on the team." In general, in many of the domains in Tommy's life, he sees himself as "bad" or "unsuccessful," which is affecting his sense of self-esteem. Themes in the semistructured interview indicated problems with anger, low self-confidence, poor peer relationships, and a lack of interest in school.

Social Cognition and Regulation

Ms. Paul reports that Tommy does not have good judgment. Often it appears that Tommy does not think through the consequences of his actions. On several occasions, Tommy has been excessively cruel to their pet dog. Ms. Paul has consistently tried to explain to Tommy that it is wrong to inflict pain on the dog, yet Tommy does not refrain from being cruel toward it. Ms. Paul also reports that Tommy has difficulty getting along with peers partly because he sees them as mean and "always bugging him." Tommy has a difficult time having successful long-term interactions with his peers.

Tommy does not appear to have reciprocal friendships. For example, he does not know anything specific about his best friend's likes or dislikes. When asked, "What is a friend?" Tommy stated, "When you are over at someone's house playing with their things." In the interview with Tommy, he recounted an incident that occurred between him and a neighborhood boy. Tommy was asked how his actions might have made the other boy feel. Tommy could not identify the feeling the other boy would have been likely to have. Tommy's social knowledge of others and his sensitivity to other people's feelings is apparently not well developed.

With regard to adaptive and self-help skills, Tommy seems to have no difficulties. Tommy functions well in terms of daily living skills—he feeds himself, brushes his teeth, and cares for his health. Ms. Paul states that sometimes Tommy has difficulty going to sleep at bedtime and has difficulty getting up in the mornings.

In the semistructured interview, Tommy was presented with a conflicted social situation and asked how he would resolve the problem. He generated two impulsive solutions and could identify only a few of the consequences associated with his solutions. In a role-playing situation that could easily incite a fight, Tommy was asked what he would say or do. His response showed he lacks the skills needed to avoid situations likely to lead to conflict.

On the social competence measure of the Child Behavior Checklist, Tommy scored within the normal range on the activities scale but above the clinical cutoff point on the social and school scales.

Social Considerations

Family Situation

Ms. Paul and Tommy live together in a low-income African American neighborhood. Ms. Paul and Tommy's father divorced two years ago. Tommy is an only child. Tommy sees his father about every two weeks. Ms. Paul states that she believes Tommy and his father have a good relationship. Ms. Paul characterized her marriage before the divorce as always in a conflict or fight over something. She reports that Mr. Paul was not abusive toward her or Tommy. Currently, Mr. Paul is contributing money toward child support, although sometimes his payments are late.

Ms. Paul recently got a new job as a sales clerk. She reports that she is happy with her new job and that she has been in good spirits lately. Ms. Paul reports frequent episodes of depression in the past. She has never been hospitalized or received treatment for depression. Although Ms. Paul is involved with her extended family, she states she feels lonely and without close friends. Ms. Paul says she loves to cook and enjoys having others over for dinner. Weekends often are spent with the relatives, fishing, or other planned activities.

Ms. Paul sees Tommy's problems as a result of his poor adjustment to the divorce. She thinks Tommy may be "hyperactive" but is not sure and does not want to put Tommy on "any drugs." Although she has problems with his behavior at home, she believes the school has not really worked with Tommy to help him. Ms. Paul made it very clear that she is not happy with Tommy's school and how it has treated him. She has become increasingly concerned about her ability to manage Tommy. She feels "completely exhausted at having to deal with him after work" and complains of extreme tiredness.

Ms. Paul and Tommy spend a lot of time with Tommy's grandparents. Ms. Paul's mother has "pitched in and helped a lot." Ms. Paul says she doesn't know what she would do without her. However, Tommy's grandfather is a concern. Ms. Paul reports that he has a long-term drinking problem and that she does not like to see Tommy around him when he has been drinking. Although she has discussed this many times with her parents, her father continues to drink sometimes when Tommy is around.

When Tommy was asked to do a family drawing, he stated, "I don't have a whole family." Tommy drew a picture of his mother cooking and him watching TV. He then drew a solid black line and drew a picture of his father. He stated that he and his father don't get to watch TV much.

Groups, Social Supports, and Contexts

Ms. Paul describes Tommy as not well liked by his peers, although he does have a few good friends. She believes Tommy's aggressive behavior affects his ability to get along well with peers. Tommy was rated above the clinical cutoff for aggressive on the Child Behavior Checklist. Ms. Paul noted the following items were of concern: aggressive, brags, cruel to others, demands attention, destroys others' things, disobeys at home, disobeys at school, poor peer relationships, impulsive, shows off, excess talk, teases, temper, and loud. Teacher reports confirm Tommy's difficulty with aggressive behavior.

Ms. Paul and Tommy interact with several social institutions that are of significance. As already noted, Ms. Paul is concerned about Tommy's school. She has gone to a number of teacher conferences, and each time she has felt that the school is unresponsive to her. She believes the teacher is angry because she has not put Tommy on any medication for his hyperactivity. Ms. Paul perceives the school as too large to respond effectively to the needs of the students. Ms. Paul describes Tommy's class as unstructured and too large for one teacher to handle. She also believes that the expectations of students there are extremely low because of where the school is located, in a low-income neighborhood that is well known for having many social problems. Drug abuse is not uncommon.

Ms. Paul and Tommy regularly go to church. Ms. Paul states this is a very important part of her life. She sees a few of her friends there but wishes

(*continues*)

APPLYING THE FRAMEWORK
(continued)

she could spend more time getting to know others in the church. Ms. Paul would like to bring better role models into Tommy's life. She is concerned that he will never have a chance at a decent life unless he sees the success some people can attain. Ms. Paul has friends, but without child care she cannot afford to spend much time away from Tommy.

Multicultural and Gender Considerations

Ms. Paul and Tommy live in an old house that is badly in need of repair in a poor, urban African American neighborhood. Ms. Paul reports that much of the paint inside and outside the house is cracked and peeling. The paint could be lead-based and might account for Tommy's hyperactive behavior (research has found a relationship between high lead levels and attention-deficit/hyperactivity disorder).

Many of Tommy's peers in the neighborhood have already had associations with the law owing to drug use and vandalism. This leaves few male peer models for Tommy. Ms. Paul is concerned about his lack of "appropriate friends and acquaintances." Much of Tommy's free time appears to be spent playing aggressive sports or watching violent TV shows. Ms. Paul reports she does not monitor the type of TV programs Tommy watches. Ms. Paul feels many of the types of activities and games Tommy plays contribute to his problems because there are no "normal recreational activities for him to play in the neighborhood."

Although Ms. Paul and Tommy live in a primarily African American neighborhood, Ms. Paul is concerned about Tommy's experiences of prejudice and discrimination. There have been long-standing conflicts among several of the ethnic groups in the nearby neighborhoods. Tommy has been in a number of fights that have occurred because of racial issues. Ms. Paul is also angry that Tommy's school is underfunded and that the teachers have such low expectations of the students.

Ms. Paul and Tommy have limited access to a number of needed resources. Although Ms. Paul has a full-time job, the minimal pay has not allowed her to receive needed health care for Tommy. Their house is crowded, and the peeling paint may be a significant health hazard. Ms. Paul's income level does not allow her to meet her and Tommy's needs adequately. Mr. Paul's late and inconsistent child-support payments make budget planning difficult.

Summary and Impressions

Tommy has several problems that have become evident from the assessment:

1. Impulsive and overactive behavior—apparently attention-deficit/hyperactivity disorder
2. Aggressive behavior—possibly conduct disorder
3. Poor school progress
4. Poor peer relationships and lack of social skills

Additional difficulties include the following:

5. Inadequate health care for Tommy
6. Inadequate and possibly unhealthful living environment
7. Inadequate recreational opportunities
8. Lack of role models

Ms. Paul and Tommy do have a number of personal strengths and resources. Ms. Paul is clearly concerned and motivated to do her best in providing for Tommy. She displays caring and concern over his difficulties. Ms. Paul has successfully provided for Tommy, to the best of her ability. She is perceived as an intelligent, hard-working person who has a lot of concern for others. Ms. Paul has better-than-average parenting skills. Tommy continues to have a successful relationship with his father following his parents' divorce. Ms. Paul also has some social support—especially from the extended family. She is involved in her church and continues to maintain a number of friendships.

Key Terms

- acculturation
- attention-deficit/hyperactivity disorder (ADHD)
- bilingual
- conservation
- cretinism
- Das-Luria model of cognitive functioning
- Ebonics
- emotional intelligence (EQ)
- externalizing problems
- gender identity
- Individualized Education Program (IEP)
- induction
- intelligence quotient
- intention-cue detection
- internalizing problems
- learned helplessness
- logical consequences
- love withdrawal
- mental age
- metacognition
- metalinguistic awareness
- natural consequences
- peer groups
- power-assertive discipline
- readiness
- reversibility
- rickets
- role-taking ability
- school phobia
- sex-role stereotypes
- social cognition
- uninformative messages
- verbal control

Online Resources

Websites

Go to http://info.wadsworth.com/ashford to find specific links to these web pages.

The Child Survivor of Traumatic Stress

Based on an annual newsletter of the same name, this site provides information for professionals who work with traumatized children. Articles on the site are selections from earlier issues of the newsletter, with some updated or expanded for online readers. Online links to other trauma-related websites also are provided.

National Clearinghouse for Bilingual Education

Provides information on language education for minority students, bilingual education, and English as a Second Language (ESL).

The United States Department of Education

Includes information on the administration's priorities, funding opportunities, student financial-aid assistance, research and statistics, news and events, and so forth.

Center for Effective Collaboration and Practice (CECP)

This site provides ways to improve services to children and youth with emotional and behavioral problems.

National Information Center for Children and Youth with Disabilities (NICHCY)

NICHCY is an information and referral center that provides free information on disabilities and disability-related issues. It provides personal responses to specific questions, publications, informational searches, and technical assistance.

InfoTrac College Edition Keywords

For interesting materials related to what you have just read, please go to the InfoTrac College Edition website and search using the following keywords:

- bilingual education
- refugee children
- sign language
- school performance
- childhood friendship
- emotional IQ

Book-Specific Resources

Book-specific resources, which can be found at http://info.wadsworth.com/ashford, include the following:

- Case studies
- Quizzes to test your knowledge
- PowerPoint presentations

CHAPTER 9
ADOLESCENCE

CHAPTER CONSULTANTS

HOLLY MATTO
Virginia Commonwealth University

DIANE DEANDA
*University of California,
Los Angeles*

DEVELOPMENTAL THEMES	
	Stage: identity versus identity confusion. Today's adolescents. Independence from parents, increased emphasis on peer-group relations, preoccupation with self, changing body image.
BIOPHYSICAL DIMENSION	
Biophysical Growth and Development	Adolescent growth spurt. Pubertal process: menstruation, secular trend. Hormonal changes. Psychological consequences of puberty.
Biophysical Strengths and Hazards	Brain development, nutrition, obesity, dysmennorhea, acne, headaches, sleep.
PSYCHOLOGICAL DIMENSION	
Cognitive Development and Information Processing	Formal operations, more abstract thinking, hypothetical reasoning, logical consistency.
Communication	Increased language ability. Use of metaphors and satire. Writing becomes more meaningful. Girls' and boys' talk becomes more differentiated. Confidentiality.
Attitudes and Emotions	Identity formation. Increased emotional intensity and fluctuation. Changes in self-esteem. Foster-care adolescents' self-images. Enhancing adolescents' self-concepts.
Social Cognition and Regulation	Identity development: psychological moratorium. Identity status theory. Youth of color and adolescent identity. Identity and independence. Social cognitive monitoring. Regulation: moral development. Kohlberg's moral development theory. Justice perspective versus care perspective. Overcoming adolescent conformist reasoning. Theoretical perspectives on moral development. Egocentrism: imaginary audience, personal fable.
Psychological Strengths and Hazards	Negative images of adolescents. Stress-resistant adolescents. Internalizing and externalizing disorders. Conduct disorder. Delinquency. Self-harm and cutting.
SOCIAL DIMENSION	
Families and Groups	Control and autonomy within the parent-adolescent relation-ship. Parent-adolescent conflict and attachment. Peers and adolescent development. Conformity. Friendship. Social skills training. Peer groups. Cliques and crowds. Gangs.
Communities and Support Systems	School influences. High school dropouts. Making family relocations smoother. Runaway youths.
Multicultural and Gender Considerations	Peer relationships and adolescents of color. Adolescent immigrants. Gender roles: androgyny. The voice of adolescent girls. Body image and depression in girls. The war against boys: suicide rates, schooling. Heterosexuality: oral sex, influences on sexual activity. AIDS prevention and adolescent males. Gay, lesbian, bisexual, and questioning youth. Castration and sexual orientation. Guidelines for adolescents coming out. Harassment.
Social Strengths and Hazards	Building youth assets. Adolescents at risk. Victimization of children. Youth employment. Adolescent pregnancy. Adolescent fathers. Sex education. Alcohol and other drug use.

DEVELOPMENTAL THEMES

On a beautiful spring evening in San Francisco, I stood at the intersection of Sutter and Polk streets, a cheerful, crowded jumble of boutiques and bookstores, head shops and bead shops, restaurants, and bars. The corner was thronged with students and tourists, straights and gays, and bunches of teenagers leaning against the window of a pizza shop. They wore uniforms and insignia of their various tribes: leather-clad punks, California surfers, eastern preppies, suburban gypsies, and born-again hippies. Boys and girls laughed and joked together, jostled and pushed one another with the rough physical affection with which kids treat their friends and fellow tribespeople.

—P. Hersch

America's adolescents attract a lot of attention in their exuberance to establish an identity. Adolescence represents the journey of discovery—Who am I? How am I different from others? What do I want to do with my life? Erikson's theory of adolescent identity recognized this almost universal phenomenon.

But what is life like for today's adolescents? Our society offers a wealth of opportunities—modern technology has brought endless hours of watching MTV, Internet connections to the world, better physical health, and improved education. Yet young people must also face head-on the ills that modern society brings with it: AIDS, violence, exposure to alcohol and drug abuse, bombardment of media images, and hopelessness.

In spite of our changing society, the tasks adolescents face have remained stable. In essence, they must carve out their place in the world. And many of the problems young people face do not stem from youth itself but result from reduced opportunities and lack of support from a caring adult (Santrock, 2002).

Adolescence is typically defined as the period of growth beginning at about 10–12 years of age and ending at around 21–22 years of age. Researchers studying adolescent development believe it is important to consider adolescence in terms of three periods: early, middle, and late (Kaplan, 2004). Early adolescence begins at puberty and continues to about age 14, and it is characterized by important physical changes and significant cognitive and social changes (see Exhibit 9.1). In particular, early adolescents place great importance on peer approval. Middle adolescence is from ages 15 to 17 and corresponds to the high school years. This period represents the adolescent's reflective and self-discovery journey. Late adolescence begins around the age of 18 and continues up to approximately 22 years of age. During late adolescence, two developmental tasks are considered important: independence from the family, and the development of personal identity. Erikson referred to this stage as one of identity versus identity confusion.

Some key aspects of adolescence as a developmental period are that young people become concerned about their physical appearance and about others' perceptions of how they look. They become aware of the fact that their bodies are developing—girls will have their first menstrual cycle, and boys may have their first nocturnal emission, or wet dream.

EXHIBIT 9.1 Developmental changes of early adolescence

Puberty
Adult appearance and size
Reproductive capacity
Timing (especially if off-time)
Internal endocrine changes
Asynchrony (among body parts, among adolescents)

Cognition
Capacity for abstract thought

Peer groups
Conformity
Pressure to try new experiences

School
Changing school structure and format

Parents
Parental responses to adult size of adolescent
Sexual stimulation of newly pubertal child
Implications for parents' aging
Impending separation

Society
Hope and expectations for youth
Occupational choices and opportunities

From "Coping with adolescence," by Anne C. Petersen et al., in Mary Ellen Colten and Susan Gore (Eds.), *Adolescent stress: Causes and consequences.* Copyright © 1991 Transaction Publishers. Reprinted with permission.

STUDY TABLE:	Developmental themes of adolescence
Developmental Themes	Adolescence represents a journey of discovery, establishing one's identity (Erikson's stage of identity versus identity confusion) and place in the world. Adolescent development is composed of three periods: early (physical changes and peer approval are prominent), middle (reflection and self-discovery are prominent), and late (familial independence and personal identity are prominent). Other key aspects include concern about physical appearance; concern about how other people perceive how they look; and awareness of their developing bodies.

BIOPHYSICAL DIMENSION

Biophysical Growth and Development

Boys and girls at this stage of development experience what is referred to as an adolescent growth spurt, where there are rapid gains in height and weight. However, the growth spurt occurs two years earlier for girls than for boys. The growth spurt for girls begins at about age 10 and lasts for about two years. For boys, it begins at age 12 and also lasts about two years. There is considerable individual variability, so girls could begin the growth spurt as early as age 7, and boys as early as 9. The rate of adolescents' weight gain corresponds with the rate at which they gain height.

The Pubertal Process

Biologically, adolescence begins with the onset of the pubertal process—the time at which young people can reproduce. **Puberty** is identified by the combination of the growth spurt, maturation of physiological mechanisms, and the development of secondary sex characteristics, such as pubic hair and breasts (Graber, Petersen, & Brooks-Gunn, 1996; Kaplan, 2004). Although menstruation is one indication of puberty for girls, there is no clear indication for boys. **Menstruation** is the cyclic shedding of the uterine lining that leads to vaginal bleeding about two weeks after an egg is released from an ovary and is not fertilized. Nocturnal emissions and facial hair can indicate puberty in boys, but they may go unnoticed. Exhibit 9.2 summarizes the changes that take place for both boys and girls in the pubertal period.

EXHIBIT 9.2 Physical changes of the pubertal period

Step	Females	Both sexes	Males
1		Apocrine gland development	
2	Increased diameter of internal pelvis	Pelvic changes	Thickening and strengthening of bone structure
3	Growth of ovaries and uterus	Growth in gonads	Growth of testes and scrotum
4		Breast enlargement	
5		Appearance of pubic hair	
6	Growth of labia and vagina	Growth of external genitalia	Growth of penis
7	Menarche	External puberty	Nocturnal emissions
8		Axillary hair	
9	Oogenesis, ovulation	True puberty	Spermatogenesis, sperm in urine and semen
10	Broadening of hips	Broadening of body frame; vocal changes	Broadening of shoulders

SOURCE: From *The process of human development*, by C. S. Schuster and S. S. Ashburn, p. 499. Copyright © 1992 J. B. Lippincott Company. Reprinted with permission.

> ## FOCUS ON MULTICULTURALISM
>
> ### THE APACHE CEREMONY OF THE CHANGING WOMAN
>
> When an Apache girl reaches childbearing years, she is honored with a traditional ceremony of the changing woman. This ceremony comes from the Apache goddess White Painted Woman, who declared this event significant in the lives of the people: "Let all the people come together. Let them eat and dance and have a good time. The Masked Dancers will come forth at night and then the People will dance with each other, side by side and face to face."
>
> The four-day celebration is one of the tribe's most private ceremonies. In preparation, the father sends announcements to friends and family. The girl undergoes instruction from an attendant who guides her in proper behavior. A special dressmaker constructs clothes based on the original garments worn by the White Painted Woman. The garments are dyed pollen yellow, a symbol of fertility. Food is gathered and made to accommodate all the guests.
>
> The ceremony begins in the morning with the washing of the maiden's hair with yucca roots. The attendant gives traditional advice: "Be happy so your people may be happy. Don't talk too much or you'll always be a talker. Don't be cross or you'll always be a nag. Don't laugh too much or your face will wrinkle soon. Don't allow water to touch your lips, or the skies will weep and everybody will not have a good time. Don't think bad thoughts or you'll have evil to the end of your days" (Mildred & Hooper, 1993, p. 64).
>
> The White Painted Woman's holy home, or wickiup, is made of four spruce poles that are lashed together. The maiden enters her home and is now the personification of White Painted Woman. She now has supernatural powers. She lies down on deerskin and is massaged to become supple and possess good health. The shaman and special dancers perform rituals. As the sun rises, the woman faces east and the shaman paints her face with white clay, using an eagle feather. She becomes "White Painted Woman" and is again painted with pollen and runs in four directions. As she leaves the wickiup for the last time, it is pulled down and pushed to the east. Favors are tossed to the children, and her parents can now accept marriage proposals.
>
> SOURCE: Mildred & Hooper (1993).

The onset of puberty for girls has been getting earlier since it was first recorded in the 1800s. This trend toward earlier maturity is known as the **secular trend**. Each new generation over the past 100-plus years has been taller and heavier, and has entered puberty earlier. Records from Norway in the 1840s show that on average, **menarche**, the first menstruation, occurred at age 17, whereas today it occurs at age 11–12. In the United States, the average age for menarche has declined to 11.5 years of age (Wattigney et al., 1999). This dramatic change in the age of menarche has decreased an average of four months every ten years for the past century. Why are girls prepared for childbirth at an earlier age today? Although there are no clear answers, most experts believe the earlier onset results from better standards of living, medical advances, and improved nutrition. One study (Wattigney, Srinivasan, Chen, Greenlund, & Berenson, 1999) comparing age of menarche in the late 1970s and in the 1990s found continued early onset that is linked to increasing obesity in adolescents. Indeed, body mass is a key factor in menarche; for it to begin and continue, fat must make up 17% of a girl's body weight. The above Focus on Multiculturalism section examines how an Apache ceremony honors the young woman who reaches the childbearing years.

Hormonal Changes in Adolescence

During adolescence, the **endocrine glands** produce **hormones** that create different bodily changes in the young person. Hormones are powerful chemical substances that regulate various organs in the body. The endocrine glands that secrete the sex hormones are the pituitary gland and the sex glands, or gonads, referred to as testes in the male and ovaries in the female. The pituitary gland, or master gland, regulates a number of the other glands. Control of the pituitary gland rests with the **hypothalamus**, which "instructs" the pituitary gland on the optimum level of hormone secretion. The hormones secreted by the pituitary gland are known as **gonadotropins**, and they activate the **testes** and **ovaries**, which are the parts of the endocrine system called the gonads. The gonads secrete hormones; **androgen** from the testes, and **estrogen** from the ovaries. Males and females produce both estrogen and testosterone, although males produce more testosterone and females produce more estrogen. These hormones have an important effect on puberty in adolescence. Their effect is gradual as the hormones are gradually secreted, and the child moves toward physical and sexual maturity. The hormonal changes take place about a year before changes in the body and sex organs are visible.

Implications for Practice: Physical Changes and Psychological Consequences

Physical changes have psychological consequences for developing boys and girls. With girls, menarche is associated with greater social maturity, improved status among peers, higher self-esteem, greater self-awareness regarding one's body, and increased self-consciousness (Brooks-Gunn, 1986; Petersen, 1987). These psychological reactions are convincingly described in this diary entry of Anne Frank (1952):

> I think what is happening to me is so wonderful, and not only what can be seen on my body, but all that is taking place inside. I never discuss myself or any of these things with anybody; that is why I have to talk to myself about them.
>
> Each time I have a period—and that has only been three times—I have the feeling that in spite of all the pain, unpleasantness, and nastiness, I have a sweet secret, and that is why, although it is nothing but a nuisance to me in a way, I always long for the time that I shall feel that secret within me again.

Puberty can be related to both positive and negative emotions; however, more recent research has found that girls do not have intense reactions to menarche but most find it mildly stressful. Most girls receive some information about menarche, and that may explain why their reactions are less intense than in the past. One factor that influences whether a girl's reaction will be positive or negative is early or late maturation.

Studies have found that, in general, it is better to be an early-maturing rather than a late-maturing boy. Research has found that early-maturing boys perceived themselves more positively, had more successful peer relationships, were more athletically oriented, and were more confident when compared with late-maturing boys (Spencer, Dupress, Swanson, & Cunningham, 1998; Simmons & Blyth, 1987). For girls, research has found early maturation to be a fairly strong risk factor. Early-maturing girls (*maturity* defined as onset of menstruation) did not do as well academically and were more likely to have behavior problems (see Spencer et al., 1998). One study (Attie & Brooks-Gunn, 1989) found the single largest impact of early sexual maturation on adjustment is body-image dissatisfaction. Early development was initially related to a positive body image, but this pattern was reversed when the girls entered the ninth grade. This may be due to the fact that early-maturing girls are shorter and stockier, whereas late-maturing girls are often taller and thinner.

These studies clearly demonstrate that the physical changes that take place in boys' and girls' bodies can lead to positive or negative reactions. An explanation for many of the negative reactions is that the young people were not prepared for the changes they were experiencing (LeCroy & Daley, 2001). Most girls describe their first period as "a little upsetting." Although girls often receive some preparation, boys receive little or no preparation for their experiences of nocturnal emissions and spontaneous erections. What can be done to better prepare young people for these impending changes in their bodies? Better information from sex-education programs or from parents could be helpful in creating a more positive adjustment for adolescents. A cross-cultural perspective indicates that for girls, menarche is a sign of womanhood; therefore, it is surprising that in the United States we do not treat a girl's first menses as a **rite of passage**. A ritualized recognition may be beneficial in helping young people experience their bodily changes as positive. Consider the ritual one girl reported in her family's reaction to her period (Shipman, 1968):

> When I discovered it, I called my mother and she showed me what to do. Then she did something I'll never forget. She told me to come with her and went to the living room to tell my father. She just looked at me and then at him and said, "Well, your little girl is a young lady now." My dad gave me a hug and congratulated me, and I felt grown up and proud that I really was a lady at last. That was one of the most exciting days of my life. I was so excited and happy (pp. 6–7).

Although puberty clearly has an impact on adolescent development, many researchers are concluding that the effect is not as strong as it was once believed to be (Kaplan, 2004). Looking at this period within the overall framework of the life cycle, it clearly has an impact; but so do other facets of the life cycle. Puberty may be no different. For some young people it is a significant stress, but for most it is not. New challenges result from the biological changes, but there are also cognitive, social, and environmental changes to be dealt with. Biological change may not be the single source of significant change we once thought it was. ■

Biophysical Strengths and Hazards

Increasingly, strengths are being recognized as an important part of the adolescent experience. For example, menstruation was previously perceived as an adverse experience for girls, but today it is known to elicit only a mild reaction. Also, much of the research on adolescent brain development is showing that the adolescent brain is not fully formed and functional but is a changing part of the biophysical development of the young person.

Adolescent Brain Development

Brain research in the past has focused on early childhood because it was believed that the brain had finished its development by puberty. Most researchers now believe that myelinization, the process in which neurons surround themselves by a fatty covering called the myelin sheath, continues throughout adolescence (Kalat, 2001). The myelin sheath insulates the wire-like fibers connecting regions of the brain, and this allows impulses to travel faster and more efficiently, leading to improved problem-solving and coordination, as well as faster reflexes.

An important implication regarding adolescent brain development is that parts of the brain related to emotions, judgment, and problem solving are later to arrive than previously believed. Indeed, a final growth spurt in the brain's gray matter occurs at around ages 11–13 in the frontal lobes of the brain—the regions that guide planning, problem solving, and judgment. Recent studies have found that one part of the brain, the amygdala, which governs emotional responses, expands in adolescence (Yurgelun-Todd, 2004). Studies have looked at how teens and adults respond to the same facial images. Looking at photographs of facial expressions depicting various emotions, such as fear, adults identified the correct emotion but surprisingly, teens got it wrong, often saying the person was angry. Conducting functional magnetic resonance imaging of the subjects' brains showed a stark difference in parts of the brain being used. Adults used the advanced prefrontal cortex and the more basic amygdala to evaluate the facial pictures. Younger adolescents relied entirely on the amygdala; older adolescents showed a shift toward using the frontal area of the brain.

The overall implication of this new brain research is that cognitive functions like problem solving, maturity, and insight are still developing in adolescence. This helps explain why a 15-year-old might get into a car driven by older friend who clearly has had too much to drink. This new understanding of the brain also raises new questions about ethics and legalities (Bowman, 2004). Should teenagers be executed for crimes they committed when they were 15 years old? Many scientists believe that emerging biological explanations that adolescent brains are different means that young people are less culpable. This new understanding about the brain influenced the recent Supreme Court's ruling that capital punishment was inappropriate for adolescents.

Common Health Hazards in Adolescence

Although adolescence is typically a period of good general health, it is also the beginning of some potentially serious health concerns. In particular, many adolescents experience problems with nutritional needs and eating habits, weight concerns, dysmenorrhea, acne, and headaches.

Nutritional Needs and Eating Habits

A proper diet and physical exercise are especially important for young people. The rapid development young people experience causes an increased need for nutrients (Lopez, Kelly, & Lopez, 2003). A familiar sight is the hungry teenager wolfing down a burger, fries, and a large shake. Adolescents need to increase their calorie intake to match their rate of growth. Their calorie intake can be so enormous that it often surprises parents who have to provide the food they need. In general, an average girl needs 2,200 calories per day and an average boy needs 2,800 calories per day (Clinton, Greenleaf, & Harrison, 2000). However, an adolescent male who is involved in sports may need as many as 6,000 calories in one day (Lopez et al., 2003). Given this large need for food intake, a critical question is whether the adolescent is getting his or her nutritional needs met. Often, adolescents do not get the proper nutritional diet. They frequently miss a meal, usually breakfast, and may fill up on high-energy snacks rather than eating a proper meal. In fact, it is estimated that up to 20% of a young person's calories come from snack foods (Haas & Massey, 2001). Although adolescents may get the calories they need, it is not uncommon for them to be lacking in the proper amount of fluid, protein, iron, and calcium. In addition to a diet that often contains too much fat, adolescents do not eat enough fruits and vegetables. One study found that only 17% of boys and 19% of girls ate the recommended amount of fruit (Munoz et al., 1998). Protein should constitute a reasonable part of adolescents' total daily energy intake. Adequate calcium intake is also a concern. Boys may not get enough calcium during periods of rapid skeletal growth, and girls, when weight conscious, may unknowingly reduce their calcium intake. Also, overconsumption of soft drinks may interfere with obtaining enough calcium, but this is primarily due to the replacement of milk with soft drinks not due to the caffeine and sugar in the soft drink. The female adolescent's iron levels may be low from blood loss during her menses. An iron supplement is often recommended.

Weight Concerns

Obesity can be a serious problem for adolescents, and it is rapidly increasing (Seidenfeld & Rickert, 2001). **Obesity** can be defined as a body weight of 20% or more above the recommended weight for one's height. Current estimates of the prevalence of obesity in adolescents as measured by the National Health and Nutrition Examination Survey range from 11% to 24% (Troiano & Flegal, 1999). It is a serious health problem that is associated with certain diseases, high blood pressure, and social and psychological problems. In adolescence, obesity is a serious social problem because of the name-calling, stigma, and rejection from peers that many young people experience. Many children prior to adolescence develop extra fat in response to the adolescent growth spurt. Once additional cells are formed, they may predispose the person toward obesity. In fact, eating behaviors established in adolescence carry into adulthood: 80% of obese adolescents become obese adults (Sigman & Flanery, 1992).

Dysmenorrhea

Dysmenorrhea is defined as cramping pain in the abdomen occurring just before or during menstruation (Coco, 1999). It is a very common experience, and prevalence rates report it is as high as 90%. Dysmenorrhea usually begins in the adolescent years. and it is too often underdiagnosed and undertreated. A study of college students found that 72% of monitored periods were painful, usually during the first day of the period (Harlow & Park, 1996). Treatment by physicians usually includes nonsteroidal anti-inflammatory medications (Coco, 1999). *Secondary dysmenorrhea* also occurs—it refers to painful menses resulting most often from endometriosis. The notion exists that menstrual pain diminishes either after the female reaches 24 years of age, when the uterus is completely mature, or after the birth of a baby, but this has not been consistently reported.

Acne

Acne occurs in more than 80% of adolescents (Russell, 2000). Acne is the result of increased androgen levels at puberty, which stimulate the production of sebum by the sebaceous glands of the body, usually the face. Most adolescents start to experience a decline in acne sometime after their 20th birthday. Acne is associated with genetic predisposition, but it is also related to accumulated oils in the body. Acne can lead to scarring of the tissue and can create embarrassment and social withdrawal. In recent years, oral and topical antibiotics have been used to greatly control the spread of acne. No research has been reported that links diet—foods such as pizza, chocolate, or soda—to acne, and studies have not found a link between stress and acne.

Headaches

By the time people reach adolescence they most likely have experienced a headache. In fact, headaches can begin to occur with some frequency—50% of adolescents who were at least 15 years of age had headaches. "Frequent" headaches were reported in 15% of those who were at least 15 years old (Lewis, 2002). Approximately 5% of boys and girls experience migraine headaches during adolescence. The common tension headache is believed to be caused by such factors as family or school stress, eyestrain, or neck and back strain. Headaches can also be related to other illnesses, such as the flu. The causes of migraine headaches are unknown and likely to be genetic.

Sleep

Sleep, or lack thereof, has become an increasing concern among professionals who work with adolescents. We know that the amount of sleep 10–18-

year-old children get each night declines from about 10 hours in middle childhood to around 8 hours by age 16 (Iglowstein et al., 2003). Sleep experts believe adolescents need about 9.25 hours of sleep every night to be in good physical and mental condition. In one study (Carskadon, 2002), approximately 50% of high school students went to bed after midnight on school nights, and 90% did so on weekends. Research has found that adolescents' circadian rhythm changes and they are more alert in the afternoons and evenings and not alert in the mornings when they require more sleep (Carskadon, 2004). Many difficulties emerge when young people fail to get enough sleep, including poor cognitive functioning, increased irritability, anxiety, and depression (Dahl & Lewin, 2002). Getting up for an early-morning schedule leaves adolescents sleep deprived and physiologically unready to perform. Unfortunately, many schools have started the school day earlier for adolescents. Research from one study found that adolescents who started the school day two hours later than typically required showed better academic performance.

STUDY TABLE: Biophysical dimension of adolescence

Biophysical Growth and Development	Adolescent boys and girls experience a growth spurt during which they gain in height and weight. Adolescence begins with the onset of puberty, which is identified by the combination of the growth spurt, maturation of psychological mechanisms, and the development of secondary sex characteristics. During puberty, girls experience menstruation, which is the cyclic shedding of the uterine lining that leads to vaginal bleeding about two weeks after an egg is released from an ovary and is not fertilized. In boys, puberty may be indicated by nocturnal emissions (wet dreams) and facial hair. Secular trend is the tendency in girls toward earlier maturity as a result of a better standard of living, medical advances, and improved nutrition. The endocrine glands that secrete sex hormones, which produce changes in the young person, are the pituitary gland and the sex glands or gonad (testes in males and ovaries in females). The hypothalamus controls the pituitary gland. The gonads secrete hormones. The testes secrete androgen and the ovaries secrete estrogen. Both males and females produce estrogen and testosterone, but males produce more testosterone and females produce more estrogen. Hormonal changes occur about a year before changes in the body and sex organs are visible. Menarche in girls is associated with greater social maturity, improved status among peers, higher self-esteem, and increased self-consciousness. Menarche may be mildly stressful for most girls. It is better for a boy to mature earlier rather than later; earlier maturation leads to more successful peer relationships, a stronger athletic orientation, and more confidence. On the other hand, early-maturing girls may be more at risk; they do not do as well academically and are more likely to have behavioral problems and a negative body image.
Biophysical Strengths and Hazards	The adolescent brain is not fully formed and functional, and cognitive functions such as problem solving, maturity, and insight are still developing. Myelinization, where neurons surround themselves by the fatty covering called a myelin sheath, continues throughout adolescence. This process leads to improved problem solving and coordination. A final growth spurt in the brain's gray matter in the frontal lobes, the regions that guide planning, problem solving, and judgment, occurs around age 11–13. The amygdala, which governs emotional responses, expands in adolescence. Adolescents need to increase their calorie intake to match their rate of growth. Often adolescents do not follow a proper diet. Adolescents need to eat

enough protein and should consume enough calcium. Female adolescents also may need to take a iron supplement due to blood loss during menses. Obesity (a body weight of 20% or more above the recommended weight for one's height) in adolescence is associated with certain diseases, high blood pressure, and social and psychological problems.

Dysmenorrhea is a cramping pain in the abdomen occurring just before or during menstruation. Acne is a result of increased androgen levels at puberty and can lead to scarring, as well as create embarrassment and social withdrawal. Headaches can begin to occur during adolescence as a result of migraine, illnesses, tension, and stress. Adolescents need about 9.25 hours of sleep per night. Adolescents' circadian rhythm changes, and they become more alert in the afternoons and evenings, and less alert in the mornings. Young people who do not get enough sleep may have poor cognitive function, increased irritability, anxiety, and depression.

CONCEPT MAP

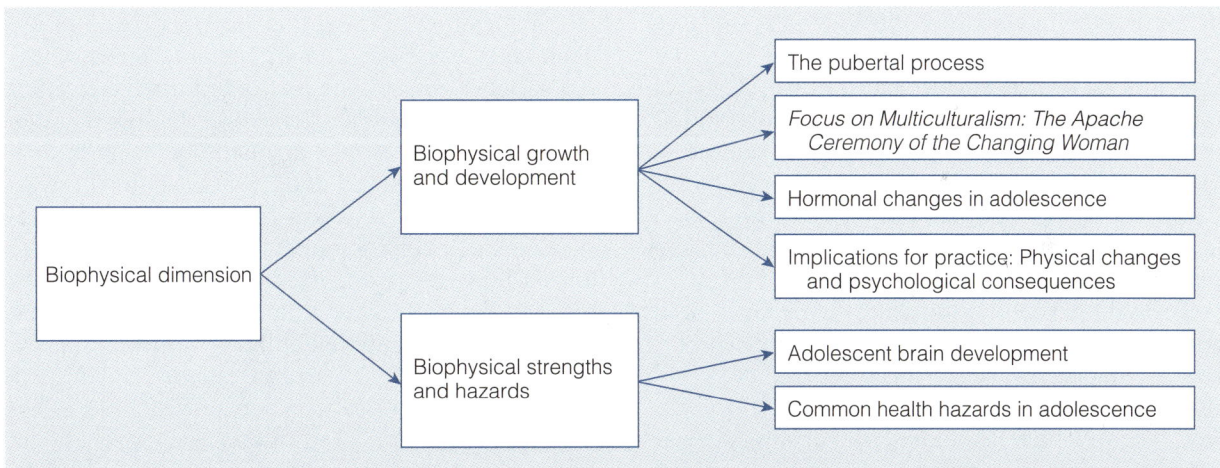

PSYCHOLOGICAL DIMENSION

Cognitive Development and Information Processing

Cognitive development in adolescence is identified with Piaget's last intellectual stage—formal operations. This period of development generally begins at around age 11 or 12. At this stage of development, the adolescent is capable of abstract thought; prior to this stage, the child could use only **concrete thinking** or **concrete operations**. Now a whole new world is opened up within the adolescent's mind—flexible and abstract thinking. Adolescents begin to understand abstract propositions and try to reason logically about them. This kind of logical problem solving is referred to as **hypothetical-deductive reasoning**. This problem-solving process uses hunches, or hypotheses, to solve a problem and follows a planned manner to test and evaluate the hypotheses until the best solution is discovered.

In fact, adolescents may begin to ponder the nature of their own thinking. They can think about why they were thinking about certain things. This kind of abstract thinking is also associated with idealism and thoughts about future possibilities.

Why do adolescents often concern themselves with such things as future life plans, their internal

EXHIBIT 9.3 Examples of formal operations and logic in adolescence

Major changes in thinking	Examples
Thinking about possibilities	"I would like to get to know her even better—she could be a good friend, or I might decide she'd be good as a girlfriend. We like each other. We can work out a closer relationship."
Testing hypotheses	"She told me she wasn't interested in being my girlfriend. After that I thought girls just don't like me, that I'm not good enough looking or cool enough. But I've had other girlfriends and other girls have shown interest in me. Not all girls are going to like me—I just need to find the right girl for me."
Thinking about the future	"I have a girlfriend now, and we get along really well, but if we stay together, I won't know what it's like to be with other girls. In order to marry the best person, it seems that you need to have a lot of girlfriends."
Thinking about thoughts	"I keep thinking about how much other people like me. Am I really popular with other kids? But even if I'm not that popular, I've got a lot of good friends. I shouldn't worry so much about whether I'm popular and just keep the good friends I have."
Expansion of thought	"I was invited to a party, but my best friend, Tyler, wasn't. John, who's giving the party, doesn't like Tyler. If I tell Tyler, then he'll be mad at John—and John told me not to let him know. But if Tyler asks me, I don't want to lie to him. I don't know if I should keep my promise to John and lie to Tyler."

life, or developing their own ideology? Piaget (1972) would argue that this thinking is caused by the characteristics of formal operational thought. They can now think beyond the real to the possible and reflect on the nature of thought itself. For example, an adolescent girl might think, "What would it be like if Jack and I were dating? I shouldn't think about Jack that way; I should think about what I want from him now."

Formal operational thought is believed to occur in two distinct stages during adolescence. The first stage is characterized by a focus on the ideal, with unlimited possibilities. This stage is referred to as *assimilation*, in which the adolescent consolidates new information into existing knowledge. During middle adolescence, a better balance is obtained through the process of *accommodation*; the adolescent must adjust to the cognitive changes that have occurred. By late formal operational thought, adolescents test their reasoning against experience and they incorporate their formal operational thinking (Lapsley, 1996). Exhibit 9.3 presents a summary of the five major changes that occur with formal operational thinking.

Although Piaget's theory emphasizes a universal understanding of thought, it is important to recognize the individual variations that occur in adolescents' cognitive development. For example, research has found that only one out of three eighth-grade students is capable of formal operational thinking and by late adolescence only about 60% of young people use formal operations (Kaplan, 2004). A critical factor in such thinking is the adolescent's experience and knowledge in certain areas (Flavell, 1985). In fact, many experts believe that Piaget's stage of formal operations reasoning is applicable only to technological societies where there is a lot of formal education and practice using such reasoning. In this manner, children and adolescents gradually build up knowledge through experience and practice in different areas.

These types of concerns led Piaget (1972) to reevaluate his theories, and he was convinced that factors such as education, vocational interests, and culture can determine one's performance on tests that assess formal operational abilities. Consider this example from a study of African Americans who play a challenging board game where players must calculate complex defense and offense moves. These are just the kind of strategies that require logical thinking representative of formal operations (Retschitzki et al., 1989). Yet experts in this game do poorly on Piagetian tests of formal operations. Why would they perform poorly on such tasks? Although they use formal operations in one context, they do not have the experience required to do well in a context of Piagetian types of problems.

Communication

Along with an improvement in thinking abilities in adolescence comes a greater capacity for effective communication. The manner of a person's thinking logically relates to his or her ability to use language. For example, the use of metaphors increases during this time period. To understand metaphors, one must think beyond concrete operations; therefore, fables or parables are not of interest to elementary school children. (A metaphor is a comparison of two ideas, such as in the statement "He has a heart of stone.")

Also of particular interest in adolescence is the use of satire or ridicule (Santrock, 2002). Adolescents typically invent satirical labels for teachers, parents, and peers. For example, peers may be better known by labels such as "klutz," "brain," or "Mr. Heavy Metal" than by their real names.

Writing becomes much more meaningful in adolescence. This is the age when many young people begin a journal to record their inner thoughts and personal experiences. Younger children have difficulty writing because they do not have the type of logical thought processes needed to organize their ideas. Adolescents are able to accentuate the important points they are trying to communicate because they can think logically about what they want to say before they write it down.

During adolescence, the nature of boys' talk and girls' talk begins to become increasingly differentiated, as described by one adolescent boy (Eckert, 1990, p. 91):

> I think girls must talk too much, you know, they—they—talk constantly between themselves and about every little thing. Guys, I don't think we talk about that much. (*What kinds of things do you talk about?*) Not much. Girls . . . cars, or parties, you know. I think girls talk about, you know, every little relationship, every little thing that's ever happened, you know.

In general, it appears that boys talk more in terms of competitive conversation, comparing knowledge and experience, whereas girls talk more about themselves, their personal feelings, and their relationships.

Adolescent Communication and Confidentiality

There is a growing need for social workers to understand the social and legal aspects of communicating consent and confidentiality to adolescents. Because adolescents engage in a variety of health-risk behaviors, they need to access services without facing significant barriers (LeCroy & Daley, 2001). Unfortunately, adolescents vastly underutilize systems of care; they seek assistance less frequently than any other age group.

Concerns about confidentiality are becoming more complex, especially for sexually active adolescents. Although information about issues such as family planning and sexually transmitted diseases is protected as belonging to "confidential medical records," separate laws aimed at child abuse require health professionals to report all sexually active adolescents younger than 18 to authorities. How this trend in increased reporting of adolescents will impact their motivation to seek other forms of help is still unknown.

A growing body of knowledge is making it clear that confidentiality is the foremost barrier in the effective treatment of adolescents. One study of a high school found that 25% of students would not seek health care if confidentiality were not assured (Cheng, Savageau, Sattler, & DeWitt, 1993). Other studies have found that adolescents will not seek care from their physician for sexuality, substance abuse, or emotional issues if their parents have to know about the office visit (Society for Adolescent Medicine, 2004).

One study (Ford, Millstein, Halpern-Felsher, & Irwin, 1997), using a randomized trial, found that adolescents were more willing to communicate with and seek health care from physicians who provided assurances of confidentiality. More dramatically, consider that one study reported that almost half of all adolescents with depressive symptoms cited concerns about confidentially as their reason for not getting help (Phillips, 1998). Some fear parental retribution, lack of understanding, and damage to their reputation or self-worth (Society for Adolescent Medicine, 2004).

Adolescents have made it clear that in order for many of them to feel comfortable receiving services they want clear communication about confidentiality. It is important to recognize that communicating directly with the adolescent alone, clarifying with whom the information will be shared, and creating a comfortable and trusting environment is needed to obtain candid information.

Attitudes and Emotions

Adolescence is an important period for the developing self-concept. Young people set out to discover "who they are" and "what they want to become." A significant part of this process results from a focus on self-reflection and thought. And indeed there is much for the young adolescent to think about. Adolescents obtain greater freedom in behavior and decision making, increased opportunities for both acceptance and rejection by peer groups, experience in dating and the awareness of their sexuality, and major decisions affecting their movement into adult life. As these experiences are explored and reflected upon, the adolescent develops a more integrated self.

The founder of developmental psychology, G. Stanley Hall, is well known for his characterization of adolescence as a time of "storm and stress." In her writings, Anna Freud argued that such storm and stress is simply a part of normal adolescence. Psychoanalyst Peter Blos also believed that adolescence was a period of uncontrolled sexual and aggressive impulses. However, these early notions about the craziness of the teenage years are now considered myths. Experts in adolescent psychology (for example, Adelson, Douvan, Offer, and Bandura) are increasingly concerned because the widespread idea that adolescence is a normal period of serious difficulty has mischaracterized the lives of millions of healthy adolescents. Daniel Offer, an adolescent psychiatrist, brought attention to this myth when he declared a "Defense of Adolescence." Although it is difficult for many people to believe, research has empirically supported the fact that the majority of adolescents are well adjusted, get along well with peers and parents, and cope well with their emotional processes and external environments. For purposes of studying the issues social workers and mental health professionals come in contact with most often, this chapter may seem to focus mostly on the deviant behaviors or alternative attitudes of teenagers. It is important for us to remember that the majority of teens are not like the ones this text uses as examples.

Adolescent Self-Esteem

Self-esteem is a global evaluation of one's self, often referred to as *self-image* or *self-concept* (Adler & Stewart, 2004). What does research on adolescent self-esteem tell us about adjustment in adolescence? In general, we find that self-esteem can vary depending on the stage of adolescence. During early adolescence (age 12 to 14 years), self-esteem appears to reach its lowest point (Kaplan, 2004; Simmons, Rosenberg, & Rosenberg, 1973). During these years, young people are highly self-conscious, and their self-perceptions are more easily influenced. This is especially true of girls making the transition to junior high school (Quatman & Watson, 2001). The lowest self-esteem occurs among girls who mature early and start to date (Simmons et al., 1973). It is important to emphasize that, overall, most adolescents emerge from this developmental phase with about the same amount of self-esteem as they had at the outset.

One interesting study attempted to examine the emotional life of adolescents during their daily activities. Researchers Csikszentmihalyi and Larson (1984) asked seventy-five adolescents to wear electronic pagers for one week. When they were signaled, about every two hours, they completed a log about where they were, how they felt, and what they were experiencing. One conclusion derived from the study was that adolescents experience a remarkable amount of diversity. They may be a student, a helper, an employee, a commuter, a child, a teammate, a friend, and more. Also remarkable is that the average adolescent can come down from extreme happiness or up from extreme sadness within forty-five minutes. Adults, by contrast, often take hours to change from one mood to the next. The researchers suggest that adolescents must learn to come to terms with the downs as well as the ups. Instead of allowing the downs to completely overtake them, they need to strive for greater balance and perspective. Many of the youth, in response to boredom, became involved in less productive and less satisfying activities like watching television. However, youth who took up more challenging activities learned the positive feelings of personal fulfillment that can result from such challenges.

Foster children, who tend to move around often from one family unit to another, may have an especially hard time adjusting to the many transitions of adolescence and therefore suffer in their self-image.

Self-Image and Adolescents in Foster Care

In adolescence, self-esteem has been shown to be influenced by parental support, control, and participation; perceptions of family cohesion; and a sense of belonging to one's family. Consistent with these findings, low self-esteem has been found to be a characteristic of foster-care children, with weakened family ties being associated with low self-esteem and identity confusion. The dismal fact is that more than 98% of foster care children enter care because of some family dysfunction (Pecora, Whittaker, Maluccio, & Barth, 2000).

There is some positive evidence that removal from a dysfunctional family may increase self-esteem because of a reduction in the inconsistent interactions and conflict that characterize many dysfunctional families. However, foster children are at a higher risk for both psychosocial and medical problems. Also, research has found that low self-esteem is related to the multiple placements and the length of time in placement that foster children often experience. There is a high incidence of behavior problems and school problems in this population. Due to these conflicting findings, there is controversy over recent social-work practice and policy, which view foster care as a last resort because of the perception that the harmful effects of removal from the home outweigh the benefits (Courtney & Barth, 1996).

The pattern of loss experienced by foster-care children, including the loss of family, peer relationships, and community, is likely to influence the way children view themselves. In fact, self-esteem, as a major determinant of general mental health, could play a role in the resilience of foster-care youths. Given the controversy over the use of foster care as an intervention and the effects that this debate has on placement decisions, it would be valuable to know how foster-care youth value themselves and see their foster-care experience.

Researchers found that the pattern of loss typically found in foster-care children is likely to influence the way children view themselves. Research shows that when family support is low, social relationships gain importance. Therefore, removal from a high-conflict family situation and placement in a foster-care situation may provide the opportunity to develop other supportive relationships that can then be used to develop a positive image.

So, what are the implications of this research? In general, foster-care placement as an intervention for older adolescents should be reconsidered as an alternative (Pecora et al., 2000). Adolescents who are experiencing deficits in the realms of family relations and mental health should have resources targeted to them to address these issues (Webb & Harden, 2003). The results also support the concern that multiple placements can create risk. Efforts aimed at stabilizing placements need to be paramount in the placement decision process. Finally, stable placements that provide opportunities for adolescents to achieve and to form supportive relationships may even be able to compensate for problems in other life areas.

Implications for Practice: Enhancing Adolescents' Self-Concepts

There are four main strategies for enhancing adolescents' self concepts: (1) encouraging achievement, (2) promoting competencies in specific areas, (3) provision of peer and

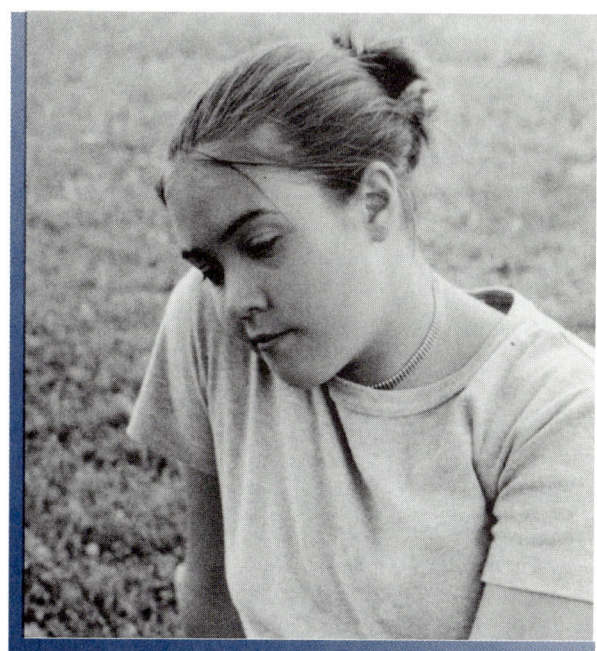

In early adolescence, young people who are self-conscious can easily develop negative self-perceptions that sometimes lead to depression, a common problem in adolescents.

parental support, and (4) developing coping skills. Adolescents can improve their self-concept so that it moves closer to their ideal self. Many young people need to challenge the realism of their ideal self. Is it realistic to hope for such high standards? Many adolescents begin the process of insisting on irrational standards of behavior. These "shoulds" and "musts" can take the place of recognizing actual accomplishments (LeCroy & Daley, 2001). Adolescents who are taught to recall positive thoughts and feelings about past events show an increase in self-esteem (LeCroy, 2004).

Adolescents can be guided to emphasize the areas in which they are more likely to succeed. A less physically coordinated young person can become more skilled in playing a game that requires intellectual skills. Assertiveness-training studies with young people have found results that show an increase in self-esteem (Stake, DeVille, & Rennell, 1983). Sometimes adolescents need to work harder at achieving their standards of excellence or to accept a good performance, as opposed to a perfect one (LeCroy & Daley, 2001).

Self-esteem is also related to other factors, such as peer-group formation. Studies find that self-esteem is improved by both peer and parental support (Robinson, 1995), and by participation in community and school experiences (Harter, 1999). Coping abilities relate to both enhanced self-esteem and reduced stress (Heatherington

> ### FOCUS ON MULTICULTURALISM
>
> #### DO AFRICAN AMERICAN ADOLESCENTS HAVE LOW SELF-ESTEEM?
>
> Although growing up as an African American adolescent might suggest low self-esteem when compared with majority white youth, such a finding is simply not true. During the period of school desegregation, it was believed that African American children suffered damage to their self-esteem because they were in segregated schools. However, research that examined this issue found there are no differences in self-esteem between African American children in segregated and desegregated schools (Cook, 1979; Gray, Little & Hafdahl, 2000; Twenge & Crocker, 2002). Adolescents of color do experience greater discrimination, poverty, and social and educational barriers than white youth do, and as a result, we can predict more negative outcomes for African American adolescents. However, as Gibbs (2003) has pointed out, social workers must be careful about overpathologizing and stereotyping all African American youth as victims of their racial identify or social-class status. The majority of African American youth cope effectively with their ethnicity and class status.

& Blechman, 1996; Lazarus, 1991). When adolescents use coping abilities to solve problems, the result is often positive self-evaluations and increased self-esteem. When taught coping strategies, adolescents learn to face problems realistically and honestly (Compas, 1995). The above Focus on Multiculturalism box examines self-esteem for a particular group, African Americans.

Social Cognition and Regulation

Adolescence is believed to be an important time for the development of identity. Young people seek to answer important questions about themselves. Who am I? What is important to me in my life? These types of questions represent the stage of life that Erikson characterized as identity versus identity confusion.

Young people enter what Erikson calls a **psychological moratorium**—a gap between childhood security and adult autonomy. Erikson's ideas were extended by James Marcia (1966), who developed a classification system for adolescent identity statuses, or modes of resolution:

- *Identity diffusion.* This is the least mature status for the adolescent to be in. These adolescents have not yet experienced a crisis; that is, they are not exploring meaningful alternatives. No commitments have been made to important attitudes, values, or plans for the future.
- *Identity foreclosure.* In this stage, adolescents have made a commitment to particular goals, values, and beliefs but have not yet experienced a crisis. Most often, in identity foreclosure, parents push a commitment on their adolescents in an authoritative manner (you will go to college or join the army). Yet adolescents have not had the needed opportunities to adequately explore their own perceptions, ideologies, and beliefs.
- *Identity moratorium.* This status describes adolescents who are currently experiencing a crisis—actively exploring values, ideologies, and beliefs. Their commitments may be either absent or only vaguely defined.
- *Identity achievement.* At this final stage, adolescents have undergone and resolved their crisis by making strong commitments to things such as an occupation, a sexual orientation, or a religious ideology.

Although the identity status theory has had an enormous influence on the field of adolescent psychology, it has become increasingly criticized (Cote & Levine, 1988; Lapsley & Power, 1988). Most of the criticism revolves around Erikson's notions of crisis and commitment. Erikson emphasized questioning perceptions and expectations and developing an autonomous position within one's society, whereas the identity status approach is concerned with simply evaluating whether one has thought about such issues. In their search for identity, young people are struggling with unresolved questions. Adams and Gullotta (1989) presented a variety of questionnaire items that represent an alternative to Marcia's interview technique in assessing identity status. Exhibit 9.4 presents examples of the questionnaire items used in measuring ego-identity status.

Recent work in identity development suggests several important considerations. The idea of *crisis* may

> ### FOCUS ON MULTICULTURALISM
>
> #### IDENTITY AND NATIVE AMERICAN YOUTH
>
> Consider the following story about a conversation between a Native American and an Anglo youth (Coles, 1986). "In school, I drew a picture of my father's horse. One of the other kids wouldn't believe that it was ours. He said, 'You don't really own that horse.' I said, 'It's a horse my father rides, and I feed it every morning.' He said, 'How come?' I said, 'My uncle and my father are good riders, and I'm pretty good.' He said, 'I can ride a horse better than you, and I'd rather be a pilot.' I told him I never thought of being a pilot."
>
> The boy is clear about the differences between himself and the Anglo youth he knows. "The Anglos I've met, they're different. I don't know why. Anglo kids, they won't let you get away with anything. Tell them something, and fast as lightning and loud as thunder, they'll say, 'I'm better than you, so there!' My father says it's always been like that."
>
> This poem of a 12-year-old youth reflects the development of his peaceful identity as a Native American youth (Coles, 1986):
>
> Rivers flow. The sea sings.
> Oceans roar. Tides rise.
>   Who am I?
> A small pebble on a giant shore;
> Who am I
> To ask who I am?
> Isn't it enough to be?
>
> SOURCE: From *Political life of children*, by Robert Coles. Copyright © 1986 Robert Coles. Used by permission of Grove/Atlantic, Inc.

be misleading, in that identity development appears to be a lengthy process. The complexity of identity formation is becoming more recognized (Marcia, 1987), as is the notion that such a process does not begin and end in adolescence. Identity development is significant in adolescence because this is when physical development, cognitive development, and social development converge, creating the opportunity for a synthesis as the young person charts a path to adulthood (Santrock, 2002).

EXHIBIT 9.4 Examples of questionnaire items used in measuring ego-identity status

Status	Item
Diffusion	I haven't chosen the occupation I really want to get into, but I'm working toward becoming a _____ until something better comes along.
Foreclosure	I've never really questioned my religion. If it's right for my parents, it must be right for me.
Moratorium	I just can't decide how capable I am as a person and what jobs I'll be right for.
Identity achievement	A person's faith is unique to each individual. I've considered and reconsidered it myself and know what I can believe.

SOURCE: Adams & Gulotta (1989), p. 241.

Marcia (1987) noted that critical issues for early adolescence are gaining confidence in parental support, the development of a sense of industry, and a self-reflective perspective about the future. However, research (Bosma, 2001) is finding that many of the most important identity changes are taking place in later adolescence, between the ages of 18 and 21. Furthermore, researchers (Bosma & Kunnen, 2001) have found that changes toward a more advanced identity status are related to personality development and to social cognitive development.

Youth of Color and Adolescent Identity

Identity in adolescence is a significant developmental task, and often it is an even more critical task for the adolescent of color. During adolescence, youth must integrate their image of being from an ethnic group while being exposed to values and images of the mainstream white culture. Young people often perceive a negative image from the white majority and then face the task of developing a positive identity as a member of an ethnic group (Yeh & Drost, 2004). Because of their cognitive maturity, adolescents of color are often quite aware of how others evaluate their minority status.

> ### FOCUS ON NARRATIVE
>
> #### AN OPEN LETTER TO THE WORLD
>
> *Dear World,*
> *I am a black child, a Black child with pride, dignity, strength and courage and intelligence.*
>
> *You wonder, "Is it possible for a black child to possess all those qualities?" And, of course, the realization that I do scares you to death. So . . . as you continue in your state of deep, never-ending denial of my will to survive, you deprive me of my heritage, misinform me of my accomplishments, omit my history from your schoolbooks, try to ban my musical education, tear down my community with drugs, disease, police brutality, and more.*
>
> *I have been oppressed and enslaved for many years. Every time you think you've won, I, and all of my brothers and sisters, rise to the occasion, and you lose again. I'm still here, and I'm still Black.*
>
> *I am a Black child, here to return my people's dignity, to retrieve my people's history and, most of all, I am today's Black child, striving to become tomorrow's black future.*
>
> —SHIELA "DA MOON" ROSE
>
> SOURCE: Carlip (1995), p. 214.

Issues that such youth face as they focus on identity development include racial stereotypes that affect their "looking-glass self"; cultural devaluation of the symbols and heroes of their group; and lack of successful role models with whom to identify (Spencer & Dornbusch, 1990). Identity development during adolescence leaves many young people making comparisons between themselves and others. Eventually, adolescents of color must reconcile their lives from the standpoint of two contrasting cultural systems—their own ethnic and cultural values, and the white majority cultural values. This often leads to three options: alienation, where youth reject the majority culture and the opportunities it provides; assimilation, where youth reject their ethnic values and strive to conform and assimilate to white majority values; and biculturalism, where youth learn to negotiate both their ethnic values and the values of the dominant culture. In this case, the value structures of both groups are available, and the young people must negotiate which standards to use depending on the situation (Yeh & Hwang, 2000). The Focus on Narrative presents the voice of an African American girl who identifies with the hip hop culture.

Implications for Practice: Identity and Independence

Independence is a related aspect of developing an identity. To help a young person successfully develop an identity, issues of independence need to be carefully reviewed. Young people face many challenges as they attempt to establish an identity—making new commitments to friends, gaining greater independence from parents, and developing more intimate friendships and relationships. Also at this time, the young person is increasingly learning to reflect on his or her actions as he or she makes increasingly important life decisions.

Parents can be important influences in the adolescent's development of identity (Santrock, 2002). Research has found that the adolescent's connectedness to parents and the presence of a family atmosphere promote individuation in the adolescent's identity development. **Connectedness** refers both to the adolescent's sensitivity to and respect for others' views and to the adolescent's openness and responsiveness to others' views. **Individuation** has two parts—separateness and self-assertion. Separateness is the expression of the individual's distinct self from others. Self-assertion refers to adolescents' expression of their viewpoints and their clear communication.

Consider the situation in which the adolescent's mother has not "let go" of her daughter. The girl is tied to the mother financially and emotionally in ways that do not let her mature independently. Under these circumstances, the girl could develop difficulties in developing mature intimate relationships and in career choices (Santrock, 2002). She may turn down important opportunities for more responsibility, doubting her abilities to be independent. Similarly, rather than confronting difficulties in her intimate relationships, she may turn to her mother for support and comfort. In working with adolescents, social workers need to be aware of their need for independence and help young people chart a course of increased maturity. This may involve working with parents or school staff on independence-granting skills in order to encourage responsibility and maturity. Too often, society sees the young person as immature and not ready for adult roles rather than systematically encouraging the young person to take increasing responsibility for mature behavior.

It is important to recognize that such notions about individuation and independence are culture bound (de Anda, 2004). In Latino families, interdependence is a more appropriate concept. Indeed, the one characteristic that many people believe is consistent in most Hispanic cultures is family commitment—based on loyalty, support, honor of the family, and duty to care for family members. These notions are in conflict with the more mainstream emphasis on individualism (Griggs & Dunn, 2004). Research studies (Black, Paz, & DeBlassie, 1991) confirm that Hispanic adolescents are more likely than white adolescents to adopt their parents' occupational preferences, lifestyle, and commitment to religious and political beliefs. The implication is that for Hispanic adolescents the move to independence may look more like interdependence, whereby the young person is less likely to move away from the family but takes on more responsibilities for the family (de Anda, 2004). For Hispanic adolescents who do have identity-related problems, a group counseling format with peers is recommended (Griggs & Dunn, 2004).

Social Cognitive Monitoring

Social cognitive monitoring is a person's ability to monitor and make sense of his or her social thoughts. This development of conscious self-awareness increases during middle childhood and adolescence. Such social awareness is indicated by thoughts like "I don't think I'm easily influenced by others" or "I'm going to have a difficult time talking to and getting to know this person." These kinds of thoughts exemplify how adolescents monitor their social world. As young people develop, they begin to recognize that social thoughts are difficult to assess. Also, experiencing different aspects of others can decrease their accuracy in assessing social thoughts. For example, witnessing another person expressing strong emotions may lead to an inaccurate understanding of that person. As this process develops, children learn that people sometimes do not think accurately about others because they have caught them in a bad mood (Flavell, 1981). Flavell (1979, p. 910) states that "In many real-life situations, the monitoring problem is not to determine how well you understand what a message means but rather to determine how much you ought to believe it or do what it says to do."

Regulation

A woman was dying of a particular type of cancer. However, there was one drug that doctors believed could save her. A druggist in the town where the woman and her husband lived had discovered this drug. Although the drug was expensive to make, the druggist was charging ten times what the drug cost him to make. He paid $200 for the drug and was charging $2,000 for a small dose of it. The woman's husband, Heinz, went to all their friends to borrow money for the drug; however, he gathered only $1,000—half the cost. He told the druggist that his wife was dying and asked him to sell it more cheaply or let him pay later. The druggist said, "No, I discovered the drug, and I am going to make money from it." So Heinz got desperate and broke into the druggist's store to steal the drug for his wife (Kohlberg, 1969).

This story raises a number of difficult moral questions. Does the husband have a duty to steal the drug for his wife if he cannot get it in another way? Did the druggist have a right to charge so much for the drug?

This story and these types of questions are a common method of investigating adolescents' moral judgments. The attempt is to find out how the adolescent thinks about moral dilemmas where there is no clear right or wrong answer. How a person reasons about whether to steal or not steal the drug would be an indication of his or her stage of moral development. **Moral development** refers to the rules of conduct people use in their interactions with others. For example, the adolescent could reason that he or she should not steal the drug because stealing is against the law. However, another line of reasoning might be that stealing the drug is acceptable because it is unfair to charge such a high price for the drug and it is worse to have the wife die from not receiving the drug than it is to steal.

Kohlberg believes that rules of conduct develop as individuals progress through stages. Each stage represents a different way of reasoning about various rules of conduct. In this model, summarized in Exhibit 9.5, there are six separate stages of moral development that begin in the preschool years and continue through adulthood. These stages can be thought of as theories of right and wrong that we carry around with us. Each stage has a different idea of what's right and a different idea of the reason a person should be good (Lickona, 2004). As people progress through each stage, they get closer to a fully developed morality. The stages correspond to the preconventional

EXHIBIT 9.5 Kohlberg's stages of moral reasoning showing sample responses to the Heinz-and-druggist dilemma

Stage of moral development	Examples of moral reasoning that support stealing the drug	Examples of moral reasoning that support not stealing the drug
Level 1: Pre-conventional reasoning		
Stage 1: Punishment and obedience	Heinz should not let his wife die, so he will stay out of trouble.	Heinz should not get caught and end up being sent to jail.
Stage 2: Instrumental-relativist	If Heinz does get caught, he should give the drug back and try to avoid a long jail sentence.	The druggist is in a business. He deserves to make money from his business.
Level 2: Conventional reasoning		
Stage 3: Interpersonal concordance, or "good boy/nice girl" stage	Heinz is being a good husband; he is doing this because he loves his wife.	Heinz cannot accept blame if his wife dies. The druggist is being selfish.
Stage 4: Law and order	If Heinz did nothing, he would be letting his wife die; it is his responsibility if she dies. He can steal the drug and pay the druggist later.	It is always wrong to steal. Heinz will suffer from lifelong guilt if he does steal the drug.
Level 3: Post-conventional reasoning		
Stage 5: Social contract; legalistic orientation	There is no law set up for these circumstances. Although stealing the drug is wrong, Heinz is justified in doing it.	These circumstances don't justify someone taking the law into their own hands. Heinz should not be guided by emotions; he should consider the long-term implications and not lose respect for himself.
Stage 6: Universal ethical principle	If Heinz steals the drug he would live up to society's rules, but he would let down his own conscience.	Heinz should think about other people who might need the drug as badly as his wife. His actions should be guided by consideration of the value of all lives involved.

and postconventional stages of moral reasoning as described by Kohlberg.

Critique of Kohlberg's Moral Development Theory

Although Kohlberg's theory of moral development has received considerable support, questions have been raised concerning the link between moral thought and behavior, the quality of the research, and gender bias. To what extent is moral judgment associated with behavior? Do people who reason differently also decide to act on the basis of their judgments? These are difficult questions, and researchers have not found consistent results (see Emler, Renwick, & Malone, 1983; Lapsley, 1990). Perhaps moral reasoning does not directly affect behavior but may provide a sense of direction and ethical standards.

Criticism concerning the quality of the research in this area tends to focus on a couple of aspects. Most criticized is how moral development is measured. Kohlberg uses a series of moral dilemmas, like the one presented above, and interviews subjects in order to determine a stage of moral development. Some researchers (Rest, 1986) would like to see alternative assessment methods used. Also, concerns have been raised about the content presented in the moral dilemmas—that is, the dilemmas do not reflect the subjects' lives. One developmentalist (Yussen, 1977) had adolescents generate their own moral dilemmas, and, indeed, the focus was more oriented toward friends, acquaintances, family, and authorities.

Another issue involving moral development has to do with gender bias. Most moral development research has been conducted with males. Carol Gilligan (1982, 1985) is well known for her criticism of Kohlberg. She contends that his theoretical perspective is based on a **justice perspective**, in which the focus is on the rights of the individual. People are characterized as standing alone in their decision making. In contrast, Gilligan offers a theory based on a **care perspective**, in which the focus is on people's connectedness to others. Her theory emphasizes attachments, allowing for both self-sacrifice and self-promotion, with connections being seen as most important (Gump, Baker, & Roll, 2000). There is more of a focus on interpersonal communication. According to Gilligan, Kohlberg has underestimated the care perspective underlying moral development for both males and females. She believes that the highest level of moral development involves a search for moral equality between oneself and others. Much research has examined the gender difference in moral development. An analysis of the combined research (Jaffee & Hyde, 2000) found very few differences between males and females in their moral reasoning, concluding that the majority of studies do not lend support to the idea that females reason in a predominantly caring manner and males in a predominantly justice-oriented manner. In fact, most people reason using both perspectives. Although Gillian's classic criticism of Kohlberg may not stand up to research, her contribution that individuals consider both justice and caring perspectives has advanced the field greatly.

Implications for Practice:
Adolescent Moral Development

To further illustrate how moral development can be used to better understand adolescence, we will use independence as an example. Most young adolescents are in stage 3, interpersonal conformity, according to Exhibit 9.6, which describes the stages of moral development and the corresponding thoughts that relate to each stage. At this stage, young people seek to be nice people—so that others will think well of them and they can think well of themselves.

A significant challenge for parents is confronting the typical conformist reasoning apparent at this stage. This is best done by teaching the value of independence and strengthening the young person's ability to be her or his

EXHIBIT 9.6 The stages of moral reasoning

Ages indicate reasonable developmental expectations for a child of normal intelligence growing up in a supportive moral environment.

Stages	What's right	Reason to be good
Stage 0: Egocentric reasoning (preschool years—around age 4)	I should get my own way.	To get rewards and avoid punishments.
Stage 1: Unquestioning obedience (around kindergarten age)	I should do what I'm told.	To stay out of trouble.
Stage 2: What's-in-it-for-me fairness (early elementary grades)	I should look out for myself but be fair to those who are fair to me.	Self-interest: What's in it for me?
Stage 3: Interpersonal conformity (middle to upper elementary grades and early to mid-teens)	I should be a nice person and live up to the expectations of people I know and care about.	So others will think well of me (social approval) and I can think well of myself (self-esteem).
Stage 4: Responsibility to "the system" (high school years or late teens)	I should fulfill my responsibilities to the social or value system I feel part of.	To keep the system from falling apart and to maintain self-respect as somebody who meets my obligations.
Stage 5: Principled conscience (young adulthood)	I should show the greatest possible respect for the rights and dignity of every individual person and should support a system that protects human rights.	The obligation of conscience to act in accordance with the principle of respect for all human beings.

SOURCE: From *Raising good children*, by Thomas Lickona, Ph.D., p. 12. Copyright © 1983 Thomas Lickona. Used by permission of Bantam Books.

own person and resist the pressures of the peer group (Lickona, 2004, 1983). Lickona presents a parent's perspective on how to challenge adolescent thinking at this stage. He presents six ways to help adolescents break free of typical conformist reasoning:

1. *Be an independent person yourself.* Parents need to model independent thinking and behavior. When young people suggest the old standby "Other parents let their kids do . . . ," parents need to resist the pressure to conform to parent peer pressure. Parents should suggest that what is important is not what others are doing but what they think is right.
2. *Talk about the value of being independent.* Parents need to help adolescents see that it is in their own interest to be independent. Lickona (1983; 2004) has recommended that parents say things such as, "Be your own person. Do what you like to do, what *you're* interested in. If you're true to yourself, you'll be happy with yourself. You can't be happy trying to be what you're not" (p. 189).
3. *Help young people think of words to say.* Parents should help young people role-play the exact words they might use in resisting peer pressure. For example, to a boyfriend who's interested in sexual relations, the young person might respond to a statement such as "Everybody's doing it," with, "Well, if everybody's doing it, then you shouldn't have any trouble finding somebody else" (Lickona, 1983, p. 189).
4. *Help young people understand themselves.* Young people will be better prepared to be independent if they understand the feelings that cause them to conform. Many young people experience feelings of inferiority, and those feelings lead them to seek peer approval through conformity.
5. *Help young people put popularity in perspective.* Peer popularity is what often keeps adolescents from being more independent. It is important for young people to realize that values change. Having a winning personality is valued at age 14 but may be less important in three or four years. Later, values such as sensitivity to others and being able to accomplish their goals will become increasingly important.
6. *Challenge the "group morality" of stage 3.* Parents can challenge adolescents' conformist reasoning by helping them see that "group morality" isn't a very good way to solve moral problems.

Lickona (1983, p. 190) presented an example of how parents can help their children move beyond group morality:

Will, who was on the junior high school baseball team, told his mother that the coach had kicked a kid off the team. Kids who thought it was unfair were talking about boycotting practice.

"Do *you* think it was unfair?" his mother asked.

"I'm not sure," Will said. "I just heard about what happened from some other kids. I didn't see it. According to them, Mr. Thompson accused Eric Miller of goofing off when he wasn't doing anything wrong. Then he just told him he was off the team."

"I see," his mother said. "So it's hard to be sure exactly what happened. What do you think of the boycott idea?"

"I don't know," Will said.

"How will you decide what to do?"

"I'll find out what other kids are going to do."

Will's mother tried to get him to examine the inadequacy of this kind of moral thinking. "What will you do then?"

Will sighed and shrugged his shoulders.

"So can you decide what's right on the basis of what the other kids are doing?"

"I guess not," Will said.

"Right," his mother said. "You have to use your own judgment. Think about what's fair, and what's going to help you, the coach, and the team. Would a boycott help matters?"

"No, not really."

"What else can be done?"

Together, Will and his mother came up with the idea that he could go to Mr. Thompson privately the next day and ask if he would call a meeting of the team to talk about what happened. ■

Moral Development: Three Theoretical Perspectives

Three common theoretical perspectives can be used to help explain and understand moral development: cognitive-developmental, learning-theory, and psychoanalytic (Adams & Gullotta, 1999). The cognitive-developmental perspective is based on the notion of reciprocity between the individual and society. There is a norm of reciprocal respect that guides the individual in his or her moral conduct. A person's moral behavior is based on the manner in which the person justifies his or her actions. Therefore, the way a person reasons directly affects his or her behavior.

In the learning-theory perspective, moral behavior results either from the reinforcement of behavior or through the observation of others' behavior (modeling). Individuals learn moral behavior through direct reinforcement and indirectly through observation of models. In the psychoanalytic perspective, moral behavior is the result of people's personalities, primarily their instinctual drives. People's instinctual drives are moderated by their ego development. Moral behavior is the result of people's personality—their early-childhood experiences that have influenced their ego development.

The perspective provided by each theory would lead the practitioner to emphasize different things. For example, in understanding a young person's violent action, a cognitive-developmental perspective would seek to examine the person's reasoning—the person's moral justification for his or her actions. A learning-theory perspective would seek to examine what elements present in the young person's environment may be reinforcing his or her actions or what role models provide vicarious reinforcement. Last, a psychoanalytic perspective would focus on parental relationships, sense of guilt, and ego development to understand how desires and impulses are controlled.

Egocentrism

"I hate eating at the swimming pool. Everyone just stares at you. I never know if I've got ice cream all over my face or if guys are just trying to look at my body," Janna said with a sense of desperation. Her friend, Anita, has a similar reaction: "I know, you can never look right at this place. I mean with wet hair and no makeup I think people are looking at me and saying, gosh, I didn't think she looked that bad. I keep thinking that guys who might think I'm reasonable looking will come here and see me and never give me a second look."

This conversation between Janna and Anita at the local swimming pool represents what David Elkind (2001) has referred to as adolescent *egocentrism*. Egocentrism refers to a type of thought that is characterized by preoccupation with one's behavior, feeling, or thoughts in a self-conscious manner. It is the onset of formal operational thinking that is believed to lead to such egocentric thought. Elkind discussed two aspects of egocentric thought—the imaginary audience and the personal fable.

The **imaginary audience** is the belief that others are as preoccupied with the adolescent's behavior as he or she is. Adolescents harbor this notion that they are "on stage" and that everyone is their audience. Adolescents' preoccupation with their own bodies may be a result of their egocentric thinking. In the conversation above, both Janna and Anita believed that everyone's attention was directed at them, and therefore they were very concerned about their appearance.

The **personal fable** reflects adolescents' sense that they are indestructible and unique. In fact, they are so unique that no one can understand what it is like to be them. In their self-focus, they also come to believe that they are indestructible. Things simply are not going to happen to "them."

Recent work in adolescent egocentrism suggests that this phenomenon may be due not only to formal thought, as Elkind hypothesized, but also to the adolescent's interpersonal understanding (Lapsley, 1991; Lapsley & Rice, 1988). Such an understanding reflects the ability to step out of oneself and perceive reactions from others in imaginative circumstances. This theoretical notion is similar to the perspective-taking theory presented earlier by Robert Selman (1980). As you will recall, Selman discussed how a child's perspective taking or role taking develops across five levels. By examining the way a child reasons according to different perspective-taking levels, you can better understand the child's behavior.

Psychological Strengths and Hazards

What is your image of the adolescent in the twenty-first century? Is it an adolescent stumbling around drunk? An emaciated teenage body? A pierced body? A pregnant teenager? Society has fallen prey to a number of negative images when it comes to our young people. Most people don't refer to adolescents as healthy, well functioning, and serious in spite of undergoing a number of stressful life changes. Yet, these healthy adolescents are likely the norm rather than the exception (Masten, 2001). A fact that many adolescent researchers have been communicating for a long time is that most adolescents develop into independent, healthy, and well-functioning adults!

Why do some adolescents become more negatively influenced by stress than others do? This question has led the way for researchers to better understand how risk factors contribute to stress-related problems and how protective factors buffer the negative impacts of stress. Adolescents who do well in spite of the stresses they face are referred to as *stress-resistant adolescents* (Rutter, 1985). These young people "bounce back" despite undergoing intense pressures that would normally have a negative impact on most young people.

What is the model for stress resilience for young people? Several studies have identified qualities of the adolescent and his or her social environment that lead to better outcomes despite impending stress (Masten, 2001; Masten & Coatsworth, 1998). Factors that appear to contribute to adolescent stress resistance include the following:

- positive and nurturant relationships with others
- caring relationships with parents
- easy temperaments, optimism, and a positive perspective about the future
- an internal locus of control and good self-regulation
- an active coping style
- good social skills and social support
- positive relationship with parents and extended family members
- good cognitive skills (problem-solving abilities) and intellectual abilities
- outside activities and hobbies

As Masten has noted, there is nothing magical here—stress-resistant adolescents have obtained important resources and use them to cope better with stress.

Internalizing and Externalizing Disorders

Chapter 8, on middle childhood, introduced the concepts of internalizing and externalizing disorders and discussed the use of the Child Behavior Checklist. Social workers interested in community mental health with children and adolescents need to become quite familiar with the problems associated with conduct disorder and delinquency (externalizing disorders) and depression and suicide (internalizing disorders), because these are major psychological hazards for young people.

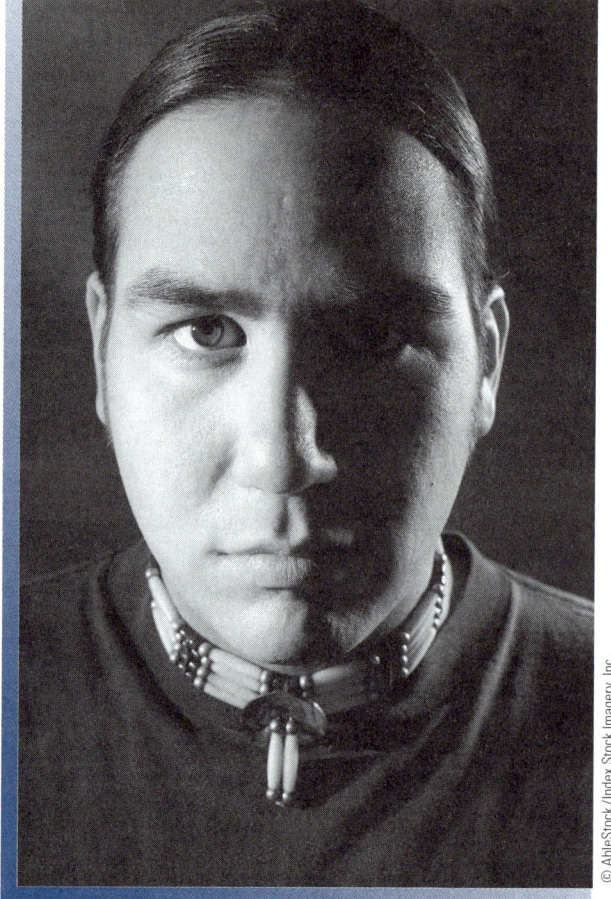

American Indian youth face a large number of risk factors and have the highest suicide rate of all ethnic groups.

A majority of psychological problems for adolescents—especially boys—involve externalizing disorders. Between the ages of 12 and 16, more than 25% of all boys and girls are referred to mental-health clinics for problems of delinquency or conduct disorder (LeProhn, Wetherbee, Lamont, Achenbach & Pecora, 2001). Internalizing disorders such as depression are also common in adolescence, and suicide is the third leading cause of death among adolescents, which means that more than 5,000 young people between the ages of 15 and 24 commit suicide each year in the United States. Surprisingly, only 20–40% of children who attempt suicide receive follow-up care after getting medical treatment (Chamberlin, 2000). The fact is, in-hospital emergency rooms rarely have mental-health or social-work services available. Depression

FOCUS ON MULTICULTURALISM

IDENTIFYING RISK FACTORS FOR SUICIDE ATTEMPTS AMONG NAVAJO ADOLESCENTS

Suicide is the third most common cause of death in adolescents. The suicide rate for youths has tripled during the past thirty years. American Indians and Alaskan natives have the highest suicide rates of all ethnic groups, more than four times higher than for adolescents of all races (Rabasca, 2000). In American Indian communities, people often form close groups and experience multigenerational difficulties that originated with efforts to force their assimilation into mainstream Western culture. Many experts believe the repression of American Indian cultures has caused a long-term trauma, often referred to as *post-colonial stress disorder*. In this instance, the trauma is caused not by a specific event but by long-term oppression. Adolescent American Indians have been raised by parents and grandparents who have experienced this long-term trauma. In a study (Grossman, Milligan, & Deyo, 1991) conducted to identify the risk factors for self-reported suicide attempts by Navajo adolescents, more than 7,000 students in sixth through twelfth grades on the Navajo reservation were surveyed. The study found that 15% of the sample ($N = 971$) reported a previous suicide attempt; more than half of those admitted to more than one attempt. The researchers wanted to discover what factors are more likely to predict suicide attempts. Controlling for age, they found the following factors predict the risk of suicide: history of mental-health problems, alienation from family and community, having a friend who attempted suicide, weekly consumption of hard liquor, a family history of suicide or attempts, poor self-perception of health, history of physical abuse, female gender, and sexual abuse. The authors concluded that efforts to prevent suicide attempts in Navajo adolescents should target individuals with the identified risk factors.

and suicide go hand in hand; depression is discussed in Chapter 10, on young adulthood.

Conduct Disorder

Debbie was very active as a young child. Her parents complained that she was difficult to manage as early as 4 years old. At that time, they believed that Debbie just would not listen and follow their instructions. Both parents used reprimands and spanked Debbie, but to no avail—she was her own boss. As she got older, Debbie became argumentative and increasingly noncompliant. When requested to be home at a certain time or to do a chore, Debbie often would exclaim, "I don't have to if I don't want to." Easily "set off," Debbie would yell at her parents and scream, "I hate you." She has been increasingly absent from school. School officials claim she is involved in a gang that sells and uses drugs. One of her girlfriends is now on probation after having been arrested for shoplifting.

Debbie's pattern of behavior would easily fit into the category of **conduct disorder** (see Exhibit 9.7), which is a constellation of behaviors that range from oppositional and noncompliant behavior to delinquent behaviors such as stealing, robbery, and physical assault (Loeber & Farrington, 2001).

It is difficult to estimate the prevalence of conduct disorder, because it represents a fairly large heterogeneous group. For example, some researchers distinguish between delinquent and nondelinquent conduct problems, and others refer only to delinquent behavior. The estimate of prevalence is between 1.5% and 3.4% in the general population (American Academy of Child and Adolescent Psychiatry, 2004). We know that each year, between 4% and 5% of young people are referred to the courts for suspected offenses other than traffic violations. However, twice as many young people come in contact with the police but are not arrested. Also, studies of "normal" children indicate that most (up to 75%) have engaged in illegal behavior (Johnson & Fennell, 1983).

Although many young people may engage in illegal behavior, for some, conduct-disorder behaviors begin early in life and follow them into adulthood. One well-known study (West & Farrington, 1973)

EXHIBIT 9.7 DSM-IV-TR diagnostic criteria for conduct disorder

A. A repetitive and persistent pattern of behavior in which the basic rights of others or major age-appropriate societal norms or rules are violated, as manifested by the presence of three (or more) of the following criteria in the past 12 months, with at least one criterion present in the past 6 months:

Aggression to people and animals
 1. Often bullies, threatens, or intimidates others
 2. Often initiates physical fights
 3. Has used a weapon that can cause serious physical harm to others (e.g., a bat, brick, broken bottle, knife, gun)
 4. Has been physically cruel to people
 5. Has been physically cruel to animals
 6. Has stolen while confronting a victim (e.g., mugging, purse snatching, extortion, armed robbery)
 7. Has forced someone into sexual activity

Destruction of property
 8. Has deliberately engaged in fire setting with the intention of causing serious damage
 9. Has deliberately destroyed others' property (other than by fire setting)

Deceitfulness or theft
 10. Has broken into someone else's house, building, or car
 11. Often lies to obtain goods or favors or to avoid obligations (i.e., "cons" others)
 12. Has stolen items of nontrivial value without confronting a victim (e.g., shoplifting, but without breaking and entering, forgery)

Serious violations of rules
 13. Often stays out at night despite parental prohibitions, beginning before age 13 years
 14. Has run away from home overnight at least twice while living in parental or parental surrogate home (or once without returning for a lengthy period)
 15. Is often truant from school, beginning before age 13 years

B. The disturbance in behavior causes clinically significant impairment in social, academic, or occupational functioning.
C. If the individual is age 18 years or older, criteria are not met for Antisocial Personality Disorder.

Specify type based on age at onset:

Childhood-Onset Type: onset of at least one criterion characteristic of Conduct Disorder prior to age 10 years
Adolescent-Onset Type: absence of any criteria characteristic of Conduct Disorder prior to age 10 years

Specify severity:

Mild: few if any conduct problems in excess of those required to make the diagnosis and conduct problems cause only minor harm to others
Moderate: number of conduct problems and effect on others intermediate between "mild" and "severe"
Severe: many conduct problems in excess of those required to make the diagnosis or conduct problems cause considerable harm to others

SOURCE: Reprinted with permission from the *Diagnostic and statistical manual of mental disorders*, Fourth Edition, Text Revision. Copyright 2000. American Psychiatric Association.

found that the aggressive and difficult behavior of 8- to 10-year-olds was a strong predictor of later delinquent behavior. For some, youth conduct disorder or delinquency is strongly related to psychological factors or personality. Almost half of all children with a diagnosis of conduct disorder will go on to develop antisocial personality disorder (American Academy of Child and Adolescent Psychiatry, 2004). Of course, there are many causes of delinquent behavior. Conduct disorder may be related to factors such as temperament or personality, deficits in moral development, family structure and environment (divorced parents, absent fathers, uncaring and abusive parents), and negative modeling. Biological factors could come into play, as conduct disorder may arise from biologically driven arousal deficits that lead to stimulation-seeking behaviors (Loeber & Farrington, 2001). What theories do you think best explain delinquency?

Delinquency

A chapter on adolescence would also not be complete without a discussion of juvenile delinquency. How many of the individuals in your social-work class do you think committed a delinquent act as a youth? If you guessed quite a lot, you are right. One recent study (Snyder, Espiritu, Huizinga, Loeber, & Petechuk, 2003) that looked at a higher-risk urban sample in two major U.S. cities found that the percentage of young people who committed theft ranged from 38 to 56%, property damage 31–51%, status offences 19–39% and burglary 6–8%. Other studies have found that more than 80% of young people commit delinquent acts (Gold & Petronio, 1980), and studies of inner-city youth found that most delinquent acts occur at around age 15 to 16 years. Delinquent acts are more common among boys than girls, but the rate of delinquency for girls has been increasing in the past several years (Underwood, 2003).

A lot of delinquent behavior is related to status in the peer group. Delinquent acts are committed both with peers and for peers. Minor delinquent acts are considered normal and appear to be motivated by the desire to be liked by peers and to enhance one's sense of self-esteem. In adolescence, when most delinquent behavior begins, young people feel an increasing pressure to conform with the peer group, beginning around age 13 (LeCroy & Daley, 2001).

When deviant behavior occurs at early ages, the problem is seen as conduct disorder. However, when the behaviors lead to illegal acts by juveniles, then the problem is identified as delinquency. Research has found that delinquency can be predicted from behavior displayed at early ages. For example, children who are identified as aggressive have a high probability of becoming delinquents in adolescence (Loeber & Farrington, 2001). It is important to understand, however, that most criminals have a history of juvenile delinquency, but most individuals with a history of juvenile delinquency do not end up as criminals (Gambrill, 1997).

Many studies have examined the different predictors of delinquency (Dryfoos, 1990; Loeber & Farrington, 2001). The predictors can be viewed from the multidimensional perspective, examining biological, psychological, and sociological antecedents to delinquent behavior. Exhibit 9.8 summarizes this literature.

A survey conducted by the U.S. Department of Justice revealed that approximately 25,000 juveniles are in state correctional facilities. Characteristics of the juveniles in these facilities include the following: 93% are male, 40% African American, and 12% Hispanic; 75% are from divorced or single-parent families; over 50% have had a family member incarcerated; and 60% already had been in jail.

Are criminals getting younger? We know they are, because the number of child delinquents entering the juvenile justice system is increasing, as evidenced by rising arrest rates and court caseloads (Loeber & Farrington, 2001). This is bad news, because child delinquents represent a more serious social problem than do juvenile delinquents. Child delinquents have two or three times greater risk than juveniles of becoming serious, violent, and chronic offenders. They also have longer offending careers than do young people who are delinquent at a later age, and they represent a greater threat to public safety (Loeber & Farrington, 2001).

Depending on the state, some of these youths are being incarcerated in adult facilities. Some states have lowered the age restrictions for admitting youths to adult prisons, and others have dropped the age restrictions entirely. And many states are spending more on prison cells and less on early intervention, family counseling, and treatment. Instead of rehabilitation, incarcerated juveniles will be exposed to deviant peer groups and become more entrenched in the criminal community (Ashford, Sales, & Reid, 2001). What does this say about how we think of juvenile offenders?

EXHIBIT 9.8 Multidimensional factors that predict delinquency

Predictive factor	Association with delinquency
Biological	
Age	Early age is a strong predictor
Gender	Males commit more delinquency
Congenital defects	Developmental conditions
Psychological	
Conduct	Behaviors such as stealing, lying, and truancy
Peer influence	Peer pressure can exert influence toward delinquency
High-risk behaviors	Early substance abuse and sexual intercourse
Psychiatric conditions	Delinquency is a co-morbid factor with ADHD, anxiety, and aggression
School commitment	Low school expectations and attachment to school
Social	
Income	Low income status
Family interactions	Low bonding, abusive family conditions
Family background	Family history of violence, substance abuse, mental illness
School grades	Low achievement and poor verbal ability
Religiosity	Low church attendance
Neighborhood conditions	High crime, dense urban areas, neighborhood blight
School conditions	Poor school conditions, poor tracking and monitoring

We support a combination of punishment and treatment, especially for first-time offenders. The following Implications for Practice section discusses various ways to deal with juvenile offenders.

Implications for Practice: Approaches to Treating Delinquent Youth

The approach to treatment of delinquent youth has gone through much change in the last twenty years. In general, treatment has moved away from a psychiatric model focusing on intrapsychic conflict, emotional disturbance, and diagnosis to treatment models based on growth, behavioral change, skill acquisition, social learning and modeling, and responsibility for one's actions (Petr, 1998). Behavioral approaches have been applied and evaluated with such youth. Treatment techniques emphasize reinforcement for appropriate behaviors, learning new social skills, token economies, modeling, and goal setting. One of the best-established treatment models is Patterson's parent-training model for aggressive children (Chamberlain & Patterson, 1985), an approach that teaches child-management techniques to parents. Parents learn to define, pinpoint, monitor, and apply consequences to various child behaviors. Feldman, Caplinger, and Wodarski (1983) found support for behavioral methods in a community-based setting, and Alexander and Parsons (1982) integrated family systems and behavioral methods for delinquent youth. Dishion & Kavanagh (2003) have introduced a family-centered approach that teaches and supports parents' skills and motivation to reduce adolescent problem behavior. Multisystemic therapy, an empirically based model, has gained in popularity as a broad-based treatment model that resembles many of the fundamental elements of social-work practice (Henggeler, Schoenwald, Rowland, & Cunningham, 2002). Behavioral methods became quite well known through the popularity of Achievement Place, behavior-modification programs for delinquent youth in a home-based residential setting (Kazdin, 2000). In the Achievement Place model, parents are taught to apply the principles of behavior modification with their children. The young people follow a set of rules based on a token economy where they earn privileges based on their daily behaviors.

One model of treatment that has fallen into disfavor is peer-based group therapy. Dishion & Andrews (1995) reported inadvertently discovering that aggregating high-risk young adolescents into group interventions actually led to increases in their substance abuse and delinquent behaviors. Their summary article, "When Interventions Harm: Peer Groups and Problem Behavior" (Dishion, McCord, & Poulin, 1999) has become a classic in the field, warning practitioners that not all interventions are helpful.

In general, six treatment methods appear to be the most widely used with delinquent youth: restitution and community service (teaches responsibility through direct or symbolic repayment of the victim); family intervention; token economies; fear, emotional shock, and avoidance training; wilderness training; and social-skills training (White, 1989). Family intervention and social-skills training appear to have the best results in reducing recidivism (Fonagy, Target, Cottrell, Phillips, & Kurtz, 2002). ■

Self-Harm and Cutting

Self-harm has become an increasing concern among professionals who work with adolescents. Self-harm is a process of "self-mutilation" defined as "the deliberate destruction or alteration of one's own body tissue without conscious suicidal intent" (Favazza, 1987, p. 225). Self-harm has increased to nearly 1% of the population (Conterio & Lader, 2000). Other research reports self-mutilation as high as 4% in the general population, 21%–61% in clinical populations (Briere & Gil, 1998; Suyemoto & Kountz, 2000), and 12% in the college population (Suyemoto & Kountz, 2000). Self-harm is usually performed in secret, and it often begins in adolescence (Russell, 2002). It evokes many strong feelings, such as shame and guilt, and can take on an addictive quality. Many experts believe self-harm occurs because of emotional expression and control, although the reasons for self-harm vary. The most commonly cited reasons include relief from feelings, a method of coping, preventing dissociation, euphoric feelings, expressing pain, communication, self-nurturing, self-punishment, reenacting abuse, and establishing control (Alderman, 1997). Self-harm has been associated with physical and sexual abuse, compulsive disorders, and body image and eating disorders, loss, alcoholism, violence, peer conflicts, and impulse-control difficulties.

FOCUS ON NARRATIVE

ONE GIRL'S ACCOUNT OF CUTTING

I was cleaning my room one day and found a broken piece of glass. I took it to my arm in the midst of me bawling my eyes out over my boyfriend and me, and I proceeded to gash away at my lower arm. I then found a razor blade. I used that instead. I sat there and watched the blood pour out of the newly made cuts, and I just thought to myself, what is my life for? Why am I here? It would be so much better if I weren't. But I didn't want to die. I covered my arm with a towel and let the blood soak through. This was not the first time I cut myself, however. I was in the fifth grade the first time I cut myself. I broke a mirror that time and used the sharp pieces to carve into my leg cause I was depressed.

My boyfriend and I talked it over and we resolved everything. Meanwhile I told my mom and friends about my cutting. I told my shrink that I did it and he referred me to the Partners Program. It's a therapy class you take instead of school. It's at the local mental ward of the hospital. I start there tomorrow.

Things with my boyfriend continued to get worse, and whenever I feel like crap, I go and cut myself some more. I do it on the same arm 'cause I promised my boyfriend I wouldn't do it anymore. But feeling the razor go through your skin, and seeing the blood pour out, is oddly soothing. It makes the mental pain go away for some time, 'cause you are too concentrated on the physical pain that's inflicted on you. But this only lasts for so long. I continue to cut my arm up. It's almost an everyday routine for me now. It's addicting, and I wish that I could stop, but honestly I don't know how I am going to. My home life sucks. My school life sucks. I have no social life anymore 'cause I sit around and cry all day 'cause my boyfriend hasn't taken the time to call me.

SOURCE: Candace (2003), n.p.

STUDY TABLE: Psychological dimension of adolescence

Cognitive Development and Information Processing	Piaget's last intellectual stage, formal operations, begins around age 11 or 12. At this stage, the adolescent is capable of abstract thought and logical reasoning. Hypothetical-deductive reasoning is characterized by understanding abstract propositions and reasoning logically about them to discover the best solution. Formal operational thought includes assimilation: the adolescent consolidates new information into existing knowledge. During middle adolescence, the process of accommodation creates a balance, and by later formal operational thought, adolescents test their reasoning against experience and incorporate their formal operational thinking.
Communication	Improvement in thinking abilities allows for a greater capacity for effective communication in adolescence. Metaphors increase, as does the use of satire or ridicule. Writing becomes more meaningful because adolescents have developed the type of logical thought processes needed to organize their ideas. Girls' talk and boys' talk become increasingly differentiated. Boys are more competitive in conversation, and girls talk more about their personal feelings and relationships. Social workers need to understand the social and legal aspects of communicating consent and confidentiality to adolescents because they are engaging in a variety of health-risk behaviors and because adolescents are more likely to seek help when provided with assurances of confidentiality.
Attitudes and Emotions	Adolescents develop a more integrated self-concept through greater freedom in behavior and decision making as they move into adult life. The idea that adolescence is a normal period of serious difficulty is a myth. The majority of adolescents are well adjusted. One problem adolescents may face is self-esteem, which is at its lowest in early adolescence. This is especially true of girls transitioning into junior high school who mature early and start to date. Adolescents experience a remarkable amount of diversity in roles and can switch between extreme moods within forty-five minutes, in contrast with adults, who often take hours to change moods. Adolescents in foster care have a harder time adjusting to moving and suffer in their self-image because they lack the parental support, parental control, parental participation, and a sense of belonging to one's family that influence self-esteem. Multiple placements can create risk, and stable placements are important for providing opportunities for adolescents to achieve and form supportive relationships. There are four main strategies for enhancing adolescents' self concept: (1) encouraging achievement, (2) promoting competencies in specific areas, (3) provision of peer and parental support, and (4) developing coping skills. Self-esteem is improved by peer and parental support and extracurricular experiences. There are no differences in self-esteem between African American children and white majority children, but African American children do experience greater discrimination, poverty, and social and education barriers than white youths do.
Social Cognition and Regulation	Adolescents enter a psychological moratorium—a gap between childhood security and adult autonomy. Adolescent identity statuses or modes of resolution include identity diffusion, identity foreclosure, identity moratorium, and identity achievement. The idea of crisis may be misleading, because identity development appears to be a lengthy, complex process. During adolescence, youths of color

must integrate their image of being from an ethnic group while being exposed to values and images of the mainstream white culture. Issues that adolescents of color face include stereotypes, cultural devaluation of the symbols and heroes of their group, and lack of successful role models. In this process three options emerge: alienation, assimilation, and biculturalism.

Social cognitive monitoring, which increases in adolescence, is a person's ability to monitor and make sense of his or her social thoughts. Moral development refers to the rules of conduct people use in their interactions with others. Kohlberg posited that rules of conduct develop as individuals progress through six separate stages, where each stage represents a different way of reasoning about various rules of conduct. Adolescents are in stage 3, "interpersonal conformity"—their reason to be good is so that others will think well of them and they can think well of themselves. By late adolescence most young people move to stage 4, "responsibility to the system." Kohlberg's view is based on a justice perspective, and Gilligan has argued a care perspective, in which the focus is on people's connectedness to others, has been underestimated.

Egocentrism refers to a type of thought characterized by preoccupation with one's behavior, feelings, or thoughts in a self-conscious manner. Formal operational thinking is believed to lead to egocentric thought. The imaginary audience (the belief that others are as preoccupied with the adolescent's behavior as he or she is) and the personal fable (adolescents' sense that they are indestructible and unique) are two aspects of egocentric thought.

Psychological Strengths and Hazards

Adolescents who do well in spite of the stresses they face are referred to as stress-resistant adolescents and are characterized by these factors: positive and nurturing relationships with others, caring relationships with parents, easy temperaments, an internal locus of control, an active coping style, good social skills, good cognitive skills and intellectual abilities, and outside activities and hobbies.

A majority of psychological problems for adolescents involve externalizing disorders. The most common are delinquency and conduct disorder. Internalizing disorders include depression and suicide. Suicide is the third leading cause of death among adolescents. American Indians and Alaskan Natives have the highest suicide rates of all ethnic groups. Delinquency can be predicted from behavior displayed at early ages. Treatment techniques emphasize reinforcement for appropriate behaviors, learning new social skills, token economies, modeling, and goal setting. For conduct disorder, peer-based group therapy may lead to increases in substance abuse and delinquent behaviors. Family intervention and social-skills training appear to have the best results in reducing recidivism. Self-harm is a process of "self-mutilation" defined as the deliberate destruction or alteration of one's own body tissue without conscious suicidal intent.

CONCEPT MAP

SOCIAL DIMENSION

Families and Groups

The transition into adolescence involves some stress in most families, for both adolescent and parent (Steinberg, 2001). This stress may be caused in part by the rapid developmental changes that take place—more occur during adolescence than any other period of the life cycle. Three key developmental tasks for the family are the development of autonomy, resolution of parent-adolescent conflict, and establishing parent-adolescent attachment (Steinberg, 2001).

Family Influences: Development of Autonomy

Consider the following interaction between a mother and daughter:

DAUGHTER: Mom, get off my back! I know what I'm supposed to do around this house. I don't need you telling me every second.

MOTHER: I have to tell you every second or it just doesn't get done. If I could trust you to do it, I wouldn't have to keep after you.

This common interaction reveals an essential theme of the parent-adolescent relationship: control versus autonomy. Much of the stress in parent-adolescent relationships relates to struggles that revolve around control and autonomy. As young people move into adolescence, they begin the process of acquiring more independence, and parents need to begin the process of granting more independence. Because parents have had full responsibility for their children up to now, the process becomes a difficult balance between letting go and still having some control. Some parents successfully adapt to the adolescent's need for independence and are able to grant the young person more decision-making authority. However, other parents do not acquire the needed skills involved in independence granting and remained locked into a need for control over decision making. What is the result of these two different styles of parenting? Parents who hold tightly to their control and are authoritarian in their decision making are more likely to produce young people who have difficulty with autonomy. A democratic family structure, where there is equal involvement of parents and adolescents, with parents retaining the final authority, appears to produce a young person with a healthy sense of autonomy.

Parent-Adolescent Conflict

The parent-adolescent relationship is not viewed as one of stress and storm, rebellion against parents, or a generation gap as it was in the past. Current thinking views the parent-adolescent relationship as a transitional one characterized by some conflicts and disagreements about the details of everyday life (Galambos & Almeida, 1992; Steinberg, 2001), yet, most adolescents have satisfying relationships with parents (Offer, Ostrov, & Howard, 1981; Steinberg, 2001). Also, it may be that perspectives on parent-adolescent conflict vary depending on who is reporting on the perceived conflict. Adolescents often report that there is little conflict and they are happy in their relationships with parents. However, parents may not see it this way. Studies (Steinberg, 2001) have reported that the "little" conflicts may not bother adolescents but are a significant source of distress to parents. Steinberg (2001) believes that parents are both more bothered by the conflicts and generate more negative affect as a result of the conflicts than do adolescents. Reactions may vary, but parent-adolescent disagreements are in fact common, and they appear to be a normative and adaptive aspect of the transition to adolescence (Smetana, 2000; Steinberg, 2001).

Researchers have discovered that conflict between parents and adolescents begins during early adolescence and is characterized by bickering and negative interactions, fewer shared activities, and less frequently expressed affection. Such conflicts often occur around the time of puberty and thus are interpreted by some to represent the family's adaptation to the adolescent's physical development (Hill, Holmbeck, Marlow, Green, & Lynch, 1985). The prevalence of conflict between parent and adolescent is about two times weekly—twice as often as a typical married couple (Montemayer, 1983). Contrary to many popular notions, conflicts are not about values, politics, or social issues but about mundane, everyday issues such as curfew, chores, and school—the same issues since studies began sixty years ago (Kaplan, 2004).

Is there a functional reason that adolescents and parents have this increase in conflicts? Many researchers believe there is, and they base their ideas on the following theories (Steinberg, 1990).

A sociobiological perspective (Steinberg, 1990) suggests that conflict during adolescence ensures that young people will spend time separated from their family of origin and mate outside the natal group. This theory is based on the observation that conflict intensifies at puberty in other species of primates and that the underlying tension may be derived from evolutionary pressures. The adolescent is forced, through the bickering, to search for intimate companionship outside the family.

From an intrapsychic perspective, the conflict may facilitate the process of individuation. Furthermore, this intrapsychic emancipation allows the young person to develop a more realistic and mature appraisal of his or her parents, leading to a more mutual relationship with them. The function of the disagreements is that adolescents must come to terms with their parents' fallibility and, as a result, release their dependence on their parents.

From a cognitive-developmental perspective (Smetana, 2000) parent-adolescent conflict can be best explained by the different manner in which adolescents and parents define family rules, events, and regulations. Conflict in adolescence is related to the development of social reasoning. For example, instead of seeing an issue as one of social convention ("Everyone in this family must keep his or her room clean"), it is perceived by the adolescent as a matter of personal choice ("This is my room, and I should decide how clean I want to keep it"). Because parents maintain a conventional stance regarding such issues, conflict results. Also significant is that at this early and middle adolescent period, young people tend to perceive social conventions as arbitrary.

Parent-Adolescent Attachment

Is it better for adolescents to become detached from parents as they move toward independence, or is it better for them to remain attached? Just as it has been

---

FOCUS ON NARRATIVE

AN ADOLESCENT'S PERSPECTIVE ON DIVORCE

"Best years of your life," someone once said. I suppose it could be true if it wasn't for your parents. I know that sounds harsh, but imagine it: a teenage kid, going through the adolescent problems of anyone my age—boys, friends, changes physically and mentally. Add to this "O"-level examinations—the piece of paper which could decide my future—at school and family pressuring me into doing well (even though I realize it's for my own good). Then suddenly it seemed as if my whole world as I knew it was collapsing around me and I couldn't do anything about it. I'm talking about divorce, affairs, and separations, the whole horrible business rolled into one.

It started when my father announced, with some bitterness I might add, that he was having an affair. It was so unexpected, so devastating even now, looking back, I can't see how my mother managed to hold herself together. She had always been so dependent on my father. Maybe that was one of the pressures which he tried to explain to me after the initial shock.

They tried desperately to save their marriage, not once but several times, leaving a trail of bitterness and heartache behind them, but it wasn't working. My dad would sometimes leave for a few days in an attempt to gather his thoughts, sometimes returning for me, as we were always close, or maybe to relieve his guilt. Yet each time he was less like the father I had known. It was killing them both, and family life became so unhappy. I can remember many a blazing row: things were hurled, words were so blatantly said, and I was stuck in the middle of them both. I tried so hard to comfort both of them. First my mother, but when I was with her I was laden with guilt for not being with my father. I thought that he might think I didn't love him anymore, and vice versa. Yet as hard as I tried, I was inadequate; he finally left. Sitting at home night after night, wondering if my father was all right. Many a time the thought of my dad, or my mother for that matter, committing suicide came into my mind. Why didn't he phone? I would sit there willing the phone to ring just so that I would know he was OK.

SOURCE: Goodings (1987), pp. 157–58.

in infancy, secure attachment is becoming increasingly recognized as critical to adolescent healthy development. Traditionally, the psychoanalytic notion has been that adolescents who remain close to their parents will not show healthy developmental progress. Yet research has found that adolescents with secure attachments to their parents do better than their peers in terms of self-reliance and independence, behavioral competence, and psychosocial well-being (Hill & Holmbeck, 1986; Maccoby & Martin, 1983; Steinberg & Silverberg, 1986). Furthermore, adolescents with secure attachments score lower on measures of social and psychological problems such as drug abuse, depression, and delinquency (McCord, 1990). As Steinberg (1990) has pointed out, this finding is robust across socioeconomic and ethnic groups. He also stated that, contrary to some clinical notions, there is no research to support the hypothesis that the parent-adolescent relationship can be so cohesive that it is enmeshing.

Implications for Practice:
The Power of Authoritative Parenting

Steinberg (2001) has suggested that the power of "authoritative" parenting (originally described by Baumrind and discussed in Chapter 7, on early childhood) can be taught. Authoritative parents are warm, involved, but firm and consistent in their parental guidelines. In adolescence, an important addition to the notion of authoritative parenting is the extent to which parents encourage their adolescent children to develop their own opinions and beliefs (Steinberg, 2001). Research has documented that adolescents with authoritative parents do better in school, report less anxiety and depression, and are less likely to engage in antisocial behavior (Steinberg, 2001).

What aspects of authoritative parenting leads to such positive outcomes? Steinberg (2001) noted three: (1) the nurturing relationship promotes parental influence; (2) the support and guidance help the adolescent develop better self-regulatory skills and promote competence; and (3) the give-and-take of the relationship engages the child in a process that promotes cognitive and social competence. These conclusions are supported by the clinical research of Patterson and colleagues at the Oregon Social Learning Center. They have developed specific treatment methods for working with families with aggressive, delinquent, and noncompliant children. Their social-learning model embraces many of the aspects of authoritative parenting: monitoring, supervision, clear limit setting and rules, and a warm relationship built on positive reinforcement. The focus of the program is on child management, not on interpersonal and underlying psychodynamics. The model teaches parents to communicate clear expectations for acceptable and unacceptable behavior, to carefully monitor target behaviors selected for modification, to consistently and contingently apply discipline (time-out), and to reinforce acceptable and positive behaviors. Research results have shown improvement in the target behaviors of children and improvement in the behavior of siblings, as well (Fonagy et al., 2002). ■

Peers and Adolescent Development

The notion of the "teenage" years is practically synonymous with peer relationships and peer groups. If we asked you to picture the first thing that comes to your mind when you hear the word *teenager* or *adolescent*, you'd probably summon one of the following scenes: a teenager talking on the telephone, two girlfriends sitting and talking with each other, a couple out on a date, a group of peers at the mall, or a group of teenagers at the movie theater. Such is the reality of most adolescents, who spend an increasing amount of time in the company of peers (Bukowski, 1998; Schneider, 2000). Research has documented that by the sixth grade, adults (excluding parents) account for only 25% of early adolescents' primary social network and even less (10%) when adolescents mature early (Garbarino, Burston, Raber, Russel, & Crouter, 1978).

Adolescents are at a point in their development where they need to spend time with peers. This interaction provides important information that is usually not available within the family; peer interaction is a critical source for personal and social competence development. Through interaction with peers, young people learn about sexual relations, compassion, leadership, conflict, mutual problem solving, and more. Locating a peer group that is supportive and compatible with one's interests is a psychological task of early adolescence. As discussed in earlier chapters, the impact of peer rejection and isolation can be critical to the adolescent's healthy development.

Good peer relations are also critical to one's popularity, and popularity is keenly sought after in adolescence. Young people strive to behave in a manner that will enhance their popularity. Many factors contribute to popularity: attractiveness, athletic ability, intellectual ability, social class, ethnic group membership, and special characteristics or talents. Attractiveness is a powerful force in determining one's popularity. This appears most critical at the extremes—either very attractive or very unattractive—and is a determinant of social acceptance or rejection (Schneider, 2000).

Peer Pressure and Conformity

As one 15-year-old stated: "Kids need to look at peer pressure and ask, 'Do I want to do this?' Whether the answer is yes or no, they need to ask why" (Clasen & Brown, 1987). Peer pressure and conformity are strong processes in adolescence and reach their peak in early adolescence, especially from the sixth to the ninth grades (Schneider, 2000). Adolescent thinking is often characterized by the logic, "If the group is doing it, it must be good and right." By late adolescence, conformity to antisocial behavior decreases and parents and peers begin to experience greater agreement. As young people move toward independence, they rely less on peer and family influence. Perhaps this period of strict conformity to peers is a normal and important task of adolescence—to gradually come to terms with the influence of groups (Steinberg, 2001). We all have to learn to balance the need for personal autonomy with the desire for group participation.

Conformity, agreeing with the group opinion when pressured, can be both positive and negative. Although we usually view adolescent peer pressure and conformity through a negative lens, it is often positive or neutral. For example, many young people conform to dress, music, and hairstyle norms. Perhaps the greatest conformity is spending time with the peer group itself. Positive conformity and constructive peer pressure are exemplified by Students Against Drunk Driving (or SADD), where students promise themselves, peers, and parents not to drink and drive.

Friendships

In adolescence, more complete friendships begin to develop. Over time, the concept of friendship enlarges for young people. When asked to describe friendship, adolescents refer to *intimacy*, *trust*, *loyalty*, and *commitment*. Perhaps most significant is the capacity for intimacy in friendship. Intimacy in friendship refers to the sharing of personal thoughts. This personal knowledge about others leads to a greater sense of closeness. Gender differences are apparent, with male friendships reflecting more shared interests and female friendships reflecting more supportive and emotional aspects of friendship. Although the intimacy of friendship is highly valued in adolescence, there are other important functions of friendship. Aspects such as companionship, stimulation, interest, and provision of ego support all begin to emerge as friendship deepens.

Consider the following description of a close friendship between two boys:

> I know everything about John, and he knows everything about me. We know where the secret places are in each other's houses, and that my mother cooks better but his father tells funnier jokes.... We always stick together because I'm good at fights, but John's the only one besides my family who knows that I sleep with my light on at night. He can jump from the high diving board but I know he's afraid of cats.... He saw me cry once, and the day he broke his arm I ran home and got his mother for him. We know what's in each other's refrigerator, which steps creak on each other's stairs, and how to get into each other's house if the door is locked. I know who he really likes, and he knows about Mary, too. John is my best friend and I am his (Zolotow, 1968).

This quote clearly outlines the many functions of friendship described above.

Implications for Practice: Social Skills Training

Because friendships and social interactions are critical for young people's healthy development, social skills can be an important asset for adolescents to posses. We know that some adolescents are unpopular, either rejected by their peers or neglected. Many of these adolescents have poor social skills (Kaplan, 2004). As a result, an increasing emphasis is being placed on a social skills or social competence model for understanding, preventing, and remediating the problems experienced by adolescents. **Social skills training** assumes that problem behavior in young people can be understood in terms of their not having acquired skills needed to cope with various situational demands. The focus is on discovering effective responses for resolving the demands of problem situations while minimizing the likelihood of future problems. This approach perceives human development as a process of confronting a series of tasks and situational demands rather than as movement through stages. The treatment model focuses on teaching the prosocial skills and competencies that are needed for day-to-day living, rather than on understanding and eliminating pathological responses. The emphasis is on new learned behavior that leads to positive consequences rather than on past behaviors that may have elicited negative consequences.

Promoting social competence in young people can be an effective strategy for helping them confront stressful and problematic situations. Adolescents need to acquire numerous social skills, because during this stage of life they develop new patterns of interpersonal relationships, confront new social experiences, and need to learn new behavioral responses. Social skills training has been applied to many different problem areas—for example, the specific problems Native American adolescents face (Okamoto, LeCroy, Dustman, Hohmann-Marriott, & Kulis, 2004), school adjustment problems (LeCroy, 2000), aggressive behavior (Feindler & Guttman, 1994), life skills for adolescent mothers (Harris & Franklin, forthcoming), preventing unwanted pregnancy (Barth, 1996), depression (Santor & Kusumakar, 2001), prevention of substance abuse (Botvin, Griffin, Diaz, & Ifill-Williams, 2001), and withdrawn behavior (Weiss & Harris, 2001). Without adequate social skills, these experiences can become avenues to problems such as pregnancy, drug use, social isolation, and loneliness.

Depending on the goals of the program and the type of problem situations being addressed, different skills would be appropriate. For example, a program for juvenile offenders might focus on skills such as giving and receiving feedback, negotiating and resisting peer pressure, and problem solving. A program for pregnancy prevention might focus on skills such as discussing birth control, asking for information, refusing unacceptable demands, and problem solving. All social-skills programs break down the skills into component parts for easy teaching. For example, beginning conversational skills might include four parts: greeting the other person, making small talk, deciding whether the other person is listening, and bringing up the main topic.

In teaching social skills, it is also important to construct social situations that demand the types of social skills you want to teach. For example, LeCroy (2001) has used the following situation in a social-skills program:

> You went to spend the afternoon with some friends but agreed to be home by 4:00 p.m. since your family has plans to have dinner with some friends. You lost track of time and did not get home until 4:45 p.m.

The process of teaching social skills includes seven basic steps that leaders should follow. Exhibit 9.9 presents these steps and outlines the process for teaching social skills (LeCroy, 2001). In each step, there is a request for group member involvement, because it is critical that group leaders involve the participants actively in the training. This keeps the learning process interesting and fun for the group members. ∎

EXHIBIT 9.9 Seven basic steps for teaching social skills

1. Present the social skill being taught.
   a. Solicit an explanation of the skill.
   b. Get group members to provide rationales for the skill.
2. Discuss the social skill.
   a. List the skill steps.
   b. Get group members to give examples of using the skill.
3. Present a problem situation and model the skill.
   a. Evaluate the performance.
   b. Get group members to discuss the model.
4. Set the stage for role playing the skill.
   a. Select the group members for role playing.
   b. Get group members to observe the role play.
5. Have group members rehearse the skill.
   a. Provide coaching if necessary.
   b. Get group members to provide feedback on verbal and nonverbal elements.
6. Practice using complex skill situations.
   a. Teach accessory skills (e.g., problem solving).
   b. Get group members to discuss situations and provide feedback.
7. Train for generalization and maintenance.
   a. Encourage practice of skills outside the group.
   b. Get group members to bring up their own problem situations.

SOURCE: LeCroy (2001).

Adolescent Peer Groups

Adolescent peer groups provide important functions that extend beyond friendship. Groups provide an organized means of participation, a collective sense of camaraderie, and group support for mastering the tasks of adolescence. Group membership allows young people to assess their individuality in light of group pressure and norms. As young people continue their search for identity, choosing to participate in a group helps answer the question "With whom do I belong?" Groups provide experience with difficult social expectations of inclusion and exclusion, as well as conformity and independence.

From late childhood through adolescence, peer groups have their greatest importance. As adolescents prepare for increasing independence, peer groups can provide needed support. For example, during this time, sexual and emotional development are critical, and peer groups help young people address these challenges.

Cliques and Crowds

Adolescents typically form small interaction-based groups in which they spend a great deal of time and develop close relationships. These groups are referred to as **cliques**. In contrast, **crowds** are larger, reputation-based collectives of similar young people who do not necessarily spend a lot of time together. *Reputation-based* refers to the adolescent's crowd affiliation, which suggests the attitudes or activities with which one is associated by peers (Brown, 1990). Typical crowds are commonly known as jocks, brains, partners, nerds, and druggies. Crowd norms reflect the stereotypic images that peers have of crowd members (Schwendinger & Schwendinger, 2004). These different types of crowds are commonly described in various studies and may be related to two basic dimensions on which adolescents could be rated: commitment to the formal reward system of the school (adult controlled) and commitment to the informal status system (peer controlled).

Gangs

Increasingly familiar are the gangs of the big cities—the Crips and Bloods of Los Angeles, or Chicago's Vice Lords and Black Gangster Disciples. Gangs across the United States have received increasing attention from the media, popular writers, and scholars; for example, films such as *Colors*, about the Crips and Bloods, and *The Gangs of New York* put the topic of gangs on the front pages of many newspapers.

No longer are gangs associated only with New York, Chicago, and Los Angeles (Huff, 2001). How can we tell whether a person is a gang member? Defining what constitutes a gang is difficult. For example, what is the difference between a gang and a group? Gangs are usually differentiated from other groups on the basis of their delinquent activity, but the distinction is not limited to delinquency. Huff (2001, p. 4) has provided a comprehensive definition of a youth **gang**: A collectivity consisting primarily of adolescents and young adults who (a) interact frequently with one another; (b) are frequently and deliberately involved in illegal activities; (c) share a common collective identity that is usually, but not

EXHIBIT 9.10 The criteria used by law-enforcement agencies to define a youth gang

Gang characteristic	Number	Percentage
Commits crime together	613	50
Has a name	228	19
Hangs out together	119	10
Claims a turf or territory	104	9
Displays/wears common colors or other insignia	101	8
Has a leader or several leaders	89	7

SOURCE: Youth gang survey, Office of Juvenile Justice and Delinquency Programs, 2000.

always, expressed through a gang name; and (d) typically express that identity by adopting certain symbols and/or claiming control over certain "turf" (persons, places, things, and/or economic markets). Exhibit 9.10 presents the rating of criteria considered important in defining a youth gang by law enforcement agencies.

Gangs seem to be related to the developmental need for young people to associate with peer groups. Indeed, adolescents who have difficulties with peer relationships are often maladjusted (Huff, 2001). Because adolescence is a time when intense peer involvement is typical, it is not surprising that gangs are an outgrowth of that involvement. According to Huff (2001), because group experience is a normal part of the adolescent subculture, gangs can be considered an extreme manifestation of the need for peer group involvement and acceptance. Gangs often play a very important function for young people by providing social support, bonding, and protection from rival gangs (Huff, 2001).

Long-term studies have found that the most important risk factor for gang membership is growing up in a neighborhood with poverty where there is little attachment to people and social institutions (Huff, 2001; Howell & Lynch, 2000). Absent parents, lack of supervision, and parental substance abuse are some of the critical risk factors related to parents. School-related risk factors include low expectations for success in school by teachers, parents, and students, and little school bonding. Of course, peers have a substantial impact, as previously discussed.

Growth in gang numbers is considerable. In Los Angeles, it is estimated that there are approximately 100,000 Crips and Bloods who account for more than

500 homicides every year. These two groups are the most discussed gangs because of their size, the extent of their violence, and their role in drug trafficking. Also, these gangs now exist throughout the United States and are not limited to Los Angeles. These gangs began as primarily African American and Hispanic street gangs in the late 1960s. The Crips are the original gang, and the Bloods formed as a means of protection against the Crips. Today, there are more than 26,000 gangs (Surgeon General, 2001) in schools all across America.

Gang members range in age from 15 to 30 years old, with the majority of gang members between ages 14 and 18. There is no centralized leadership, but groupings are based on different factors, such as location. Gangs are often discussed in terms of three primary groupings: (a) leaders or original gangsters; (b) hard-cores, members committed to the gang and its criminal activities; and (c) wannabes, usually younger youth who want to be hard-core gang members. In a national survey of students ages 12–19, more than one-third reported gangs at their schools (Howell & Lynch, 2000).

Gangs are not limited to males. Female gang involvement is reported by law-enforcement agencies to be about 8%–11% (National Youth Gang Center, 2000). However, this figure may underrepresent the population, as some agencies may not report female gang members. Self-identified female gang membership ranges from 9%–22%. Why are girls joining gangs? Traditional theories about female gang participation focus on girls' social ineptness, physical unattractiveness, or psychological impairments. Does this mean that personal maladjustments create a female delinquent? Research (Moore & Hagedorn, 2001) has shown that the traditional theories do not show the entire picture. Themes that emerged included the lack of formal education because of falling through the cracks in the school system, as well as a severely dysfunctional family life, including domestic violence, divorce and remarriage, the birth parents never having married, extensive alcohol and drug abuse by parents and extended family members, and severe physical or sexual abuse by relatives beginning at an early age. In addition, the majority of the young women's neighborhoods had widespread poverty, alcohol and drug use and distribution, and gang violence.

It is important to understand that many members of gangs are actually victims long before they "choose" to join a gang. Interventions must start at an early age, before middle school, and must be focused on the family and community.

Communities and Support Systems

School Influences

A functional match between schools and the adolescent is becoming an increasingly recognized idea that needs attention and reform. Indeed, many researchers and professionals believe that the middle school is not an effective institution for young people. Eccles, Barber, Jozefowicz, Malenchuk, and Vida (1999) argued that a serious mismatch exists between the organization and curriculum of middle schools and the intellectual, social, and emotional needs of young adolescents. Studies (Watt, 2000) have found that there is a decline in students' academic motivation, attitudes toward subjects being studied, and an increase in conduct disorders. To address many of the educational issues of adolescents, we will examine three themes: the effect of schooling on adolescent development; the ecology of schools; and a life-course perspective about schools.

Schooling has played an important role in influencing adolescent development. Perhaps most significant was the movement to make secondary schooling compulsory, putting adolescents in a submissive position and keeping them from the workforce in order to make employment more manageable. Although the emphasis in schools has changed over time, the basic function has remained stable since the 1900s. That function is to provide a comprehensive curriculum to prepare young people for the diverse aspects of life. How this "comprehensive curriculum" is structured is a source of debate. For instance, the back-to-basics movement has gained prominence, but opponents argue that schools must also be responsive to young people's social and emotional lives.

Whatever the curriculum, the numerous hours that young people spend in school expose them to significant and life-changing events and experiences. Their identity formation, competence in social and academic abilities, career paths, and social relationships all are affected by their experience in school. In spite of this influence, many people have questioned whether schooling is effective. This question is evaluated from two vantage points: Does school affect cognitive abilities? and Can schools compensate for the negative effects of poverty? (Santrock, 2002). Research suggests that schooled children can outperform unschooled children (Wagner & Stevenson, 1982). However, it is also true that in high school, average achievement-test gains are small and grades often decline (Alspaugh, 1998). With regard to the second question, there is evidence, although not without controversy, that schools have little impact on the cognitive development of students living in poverty. Furthermore, the effect of school quality produces small differences in students' achievements.

Our previous discussion focused on how young people's backgrounds and personal characteristics influence their school success, but also important are the social and organizational characteristics that influence adolescent development (Kaplan, 2004; Pawlak & Cousins, 1999). One of the major organizational factors that influences the relationship between school and adolescent development is the transition from elementary school to middle school and from middle school to high school.

In most schools, the ninth grade has been included in the high school system, and most school systems now have middle schools that include either the seventh and eighth grades or the sixth, seventh, and eighth grades. The transition from elementary school to middle school is often a stressful one. As the Carnegie Council on Adolescent Development (1989) has pointed out, this transition often represents a move from a small neighborhood school and the stability of one classroom to a large, impersonal institution, often more complex and bureaucratic, and a period class schedule with multiple teachers. This shift may disrupt important support and comfort from peer groups and caring relationships from school teachers and staff. Furthermore, this transition occurs in tandem with puberty and other emotional and social changes (e.g., concerns about body image, decreased dependency on parents, and changes in social cognition).

This stressful transition may be explained in part by the top-dog phenomenon observed by Simmons and Blyth (1987) in their study on the transition into adolescence. These researchers found that stress increases for young people as they move from being "top dog" (biggest, oldest, most powerful) in the elementary school to being "bottom dog" (smallest, youngest, least powerful) in the middle school. This study also compared the self-esteem of seventh-grade girls who had transitioned to junior high with girls who remained in a K–8 school. The junior high students were negatively affected by the transition: They had lower self-esteem, negative attitudes toward school, fewer leadership roles, and more victimization by boys. Despite the trend toward creating separate middle schools, there is no good evidence to support this change; in fact, some research suggests it would be better to keep the old school system of grades K–8 and 9–12.

The Carnegie Council on Adolescent Development has been extremely critical of the organization and curriculum of middle schools. Thus, some districts have begun to eliminate middle schools and use the kindergarten-through-eighth-grade structure (Schouten, 2002). The Council found that middle schools fall short of meeting the educational, health, and social needs of young adolescents. They identified three essential qualities schools need to create a community for learning: (1) schools need to be restructured to a more human scale, which means creating smaller learning environments; (2) schools need to create a small group of caring adults who work with each other to develop coordinated, meaningful, and challenging educational experiences and provide some stability with peer groups; and (3) schools need to create opportunities for each student to interact with at least one adult who can provide the youth with advice about academic matters and personal problems and emphasize the importance of succeeding in the middle school.

The high school also is not beyond criticism. One of the most prevalent images of the high school is that of the "shopping mall" (Powell, Farrar, & Cohen, 1985). Just as many shoppers wander aimlessly in the mall, the average high school student is lost within the corridors and classrooms of the high school. This image arose from an extensive study of fifteen diverse high schools. Although the high schools offered variety and choice, the result was a curriculum that is watered down and lacking in substance for most of the students. The researchers claimed that the average students—those neither on a "high" track nor a "low" track—were overlooked in the high schools. Thus the shopping mall high school promotes individualization but does not provide personalization. It is widely accepted that the high school experience is one where students are less engaged than previously and are in an even less friendly environment than in middle school.

Some researchers (Aronson, 2000) believe problems like those experienced at Columbine (the mass killing in Colorado of high school classmates) directly relate to the impersonal and negative environments that exist in high schools. Aronson (2000) wrote that schools must work harder to create environments where understanding and compassion exist. In his book *Nobody Left to Hate*, he outlined a series of interventions that can transform schools. He included targets such as reduction of bullying, promotion of social skills, conflict resolution, empathy training, and structural changes in the schools. In Aronson's view, we must break down existing peer barriers through the use of cooperative learning strategies.

High School Dropouts

Although high school dropouts remain a serious problem, the percentage of youths who do not finish high school has decreased considerably over the years. Fifty years ago, more than 60% of students overall did not finish high school. In the year 2001, 91% of white students, 84% of African American students, and a dismal 63% of Hispanic students completed high school (National Center for Education Statistics). The poor academic preparation and disadvantaged economic background of students of color appear to account for their higher dropout rates.

Also, dropout rates vary dramatically depending on the city and region of the country. In Chicago, the dropout rate can be as high as 55%.

Studies of the characteristics of dropouts have found several factors that predict dropout: poor attendance, disinterest in school, living in poverty, single-parent families, parents who do not participate in decision making concerning the student, conduct problems in school, grade retention, poor grades, pregnancy, more than fifteen hours of work per week, and urban lifestyle (National Research Council, 1993). Dropping out is not usually a response to a lack of ability—these students have average intelligence scores. In general, the pattern that emerges is one of students who disengage from school. Dropout prevention programs have focused on targeting at-risk students and improving academic performance, changing attitudes about school, and reducing absenteeism. Very few dropout prevention programs have been evaluated for their effectiveness. However, the trend is to begin dropout prevention strategies earlier than high school by focusing on middle schools and elementary schools. Also, because dropout rates in some schools are so high, the strategy is to improve the school overall in order to prevent dropout. An individualized approach is no longer feasible. The current focus of prevention is on schoolwide practices that can reduce alienation from the educational process and increase motivation and interest in learning. One major change that can impact a young person's adjustment to school is a move from a familiar community to a new one.

Implications for Practice: Recommendations for a Smoother Family Relocation

Today's United States seems to be getting smaller. Workers increasingly move their families from one state to another because of downsizing or company mergers. Extended family members live farther from one another and therefore are often unable to act as the natural support system they are meant to be. According to the U.S. Census Bureau, each year more than 9 million children are uprooted as 17% of families change residence (Seppa, 1996). Several research findings generalize the effects on children of leaving home, school, friends, and being forced to start over. For many children, stresses are short-term. However, relocation can have consequences later in life for at-risk children who have social adjustment problems, are slow in school, or move because of a family crisis, such as divorce. Fortunately, at-risk children who have even a slight amount of special care given to them in their new school adapt better than those left to do the best they can by themselves. This special care could take the form of a designated "special friend" who shows the new student around school and introduces him or her to peers. Or the care could go further, to include special tutoring at school and at home to ensure that the new student does not fall behind.

What age of children are affected the most? Preschool children can have problems adjusting because they have not developed coping skills and cannot comprehend the reasons for the move. However, as a general rule, the older the child, the harder the transition. Older children and teens may understand the reasons for the move too well. In situations such as divorce, teens may feel pressure to support the parent they are moving with and therefore alienate the other parent. Research (Seppa, 1996) has found that teens whose mothers had negative attitudes about moving scored higher for depression than did other adolescents. And because adolescents are peer oriented, depression further isolates them by diminishing their motivation to make new friends.

Although research indicates that moving is a stressful life event that can hinder a teen's adjustment, researchers note that any long-term effects are inconclusive. Regardless, interventions can only help a teen transition during this time. The following are some suggestions for adults who relocate a family:

- Give adolescents three months' notice of an upcoming move.
- Minimize other upheavals in family life.
- Involve the children in the move with projects, such as gathering information about the new location.
- Move during the summer, if possible, to minimize school stresses.
- Recognize your own stress level and do not take on more than you can handle.
- Help teens explore social opportunities in the new environment, and resist the temptation to be overprotective. ■

Homeless youth are becoming an increasingly serious problem in today's society.

Runaway Youths

Tim, at age 16, knows what it is like to be homeless. He's lived that way for the last five years. Where would you be most likely to find him? Look in abandoned buildings in downtown Phoenix, under highway overpasses, or in alleys filled with homeless men and women in the worst parts of the city. Tim is only 1 of an estimated 1.7 million runaway/thrownaway youth (Hammer, Finkelhor, & Sedlak, 2002). What kinds of difficulties do these young people face? Do most runaway youth share common problems?

This section includes information on children who are gone from their homes either because they have run away or because they have been thrown out by their caretakers. Based on a series of national studies (Hanmer et al., 2002), such homeless youth are frequently afflicted with drug and alcohol abuse, sexual or physical abuse, criminal activity, and thoughts of suicide. The most prevalent characteristic of the runaway episode is that the young person had been physically or sexually abused at home in the year prior to the episode (see Exhibit 9.11 for details related to the runaway episode). Two-thirds of the youth with runaway/thrownaway episodes are between the ages of 15 and 17, and they are equally split among males and females.

EXHIBIT 9.11 Percent of runaway/thrownaway youth with endangered episodes

Characteristic of episode	Estimate	Percentage
Child had been physically or sexually abused at home in the year prior to the episode or was afraid of abuse on return	350,400	21
Child was substance dependent	317,800	19
Child was 13 years old or younger	305,300	18
Child was in the company of someone known to be abusing drugs	302,100	18
Child was using hard drugs	292,000	17
Child spend time in a place where criminal activity was occurring	256,900	12
Child engaged in criminal activity during the course of the episode	197,400	11
Child was a violent person	125,400	7
Child had previously attempted suicide	70,500	4
Child was enrolled in school at the time and missed at least 5 days	70,500	4
Child was physically assaulted or someone attempted to physically assault child during course of the episode	69,100	4

SOURCE: Hanmer, Finkelhor, & Sedlak (2002).

> ## FOCUS ON NARRATIVE
>
> ### HOMELESS YOUTH
>
> It's strange, but I really like it when the lights go off in the movies because then I'm no longer a "homeless kid." I'm just a person watching the movie like everyone else.
>
> A lot of the children at the hotel believe that they are "hotel kids." They've been told by so many people for so long that they are not important, they live up to what is expected of them. It gets so some children have no dreams and live in a nightmare because they believe that they are "hotel kids." It's worse than being in jail. In jail you can see the bars and you know when you're getting out. In the hotel you can't see the bars because they're inside of you and you don't know when you're getting out.
>
> SOURCE: Berck (1992), p. 6.

Clearly, runaway youth face many health and social problems. Unfortunately, very few of them have the needed resources to address the problems they face. Most have no medical coverage. Although many of these young people are in state care, many have fallen out of care and are not receiving benefits they are entitled to through the state. Runaway shelters provide a limited means of protection. Many young people stay for a short time and end up back on the street, where they again face issues of substance abuse, unprotected sex, isolation, and feelings of hopelessness. The above Focus on Narrative section presents the voice of homeless youth.

Multicultural and Gender Considerations

There are many multicultural and gender considerations in adolescence (Gibbs, 2003). As young people experience a broader world, they become more aware of their unique qualities—what it means to be a person of color, an immigrant from another country, a boy or girl, or a heterosexual or a gay or lesbian or bisexual person.

Peer Relationships and Adolescents of Color

In adolescence, young people of color begin to interact with a more heterogeneous population, and as a result they become more aware of their ethnic status. Adolescents from a minority group begin to develop an ethnic or racial identity. Such an ethnic identity is important because it relates to a stronger sense of purpose, self-confidence, and social competence (Gibbs, 2003; Martinez & Dukes, 1997).

Minority youth often confront living in two different cultures—the dominant culture, and a culture shaped by their ethnic or racial status. Living in two cultures is a challenging background for development, especially when the two cultures clash. For example, one culture may value individual achievement, whereas the other may focus more on group-oriented achievement (Kaplan, 2004).

Adolescents of color often have two sets of peer relationships: one at school, and another in their neighborhoods (Santrock, 2002). Neighborhood peers are more likely to be from their own ethnic group. In a study by Brown and Mounts (1989) of multiethnic high schools, between one-third and one-half of students of color were associated by peers with ethnically defined crowds—for example, rappers. The remaining students, two-thirds to one-half, were classified into reputation-based groups such as populars or New Wavers. Because adolescents of color may have two sets of peers, it is important to inquire about relationships both in school and in the neighborhood. Adolescents who may be isolated and rejected in school could be neighborhood stars (Gibbs, 2003).

The Adolescent Immigrant

Thousands of adolescents immigrate to the United States with their families each year, from countries all over the world—Mexico, Thailand, Vietnam, and Haiti, to name a few. How does immigration affect their long-term adjustment to a new country? Several factors are important for their satisfactory long-term adjustment to a new country (Potocky-Tripodi, 2003). Adolescents must address the issue of belonging versus estrangement. Many adolescent immigrants get quick exposure to racial and ethnic discrimination. Their minority status is heightened by differences in appearance, dress, and language. A sense of belonging can be developed through participation in their immediate community or through participation in educational and political activities. Critical to their adjustment is reliance on their earlier primary group's cultural values, because this can provide a foundation for their adjustment. By using their identification with earlier values, they can make new accommodations without the need to reject basic values. Last, supportiveness of family relationships is necessary to provide positive expectations about their new adjustments to a different way of life. Encouragement that they can be successful and achieve reduces the sense of self-doubt and feelings of being marginal and provides a basis for them to realize their aspirations. Immigrating adolescents face many unique challenges in successful acculturation.

Gender Roles

What does it mean to be a boy or girl in today's society? In the past, there were more clear indications about what a boy did compared with a girl—boys played rough and got dirty, whereas girls played quietly and kept clean. In today's culture, there is greater diversity in gender roles and an increasing emphasis on equality or role sharing. Much of this change in gender roles is characterized as a move toward **androgyny**, which is the combination of masculine and feminine behaviors in the same person (Bem, 1977). An androgynous male adolescent is someone who is both assertive and sensitive to others; an androgynous female is dominant and assertive as well as nurturing. Various research studies on gender roles suggest that, in general, changes are taking place in the direction of greater role sharing.

Do you think you are an androgynous person? A widely used measure of sex roles, the Bem Sex Role Inventory, is presented in Exhibit 9.12, so you can make an assessment of yourself. There are four major gender-role classifications: androgynous, masculine, feminine, and undifferentiated. We have already defined *androgynous*, you are familiar with the notions of masculine and feminine, and the undifferentiated classification refers to a person who has neither masculine nor feminine characteristics. Although androgyny is a useful concept, researchers have had a difficult time specifying the concept. Also, we must consider how the concept reflects the developmental level of the child (Santrock, 2002). What is feminine for a 4-year-old girl will be quite different than for a 15-year-old. What aspects do you think best characterize masculinity and femininity during adolescence?

The Voice of Adolescent Girls

Carol Gilligan is well known for her feminist work *In a Different Voice*, which changed the way researchers view women's development. In her new work *Meeting at the Crossroads*, with Lyn Mikel Brown, she examines the lives of adolescent girls and provides a new perspective about their development. The central question the researchers sought to answer was, "What, on the way to womanhood, does a girl give up?" The way to womanhood was found to be accompanied by a falling away of the self. The researchers found that younger, preadolescent girls perceived conflict as a sign of healthy relationships, and they could more easily speak about their thoughts and feelings. At this stage of development, these girls were comfortable with feelings of anger, fighting in relationships, and disagreements. In contrast, girls approaching adolescence struggled with a preoccupation with perfection and were engulfed with idealized relationships. Gilligan and Brown found that at this age girls desire attention, love, and popularity, and in their pursuit to build relationships, they are expected to give up something—for example, expression of their real feelings of anger. These girls' accounts are documented with vivid anecdotes as they describe their losses and their inability to express themselves. The researchers refer to this phenomenon as a form of psychological repression. For example, Gail reflects on her life over the past year: "I think I've gotten along better with people . . . I don't disagree as much . . . and I don't get into fights as much. Like arguments with my friends." When the interviewer asked why, she responded, "Maybe because I can understand how they think now and accept them . . . accept what they think, instead of being just one-minded . . . I realized that I went along with that and I realized I was experienced I guess, because I realized that I should understand what they think also." Then the interviewer asked, "Do you think fighting or arguing is worthless?" and Gail offered a confusing statement and then concluded that yes, fighting is worthless because she's stopped fighting and she doesn't "have to think." In this example, Brown and Gilligan (1992, p. 93) commented:

> Gail's response to her interviewer's questions about arguing exemplifies the intricate and subtle relationship between Gail's developing capacity to understand and appreciate and take in viewpoints different from her own and the fear that by continuing to speak in the presence of difference she will lose her relationship with her friends." Brown and Gilligan have encouraged

EXHIBIT 9.12 The Bem sex role inventory

Instructions: Rate each item on the scale from 1 (never or almost never true) to 7 (always or almost always true).

1. self-reliant
2. yielding
3. helpful
4. defends own beliefs
5. cheerful
6. moody
7. independent
8. shy
9. conscientious
10. athletic
11. affectionate
12. theatrical
13. assertive
14. flatterable
15. happy
16. strong personality
17. loyal
18. unpredictable
19. forceful
20. feminine
21. reliable
22. analytical
23. sympathetic
24. jealous
25. has leadership abilities
26. sensitive to the needs of others
27. truthful
28. willing to take risks
29. understanding
30. secretive
31. makes decisions easily
32. compassionate
33. sincere
34. self-sufficient
35. eager to soothe hurt
36. conceited
37. dominant
38. soft-spoken
39. likable
40. masculine
41. warm
42. solemn
43. willing to take a stand
44. tender
45. friendly
46. aggressive
47. gullible
48. inefficient
49. acts as a leader
50. childlike
51. adaptable
52. individualistic
53. does not use harsh language
54. unsystematic
55. competitive
56. loves children
57. tactful
58. ambitious
59. gentle
60. conventional

Scoring: Masculinity score—add up ratings for 1, 4, 7, 10, 13, 16, 19, 22, 25, 28, 31, 34, 37, 40, 43, 46, 49, 52, 55, and 58. Divide the total by 20. The result is your masculinity score.

Femininity score—add up ratings for 2, 5, 8, 11, 14, 17, 20, 23, 26, 29, 32, 35, 38, 41, 44, 47, 50, 53, 56, and 59. Divide by 20. That is your femininity score.

Note: If your masculinity score is above 4.9 (the median score) and your femininity score is above 4.9 (the median score), then you would be classified as androgynous on Bem's scale.

SOURCE: From *Half the human experience: The psychology of women*, 3rd ed., by J. S. Hyde. Copyright © 1985 D. C. Heath & Company. Reprinted with permission of Houghton Mifflin Company. Material originally from Bem (1974, 1977); Hyde & Phillis (1979).

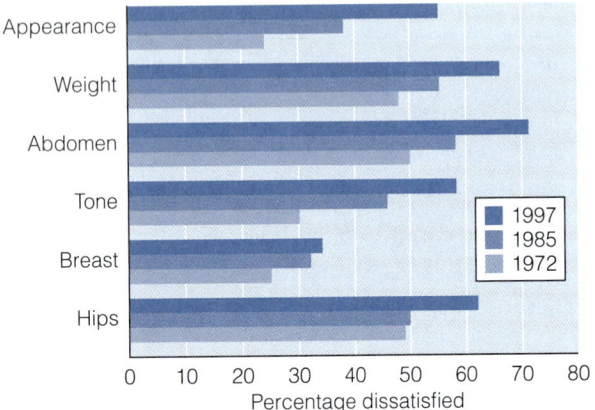

EXHIBIT 9.13 Women's body dissatisfaction across three time periods
SOURCE: Adapted from Gardner (1997).

practitioners to help strengthen healthy resistance and courage in girls. The major lesson is the importance of helping girls discovers their lost voices.

Body Image and Adolescent Depression for Girls

In childhood up to puberty, more boys than girls are depressed. Suddenly, in late adolescence, the number of girls experiencing depression is twice that of boys—a disparity that continues through adulthood (Marcotte, Fortin, Potvin, & Papillon, 2002).

Research has examined a number of possible factors that could account for such differences, including life events, popularity, and sex roles. However, the most significant factor related to depression is body image. Girls interpret their maturing bodies negatively, whereas boys perceive their own body changes as positive—as the development of more muscles.

Media exposure can have a profound effect on one's body image. Exhibit 9.13 presents a summary of women's dissatisfaction with their bodies over three time periods, and the clear trend is that dissatisfaction has been growing during the last thirty years.

Girls and boys are equally likely to be depressed because of life events, but girls unhappy with their body images are more likely to be depressed. Also, girls who spend more time in "feminine activities"—such as makeup, cooking, shopping—are more inclined to be depressed. Furthermore, because stereotypically feminine activities tend to be passive and may provide less mastery and autonomy, they may contribute to a tendency to depression (LeCroy & Daley, 2001).

FOCUS ON NARRATIVE

THE DIFFICULTY OF BEING A GIRL IN TODAY'S SOCIETY

I cannot stop crying. Why won't the tears stop flowing? When I was little I'd just think of something and then I'd be ok, but no happy thoughts pop into my mind at the moment. Crying is pointless. It gives me a headache, makes my eyes burn, makes my nose run, and causes people to ask, "What's the matter?" What do you expect me to say? Where would I begin?

How could I possibly explain how awful I feel about myself; how I can't remember the last time I was actually proud of myself; how I can't stand any of the people I used to call my "friends"; how I feel guilty about everything I do; how I hate being fat but wish I were thin; how I wish boys would like me even though I'm fat so I'd be happy with myself; how I wish I didn't depend on boys to raise my self-esteem; how I hate boys but want them anyway; how I know you don't really care what's the matter with me. Nobody cares. Maybe that's why I'm crying. Would you understand this? NO, BECAUSE YOU'RE SELF-CONFIDENT, POPULAR, AND THIN! YOU HAVE NO IDEA WHAT IT FEELS LIKE TO BE SO INFERIOR TO EVERYONE AROUND YOU! SO SHUT THE FUCK UP, WALK AWAY FROM ME, AND LET ME CRY IN PEACE!

Source: Carlip (1995), p. 53.

Implications for Practice: A Prevention Program for Adolescent Girls

The "Go Grrrls" program (LeCroy & Daley, 2001) seeks to address the unique challenges early-adolescent girls encounter by providing them with practical instruction and skill-building exercises. The target population is seventh graders, and the hope is that the program will provide a sort of inoculation of knowledge and skill early enough that girls may resist some of the common hazards of growing up in a culture that seems, in many respects, to be toxic to females. The program includes topics such as being a girl in today's society, establishing a positive self-image, developing an acceptable body image, assertiveness, problem solving, friendship skills, finding help, and planning for the future.

Some of the group sessions (such as the session on problem-solving) emphasize skill building in areas equally pertinent to boys and girls, but the examples and role-plays used to illustrate the skills emphasize girls as the major actors. Other sessions (such as the session on being a girl in today's society) are designed to address areas of special concern to adolescent girls—the profusion of negative images of women and girls in popular media, and the ability and confidence to critically challenge these cultural stereotypes. A randomized control-group experiment found the program enhanced the skills and abilities of the participants significantly (LeCroy, 2004). ■

The War against Boys

In a direct challenge to Gilligan's work on adolescent girls, Sommers (2000) has put forth her new book *The War Against Boys*. In this work, Sommers critiques the research that suggests there is a "crisis of adolescent girls." For example, Pipher's well-known and often-quoted book *Reviving Ophelia* laments the dramatic increase in suicide rates for girls—a 57% increase. Sommers dug deeper into the statistics and found that the suicide rate for boys increased 71% and for girls 27%. But she was most convincing in her analysis of data regarding schooling and adolescent boys. Here, Sommers pointed out that it is boys, not girls, who need dramatic help. As she noted, girls get better grades, do more homework, engage in more extracurricular activities, enroll in more advanced-placement classes, and go to college in greater numbers. Her point is well taken—boys are being neglected, especially in the educational realm. And like our recent efforts to promote the healthy development of girls, equal effort should be made on behalf of boys.

Adolescent Heterosexuality

No discussion of adolescence would be complete without a section on adolescent sexuality. In adolescence, formation of a sexual identity is a major developmental task. From adolescence to young adulthood, young people begin the process of sexual exploration—a search for their sexual identities. Although this may sound like a gender stereotype, it is during this time that boys aggressively search for sexual experience with girls and girls eagerly desire romantic involvement with boys. More girls than boys report being in love as the main reason for engaging in sexual intercourse (Kaplan, 2004). Adolescent boys recognize this socialization and, as a result, profess to be "in love" with a large number of girls. However, changes in sexual behavior in the last twenty years do show a decline in the sexual double standard. Sexual intercourse for adolescent girls has increased more rapidly than for boys, indicating greater acceptance of girls being sexually active. However, research on attitudes and feelings about sexual intercourse has found that more boys than girls report positive feelings about their sexual experiences (Santrock, 2002). Also, both male and female adolescents accept that the role of the male adolescent is to be the aggressor in sexual relations and that the female adolescent's role is to set limits on this behavior. Many aspects of adolescent sexuality have undergone rapid and considerable change, yet many other aspects have remained unchanged.

How sexually active are adolescents? Recent data suggest that they are quite active. Most people believe the statistics underestimate the extent of adolescent sexual behavior. Of particular attention recently has been the number of adolescents engaging in oral sex.

Recent media reports have popularized the notion that adolescents are engaging in oral sex because it isn't "real" sex. Many of the reports focused on what was labeled a fad among suburban middle school students. Because of the complexity in conducting research on such sensitive topics with young adolescents, there is little data to verify these media reports. Still, it would appear that there is an increase in such sexual behaviors, but it is difficult to know the extent of the behavior. As one expert put it, "Middle school girls sometimes look at oral sex as an absolute bargain—you don't get pregnant, they think you don't get diseases, you're still a virgin and you're in control since it's something that they can do to boys" (CDC, 2003). There is also the perception that oral sex is something you can do with someone you are not intimate with, intercourse being reserved for that special person. Adolescent health professionals will need to address these issues as they continue to work on improving the health status of young people. If nothing else, oral sex has helped everyone recognize that we need a broader definition of sex—it is not just a single act but a wide range of behaviors.

As might be expected, several factors influence the incidence of sexual activity among adolescents. For example, sexual activity is lowest for white adolescents, followed by Hispanic, and then African American adolescents. The following are some key factors that have been found to significantly influence adolescents' sexual activity (American Academy of Pediatrics, 1999):

- Living in a single-parent household is related to a higher incidence of sexual activity.
- Attending church and doing well in school discourage sexual activity.
- Good parent-adolescent communication discourages sexual activity.
- Early dating experience encourages sexual activity.
- Parental discipline—either too permissive or too strict—encourages sexual activity.

Petersen and Crockett (1992) have identified four influences that they believe are associated with early sexual behavior and subsequent pregnancy:

1. *Biological influences.* Puberty is hypothesized to have a major influence on adolescent sexual behavior, leading to greater risk of pregnancy and childbearing. Pubertal development may affect adolescent sexual behavior in two ways: directly through hormonal effects on the brain, and more indirectly through somatic changes that stimulate a more mature physical appearance, which in turn suggests expectations about more mature sexual behavior.
2. *Sexual abuse.* Prepubertal sexual abuse may have a significant effect on girls' subsequent sexual behavior. It is hypothesized that prepubertal sexual abuse is linked to earlier sexual behavior, earlier pregnancy, and earlier childbearing and that it is related to difficulties with child-rearing skills. The reasons for these connections are complicated and not well understood.
3. *Deviance or problem behavior.* Adolescents who are involved in problem behaviors are more likely to have earlier sexual behavior and earlier pregnancy. Jessor (1992) has identified sexual behavior as one part of the problem-behavior syndrome and speculated that involvement in problem behavior is related to psychological readiness to participate in adult behaviors. Or participation in one problem behavior may bring young people into contact with peer groups where additional problem behaviors are modeled and encouraged. More simply, pregnancy and the sexual behavior of adolescents appear to be part of a "deviant lifestyle" characterized by multiple problem behaviors (McWhirter et al., 1998).
4. *Normative expectations.* Transitions to subsequent life stages may be influenced by societal expectations. In other words, if an adolescent is ex-

FOCUS ON NARRATIVE

ADOLESCENTS' VIEWS ON SEX

Santrock (1996, p. 384) has quoted several adolescents about their sexual experiences:

> I am 16 years old and I really like this one girl. She wants to be a virgin until she marries. We went out last night and she let me go pretty far, but not all the way . . . It's getting hard for me to handle . . . I feel I am ready to have sex. I have to admit I think about having sex with other girls too . . . (Frank C.)
>
> I'm 14 years old. I have a lot of sexy thoughts. Sometimes just before I drift off to sleep at night I think about this hunk who is 16 years old and plays on the football team. He is so gorgeous and I can feel him holding me in his arms and kissing and hugging me . . . (Amy S.)
>
> Is it weird to be a 17-year-old guy and still be a virgin? Sometimes I feel like the only 17-year-old male on the planet who has not had sex. I feel like I am missing out on something great, or at least that's what I hear. I'm pretty religious and I sometimes feel guilty when I think about sex . . . (Tom B.)
>
> I'm 15 years old and I had sex for the first time recently. I had all of these expectations about how great it was going to be . . . We were both pretty scared about the whole thing. It was all over in a hurry. My first thought was, "Is this all there is?" It was a very disappointing experience. (Claire T.)

pected to complete college, then marry, and then have children, these expectations are likely to influence the course of such events. Petersen and Crockett (1992) found that girls who are sexually active in junior high school anticipate making several adult transitions, such as finishing their education, starting a job, and marrying, at earlier ages than do girls who are not yet sexually active. Also interesting is the finding of familial transmission of these expectations. Several studies have found a relationship between mothers' sexual experience as adolescents and the sexual experience of their adolescent child. This may be due to a permissive attitude toward sex, or it could be due to early maturity by both mother and daughter. The accompanying Focus on Narrative presents several adolescents' viewpoints about sex.

AIDS Prevention and Adolescent Males

Given the high rate of sexual intercourse among adolescent boys, there is a great need for AIDS prevention among this population. AIDS, or acquired immune deficiency syndrome, is caused by the **human immunodeficiency virus (HIV)**. This virus destroys the human immune system and leads to opportunistic infections by agents such as bacteria and viruses that are usually harmless to a healthy individual. In the immune-compromised individual, however, these agents produce illness and, ultimately, death. Infection with HIV leads to a classification of the person as HIV-positive. The rate of infection from this virus continues to be a serious health concern. AIDS is the sixth leading cause of death among people aged 15–24 years (National Center for Health Statistics, 2003). Because of the long incubation period for the HIV infection (it averages 11 years), many people are infected with HIV as adolescents and will develop AIDS in their 20s or 30s. Of the new AIDS cases in young people, the majority were in young men who have sex with men. A serious issue is that many young people with HIV infection continue to engage in risky behavior even after the infection has been diagnosed (Diamond & Buskin, 2000).

It appears, however, that AIDS prevention is responding to the AIDS epidemic. The proportion of sexually active adolescents using condoms has increased. For example, the percentage of youth using condoms during their last sexual intercourse has increased from a low in 1991 of 46% to 63% in 2003.

Less encouraging is that young gay men aren't consistently practicing safe sex, although a majority of older gay men have changed to safe-sex behavior. In one study of young gay men, 36% indicated they had unprotected anal sex during the prior two months. Younger gay men see AIDS as something that happens to older gay men. Also, homeless and runaway youths are at higher risk for AIDS. Because they are more concerned with daily survival, protecting themselves against AIDS is not seen as a priority.

Gay, Lesbian, Bisexual, and Questioning Youth

Consider the following quotations from gay and lesbian adolescents (Hersch, 1990):

> When all the guys are discussing their latest crushes, I play along. What a body Carol has. Look at those great tits on Marge. How can I tell them I dream of Dave? It would be all over the school in a flash. I'd be dead meat.

> It's difficult to know what to wear, what to say, how to act with different people. You are so scared of being found out that you never know if you will ever be able to be yourself.

> I don't understand what is going on with me. I want to kill myself. I'm scared of who I am. There is no one else like me. What am I going to do? It's not normal to be gay—normal is a man and a woman. Am I the only one?

These are the words of gay and lesbian adolescents. The term *gay* refers to both men and women whose sexual orientation is toward members of the same sex. The term *lesbian* is used to describe women. The term *bisexual* is used to describe sexual behavior that is directed to members of the same and opposite sex. The word *transgendered* is a person whose identity differs from conventional expectations for their physical sex. Transgendered people can include transsexuals, drag queens/kings, cross-dressers, and so forth, and transgendered people can be gay, lesbian, bisexual, or straight. Often gay and transgendered people are referred to together as LGBT (lesbian, gay, bisexual and transgendered) or LGBTQ (with the addition of questioning). The word *homosexual* refers to both gay men and lesbians but is often not the preferred language, as homosexual has been associated with negative stereotypes. These labels are also words of secrecy and fear—a world that gay adolescents must learn to live within. Life can be difficult, if not dangerous, for many gay adolescents, who experience violence because of their sexual orientation. Indeed, gay adolescents present our society with many challenges. As Hersch (1990) aptly put it, "to a culture already uncomfortable about adult sex, worried about adolescent sex, and downright hostile about homosexual sex, gay and lesbian adolescents pose a compounded threat—children who are sexual *and* deviant." Society has a difficult time accepting adolescents as sexually active and would rather deny the existence of gay adolescents. Even sex-education programs fail to address gay adolescents' needs or acknowledge their sexuality. This increases their sexual confusion and isolation and may make them feel that their sexuality does not exist.

Yet gay, lesbian, bisexual, and questioning adolescents do exist. Studies confirm that 3%–10% of men define themselves as gay and between 1%–3% of women define themselves as lesbian (Strong & DeVault, 2004). However, those statistics were gathered more than 15 years ago. Today some experts estimate the gay and lesbian population at about 10% (Isay, 1997). The basis for homosexuality is controversial. However, it is likely to have a genetic component; when one twin is gay, the other twin is gay more than 50% of the time. No matter what the origin of homosexuality, the estimated 4 million gay adolescents in the United States must confront many social difficulties.

Perhaps of most concern among GLBTQ adolescents are isolation, depression, and potential for suicide. These young people are two to three times as likely to attempt suicide as are other youth (Kaplan, 2004). A significant number of the suicide attempts relate to personal turmoil about being gay. Many of these young people have a difficult time confronting the social isolation they experience, their concern about secrecy, and their fear of violence. Other risks include low self-esteem, substance abuse, and harassment.

Several authors have explored the unique developmental challenges faced by gay youth in relation to the coming-out process. Adaptation to a gay identity is commonly conceived to span four stages, often sequentially, though progression may cease at any stage. It is important to remember that although frameworks provide a helpful generic description of the developmental transition, the process is highly variable and rarely unfolds in an orderly, linear fashion. It is characterized by diversions and detours and by individual differences, sex differences, and the historical context.

Homosexual adolescents often experience alienation and face developmental problems because they may repress their identity, face peer rejection, and feel the pressure of cultural sanctions against intimate homosexual relations.

Troiden (1989) has referred to the first stage of adaptation as *sensitization*, during which the individual becomes aware of feelings that make him or her different according to social definitions. The next stage is *identity confusion*, where the person struggles with the implications of a gay identity. At this stage, individuals often try to make sense of their feelings without the advantage of accurate information and are informed only by the negative and erroneous stereotypes of the dominant culture. Eventually, the strength of the feelings associated with sexual attraction lead to some degree of self-redefinition that may be associated with behaviors consistent with a gay identity. Troiden referred to this stage as *identity assumption*. Troiden described the final stage as *commitment*, which involves restructuring of the individual's social life to include a sustained, positive association with a community of like others.

Unfortunately, many gay youths do not learn to accept or feel comfortable with their sexual identity. In addition to the concern about depression and suicide, gay adolescents face a number of increased risks, such as destructive alcohol and drug abuse, being victims of crime, sexual diseases including AIDS, and school dropout. These risks can be compounded if the youth is a minority. Gay and lesbian youth of color live within three communities: their ethnic community, the gay and lesbian community, and the majority community. They are thus susceptible to two types of prejudice: racism and homophobia. A gay person can feel as if she or he lives in three different worlds—and too often none of the worlds provides the support that is needed.

Can Changing a Child's Sex Change His Sexual Orientation?

He was one of a set of infant twin boys when, in 1963, his penis was damaged beyond repair by a circumcision that went awry. After seeking expert advice at Johns Hopkins Medical School, the parents decided that the child's best shot at a normal life was as an anatomically correct woman. The baby was castrated, and surgeons fashioned a kind of vagina out of the remaining tissue. When "she" grew older, hormone treatments would complete the transformation from boy to girl.

In the 1960s and 1970s, doctors believed that sexual identity existed on a continuum and that nurture was more important than nature in determining gender roles (Bradley, Oliver, Chernick, & Zucker, 1998). Basically, experts believed that babies were born gender neutral, and if they were indoctrinated early enough, they could become either gender. Unfortunately for the child called "Joan," this theory did not hold true. Joan never really adjusted to her assigned gender. She spent her childhood and early adolescence rejecting life as a girl; as a toddler she ripped off her dresses; she played only with boys and with stereotypical boys' toys; and she urinated standing up. Joan was sure she was a boy. But her doctors and psychiatrists kept pressuring her to act more feminine. At the age of 14, Joan gave up and decided she could either kill herself or live her life as a male. When she confronted her father, he tearfully told her the true story of her birth and sex change. "All of a sudden everything clicked . . . for the first time things made sense, and I understood who and what I was" (p. 83). With the support of her parents and different doctors, Joan underwent several surgeries to reconstruct a penis. "Joan" is now John, a happily married father of three adopted children.

This original landmark of modern science was, in actuality, a disaster. Although Joan became John in the late 1970s, no follow-up study reporting John's rejection of his original sex change was published. Dozens of other boys over the years have been needlessly "castrated" because of Joan's assumed success. Today's experts expect these boys-made-girls will reject their female identity by the time they reach puberty. But others are not so sure we have the answers.

Implications for Practice: Guidelines for Adolescents Who Want to Consider Coming Out

Many gay and lesbian adolescents will confront the decision about whether or not to come out and discuss being gay. This is a difficult decision with a lot of serious consequences. More than twenty years ago, Sauerman produced a pamphlet for the Federation of Parents and Friends of Lesbians and Gays about coming out, and Pope (2004) has updated these guidelines for coming out to one's parents:

1. Be clear yourself. Tell them when you have accepted your own sexual orientation and are comfortable and happy with it. Then it is important to express this to your parents. If you are not comfortable or happy, they will perceive this incongruity between your words and feelings and they will want to try to change you.
2. Tell them about your sexual orientation when things are going well for both you and them, or during a period when there is relative tranquility in your lives.
3. Do not come out during an argument, because this knowledge may then become a weapon to be used to cause pain to everyone.
4. It is okay to tell only one parent initially if that is easier or more comfortable for you. It is important that both parents know eventually.
5. Begin by telling your parents that you love them. If you do not usually say these things, then find other positive thoughts to share.
6. Be prepared for your parents to be upset and hurt by this news. Your parents may respond with anger, but try not to be defensive and angry also. Be prepared also for your parents to say, "I've known this for many years," or to say nothing. Different parents react differently.
7. Give them the time and distance they need to assimilate this information.
8. Tell them that you are still the same person and you hope they will continue to love you.
9. Try to maintain open lines of communication. Your parents are going to go through a period of adjustment as well—feelings of guilt, lost dreams, and greater uncertainty of the future. Sometimes they just need time.
10. Get reading material and share it with your parents. Get the address and phone number of the local Parents and Friends of Lesbians and Gays (PFLAG) and give it to your parents.
11. Coming out to your parents is probably more important for you than it is for them. Do not force the discussion further if your parents are not ready to continue the dialogue at this time. Sometimes they just

> **FOCUS ON NARRATIVE**
>
> ### BEING GAY IN HIGH SCHOOL
>
> "DYKE!"
>
> From behind my back, I hear the slur for the umpteenth time. "I'm not going to let it go this time," I think to myself. "Let's see who's so tough and brave now." I whip around to face four boys who like to think of themselves as men.
>
> "Who said that?" Four heads bow dumbly at their desk. "I asked you, who said that?" Not one of those pairs of "tough" eyes dares to look into mine. "You're all a bunch of cowards," I say with exasperation and walk away.
>
> As soon as I walk away, frustration, disappointment and anger well up inside of me and I explode with unanswerable questions. I'm a good person and I don't try to hurt other people. Why can't they just leave me alone? Do they hate themselves so much that they hate me too? Do they fear me? What do they know about the real me? They don't even know who I am.
>
> This was not an isolated incident. I've experienced this harassment throughout high school. I have always been able to stand up for myself, but I've always been left with a vague angry feeling . . .
>
> Source: Carlip (1995), pp. 93–94.

need some time and space to process this information and gain some perspective. ■

Harassment

Harassment is becoming an increasing concern among school officials. On average, about 80% of adolescent boys and girls report being sexually harassed by their peers (American Association of University Women, 2001). In the AAUW report *Hostile Hallways: Bullying, Teasing and Sexual Harassment in Schools*, one-third of students fear being sexually harassed in school, whereas less than half report never being afraid when they go to school. More than one quarter of the students surveyed report they often experience sexual harassment. This report discusses the negative ramifications of harassment for girls, who describe feeling self-conscious, embarrassed, and less confident when experiencing sexual harassment. Other research indicates that students with disabilities are more likely to be sexually harassed than their peers and that lesbian, gay, bisexual and transgendered (LGBT) youth can experience intense harassment (Smith, 2001). Surprisingly, much of the harassment is taking place in front of teachers and school officials despite the fact that since Title IX of the 1972 Education Amendments, schools are legally liable when they know of sexual harassment but do not act on it.

What needs to happen to curb the incidence of such harassment? Experts agree that first, social workers should become aware of any existing policies in the schools; if there are none, policies need to be created. Second, make sure the school has a plan for what to do when an incident is reported to a school official and that everyone is clear about how a student can file a complaint. Third, all school staff need to be trained in sexual-harassment policies and principles. Fourth, whenever harassment occurs, it should be addressed immediately. And lastly, build a supportive community of parents who can help ensure that policies and practices are consistently implemented.

Social Strengths and Hazards

Building ASSETS for Youth: A Strength and Community-Based Approach

Peter Benson, president of the Search Institute, has led a nationwide effort to promote positive youth development. His work began with research describing assets and their impact on the at-risk behavior of youth described in the report *The Troubled Journey* (Benson, 1990). His subsequent work has used this research to promote strategies that communities can use to build the assets of children and adolescents (Benson & Lerner, 2003). This approach attempts to shift the current emphasis on the crisis and problems of youth and concentrate on building assets for and with young people. According to Benson, too much focus has been placed on trying to stop or prevent problems rather than on increasing young people's exposure to positive and constructive activities as a way to build stronger communities. The research on ASSETS comes from more than 600 communities and is based on almost 50,000 young people. The survey (Exhibit 9.14) examined the presence of thirty assets.

The findings are revealing: high school students with only one to ten of the thirty assets in their lives

EXHIBIT 9.14 Forty developmental assets for youth

External assets

Support	Empowerment	Boundaries and expectations	Constructive use of time\
1. Family support	7. Community values youth	11. Family boundaries	17. Creative activities
2. Positive family communication	8. Youth as resources	12. School boundaries	18. Youth programs
3. Other adult relationships	9. Service to others	13. Neighborhood boundaries	19. Religious community
4. Caring neighborhood	10. Safety	14. Adult role models	20. Time at home
5. Caring school climate		15. Positive peer influence	16. High expectations
6. Parent involvement in schooling			

Internal assets

Commitment to learning	Positive values	Social competencies	Positive identity
21. Achievement motivation	26. Caring	32. Planning and decision making	37. Personal power
22. School engagement	27. Equality and social justice	33. Interpersonal competence	38. Self-esteem
23. Homework	28. Integrity	34. Cultural competence	39. Sense of purpose
24. Bonding to school	29. Honesty	35. Resistance skills	40. Positive view of personal future
25. Reading for pleasure	30. Responsibility	36. Peaceful conflict resolution	
	31. Restraint		

SOURCE: The list of 40 Developmental Assets™ is reprinted with permission. Copyright © 1997 by Search Institute℠. All rights reserved. No other use is permitted without prior permission from Search Institute, 615 First Avenue NE, Minneapolis, MN 55413; 800-888-7828; www.search-institute.org. Search Institute℠ and Developmental Assets™ are trademarks of Search Institute.

are involved in an average of 5.8 of 20 risk behaviors. However, youth with between eleven and twenty assets are involved in half as many risk behaviors, only 3.4. Furthermore, youth with twenty-six to thirty assets show very little risk behavior at all. Examination of one of the risk behaviors will clarify the relationship between assets and risk. Exhibit 9.15 shows that young people with the smallest number of assets have the highest alcohol use and that youth with the most assets represent only 3% of youth with alcohol problems (Youth Update, 1994).

The approach to building assets is a growing movement across the country (Lerner & Benson, 2003). Many communities, schools, and task forces are working together to develop a vision for positive youth development and to implement ways to build assets for youth.

Adolescent Risk Behaviors

How can we understand the various factors that play a significant role in leading to adolescent risk behaviors or lifestyles? For several years, Richard Jessor (1992; 1998) has been studying adolescent problem

This chart illustrates how building assets reduces problem alcohol use. Similar patterns occur for other at-risk behaviors as well.

*At risk in alcohol use is defined as drinking six or more times in the past month and/or having five or more drinks in a row, once or more in the past two weeks.

EXHIBIT 9.15 Building assets reduces alcohol abuse

SOURCE: Reprinted with permission from *The Asset Approach: 40 Elements of Healthy Development.* Copyright © 2002 by Search Institute℠, Minneapolis, MN; www.search-institute.org. All rights reserved.

behavior. Jessor's theory identifies five protective and risk factors that influence adolescent risk behavior: biology/genetics, social environment, perceived environment, personality, and behavior. Within each of these categories is a set of risk and protective factors. For example, in the social environment, the risk factors are poverty, normative anomie, racial inequality, and illegitimate opportunity; the protective factors are quality schools, cohesive family, neighborhood resources, and interested adults. It is important to point out that the influence of these concepts is bidirectional. Recent studies (Farmer et al., 2004) have examined risk behavior in samples of African American adolescents and found that a single risk in early adolescence is related to increased levels of school dropout and criminal arrests.

Before we begin to address various social hazards of adolescence, it is important to recognize that many children and adolescents today are growing and developing in a violent world. The problem of exposure to violence and its effect on the development of young people began in the late 1980s and early 1990s, with a series of studies showing how widespread exposure to violence was especially harmful for urban children (Ozer, Richards, & Kliewer, 2004). Children and adolescents are being victimized on a daily basis—more than we realize. In school, violence is a national problem. The media have recently focused on school violence as an epidemic, showing schools as places where students are barraged by rapes, shootings, stabbings, and beatings. Consistent with the media's evaluation of the condition of schools, the American public also has viewed violence as the most important problem that schools face. Almost half of all adolescents believe their schools are becoming more violent. Some young people are afraid of being hurt or shot by classmates who have weapons (10%), and twice as many youth (20%) fear going into restrooms (Safe Schools, 2002). This fear is backed up by studies that have found that 70% of middle school students and 66% of high school students physically hit another student in the last year because they were angry (Josephson Institute of Ethics, 2001). Between 14 and 24% of female adolescents and 3 to 9% of male adolescents reported experiencing physical and/or sexual violence in their dating relationships (Molidor, Tolman, & Kober, 2000). Violence in schools is a significant concern, but the incidence of violent deaths, although always tragic, remains small (.068 per 100,000; see Anderson et al., 2001).

Because people are in schools for a significant portion of their childhood, this research leads to the observation that children are potentially subjected to much more violence than are adults. In fact, rates of assault, rape, and robbery against those aged 12–19 years are two to three times higher than for the adult population as a whole. Homicide is the only violent crime to which teens are somewhat less vulnerable than adults. Yet there are huge racial disparities—for African American youth, the homicide rate has been found to be up to ten times higher (Najem, Aslam, Davidow, & Elliot, 2004). This is believed to be due to the low levels of opportunity, low education, and high levels of urbanization and poverty that exist in many African American communities.

So, who is hurting our nation's children? Sadly, it is their families. Adults report that they inflicted almost twice as much severe violence (which included beating up, kicking, hitting with fist or object) against a child in their household than they did against their adult partner. Taking into account that many acts of family violence go unreported, this is shocking. Child prostitution is another national shame which has no reliable statistics.

When the victimization of children is considered as a whole, it prompts a number of questions. First, why is child victimization so common? Although this is a complex issue, some generalizations may apply (Finkelhor & Dziuba-Leatherman, 1994). Certainly the weakness and small stature of children and their dependency status put them at greater risk. They cannot retaliate or deter victimization as effectively as can those with more strength and power. The social toleration of child victimization plays a role. Society has an influential set of institutions, the police and criminal justice system, to enforce its relatively strong prohibitions against many kinds of crime, but much of the victimization of children is considered outside the purview of this system. A final generalization is that children have little choice about whom they associate with, less choice perhaps than any segment of the population besides prisoners.

Youth Employment

Most young people today will have had a part-time job by the time they finish high school. In today's world, adolescents juggle school, friends, boyfriends or girlfriends, family, and work (Kaplan, 2004). But is it good for teenagers to work? Research has found that the amount of hours involved in work can have positive or negative effects on adolescents. In general, working fifteen to twenty hours per week improves a student's self-esteem and school satisfaction and the student's grade-point average is higher than those of nonworking peers (Steinberg et al., 1993). Research has found that adolescents working more than twenty hours per week face negative effects. Adolescents who work this much show elevated levels of psychological distress, including low self-esteem (Steinberg et al., 1993). These youth are more likely to get in trouble with the police and use drugs and alcohol. In conclusion, adolescents who are involved in some work derive benefits which may encourage responsibility and autonomy and may provide important new opportunities in the future.

Adolescent Pregnancy and Childbirth

A significant social hazard of the adolescent years is teenage pregnancy—a topic that many people in our society discuss. Teenage pregnancy has become a national concern.

The act of being sexually active can take a young person down many new roads. Once an unplanned pregnancy occurs, there are many difficult decisions to confront: Should I have this baby? Should I give this baby up for adoption? Should I consider an abortion? The result of an unplanned pregnancy has many implications for the future of the young woman: involving the father, getting married, finishing school, parent relationships—all of these things must be attended to. It is as if the young person is thrust into a completely new reality. This section will examine the prevalence of adolescent pregnancy, the consequences of adolescent pregnancy, the adolescent father, and implications for reducing adolescent pregnancy.

Prevalence of Adolescent Pregnancy

When examining the prevalence of adolescent pregnancy, several factors come into play. First, how many adolescents are sexually active? Second, how many of the sexually active adolescents are effectively using contraception? Third, if early pregnancy does occur, how many adolescents are obtaining abortions? Given all these factors, it is easier to understand that the actual rate of births to adolescent parents has been decreasing over the last several years. Exhibit 9.16 shows the prevalence of various sexual behaviors in ninth through twelfth graders across three time periods. The birthrate for female adolescents has declined 25% from 1991 to 2003, to the lowest rate in the sixty years that data on adolescent births has been collected. Also, the birthrate has declined among all ethnic and racial groups. For example, the birthrate for African American adolescents has declined 37% since 1991. But why is the birthrate declining? Reasons are many, and it is difficult to know what factors have had the most influence. Potential factors include less sexual activity among adolescents, higher rates of abstinence, increased use of contraception, and better sex education in the schools to address the spread of HIV (CDC, 2001).

Still, about 10% of American adolescent girls between the ages of 15 and 19 will become pregnant each year, contributing to the nearly one million teen pregnancies. It is startling to consider that one in five 14-year-old girls become pregnant before reaching the age of 18 (CDC, 2001). It is estimated that about one in four sexually active adolescents experience a pregnancy each year. Even with the recent decline, the United States has one of the highest teen birthrates of all developed countries. And once a young woman becomes pregnant, the risk of a second pregnancy increases. About one-third of adolescent mothers have

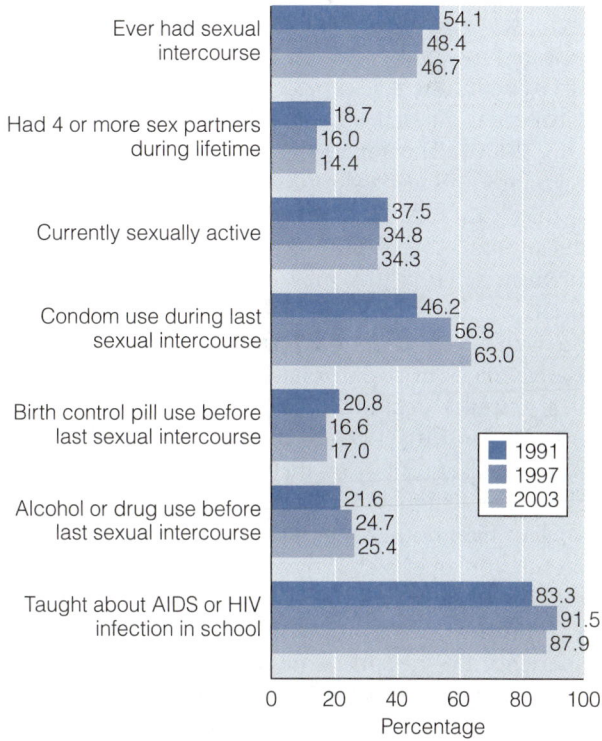

EXHIBIT 9.16 Trends in the prevalence of sexual behaviors in ninth through twelfth graders

SOURCE: YRBSS National Youth Risk Behavior Survey 1991–2003 (www.cdc.gov/yrbss), Department of Health and Human Services, Centers for Disease Control and Prevention.

a repeat pregnancy within two years (Kaplan, 2004). This sobering fact suggests the ongoing need to address birth control among young people.

What is the greatest risk factor for a teenager becoming pregnant? If you guessed poverty, you are correct (Santelli et al., 2000). With poverty comes less education, poor medical care, less opportunity, higher drop-out rates, a sense of hopelessness and isolation, and a greater likelihood that the age of first intercourse will be younger. And, not surprisingly, the younger the age at first intercourse, the less likely the teen is to use contraceptives. Often, engaging in sex and becoming pregnant is a response to the limited opportunities many of these young girls have (Coard et al., 2000).

Consequences of Adolescent Pregnancy

The consequences of early pregnancy impact both the mother and the child. For the infant, low birth weight and an increased likelihood of infant mortality are consequences. Prenatal care is obtained by only one out of every five of all mothers during the critical first three months of pregnancy. For the mother, especially young mothers, there are increased risks of complications and mortality. There is also a greater likelihood for young mothers to experience complications such as toxemia, anemia, and prolonged labor (Santelli et al., 2000). The long-term consequences of early pregnancy find teenage mothers suffering many critical disadvantages. Not surprisingly, there is reduced educational achievement, due mostly to early drop-out from school. This may contribute to the additional problems of low-status jobs, lower income, and welfare dependency. There are equally critical disadvantages in social relationships—high divorce rates, unstable relationships, and more subsequent unintended births. Long-term consequences for children of adolescents can include lower educational achievement, behavioral and emotional problems, a greater likelihood of themselves becoming teenage parents, and an existence based in poverty (Corcoran, Franklin, & Bennett, 2000).

Young women who terminate their pregnancy experience few negative consequences, although the later in the pregnancy the abortion occurs, the greater the risk of complications. The literature has not found significant psychological consequences associated with abortion. Similarly, there appear not to be any serious psychological consequences associated with adoption, although adoption is rarely an alternative selected by teenage mothers.

Adolescent pregnancy is an important risk factor because it decreases the likelihood that the mother will complete school and significantly reduces her chances for economic self-sufficiency.

Adolescent Fathers

The adolescent father is gaining increasing attention from society (Gottfried, 2001). What do we know about the adolescent father? A prevalent myth is that teenage fathers don't want anything to do with their girlfriends or the baby once they find out about the pregnancy. Recent findings, however, are showing that an increasing number of fathers do not want to abandon their babies. In general, adolescent fathers may be more involved in parenting than previously thought. Research (Danziger & Radin, 1989) has found that these fathers are willing and interested in participating in parenting. Many adolescent fathers have daily contact with their children and have a close relationship with the mother and the child (Gottfried, 2001). Nonetheless, these young fathers often face hostility from their girlfriends' parents, and the mother and her family often make all the decisions regarding the baby. Social workers need to consider including teenage fathers when decisions are being made.

Being an adolescent father is associated with several disadvantages. For one, many adolescent fathers decide to provide financial support, and often this means quitting school. Having quit school, these fathers are eligible only for low-paying jobs.

Only recently have social-service agencies recognized the need to respond to adolescent fathers. However, programs are springing up around the country that are specifically designed to help adolescent fathers cope and function effectively in their new role. One such program focuses exclusively on African American fathers; the young men get together to take their children out for the day, provide emotional support to one another, and receive education about fathering and being an effective parent.

Unfortunately, adolescent fathers' involvement tends to taper off after the first year of the child's life, when the demands of hard work (required for supporting the child and girlfriend) and raising the child become too much for them to handle. It is important, therefore, that social workers pay attention to teenage fathers and offer them services during the second year of the baby's life, as well. New programs are being offered that teach teenage fathers about nutrition and child care. Previously these classes were offered only to mothers; however, a recent trend is to offer coed classes.

Implications for Practice: Reducing Adolescent Pregnancy

The consequences of adolescent pregnancy point to the need for a more effective means to reduce its incidence. How can it be done? A comprehensive approach at several levels is needed. The following are a few of the suggested approaches:

1. *Expanded sex education efforts.* The best model for sex education and the best data supporting the influence of the model on rates of pregnancy come from efforts outside the United States. The adolescent pregnancy rate in this country is the highest in the Western world—twice as high, for example, as in England or Canada, and three times higher than in Sweden. Yet, United States adolescents are not any more sexually active than those in other countries. In fact, Swedish adolescents are more sexually active at an earlier age and are more exposed to sexual activities through television. One difference may be that all children in Sweden, beginning at age 7, are exposed to a sex-education curriculum. The majority of parents in the U.S. appear to favor sex education in the schools. In addition to sex education, there is the need for a specific emphasis on decision-making skills, life skills, and life planning. Many school-based curricula are available and emphasize the need to teach young people problem-solving and assertiveness skills for situations where there is risk for pregnancy.

2. *Increased access to birth control.* Many people believe that increased access to contraceptive devices would likely reduce the number of unwanted pregnancies. School-based clinics appear to be ideal, because they can be community based, they can reduce stigma by providing a wide range of services, and their staff can work closely with other school officials and outside social-service workers. A well-known example is Health Start, a program in which primary and preventive services (physicals, emergency care, mental health care, and social-work counseling) are offered during school hours at schools.

3. *Provide greater "life options" for young people.* Because a lot of adolescent pregnancy is associated with social disadvantage, the implication is that changes in the social environment may be needed in order to expand "life options" (Dryfoos, 1990). Increasingly, professionals are recognizing that adolescents have to become motivated to reduce their risk of pregnancy (Santrock, 2002). Edelman (1987) stated the point succinctly: "The best contraceptive is a future."

4. *Enhance community involvement and support.* Too often, sex education and advice are seen as the responsibility of parents and schools. Studies have shown that very little sex education comes from parents (Kaplan, 2004). We know that contraceptive use increases when there is greater communication between parent and adolescent about sex, but our efforts must be directed on a communitywide level. If we can change attitudes about sex education, we can enhance access to family planning services. In European countries where sex education is more open and without such conflict, adolescent pregnancy rates are much lower. ■

Sex Education and Adolescent Development

Does the adolescent's cognitive development have an influence on the success of sex education? Joan Lipsitz (1980) believes it does, because giving adolescents contraceptives is not enough. What does matter is adolescents' acceptance of themselves and their sexuality, and this acceptance depends on their emotional and cognitive development, or maturity. The prevention of adolescent pregnancy embraces some very complicated features, including the abilities to approach problem solving in a planned and organized way, to anticipate consequences, to delay gratification, and to communicate in a direct manner.

However, many of these capabilities require the capacity to solve problems and anticipate consequences—cognitive skills that many adolescents are just beginning to develop. As a result, much of the current content of prevention programs may not be appropriate for early adolescents. In late adolescence, there is some realistic and future-oriented thinking about sexual experiences. In middle adolescence, there is often much romanticizing about sexuality. And in early adolescence, sexuality is depersonalized in a manner that gives way to anxiety and denial.

Some researchers (LeCroy & Daley, 2001) have recognized these differences in sexual maturity and asserted that prevention programs should address sexual readiness and emerging sexual identities and orientations in order to be effective. Programs that teach "abstinence only" may be effective only for adolescents who refrain from sex anyway. Abstinence-only programs also fail to educate sexually active students about responsibility. Precisely because adolescence is a time of sexual awakening, sexual feelings should be discussed, not ignored. Educators must realize that pubescent children need to understand their sexual feelings and changing bodies. Otherwise, unexplored, ill-defined sexuality can lead to frustration and irresponsible sexual behavior.

Alcohol and Other Drug Use

No discussion of adolescent social hazards would be complete without a section on alcohol and other drug use. For many—parents, teachers, and human-service professionals—this is the number-one social issue facing young people today. Drinking is a big part of being an adolescent in today's world. The rate of alcohol and drug use has been followed since 1991 by the Monitoring the Future studies (Johnston, O'Malley, Bachman, & Schulenberg, 2003). The most recent data find that the majority (76%) of high school students report using alcohol and that almost half (47%) report having used alcohol within the thirty days prior to the study (Johnston et al., 2003). Marijuana use, in the thirty days before the study, among

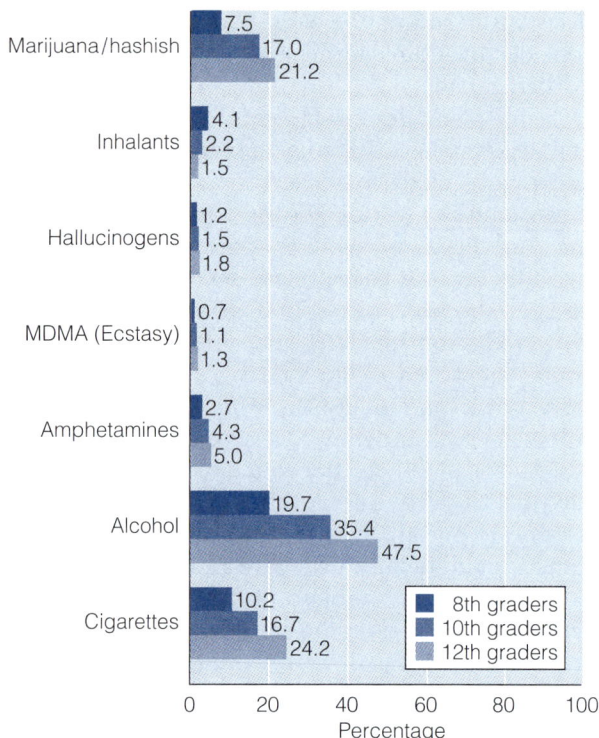

EXHIBIT 9.17 Trends in the thirty-day prevalence of use of various drugs for eighth, tenth, and twelfth graders
SOURCE: The Monitoring the Future Study, the University of Michigan.

high school seniors was 21%. Exhibit 9.17 shows the percent of use across several drugs for eighth, tenth, and twelfth graders for the most recent survey data. Most of the drug trends from 2002 to 2003 show decreases, a promising sign. The most disturbing trend in studying drug use is that adolescents are becoming involved in drugs at an earlier age. Substance use has increased substantially for young adolescents—those in the sixth through ninth grades (Johnston et al., 2002). It was found that 17% of eighth-grade students had tried marijuana and 7% had used it in the last thirty days. For alcohol, 20% of eighth graders reported use within in the last thirty days.

Binge drinking, typically defined as having five or more drinks in a row, is a common problem behavior during adolescence and young adulthood (Schulenberg et al., 1996). A survey revealed that 28% of the nation's high school seniors and 40% of 21- to 22-year-olds had engaged in binge drinking at least once within the previous two weeks (Johnston, O'Malley, & Bachman, 1994). In the last survey (Johnston et al., 2003), 10.2% of eighth graders reported they had "been drunk" in the last thirty days, as did 18.2% of tenth graders and 30.9% of twelfth graders. There is little doubt that binge drinking, particularly if frequent, is an important health-compromising behavior. It makes one vulnerable to ongoing problems with alcohol, as well as other health-compromising behaviors, such as violence, use of illicit drugs, unprotected or unwanted sex, and driving while intoxicated, and it may reflect difficulties with the transition into young adulthood.

What causes young people to be more likely to abuse drugs? This question has undergone extensive research, and several different factors play a significant role in drug use. In general, drug use by peers, drug use by parents, the belief that drugs lead to tension reduction, delinquent behavior, stress, a sense of power, and low self-esteem are often cited as key factors. Jessor (1987) suggested that problem behavior such as drug use is linked to adolescents' attempt to assert their independence and become more adult. Also, drinking may be a learned mechanism for coping with frustration at the failure to attain more conventional goals.

Have you ever heard a parent proclaim, "Other teens drink, but not my kid." Are these parents stating a fact, or a wish? Researchers in the Midwest (Bogenschneider, Wu, Raffaelli, & Tsay, 1998) studied almost 350 teens and their parents. All of the teens admitted to regular alcohol use, but less than a third of the parents were aware of it. In families with parents who were aware of alcohol use, teens and their parents were more likely to discuss the risky behaviors associated with alcohol use, and parents were more likely to be realistic about their teen's friends' drinking behaviors. Do you think parental awareness helps protect teens from risky consequences?

In a twelve-year longitudinal study of problem drinking among adolescents, Jessor (1987) found that three factors differentiated problem drinkers from other adolescents: their personal qualities, their social environment, and their other patterns of behavior.

In terms of personal qualities, problem drinkers were clearly alienated from conventional values. For example, they did not value academic achievement, religion, or conventional nondeviant behavior. In terms of their social environment, they perceived large differences between their parents' values and their friends' values, were more influenced by friends than parents, and had peers who also engaged in problem drinking.

Thus, problem drinking occurs within the context of other problem behaviors. In other words, problem drinkers were more likely than other adolescents to engage in additional problem behaviors, such as sexual activity and delinquency. Their behavior is part of a larger syndrome of norm-breaking problem behaviors. Therefore, adolescent drinking would predict other adolescent problem behaviors as well.

Implications for Practice: Substance Use Prevention

But what about intervention programs aimed at preventing a variety of these problem behaviors? D.A.R.E. (Drug Abuse Resistance Education) is being used in 80% of America's school districts (Biema, 1996). In this program, police officers present seventeen sessions on specific drugs and resisting peer pressure. Unfortunately, although it is immediately successful in preventing drug use, D.A.R.E. may not have a sustained effect on preventing drug use as the students grow older. What is the best method of prevention? A variety of approaches reflecting different theoretical orientations have been utilized in the prevention of youth substance abuse, including knowledge-based, affective, social-skills, family-skills-training, and peer-refusal approaches, and a number of these have been identified as effective (LeCroy & Mann, 2004). Typically, the targets of these prevention approaches have included the individual, the peer group, the school, or community. Although no single best prevention approach exists, research has demonstrated that effective prevention involves strengthening protective factors such as social skills, family bonds, and attachment to school while reducing risk factors that increase vulnerability to drug use. Recent research (Fishbein, Hyde, Coe, & Paschall, 2004) found that assessing the cognitive functioning of adolescents can be critical in designing effective prevention and intervention programs. Reviews of prevention research underscore that risk and protective factors should be the primary targets of intervention, and that a risk/protective factor-enhancement model provides an important framework for the prevention of adolescent substance abuse. ■

Developmental Guidelines for Assessment in Adolescence

Exhibit 9.18 presents the developmental guidelines for adolescence. These guidelines are meant to be helpful to social workers who need to understand development when making assessments.

EXHIBIT 9.18 Developmental considerations in assessment for adolescence

Routine observations
Brain development and abstract thought
Peer groups
Body image
Sense of morality
Independence
Sexual identity
Romantic involvements
Focus on physical appearance
Increased caloric intake
Hormonal changes
Menstruation (girls) and nocturnal emission (boys)

Strengths and landmarks of development
Increased resilience
Development of autonomy and independence
Increased influence of peers
Enhancing parent-adolescent relationships
Peer support
Egocentrism

Developmental issues (not problems)
Excessive concern with body image
Spending too much time alone
Negative peer influence
Decreased interest in school
Academic difficulties
Moodiness
Sexual behavior
Transition to middle school
Parent conflict
Late maturing girls
Risk behaviors (e.g., automobile safety)

Developmental observations requiring attention
Eating disorders
Depression (stability of moods)
Pregnancy
Sex abuse and rape
Substance use
Violent behaviors and exposure to violence
Firearm exposure/use
Conduct disorder and delinquency

STUDY TABLE: Social dimension in adolescence

Families and Groups	The transition into adolescence involves some stress in most families. Three developmental tasks for the family are (1) development of autonomy, (2) resolution of parent-adolescent conflict, and (3) parent-adolescent attachment. Parents and adolescents often struggle over control and independence. Parents who hold tightly to their control and are authoritarian in their decision making are more likely to produce young people who have difficulty with autonomy. A democratic family structure appears to produce a young person with a healthy sense of autonomy. Negative interactions, mostly conflicts about everyday issues between parents and adolescents, begin in early adolescence, around the time of puberty. Adolescents with secure parental attachments do better than peers in terms of self-reliance and independence, behavioral competence, and psychosocial well-being. Authoritative parents are warm and involved, but firm and consistent. Adolescents are at a point in their development where they need to spend time with peers because this interaction provides important information about sexual relations, compassion, leadership, and conflict that may not be available within the family. Peer pressure is strongest in early adolescence and decreases as the young person moves toward independence. Boys' friendships reflect more shared interests, whereas female friendships reflect more support-

ive and emotional aspects. Social-skills training emphasizes new learned behavior and focuses on teaching the prosocial skills and competencies that are needed. Adolescent peer groups allow young people to assess their individuality in light of group pressure and norms and provide needed support. Cliques are small, interaction-based groups with close relationships. Crowds are larger, reputation-based collectives of similar young people who do not necessarily spend a lot of time together. Gangs are differentiated from other groups on the basis of their delinquent activity. The most important risk factor for gang membership is growing up in a neighborhood with poverty where there is little attachment to people and social institutions. Gang interventions must start at an early age and must be focused on the family and community.

Communities and Support Systems	The transition from elementary school to middle school may be stressful due to a new impersonal school environment and the top-dog phenomenon. Middle school may not be an effective institution for young people, because a mismatch exists between the organization and curriculum of middle schools and the intellectual, social, and emotional needs of adolescents. To create a community for learning, schools need to be smaller learning environments; include caring adults who work together and provide some stability with peer groups; and create opportunities for each student to interact with at least one adult who can provide the youth with advice about academic matters and personal problems. High school dropout rates have decreased. Factors that predict dropout include poor attendance, disinterest in school, living in poverty, single-parent families, conduct problems, poor grades, and pregnancy. Most children who relocate experience short stresses, but relocation can have consequences later in life for at-risk children who have social-adjustment problems. Homeless youth who have run away or who have been thrown out by their caretakers are more likely to engage in drug and alcohol abuse, experience sexual or physical abuse, participate in criminal activity, and have thoughts of suicide. Runaways are likely to have been physically or sexually abused at home in the year prior to running away.
Multicultural and Gender Considerations	In adolescence, young people of color become more aware of their ethnic status and begin to develop an ethnic identity. Ethnic identity is related to a stronger sense of purpose, and increased self-confidence and social competence. Adolescents of color also often have two sets of peer relationships: school peers and neighborhood peers. There are several factors that affect adolescent immigrants' long-term adjustment to a new country. Relying on their earlier primary group's cultural values can provide a foundation for their adjustment. Adolescents are becoming increasingly identified with their gender roles; however, there is more acceptance of androgyny. Adolescent girls may lose their "voice" or sense of self. Depression is more common for girls and often revolves around body image. Sexual identity is a major task during this period. Boys face critical issues around schooling and education. Although there has been a decrease in the number of adolescents having sexual intercourse, about half are sexually active at the end of the adolescent years. Some key factors related to sexual activity in adolescents include (1) living in a single-parent household; (2) early dating experience; and (3) parental discipline—either too permissive or too strict. Factors that have been found

(continues)

STUDY TABLE: Social dimension in adolescence *(continued)*

	to discourage sexual activity are (1) attending church; (2) doing well in school; and (3) good parent-adolescent communication. Four major influences on early sexual behavior are biology, sexual abuse, problem behavior, and normative expectations. AIDS is caused by the human immunodeficiency virus (HIV), which destroys the human immune system and leads to opportunistic infections. AIDS is the sixth leading cause of death among people aged 15–24. The proportion of sexually active adolescents using condoms has increased. Homeless and runaway youth are at higher risk for AIDS. Life is difficult for gay adolescents, and many gay adolescents experience social difficulties and even violence because of their sexual orientation. Gay adolescents experience many risk factors and are likely to feel isolated and depressed, and they are two to three times more likely than heterosexual youths to attempt suicide. Adaptation to a gay identity has four stages: sensitization, identity confusion, identity assumption, and commitment.
Social Strengths and Hazards	Most adolescents have few assets and many more risk factors. Prevention efforts have sought to increase the number of assets youth possess. Although school violence has been a recent media focus, the incidence of violent deaths remains small. Children are potentially subject to more violence than adults, and homicide is the only violent crime to which teens are somewhat less vulnerable than adults. Huge racial disparities exist in the experience of violence, particularly for African American youth. Working fifteen to twenty hours per week may improve a student's self-esteem, but adolescents working more than this face negative effects. Birthrate for female adolescents among all ethnic and racial groups has declined. Potential factors for this decline include less sexual activity among adolescents, higher rates of abstinence, and increased use of contraception. About 10% of American adolescent girls will become pregnant. The greatest risk factor for a teenager becoming pregnant is poverty. Infants born to young mothers have low birth weight and an increased likelihood of infant mortality. Young mothers have increased risks of complications, such as toxemia, anemia, prolonged labor, and mortality. Teenage mothers also face reduced education achievement, low-status jobs, lower income, and welfare dependency. Adolescent fathers may be involved in more parenting than previously thought. The fathers' involvement tends to taper off after the first year of the child's life, when the demands of hard work and raising the child become too much for them to handle. Efforts to reduce adolescent pregnancy include expanding sex-education efforts; specifically emphasizing decision-making skills, life skills, and life planning; increasing access to birth control; providing greater "life options"; and increasing community involvement and support. Adolescents become involved in drugs at an earlier age, and substance use has increased substantially for young adolescents in sixth through ninth grades. Binge drinking, defined as having five or more drinks in a row, is a common problem during adolescence and young adulthood. Frequent binge drinking can compromise health and can make one vulnerable to ongoing problems with alcohol, violence, use of illicit drugs, unprotected or unwanted sex, and driving while intoxicated. Effective prevention involves strengthening protective factors such as social skills, family bonds, and attachment to school while reducing risk factors that increase vulnerability to drug use.

CONCEPT MAP

APPLYING THE FRAMEWORK

A Depressed Adolescent

Developmental History

Susie Lee, a 13-year-old Chinese American female, was brought to the agency by her biological parents. Susie's parents are third-generation Chinese Americans and live according to American cultural norms and values. Susie has two brothers and one sister, all younger than her.

Susie's parents discussed her early development, including pregnancy and childhood illnesses. Susie's mother reported that her pregnancy was normal with no complications. She also states that she was very careful throughout her pregnancy to avoid food, drink, medication, or illegal substances that could harm her developing fetus. The only medical problems out of the ordinary were Susie's seizures at the age of 5 as a result of influenza. Her mother reported no developmental delays and that Susie crawled, walked, and talked at the appropriate times.

Biophysical Considerations

Susie often has trouble sleeping at night and reports periodic nightmares (one or two per month). She also has experienced *night eating syndrome*—being unable to sleep at night, she eats. Then by morning she does not feel like eating breakfast. She has a tendency to consume a large amount of food quickly and feels bad about having done so afterward. She does not eat a balanced diet. She denies any self-induced vomiting. This sequence of events often leads to severe self-criticism. Susie was an early-maturing female who had her first menses at 11 years of age. She has been diagnosed with *dysmenorrhea* (painful menstruation) and often complains about having stomachaches.

Psychological Considerations

Cognitive Development and Information Processing

Susie appears to be of average intelligence and performs well academically. Last year she had above-average grades of As and Bs. In discussing her self-criticism, Susie demonstrated abstract thinking ability as she commented introspectively about her own thought processes. She demonstrates complex thinking about the psychological processes she is experiencing. However, Susie is often unable to make simple decisions because she is literally thinking too much about a decision. Susie believes she is invulnerable—that no harm can come to her. Although this is an aspect of normal cognitive development, it can lead to negative outcomes if her thinking influences her behavior.

Communication

One of Susie's strengths is her ability to communicate her thoughts and feelings clearly and directly. She expresses concern about her eating habits and about feeling down and irritable much of the time.

Attitudes and Emotions

Susie expresses intense emotions that range from extreme anger to hopelessness. She describes feeling sad, irritable, touchy, "on edge," and depressed. She described some of her feelings: "I feel like I'm falling into a dark tunnel that I cannot climb out of; screaming all the way down but no one hears me." Sometimes she's deeply sad and spends a lot of time crying. Other days she's extremely irritable—everybody and everything bothers her. When asked about how she perceives herself, she reports feeling like the ugliest girl at school. She often looks in the mirror and sees a fat, ugly person. She is extremely preoccupied with how "bad" she thinks she looks. "I hate my body," she reports. A lot of her self-criticism is related to her binge eating and her negative body image.

Susie scored in the depressed range on the Beck Depression Inventory. She admitted that she thought about suicide previously—especially after a friend had committed suicide. At present she denies any thoughts of suicide. She does not have access to a gun.

Social Cognition and Regulation

Susie expresses strong egocentric thoughts. She is preoccupied with her feelings and behaviors in a self-conscious manner. This is demonstrated in her body perceptions—she is very concerned about how others are going to view her body and looks. She feels self-conscious about not having a boyfriend at the present time. This style of thinking is an entry to more intensely self-critical statements. She reports being quite concerned about what her peers are saying and doing and has difficulty expressing any independence around them. Her parents report that she "gives in to peer pressure all the time and that this gets her into a lot of trouble." Her mother expressed specific concern that she would not be able to say no to sexual advances by boys. In the one-to-one interview, Susie discussed having been sexually active with a previous boyfriend. She reports inconsistent use of birth-control methods.

Social Considerations

Family Situation

Susie experiences serious family conflict, including a highly conflict-ridden relationship and lack of closeness with her father—her father still spanks her. Furthermore, Susie suffered a major loss when her favorite grandfather died last year of cancer. In addition, she started junior high school this school year, and this has been a difficult transition for her.

Susie expressed concern over her inability to get along with her family. In particular, fairness is a big issue with Susie. She reports that her siblings are treated more fairly than she is. Her parents describe situations where Susie feels she is being treated unfairly and throws a temper tantrum. For example, last week she found a box from a fast-food meal that had been her brother's lunch, stating it wasn't fair that he got one and she did not. She threw things around the living room, started yelling, and ran to her room crying. Susie reports being gruff and harsh with family members on a daily basis. Her oppositional behavior is also evident on a regular, but not daily, basis when she lies, loses her temper, argues with her parents, fights with her siblings, or refuses to do her chores. She says she "feels unimportant to this family" and that everyone sees her as a "bad" kid. She is angry at her father and believes he mistreats her—especially by spanking her. She also believes that her parents, particularly her father, do not love her.

Groups, Social Supports, and Communities

Susie feels like an outsider at school, although she has three or four friends she regularly interacts with. Recently Susie has found it difficult to go to school. When she is in school, she feels empty and dull. Although she used to be involved in after-school activities, she has no extracurricular activities now. When asked if she has an adult she is close to, she said there was no one for her to talk with, especially since her grandfather died. Her parents are frustrated with her and do not provide her with much emotional support.

Multicultural and Gender Considerations

Susie disclosed concern regarding her identity. Although her family is very acculturated, she has recently been questioning the significance of her Chinese American background since meeting a student at school who is very involved in Chinese culture. She has expressed concern about how others view her. For example, at school she believes teachers expect more from her than other students when she turns in assignments or takes exams. She resents the additional pressure she feels from her teachers and her parents. She wants to be treated "just like everyone else." Her parents fear that they are losing control over her, and Susie complains that her parents are not giving her enough freedom. In spite of their acculturation, they are having a difficult time reconciling their family values with the values and norms of the dominant society.

Summary and Impressions

As a result of assessment, it is apparent that Susie has several problems that need to be addressed:

1. Depression
2. Irritable, with extreme mood swings

(continues)

APPLYING THE FRAMEWORK
(continued)

3. Resentful behavior toward siblings
4. Uncontrolled anger outbursts
5. Poor family relationships
6. Possible unresolved grief
7. Adjustment issues involving her developmental stage (e.g., identity concerns)
8. High-risk behaviors such as unprotected sexual intercourse

Although the family members are experiencing difficulties, they do provide a stable, predictable living situation for Susie and her siblings. Susie's father earns a steady income that provides adequate resources. Susie's mother works part-time while the children are at school and states that she is usually home when they return from school. They have lived in the community for five years and have established a network of family friends and church support. In addition, both parents appear genuinely concerned and willing to evaluate their parenting techniques in order to work toward a positive outcome. Susie's strengths include her intellect and thoughtfulness, her good communication skills, and her desire for improved family relationships.

KEY TERMS

androgen
androgyny
care perspective
cliques
concrete thinking
concrete operations
conduct disorder
connectedness
crowds
dysmenorrhea
endocrine glands
estrogen
formal operational thought
gang
gonadotropins
hormones
human immunodeficiency virus (HIV)
hypothalamus
hypothetical-deductive reasoning
imaginary audience
individuation
justice perspective
menarche
moral development
obesity
ovaries
personal fable
psychological moratorium
puberty
rite of passage
secular trend
self-esteem
social cognitive monitoring
social skills training
testes

ONLINE RESOURCES

Websites

Go to the following web page http://info.wadsworth.com/ashford for specific links to these web resources.

Center for Adolescent and Family Studies: Indiana University

This online directory is an electronic guide to information on adolescent issues, sponsored by the Center for Adolescent Studies at Indiana University.

The American Academy of Child and Adolescent Psychiatry

This site contains information on recent news, facts for families, clinical practice and managed care, and research and training.

Girls Incorporated

This national organization offers technical assistance to community leaders who wish to start local Girls Inc. groups.

Studies in Moral Development and Education

This page links educators, scholars, and citizens who want to share their work and learn more about research, practices, and activities in the area of moral development and education.

Office of Juvenile Justice and Delinquency Prevention

The Office of Juvenile Justice and Delinquency Prevention offers fact sheets and full reports on gang activity and community initiatives to suppress it.

American Refugee Committee

The American Refugee Committee (ARC), works to aid refugees and other war-affected displaced persons. The site includes information on its programs, as well as press releases and refugee interviews and stories.

National Clearinghouse on Runaway and Homeless Youth (NCRHY)

A central information source on runaway and homeless youth issues.

Free to Be Me

"Becoming the person I want to be." FAQs about youth sexual orientation.

InfoTrac College Edition Key Words

For interesting materials related to what you have just read, please go to the InfoTrac College Edition website and search using the following keywords:

adolescent peer groups
high school dropouts
adolescent body image
adolescent suicide
adolescent ethnicity
delinquency

Book-Specific Resources

Book-specific resources can be found online at http://info.wadsworth.com/ashford and include the following:

Case studies
Quizzes to test your knowledge
PowerPoint presentations

CHAPTER 10
Young Adulthood

CHAPTER CONSULTANT

SUZANNE BUSHFIELD
Arizona State University West

DEVELOPMENTAL THEMES	
	Stage: intimacy versus isolation. Economic independence; independent decision making. Emerging adulthood.
BIOPHYSICAL DIMENSION	
Biophysical Growth and Development	Peak of physical development, loss of muscle and increase in fat weight, and development of health patterns. Changes in reproductive systems during early adulthood. The impact of hormones on women.
Biophysical Strengths and Hazards	Physical endurance. Cancer and self-examinations. Health disparities and minority men.
PSYCHOLOGICAL DIMENSION	
Cognitive Development and Information Processing	Formal operational thought. Postformal thought. Wisdom.
Communication	Miscommunication. Gender and communication. Styles of communication. Communication skills for men and for women. Nonverbal communication. Communicating with the deaf.
Attitudes and Emotions	Development of intimacy. Love: myths and theories. Possibility of isolation and loneliness.
Social Cognition and Regulation	Intimacy and independence. Moral development. Morality of justice; morality of care.
Psychological Strengths and Hazards	Major life decisions. Serious mental illness. Depression. Depression and women.
SOCIAL DIMENSION	
Families and Groups	Marriage: selecting a partner, adjustment to marriage, expectations and myths, satisfaction and conflict. Empowering African American families. Diversity in companionship. Remaining or becoming single. Gay relationships. Homophobia; internalized homophobia. Transition to parenthood. Gay and lesbian parents. Voluntary childlessness. Infertility. Miscarriage.
Communities and Support Systems	Work life. Women and work. Peer relationships and forming mentorships. Volunteerism and social services.
Multicultural and Gender Considerations	Career and multicultural challenges. Blending religions. Gender roles. Motherhood mandates.
Social Strengths and Hazards	"Social capital." Extension of young adulthood: earnings losses, supporting a family. Welfare reform. Families with a disabled member. Divorce. Sexual harassment. Sexually transmitted diseases. AIDS prevention; medication for AIDS. Rape and sexual assault. Domestic violence and effects on the family. Social workers in managed-care systems. Alcohol, tobacco, and other drugs. Alcohol use among college students.

Developmental Themes

Young adulthood, which is considered a major life transition, is a critical period that spans the ages of 22 to 34 years. In young adulthood, significant life roles become established. Young people move from a preoccupation with the self to a focus on intimacy that often leads to marriage, children, and the need to establish a stable career path. In many ways, everything that has taken place before this stage can be considered preparation for adulthood.

Perhaps two of the most critical developmental tasks at this age are economic independence and independent decision making. Often these two aspects are considered to be the hallmarks of the transition from adolescence to young adulthood. Economic independence occurs as young people move from high school or college into the workforce on a full-time basis. This change entails major life changes, because living independently carries with it new responsibilities. Many of these new responsibilities lead to independent decision making: where to work, where to live, how to budget income, what kind of dates to go on, when to get married, and so forth.

Emerging Adulthood

"When our mothers were our age, they were engaged . . . they at least had some idea what they were going to do with their lives . . . I, on the other hand, will have a dual degree in majors that are ambiguous at best and impractical at worst (English and political science), no ring on my finger and no idea who I am, much less what I want to do . . . Under duress, I will admit that this is a pretty exciting time. Sometimes, when I look out across the wide expanse that is my future, I can see beyond the void. I realize that having nothing ahead to count on means I now have to count on myself; that having no direction means forging one of my own.

—Kristen, age 22 (in Arnett, 2000)

Does this quote sound more like an adolescent or a young adult? It may be difficult to tell. Today, the field of young adulthood is being challenged by definitions of what constitutes the transition into adulthood. Is young adulthood defined by age, or by social and economic factors? Many experts adhere to the traditional notions set forth by G. Stanley Hall (who gave us the popular notion of adolescence) and Erik Erickson, who established the stages of development.

For Erikson, young adulthood was a stage of intimacy versus isolation confusion. But both Hall and Erikson had in mind adulthood as reaching maturity, leaving home, and taking on new adult responsibilities. Today, the transition into maturity and leaving home is looking quite different. Young adults are now getting married at an average age of 25 for women and 26.8 for men—four years later than just thirty years ago (Arnett, 2004). Also, a larger percentage of young adults are living at home with their families. The U.S. Census (2004) reports that more than 50% of men ages 18–24, and almost half of women that age, lived with their parents in the last year. Have these young people entered adulthood, or are they in an extended period of adolescence? Regardless of how one answers this question, the point is clear: many "young adults" are still in a transition stage from adolescence to adulthood. This transition is being increasingly recognized. The Society for Adolescent Medicine says it cares for people "10–26 years of age." The "Transitions to Adulthood" project sponsored by the MacArthur foundation extends into the later young-adulthood phase.

Overall, this period of transition is becoming known as **emerging adulthood**. According to Arnett (2000, 2004), who is a leading proponent of this conceptualization, emerging adulthood is "neither adolescence nor young adulthood but is theoretically and empirically distinct from them both" (Arnett, 2000, p. 469). It is characterized by a period of transition into adult roles but constitutes a distinct period of the life course that emphasizes change and exploration of possible life directions in love, work, and worldviews.

At this stage, the most common response to the question "Do you feel you have reached adulthood?" is "In some respects yes, in some respects no."

Theories of Adulthood

Whereas adolescents are preoccupied with the self, young adults turn outward and focus on social and intimate relationships with others, as described by Erikson (1974):

> In youth you find out what you care to do and who you care to be—even in changing roles. In young adulthood you learn whom you care to be with—at

EXHIBIT 10.1 Levinson's eight stages of adult development

Levinson and his colleagues (1978) were instrumental in developing a theory of adult development. On the basis of intensive interviews with adult men at different stages in the life cycle, Levinson set forth his ideas about the stages adults go through. More recently he has expanded his theory to include adult women (Levinson, 1985, 1986). Levinson outlined eight developmental stages in young and middle adulthood. Fundamental to his theory is his notion of "life structure." A life structure represents a basic pattern of an adult's life at a particular time. A person's life structure reflects the choices a person makes, such as marriage, childrearing, career, and so forth. According to Levinson, the stages of the adult life cycle alternate between stability and turmoil and transition. The stages are summarized as follows:

1. *Ages 17 to 22*: Leave adolescence; make preliminary choices for adult life.
2. *Ages 22 to 28*: Initial choices in love, occupation, friendship, values, lifestyle.
3. *Ages 28 to 33*: Change in life structure, either a moderate change or, more often, a severe and stressful crisis.
4. *Ages 33 to 40*: Establish a niche in society; progress on a timetable, both in family and in career accomplishments.
5. *Ages 40 to 45*: Life structure comes into question; usually a time of crisis in the meaning, direction, and value of each person's life; neglected parts of the self (talents, desires, aspirations) seek expression.
6. *Ages 45 to 50*: Choices must be made and a new life structure formed; the person must commit to new tasks.
7. *Ages 50 to 55*: Further questioning and modification of the life structure; men who did not have a crisis at age 40 are likely to have one now.
8. *Ages 55 to 60*: Build a new life structure; can be a time of great fulfillment.

SOURCE: Levinson (1986).

work and in private life, not only exchanging intimacies but also sharing intimacy. In adulthood, however, you learn to know what and whom you can take care of (p. 124).

Erikson was astute in his observation that in industrialized countries, many young people experience a prolonged adolescence represented by role experimentation.

An additional major theory of adult development comes from Daniel Levinson (1986). He describes young adulthood (ages 17–33) as focusing on choices in love, occupation, friendship, values, and lifestyle. He has referred to the *novice* phase of development, where the primary task is to move into the adult world and build a stable life structure. In accomplishing this life task, the young person experiences change and instability. Levinson's notions mirror Erikson's ideas of role experimentation. Exhibit 10.1 presents a summary of Levinson's eight stages of adult development.

STUDY TABLE: Developmental themes of young adulthood

Developmental Themes	The two most critical developmental tasks during the age of young adulthood are economic independence and independent decision making. Adulthood is seen as reaching maturity, leaving home, and taking on new responsibilities. Although this transition can be recognized in many ways, many "young adults" are still in a transition stage from adolescence to adulthood. This transition is increasingly becoming known as emerging adulthood. Those emerging into adulthood do not see themselves as adolescents or entirely as adults but as somewhere in between. Young adulthood involves role experimentation with choices involving love, occupation, friendship, values, and lifestyle.

BIOPHYSICAL DIMENSION

Biophysical Growth and Development

Physical development in young adulthood represents both the peak of physical development and its slow decline as the body gets older. Our physical performance is usually the strongest during the early 20s. An easy way to assess the body's performance is to examine the average ages of Olympic gold medalists. Only about 15% of Olympic medalists are over the age of 30 (Santrock, 2002). The peak of muscular strength occurs between age 25 and 30 years and decreases about 10% between age 30 and 60 years. As a result, the mid-20s are a good age for speed and agility. However, professional athletes perform well into their 30s if they are competing in endurance sports, such as long-distance running and weight lifting.

In young adulthood, many individuals begin a pattern of health-conscious behavior. Indeed, the workout frenzy is very popular among this age group. This is a particularly good time to begin a healthy lifestyle. Many individuals at this age realize their once-teenage metabolism is slowing down, and they start putting on weight and may struggle to avoid excessive weight gain and obesity. During early adulthood, the percentage of body weight composed of muscle decreases. This represents not a loss of muscle but an increase in fat weight. It is recommended that body fat be 15% to 18% for men and 20% to 25% for women. Women typically have more fat deposits in the buttocks, thighs, breasts, and shoulders, whereas men distribute their fat more evenly. Body composition reflects an individual's overall physical health.

Fat in the body is stored in adipose cells. As these cells fill, your hunger is satisfied. If the cells are empty, you will be hungry. As people gain weight, they increase the size of fat cells in the body—and at this point, it becomes difficult to make them shrink. Obese people have an excessive amount of fat cells in their bodies. One reason that we gain more weight as we age is that our **basal metabolism rate**, which is the minimum amount of energy that we use in our resting state, decreases. The implication of the decrease is this: To maintain the same weight we had in the past, we must eat less.

Although restrictive diets are popular, exercise combined with proper diet is a more effective means by which to lose weight. Exercise is important because it burns up calories and continues to raise the metabolic rate for several hours after the exercise. Exercise can be effective in weight loss because it lowers the body's set point for weight and makes it easier to maintain a lower weight. The most effective means to lose weight is to exercise and eat a healthy diet. The American Dietetic Association recommends the following: 10–15 grams of fiber per day, limiting intake to 30% of daily calories from fat, and increasing to 50–60% the daily calories derived from complex carbohydrates such as fruits, vegetables, and grains.

Reproductive System during Early Adulthood

This stage of development is considered the best period for a woman to become pregnant. A woman in her early 20s has a mature reproductive system and is likely to produce fertile eggs. Also, her hormone production is relatively regular. Because her physical abilities are at her peak and her uterus is receptive to a pregnancy, this is an ideal time for a safe and healthy delivery of a baby.

Effect of Hormones on Women

Although hormones influence both men and women, their effect on women is stronger. As women progress through the menstrual cycle, their hormones fluctuate. In the **menstrual cycle**, estrogen levels rise to their highest point when a woman is ovulating and then begin to decline as she approaches her menstrual period. After ovulation, progesterone levels begin to increase. When progesterone production is at its highest, about ten days before the beginning of the menstrual cycle, a majority of women (85%) experience the set of symptoms known as **premenstrual syndrome (PMS)** (Dickerson, Mazyck, & Hunter, 2003). PMS is associated with breast tenderness, a bloated feeling, irritability, and negative moods occurring just before the menstrual period.

Although women are affected by PMS, most are not incapacitated. However, some women (up to 10%) experience **premenstrual dysphoric disorder**, or PMDD, a severe form of PMS. The symptoms of PMDD include (1) sadness and crying, (2) nervous-

EXHIBIT 10.2 Example of a daily symptom calendar for monitoring PMS

Name: _____ Month: _____

Daily Symptom Calendar

	Days of the Month														
Symptom	1	2	3	4	5	6	7	8	9	10	11	12	13	14	15
Depression or sadness															
Tension or irritability															
Anxiety or nervousness															
Anger, aggression, or short temper															
Crying spells															
Swelling of hands or feet															
Tenderness or fullness of breasts															
Abdominal bloating															
Lower abdominal cramping															
Generalized aches and pains															
Low backache															
Headaches															
Fatigue															
Increased or decreased appetite															
Cravings for sweet or salty foods															
Insomnia															
Other (specify)															

SOURCE: From "Treatment strategies for premenstrual syndrom," by J. Daugherty, in *American Family Physician*, July 1998.

ness, anxiousness, and irritability, (3) craving of certain foods, (4) problems concentrating, (5) physical problems (breast tenderness, headaches, joint or muscle pain, swelling, and bloating), and (6) trouble sleeping (American Family Physician, 2002). Exhibit 10.2 presents a daily symptom calendar that is often used in the assessment of PMDD.

One particularly fascinating study sheds some light on the social and biological factors that influence premenstrual and menstrual symptoms. In a study of college women, Englander-Golden, Sonleitner, Whitmore, and Corbley (1986) found that women report more symptom changes over a month if they know that their menstrual cycles are being studied than if they are just reporting how they feel on certain days with no reference to their menstrual cycle. The implication of this research is that stereotypes of what women "should" experience during menstruation affect what they actually experience and subsequently report. Related research has found that women who fill more traditional roles report more negative emotions during premenstrual and menstrual cycles than do women in nontraditional occupations or women who are highly educated (Brown & Woods, 1986). However, significant symptoms should not be discounted.

Biophysical Strengths and Hazards

As discussed in the biophysical-development section, a clear strength for anyone in this age group is physical endurance. During this age, important health behaviors and interests can be established and have an influence throughout the life course. Becoming physically fit and developing an interest in fitness, exercise, and sport activities can be important biophysical tasks in young adulthood.

Cancer

An important health hazard of the reproductive system for both women and men is cancer. Breast cancer is the second most commonly diagnosed cancer among women, after skin cancer (Apantaku, 2000), and it is often fatal: it is the second leading cause of cancer death in women. (Lung cancer is the first.) More than one in nine women will develop breast cancer in her lifetime (Javroff, 1996). The young adult years are a good time to develop the habit of breast self-examination. The exam is easy; women should choose the same time each month to conduct the exam, preferably after the menstrual period has ended. This time frame is important because the breasts vary in size and texture during the menstrual cycle, but after the menstrual period they are not swollen. Health professionals can instruct women how to conduct the exam, and the American Cancer Society has brochures that describe the procedure. Detection of a breast mass is common; however, approximately 90% of masses are caused by benign lesions.

Men are encouraged to conduct a self-examination of the testes. Testicular cancer is a common disease for men between 15 and 35 years old and is the leading cause of cancer death among young adult males. Self-examination is important because, when detected, testicular cancer is second only to skin cancer in terms of successful cure rate. Men should be taught by a health professional how to perform the exam.

Health Disparities and Minority Men

One fact stands out when looking at health care statistics: poor men of color have the worst health. They have higher rates of illness and mortality than nonminorities. In general, men are sicker and die sooner than women, in virtually every country worldwide (Williams, 2003a). This disparity is especially true among African American men. The Focus on Multiculturalism box presents a list of health facts that show the disparities between men of color and white men. One of the strongest determinants of health is socioeconomic status (SES). Research has found that smoking, alcohol and drug use, and unprotected sex are all less common among those with higher income and education. Stress, which is also linked to health, is lower as one climbs the SES scale.

Race also plays an important role (Williams, 2001). The difficulty in finding well-paying and meaningful work is more pronounced in men of color. Research has found that even when men have the same job titles and advancements, men of color are more likely to experience occupational hazards and stress (Williams, 2003a). Consider this revealing study: Out of 171 large cities, there was not one city where the average African American neighborhood was better, in terms of quality and living conditions, than the worst white neighborhood (Williams, 2003b). Men of color face a complex social structure that impacts their health. For example, smoking can provide relief from stress. Stress being higher in minority communities, it is not surprising to see higher rates of smoking in them. Low-income and minority neighborhoods are also targeted by billboard advertisements for cigarettes and alcohol and by small businesses that provide such goods.

Lastly, cultural beliefs, such as masculinity, can impact health (Williams, 2003a). Women are more likely than men to seek and use health care. Furthermore, women are more effective in using coping mechanisms and social support, whereas men are more likely to use alcohol, drugs, and tobacco in response to stress. Men who do have gainful employment are likely to make that a first priority. As a result, they do not prioritize health (especially health-promoting activities) unless they are seriously ill. Too often, men postpone their health care, compromising health outcomes later in life.

STUDY TABLE: Biophysical dimension of young adulthood

Biophysical Growth and Development	Young adulthood is characterized in terms of physical development as both the peak of physical development and its slow decline as the body gets older. As the metabolism slows down, young adults start putting on weight, as a result of an increase in fat stored in the body's adipose cells. A female in her early 20s has a mature reproductive system and is likely to produce fertile eggs, and hormone production is regular. Because her physical abilities are at her peak and her uterus is receptive to a pregnancy, this is an ideal time for a safe and healthy delivery of a baby. Many women (85%) experience premenstrual syndrome (PMS) or Premenstrual Dysphoric Disorder (10%), as a result of increased levels of progesterone during the menstrual cycle.
Biophysical Strengths and Hazards	Becoming physically fit and developing an interest in exercise and sport activities can be important biophysical tasks in young adulthood. Skin cancer is the most common cancer for women, followed by breast cancer, which one in nine women develop in their lifetimes. Testicular cancer is the most common cause of cancer death among young-adult males. In general, men die earlier than women, in virtually every country—especially African American men. Socioeconomic status, income, and education also play contributing roles in health in relation to smoking, alcohol, drug use, unprotected sex, and stress. Cultural identification related to masculinity highlights a higher use of alcohol, drugs, tobacco, and not seeking health care.

CONCEPT MAP

PSYCHOLOGICAL DIMENSION

Cognitive Development and Information Processing

Formal Operational Thought

According to Piaget, the formal operational thinking that occurs in adolescence is the last stage of cognitive development. Therefore, young adulthood is characterized by the same mechanisms of formal operational thought. You will recall that Piaget (1972) believed that formal operational thought consists of conceiving abstract concepts, systematic thinking, and step-by-step logic. In late adolescence and young adulthood, people refine their formal-operational approach to problem solving. The cognitive changes that take place in adulthood consist of operations applied to increasingly complex situations and problems.

Adults are better able to harness formal operational thinking because of their reduced egocentrism, and therefore, adults approach problems with greater objectivity. Adults also are able to more effectively access past experiences and education in using the cognitive operations that are present. Gisella Labouvie-Vief (2003) has suggested that a new integration in thought occurs in adulthood, but she believes that adulthood carries a pragmatic adaptive strategy that leads to decreased emphasis on the logical approach characterized in adolescence. Perhaps this pragmatic approach provides experience for adults in generating and considering an increased number of options and realistically hypothesizing the potential effects of each option—a facet of multidimensional thinking (Labouvie-Vief, 1994).

Many people do not achieve the level of formal operational thinking. This could be the result of many factors, such as genetic limitations on their cognitive abilities or poor cognitive stimulation as children. Studies have shown that only 60–75% of adolescents can solve any formal operational problems (Neimark, 1975) and no more than 30% of adults ever complete the transition to the highest levels of formal operational thought (Kuhn, Kohlberg, Langer, & Haan, 1977). These findings suggest that formal operational thinking is not universal and instead is achieved only by certain people who are perhaps trained in this type of thinking.

Development of Postformal Thought

What is the difference between adolescent thought and adult thought? Researchers who study postformal thought look at cognitive development beyond Piaget's formal operational stage. One well-known theory of adult cognition is represented by Labouvie-Vief (2003), who has looked at the development of pragmatic thought, where logic becomes a tool for solving real-life problems. In her original research, she used a scenario to examine the differences between adolescent and adult thinking. Compare the adult and adolescent responses to the following scenario (Labouvie-Vief, 1985). How is the thinking different?

John is known to be a heavy drinker, especially when he goes to parties. Mary, John's wife, warns him that if he gets drunk one more time, she will leave him and take the children. Tonight John is out late at an office party. John comes home drunk (p. 13).

Does Mary leave John? How certain are you of your answer?

The adolescent response is as follows (Labouvie-Vief, 1985).

It's a good chance that she would leave him because she warns him that she will leave him and take the children, but warning isn't an absolute thing. . . . And, I'd be absolutely sure that, well let's see . . . I'm trying to go all the way. I'm trying to think of putting everything [together] so I can be absolutely certain of an answer. . . . It's hard to be absolutely certain. "If he gets drunk, then she'll leave and take the children." I want to say yes 'cause everything's in that favor, in that direction, but I don't know how I can conclude that she does leave John (pp. 17–18).

Here is the adult response (Labouvie-Vief, 1985):

There was no right or wrong answer. You could get logically to both answers [yes or no]. . . It depends on the steps they take to their answer. If they base it on what they feel, what they know, and they have certain steps to get an answer, it can be logical (p. 41).

Which response seems more characteristic of formal operational thinking? In the adolescent response, there is an understanding of the ambiguity of the situation but also the need to search for the correct answer. The adult response does not search for a correct answer—there is tolerance of the ambiguity. It also presents a combination of logic and feeling in understanding the situation.

As Labouvie-Vief (1985) pointed out in this example, the adult would be scored as not having reached formal operational thought in this example. Does this mean that there is a decline in formal operational thought as one gets older? Perhaps it is not so much a decline as a qualitative shift in one's way of thinking.

Wisdom and Cognitive Development

What makes a person "wise"? Is it age? Or is it the development of thought, or the integration of thought and action? Most people consider wisdom to include factors such as the extent of practical knowledge, the ability to reflect on knowledge, and emotional maturity. More precisely, Baltes and Staudinger (2000, p. 124) defined wisdom as "expertise in the conduct and meaning of life." Prewitt (2002, p. 10) defined it as "thoughtful judgment or decisions made when no heuristics exist for a conflict with social consequences." Many people assume that age and wisdom go hand in hand, but it may not be that simple. In one study (Staudinger, 1999) of the development of wisdom, adults, aged 20–89, were given situations such as, what would you do if a good friend is about to commit suicide? Responses were rated for wisdom using five criteria:

Knowledge of human nature, social relations, and emotions
Strategies for applying knowledge to making life decisions, handling conflict, and giving advice
A broad view that considers the multiple demands on people in their life context
A concern with human values and a respect for individual differences
Awareness and management of the uncertainties in life

Age did not predict wisdom in this study. Wisdom proved to be elusive to study, but in many respects, life experience predicted wisdom. Therefore, human-services people did much better with the above scenario than did people from other occupations. Wisdom offers much in terms of cognitive development throughout the life course. Important research is being conducted on developing strategies to teach young people how to think about life questions and make decisions wisely, concentrating on adolescence and young adulthood (Sternberg, 2001).

Communication

In young adulthood, perhaps what is most pronounced about communication is the notion of miscommunication; young men and women can become quite focused on the differences in the way they communicate. Indeed, this notion is reflected in popular culture. For example, Deborah Tannen's (1991) classic book *You Just Don't Understand: Women and Men in Conversation*, and her more recent book (2001), *I Only Say This Because I Love You: How the Way We Talk Can Make or Break Family Relationships Throughout Our Lives*, point out many of the significant ways in which women and men differ in their relationships with each other. Although gender differences do exist, much of our understanding of the differences between men and women boils down to sexual stereotyping. Often the prescription regarding differences is reduced to two conclusions: Men are in pursuit of power, and women are in pursuit of relationships. Such generalizations have yet to be supported by good studies.

However, many people have written about the different communication styles of men and women. Women obtain a much greater level of intimate communication with each other than men do. Women discuss more intimate topics and confide their personal lives more than men do. In fact, women often complain about their lack of intimate conversations with men. Studies of "divorce talk" have found that most of the women, and very few of the men, report that lack of communication was a major reason for the divorce. When men are with men, they seldom maintain an intimate conversation. Men rarely confide in each other about their private lives in the same way women do.

Why do men and women have such different styles of communication? Tannen believes that it is the "talk of the sandbox that prepares us for life at the office." Tannen has described critical differences in boys' and girls' sports behavior and drawn exact parallels to behavior in offices. Boys often search for one or two star players in a team sport; girls play in a more leaderless manner. Boys are committed to looking good, whereas girls more often search for common ground. Boys often refuse to say "I'm sorry," but girls communicate "I'm sorry" to express a true sense of empathy. Research supports some of Tannen's assumptions. She found that conflicts involving preschool girls and boys differed; boys who fought tended to pursue their own goals, whereas girls tended to balance their own interests with those of the other girls through complex verbal negotiations. Tannen believes that all of these childhood socialization experiences set the stage for adult communication.

These gender differences in communication are often the source of much frustration and anger between men and women. Because men are socialized to see the social world as basically hierarchical, men approach conversations as "negotiations in which people try to achieve and maintain the upper hand if they can and protect themselves from others' attempts to put them down and push them around" (Tannen, 2001, p. 25). In contrast, women are socialized to see the world as a community and to focus on their connections with others in the community. As a result, women approach conversations as "negotiations for closeness in which people try to seek and give confirmation and support, and to reach consensus. They try to protect themselves from others' attempts to push them away" (Tannen, 2001, p. 25). The end result: Neither understands the other. The overriding conclusion of Tannen's work is that men and women seem to speak different languages, but actually they don't. It is mostly a matter of misunderstandings that emerge from how we learn to communicate throughout life.

Styles of Communication

Some researchers identify men as using an instrumental style of communication and women as using an expressive style of communication. **Instrumental communication** refers to having a focus on identifying goals and finding solutions. **Expressive communication** involves the expression of emotions and having a perspective that is sensitive to how others feel. In general, men are more interested in having rational discussions and solving problems, and women are more interested in expressing emotions and feeling listened to and provided with support. The following scenario is a typical example of this kind of mismatch.

A young mother describes her worries and frustrations concerning appropriate child care for her son. She is using an expressive style and is most interested in having her partner listen to her and provide some support. However, the husband, using an instrumental style of communication, assumes she wants to solve a problem and begins to search for solutions. This mismatch in communication leads to serious problems. Because her husband is not listening to her and hence not providing her with the support she desires, she assumes he doesn't have any sympathy for her concerns. He is frustrated by what he perceives as her complaining and her inability to simply solve the problem.

This situation represents a classic mismatch. Each person is attempting to respond appropriately. However, each is frustrating the other; she wants his sympathy, and he wants to help her solve a problem. In this context, each partner assumes that he or she knows what the other person wants, but this is clearly not the case.

Other differences in communication, according to Tannen (1991), include women's use of **rapport talk**, which involves discussing similarities and matching experiences, and men's use of **report talk**, which involves discussing knowledge and displaying skill. What men and women talk about also varies considerably. Women usually prefer discussions about their personal lives and feelings, whereas men seem to prefer discussions about activities and events.

Differences also emerge in mixed-sex conversations, where women are more often listeners and men are more often lecturers. Tannen explains these differences by suggesting that they parallel games learned in childhood. For men the game is "do you respect me?" and for women the game is "do you like me?" According to Tannen, mixed-sex conversation places a woman in a double bind, because she will be evaluated negatively if she adopts either a male or a female style. Tannen (1991) explained that "if they speak in ways expected of women, they are seen as inadequate leaders. If they speak in ways expected of leaders, they are seen as inadequate women" (p. 244).

Implications for Practice: Communication Skills for Men and Women

Communication Skills for Women

Often, in a discussion among men and women, men dominate the discussion. Women may need to "jump into" the conversation more forcefully than they are accustomed to doing. Good use of nonverbal behavior can be critical: making eye contact, using appropriate vocal tone and pitch, and maintaining good posture and orientation in space will command attention. When the content of a spoken message is inconsistent with the nonverbal message, the nonverbal message will have the greatest effect. Because nonverbal behavior can be so powerful, women should use both nonverbal and spoken messages to convey positive responses and should rely more on oral communication to express negative responses. Use of personal space also can influence the effect of a message. Many women need to become more visible by obtaining a good position for interaction with others.

Women are often less comfortable than men are in talking about themselves and their accomplishments. Women for whom this is a problem might want to script a short biography that describes their specific accomplishments and states their areas of expertise. To feel more comfortable about sharing their point of view, women also can practice expressing opinions on a variety of topics.

Communication Skills for Men

Because men often tend to dominate a conversation, they should observe their patterns of communication and evaluate their tendency to dominate. If this is a problem for them, they can learn to catch themselves interrupting and politely encourage the other person to continue with his or her thoughts. Men can sometimes be difficult to talk with because they don't "carry" enough of the conversation; for example, they might provide only short answers to questions. Some men also need to work at being more conversational. A good technique to use for improving conversational skill is the two-question rule (Stuart, 1980). This rule keeps the conversation focused on the other person. It requires a speaker to ask an opening question and then to follow up that question with another inquiry. Often, people ask just one question, such as "How did you feel about that meeting?" and then proceed with their own analysis and reaction to the meeting. By contrast, asking a second, follow-up question demonstrates good listening and helps to keep the dominant person from launching into a lengthy monologue. Too often, women feel "talked at" by men rather than "talked with." Many men need to practice being good listeners. Good listening requires concentration and sustained effort, but a balance of conversational give-and-take will facilitate good communication between men and women.

Men who do not usually use an expressive communication style can practice discussing their interests, feelings, and thoughts. To do so, rather than approach a conversation as an interaction about events and activities, men can focus on their feelings about various subjects. ∎

Nonverbal Communication

In well-known studies of nonverbal communication, Mehrabian (1969) and others have shown three dimensions represented in nonverbal expressions. (1) The like-dislike dimension is expressed through closeness or distance—for example, looking at or away from a person; (2) the potency dimension is expressed through one's expression—for example, standing straight rather than slumped, or using rapid versus slow movements; (3) the responsiveness dimension is expressed through one's facial movements, voice tone, and voice volume. Mehrabian (1972) is often noted for his observation that, of a total feeling conveyed in a message, 7% is verbal feeling, 38% is vocal feeling, and 55% is facial feeling. What's important about this observation is that, although we may restrict what we say in words, it is often more difficult to restrict our feelings from influencing our nonverbal responses. Therefore, nonverbal responses may contradict our verbal message. It is the nonverbal part of the message that will qualify what we are attempting to communicate verbally.

Problems in communication are of particular concern to couples. Communication problems are one of the most frequently identified issues of couples seeking counseling (Christensen & Jacobson, 2000). Research (Fowers & Olson, 1989) has also found that happy and unhappy couples can be distinguished on the basis of three aspects of communication: comfort in sharing information with the other person, willingness to recognize and resolve conflicts as they occur, and quality of the couple's sexual life.

In a study that attempted to predict the likelihood of divorce, Buehlman, Gottman, and Katz (1992) studied communication and interaction styles while the couples discussed problem areas. Primarily on the basis of how the partners related to each other, the researchers were able to predict, with an accuracy rate of 94%, which couples would divorce three years later.

Communication is the center of many of the issues critical to good social work practice. Indeed, practitioners need to understand communication with a diverse range of clients. The following section looks at communication with deaf individuals.

Communicating with the Deaf

Social workers who work with deaf clients know that just using an interpreter does not address the whole picture: communicating with the deaf requires more than just signs. Deaf people represent a linguistic minority with a separate language—ASL (American Sign Language). Research in psycholinguistics has found that signing is not just gesticulation but has its own syntax and is well formed like other languages. What makes social-work practice with deaf clients difficult is that one is working in a language that is not one's own. Also, many cultural, educational, and service issues are specific to deaf people. For instance, a common error in the assessment of deaf individuals lies in not understanding that they often read and write English at a much lower level than do hearing students at the same age level. For example, a deaf high school graduate may have only a fourth-grade reading level, in which case a social worker needs to know how to evaluate a person with poor reading skills. Writing is also very different for the deaf, because ASL and English have very different structures, styles, and syntax. As a result, deaf people can appear mentally disoriented when in fact they are not. There is a need for social-work professionals who specialize in deafness; however, few programs offer a subspecialty in deafness.

Attitudes and Emotions

A major psychosocial task in young adulthood is the development of intimacy with others. Erikson referred to this stage as "intimacy versus isolation." Indeed, many young adults become quite focused on building intimate relationships with others. *Intimacy* in this context refers to the ability to share one's true self—both the good and the bad parts. Developing intimacy involves taking a risk, sharing things about yourself while knowing that the other person can make judgments about what you share. Kiefer (1988, p. 131) described the complexities involved in intimacy: "Any close relationship involves the exchange of demands and expectations, some of which are difficult and unpleasant. More importantly, getting to know someone intimately always involves hurt when illusions are dashed or expectations unfulfilled; and it always involves unpleasant insight into one's own weaknesses."

Love

One of the most prevalent emotions in young adulthood is love. Love takes on particular significance for the young adult, who begins to experience many meaningful emotional relationships (and emotions of love are likely to lead to marriage in young adulthood). Erik Erikson identified the core task of the early adult years as intimacy. As the task of identity is addressed, the individual moves toward preparation for intimacy. Those who cannot effectively resolve the tasks of intimacy are left to isolation and lack the ability to form reciprocal exchanges based on understanding, empathy, and support. A major developmental task of the young adult is to develop emotionally satisfying relationships—to experience love.

But what is love? This is a critical question asked by many young adults. A typical young-adult scenario could be the following: Two young people meet, and they begin seeing each other. As their interest and excitement grows, each becomes increasingly obsessed with the other. They want to spend increasing amounts of time with each other, and their sexual desires cannot be entirely fulfilled, no matter how much they try. Yet although they are sharing what seem to be immense parts of themselves with each other, they do not know if this is really love. They realize that to keep the relationship going entails a certain amount of sacrifice and personal risk. They are unsure whether they should take the plunge and exclaim "I love you" to each other. They face extremely difficult questions that young adults commonly ask: Is this love? How can I tell?

Is love something we can define and study? In the last twenty years, many researchers have set out to study love and achieve a more exacting understanding of this emotion. Most researchers begin by differentiating romantic love from "true" love. Robert Solomon (1988) described three features common to romantic love: (1) it is sexual in origin and motivation; (2) it is spontaneous and voluntary—and not directly under our control; and (3) it is an emotion appropriate only between equals (for example, not between a mother and child).

Recent research (Bartels & Zeki, 2004) examined the effect of love on brain activity. Interestingly, this research supports the old adage "Love is blind." It appears that feelings of love suppress the activity in the brain that is responsible for controlling critical thought. Both romantic love and maternal love produced the same effect on the brain. This function may make it easier for people to "couple" and at the same time the emotions of love bond individuals through the brain's "reward system" of positive emotion. Still, some would argue that emotions are evaluative judgments and that we in essence choose our emotions (Solomon, 2003). Whatever the process that leads us to love, many individuals do not cope very effectively with this age-old emotion, in part, because of the many myths that surround it.

Some common myths that have resulted from our idealized concept of love include the following:

- Myth 1: When you fall in love, you'll know it.
- Myth 2: You have no control over love.
- Myth 3: Love is a completely positive experience.
- Myth 4: True love will last forever.
- Myth 5: Love can conquer all problems.

Some new theories of love may shed light on how we can better understand this elusive concept. Sternberg's triangular theory of love (1998) suggests that love has three components: intimacy, passion, and commitment. In this theory, *intimacy* refers to the warmth and closeness shared in a relationship; *passion* refers to the intense feelings (both positive and negative) experienced in love relationships, including sexual desire; and *commitment* refers to the deci-

EXHIBIT 10.3 The triangular theory of love
The triangular theory of love includes three basic components: intimacy, passion, and commitment. The figure shows the three basic components and possible combinations.
SOURCE: Sternberg (1986).

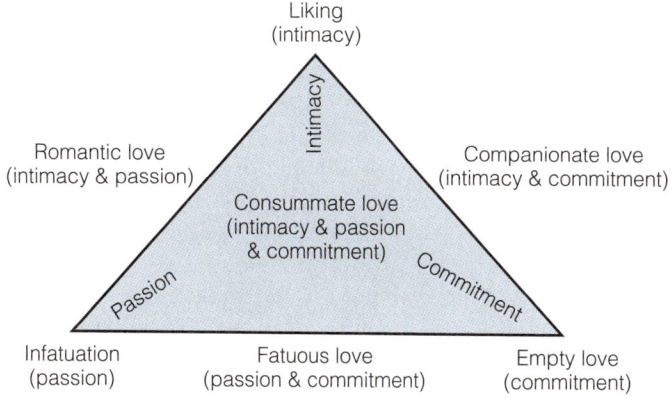

sion and intent to maintain a relationship in spite of the difficulties encountered. The triangular theory of love posits eight types of relationships that emerge from the presence or absence of the three components of love (see Exhibit 10.3) (based on Sternberg, 1997; 1998):

- Nonlove is the absence of all of the three components and reflects casual interactions.
- Liking involves the experience of only one component of love—intimacy. We feel close but not passionate toward the other.
- Infatuation involves the experience of only one component of love—passion. In infatuation, the person who is loved is viewed as an idealized object rather than a real person.
- Empty love involves having commitment but none of the other essential ingredients of love.
- Fatuous love is the combination of passion and commitment. An example is people who become quickly and intensely involved with each other and decide to marry.
- Romantic love is the combination of intimacy and passion. Romantic lovers are drawn to each other in an intimate way and have lots of passion, but there is no commitment. Romantic love may begin as infatuation.
- Companionate love is the combination of intimacy and commitment. This type of love is observed in long-term marriages where passion is no longer present. Most romantic love relationships will eventually become companionate love relationships as passion fades.
- Consummate love is the result of all three components of love—intimacy, passion, and commitment. Although most of us seek consummate love relationships, maintaining such relationships is quite difficult.

Sternberg believes that in a particular relationship the components of love take different courses. For example, in a long-term relationship, passion often decreases but intimacy keeps increasing. Furthermore, two partners may not emphasize the same elements at the same time. Of course, a successful relationship means resolving these differences.

Isolation and Loneliness

The counterpoint to intimacy is isolation—the inability to share intimately with others. With a lack of such exchanges, you are robbed of the experience of having another person understand you from your point of view, as well as insight and understanding of yourself, and support and encouragement concerning your actions and thoughts. Such isolation may lead to a deep sense of loneliness.

Although many young adults actively seek emotionally satisfying friendships and romantic relationships, many others experience feelings of loneliness. In fact, research on the prevalence of loneliness (1) identifies adolescence and young adulthood as the loneliest age groups and (2) finds that loneliness decreases with age, at least until late adulthood, when marriage partners and friends begin to die (Rokach, 2001).

Loneliness is a subjective feeling, and it is not the same as social isolation, although the two are associated. **Loneliness** is best defined as having fewer interpersonal relationships than desired, or not obtaining the desired level of personal satisfaction from interpersonal relationships. Loneliness, therefore, is not the same as spending time alone. Many people experience loneliness even though they may have many personal "friendships." However, many people desire solitude and want few personal relationships.

Loneliness is not one-dimensional; it appears to occur in different areas of one's life. For example, you could be satisfied with your relationship with your partner but not with your friendships. There are different areas where loneliness can be a problem: (1) romantic relationships, (2) friendship relationships, (3) family relationships, and (4) community relationships. Therefore, knowing what areas of loneliness are particularly problematic suggests a different focus for learning how to best address feelings of loneliness.

Implications for Practice: Coping with Loneliness

Most of the interventions developed to help people cope with loneliness focus on three areas: cognitive restructuring or changing negative self-talk; reducing anxiety and increasing comfort to help people stay engaged in social situations; and teaching people social skills, such as how to start and maintain a conversation. The appropriate intervention depends on the particular cause of the loneliness.

Young (1982) identified a variety of different kinds of cognitions or self-talk that contribute to feelings of loneliness. His research identified six clusters of cognitions that lead to different kinds of irrational cognitions and subsequent behaviors (see Exhibit 10.4). Understanding a client's thinking processes can be helpful in planning different intervention strategies.

Social Cognition and Regulation

Intimacy and Independence

Although intimacy is a primary focus in young adulthood, independence also becomes an important developmental task. Although young adults are exploring aspects of intimacy, they are also recognizing their need for independence and freedom. Maturity and growth are reflected in the ability to experience both intimacy and dependence, and freedom and independence.

In adolescence, young people are working to develop their identity; in young adulthood they are trying to establish their identity. This establishment often takes place as young adults begin to strengthen their own inner identity and clarify their beliefs and values (Cote, 2000). The key issues revolve around vocational directions, as well as political, religious, interpersonal, sexual, and life-philosophy values (Kroger, 1999). Still, it is common for people in this stage to struggle with doubts about independent decisions they must make. For example, they may be concerned about career choices or relationship commitments they are making. In moving from early to mature adulthood, goals and values may change frequently. Cote (2000) has referred to young adulthood as "arrested adulthood," given the changing nature of identity experienced by young people.

This process of developing one's identity is often facilitated by how the young adult begins to shape a "dream." According to Levinson (1978), such dreams reflect what a person would like to accomplish as an adult. These dreams often start out being concrete and overly simplistic; then they mature into clear and realistic visions. Men's dreams tend to focus more on

EXHIBIT 10.4 Cognitions and behaviors that lead to loneliness

Cognitive clusters	Behaviors
I'm undesirable. I'm dull and boring.	Avoidance of friendships
I can't communicate with others. My thoughts and feelings are bottled up inside.	Minimal self-disclosure
I'm not a good lover. I can't relax, be spontaneous, and enjoy sex.	Avoidance of sexual relationships
I can't seem to get what I want from this relationship.	Lack of assertiveness in relationships
I won't risk being hurt again. I'd screw up any relationship.	Avoidance of potentially intimate relationships
I don't know how to act in this situation. I'll make a fool of myself.	Avoidance of other people

SOURCE: From "Loneliness, depression and cognitive therapy: Theory and application," by J. E. Young, in L. A. Peplau and D. Perlman (Eds.), *Loneliness: A sourcebook of current theory, research, and therapy.* Copyright © 1982 John Wiley & Sons, Inc. Reprinted with permission of John Wiley & Sons, Inc.

occupational goals, whereas women's dreams often include visions of both career and family (Levinson, 1986; Roberts & Newton, 1987).

Problems, however, can occur when people fail to establish their own identities. How can young people develop independent identities when they are still dependent on their parents for financial, personal, and emotional needs? Such dependency may lead to problems in developing intimate relationships with others or in developing independent career opportunities.

Moral Development and Gender

Kohlberg's theory of moral development was introduced in Chapter 9, on adolescence. In young adulthood, moral development is further refined as young adults address the cognitive complexities involved in resolving moral dilemmas.

Widely recognized in moral-development theory is the controversy about whether there is a gender bias. Carol Gilligan (1982) is well known for her criticism of Kohlberg. She pointed out that most of Kohlberg's interviews regarding morality were conducted with men, and the results of the interviews showed that women reason more at stage 3, whereas men reason more at stage 4. Gilligan challenged this finding because it suggested that women are considered morally inferior to men.

But what could account for these differences between men and women's moral thinking? Gilligan looked to the differences between how boys and girls are socialized. Boys are taught to be assertive, independent, and achievement oriented, and this may lead them to perceive moral dilemmas as the result of conflicts between the rights of different parties (representative of stage 4). Girls, in contrast, are raised to be nurturing, concerned about the needs of others, and empathic, and this may lead them to perceive moral dilemmas as conflicts between individual needs, and the needs and desires of others (representative of stage 3). Gilligan (1982) theorized that these differences show a male perspective that emphasizes justice, and a female perspective that emphasizes care. These contrasting approaches view morality in terms of laws that define rights and responsibilities as preeminent (male perspective), or in terms whereby the welfare of people is central (female perspective).

Gilligan first set out to examine women's morality in her study of pregnant women facing the dilemma of whether to keep their babies or have abortions. She identified a series of stages that women go through:

- Stage 1: Self-interest is the key factor in decision making.
- Stage 2: Sacrificing self-interest for the welfare of others is the deciding influence.
- Stage 3: Avoiding hurting either the self or others is the guiding principle.

The last stage represents a morality of care or responsibility. An example of this stage of thinking would be as follows:

> I would not be doing myself or the child a favor by having this child.... I don't need to pay off my imaginary debts to the world through this child, and I don't think that it is right to bring a child into the world and use it for that purpose (Gilligan, 1977, p. 505).

The gender bias in moral thinking is still a controversy, and it has not been proved that Kohlberg's theory is biased against women (Sigelman & Rider, 2002). Some studies have found that women do reason in a similar manner to men (Walker, 1995; Wark & Krebs, 1996). In fact, one study (Garmon et al., 1996) found that females were quicker than males to reach the conventional level of moral reasoning. Nonetheless, Gilligan's work has raised awareness about the importance of considering gender in interpreting research results and has provided an important new direction in studying morality—an examination of both a morality of justice and a morality of care. For example, Gilgun (1995) examined the moral thinking of incest perpetrators using the concepts of both justice and care.

Psychological Strengths and Hazards

Young adulthood is an interesting combination of true psychological strength and hazards. In many respects, young adults are at the top of their game. They are physically strong and capable, cognitively advanced, and often seizing upon career advancement. Young adults are in the process of achieving their long-term goals. As they move toward psychological and economic independence, their decisions have an enormous impact on the trajectory of their functioning into late adulthood. However, on the other side of these strengths are growing responsibilities that can create stress and problems for the young adult.

Robert Havighurst (1972), a researcher who studies adulthood, has noted that the young-adult years are one of the most difficult periods in a person's life. Young adults must make major decisions that include career and job choices, selecting a mate, extending education, and bearing and rearing children—these are major responsibilities for someone who is just entering adulthood. Many young adults become easily frustrated because they have not been adequately prepared for the life challenges they now face. The large number of frustrations, coupled with immense responsibilities, often cause psychological problems. One devastating problem that a young person could have to face is learning to cope with a major mental illness.

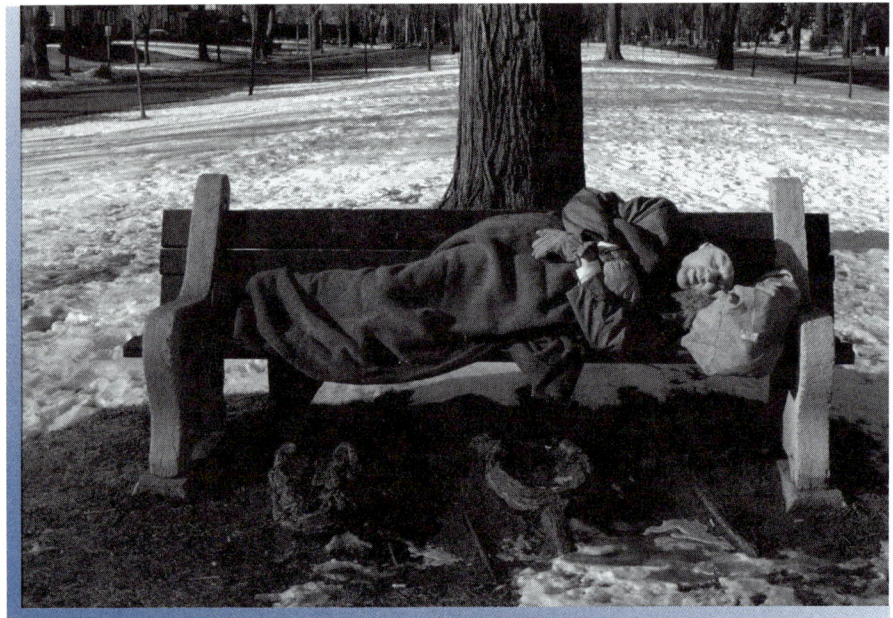

Serious mental illness—from which people can suffer throughout their adult life—often makes its first appearance in young adulthood. Proper care and treatment for people with mental illness are enhanced through case management services.

Serious Mental Illness

Many of the major mental illnesses—in particular, schizophrenia—become evident in late adolescence and early adulthood. **Schizophrenia** is a prominent thought disorder that includes delusions, inappropriate affect or silly affect, and disorganized speech. Those who suffer from schizophrenia can be grouped into three broad categories: (1) treated successfully with a full recovery, (2) partial recovery with a reasonably normal life, and (3) little or no recovery with repeated hospitalizations.

When a person suffers from an illness like schizophrenia, what factors might produce a favorable prognosis? Lehmann and Cancro (1985) have identified four factors that suggest the promise for recovery: (1) sudden rather than gradual onset, (2) onset that occurs at a later age, (3) good social and work environment before the onset of the disorder, and (4) an informal support system within the patient's family.

What leads a person to develop a serious mental illness like schizophrenia? Most of the evidence points to heredity as the major explanation (Torrey, 2001). Studies have shown that relatives of a person with schizophrenia have an increased risk for developing schizophrenia, and the closer the relationship, the higher the risk. Exhibit 10.5 shows the association between the kind of relationship, the genetic relatedness, and the concordance rate, or lifetime risk. Being an identical twin of a schizophrenic person or the offspring of two schizophrenic parents creates an almost 50% risk for developing schizophrenia (Gottesman, 1991).

What physical mechanisms are involved in schizophrenia? Many researchers now look to the influence of neurochemical factors. Schizophrenia and other mood disorders are accompanied by changes in neurotransmitter activity, and most of the drugs that are effective in controlling the symptoms of schizophrenia act to restrain dopamine activity in the brain. Therefore, excess dopamine is believed to be the most likely cause of schizophrenia. Research (Davis et al., 1991) has linked schizophrenia to excessively high dopamine activity in subcortical areas of the brain but abnormally low dopamine activity in the prefrontal cortex area.

The National Alliance for the Mentally Ill (NAMI) has become a powerful advocacy group that promotes the well-being of people with schizophrenia and their

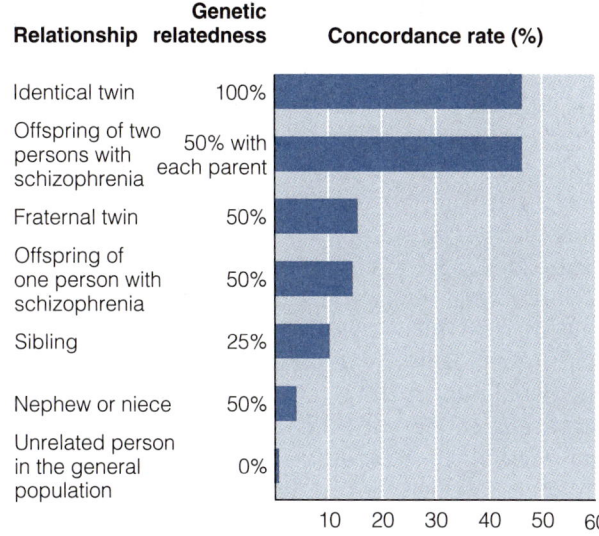

EXHIBIT 10.5 Genetic vulnerability to schizophrenic disorders

SOURCE: From "Clues to the genetics and neurobiology of schizophrenia," by S. E. Nicol and I. I. Gottesman (1983), *American Scientist*, 71, 398–404. Copyright © 1983 The Scientific Research Society. Reprinted with permission.

families. Formed from a grassroots organization in 1979, today NAMI has chapters in most cities across the country. The organization is designed to serve in an advocacy role, bringing problems and issues to the attention of local, state, and government agencies. For example, NAMI is particularly interested in research that would identify new ways to help clients readjust to the community, using the least restrictive environment as a guiding principle. NAMI is also involved in finding ways that would enable families to function more effectively and with less overall stress.

Implications for Practice: Assessment of Clients with Mental Illness

Social workers often are called on to provide necessary services for clients with mental illness. Understanding the multifaceted nature of mental illness is critical in designing and coordinating services. Some of the factors that social workers might want to consider in assessing the clients and their social situation are as follows (adapted from the National Institute of Mental Health, 1991):

Physical health status
Physical functioning
Ability to perform activities for daily living
Extent of bodily pain
Quality of sleep
Level of energy and fatigue
Quality of life
Access to resources and opportunities
Fulfillment of life's roles and tasks
Overall well-being or life satisfaction
Family and peer relationships
Ability to maintain and develop relationships with others
Ability to maintain and develop relationships with family members
Extent of the family's burden
Rehabilitation status
Social skills
Vocational status
Independent-living skills

Although not complete, the preceding assessment list gives some idea of the complexity involved in working with people with mental illness. Understanding and helping these clients involves assessing multiple aspects of the social environment. There is also growing evidence that hope, or positive expectation, has an influence on the person with mental illness and his/her adaptation to living with mental illness. ■

Depression and Young Adulthood

For young people, depression is a common psychological hazard—so common that today's universities are focusing on ways to combat the problem. A growing number of college students are suffering from depression. A survey of college mental-health counselors found that the percentage of students who had psychological problems and are taking psychotropic medication increased from 7% in 1992 to 18% in 2001 (Kluger, 2003). The survey also reported that during the previous five years, counseling centers had an 85% increase in students with severe psychological problems. For whatever reasons, college students appear to be feeling increased pressures that are taking their toll. Some experts have reported that college students are less comfortable than students in the past in seeking support from friends, primarily because other students are seen as competition, not as friends. Others have found that students rely on medical solutions such as antidepressants, which may weaken their ability to develop and use critical coping skills. In spite of increased problems with depression, suicide rates have fallen, and this decline may be due to the increased use of medication.

Depression and Women

Depression is one of the leading mental-health problems for women in the United States. It is estimated that more than 7 million women have diagnosable depression; indeed, women constitute 70% of those with depression. Unfortunately, many of these women will go without proper treatment, in spite of new treatment technologies that have reduced depressive symptoms in women by 80–90%. Why do women experience such high rates of depression? This question, as you might imagine, generates a number of explanations.

Most experts now agree that depression in women can be explained only from a biopsychosocial perspective. Research has identified a multitude of factors that influence the prevalence of depression, such as personal styles characterized as avoidant, passive, and pessimistic (LeCroy & Daley, 2001). These characteristics are related to sex-role expectations and socialization experiences. Also, women who suffer from depression often focus on their feelings, neglecting to take action to gain a sense of control over the conditions that may be leading to the depression. Whereas men are more likely to distract themselves, women tend to ruminate on their mood. This rumination is believed to amplify negative emotions and reinforce the negative mood state (Nolen-Hoeksema, 2003). This internal attributional style also can lead to increased feelings of helplessness.

Additional research has found that being unhappily married increases the chances for depression. For women, being in an unhappy marriage increases the likelihood of depression threefold. When there are young children to care for in the home, women are more likely to be depressed. Similarly, the more children a woman has, the greater the likelihood of depression.

Other factors for depression include any physical and emotional abuse that a woman may have experienced. Also, many women in this country live in extreme poverty, and such adverse economic conditions contribute to persistent depression. Other women may be further marginalized or socially stigmatized by their age, ethnicity, or sexual orientation, or by drug dependence.

STUDY TABLE: Psychological dimension of young adulthood

Cognitive Development and Information Processing	Piaget believed that formal operational thought (the last stage of cognitive development, which consists of conceiving abstract concepts, systematic thinking, and step-by-step logic) is refined in late adolescence and young adulthood, although not everyone achieves formal operational thinking. Beyond Piaget's formal operational stage is Gisella Labouvie-Vief's theory of adult cognition, which describes the development of pragmatic thought, where logic becomes a tool for solving real-life problems.
Communication	There are significant differences in the ways in which women and men differ in their relationships with each other. The differences between men's and women's communication are attributed to sexual stereotyping; childhood socialization experiences set the stage for adult communication. Stereotypes include communication styles; women obtain much greater levels of intimacy in communication and use an expressive style, whereas men use an instrumental style. Differences also emerge in mixed-sex conversations, where women are more often listeners and men are more often lecturers. Studies of nonverbal communication show three dimensions represented in nonverbal expressions. (1) The like-dislike dimension is expressed through closeness or distance—for example, looking at or away from a person; (2) the potency dimension is expressed through one's expression—for example, standing straight rather than slumped, or rapid versus

slow movements; (3) the responsiveness dimension is expressed through one's facial movements, voice tone, and voice volume. Evaluations of students who are deaf need to accommodate the fact that deaf students read and write English at a lower level than do hearing students.

Attitudes and Emotions	Erikson referred to this stage as intimacy versus isolation. Intimacy in this context refers to the ability to share one's true self—both the good and the bad parts. As the task of identity is addressed, the individual moves toward preparation for intimacy. There are three features to romantic love: (1) it is sexual in origin and motivation; (2) it is spontaneous and voluntary; and (3) it is an emotion appropriate only between equals. Both romantic love and maternal love produce the same effect on brain activity. Sternberg's triangular theory of love (1998) suggests that love has three components: intimacy, passion, and commitment. Adolescents and young adults are the loneliest age group, and loneliness decreases with age, at least until late adulthood, when marriage partners and friends begin to die. There are different areas where loneliness can be a problem—e.g., romantic relationships or friendship relationships. Interventions to help people cope with loneliness focus on three areas: cognitive restructuring or changing negative self-talk; reducing anxiety and increasing comfort to help people stay engaged in social situations; and teaching people social skills such as starting and maintaining a conversation.
Social Cognition and Regulation	Although young adults are exploring aspects of intimacy, they also are recognizing their need for independence and freedom. While establishing their identity, young adults begin to strengthen their own inner identity and clarify their own beliefs and values. The key issues revolve around the domains of vocational directions, and political, religious, interpersonal, sexual, and life-philosophy values. Moral development is further refined as young adults are able to address the cognitive complexities involved in resolving moral dilemmas. Gilligan's work has raised awareness about the importance of considering gender in interpreting research results and has found that both a morality of justice and a morality of care are important.
Psychological Strengths and Hazards	Young adults are physically strong and capable, cognitively advanced, and able to seize on career opportunities. Still, the young-adult years are one of the most difficult periods in a person's life. Many major mental illnesses become evident in late adolescence and early adulthood. Evidence points to heredity as the major explanation of development of serious mental illness. Depression is a common hazard for young people. It has increased among college students. It is one of the leading mental-health problems for women. Of those with depression, 70% are women. This overrepresentation is likely due to sex-role expectations and socialization experiences. Also, women's tendency to ruminate amplifies their negative mood state and can lead to feelings of helplessness.

CONCEPT MAP

SOCIAL DIMENSION

Families and Groups

Marriage and the emergence of the "family" become one of the most significant life changes in young adulthood. Decisions regarding whether to get married and to have children are fundamental struggles in this period. Newman and Newman (2002, p. 523) have described the importance of these decisions:

> The most important social factors contributing to the creation of a lifestyle are whether one marries, the characteristics of one's marriage or intimate life partner, whether one has children and the characteristics of those children, and one's work. The extent to which one has a choice about each of these factors depends on cultural values and restrictions, societal norms and barriers, and socioeconomic factors, especially educational attainment. Each factor interacts with personality, interests, and life goals to shape a lifestyle.

Marriage

Although the institution of marriage has changed considerably over the past thirty or forty years, most Americans still opt for marriage at least once in their lives. However, recent census data do show a rise in the percentage of women who do not choose marriage—in 2002, 14.7% of women between the ages of 35 and 39 reported never having been married (U.S. Bureau of the Census, 2002). Some distinctive changes have taken place with regard to marriage. Perhaps most significant is that young adults are postponing marriage until their late 20s; the percentage of single women between the ages of 20 and 24 has risen dramatically, from 35.8% in 1970 to 85.4% in 2002 (U.S. Bureau of the Census, 2002). In addition to the increase in the number of single women, there also has been an increase in the number of couples who choose to cohabit and not get married. The upward trend in the divorce rate also has changed the way we view marriage. Marriage now takes place within the context of each marriage partner's own personal growth. As a result, people are less willing to sacrifice for the sake of the marriage. Today, fewer stigmas are associated with divorce than in the past, partly because of the sheer numbers of people who eventually divorce. It is estimated that two out of every three marriages will end in divorce or separation.

These recent changes suggest that the influence of parental divorce on the marriage choices of children is likely to exert an influence. The long-term impact of divorce on adult children is being increasingly studied, as is the growing trend of divorce in more long-term marriages.

In spite of these trends, many people still have an idealized notion of the "nuclear" family: a married couple with two or more children, the husband as the primary breadwinner, and the woman as the homemaker. Yet it has been estimated that very few American families achieve this ideal. Our image of the American family needs to change. We need to recognize the influence of single-parent families, childless families, unwed parents, gay couples, and dual-career families, which reflect the reality of the diversity of families. Also, it is important to recognize that this diversity may be related to the larger influence of the economy and broader social changes.

Selecting a Partner

Finding a partner to whom you are willing to make a serious commitment is usually a gradual process. This process involves moving through a series of phases that leads to a deepening attraction and commitment. Adams (1986) identified four phases that lead to marriage:

- Phase I: Opportunity, physical attraction, valued behaviors
- Phase II: Positive self-disclosure, rapport, sexuality, value concerns, salient homogeneity, similarity
- Phase III: Role compatibility, empathy
- Phase IV: The "right one" relationship, commitment escalators

In phase I, opportunity plays a critical role in determining who is available to choose from as a partner. Opportunity will be influenced by the values of the young person's culture, family, and social class. For example, such cultural influences may produce opportunities for selecting a partner based on attendance at private schools, church groups, sporting events, or local neighborhood events. In the early stages, physical attraction and behaviors that are valued (for example, being outgoing) are also important determinants in the selection process.

By the time young people move to phase II, they are focusing on a process of more intimate discovery. They might reflect on such questions as, Who is this person, really? Is he or she similar to me? Through reciprocal self-disclosure, each person learns more about the other. The information gained often is assessed in terms of similarities. For example, many people would consider similarity in religious faith to be an important factor in selecting a mate.

The transition to phase III is similar but involves a deeper level of disclosure. Couples may share aspects about their sexual desires, personal fears, and life's dreams. In this phase, there is more trust and a greater level of risk as one shares increasingly intimate aspects of the self. This sharing leads to two central processes: role compatibility and empathy. The couple learns about the extent to which they are truly compatible and deepen their level of understanding about each other.

Finally, the couple reaches phase IV, where each partner is persuaded that this is the "right" relationship, and each person take steps to deepen his or her commitment to the other. Each partner has developed comfortable feelings and predictability. Furthermore, the couple is socially defined as being "together," so the costs of ending the relationship become much greater. Selecting a partner is complicated for any of

> ## FOCUS ON MULTICULTURALISM
>
> ### MARRIAGE AND MENTAL RETARDATION
>
> Getting to the church on time is the least of the obstacles facing Roger Drake Meyers and Virginia Rae Hensler on their wedding day, but you would never know it. Roger and Virginia, both born with mental retardation, are challenging the previously designated dependent role of adults with mental retardation (Myers, 1978). Their marriage is a reflection of their commitment to each other and their desire to free themselves from the often inaccurate labels society imposes on individuals with mental retardation.
>
> Determination of mental retardation is frequently based on IQ and social adjustment; difficulties in both areas appear before age 18 in people determined to have some form of retardation. About 89% of individuals with mental retardation have mild retardation and can lead, with some assistance, an independent life. Early-intervention programs involving intellectual and motor stimulation may enhance potential for this population.
>
> Even with early developmental attention, how can we be sure that people like Roger and Virginia are ready for the rigors of marriage? In reality, we can never be sure that any couple, whatever its characteristics, is marriage-ready. The statistics suggest, however, that mildly retarded couples have as good a chance of navigating marriage as do other couples. Marriage between such people occurs at roughly the same rate as marriage between members of any group within the nonaffected population. Couples' descriptions of their marriages are diverse: Some report creative, satisfying marriages; some describe a relationship characterized by poverty, depression, and violence; others see marriage as a "badge of normality and a way to 'pass' into the nonretarded community" (Meyers, 1978, p. 107).
>
> Roger and Virginia see marriage as one way of finding a place within the larger community. In working toward complying with societal norms, they face many difficult marital issues. For example, they must decide whether to have children. Because neither Roger nor Virginia has congenital retardation, their children would have as much of a chance of not being retarded as would a child born to parents who have no retardation. Other difficulties relate to handling the well-intentioned but troublesome interference of their in-laws. With the help of a counselor, Roger and Virginia are able to address these issues effectively.
>
> Both individually and as a couple, Roger and Virginia are excellent models of people who learn to work with and around a disability. They demonstrate the power of developing an individual's potential and of using personal strengths to move beyond societal labels.
>
> SOURCE: Based on Myers (1978).

us but the same is true for mentally retarded couples who may also be interested in marriage.

Adjustment to Marriage

Once a person has found the "right" partner, both must come together and begin the process of making an adjustment to marriage. This adjustment can be challenging, because it includes adapting to myths and expectations of marriage, learning how to effectively communicate with one's spouse, deriving satisfaction from one's relationship and learning how to deal with conflict, and negotiating gender differences in how men and women relate to marriage.

Marital Expectations and Myths

Addressing marital expectations and myths is often a good place for couples to start adjusting to marriage. Too often, marriages go awry because one or both partners have unrealistic expectations. Larson (1988) found that many college students are influenced by myths about marriage, and he developed a marriage quiz to assess such myths. The quiz includes items that are evaluated as either true or false. Some sample questions from the quiz are as follows:

1. A husband's marital satisfaction is usually lower if his wife is employed full-time than if she is a full-time homemaker.

2. In most marriages, having a child improves marital satisfaction for both spouses.
3. For most couples, marital satisfaction gradually increases from the first year of marriage through the childbearing years, the teen years, the empty-nest period, and retirement.

All of these items are false. Larson (1988) found that young adults answered almost half of the items on the marriage quiz incorrectly. Based on an understanding of such myths, Larson (2002) developed a program to help couples overcome fundamental myths about marriage.

PREPARE (Premarital Personal and Relationship Evaluation) (Gleick, 1995) is a set of 125 questions used to assess a couple's compatibility, and it has been used with 500,000 couples for premarital counseling. The results are computer scored and can determine with 80% to 85% accuracy which couples will divorce.

Individuals are asked if they "Agree Strongly," "Agree," are "Undecided," "Disagree," or "Disagree Strongly" with statements such as the following:

- I believe most disagreements we currently have will decrease after marriage.
- I expect that some romantic love will fade after marriage.
- I am concerned about my partner's drinking/smoking.
- I wish my partner was more careful in spending money.
- I am satisfied with the amount of affection I receive from my partner.
- My partner and I sometimes disagree regarding our interest in sex.
- I have some concerns about how my partner will be as a parent.
- We disagree on whether the husband's occupation should be a top priority in deciding where we live.
- I can easily share my positive and negative feelings with my partner.
- My partner is less interested in talking about our relationship than I am.
- We have some important disagreements that never seem to get resolved.
- I enjoy spending some time alone without my partner.
- At times I feel pressure to participate in activities my partner enjoys.
- My partner and I agree on how much we will share the household chores.
- We sometimes disagree on how to practice our religious beliefs.

Ten percent of couples who take the test are shocked by their poor scores and break their engagement (Gleick, 1995). Although this is painful, the immediate anguish is much less excruciating than a divorce after the birth of two children. These results confirm the notion that young adults may not be properly prepared to enter marriage with a realistic point of view. Adjustment to a new marriage requires a multitude of new tasks for each person. For example, establishing new routines for daily living, building new friendships as a couple, creating common goals, learning how to negotiate, and establishing a family budget are just a few of the many tasks couples must master.

Satisfaction and Conflict in Marriage

What factors predict marital satisfaction? Researchers have attempted to answer this question for years. However, notions such as marital "satisfaction" or "success" are difficult to define. In spite of this problem, researchers have generally found the following factors to correlate positively with marital satisfaction:

- People whose parents were divorced are more likely to experience divorce themselves (White, 1990).
- Couples who marry young have a higher divorce rate (White, 1990).
- The longer the courtship, the greater the likelihood of marital success (Grover et al., 1985).
- Divorce is more common among the working and lower classes than among middle and upper classes, probably because of the greater financial stress in the world of the working and lower classes (Conger et al., 1990).

Is compatibility critical to marital success? Is the reduction of conflict critical to saving troubled marriages? Although many social-work practitioners would answer yes, recent research found a different answer. Research by Gottman (1994) found that "it isn't the lack of compatibility that predicts divorce but the way couples handle their inevitable incompatibilities, not whether they fight all the time or never fight at all but the way they resolve conflicts and the overall quality of their emotional interactions" (p. 44). Gottman and associates discovered that what is critical in a marriage is the balance between the couple's positive and negative interactions—this is what determines their satisfaction. In fact, their research has shown that you can quantify the ratio of positive to negative interactions needed to maintain a healthy marriage. Gottman (1994) believes that "satisfied couples, no matter how their marriages stacked up against the ideal, were those who maintained a five-to-one ratio of positive to negative moments" (p. 44).

Conflict and fighting are part of married life. All marriages, including good ones, have a degree of conflict. It may be that such negativity serves a function, in that it keeps the marriage dynamic rather than static. Gottman (1994) suggested that anger, if it is directed at a specific issue and expressed without contempt, can be healthy for marriages. However, not all negativity is equal, and the four factors that seem to lead to the worst outcomes for married couples include criticism, defensiveness, contempt, and stonewalling. In a functional marriage, anger and disagreements are directed at the other person's specific actions, whereas in a troubled relationship, criticism and contempt are directed at the person, rather than his or her actions. So it is not necessarily the anger but the insulting manner in which the anger is directed that makes the difference.

Insulting remarks often lead to intense fighting, and one spouse is likely to adopt the other processes that contribute to the negativity—for instance, stonewalling. Gottman (1994) found that about 85% of the stonewallers are male, and he believes this may be because of men's physiological reaction to conflict. When men face conflict, they get more intensely upset physiologically than women do—they experience increased heart rate and blood pressure and remain upset for longer periods of time. One explanation for this difference is that the male response may have produced some evolutionary survival benefits: To protect the female and her young, perhaps men needed to remain physiologically responsive to external danger. However, as Gottman (1994) pointed out:

> In modern life, the propensity to higher arousal is not nearly so adaptive; it feels terrible, and to avoid the acute distress it causes, men are likely simply to shut themselves down, refuse to respond, try, as much as possible, to turn themselves into unfeeling stone (p. 46).

This physiological gender difference may help us understand why men and women have such different approaches to conflict: women pursue the conflict with emotion, and men avoid the conflict through rationalizations, the "silent" treatment, and physical withdrawal. When there is conflict in families, social workers should consider the potential benefit of working with both couples and their extended families, especially in African American families, as the next section describes.

Empowering African American Families

To increase their effectiveness in working with African Americans, social workers need to recognize the potential of the client's extended family, spirituality, religion, and the African American community as a whole. Many practitioners who work with African American clients are treating the wrong people. The people who come into therapy, women and children, may be the least likely to effect change in the family. Instead, members of the extended family—the grandmothers and grandfathers, aunts and uncles, and fathers and boyfriends—should be targeted for change. For practitioners to increase their effectiveness, they must work with the people who traditionally have the power in African American families. Unfortunately, many African Americans view therapy as something that "crazy, sick, white, or rich people" do—everyone but them. The challenge for social workers is to demonstrate to African Americans that they have something to offer them. How can this be done? Two approaches are bringing spirituality and religion into practice and bringing families together as a key source of help.

For many African American families, the psyche and the spirit are one. Therefore, some African Americans view psychotherapy as antispiritual, because its theories do not include spirituality. Exploring religion in therapy and using it to help clients cope with trauma can be a key to working effectively with African American families.

The pervasive threat of crime in poor African American communities is a crisis that leaves people feeling increasingly vulnerable and isolated. It is not enough for practitioners to do family therapy one family at a time. The challenge for social workers is to find a way to bring families closer together and capitalize on the strengths of the African American community (Martin, 1995).

Diversity in Companionship

Although marriage is a major developmental task for many young adults, increasing numbers of young adults are choosing alternatives to the traditional pathway of marriage and children. Many young adults choose to remain single, go through divorce and remarriage, become part of a stepfamily, develop a committed relationship with a partner of the same sex, or cohabitate. There are many ways that young adults can meet their needs for companionship.

Remaining or Becoming Single

Many adults will remain single throughout their life time. Schwartzberg, Berliner, and Jacob (1995) validated the life stage of always single, in their now classic book *Single in a Married World: A Life Cycle Framework for Working with the Unmarried Adult*. Although some young adults remain single throughout their lives, many become single after being widowed, separated, or divorced. For whatever reason, being single has increased dramatically over the last twenty-five years. In the early 20s and mid- to late-20s age groups, the percentage of men and women who remain single has more than doubled. Several factors have created this trend. For example, young adults have increasingly delayed the age at which they marry, and this has increased the number of people who remain single before marriage. Also, the increased rate of divorce and separation has contributed to a larger number of men and women becoming single.

Many young adults who are single face difficult stereotypes and pressures. When the majority of the population marries, the question many single adults must confront is, "Why haven't you married?" There are many stereotypes about remaining single as an adult (Lewis, 2000). For example, the assumption is either that the single people are uncommitted so they can pursue promiscuity, or they are single because they were not "good enough" to attract a mate.

Research studies have attempted to examine the differences between single and married people. Although research has shown that single women are happier than single men (Glenn & Weaver, 1988), overall, single people do rate themselves as less happy than married people (Lee, Secombe, & Shehan, 1991; Waite & Gallagher, 2000). This finding seems to reflect the social expectation that it is better to be married. Despite changes in marriage as an institution, the advantages of being married have been touted recently in the book *The Case for Marriage: Why Married People Are Happier, Healthier, and Better Off Financially* (Waite & Gallagher, 2000).

Being single may require some special adaptations. For example, socializing often occurs in couples, and the single person may feel left out. Many single people feel lonely because they lack the constant companionship available in a marriage or a committed relationship. Single people often complain about not wanting to go places or do things alone. A good network of friends can help eliminate these concerns. Lewis (2000) outlined the tasks that identify predictable issues for single adults, such as meeting basic needs, making a decision about children, intimacy, making peace with one's parents, and preparing for old age.

Gay Relationships

In the late 1940s and early 1950s, Alfred Kinsey reported the sexual histories of thousands of Americans. His research found that 8% of men and 4% of women were exclusively homosexual or gay (*gay* refers broadly to gay men and lesbian women) for at least a period of three years. In addition, 4% of men and 2% of women were exclusively gay after adolescence. A much larger percentage of the population had some previous experience with gay behavior—37% of the men and 20% of the women reported at least one gay experience that led to orgasm.

The myth exists that individuals are either gay or heterosexual. However, Kinsey's sexual-behavior studies showed that one should view homosexuality and heterosexuality as a continuum. Exhibit 10.6

EXHIBIT 10.6
Continuum of heterosexuality and homosexuality

Heterosexual		Questioning	Bisexual		Gay or Lesbian	
0 Exclusively heterosexual behavior	1 Incidental homosexual behavior	2 More than incidental homosexual behavior	3 Equal homosexual and heterosexual behavior	4 More than incidental heterosexual behavior	5 Incidental heterosexual behavior	6 Exclusively homosexual behavior

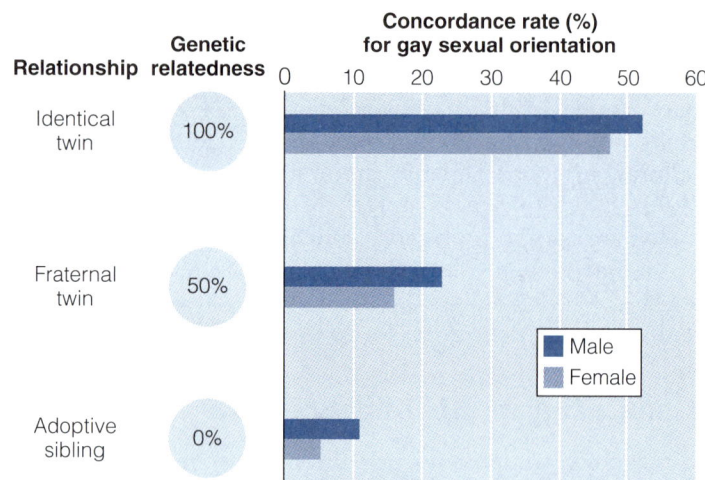

EXHIBIT 10.7 Concordance rate for sexual orientation

SOURCE: Based on data from Bailey et al. (1993).

illustrates Kinsey's original idea that sexual orientation represented a seven-point scale.

More representative studies of the general population have estimated lower rates of gay behavior than did the early Kinsey studies. For example, the National Health and Social Life Survey found 2.8% of men and 1.4% of women identified themselves as gay, lesbian, or bisexual (Black, Gates, & Sanders, 2000). Many experts believe that these estimates are low because the tremendous amount of social prejudice against homosexuals would preclude many from self-reporting homosexuality. Many experts place the estimate of the incidence of homosexuality as high as 10% for both sexes. Furthermore, the way one defines homosexual behavior is going to have a large influence on how the prevalence is estimated. Individuals who do identify themselves as gay tend to be well educated. In fact, twice as many college-educated as high-school-educated men, and eight times as many college-educated as high-school-educated women stated they were gay. This difference may reflect the more liberal orientation among more educated individuals.

What determines sexual orientation? Some therapists believe it is biologically based, dependent on, for example, hormones and neurological factors. Other researchers have focused on genetic factors as determinants of sexual orientation, and they have shown that the concordance rates for homosexuality in identical twins far exceed that of fraternal twins or adoptive siblings (see Exhibit 10.7).

Many different studies have been conducted to determine whether gays have a greater degree of psychopathology than do heterosexuals. Most studies using various methodologies have failed to find any differences (Gonsiorek, 1991). Furthermore, research on specific disorders, such as the sexual abuse of children, has not found an increased frequency of homosexual perpetrators (Groth & Birnbaum, 1978). This information has not provided support for the once-popular notion that detached or hostile fathers and castrating mothers are the link to men who become gay. Instead, most experts recognize that the origins of sexual orientation are multiple and diverse.

There may be as many as 25 million gay people in the United States. How do gay couples differ from their heterosexual counterparts? A study by Peplau (1991) compared gay men and women and heterosexual men and women on what aspects of intimacy they valued and found that heterosexual men and women were quite similar to gay men and women.

Studies (Brooks, 2000) have found that the majority of Americans support civil liberties and equal-employment opportunities for gay men, lesbians, and bisexuals. Polls have measured increasing levels of acceptance toward gays during the past decade. Although most Americans disapprove of sexual relations between two people of the same sex, in one study, one-third of respondents indicated "homosexuality is not wrong at all" (Loftus, 2001).

Gay couples, however, do have to face a different reality concerning their relationship. Many couples want to legally bind their commitment but are unable to do so. Legal marriage is a nonreligious contract designed to support, encourage, and protect intimate relationships. Marriage law touches nearly every aspect of monogamous relationships, including domestic partner benefits, rights of visitation, medical decision making, survivorship, child custody, immigration, and funerals. Because many couples have accepted the responsibilities of marriage, they feel they should get the rights, as well. However, almost all states prohibit gay couples from legally marrying. Currently, employment benefits for domestic partners do not provide for full equity, and child custody and inheritance also are not covered. As a result, gay couples do not get the same economic benefits that heterosexual couples do.

Homophobia

Homophobia is an irrationally negative attitude toward gay people. Gay and lesbian people often are depicted in terms of negative stereotypes; however, as noted earlier, this tendency recently may have begun to lessen. Still, a majority of people indicate that they would prefer not to be in a work setting with gays (Herek, 1991). Factors that appear to be related to homophobia include authoritarian perspectives, highly religious views, being with others who share negative views toward gays, and not having had any personal contact with gay or lesbian people. In recent years, homophobic attitudes, as well as the fear of AIDS, have led to many gays being harassed or even assaulted.

Homophobia exists in all aspects of society. Many gay professionals, including doctors, social workers, and lawyers, believe that they need to conceal their gay identity. One study (Wisniewski & Toomey, 1987) found that social workers, like many other professional groups, show evidence of homophobia.

The spread of AIDS has increased the visibility of gays and added fuel to gay rights. Efforts such as AIDS prevention, access to health care, and the cost of drug treatment have focused attention on the needs and civil rights of gay people. In fact, in some ways AIDS has facilitated the process of coming out because individuals must address the consequences of the disease. What has changed is the way people come out. The past image of gay men descending on the gay bar scene in search of sex is giving way to a stronger desire by gay men for more long-lasting relationships.

Internalized Homophobia

Why do some lesbians, gay men, and bisexuals seem to easily ignore society's prejudices toward their sexuality, whereas others absorb the bigotry to the point of self-loathing? This self-loathing, called **internalized homophobia**, exists when a gay man or lesbian has negative feelings about his or her own homosexuality or bisexuality. It can be associated with depression, low self-esteem, or extreme defensiveness, and it can impair a person's capacity for intimacy. Researchers (Sleek, 1996) have identified populations that have lower rates of internalized homophobia. They are (1) people who are more open about being gay or bisexual with their friends and acquaintances, particularly with heterosexuals; (2) women who have told their partners about their sexual orientation; (3) people who have a strong support system both within and outside the gay and lesbian communities; and (4) gay and bisexual men who told their mothers about their sexual orientation. Researchers note that internalized homophobia may actually be a common, albeit painful, path of development for gays, lesbians, and bisexuals living in a homophobic society.

How can social workers help clients with internalized homophobia? Some approaches (Sleek, 1996) may include the following:

1. Discuss the patient's early experience and the ways he or she adapted to or repressed his or her gay feelings.
2. Challenge the client's assumptions or beliefs about gender roles.
3. Examine your own assumptions about gender roles, to make sure you are not presenting a traditional role as the only acceptable alternative for the client.
4. Be a role model. If you are gay or lesbian and have dealt with and overcome your own internalized homophobia or self-contempt, you provide a positive model for a gay client struggling with similar issues.

Researchers admit that more research is needed on internalized homophobia to explore ethnic, cultural, and socioeconomic differences in internalized homophobia, as well as the role it plays in substance abuse, domestic violence, and suicide among gay men and lesbians.

Transition to Parenthood

Carrying the baby horizontally across my chest like a football usually calms him and often puts him to sleep. But not tonight. He's still crying, cycling through his whole repertoire: the screechy fear cry; the lower, throaty demand cry; the pitiable gasping interspersed with slobbery whimpers. Kapa nursed him an hour ago at midnight, so he isn't hungry. Teething—always a suspect—doesn't seem to be the problem tonight: he isn't drooling much, nor is he clawing at his ears. I may give him a dropperful of Tylenol anyway, to help me relax.

—C. Goodrich

As this scene depicts, the transition to parenthood brings many changes and new challenges. Consider all the adaptations the new parent must make. Parents must now accommodate changes in priorities, as they have less time to spend on career and personal interests. Indeed, the loss of free time appears to be one of the most difficult adjustments for parents. How will the new household tasks be divided between the parents? Many parents struggle to find the time and energy needed to keep their own relationship satisfying in terms of intimacy and companionship. The transition also must include their adaptation to a new role—that of parent. What makes a good parent? What kind of parents do they want to be?

These life changes are usually accompanied by a significant increase in stress (Cowan & Cowan, 2000). The crying baby and the new demands of diapers, bottles, and laundry combine to create a stressful environment for many new parents. Mothers can be uniquely affected, and they often enter parenthood exhausted from the birth process. For older mothers and working mothers, the transition to parenthood often is more difficult. Women are particularly vulnerable to distress when they are the infant's major caretaker and when they have babies with difficult temperaments. Curran (1985) surveyed married couples and single mothers to identify what parents perceive to be the most stressful aspects of their lives. He identified the following top ten stressors, listed in order of priority:

1. Economics, finances, budgeting
2. Children's behavior, discipline, sibling fighting
3. Insufficient couple time
4. Lack of shared responsibilities in the family
5. Communicating with children
6. Insufficient "me" time
7. Guilt for not accomplishing more
8. Spousal relationships (communication, friendship, sex)
9. Insufficient family playtime
10. Overscheduled family calendar

Implications for Practice: Preparing for the Transition to Parenthood

How can we make the transition to parenthood less stressful? Jay Belsky (1985) has recommended that parents be helped to reach realistic expectations about parental responsibilities. This recommendation is based on the finding that stress is highest in new mothers who have overestimated the benefits of their new mothering role and underestimated the difficulties associated with their new role. Mothers with optimistic perspectives about what it is like to be a parent tend to experience more distress, because their expectations need the greatest amount of realignment. Prospective parents could be greatly helped by better education about what parenting is like. Once parents understand that although children are "bundles of joy," they can also be "bundles of stress," they can develop more realistic expectations and be in a better position to cope effectively with their new role as parents.

One factor that is particularly powerful during this time is social support. When a mother has a good supportive relationship with her husband or partner, and he shares the burden of care and household responsibilities, stress is significantly lower than when the mother has no partner or an unsupportive one (Demo & Cox, 2000). Social support from family and friends is also a buffer to the stress new parents experience. The importance of fathers is being increasingly documented as an important source of support.

Social work and public policy have traditionally ignored fathers, other than for their role in financial support. New research has identified distinct contributions of both mothers and fathers, and it has discovered the importance of parenting classes for fathers and mothers. ■

Gay and Lesbian Parents

An increasing number of parents do not fit the stereotypical mold of "mom" and "dad." Today, several million gay men and lesbians are parents. Many have children from a previous heterosexual relationship that did not work out, but an increasing number of gay parents have emerged because of adoption and new reproductive technologies (Patterson, 2002). In addition, the practice of divorce judges giving custody automatically to the heterosexual parent is decreasing, as many states have issued opinions that sexual orientation is not relevant in making custody decisions (Berk, 2004).

Much debate has centered on whether gay or lesbian parents could be adequate parents because of their sexual orientation. With increased acceptance of gay and lesbian lifestyles and ongoing research, this question is being asked much less frequently. Research studies have shown that gay and lesbian parents are as committed to and as effective with children as are heterosexual parents. Children of gay couples are no more likely than children of heterosexual parents to develop a gay or bisexual orientation—more than 90% of the children of gay couples are heterosexual (Golomobok & Tasker, 1996). One study (Bigner & Jacobsen, 1989) found that gay fathers were more responsive to their children's needs than were heterosexual fathers. The authors theorized that the gay men's less traditional gender identity allowed for a greater involvement with the children.

In summary, parenting by gay men or lesbians is similar to that of heterosexual parents. However, gay parents do experience less social support for their parenting (Berk, 2004). The major issue today with gay and lesbian parenting is the likely stigma that the children will receive because of ongoing prejudice toward gays.

Of course, regardless of sexual orientation, not all couples are interested in having children. A large number of couples choose not to have children.

Voluntary Childlessness

An increasing number of married couples choose not to have children. This change is most likely the result of women seeking career opportunities and marrying at a later age. The percentage of women who never expect to bear children is about 10%, according to U.S. Census data. Given that a large number of couples decide to be voluntarily childless, how do they compare with couples who have had children? Overall, they do quite well. For example, their marital satisfaction is higher than that of couples with children during the childrearing years (Kurdek, 1999). Furthermore, middle-aged and elderly childless couples are equally satisfied with their lives when compared with similar couples that had children (Allen, Blieszner, & Roberto, 2000). However, elderly women who are both childless and widowed often find themselves without needed support.

Infertility

Infertility is defined as the inability to achieve pregnancy after one year of sexual intercourse with no contraception. The latest figures indicate that 20% to 25% of couples are infertile. This number is a significant increase over the 10% of couples unable to conceive only a generation ago. This rise in infertility is attributable to an increase in sexually transmitted diseases, which result in pelvic inflammation and adhesions, and also to the fact that couples now delay childbearing into their 30s. Female fertility decreases after age 30, and male fertility drops after age 45. Thus, couples who delay childbearing may pass up their most fertile years and later experience difficulties conceiving.

Infertility has several causes. Male abnormalities contribute to 40% of the cases of infertility, and female problems constitute another 40%; in the remaining 20% of cases, there is no ascertainable reason the couple cannot conceive. In males, the problems of infertility involve having a low sperm count, having abnormally formed sperm, or having sperm with low motility (that is, the sperm are unable to make the journey through the cervix and uterus to the fallopian tube).

In females, menstrual cycles can result in infrequent or absent ovulation. Cervical mucus, which is hostile to sperm, can prevent migration of the sperm through the cervix. The fallopian tubes may become blocked, from past pelvic infection or inflammation from gonorrheal salpingitis, or from the pelvic adhesions of endometriosis (a condition that arises when pieces of the lining of the uterus become attached to structures in the abdominal cavity, including the fallopian tubes). Uterine problems such as fibroids, congenital malformations, and intrauterine adhesions can keep a fertilized egg from implanting.

Implications for Practice: The Infertile Couple

Julie had always planned on having children. She had assumed she would get her degree, marry her boyfriend, work awhile, and have a couple of children. After college, though, she went to graduate school and then began an exciting career. After eight years of an on-again, off-again relationship, her boyfriend left. After a couple of years of dating, at the age of 34, Julie fell in love, got married, and stopped taking birth-control pills. Two years later, Julie has not conceived. At first she attributed her failure to conceive to having taken the pill for so long. But now, each month when she gets her period, Julie is increasingly worried. An infertility workup disclosed that her husband has a low sperm count. The couple's relationship is becoming strained as they consider their options for having a child.

Couples who receive the diagnosis of infertility may be in a crisis situation, and their emotions and reactions should be considered from this viewpoint. They are facing the loss of a lifelong dream—the end to their hopes and dreams of having a family. Often the first reaction is shock, followed by denial ("This can't happen to us"). The practitioner should allow the couple to express their feelings of isolation, guilt, depression, and anger. Because of the economic and emotional cost and low success rate of infertility treatment, Paulson and Sauer (1991) have urged that counseling the couple should, from the beginning, include the option to stop the treatment. The social worker should help the couple differentiate treatment failure from personal failure. The practitioner's challenge is to reframe the meaning of infertility and the partners' view of themselves (Olshansky, 1992). Although the drive to become a biological parent may be strong, other options for fulfilling the need to nurture should be explored with the couple. The social worker should discuss the options of adoption and of leading a fulfilling life as a childless couple.

Ken Daniels feels that "social work, with its focus on the interaction of person/problem/situation, is ideally suited to respond to the psychosocial needs arising from infertility" (1993, p. 507). According to Daniels:

> A social worker providing counseling from a psychosocial perspective will be aware of the importance of the couple's support system and seek to enable them to utilize this vital source of support. This is in contrast to more traditional infertility counseling, where the focus is more likely to be on the individual or couple alone (p. 509).

In addition to counseling for their emotional needs, the partners need assistance in using their social-support system to help them through this crisis. The couple may have problems communicating with parents or employers at this time when they most need to talk with others. The social worker may need to hold sessions with the couple and with members of their extended family. Through role playing and problem solving, the social worker also can enable the partners to explain to employers any work-related problems caused by the infertility treatment. Recent advances in technology have only increased the issues involved with surrogate parenthood. Today, many social workers face complex ethical dilemmas because of the many "parents" who can be involved in the creation of an infant (for example, shared embryos).

Many pregnancies, however, terminate prematurely, and families must confront the sadness of fetal loss. The following section examines what happens when a couple loses a baby.

Miscarriage

Mei Ling and Kim were thrilled when they learned that Mei Ling was pregnant. Mei Ling told everyone—her co-workers, her friends, neighbors, and family—that she was pregnant. The couple began to look at baby items in stores and to plan how they would decorate the nursery. Eleven weeks into the pregnancy, however, late one afternoon at work, Mei Ling experienced some lower abdominal cramping. After dinner that night, she felt increased cramping and began to have vaginal bleeding. Mei Ling called her doctor, who told her to go to the hospital. There, later that evening, Mei Ling miscarried. Mei Ling and Kim were devastated by the loss, but their doctor assured them that they were young and could try again soon. The nurses gave Mei Ling a booklet about coping with fetal death, the number of a support group to call, and a satin-covered box containing a small gold ring. The couple was encouraged to name the baby and to have some kind of memorial. They hardly had time to cry. Kim returned to work two days later, and Mei Ling took a few days to recover. Two weeks after the loss, friends and family stopped asking Mei Ling how she felt. One month later, the couple had a major argument after Mei Ling accused Kim of not caring about their baby. After this blowup, they decided to attend the support group. Their first question was, "How long does this pain last?"

Often in a hospital or a clinical setting, a social worker is called on to support families who suffer a fetal loss. To many couples, an early miscarriage can signify the loss of a child. Even at the beginning of pregnancy, most couples have dreamed of and planned for their expected child. The mother, especially, has fantasized about the baby she will have, and the loss of that dream is very real and painful. At any stage of pregnancy, mourning a perinatal loss is difficult, though, because there is so little concrete evidence of the child's existence. It is hard for a mother to identify with a child she has only interacted with through fantasy. It is hard for friends and family to understand the pain of the loss of someone they never knew. It is difficult to grieve for someone who never lived. As a consequence, many couples who experience a fetal loss lose not only their dream but also their right to mourn.

Often, because this situation involves coping not only with one's own grief but that of one's spouse, partners experience at least one episode of intense conflict following perinatal loss (Gilbert, 1989). Men and women grieve a fetal loss in different ways. Fathers report that intense grieving lasts less than one month, whereas mothers' intense grieving lasts up to one year (Hughes & Page-Lieberman, 1989). Because of the shorter period of intense grief that fathers experience, mothers may believe that their partner is unfeeling and not adequately mourning the loss, and fathers may conclude that their partner is dwelling on her grief instead of getting on with life (Hughes & Page-Lieberman, 1989).

The couple needs to recognize that the fetal loss is the loss of a real baby and all the dreams and fantasies surrounding it. The couple should be encouraged to mourn adequately before attempting another pregnancy. Attempting to have a second pregnancy to replace a perinatal loss is likely to result in unresolved grief. First, the couple should be encouraged to see the body, name the baby, make a book of memories, and have a memorial service (Leon, 1986). The hospital can attempt to provide the family with evidence of the child's existence by providing a photograph, a lock of hair, a footprint, or whatever the couple wishes to keep. Most important, the couple should be allowed the time and opportunity to express their feelings about the loss. They should be helped to understand and accept that each person grieves loss in his or her own way. But for some who ask, "How long will the pain last?" the answer is often, "A long time."

Communities and Support Systems

Work Life

In young adulthood, a person's career or job can become a significant part of the person's self-identity. Often a person's self-definition is related to what he or she does. Levinson (1978) describes the process of young adults entering an occupation whereby they must develop an occupational identity and establish themselves in the work world. Each job carries with it a set of components that must be adapted to for successful adjustment in the workplace. Newman and Newman (2002) describe four of these components: the use of technical skills; the development of authority relations; adapting to special demands and hazards; and the development of interpersonal relationships with peers. As young adults make important inroads in their careers, they may also be starting a family. Achieving a balance among one's career, leisure, and family lives is a developmental task that needs to be addressed during this period.

The psychological importance of what people do varies, and it is important to understand the difference between a job and a career. Many people pursue a job in order to earn a living. Therefore, their job may not have much value to them from a psychological perspective. Other people pursue a career more as a way of life. Their career may have significant value to them because it is a central aspect of their identity. Not everyone has the opportunity to pursue a career, so adapting to young adulthood can be very different depending on whether one is entering the workforce for a "job" or a "career."

Women and Work

The role of women in the workplace has changed dramatically in recent decades. The majority of married women with children under the age of 6 work outside the home (U.S. Bureau of the Census, 2004). Although the role of women has changed dramatically, the reality is that the workplace is still quite different for men than for women. Discrimination and inadequate opportunities remain significant obstacles for women. Particularly significant is the fact that women still experience job segregation on the basis of gender. Some jobs are considered "male," and some are considered "female." Many of the major professions—computer programming, electrical engineering, accounting, and law—are dominated by men. And, of course, employees in female-dominated professions earn less than employees in male-dominated professions, even when skill levels and responsibilities are similar. The separation between men's and women's work evokes many questions about larger issues. Is this a result of the economics of capitalism? Or is it, as some assume, part of the need for women to be a part of an underclass that supports our current economic structure?

Peer Relationships and Forming Mentorships

Levinson's theory of adult development describes the stage of entering the adult world. During this phase the person begins to shape his or her "dream," or vision of what the person would like to accomplish as an adult. Often during this phase a special relationship is formed with a mentor—a person who serves as a role model, teacher, and adviser. This most often occurs in a work setting with a colleague. Mentors are usually about 10–15 years older than the individual and play a critical role in helping the young adult refine and achieve his or her dream. The use of mentors occurs more often for men than for women. Studies have found that, for career women, professional mentoring is less likely (Noe, 1988). This may be due to the lack of available mentors for young professional women or inequality in the workplace, whereby professional socialization is available for men but not for women.

However, women have indicated that they often perceive older friends or relatives as role models. Often people volunteer to be a mentor for someone else. The following section discusses volunteerism as a vital societal movement.

Volunteerism and Social Services

Have you ever felt the satisfaction of knowing that you helped someone by your volunteer efforts? You are not alone. There are an estimated 93 million volunteers in America (Gerson, 1997). Volunteering confers many acknowledged benefits. It helps build a sense of community, breaks down barriers between people, and often raises quality of life for all involved. Some types of volunteer activities seem consistently successful, the most obvious example being the outpouring of help that occurs after natural disasters.

The role of women in the workplace has changed dramatically.

But we have to ask: If there are really almost 100 million volunteers in our country, why are our cities in worse shape than they have ever been? Few of those millions of volunteers, just 8.4%, work in "human services," a broad category that includes aiding the homeless, family counseling, and serving as tutors or mentors. But the problems of troubled children, needy seniors, and the poor require exactly this kind of volunteering. It must be performed one-on-one, over a long period of time, and often in low-income neighborhoods. And for this type of assistance, there is a shortage of volunteers.

Why are supply and demand so misaligned? The simplest explanation is that volunteers sign up for reasons other than the urgency of social problems. Volunteers say they participate because (1) they were asked by someone, (2) they learned of an opportunity through an organization to which they belonged, or (3) a family member or friend would benefit as a result.

Economic realities also shape the choices volunteers can make. The backbone of volunteer involvement in the past was stay-at-home mothers with flexible schedules. Now many families have both parents working, and whatever spare time is left over must go to the kids. "I don't think it is a question of people not wanting to volunteer; it is a question of how, where, and can I do it in a way that fits in my schedule," according to the vice chairwoman of City Cares of America, a group that matches busy people with appropriate volunteer opportunities (Gerson, 1997, p. 29).

Partly because the number, 100 million volunteers, is so impressive and inspiring, some politicians think that churches and charities, not government, should provide more of the social safety net for welfare reform. Supporters of turning over social programs to churches and charities say their plan will reawaken American passion. Religion, they say, is often crucial to turning lives around, and charitable organizations are often more efficient and effective than government programs. Furthermore, Americans give billions of dollars to charities, and the amount of giving has increased over the past decade. Opponents contend that counting on charity would ignore history. The social safety net grew precisely because churches and charities could no longer deal with the entrenched poverty. Additionally, charities are already overburdened trying to respond to existing cuts in government spending for the poor, disabled, and needy. Finally, nonprofit organizations are not a substitute for government, because government already provides about one-third of the funding for charities.

It is one thing to celebrate volunteers. It is another thing to depend on them to fill the gaps in welfare and other government programs. In this light, it is not the thought that counts. Volunteerism is often understood as a virtue, but now it should also be understood as a market. And viewed that way, it is an inefficient one. Most volunteers are not deployed effectively to solve the hardest and most critical problems. In fact, the majority of the 93 million volunteers do informal volunteering: babysitting for a neighbor, baking cookies for a school event, singing in the church choir, or serving on community boards. Volunteer management is often poor, and amazingly little is known about which volunteer programs really work. To an extent rarely acknowledged publicly, the volunteer sector is not ready for the responsibilities politicians want to thrust upon it.

Multicultural and Gender Considerations

Multicultural aspects of young adulthood are many and varied across different cultures. However, the development of one's career or livelihood is an important task that has clear multicultural aspects. In particular, unemployment rates are critical among African Americans, Hispanics, and Native Americans. Many young adults in these groups value the family but are frustrated in their attempts to provide for their families because of limited opportunities. Baruth and Manning (1991) described the following additional issues among different cultures as their members face adulthood: alcoholism among Native Americans; acculturation for Asian Americans; the stereotype of the African American as violent; and the increasing significance of African American females as the head of household. Exhibit 10.8 presents some of the unique challenges that confront Native American, African American, Hispanic American, and Asian American adults.

EXHIBIT 10.8 Challenges confronting ethnic or racial groups

Ethnic or racial group	Unique challenges confronting adults
Native Americans	Many of their unique problems stem from a history of discrimination, broken treaties, and prejudice. Poor academic attainments (only 57% are high school graduates). Extremely high unemployment rates. Language problems have affected progress. Stereotypes promoted by TV and movies.
African Americans	Dialect differences have challenged them. The stereotype of the "violent black" is influencing their social progress. Poor academic progress and lack of social progress. Social conditions that are detrimental to self-improvement like discrimination, racism, lack of opportunities.
Asian Americans	Language problems have been a challenge. The "model minority" stereotype. With acculturation, family roles and expectations can conflict with the white American culture. Value changes in family relationships can lead to a schism between younger and older generations.
Hispanic Americans	Language problems are critical because many Hispanics speak only Spanish. Poor academic progress and lack of social progress. Improvement in middle-paying and high-paying jobs. Lack of appropriate skills for coping in the dominant white society and with discrimination and prejudice.

SOURCE: Adapted from Baruth & Manning (1991).

Blending Religions

The variety and abundance of the world's major religions seems to show that there are many paths to God. For the last 2,000 years, when most people lived in villages, if those paths crossed, a holy war was more likely to break out than a wedding. But in America today we have a unique society in which the person next door may believe in one of many religious beliefs; our "paths" are crossing more than ever. For example, the proportion of Jews who married Gentiles—about one in ten around the first half of the twentieth century—doubled by 1960, doubled again by the early 1970s, and in this decade has leveled off at around 50%. Currently, one in three American Jews lives in an interfaith household. The comparable figure for Catholics is 21%; Mormons, 30%; and Muslims, 40% (Adler, 1997). And as these couples raise their children, they are, in effect, creating a new form of religious identity in America.

Expecting children to choose either their mother's or father's religion may put them in the position of rejecting one of their parents. These children also may feel inferior to their cousins or friends whose families share a single religion (Adler, 1997). To remedy these dilemmas, some couples choose one religion to raise their children in, others expose the children to both or to a variety and let the children choose, and still others blend their religions to make a third one. This dilemma is well stated in the following quote (Sparrowe, 1997, p. 4):

> The problem was, by the time I became a mother, I did not know what beliefs to 'subject' them to. I had thrown out my religious roots and did not know how to replace them. Even more to the point, I did not know how to define or talk about the spiritual connections I did feel . . . So our challenge became . . . how to raise two children to be compassionate, moral, and ethical people without returning to the very traditions we had rejected years ago.

A complicated aspect of parenting is finding how to integrate what both parents believe religiously into an agreeable plan for the whole family.

Gender Roles

In young adulthood, women confront two significant role expectations (Weiten & Lloyd, 2002): the marriage mandate and the motherhood mandate.

The marriage mandate says that, to be a successful heterosexual female, you must find a marriage partner. In fact, part of being a young adult is that you have gotten married. Some researchers believe that the fact that a significant number of lesbians previously were married is evidence of the power of the marriage mandate.

The motherhood mandate says that a successful adult woman also must bear children and become a mother. The mandate further suggests that it is important to have two children, with one of them being a son. The woman also should be a "good mother."

What is it like for women who do stay home to take care of the house and children? Tavris and Wade (1984), in their classic work, referred to this scenario as the "housewife syndrome." In general, women who stay at home have greater psychological adjustment problems compared with either employed husbands or employed wives (Steil & Turetsky, 1987). Women who experience the housewife syndrome have been found to be less happy, feel more discouraged, and be more self-critical than are employed single or married women (Nickerson & Pitochelli, 1978).

Two factors may help explain why women are less happy when they occupy the homemaker role. First, these women are socially isolated. It may be difficult, especially in our postmodern world, for them to find meaningful connections with others on a day-to-day basis. Second, the important role of homemaker and mother, rather than being highly valued by our society, carries a negative connotation, and therefore the status of the homemaker is low.

Gender expectations and stereotypes can be negative and destructive for women and men. Many young adults are committed to discarding such expectations, focusing instead on qualities that are valued by everyone. For example, Carol Tavris (1992), in her book *The Mismeasure of Women*, has examined the dominant male viewpoint and challenged this as a standard for what is normal for both men and women. She argued for an expanded view of what it means to be human and recommended a move away from the typical "us/them" perspective used when discussing gender issues.

Housework—Are Men Doing Their Fair Share?

Because the roles men and women play in the family have changed dramatically in the last 30–40 years, many experts look to changes in child care and

Social Strengths and Hazards

Young adults embrace many aspects of their social world. Building stronger friendships, establishing intimacy and perhaps marriage with another person, engaging in the world of work, and forming families: these are all important social strengths. Young adults can build good communication skills that will help them obtain stronger and longer-lasting marriages, and form friendships and mentorships that will lead to a stronger positive sense of self. Erikson's notion of intimacy versus isolation provides a guideline for consideration of strength. Much can result from reaching out to others and building relationships that help the young adult confront many of the demanding tasks that lie ahead of them. The "social capital" of this life stage comes from such relationships, as they provide individual, psychological, and social benefits.

This chapter on young adulthood began with a description of a new phase in the life cycle—emerging adulthood, or early adulthood. It is fitting to end the chapter's section on social hazards with some information about one of the main reasons why young adulthood has been extended. Work by economists Smeeding and Phillips (2002) found that 70% of American men aged 24–28 earned enough income to support themselves, but fewer than 50% earned enough to support a family of three. The social significance of this is clear: to obtain a decent standard of living requires a college education. One of the main reasons for a prolonged early adulthood is that it takes longer to secure a full-time job that will provide enough income to support a family (Furstenberg, Kennedy, Mcloyd, Rumbaut, & Settersten Jr., 2004). Groundbreaking work by the William T. Grant Foundation (1988) examined how well American young people are making the transition from school to adult roles in work and family life. The results of their study found that the transition was particularly difficult for the forgotten half—the non-college-bound youth. A major focus of the study was on the declining economic fortunes of young adults. A disturbing finding was that "virtually all young male workers, despite their educational achievements, are, on average, far worse off than they were a decade ago, and minorities are substantially worse off than whites" (William T. Grant Foundation, 1988, p. 21). All males (except young African American college graduates) suffered substantial earnings losses. This decline in earnings is

---

> **FOCUS ON MULTICULTURALISM**
>
> ### WHEN WILL WOMEN AND MEN BE EQUAL?
>
> According to the results of a survey, it may take another 1,000 years for women to match the political and economic clout of men. Based on the current rate of progress, it will take 500 years for women to hold equal managerial jobs and 475 years more for women to reach equal political and economic status. These findings are based on the following types of statistical data:
>
> - Women hold 41% of management jobs in the United States—11% of high-ranking, and 3% of top-level positions.
> - Women hold 40% of management jobs in Canada and Australia, 8.3% in Japan, and 4% in South Korea.
> - Greece and Paraguay had a decrease in women managers.
> - Only 6 of 179 members of the United Nations have a female head of state.
> - Women occupy 3.5% of government cabinet posts worldwide.
>
> SOURCE: Sanchez (1994).

---

housework when assessing the significance of the changes. Do men share a greater role in child care and housework than they did in the past? Studies of the family in the late 1960s found that a husband's participation in family work was 1.1–1.6 hours per day, whereas housewives worked for the family 7.6 to 8.1 hours per day. But what if the wives were working outside the house? When their wives were employed, husbands increased their participation by 0.1 hours per day (Robinson, 1977). A few changes were noted in the 1970s. For example, Pleck (1985) found that husbands did family work 1.8 hours per day and housewives did family work 6.8 hours per day; employed wives did family work 4.0 hours per day. Studies have found that, yes, husbands have increased the amount of time they spend doing family work, by about 25%. However, husbands' participation in family work continues to be about one-third that of their wives.

a result of changes in the economy that have created a deterioration in real earnings.

How can there be earnings losses for Americans? This happens when the amount of money someone earns does not keep up with living costs. It simply costs a lot more to live today than it did ten to thirty years ago—and how much you can buy for your money is substantially less. For example, thirty years ago a low-income family spent about 35% of their income on rent and utilities, but today those essentials cost families about 50% of their family income. The same is true for those who can afford a house—whereas mortgage payments used to cost about 25% of one's income, today 50% or more of one's monthly income may go to the mortgage.

These facts mean that supporting a family is a lot harder for a larger percentage of American society today than it was in the past, particularly for young people who are not college bound. Coupled with this loss of earnings is the fact that good job opportunities are shrinking for young people, and this is especially true for minority youth. Decline in earnings is the primary reason the percentage of minority families that live below the poverty line has increased so dramatically.

American society needs to work toward better compensation for non-college-educated youth. The William T. Grant Foundation (1988, p. 24) concluded that "the American people should set as a conscious goal of public policy the improvement of employment and earnings levels for all workers, not the least those lacking college education." This point is even more urgent today, because in addition to a loss of buying power come longer work hours to make up for the lost income, less jobs because of outsourcing, and fewer good jobs for those who lack a college education.

Welfare Reform

Millions of American families hold two or three jobs but still cannot afford necessities, and they see little relief ahead. "Welfare reform" is on many people's lips, but the working poor receive little or no attention from politicians or policies. Although welfare reform has lifted millions of people off the dole and into the workforce, many will join the 10 million Americans who hover one rung above poverty on the nation's ladder of opportunity. The difficulties of living on a low income were well described in Barbara Ehrenreich's (2001) book *Nickel and Dimed: On (Not) Getting by in America*. She set out to experience how to get by on a low-income wage. The bottom line: it wasn't easy. People with low income must stretch groceries from one paycheck to another and have no savings. They ride the bus to discount stores and do not bother to clip coupons because the generic products are still cheaper. And, because they cannot afford health insurance, they can be wiped out and pushed into poverty by even a minor medical problem. (Two-thirds of the over 40 million Americans with no health insurance live in families with full-time workers.)

In some cities, one-quarter of the people who call local homeless hotlines are employed: they include schoolteachers, chefs, computer maintenance workers, and airline flight attendants. The standard recommendation is that a family should budget 30% of its income for housing. Among the working poor, 70% is more typical. The working poor may not expect much from government, but at a minimum, they wish the government would not make their hard lives even harder. Unfortunately, many of the working poor say that they are too discouraged to go out and vote because it is so easy for politicians to ignore them. As some people feel, "Now everything goes up except people's wages. Either you're rich or you're poor" (Gibbs, 1995, p. 17). Unfortunately, most people fail to recognize that poverty affects us all (Rank, 2004).

Families and Children with Disabilities

Families that have a child with a disability often face especially trying financial circumstances. The care of a child with a disability often restructures the family's intentions and plans. The mother, who perhaps was looking forward to returning to work, may now decide that she needs to stay home to provide special care for the child. This decision, in turn, affects the financial status of the family and may compel the father to seek additional work to compensate for the loss of income. However, the father may also feel a need to be more available to the family. The family may decide that services are not adequate in the area where they live and may seek a new location that can better provide for the child. Many sacrifices are made as the family attempts to adapt to the new demands placed on it.

The mother is often under enormous pressure and may become physically exhausted. She is often the person who must spend hours traveling to doctor's offices, following up on health insurance claims, seeking special education programs, and so forth. Going on a simple outing may require taking special equipment such as a wheelchair, special eating utensils, and medications. Caring for a child with a severe disability is demanding and often leaves the mother stressed, socially isolated, and exhausted from the hard work. Much of the stress results from the mother's inability to develop interests beyond the child's care. Critical to successful adjustment is the emotional support she can receive from her husband or significant others.

Parents of children with disabilities can benefit from respite service, so the parents can leave the child with others and get some time away. However, these services are not always available. And some parents have had so little time to themselves that, when they do get away, they do not know what to do. The parents may spend their time fighting, because they have not had any opportunity in their regular schedules to address their problems. For adjustment to take place, parents need to recognize their responsibilities to each other as a couple, as well as their responsibilities to the child as parents.

Does the increased pressure result in a higher divorce rate among couples with a child with a disability compared with couples without such children? Although it would be logical to assume so, this is not the case. When divorce does occur, it is usually because of preexisting problems (Simons, 1987). Thomas (1987), who has studied family adaptation, reports that a common response among parents of children with a disability is a strengthening of their relationship and a perception that the experience of raising a child with a disability has helped them grow as individuals.

A family with a child who has a disability needs to make special efforts to provide the child with normal social experiences.

Divorce

After years of climbing, the divorce rate began a slight decline in the mid-1980s. This decline is most likely due to the rising age of marriage (Heaton, 2002). Overall, about half of all marriages end in divorce. The United States has the highest divorce rate in the world. The old notion of a "seven-year itch" has some validity, as most divorces occur within seven years of marriage. This span is long enough, however, so that half of all divorces involve children. In fact, at any given time, one-fourth of American children live in single-parent households. Although most children live with their mothers, the percentage of father-headed households has increased to about 12% (Heatherington & Stanley-Hagan, 2002). Divorce is also common during the midlife phase, when parents have adolescent children. This life phase is known for low marital satisfaction. In spite of these high percentages of divorce, most divorced Americans will remarry, about three-fourths. And during the first few years of remarriage, the divorce rate is even higher for second marriages than for first marriages. Exhibit 10.9 presents the top ten reasons men and women obtain a divorce.

Whatever the cause of a divorce, its emotional consequences are often dire for both men and women. It is a dramatic change in one's life to go

EXHIBIT 10.9 Reasons for divorce for men and women
SOURCE: Cleek & Pearson (1985).

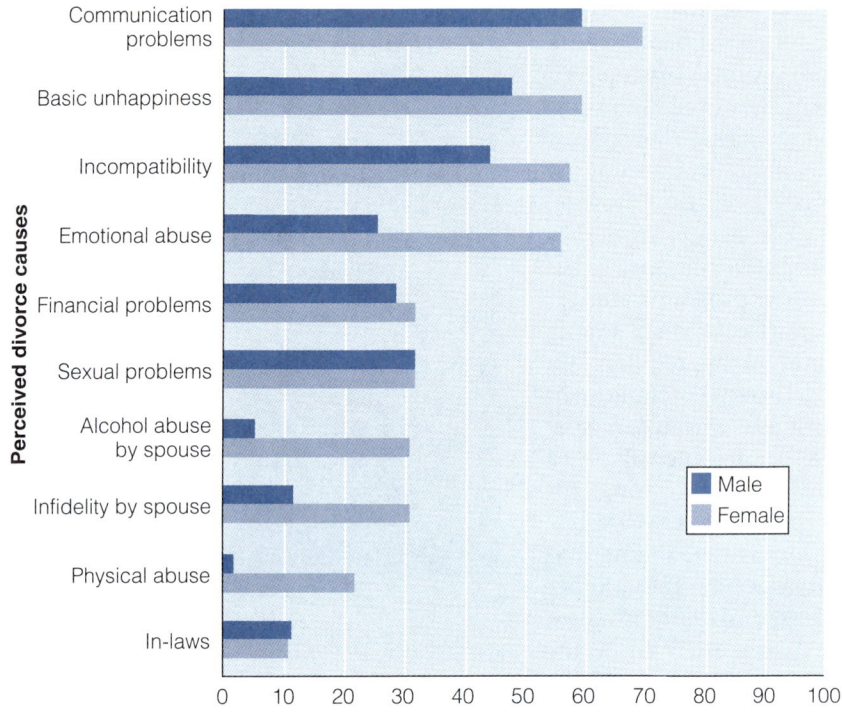

from being married to being divorced. Consider the following statement from a divorced man in Weiss's (1975) well-known study on marital separation: "And then all of a sudden every goddamn thing, I'm back to zero. I have no house. I don't have a child. I don't have a wife. I don't have the same family. My economic position has been shattered. And nothing is recoverable. All these goals which I had struggled for, every goddamn one of them, is gone" (p. 75). Indeed, we now know that divorce is not a single event; it is a series of stressful events for the entire family and encompasses life changes and ongoing efforts for family members to reorganize their lives (Amato, 2000).

Research supports the negativity of divorce on husbands, wives, and their children. Chapter 8 discussed the impact of divorce on children, but how does divorce affect husbands and wives? The overall reaction from both husbands and wives is that divorcing leads to overwhelming stress. It is a period of disruption that lasts at least one and often two years (Amato, 2000). The husband and wife often have similar feelings of anger and depression but for different reasons. The wife often feels anger for having to take on all the custody responsibility and depressed and overwhelmed by the responsibilities. The husband is angry, especially if he did not want the divorce, and depressed over not having access to his children at all times. For both men and women, adjustment to divorce involves redefining themselves as single individuals and discovering new ways to relate to the former partner, especially if children are involved. Both are likely to feel isolated, alone, and unsure of themselves as they explore new relationships. Divorced women with children will most likely struggle to get by with considerably less income (Amato, 2000).

All of these stressors lead to divorced adults that are at higher risk for depression, psychological distress, physical health problems, and substance abuse (Amato, 2000). Outcomes are worse for individuals who did not initiate the divorce, have little income, and do not find any new supportive relationships (Wang & Amato, 2000). Of course, there are positive aspects of the divorce—many individuals feel more in control of their lives and less miserable on a day-to-day basis.

Why do people divorce? Answers to this complex question must take into consideration a multitude of factors. One explanation has to do with the social changes that have occurred regarding the stigma associated with divorce. Divorce is not the evil phenomenon it was fifty years ago. Society as a whole has become increasingly tolerant of divorce—partly because of the increasing numbers of people who have experienced it. The institution of marriage underwent a particularly dramatic shift when women entered the workforce. People no longer necessarily have to stay married because of economic forces. According to researchers, we are in the midst of trying to renegotiate what the marriage contract is—what men and women are supposed to do as partners. Families have changed, as well: The decline in fertility rates and smaller families enhance the likelihood of divorce when problems arise. Legal barriers to divorce have been reduced, and men and women are more likely to seek their own self-fulfillment rather than make sacrifices for each other (Yankelovich, 1981).

However, not all couples are calling it quits at the first sign of marital stress. As couples see the havoc divorce wreaks on divorced friends and acquaintances, many are now asserting a new effort to fight for their marriage. Also, many younger couples have lived through their own parents' divorce and are now less likely to pursue divorce themselves. There is a growing recognition that marriages are not to be entered into—or dissolved—lightly because of the enormous social and economic costs.

Almost no one disputes the many valid reasons for divorce—among them, domestic violence, child abuse, and substance abuse. Mere incompatibility seems reason enough, when no children are involved. But the breakup of families is not considered to be only a social crisis. In the United States, the byproduct of what remains the world's highest divorce rate is millions of children thrown into poverty; despite their work outside the home, many women still suffer a severe income drop after divorce.

This may be why, suddenly, there seems to be so much attention being paid to preventing divorce. The past few years have seen a rise in the number of couples doing more to preserve and strengthen relationships. Some 4.6 million couples a year visit 50,000 licensed family therapists, up from 1.2 million in 1980 (Gleick, 1995).

But what happens to couples whose relationship is not recognized by society? The following section explores what happens when gay and lesbian couples break up.

When Lesbian and Gay Couples Break Up*

Surveys typically find that about 60% of all gay and lesbian adults are in couple relationships. In one survey of 1,266 same-sex couples, about three-quarters subscribed to a lifelong commitment, and most of the remainder were committed "for a long time"—not unlike heterosexuals.

But lesbian and gay couples face many more obstacles than heterosexuals do in maintaining a relationship. Separation poses special burdens, as well. Some couples must remain "invisible," a response to the threat of violence or lost jobs. Too often they enter relationships with problems, such as substance abuse and low self-esteem, that result from experiences of oppression.

Gay and lesbian couples also frequently lack support from immediate family. Instead of the typical blessings and presents awarded heterosexual unions, a same-sex wedding announcement may result in abandonment. Even the gay community has been slow to take these marriages seriously. As one woman put it, "Gay friends I haven't seen in a while ask if we're still together—not 'How are you doing?'"

When relationships end, same-sex couples face the gender-blind pain of separation, property division, and lost contact with "in-laws" and common friends. Legally, they can mark the split by revising or destroying any documents that may have marked the relationship, such as powers of attorney, wills, and domestic partnership affidavits.

We people believe that lesbian and gay couples deserve the option to marry. Many already behave as married couples, but legalizing same-sex marriage would change the world around them and, we believe, make separation and divorce less likely.

Sexual Harassment

Sexual harassment is defined as unwelcome sexually oriented behavior. The behavior in question may be glares or "checking someone out," or it may involve physical touching, pressuring someone into sex, or sexual assault. It is recognized as a problem, and it

---

* From "When lesbian and gay couples break up," by S. Bryant and Demian, 1990, *Partners Newsletter for Gay and Lesbian Couples*, May/June. Copyright © 1990 Partners Task Force for Gay & Lesbian Couples. Reprinted with permission

extends beyond the work setting—although this is where it usually occurs.

It is difficult to obtain accurate information about the prevalence of sexual harassment because many people don't recognize it and thus hesitate to report it. However, it has been estimated that as many as 50% to 75% of women have experienced sexual harassment on the job (Fain & Anderson, 1987), and 17% to 38% of women on college campuses report an experience with harassment (Dziech & Weiner, 1991).

From a legal viewpoint, there are two types of sexual harassment: quid pro quo and environmental harassment. *Quid pro quo* is a Latin phrase that means one thing is exchanged for something else. In **quid pro quo harassment**, a person in a position of power subjects a person of lower status to unwanted sexual advances. Furthermore, the person in power requires certain behaviors in exchange for a job, a promotion, a higher grade, and so forth. Essentially, some aspect of the person's job depends on her or his agreement to engage in some form of unwanted sex.

Environmental harassment occurs when a hostile work environment is created by the person in power as a result of some unwanted sexual behavior. For example, telling work colleagues sexual jokes may create a hostile work environment.

Sexual harassment is not limited to sexual acts such as intercourse. It includes a wide range of unsolicited and unwelcome actions like flirting, comments about another person's dress or anatomy, intrusive questions about another person's personal life, and descriptions of the harasser's own sexual experiences. Unwanted physical contact also includes a wide range of unwelcome behaviors, such as touching, hugging, pinching, and slapping. Fundamentally, sexual harassment is an abuse of power by someone in a position of authority.

Sexually Transmitted Diseases

Sexually transmitted diseases (STDs) are illnesses that are transmitted through sexual contact. STDs are being increasingly recognized as a serious social problem for adolescents and young adults. Many people think of STDs as one of three diseases: AIDS, syphilis, and gonorrhea. Actually, there are approximately twenty sexually transmitted diseases. Some can be easily treated; others cannot. Most, but not all, are transmitted through genital, oral-genital, or genital-anal contact; some do not require intercourse for transmission. The overall rate of STDs is higher among women than men. This is because it is twice as easy for a man to infect a women with any STD, including AIDS, as it is for a woman to infect a man (U.S. Centers for Disease Control, 2001).

The rate of STDs is increasing, and there are more than 13 million new cases each year. It is estimated that one in four Americans are likely to contract an STD sometime in their lives (U.S. Centers for Disease Control, 2001). Exhibit 10.10 describes the common sexually transmitted diseases.

AIDS and Prevention

A culturally specific intervention was developed to reduce the frequency of unsafe sex practices among African American gay and bisexual men. Researchers believed that low self-esteem can promote riskier sexual behavior (Freiberg, 1998). In this study, researchers worked with 318 participants teaching assertiveness training, negotiation skills, and game-playing to improve knowledge of safe sex and effective condom use. Researchers reported that participants in the triple-session intervention greatly reduced their frequency of unprotected anal intercourse—from 46% to 20%. This reduction continued through the twelve-month follow-up evaluation. The study demonstrated that African American gay and bisexual men can reduce risky behavior if they are exposed to culturally relevant prevention messages (Freiberg, 1998).

Other AIDS prevention programs are designed specifically for women. One particular program (Freiberg, 1998) focused on teaching women negotiating skills, condom use, and the risks and barriers associated with their relationships with men. More than 200 single, pregnant inner-city women (57% African American, 40% Caucasian, 3% other) were assigned to either an AIDS prevention group or one of two control groups—a general health-promotion group or a no-intervention group. The prevention group helped the women develop a health plan to curb their risk for HIV infection; the other group focused more broadly on improving the participants' general health. Women practiced assertiveness and negotiation skills with their partners and "cognitive rehearsal," imagining how they would solve a problem. Results indicated significantly greater condom use for the AIDS prevention group than for the no-intervention group; the health-promotion group

> **EXHIBIT 10.10** Common sexually transmitted diseases
>
> **STD/Transmission/Symptoms**
>
> Acquired immune deficiency syndrome (AIDS): Spread by sexual intercourse or anal intercourse. Can be spread by oral-genital sex, especially when semen is swallowed. Spread by nonsexual interaction through contaminated blood—for example, by sharing hypodermic needles used for drug injection. Typically there are no symptoms for approximately five years. After symptoms appear, death occurs soon afterward.
>
> Bacterial vaginosis: Most common is the transmission of *Gardnerella vaginalis* by sexual intercourse. Women experience a thin, musty-smelling discharge. Most men are asymptomatic.
>
> Candidiasis: The growth of this fungus accelerates when the chemical balance of the vagina is disturbed; it can be transmitted through sexual intercourse. Described as a white, "cheesy" discharge from the vagina, irritation of the vaginal tissue.
>
> Trichomoniasis: Can be transmitted through genital sexual contact or through less direct means—for example, from towels or bathtubs of infected people. Vaginal discharge that is white or yellow; unpleasant odor; vagina is sore and irritated.
>
> Chlamydial infection: The bacterium is transmitted primarily through sexual contact. It can be spread by fingers from one body part to another. For women, pelvic inflammatory disease can occur. This can disrupt the menstrual periods; elevate body temperature; lead to abdominal pain, nausea, vomiting, and headaches. In men, it can cause discharge from the penis and a burning sensation during urination. May be accompanied by heaviness in the affected testicles, inflammation of the scrotal skin, and swelling at the bottom of the testicle.
>
> Gonorrhea: The bacterium is spread through genital, oral-genital, and genital-anal contact. In women, a greenish/yellow discharge; however, it often goes undetected. At a later stage, pelvic inflammatory disease may develop. In men, discharge from the penis and burning sensation during urination. Untreated complications can include inflammation of the scrotal skin and swelling at the base of the testicle.
>
> Syphilis: The bacterium is transmitted from open lesions during genital, oral-genital, or genital-anal contact. In the primary stage, a chancre appears where the spirochetes entered the body. In the secondary stage, the chancre disappears, and a generalized skin rash appears. In the latent stages, there are often no observable symptoms. In the tertiary stage, serious symptoms occur: heart failure, blindness, eventually death.
>
> Pubic lice: Pubic lice are easily spread through body contact or through shared clothing or bedding. Lice invade the pubic-hair area and cause persistent itching.
>
> Herpes: The virus is transmitted primarily by genital, oral-genital, or genital-anal contact. An oral herpes virus is transmitted by kissing. Genital area develops small red, painful bumps. These papules are painful blisters that will rupture and form open sores.
>
> Genital warts: The virus is spread primarily through genital, oral-genital, and genital-anal contact. Warts develop in the affected areas as hard, yellow-gray bumps or soft, pinkish, cauliflower-like bumps in moist areas.

obtained more condoms than the no-intervention group but fewer than the AIDS prevention group. With the large increase in AIDS among women during the past twenty years, from 7% to 19%, prevention efforts aimed at women are needed (Hader et al., 2001). The female condom may offer some hope because it is the only alternative to the male condom as a means of protection against both pregnancy and STDs. In spite of this, acceptance and use of the female condom has been limited (Hoffman, Mantell, Exner, & Stein, 2004).

AIDS and Medication

AIDS is no longer the disease it used to be with the highly active antiretroviral therapy (HAART) that became the treatment of choice fifteen years ago. This medication can virtually stop the virus in its tracks, turning the disease that was once a clear death sentence into a chronic illness. However, getting AIDS clients to comply with the medication is a difficult and often overlooked task of therapy. It is recommended that adherence rates of 95% are needed

FOCUS ON NARRATIVE

SPIRITUAL GROWTH IN WOMEN WITH AIDS

By failing to recognize the personal growth experienced by some women with HIV, social-work professionals can inadvertently minimize the strengths and power of their clients. This mindset tends to keep clients as victims and may impede ethical social-work practice, which includes primacy of clients' interests, rights, and prerogatives.

When asked whether they had discovered any unexpected positive outcomes in the face of this very serious illness, 82% of infected women answered yes. These women spoke of rebuilt relationships, newfound values, a new sense of meaning and purpose, profound self-awareness and self-acceptance, and discoveries of connections with nature, God, and higher powers. They reported being able to use the pain and despair of the HIV diagnosis as an opportunity for self-awareness and growth, and some women described a profound healing in their lives that made room for a richer existence.

Five themes emerged: reckoning with death, life affirmation, creation of meanings, self-affirmation, and redefining relationships. The following are some quotes that express these themes (Dunbar et al., 1988):

Reckoning with death: "The only difference between me and you at this point... is that I know I might leave my body sooner that I thought I might. It only puts me closer to knowing that I'm mortal... I think AIDS brought the reality of death right home."

Life affirmation: "I went though a process where I would see beauty in real simple things: flowers, a rainbow, these mountains, a rainstorm, a pond, a river. I never stopped to notice these things before. Yeah, you saw a rainbow, but now a rainbow represents to me the entire life force. It's a deeper appreciation... I think I've been on a steady course of becoming less materialistic... that is just not important anymore."

Creation of meaning: "Well, we're in a body, here on this earth. We have some sort of purpose for being here; it may not be clear to us in this whole lifetime what the purpose is, but we have a purpose. And it may not be some huge purpose. It may be only to learn patience, virtue, kindness."

Self-affirmation: "You know, I think as a mother, as a woman, as a wife, I am always taking care of everybody else... But I finally realized that... if I don't start taking care of my own self, then I am not going to be around to take care of anybody else."

Redefining relationships: "I am a lot harder on myself and on other people that I see... I don't try to fix people anymore... I don't wait around for it to happen... I'm very intolerant with people that I feel are wasting their life away... Who I choose as friends is different."

Many and probably most women living with HIV can describe positive psychological and spiritual growth, consistent with these five themes. These findings have direct implication for social workers, particularly those in clinical practice. There are at least seven ways a practitioner can help a client with a terminal illness: (1) anticipate, recognize, and encourage growth; (2) assist clients with death and dying issues; (3) identify and facilitate life affirmation; (4) recognize the importance of spiritual well-being and the creation of meaning; (5) encourage self-evaluation, self-affirmation, and self-care; (6) facilitate relationship resolution and the development of new relationships; and (7) keep biases in check (Dunbar et al., 1998).

SOURCE: Excerpts from Dunbar et al. (1998). Copyright 1998, National Association of Social Workers, Inc.

---

for the medication to work. Critical to this demand is the fact that failure to adhere to medication can cause the virus to multiply rapidly and become drug resistant. Yet a 95% adherence rate is difficult to meet under any circumstances. Recent work has centered on developing interventions to improve medication adherence.

Studies on adherence found that substance users or depressed clients were less likely to adhere to the medication requirements (Crawford, 2003). This led to recommendations that prior to HAART initiation, clients should receive treatment for substance use or depression. Also, it became clear that greater adherence could be obtained when substance abusers had support and contact with staff. Additional work published in *AIDS Care* found that clinic staff were not counseling the AIDS clients enough. It is one thing to give the client a pharmacy bag of drugs and another to sit down and work out a plan for integrating the medication into daily life. Efforts to improve adherence focused on several things: making sure the client understands the regimen, developing a clear plan for daily and weekly efforts, setting up cues or reminders to take medications, and discussing how to handle missed doses. New research is looking into the use of beepers to increase adherence.

Rape and Sexual Assault

There is no justification in this world for hurting me, for taking away what he tried to take away from me. . . .
I cried, I know what rage lives inside of me. It's always been there—it always will be. It's OK. I went out and danced and got plowed last night. . . . I was drained the rest of the day and felt cruddy cuz of my hangover. . . . Tonight is my first night alone and I battle the "caged in" feeling. . . . I screamed in a loud voice in my front yard, "I am mad at the whole world."
—From the diary of a 26-year-old rape victim

The prevalence of rape is so high that it is likely to touch everyone. It is now estimated that one of every seven women has been raped in her lifetime (Kilpatrick & Ruggiero, 2004). Other experts estimate that up to 50% of women in the United States will be raped or subjected to attempted rape in their lifetime (Matsakis, 2003). Victims of rape are likely to be young, and only 20% of all rapes are committed by strangers. A recent study (Mohler-Kuo, Dowdall, Koss, & Wechsler, 2004) of 24,000 college students found that one in every twenty college women is raped each year. More than 70% of these women are raped while they are too intoxicated to give consent.

The fear of rape has a direct effect on the quality of all women's lives. In their daily lives, women must take precautionary actions because of the possibility of rape. In particular, women often must isolate themselves, by not going out after dark and certainly not going out alone at night.

Although victims of rape are predominantly women, men can be victims. Men raped by men suffer traumatic and long-term consequences, especially because they have never thought of themselves as possible rape victims. Also, rape is usually discussed in a heterosexual context, but gays are also victims of rape. And, increasingly, men have reported being raped by women.

Two types of rape have been distinguished: acquaintance rape and date rape (Weiten & Lloyd, 2002). **Acquaintance rape** occurs when a woman is raped by someone she knows; **date rape** occurs when she is raped by someone she is dating. Date rape is different from the act of seduction. Seduction occurs when a woman is persuaded and agrees to have sex. Date rape occurs when a woman is forced into sexual intercourse without her consent.

Both men and women often fail to acknowledge that date rape has occurred. In one study (Koss, Gidycz, & Wisniewski, 1987) of men who admitted forcing a woman to have intercourse, none perceived this act as rape. Of the women who indicated sexual aggression that constituted a legal definition of rape, only 27% actually said that they had been raped. Thus, this kind of rape has been referred to as a "hidden crime." Why is there so little recognition that rape has occurred in these instances? Part of the answer lies in the myth that, for rape to occur, it has to be perpetrated by a stranger; this myth helps men deny their responsibility and causes women who have been raped to doubt the man's intentions. However, stranger rape is less frequent than rape by an acquaintance or by a person the victim is dating.

Implications for Practice: Rape Trauma Syndrome

Regardless of the type of rape women experience, a common reaction is the **rape trauma syndrome**. As the quote at the beginning of the previous section reveals, women experience many intense emotions and reactions about being physically forced to have sex against their will. The crime may be life threatening; the victim is helpless. She experiences a loss of control, and she has become the object of another person's rage. These reactions lead to overwhelming feelings of fear and stress. Women may develop a number of fears: fear of being alone, fear of men, inability to trust a dating partner. Common feelings associated with rape include depression, anger, guilt, shame, and anxiety. Most rape survivors experience some of the following clusters of symptoms (Matsakis, 2003):

- **Disorganization phase**: This phase reflects the woman's immediate expressed or controlled physical and emotional reactions to the trauma. Common feelings in this phase are most likely fright, anger, and disbelief. A common reaction is "second guessing"—for example, asking, "What could I have done to avoid this?" Such questioning can lead to intense feelings of guilt and self-blame.

FOCUS ON MULTICULTURALISM

THE GLOBAL WAR AGAINST WOMEN

Violence against women—including assault, mutilation, murder, infanticide, rape, and cruel neglect—is perhaps the most pervasive yet least recognized human-rights issue in the world. It is also a profound health problem, sapping women's physical and emotional vitality and undermining their confidence—both of which are vital to achieving important social goals, especially in the Third World.

In Bangkok, Thailand, a reported 50% of married women are beaten regularly by their husbands. In the barrios of Quito, Ecuador, 80% of women are said to have been physically abused. And in Nicaragua, 44% of men admit to beating their wives or girlfriends. Equally shocking statistics can be found in the industrial world. There are also less recognized forms of violence. In Nepal, female babies die from neglect because parents value sons over daughters; in Sudan, girls' genitals are mutilated to ensure virginity until marriage; and in India, young brides are murdered by their husbands when parents fail to provide enough dowry. This is not random violence. In all these instances, women are targets of violence or abuse because of their sex; the risk factor is being female. Most of these abuses have been reported in one or another country, at one or another time. But it is only when one begins to amass statistics and reports from around the world that the horrifying dimensions of this global war on women come into focus.

For me, the revelation came only recently after talking with scores of women throughout the world. I never intended to investigate violence; I was researching maternal and child health issues overseas. But I would commonly begin my interviews with a simple question: "What is your biggest problem?" With unnerving frequency the answer came back: "My husband beats me."

SOURCE: Reprinted from "The global war against women," by Lori Heise in the March/April 1989 issue of *World Watch* magazine with permission of World Watch Institute, Washington, D.C., copyright © 1989.

- **Controlled reaction**: In this phase, the rape victim achieves a more composed and calm perspective following the trauma. Although some women react in a physical manner, by crying, shaking, and behaving hysterically, other women do not. Even though the woman is experiencing a controlled reaction, she is still suffering from the trauma.
- **Reorganization phase**: This phase reflects the adjustment and adaptation necessary following the rape. In one study (Burgess & Holmstromm, 1985) of rape victims four years after the rape, three-quarters of the women felt recovered. Half the women felt recovered after several months; the other half indicated it took them years to recover following the trauma. A quarter of the women still did not feel recovered after four years. Reorganization needs to take place as women attempt to regain equilibrium in physical, psychological, social, and sexual areas.

The recovery process follows a pattern similar to that of people who must adjust to grief. Matsakis (2003) has identified four issues that are important to the rape victim during the reorganization process:

1. Regaining a feeling of physical well-being and safety
2. Working through fears and phobias
3. Coming to terms with losses, such as loss of trust
4. Redefining a new sense of self

For many women, being in a support group is helpful because they can "tell their story" and begin the process of accepting what happened to them and learn how to assimilate their experience into their sense of self. However, many family therapists believe that the family can critically affect a rape victim's ability to recover from a trauma. For example, Pauline Boss has noted, "I've come to believe that trauma survivors need more than to tell their story to the therapist . . . they have to tell it to someone who matters to them, someone who is willing to validate their pain" (cited in Markowitz, 1991). Often that person is a family member. According to Markowitz (1991), "the most powerful healing from a trauma comes from the love and support of family. Knowing they have someone they can count on, who loves them no matter what, helps survivors regain their confidence and trust in the world after a debilitating setback" (p. 32).

> **EXHIBIT 10.11** Violence against women in the United States

Murder: Every day four women die as a result of domestic violence; this adds up to approximately 1,400 women a year. The number of women murdered by intimate partners exceeds the number of soldiers killed in the Vietnam War.

Battering: There are 572,000 reports of assault by intimate partners each year. A conservative estimate is that 2 to 4 million women are battered each year. Approximately 170,000 of those violent acts are so severe that women seek hospitalization, emergency room visits, or need a doctor's assessment.

Sexual assault: It is estimated that 132,000 women have been victims of rape or attempted rape, and more than half know their attackers. Anywhere from two to six times as many rapes are likely to happen that don't get reported. When one's former spouse or partner is the perpetrator, then the number of forcible rapes increased to 1.2 million.

The targets: Women are more than ten times more likely to be victims of violence perpetrated by an intimate than by a stranger. Women who are young, separated, divorced, single, low income, and African-American are more likely to be victims of assault and rape. Poverty is a significant factor in domestic violence, and spouse abuse is twice as likely when the spouse is unemployed. Violent attacks on lesbians and gays are growing at a very fast rate.

Effect on children: Violent juvenile offenders are four times more likely to have grown up in homes where there was a history of violence. Child witnesses of violence are reported to be five times more likely to commit or suffer violence when they become adults.

Effect on health and social services: Battered women need more than twice the health care as nonbattered counterparts. Pregnant women who become battered (17% report being battered) are at risk for poor health outcomes such as miscarriages, stillbirths, and low-birth-weight babies.

Legislation: NOW, the National Organization for Women, helped secure passage of the Violence Against Women Act, which provides new revenue for addressing the issues of violence against women.

SOURCE: From "Violence against women in the United States," copyright © 1995 National Organization for Women. Reprinted with permission.

Domestic Violence in the Family

Domestic violence is a serious problem in the United States. Families, often suffering from intense stress, conflicts, and maladaptive coping, fall prey to acts of violence (see Exhibit 10.11). It is estimated that one out of three women experiences at least one physical assault by a partner during adulthood. In many cases, the battering is life threatening; 2,000 to 4,000 women are beaten to death every year (Browne, 1987). Women are more likely to be killed by a husband, ex-husband, boyfriend, or acquaintance. Also, spouses and ex-spouses commit a much larger percentage of the homicides (18%) than do strangers (8.8%) (U.S. Department of Justice, 2002). Women aged 19 to 29 and women with incomes below $10,000 are more likely than other women to be victims of violence by a spouse or intimate (U.S. Department of Justice, 1995). Such violence often leads to homelessness when women flee violent home situations. As many as one-third of homeless women have suffered domestic violence (National Council on Homelessness, 2003). All of these facts support the finding that 92% of American women rank domestic violence as one of their top worries (National Coalition Against Domestic Violence, 2003).

Domestic violence is estimated to occur to approximately one-half of women over the course of their lives.

What would cause spouses and partners to resort to such gross mistreatment of each other? Of course, many factors relate to family violence, including intergenerational transmission of violence, poverty, social pressure and stress, social isolation and a lack of community involvement, serious personality problems, and psychopathology. When multiple risk factors are present, the family is vulnerable to maladaptive coping behaviors, and the family's welfare becomes threatened. Increasingly, researchers find that the minor, mutual slaps, kicks, and shoves depicted in television, movies, and comic strips are an all-too-common feature of real-life love and marriage. Even though such acts may seem trivial compared with the type of assaults that force women to seek safety in battered women's shelters, they are still abusive—to the psyche, if not to the body. This initial type of aggression may lead to outright battering, in which the man usually has the physical advantage. Yet shockingly, many couples regard such actions as innocuous, even normal in any loving relationship. Even for mutually violent partners, therapy should focus first and foremost on ending the man's violent behavior, mainly because he can usually inflict more physical and psychological harm than the woman can. However, a practitioner should never question the spouses' strong bond with each other. The couple often still shows evidence of mutual affection, empathy, and commitment.

Research (Sleek, 1998) has found similarities among romantic partners who exchange minor physical blows. They tend to (1) express a strong commitment to the relationship; (2) also engage in psychological abuse, such as insults and verbal threats; and (3) dismiss the physical fighting as minor, infrequent, or secondary to other problems.

If we could look back in time, we would see that many of these couples started exchanging shoves and slaps long before they exchanged vows. For this reason, reducing violence in dating relationships should be a focus for researchers and practitioners. Young people need to know how to resolve conflicts peacefully, become intolerant of physical abuse in romantic arguments, and minimize dominating and jealous behaviors toward a partner.

In addition to providing shelter to protect women from violence, many communities are attempting rehabilitation of the man who was the perpetrator. Increasingly, social-service agencies are addressing the impact of domestic violence on children who witness violent acts (Graham-Bermann & Edleson, 2001).

Social Workers in Managed-Care Systems

Managed care, as a cost-containing system of health care administration, is here to stay. However, this leaves the most vulnerable populations—poor people, people of color, women and children, and seniors—on the periphery. The populations in greatest need are often selected out of managed care systems because their high-risk status (poor nutrition, inadequate income, lack of prenatal care, substandard housing, minimal preventive care, and so on) ensures increased costs of care (Resnick & Tighe, 1997). Specific communities (certain rural and urban areas) are less likely to be served.

So what can social workers do? Between 20% and 80% of primary care visits involve the medicalization of presenting problems that are frequently psychosocial in origin (Resnick & Tighe, 1997). As Resnick and Tighe (1997) pointed out, physicians spend an excessive amount of time dealing with patients' psychological, social, and environmental concerns when their preference is to refer nonmedical issues to mental-health practitioners. Physicians could make more effective use of their time by referring clients with the appropriate issues to social workers. Some of these issues include those related to family, resources, mental health, behavioral problems, and medical noncompliance. Other issues involve children, older adults, and people with mental retardation. In sum, social workers can play many vital roles as interdisciplinary team members working in community clinics under a managed health care system. Redirection of emotional, psychological, familial, and social concerns to social-work professionals relieves other primary-care staff from dealing with issues that may not best fit their area of expertise. Additionally, social-work screening and case finding lessen the inappropriate use of valuable interdisciplinary professional time, thus increasing patient satisfaction.

Alcohol, Tobacco, and Other Drugs

In studies nationwide, alcohol, more than any other drug, has been closely associated with violence and aggression. In one study, respondents reporting either physical abuse or neglect of children were five times more likely to report alcohol abuse or dependence than were those who did not often report physical abuse or neglect. Alcohol also is involved in more than half of all rapes. Substance abuse brings out the worst in people and makes victims of us all.

This section focuses on issues compounded by substance abuse. The following facts and statistics make clear the need for preventing alcohol and other drug problems (adapted from the Center for Substance Abuse Prevention):

- After alcohol, tobacco, and marijuana are the most frequently used drugs on college campuses. And the past few years have seen an increase in the use of LSD among college students.
- Alcoholism and child abuse, including incest, seem tightly intertwined. Not only do abusers tend to be heavy drinkers, but those who have been abused are subject to an increased risk of abusing alcohol and other drugs over the course of their lifetimes.
- Alcohol consistently emerges as a significant predictor of marital violence. Alcoholic women have been found to be significantly more likely to have experienced negative verbal conflict with spouses than were nonalcoholic women. They were also more likely to have experienced a range of moderate and severe physical violence.
- Alcohol is present in more than 50% of all incidents of domestic violence.
- Alcohol, tobacco, and other drugs (ATOD) have been implicated as factors in many of the United States' most serious and expensive problems, including domestic violence, injury, HIV/AIDS and other sexually transmitted diseases, teen pregnancy, school failure, car crashes, escalating health care costs, low worker productivity, and homelessness.
- A large part of the U.S. national health care bill is for ATOD-related medical expenses. For example, 25% to 40% of all Americans in general hospital beds are being treated for complications of alcoholism.
- Alcohol is the drug most frequently used by 12- to 17-year-olds, and it causes the most negative health consequences. More than 4 million adolescents under the legal drinking age consume alcohol in any given month. Alcohol-related car crashes are the number-one killer of teens.
- ATOD prevention does work; however, different ATOD prevention programs yield economic benefits at various times. For example, if alcohol- and drug-taking behavior is reduced among pregnant women, the payoff will be realized within a year. In contrast, the benefits of a successful preschool program may not accrue to society for a decade or more—when these youngsters become adolescents and begin making choices about ATOD use.
- The effect of ATOD-related injuries and deaths takes a tremendous toll on our society. The number of potential years of life lost to ATOD-related injuries equals those lost to cancer and surpasses those lost to heart disease, the two leading causes of death in the United States. The cost of alcohol-related injuries exceeds $50 billion annually.
- Approximately 10% of adult dementia in the United States is a result of alcohol-related brain damage.
- At least 90% of alcoholics are nicotine dependent.
- Alcohol consumption by a pregnant woman can result in her child being born with Fetal Alcohol Syndrome (FAS), the most preventable cause of mental, physical, and psychological impairment in the Western world. According to research estimates, 1–3 of every 1,000 babies are born with FAS. There is no known safe level of alcohol consumption for a pregnant woman.
- Maternal smoking is a contributing factor in 14% of premature deliveries in the United States. There is also a direct correlation between the amount of smoking during pregnancy and the frequency of spontaneous abortion and fetal death.
- Adverse effects of secondhand smoke on children include respiratory infections such as bronchitis and pneumonia, increased prevalence of fluid in the middle ear, reduced lung function, increased frequency and severity of symptoms in asthmatic children, and increased risk for asthma in children with no previous symptoms.
- Alcohol and other drug use may interfere with a parent's caregiver role; 50% to 80% of all child abuse and neglect cases substantiated by Child Protective Services involve some degree of alcohol and other drug use by the child's parents.
- ATOD weaken the immune system, thereby increasing susceptibility to infection and disease.
- More than half of the new cases of HIV infection are related to drug use.
- High rates of alcohol involvement have been found among suicide victims who use firearms.

- Recent studies suggest that alcohol tends to be associated with impulsive rather than premeditated suicides.
- Crime is inextricably related to alcohol and other drugs. More than 1.1 million annual arrests for illicit drug violations, almost 1.4 million arrests for driving while intoxicated, 480,000 arrests for liquor law violations, and 704,000 arrests for drunkenness make a total of 4.3 million arrests for alcohol and other drug statutory crimes. The total accounts for more than one-third of all arrests in this country.
- Alcohol is a key factor in up to 68% of manslaughter cases, 62% of assaults, 54% of murders/attempted murders, 48% of robberies, and 44% of burglaries.
- Some women develop drug or alcohol dependencies as a way of coping with past abuse. For example, childhood sexual abuse is a strong predictor of later problem drinking.
- Workplace alcohol-, tobacco-, and other drug-related problems cost U.S. companies more than $100 billion each year.
- Up to 40% of industrial fatalities can be linked to alcohol consumption and alcoholism.
- Over a lifetime, each cigarette smoker requires approximately $10,000 more in medical expenditures than does a nonsmoker.

This exhaustive list suggests one clear fact: alcohol and drugs take an incredible toll on the lives of all of us. Social workers need to learn much more about the effects of drugs and become increasingly skilled in prevention and rehabilitation efforts of alcohol, tobacco, and other drugs.

Alcohol Use among College Students

Loaded. Plastered. Tanked. Smashed. College entrance-exam vocabulary words? Guess again. These are colloquial terms for the all-too-familiar collegiate phenomenon of getting drunk. Although research indicates that most students successfully mature past the period of heavy drinking, the college period is one of heightened vulnerability to the pressures associated with alcohol consumption. Traditional prevention efforts have relied on educating the population about the potential dangers of abusing alcohol, assuming that the individual will apply this information to his or her own personal situation. Recently, prevention has taken on a new focus: affecting people's motivation and desire to drink. This approach is being implemented on college campuses and in small towns.

From laboratory data collected over more than ten years, researcher Alan Marlatt has found that "peer pressure and expectancies about sexual arousal and social acceptance could increase the reported amount people drink" (Azar, 1995, p. 20). Marlatt also found factors that could decrease the reported amount people drink: exercise, meditation, and participation in community activities. Marlatt is now using the information he discovered in his field research. His energies are aimed not at preventing drinking but at preventing development of drinking problems and ensuing injuries in those individuals who already drink.

With these goals in mind, Marlatt developed a six-week cognitive-behavioral program that (1) challenges the glamorous portrayal of the effects of alcohol; (2) emphasizes awareness of one's drinking habits as a safety precaution; and (3) suggests plausible alternatives to drinking—exercise, nonalcoholic parties, and community work. A one-hour motivational interview emphasizing these areas was effective in reducing binge drinking among small groups of college students.

On the basis of this success, Marlatt and his colleagues began a longitudinal study in which they followed 500 college students identified as high-risk for problem drinking when they were high school seniors. Half the sample received no treatment, and the other half underwent the one-hour motivational interview when they started college. Students whose drinking problems persisted received the six-week program, and any students who showed signs of severe drinking problems were taken out of the study and given a referral for treatment.

Annual evaluations, even after three years, show that the program makes a significant difference in helping to accelerate "maturing out of drinking behavior." Marlatt has now targeted fraternities and sororities with the hope that the group format will foster group pressure toward behavior change.

Developmental Guidelines for Assessment in Young Adulthood

Exhibit 10.12 presents the developmental guidelines for assessment in young adulthood. These guidelines are meant to be helpful to social workers who need to understand development when making assessments.

EXHIBIT 10.12 Developmental considerations for assessment in young adulthood

Developmental milestones	**Developmental issues (not problems)**

Developmental milestones
Emerging adulthood
Vocational and career development
Independent living
Economic independence
Cohabitation or marriage
Childbearing and rearing
Adult friendships form

Strengths and landmarks of development
Motor skills and physical development peak
Development of expertise
Improved mental functioning (formal operational thinking)
Development of adult intimacy
Development of mentorships
Establishment of religious practices

Developmental issues (not problems)
Increased sexual activity
Fertility difficulties
Adjustment to marriage or gay lifestyle
Remaining or becoming single
Transition to parenthood
Divorce and new family arrangements

Developmental observations requiring attention
Premenstrual syndrome
Early health problems (especially cancer)
Isolation and loneliness
Abnormal behavior indicative of mental illness
Sexually transmitted diseases
Sexual harassment and rape
Family violence
Alcohol, tobacco, and drug use

STUDY TABLE: Social dimension in young adulthood

Families and Groups	Marriage and beginning a family are among the most significant life changes in young adulthood. Very few American families fit the definition of the "nuclear" family, so it is important to recognize the diversity of families; single-parent families, childless families, unwed parents, gay couples, and dual-career families. Four phases that lead to marriage are Phase I: opportunity, physical attraction, valued behaviors; Phase II: positive self-disclosure, rapport, sexuality, value concerns, salient homogeneity, similarity; Phase III: role compatibility, empathy; and Phase IV: the "right one" relationship, commitment escalators. The following factors influence the outcome of marriage: having parents who divorced, getting married young, having a longer courtship, being lower- or working-class. A balance of positive to negative interactions is important, and a five-to-one ratio leads to more satisfaction. Not all negativity is equal, and the four factors that seem to lead to the worst outcomes for married couples are criticism, defensiveness, contempt, and stonewalling. Social workers need to recognize the potential of the African American's extended family, spirituality, and religion, and the African American community as a whole. Most experts recognize that the origins of sexual orientation are multiple and diverse. Social workers, like many other professional groups, show evidence of homophobia. Factors that appear to be related to homophobia include authoritarian perspectives, highly religious views, being with people who have negative views of gays. Efforts such as AIDS prevention, access to health care, and the cost of drug treatment have focused attention on the needs and civil rights of gay people. Some lesbians, gay men, and bisexuals seem to easily ignore society's prejudices toward their sexuality, whereas others absorb the bigotry to the point of self-loathing referred to as internalized homophobia. The transition to parenthood brings many changes and new challenges and is usually accompanied by a significant increase in stress. There are currently several million gay men and lesbians who are parents, and many have emerged because of adoption and new reproductive technologies.

(continues)

STUDY TABLE: Social Dimension in Young Adulthood *(continued)*

Communities and Support Systems	A person's career or job can become a significant part of self-identity. Young adulthood can be very different depending on whether one is entering the workforce for a "job" or a "career." The majority of married women with children under the age of 6 work outside the home. Unequal pay rates and job segregation on the basis of gender are contributing hardships for women. Although there are an estimated 93 million volunteers in America, only 8.4% work in "human services," a broad category that includes aiding the homeless, family counseling, and serving as tutors or mentors.
Multicultural and Gender Considerations	Many young adults in these groups value the family but are frustrated in their attempts to provide for their families because of limited opportunities. Unemployment rates are critical for the African American, Hispanic, and Native American groups. Expecting children to choose their mother's or father's religions may put them in the position of rejecting one of their parents. To remedy this dilemma, some couples chose one religion to raise their children in, others expose the children to both or to a variety and let the children choose, and still others blend their religions. Women confront two significant roles, the marriage mandate and the motherhood mandate.
Social Strengths and Hazards	Reaching out and building social capital can provide significant benefits. One of the main reasons for a prolonged early adulthood is that it takes longer to secure a full-time job that will provide enough income to support a family. The United States has the highest divorce rate in the world; about half of all marriages end in divorce. Most divorces occur within seven years of marriage. Of those that do divorce, about three-fourths will remarry. About 60% of gay and lesbian adults are in couple relationships. Many face obstacles in maintaining a relationship. Legally, there are two types of sexual harassment: quid pro quo harassment, and environmental harassment. There are approximately twenty sexually transmitted diseases, including AIDS, syphilis, and gonorrhea. It is estimated that one in four Americans are likely to contract an STD sometime in their lives. Culturally relevant prevention messages are shown to be effective and can reduce risky behavior. AIDS is now treated with antiretroviral therapy that stops the virus. One of every seven women has been forcibly raped in her lifetime. Estimates are that up to 50% of women in the United States will be raped or subjected to attempted rape in their lifetime. Two types of rape have been distinguished, acquaintance rape and date rape. Rape survivors experience three phases: disorganization, controlled reaction, and reorganization phase. Violence against women—including assault, mutilation, murder, infanticide, rape, and cruel neglect—is perhaps the most pervasive yet least recognized human-rights issue in the world. It is estimated that one out of three women experiences at least one physical assault by a partner during adulthood. Many factors relate to family violence, including intergenerational transmission of violence, poverty, social pressure and stress, social isolation and a lack of community involvement, serious personality problems, and psychopathology. The college period is one of heightened vulnerability to the pressures of alcohol consumption. Alcohol is present in more than 50% of all incidents of domestic violence. Alcohol-related car crashes are the number-one killer of teens.

CONCEPT MAP

Social dimension

- **Families and groups**
  - Marriage
  - Selecting a partner
  - *Focus on Multiculturalism: Marriage and Mental Retardation*
  - Adjustment to marriage
  - Marital expectations and myths
  - Satisfaction and conflict in marriage
  - Empowering African American families
  - Diversity in companionship
  - Remaining or becoming single
  - Gay relationships
  - Homophobia
  - Internalized homophobia
  - Transition to parenthood
  - Implications for practice: Preparing for the transition to parenthood
  - Gay and lesbian parents
  - Voluntary childlessness
  - Infertility
  - Implications for practice: The infertile couple
  - Miscarriage

- **Support systems and communities**
  - Work life
  - Women and work
  - Peer relationships and forming mentorships
  - Volunteerism and social services

- **Multicultural and gender considerations**
  - Blending religions
  - Gender roles
  - *Focus on Multiculturalism: When Will Women and Men Be Equal?*

- **Social strengths and hazards**
  - Welfare reform
  - Families and children with disabilities
  - Divorce
  - When lesbian and gay couples break up
  - Sexual harassment
  - Sexually transmitted diseases
  - AIDS and prevention
  - AIDS and medication
  - *Focus on Narrative: Spiritual Growth in Women with AIDS*
  - Rape and sexual assault
  - Implications for practice: Rape trauma syndrome
  - *Focus on Multiculturalism: The Global War against Women*
  - Domestic violence in the family
  - Social workers in managed-care systems
  - Alcohol, tobacco, and other drugs
  - Alcohol use among college students
  - Developmental guidelines assessment in young adulthood

APPLYING THE FRAMEWORK

SCHIZOPHRENIA

Maria is a 24-year-old single woman who looks older than her stated age. She presented with symptoms of schizophrenia—prominent thought disorder, delusions, inappropriate affect or silly affect, and disorganized speech. The police brought Maria to the emergency room after neighbors complained of a young woman, who they feared might be dangerous, walking down the street, laughing and talking to herself. Several days later, her brother called the police and reported Maria as a missing person. The police informed her brother that a young woman fitting his sister's description had been taken to the hospital and admitted to the psychiatric ward a few days earlier.

Maria's family history revealed that she came from a problematic family. She was the second of three children and was often the victim of criticism and abuse from her father. Her father was abusive when he came home drunk. Maria's mother died when she was 13 years old, and Maria never "recovered." While she was living, Maria's mother had tried to protect the children from their father. Maria and her mother had been particularly close. When Maria's mother died, the children were placed in the custody of the state because of their father's inability to take care of them. The children were separated on several occasions during their tenure in foster homes, and separation took its toll on Maria.

Even when Maria was a young child, she experienced problems adjusting to minor changes and withdrew from her normal activities. Her school records recorded problems Maria had in trying to adjust to school routines and how traumatic it was for Maria to leave home and go to school. She had to compete with different children of different age groups while living in foster homes. She was beaten by some of these children and by some of the foster parents. Even before the foster homes, Maria had a history of "bizarre behavior" and was highly withdrawn. Her mother was hospitalized twice before she died, according to Maria's older sister. She told the attending physician: "My mother had emotional problems and was sent away."

Developmental Considerations

Maria's problems started when she was very young—physical and psychological abuse, placement in foster homes, and lack of a sense of security. The first signs of her disorder were not detected until adulthood. However, she had a number of developmental issues often noted in the histories of people who develop schizophrenia. Her early childhood and adolescence indicate that she had issues involving trust versus mistrust, separation-individuation, evidence of possible bonding difficulties, and identity difficulties during adolescence. The loss of her mother had a profound effect on Maria because her mother was Maria's only support system. Maria's symptoms of schizophrenia were undetected before the presentation of active psychotic symptoms. Her history of poor functioning in school and at work and her inability to adjust to life events contributed to Maria's disorder. Her disorder had an early and insidious onset. Given the characteristics of the onset, Maria was untreated until she moved into the active phase of schizophrenia.

Biophysical Considerations

Maria's episode with schizophrenia may suggest that she had a predisposition for schizophrenia (genetic), which is supported by the finding that her mother had been hospitalized for emotional problems. Because structural changes in the brain are likely in neurotransmitter systems (namely dopamine), further confirmation for biophysical hypotheses can be found if brain imagery techniques show evidence of cortical atrophy.

Psychological Considerations

Maria manifested some deficits in the cognitive, affective, and behavioral domains. During the active phase of her disorder, she presented with disorganized speech, distorted perceptions (delusions and hallucinations), and distorted thought processes in the cognitive area. Her affective state is best characterized as inappropriate or silly. She laughed inappropriately throughout the admission process.

Communication

The communication process within Maria's family is unclear. The family demonstrates some signs of limited communication abilities within the family. Her bizarre behavior further aggravates her communication competence. She smiles inappropriately and does not demonstrate that she can share what she is experiencing.

Attitudes and Emotions

It is difficult at this time to assess Maria's attitudes and emotions; she is currently in the active phase of her illness, and the medication has not reduced her symptoms. Usually, her type of schizophrenia has a poor prognosis with a chronic course. Maria has isolated herself and rarely interacts with others. She does not appear to hold suspicious or bizarre delusions.

Family

Maria is 24. Before her mother died, Maria lived with her parents and two siblings. Maria's father was particularly abusive to her. The family believes that he singled her out because she looks like his paternal grandmother. Maria and her siblings lived in foster homes for about five years. Her sister, Ester, is eighteen months her senior, and her brother, Mario, with whom she presently lives, is the youngest member of the family. She has no contact with her extended family.

Social Support

The most consistent support Maria ever had was her mother, who died when Maria was 13 years of age. Her mother's death undoubtedly contributed to many of Maria's problems in later life.

Summary and Impressions

Maria is experiencing the following:

1. She developed schizophrenia, and the symptoms are currently in the active phase.
2. She had a prolonged history of social and psychological problems.
3. She was a victim of physical and psychological abuse.
4. The course of her disorder suggests a poor prognosis.
5. Her responses to neuroleptic medications have been marginal at best.
6. Her past medical record was essentially unremarkable.

Maria is a young adult who has developed a severe mental disorder known as schizophrenia, disorganized type. Her prognosis is poor with a chronic course. Her disorder is associated with possible structural changes in the brain—type II schizophrenia. The etiology is unknown at this time. She may have had a predisposition for this disorder, as indicated by her family history. Her problems have been exacerbated by the interaction of biological, social, and psychological factors. These factors proved too much for her to handle. She cannot cope with changes nor handle many other demands.

In the event of her discharge, she will need supervision and social support. It is imperative that her physician closely supervise her medication and be kept informed of Maria's status/relapse by those in charge of her custody. Her caregivers should be educated about Maria's disorder and attend at least some of her group sessions. Finally, it is critical that Maria's cultural background be taken into account in planning support services.

Hubert Johnston

Key Terms

- acquaintance rape
- basal metabolism rate
- controlled reaction
- date rape
- disorganization phase
- emerging adulthood
- environmental harassment
- expressive communication
- homophobia
- infertility
- instrumental communication
- internalized homophobia
- loneliness
- menstrual cycle
- premenstrual dysphoric disorder
- premenstrual syndrome (PMS)
- quid pro quo harassment
- rape trauma syndrome
- rapport talk
- reorganization phase
- report talk
- schizophrenia
- sexual harassment
- sexually transmitted diseases (STDs)

Online Resources

Websites

See http://info.wadsworth.com/ashford for specific links to these web pages.

Cooperative Communication Skills—Internet Resource Center

Self-help information, encouragement, and teaching materials for better communication in work, family, friendship, and community.

Gay and Lesbian Alliance Against Defamation

Working with the media, GLAAD aims to improve the public's attitudes toward homosexuals and put an end to violence and discrimination against lesbians and gay men. In English and Spanish, this website provides media alerts, policy updates, and links to other sites.

Planned Parenthood

The official website of Planned Parenthood Federation of America. Planned Parenthood provides high-quality, affordable reproductive health care and sexual-health information.

The International Council on Infertility Information Dissemination

This site provides current information regarding the diagnosis, treatment, and prevention of infertility and pregnancy loss, as well as links to related websites.

National Domestic Violence Hotline

Links individuals to help in their area using a nationwide database that includes detailed information on domestic violence shelters, other emergency shelters, legal advocacy and assistance programs, and social-service programs.

InfoTrac College Edition Keywords

For interesting materials related to what you have just read, please go to the InfoTrac College Edition website and search using the following keywords:

- serious mental illness
- rape
- premenstrual syndrome
- infertility
- divorce

Book-Specific Resources

Book-specific resources can be found at http://info.wadsworth.com/ashford and include the following:

- Case studies
- Quizzes for testing your knowledge
- PowerPoint presentations

CHAPTER 11
MIDDLE ADULTHOOD

CHAPTER CONSULTANTS

Ski Hunter
University of Texas at Arlington

Jill Jones
University of Nevada–Las Vegas

DEVELOPMENTAL THEMES	Stage: generativity versus stagnation. Life expectancy. Midlife as a crossroads. Stage theories.
BIOPHYSICAL DIMENSION	
Biophysical Growth and Development	Adaptation to physical changes; changes in physical appearance. Personality type and disease. Menopause. Ethnicity and menopause. Estrogen-replacement therapy. Sexuality in middle adulthood.
Biophysical Strengths and Hazards	Physical fitness. Breast and prostate cancer. Family-systems approach to couples and illness. Psychological interventions for the seriously ill. Women and health care. Overweight and exercise. Brain injury.
PSYCHOLOGICAL DIMENSION	
Cognitive Development and Information Processing	Stability of intellectual functioning. Concern over professional adolescence.
Communication	Reconnection with one's partner or spouse. Communication on a deeper level. Forgiveness. Execution and therapeutic revenge. Concerns about illiteracy. Communication with nonspeaking adults. The hard-of-hearing adult. Title V.
Attitudes and Emotions	Well-being and anxiety. Midlife as a crisis.
Social Cognition and Regulation	Development of caring and socially responsible behaviors. Crystallized intelligence; fluid intelligence.
Psychological Strengths and Hazards	Developing optimism and happiness. Alcohol and drug addiction. Women and drugs. Codependency. Need for professional help. False memory syndrome.
SOCIAL DIMENSION	
Families and Groups	Blended families. Marriage at midlife. Marital satisfaction among African Americans. Extramarital affairs. Impact of adolescent children on middle-aged parents. Changing relationships with adult children. Addressing the needs of aging parents. Families of adults with mental retardation. Caregiving. Grandparenthood. Grandparents raising their grandchildren.
Communities and Support Systems	Decline of civic engagement. Career development and job satisfaction. Work as a way of life. Spirituality in work. Career changes at midlife.
Multicultural and Gender Considerations	Ethnic identity in adulthood. Problems with generalizing adult-development theories to women. Gender differences at midlife. Role strain and role conflict for women. African American women at midlife. The men's movement. Men in therapy. Gender, work, and the family.
Social Strengths and Hazards	Variety in social roles. Launching children. Occupational advantages in midlife. Joblessness. Homelessness. Adapting to midlife.

DEVELOPMENTAL THEMES

Less than 100 years ago, only half of all Americans who reached age 20 lived to see the age of 65. And because their ancestors had little chance of living past 40, the concept of "middle age" as we now know it is new. In America today, most people survive well into their 70s or 80s. But midlife remains a mystery. The myths about psychological landmarks of midlife, such as the "empty-nest syndrome," the "midlife crisis," and the menopausal "change of life" continue to thrive in our society, however (Hunter, Sundel, & Sundel, 2002). Middle adulthood is often characterized as a time of questioning and "a time of change to an internal focus that provides wisdom for the later years" (Dziegielewski, Heymann, Green, & Gichia, 2002, p. 65). Many adults truly feel that they are at a crossroads at midlife, as aptly described by Margaret Atwood (1991) in her novel *Cat's Eye*:

> This is the middle of my life. I think of it as a place, like the middle of a river, the middle of a bridge, halfway across, halfway over. I'm supposed to have accumulated things by now: possessions, responsibilities, achievements, experience and wisdom (p. 13).

Midlife is different from other developmental phases in that it is less affected by biological maturation. Indeed, adults are most affected by their own experiences—and how they time those experiences. Even success or failure in life is shaped by personal and social factors. For some, midlife involves "launching" children and focusing on career development; for others, it may involve beginning a family and postponing career development. The effect of chronological age seems to become a less reliable indicator of what men and women are like at various points in their lives.

Midlife is often considered to begin at age 35 and continue until age 60—a span of twenty-five years. However, midlife is different for men and for women because of their differences in life expectancy. Therefore, more accurately, midlife begins at age 35 for men and age 39 for women (Baruch & Brooks-Gunn, 1984). For some, middle age has been pushed forward all the way to the 50s because we are living so much longer. These changes have led to a reconceptualization of the life course in adulthood, beginning with provisional adulthood (18–30), followed by first adulthood (30–34), and ending in second adulthood (45–85+) (Sheehy, 1996). Imagine: young people today are likely to turn 45 years old and begin their second adulthood; they will face the question of how they want to live in this new phase of adulthood. Many adults will choose to make critical changes built on this notion of a second life.

Adults at midlife are most typically characterized by a new perspective of who they are and a new perspective about their world, including a new definition of self, new expectations about what they want to accomplish, and new satisfactions in living. Erikson (1974) referred to this period as one of generativity versus stagnation. Generativity represents reaching out to others in ways that guide future generations. Because there is so much diversity in midlife, many experts refuse to identify a timetable for adult development. However, Gail Sheehy's (1976) classic book *Passages* reinforced the notion that adult lives are predictable and based on age-linked stages. In fact, the profound influence of Sheehy's book was that it set out a normative expectation that in middle adulthood there is a "midlife crisis" phase.

What led to the enormous success of *Passages*? Many people want predictability and could relate to one of the phases Sheehy described. However, as midlife was studied further, the picture of development in adulthood grew more complex. Today, most experts note many of the problems identified in previous stage theories, and the idea of a universal midlife crisis has not found much empirical support. One study (McQuaide, 1998) found that 72% of women in midlife described themselves as happy or very happy—far from being in a crisis stage.

Although stage theories have been commonly used to examine the life course (and midlife in particular), they are becoming increasingly less relevant. Many of the stages are simply not connected with the age ranges originally intended. For example, much of the identity crisis Erikson referred to for adolescence is not resolved until the 20s (Arnett, 2004). Furthermore, societal changes for women have disrupted ideas of a life-stage approach. Women entering the workplace, delays in having children, changing patterns of career development—all these factors have wreaked havoc with attempts to generalize women's life patterns. As Schlossberg (cited in Goldstein & Landau, 1990) noted, "Give me a room of 40-year-old women and you have told me nothing" (p. 20).

Complicating the picture even further is the work of Neugarten, who has focused on the importance of changing times and how different expectations influence various "cohorts"—groups of people who are born in the same year or time period. For example, if you were born during the Great Depression, your perspective on midlife may be different than if you were born during more optimistic times. Neugarten has argued that the social environment of a particular cohort will influence the timetable of when people expect to accomplish major life tasks, such as having children or selecting a career. This situation implies that findings from one cohort may not apply to other cohorts. For this reason, it is difficult to make generalizations about people in middle age. In this chapter, then, we will attempt to explore the various ways individuals experience their middle years of life.

STUDY TABLE: Developmental themes and biophysical dimension of middle adulthood

Developmental Themes	Midlife is different from other developmental phases in that it is less affected by biological maturation. During middle adulthood, chronological age seems to become a less reliable indicator of what men and women are like. Midlife is different for men and for women because of their differences in life expectancy; midlife begins at age 35 for men and age 39 for women. Although midlife is a time of reflection, there is not much empirical support for the popular notion of a midlife crisis. Erikson referred to this stage as generativity versus stagnation. For many adults, midlife is a time for launching children and focusing on career development.

BIOPHYSICAL DIMENSION

Biophysical Growth and Development

In middle adulthood, individuals often look back to their life in young adulthood and for the first time see and feel significant changes in themselves physically. Most individuals in middle adulthood are less fit; they have a fuller body shape. And anyone who has been to a twenty- or thirty-year high school reunion will remark that those additional years have created many gray heads, lots of bald heads, and lined faces. A quick glance around the room always finds plenty of people peering through reading glasses as they attempt to find out who has won the awards for most children, person with the youngest child, and most traveled. Discussion at that reunion also will include remembering or discussing individuals who have been challenged by life-threatening events, most likely cancer or heart disease. All of this adds up to a revision of the physical self-image that takes place in midlife (Berk, 2004). Many people at this age confess fears of disease and decline. However, an increasing number of middle adults also pursue health with a newfound passion, as they get ready for late adulthood by developing a physical fitness routine and increasing mental preparedness for late adulthood.

Personality Type and Disease

Although the leading causes of death during middle age are cancer and heart disease, evidence suggests that these illnesses may not be purely physiological in origin. What other factor could be so powerful that it influences how a disease presents itself? Stress has been part of the discussion for a long time. Stress is linked to physical illness and may have an effect on how illness affects an individual.

A classic study sought to discover the causes of coronary disease. Friedman and Rosenman (1974) found that some individuals who were in good physical shape and should have avoided heart disease didn't, and others who were in bad physical shape successfully avoided heart disease. Eventually, they discovered that physical shape in addition to personality factors influenced the course of heart disease. They found people are of two personality types: **type**

A **personality**—competitive, impatient, and sometimes hostile perfectionists; and **type B personality**—relaxed, easygoing, and generally amicable individuals. Type B personalities are less easily agitated than Type A personalities are.

More recent research today suggests that the key factor leading to health problems is most likely **cynical hostility**, characterized by angry outbursts, disagreeable behavior, and criticism, and feelings of contempt toward others (Aldwin et al., 2001; Williams, 2000).

An important criticism of the studies on type A personality and heart disease is that they have been limited primarily to people who were already ill. As a result, it is not clear whether the personality led to the disease or the disease led to the development of the personality. Groundbreaking research by Ronald Grossarth-Maticek (cited in Eysenck, 1989) examined a large group of individuals by administering personality tests and following them for ten years or more to see what health problems they might develop. This research identified different personality types: type 1, cancer-prone; type 2, coronary-heart-disease-prone; and types 3 and 4, healthy individuals who cope with stress in a nondestructive fashion. It also uncovered a strong relationship between personality and various health outcomes. For example, Grossarth-Maticek was able to achieve 50% accuracy in predicting death from cancer. More specifically, he found that of the type 1 individuals who died, half died from cancer and fewer than one-tenth died from heart disease. Of the type 2 individuals, one-third died from cancer and one-fifth died from heart disease. However, individuals of types 3 and 4 showed few deaths. These basic conclusions have been replicated in other studies.

If we can understand more about why certain individuals develop health problems, can we prevent the problems? Eysenck and Grossarth-Maticek believe the answer is yes. They conducted an experimental study in which they taught cancer- and heart-disease-prone people to express their emotions more readily, use coping skills for stress, reduce their emotional dependencies, and become more self-reliant. In the study, they assigned fifty cancer-prone people to the therapy and fifty to a no-therapy condition. Their results showed a dramatic influence: In a thirteen-year follow-up, forty-five of the original fifty in the therapy group were alive, but only nineteen of the fifty in the no-therapy group were still living. They replicated these results with heart-disease-prone individuals and then again with women who had terminal breast cancer.

Menopause

You know, it's kind of like when I was 10 years old, before puberty. I don't have to deal with all that female, sexual stuff anymore. I'm just me again.
　　—A woman discussing her experience of menopause

Menopause occurs when a woman has not experienced a menstrual cycle for one year. Attitudes toward this event vary, depending on cultural connotations and on women's individual expectations. In societies in which the woman's role is mostly reproductive, inability to bear any more children is a loss of status. In cultures in which the wisdom and experience of older women is valued, menopause is seen as a positive life event (Adler et al., 2000). In general, young women and men view menopause more negatively, whereas women who have gone through the experience view it more positively. Individually, some women view the cessation of their monthly period as a sign of impending old age and mourn the loss of youth and beauty. Other women, as the one quoted above, are glad to be rid of it.

Menopause occurs when the ovaries stop functioning and no longer produce the hormones estrogen and progesterone. It is a gradual process that can take from five to twenty years. During perimenopause, the time when hormone levels begin to fall until menstrual cycles stop, a woman may notice several changes: her menstrual cycles may become irregular; she may experience a decreased monthly flow as well as increased spotting; and symptoms of premenstrual tension, such as breast tenderness and fluid retention, may increase. The average age of menopause is 51 years old; the vast majority of women reach menopause between 45 and 55 years of age (Barbach, 2000). Women who are childless and women who smoke are more likely to reach menopause earlier (Avis, Crawford, & Johannes, 2002). This is critical, because women who undergo early menopause, with the onset before about age 50, are at greater risk for developing heart disease, osteoporosis, and other chronic diseases than are women who reach menopause later (DeAngelis, 1997b). For men, testosterone production declines gradually with age but the change is minimal, especially for men who continue sexual activity, which stimulates the cells that release testosterone. Therefore, many people believe that no

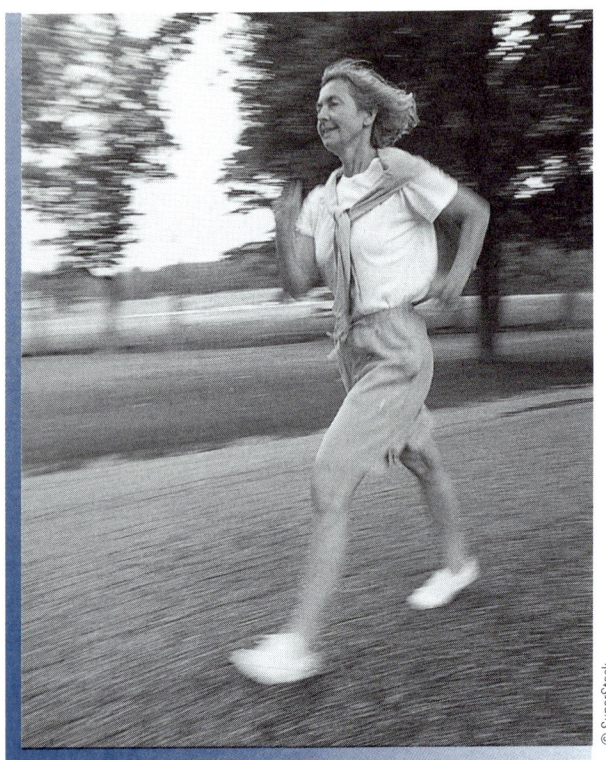

In general, women who have gone through menopause view it more positively than do men and younger women. Some women report increases in energy, self-confidence, and assertiveness.

male counterpart for menopause exists; however, the notion of male menopause (or andropause) is often discussed.

Falling estrogen levels affect women in different ways. The most universal change is the **hot flash**; a wave of heat rises from the woman's chest to her neck, face, and arms. This feeling of heat may last from a few seconds to a minute or more, often followed by a cold shiver (Bromberger et al., 2001). Hot flashes affect about 75% of women in industrial nations. Hot flashes frequently occur at night, causing "night sweats." Recurrent night sweats can interfere with sleep—a common complaint among women. Another effect of estrogen loss is thinning and drying of the vaginal membranes. This problem occurs with less severity, though, if a woman stays sexually active. Loss of estrogen also affects the urinary tract and can result in an increase in the frequency of urination, as well as incontinence. This means that when a menopausal woman coughs, sneezes, or laughs, she may inadvertently lose urine (Voda, 1993). Other physical changes include dry, itching skin and dry hair, and a heightened sense of touch (see Exhibit 11.1). But the major physical effects of estrogen loss are cardiovascular changes, which put postmenopausal women at greater risk of heart disease, and increased bone loss, which puts them at risk of **osteoporosis** (thinning and weakening of the bones). As a result of this bone loss, postmenopausal women are at increased risk of bone fractures, especially of the hip, and vertebral fractures (in the spine). Women most at risk of osteoporosis are white, slender smokers with low calcium intake who don't exercise regularly. Although increased calcium intake can help prevent osteoporosis, the amount of calcium the body can use is limited without estrogen. Bone-density testing is often recommended for women entering menopause.

Psychological effects of menopause are unclear. Some women report increased energy, often referred to as "postmenopausal zest" (PMZ). Some attribute this increase in energy, confidence, and assertiveness not to biological events but to "the crisis and resolution of midlife women's psyche" (Apter, 1995, p. 201). In other words, menopausal women are struck by a sense of unmet goals or unfulfilled potential and experience "an increased capacity to resolve old conflicts and satisfy suppressed desires" (p. 202). Also, menopausal women no longer have a monthly loss of blood, so their levels of iron may increase. Plus, they no longer have periodic hormonal fluctuations and no longer have to deal with premenstrual syndrome. Jones (1999) has recommended that workers not refer to menopausal "symptoms," because this term reinforces social attitudes that menopause is a disease in need of medical treatment. Instead, one can describe the "changes" that are likely to take place.

A critical question is this: Do women become depressed and irritable at menopause? Because menopause occurs at a time in life when women may feel they are "getting old," it is difficult to differentiate the effects of menopause from the effects of aging (Dan & Bernhard, 1989). Apter (1995) stated:

> Current research has found no significant changes in anger, anxiety, depression, self-consciousness, or worry about the body between women observed from the time they were premenopausal to the time they had become postmenopausal. This means that, in general, a woman's mood is not determined by menopause; but an individual woman may respond to it with increases in anger, anxiety, depression, or self-consciousness because of how she experiences or perceives its meaning (p. 215).

Some research has found that women who expect menopause to be a negative experience do indeed

EXHIBIT 11.1 The changes of menopause

When	Symptom	Comments
Before menopause	Irregular periods	Cycle may shorten or lengthen; flow may increase or decrease.
During menopause	Periods stop	
	Hot flashes	Skin temperature rises, then falls. Accompanied by sweating and sometimes heart palpitations, nausea, and anxiety. Occur anywhere from once a month to several times an hour. May begin 12–18 months before menopause and continue for some years thereafter.
	Insomnia	Sometimes caused by nightly bouts of hot flashes. Dream-rich REM sleep may also decrease, disturbing sleep.
	Psychological effects	Irritability, short-term memory loss, and problems with concentration are common. These symptoms may simply result from sleep deprivation.
After menopause	Changes in nervous system	The perception of touch can become more or less sensitive.
	Dry skin and hair	The skin can become thin, dry, and itchy. Hair may thin out. Facial hair may increase.
	Incontinence	Tissue shrinkage in the bladder and weakening pelvic muscles may lead to problems with bladder control.
	Vaginal dryness	The mucous membranes and walls of the vagina become thinner, which may lead to pain on intercourse and susceptibility to infections.
	Bone loss	Increases dramatically.
	Cardiovascular changes	Blood vessels become less flexible. Cholesterol and triglyceride levels rise.

SOURCE: Adapted with permission from "The changes of menopause," by Lisa Davis, *Hippocrates*, May/June 1989. Copyright © 1989 The Health Publishing Group.

find it to be a negative experience (Matthews, 1992). Others believe that depression may occur as a result of the changes in a woman's life (no longer feeling young, children leaving the home) rather than because of hormonal loss. However, overall, for most women menopause is not a critical event.

No matter what happens physically to women during menopause, it represents an important marker of aging (Jones, 1994; 1997). Many women seek the facts to understand menopause, but they also want to explore the personal and social meaning associated with it. For them, menopause is a symbol of changing health, physical appearance, sexuality, and aging in general (Jones, 2004). No longer is menopause considered a time-limited physiological condition, as it is increasingly recognized that it represents a significant life-stage developmental change.

Ethnicity and Menopause

Researchers from the Study of Women's Health Across the Nation (SWAN) have noted that, at present, the base for understanding menopause is Caucasian women. SWAN researchers have found that women in different ethnic groups vary in the kinds and degree of menopausal symptoms they report. SWAN looked at two kinds of symptom clusters: estrogen-related symptoms, including hot flashes, night sweats, vaginal dryness, and urine leakage; and somatic symptoms, including difficulties in sleeping, headaches, a racing heart, and stiffness and soreness in the joints, neck, or shoulders. Exhibit 11.2 presents generalizations of the findings within various ethnic and lifestyle groups.

SWAN also found that women's attitudes toward aging may explain who uses hormones and who does not (DeAngelis, 1997). Caucasian women may use hormones to slow down the physical signs of aging. Interestingly, women of color get hysterectomies more often than Caucasian women do. In particular, African American women, for whom fibroid tumors are common, are twice as likely to have hysterectomies as white women. Hysterectomies also are common in women with less education. In sum, white, highly educated women are more likely to use hormone-replacement therapy than are women of color.

EXHIBIT 11.2 Menopause symptoms of ethnic and lifestyle groups

Ethnic or lifestyle group	Symptoms
African American	Report more estrogen-related symptoms and fewer somatic symptoms than all other ethnic groups.
Hispanic	Report more urinary leakage and racing-heart symptoms than all other ethnic groups.
Asian American	Report fewer symptoms than all others.
Smokers	Within all ethnic groups, report more of both estrogen-related and somatic symptoms.
Education level	Less-educated women have more estrogen-related symptoms and more racing-heart symptoms than others.
Physical activity	Women who report getting less physical activity have more of all types of symptoms.

Source: Adapted from DeAngelis (1997).

Some women pass through menopause with few symptoms or effects; others experience severe problems. Although the occurrence of psychological changes at menopause is debatable, a woman experiencing any of these symptoms needs to believe that, whatever the cause, her complaints are being taken seriously and not being passed off as "all in her head." Women with physical symptoms may benefit from **estrogen replacement therapy (ERT)**, in which synthetic estrogen is taken to replace that lost through menopause.

Estrogen Replacement Therapy

Recently, some literature has been encouraging women to accept menopause as a natural part of the life cycle. The writers claim that the medical profession has described menopause as a deficiency disease for which medication is prescribed. Such authors suggest that the cessation of menstruation is not an illness that needs to be treated but a part of the rhythm and flow of a woman's life. Some even claim an evolutionary advantage to menopause, in that women can stop bearing children when they are still young enough and energetic enough to participate in raising older children (Dan & Bernhard, 1989).

This attitude, however, overlooks the fact that, as recently as the nineteenth century, the average life expectancy of a woman was 48 years. So women who experienced the natural process of menopause may not have lived many years beyond that experience. Today, a healthy woman undergoing menopause at 52 can expect to live another thirty or more years.

And some research indicates that, as these years pass, the reduction in estrogen that occurs at menopause increases a woman's risk of heart disease, stroke, and osteoporosis. To reduce the symptoms of menopause and to protect women from other difficulties due to estrogen loss, doctors have used **hormone therapy**, which is daily dosages of estrogen. The treatment can include estrogen alone, or estrogen-replacement therapy (ERT). The treatment is complicated, in part because taking estrogen increases the changes of cancer but combining estrogen and progesterone lessons the risk. Initial research on estrogen replacement therapy (ERT) found it greatly reduced a woman's risk for all these problems (Grodstein et al., 2000). It also offers some protection against bone deterioration and colon cancer (Nelson, Humphrey, Nygren, Teutsch, & Allan., 2002). ERT is prescribed most for its help with the symptoms of hot flashes and vaginal dryness, too, but many women find these symptoms to be mild and easily remedied without the addition of daily hormones.

Recent concerns about HRT emerged after a large-scale experiment where women were randomly assigned to take HRT or a placebo. After five years of follow-up data, two negative results were revealed. First, although HRT is thought to reduce heart disease, there was a slight increase in heart attacks, stroke, and blood clots. Second, there was an increase in breast cancer among women who took HRT (Women's health initiative, 2002). Furthermore, additional studies revealed slightly elevated cognitive impairments among the HRT group (Rapp et al., 2003). The fate of HRT is unclear. The choice should be up to the individual patient, depending on the severity of her symptoms and her risk of heart disease and osteoporosis. In particular, women also should consider their personal risk of developing breast cancer when considering HRT. Also, recent research is being conducted on alternative medications to treat menopause symptoms, such as migraine-headache treatment and antidepressant medications, which reduce hot flashes (Guttuso, Kurlan, McDermott, & Kieburtz, 2003).

Sexuality in Middle Adulthood

The midlife years often can lead to problems for marital couples who do not understand some of the changes they are going through. Maggie Scarf (1992) has noted the different physical changes that men and women go through during the middle years. A man's aging crisis can be related to the pressure he feels to "make it," and a woman's aging crisis can be related to concerns and anxiety she feels about her physical appearance. These changes have direct implications for their sexual relationship. Scarf (1992) described how such changes affect the **sexual response cycle**, which includes three phases: desire, excitement, and orgasm. First, desire, being sexually motivated, can be affected by aging. For example, the side effects of diseases (such as diabetes or hyperthyroidism), of psychological difficulties (such as depression), or of medical concerns (such as hypertension) that require drug treatment all can negatively affect desire. In general, over time the sex drive declines, particularly for men. The male sex drive is also affected by a drop in testosterone, the male hormone.

Excitement, the second phase of the sexual response cycle, is the first physiological reaction to stimulation and results in blood engorgement of the genitals. As Scarf (1992) pointed out, "while earlier the mere thought of having sex might have made him erect, later on in life he will often require both psychological and tactile stimulation" (p. 54). This can make the man feel more vulnerable. In fact, without successful adaptation, both partners may end up humiliated—the man, who has to confront his slowed sexual response, and the woman, who may perceive his slowness as a sign of rejection and of her lack of attractiveness.

The last phase of the sexual response cycle, orgasm, also changes dramatically with age, primarily in the area known as the **refractory period**—the time between one orgasm and the physical capabil-

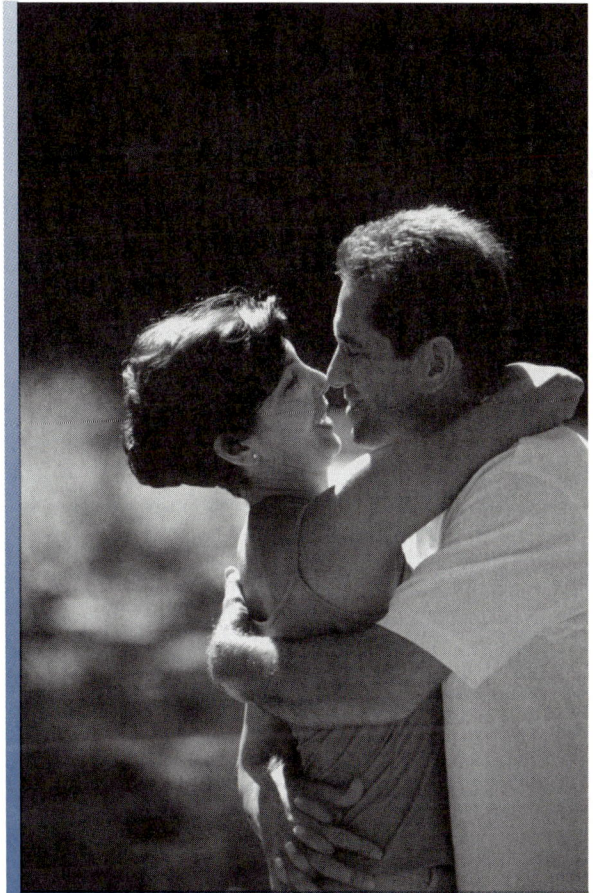

Understanding the physical changes that affect sexuality in midlife can help men and women adapt and adjust.

ity to achieve another orgasm. The adolescent male can have as many as two orgasms per minute, but the midlife male may need as long as twenty-four to forty-eight hours between orgasms. Most often for men, the difficulties experienced are a delay in erection and ejaculation during sexual intercourse due to reduced blood flow to the penis. These difficulties can affect 25% of men by age 60 (Blanker et al., 2001). The well-known drug Viagra works by increasing blood flow to the penis.

For the midlife woman, the sexual profile is quite different. Indeed, erotic interest often increases in the desire phase, primarily in response to changes in her biological makeup. When estrogen, the female hormone, declines, it allows her testosterone to have more of an influence. During menopause, the ovaries continue to produce small amounts of testosterone, and given the decline of estrogen, the effect of the testosterone is greater, leading to increased sexual desire. However, in the excitement phase, lack of estrogen often leads to problems with vaginal dryness. Without proper treatment for this dryness, the sexual experience can be adversely affected. During the last phase, orgasm, the woman—unlike her male counterpart—has no refractory period and can have multiple orgasms. All the changes we have mentioned can make life difficult for sexual partners. As our sexual response system changes, we must be prepared to accommodate the changes and learn new ways of remaining sexually active.

Biophysical Strengths and Hazards

Middle adulthood is a time of many biophysical strengths and hazards. Although we are often quick to consider the development of a fatal disease, becoming too ill to manage one's affairs, or losing some mental capacities, midlife also can be a time of great energetic physical health and positive development.

Becoming Physically Fit in Midlife

As adults mature and begin to think about their lives differently, becoming physically healthy often takes on greater importance. Middle-age adults may be developing a new definition of who they are as a physical self and set new expectations about what they want to accomplish. Indeed, many midlife adults become passionate about yoga, spinning classes, or vigorous walks—and such interests can take on increasing importance as one grows older.

One outcome of developing a regular exercise program is that it can increase one's self-efficacy—an individual's sense of effectiveness as a physical person. This in turn promotes more physical activity (McAuley & Blissmer, 2000). The end result is often an increase in the person's "physical self-esteem": a positive sense of one's body conditioning and body attractiveness. Developing these characteristics is important given today's sedentary lifestyles. As a society we need to develop new opportunities for developing exercise environments where there are few barriers and increased incentives for getting out—to walk, bike, hike, or climb. For instance, researchers have documented that people can be cued to get more exercise simply by posting "take the stairs" signs by escalators (Blamey, Mutrie, & Aitchison, 1995).

Cancer

In midlife, concerns about cancer are common. Cancer is only second to heart disease as the most common cause of death in men and women. In fact, more than 12 million people have a diagnosis of cancer at any given time in the United States.

In the end, cancer will have taken the lives of one of every four Americans. But chances of recovery have risen from one out of two, ten years ago, to three out of four today. Although many people still believe cancer is incurable, increasingly the public is recognizing that many people survive cancer. Lance Armstrong, the famous bicyclist, suffered from cancer, received treatment, returned to biking, and won the grueling Tour de France bike race a record six consecutive times. This and other public-awareness campaigns have reduced some of the stigma associated with cancer. Overall, about 40% of people with cancer are cured, that is, free of the disease for five or more years. The incidence of cancer has fallen during the past several years, but much of this decline is attributed to the increasing numbers of people who have quit smoking. Exhibit 11.3 shows the percentage of total cancer incidence among men and women in the United States.

How does cancer occur? Cancer occurs when a cell is disrupted and begins uncontrolled growth and spread of abnormal cells that crowd out normal tissues and organs. It is believed that damage to gene p53, which keeps cells with defective DNA from multiplying, is involved in 60% of cancers. New cancer therapy is targeting the p53 gene and shows promise in reducing tumor growth (Fisher, 2001).

One of the biggest health fears of middle-aged women is breast cancer. Almost 200,000 women were diagnosed with breast cancer, and about 50,000 women died of this disease. Women who live to age 85 have a one-in-nine chance of developing cancer of the breast in their lifetime (Greenlee, 2000). Not only is this risk high, it also represents a dramatic increase in breast cancer risk; in 1970, the risk was one in sixteen. What is causing this alarming increase?

Some medical experts believe that the increase is the result of heightened awareness of and earlier detection of the disease. This explanation might account for the fact that, although the rate of breast cancer has increased, earlier detection of the disease has improved the survival rates—so the mortality rate has remained stable or in some areas decreased (Greenlee, 2000). Others argue that the increased incidence

EXHIBIT 11.3 Percentage of cancer by men and women

SOURCE: Adapted from Greenlee (2000), p. 16.

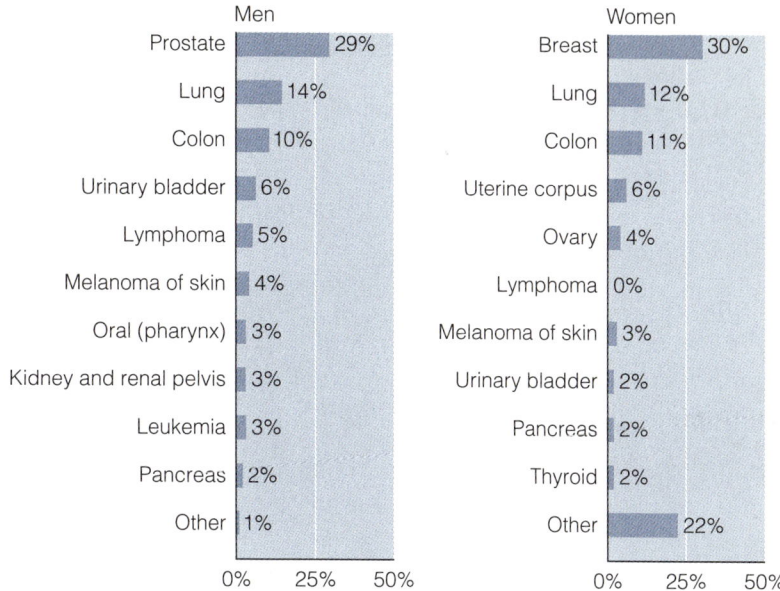

of breast cancer is the result of environmental factors. Some support for this idea comes from the fact that women who move from an area with low breast cancer rates to an area with high breast cancer rates experience an increase in their personal risk. Environmental factors that have been suggested as contributing to breast cancer include a diet high in fat, the presence of pesticides and other toxic chemicals in food and water, exposure to radiation from nuclear testing in the 1950s, and increased levels of stress.

Several factors that increase a woman's personal risk for breast cancer have been identified. One is age. Although the overall chance of developing breast cancer is 1 in 9, this risk applies to an 85-year-old woman. A woman at age 30 has only a 1-in-2,500 chance, and a woman at menopausal age has a 1-in-50 chance (Winawer & Shike, 1995). Other risk factors include having a family history of breast cancer, undergoing menarche (the onset of menstrual periods) before age 12 or menopause after age 50, being childless or having a first child after age 30, being overweight, having a sedentary lifestyle, drinking alcohol, and eating a diet high in fat.

Women are now encouraged to decrease their risk of breast cancer by lowering their intake of dietary fat, increasing their physical activity, performing monthly breast examinations, and having annual mammograms (screening X-rays of the breasts) after menopause (Greenlee, 2000).

Early detection of breast cancer can reduce the need for extensive surgical intervention. In many instances, however, the treatment for breast cancer involves the surgical removal of part or all of the breast. Because of this disfiguring treatment, a woman may perceive breast cancer as a threat to her sense of herself as a feminine, sexual, nurturing being. The psychosocial/psychosexual adjustments to the disease may be more difficult for a woman than the actual physical recovery from the surgery (Winawer & Shike, 1995). Women with breast cancer need support for their emotional as well as their physical well-being. Many women benefit from support groups for breast cancer patients. But some research suggests that the most important source of support is the family, in particular the woman's partner (Pistrang, 1995). The woman needs to be able to maintain good communication with her partner and to feel that her partner is empathic and will not withdraw from her because of disfiguring treatments. To mediate the psychological stress of breast cancer, social workers can help partners to continue to communicate with and support each other.

The implications of a diagnosis of breast cancer for women who lack a partner or other significant support are described in the following Focus section.

Prostate Cancer

A disturbing silent issue for middle-aged men is prostate cancer. Although one in five American men will develop prostate cancer in his lifetime, most are only vaguely aware of the disease, its treatment, and its

FOCUS ON NARRATIVE

AN AFRICAN AMERICAN WOMAN'S EXPERIENCE WITH BREAST CANCER

In July 1991, I was taking a shower, and all of a sudden there was this lump in my right breast. I'm fortunate because I only had a lumpectomy [the lump removed, instead of the whole breast]. It just put a little crease in the upper part of my right breast. They also took 25 lymph nodes out. Only two of them were cancerous, which was absolutely great. Then, I was in a state of denial, thinking, I'm fine now. But the doctors said, 'You have to have radiation and chemotherapy.'

So I went for a bone scan. I'm looking up, and I see all these frigging signs that say, 'You are now entering a radiation zone.' That's when I became aware of what was really wrong with me. I started crying and could not stop. The doctor was totally detached. He was like: 'What's wrong with you? Why are you crying?'

No one was with me. Girlfriend, this whole thing has been by myself. My mother had to work. My friends had to work. My daughter had to work. My children—two daughters and a son—couldn't really deal with it. I was dating a doctor at the time. He had been very supportive, but when I had my surgery, it took him an extra day to show up. I got out of the hospital, and he stopped communicating with me. I had to go through this alone.

I got angry, because I kept getting these calls to go to support groups out of my area. All the groups that were available to women in Los Angeles are either on Wilshire Boulevard, which is in the financial district, or in Santa Monica, which is a good 20 miles from South Central L.A., where I live. It takes two hours to get to Santa Monica on a bus.

My issues are different from the issues in the white community. My experience is, right now, all my bills are due. Some black women just started a job, won't get a paycheck for three weeks, and have no transportation. If women with children leave them at home, they have to pay someone.

During my treatment, I started the Women of Color Breast Cancer Survivors' Support Group, which now has four sites in Central and South Central L.A. Our groups have three facilitators and me, trained through the National Black Women's Health Project. I make presentations about prevention. In the underserved community, you have women whose health gets pushed to the side. I enlighten them. It's about care of one's body. They don't even know they're at risk.

And I want them to see my attitude. I'm overweight from the chemo, but you cannot tell I've had cancer, because everything about me exudes health, energy, and life.

SOURCE: Adapted with permission from "The politics of breast cancer," by P. J. Viviansayles, Ms. (May/June 1993), 54–55. Copyright © 1993 Ms. Magazine.

---

consequences. Unlike women, who often talk freely among themselves about intimate health problems, most men shy away from discussion of their physical disorders, let alone problems involving a gland that produces seminal fluid and affects urinary flow. And they prefer not to undergo, or even think about, the digital rectal exam—the traditional test for detecting prostate problems.

However, whether a man is comfortable with these issues or not, the fact remains that prostate cancer is common and deadly. The American Cancer Society estimated that almost 50,000 men will die each year, about the same number as women who will die from breast cancer. Why are so many Americans developing cancer? Simply put, as the life span of Americans increases, so do the rates of cancers. More men are afflicted with prostate cancer because men are living longer, into the 70s and 80s, when the disease most often strikes. As men live longer and do not succumb to heart disease and stroke, more will die from prostate cancer.

The biggest factor in the high prostate-cancer diagnosis rate is the PSA test, which is a screening test for prostate-specific antigen in the blood, which in many cases can detect the disease early in its course, long before the tumor becomes palpable. Early detection and treatment will help reduce the number of prostate cancer deaths.

The prostate gland naturally begins to enlarge in a 50-year-old man, and the growing number of cells

FOCUS ON NARRATIVE

CANCER AFFECTS US ALL

Two women discuss their experience with cancer and how painting helped them cope.

In 1990, cancer became a catalyst for change in my family when my mother was diagnosed with an advanced endometrial tumor. Watching her struggle to maintain the consistency of her life against the inevitable force of her cancer was, for me, a difficult and unforgettable passage. In the aftermath of her death, I began to make paintings of my mother as a child, as a young woman, as an older woman, when she was ill. These reconstructed paintings not only helped me to deal with my grief, but they were also a tribute to her memory and a reminder of what there is both to lose and cherish.

— GAIL SKUDERA

It took enormous discipline to alter my attitude more toward the positive, having suffered four cancer surgeries and follow-up treatments over a 20-year period. But I am now functioning better than ever, lavishing in my health. I paint as though I have only this day to touch paint and see color. I constantly make new discoveries by thoroughly indulging my curiosities.

My paintings, better seasonal as I finally realize, document time through my study of color in the landscape. My reaction to facing the unknown, suddenly, and not recognizing myself in the mirror, and having pain, was to paint as though there was no tomorrow.

—LORNA RITZ

SOURCE: *APA Monitor*, 30 (June 1999).

contribute to what is generally a steady but slight rise in the PSA count. But if the prostate cells become cancerous and begin multiplying, the PSA level jumps dramatically.

Because the average prostate cancer takes a decade to develop symptoms that seriously affect the quality of life, men either take a "watchful waiting" approach or receive treatment. Watchful waiting includes frequent blood tests, rectal exams, and an occasional biopsy, but no intervention unless the cancer becomes more aggressive. For those men who choose treatment, the options create dilemmas: Virtually all of them affect quality of life: hormones, radiation, cryotherapy (freezing the cancerous cells), and surgery may cause impotency, incontinence, or both. Although the decisions are ultimately the man's, doctors urge men whose life expectancy is ten years or more to get treatment.

A Family-Systems Look at Couples and Illness

When one spouse is sick, is it a family affair? It is, according to researchers Howard Liddle and Gail Dakov. Liddle and Dakov studied patterns of coping in couples in which one spouse had cancer. Contrary to popular belief, they found that openly talking about the illness is not always the best coping mechanism. Instead, Liddle and Dakov conclude that what is important is not how much the couple communicates about illness-related concerns but how much "their desire to share is similar." This means that adjustment of partners who do not wish to discuss the illness is just as good as adjustment of spouses who wish to discuss concerns openly. Adjustment problems occur, however, when partners experience different levels of desire to talk about the illness.

Liddle and Dakov note that couples' adjustment to cancer is not based solely on communication styles but is also related to other factors. Relationship history, for example, plays a role in how couples adjust to illness. In many troubled couples, partners showed hostility toward each other after diagnosis. In happier couples, diagnosis reportedly brought spouses closer together.

Other research on couples in which the husband had a heart attack six months earlier looked at the emergence of overprotectiveness within the relationship. Researchers found that overprotectiveness, commonly thought to be hostile in origin, is actually a response to the well partner's desire to help when illness threatens a close relationship. The illness becomes an integral part of the system and emphasizes the interdependence of partners as key in understanding the dynamics of the dyad.

Implications for Practice: Psychological Interventions for the Seriously Ill

Social workers would be quick to tell us that although medical care for cancer patients has improved, psychosocial support is lacking. Such a conclusion is confirmed in the report *Ensuring Quality Cancer Care* (1999), which found important differences in care provided by health care systems, health care providers, and insurance companies. Too often, physicians do not recognize the psychological long-term effects of cancer and its treatment. For example, physicians do not accurately assess depression among cancer patients. Increasingly, it has become recognized that pain management has been inadequate to meet patients' needs.

A difficult task that patients struggle with is coming to terms with a serious illness.

Can stress management or psychosocial interventions slow down the progression of AIDS or cancer? It can, according to researchers throughout the United States. Psychological interventions such as teaching stress management, coping skills, relaxation training, problem solving, and fatigue management, as well as group support and social support, were tested in several states (DeAngelis, 1995; Sleek, 1995). The biological theory behind this holistic approach to healing is based on the hypothesis that discovering one has HIV or cancer may lead to social isolation and poor coping strategies that could suppress the immune system. Researchers have linked the amount of social support to changes in white blood cell (the natural "killer cell") activity, an indicator of how well the immune system is handling stress. Research also shows that relaxation techniques taught to cancer patients improve their moods, reduce emotional distress, and improve their ability to cope with their illness. For example, for women with breast or cervical cancer, group therapy allows them to express their feelings about their illness and treatment in a context of mutual support. By receiving group therapy as part of a medical treatment, women comply better with their treatment regimen and engage in healthier behaviors.

Group support and treatment is being widely used for cancer patients across the country. Studies have found that such treatment can improve the patient's quality of life, instilling a more positive mood, creating better interactions with family members, and increasing energy levels (Spiegel, 1999). In fact, one study (Spiegel, 1993) found that group treatment increased survival by eighteen months for women with metastatic breast cancer. However, a replication of this study (Cunningham et al., 1998) did not find a longer survival rate for group therapy participants. At this point, additional studies are needed to confirm if group treatment can enhance a person's longevity.

Even homebound clients may want to participate in group therapy. Yvette Colon, a social worker, provides a telephone and online support group (Murray, 1999). She has described how people's increasing comfort with technology is expanding the available means of delivering client support. Telephone and online groups provide a forum for clients to address coping ability, emotional overload, fatigue, loss, and death.

For unknown reasons, not all women consider their health care in the same manner. In particular, low-income minority women have lower rates of follow-up care than do higher-income white women (Cancer Rates, 1998). This low follow-up rate may be a primary reason for the significant late-stage diagnosis and cancer fatalities among the low-income minority population. Group support and therapy that take into account the cultural, psychosocial, and systematic barriers encountered by these women as they obtain additional health care could greatly affect their chances for survival.

In general, stress-management and related interventions help patients to raise their awareness of stress symptoms and to challenge their negative thinking to better combat stress. Such interventions do not necessarily help people live longer or reverse the effects of serious diseases. However, research has shown that they help people to better cope with their illness and boost their immune functioning, which can improve quality of life for many people.

Unlike other research with social implications, there are hard outcomes to this type of health psychology, because a person either has a disease or does not. Unfortunately, insurance plans often refuse to cover psychological services, even when the interventions are proven to be successful. Social workers and mental-health professionals should lobby on clients' behalf for more holistic treatments. A healthy state of mind may be humankind's best medicine. Health care for women has undergone much change. The following section examines some of these dramatic changes. ■

Women and Health Care: A Short History

Health care for women has changed dramatically in the last twenty-five to thirty-five years (Boston Women's Health Book Collective, 1992). Imagine the following: a woman being told that childbirth is better experienced in an unconscious state, natural childbirth being considered too dangerous, and a friend—unexpectedly pregnant—having to fly to Mexico to obtain an abortion that is illegal in the United States (Boston's Women's Health Book Collective, 1992). These are the kinds of events that led to the 1970 publication of *Our Bodies, Ourselves*. This classic, first priced at 75 cents, sold more than 250,000 copies before it was commercially published. Women embraced the idea that they could be experts on their own bodies and guide their own health care. They began to take action on policies that directly affected their health. For example, congressional hearings were disrupted when women voiced complaints about the side effects of the Pill. This crusade led to the development of a self-help movement that inspired the opening of dozens of women-controlled health centers. These efforts were largely in the service of white, middle-class women, but by the 1980s, women of color began to use their voices for change. They addressed issues such as the high incidence of sterilization abuse against poor women, especially women of color. By 1981, Bylle Avery, an African American woman, was elected to the board of directors of the National Women's Health Network. Today, there are more than 150 chapters of the National Black Women's Health Project, as well as many chapters of associations such as the National Latina Health Organization, the Native-American Women's Health Education Resource Center, and the Asian Health Project—all the result of the grassroots effort to organize women at the community level with a commitment to self-help.

The results of this early movement led to changes that directly influence the lives of individual women. For example, midwives and nurse practitioners deliver babies in women's homes; the birth control pill no longer has excessive amounts of estrogen; women with breast cancer do not automatically lose their breasts; DES (diethylstilbestrol, a drug that produced offspring with increased cancer rates) is no longer given during pregnancy; abortions are readily available; and silicone breast implants are being phased out in favor of saline implants. Today, much of this tradition on women's health care is carried forward by the Women's Health Initiative, which has conducted groundbreaking studies related to the use of hormones. It represents a major breakthrough in terms of federally funded research on women's health.

Midlife and the Widening Midsection

"Super size"; "double gulp." Have you noticed how large American's food portions are? How many fast-food eateries do you drive by on your way to work? When was the last time that an eight-ounce carbonated beverage satisfied your thirst? According to the Agriculture Department, the food and restaurant industries spend $36 billion a year on advertisements designed to entice hungry people to abandon fruits and vegetables for chips, sodas, and Happy Meals. The average American watches 10,000 food ads on TV a year. What does this matter? Well, Americans are listening to the advertisements and getting fatter in the process. Drive-through windows and convenience stores have contributed to our expanding waistlines. Why? (1) Take-out food tends to be high in fat, carbohydrates, sodium, and calories; (2) it tends to be eaten quickly, which means more of it is consumed; and (3) it tends to get eaten, all of it, no matter how much of it there is.

The number of Americans who are overweight has steadily increased over the last thirty to forty years. The median weight gain since the 1980s is 7.6 pounds for both men and women (Dziegielewski et al., 2002). Currently, some 58 million people in the United States weigh at least 20% more than their ideal body weight, making them obese. Just when the country needs to reduce its health care bills, our eating habits may be pushing the costs higher. Overweight people are at a higher risk for diabetes, hypertension, heart disease, stroke, gout, arthritis, and some forms of cancer.

But all this talk of food ignores the other side of the weight-gain equation. Most Americans are bulging not because they consume too many calories but also because they burn off too few. A century of industrialization and invention, and with it new technology, has taken people out of the fields and put them behind desks and in front of computers. We are doing less manual work. Any exercise we get must be purposeful, and therefore scheduled into our hectic lives.

Are people taking the time to burn off those fast-food calories? Not many are. In one survey, about half of U.S. adults said they exercised sporadically or not at all. The inactivity was especially marked among African Americans, Hispanics, people with low income, and the unemployed. The prevalence of obesity was nearly 50% for black and Hispanic women, compared with 35.5% for white women. In some Native American communities, up to 70% of the adults are dangerously overweight. In all groups, genetic factors play a role. For example, scientists have known for years that identical twins separated at birth are far more likely to grow into the body types of their biological parents than of their adoptive parents.

So if we aren't exercising, what are we doing to try to fight the fat? Each year an estimated 80 million people go on a diet, but unfortunately, no matter how much weight they lose, 95% of them gain it back within five years. How can one teach people to listen to their body? To eat when they're hungry, to eat appropriate portions, to move and stretch? A major problem, nutritionists agree, is that most people think of diets as temporary restrictions imposed from the outside, and so they do not internalize their behavior change.

In middle adulthood, exercise may be particularly important to one's well-being. Taking steps to improve health is a good predictor of psychological well-being. In one study (Ransford & Palisi, 1996) engaging in regular exercise such as walking, dancing or swimming was more strongly associated with self-rated health and positive outlook in older than younger adults. A regular exercise outlet for middle-aged adults enhances their perception of being active for their age and creates a special sense of accomplishment. Also, exercise is likely to reduce the feelings of vulnerability to illness that increase with age, providing further psychological benefits (Berk, 2004). Some biophysical hazards come not from health behavior but are the tragic result of accidents. The following section looks at what happens to families when one family member suffers from a brain injury.

Effects of Brain Injury on the Family

In the movie *Regarding Henry*, a ruthless, high-priced lawyer suffers brain damage after being shot in the head. Following the injury, he remembers little of his former self or life. He is a very different man—one who moves slower, thinks slower, and cannot even remember how to read. He is unable to take up his old life again. At one point he comments, "I thought I could go back to my life . . . but I don't fit in." Henry cannot function as before in his job and ultimately quits. He loses most of his old friends, who cannot get used to the new Henry. Commenting on his recovery, his friends whisper at a party, "One minute you're an attorney. The next you're an imbecile." Henry and his family must learn to cope with a very different life.

What is the best way to cope with the brain injury of a loved one? Research suggests that there is no simple answer to this question. According to Betsy Zeigler, families who adjust well to the situation learn to see the post-injury person as distinct from the individual they previously knew. They are then able to let go of the old image of the family member and to integrate the new person into the family system. Although this perspective provides a practical goal for the family, the nature of brain injury makes this task difficult. The loss felt after a brain injury is in some ways harder to reconcile than the death of a loved one. Death is finite, but the extent and permanence of the loss with brain injury remains unclear. This fosters hope for recovery, but it also leaves family members in limbo: "After a death, you eventually get on with your life. [Brain injury] goes on forever, and you're dealing with it in one stage or another for the rest of your life" (Souza, cited in Mitiguy, 1990, p. 12).

Family members' grief may never quite be resolved, because of the unpredictable nature of brain injury. The injured individual remains a constant reminder of loss for family members, but society may not recognize the family's grief because the injured individual remains present in a physically familiar form.

Familial responses include denial and hope. Reactions to brain injury are not the same for any two individuals, but research suggests certain parental, sibling, son/daughter, and spousal similarities. For parents, children represent immortality through the perpetuation of family traditions and values. Although returning to the role of caregiver for a child with brain injury may recall an earlier nurturing role, this change in dynamics may also lead to overprotectiveness on a parent's part. Responses of mothers and fathers may differ, owing to the differing nature of parent-child relationships. Injury can be both a binding and a divisive factor for parents.

Siblings' reactions to brain injury tend to vary according to age, prior relationship with the injured sibling, and role in the family. Sons and daughters of brain-injured parents also have diverse experiences, dependent on age, relationship with both the healthy and the brain-injured parent, and role changes within the family. Spouses of brain-injured individuals face challenges associated with the emotional, social, and physical aspects of the marital bond.

Although their feelings may not ever be completely resolved, many families do achieve a level of adjustment that incorporates a realistic perspective of the nature and the duration of loss. This realism facilitates the functioning of a family system that includes and changes with the brain-injured person.

STUDY TABLE: Biophysical dimension of middle adulthood

Biophysical Growth and Development	At this stage, individuals see and feel significant changes in themselves physically. Most individuals in middle adulthood are less fit and have a fuller body shape. Revision of the physical self-image takes place in midlife, and many people at this age confess fears of disease and decline. The leading causes of death during middle age are cancer and heart disease. People can be classified into two personality types, type A and B, and these individuals develop physical illness differently as a result of stress. Most critical are personality characteristics that represent *hostility*, characterized by angry outbursts, disagreeable behavior, and criticism and feelings of contempt toward others; hostility leads to greater health problems. Menopause is a gradual process that occurs when a woman (average age 51) has not experienced a menstrual cycle for one year and the ovaries stop functioning and no longer produce the hormones estrogen and progesterone. These hormonal changes may lead to hot flashes, night sweats, incontinence, and vaginal dryness, as well as health concerns such as risk of heart disease and osteoporosis. Reactions to menopause can be positive or negative. No significant changes in anger, anxiety, depression, self-consciousness, or worry about the body have been found to occur with menopause. Women of color are more likely than white women to get hormone replacement therapy. Estrogen replacement therapy has been used to protect women against health risks and treat the negative symptoms of menopause. Recent studies have reported negative outcomes from HRT. The physical changes of middle adulthood also lead to changes in the sexual response cycle.

(continues)

STUDY TABLE: Biophysical dimension of middle adulthood *(continued)*

Biophysical Strengths and Hazards	As adults mature, becoming physically healthy often takes on greater importance. Developing a regular exercise program can increase one's self-efficacy. Cancer is second to heart disease as the most common cause of death in men and women. Many women experience breast cancer (1 in 9), and men face prostate cancer (1 in 5) as they get older. Coping with cancer is difficult, and research suggests that couples openly talking about it may not be the best coping mechanism. However, stress management or psychosocial interventions have been shown to slow down the progression of AIDS and cancer. The number of Americans who are overweight has steadily increased over the last 30–40 years. This epidemic is linked to overeating, lack of exercise, and biology. Physical injuries, such as brain injuries, can take a toll on families as they try to let go of their old image of the person and integrate the "new" person into the family system.

CONCEPT MAP

PSYCHOLOGICAL DIMENSION

Cognitive Development and Information Processing

Adult Development

Past researchers have attempted to study adult cognitive development based on the seminal ideas of Piaget. However, recent researchers interested in adult development have discovered that using Piaget's child-oriented theory may not be the best approach for studying adult development. In fact, Piaget's work has contributed to the accepted social stereotype that childhood is the primary period for intellectual development (Willis & Schaie, 1999). Childhood and adolescence have been seen as the time periods for acquiring the knowledge needed to operate successfully in adulthood. For a long time, it was believed that cognitive development or intelligence peaked in late adolescence and early adulthood. Of course, this belief appeared logical because there is an obvious shift of biological aging in middle adulthood, signaled most obviously by one's graying hair. A critical question related to the attempt to understand how cognitive development changes over the life course is this: Do individuals' cognitive abilities decline after young adulthood, as some stereotypes suggest?

A series of studies by Schaie has dramatically changed the way many people view cognitive development in middle adulthood. Schaie conducted longitudinal studies that discovered, for example, that verbal ability actually peaks in late middle age (Willis & Schaie, 1999). Exhibit 11.4 shows changes across the life span in five different aspects of cognitive ability: spatial visualization, reasoning, verbal ability, word fluency, and number ability. The overall conclusion from this data is that intellectual functioning is stable in middle age. Decline in intellectual ability begins only after age 60. Other interesting findings suggest that age-related declines occur earlier for some abilities—for example, numerical computations and spatial reasoning. The gender differences show that men perform at a somewhat higher level than women on spatial ability, but women perform at a somewhat higher level on reasoning ability.

The results of these findings probably will be comforting to the many men and women at midlife who are required to perform at a very high level of intellectual competence. Adults in middle age assume major family, professional, and social responsibilities that demand sharp minds and the ability to acquire new skills and information. Schaie (1994) has contended that although we examine children's cognitive functioning by studying how information is acquired, to understand adult intellect, we need to examine how information is used. During adulthood, individuals are not exclusively concerned with acquiring skills but are concentrating more on achieving goals. This means that a majority of their cognitive abilities are focused on applying knowledge to real-world problems, which requires a new set of cognitive abilities—social and abstract cognitive skills. Schaie (1983a) argued that cognitive and social functioning merge dramatically in midlife, when tasks have what Schaie calls "role-related achievement potential." Adults perform better at these tasks because the tasks are strongly related to the roles adults are assuming. This merging of social and cognitive functioning is also related to adults at midlife who are assuming more responsibility for others. Many adults become increasingly involved in civic and community organizations. Schaie's theory suggests that young adults move from "What should I know?" to the middle-adulthood focus of "How should I use what I know?" to later adulthood, when the emphasis is "Why should I know?" (Schaie, 1977, p. 135).

Effect of Professional Obsolescence

The concept of professional obsolescence may be particularly relevant during the midlife years (Willis, 1989). **Professional obsolescence** refers to the use of information, theories, and technology that are less useful in performing tasks than what is currently available in one's field of practice. Obsolescence is not linked to age-related loss of ability but rather to an inability to learn and apply new information and techniques.

In our rapidly changing information society, it is critical to keep up with relevant knowledge. Adults in midlife have finished schooling but may need additional training to remain current on the job. As people's life span grows, so does their longevity in the

EXHIBIT 11.4 Intellectual performance across late adulthood

Source: From *Longitudinal studies of adult psychological development*, by K. W. Schaie. Copyright © 1983 The Guilford Press. Reprinted by permission.

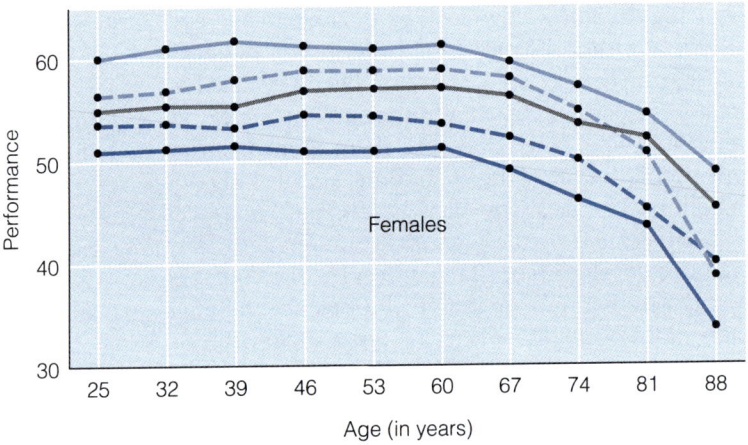

workforce. As a result, special efforts may be required to prevent professional obsolescence.

A person's professional half-life may be getting increasingly shorter as the information explosion expands. One's **professional half-life** is the time it takes for 50% of one's professional knowledge to become invalid or obsolete (Dubin, 1972). This time varies according to one's career; for example, the professional half-life of a computer scientist is perhaps only two or three years. We can see that "learning is, indeed, becoming a lifelong process" (Willis, 1989, p. 109). Midlife adults recognize this, and many are returning to college to further their careers and education (U.S. Department of Education, 2002). Such "nontraditional" students are requiring schools to consider new ways to provide needed support in their efforts.

Communication

By midlife, the process of communication is clearly established. Communication at this stage is dominated by family and by friends. In terms of the family, this may be the period in life when one can truly reconnect with one's partner or spouse. After many years of raising children, midlife adults often are ready to establish more meaningful relationships with their spouse, adult children, and friends. Before middle adulthood, many adults are simply too busy managing family life to establish a strong network of friends. Also, at midlife, adults begin the process of "life review"; they may reflect on communications that they would like to mend or at least make better. Midlife adults seek more meaning in their lives, and as a consequence, they are interested in communication on a deeper level. The friendships developed at this time are based on values such as honesty, sincerity, closeness, and mutual support.

The Forgiveness Process

In fact, many adults may become increasingly interested in engaging in the process of forgiveness as they reflect on relationships that may not have progressed the way they wanted. Research studies are beginning to support the social and psychological benefits of forgiveness (Enright & Fitzgibbons, 2000). Forgiveness can be a helpful process for individuals who are seeking help with questions like the following: How long should a woman maintain anger at a husband who leaves her for a younger woman? Should she express rage toward the husband, and, if so, for how long after their divorce? How can she make things right in her own life after this unforgivable act?

By midlife, many people have accumulated a history of harms from people with whom they have had close relationships. We have all heard of individuals who are not communicating with a sister, brother, child, parent, or close friend because of some unforgivable act. Forgiveness is an essential mechanism for righting such wrongs. Many people are not at peace with themselves for not having asked the forgiveness of a loved one. Others remain angry at themselves for not being able to forgive a friend or a relative for some harmful action. If practitioners desire to help clients with forgiveness issues, they should have some understanding of the forgiveness process.

Robert Enright (2001), a leader in the forgiveness field, has written a self-directed book that examines the process of forgiveness. He identified a four-stage process:

1. Uncovering anger
2. Deciding to forgive
3. Working on forgiveness
4. Discovery and release

This process of forgiving ends with the emergence of a new self. Although many people begin this process, not everyone finishes it. Forgiveness will not occur without a person making significant changes in his or her feelings and beliefs. "Forgiveness is a rational process; it is a conversion in the way you have thought about yourself and other people and about harm and vulnerability" (Flanigan, 1992, p. 72). At the end of this process, individuals do not wish any harm on their injurers and develop a new perspective about the causes of events in their lives.

In addition, research (Enright & Fitzgibbons, 2000; Enright, 2001) shows that people who forgive someone who has hurt them seem to reap significant mental-health benefits. And the act of forgiving appears to be one of the basic processes that keeps personal relationships functioning, according to studies of long-married couples. Forgiveness takes conscious effort, whereas the defensive mechanisms of resentment or revenge are somewhat automatic. Forgiveness is not the same as reconciliation. Forgiveness involves only the person who was hurt. Reconciliation takes both people and requires a change in the person who did the hurting. Forgiving can be liberating. Carrying around a desire for revenge or a need to avoid someone is not healthy. Hostility and aggression are linked to a multitude of health problems. However, people who are able to forgive benefit through a decrease in anxiety, depression, and hostility and an increase in hope, self-esteem, and existential well-being.

So what is the key to forgiveness? How do we begin to forgive someone who has hurt us deeply? Empathy motivates forgiveness: people who feel empathy for the person who offended them are more able to forgive than people who do not. People are also more likely to forgive an offender if the offender apologizes—because the apology encourages empathy. In sum, an apology leads to empathy, and empathy mediates forgiveness.

But are there some situations in which not forgiveness but revenge lets people heal? The following section discusses how many grieving families try to find comfort and closure in the execution of a loved one's murderer.

Execution and Therapeutic Revenge

A murderer, strapped to a gurney, hooked up to intravenous tubes, and waiting for the deadly drugs to flow into his body turns to the grieving family of his victim and says, "I hope you can go on with your lives and we can put an end to this" (Brownlee, McGraw, & Vest, 1997). This is what many victims' family members hope to get out of an execution: an end to their suffering and grief. But do they find it?

Consistently since 1987, more than 70% of Americans polled say they support the death penalty. Although the percentages regarding capital punishment have not changed much within the last decade, the nature of the discussion has. The discussion used to be formed in terms of practicality: Was the death penalty effective in deterring crime? Was killing an offender the best way to protect society? But recently, the argument for the death penalty has centered not on the criminal's "debt" to society but on the right of a victim's loved ones to gain peace of mind through his or her death. This is, in effect, therapeutic vengeance.

The impulse for revenge is potent and natural. The grieving process for a murder victim is similar to the grieving process many go through when they loose a loved one: disbelief, anger, grief, and finally, for some, acceptance. But loved ones of homicide victims rarely move through these stages easily. "Murder often taps a well of rage that can drown out all other emotions" (Browne, McGraw, & Vest, 1997, p. 28). Survivors often mistakenly think that if "justice is served" and the murderer is executed, they can move past the rage and get on with their lives.

In recent years, a victims'-rights movement has lobbied to let victims testify directly to the accused during the trial and make statements about their pain and suffering during sentencing, and to allow victims' families to view executions. In some cases, allowing these rights does help the survivors heal, but, in others, survivors realize that revenge is not so sweet. In order to resolve such deeply held feelings, communication is a key process. For some adults, the effectiveness of communication is hampered by illiteracy. For example, sometimes families use letter writing in order to more easily express their feelings, but this requires writing skills that the illiterate adult often does not have.

The Illiterate Adult

Many of us take for granted our ability to communicate through writing, reading, and speaking. However, as many as 20% of adults in the United States are functionally **illiterate**—they cannot read and write well enough to participate in society. The National Institute for Literacy (1998) estimates that 40 million or more American adults do not possess the reading skills needed to function independently. As modern society becomes more complex, concerns about illiteracy become increasingly critical.

The notion of being functionally literate originated in World War I when the U.S. Army found that many soldiers could read and write but not to an extent that would make them effective soldiers (Radwin, 1993). Programs were started to teach soldiers to be functionally literate.

What does it mean to be functionally literate? Definitions of functional literacy vary widely. The U.S. Bureau of the Census defines **functional literacy** as a sixth-grade reading level. The most common definition of functional literacy is the ability to perform everyday reading, writing, and arithmetic tasks. These different definitions produce different estimates of functional illiteracy that range from 13% to 50% (Radwin, 1993). Whatever the exact percentage, we do know that illiteracy afflicts mainly people who are poor, uneducated, undereducated, and belonging to a minority. Many illiterate adults grew up in socioeconomically disadvantaged areas with family members who did not encourage reading and with no one else to help them learn essential literacy skills. Illiterate adults may have completed elementary school, and many even received a high school diploma. However, in school they did not learn some essential skills, such as writing letters, filling out applications, reading instructions on a package, reading the newspaper, and writing a check.

Functionally illiterate adults are often embarrassed that they do not understand essential communication. They are often concerned that people will "discover" that they are illiterate, and therefore they hide their inability to read and write. Disabled people may be illiterate because they were denied proper educational services as a child. Parents may have lacked confidence that the child could learn and so inadvertently contributed toward his or her illiteracy.

Non-English-Speaking Adults

In many respects, adults living in the United States who do not speak English may face difficulties similar to those encountered by adults who are illiterate. Often, immigrants who do not speak English face discrimination in employment. They may be highly educated and competent in their native language but unable to communicate in English, and thus find themselves forced into low-paying jobs and lives of poverty. The immigrant may not have important functional skills such as reading street signs, advertisements, newspaper want ads, and so forth. Being shut off from one's surrounding world can lead to anger, frustration, and depression. Often, non-English-speaking persons must become dependent on others to translate and communicate for them. This can lead to relationship problems and a difficult lifestyle wherein one cannot communicate with other people. Imagine what it would be like to have to keep your fears, successes, and observations all to yourself—it would make for a lonely existence.

The Hard-of-Hearing Adult

Imagine being 36 years old and noticing that you are having trouble understanding your friend when you are speaking on the telephone. At first you ask the speaker to repeat his statement, but as time goes on and friends and co-workers wonder why you are always so absent-minded, you find it easier not to initiate conversation. Such slow loss of hearing is a fact of life for many people in the United States.

The estimates of the number of people who are deaf and hard of hearing range from 22 to 28 million (Berke, 2004; Seppa, 1997). The incidence of self-reported trouble with hearing is 33% for people aged 65 to 74, and 62% for people older than age 85. In contrast to the high prevalence of hearing impairment, only 1% of the population is profoundly deaf, and, of those, only 22% lost their hearing before age 19. People who were born deaf, then, actually constitute a small percentage of the hearing-impaired population (Luey, Glass, & Elliott, 1995).

Sadly, despite greater social acceptance and mainstreaming of people with disabilities, the stigma of hearing loss has endured over the years. Hearing loss and hearing aids are commonly associated with aging, being inadequate, or being incompetent (Seppa, 1997). Therefore, people often deny their hearing loss or avoid doing something about it. Practitioners can alert families to basic techniques that improve the lives of people with hearing problems, such as talking directly at them so they can see the speaker's face and read his or her expressions and lips. Speaking clearly and at an unrushed pace also helps the partially deaf to understand conversation. Connecting hard-of-hearing people with others who face the same disability provides a peer network of people who are not deaf but are not fully hearing.

Implications for Practice: Clients with Hearing Loss

Hearing impairment is one of the most common of all chronic disabilities, and it affects people's lives in profound ways. People with hearing loss are subject not only to the particular difficulties that their disability creates but also to any social or psychological problems that might require social-work intervention. It is important, then, that all social workers understand the differences among deaf and hearing-impaired people and have the tools for assessing the meaning of hearing loss for a particular client (Luey, Glass, & Elliott, 1995).

Hard-of-hearing people have little in common with profoundly deaf people, many of whom were born unable to hear, live in a deaf society, use sign language, and flourish in a rich culture of their own. On the contrary, hard-of-hearing people are at risk of isolation and withdrawal from society. They confront psychological issues different from those dealt with by deaf people, including the frustrations of having cultural and personal links to the hearing world slip away.

The most damaging thing about hearing loss is that it interferes with communication. Some people with hearing loss are able to understand speech by discerning meaning from fragments of sound, supplemented by visual clues from people's lip movements and facial expressions. This skill is called speechreading, and some people seem to have a talent for it, yet others do not. At best, however, speechreading is demanding, tiring, and only partially accurate. Generally, the worse hearing becomes, the harder it is to speechread and the more likely it is for people to think of themselves as deaf rather than hard of hearing (Luey, Glass, & Elliott, 1995).

Whereas people who are hard of hearing tend to become isolated, people whose primary language is ASL tend to come together. Such groups have existed for many generations and have established a particular culture. Many people tend to marry within the culture and affiliate with formal and informal organizations that are a part of it. In addition to language, the culture includes particular behaviors, norms, and beliefs (Berke, 2004).

Another significant difference between culturally deaf people and those that have become hard of hearing are their feelings about deafness itself. People in the deaf community and culture tend to perceive deafness not as a disability but as an alternative lifestyle and culture. In contrast, those who become deaf miss their earlier access to spoken communication, and they miss sound. For them, deafness is both a disability and a loss; it is something to be mourned.

In recent years, people with onset hearing loss have formed groups and organizations to address their social, cultural, and political interests. The best-known group for this is Self Help for Hard of Hearing People (SHHH), an international, educational consumer organization devoted to hard-of-hearing people and their relatives and friends who still want to participate in the hearing world. Self Help for Hard of Hearing People (SHHH) largely comprises culturally hearing people with relatively severe hearing losses. SHHH members usually are not comfortable with the word "deaf" and generally communicate by speechreading aided by special amplifying devices. Few SHHH members use manual communication of any form, though some of them are beginning to use speech-to-text technology. SHHH members are largely middle-class and middle-aged or older.

So where do social workers come in? The first thing a social worker needs to do when meeting a deaf or hard-of-hearing client is to establish a way to communicate. What language does the client know and prefer? Because most hearing-impaired people are not culturally deaf, most clients with hearing loss will have good speech ability and prefer English or the spoken language of their culture. If the client speechreads, the social worker can help by finding a quiet, well-lit place to talk. He or she should face the client; speak slowly and clearly; rephrase anything the client misunderstands; and offer to write key words, names, or specific information. Some clients with good speech and knowledge of English prefer to involve an interpreter for important interactions, and they are entitled to that accommodation. Professional interpreters for the deaf are able to use both signed English and ASL and to select the language suited to the individual and the situation. Because hearing loss impacts so many people over the life course, understanding the legal implications of disabilities is important for social workers. ■

Legal Implications: Title V

The U.S. Rehabilitation Act of 1973 addressed the needs of disabled people at different ages. Title V was designed to ensure that programs receiving federal funds could be used by disabled individuals. The four major sections of Title V prohibit discrimination and require accessibility in employment; education; and health, welfare, and social services (McEntee, 1995).

To increase access to services, U.S. federal laws dictate the use of interpreters in mental-health settings. Despite this, a survey of all mental-health centers in one state found that 29% of the twenty-eight respondents flatly stated that they were not accessible to deaf people. Additionally, 39% stated that they did not provide interpreters, even though 72% of the agencies indicated that they had served deaf individuals; of these 72%, only 25% had used certified interpreters (McEntee, 1995).

To be effective advocates, social workers need to be aware of the various pieces of legislation that affect the lives of clients. The profession also needs to be aware that services must be rendered in a different manner for deaf people and for hard-of-hearing people. Social workers need to be aware of their own communication modes and how to use support personnel and equipment.

Attitudes and Emotions

Well-Being and Anxiety

To better understand the impact of attitudes and emotions on midlife adults, an understanding of well-being is essential (Dziegielewski et al., 2002). **Well-being** is most often defined as a person's emotional and psychological capacity to cope with demands across time, circumstance, and setting. For example, feelings about deteriorating health, worries about the future, and stress are some concerns that may emerge in midlife (Hunter et al., 2002).

Two emotions that can take on a more prominent position in midlife are fear and anxiety. According to Dziegielewski et al. (2002), fear is common for both men and women in midlife. The foundation of the fear is the process of aging and the related potential for loss of mental and physical abilities. For women, a loss in their sense of desirability can be a factor; for men, a loss in their sexual prowess can be important. A lot of the fear is created and supported by the media, which promote a relentless drive for eternal youth and beauty (Jones, 2004). Society has created and promotes solutions to these difficulties of middle age—Viagra to enhance men's sexual performance, and Botox to eliminate facial wrinkles on women (Jones, 2004). Both men and women express fear of death and being alone in their later years. Also, career-oriented men and women fear that youthfulness, flexibility, and excessive work hours will be more valued and rewarded than experience and wisdom. Midlife adults often consider the impact of losing their professional abilities and fear job loss.

Such fears can turn into anxiety. Women may begin to have increased anxiety following the early stages of menopause as they adapt to physical and psychological changes. Social workers need to consider that women in midlife benefit from a better understanding of this life stage and such knowledge can reduce fear and anxiety (Dziegielewski et al., 2002). Men have been socialized to believe that age leads to impotence and decreased influence and power. In fact, some men can be driven to suicide as they consider the impact of less success and hampered sexual functioning (Clarke, Shute, & Kelly, 2000).

Midlife as a Crisis

Many theorists believe that a midlife identity change takes place for most adults. Adults may begin to ask themselves, "What do I want to spend the rest of my life doing?" or "Are my relationships giving me the kind of satisfaction I want?" Such questions reflect identity changes that can have a strong influence on emotions.

Carl Jung, an early psychoanalyst, wrote extensively on midlife and has influenced contemporary psychotherapists and writers who believe this to be a time when forgotten or denied aspects of the personality begin to bubble to the surface. Jungian theory sees the midlife crisis as symptoms that occur when these aspects of the person's self that were not allowed to be experienced or expressed, whether because of family, social, occupational or internal pressures to conform or succeed, can no longer be controlled. We are vulnerable at midlife when many of the goals that motivated us in youth and early adulthood either have been achieved or discarded, roles we played may no longer be appropriate or satisfying, and we are increasingly aware that time remaining is finite. Jung characterized the roles we play in adult life as *personae*, Latin for "mask"; our personae are only a part of who we are and may not let us show our true selves.

Is there really such thing as a midlife crisis? The answer to this question is complex. Levinson's (1978) theory of adult development suggests that crisis is a normal part of adult development. However, work by Vallant (1977) found that only a small percentage of adults experience a midlife crisis. Hunter et al. (2002) added to the literature on women in midlife and concluded that at midlife a crisis is likely to occur and includes a period of reflection and self-questioning. She suggested that men may no longer experience the midlife crisis but that women today engage in crisis as a normal developmental stage. Neugarten (1986) reminded us that development may be different, depending on the cohort; therefore, past studies may have reflected a cohort phenomenon rather than a universal life stage. And although not all midlife adults will experience a "crisis," this period of life does seem to be a time for intense self-reflection.

So, particularly during middle age, adults are in a position to reflect on their lives. This reflection often influences important actions they may take. Levinson (1978) has presented the most compelling theory about the influence of such reflection on the behavior of men at midlife:

> A profound reappraisal of this kind cannot be a cool, intellectual process. It must involve emotional turmoil, despair, the sense of not knowing where to turn or of being stagnant and unable to move at all. A man in this state often makes false starts. He tentatively tests a variety of new choices, not only out of impulsiveness but, equally, out of a need to explore, to see what is possible, to find out how it feels to engage in a particular love relationship, occupation, or solitary pursuit. Every genuine reappraisal must be agonizing, because it challenges the illusions and vested interests on which the existing structure is based (p. 23).

Why do midlife adults reflect on the importance of meaning in their lives? The process begins with recognition that youthful qualities are being lost, bringing reminders that one's physical functioning is decreasing while contact with problems of illness and exposure to death are increasing. Levinson suggested that much of this cognitive processing is in response to a subtle reflection of one's mortality.

Midlife can become painful for adults as a result of the growing realization of their mortality. As they reflect on the fact that their life will eventually end, they feel a corresponding concern about its meaning. Reflecting on their life, they have many questions and doubts about how meaningfully they have pursued it.

Social Cognition and Regulation

Although the preceding theories seem to suggest that at midlife there is a strong internal focus on oneself in which change is experienced as a crisis, Maas (1989) has argued that midlife represents an increased opportunity to branch out and become involved in socially responsible activities. This branching out to more socially responsible behavior results from the natural transitions that occur in midlife. For example, children often leave the home, and spouses become increasingly removed from their roles as mother and father.

The major theorists on adult development discuss this emphasis on social responsibility. Early on, Havighurst (1952) suggested that at midlife the major task was one of civic and social responsibility. Erikson's task of ego integrity reflects an emphasis on actions directed toward social causes. It is "an emotional integration which permits participation by followership as well as acceptance of the responsibility of leadership: both must be learned and practiced in religion and in politics, in the economic order and in technology" (Erikson, 1959, p. 97). Maslow (1962) described the feelings of gratitude that arise following an individual's "peak experience" and which often result in the person's desire to do something good for the world.

Maas (1989) defined the essence of social responsibility as based on two aspects. The first is the person's sense of obligation. Midlife adults can move beyond their narrow self-interest and begin to consider the general interest of others. "The obligation is based on a keen awareness of one's group memberships—ultimately, the human race—and of human interdependence in society" (Maas, 1989, p. 260). The second aspect of social responsibility is the person's ability to carry out his or her sense of obligation. By midlife, most adults have obtained a level of competence that allows them to be effective in undertaking their obligations. Over time, they develop the capacity to become socially responsible and fulfill their sense of obligation to society.

A review of past research on changes in mental abilities during middle age will show a focus on deficits, and they are an area of concern, but there is evidence of noteworthy cognitive stability and gains in midlife (Berk, 2004). Two aspects of mental abilities are often discussed. **Crystallized intelligence** refers to skills that depend on accumulated experience and knowledge, the exercise of good judgment, and social competence. Many people associate practical problem solving—sizing up real-world situations and analyzing how to achieve goals—as one aspect of the adult's crystallized intelligence. This form of intelligence increases with age. In contrast, **fluid intelligence** involves more basic information-processing skills, such as the speed of analyzing information, detecting relationships among stimuli, and ability to use working memory. Research has shown that although crystallized intelligence increased through midlife, fluid intelligence begins to decline in the 20s. The longer such cognitive skills are used the longer they will be maintained.

Psychological Strengths and Hazards

As many adult-development theories point out, midlife can be a difficult period, requiring many new adjustments. The new roles one must adapt to, the intense reflection about one's accomplishments, and the search for new meaning can lead either to psychological strengths or psychological hazards.

Developing Optimism and Happiness

Our ability to cope with the demands of life changes depends in part on our perspective. Developing optimism and happiness is a viable strategy that fits with the midlife search for more meaning and quality in life.

In the same manner that social work began its emphasis on the "strengths model," psychology has an emphasis on "positive psychology." Many psychologists are recognizing the limits of the deficit or disease model of mental health. Much of the positive psychology movement is related to Seligman's (2002) work on authentic happiness. Seligman discussed three fundamental aspects we need to change to create this emotional state:

1. Being happier about our past. This occurs by resolving false past beliefs that negative experiences determine your present and future, as well as increasing your gratitude about the good things that did occur in your past and forgiving past wrongs.
2. Being happier about our present. This is done by knowing the difference between pleasures and gratifications. Pleasures are sensory delights but gratifications are things we like to do but

not necessarily because of the sensory feelings that emerge. Gratifications are tied directly to strengths and virtues.
3. Being happier about our future. This occurs when we change our explanatory style and learn to become more optimistic and hopeful. Much of one's authentic happiness emerges from focusing on identifying and developing one's "signature strengths." Midlife is an excellent time to reflect and *act* in a way to bring these new positive psychology discoveries into daily living. In midlife, psychological hazards can take a toll; alcohol and drug addiction are some of the most serious of these hazards.

Alcohol and Drug Addiction

Alcoholism is the consumption of alcoholic beverages to the extent that major aspects of a person's life, such as work, family, and friends, are affected. Alcoholism is considered a disease by many, meaning that it follows a prescribed course of physical, psychological, and social symptoms. Alcoholism is a progressive problem that can lead to irreversible damage and, ultimately, death. When an alcoholic person abstains from drinking, he or she is said to be "recovering."

An estimated 8.4% of the population, or 17.6 million people, abuse alcohol (National Institute on Alcohol Abuse and Alcoholism, 2004). This number is much higher than the 13.8 million reported ten years ago. However, the number of people classified as alcoholics was down from 4.38% in 1992 to 3.8% in 2004. Alcoholism touches all age groups and all sociocultural and economic groups. It is currently estimated that, of all alcoholics, the majority (75%) are men and a quarter (25%) are women. Alcoholism is one of the most serious social problems facing Americans. Weiten and Lloyd (2002) have noted that alcohol misuse is blamed in 64% of murders, 41% of assaults, 30% of suicides, 60% of child abuse incidents, 45% of drownings, and 55% of arrests. Alcohol contributes to 100,000 deaths annually, making it the third leading cause of preventable mortality in the United States, after tobacco and diet activity patterns. It is estimated that as many as one family in three is affected in some way by a drinking problem.

Identification and assessment of alcoholism are complex. Not all alcoholics drink every day, and many people who do have one or two drinks every day would not be considered alcoholics. Some people will react to a personal crisis and abuse alcohol as a means of coping for a period of time but not become alcoholics. Indeed, many young adults will abuse alcohol for a short time period but eventually develop a healthy pattern of social drinking. Distinguishing heavy drinking from the early stages of alcoholism sometimes can be difficult.

Assessment usually begins with a person's consumption levels and personal or family history of alcohol-related problems. Common assessment questions include (National Institute on Alcohol Abuse and Alcoholism, 2004): How long have you been drinking this amount? How many times a week (or month) do you have four or more drinks on one occasion? What is the most you have consumed on one occasion during the past year? And a family-history question: Have you or anyone in your immediate family ever had a drinking problem?

When individuals are currently experiencing alcohol-related problems and need to be assessed for alcohol dependence, the CAGE is often used as an assessment instrument (National Institute on Alcohol Abuse and Alcoholism, 2004). Indications of dependence are three or four positive responses to the CAGE's four questions:

C—Have you ever thought you should *cut down* on your drinking?
A—Have you ever felt *annoyed* by others' criticism of your drinking?
G—Have you ever felt *guilty* about your drinking?
E—Do you ever have an *eye opener* in the morning?

Some common signs suggest someone is moving into the early stages of alcoholism. Many people increasingly use alcohol to cope with their personal problems. Others experience memory lapses or "blackouts" while drinking, craving for alcohol, and an increase in tolerance for alcohol. In the middle stages of alcoholism, there is an increase in memory problems from blackouts, and the person becomes increasingly physically dependent on alcohol. This dependence is first suggested when the person experiences early-morning tremors and agitation that require a drink for relief. In the later and final stages, there are regular drinking bouts. Also during this stage, alcoholics experience **delirium tremens (DTs)**, a withdrawal syndrome with symptoms including agitation, tremor, hallucination, and sometimes seizures.

Researchers still do not understand the causes of alcoholism; however, it is likely to include a combination of biological, psychological, and social factors. Recent attention has been directed to the incidence of alcoholism in families. Studies based on twins support a genetic contribution to alcoholism (Tsuang et al., 2001). It is estimated that 50–80% of all alcoholics have a close relative who is alcoholic (Littrell, 1991). As a result, researchers have begun to search for an inherited physical predisposition to alcohol addiction. Some research has suggested that alcoholism is related to a particular gene on chromosome 11. This gene is related to the production of receptor sites, on brain cells, of the neurotransmitter dopamine.

Many researchers have attempted to find a particular personality that would lead to the development of alcoholism, but results have not been encouraging. However, alcoholism does appear to be related to various types of emotional problems. For example, many alcoholics drink to help them cope with feelings of depression or anxiety. Other individuals drink as a means to release their inhibited feelings. Alcoholics may experience role conflicts in their work and family life.

Although in the United States many substance-abuse problems are related to alcohol, serious consequences are also associated with drug dependence. Drug dependence, or drug addiction, is defined by three characteristics (Goode, 1993). First, it is related to the length of time a person has been using the drug. Just how long a time is required to develop dependence is difficult to say and is related to the particular type of drug and the particular user's characteristics. Second, individuals who are dependent find it difficult to stop using the drug. Continuing to use it requires a lot of effort, even including stealing to get needed money. Third, when dependent drug users do refrain from using, they experience physical pain or psychological stress, referred to as the withdrawal syndrome.

Drug dependence is associated with a large number of different drugs, including nicotine found in tobacco products, Valium used as a sedative, angel dust (a street drug derived from horse tranquilizer), and hallucinogenic drugs (such as LSD and mescaline), to name only a few. There are six primary classifications of drugs: narcotics, such as heroin and morphine; sedatives, such as Seconal and Quaaludes, which include barbiturates and nonbarbiturates; stimulants, such as amphetamines and cocaine; hallucinogens, such as LSD and mescaline; cannabis, such as marijuana and hashish; and alcohol, including wine and scotch. Do alcohol and drugs affect women differently than men? The next section looks at the special case of women and drugs.

Women and Drugs

When you think of a "druggie," is the picture that first comes to your mind a woman? Probably not. However, the use of alcohol, tobacco, and other drugs (ATOD) by women is a significant problem (Kauffman, Silver, & Poulin, 1997). It is estimated that 4.6 million women in the United States are alcohol dependent. Additional estimates are that 5% of American women have used an illicit substance in the past thirty days. However, although the number of women abusing substances is significant, women appear to be less susceptible than men are to addiction to illicit substances. Interestingly, current evidence suggests that women view substance abuse more negatively and tend to be less tolerant of it than men. This may help explain why our idea of a drug addict rarely includes women.

Psychosocial factors associated with ATOD use and abuse also appear to be different for men and women. Addicted women are more likely than addicted men to suffer from affective disorders; are more likely to experience guilt, anxiety, and depression; and typically have lower self-esteem. Addicted women are more likely to have lower life expectations, less education, fewer job skills, and fewer financial resources. For these reasons, women in recovery may be better helped by groups that focus on building self-esteem and perceptions of personal power and that challenge sex-role stereotyping.

Many previously nonalcoholic young women typically began as "social drinkers." Therefore, to be effective, ATOD prevention must address the target population's beliefs about vulnerability to substance abuse. Women tend to believe that substance abuse is caused by biological and environmental influences. They view genetic disposition and family history as more strongly contributing to substance abuse. Similarly, women commonly identify relationship problems and stress as situational or environmental causes of substance abuse. Because women are more receptive to ideas about the influence of environmental and genetic factors in substance abuse, prevention programs should provide the opportunity to explore these issues in detail, especially those that influence

FOCUS ON NARRATIVE

GOODBYE, JOHNNIE WALKER

In the past year, I started drinking in the shower each morning. I was drunk by nine, drunk at noon, drunk at three, drunk at seven, and drunk at ten o'clock. I had pretty much stopped eating, although I still made dinner for my wife, our dogs, and myself and pretended to enjoy a fine meal in a fine little house on a pretty street in a nice little town. Eventually, my body started eating itself to stay alive. Ketosis is the medical term.

Why my drinking got so out of control after so many years of my being a functioning and productive alcoholic remains a mystery to me. I just know that I had become (and still am) one sick son of a bitch just a step away from the grave because I suffer from the disease of alcoholism. I drank too much. It is as simple and as difficult as that. I find most books that deal with drinking and rehab somewhat smug and self-congratulatory. I am neither confident enough or sufficiently proud of getting through a day sober to take that attitude. Truth be told, I am confident only that I will have another drink at some point in my life. Maybe today."

SOURCE: Davidson (1998), p. 18.

---

women to initiate substance abuse. Examining how interpersonal influences increase women's vulnerability should be an integral part of prevention strategies. Additionally, given the reported incidence of addiction to psychotropic medications among women, an important aspect of prevention programs would be raising women's consciousness about addiction to these medications.

Implications for Practice: Addiction and AA's Twelve-Step Program

The twelve-step approach to addiction is so popular that it is now referred to as a social movement (Herman, 1988). In the twelve-step approach—the core of Alcoholics Anonymous (AA)—people follow twelve carefully devised steps on the road to recovery (Alcoholics Anonymous, 2002). What exactly is the twelve-step program, and how does it work?

The twelve-step program is straightforward in its approach to alcoholism (Alcoholics Anonymous, 2000). Part of its success may be related to the clear model it sets out as necessary for the road to recovery. Essentially, members are expected to "work the steps." In the process, individuals must admit wrongdoing, admit their powerlessness, pray and meditate, and meet with sponsors outside the group meetings. AA is famous for its helpful slogans, such as "Live one day at a time" and "Let go and let God."

The program is delivered through a series of weekly meetings. Members are encouraged to go to the meetings, and many people keep a daily schedule of meeting attendance. Most meetings begin with an opening statement; then a speaker addresses the group, telling his or her own personal story. Next, the members are invited to share, and last there is a closing statement. Members may speak about whatever they want, and the group must listen without interruption or subsequent comment.

Members are also encouraged to get involved with a sponsor. The sponsor is a kind of "buddy" who helps the member by providing advice and counsel about the program philosophy and structure. There is a strong emphasis on providing members with support. Sponsors and other members make themselves available twenty-four hours a day to help the person during times of crisis.

Although AA is recognized as one of the more effective approaches to alcoholism, it has come under increasing criticism. First, few studies have been able to clearly document AA's effectiveness, so many researchers are leery about its overall "success" rate. Equally critical are individuals who do not like AA's emphasis on religion and individual responsibility. For example, one of the twelve steps states, "[We have] made a decision to turn our will and our lives over to the care of God, *as we understood Him*" [italics added]. Many individuals also do not like the emphasis of putting the alcoholic's addiction completely on the alcoholic's shoulders. Because AA accepts a disease concept of alcoholism, the responsibility for both the disease and recovery rests with the individual.

What other contextual factors might relate to people becoming addicted? Increasing research is providing some support for the notion that there may be a genetic predisposition toward alcoholism. These explanations are not consistent with the AA philosophy. Because AA members must admit to "powerlessness," it is difficult to promote notions of empowerment with AA members.

Critics offer additional questions for thought: "Can all human pain be collected into one big bundle labeled addiction? Should it be? What about the feelings of pleasure that people derive from food, drugs, alcohol, sex, and a host of other substances and activities?" (Herman, 1988, p. 59). This "movement" of disease-related addictions raises concerns about turning self-destructive behaviors into diseases and normal people (with problems) into victims rather than promoting empowerment of the individual as a socially responsible member of society. Some of the dissatisfaction with the AA model has inspired new but related approaches, such as Rational Recovery, Secular Organization for Sobriety, and Women for Sobriety. Fingarette (1988), an outspoken critic of the AA model, has argued that alcoholism is a mythical disease. He noted that "what seems to be compassion done in the name of a 'disease' turns out to subvert the drinker's autonomy and will to change, and to exacerbate a serious social problem" (p. 64).

If there are so many problems with AA's model of addiction, why do so many professionals believe that it is an effective alternative for alcoholics? Regardless of all the criticism, AA does attract a large number of individuals who are looking for help and offers them something that appeals to their needs. There may be three primary reasons why AA works, at least for some people (Bufe, 1987; Herman, 1988):

1. It provides a needed social context for addressing the problem. In this social context is a safe haven for people to be understood and to be accepted for who they are. Many people are demoralized and lonely, and any program that can address those issues will be helpful to people.
2. It provides a group setting for social support. In most groups, a critical factor to success is having the feeling that you are not alone—that you are not unique. By expressing feelings and receiving emotional support, people gain confidence that they can take action to solve their problems.
3. It provides a clear structure—a path to follow. There is a self-determined behavioral routine that members

Twelve-step programs, which attract many people who are seeking help, offer a social context for addressing problems, a group setting for social support, and a clear structure.

follow, and this can be critical when your life is turned upside-down. The steps provide a mechanism to focus one's energy.

Codependency

As part of the self-help movement, the codependency movement has become very popular—"the chic neurosis of our time" (Lyon & Greenberg, 1991, p. 435). The term *codependency* refers to a pattern of behavior in which a person's sense of self-worth is based on external referents. Codependents have a strong need for personal validation that is met by excessive caretaking of others, often to the neglect of their own best interests. The excessive caretaking often results in a preoccupation with the other person's feelings. The end result is excessive guilt when the codependent does not act assertive, fears of abandonment, and anxiety over not hurting another's feelings. The term *codependency* was originally applied to the wives of alcoholic husbands who got enmeshed in their spouses' addictions in ways that supported their addiction. For example, a wife may lie to her husband's supervisor, who calls to find out why her husband has not yet arrived for work. In essence, she protects him from the natural consequences of his addiction. Today, the term is used very broadly to refer to the general tendency to be preoccupied with another person's needs to the exclusion of one's own (Weiten & Lloyd, 2002).

Why would someone become codependent? The major theorists believe that codependents seek out dysfunctional relationships with troubled individuals so they can fulfill their need for excessive caretaking. Codependency is particularly a concern for women who have an overly strong need for affection and approval. Haaken (1990) suggests that women are more vulnerable than are men to codependency because they are socialized to value support, selflessness, and caretaking.

Similar to AA groups is Codependents Anonymous, a recovery program for people afflicted with codependency. In this context, codependency is seen as a disease, and recovery takes place when individuals admit that they have lost control over the disease (Weiten & Lloyd, 2002).

Weiten and Lloyd (2002, p.8) have reviewed literature on the codependency movement and summarized a number of criticisms that are worth noting:

1. There is no clear definition of codependency. In fact, Whitfield (1991) found 23 different definitions. The implication of this discrepancy is that it is difficult to determine who is codependent and who is not.
2. At present, no good empirical studies exist to support many of the basic concepts of codependency. Also, it is difficult to determine whether codependency is equally relevant across different types of problems. Does codependency operate in the same way for people who are addicted to food, love, or sex?
3. Kaminer (1992) asserted that "every conceivable form of arguably compulsive behavior is classified as an addiction. We are a nation of sexaholics, rage-aholics, shopaholics, and rushaholics" (p. 10). This perspective may demean the concept of addiction.
4. All problems end up being traced back to codependency. For example, Beattie's (1987) book *Codependent No More* lists 234 symptoms of codependency. This is considered an oversimplification of a complex problem, because it seems unlikely that everything can be explained by the processes of addiction and codependency.
5. Some women have raised concerns about the label of codependency as it is applied to women. It may contribute to a pattern of self-blame regarding their own suffering, problems with men, and their husband's problems (Tavris, 1992).
6. Although recovery groups are suggested as the only viable treatment, alternative further research may uncover additional treatment strategies that are helpful. Perhaps certain people will do better with recovery groups, and others will need to find alternative treatments.

Given these criticisms, is codependency a useful concept? The answer depends on one's perspective. However, it has helped practitioners to better understand complex relationships and how they are tied to addictive behaviors. Certainly, codependency is a popular concept, and to some extent it has accurately described the conflicts that many people feel. Furthermore, recovery groups like AA are likely to provide participants with needed social support to get additional help or learn how to cope better with their problems. Part of that help may be obtained through professional guidance from a social worker or other health professional.

Implications for Practice: When to Seek Professional Help

Under what circumstances would you recommend a person seek professional help? In general, individuals should be encouraged to seek professional treatment when they are under serious psychological distress. First, consider that other forms of social support may be helpful to the individual, including family members, church members, and personal friends. Sometimes a person's distress or conflict can be effectively dealt with by these types of natural helpers. However, other times it is best to encourage the person to turn to a professional. The type of help called for—individual therapy, group therapy, or family therapy—varies depending on the nature of the concern. Some general guidelines for when to get help might include the following (Bruckner-Gordon, Gangi, & Wallman, 1988):

- There are no friends or acquaintances to talk to the person or help with his or her problem.
- The friends or acquaintances indicate that the person's problems are too difficult for them to handle.
- The person feels extremely overwhelmed and helpless.
- The person's daily life is affected by his or her psychological distress.

However, given the complexities we all face in modern life, individuals often seek professional help because they feel dissatisfied. The following section examines the controversial false memory syndrome, stimulated by the large number of women who sought help for having been sexually abused as a child. ■

False Memory Syndrome

One of the fascinating stories of the 1990s is the emergence of the False Memory Syndrome Foundation (FMSF). This foundation was established after thousands of women revealed that they had been sexually abused as children. In 1985, a *Los Angeles Times* poll reported that 22% of those sampled had been sexually abused before the age of 18. Many of these women sought refuge in *The Courage to Heal* (Bass & Davis, 1994), a self-help book that profiles more than 100 interviews with survivors of sexual abuse. Although this revelation shocked the country, a new development became equally shocking—the organization of a group of parents who believed that they had been falsely accused of sexual abuse. By 1992, more than 8,000 accused parents were involved with the False Memory Syndrome Foundation. These parents claimed their innocence and were exasperated in their attempts to meet with their sons' and daughters' therapists to tell their part of the story. They were angry about having become completely ostracized by their children and sought some scientific evidence that might help explain their sons' and daughters' misperceived judgments.

The interest in false memory syndrome intensified as several books were published, such as Elizabeth Loftus's *The Myth of Repressed Memory*, Richard Ofshe's *Making Monsters*, and Mark Pendergrast's *Victims of Memory* (Pendergrast was a father accused of sexual abuse). As Butler (1995) described it, "the 'incest recovery movement' turned into the 'recovered memory movement.'" Also contributing to the growing interest in false memory syndrome (FMS) were the court cases won by the parents accused of sexual abuse against the therapists of women who recalled memories of sexual abuse. The validity of the memories were challenged, with the defense that many of the recollections were false creations, born of the patients' suggestibility and their therapists' leading questions. Indeed, the therapists were found to have reinforced the false memories of their clients. By 1994, more than 300 women and men had "recanted" accusations of parental sexual abuse and contacted the False Memory Syndrome Foundation. Not surprisingly, these events raised far more questions than answers. Butler (1995) asked: "Why are a relatively small group of accused parents so close to setting the clinical agenda for millions of genuine abuse survivors and eclipsing public awareness of the more than 130,000 children who are newly sexually victimized each year?" (p. 43).

Butler concluded that these events may be partly the result of a backlash against therapy—against the idea that anybody can be a victim. And although many therapists may be contributing to this backlash through their ineffective practice, incest cannot be explained by bad therapy alone. As Butler (1995) stated, "It may be easier for the culture to focus its outrage on therapy than to face the larger issue—its failure to protect children, both yesterday's and today's, from real abuse" (p. 79). Child abuse is a real and enormous problem. More than 400,000 reports of verified sexual assaults are filed with authorities each year by teachers and doctors who deal with obviously battered and traumatized youngsters. Efforts to bridge the gap between victims of abuse and victims of false memory may help discover a balanced truth (Davies & Dalgleish, 2002).

STUDY TABLE: Psychological dimension of middle adulthood

Cognitive Development and Information Processing	Verbal ability actually peaks in late middle age. Therefore, cognitive abilities do not decline after young adulthood. Adult intelligence is more related to performing role-related tasks. Professional obsolescence may become relevant during this life stage.
Communication	Communication patterns often change as adults reconnect with their partner or spouse. As adults move closer to doing a "life review" or seeking more meaning,

they reassess their communication with others. There are social and psychological benefits to forgiveness. Most Americans support the death penalty. Attitudes have changed, and support for the death penalty centers not on the criminal's "debt" to society but on the right of a victim's loved ones. This is therapeutic vengeance, the gaining of peace of mind through another's death, but often it fails. As many as 20% of the adults in our society must adjust to being functionally illiterate. Many illiterate adults grew up in socioeconomically disadvantaged areas with family members who did not encourage reading and with no one else to help them learn essential literacy skills. Adults who do not speak English may face similar difficulties, such as discrimination in employment. They may be highly educated and competent in their native language but unable to communicate in English, thus forced into low-paying jobs and lives of poverty. Hard-of-hearing people are at risk of isolation and withdrawal from society, as well as the frustration of having cultural and personal links to the hearing world dissipate. Interference with communication is the most damaging aspect of hearing loss. Title V was designed to address the needs of individuals with disabilities like deafness.

Attitudes and Emotions	The midlife adult's well-being is most often defined as a person's emotional and psychological capacity to cope with the demands across time, circumstances, and settings. Fear and anxiety are two emotions that become more prominent in midlife. Both men and women express fear of death and being alone during their later years. Although midlife does not usually result in a midlife crisis, it frequently involves a period of reflection.
Social Cognition and Regulation	Midlife often represents an opportunity for people to reach out and become involved in socially responsible activities. Two aspects of mental abilities are often discussed regarding midlife. Crystallized intelligence depends on accumulated experience and knowledge, the exercise of good judgment, and social competence. Fluid intelligence is basic information-processing skills, such as the speed of analyzing information, detecting relationships among stimuli, and the ability to use working memory.
Psychological Strengths and Hazards	Our ability to cope depends in part on our perspective. Optimism and happiness play a significant role in the midlife search for more meaning and quality in life. An estimated 8.4% of the population abuse alcohol; a problem that touches all age and sociocultural and economic groups, but the majority of alcohol abusers are men (75%). Screening instruments such as the CAGE help identify when an individual is having problems with alcoholism. Alcoholics Anonymous is a popular approach to alcohol dependency that uses a social context, a group setting, and a twelve-step structure in its treatment design. Drug dependence is related to one of six classifications of drugs. Codependency refers to a pattern of behavior in which a person's sense of self-worth is based on external referents. Many criticisms have been identified with the notion of codependency. False memory syndrome refers to the belief that many therapists provided clients with leading questions to create "false memories" of past childhood problems such as abuse.

CONCEPT MAP

SOCIAL DIMENSION

Families and Groups

Family diversity was discussed in the chapter on young adulthood, the stage when many adults are beginning their families. Divorce also was addressed, but divorce often leads to new relationships and new marriages—with the end result of a blended family or stepfamily. A **stepfamily** is a newly formed unit consisting of a husband and a wife, one or both of whom have children from a previous marriage. Stepfamilies are a norm in our society today. In middle adulthood, many divorces and remarriages take place, creating blended or stepfamilies. More than 33% of all U.S. children are expected to live in a stepfamily before they reach the age of 18 (Ganong & Coleman, 2004). Adapting to a stepfamily may require facing unique tasks, because many changes must be confronted. Children, after witnessing conflict, loss, new commitment, and overall transition after a divorce, are at a higher risk for emotional and behavioral problems (Amato, 2000).

Blended Families or Stepfamilies

As we have seen, divorce and subsequent remarriage is increasingly common, and 60% of partners who divorce have children and become single parents. However, most single parents do not remain so for long. Within five years of a divorce, three-quarters of single-parent families will become blended families, or stepfamilies (Ganong & Coleman, 2004). Stepfamilies are families whose kinship is determined by remarriage. Many stepfamilies will procreate to add to the family.

Stepfamilies face significant changes, as they must adapt to a new marital relationship, continue relationships with prior spouses, and help the children adjust to a difficult family transition. Families must begin with acceptance of loss and changes, readjust expectations about what a family is, facilitate role adjustment for all family members, and coordinate a lifestyle that juggles two family households.

How do such changes affect the children in stepfamilies? Research is just beginning to shed light on this question. In general, following remarriage of their parents, many children develop behavior problems as they adjust to new family roles (Heatherington & Stanley-Hagan, 2000). Behavior problems are more likely in boys, whereas girls often experience an increase in emotional problems. Adolescents can pose special problems for the stepfamily because they are moving toward independence, and the increased stress associated with the stepfamily may adversely affect them. Younger adolescents (ages 10–14) have the most difficult time adjusting because they are wrestling with identity formation issues and tend to be oppositional. Older adolescents (ages 15 and up) need less parenting and have less investment in family life. Younger children are the most accepting of a new adult, particularly if he or she is a positive influence on the newly formed family.

Of course, some benefits are also associated with a stepfamily. Moving from a single-parent family to a family with a stepfather or a stepmother can add a significant new relationship to the life of the child. In fact, boys seem to do less well in single-parent families than girls do, and when they gain a stepfather, they become less anxious, experience increased self-esteem, and make a better adjustment in general (Ganong & Coleman, 2004). Girls do not seem to benefit as much in gaining a stepfather. Still, over time both boys and girls make an adjustment to being part of a stepfamily.

Research (Heatherington & Stanley-Hagan, 2000; Ganong & Coleman, 2004) suggests that the stepfather is most likely to gain acceptance by his stepchildren if he refrains from directly controlling the child's behavior; this is better left to the mother of the child. "Instead, the new father should first work at establishing a relationship with the child and support the mother in her parenting" (Heatherington, 1988, p. 311). After a stronger relationship is established, then the stepfather can engage in more authoritative parenting.

Adapting to the new stepfamily can be complex and may be assisted by professional counseling services. Couples need to bolster their marital relationship and work to adapt to the changes. Wald (1989) wrote that it is essential for social workers to "understand that the characteristics inherent in the stepfamily do not reflect pathological dynamics but rather normal and transitional adjustments to a new situation" (p. 560). Even under the best conditions within the new family, it may take two to four years for the

EXHIBIT 11.5 Stepfamily issues, coping strategies, and suggestions

Issues	Coping strategies	Suggestions
Planning for remarriage	Financial and living arrangements	Couples who hold a "one pot" philosophy about family money and move into a new home together report greater satisfaction.
	Resolve feelings with the previous marriage	Ex-spouses who reframe a remarriage as a "final emotional divorce" prevent further hurt and allow the new couple a fresh start.
	Anticipate parenting changes and decisions	Making decisions as a team will strengthen the new marital bond and defray some future conflicts.
Marriage quality	Give priority to building the marital bond	Couples who create a strong bond first will ultimately benefit the children by creating a stable home environment.
Parenting in stepfamilies	Recognize children's needs	The new stepparent should act as a "buddy" until a solid bond is formed. Negotiating family rules frees the stepparent from acting as disciplinarian.
Stepparent-child relations	Consider children's gender	Both boys and girls prefer verbal affection such as praises and compliments. Girls are uncomfortable with physical closeness. Boys accept a stepfather more quickly than girls do.
Noncustodial parent issues	Maintain positive relationship	The less a parent visits, the more abandoned a child will feel. Speaking against an ex-spouse undermines a child's self-esteem and puts the child in the unjust position of having to defend a parent.

SOURCE: Martin (1995).

new family members to adjust to one another (Ganong & Coleman, 2003).

Bray (1999) conducted a nine-year longitudinal study to find out how mental-health professionals can help families cope with the transition into a blended family. Five specific themes emerged from his study: planning for remarriage, marital relationships, parenting in stepfamilies, stepparent-child relationships, and noncustodial-parent issues. Exhibit 11.5 presents a summary of these five coping strategies for newly blended families.

Marriage and Intimate Relationships at Midlife

Many couples at midlife are launching their children into adulthood. For the partners who have been parents throughout much of their lives, this signals a significant change—often referred to as the empty-nest syndrome. However, this reference confers some outdated notions on this stage of life. Originally, the empty nest syndrome was of particular concern for the mother who had devoted herself full-time to raising children. Of course, that picture has changed with the large increase in the number of working mothers. Studies have found that, rather than being "empty," this stage can be fulfilling for both men and women. So, rather than seeing marital satisfaction decline, research has found that it begins a steady climb in the post-childbearing years (Ganong et al., 1999).

Why would satisfaction increase as children are launched into adulthood? Most likely the stresses associated with children are due to "roles overload," whereby parents with children at home neglect their roles as married partners, and that this situation has a negative effect on marital satisfaction. Overload occurs in these families because communication and companionship are sacrificed in order to respond to the caregiving role as parents. The implication is that professional helpers can be alert to marital problems of their clients at midlife that are related to poor communication and lack of companionship (Hunter, Sundel, & Sundel, 2002).

How do love and intimate relationships change at midlife? One common explanation is that the nature of intimacy changes and couples develop more affectionate and companionate love. Whereas in young adulthood much of the focus on intimacy revolves around romantic love, physical attraction, and passion, by midlife many adults are more concerned about maintaining relationships from the perspective of mutual sharing, security, and loyalty. Indeed, by midlife, the marital relationship is central in the lives of men and women. As is well advertised by those that promote marriage—married adults are happier, healthier, and better off financially than other adults (Waite & Gallagher, 2000). The trick is to manage their relationship in bad times so they can reap the rewards that can come with a good marriage.

Is there such a thing as a good marriage that has survived? Judith Wallerstein (1995) has noted that many people claim they have never seen a good marriage and cannot imagine how one would look. Her research examined the lives of affluent married couples who have experienced satisfying, enduring marriages. What she offers is confirmation that a good marriage requires a lot of hard work and dedication. Without a strong appreciation for the other person, a sense of companionship and loyalty, sexual attraction, and empathy, you are less likely to have a successful marriage.

Of course, many middle adults' lives move in different directions, and this creates distance between them. Each partner may be seeking different goals and commitments that make the development of mutual sharing difficult. For example, the wife may be seeking growth through work and other commitments, and the husband may be seeking stronger emotional support and shared activities. As Wallerstein (1995) points out, the survival of the marriage may depend on the commitment level each spouse has attained over the years and each one's ability to appreciate and understand the other person's needs. In many respects, it is during middle adulthood that the couple may want to review and renew their commitment to the marriage. Although a couple may face important changes, divorce is much less likely to occur at midlife than at an earlier point in life.

Marital Satisfaction among African Americans

Most of the research on marital satisfaction has been conducted with couples who are white, middle-class, and affluent. However, African Americans have a higher divorce rate compared with whites at every income level. Research by Broman (1993) sought to examine what factors predict marital quality among African Americans. Results found that, for both husbands and wives, the perception that family income was adequate to meet the family's needs was predictive of marital satisfaction. For African American women, economic adequacy was related to how positively they assessed their husband's role performance. In addition to economic adequacy, the following factors also were considered important: providing emotional support predicted marital satisfaction and harmony for both men and women; for African American men, having a smaller number of children was related to greater marital satisfaction, but for African American women, it wasn't the number of children but the degree of problems associated with raising the children; personal development and the opportunity to express individual freedoms were positively related to marital satisfaction for both husbands and wives; and for African American women, job satisfaction was correlated with marital satisfaction.

Extramarital Affairs

A discussion about marriage wouldn't be complete without a discussion about extramarital affairs. For many men and women who struggle with changes in midlife, an extramarital affair offers an opportunity to rediscover themselves. Married couples often have established routine patterns that become unexciting and boring. At midlife, they are often searching for something new and different, and an affair may offer them a unique opportunity to rediscover different aspects of themselves. Such affairs may be related to seeking greater fulfillment in personal relationships. An affair may emerge out of anxiety over physical aging and a need to perceive oneself as still attractive. For men, an affair may be an opportunity to deny their declining sexual performance. As Goldstein and Landau (1990) aptly put it, "if either a man or a woman is haunted by the sense of time running out, if either abruptly realizes that they have spent much of their lives doing what others wanted them to do, then either one is a likely candidate to follow wherever a forbidden impulse leads" (p. 189).

Today there is more opportunity than ever for individuals to get involved in extramarital affairs, especially with the increased number of women working and the Internet (Glass, 2003). Most experts agree that affairs often occur not because of a bad marriage or unhappiness but out of a desire for variety and excitement. Glass (2003) found in a study of 350 couples who had affairs that 83% of women and 58% of men reported a strong emotional attachment to the marriage partner. And conversely she found

26% of the men and 3% of the women reported having extramarital sex with no emotional attachment. Furthermore, men who were involved in affairs were as satisfied in their marriages as men who were not involved in affairs, whereas women who had affairs were less happy in their marriages than women not involved in affairs. Santrock (2003) has stated that for the next generation of midlife women, sexual relationships outside of marriage are likely to continue to increase because of such factors as greater acceptance of women as sexual beings, family changes that leave many women without men, men's shorter life expectancy, and the changing role of women in the workforce.

How common are extramarital affairs or instances of nonmonogamy in couple relationships? Affairs are estimated to occur in 50–60% of marriages for men, and 45–55% of marriages for women (Americans for Divorce Reform, 2004). For gay men, nonmonogamous relationships were extremely common—more than 80% report instances of such relationships. Lesbians were only a little more likely to have nonmonogamous relationships (28%) when compared with husbands and wives.

Parent/Adult-Child Relationships

Any discussion of the family in middle adulthood must address two aspects: how middle-aged parents relate to their adult children and how middle-aged parents relate to their aging parents. For this reason, middle adulthood is seen as the phase in life that provides continuity in the family's identity. Middle-aged adults become the critical link between their aging parents and their young-adult children.

As in other stages in the family life cycle, the family continues to be a primary source of social support, with parents and their children providing important mutual assistance to one another (Lemme, 2001). The mutual support comes in a variety of ways; for example, parents may provide needed baby-sitting when grandchildren are small, and children may provide needed care to parents during times of illness or hospitalization. As Lemme (2001) pointed out, "this reciprocal assistance may shift in direction over the life of the family, focusing more on children in the earlier stages and flowing more toward parents as they age" (p. 283). Social support is a critical link in the long-term relationship between middle-aged parents and their children, and between middle-aged adults and their aging parents.

Middle-Aged Parents and Their Adolescent Children

When I was a boy of 14 my father was so ignorant I could hardly stand to have the man around. But when I got to be 21, I was astonished at how much he learnt in 7 years.

—Mark Twain

Small children tend to see parents as all-powerful and all-knowing. When those children become adolescents, suddenly their parents no longer seem so competent or knowledgeable. Throughout this book, we have been concentrating on how parents influence their children's development; but how do children, especially adolescent children, influence their middle-aged parents?

Research by Laurence Steinberg (2004) has found that the most difficult time for parents is when their children are between the ages of 11 and 14. Steinberg states that parents' midlife crises develop most often when their children reach this age. In fact, 40% of parents experience a decrease in psychological well-being during their children's adolescence. Also, marital satisfaction declines during this time. What changes in the parents and the children account for these midlife problems?

For one thing, parents experience more economic problems during their children's adolescence because teenage children cost more. Parents may be dealing with career decisions and questioning life goals during this time. They also may be concerned with their health and appearance. Middle-aged parents may feel they are becoming less attractive while watching their adolescents become more attractive. One mother remarked, "You know you are a middle-aged woman when you go out in public and the men who used to flirt with you now flirt with your daughter."

Children also are going through changes at this time. Whereas younger children are more compliant and easy to handle, adolescent children become noncompliant, oppositional, and resistant to parental standards. They may question parental demands and challenge decisions. The child may become oversensitive to adult remarks. Adolescents begin to push for more independence and autonomy from parental control. Many adolescents become larger than their parents. A single mother may wonder how to control a son who towers over her.

All these changes lead to conflict and power struggles between adolescents and their middle-aged parents. And this conflict increases the stress level in the lives of these middle-aged adults. Steinberg has found that these problems occur in all types of families. Single mothers have more problems with their sons, and they tend to let their sons go their own way when power struggles arise. In stepfamilies, more problems exist with daughters, who may feel a loss of closeness with the mother when she remarries. And in intact two-parent families, both parents may face a loss of control of their children, jealousy of their children's accomplishments, or fear of the children making the same mistakes the parents made.

Life course research has found that the most difficult time for parents is when their children are between 11 and 14 years old.

Steinberg has found that being involved in a satisfying career and having outside interests and activities help middle-aged parents cope with this difficult time (Steinberg, 1995). Patience and understanding become critical when parenting adolescents.

Middle-Aged Parents and Their Adult Children

By midlife, many parents have raised their children and now must shift their relationship from one of parent-child to one of parent-friend. In large part as a result of longevity, parents and their children are likely to grow old together. This change is positive; most parents report an improved relationship with their sons and daughters as they become young adults. Most adult children feel "close" or "very close" to their parents, especially when close relationships existed in middle childhood and adolescence (Ryff, Singer, & Seltzer, 2002). Middle-aged parents and their adult children have frequent contact and emotionally satisfying relationships.

However, at midlife, parents are often in the ironic situation of addressing the difficulties of raising children and at the same time discussing shared difficulties with difficult and impossible parents. Thus middle-aged adults often are referred to as the *sandwich generation*. Although many parents may perceive their children as friends when they become adults, does having a good relationship with one's parents make a difference on a young adult's psychological adjustment?

One study of middle-aged women (Baruch and Barnett, 1983) examined how a woman's overall well-being was related to her relationship with her mother. The results showed that middle-aged women are better adjusted psychologically when they have a positive relationship with their mothers. In particular, those women with positive relationships had greater self-esteem and were less anxious and less depressed than women who did not have satisfactory relationships with their mothers.

Middle-aged women also play an important role as *kinkeeper*, keeping the ties between families. It often becomes the middle-aged woman's role to bring the family together for family traditions and celebrations. This role is probably related to the strong mother-daughter bond that is consistent over the life span (Ryff et al., 2002). Adult daughters are more likely than adult sons to live nearby and to exchange help with their mothers. Daughters also are more likely to be the keepers of family symbols, photographs, and heirlooms than are sons.

Middle-Aged Adults and Their Aging Parents

It is too late to turn back. I have set in motion events that are tumbling me along like a broken branch in floodtide. I have run out of choices. I look at my 94-year-old mother. Her thin, hunched body is dwarfed amid a welter of crates, cartons of books, piles of possessions to take to the Salvation Army, and other stacks of worthless items too precious to leave behind. Her expression matches the disheveled room. She doesn't know it yet, but by this time next week, she will be in a nursing home in Colorado, a thousand miles from here, whatever life remains to her drastically changed. The cost of dying, particularly if one does it slowly, is prohibitive in California.

—L. Hartney*

As the above quote points out, middle-aged adults must face the task of caring for their aging parents—a task that can sometimes be very difficult. With the increase in life expectancy, there is a greater need for adult children to care for their aging parents, who may need assistance with daily activities such as eating, dressing, housework, and finances. A large number of midlife adults, in fact 20%, are involved in caring for an aging parent with a chronic illness or disability (Takamura & Williams, 2002). Most often when an elderly parent needs some assistance, family members provide the needed medical and personal care.

Not only has the number of older people who need caregiving increased, but the nature of caregiving also is changing. Because of rapid medical advances, individuals are much less likely to die from acute causes and instead are more likely to die from a chronic illness, such as cancer (Lemme, 2001). Furthermore, when an individual gets a chronic illness, he or she is more likely to live longer than in the past. The implication for middle-aged adults is that the caretaking role is extended over a longer period of time. Therefore, adult children provide not only longer care to their parents but also more difficult care.

Providing needed assistance is a shared expectation of both adult children and their aging parents. Harmon and Blieszner (1990) found that more than 85% of adult children agreed they should assume the following responsibilities: help understand resources, give emotional support, talk over matters of importance, make room in home for emergency, sacrifice personal freedom, and be together on special occasions. Aging parents endorsed these same responsibilities, but adult children had a greater sense of obligation than their parents expected of them.

Parent caring, as it is sometimes called, is most often left to the daughter in the family. In this culture, women are expected to assume the role of caretaker, managing and nurturing the family. Many women assume dual roles of both mother and grandmother, caring for elderly parents and helping adult children manage their families (Hunter et al., 2002). Most often, women play an essential role in making sure family members receive proper health care, providing transportation, arranging and planning family gatherings, providing emotional support to aging parents, and talking with family members to keep everyone abreast of new developments in the family.

This picture of the adult child caring for elderly parents has been refuted by media reports, which too often have portrayed the adult child as neglecting or abandoning his or her parents. Gerontologists have pointed to research that shows children attending to parents' needs and providing essential caregiving functions. Also, most of what we know about caregiving comes from research on middle-class European Americans, and there may be similarities and differences depending on the ethnic group studies. For example, Pueblo Indian caregivers report similar experiences of role strain (Hennessy & John, 1995), conflict with the family, and difficulties in managing care. However, the Indian caregivers do not experience social constraints, limits on personal freedom, or embarrassment.

Although we are emphasizing caregiving here, many older people remain in good or excellent health. Only 5% of adults who are 65 years and older suffer from organic brain syndrome, and only 10% show signs of dementia. Older people like living alone and want to function independently (Lemme, 2001). In fact, research by Stueve and O'Donnell (1984) found that the notion of "caught in the middle" may be inaccurate for our understanding of parent-child relationships. This notion makes sense only in the context of a traditional life-cycle approach, and, as these

---

*Quotation from "My mother's keeper," by L. L. Hartney, *Family Therapy Networker*, Sept./Oct. 1989, 38–41.

researchers found, many women today do not fit into the typical life-cycle stages. For example, many women in their 40s and 50s may be parenting adolescent children, but an increasing number of women in their 40s also are just beginning their families. Still, women are expected to provide care for elderly parents and often for other elderly kin, as well—including parents-in-law.

Parent care is best conceptualized as an unexpected career. A **caregiving career** often includes caring for children, caring for elderly parents and relatives, and providing care for a dependent husband. Caregiving is not simply a one-time, limited episode; indeed, caregiving has important implications for women, who provide this care without receipt of wages, pension benefits, or other resources (Lemme, 2001). How the caregiving duties of middle-aged women affects their participation in the labor force is an important consideration for their future. Beck (cited in Lemme, 2001) states that the average woman will spend seventeen years caring for children and eighteen years caring for aging parents.

A significant life task of many midlife adults is successful coping with the loss of their parents. Many midlife adults lose their parents during this life stage and must grieve and reevaluate their lives without their parents. For many it is a difficult adjustment. In fact, psychologist Bruno Bettelheim asserted that no one is truly an adult until they have lost both of their parents. The change is dramatic for many adults—they can no longer share accomplishments with the people they care for the most, their sense of family is shattered, and they lose a quality of intimacy that cannot be replaced.

Families of Adults with Mental Retardation

Many social workers work with adults with disabilities in institutional settings. Have you ever thought about people who are being cared for in their parents' home, long after they reach adulthood? Of the estimated 2 million people with developmental disabilities living in the United States, only 15.6% live in institutional settings. Of those living in noninstitutional settings, the majority will live with their families. Consequently, families play a significant role in the service-delivery system. Family living often promotes community integration, employment, social relationships, and other benefits that are not easily provided in the social-services system.

There are several reasons to become more knowledgeable about families who continue to care for their child past the age of 21 (Hayden & Goldman, 1996). First, researchers have found that, although older caregivers of adults with mental retardation experience stress and personal burden, they have greater stability, better morale, and better health than caregivers of elderly people. Support resources have been found to play a significant role in reducing perceived caregiver burden. It has long been known that strong formal or informal social supports can buffer the effects of stress. Research has shown that support services can have a positive influence on the family's ability to provide care to a child with developmental disabilities and can postpone the need for out-of-home placement.

There are several implications for social workers who work with families of adults with mental retardation and other developmental disabilities. First, social workers employed by public agencies must continue to identify and serve the families with the greatest needs. Second, social workers must learn to listen to how the families define their situations, explore with them resources that are available to them, and support them in deciding which resources would be most beneficial. Third, social workers can connect families with parent support groups; these groups provide emotional support and teach parents to use their own strengths and develop coping skills that help them face their particular difficulties. Finally, social workers can serve as advocates for the development of services and support for families of adult children with mental retardation. Social workers can advocate within the social-services agency on behalf of the families, connect families with legal advocates or attorneys, provide families with information, and train families to advocate on their own behalf.

Implications for Practice: Adjusting to the Role of Caregiver

Although being a caregiver is most often a satisfying experience, it is also the kind of experience that provides constant stress and often produces mental and physical consequences for the caregiver (Ingersoll-Dayton, Neal, & Hammer, 2001). Twenty years ago, little was known about effective caregiving. Mace and Rabins' *The 36-Hour Day* (1981) was a breakthrough in documenting the difficulties of caring for a family member with dementia. Because so many older people will need caregivers in the future, Peak and Toseland (1999) refer to caregiving as a social problem. As they note, many caregivers are unprepared for their role. Also, depending on the nature of the illness, caregivers may need to be prepared for rapid degeneration of the person being cared for. Daily routines such as helping with feeding, toileting, and lifting can become difficult. From a psychosocial perspective, caregivers often feel abandoned by their friends and family members and may have feelings of depression, anxiety, self-blame, and general stress (Peak & Toseland, 1999).

An important resource for caregivers is a social support group. Such a group may provide needed emotional support, teach coping skills, and reduce anxiety and stress. Toseland and Rossiter (1989) suggested that a support group can provide the following functions to caregivers:

- Provide a much-needed respite from caregiving
- Reduce isolation and loneliness
- Provide an opportunity to share feelings and experiences in a supportive atmosphere
- Affirm and validate feelings and thoughts about the caregiving situation
- Instill hope
- Educate caregivers about the effects of chronic disabilities and available community resources
- Encourage a mutual sharing of information about effective coping strategies
- Help caregivers to become motivated to use systematic problem-solving procedures and coping strategies to reduce or eliminate the stress they are experiencing

In caregiving support groups, social workers are expected to provide supportive interventions that emphasize skills such as ventilation of stressful experiences in an understanding and supportive environment, validation and confirmation of similar caregiving experiences, affirmation of members' ability to cope with the situation, praise for providing the care, and support and understanding of members' struggles with difficult situations (Peak & Toseland, 1999).

Grandparenthood

Many parents have the opportunity to be grandparents. Indeed, given the longevity of older adults, most will live long enough to be involved with grandchildren, and some will live long enough to be involved with their great-grandchildren. The average age of first-time grandparenthood is 47 (Conner, 2000).

Grandparents approach their new roles from different perspectives. Some are interested more in being fun-seekers, having mostly informal and playful interactions, and others are surrogate parents, assuming major child-care responsibilities. Grandparents can serve as important role models of aging and integrity. They offer the family a sense of continuity.

The role shift to grandparents can require relearning old skills and adapting to new ways of parenting. Grandparents may be called on to help calm a fussy baby, change a diaper, heat a bottle of milk, and teach toilet training to a toddler. Often the grandparent's approach is different from that of the parent, and the differences between them need to be worked out. Being a grandparent, therefore, involves new roles that affect family relationships (Conner, 2000). Grandparenting can be very rewarding if it is approached with experience and wisdom.

Being a grandparent may offer a sense of completion to the middle-aged adult. Being a grandparent may reflect a person's influence across the generations, providing to him or her an affirmation of values and a sense of general satisfaction (Cherlin & Furstenberg, 1986). Grandparents often are able to share their experience and wisdom in childrearing, offer emotional support to the parents, and achieve satisfaction in their grandchildren's accomplishments. This new role offers new opportunities and new learning. The tasks of grandparenting can lead to self-reflection on one's own parenting history and call for new competencies.

Grandparents Raising Their Grandchildren

> "It's like turning back the clock to 20 years ago, yet we're a lot older. We're back to finding a sitter if we have to go out. We're back to having very little, or should I say, no time to ourselves. I am too old for the young mothers, and the people I grew old with do not have grandchildren with them all the time. We have nothing in common anymore. This situation makes me feel like a misfit. I should be going to senior citizens' activities instead of parent-teacher meetings. What worries me most is what should happen to him if I should die" (Kelly, 1993, p. 331).

When young parents cannot care for their children because of factors such as substance abuse, mental illness, criminal activity, poverty, homelessness, or AIDS, frequently the grandparents end up raising the children. Though many grandparents willingly accept the responsibility for their children's children, this responsibility often brings added stress, discussed by Kelly (1993):

- Older adults raising their children's children face increased family stress at all levels. These grandparents may worry about their own children, who may be in trouble with addiction or illness. These older adults also may be coping with their own elderly parents who need care. Now they have small children to raise who may have been abused or neglected. These children may need extra care and support.
- In general, social support mediates stress for parents. But grandparents raising their grandchildren may lose their support network. They often are isolated from their peers, who are no longer raising children.
- The grandparents may worry about living long enough to raise their grandchildren or about becoming ill and being unable to care for their grandchildren.

Because of such stress factors, grandparents may experience problems in relating to their grandchildren. Such stress can lead to a decrease in caregiver-child interactions, which can then affect the children's development (Crnic & Greenberg, 1990).

Organizations such as the American Association of Retired Persons (AARP) have established formal support systems for grandparents raising grandchildren. AARP publishes a newsletter and offers a grandparent information center. The notion of "kinship care" has gathered a lot of support as it is increasingly recognized. Across the country, kinship care centers are starting to take hold as the needs of grandparents caring for children are recognized. Many services are used by grandparents, including support groups, advice on obtaining guardianship, counseling, and parent-skills training.

In general, grandparenting can play a critical role in adapting to the aging process. For many grandparents, this new role replaces impending retirement and concern over loss of responsibilities. Being a grandparent contributes to one's personal influence across the generations, and in this sense it may help grandparents become more comfortable with their own death. It provides an acceptable opportunity to pass on one's cultural heritage and communicate special meanings to grandchildren.

Communities and Support Systems

Robert Putnam's book *Bowling Alone* struck a chord with many midlife Americans. "Bowling alone" refers to the fact that the number of people who bowled in leagues has sharply dropped, despite the popularity of bowling. Why would this trend occur? Putnam wrote that this symbolized a troubling trend—the erosion of community ties, social networks, informal bonds, and political involvements. In total, this represents a decline in "social capital." Building a successful community involves capitalizing on the social connections between people. Putman found that many aspects of civic engagement were on the decline—national organizations such as the American Legion, the AFL-CIO, and PTA have seen losses in membership. Fewer people are giving dinner parties, playing card games, and visiting with friends, family, and neighbors. Putnam outlined four critical reasons for these societal changes:

1. Urban sprawl has increased the time spent commuting and decreased neighborhood and town identities.
2. Women's movement into the workforce has created less time for volunteer associations and neighborhood interactions.
3. Use of—some would say addiction to—television has increased and created a "cocooning" effect where we are passive consumers rather than actively engaging with others.
4. Later generations have moved away from social engagement. The baby boomers (born 1946–64) and now generation Xers (born 1965–80) display a trend away from social engagement.

Putnam has systematically gathered data to support his notion that things have indeed changed in how we act upon our social and community life. However, other activities may have replaced the social engagements that have declined—there are more soccer leagues, self-help groups abound, and the Internet is a source of virtual connection to a growing number of people. What remains clear is that we need civic engagement for a healthy society, and an important task is to learn new ways to reinvigorate communities. In addition to needing civic engagement, middle adults also look to enhanced career development and job satisfaction.

Career Development and Job Satisfaction

Consider the following comments from Kyle, a 51-year-old man (Bergoquist, Greenberg, & Klaum, 1993):

> I have come through the printing industry, from apprentice to journeyman, learning the trade and going through the changes we have experienced in the industry. It's been quite an experience. But my success was moving through the management part of the job, and this has been most rewarding to me. It certainly broadened my scope, and being part of the challenges of the future has been a great lesson. . . . I'm where I am today because of the way I do my job, and I feel I have been recognized for that. This job is a continuing learning process. I don't happen to think that, just because I have this job, I have reached the goal I set for myself in life. I feel that there is a lot more for me to do and still a lot more for me to learn (pp. 120–21).

Development in work and career is a major context for adult development (Newman & Newman, 2002). Regardless of the nature of the work, unskilled or professional, it becomes a central focus around which adult life revolves. Indeed, work often provides a growing sense of satisfaction as one gets older (Lemme, 2001). Our jobs may mean more to us, and as a consequence, we are more serious about our work and derive more satisfaction from it—a situation aptly described in the preceding quote.

Unfortunately, more and more husbands and wives are in conflict over the amount of time men put into their work. Waters and Saunders (1996) considered this a conflict because families are no longer willing to consider the husband's contribution to the family in terms of financial support only. More and more men are uncomfortable with this concept, as well, although they do not know how to "back off" from work without feeling like less of a man. When put in the context of today's working world, which seems to demand "more for less," men's awareness that they need to be more accountable to their spouses and families for both active contributions and emotional awareness has the effect of putting them "right in the middle." Many men realize that they are less willing to brush off family needs for work demands, and at the same time, families are less willing to be brushed off.

Too often, men tend to confuse what they do with who they are. Historically, men have been able to express their manhood through their work. Consider this man's dilemma: "If I put myself and my family seriously in the picture, I feel like I'm just not really trying at work, like everyone else is going to get ahead of me and I'm washed up. I know it's illogical, but it's like work is all or nothing—either I go 100% or I'm a has-been" (Waters & Saunders, 1996, p. 47).

Work as a Way of Life

What you do in your job is likely to have a major effect on your overall lifestyle. First, work is going to determine your socioeconomic status. **Socioeconomic status** is a common research variable that combines economic status or level of income, social status or level of education, and work status as measured by your occupation. Our world is centered on our work—it frequently determines where we live, who we socialize with, and what schools we take our children to, and it contributes to our sense of self.

Our work also sets forth the kind of expectations that society has for us. It determines the social appropriateness of how we dress, behave, and evaluate ourselves (Lemme, 2001). So, our work is certainly more than just a job; it gives direction to our overall lifestyle and is central to our identity. Studs Terkel (1974), who interviewed men and women about their work, concluded that work is

> a search for daily meaning as well as daily bread, for recognition as well as cash, for astonishment rather than torpor; in short, for a sort of life rather than a Monday through Friday sort of dying. Perhaps immortality, too, is part of the quest (p. xiii).

The Spirituality of Work

Matthew Fox, a priest and director of the Institute in Culture and Creation Spirituality, has provided an outline of a spirituality of work in his book *The Reinvention of Work* (1995), discussing how work and life are part and parcel of the same thing:

> Life and livelihood should not be separated but flow from the same source, which is spirit, for both life and livelihood are about spirit. Spirit means life, and both life and livelihood are about living in depth, living with meaning, purpose, joy and a sense of contributing to the greater community (p. 206).

For Fox, developing a spirituality of work consists of bringing life and livelihood back together again. As Thomas Aquinas said, "To live well is to work well."

Fox developed a questionnaire that helps people consider the role of spirituality in their work. Some of the questions include the following (Fox, 1995, pp. 309–10):

1. Do I experience joy in my work?
2. Do others experience joy as a result of my work?
3. Is my work actively creating good work for others?
4. How does my work connect to the Great Work of the Universe?
5. What inner work have I been involved in over the past five years?
6. What do I learn at work?
7. If I suddenly received an inheritance of $300,000, would I immediately cease my work?
8. What am I doing to reinvent the profession in which I work?
9. How can my family and I lead a simpler lifestyle, get along on less, and enjoy life more?
10. What is sacred about the work I do?

These are only ten of thirty questions in the spirituality-of-work questionnaire. However, these questions do allow one to examine one's attitude toward spirituality and work.

Career Changes at Midlife

The popular idea holds that many individuals change their careers at midlife. Indeed, many fascinating stories have been written about people who gave up jobs earning hundreds of thousands of dollars to move to the country and reconsider their values. But how many people really make such dramatic life changes? Estimates are that only about 10% of men and women change jobs at midlife. What are some of the reasons that motivate men and women to change careers?

Newman and Newman (2001) have identified five reasons that work-related goals may change. First, some careers may just end during middle adulthood; the individual cannot perform the duties of the job—for example, professional athletes retire or change jobs relatively young. The second reason reflects the popular stereotype of the midlife crisis—that adults decide that their work is not meaningful to them anymore and go in search of a different, more meaningful, career. Third, midlife career change can occur because the individual believes he or she has succeeded as much as possible in a job, perhaps because changing technology has created the need for specialized training to keep up with the job. Fourth, particularly for women, a career change may come when children are "launched" and there is more time to commit to a career. Also, women may become **displaced homemakers**, forced into the job market by the circumstances of divorce or widowhood. Fifth, because of economic pressures, the workforce may be restructured, requiring that some workers be laid off.

The idea of the midlife career change is a central thesis in Levinson's (1978) theory of adult development. Levinson suggests that many adults become reflective about their experience in a job and must reconcile their idealistic hopes with realistic possibilities. Given the amount of time left in a career, can the individual reach his or her goals? When this issue becomes a central focus, it can be the motivating factor behind serious midlife changes, such as career changes, extramarital affairs, divorce, and alcoholism.

Multicultural and Gender Considerations

Cavanaugh (1997) raised the question, "To what extent is it important or beneficial to maintain ethnic identity across adulthood?" (p. 52). In many respects, the notion of ethnic identity is contrary to the idea of assimilation into the larger society. Research among older adults has found that at the point in life when people are becoming increasingly removed from society, ethnic identity is likely to provide a strong source of support. Indeed, research by Luborsky and Rubinstein (1987; 1990) found that ethnic identity became more important later in life than it was in early adulthood. Qualitative interviews with older widows uncovered the manner in which ethnic identity became stronger as the individual aged. For example, individuals discussed how, after the death of a spouse, they adopted the role of family historian. As a consequence, they reflected on the importance of family heritage and traditions, which often led to a rediscovery of the significance of their ethnic roots. Also, individuals discussed how reexamining the past had to be integrated with their current selves. This process becomes increasingly important as people age and move toward an overall sense of integrity in their life.

The following Focus section describes a Puerto Rican American woman's experience of being a person of color who is a professional social worker.

> ## FOCUS ON NARRATIVE
>
> ### A BICULTURAL LIFE—LIVING IN TWO WORLDS
>
> It is strange to have lived in the country for almost 40 years and have someone I've just met ask me, "Where do you come from?" as if I had just arrived from the island. At those moments, I feel a sudden split in my being. How do I explain that I come from two worlds, and that most of the time I feel I am on a bridge shuttling back and forth between them? Despite my lush memories of growing up in Puerto Rico—the smell of the ocean, the sound of the breeze, and the taste of cornmeal with coconut milk and ripe plantains—sometimes it seems I have become a gringa in the way I think and live my life. Yet, that question about where I come from always reminds me that others see me as a foreigner, as someone who doesn't belong . . .
>
> It was not until I was 26 that I finally realized that much of my life would not be lived fully in either world but on the bridge. Most Latinos marry early and have children right away and that was what my Puerto Rican fiancé wanted. Instead, I decided to go to graduate school, even though that meant abandoning rules I had learned growing up about being a Latina. Despite the shame I felt admitting to my fiancé—and myself—that I did not immediately want children and my mother's life, my choice marked my liberation from the world of my childhood and my embrace of the part of me that had become a gringa . . .
>
> While I can't remember experiencing outright discrimination as a professional because of my race or culture, I have felt the subtleties of prejudice and the discomfort of tokenism. When I am asked to present at national conferences, or to be active in professional organizations, it is never clear to me whether I'm being asked for myself or because I represent a "minority" group. Recently, while giving information about my professional experience over the phone to someone from a national professional organization, I had to explain over and over that my work as a family therapist wasn't limited to Latinos and that I gained my expertise working with adolescents and their families while directing an adolescent day hospital at a major mental-health center . . .
>
> What I offer, beyond my skill as a therapist and my own experience of immigration, is my optimism. While never easy, I know it is possible to shuttle between these two worlds. When I help people construct the bridges they need for this journey between cultures, my own bridge becomes sturdier and wider.
>
> SOURCE: From "On the bridge," by N. Garcia-Preto, *Family Therapy Networker*. Reprinted with permission..

Gender Concerns

Perhaps nowhere in the life cycle is the issue of gender differences more pronounced than in middle adulthood. Part of the reason for this disparity is that the classical research in this area was based exclusively on men but was generalized to women. For example, Daniel Levinson's well-known work on adult development is based on a small sample of all men. Yet, the purpose of his study was to create an overarching conception of development that would encompass the biological, psychological, and social factors that influence adult development. Carol Gilligan, in her work on women's development, examined many well-known theories and ideas about adult development and found clear examples of sexual stereotypes that emphasized either love or work. Expressive capacities are assigned to women, whereas instrumental abilities are assigned to men.

What, if any, are the differences between women and men when they reach midlife? Apter (1995) argued that women experience a crisis at midlife that is a normal part of their developmental growth, whereas the midlife crisis is relevant to only a minority of men. Although women must suffer through some doubt and despair, a hope of new development sustains them. Apter (1995) explained it this way:

> When women are freed of the supposition that someone else has the answer, when they are no longer shadowed by a need to please a parent, when they are less anxious about standing in opposition to a partner, when the fantasy of the ideal of who they should be is shattered by the mature reflection in the mirror, they

grow strong enough to listen to their own answers to the questions they pose (p. 23).

Therefore, even though there is a crisis, women become empowered to come up with their own answers. This newfound energy and self-assertion is what Apter refers to as the "secret path that women achieve at midlife."

A major difference between men and women is that men often are focused on their one primary role—whether it be worker, father, or lover—in midlife. They often find a new sense of relaxation about life, more expressiveness, and a general enjoyment of the fruits of their labor. In contrast, women's roles in midlife are characterized by their multiple roles—mother, wife, daughter, worker. Bateson (1990) referred to how women "compose a life" as they develop different themes. These themes result in more change over the life course in comparison with men. They move from their crisis to liberation and newfound energy as they confront a critical question: "Why did it take me so long to trust myself?" (Apter, 1995, p. 27).

To answer this question, women must do a lot of "midlife reconstruction." Men, however, appear not to have this need for integration among the various parts of their selves. Their needs are less likely to conflict, whereas women must address conflicting needs—for example, pleasing self versus pleasing others, and private time versus development of outside relationships.

From a more theoretical perspective, women at midlife may be dealing with role strain and role conflict. Since women are searching for greater integration, this is likely to reflect attempts to adapt to each role and to the many segments of each social circle subscribed to that role. Indeed, women are often committed to four major roles: wife, homemaker, mother, and employee. In addition, women must relate to other roles—such as daughter, daughter-in-law, neighbor, and friend—which can lead to role conflict (Hunter et al., 2002). (Exhibit 11.6 presents the four major social roles of women in American society.) However, many men and women in midlife relinquish the role of parents, and, as the major duties of parenting decline, they are more free to break out of traditional sex roles.

Although many similarities exist between middle-adult men and women of different ethnicities, there are some distinctions that can have important implications. For example, Cavanaugh (1997) discussed some of the similarities and differences between African American men and women and white men and women at midlife. He referred to research by that found African Americans to be more likely than whites to come from backgrounds of poverty and to be more likely to age quickly and to be vulnerable to disorders related to poverty. Among all African Americans across lower- and upper-income classes, hypertension is a common disorder in the middle-adult years (Gaston & Porter, 2001). Brice (2003) outlined the midlife experience for African American women.

The fate of African American men has an effect on African American women. Because African American men are more likely to suffer from poor health, African American women are more likely than white women to face midlife as widows. Furthermore, African American women have fewer opportunities for remarriage when compared with their white counterparts. These factors, and others, mean that many African American women are single.

In addition, for many African American women, midlife is a period of mothering—of her grandchildren or other children related to the extended family. Perhaps most significant is the fact that the "overwhelming majority of black women arrive at and live through the middle years burdened by economic problems" (Spurlock, 1984, p. 255).

The Men's Movement

Almost everyone is familiar with the women's movement and its influence on American society, but we have only recently been exposed to the men's movement. Although the men's movement is current, it emerged in a different way from the women's movement. In particular, the men's movement seems aimed more toward personal change rather than external change (Grove & Burnaugh, 2002). Perhaps best known in the men's movement is Robert Bly's book *Iron John* (1992). The story of Iron John is about a boy who helps a primitive man escape from the adults who are holding him captive and goes with him to a journey in the woods. Here the boy grows to manhood. This story is about the unavailability and the distance many men feel in their relationships with their fathers. Bly addressed the influence of his own abusive and alcoholic father and was concerned about the contemporary separation of boys from their fathers. He contended that many mothers look to their sons for the emotional satisfaction their husbands deny them. The son feels ashamed when he

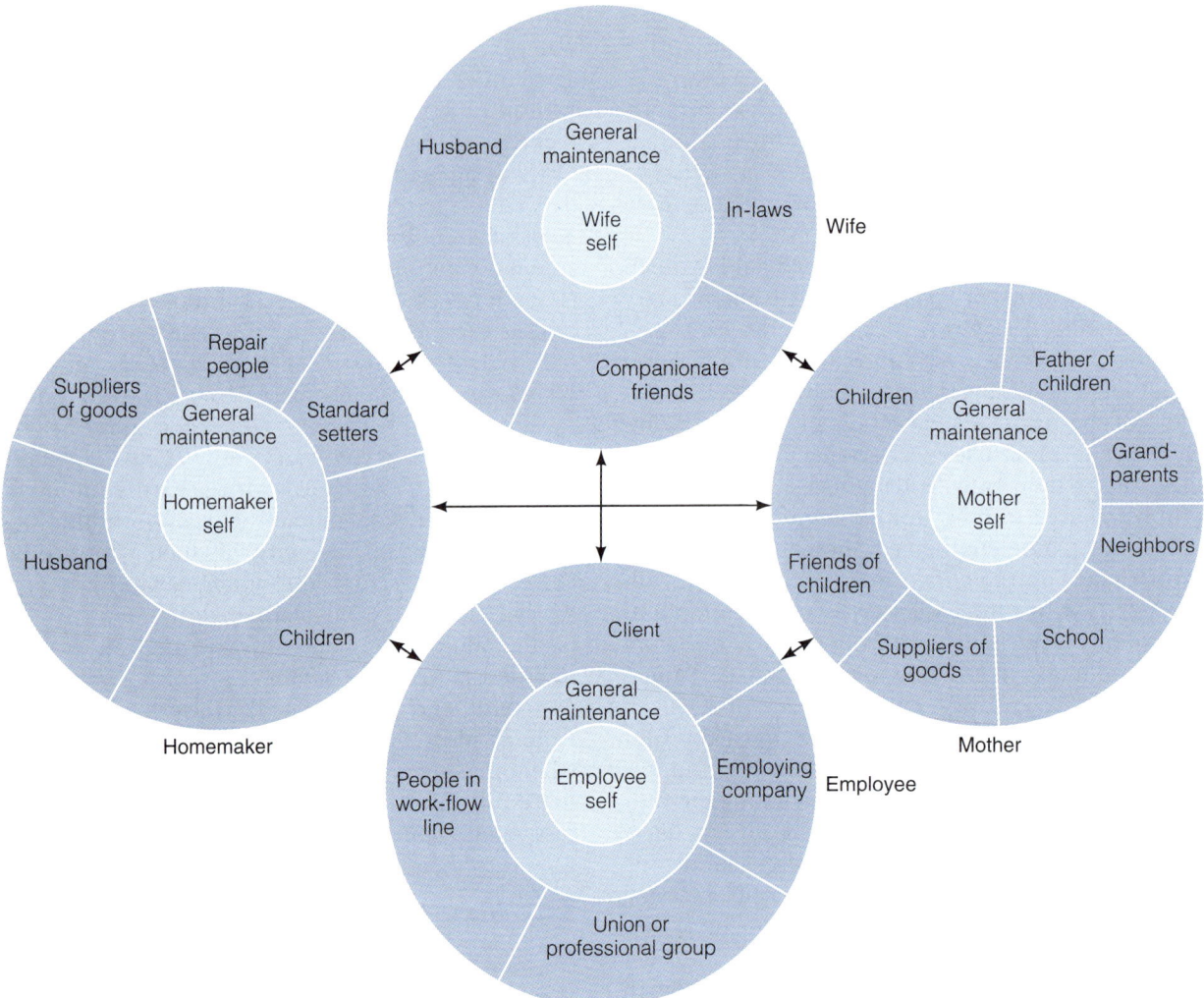

EXHIBIT 11.6 Four major social roles of women

SOURCE: From "The middle years: Changes and variations in social role commitments," by H. Z. Lopata and D. Barnewolt. In G. Baruch and J. Brooks-Gunn (Eds.), *Women in midlife*, p. 85. Copyright © 1984 Plenum Publishing. Reprinted with permission.

realizes he cannot soothe his mother, and at the same time he distrusts his father and other men. Bly's book highlighted how our culture contributes to the separation of boys from their fathers, which has led to an absence of appropriate masculine identity, and has spawned a movement of men denouncing contemporary culture and rediscovering their lost masculine identity.

Similarly, Sam Keen's (1991) *Fire in the Belly* is about the process of being a man. Keen, like Bly, suggested that men must break free of cultural boundaries in order to reassert their masculinity and male role. Keen stated than men's problems result from the "primal power that women wielded over men because of the imperfect separation of man from the mother" (p. 17). Many theorists believe that, in childhood, boys prematurely dissociate from their mothers and enter the aggressive, competitive world of men. The boy desires to turn to his father but finds him emotionally distant and unavailable. The result is that his developing masculinity is defined by turning away from anything feminine.

The previous popular image was of the sensitive man. As Graham (1992) noted, "the sensitive-man model was accepted and emulated by few men, and it did not seem that many women found it completely satisfying" (p. 840). To Bly, this image of the sensitive man is what has robbed men of their righteous anger and their ability to act with certainty and has disconnected them from their identity and their instincts toward manhood (Graham, 1992).

The interest in men's issues is also being examined within specific ethnic groups. For example, there is a National Council of African-American Men, an organization that fosters understanding of black males. The Million Man March, where African American men bonded together and marched in Washington, D.C., was a historic event representing men's issues from a particular ethnic group. One program receiving increasing attention is the Afrocentric socialization model, whereby black youth are matched with positive black male role models to help them develop more effective coping responses.

African American men are actively examining positive black male role models.

Implications for Practice: Men in Therapy

Male and female stereotypes of men can have a significant effect on a man's use of social services. As Sleek (1994) stated, "Men are about as comfortable in therapy as penguins in the desert" (p. 6). Men seek mental-health services about half as frequently as women do. When men do enter treatment, they often are uncomfortable with self-disclosure and emotional exploration (Grove & Burnaugh, 2002). Bogard (1991) described her experience of reaching an impasse with a defensive male client. She confronted her stereotype that "men can't do more" when a colleague confronted her about why she stopped challenging the client. Bogard now argues that men's ability to grow is seriously untapped by mental-health practitioners. Female practitioners often describe male clients as dependent, childlike, and distant. She found that women often do the emotional work for their male clients rather than challenging them to articulate their feelings.

Male practitioners also have negative stereotypes about their male clients. In one study (McPhee, cited in Sleek, 1994), therapists were asked to diagnose, based on individual vignettes, male and female potential clients with different jobs and income. Both male and female therapists diagnosed more serious problems—for example, affective or personality disorders—in the men than in the women, even though the vignettes described symptoms characteristic of adjustment disorder.

Mental health practitioners are now realizing the need to make treatment male-friendly. This can be accomplished through several avenues, such as helping the reluctant male client move toward instrumental changes rather than stressing emotional expression. And the process of seeking treatment can be reframed as a sign of strength. Also, many practitioners believe that men's therapy groups work better than individual therapy for many men. Several books, such as *Men in Groups* (Andronico, 1997), *A New Psychotherapy for Traditional Men* (Brooks, 1998), and *Invisible Men* (Grove & Burnaugh, 2002) have documented the increasing emphasis on group work with men. Wisch, Mahalik, Hayes, & Nutt (1995) discussed tailoring therapy to make it more appealing to men by using more task-oriented approaches. For example, research suggests men may be more open to cognitive-behavioral approaches than to psychodynamic or more emotionally focused strategies. Brooks (1998) also suggested taking advantage of a "traditional" man's interests in therapy by using examples to which a man might better relate, such as sports or news events. In group work with men, Brooks observed that discussions that might begin as male banter can often bridge into deeper issues and allow for more self-disclosure.

Attempts to make treatment more accessible to men may be critical to creating successful adjustment for many men. A program by Ivanoff (High Rate of Suicide among New York City Police, 1994) attempted to respond to the high rate of suicide among personnel of the New York police department. Because most police officers are male, Ivanoff had to respond to the resistance of the officers to seeking treatment. Indeed, Ivanoff found that officers are trained not to show signs of weakness and not to discuss problems or feelings. The project had to encourage officers who needed help to seek it. The methods used to address officers' reluctance included viewing a film that examines the lives of three officers who considered suicide. The reluctant officers reported that they were more willing to seek help for themselves and for fellow officers after having viewed this film and having participated in a training session. ■

Gender, Work, and the Family

Typically, men have pursued a narrow career pathway for most of their adult lives. At midlife, they may begin to question their accomplishments at work, but they may also question their contribution to the family. At midlife, a common male reaction is to re-evaluate one's role in the family in relation to one's commitment to work. Men may regret not having spent more time with their children. For example, the reflections of Alex, a 50-year-old, are common: "We had a good family. It could have been much better if I had put much more into it. I've learned to take the important things more seriously than I had before. Too many times my family took a back seat to my work" (Bergquist, Greenberg, & Klaum, 1993, p. 93).

For women, the potential for midlife career changes is greater because they have not had such a narrow career pathway. Many women have had an **interrupted career** that began before motherhood, was interrupted by childrearing, and was then re-established when full-time work resumed (Hunter et al., 2002). Other women start professional training while raising children and then move into a full-time career. The implication for this pattern is significant in terms of career progress and earning potential for later life. Because retirement income is directly related to work history, women's earning potential has long-term economic consequences for them. This fact, coupled with increasing caregiving functions, is likely to contribute to poverty among older women.

When a midlife career or schooling change does take place, it is likely to have special significance. A number of benefits are enjoyed by many women who return to or start a career. Apter (1995), in her study of midlife women, explained it this way:

> They not only learned new facts, but gained new perspectives. In learning how to run a business, for example, some women felt they were gaining access to an entire range of concepts that they had previously thought themselves incapable of mastering. In studying social theory or psychology or literature, they gathered new tools for reflecting on the problems that had long plagued them. Moreover, the new knowledge and new skills would, they hoped, lead to new opportunities for further friendships, further self-confirming experiences, and make further knowledge possible (p. 154).

Many women at midlife pursue schooling as a means of continued growth and change. The pursuit of learning does not just enhance one's education. It reflects something more personal—an opportunity to rediscover strengths and become empowered (Hohman, 1995).

These kinds of changes may create conflict within the family. This may be particularly true when a husband is pulling back from his career and wants to spend more time with his family and his wife wants to spend more time pursuing school or a career. Also, the woman's shift in direction may mean that she will put less emphasis on other more family-oriented roles. The extent to which work and family roles conflict depends in part on how the partners view each other's participation in the world of work (Newman & Newman, 2001). For example, in a traditional household, a husband may support his wife's new career as long as it is viewed as supplementary to his own career. Successful adaptation will depend on how partners resolve the changes in roles and the flexibility with which they approach these changes.

Social Strengths and Hazards

Of the many changes experienced in midlife, the variety of social roles that adults can embrace is a significant source of satisfaction and strength. The growing maturity of those around the midlife adult provides new opportunities for friendships and a stronger sense of support. For many midlife adults, friendships grow as they seek relationships that are increasingly mutual, loyal, and offer true companionship. Studies (McQuaide, 1998) show that being more social—having a group of friends or a confidante—is predictive of midlife satisfaction for women.

Midlife adults move from being parents to being friends with their children, who are becoming mature adults. Launching children into adulthood leads to feelings of joy and pride for most midlife adults. Recent research has found that contrary to the "empty nest" syndrome that is characterized as negative, midlife adults capitalize on greater freedom, reconnections with spouses or friends, and more time to pursue their own goals and interests (Fingerman, 2002). For women, these positive changes may reflect the larger number of roles they play outside of the home. Also, parents are experiencing an improved relationship with their children when they leave home.

An additional strength in midlife is the occupational advantage of being over 40 (Dziegielewski, et al., 2002). Many high-paying and high-status jobs come only after midlife. Top administrative positions often are left to older, experienced employees. Political appointments typically are given to adults who have established themselves throughout their careers. Employment of older midlife adults comes with little or no decline in cognitive functioning. Research has documented that verbal ability, numerical ability, reasoning, and verbal memories all improve by midlife (Willis, Willis, & Reid, 1999). The only decline is perceptual speed, the ability to see differences between two objects quickly. Because midlife often is associated with career success, however, the loss of a job can be a significant social hazard.

Joblessness

Employment is an important aspect of most adults' meaningful participation in life. Therefore, when adults become jobless, it can have significant physical, psychological, and social consequences. The individual's sense of worth and hope about the future decline. For men, employment has a strong cultural significance—this is how a man cares for his family. Loss of a job can be embarrassing and socially uncomfortable, especially given this country's emphasis on productivity. Joblessness can stimulate feelings of anger, guilt, and shame (Newman & Newman, 2001).

African Americans and Hispanic/Latino Americans are more likely to experience unemployment—often chronic unemployment—than are white Americans.

Joblessness affects the entire community. For example, one study (Janosik, 1986) found that a 1% increase in unemployment resulted in the following consequences for the community: 5% more suicides, a 3–4% increase in hospitalizations for mental illness, a 4–6% increase in homicides, a 6–7% increase in prison incarcerations, and a 2% increase in the overall death rate. Studies that have compared men who became unemployed with employed men often reveal the psychological effect of unemployment (Berk, 2004). The men felt unwanted and insignificant, lacking a role in society. Many of the men harbored feelings of anger and bitterness. They felt isolated and looked down on by their friends. Particularly revealing was the finding that even after becoming reemployed, they continued to suffer from feelings of low self-esteem. Job loss can impact the major tasks of midlife, such as generativity and the reappraisal of life goals and accomplishments (Berk, 2004).

The effects of joblessness are felt not just by the unemployed individual. If a family is involved, members face problems of increased conflict, loss of morale, violence, feelings of deprivation, and loss of roles. The family's ability to cope with adversity is tested. Children can also be affected because they may no longer have the money to participate in special events or buy new clothes. Children may become depressed at their situation or angry toward their parents for not being able to provide them with certain necessities. Joblessness often leads to homelessness, a major social problem in America.

Homelessness

Imagine what it would be like to have no permanent place to call home. For many people, "home" is a makeshift structure in a washout in the desert, a county jail cell, or even a storm drain. Yet, every night almost a half-million people are homeless and end up sleeping wherever they can—often in public parks, bus stops, homeless shelters, or just in the street (The Urban Institute, 2000). The prevalence of homelessness is often debated, but one estimate states that from 2 to 3.5 million people who experience homelessness in a given year in the United States (The Urban Institute, 2000).

The problem of homelessness has grown in recent years. A wide range of people can become homeless; common reasons for homelessness include loss of job, lack of family support, avoidance, substance abuse, and mental illness.

Who are the homeless? The homeless are a diverse group of men and women that includes young people, single men and women, families, adults with mental illness, and older adults. They are often disabled or chronically sick individuals without support for housing, older people on fixed incomes who have no family support, Vietnam veterans who have not adjusted to society, documented and undocumented immigrants, ex-prisoners without support for their return to society, and unemployed people without adequate income (Hopper, 2003). According to studies conducted in homeless shelters, the majority of the homeless population is white, although African Americans and Hispanic/Latino Americans are overrepresented. And homeless people no longer fit the stereotype of the middle-aged alcoholic male; instead they are a heterogeneous group. In fact, owing in part to poor wages and a loss of buying power over the last several years, families are the fastest-growing group among the homeless.

What factors contribute to homelessness? The reasons for homelessness are as diverse as the homeless population. In general, homeless people get to that state after a long series of crises, poor decision making, and missed opportunities. Other factors that push people into the streets include drug abuse, deinstitutionalization of the mentally ill, joblessness, need to flee from violence, reduced welfare benefits, lack of family support, and the destruction of skid rows.

The difficulties of the homeless are great. Efforts to reduce and resolve homelessness need increasing amounts of support if progress is to be made on this devastating social problem. Policy analysts, experts and advocates recommend a variety of solutions: day-labor opportunities for those who can work, subsidized housing for families, cubicle "hotels" to provide privacy and stability, improved disability benefits for those who cannot work, and vouchers to allow homeless individuals to select support services they feel are worthwhile (Jencks, 1995; The Urban Institute, 2000; Hopper, 2003).

Mental illness among the homeless is a serious problem in this country (Hopper, 2003). Many people with mental illness have become homeless through failures in the mental-health care system, the disabling effects of mental illness that has gone untreated, the combined influence of substance abuse and mental illness, and the inability of many people with mental illness to set realistic life goals. Also relevant are a loss of adequate income and diminished social supports. Many of the current problems of this segment of the homeless population are related to the effects of deinstitutionalization. When people with mental illness were categorically released from hospitals and care facilities, they were not provided adequate community support programs. E. F. Torrey (1988) has studied mental illness for years and has pointed out many of the problems of deinstitutionalization:

- There are twice as many people living on the streets and in shelters as there are in public psychiatric hospitals.
- There are increasing numbers of people with serious mental illness in the nation's jails and prisons.
- People with serious mental illness are regularly released from hospitals with little or no provision for aftercare or follow-up treatment.
- Violent acts perpetrated by people with untreated mental illness are increasing.

- Housing and living conditions for people with mental illness in the community are grossly inadequate.
- Community mental-health centers, originally funded to provide community care so people with mental illness would no longer have to go to state psychiatric hospitals, are almost complete failures.
- Laws designed to protect the rights of people with serious mental illness primarily protect their right to remain ill.
- The majority of the people with mental illness who were discharged from hospitals have been officially "lost."

Predictors and Prevention for Inner-City Homeless Individuals

A major study funded by the National Institute of Mental Health (NIMH) engaged almost 400 homeless people in inner-city Los Angeles in extensive individual interviews to learn about homelessness (Koegel, 1989). Using this sample as representative of the skid row homeless population, researchers sought to gain insight into these individuals' experiences and characteristics, to learn the incidence of specific psychiatric disorders in this population, and to discover differences between homeless individuals with chronic mental illness and those who do not have mental illness.

Data from this study suggest that mental illness is more prevalent in the inner-city homeless population than in the greater Los Angeles community. About 28% of the targeted population suffered from "severe and chronic major mental illness," such as schizophrenia or bipolar disorder (Koegel, 1989, p. 16). Nearly half of these individuals were also chronic substance abusers. In addition, 34% of the population abused substances but did not have a major mental illness. This finding suggests an overall chronic substance abuse rate of 46%. Individuals who abused substances and/or had chronic mental illness were homeless more often and for longer duration than those without either condition.

Yet substance abuse and mental illness should not be isolated as the only causes of homelessness. Urban demographics contribute, as well: As the number of both employed and unemployed poor is increasing, the availability of low-income housing is decreasing. Poverty and the lack of affordable housing cause homelessness; mental illness and substance abuse increase vulnerability to homelessness.

This complex interaction of factors leading to homelessness suggests that effective intervention must take a comprehensive approach to helping this population. Mental-health programs should take preventive steps on behalf of vulnerable individuals. In addition, attention must be given to the broader social issues that affect this population, such as social welfare and affordable housing. Effective outreach is critical to helping vulnerable populations. Even when the extraordinary challenges of homelessness are not involved, special skills often are needed in order to making a successful adaptation to midlife.

Adapting to Midlife

The experience of reaching midlife affects individuals in different ways, depending on their expectations and their own life experiences. Some people may greet the approach of their later years with anxiety and dread, as exemplified by the following quote from Apter (1995):

> From the very beginning of my awareness that this person who was "me" would grow older, the prospect brought no eagerness, only dread. At some prehistory of the self, as I was attempting to adapt to a grotesquely conceived future, I plotted my escape from aging. The simple solution I came to was that when I discovered my first grey hair, I would pull it out and then kill myself. I imagined how I would lie on the carpet of my childhood bedroom where this chill thought found me. I would be discovered, dead, before anyone could disclose the evil secret of my maturity (p. 51).

Yet for others, the prospect of maturity means renewal and opportunity—not a last chance, but a continuing chance to develop and grow, to leave one's mark in the world. In many instances, the old saying holds true: "Life begins at 40." As people's longevity increases, expectations of their productivity also increase, and they do more and demand more from midlife.

Developmental Guidelines for Middle Adulthood

Exhibit 11.7 presents the developmental guidelines for middle adulthood. These guidelines are meant to be helpful to social workers, who need to understand development when making assessments.

EXHIBIT 11.7 Developmental considerations in assessment for middle adulthood

Developmental milestones
Physical aging (gray hair, wrinkles, sight/hearing loss)
Grandparent role
Parent-child adult friendships emerge
For women, menopause
For men, testosterone declines
Retirement
Self-reflection or "life review"

Strengths and landmarks of development
Crystallized intelligence
Increased role-related achievement
More purposeful living
Generativity increases
Job satisfaction
Enhanced friendships
Enhanced marital or partner relationships
Focus on physical fitness

Developmental issues (not problems)
Reduced sexual interaction
More stimulation for erection
Empty-nest syndrome—launch children
Increased weight gain
Caretaking and kinkeeper roles expanded
Adaptation to menopause

Developmental observations requiring attention
Cancer and cardiovascular disease
Menopausal symptoms
General well-being
Increased fear and anxiety
Alcohol and drug use
Role overload
Impact of caretaking
Reduced income
Long-term effects of homelessness or mental illness

STUDY TABLE: Social dimension in middle adulthood

Families and Groups	Many middle-aged adults join blended or stepfamilies—33% will live in a stepfamily by age 18. Individuals in stepfamilies face significant change. Love and intimate relationships often change at midlife; for example, the nature of intimacy changes and couples develop more affectionate and companionate love. During middle adulthood, the couple may want to review and renew their commitment to the marriage. For African Americans the divorce rate is higher compared with whites at every income level. At midlife, adults are often searching for something new and different, and an affair may offer them a unique opportunity to rediscover different aspects of themselves. Affairs occur in approximately half of marriages for men and women. Middle-aged adults become the link between the generations, often serving as kinkeepers. In the family life cycle, the family continues to be a primary source of social support; parents may provide needed babysitting when grandchildren are small, and adult children, particularly women, may provide needed care to parents during times of illness or hospitalization. A significant life task for midlife adults is coping with the loss of their parents. Families of adults with mental retardation take on extra burdens of caregiving. Because caregiving can be stressful, resources such as support groups are becoming increasingly available. The experience of being a grandparent may offer a sense of completion to the middle-aged adult; however, sometimes grandparents end up raising their grandchildren, and this can lead to special difficulties.

Communitiess and Support Systems	Civic engagement may be on the decrease in America, so that less "social capital" is available. The men's movement has provided new alternatives in the ways men see their roles and responsibilities; for many men, it has provided a new type of masculine identity. One's work or career can lead to different pathways for men and women. At midlife, men are often stepping back from their work, whereas women may be investing time in a new job or returning to school. Men often have confused what they do with who they are, making a work shift difficult. Because many men have invested heavily in work, by late midlife they may reevaluate their role in the family. Women look at career as an opportunity because they have often had more narrow career pathways. Because of the importance of work in our lives, the spirituality of work is one perspective that helps to integrate work with who we are.
Multicultural and Gender Considerations	Ethnic identity can provide a source of support in midlife. Gender differences are more pronounced in middle adulthood. Many of the original theories of adult development were based on men. Men often focus on one primary role, whereas women often juggle multiple roles. These multiple roles may lead women to search for a sense of integration in midlife.
Social Strengths and Hazards	Midlife adults enjoy a variety of social roles. There are new opportunities for friendships and more meaningful relationships with adult children. There also can be occupational advantages to midlife. Adults can face significant hazards. Joblessness takes a strong social and psychological toll. Homelessness can emerge with decreased opportunities. In particular, homeless adults with mental illness who were deinstitutionalized face difficult adjustments in the community. Poverty and the lack of affordable housing can cause homelessness; mental illness and substance abuse can increase vulnerability to homelessness.

CHAPTER ELEVEN

CONCEPT MAP

APPLYING THE FRAMEWORK

ALCOHOLISM IN MIDDLE AGE

Lee Park is a 54-year-old man who has an alcohol addiction. He began treatment at the Harborview Medical Center after his wife and children worked with a substance-abuse counselor who coached them in how to perform an "intervention" on Lee. The "intervention" consisted of a meeting among Lee, his wife, and their two children, in which they expressed to him their concern about his drinking and the negative consequences it had for them. Each family member spoke frankly about his or her fears and anxieties over Lee's drinking behavior. They gave carefully constructed examples of when he had acted inappropriately because of his drinking. They also pressured Lee to seek immediate treatment, and he agreed to go with them to the Harborview Medical Center, which specializes in alcoholism treatment.

Developmental Considerations

Lee began drinking socially as a young adult. He enjoyed entertaining and being in the company of others. His social drinking continued, and slowly, over time, it grew more and more serious. Lee also has experienced bouts of depression. He becomes very withdrawn and loses all motivation for work. He becomes irritable and often does not get enough sleep during the night, and then he feels drowsy during the day.

Lee describes an eventful history that seems to have preceded his move into a serious drinking problem. Throughout his career, Lee had been loyal to one company and performed adequately as an electrical engineer. Slowly his job performance deteriorated, and although Lee still adequately conducted his job, his employer was unhappy with his results. Eventually Lee was "let go" from his job, and at 54 years of age, he did not have an easy time seeking new employment. Lee was unemployed for more than one year. At that time, he desperately searched for a new position; however, it seemed that employers were interested in hiring only younger workers. Lee's frustration at not being able to find work led to an increase in his rate of drinking. Drinking became a way for him to calm his anxieties and move from very unpleasant feelings of worry and concern to more pleasant feelings. Lee was able to start a small business successfully, and it has been going well, although Lee reports feeling extremely nervous about his potential for continued success.

Biophysical Considerations

Lee's alcoholism has developed into a physical dependence. His abstinence from alcohol in the hospital led to alcohol withdrawal, suggesting physical tolerance. He was observed to have coarse tremors of the hands. Family members report the presence of chemically induced alcoholic blackouts. Additional symptoms included insomnia and daytime drowsiness, increased psychomotor activity, and increased blood pressure.

Lee has been drinking for almost thirty years. He began drinking in his 20s, and it has gotten steadily more frequent and more intense. He drinks every day but most heavily on weekends. Lee primarily drinks scotch but also consumes beer. He estimated his drinking to be about "a pint of scotch" a day.

In spite of a long history of drinking, Lee's general health was rated satisfactory by the physician. He has a tendency toward high blood pressure, but the doctor does not consider it to be a medical concern at this time. Lee is twenty-five pounds overweight, owing primarily to a lack of exercise and excess calories obtained from drinking. All indications suggest Lee does not have any other physical concerns.

Psychological Considerations

Cognitive Development and Information Processing

Lee is a college graduate with a BA degree in engineering. He presents himself as someone who has the capacity for good intellectual functioning.

(continues)

APPLYING THE FRAMEWORK

(*continued*)

However, this is difficult to assess at times because of his lack of motivation and flat affect. In discussing his current work situation, Lee is able to articulate difficult business decisions he is grappling with. Moreover, he displays reasonable problem-solving abilities in relation to the tasks he is currently working on. For example, he recognizes that one of his difficulties is retaining good employees and keeping them motivated to work. Because he is feeling unmotivated, he is concerned about how his employees may be reacting to his lack of motivation. He has described several ideas for how to address this problem. In general, Lee's judgment about work issues shows careful consideration of consequences and forethought about the implications of his actions.

When discussing more personal issues, Lee appears to have difficulties with cognitive flexibility. In particular, he displays thinking styles characteristic of a depressed person. For example, when asked about how he could reach out to establish some new relationships with other men, he could think of no alternatives. And when asked about past relationships, he exclaimed, "I should have friends but no one really feels close to me." Such thoughts show minimization and all-or-nothing thinking patterns.

Communication

Lee has serious communication difficulties, particularly in the context of his family. He is reserved and has a timid, unassertive personality style. In family sessions, he often turns to his wife to let her speak for him. His wife describes frustrating attempts to simply "talk to Lee about what is going on with him." He recognizes this and describes difficulties in "expressing my thoughts to my wife and children." Because the children have recently moved out on their own, Lee and his wife are adjusting to having more time by themselves and with each other. Lee's wife wants him to become more involved with social activities and is motivated to push him to confront his drinking problem so "they can return to a normal life."

Attitudes and Emotions

Although alcohol drinking has been consistent since young adulthood, it became more frequent and more intense after Lee lost his employment. This loss was significant for Lee, because he felt he no longer had a significant role in his family. He reports feeling guilty about not being able to provide for the family. Lee reported a general sense of failure and hopelessness about the future following his employment loss. Although he now has a financially stable business, he reports feeling anxious and nervous about his future. Lee complains often of "low energy" and believes he is depressed much of the time. He states, "I do not have anything to look forward to." Lee is also beginning to wonder what the meaning of his life has been. He describes much of his life to date as "a failure." When asked what he would like to accomplish, he responded, "I don't feel I have anything I can accomplish or look forward to."

Social Cognition and Regulation

Lee's sense of self, or self-concept, is negative. He is focused on his limitations and inadequacies and has a great deal of difficulty when asked to discuss any positive attributes. This is probably related to his depression, as described above.

Lee is beginning to accept the notion that he has a drinking problem. In the past when confronted with concerns about his drinking, he immediately expressed denial of any problems. In the last five years, his wife has been increasingly concerned and confrontational about his drinking. About one year ago, Lee had an alcohol-related accident; fortunately, no one was hurt. At one point, his wife challenged him to quit for three months to prove that he did not have a drinking problem. Lee was unable to meet the challenge. Also, family members, especially after working with a counselor, became better at letting Lee experience the consequences of his drinking behavior rather than covering up for him and assuming caretaking and enabling roles for him. Lee does acknowledge that his drinking is "a problem for other people in my family."

Lee does express much concern over "what he has left in his life." He appears concerned that family members and others perceive him as having made an important contribution. With regard to this issue, he expresses intense dissatisfaction: "I want others to feel I have done right by them, and I should get my act together for the benefit of others." He can express his frustration over wanting to "get more out of life," and it appears he is consistently thoughtful about what he wants to achieve in the future.

Social Considerations

Family

Lee has been married for thirty years and feels his marriage is one of convenience. He gets along with his wife, but she "isn't able to really understand my problems or help me." Although he presents the marriage in a negative light, he is observed to be caring and concerned with discussing his problems with his wife. She has been putting increasing pressure on Lee, which has resulted in an increasing conflict between them. She stated, "I told Lee I was tired of this and I did not want to live under these circumstances."

Lee's relationship with his children also has become increasingly strained. The children and his wife have been more confrontational, and this may explain the increase in family conflict. Lee believes the children should "stay out of this" and does not want them to be involved in his treatment. He appears embarrassed to admit that he has a problem and needs help. The children report feeling "cut off" from their father and "do not know how to separate who he is from his drinking problem."

Lee's parents live far away, and he has not been very involved with them in the past even though he is an only child. However, recently his father had a heart attack and he went to visit them. When he returned, he said he was "shocked" to see how old they were getting and realized that they may need help in the next several years. He reports additional stress and feels that this is not a burden he can take on right now.

Social Support

Lee's greatest social support is from his family. His wife and children are concerned about his behavior and are motivated to help him quit drinking. And even though he describes his relationships as strained, they are what he appears to care the most about. Lee has a strong sense of social responsibility toward his family, and he wants them to see him as a competent and effective husband and father.

Outside his family, Lee has one business friend that he spends a lot of time with. He describes this person as his only friend. His wife has encouraged him to attend AA meetings in the past, and within the last six months, he did attend AA meetings for about a month. He quit going, complaining that they were too religious and that the people there were "too screwed up to be of any help to me."

Multicultural and Gender Considerations

Lee comes from a family that has always been accepting and open toward drinking. He can remember drinking with his family of origin when he was only 17 years old. Both of his parents drank alcohol, but he says neither of them had a drinking problem.

Lee also comes from a middle-class family that values success through hard work. It is difficult to determine exactly when Lee's drinking became serious enough to constitute alcoholism. However, his loss of employment was very significant in his life, and he describes his most serious problems as having begun when he lost his job. For Lee, work gave him an acceptable role to play in his family and helped him feel he was making a contribution to society. When he lost that ability, he was not able to cope effectively and turned to alcohol for relief.

Summary and Impressions

Lee is experiencing the following problems:

1. He has an alcohol addiction.
2. He has mild to moderate denial regarding the negative aspects of his alcohol use.
3. He is experiencing clinical depression.
4. He has serious self-doubts concerning his self-worth and experiences worry and anxiety over his future.
5. He needs to reestablish his relationship with his wife and children.

(continues)

> **APPLYING THE FRAMEWORK**
> *(continued)*
>
> 6. He has difficulty expressing himself and being assertive.
>
> Lee is a high-functioning midlife male who has an alcohol addiction and is experiencing depression. It is difficult to assess the relationship between his feeling depressed and his drinking. He may have developed a serious drinking problem in his effort to use alcohol to cope with his depressive feelings. Lee's family is experiencing many concerns related to Lee's drinking and is actively involved in his treatment. They can offer him needed support and reassurance throughout his recovery. Although Lee has entered Harborview Medical Center for his alcoholism, he is still experiencing denial in relation to his alcohol use.
>
> Exacerbating his problems are concerns that Lee has regarding his future and worries about his ability to succeed in life. He is increasingly concerned about his contribution in life. Lee's difficulties in communication and assertiveness make it difficult for him to make his needs known. Lee has some important strengths that will help his prognosis for treatment. He is an intellectually competent man with a successful business. His family is supportive and involved in his treatment. He is making progress on his denial and has agreed to a first step of seeking inpatient treatment.

Key Terms

alcoholism
caregiving career
crystallized intelligence
cynical hostility
delirium tremens (DTs)
displaced homemakers
estrogen replacement therapy (ERT)
fluid intelligence
functional literacy
hormone therapy
hot flash
illiterate
interrupted career
menopause
osteoporosis
professional half-life
professional obsolescence
refractory period
sexual response cycle
socioeconomic status
stepfamily
type A personality
type B personality
well-being

Online Resources

Websites

See http://info.wadsworth.com/ashford for specific links to the following websites.

The American Institute of Stress

The American Institute of Stress provides information on the role that stress plays in health and disease. The site is a clearinghouse for information on stress-related subjects.

National Organization for Women (NOW)

This site is maintained by NOW and provides information about women and advocacy efforts to prevent violence.

National Institute on Alcohol Abuse and Alcoholism (NIAAA)

NIAAA is the information service of the Center for Substance Abuse Prevention of the Substance Abuse and Mental Health Services Administration in the U.S. Department of Health and Human Services.

Alcoholics Anonymous (AA)

This site provides a self-recovery program for alcoholics. It also includes information for professionals.

American Cancer Society

This site has information on research, new findings, statistics, and a searchable database on cancer-related topics.

The Kinsey Institute for Research in Sex, Gender, and Reproduction

This site is from the famous Kinsey Institute. It includes research, publication papers, and links to other sites.

The National American Menopause Society

This site provides information about menopause. It includes information about the organization, suggested readings, and research.

American Men's Studies Association

This site is a not-for-profit organization for people interested in the exploration of masculinity in modern society.

InfoTrac College Edition Keywords

For interesting materials related to what you have just read, please go to the InfoTrac College Edition website and search using the following keywords:

menopause
forgiveness
hearing loss
false memory syndrome
caregivers
homelessness

Book-Specific Resources

Book specific resources can be found at http://info.wadsworth.com/ashford and include the following:

Case studies
Quizzes to test your knowledge
PowerPoint presentations

CHAPTER 12

LATE ADULTHOOD

CHAPTER AUTHOR

KATHRYN BETTS ADAMS, MSW, PH.D.
Mandel School of Applied Social Sciences and University Memory and Aging Center, Case Western Reserve University

CHAPTER CONSULTANTS

ELLEN NETTING
Virginia Commonwealth University

VIRGINIA RICHARDSON
Ohio State University

	DEVELOPMENTAL THEMES
	Stage: integrity versus despair. Phases of late adulthood. Growth of aging segment of population. Older minorities. Life-course perspective. Functional age. Theories of aging. Defining "successful aging."
	BIOPHYSICAL DIMENSION
Biophysical Growth and Development	Life span and life expectancy. Age-related changes. Exercise and nutrition. Health care and medications. Changes in sexuality and sexual relations.
Biophysical Strengths and Hazards	Chronic health problems. Arthritis. Hypertension. Death and dying. Advance directives for health care. End-of-life care.
	PSYCHOLOGICAL DIMENSION
Cognitive Development and Information Processing	Elderhostel programs. Cognitive theories of aging. Fluid and crystallized intelligence. Adjustment to normal changes in memory and learning. Concerns about dementia.
Communication	Sensory limitations; disorders; isolation. Dementia and communication. Elderspeak.
Attitudes and Emotions	Complexity of emotional experiences. Loss, grief, and mourning. Loneliness.
Social Cognition and Regulation	Maintenance of a stable sense of self. Reminiscence.
Psychological Strengths and Hazards	Wisdom. Spirituality and religious beliefs. Alzheimer's disease and other dementia. Mental illness. Depression. Suicide. Dependence on alcohol and other drugs.
	SOCIAL DIMENSION
Families and Groups	Families. Couples. Gay and lesbian elders. Widowhood. Parent-child relationships. Grandparenthood.
Communities and Support Systems	Friendships and social networks. Work, retirement, and volunteering. Gender differences in retirement. Living on a fixed income. Continuum of care. Housing options.
Multicultural and Gender Considerations	Ethnic and racial minority groups. Extended-family relationships. Social work and cultural competence. Gender issues. Ageism.
Social Strengths and Hazards	Social support for older adults. Elder abuse and neglect.

DEVELOPMENTAL THEMES

There are certain pursuits adapted to childhood: do young men miss them? There are others suited to early manhood: does that settled time of life called "middle age" ask for them? There are others, again, suited to that age, but not looked for in old age. There are, finally, some which belong to old age. Therefore, as the pursuits of the earlier ages have their time for disappearing, so also have those of old age. And when that takes place, a satiety of life brings on the ripe time for death.

—Roman Philosopher Cicero, 106–43 B.C., "On Old Age"

The years from age 60 until death are considered late adulthood. Erik Erikson (1959/1980) termed this eighth life stage "old age," characterized by the developmental task of integrity versus despair. Erikson and fellow psychoanalyst Carl Jung noted that people tend to become more reflective and introspective as they age. Here, **integrity** refers to the ability to integrate or satisfactorily blend one's history and experience with the task of evaluating and accepting one's life. In later life, as people reflect back and find that their life has been meaningful and rewarding, they experience satisfaction and develop integrity. If, however, they are disappointed because of missed opportunities and unresolved conflicts, they may be vulnerable to despair.

Some theorists have argued that one stage is not enough to encompass all of life from age 60 till death. Developmental psychologists Newman and Newman (1998) have revised Erikson's stages, dividing later life into two developmental stages rather than one: late adulthood (ages 60 to 75) and very old age (75 until death). Joan Erikson, widow and former collaborator with Erik, also added a ninth stage to late life, to apply to the stage of increasing frailty of the late 80s and beyond (Erikson & Erikson, 1998). Another way some refer to late life is to differentiate the "third age" (those who are young-old, or from their 60s to early 80s) from the "fourth age"—the oldest old. Despite the diversity in the experience of late life, some common tasks for each decade of late life can be identified (see Exhibit 12.1).

Scholars and philosophers have long been interested in aging. Cicero, a Roman philosopher born in 106 B.C., wrote about his "old age" even though he lived to be only 63. Shakespeare, too, dealt with aging in many of his plays, including *King Lear* and *As You Like It*. It was in the 1950s that the interdisciplinary social science of gerontology—the study of aging and old age—really heated up. And now in the new millennium, we are faced with a "demographic imperative"—the graying of America and many other nations in the world—which will require an overhaul in our medical and social services. As people live longer, with access to better health and personal care, what we think of as "old" keeps getting older. And consequently, the stage of "old age" keeps lasting longer. The first of the "baby boomer" generation will reach age 65 beginning in 2011. Currently, there are approximately 36 million people over the age of 65, or approximately 12.4% of the population in the United States, and it is expected there will be 86 million by 2050 (U.S. Census Bureau, 2004). But it is those who are 85 and older who make up the fastest-growing segment of the population in the United States and other industrialized nations. The U.S. Census Bureau projects that by the year 2050, there will be 20.8 million Americans 85 years or older, or 5% of the U.S. population (U.S. Census Bureau, 2004).

Members of minority groups represented 13.2% of those over age 65 in 2000. By 2030, minority groups are projected to nearly double their proportion of the older population, to 25%. The numbers of older minorities are increasing faster than those of whites. Between 2000 and 2030, the white population 65 years and older is projected to increase by 77%, compared with 223% for older minorities, including African Americans, Latinos, Asian Americans, American Indians, and Pacific Islanders (see Exhibit 12.2; Administration on Aging, 2004a). Social work is among the key disciplines responding to this imperative. "As Baby Boomers reach age 65, there will be a greater need for social workers to use their skills to enhance the quality of life for older adults and their families and to assist them in navigating ever-changing and increasingly complex health, mental health, social service, and community environments." (Council on Social Work Education, 2001).

Younger people naturally tend to think that all older people are more alike than different, but the fact is, when people live longer, they have more opportunities to develop differently. With increased life expectancy, it is not uncommon for individuals to live nearly a third of their lives in the arena of late adulthood. Because of differences in older people's income, health, ethnicity, and social supports, today's older adults form a very heterogeneous group (Administra-

EXHIBIT 12.1 General characteristics of older adults by subperiod

Subperiod	Characteristics
Young-old (65–74)	The young-old typically remain active in the community and maintain strong ties with families and friends; some may increase their recreation, adult education, and volunteer activities; many may still be employed full- or part-time because of financial need or the personal desire to work; the phenomenon of women outliving their spouses begins to emerge. Those young-old with adequate health and financial resources may be experiencing their first decade without parenting responsibilities and may travel or relocate, though many in this age group may assume or continue the caregiver role to a grandchild, an elderly relative, or a spouse. For some, retirement means new freedoms, but for others it can bring losses, including loss of status and income, loss of being needed, or loss of meaning in life. Loss through death of mates, friends, family members, and coworkers becomes more frequent. Chronic illness may develop and/or become more debilitating, and some young-old experience depression, but most individuals in this age group maintain a good capacity to cope and use their talents productively.
Middle-old (75–84)	More in this age group experience chronic disease (arthritis, cardiovascular, respiratory, circulatory) and added stresses through widowhood, deaths of friends, relatives, and adult children. Generally, people in this age cohort tend to experience more physiological changes in terms of impairments in vision or hearing; problems with balance that may lead to loss of mobility (for example, walking, driving); and slowing of response time and judgment of spatial relationships. Growing numbers of people in this age range, however, continue to manage well and contribute to their families and communities. They are socially and physically active, in relatively good health, and able to function independently. Because of the noticeably different rates of change of individuals in this age group, they are even more diverse than are the young-old.
Old-old (85+)	A predominant number of this group is dependent, frail, and experiencing more disabilities and chronic illnesses. Mobility is more likely to be limited, and very few are employed, though some work independently or use their creative capacities for fulfillment. Social isolation tends to become greater for this cohort because they have more physical decrements, many can no longer drive themselves, and many are widowed. The prevalence of dementia, such as Alzheimer's disease, increases with age—up to 50% of the 85+ group show evidence of brain disorders or some form of dementia. Those elderly who have survived well continue to maintain daily routines and live independently or with families, although the ratio of women to men who have survived to this age (265:100) is much greater.

SOURCE: Based on Hartford (1985).

EXHIBIT 12.2 Projected rate of growth of ethnic older people (65+) between 2000 and 2030

Ethnic group	Percent increase
White non-Hispanic	77%
Hispanic	342
Non-Hispanic Blacks	164
American Indians, Eskimos, Aleuts	207
Asians, Pacific Islanders	302

SOURCE: Based on Administration on Aging (2004a).

tion on Aging, 2004a). The **life course perspective** takes into account one's cohort in history, racial and cultural background, gender and sexual preference, economic and social status, and level of education and employment to understand the experience of older adults (Stoller & Gibson, 2000). Added to that, genetic strengths and vulnerabilities, availability of supportive family and significant others, and just luck all combine to make each older adult's situation unique.

It follows that chronological age is only one factor in considering the life situation of older adults. To some extent, the old adage "You're as young as you feel" is true, though it may be more accurately stated, "You're as young as you can function." Practitioners' assessment of **functional age** takes into account the person's physical impairments; ability to perform activities of daily living (ADLs), such as personal care and food preparation; psychological strengths, such as flexibility and good reality testing; and family and social supports (Greene, 2000). For example, two women who came to the attention of social workers recently, both chronologically in their early 80s, are in radically different circumstances. Helen is a white, middle-class married woman who comes to the local senior center regularly to socialize and play cards. She lives at home with her husband and considers their relationship to be the high point of her life. Their two grown children live in the area and help when needed. Helen still drives, buys groceries and prepares meals, and keeps her own house. Old age has taken a toll on Helen in two ways: she has some painful arthritis that slows her down at times, and many of her closest friends have died. Nevertheless, Helen stays active and optimistic. She says, "When you are a kid, you seem invincible, untouchable even. As you grow up and start to care for others, you realize that life is a precious gift that should not be wasted. I am very blessed that I have been able to live my life fully with someone I dearly love." Although she enjoys chatting with the social worker at the senior center, Helen isn't in need of social work services at the present time.

In contrast, Ann is a recently widowed African American woman whose family reports that she has become more forgetful and anxious. Without anyone else in the home, they worry about her safety and well-being. The family has no extra money and lacks the stability of employment or residence to provide Ann with the help and supervision she needs. She will most likely need to sell her heavily mortgaged home and move to a facility where Medicaid will pay for her care. Ann is constantly worried and sometimes finds it difficult to get out of bed in the mornings because she feels so overwhelmed. Ann needs significant help from social workers to evaluate her needs, refer her for psychiatric assessment and treatment, offer her emotional support, and work with her family on the upcoming move. Clearly, assessment of functional age gives a more complete picture than chronological age in these two older women.

Despite the difficulties inherent in trying to identify specific common tasks in the stage of life we commonly call "old age," social gerontologists have tried to do so. There are a number of theories of aging that address how people change or do not change with advancing age, how late life differs from earlier adulthood, and characteristics of normal or successful aging—theories that can help us understand aging and inform our social work practice with older adults and their families.

Continuity theory (Atchley, 1989) emphasizes that people change less with aging than they stay the same. The theory states that adaptation to changes that occur with age is done using familiar strategies from the individual's past repertoire. "Because of continuity, human development in later life is subtle" (Atchley, p. 184). The theory is based in part on longitudinal studies of adult personality that have found the relative stability of personality traits from young adulthood into old age. The traits of conscientiousness, neuroticism, extraversion, agreeability, and openness to new experience constitute a five-factor personality model developed from one of these studies (Costa, Metter, & McCrae, 1994). Age-related changes are incremental, and the integrity of the person's identity remains stable. What are some potential practice implications of continuity theory when working with older adults?

Other theories of aging have focused more on change than continuity. The best-known and oldest of these were activity theory (Havighurst, 1961) and disengagement theory (Cumming & Henry, 1961). In the ensuing years, these rival theories fueled both debate and research, and they have led to newer theories that encompass contemporary clinical and research findings.

Activity theory applies social role theory to late life. The central assumption of this theory is simply that older people experience greater subjective well-being when they continue to be active in many roles. According to this theory, successful aging depends on adaptation through substitution for roles that are no longer available.

Disengagement theory argues that disengagement occurs in late adulthood through the process of mutual withdrawal of the person and of society, and the process could begin from either side. The theory was based in part on Jung and Erikson's notion that introspection seems to increase as we age, as well as research that showed the decrease in social roles and social contacts that accompanied aging. Withdrawal was not viewed as a uniform pattern—for example, some people might be forced to retire rather than choose to retire. Moreover, even with cultural and individual variations in timing, the process of disengagement was seen as universal and inevitable.

These two theories are no longer accepted wholesale—both have been widely criticized. As a theory of successful aging, activity theory may have been overly simplistic. For instance, can we be sure that it is activity that leads to satisfaction and well-being, or is it possible that those older adults who are naturally more healthy and optimistic happen to engage in more activities? Whereas concerns about activity theory were fairly benign, disengagement theory became very controversial, as it seemed to suggest that society and practitioners should abandon older adults. This controversy led to a backlash against attempts to determine how older adults may differ from younger adults (Achenbaum & Bengtson, 1994).

> ## FOCUS ON NARRATIVE
>
> ### LIFE IS SO GOOD
>
> George Dawson (1898–2001) cowrote his memoir, *Life Is So Good* (Dawson & Glaubman, 2001), at the age of 101. An African American who was the grandson of slaves, George had to work on his family's Texas farm and never attended school as a boy. Despite a harsh early life marked by discrimination, his family gave him the skills to survive and even thrive in the world. Blessed with an optimistic spirit and a quick mind, George lived a long and happy life, much of which he recounts in his memoir. One of the most remarkable things about this story is how, long after his retirement as a laborer, George decided to attend literacy classes in Dallas, Texas, at the age of 98. He learned to read and write and then went on to publish his life story, offering an amazing example of successful aging!

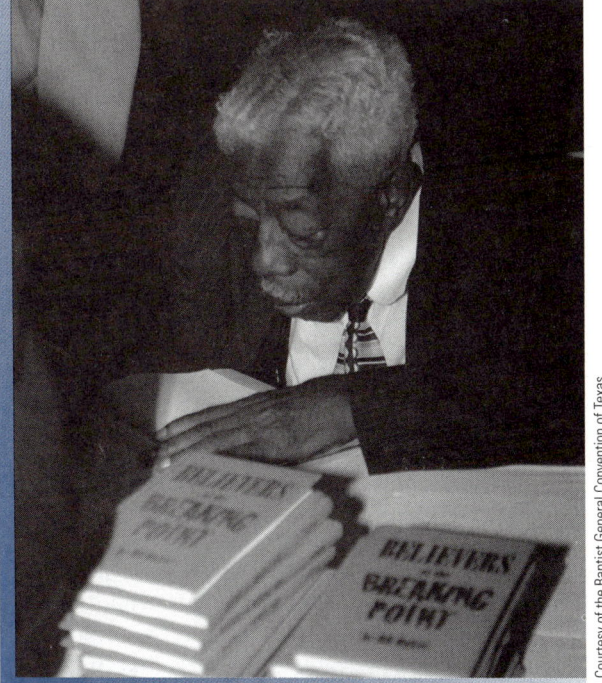

George Dawson after he learned to read and write at the age of 98.

Newer theories of aging have returned to the themes of activity and disengagement in different ways. One branch of inquiry launched an ambitious attempt to identify factors that lead to successful aging. The results of this longitudinal research were summarized by Rowe and Kahn in their book *Successful Aging* (1998). They focused on three main areas that appear to contribute to successful aging: (1) maintaining cognitive abilities, (2) avoiding disease and maintaining physical functioning, and (3) maintaining active engagement with life. A major message of the study and the book is that many factors are in the individual's personal control, such as the choice to smoke or not, to exercise and maintain a healthy weight, to reach out to others and stay actively involved. Critics of the successful-aging paradigm have pointed out that because of inequalities experienced by ethnic minority and female elders, who are more highly represented among the poor, the uninsured, and the uneducated, successful aging is not equally attainable by everyone (Holstein & Minkler, 2003). Another major criticism is that there appears to be a lack of room to consider those who are disabled, cognitively impaired, or frail as "successful agers" (Holstein & Minkler, 2003). Others have advocated for inclusion of the inner life, or a spiritual component to round out the successful-aging concept (Crowther, Parker, Achenbaum, Larimore, & Koenig, 2002).

One way to study successful aging is to ask older adults what they think. Researchers in Australia interviewed sixty participants over age 70 about how they defined successful aging and obtained some very interesting results (Knight & Ricciardelli, 2003). The respondents identified several major themes: health, personal growth, contentment, good relationships, and maintaining independence. Another question asked how they deal with age-related losses and changes, and their responses identified these themes: compensation for lost roles and relationships, acceptance, faith or religious involvement, keeping active, and maintaining relationships.

Two new theories of aging, socioemotional selectivity (Carstensen, 1992) and gerotranscendence (Tornstam, 2000), have emerged within the past dozen years or so. These theories draw upon some of the ideas from disengagement theory to address psychological and social changes that accompany the aging process. **Socioemotional selectivity**, based on a number of research studies, asserts that as people age, familiar and reliable relationships become more important. Older adults regulate emotions and conserve energy by selecting with whom and how to invest their emotional energies, so that novelty and newer friends become less important than old friends and family members. Gerotranscendence theory argues that optimal aging has a contemplative, spiritual component that allows the older adult to transcend concerns about the deteriorating physical body or materialism of everyday life and instead focus on concerns about connectedness with others and the spiritual realm. Both of these theories go somewhat against the universal prescription for older adults to be active, instead acknowledging the importance of changes in their need for solitude, choice, and meaningful relationships.

With all these different theories, is there anything we can say for sure about how people change as they age, or common characteristics of older adults? There are some qualities typical of older adults that most practitioners and researchers can agree upon (Butler, Lewis and Sunderland, 1998):

- Concern with leaving a legacy—the meaning of their life in some tangible form, whether it is their offspring and grandchildren, examples of their work, or personal mementos that they wish to pass on to younger friends and family.
- A change in the sense of time: older adults tend to live in the present and experience "now."
- Wanting to fulfill the "elder" function, which is closely associated with the notion of legacy, in that older people have a predilection for sharing a wealth of accumulated knowledge, experience, and wisdom with the young.
- Attachment to familiar objects, which means an increasing emotional investment in familiar household objects, heirlooms, keepsakes, photo albums, letters, and pets which provide a sense of continuity, assist the memory, and provide both comfort and security.
- Creativity, curiosity, and surprise, which suggest that, with continued good health and adequate social and environmental supports, many older people retain a curiosity about life and all living things, and some develop or discover creative abilities.

EXHIBIT 12.3 Exploring attitudes about age and aging

1. When is a person "old"?
2. When will you be "old"?
3. How should you refer to a person who is "old"?
4. List some common stereotypes about "old" people.
5. What are some changes we will all experience as we become "old"?
6. What is the worst and best part of growing older?
7. How do you define "successful aging"?

SOURCE: Adapted from http://ist-socrates.berkeley.edu/~aging/ModuleAgeism.html.

Can you see how some of these characteristics relate to the theories mentioned above? Do you know some older adults who represent "successful aging" to you? Try the thought-provoking questions in Exhibit 12.3. Before going on to learn about biological, psychological, and social issues in late adulthood, read what Dr. Margaret A. Noel (2000), a geriatric physician, has written about "successful aging":

> I regard my patients and older friends as repositories of the secrets of aging well ... Battling the visual effect of time and gravity is a rapidly growing industry, but those I want to imitate appreciate youth and beauty as a season and would not exchange the work of time upon their character to have that season back. Long lives portioned with worldly success and failure, joy and grief, giving and receiving, have distilled and refined their spirit. It shines through frailty, through physical and cognitive decline, and continues to be reflected by those who love them, who bear witness to their lives.

STUDY TABLE: Developmental Themes of Late Adulthood

Developmental Themes	Late life is represented by integrity versus despair. Two or even three stages constitute late adulthood as life expectancy increases. The oldest old and minority elders are the fastest-growing groups. Vast differences characterize older adults; one way to assess is by functional age. Continuity theory suggests personality is fairly stable across adulthood. The concept of "successful aging" is currently being debated—maintaining health and independence is one measure of success but may leave out frail and disabled elders. Socioemotional selectivity is a newer theory addressing older adults' need for solitude, choice, and meaningful relationships. Leaving a legacy is an important goal for many in late life.

BIOPHYSICAL DIMENSION

Biophysical Growth and Development

Given successful treatment of illnesses and accidental injuries, the maximum human life span appears to be about 120 years of age (Hooyman & Kiyak, 2002). Although **life span** represents the upper limit of human age, **life expectancy** refers to the number of years the average person who was born in a particular year may live. Because of healthier lifestyles, better nutrition, and technological advances in medicine, life expectancy has increased significantly in the last several decades. For babies born in the year 2000, average life expectancy is 76.9 years. To get an idea of how far we've come, the average life expectancy for babies born in 1900 was only 49 years (National Institutes on Aging, 2001). Data drawn from the Federal Interagency Forum on Aging-Related Statistics (2004) indicate that people who reached age 65 in 2000 had an average life expectancy of an additional 17.9 years—19.2 years for females and 16.3 years for males. Because women tend to outlive men, the ratio of women to men increases with age, ranging from 122:100 at ages 65–69 to 256:100 after 85. Life expectancy for blacks is about 3 years less than for whites at age 65, but is about equal by age 85.

Scientists are finding that the rule for biological aging is "heterogeneity," or differences among individuals. There is as much variation among older people in the physical changes that occur with age as there is with their developmental tasks generally. There are a number of theories of biological aging, including some better-known ones, such as the "wear and tear" theory, which states that the body, like an automobile, is genetically programmed to wear out after a given time; the "cross links and free radical" theory, focused on unstable oxygen molecules that impair healthy cells in the body; and an "immunological" theory of aging, which attributes most biological change to the fact that the immune system deteriorates and produces fewer antibodies to attack disease with age.

According to one of the directors of the National Institute on Aging's Biology of Aging program,

> There is no single theory to explain aging... It's possible that some age-related changes are genetically programmed while others involve the effects of less predictable activity, such as free radical damage to cells or other insults that seem to occur with age (National Institute on Aging, 2001, p. 5).

Despite the lack of a single grand theory of biological aging, no one denies that a predictable pattern of some physical decline, called **senescence**, naturally occurs in the human organism with age. One of the difficulties with studying physiological aging is that advanced age increases the vulnerability to disease, and thus it is a challenge to distinguish the effects of aging processes from the effects of disease processes.

Because the rate of physical change due to aging varies from individual to individual and for different organs and tissues within individuals, chronological age cannot be used as an absolute marker for biophysical change. Inevitably, however, physical change does occur in all of the major organ systems of the body. As shown in Exhibit 12.4, there is virtually no part of us that remains unaffected by aging, but the good news is that along with the increasing longevity, medical, biological, and social scientists have been focusing on ways for older adults to live a healthier, higher-quality life into advanced age.

Discovering ways for older people to maintain higher functioning and avoid disability until shortly before death increases the compression of morbidity—where morbidity means illness and disability. These efforts have resulted in some significant findings about ways to slow and, in some cases, even counteract the physical decline that occurs with age. According to a report from the Centers for Disease Control (2001), exercise is perhaps the number-one key to a healthier late life: "Being physically active reduces the risk of coronary heart disease, colon cancer, diabetes, and high blood pressure. Regular physical activity also helps older people reduce their risk of falls, reduce anxiety and depression, maintain a healthy body weight, and maintain joint strength and mobility... Physical activity is the crux of healthy aging." As we age, muscle is gradually replaced with fat, which reduces strength and also reduces the rate of metabolism, because fat burns fewer calories than muscle at rest, thus leading to weight gain. Researchers have found that strength training can reverse this age-related muscle wasting, called *sarcopenia*. Small studies in the early 1990s started to show the amazing ability of even the very frail oldest-old nursing home residents to make significant gains in muscle

EXHIBIT 12.4 Age-related changes in biological systems

Skeletal system	Height peaks in a person's late thirties, and by age 75 most people have lost 5 cm in height, owing to decline of spinal discs, osteoporosis, and other age-related changes. The chest cavity also becomes deeper and less wide. Bones become less dense due to osteoporosis—a gradual loss of bone mass (more accelerated in women owing to estrogen loss). Joints are more restricted, resulting in a diminished range of motion in the upper arms, lower back, hips, knees, and feet. Arthritis is known to affect approximately 58% of all people aged 70 or older. Foot problems (non-disease-related) may include bunions, heel spurs, hammer toes, and calluses.
Muscle system	Lean body mass decreases with the beginning of middle age, and body fat increases in males (50%) and females (33%); fat redistributes, with more in the midsection. The power and speed of muscular contractions gradually decrease with age; without exercise, there is a gradual decline in muscle strength and endurance.
Brain and nervous system	With age there is a loss of neurons (estimated to be between 5% and 10% until the 70s—may accelerate subsequently), the basic cellular unit of the nervous system; unless the blood supply is blocked, there may be little functional change. If, for example, there is diminished flow of blood to the brain, neurotransmitter changes, accumulations of cholesterol, and so on, these changes may affect reaction time and interfere with perception and cognition.
Sensory system	Gait and balance may be affected by the combined effects of muscular, skeletal, and neurological changes, which may result in an increase in accidents and falls. Reduced tactile sensitivity results from a gradual toughening of the skin, older people develop a higher pain threshold. There is a decline in a sense of smell owing to gradual degenerative changes in olfactory cells, which is accompanied by a decrease in sense of taste. Age-related changes in vision increase with age, often as the result of a reduction of the quality or intensity of light reaching the retina. Very old age may be accompanied by degenerative changes in the retina, impairing one's ability to see; the ratio of legal blindness is 100:100,000 in individuals under age 21, but it increases to 1,400:100,000 in individuals age 69 and above. Significant hearing impairment occurs with increasing age when degenerative changes affect the compartments of the ear and the auditory nerve pathway; high-pitched sounds are not heard as well, resulting in jumbled or distorted words and sentences.
Circulatory system	Age-related changes appear to include a slight enlargement of the left ventricle of the heart and thickening of the atrial endocardium and atrial ventricular valves. Changes in the arteries (an increase in collagen and calcification of elastin fibers) make the arterial walls more vulnerable to disorders that cause their hardening and thickening (for example, the most common form of arteriosclerosis). Factors such as obesity, lack of exercise, anxiety, illness, and hardening of blood vessels may cause an increase in blood pressure, and with increasing age, veins become less elastic, thicker, and more dilated, causing valves in the large leg vein to become less efficient in returning blood to the heart.
Respiratory system	Between the ages of 20 and 80, lung capacity decreases 40%, even in the absence of disease; lungs lose elasticity, the chest decreases in size, and the diaphragm weakens; mouth breathing and snoring result from connective tissue changes that cause the nose to have a retracted septum.
Integumentary system	Aging skin becomes dryer, thinner, irregularly pigmented, and subject to mostly harmless growths and lesions. Without as much connective-tissue support, skin is more easily bruised or injured in old age. Skin has diminished collagen content and less elasticity, resulting in wrinkling and sagging. Fingernails and toenails may thicken; hair thins and loses it pigment; loss of body hair is progressively experienced by men and women in the pubic and armpit area; coarse hair, caused in part by hormonal changes, may grow on the upper lip and lower face of older women and the ears, nostrils, and eyebrows of older men.

SOURCE: Based on Schaie & Willis (2002); McInnes-Dittrich (2005).

strength with proper training. A recent controlled study (Baum, Jarjoura, Polen, Faur, & Rutecki, 2003) randomly assigned groups of long-term care residents aged 75 to 99 to a strength-and-flexibility exercise regime three times per week or a recreational session of a sedentary activity such as painting of the same duration. The exercise condition was shown to increase flexibility and strength, and also increased average scores on the Mini-Mental Status Exam (MMSE), a test of cognitive ability, by three points. Maintaining

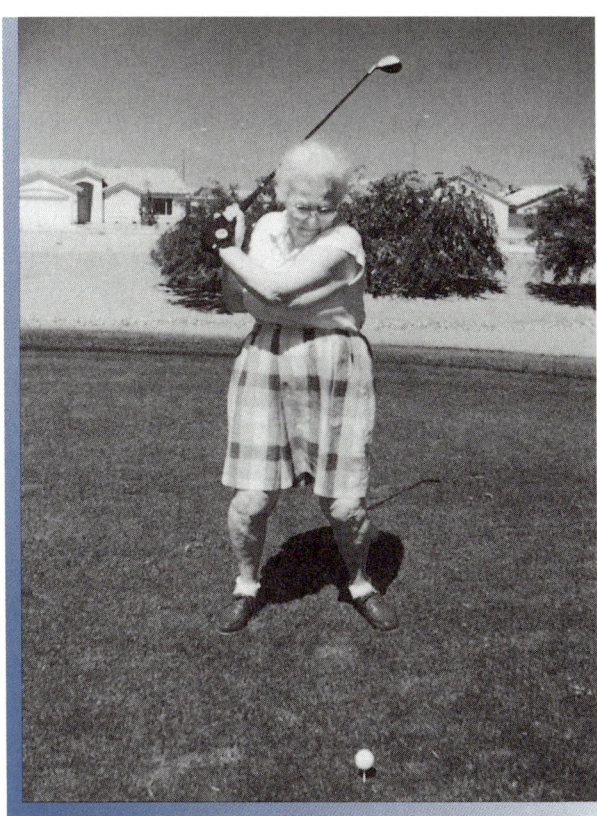

Regular exercise helps older adults maintain or improve their physical and mental well-being.

the body's lean muscle helps avoid frailty and disability, and this study and others like it demonstrate that it is literally never too late to start. Aerobic activity, such as brisk walking, swimming, or other "moving" activities (some of which can even be done by those who are wheelchair-bound), helps maintain healthy heart and lungs, tones muscles, burns calories, and enhances mood. Both types of exercise also reduce the loss of bone mass that occurs through normal aging, or more severely, through *osteoporosis*, a condition in which the bones become weak and porous. Two common reasons that older adults avoid physical activity are foot and joint pain due to arthritis or other conditions, and a fear of falling and its possibly serious consequences (Yardley & Smith, 2002). For these reasons, special exercise programs that go at a slow pace, with considerations for the special safety concerns of older adults, are in place in many congregate living facilities.

Along with physical activity, adequate nutrition promotes a higher level of wellness in late adulthood. Although nutrition requirements of older adults are not significantly different from those of middle-aged people, it is crucial that they eat high-quality diets that are lower in fat and higher in protein than that of a similar-sized young adult (Webdietitian.com, 2004). Nutritional issues for older people include their reduced ability to smell and taste, which can result in a lowered appetite and a fondness for sweet and salty foods. Gastrointestinal changes can occur because of a natural reduction in the production of digestive juices in the stomach (Webdietitian.com, 2004). Older adults also experience changes in the body's ability to metabolize nutrients and water, so they can become more susceptible to dehydration in warm weather or after exertion. Low-income elders, those who are functionally impaired, and the oldest old who live alone often face financial limitations, mobility problems, or both, that make it difficult to obtain and prepare the foods necessary for a healthy diet.

Health Care and Medications

Americans over age 65 were hospitalized during 2002 at a rate approximately three times the rate for people aged 45–65. And once admitted, older people tend to stay longer in the hospital—on average, 5.8 days, compared with 5.0 days for people under 65 (Administration on Aging, 2004a). In addition, those over 65 averaged more contacts with doctors—6.2 visits annually in 2001 for people aged 65–74; 7.4 visits for those aged 75 or over; and just 3.8 visits for adults 45–65. A disproportionate amount of total personal health-care expenditures are attributable to this age group. In 2001, the average noninstitutionalized older adult spent $1,886 for health-insurance premiums, $955 for medications, $582 for medical services, and $163 for medical supplies (Administration on Aging, 2004a).

The greater number of physiological problems and co-occurring chronic conditions in older adults means they consume a greater number of prescription and over-the-counter medications than do younger adults (Feinberg, 2000), estimated at four prescription medications and two over-the-counter medications per person over the age of 65 (Beers, 2000). Although many of these medications are literally "life-savers" that help older people control critical physical functions such as blood pressure, blood sugar, cholesterol, and heart functioning, the proliferation of available medications leads to a greater risk of medication-related side effects and problems. There is a situation known as the "prescribing cascade," in which a medication causes an adverse side effect that is mistaken as a different illness, leading the physician to prescribe another medication, and so on (Cameron & Richardson, 2000). Older people's bodies process medications differently from younger people's. Decreased liver and kidney functioning in late life mean that the elimination of medications from the body is not as efficient, and this difference causes older people's reduced tolerance to the usual dosages of many types of medication. This is a particularly serious concern with antianxiety or other sedating medications (Beers, 2000). Appropriate use of medications is an issue affecting many older adults that should be of concern to the providers who work with them. Issues regarding sexuality in older adults are less likely to be discussed by providers yet may be equally important to the quality of life for many older people.

Sexuality

The capacity for sexual expression continues into late adulthood, although the frequency of sexual activity decreases because of ill health or lack of access to suitable partners. The first large-scale research on sexual behavior in males (Kinsey et al., 1948) and females (Kinsey et al., 1953) suggested that older adults maintain an active interest in sexual relationships in later life. Subsequent research has confirmed that older adults are interested in sexual expression, but that the frequency of sexual intercourse gradually declines in later life (Walz, 2002). In the late 1990s, two groundbreaking surveys focusing on sexuality in older adults were conducted. The first, a large-scale survey by the National Council on Aging (Cutler, 2001) of 1,292 adults aged 60 and older found that 48% (61% of men and 37% of women) reported being sexually active. The proportions were higher for those in their 60s (71% for men and 51% for women) and lower for those in their 70s and 80s. This particular survey tells only part of the story—the researchers specifically asked for information on sexual practices, such as vaginal or anal intercourse, oral sex, or masturbation, to define "sexually active." But information about intimate relationships that do not involve those specific sexual practices, or how many wish for a sexual partner but do not have one, was not included. The second survey looked at self-rated sexual interest, sexual participation, and sexual satisfaction in more than 1,300 older adults (Johnson, 2001), with results suggesting men were somewhat more interested, active, and satisfied than women, on average.

Walz (2002) has argued that our youth-oriented society is uncomfortable with the idea of sexuality in late life, and he noted that depictions of sexual intimacy between two older people are very seldom seen in contemporary movies or fiction. In popular culture, Walz asserts, sexual interest on the part of older adults is often considered funny, pathetic, or frightening (e.g., "dirty old men"). As of this writing, there have been a number of magazine and television ads for medications to treat male erectile dysfunction such as Viagra and Cialis. Interestingly, most of the men and women appearing in romantic situations in those ads appear to be in their early 50s, the age of a large number of baby boomers, but it has been rarer to see images of men in these ads who are in their 60s or older, despite the fact that the older men are more likely to have a significant problem with sexual impotence. Likewise, there has been an increased interest in how women's sexuality may be affected by menopause now that the baby boomers are in the midst of that stage of life, but older women are less visible. Clearly, with the aging of the baby-boomer cohort, the issue of sexuality among older adults may come out from under the covers within the next two decades, as it is unlikely that the generation that participated in Woodstock will accept being stereotyped as asexual.

Physiological Changes and Sexual Activity

The majority of older men and women in good health can expect to continue sexual activities well into later life. Nevertheless, physiological changes affect both female and male sexual functioning in old age. As discussed in the last chapter, menopause in women brings about a reduction in the levels of estrogen and other hormones, called androgens, and with that reduction, some women experience reduced interest or pleasure in sexual activity. The loss of hormones and changes to the aging skin cause the vaginal walls to become thinner and less moist, which can make sexual intercourse or stimulation uncomfortable for some older women. Older women who have been inactive sexually for a time, for example because of widowhood, may find it particularly uncomfortable when they recommence sexual activity (Zeiss & Kasl-Godley, 2001). Fortunately, a number of over-the-counter or prescription lubricants and other medications can help. Side effects of medications, including some that treat high blood pressure, depression, anxiety, and diabetes, can also diminish older women's ability to achieve orgasm. And finally, urinary incontinence is an embarrassing problem that is more common for older women. Although it can usually be treated medically, it may erode a woman's confidence about becoming sexually intimate (National Institute on Aging, 2002).

Older men typically are able to engage in sexual activity well into their 70s, 80s, and beyond. However, an estimated 15–25% of men over the age of 65 experience sexual impotence, the inability to achieve or maintain an erection, at least a quarter of the time (National Institute on Aging, 2002). Most erectile dysfunction in older men can be directly attributed to a chronic illness such as hypertension, heart disease, or diabetes, or to the side effects of drugs such as antihypertensive medication, tranquilizers, and antidepressants. Prostate surgery, whether for cancer or the benign condition of an enlarged prostate, is a common procedure for older men and also sometimes results in erectile dysfunction (National Institute on Aging, 2002). Healthy older men require more time and direct stimulation of the penis to initiate sexual activity than they did when they were younger. Other changes due to normal aging include a reduction in the volume of seminal fluid, so that orgasms may be shorter and less intense than earlier in life. It also may take from 12 to 24 hours for older men to achieve another erection following ejaculation. Recent years have brought a proliferation of medications, such as Viagra, designed to enhance the ability to achieve and maintain an erection. These medications work by increasing the blood flow to the area of the penis; they have some side effects and are not recommended for men with certain medical conditions, so they should not be considered a panacea for older men. Nevertheless, their popularity suggests that many middle-aged and older men have some concerns with their sexual functioning and welcome the possibility of improved performance.

Implications for Practice: Sexuality in Late Adulthood

After puberty, sexuality is closely related to a sense of self-esteem and self-identity in most people, whether male or female, straight or gay, young or old. Changes in one's sexual functioning, concerns about being unable to function, and the loss of a sexual partner through death, illness, or disability all can be very difficult transitions for older adults. Lack of opportunity may be the biggest problem for single older adults; lack of privacy may be a problem for those living in long-term care. Concerns about how aging affects one's attractiveness and physical capacities are not uncommon, especially in a culture that highly values both youth and sexuality. In practice with older adults, depending on the situation, it is often appropriate to inquire about sexual interest and activity as part of a comprehensive biopsychosocial assessment. For example, McInnes-Dittrich (2005) has suggested that the social worker may wish to ask about intimate relationships in a matter-of-fact way, such as, "Many older adults continue to be sexually active. Is this important to you?" That type of question opens the door for the client to discuss his or her concerns. Another critical social-work role is to educate midlife and older adults about HIV/AIDS prevention. Approximately 11–15% of new AIDS cases in the U.S. occur in adults over age 50, and about 3% over age 60, and those cases are expected to increase (HIVoverfifty.org, 2004). Condom use, asking a new partner about his or her sexual and drug abuse history, and testing for HIV all are recommended for sexually active older adults.

Biophysical Strengths and Hazards

Chronic Health Problems

Physiological aging increases the individual's vulnerability to chronic health conditions. Most older people have at least one chronic condition, and the older one becomes, the more likely one is to have multiple conditions. Although chronic diseases increase an older adult's risk of frailty and disability, it is important to remember that the majority of older adults with chronic conditions do not experience significantly impaired functioning. Many older people with chronic conditions manage to live normal lives and cope very well. The two most common types of chronic health conditions experienced by people over age 65 are hypertension (49.2%) and arthritis (36.1%), followed by all types of heart disease (31.1%), sinusitis (15.1%), and diabetes (15.0%) (Administration on Aging, 2003). In addition, because cancer becomes more common as people age, and current treatments allow older adults to live a number of years with some types of cancer, many cancers are now more like chronic, rather than acute, conditions. In 2001, approximately 20% of older adults had some sort of cancer. Percentages of older people with various health conditions are shown in Exhibit 12.5.

Osteoarthritis, a degenerative joint disease, is the most common type of arthritis and is the largest cause

EXHIBIT 12.5 Percentage of older people with chronic health conditions in 1995

Condition	Males (%)	Females (%)	Total (%)
Arthritis	49.5	63.8	58.1
Diabetes	12.9	11.5	12.0
Cancer	23.4	16.7	19.4
Stroke	10.4	7.9	8.9
Hypertension	40.5	48.0	45.0
Heart disease	24.7	19.2	21.4

SOURCE: Adapted from the Federal Interagency Forum on Aging-Related Statistics; available at http://www.agingstats.gov.

of disability after age 65 in the United States (Lane & Wallace, 2002). Osteoarthritis is the result of repeated trauma or wear and tear on tissue, primarily in large joints such as the shoulder, knee, hip, and ankle. It involves the loss and destruction of cartilage that serves as a buffer between bones where they have contact with each other. Cartilage loss results in severe pain and impaired joint function (Lane & Wallace, 2002). Osteoarthritis affects men and women equally. Rheumatoid arthritis is an inflammatory joint disease that affects all ages and is more common in females than in males. Arthritis can affect older adults' ability to function independently. Of those over 70 years old who have arthritis, 50% require assistance with at least one activity of daily living (ADL), whereas 23% of those in that age range without arthritis require any assistance (National Academy on an Aging Society, 2000a). Experts caution that avoiding activity because of arthritis will only cause the joints to become more stiff and painful over time. A moderate exercise program, use of anti-inflammatory medicines, and special shoes or other assistive devices help to maintain the independent functioning of older adults with arthritis.

The National Institute on Aging (2002) has reported that only an estimated 25% of adults over age 60 have their blood pressure under control. Hypertension (high blood pressure [BP], defined as greater than 140/90mmHg) predisposes older people to stroke and heart attacks (National Institute on Aging, 2002), and recent research has shown that the top number, the systolic BP, is more important than the lower number as a risk for cardiovascular disease (Chobanian et al., 2003). Risk factors for high blood pressure include obesity, high cholesterol, smoking, excessive alcohol use, and lack of exercise (National Academy on an Aging Society, 2000c). Hypertension in older people is most commonly caused by arteriosclerosis (hardening of the arteries) or atherosclerosis (clogging of the arteries with fatty deposits) and may affect the kidneys and blood vessels. Medications and lifestyle changes, such as following a low-salt, low-fat diet, are used to treat the problem (Chobanian

---

FOCUS ON MULTICULTURALISM

HEALTH DISPARITIES FOR OLDER MEMBERS OF MINORITY GROUPS

Although the health of racial and ethnic minority elders has continued to improve since the 1960s, significant health disparities remain between older whites and people of color, a very important fact in light of the diversity of the coming cohorts of older adults. Particular areas of difference include overall self-rated health status, life expectancy, and the prevalence and associated complications of diabetes, hypertension, and certain kinds of cancer. For example, African Americans are 1.7 times more likely than Hispanic Americans to report poor health status, and Hispanics are 1.4 times more likely than whites to report poor health; African Americans are about twice as likely as whites to have diabetes, and Native American elders die from diabetes at a rate that is twice that for older whites (Johnson & Smith, 2002). Research has suggested that the interrelationships of genetic, social, cultural, and lifestyle differences, as well as different levels of health literacy and access to information, are at work in producing these disparities (National Institute on Aging, 2002). Unfortunately, access and quality of care has been shown to be better for whites than for nonwhites in recent large studies (Johnson & Smith, 2002). Language and cultural barriers affect older Hispanics, Asian Americans, and Pacific Islanders, and higher rates of poverty affect elders in the Hispanic/Latino, Native American, and African American communities (AARP, 2004a). Provider and institutional factors that contribute to differential access and care include racial and cultural biases, ineffective communication, and lack of transportation or outreach to minority elders (Johnson & Smith, 2002).

et al., 2003). High blood pressure is more common and severe in African Americans than in whites (National Academy on an Aging Society, 2000c). The focus section on page 580 discusses health disparities for minority elders.

Death and Dying

Eventually, death is a hazard of living that we can no longer avoid. The median age of death in the United States was 77 years in 2000. The latest information on the causes of death for Americans 65 years of age and older puts heart disease as the most frequent cause, followed by cancer, cerebrovascular disease (stroke), lung diseases, pneumonia and influenza, and diabetes (Federal Interagency Forum on Aging-related Statistics, 2004). Another major cause of death that does not show up on this list is Alzheimer's disease, because many families, nursing homes, and physicians choose to indicate another, more immediate cause of death (e.g., pneumonia) when a person with advanced Alzheimer's disease dies. Several of these causes of death are chronic conditions in the elderly with unpredictable clinical courses and prognoses, so that it is somewhat unusual for older adults to be experiencing a "terminal illness" until shortly before their death.

Although nearly 80% of people who die in the U.S. are over age 65 (Sheehan & Schirm, 2003), much of what we have learned about the process people go through when facing imminent death has been based on research or interviews with younger adults with terminal cancer or other prolonged illnesses. Perhaps the best-known investigator of the process of dying is Elisabeth Kübler-Ross, a Swiss-born psychiatrist who began a systematic study of death and dying at the University of Chicago's teaching-research hospital. Kübler-Ross's classic work (1969) identified five stages in the dying process: (1) denial and isolation, (2) anger, (3) bargaining, (4) depression, and (5) acceptance.

Preparing for death often means addressing emotional pain, grief, and indignity. Grieving the loss of family and friends, as well as the loss of life, is part of the dying process.

What does the dying process for an older person look like? Although death from a stroke or heart attack may occur very quickly, an older person's death from cancer or chronic illness such as congestive heart failure may take weeks or months. At first, the individual will become noticeably weaker, and at the same time, more socially withdrawn. He or she will begin to sleep more and to interact with friends and family less. Appetite and the ability to take any food or fluids will decrease. The actual dying process begins about one to two weeks before death occurs. The dying person may become intermittently disoriented and confused. He or she may become agitated and pick at the bedclothes. Sleep increases, and food consumption falls to very little. The dying person may perspire more, and his or her skin color may change to pale yellow with bluish hands and feet. Breathing and pulse become irregular. If the kidneys are failing, the person will become bloated with excess fluids. Just before death, the person may slip into a coma. Hands, feet, and legs may become blotchy and purplish. Breathing becomes very irregular, with long pauses between breaths and, eventually, a characteristic rattling from fluid in the lungs. Then the dying person becomes unresponsive and breathing stops.

In industrialized societies, our institutions tend to embrace the medical model and its goals of curing disease and extending life. In these settings, death tends to be viewed as an unnatural interruption of life, an undesirable outcome. The array of medical technologies that are available makes it difficult for medical personnel and families to "give up" and promote positive end-of-life care. Yet up until World War II, death was a part of the human experience and of the life of the community. People died at home in the presence of friends and family. Today, many people live in areas separated from extended family. Many adults have never seen a dying person or experienced a death.

Efforts to provide an alternative to hospital death resulted in the **hospice** movement. Hospices became important in treating terminal patients when families, patients, and caregivers found hospitals were not meeting their needs. In contrast to the goals of a hospital, the aim of hospice care is to care for and support the dying by providing what is known as **palliative care**, care that focuses on comfort, not cure. Individuals are eligible for hospice care when they have less than a six-month life expectancy and agree to give up seeking a cure for their illness. Hospice care is provided in the patient's home, in a nursing home, or in a special hospice unit in a hospital or community agency. Many hospice patients are older persons, and many are dying of cancer. But, increasingly, hospice patients are young people with AIDS.

> **FOCUS ON MULTICULTURALISM**
>
> **DEATH AS A NATURAL PROCESS**
>
> This poem illustrates a traditional culture's view of death as a natural part of the process of life.
>
> **A Native-American Elder Contemplates Life's End**
>
> Today is a very good day to die.
> Every living thing is in harmony with me.
> Every voice sings a chorus within me.
> All beauty has come to rest in my eyes.
> All bad thoughts have departed from me.
> Today is a very good day to die.
> My land is peaceful around me.
> My fields have been turned for the last time.
> My house is filled with laughter.
> My children have come home.
> Yes, today is a very good day to die.
>
> SOURCE: From *Many winters*, by Nancy Wood, p. 31. Copyright © 1974 by Nancy Wood, Illustrations © 1974 by Frank Howell. Used by permission of Bantam Doubleday Dell Books for Young Readers.

Advance Directives for Health Care

Because technological advances in medical care have complicated the dying process in the last several decades, quality of life at the end of life is an issue that will affect many older adults. There are several types of legal documents, called **advance directives**, that may be completed to make one's wishes known about healthcare decisions if one should become incapacitated. One common type is a living will. This is a document, used in the event a person has an irreversible terminal illness, stating that the individual does not want to be kept alive by artificial means but instead desires comfort care only. A common directive within these documents is a do not resuscitate (DNR) statement, also known as "no code" in most hospitals and nursing homes, which means the individual does not wish to receive cardiopulmonary resuscitation if breathing stops or the heart stops beating. Although prolongation of life is the most common and perhaps dramatic issue covered in a living will, there are a number of other concerns that arise in caring for very ill elders, including decisions about administration of antibiotics for infections, use of a mechanical ventilator to assist breathing, insertion of a feeding tube or an intravenous line for fluids, and even whether or not to perform surgeries. It is not always clear when the time is appropriate to stop active treatment of a disease or symptom and begin palliative care. Because health care has become so complex, a living will may not be able to cover every eventuality, and it is a good idea to designate one close family member or friend to be one's advocate and have decision-making power in the event serious illness or cognitive impairment renders one incapable of making their own decisions.

A **durable power of attorney for health care** is a document that is used to legally designate someone to have the authority to make health-care decisions should the person become incapacitated. Since the Patient Self-Determination Act of 1990, federal law requires all medical facilities that receive Medicare or Medicaid funding to inform patients about their rights to complete these documents upon entry to the facility. Many states now have advance-directive forms that include both a living will section where one can write one's wishes, and the designation of a person to have durable power of attorney for health care. These forms are recommended because they tend to cover more of the key issues that arise for very ill or dying people (Gunter-Hunt, Mahoney & Sieger, 2002).

Implications for Practice: End-of-Life Care

Current statistics show that nearly 50% of deaths occur in hospitals, and another 20–25% occur in nursing homes or other long-term care facilities. Clearly, end-of-life care often occurs in institutional settings. Social workers in all types of health-care facilities have important roles to play in assisting and advocating for the dying and their families within these institutions. The situation is complicated for older adults, by the nature of chronic illness in older persons and difficulty in predicting the timing of death (Sheehan & Schrim, 2003). In addition, because they were designed to maintain and enhance residents' health, the regulations and procedures in nursing homes do not tend to address the needs of dying people. It is not uncommon for persons with incurable, advanced illness to be treated as if they are still going to recover, because the decision to stop treatment and commence comfort care is not routinely made (Sheehan & Schrim, 2003). In hospitals, emergency treatments may be administered to dying patients unless there is a specific directive or family member who says not to. Once treatments are started, it is sometimes very difficult for families to decide to stop them. Such an instance is described by a hospital social worker working with the family of a 79-year-old woman with advanced dementia, pneumonia, and severe respiratory distress (Kaufman, 1998):

> Mrs. A was brought by ambulance with high-flow oxygen to the hospital emergency room and intubated (put on a mechanical ventilator). I was informed by ICU staff that her son was with her when she arrived on the unit. He was "very concerned" and wanted "everything done." . . . He told me that the doctors in the emergency room needed to know from him if they should intubate her because without mechanical ventilation she would have died immediately. With tears in his eyes he reported that he had said "yes, go ahead," because he wanted her to live, was hopeful she would stabilize, and could not possibly be singled out to be responsible for her death at that moment . . . [Two days later, the son agreed to make his mother DNR (Do Not Resuscitate) in case of cardiac arrest] but she was still receiving mechanical ventilation and intravenous medication and nutrition . . . Ten days after admission, Mrs. A's son continued to want "aggressive care" . . . for the recalcitrant pneumonia . . . I spoke again with her son and with her daughter who had just arrived from another state. They both repeated to me that they would not want their mother to be on life support; however, they did not understand that what they were viewing—a woman intubated to receive mechanical ventilation—was indeed life support. Two days later, 12 days after she was hospitalized in the ICU, Mrs. A's kidneys and other organs began to fail. Her doctor discussed her failing condition with her son and daughter at length . . . They agreed to let her die. She died shortly after the ventilator was withdrawn, with her children [and] the family doctor at her bedside (p. 718).

In this case, the social worker was involved after treatment had already begun with Mrs. A and her role was one of helping to educate the family about the situation and to hear out their feelings and concerns about the decisions that needed to be made. Another social worker in the nursing home may have been involved before this crisis to alert the family to the imminent possibilities for Mrs. A because of her deteriorating condition, and to help the son prepare to let his mother die.

The following points (adapted from Kayser-Jones, 2002) outline the basic needs of older people who are near death—needs that medical personnel and social workers can and should provide:

- A dying person needs adequate pain management and medical management of other distressing symptoms, such as shortness of breath. Pain is a physical phenomenon that can be assessed in those who are mentally alert by a simple numeric rating (e.g., "If 0 is no pain and 10 is excruciating pain, how are you feeling now?") or a visual analog scale, where the person is asked to mark or point to the place along a line where the level of pain is.
- The dying person needs competent, gentle physical care to maintain comfort, cleanliness, and personal dignity.
- The dying person and the family need straightforward information about their situation and any options for care—and help to make decisions. This is an area where social workers can be instrumental in helping

ease the communication between medical professionals and the patient and family.
- Suffering, more global than physical pain, may occur during the dying process because of anxiety, fears, or regrets. The dying person and his or her family need reassurance and support to ease the emotional distress and anxiety common in their situation. The mentally alert dying person needs the opportunity to talk about fears, unfinished business from the past, and concerns for the future of loved ones. The social worker can spend time allowing the dying person to voice these concerns and may use the technique of Life Review if the person has the strength for longer conversations. This technique helps the person to look back on the major events of his or her life and evaluate them. Visualization and relaxation techniques are often helpful. Ideally, the person's loved ones can be encouraged both to talk about these issues and to listen.
- The dying person and the family need the opportunity to receive spiritual support and to engage in the comforting rituals particular to their religion or culture. ∎

STUDY TABLE: Biophysical dimension of late adulthood

Biophysical Growth and Development	The maximum lifespan is about 120 years. Biological theories attempt to explain senescence, the decline seen in the body and its components with age. Compression of morbidity is the goal to keep older people well so they avoid disability until shortly before death. Exercise is an effective way for older people to maintain muscle mass, flexibility and even cognitive abilities. Older adults are hospitalized at three times the rate of younger adults, and they stay longer. They also use more medications. Differences in metabolism with age increase the risks for side effects and drug interactions. Interest in sexual expression continues for a majority of older adults. Frequency of sexual activity decreases due to health conditions and lack of available partners. Popular culture stereotypes sexuality of older adults and has a relatively negative view. Normal physical changes affect both female and male sexual functioning with age. Social workers may want to broach the topic of sexuality in assessments with older clients to support their interest in remaining sexually active and to provide education about HIV/AIDS prevention.
Biophysical Strengths and Hazards	Chronic health conditions increase with age, and many older adults have more than one condition, yet the majority continues to function independently. Many cancers are now considered chronic conditions for older adults, about 20% of whom have some sort of cancer. Hypertension and arthritis are the most common chronic health conditions. Arthritis causes impaired functioning in approximately 50% of sufferers over age 70. Hypertension, or high blood pressure, is very common and associated with higher risk for stroke and heart attacks. Medications and lifestyle changes are used to treat the problem. Minority elders experience significant disparities in terms of health conditions and health care. Nearly 80% of deaths in the U.S. are among people over age 65. Most deaths occur in hospitals or nursing homes. The hospice model provides comfort care and support to dying people and their families. Advance directives for health care include living wills and durable power of attorney for health care. Social workers are often involved in the process of completing advance directives and in end-of-life care decisions for patients and families, and they may participate with a healthcare team to provide adequate pain management, gentle personal care, complete information about options available, psychological reassurance and support, and access to spiritual support and guidance.

CONCEPT MAP

PSYCHOLOGICAL DIMENSION

Cognitive Development and Information Processing

All over the United States, and in about ninety other countries, there are classrooms filled with eager, enthusiastic students who spend a week or two at a college campus or state park to learn about topics as diverse as bluegrass music, the current state of the media, or the biography of Thomas Jefferson. The interesting thing about these students is that they are attending Elderhostel programs, so most of them are over the age of 55, and many are in their 70s, 80s, and 90s. Elderhostel is a nonprofit organization that promotes late-life learning by sponsoring approximately 10,000 one- or two-week programs yearly (www.elderhostel.org). Each program includes three or four noncredit courses, most taught by university-level faculty, many of whom are retired. Program fees include tuition, food, and lodging, and are usually far less than a week at a hotel or resort. The growth and success of the Elderhostel program attests to the fact that many older adults are eager to continue learning new things.

Whether older people think or learn differently from younger adults is a complex question. Schaie and Willis (2000) have outlined six stages of cognitive development across the adult lifespan, two of which apply to later life. Schaie proposed that in the young-old, the need to acquire and monitor information lessens, leading to a reorganizational stage, in which the individual rearranges and reallocates intellectual abilities to meet changing roles and changing personal needs. For those in late old age, the cognitive stage is called reintegration; this stage corresponds to Erikson's idea of integration versus despair. Accordingly, "the information that elderly people acquire and the knowledge they apply is, to a greater extent than earlier in life, a function of their interests, attitudes, and values. It requires, in fact, the reintegration of all of these" (Schaie & Willis, 2002, p. 349).

Another related cognitive theory of aging is **selective optimization and compensation** (Baltes & Baltes, 1990), which focuses on ways the older self is able to cope and maintain integrity despite declines in reserve capacities. The need to adapt to declines in functioning encompasses the *selection* component of the model, in which the older person determines which tasks or activities are most important and decides to drop others from the repertoire. *Optimization* comes with a concerted effort to make the best use of one's remaining strengths, skills, and energies, and *compensation* arises when a narrowing of the range of capacities requires that behaviors be altered to fit current levels of functioning. Research on cognitive development in older adults has attempted to test these and other similar theories. For example, in a cross-sectional study that looked at both cognitive and social developmental issues, a sample of older adults was asked to rate whether they had become more interested, less interested, or retained about the same level of interest in a set of activities and pastimes. Adams (2004) found that investment decreased in activities requiring physical and social effort, such as entertaining in one's home, attending social events with strangers, or shopping and buying things, but that interest in intellectually and emotionally satisfying activities over which the older adult has some control remained high. A majority of the sample remained invested in receiving calls or visits from family and friends, participating in some form of prayer or spiritual life, reading, puzzles or computer activities, and keeping up with current events.

Normal aging has an effect on the brain and its functions through a number of pathways, including changes in the size of the brain, neurological changes, changes in glucose metabolism, and blood flow to the brain (Piguet et al., 2002). Yet it appears that these changes do not always affect cognitive functioning to an equal degree in older individuals. Determining the nature of the change in intellectual function that occurs in late adulthood is a complex issue. A classic study by Horn (1982) used cross-sectional data to conclude that **fluid intelligence** (abstract reasoning ability or "native intelligence") decreases with age, but **crystallized intelligence** (accumulated information and verbal skills) remains stable or may even increase with age. This theory is intuitively appealing and has influenced subsequent research and practice in the area of cognitive development with older adults. Another recent cross-sectional study done in Australia with persons age 80 and above concluded that changes seen in **executive functioning**—the cognitive abilities of organization and task performance—were not caused by aging per se, but rather by age-related specific conditions that may cause cognitive impairment (Piguet et al., 2002).

Cross-sectional studies can offer reliable information about age differences at any point in time, but longitudinal studies offer more reliable information about age changes over the life span (Schaie & Hofer, 2001). The Seattle Longitudinal Study (SLS; Schaie, 1996) began in 1956 and has conducted assessments every seven years. In the SLS, five primary mental abilities of respondents were tested, including verbal meaning, reasoning ability, word fluency, numerical ability, and spatial visualization. Findings covering a span of thirty-five years indicate that abilities varied greatly in areas tested; however, by age 67, there was no more than a 25% decline; by age 74, there was about a 33% decline; and by age 81, decline had risen to about 40%. The declines that occurred were very gradual until the respondents reached their late 80s or early 90s, at which time declines were seen to occur much more rapidly and uniformly. The investigators pointed out that the large proportion remaining stable and the few who increased performance on some measures was remarkable. Although the state of knowledge of intellectual decline is imperfect, it appears likely that decline is not a given with advancing age and that there is considerable variation in the loss of mental abilities.

It is well established that information processing speed declines with age (Schaie & Willis, 2002; Salthouse, 2000). Studies of learning in animal models show that older animals can learn as well as younger ones, but they learn more slowly (National Institute on Aging, 2001). The time it takes to retrieve knowledge is dependent on sensory inputs from the eyes, ears, and other sensory organs. With age, the eye's ability to focus on nearby objects decreases, the amount of light required increases, and there is impairment in the ability to adapt from light to darkness and back to light. The ability to hear, particularly high frequencies, also decreases (Fozard & Gordon-Salant, 2001). With sensory deficits, age seems to affect the quality of perception and the ability to receive, process, and act on information. This change tends to lead to a slowing of behavioral responses or reaction time in late adulthood (Madden, 2001; Salthouse, 2000).

Perhaps the most common change in cognitive abilities associated with getting older is memory loss, usually in the form of recall. Word-finding, retrieval of nouns in particular, appears to accompany normal aging, and is characterized by that "tip of the tongue" experience (National Institute on Aging, 2001). There is an interrelationship between memory and learning; that is, memory is the ability to retain (or encode) and recall (or retrieve) what has been learned. Psychologists have identified a number of types of memory. Long-term memory consists of four subtypes (episodic, semantic, procedural, and prospective) and generally remains intact with age,

EXHIBIT 12.6 Common Myths Associated with Mental Impairment

Is it normal or is it dementia?

Normal	Possibly Alzheimer's disease or other dementia
1. Temporarily forgetting a colleague's name.	Not being able to recall the name later.
2. Having a word on the tip of the tongue.	Substituting strange words for forgotten words.
3. Misplacing objects in moments of distraction.	Misplacing things in unusual places and having no memory of putting them there.
4. Forgetting for a moment where you're going.	Getting lost on your own street.
5. Having trouble balancing the checkbook accurately.	Forgetting how to add or subtract numbers.
6. Not feeling like doing a chore.	Not knowing or caring that the chore needs to be done.
7. Temporarily forgetting the day of the week.	Not knowing what season or year it is, even after thinking about them.

SOURCE: Adapted from the Alzheimer's Association (www.alz.org).

although episodic memory, the ability to remember things associated with a particular time or place, is subject to heavier processing demands and shows some age-related reduction (Schaie & Willis, 2002). Short-term memory consists of two main types: primary memory, referring to the "storage space" available for short-term memories, and working memory, the capacity to hold on to a piece of information while mentally manipulating it. In the normal aging process, primary memory loss rarely occurs, whereas both the encoding and retrieval abilities associated with working memory are shown to decline with age (Backman, Small, & Wahlin, 2001).

Difficulties or impairments in memory may be caused by problems of perception, attention, or motivation. The state of emotional and physical health can have a significant effect on memory functions, and conditions such as diabetes, high blood pressure, cardiovascular problems, and depression all have been shown to negatively impact memory (Backman, Small, & Wahlin, 2001). Some memory impairments may be misdiagnosed when, as is often the case, they are transitory or reversible. In addition, a variety of medications and some vitamin deficiencies may affect memory function or mimic certain brain disorders (Butler, Lewis, & Sunderland, 1998; Backman, Small, & Wahlin, 2001).

Methods of retraining have been developed to assist older adults in sharpening their cognitive skills. For instance, older adults' ability to remember new material improves after they are shown how to use organizational strategies (Schaie & Willis, 2002). In one classic study, Willis and Nesselroade (1990) used modeling, individual practice, feedback, and group discussion to train older adults how to identify the rule or pattern in problem solutions. Following the cognitive training, in this seven-year longitudinal study, 70- and 80-year-old adults performed at a higher level than they had in their late 60s. The results of this and other studies suggest that cognitive declines due to normal aging may be reversible.

Cognitive well-being is an overriding concern for older people and their families. The risk for cognitive impairments is known to increase with age (National Institute on Aging, 2001), and with the graying of the baby boomers, longer life spans, and greater visibility of Alzheimer's disease and other dementias in the media, a growing phenomenon among middle-aged and older adults is anxiety about getting or having Alzheimer's disease (Hodgson & Cutler, 2003). The term "senior moment," describing a lapse in memory, has become popular in the past few years, reflecting both a stereotype (i.e., that aging automatically brings poor memory or only older persons are forgetful) and the high level of anxiety in our society about getting old and losing one's cognitive abilities (Bonnesen & Burgess, 2004). A recent study done in Britain interviewed older adults about their views of dementia and found that many were uncertain about the difference between normal aging and dementia (Corner & Bond, 2004). The interviewees expressed considerable anxiety about becoming "senile" and focused on anxiety about "loss of independence, control, identity, and dignity" (Corner & Bond, 2004, p. 150). Fortunately, there are guidelines to help distinguish normal cognitive changes from a possible dementia (see Exhibit 12.6). We discuss Alzheimer's disease in detail later in this chapter.

Communication

Communication in late life may be affected by sensory limitations, such as loss of hearing or failing eyesight, or by cognitive impairments or mood disorders. Disorders such as Parkinson's disease affect speech, causing the person to be very soft-spoken by later in the illness. In the oldest old, even those who do not suffer from a particular disorder tend to speak more slowly, with greater response latency in conversation. Some elders suffer from social isolation, particularly frail older people who live alone. There may be no one whom they see and talk with regularly other than helpers such as the volunteer who delivers Meals on Wheels, or the aide who comes to help with personal care. For many older adults who have few family members close by, or who have difficulty getting out on their own, the telephone and often the Internet provide important links to distant loved ones and to the outside world.

Communication with cognitively impaired elders can be very challenging, yet it is important for family members and professionals to continue communicating with them in positive ways. In the 1960s, validation therapy was developed by a social worker who argued that it is most helpful to try and understand the needs and feelings of a confused elder, so that rather than constantly orienting the person to the present, the validation therapy–trained worker will go along with the person's view of reality and ask questions in order to try to interpret his or her needs and messages. The emphasis of the method is listening empathically to the feelings being expressed by the person with dementia (Feil & Altman, 2004). Even hostile or "acting out" behaviors are seen in this approach as forms of communication that need to be listened to by people interacting with the individual. This method has gradually become accepted in many institutions that serve persons with Alzheimer's disease and other dementias, although it is seldom used in pure form; most long-term care settings continue to post the date and season and introduce some current reality into activities with residents with dementia.

Elderspeak is the term for the particular manner in which people commonly tend to address older adults, both those with dementia and those who do not have dementia, in order to be better understood by the older person; this style of communication has been found in a number of research studies in a variety of settings (Kemper & Mitzner, 2001). Elderspeak can be characterized by "a simplified speech register with exaggerated pitch and intonation, simplified grammar, limited vocabulary, and slow rate of delivery" (Kemper & Mitzner, 2001, p. 391) and resembles the way adults sometimes speak to small children. There is debate about the relative harms and benefits of the use of elderspeak. Elderspeak may appear to be disrespectful and may serve to undermine the self-esteem and independence of older adults, particularly those in nursing homes, yet some research has found elderspeak provides benefits in terms of increased comprehension for the older person (Kemper & Mitzner, 2001).

Attitudes and Emotions

Research on emotions in later life has found a few minor differences between younger and older adults in terms of affective intensity, qualities of emotions experienced, and specific emotions that are more prevalent (Magai, 2001). For instance, in the very oldest old, a reduction in positive affect is typically seen, but otherwise, emotional intensity of positive and negative affect appears to be relatively stable, although there appears to be a small decrease in the frequency with which older adults experience anger and sadness (Magai, 2001). The complexity of emotional experience has been found to be greater in older adults than younger adults (Carstensen, Pasupathi, & Mayr, 2000). This study found that the older people in their sample typically experienced more poignant or bittersweet emotions than the younger people. The authors speculated that an awareness of limited time remaining adds to this appreciation of the mixed qualities of many everyday experiences. Two theories mentioned earlier in this chapter, socioemotional selectivity, and selective optimization and compensation, were developed through studies of emotional life of older adults and reflect several of the findings of these studies. Both of these theories involve the older adult making choices to achieve optimal affect regulation and an appropriate blend of stimulation and comfort, while avoiding negative affect (Magai, 2001).

Loss, Grief, and Mourning

Experiences of loss, anticipation of loss, and adaptation to loss tend to characterize the emotional fabric of late life. In every aspect of late adulthood, losses occur: death of loved ones; decline in health; loss of youth; loss of customary social roles and perhaps their

EXHIBIT 12.7 Factors that may affect experience, behavior, and adaptation in loss

Environmental or Extrinsic Factors

Personal losses or gain: marital partners; other loved and significant figures (friends, children)

Social forces (losses or gain): status changes, prestige changes: in social groups other than family

Socioeconomic adversities: income drop, inflation

Unwanted retirement: arbitrary retirement policies

Cultural devaluation of older persons: sense of uselessness, therapeutic pessimism, forced isolation, forced segregation

Intrinsic Factors

Nature of personality: character structure (defensive and integrative mechanisms), life history, survival characteristics

Physical diseases: disease of any organ system; perceptual decrements; sexual losses; disease of integrative systems (hormonal, vascular, and central nervous systems); brain damage; arteriosclerosis; senile dementia, and so on; physical limitations (such as arthritis)

Age-specific changes (largely obscure and mysterious, but inexorable with the passage of time): losses of speed of processing and response; involuntary processes; others (heredity, survival qualities); changes in body size and appearance

Experience of bodily dissolution and approaching death (subjective passage of time)

SOURCE: From Aging and mental health: Positive psychosocial and biomedical approaches, Fourth Edition, by R. N. Butler, M. Lewis, and T. Suderland, p. 89. Copyright © 1991 by Allyn & Bacon. Reprinted by permission.

---

status and prestige; and, for some, loss of aspects of independent functioning. Multiple losses at any one point in time are not uncommon, and the fact that many of these losses were expected may not make them any easier for the person who is experiencing the losses, yet family and friends may minimize the impact of losses on older adults (Knight, 2004). Exhibit 12.7 shows some of the factors that affect older adults' ability to adapt to loss.

Grief is the normative emotional reaction in response to the death of a loved one that may be expressed both physiologically and emotionally. Physiological expressions of grief often include emptiness in the pit of the stomach, a feeling of shortness of breath, tightness in the throat, muscle weakness and fatigue, sensitivity to noise, and a dry mouth (Worden, 2002). Emotional expressions of grief normally may include sadness, anger, self-reproach, anxiety, loneliness, helplessness, numbness, and, at times, relief or emancipation (Worden, 2002). The loss of a spouse or a partner or other loved ones through death may have a profound effect on older survivors, partly because there is less likelihood that the lost relationships will be replaced.

William Worden (2002) has discussed the importance of working through grief. When people who experience the loss of a loved one do not deal with their pain and loss, problems can arise years down the road. Worden outlined four tasks essential to mourning a loss:

- Accept the loss. Initially, people deny the reality of a death, so the first task is to accept that the loved one is gone and will not return. Often people display searching behaviors, seeing the loved one in a crowd or hearing his or her voice.
- Feel the pain. Many ask after the death of a loved one, "When does this pain go away?" Many simply do not want to hurt so much, so they busy themselves with activities or go on a trip to avoid their feelings. But pain cannot be avoided, and, if not dealt with at the time of death, it may resurface later when another loss occurs. Bereaved individuals need to externalize the pain by talking about the death and the loved one. Group therapy situations are helpful.
- Adjust to the new environment. External adjustments include dealing with practical realities and loss of social roles; internal adjustments may relate to the person's identity as a child or a partner of the person who is deceased; and spiritual adjustments, coming to some understanding of the meaning of the person's life and the loss, need to be made.

- Find an appropriate way to maintain connection with the deceased, yet move on with life.*

Rather than expecting bereaved people to withdraw their emotions from the lost person, Worden suggested thinking of this final step as "relocating" the deceased in one's life.

In recent years, a variation on traditional stage models of grief, called the "dual process model of coping with bereavement," has been introduced (Stroebe & Schut, 1999). In this model, it is acknowledged that the grieving occurs on two levels, termed *loss-oriented* and *restoration-oriented* coping. Loss-oriented coping focuses on the negative feelings, such as yearning, despair and the memories of the deceased, and restoration-oriented coping focuses on distractions from grief, including new roles and new relationships. The model proposes that these two means of coping go on simultaneously and serially, so that the painful "grief work" is not done all at once, nor without breaks for finding new positive aspects of living. Richardson (2003) found support for this model from a study of 276 bereaved husbands and wives. One interesting result was that the more the respondent reported mentally going over the circumstances of the death, the lower the well-being; that is to say, rumination over the negative events surrounding the death was not helpful in the long run. Early in the bereavement process, loss-oriented coping dominated, and later, restoration coping was more prevalent in the study.

Loneliness

Bereavement in late adulthood may lead to loneliness (Adams, Sanders & Auth, 2004). **Loneliness** has been defined as an unpleasant subjective state in which the person senses a discrepancy between the desired amount of companionship or emotional support and that which is available (Blazer, 2002b). A person may be socially lonely—there simply isn't enough companionship available from anyone—or lonely for a specific intimate other. Other common age-related losses and transitions, such as moving to a new residence or a change in health that necessitates a change in routine, also may cause loneliness. In a review of 149 studies examining loneliness in older people, women, those over 80, and those with lower incomes were more likely to be lonely (Pinquart & Sorensen, 2001). Loneliness is sometimes a precursor to or a symptom of depression (Blazer, 2002b). For older adults in congregate living or long-term care facilities, attendance at organized social activities does not appear to inoculate against loneliness (Adams, Sanders & Auth, 2004). Possible social-work interventions to prevent or alleviate loneliness in older adults in various settings might include the following:

- Social-skills groups for residents in congregate living facilities; in these groups, members learn how to be more sociable, at the same time getting to know one another better.
- Friendly visitor programs for the homebound in the community.
- Family therapy with a focus on mobilizing social and emotional support for a lonely older family member.
- Arranging special social events involving friends or family who reside outside of a long-term care or congregate living facility, to help residents maintain ties to the community.
- Bereavement support groups in which the recently widowed are given the opportunity to talk about the spouse they have lost.

Social Cognition and Regulation

Age and Self-Concept

I do not live in the past; it is the past which is alive in me.

—Rene Dubos

Older adults resist thinking of themselves as old. A recent study found that, on average, a sample of adults aged 51–92 reported feeling eight years younger and believing that people think them to be seven years younger than their actual age (Kaufman & Elder, 2002), and another examined the ways older women negotiate their identities while distancing themselves from stereotyped notions of being old (Hurd, 1999). There are numerous anecdotes about this phenomenon: A social worker speaking at a weekly social meeting of a senior citizens' group where all the participants were at least 70 years old asked how many

---

*Used by permission from *Grief counseling and grief therapy: A handbook for the mental health practitioner*, by W. Worden. Copyright © 1991 Springer Publishing Company, Inc., New York 10036.

people present considered themselves "older adults." Not a single person raised a hand! A woman in her early 70s complained to her daughter-in-law when they visited a retirement home, "There are so many OLD people here!" And this author's paternal grandmother, who lived to be 96, had two pet phrases on the topic of growing old. The first reflected the many challenges of aging she had to face. She'd say emphatically, "Old age ain't for sissies!" But she'd also say, "I swear I feel about 35 inside!"

Many older adults tend to think of themselves in terms of their former occupation or social role. When introduced, many state what job they retired from. And those who have retired may find they engage in volunteer work or other pastimes that reflect those prior roles. This fits with continuity theory, which was discussed earlier in this chapter. As people age, their basic personality or core sense of self does not change, although their psychosocial needs may change, along with their physical bodies and social roles. Reminiscence, a part of the life-review process (Butler, 1963), is one way older people maintain a sense of self. **Reminiscence** is designed to help the older adult retrieve positive memories from the past, with the goal of improving mood, but unlike life review, reminiscence is not geared toward gaining insight or resolving earlier conflicts (McInnes-Dittrich, 2005). As aging brings loss of some of the roles and relationships that were important in creating the individual's personal identity, thinking over and talking about important past roles, events, and people helps keep these memories alive and literally helps maintain the identity of the person. Reminiscing is part of the process of putting meaning to our lives. But there may be more to sharing memories for older people. Reminiscence can be a socialization tool, as memories are shared with friends and relatives. It can help an older person orient to the present by getting a "good grip" on the past. As one reviews the events of one's life, past accomplishments and successes may be more appreciated in hindsight, whereas weaknesses and mistakes don't seem as serious as they did decades ago.

Implications for Practice: Reminiscence Groups in Long-Term Care

Groups convened for the purpose of reminiscence are common in long-term care. Group settings facilitate socialization and skills acquisition along with the more general goals of improving mood and self-esteem. McInnes-Dittrich (2005) has offered a number of suggestions for these groups:

- One possible way to structure a reminiscence group is to go through the life span chronologically, beginning with childhood and spending a couple of sessions on each major developmental period.
- Allow group members to have a role in choosing the specific topics they wish to focus on.
- Avoid a focus on "firsts," such as first dates, first kisses, or first jobs, because these topics tend to be less uniformly good memories. General topics such as pets, holiday traditions, or favorite foods from early life are recommended.
- Take into consideration the cultural origins, gender, and functional level of the group's members when planning topics and activities.
- Music and photos from the era of the childhood and young adulthood of group members may trigger fond memories, even among residents with dementia.
- Structured activities such as creating scrapbooks, writing memoirs, and constructing a family tree or group cookbook may be used with high-functioning older adults in a number of settings.

Psychological Strengths and Hazards

Psychological well-being in late life brings us back to "successful aging"—older people who have kept their minds and bodies active are more likely to age successfully and avoid some of the hazards of aging, including psychological ones. Numerous studies have shown that psychological well-being in later life is associated with a flexible attitude and the ability to adapt to the changes that aging brings (Greene, 2000). Although adaptability is a positive quality, a sense of personal mastery, or control over the environment, is a strength also shown to be important to the psychological well-being of older people (Jang, Haley, Small, & Mortimer, 2002). Older residents of nursing homes and others who are disabled often experience greatly diminished personal control and mastery, and thus are particularly vulnerable to depression. Offering choices to functionally impaired older adults and helping them to maintain their current level of functioning will help them with their sense of mastery and enhance their psychological well-being.

Wisdom

As we know, Erikson's developmental crisis for the final stage of life is integrity versus despair, but the strength he saw resulting from successful resolution of the crisis is **wisdom**. Much has been written about wisdom but, as Schaie and Willis note, the concept is still an elusive one (2002). How would you define wisdom? Do you think older adults seem wiser than younger people? One review of the literature on wisdom defines it as "the application of tacit knowledge [practical knowledge, or knowing *how*] toward the achievement of a common good through a balance among intrapersonal, interpersonal and extrapersonal interests" (Sternberg & Lubart, 2001, p. 507). The association of the concept of wisdom with growing older equates accumulated life experience with becoming wiser. Paul Baltes and his colleagues in Berlin have devoted much attention to the concept of wisdom, mostly through a series of studies that asked adult participants open-ended questions about life-management problems. They have developed a five-component model of what constitutes a wise response, summarized in one of their most recent publications (Baltes & Staudinger, 2000), as follows:

- rich factual knowledge about life
- rich procedural knowledge about life
- putting things into a lifespan context
- relativism of values (appreciating others' values)
- recognition of uncertainty

Data from Baltes's work has shown that wisdom-related responses remained stable from young adulthood up till about age 75, disappointing those who would like to see a true increase in wisdom with age (Baltes & Staudinger, 2000).

Spirituality and Religious Beliefs

There is a growing awareness of the significance and positive roles of religion and spirituality in the lives of older people. Religious beliefs tend to remain stable until about age 60 and then increase (Hooyman & Kiyak, 2002), although attendance at religious services decreases with the onset of chronic illnesses (Benjamins, Musick, Gold, & George, 2003). A sense of meaning in life that comes from religious beliefs has been found to be associated with greater subjective well-being in older adults (Krause, 2003). Spirituality is considered separate from religious behavior, although the two often may be linked (Ortiz & Langer, 2002). **Spirituality** can be defined as faith that there is a greater power than oneself and the possibility of coping through trust in and prayer to that greater power (Hooyman & Kiyak, 2002). Spirituality connotes a level of awareness that goes beyond ordinary physical and spatial boundaries. Studies have found an association of religiosity, private prayer, or spiritual beliefs with physical health (Musick, Traphagen, Koenig, & Larson, 2000) and even with length of survival (Helm, Hays, Flint, Koenig, & Blazer, 2000). Spiritual beliefs are associated with indicators of well-being, such as quality-of-life ratings, and with both the will to live and the acceptance of the inevitability of death (Hooyman & Kiyak, 2002).

There has been a recent interest in expanding the biopsychosocial model of social-work assessment with older people to include spirituality (Ortiz & Langer, 2002). An awareness of both the religious beliefs and the spiritual needs of our clients is particularly important in residential long-term care, hospitals, end-of-life care, and individual mental-health treatment. A brief "spiritual assessment protocol" has been proposed, which can be used by social workers to open discussion of spiritual practices, beliefs, and needs perceived by the older clients, whether or not they participate in organized religious faiths (Ortiz & Langer, 2002).

Cognitive Impairment: Alzheimer's Disease and Other Dementias

It is estimated that there were 4.5 million individuals in the United States with Alzheimer's disease (AD) in 2000, and it is projected that by 2050, approximately 13.2 million people will suffer from this disease (Hebert, Scherr, Bienias, Bennett, & Evans, 2003). Approximately 10% of all people in the United States over age 65 and 50% of those over age 85 are afflicted with AD (Naditz, 2003). The disorder starts with loss of short-term memory, eventually progressing to interfere with all of the brain's functions (Naditz, 2003). Behavioral and emotional changes are common in people with AD; lack of motivation, or apathy, is part of the usual presentation in the early stages, so that the person with AD becomes dependent on others and lacks interest or emotional reactivity (Landes, Sperry, Strauss, & Geldmacher, 2001). By the middle or moderately severe stages, about 50% of those with the disease experience symptoms such as delusions or hallucinations, agitation, verbal and physical ag-

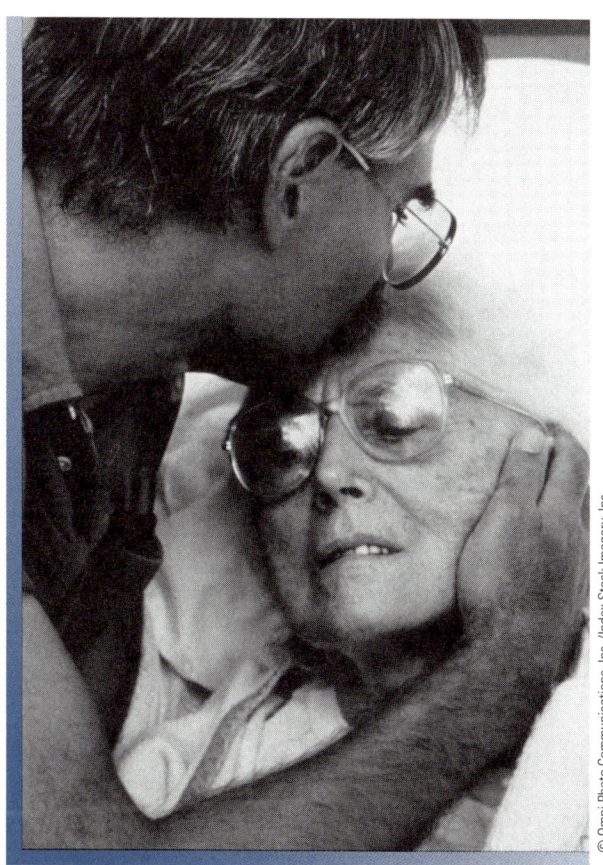

Alzheimer's disease brings significant challenges to the caregiver and family members because of the sufferer's extensive loss of memory, personality changes, loss of communication, and relinquishing of inhibitions.

gression, or uncooperativeness with care (Schneider, Porsteinsson, Peskin, & Pfeiffer, 2003).

Diagnosis of Alzheimer's Disease

The term **dementia** usually refers to irreversible changes in the brain that affect memory, personality, and functioning. Alzheimer's disease is the most common form of dementia, accounting for about 60–70% of the dementia disorders in older adults (Schneider et al., 2003). There are several other types of dementia with somewhat similar symptom presentation but different etiologies, including vascular dementia, Lewy body dementia, and frontal lobe dementia. Other problems, such as substance abuse and Parkinson's disease, can sometimes cause dementia, complicating the diagnosis of AD. In addition, because of the apathy present in AD and the cognitive symptoms that accompany late-life depression, early-stage Alzheimer's might "look like" depression, and vice versa (Schneider et al., 2003). Although at this time autopsy is the only absolutely definitive method of diagnosing AD, to see whether the characteristic amyloid plaques and neurofibrillary tangles can be seen in the brain, cognitive and neurological tests and a detailed history of the presenting symptoms can identify "probable AD" or another type of dementia in a vast majority of cases. Efforts are under way to refine brain-imaging techniques and biological markers for diagnosis of AD (Naditz, 2003).

In recent years, health practitioners and researchers have placed an emphasis on early diagnosis of AD and other dementias. The early disclosure to patients and their families allows early treatment to commence, particularly drug therapies, but also carries some inherent risks, such as the possibility of a false positive, wherein the person actually does not have progressive dementia (Iliffe & Manthorpe, 2004). Moreover, even the person who actually does have early dementia then faces the psychological issues that accompany knowing one has a serious progressive terminal condition, exposure to new medications with side effects, and the possibility that relationships with friends and family will be altered as they start to treat the affected person differently (Iliffe & Manthorpe, 2004).

Another new phenomenon is the increasing frequency with which people are now being diagnosed with mild cognitive impairment, or MCI, a designation first appearing in 1990 (Bennett, 2004). Although there has been some blurring between the diagnosis of MCI and early dementia, MCI is generally used when the person has cognitive deficits reflected in test scores that are greater than one would expect with normal aging, yet lacks functional impairment and behavioral symptoms that mark AD and related dementias (Bennett, 2004). Research is so far unclear as to whether MCI is a distinct condition or simply a precursor to dementia (Davis & Rockwood, 2004), though in one study, 80% of those diagnosed with MCI went on to develop AD within eight years (National Institute on Aging, 2001). The uncertain future with MCI can make this a particularly troublesome diagnosis for older adults and their family members.

Risk Factors for Alzheimer's Disease

Getting older is the greatest risk factor for development of AD and other dementias, so in one sense, all older adults are at risk. Family history is another known risk factor. Scientists have already found certain inherited abnormal genes that predispose an individual to familial or early-onset AD, a very rare form of the disease in a small number of families, where many family members are afflicted at relatively early ages. Most AD, however, is late-onset and its inheritance is sporadic, meaning that it appears once or twice in the same family over the generations, but not in a predictable way. For sporadic AD, genes are thought to play a role, but not in any straightforward manner. Much of the research to date has focused on one gene, called APOE, that has been shown to influence susceptibility to Alzheimer's disease (Alzheimer's Association, 2003b). Other established risk factors are suffering a head injury and elevated cholesterol levels (National Institute on Aging, 2001). Other predisposing factors, such as lower IQ level or verbal ability in the early teens and lower activity levels in middle adulthood, have been investigated and shown to play a role in developing dementia. The book *Aging with Grace* (Snowden, 2001) describes research with an order of nuns that led to some of these discoveries about the connection between early mental abilities and later development of AD.

Treatments

Two classes of medications have been approved by the Federal Drug Administration (FDA) for Alzheimer's disease or other types of dementia. The first class consists of cholinesterase inhibitors, designed to prevent the breakdown of acetylcholine in the brain, a chemical that affects thinking and memory. These include donepezil (Aricept®), approved in 1996, and at least two newer drugs that are usually prescribed in the mild to moderate stage of the disease (Alzheimer's Association, 2004). The effectiveness at stabilizing cognitive symptoms is relatively modest and seldom lasts more than six to twelve months (Schneider et al., 2003). The second class of drugs is represented by memantine (Namenda®), which has been approved for patient use since late 2003. Memantine is approved for use in moderate to severe AD, and studies are under way for use in the early stages of AD (Marksteiner & Schmidt, 2004). The drug works by regulating glutamate, a chemical that plays a role in the processing and storage of information in the brain (Alzheimer's Association, 2004). Also being researched are anti-inflammatory drugs, such as aspirin or ibuprofen, which have been shown in large epidemiological studies to be associated with lower rates of dementia but so far are not proven as an effective treatment after diagnosis (Marksteiner & Schmidt, 2004). Similarly, cholesterol-lowering drugs, called statins, are currently under study as possible treatments for AD and related dementias because they appear to have some preventive influence (National Institute on Aging, 2001). And finally, the behavioral and depressive symptoms in AD are normally treated with antipsychotic and antidepressant medications (Marksteiner & Schmidt, 2004).

Psychosocial treatments for Alzheimer's disease usually aim to improve mood and adjustment in people with mild or early disease, or focus on alleviating problematic behaviors in people with later-stage disease. A recent trend is psychoeducational groups for both the person with early AD and a caregiver, or care partner. One example is called Memory Club, a ten-session group model that has been reported to build

---

FOCUS ON MULTICULTURALISM

ALZHEIMER'S DISEASE IN AFRICAN AMERICANS

Evidence is accumulating that AD and related dementias affect the African American community disproportionately. Although rates vary among studies, there is from a 14% to 100% higher incidence of dementia among African Americans than whites. Genetic predisposition in blacks appears to differ from that in whites, and probably is not limited to the APOE gene. (Risk among first-degree relatives of someone with AD has been found to be 43.7%, and for spouses, who share environment, but not genetics, 18.4%.) The higher incidence of vascular problems and related disorders, such as hypertension, type 2 diabetes, and high cholesterol, among African Americans may be one reason why this group also has higher rates of AD and related dementias. Access to good health care and possible distrust of the established health-care system may contribute to the fact that African Americans tend to be diagnosed later in the dementia process than their white counterparts. There are significant efforts to recruit larger numbers of older African Americans to major AD research centers for diagnosis and participation in research.

SOURCE: Compiled from the Alzheimer's Association, www.alz.org (2003a).

social support among group members and to help the dyads (either spouses or parent-child) deal with immediate issues brought about by AD and make plans for the future (Zarit, Femia, Watson, Rice-Oeschger, & Kakos, 2004). Validation therapy, mentioned earlier in this chapter, is an example of a treatment strategy frequently used in the later stages of dementia. Recent evidence also points to the potential to assist mildly impaired persons with AD to improve their cognitive abilities with cognitive rehabilitation (NIH News, 2004), although this approach is not widely utilized as of this writing.

Dementia Caregiving

In a church fellowship hall, a support group for the spouses of people with Alzheimer's disease meets with two social workers. Most cradle Styrofoam coffee cups and cookies as they share their stories. Their comments revolve around common themes—"She just doesn't want to do anything." "I have to say it's for *me*, then she'll come with me on a walk." "He watches TV, but he can't read anymore . . . or at least, he'll look at the newspaper, but I don't think he can read." "I think he knows he's got a problem, but we don't talk about it." In every instance, the people attending this group are witnessing the gradual loss of their spouse, for Alzheimer's disease is a slow thief—of memory, motivation, reasoning, and, finally, physical functioning of the unique qualities of intimate relationships.

In people with moderate or midstage Alzheimer's disease, behavioral changes such as physical and verbal aggression, delusions, suspiciousness, uncontrollable agitation, and wandering can make living with and caring for the individual very challenging. A recent review of the research on dementia caregiving put it this way: "For some individuals, the caregiving role lasts many years, even decades, and caregivers are increasingly being asked to perform complex tasks similar to those carried out by paid health or social service providers" (Schultz & Martire, 2004). Some common formal services directed at the caregiver consist of support groups such as the one mentioned above, cognitive-behavioral group therapy (Akkerman & Ostwald, 2004), and individual counseling or psychotherapy. Recently, online support groups have become feasible and present opportunities for caregivers to communicate with others in similar situations without leaving their homes or offices (Smyth, Feinstein, & Kacerek, 1997). Adult daycare programs for the person with dementia to relieve the caregiver during day hours, or respite care, usually a service providing overnight in-home care while family members are unable to be at home, are other services that are frequently available. Residential care, such as nursing-home placement, is often seen as a last resort by families and is more often chosen when the person with dementia lives alone, or at the point when problems such as wandering or incontinence become unmanageable.

The effects of caring for someone with dementia have been the focus of a great deal of research since the early 1980s. The earliest studies looked primarily at the considerable stress and burden experienced by family caregivers (e.g., Zarit, 1980) and spurred development of psychosocial interventions to help caregivers. In general, caregivers appear to suffer from higher depression levels and other physical and emotional disorders, yet some individuals do well whereas others do poorly, leading to an effort to identify reasons for these differences. Psychological and social resources, such as personality and the availability of social support, are established factors that impact caregivers' ability to cope (Pearlin, Mullan, Semple, & Skaff, 1990). Another research focus has been an appreciation of some of the positive gains from caregiving, because it appears that for many family members, the caregiving role offers gains such as feeling useful, building self-confidence, and repaying debts to their loved one (Kramer, 1997). Recently, a model of caregiver grief has been developed (Meuser & Marwit, 2001). Clinicians and researchers working with caregivers have realized that stress and burden from caregiving tasks is not always the main cause of distress among caregivers, but rather that grief—due to the many (and ambiguous) losses that occur when a close family member has AD—is a very real and significant contributor to the high levels of depression in caregivers (Adams & Sanders, 2004).

Mental Illness in Late Life

When an older adult presents for help, a variety of factors (for example, physical, cognitive, social, and emotional difficulties) may combine in such a way that diagnosis of a mental disorder is confounded. For instance, there is considerable overlap between physical symptoms and emotional symptoms, between normal bereavement and depression, and between cognitive impairment of early dementia and many other mental disorders. Current cohorts of older adults seek help less frequently for emotional or mental conditions than do younger people, in part because they tend to identify their problems as physical or environmental rather than psychological in origin (Knight, 2004). Even when older adults present with mental-health concerns, they generally receive less psychotherapy than younger adults, instead receiving services such as medication or custodial care (Schaie & Willis, 2002). Among older adults who are seen for mental-health services, some have had a longstanding serious mental disorder such as schizophrenia or bipolar disorder. Other older adults have personality disorders, such as narcissistic, dependent, obsessive-compulsive, or borderline. It is not unusual to see an older person with a personality disorder whose functioning has been acceptable during middle adulthood but who is not dealing well with age-related transitions and losses (Segal, Coolidge, & Rosowsky, 2000). In these situations, the person may experience a depressive episode or anxiety overlaid upon the preexisting personality disorder and may seek help or may cause his or her family so much distress that they seek help. In addition, many older adults experience a psychological problem for the first time late in life, sometimes in conjunction with bereavement or with a physical illness. Many will seek help from primary-care physicians. These late-onset disorders are most commonly some form of depression or anxiety, though a few older adults develop paranoia or other psychotic thinking for the first time in late life.

Depression

A relatively small percentage, estimated at 1% to 4%, of older people living in the community have major depressive disorders as classified by the DSM-IV (Blazer, 2003), yet approximately 2 million people over age 65 are estimated to have a depressive illness (National Institute of Mental Health, 2003). Studies conducted in long-term care settings have found rates of depression among residents to be over 30% (Blazer, 2002a). Minor or "subthreshold" depressions are more common in late adulthood, affecting up to 5 million older adults (NIMH, 2003), with prevalence estimates ranging from 4% to up to 30% (Blazer, 2002a). Both depressive disorders and subthreshold depressive symptoms in older adults are associated with clinically significant impairments in functioning (Hybels, Blazer, & Pieper, 2001).

Depression is not the same as the unhappiness felt by people confronting everyday life. Symptoms of depression may include feelings of sadness, but in older adults, depression may not be presented as sadness at all (Gallo & Rabins, 1999). **Anhedonia**, the loss of pleasure in things that used to be pleasurable, is a hallmark of late-life depression, along with feelings of emptiness, excessive social withdrawal, loss of interest in usual activities, self-neglect, changes in appetite, sleep problems, and expressions of worthlessness, such as concerns about being a burden. And finally, older adults tend to somaticize more than other age groups—meaning they express their psychological distress through concerns with physical symptoms, such as weakness, dizziness, vague pain, or constipation, that don't have an underlying physical cause (Scanlon, 2003). In addition, a number of medical conditions, including hypertension, diabetes, Parkinson's disease, and cancer, as well as major health events such as heart attacks and strokes, commonly predispose elders to depression (Blazer, 2002b).

There are a number of short assessment tools used by social workers with older adults, including those that assess activities of daily living, cognitive impairment, and mood states (Berkman, Maramaldi, Breon, & Howe, 2002). One quick measure for assessing potential depression in older people is the Geriatric Depression Scale (GDS), a 30-item validated scale (see Exhibit 12.8).

Implications for Practice: Helping Depressed Older People

Social workers see depressed older people in a number of settings. Enlisting help from family members and involved friends is a useful strategy to build up a supportive network for the depressed older person. Prescription antidepressants are often highly effective for older adults, and it is appropriate to arrange a referral for medication evaluation when the person's depression impairs functioning or seems severe. The best treatment approaches may be a combination of medication and "talk therapy." Supportive social-work practice with depressed older adults combines (1) establishing a relationship, (2) identifying and mobilizing the individual's strengths, (3) facilitating exploration of negative events that may have precipitated the depression and expression of the accompanying feelings such as grief, and (4) encouraging the client to engage in self-care and feasible activities that were previously enjoyable. There also has been considerable success in using more formal cognitive behavioral approaches that assist the depressed client in identifying and changing depression-generating negative thoughts.

EXHIBIT 12.8 The Geriatric Depression Scale (GDS)

Please answer the following questions by circling yes or no.

1. Are you basically satisfied with your life?	Yes	No
2. Have you dropped many of your activities and interests?	Yes	No
3. Do you feel that your life is empty?	Yes	No
4. Do you often get bored?	Yes	No
5. Are you hopeful about the future?	Yes	No
6. Are you bothered by thoughts that you can't get out of your head?	Yes	No
7. Are you in good spirits most of the time?	Yes	No
8. Are you afraid that something bad is going to happen to you?	Yes	No
9. Do you feel happy most of the time?	Yes	No
10. Do you often feel helpless?	Yes	No
11. Do you often get restless and fidgety?	Yes	No
12. Do you prefer to stay at home, rather than going out and doing new things?	Yes	No
13. Do you frequently worry about the future?	Yes	No
14. Do you feel you have more problems with memory than most?	Yes	No
15. Do you think it is wonderful to be alive now?	Yes	No
16. Do you feel downhearted and blue?	Yes	No
17. Do you feel pretty worthless the way you are now?	Yes	No
18. Do you worry a lot about the past?	Yes	No
19. Do you find life very exciting?	Yes	No
20. Is it hard for you to get started on new projects?	Yes	No
21. Do you feel full of energy?	Yes	No
22. Do you feel that your situation is hopeless?	Yes	No
23. Do you feel that most people are better off than you are?	Yes	No
24. Do you frequently get upset over little things?	Yes	No
25. Do you often feel like crying?	Yes	No
26. Do you have trouble concentrating?	Yes	No
27. Do you enjoy getting up in the morning?	Yes	No
28. Do you prefer to avoid social gatherings?	Yes	No
29. Is it easy for you to make a decision?	Yes	No
30. Is your mind as clear as it used to be?	Yes	No

Items 1, 5, 9, 15, 19, 21, 27, 29, and 30 are reverse scored. Score 1 point for each item in the depressed direction. Scores of 11 or more indicate possible depression.

EXHIBIT 12.9 Suicide rates in the United States by age and gender for 2001 (deaths per 100,000 residents)

Age	Females (all races)	Males (all races)	White females	White males
15–24	2.9	16.6	3.1	19.6
25–44	5.5	22.1	6.2	26.4
45–64	6.6	22.5	7.3	25.9
65 +	3.9	31.5	4.1	34.4
65–74	3.9	24.6	NA	26.3
75–84	4.0	37.8	NA	40.2
85 +	3.4	51.1	NA	55.0

SOURCE: Adapted from the Centers for Disease Control (2003).

Suicide

Sadly, a disproportionate number of older adults are desperate enough to commit suicide each year. Suicide is a significant problem in late adulthood that is difficult to generalize about because the older population itself is so heterogeneous (Duberstein & Conwell, 2000). Most serious suicide attempts are made by depressed people, but other diagnosable psychiatric disorders, physical illnesses, and substance-abuse problems (even if the person is sober) also increase the relative risk for suicide in an older adult (Duberstein & Conwell, 2000). Socially isolated elders, particularly those who live alone and are widowed or divorced, also have higher suicide rates than married or co-residing elders (Harwood, Hawton, Hope, & Jacoby, 2000). The prevalence of suicide in any group is difficult to determine with accuracy because suicides may be masked, for instance, as accidents or natural causes. However, data consistently show that suicide rates in the U.S. are higher among older adults than younger adults, and are highest for white males over age 85 (see Exhibit 12.9). Although suicide attempts are very difficult to predict, Roff (2001) has summarized clues older adults may provide to family members, service providers, or other informants, including behavioral clues, such as increased isolation or giving away possessions, and verbal clues, such as threats of suicide, wishes to die, saying goodbye, or expressions of worthlessness or hopelessness. Suicides may be prevented by providing adequate mental-health and substance-abuse screening services for older adults in settings where they normally go. In some instances, older adults require in-home treatment for mental illness, but these services are not available in every community (Kohn, Goldsmith, Sedgwick, & Markowitz, 2004). Publicizing the nature of depression among older people and advertising that treatments are available is another strategy that is currently a focus of the National Institute of Mental Illness (NIMH, 2003).

Alcohol and Other Drug Use in Late Adulthood

A recent epidemiological study estimated that 1.7 million older adults were in need of substance-abuse treatment in 2001, and by 2020, with the aging of the baby boomers, there will be 4.4 million older adults with substance-use disorders (Gfroerer, Penne, Pemberton, & Folsom, 2003). The most-used substance is alcohol. Data from a large household survey found that 38% of older adults reported using alcohol in the past month, 9% reported binge drinking (five or more alcoholic beverages in a sitting), and 2% reported binge drinking five or more times during the month (SAMHSA, 2001). The amount of alcohol consumption that is associated with problem use is usually less for older people because metabolic changes associated with aging allow alcohol to be absorbed into the bloodstream much more rapidly (Sattar, Petty, & Burke, 2003). Alcohol also interacts adversely with a number of prescription medications commonly taken by older people. For these reasons, the National Institute of Alcohol and Alcoholism has published guidelines suggesting that adults over age 65 should limit alcohol consumption to one drink per day or seven drinks per week (Sattar, Petty, & Burke, 2003). It has become clear that the

> **EXHIBIT 12.10** Short Michigan Alcoholism Screening Test—Geriatric Version
>
> 1. When talking with others, do you ever underestimate how much you actually drink?
> 2. After a few drinks, have you sometimes not eaten or been able to skip a meal because you didn't feel hungry?
> 3. Does having a few drinks help decrease your shakiness or tremors?
> 4. Does alcohol sometimes make it hard for you to remember parts of the day or night?
> 5. Do you usually take a drink to relax or calm your nerves?
> 6. Do you drink to take your mind off your problems?
> 7. Have you ever increased your drinking after experiencing a loss in your life?
> 8. Has a doctor or nurse ever said they were worried or concerned about your drinking?
> 9. Have you ever made rules to manage your drinking?
> 10. When you feel lonely, does drinking help?
>
> Scoring: Two or more "yes" responses indicate an alcohol problem.
>
> SOURCE: Blow, Brower, Schulenberg, Demo-Dananberg, Young, & Beresford (1992).

only safe drinking for older persons is light drinking. Undoubtedly, a large number of older people who do not meet criteria for alcoholism or alcohol dependence nevertheless may be drinking in excess of these recommended amounts.

Alcohol use often progresses with age, so that a regular moderate drinker may become a heavy drinker in later life. It is estimated that approximately two-thirds of older people with alcohol dependence have been drinkers during their entire adult life (Sattar, Petty, & Burke, 2003). The other one-third began drinking regularly in their 50s or 60s, often in response to a significant loss or retirement. Both groups of older people with alcohol dependence tend to live alone, may suffer from anxiety or depression, and have more medical problems than do nondrinkers or light drinkers (O'Connell, Chin, Cunningham, & Lawlor, 2003).

How can we identify older alcoholics? In practice, alcohol problems among older adults often go undetected because clinicians may assume presenting symptoms are age-related rather than substance-related (O'Connell, Chin, Cunningham, & Lawlor, 2003). Symptoms of alcoholism can masquerade as depression, dementia, or other problems associated with aging, and alcohol misuse commonly co-occurs with a number of physical or emotional problems. Older women are particularly likely to be overlooked for alcohol screening. Alcohol screening scales designed specifically for older adults can be very helpful in determining the extent of the problem. One of the best known is the Michigan Alcoholism Screening Test–Geriatric Version (MAST-G; Blow et al., 1992), which has a full-length and a brief ten-item version (see Exhibit 12.10).

Older alcoholics often respond well to treatment (Atkinson, Misra, Ryan, & Turner, 2003). They generally have fewer drinking-related social, legal, and occupational problems to contend with than younger alcoholics. Those with late-onset alcohol misuse may be able to cut down on or stop drinking when their losses are acknowledged and they receive needed social and emotional support, usually in an outpatient setting. Those with a lifelong drinking problem or a co-occurring psychiatric disorder may be less compliant and usually require higher levels of care, perhaps even repeated inpatient treatment stays, before they are able to sustain sobriety in the community. Attending AA meetings is a way to reduce their sense of social isolation, and finding a ready-made social group can be very helpful. Many experts believe that older people need elder-specific treatment. For example, some inpatient hospital units and Alcoholics Anonymous (AA) groups cater primarily to older people. Although such programs can have added benefits for older drinkers, requirements of effective treatment of older people with alcohol dependence in any setting will be age sensitivity and an understanding of the unique medical vulnerabilities of older adults. A strengths-based approach can be effective with older alcohol abusers. Perkins and Tice (1999) presented a treatment model for alcohol problems among older adults that emphasizes prior coping, dealing with the losses and feelings masked by the alcohol use, and empowering the client to make important decisions about his or her recovery.

STUDY TABLE: Psychological dimension of late adulthood

Cognitive Development and Information Processing	Many older adults pursue lifelong learning, for example Elderhostel programs provide older adults with opportunities for learning and travel. Stages of cognitive development called reorganization and reintegration characterize some of the cognitive differences found in late adulthood. Selective optimization and compensation theory proposes that older adults adapt to declines by purposefully selecting tasks or activities, optimizing their remaining skills and abilities, and compensating for skills that are lost. Apparent effects of normal aging on cognitive abilities differ according to cross-sectional or longitudinal research methods. Declines in five primary mental abilities are very gradual up until the late 80s; information-processing speed and memory decrease with age. Perceptual, attention, and physical health issues can affect cognitive abilities in late life. Retraining methods are available to help older people maintain their abilities or even reverse cognitive decline. Many elders are concerned about becoming cognitively impaired.
Communication	Communication may be impacted by sensory limitations, cognitive impairment, some health conditions, and social isolation. Validation therapy, a mode of communication with people with Alzheimer's disease or other dementia, attempts to get to the underlying feelings and needs being expressed. Elderspeak is a way of talking to older adults as though they were small children. Although this means of talking sometimes helps the older person comprehend better, generally elderspeak undermines self-esteem and dignity of older adults.
Attitudes and Emotions	Among the oldest old, positive emotions, anger, and sadness are a little less frequently experienced than in younger persons. Emotions in late life may tend to be more complex—e.g., poignant or bittersweet. Loss is a major theme of late life. Grief affects older adults who experience losses, even though they may be "normal" for this stage of life. Grief must be worked through in order to avoid emotional problems. A dual-process model of coping with bereavement proposes that grief operates on two levels that operate simultaneously and serially. Older people who are bereaved, who have moved to a new location, or who lost some important health and functioning may be vulnerable to loneliness, also a risk factor for depression.
Social Cognition and Regulation	Older people resist thinking of themselves as old. Identity in late life often rests on former social or occupational roles. Reminiscence is a way to maintain a sense of self, and groups to help residents of long-term care retrieve and share positive memories enhance socialization and improve morale in these settings.
Psychological Strengths and Hazards	Flexibility and adaptability, along with a strong sense of personal mastery, are important psychological strengths for older people. Wisdom is an elusive concept that many believe is associated with growing older, but studies have found wisdom to be stable from young adulthood to age 75. Spirituality and religious beliefs have positive and significant roles in the lives of many older adults and association with greater health and well-being. Alzheimer's disease (AD) affects approximately 4.5 million people, or about 10% of older adults. Diagnosis of probable AD is based on neurological tests and detailed history of presenting symptoms, although it is sometimes difficult

to distinguish early AD from depression, or symptoms of another problem such as Parkinson's disease. Early diagnosis is now emphasized because of the available medications to treat symptoms of AD. Another diagnosis, mild cognitive impairment (MCI), is becoming more common. People diagnosed with either early AD or MCI need to deal with the anxieties and possible loss of morale inherent in knowing they have a condition that may be progressive and terminal. Increasing age is the biggest risk factor for AD. Most AD is late-onset and not predictably inherited. Medications for AD are used to stabilize cognitive decline; their effectiveness is relatively modest and may not last beyond a year. Other new drugs, including statins, are being investigated as promising preventatives for AD. Psychosocial treatments aimed at the person with early dementia seek to improve mood and adjustment; some newer models of psychosocial groups include both the person with dementia and a family member/caregiver to deal with the disease's effects and plan for the future. Behavioral, cognitive, and emotional changes of AD are challenging and stressful for families. Support groups, group therapy, and online support are all formal services offered to families. Caregivers of someone with dementia suffer from higher levels of depressive symptoms and health problems than noncaregivers, although there are psychological gains as well. Grief is a new focus in dementia caregiving, as families deal with the ambiguous losses involved.

Diagnosis of mental disorders in late life is challenging; older adults seek help for emotional or psychological problems less often than for physical problems. Older adults with longstanding mental disorders may have difficulties adjusting to losses and physical changes of aging. Depression, anxiety, and paranoid thinking represent common late-onset disorders. Depression affects approximately 2 million older adults; many suffer from lower-level depression, but also experience impaired functioning. Depression in older people may not include expressions of sadness; anhedonia, lack of interest, social withdrawal, self-neglect, expressions of worthlessness, and unexplained somatic symptoms are all possible indicators of depression. Social workers see many depressed elders in practice. Treatment is often effective with supportive psychotherapy alone, though it is appropriate to refer for a medication evaluation if the depression is severe or progress is not occurring. Suicide is a significant problem among older adults, particularly men over age 85. Most suicides are completed by depressed people, though social isolation, physical illness, substance abuse, and other psychiatric illnesses are all risk factors for suicide attempts. Suicidal elders may give family and professionals behavioral and verbal clues that should be taken seriously.

The number of older adults with substance-abuse problems is increasing. Metabolic changes with aging mean that the amount of alcohol that can be consumed safely is only about one drink per day or seven drinks per week. Two-thirds of older alcoholics are lifelong drinkers, and one-third developed alcohol dependence late in life, usually in response to a loss. Substance abusers tend to live alone and often have anxiety or depression. Detection of older alcoholics is difficult because the symptoms may look like another common problem of old age. The Short MAST-G is a good brief screening tool for older persons suspected of an alcohol problem. Treatment is often effective; late-onset problem drinkers respond to social and emotional support and information about the dangers of heavy drinking. Lifelong drinkers may require special inpatient units. An age-sensitive, strengths-based approach is useful for older alcoholics.

CONCEPT MAP

SOCIAL DIMENSION

Families and Groups

As was discussed earlier in this text, an ecological approach to human behavior looks at individuals in the context of their physical and social surroundings. The person cannot really be considered separately from his or her environment—culture, community, neighborhood, family, and residence. Today's young-old, middle-old, and oldest-old adults have been influenced by their families of origin and the home environments of their childhoods, the way they were parented and taught in school, and the families, friendships, and lifestyles they have created over the life span. A life course approach to human behavior focuses on how, aside from their personal histories, individuals have witnessed and been a part of historic events at unique points in time in their development, influenced by an interaction of history and age (Stoller & Gibson, 2000). From all of these earlier experiences, older people have developed certain sets of values, beliefs, and varied ways of interacting with others and with their environments. And in turn, the social and physical environment continues to be important to older people's continued growth and development.

Families

The great majority of older adults have some family, and family is the first line of support when older adults need assistance (Hooyman & Kiyak, 2002). With longer life spans, the presence of multiple generations in one family is an increasing phenomenon, and intergenerational relationships provide an important source of reciprocal support (Hooyman & Kiyak, 2002). Never before in history has there been such a large number of retirement-age "children" who still have one or more living parents. Older people who have them tend to obtain the most emotional support from their spouses, followed by adult children, and then siblings. Sibling relationships frequently become more important in old age, after the parents have died, and possibly after one or both siblings have been widowed, as the narrative on this page illustrates.

Social-work family theorists Hartman and Laird (1987) have defined two types of families, one that is created and one that is inherited: "A family is created when two or more people construct an intimate environment that they define as a family, an environment in which they generally will share a living space, commitment, and a variety of roles and functions usually considered part of family life" (p. 576). Research on late-life families with "postmodern" theoretical perspectives such as feminist, life-course, and constructivist, which focuses on the meaning each individual makes of his or her own life story, has brought to light an incredible diversity and complexity of intergenerational family forms and connections (Allen, Blieszner, & Roberto, 2000a). Some older adults live with their spouses of forty years or more; others are newlyweds; some are widowed, single, or never

> ### FOCUS ON NARRATIVE
>
> #### MARYLAND SISTERS STILL SIDE BY SIDE
>
> They are roommates, prone to the occasional spats that erupt when two people live in close proximity to each other. And they are sisters, united by genes and memories tugging back more than 80 years. Both facts matter equally within the small space that Thelma and Margaret share, a downstairs corner room at Manor Care nursing home. Each has her own television (the two sets are side by side) because Thelma likes watching Lawrence Welk reruns and Margaret prefers soaps and *The Price Is Right*. Each harbors her own candy drawer because one can eat Cadbury while the other (who has diabetes) must stick to sugar-free treats. But the fading photos on the walls illustrate the common markers of their lives—the dapper man Margaret still calls Pop, the demure-looking woman who was Mother, the modest Methodist church they attended while growing up. "We get along all right," Thelma said, although she allows that things "get a little rough once in a while." Specifically, there has been laundry thrown. The sisters both grin. "Nobody ever got hurt with laundry," Thelma scoffed.
>
> BY SUSAN LEVINE
>
> SOURCE: Excerpted from *The Washington Post*, September 2, 1999.

married; and others are gay men or lesbians. In a sense, those who reside in nursing homes can count other residents and staff as family, as well as adult children and other relatives. In a complex society in which multiple marriages and family relocations are common, older adults frequently use "kin upgrading," in which a more distant relative with whom they have more involvement or connection becomes "like a son" or "like a daughter" to them (Allen, Blieszner, & Roberto, 2000b). Another related phenomenon is that of **fictive kin**—many older adults who may lack a spouse or close adult child develop close relationships with friends or neighbors, who become the primary family for them (Barranti & Cohen, 2000).

Couples

In 2002, statistics on marriage for older adults showed 56.7% of women over 65 were married and 32.2% were widowed, whereas 75.7% of men were married and 13.9% were widowed (www.agingstats.gov). Of those aged 85 or older, only 28% of women were married (64.8% were widowed), but 60.1% of men were married and 33.8% were widowed. Smaller numbers of both men and women, of course, were divorced (from 3% to 9%) or never married (from 3% to 4.4%). The differences in the rates of marriage and widowhood for men and women in late life reflect the fact that women have a somewhat higher life expectancy than men, and cultural norms, particularly in the current cohorts of older adults, have promoted marriages in which the man is older than the woman (Schaie & Willis, 2002). The result is that unattached older women are plentiful, whereas unattached older men are in relatively short supply.

Several studies have focused on the effects of the youngest child leaving home (i.e., the "empty nest") and retirement from work on marriages. In general, both of those important events may cause an increased focus on the marital relationship, but depending on the underlying strength of the bond, the outcome may be either increased strain or increased satisfaction (Barnes & Parry, 2004). Overall, much of the literature has concluded that late-life marriages may be characterized by a decrease in disagreements and an increase in satisfaction from midlife; however, most of the studies on satisfaction with marital relationships have used cross-sectional approaches, which tend to measure cohort differences rather than relationships over time (Schaie & Willis, 2002). Hatch & Bulcroft (2004) recently published a study concluding that longer duration of marriage may actually lead to an increase in disagreements but that other factors outweigh the length of marriage or the ages of the partners. Bookwala and Jacobs (2004) compared negative processes such as disagreements, marital satisfaction, and depressive symptoms of young, middle-aged, and older (over age 60) married couples. They found that older couples reported higher levels of marital satisfaction despite having similar levels of negative processes, and that marital satisfaction was related to their level of depression. This ability of the older couples to "overlook" the negatives and experience high marital satisfaction was attributed to socioemotional selectivity theory (Carstensen, 1992), described earlier in this chapter, which states that as people age, they attempt to regulate their emotions by choosing to focus on comfortable and reliable social partners. Bookwala and Jacobs proposed that older marriages are similarly characterized by the choice to focus on the positive aspects of the marital relationship (2004). This is important, because marital satisfaction, perhaps even more than health, predicts life satisfaction and quality of life for older people who are married, offering the partners "intimacy, interdependence, and a sense of belonging" (Hooyman & Kiyak, 2002, p. 282).

As couples grow older, the risk increases that one or both of the partners will become ill with a serious chronic or acute condition. Studies have shown that when one of the marital partners becomes ill, the other partner's morale declines (Schulz & Martire, 2004). In fact, in later life, partners tend to resemble each other in terms of subjective well-being and affective states, such as depression (Townsend, Miller, & Guo, 2001). Social workers in hospitals and other health settings often see couples when one of the partners is ill or newly disabled and in the context of a crisis, or at least a transition to a new phase of their lives, that may involve mutual decision making. For married people, the spouse is usually the first and primary caregiver unless the duties involved become too difficult (Hooyman & Kiyak, 2002). Many spouses obtain satisfaction in being able to help their partners, yet it can become physically and emotionally draining if the care required is long-lasting and intensive. Nevertheless, older couples have an advantage over singles or widows, as they can often compensate for each other's impairments—one can no longer drive, but the other does; one can't walk well, but the other can help or even push the wheelchair; one can no longer read the fine print, but the other can; one can't remember to take important medicines, but the other can keep track—and they offer each other reciprocal help that allows them to continue to function independently as a couple.

The marital relationship may become strained when one or both partners become impaired in some way and the old styles and forms of communication no longer work, leading to isolation or hostility between the partners (McInnes-Dittrich, 2005). As an example, hearing loss in one of the partners, a common impairment in later life, can be a factor in the well-being of the other partner, affecting the ability to communicate or share pleasant experiences (Wallhagen, Strawbridge, Shema, & Kaplan, 2004). Couples trying to navigate life transitions have the added complications of dealing with issues of the partner along with their own. This was illustrated when the Edwardses, a good-looking couple in their mid-80s, both walking with canes, presented to the admissions office of an assisted-living community. Mrs. Edwards seemed very sociable and talked quite freely, and it didn't take long for her to let the social worker know, in her pleasant soft voice, that her husband, who was not saying much, was very hard of hearing. She stated very definitely that they were there to see the facilities because they wished to obtain an apartment there. Mrs. Edwards needed to use the restroom at one point, and while she was away from her seat, her husband leaned over and spoke, in the loud way of the deaf, confiding that his wife had been diagnosed with Alzheimer's disease and her short-term memory was very poor. Mr. Edwards admitted not hearing well, though he took out of a small case a sort of amplifying earphone device that he used to better hear the conversation. He told the social worker that he didn't think they'd need the services offered at this facility; although his wife wished to move to an assisted-living apartment, he wanted to stay in their home because he loved to garden and work outside. He said, "With my bad hearing and her bad memory, we may need some help, but I'm not ready to give up my yard!" When his wife returned, Mr. Edwards again fell silent and did not express his hesitations about making a move. It would be a challenge for this couple to negotiate the issue about moving from their home. McInnes-Dittrich recommends communications skills training for older couples who need to adapt to sensory and health changes, so they may successfully decide about lifestyle changes and procurement of services while avoiding the deterioration of their personal relationship.

Gay Male and Lesbian Elders

Estimates of the proportion of gay men and lesbians in the over-65 population range from 3% to 8% (Cahill, South, & Spade, 2000). Older homosexuals are very similar to older heterosexuals, except that to varying degrees they have suffered oppression and hostility due to their sexual orientation (Hooyman & Kiyak, 2002). Because older gays and lesbians grew up in a time before gay liberation of the late 1960s and early 1970s, many of them feel more comfortable keeping their sexual orientation secret and may not be open even with family members. Thus, there is a danger that the unique needs of gays and lesbians, such as the important role of a same-sex partner, may remain invisible to health and social-service providers (Brotman, Ryan, & Cormier, 2003). Research with this population is difficult, and reliable figures are not available to indicate the numbers or proportion involved in a committed or cohabiting relationship (Blando, 2001), although in one pilot study of gays, lesbians, bisexuals, and transgendered individuals over age 50, 59% of the respondents reported being in an intimate relationship (McFarland & Sanders, 2003). Older gays and lesbians tend to have close-knit friendship groups and to rely on these "created families" in times of need, particularly if they are childless and/or unable to rely on support from their own family of origin. Close, familylike relationships are important sources of support for older people, whether gay or straight, partnered or not.

Widowhood

Adjustment of older women and men after the death of a spouse or committed partner can vary widely. In our society, nuclear families are often quite independent from the extended family or wider community, and spouses rely on each other to make everyday decisions, share responsibilities and tasks, and provide emotional support. Thus, when one spouse dies, the remaining spouse grieves for the loss of the unique person, a sexual partner, a confidant, but also loses the contributions of that partner to their home, their extended family, and their relationship (Carr et al., 2000). Researchers have found that adjustment to widowhood is harder, and the widowed partner more susceptible to depression, when the marriage was particularly warm and intimate, and when he or she relied heavily on the partner for instrumental help (Carr et al., 2000). Those widows and widowers without adequate family and social support tend to have a poorer and slower adjustment; some may turn to alcohol dependence (Lee & Bakk, 2001). Older men who experience the death of a spouse are thought to have more difficulties, such as depression, in part because their situation is less common, yet one study has found that this difference is due to the fact that men are less depressed than women up until the loss of a spouse, at which time their depression levels become very similar to women's (Lee, DeMaris, Bavin, & Sullivan, 2001). Psychosocial adjustment of older widows and widowers also depends upon several "existential factors" (the personal meaning they ascribe to life, and spirituality and religious beliefs), such that those who are able to find a reason to live that goes beyond the individual lost relationship appear to do better (Fry, 2001).

Eighty-five percent of wives outlive their husbands, more than three times the rate of widowhood for men (Hooyman & Kiyak, 2002). This fact means that the world of older people, particularly among the oldest old, is a world in which women, especially unattached women, vastly outnumber men. Accordingly, it is seven times more likely for widowed older men to remarry than for widowed older women to do so (Hooyman & Kiyak, 2002). For older women in relatively good health and financial situations, widowhood may actually signify a time for growth as they call upon their own resources for the first time, and they may not be eager to remarry. In a recent study that interviewed older people two years after the death of their spouses, the widows expressed little interest in finding a new partner and mentioned relishing their current freedom, whereas the widowers in the sample did not mention freedom and expressed strong interest in finding a new mate (Davidson, 2001).

Parent-Child Relationships

Increased health and longevity have complicated parent-child relationships. Older adults generally remain in frequent contact with their grown children, whether they live nearby or at a distance, and their relationships are characterized by continuity from earlier life stages (Allen, Blieszner, & Roberto, 2000a). Researchers have proposed two somewhat divergent theories to describe family ties in later life: solidarity, focusing on the strength of these intergenerational ties throughout the life course, and the expectation of mutual assistance; and ambivalence, focusing on the mixed feelings and conflicts that arise (Connidis & McMullin, 2002). Practitioners working with older families certainly can attest to the fact that these parent-child relationships in late life appear to be characterized by strong bonds and sense of responsibility, but that there is considerable ambivalence about giving and receiving help, the time it involves, and changing roles that occur when the parents become frail or need additional assistance. When aging parents become newly dependent upon adult children, the role reversals can be upsetting to all involved, heightening the ambivalence felt by both parties. Because family connections and support are so important, Greene (2000) has recommended family assessment and family consultation as part of any social-work practice with older adults.

Grown children who themselves are parenting teenagers, working at demanding jobs, or approaching retirement age frequently find they need to be involved in providing support to older parents, as well. One study identified the types of support typically given by adult children to their older parents: emotional support, such as phoning, offering assistance, affection, and listening; instrumental support, such as transportation, chores, and other tasks; and management of medical conditions, such as helping with blood-sugar testing, medications, and so on (Spitze & Gallant, 2004). This becomes more complicated when families are separated geographically, although many families are in this situation and communicate regularly by phone and e-mail, with visits once or twice per year. In recent years, it has become more common for older adults to relocate to live with or near an adult child. Such a move to be closer to family can have positive effects. The adult children may get help with caring for the grandchildren, and the older parents gain a sense of security at a time of vulnerability. However, these multigenerational families often struggle with how to set boundaries in the situation, and the older parent, who usually has few other social supports in his or her new area, may feel isolated with only the extended family to rely upon.

Caregiving is a very broad term that may describe hands-on assistance with activities of daily living, helping to hire and manage professional caregivers, making decisions about care for a parent who needs help, or overseeing the care a parent receives in a nursing home. Although physical caregiving is obviously burdensome and time-consuming, managing someone's care also can be very stressful for families. Research from the 1980s and 1990s consistently showed that daughters were more likely than sons to become the primary caregiver of an older parent (Franks, Pierce, & Dwyer, 2003), but today, some investigators (e.g., Sanders & McFarland, 2002) have begun to examine the role of sons as primary caregivers. When wives, daughters, or daughters-in-law are not available nearby, sons are more likely to become a primary caregiver to the dependent elder. Caregiving can be stressful for any adult child, but researchers have identified some factors that add to the resilience of some caregivers (see Exhibit 12.11).

The burdens for low-income families and for single adults caring for an older parent may exceed those of other adult children. Take, for example, the

EXHIBIT 12.11 Contributors to resilience in family caregivers

Distancing from the care situation, physically and emotionally

Regular physical exercise

Keeping up personal hobbies

Having at least one close confidant for emotional support

Personal religious beliefs

A philosophy of duty toward the parent

Sense of humor

SOURCE: Adapted from Ross, Holliman, & Dixon (2003).

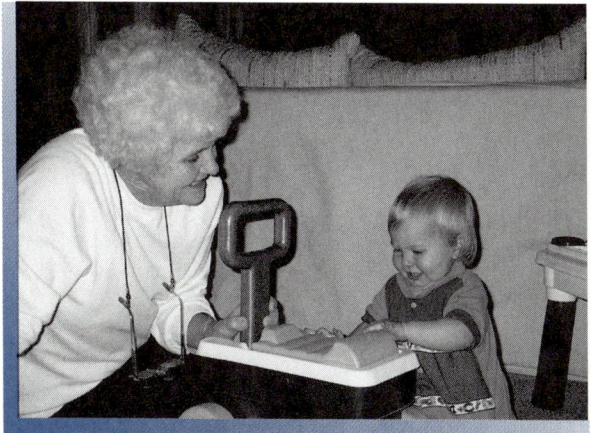

Grandparents can be important figures in a child's life and can play a significant role in transmitting cultural and family values to children.

situation of a 57-year-old gay man who cares for his 90-year-old mother in the home. Ricardo, as we will call him, has schizophrenia, is stabilized on medication and supportive treatment, and has fifteen years of sobriety from alcoholism. His mother is bedridden and needs constant personal care. According to his social worker, Ricardo and his mother live in the family home and are supported by their disability and Social Security income. Ricardo is a bright, well-read, articulate individual who cultivates a large vegetable garden each year and cares for his mother with tenderness and concern. Ricardo's caregiving role has kept him from pursuing other interests and relationships, but he does not complain. There are times when he speculates about what will happen after the death of his mother and when he reaches old age. There will be no one left in the family to call on.

Grandparenthood

For many older adults, the arrival of a first grandchild is an event that rivals the birth of their own first child in level of excitement, pride, and emotionality, as it provides another opportunity to leave a personal legacy in the world. Relationships with grandchildren tend to be mediated by the adult child/parent when the children are young and continue to evolve as the children mature (Hooyman & Kiyak, 2002). When the parent is present and functioning, grandparents are free to be more like friends or confidants to their grandchildren rather than disciplinarians; the stereotype of the grandmother spoiling the kids is based on this premise. For the older adult, positive interactions with grandchildren can contribute to a younger age identity (Kaufman & Elder, 2003).

Grandparenting appears to have different functions for different families, depending on factors such as the ages of the family members, geographic location, ethnicity, and culture. For instance, a recent study identified five distinct grandparenting styles: (1) influential, (2) supportive, (3) passive, (4) authoritarian, and (5) detached (Mueller, Wilhelm, & Elder, 2002). The most common type, those who were influential, were most intimately involved with their grandchildren, tended to live close by, and provided material support as well as advice and emotional support. Ties through the maternal lines tend to be stronger than those through the paternal lines, so that grandmothers are closer to both their children and grandchildren than grandfathers and provide more personal advice to them (Mueller, Wilhelm, & Elder, 2002), but in recent cohorts in which fathers have been more involved in childrearing, this may change. Not surprisingly, geographic distance has been found to be a major factor in the level of contact and exchange of assistance shared by grandparents and grandchildren, although not necessarily on the quality of the relationship (Kivett, 1996). Organizations such as AARP (www.aarp.org) and the Grandparent Foundation (www.grandparenting.org) provide a forum for narratives and advice on the ways grandparents, particularly those who live at a distance, can create and maintain positive connections with grandchildren at every age.

Many grandparents provide hands-on care and supervision for their grandchildren. A study of noncustodial grandparents providing care found that

7% of a large representative sample of grandparents cared for a grandchild more than thirty hours per week or for ninety overnights per year (Fuller-Thomson & Minkler, 2001). Moreover, according to the 2000 U.S. Census, approximately 4.5 million American children, 6.3% of all children under age 18, lived full-time in the home of a grandparent. This was nearly a 30% increase from the number of children living with grandparents reported in the 1990 Census (AARP, 2004b). Some of the first literature on grandparents providing what is called *kinship care* looked at African American urban families where the grandparents substituted for crack-addicted parents (e.g., Minkler & Roe, 1993), but grandparents caring for their grandchildren is a phenomenon that spans urban, suburban, and rural areas and all racial and ethnic groups in the United States (Allen, Blieszner, & Roberto, 2000a). Financial, social, and interpersonal aspects of providing kinship care can be quite stressful. Many of these grandparents live on fixed incomes, have low-paying jobs or are unemployed, and must rely on public social agencies to provide money and services for their grandchildren (Gibson, 2002).

Communities and Support Systems

Friendships, Neighbors, and Support Networks

Friends play a very important role in old age, offering emotional support and shared experiences. Sandmaier (1995) has noted that because the bond of friendship is elective, it is more fragile than ties with kin and has no formalized rituals. She also pointed out that, "as we move through our lives, the friends we've made and kept over time take on an increasingly vital role as curators of our emotional histories" (p. 34). Although it is true that younger people socialize more frequently than older people, the contacts tend to be acquaintances and colleagues from work. According to socioemotional selectivity theory, discussed earlier in this chapter, older adults, by comparison, seek social contact with a select few close friends and family members whom they can relate to reliably and comfortably. Adams, Blieszner, and deVries (2000) have explored how older adults define friendships. They found the first criterion to determine whether a person is a friend to be the behavioral or concrete aspects, such as sharing activities, self-disclosure in conversation, and offering assistance, followed by cognitive aspects such as trustworthiness, loyalty, and interests shared, and lastly according to length of time known and nearness of residence.

Although we think of family support and family ties as very important to well-being of older adults, friendships may have a special meaning and provide qualitatively different kinds of support. For instance, a study with residents in retirement housing found that more visits from friends, but not from family members or neighbors, were associated with less loneliness among the residents surveyed (Adams, Sanders, & Auth, 2004). Another recent study found that among a group of men and women ages 55–84, the happiest were those who had the most friends with similar marital status and life situation to their own (Blieszner, 2001). Older adults tend to obtain the most emotional support from confidants close to their own age (Hooyman & Kiyak, 2002). The support of friends and neighbors also has special significance for the 30% of adults over 65, and 46% of those over 85, who live alone, as well as for the approximately 20% of older adults who are childless (Hooyman & Kiyak, 2002). Older adults who live alone or who are without family ties are at high risk for social isolation unless they build a personal support network of friends, neighbors, and formal services when they are needed.

Offering care and support to others is important to many older adults. Thus, older people are not only recipients of care, but provide a remarkable amount of support and help to relatives, friends and neighbors. As noted earlier in the chapter, spouses care for each other, sometimes into late old age, retired "children" must care for their oldest-old parents while also supporting fledgling young-adult children, older siblings help one another and provide emotional support, neighbors look in on each other, and residents of congregate housing tend to form informal networks to provide assistance when other residents experience a loss or become ill. Even older people who may need assistance with some of their activities of daily living often offer assistance to others and find that this informal helping provides meaning to their lives. For example, it is not uncommon to see residents in a nursing home, who themselves may need a cane or have some physical frailty, voluntarily assist fellow residents who are wheelchair-bound.

Churches, senior centers, and volunteer programs that recruit older adults are among the many ex-

> ## FOCUS ON NARRATIVE
>
> ### THE CHURCH LADIES
>
> The "Church Ladies," a group of seven women friends whose ages span from 70 to the mid-80s, attend the same church in Eau Claire, Wisconsin. None of the women is married—they are widows and divorcées—and several are childless. Almost every Sunday, they go for brunch after church at a pancake restaurant, and on Fridays, they meet at a local seafood buffet for dinner, or for lunch in the winter, because it is difficult to drive after dark. Occasionally, they go to a play or a special event as a group. Most of the women have known one another a long time, but their group gradually evolved in just the past few years. With advancing age, there have been health problems; one woman has macular degeneration and has become legally blind. The group makes sure someone will give her a ride when she needs it. As long as they are able, they continue to share good times and look out for one another.

amples of organizations in the community that offer social services and social opportunities to older adults. Many programs specifically targeted to older adults are funded through the Administration on Aging (AoA), a federal agency established in the mid-1960s. The AoA allocates monies to states and localities to fund local Area Agencies on Aging, which in turn fund senior centers, congregate meal programs, and numerous other programs for older people in the community.

Retirement, Work, and Volunteering

Retirement may be defined as the time when the individual begins receiving pension benefits, reduces or stops paid employment, and identifies him- or herself as retired (Atchley, 2000). Although most people think of retirement as occurring around age 65, a substantial portion of older adults retire early, sometimes attracted by company incentives that give them severance pay and continued health benefits, and often because health conditions begin to interfere with job performance or satisfaction. On the other hand, with the lifting of mandatory retirement laws in the U.S. through the Age Discrimination in Employment Amendments of 1986, a new phenomenon has become common: women and men who work as long as they want to, well into their 70s and 80s. U.S. Bureau of Labor and Statistics for 2003 show that 32.8% of men and 22.7% of women aged 65 to 69 participated in the labor force, compared with 18.8% of men and 11.2% of women aged 70 to 74, and 8.3% of men and 4.1% of women over age 75 (Rix, 2004). Those in the current cohort over 65 who continue to work tend to be highly educated and hold jobs with moderate levels of stress, relative flexibility, and high satisfaction, clustering in the professions and the self-employed (Meadows, 2003). And the trend for late-life working appears to be continuing among those who are now in their late 50s and 60s. In a 2003 survey of people aged 50 to 70 in the workforce, only 29% said they plan to give up all paid employment when they eventually retire, and 68% expect they will work part-time or full-time indefinitely (AARP, 2003b). The top reasons given by a group of 364 older workers for working after retirement age were the need for more money (35%), wanting to remain productive or useful (14%), and wanting to stay mentally active (10%) (AARP, 2003b). More than half indicated they are in a field quite different from their previous employment (AARP, 2003b). The occupations in which older workers are most likely to be employed include teaching, consulting, real estate, office work, management, or courier work, and about 20% are self-employed (AARP, 2003b).

Many older adults also engage in unpaid work after retirement. Hospitals, nursing homes, senior centers, theaters, art galleries, and even schools across the country have many older-adult volunteers who spend their time helping others. About 40% of older adults engage in volunteer work, and those who do tend to work more volunteer hours than younger adults because they have more free time (Hooyman & Kiyak, 2002). Volunteering provides older adults with meaningful social roles and can enhance their life satisfaction. Fried and colleagues (2004) also provided recent evidence that older volunteers who helped in elementary school classrooms in Baltimore, Maryland, experienced improved physical, cognitive and social functioning in comparison to a control group.

Retirement involves a major shift in one's family roles, daily activity, social interactions, and financial resources. How one anticipates these changes can affect how successfully one retires. Most people who are thinking ahead to their retirement envision the opportunity to spend more time with friends and family, relax, have more fun, travel, and engage in volunteer work (AARP, 2003b). Atchley (2000) has characterized retirement as a process in several phases, beginning with the preretirement phase, during which people imagine their retirement and make plans. Just after retirement, individuals often move into a honeymoon phase, savoring their newfound freedom. Not surprisingly, the honeymoon phase ends and leads to a disenchantment phase, wherein retirement does not seem as pleasant as before. Next in this process, the individual moves to a reorientation phase and becomes more realistic about retirement and learns to make the necessary adaptations. This may involve finding new part-time or full-time work, starting to volunteer, or taking up new hobbies. Finally, the individual establishes a routine whereby retirement has become the normal way of life.

Often older adults live on a fixed income—for many this means poverty.

Gender Differences in Retirement

A recent longitudinal study of retirement in married couples (Kim & Moen, 2002) has found that the men reacted according to the Atchley (2000) model—they experienced an upsurge in subjective well-being early in retirement, which leveled off after two years, but there was no consistent difference for the women in their well-being from early to later retirement. Other factors, such as health status and perceived income adequacy, were predictive of well-being after retirement for both men and women (Kim & Moen, 2002). Price (2000) has examined responses to retirement among professional women and has found that the loss of professional identity can make their adjustment to retirement very difficult. Barnes & Parry (2004) also report that the ability to formulate an adequate new identity after retirement is predictive of well-being for either sex.

Living on a Fixed Income

Retirement is made more difficult for individuals who have little income to begin with and must then adjust to a reduction in income. Individuals in other stages of life can look to the future with the hope of increasing their income in various ways (promotion, new job, spouse returns to work, kids leave home). But for many older people, retirement means living on a fixed income, which does not increase from year to year, and adjusting their lifestyles to cope with the reduced availability of financial resources. Adjustments range from eating out less often to substantially reducing food intake; from moving to a smaller home to forgoing necessary home repairs and doing without heat or air-conditioning. Even those who saved money for retirement may find their resources greatly reduced after a prolonged illness.

In 2002, 10.4% of Americans over age 65, or about 3.6 million older people, lived below the poverty level (U.S. Census Bureau, 2004). Because of their reduced resources and potential for earnings, if older people fall into poverty, they are more likely to stay in poverty than younger adults (AARP, 2003a). Older women are more likely than their male counterparts to be in poverty and to stay in poverty (AARP, 2003a). Particularly hard hit are women of color and others who have worked at part-time or low-paying jobs that were not covered by Social Security benefits. They may be eligible for other public benefits, but the typical monetary amounts are very low.

Housing Options

Many older adults prefer to "age in place"—staying in their own homes and in their own neighborhoods indefinitely. In many urban, rural, and older suburban areas, the aging in place of the generation that moved into homes and apartments in the 1960s and 1970s has brought about a phenomenon known as NORCs, or naturally occurring retirement communities. These communities tend to have a high density of older adults, some of whom are frail and require in-home services, and it is becoming more common for residents on a street or in an apartment building to join together to share service providers. Complications arise when people develop age-related chronic conditions or disabilities and may no longer be able to drive, shop for food, or get around easily. Then the single-family homes that worked so well throughout raising a family and later adulthood become too large to manage, with stairs that can be difficult or impossible, yards requiring too much maintenance, and neighborhoods that are not easily navigated and may not feel safe. It has been proposed that older women, in particular, have an attachment to their homes and possessions that derives from their investment in the homemaking role; thus, many widows remain in homes that are larger than required and ill-suited to their practical needs (Shenk, Kuwahara, & Zablotsky, 2004).

Influential gerontologist M. Powell Lawton studied issues of older adults and their physical environment, and developed a model that stresses person-environment congruence and the concept of environmental press (Lawton, 1975). The model proposes that there is an optimal level of stimulation and challenge for each individual provided by the environment. As people age, the balance of stimulation and competence may change, and they may require assistance or a move to a different environment. This model has been important in the field of environmental gerontology, which focuses on modifications to homes and other environments to make them safer and more appropriate for older people with sensory and mobility impairments (Wahl & Weisman, 2003). Community-wide efforts to identify what makes a neighborhood "elder-friendly" have been based on some of these same concepts. For example, in Cleveland, Ohio, the Successful Aging Initiative has been launched (www.successfulaging.org) to develop five-year plans to address transportation, housing, and health-services needs for older adults.

The Continuum of Care

Long-term care can be defined as medical and social interventions for those who have chronic illnesses or impairments. These interventions are geared toward helping a patient live as satisfactorily as possible in an appropriate setting. Long-term care once was synonymous with nursing homes. Nowadays, much long-term care occurs in other settings, starting with regular homes. These home- and community-based services (HCBS) are available through a number of pathways—from private home-care agencies that send companions or nursing assistants for an hourly rate, to long-term-care services covered by Medicare or Medicaid—that can help older persons remain in their homes. A relatively new profession, the geriatric care manager, usually a trained social worker or a registered nurse, works with older adults and their families to assess their living arrangements and service needs and to arrange for needed care. The geriatric care manager helps the family decide whether remaining in the home is practical or whether a move to another type of housing or long-term care is needed. There are often ethical as well as practical considerations involved in making these recommendations, as the tension between the older person's independence and autonomy is balanced with his or her safety, security, and health.

Because of the array of options for older adults who either cannot stay or choose not to stay in their own homes, there is a blur between the areas of senior housing and long-term care. Among the least restrictive and service-intensive options, there are several types of congregate housing, most of them age-segregated, that offer the residents an independent apartment along with planned social events, recreation, some or all meals, transportation, and selected social and medical services onsite. A recent study compared residents of congregate senior housing and those living in a large apartment building that was a NORC (see above), both in New York City, and found those in the senior housing used more social and assistive services and expressed higher satisfaction with their environments (Rinehart, 2002). Approximately 5% of older adults live in some kind of senior housing, and another 5% live in nursing homes (Administration on Aging, 2004a). The following list outlines the array of senior living and residential care options that are available:

- *Independent living senior apartments* usually consist of just one or two buildings that offer residences for older adults who can function independently in their personal care needs, but who wish to be in a sheltered environment where other services are offered.
- *Low-income-housing tax credit* properties provide affordable rental housing for older adults who meet a financial-needs test. Most of these properties have long waiting lists. More than half don't provide any special services, but they may have accessibility features for residents such as grab bars in bathrooms (AARP, 2002).
- Board and care homes or *adult foster homes* are usually small, independently operated homes for older or disabled adults housing three to ten older people in a familylike environment; some specialize in older adults with mental disorders.
- Freestanding *assisted-living facilities* generally offer private apartments designed for older people who need some assistance with personal care but don't require constant supervision or the degree of medical attention they would receive in a nursing home (Hooyman & Kiyak, 2002). Usually they provide all meals, help with personal care and medication, and offer a number of social services and activities. Assisted-living homes are overseen and licensed by states, so the offerings differ widely. Monthly costs are usually quite high, but some states are experimenting with Medicaid waivers to cover costs for eligible residents.
- *Continuing care retirement communities*, or CCRCs, offer independent living residences, along with a continuum of care onsite, such as an assisted-living wing or floor, for those who need more help with personal care, and a health facility for those who require skilled nursing care. Financial arrangements to enter CCRCs vary, but the usual way is for the individual or couple to pay an amount comparable to purchasing a small house, in order to "buy in" to the community. From there, they are charged a monthly maintenance and meals fee, but they are guaranteed access to all of the services and medical-care facilities at the CCRC. Older adults who can afford to enter these communities like them because they offer peace of mind for the future, as well as many social benefits and services.
- *Nursing homes* provide skilled medical care and rehabilitation services, though many also offer so-called "custodial" care, assistance with personal care and supervision. Some nursing homes have specialized units for people with dementia. Although only 5% of older people live in nursing homes in the United States, that number rises to nearly 20% of people over age 85 (Hooyman & Kiyak, 2002). Many nursing homes are based on a hospital-like medical model, there is a growing movement called "The Eden Alternative" to humanize and personalize these facilities through the addition of plants, pets, and less rigid scheduling and use of space to enhance quality of life (see www.edenalt.com).

The decision to move to a nursing home can be a difficult one for families and individuals. Most older adults wish to remain independent as long as possible, and family members usually try to provide care at home for as long as possible. However, when an older adult requires round-the-clock supervision, is incontinent, or is bedridden, placement in a nursing home may become necessary. Most nursing homes employ social workers who assist families and residents with the transition into the facility, offer emotional support, and advocate for their needs during the resident's stay.

Multicultural and Gender Considerations

Older Racial or Ethnic Minorities

Older members of racial or ethnic minorities often have histories of social oppression and reduced educational and employment opportunities, and many continue to be disadvantaged today (Beckett & Dungee-Anderson, 2000). For instance, the life-course perspective reminds us that social conditions during the youth of today's older African Americans were not only very different than today, but certainly very different from those of their white-majority counterparts. Those born before the 1950s lived in the time before Civil Rights were won, when racial discrimination was an accepted part of American society. Today, some of them see their children or grandchildren still fighting racism and social oppression, and they continue to have higher rates of poverty in late life (AARP, 2003a). Likewise, Native Americans may have experienced their whole lives on a reservation. Although they may take pride in their traditions and accomplishments, they have lived with restricted access to and opportunities in the greater society. Today, their children and grandchildren disproportionately face poverty and social ills such as high rates of alcohol and drug abuse. Recent immigrant elders, on the other hand, even those who are well educated and financially comfortable, may have lived under oppressive governments in their homelands. Their opportunities for social integration in the U.S. may be limited by language and cultural differences (Wilmoth & Chen, 2003; Burr & Mutchler, 2003). All of these stresses and hardships have an effect on how these older people view the world and themselves (Beckett & Dungee-Anderson, 2000), and on how they respond to the dominant culture.

In general, the ethnic minority cultures prominent in the U.S. value extended-family relationships and mutual assistance among family members of different generations (Becker, Beyene, Newsom, & Mayen, 2003). With less emphasis on the stand-alone nuclear-family structure, there are usually important roles for older adults within the family. Latino, Native American, and Asian American cultures traditionally honor and provide for older persons, although modern life may change the ways that families enact or follow these traditions. About 40% of Native American households are headed by older women who have a strong role in offering support and guidance to young families (Hooyman & Kiyak, 2002). Many Latino and Asian American extended families also live together so that the grandparents can provide child care while the parents work. Becker and colleagues (2003) conducted interviews with elders from four ethnic groups and uncovered some differences in the way different groups tend to provide support within families. They found that although the Latino elders provided help and child care to their families, they also expected help and financial support from their grown children and were unhappy when it wasn't available; the Asian (Cambodian and Filipino) elders were more invested in living with their grown children, which they saw as a sign of their children's devotion to them, and many of the African American elders were in the position of helping out their grown children and grandchildren financially and by providing them with a place to live (Becker et al., 2003).

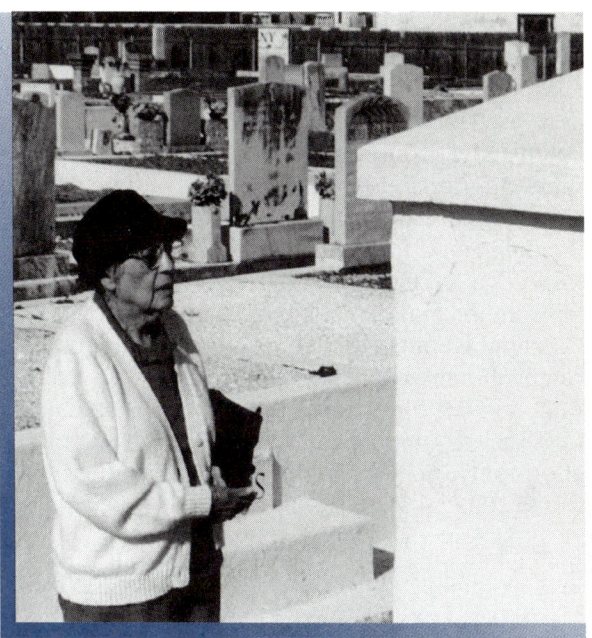

This woman, from French-speaking Louisiana, is confronting a personal problem: her husband has died. Her responses are influenced by socially prescribed customs and coping styles related to death and burial practices.

African American elders live alone, and live with grandchildren and nonrelatives, more often than the other groups (Peek, Koropeckyj-Cox, Zsembik, & Coward, 2004). In the African American community, because of high divorce rates, high death rates among African American men, lack of employment opportunities, and welfare policies that discouraged marriage starting in the 1960s, there are fewer married elders (Hooyman & Kiyak, 2002). With large numbers of African American elders unmarried and living alone, some may be left without any family support when care is needed (Peng, Navaie-Waliser, & Feldman, 2003). However, African Americans also have more active informal support networks than whites, often linked with their churches, whose members may assume the role of fictive kin (Williams & Dilworth-Anderson, 2002).

With the anticipated increase in the diversity among elders in the coming decades, particularly those from Hispanic and Asian cultures, social work as a profession has an increased need for cultural competence—the need to become informed about other cultures, to coordinate services with indigenous workers and native speakers, and to espouse sensitivity and respect for the values and traditions that are important to clients with backgrounds that may differ from the majority culture. As Yee has aptly stated, "Cultural competence is not a tonic or product that can be dispensed at a workshop or noted on a certificate. Cultural competence is a set of skills or perspectives that require lifelong learning and a disciplined effort to try on new and often uncomfortable behaviors." (2002, p. 7).

Gender Issues

Like older people from underprivileged minorities, older women came of age during a time when girls and young women were disadvantaged in terms of educational and employment opportunities. Older women are more likely to live in poverty than older men, in part because of these cumulative disadvantages, and also because of their predominant roles as wives and homemakers (Browne, 1998). As has been noted earlier in this chapter, women have a longer life expectancy than men do; there are currently about 20.8 million women over the age of 65, and only 14.8 million men, and at age 85, the ratio of women to men is 230 to 1 (Administration on Aging, 2004a). This fact of women's longevity contributes to them living alone in greater proportion (fully half the women who are 75 or older live alone), and suffering from more chronic disabilities than men (who may die from other causes before these disabilities set in), which combine to put them at much greater risk for nursing-home placement as they become older.

Ageism is the stereotyping of older people, or prejudice and discrimination against older persons solely because of their age. In our culture, which prizes youthful feminine beauty and physical fitness, older women are particularly vulnerable to ageist attitudes, including some that they believe themselves. According to research by Morell (2003), older women tend to reject their aging bodies, to subtly disavow the physical self as it becomes weaker, less able, and less like the culture's norms for beauty. Women resist being identified with old age, disability, and death, yet it is difficult to deny the realities of how they really function, feel, and look in the mirror. Morell (2003) recommends that social workers help older women to accept the age-related changes they inevitably experience without the need to apologize for themselves or incorporate negative self-images and self-assessments.

Older women deal with the double jeopardy of aging and being female—ageism and sexism—and older women from minority groups may suffer the triple burden of ageism, sexism, and racism. How gender and race combine to contribute to disadvantaged status is evident in poverty statistics (AARP, 2003a). Older women of all races combined have a higher poverty rate than older men (12.4% compared to 7.7%). Older people living alone have a poverty rate of 19.2%. However, older African Americans of both sexes have a poverty rate of 23.8% and older Latinos have a rate of 21.4%. The highest poverty rate is for older Latinas; over 40% are in poverty.

Social Strengths and Hazards

Social Support for Older Adults

As we have seen throughout this section, older adults with extended family, with involved grown children, with good friends and neighbors, who are married or partnered with a significant other, who have planned for retirement and have adequate finances, and who are able to continue to get around and enjoy volunteer work and social activities—these are the older adults who have the most social support available to them. Should they require assistance, they are likely to be able to obtain the help and services they need, when they need them, at a cost they can afford. In addition, the personal flexibility to adjust to and accept growing dependence on others, if and when the time comes that independence becomes limited, is an invaluable strength. However, many of these factors are not under the control of the individual. Older adults who live alone, who may not have living children or extended family, those over age 85, and those who live in poverty, in inappropriate or unsafe settings—these are the adults who are particularly vulnerable to social isolation, to loneliness, to nutritional insufficiency, and to unmet healthcare needs, and who may need social work interventions the most.

Elder Abuse and Neglect

With reduced physical strength and independence, older adults may become vulnerable to a social hazard that has increasingly come to the attention of social-work and health-care practitioners—**elder abuse**. The definition of elder abuse includes any mistreatment of older adults, whether abuse or neglect, intentional or unintentional, and includes physical, emotional and financial mistreatment resulting in suffering, pain, or loss for the victim (Wolf, 2000). Categories of elder abuse and neglect include such diverse harmful acts as hitting the person, withholding food or water, bullying and threatening, abandoning them when they cannot care for themselves, rape or unwanted sexual touching, or taking their material goods without permission, and involve elders in their homes or in residential care (Wolf, 2000). Self-neglect occurs when an independent older person is incapable of necessary self-care, so may be malnourished, dehydrated, dirty, ill, or living in a cluttered, unsafe environment. Usually, self-neglect relates to dementia or psychiatric illness of an older person who lacks involved family nearby. In some cases, legal guardianship procedures and placement of the individual must go through the courts.

A major study of the incidence of elder abuse and neglect conducted in 1998 found that approximately 450,000 people aged 60 or over experienced either abuse or neglect, and another 110,000 experienced self-neglect in the course of one year, and only one in four incidents were reported to officials (Administration on Aging, 2004b). Adult Protective Services (APS) is the organization charged with investigating reports of elder abuse and neglect; 75% of the states have dedicated agencies specifically for elder abuse, the remaining 25% run their APS services from state aging agencies (McInnes-Dittrich, 2005). Much like Child Protective Services, after a call comes in reporting suspected mistreatment, APS workers visit the alleged victim to try to determine whether abuse or neglect has taken place, whether an emergency move to protective custody or another facility is needed, and what other social, legal, and medical services may be appropriate so that the abuse or neglect doesn't continue.

Approximately 90% of abuse and neglect is perpetrated by family members or relatives, two-thirds by the spouse or adult child of the victim (Administration on Aging, 2004b). Females and those over age 80 are disproportionately represented in the victim profiles (National Center on Elder Abuse, 2004). Practitioners and researchers have noted two paths that appear to explain what causes elder abuse: caregiver stress and caregiver impairment (Brownell & Wolden, 2002). Caregiver stress as a cause of elder abuse refers to situations in which the caregiver becomes overwhelmed by the demands of the dependent older person and may either perpetrate violence in a moment of anger and stress, or may neglect the person's needs, sometimes through a combination of ignorance, denial, and outright inability to meet those needs. Caregiver impairment refers to a caregiver's mental illness, personality disorder, or substance abuse, and may involve more serious harms that are perpetrated repeatedly. According to Wolf (2000), there is a growing body of evidence that caregiver stress alone does not cause a great deal of elder abuse and neglect, but that there are multiple risk factors, including the earlier relationship of the victim and abuser, the abuser's mental state, and the lack of appropriate alternative services or caregivers. An ecological model of elder abuse, therefore, sees the problem as multidimensional and linked to other social problems. Brandl (2000) has contended that caregiver stress is not an excuse and should not be considered an adequate explanation for elder abuse and neglect in most cases, citing the sense of entitlement of many abusers. A number of specific risk factors and signs of elder abuse and neglect have been identified that may be helpful for social workers as they work with dependent elders in the community (McInnes-Dittrich, 2005), including the following:

- Presence of family member's mental illness, or drug or alcohol abuse
- Stressful life events for the family, such as financial loss, death, divorce
- Cognitive impairment of the older person (more likely to be neglected)
- Physical impairment/dependence on others for physical needs (more likely to be abused)
- Older person's social isolation
- Poor hygiene and nutritional status; obvious lack of care
- The older person appears hypervigilant or nervous
- The caregiver displays hostility and impatience toward the elder

Social workers have important roles to play in the identification and psychosocial treatment of elder abuse and neglect. Anetzberger (2000) proposed an integrative framework to address elder abuse that consists of protection, empowerment and advocacy, working with the victim-perpetrator dyad within the family system, and providing emergency support as needed to treat the victim and prevent further abuse. Brandl (2000) offered specific interventions to empower older victims of domestic abuse, including empathic listening and sensitive questioning to identify the nature of the abuse, minimizing potential danger through appropriate security measures, safety planning, evaluating options (such as a move to another relative's home, or pressing charges on the abuser), holding the perpetrator responsible for his actions, and providing hope and support.

Developmental Guidelines for Assessment in Late Adulthood

Exhibit 12.12 presents the developmental guidelines for late adulthood. These guidelines are meant to be helpful to social workers who need to understand development when making assessments.

EXHIBIT 12.12 – Developmental considerations in assessment in late adulthood

Routine Observations
Chronic health conditions
Availability of appropriate health care
Functioning in activities of daily living
Medications used and their side effects
Ability to obtain nutritious meals
Opportunities for exercise
Alcohol or other drug use
Mental status: Memory, judgment
Emotional expression
Availability of companionship, friendship
Family support or family conflicts
Caring for others: spouse, family, grandchildren
Neighborhood safety
Transportation issues
Home safety and appropriateness
Employment or volunteer opportunities
Social and community opportunities

Strengths and Landmarks of Development
Maintaining interests and activities according to capability
Interest in remaining as independent as possible
Interest in sexual expression and companionship
Desire to leave a legacy—e.g., creative work, possessions, or family
Desire to maintain family and friendship connections
Adapting to new roles
May be more reflective or introverted
May take comfort in religious beliefs or spirituality

Development Issues (Not Problems)
Physical vulnerability due to senescence of bodily systems
Continuity of personality traits from earlier adulthood
Cognitive processing speed decreases
Short-term storage and recall memory decreases
Strengthening of religious beliefs (sometimes)
Preference for reliable, comfortable relationships
Selective about appropriate activities and interests
Resisting "old" identity
Role relinquishment as necessary
Recent bereavement or other losses experienced
May need to give up driving
May need assistance with daily activities
May need residential placement
May need supportive end of life care

Development Observations Requiring Attention
Little affect; lack of interest or enjoyment
Talks of being worthless or being a burden
Persistent loneliness
Social isolation
Paranoid ideation or delusions
Slurred speech or otherwise not alert; can't stay awake
Walking unsteadily but without cane or walker
Multiple medications with possible interactions
Possible alcohol misuse
Repeats same questions, gets lost, obvious memory loss
Unsafe living situation
Signs of physical neglect—dirty, unkempt, bedsores
Signs of physical abuse—unusual bruises or bleeding, fearfulness
Signs of nutritional deficiency—too thin, little food in the house, etc.

STUDY TABLE: Social Dimension in Late Adulthood

Families and Groups	Older adults are a product of their backgrounds, their culture, parenting, neighborhoods, etc. The physical and social environments continue to impact older people's growth and development. Family is the first line of support when older people need help. With longer life spans, there are many multigenerational families. Spouses, adult children, and then siblings provide most support for older adults. There are many forms of family; some are created by upgrading neighbors or friends to a "fictive kin" role. More men than women are married in later life. Unattached older women are plentiful, and unattached older men are more scarce. Late-life marriages are characterized by fewer disagreements and increased satisfaction. Marital satisfaction predicts life satisfaction for married older people; research has found older marrieds are better able to overlook disagreements and remain satisfied. Illness or disability in one of the partners affects the other partner. Spouses usually serve as primary caregiver as long as possible. Couples compensate for each other's physical and sensory impairments. Older homosexuals may have suffered oppression and hostility because of their sexual preferences. They may not be "out" even to family, and some of their unique needs may be overlooked by service providers. Adjustment to widowhood varies widely. A warm, intimate relationship and reliance on the partner for instrumental tasks predict a harder adjustment, as does lack of adequate family and social support. Because older widows outnumber older widowers, remarriage is much more common for men who lose a spouse. Women who are widowed sometimes relish their independence after the period of bereavement. Two divergent theories of parent-child ties in later life are solidarity and ambivalence. Most older adults are in frequent contact with their grown children, and social workers often include family members in assessment and treatment of older people. Grown children with many other responsibilities provide several types of support to older parents. When separated geographically, these are more limited but still very important. Caregiving ranges from hands-on assistance to management of hired help, decision making, or overseeing care received in a nursing home. Daughters are usually elected to be the primary caregivers, but sons also provide a lot of informal care to older parents. Becoming a grandparent allows an opportunity to leave a legacy. The relationship is mediated by the adult child but will change as the grandchild grows. Grandparenting styles vary according to many factors, such as geographic location, and stronger links may exist with maternal relatives. Many grandparents care for grandchildren, and many have custody, providing kinship care for children when the parents cannot.
Communities and Support Systems	Friends play important roles in old age as curators of emotional history. Friends of similar age and marital status tend to provide the most important sources of support and are especially important to elders who live alone or are childless. Older people like to help and support others, and many find great satisfaction from formal and informal caring for friends, family, and neighbors. Although some older adults retire early to pursue other interests or because of attractive pension offers, many older adults work beyond normal retirement age. Many retirees work because they need money, but others report they want to remain productive. Forty percent of older people do volunteer work, and many experience enhanced well-being. Retirement is a major transition and can be seen as a process from honeymoon through disenchantment, to reorientation and routine. Health and income adequacy are important predictors of successful adjustment. Living on a fixed income can make life difficult for some retirees who may not have adequate savings or other sources of income. More than 10% of older adults live below the poverty level and are more

(continues)

STUDY TABLE: Social Dimension in Late Adulthood (*continued*)

	likely to stay there. Older women, women of color, and those who worked at low-paying or part-time jobs are hardest hit. Many older people wish to age in place. Difficulties arise when health conditions or disabilities make living at home impractical or impossible. NORCS have arisen in many established neighborhoods, where older people remain in their homes and start to require in-home services. Person-environment congruence refers to the fit of an older person and his or her residence; environmental press means that the level of challenge in the environment has become too intense. Long-term care is provided in many settings, including regular homes. Home- and community-based services (HCBS) are available through various agencies and programs. Geriatric care managers help families determine appropriate services and when a move out of the home may be needed. Senior housing and long-term care often overlap. Age-segregated congregate housing provides many services for residents. Options include independent-living apartments, adult foster-care homes, assisted-living facilities, or continuing care retirement communities (CCRCs). Nursing homes house approximately 5% of older adults, but 20% over age 85. Newer models of nursing homes provide more homelike environments. Social workers play important roles in nursing-home admissions and adjustment of residents and families after they move in.
Multicultural and Gender Considerations	Older adults of color have a history of social oppression and reduced opportunities that affect their perspectives today and contribute to higher rates of poverty in late life. Recent immigrants may have poor English-language skills and lack social integration. Ethnic minority cultures tend to value extended family and mutual assistance among members of different generations. This allows older adults to maintain important family roles. A higher proportion of African American elders are unmarried and live alone; they receive support from extended family and fictive kin from church and neighborhood. Cultural competence is crucial for social workers. Older women are disproportionately in poverty, unmarried, and living alone. Their longevity leaves them susceptible to higher rates of chronic illness and institutionalization. Ageism, sexism, and racism all operate to keep poverty rates high for older women of color. Our youth-oriented society makes it difficult for older women to feel positive about their physical selves as they age and experience disabilities.
Social Strengths and Hazards	Having the support of family, spouses or partners, friends, or neighbors, as well as having planned for retirement and possessing adequate finances, constitute social strengths for older adults. The mobility to participate in paid or volunteer work and to socialize with friends and family are other strengths. Accepting dependency should it arise is another strength that helps older adults adjust well and avoid social isolation. Elder abuse includes physical, emotional, financial, or sexual mistreatment, or neglect of needs. Self-neglect occurs when an independent older person is incapable of necessary self-care. An estimated one in four incidents of elder abuse is reported to authorities. Adult Protective Services (APS) operates much like Child Protective Services to investigate reports of elder abuse and to take appropriate action to stop abuse or neglect from occurring. Most abusers are family members. Caregiver impairments play a major role in elder abuse. After establishing that there is abuse or neglect and assuring the victim's safety, social workers use several treatment frameworks for dealing with elder abuse, including family systems and empowerment.

CONCEPT MAP

- **Social dimension**
  - **Families and groups**
    - Families
    - *Focus on Narrative: Maryland Sisters Still Side by Side*
    - Couples
    - Gay male and lesbian elders
    - Widowhood
    - Parent-child relationships
    - Grandparenthood
  - **Communities and support systems**
    - Friendships, neighbors, and support networks
    - *Focus on Narrative: The Church Ladies*
    - Retirement, work, and volunteering
    - Housing options
    - The continuum of care
  - **Multicultural and gender considerations**
    - Older racial or ethnic minorities
    - Gender issues
  - **Social strengths and hazards**
    - Social support for older adults
    - Elder abuse and neglect

APPLYING THE FRAMEWORK

DEPRESSION IN AN OLDER WOMAN

Esther Rodriguez is a 77-year-old widow who broke her hip three months ago. After a two-week hospital stay for emergency hip-replacement surgery and four weeks in a convalescent facility for strengthening and mobility training, she is staying in her daughter and son-in-law's home because she was not fully capable of caring for herself independently when her need for skilled services (and thus her Medicare coverage) ended at the convalescent facility. She was referred to Catholic Social Services by her daughter, who wanted help in making long-range plans for her mother's care.

Mrs. Rodriguez has lived in the same house for nearly fifty years. She raised two sons and a daughter there. Her husband, who died five years

(*continues*)

APPLYING THE FRAMEWORK

(continued)

ago, worked for the railroad. Mrs. Rodriguez was primarily a homemaker, but she supplemented the family income by selling her homemade tortillas and tamales to neighborhood restaurants. Mrs. Rodriguez's older son died of cancer two years ago, at age 52. Her younger son lives in another state with his second wife and their children. Mrs. Rodriguez's daughter, Ana Clark, 50, and Ana's husband, Joe Clark, are purchasing the modern townhouse that they moved into five years ago. It is located on the opposite side of town from Mrs. Rodriguez. Ana is a self-employed CPA. She and her husband own their own accounting firm. They have two grown children and three grandchildren. One of their sons, age 24, is living in their home while he seeks employment.

Developmental History

Mr. and Mrs. Rodriguez had made a comfortable adjustment to retirement and had about seven years together before his death five years ago. Mrs. Rodriguez's activities had not changed as much as her husband's, but she spent less time in church activities with the other women and more time gardening and working around the house with her husband. Once a week, however, she had lunch with three of her best high school friends while her husband played bingo with his retired friends at church. On Sundays, her daughter Ana and son-in-law Joe came for dinner. Her husband's death was very hard for her. It took her nearly two years before she felt she could wake up and not ache from feeling lonely. Following her son's death two years ago, she again had a very hard time. Ana reported that her mother never seemed to be her old self after that.

The current circumstances of Mrs. Rodriguez and her daughter's family have put a strain on the natural stages of family and individual life-cycle development. Mrs. Rodriguez's role with her older son (wise parent, loving mother) has been prematurely interrupted, as has his role with her and his sister (responsible son who can help with maintenance of family home, validation of parental wisdom and elder's value). Ana is just into the stage of launching children and moving on, but her son's return home and now her mother's living with her is requiring a return to more caretaking and home-management demands. Ana and her mother have been arguing daily about Mrs. Rodriguez returning to her own home. Ana is worried that her mother will forget to take her blood-pressure medicine, fall down, or even wander away. She doesn't think her mother will bother with eating or, worse still, may forget to turn off the stove and set fire to her house. This role reversal with her mother (daughter taking more parental responsibility for adult parent, and parent being more dependent) is magnified by the fact that her mother is living in Ana's home, and it is hard for Ana to learn to support her mother without overfunctioning for her. Their arguing represents what a considerable strain this is for both mother and daughter. Ana also has admitted that she and her husband have been arguing frequently. They are renegotiating their marital relationship to accommodate both the younger and older generation living in their family space. Ana is also feeling pressure to put in more hours at work as tax season is approaching, and her husband is expecting her to keep up with her part of their business.

Ana becomes tearful as she confesses to feeling "trapped." She is worried about her mother's current well-being, but she is also fearful that Mrs. Rodriguez may have an incurable problem, such as Alzheimer's disease, and that she will never be able to return to living in her own home. Ana seems to be feeling some resentment over the fact that she has become her mother's chief caretaker, even though she works full-time, has raised her own children, and has a brother who should be equally responsible for their mother. Ana has had several telephone conversations with her brother to discuss living arrangements for Mrs. Rodriguez. Her brother expresses concern, but he poses distance and his own family responsibilities as barriers to his being an integral part of any solution. He has offered some limited financial help and has given his approval to whatever plan his sister and mother work out.

Biophysical Considerations

Mrs. Rodriguez is not frail and is of above-average intelligence. She had been completely independent in her own home before she broke her hip.

She was able to do all her activities of daily living in her familiar environment. She needed partial help with only two instrumental activities of daily living. Following her husband's death, she had asked Ana to help her manage the lump-sum life-insurance money from her husband's railroad life policy, and she needed help with transportation for shopping because she had never learned to drive.

Chronic medical problems for Mrs. Rodriguez include arthritis, hearing loss, high blood pressure, digestive difficulties, and osteoporosis. The osteoporosis was a major factor contributing to her broken hip. Whether she fell and the soft bone in her hip broke or whether the hip broke and caused her to fall is not known; either way, the brittleness of her bones puts her at great risk for further broken bones resulting from slight falls and for compression fractures in her spine, which can occur without provocation.

Mrs. Rodriguez is well known to her family doctor, whose office is in her neighborhood. He has treated her for several years, and his late father was her doctor before him. A telephone conversation with the doctor has revealed that Mrs. Rodriguez has managed her chronic medical problems well. She has been compliant in taking her blood-pressure medication and comes in for periodic checkups. Her chronic conditions are stable. However, since being at Ana's, Mrs. Rodriguez complains of chronic pain "all over." She frequently refuses to take her daily walk, citing pain in her (artificial) hip as the reason. She has frequent headaches and seems tired most of the time. Ana reports that the orthopedic surgeon who replaced her mother's hip states she is healing well and, with time and normal activity, the soreness in her hip should decrease. Because Mrs. Rodriguez is now so far away from her doctor's office, she has not seen her regular doctor since she left the hospital. Ana is trying to decide whether to find a doctor near her own home to take over her mother's care or to transport her mother across town to see her regular doctor.

Cognitive Development and Psychological Hazards

Ana reports that her mother "is just not with it." She had always enjoyed watching the news and discussing current events with others, but Ana can no longer engage her in discussion. Mrs. Rodriguez cannot seem to concentrate on the news stories, and she becomes agitated and frustrated when Ana tries to talk with her. "She just doesn't seem to care about anything," Ana says. Ana also reports that her mother has significant short-term memory deficits. She becomes upset with Ana if Ana is late getting home from work, even after Ana calls before leaving the office to tell her that she's stopping for groceries. She often asks what day it is, only to ask the same question ten minutes later. She tells Ana that she ate the meal Ana left for her, although Ana finds it untouched in the refrigerator. Ana reports that her mother began exhibiting these memory problems a few weeks after she entered the nursing home.

In an effort to sort out whether Mrs. Rodriguez's cognitive difficulties are organic or more psychological and related to a significant depression, the social worker completed a Mini-Mental Status Exam. At first, Mrs. Rodriguez had difficulty comprehending what was being asked of her, but then the social worker decided that perhaps a part of the problem was Mrs. Rodriguez's hearing loss. The social worker began using a voice amplifier attached to earphones that Mrs. Rodriguez was asked to wear, and Mrs. Rodriguez responded much better to the questions and appeared much brighter. She scored 25 out of a possible 30 points. She had the most difficulty with attention/calculation and recall sections. This score is strongly suggestive of a pseudodementia caused by depression, rather than an organic, irreversible dementia.

When the social worker asked Mrs. Rodriguez to take the self-administered Geriatric Depression Scale, she scored 12, which suggests that depression may be the root of her cognitive difficulties.

Attitudes and Emotions

The significant losses that Mrs. Rodriguez has experienced in the last few years (losing her husband and eldest son to death; another son to distance; her hearing; and now her mobility) have taxed her abilities to adjust and cope. One coping strategy she has used is to maintain a sense of normality by continuing to perform routine activities of housekeeping, gardening, going to church, and visiting neighbors. These are now difficult for her

(continues)

APPLYING THE FRAMEWORK
(continued)

because of her physical limitations and because she resides in a household that is not her own. The loss of her husband, though devastating, was more in the expected process of life, whereas the son's death before her own is more unnatural. This fact makes bereavement more complicated for Mrs. Rodriguez. She often said she would much rather have gotten cancer herself and gone to be with her husband than for her son to have to leave this life so soon.

Ana believes that her son, who is recovering from substance abuse, may be using his grandmother as an excuse to avoid looking for employment. However, Mrs. Rodriguez states that she has developed a "new" and close relationship with this 24-year-old grandson. They have shared a common struggle to recover from different difficulties, and both are concerned that the other succeeds. They may be a newfound resource for each other to cope with loss and the new challenges in their lives.

Support Systems, Contexts, and Multicultural and Gender Issues

Mrs. Rodriguez's home is in a historic part of town, populated by mostly Latino families. Many of these families have lived in the neighborhood for three or more generations. Mrs. Rodriguez has many friends in the neighborhood, which remains largely intact with a corner grocery, a pharmacy, a school, and an active Catholic church. Mrs. Rodriguez has enjoyed cooking with the churchwomen who provide food for weddings, funerals, and special celebrations. She still takes pride in her tortilla making. She has a number of close neighbors who have known her for years. She has provided them with support (babysitting, cooking, emotional support) many times in the past.

The church remains a central focus for the life of this community as well as for Mrs. Rodriguez. Attending mass on Sundays and religious holidays has always been an important part of her self-identity. She considers the parish priest her adviser on all matters of living and has spoken to him several times about personal matters since her husband died.

Ana's husband is white. Ana has left much of her cultural upbringing behind but continues to attend a Catholic church near her current home. Ana's children have become even more assimilated into the dominant culture. Although Ana and her mother are bilingual, Ana rarely speaks Spanish to her mother because she feels this would be inconsiderate to her husband and son, who speak only English. These cultural differences make Ana's home unfamiliar and, in many ways, uncomfortable for Mrs. Rodriguez. Mrs. Rodriguez's presence in Ana's home has brought up old conflicts for Ana around her Hispanic identity and heritage that Ana thought she had put to rest long ago.

Ecomaps demonstrate the changes in Mrs. Rodriguez's life context from before her husband died (see Exhibit 12.13) to the present time (see Exhibit 12.14). This assessment tool shows the severe constriction of her life space since her husband's death and her surgery. Many nurturing support systems—priest, church, friends, neighbors—and activities are no longer a part of her everyday existence. These accumulated losses will add to her depression and confusion, and her current living situation will only exacerbate the stressful relationship between Mrs. Rodriguez and her daughter, Ana. Restoration of Mrs. Rodriguez to her home and neighborhood, with appropriate formal supports, is the preferred goal of treatment.

Social Hazards

Impoverishment may be a hazard for Mrs. Rodriguez. She owns her home and has several thousand dollars in a savings account, but her income is fixed and just meets her regular expenses. She has Medicare but has not felt she could afford the cost of a supplemental health-insurance policy on her fixed income. She has been able to manage comfortably, but added expenses for a prolonged period could quickly deplete her savings and leave her home as her only financial asset.

EXHIBIT 12.13 Ecomap before husband's death

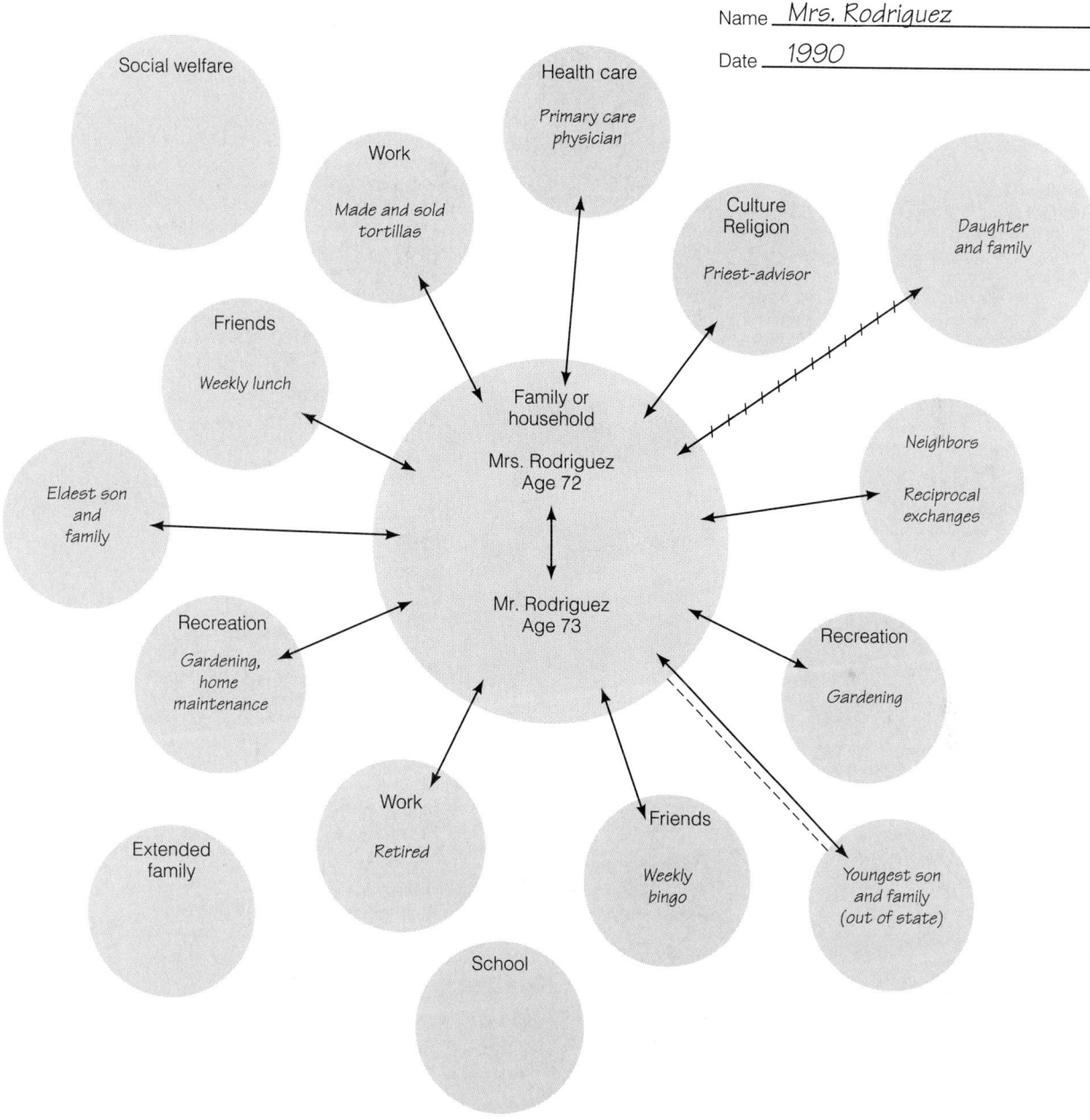

Fill in connections where they exist.
Indicate nature of connections with a descriptive word or by drawing different kinds of lines:
————— for strong, - - - - - for tenuous, —+—+— for stressful.
Draw arrows along lines to signify flow of energy, resources, etc. ⟶ ⟶ ⟶
Identify significant people and fill in empty circles as needed.

SOURCE: Hartman (1978).

EXHIBIT 12.14 Ecomap at present

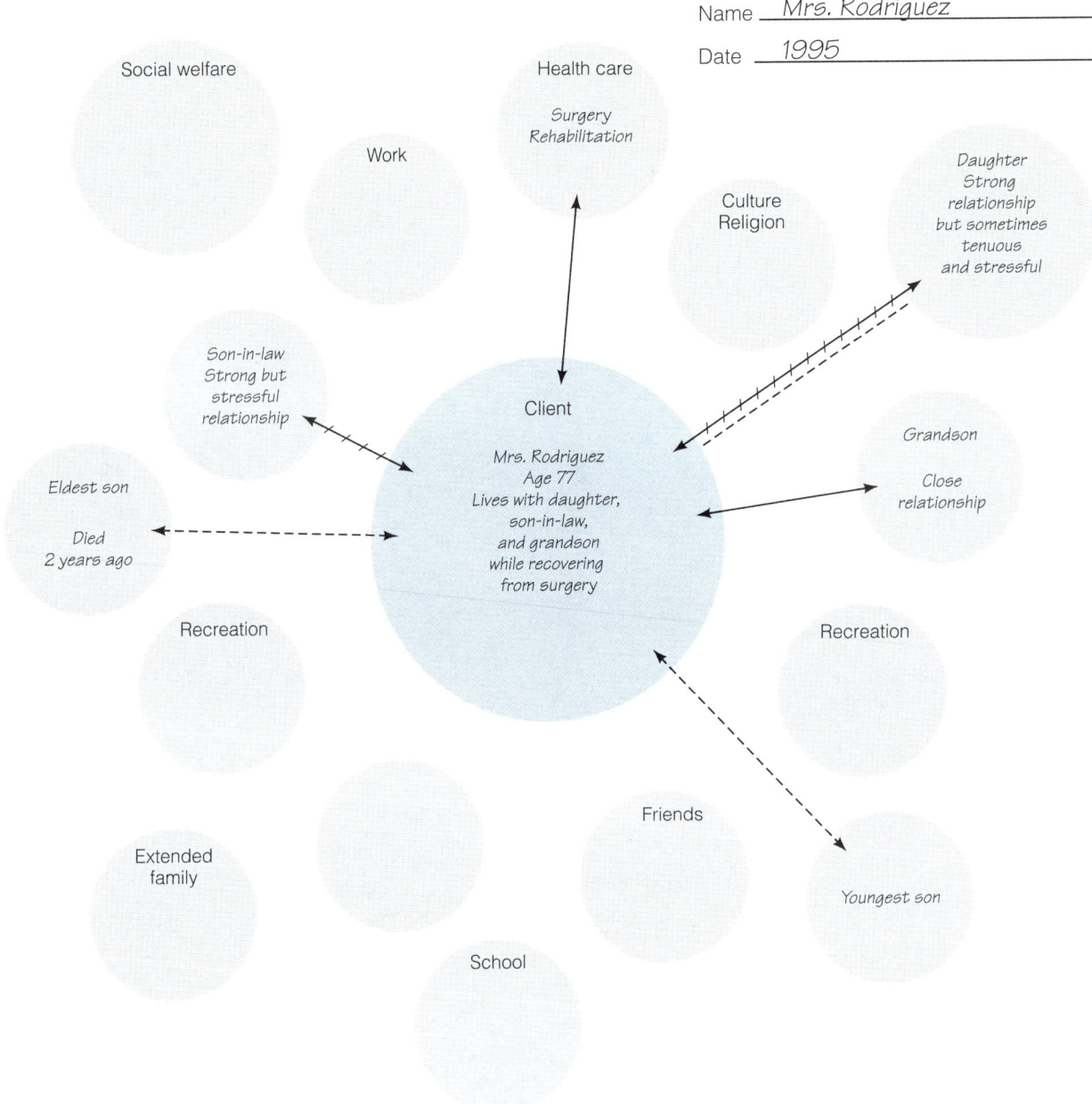

Fill in connections where they exist.
Indicate nature of connections with a descriptive word or by drawing different kinds of lines:
———— for strong, — — — — for tenuous, ⧸⧸⧸⧸ for stressful.
Draw arrows along lines to signify flow of energy, resources, etc. ⟶⟶⟶
Identify significant people and fill in empty circles as needed.

SOURCE: Hartman (1978).

Summary and Impressions

Problems needing intervention:

- It is likely that depression has caused Mrs. Rodriguez's cognitive deterioration. Both medical and psychosocial interventions are suggested, because there are important issues of loss and grief that Mrs. Rodriguez needs help in resolving, as well as physical signs of depression. With treatment for her depression, Mrs. Rodriguez should suffer less from "generalized pain," be motivated to continue rehabilitating her hip, and be able to make the necessary adjustments to continue her independent living, though with more supports.
- Hearing impairment may be creating more cognitive deficits and adding to Mrs. Rodriguez's depression. This needs to be further evaluated through an audiologist.
- Confusion as to the source of Mrs. Rodriguez's memory and concentration problems has produced anxiety and catastrophic thinking in Ana and hindered her ability to appropriately plan for her mother's future needs.
- Mrs. Rodriguez will need help with certain activities of daily living, such as bathing, dressing, and heavy housework, because her mobility is still limited from the hip surgery.
- Ana is experiencing increasing stress owing to physical and time demands of caring for her mother and managing all of her other responsibilities.
- Ana's family is experiencing stress and role strain with the new demands on Ana at a time when the family is facing other demands in the business and the need of the younger son for emotional support to progress to the next stage in his life.
- Ana and Mrs. Rodriguez are experiencing role strain as Mrs. Rodriguez becomes more dependent.

Strengths identified:

- There is a strong family bond and commitment to looking for solutions that address everyone's needs.
- Mrs. Rodriguez has been flexible in adapting to earlier changes in her life and has coping skills that should continue to help her adapt.
- Mrs. Rodriguez lives in a supportive, close, culturally homogeneous neighborhood where she feels safe and important.
- Mrs. Rodriguez has built many reciprocal relationships among her neighbors, which may make it more probable that they can help her in ways that can enable her to return to living in her own home.
- Mrs. Rodriguez has a close relationship with former high school friends with whom she enjoys leisure-time activities.

Epilogue: The Journey of Life

We have now come to the final pages of this book—moving from birth to death. We hope that the framework and information we have provided can help you make some sense of this lifelong progression. And yet, on a deeper level, is it possible for us to make sense of life? After taking this journey, perhaps this is an appropriate time to pause and reflect on the meaning of life. What is the real sense of it all?

Great minds have struggled with this question. Kierkegaard informed us that "life is lived forward, but understood backwards." Socrates was cheerful in his answer to this question—we are here to be happy. And for Socrates, the path to happiness was through knowledge. Other philosophers, such as Epicurus, would simply state that our existence is to cultivate pleasures. Religious philosophers have placed the focus of our existence on faith. If we have faith, we can be assured to have a special place in God's kingdom. According to Lao-tzu, our existence should be focused on knowing the inner harmony of nature's way. And Bob Dylan sang, "All ya can do is do what you must. / You do what you must do and ya do it well."

Though we can present the facts and theories of human development in the social environment, and philosophize at length, defining the purpose of life is a difficult task—maybe a lifelong task. In the end, perhaps it is up to us individually to make sense of our lives and to make life something very real and very meaningful. As we pause, then our personal reflections on life may provide our own sense of meaning. These reflections might bring forth images about our origin and our start in life, our growth and struggles throughout life, our hopes and our fears, our achievements, our love, and ultimately our death:

> *We whisper a new baby's name to the rising sun,*
> *we laugh as the child mistakes a cow for a dog,*
> *we call each other "buttface,"*
> *we learn and grow,*
> *we dye our hair purple as we struggle to establish a unique identity,*
> *we work and we love and sometimes we cry,*
> *we stand at the crossroads and hesitate for just a moment before moving on,*
> *we stare as the shoreline recedes and the ship sails away before finally turning to hear the voices calling from the other shore . . .*

Key Terms

- activity theory
- advance directives
- ageism
- anhedonia
- continuity theory
- crystallized intelligence
- dementia
- disengagement theory
- durable power of attorney for health care
- elder abuse
- elderspeak
- executive functioning
- fictive kin
- fluid intelligence
- functional age
- grief
- hospice
- integrity
- life course perspective
- life expectancy
- life span
- loneliness
- long-term care
- palliative care
- reminiscence
- retirement
- selective optimization and compensation
- senescence
- socioemotional selectivity
- spirituality
- wisdom

Online Resources

Websites

See web page http://finfo.wadsworth.com/ashford for specific links to the following websites.

The Administration on Aging (AoA)

This federal-government website includes numerous news items, features, and links about issues and services for older adults and their caregivers.

American Association for Retired Persons

The nation's leading advocacy organization for people ages 50 and older, the site features a wealth of features and research. Health, security, housing, consumer issues, technology, work, and economic topics are covered.

The Alzheimer's Association

A comprehensive information resource with the latest news and research about Alzheimer's disease and dementia caregiving, with links to local Alzheimer's Association chapters.

The American Society on Aging

This organization serves health and mental-health practitioners who work with older adults.

Eldercare Web

Online sourcebook with more than 4,000 reviewed links to information about health financing, housing, aging, and other issues related to the care of the frail elderly.

InfoTrac College Edition Keywords

For interesting materials related to what you have just read, please go to the InfoTrac College Edition website and search using the following keywords:

- elder abuse
- depression elderly
- widowhood
- ageism
- long-term care

Book-Specific Resources

Book-specific resources can be found at http://info.wadsworth.com/ashford and include the following:

- Case studies
- Quizzes to test your knowledge
- PowerPoint presentations

GLOSSARY

Abstraction The ability to recognize the meaning of symbols.

Accommodation The cognitive process of modifying existing cognitive schema to allow for the admission of new information.

Acquaintance rape Rape by someone the victim knows.

Activity theory A theory of aging that holds that older people who remain active and involved experience greater life satisfaction.

Adaptation The ability to respond to the demands of the environment. Includes the processes of assimilation and accommodation.

Adolescent-limited delinquency Delinquency or a crime pathway that stops after an individual grows out of adolescence.

Advance directives Instructions for doctors and other medical providers that describe the kind of care a person would like to have if unable to make medical decisions due to physical incapacitation.

Affect A person's instant emotional state.

Ageism Prejudice against and stereotypes applied to people on the basis of their age.

Agency A technical term; includes the idea that goal-oriented people act in intentional ways.

Aggression Acts intended to hurt another.

AGIL scheme Describes the basic functions of the social system as defined by Talcott Parsons.

Alcoholism The consumption of alcoholic beverages to the extent that major aspects of a person's life, such as work, family, and friends, are affected.

Allele One of a pair of genes for a specific trait.

Allostasis The process of maintaining stability through change.

Allostatic load The cumulative cost to the body of allostasis; allostatic overload is a state in which serious pathophysiology can occur.

Alpha-fetoprotein blood screening Blood test used to detect neural-tube defects.

Altruism Helpful behaviors that arise out of concern for the welfare of others, without regard for personal gain.

Amino acids A group of nitrogen-containing organic compounds that serve as the units of structure associated with proteins.

Amniocentesis A prenatal screening procedure in which a needle is inserted through the mother's abdomen into the uterus to collect a sample of amniotic fluid for chromosome testing.

Androcentricity A perspective in which men are considered the norm.

Androgen The hormone secreted from the testes.

Androgyny The combination of masculine and feminine behaviors in the same person.

Angina pectoris A coronary condition involving pain and tightness in the chest.

Anhedonia A mood characterized by a pervasive inability to perceive and experience pleasure in action and events that are normally satisfying or pleasurable.

Anoxia Insufficient oxygen to the fetus during delivery.

Apgar score A newborn assessment scale developed by Virginia Apgar that looks at the newborn's adaptation to life in the first minutes after birth. Scores are recorded at 1 minute and 5 minutes after delivery.

Assimilation The cognitive process of consolidation of new information into existing knowledge.

Assisted suicide Helping to provide the means for an individual with a terminal illness to end his or her life.

Associationism One of the oldest constructs in psychology. It involves the formation of mental associations that are registered or stored in the mind.

Asthma A respiratory illness that makes breathing difficult because of narrowing of the bronchial tubes.

Attachment The process by which an infant forms a strong emotional tie to a caregiver.

Attention The ability to focus on a specific stimulus without distraction by irrelevant stimuli.

Attention-deficit/hyperactivity disorder (ADHD) A psychiatric disorder in which a person shows signs of developmentally inappropriate inattention, impulsivity, and hyperactivity.

Attitude A learned evaluative response.

Authoritarian parenting A parenting style based on low levels of warmth and a demanding, restrictive, and punitive approach.

Authoritative parenting A parenting style that encourages warmth and affection; encourages independence but with limits and controls on the child.

Autism Pervasive developmental disorder in which children suffer psychological, cognitive, and social deficits that impair functioning in almost all areas of life.

Autosomes Chromosomes other than sex chromosomes.

Aversive racism The denial of personal prejudice but overlooking the presence of underlying unconscious negative feelings and beliefs.

Avoidant disorder Fear of strangers and strange or new situations.

Axons Long fibers that carry impulses from the cell body of a neuron to other cells.

Babbling Early communication in which a baby puts vowel and consonant sounds together and repeats them over and over.

Basal metabolism rate The minimum amount of energy that we use in our resting state.

Behavioral genetics A field of psychology that asserts that all human behavioral traits are heritable.

Behavioral intention Our subjective estimate of how likely we are to engage in a specific behavior.

Beliefs In social psychology, information about objects.

Bilingualism Ability to speak two languages.

Biography In the life-course perspective, changes in roles as they are taken up and discarded in the passage from one age group to the next over the course of an individual's lifetime.

Biophysical dimension The biochemical, cell, organ, and physiological systems that represent the material substance of a person.

Blended family A newly formed unit consisting of a husband and wife, one or both of whom have children from a previous marriage.

Brazelton Neonatal Assessment Scale (BNAS) Newborn assessment used to measure the baby's muscle tone and reflexes and how the baby responds to and controls stimulation.

Bronchopulmonary dysplasia A chronic lung disease of infancy characterized by inflammation and scarring in the lungs; involves abnormal development of lung tissue.

Bureaucracy An organization that is ruled by officials.

Canalization The process by which people inherit general pathways that constrain their growth and developmental processes.

Care perspective Reasoning about moral dilemmas, with a focus on the connectedness to others; concern for others is paramount.

Caregiving career The substantial caregiving functions women have, including caring for children, elderly parents, and a dependent husband.

Categorization The ability to place objects into groups on the basis of their similarities.

Central nervous system The brain and spinal cord.

Cephalocaudal Development that progresses from the head to the feet.

Cerebral palsy Brain damage resulting from lack of oxygen during birth or from bleeding in the brain. Can cause paralysis, muscle weakness, and incoordination. Also may result in mental retardation and speech difficulties.

Cesarean section Delivery of a baby through an incision in the mother's abdomen.

Child abuse Child maltreatment that includes physical abuse, sexual abuse, physical neglect, educational neglect, and psychological abuse.

Chorionic villus sample (CVS) A prenatal screening procedure in which a catheter is inserted into the uterus through the vagina to obtain a piece of the developing placenta.

Chromosome disorders Abnormalities or defects caused by errors in an entire chromosome or part of a chromosome.

Circular influences Process by which family interactions affect interactions with the infant and affect the infant's interactions with the caregivers, which then affect family interactions.

Classical conditioning The strengthening of an association between a stimulus and a response through the presentation of a second stimulus.

Cliques Small interaction-based groups with close relationships.

Codependency A pattern of behavior in which a person's sense of self-worth is based on external referents.

Cognition Obtaining, organizing, and utilizing sensory and perceptual information from activities such as plans and strategies.

Cohesive group A group in which individual members have strong bonds with one another and to the group itself.

Cohort A group of people of about the same age, born around the same time.

Cohort (period) effects The changes in behavior influenced by being a member of a cohort or being born in a particular period of time.

Colic Uncontrollable, extended crying in a baby who is otherwise healthy and well fed.

Communication patterns How members of a group communicate verbally and nonverbally.

Communitarian agenda Commitment to correcting the current imbalance between rights and responsibilities at the societal or community level.

Concentration A person's ability to sustain inner mental operations without disruption.

Concrete thinking The ability to perform operations such as logical reasoning, which replaces intuitive thought as long as it is applied to concrete examples.

Conduct disorder DSM-IV term that refers to a cluster of behaviors that reflect oppositional, noncompliant, and delinquent actions, such as stealing, robbery, and assault.

Connectedness A person's sensitivity to and respect for others' views.

Conscience In Freudian theory, a component of the superego that causes guilt when its standards are not met; involves internalized mental representations of conduct that are subject to punishment.

Consciousness Awareness of internal and external stimuli.

Conservation The recognition that properties of a substance do not change when its appearance is altered in some manner.

Continuity Associations made because two events occur together in time or space.

Controlled reaction A phase of rape trauma syndrome in which the rape victim assumes a more composed and calm perspective following the trauma.

Coping Active efforts to master, reduce, or tolerate the demands created by stress.

Creolization The process of maintaining original identities but incorporating customs and practices from other groups or cultures into the original identities.

Cretinism A chronic disease due to absence of, or deficiency in, normal thyroid secretion. Cretinism is characterized by physical deformity and dwarfism.

Crisis A decisive point produced by stress or other types of biopsychosocial demands of life that lead to positive or negative outcomes. For Erikson, a crisis was considered a challenge or turning point at which there are opportunities for individuals to choose between polarities associated with key developmental tasks.

Crisis theory A theory for intervention in the crises of people who are having difficulties coping with various stressors and other demands of life.

Cross-modal transfer The ability to transfer information gained from one sense to another sense. An example would be picking out a picture of something you had only felt with your hands.

Crossover A division process that involves an exchange of chromosome parts.

Crowds Reputation-based groups of similar young people who do not necessarily spend a lot of time together; larger than cliques.

Crystallized intelligence Accumulated information and verbal skills.

Cultural competency The values, principles, beliefs, and behaviors that allow professionals to practice effectively cross-culturally.

Culture A system of meanings and values shared by a population and transmitted to future generations.

Cumulative continuity An important issue in the life-course tradition that focuses on the way in which behavior at one point in life has consequences that increase the likelihood of continued behavior. For instance, being labeled a troublemaker early in life may prevent a youth from associating with good kids and increase the likelihood of continued delinquency.

Current perspective In the multidimensional integrative approach, assessing how biological, psychological, and social systems influence current states of affairs.

Cynical hostility Tendency toward being resentful, moody, and generally distrusting. Related to an increased tendency toward coronary disease, hypertension, and early mortality.

Cystic fibrosis A serious disease of the exocrine gland that causes secretion of excess, thick body fluids.

Das-Luria model of cognitive functioning A view of cognitive functioning based on two modes of processing information: simultaneous meanings and successive processing.

Date rape Rape by someone the victim is dating.

Deillusionment The process of giving up illusions from earlier periods of life.

Delirium tremens (DTs) A withdrawal syndrome from alcoholism that includes agitation, tremor, hallucination, and sometimes seizures.

Dementia Impairment or loss of cognitive abilities, including memory impairment.

Dendrites The branched fibers on the cell body that bring messages to the cell body of the neuron.

Development The refinement or improvement of body components.

Developmental perspective In the multidimensional approach, assessment of how the dimensions interact in leading up to the current state of affairs or developmental outcome.

Developmental waves The idea that children learn in overlapping waves instead of in steps.

Diastolic pressure The measure of the blood's flow during the relaxation of the heart.

Differentiation theory The view that all information needed to interpret sensory input is contained in the sensations themselves.

Difficult child A baby characterized by unpredictable daily habits, negative, intense mood, and slow adaptability.
Discrimination Prejudice or bias applied to a person on the basis of some particular characteristic.
Disengagement theory A theory of aging that holds that people and society withdraw from each other in old age—people because of their diminished capacity and society to make room for younger people.
Dishabituation The process by which an individual attends to a new stimulus after habituating to a previous stimulus.
Disorganization phase A phase of rape trauma syndrome that reflects the woman's immediate expressed or controlled reactions, physical reactions, and emotional reactions to the trauma.
Disoriented states The experience of significant deviations in an individual's levels of awareness of time, place, and person.
Displaced homemakers Women who are forced into the job market because of divorce or widowhood.
Dominant gene A gene that is always expressed for a trait, in paired genes.
Down syndrome A disorder, characterized by mental retardation, that is associated with the presence of three chromosomes, rather than a pair, for chromosome 21.
Durable power of attorney A document that allows a person appointed by you to act as your agent to continue to act on your behalf even after you have become incapacitated.
Easy child A baby characterized by regular, positive responses to new stimuli, high adaptability to change, and mild or moderately intense mood, which is usually positive.
Ebonics A form of dialect referred to as Black English or Black English Vernacular.
Echolalia Repetition of words, songs, and phrases heard in other people's communications.
Ecomap A tool used in social work to highlight the points of connection between systems influencing a person's life.
Ego According to Freud, the executive branch of one's personality that makes rational decisions.
Ego-ideal In Freudian theory, the mental representation of conduct that is positively valued by the environment.
Ego psychology (self theory) Unlike dynamic psychology, ego psychology focuses on the contributions of the ego or self in determining all aspects of human behavior.
Egocentrism Inability to distinguish between one's own perspective and another's.
Elder abuse Maltreatment of older people, which can include physical abuse, psychological abuse, material abuse, active neglect, and passive abuse.
Elderspeak Using baby talk in communicating with seniors.
Emerging adulthood A distinct stage of development that is neither adolescence nor young adulthood.
Emotion-focused coping This form of coping focuses on psychological and emotional responses to stress.
Emotional intelligence (EQ) The area of psychology that deals with measuring people's ability to identify their own and others' feelings and to solve problems involving emotional issues.
Empathy The ability to understand the feelings and attitudes of others.
Encopresis Lack of bowel control after age 4.
Endocarditis An infection or other factor that damages the heart's valves.
Endocrine glands Glands, namely the pituitary gland and male and female gonads, that secrete into the bloodstream chemicals that help control bodily functioning.
Endorphins Substances in the brain that are related to feeling good.
Enrichment theory The view that the information we receive through our senses is formless and we must augment this information to make sense of it.
Enuresis Lack of bladder control after the age of 5, which results in bedwetting or daytime accidents.

Environmental harassment A hostile work environment that results from unwanted sexual behavior by the person in power.
Environmental paths The various paths followed by people in their social environment—such as work, intimacy, and education.
Epigenetic principle The biological blueprint that dictates how an organism grows and reaches maturity.
Estrogen The hormone secreted from the ovaries.
Estrogen replacement therapy (ERT) A synthetic estrogen that is given to women to replace that lost through menopause.
Etiology The branch of science that deals with understanding causes of behavior.
Euthanasia The act of assisting the death of those with painfully debilitating or terminal illness.
Executive functioning The brain's capacity to absorb and interpret information and make decisions based on it.
Exosystems The larger institutions of society that influence our personal systems.
Explicit memory A memory of an event that occurred in the distant or immediate past.
Expressive communication The expression of emotions and possession of a perspective that is sensitive to how others feel.
Expressive language disorder Includes limited speech and vocabulary, shortened sentences, difficulty learning new words, misuse of words, limited or simple grammar, and slowed language acquisition.
Externalizing problems Problems of undercontrol, such as aggressive behavior, fighting, and overactivity.
Extinction The systematic withholding of the reinforcers that had previously maintained a behavior.
Failure to thrive Condition in which a child's weight falls below the 5th percentile for the child's age.
Family A composition of people who decide to live together.
Family structure The manner in which each family organizes itself into interactional patterns.
Fetal alcohol syndrome (FAS) A set of birth defects that occur when a pregnant woman consumes alcohol. It is the leading known cause of mental retardation. Physical signs include small head, small eyes, thin upper lip, short nose, flattened midfacial area, and poorly developed philtrum (the part of the face between the nose and upper lip).
Fictive kin Individuals who are unrelated by either birth or marriage, who have an emotionally significant relationship with another individual that would take on the characteristics of a family relationship.
Fixed income Income that does not increase from year to year though inflation and other factors may raise the cost of living.
Floating family A family with a formless array of familial relationships that are in a continuous state of flux.
Fluid intelligence Abstract reasoning ability.
Folkways Group ways of solving problems and of doing things.
Formal operational thought Thought processes characterized by adolescents' abilities to think about their own thought and to recognize both possibility and actuality.
Formal organization Any large social group that is designed to rationally achieve a specific objective.
Formed groups Groups created by an outside influence or intervention and convened for a particular purpose.
Fragile X syndrome A serious form of mental retardation that is identified in karyotype studies by a constriction at the end of the long arm of the X chromosome.
Frontal lobe The portion of the brain that participates in body movements, thinking, feeling, imagining, and making decisions.
Functional literacy The ability to perform everyday reading, writing, and arithmetic tasks.
Funnel theory Any theory supporting the hypothesis, from early developmental theory, that change tends to contract over time.
Gang "A collectivity consisting primarily of adolescents and young adults who (a) interact frequently with one another; (b) are frequently and deliberately involved in illegal activities; (c) share a common identity that is usually, but not always, expressed through a gang name; and

(d) typically express that identity by adopting certain symbols and/or claiming control over certain 'turf'—persons, places, things, and/or economic markets" (Huff, 1993, p. 4).

Gender   The social definitions of male and female.

Gender identity   Gender identity is the developmental process by which culturally assigned values and behaviors are considered appropriate for members of that sex.

Gender polarization   The organizing of social life around male and female distinctions.

General adaptation syndrome (GAS)   A series of bodily reactions to prolonged stress that occur in three stages: alarm, resistance, and exhaustion.

Genotype   The actual genes an individual carries for a specific trait.

Gestation   Length of time in the womb or fetal age. Full term is 38–41 weeks, premature is before 38 weeks, postmature is longer than 41 weeks.

Gestational diabetes   High blood sugar (glucose) levels during pregnancy, in a woman who has never had diabetes before.

Glia   The supporting cells that make up the bulk of the brain.

Goal-directed behavior   A series of actions put together to achieve a desired result.

Gonadotropins   Hormones secreted by the pituitary gland that activate the testes and ovaries.

Goodness of fit   How well the demands of the environment match the child's behavioral style.

Grammar   A set of rules for combining language units into meaningful speech or writing.

Gray matter   Areas of the nervous system with a high density of cell bodies and dendrites with few myelinated axons.

Grief   The normal, emotional reaction to loss.

Group socialization theory   A theory that believes that peer and community influences have the most impact on a child's identity.

Groupthink   An emphasis in a cohesive group on consensus at the expense of critical thinking.

Growth   A technical term that refers to the addition of new biophysical components, such as new cells or an increase in body size.

Habitat   The place where groups of people are normally found.

Habituation   The process by which an individual stops responding to a stimulus.

Hemophilia   A condition that is due to a defective gene on the X chromosome that causes a deficiency in the blood coagulation factor VIII.

Heterosexuality   The assumption that women and men are innately attracted to each other emotionally and sexually and that heterosexuality is normal and universal.

Heterozygous genes   Two genes in a specific pair that are different for a specific trait.

Hierarchy   Dimension of social space that includes all the elements in a society's system of social stratification.

Holism   The philosophy that focuses on principles of interdependence and on relationships, rather than on reducing elements to their constituent parts.

Holophrastic speech   The use of one word to express the meaning of a whole sentence.

Homophobia   An irrationally negative attitude toward gay people.

Homozygous genes   Two genes in a specific pair that are the same for a specific trait.

Hormones   Chemical substances in the body that regulate various body organs.

Hospice   An alternative to hospital care for terminally ill patients. Hospice focuses on comfort and relief of symptoms instead of cure.

Hostile aggression   Behaviors derived from the desire to hurt another.

Hot flash   A sudden feeling of heat experienced by some women during menopause.

Human capital   The form of capital based on an individual's personal assets that lead to increased forms of value.

Human immunodeficiency virus (HIV)   A virus that destroys the human immune system and leads to the set of opportunistic infections commonly referred to as acquired immune deficiency syndrome, or AIDS.

Human plasticity   The changeability of human structures and outcomes.

Human relations school   A school of organizational theory that focuses on understanding the influences of informal networks on all forms of organizational activities.

Huntington's chorea   A disorder involving a dominant autosomal gene and characterized by progressive chorea (purposeless motions) and the eventual development of dementia (mental deterioration).

Hyperemesis gravidarum   Persistent and unrelenting vomiting during pregnancy.

Hyperplasia   The type of growth that involves an increase in the number of cells.

Hypertrophic growth   The type of growth in which increases are observed in the size of cells.

Hypervigilance   An excessive focus on outward factors in the environment.

Hypothalamus   The part of the brain that controls the level of hormone secretion from the pituitary gland.

Hypothetical-deductive reasoning   The problem-solving process that tests and evaluates hypotheses to find the best solution.

Id   According to Freud, the instinctive component of personality that operates from the basis of the pleasure principle.

Ideal type   An abstract description derived from real cases that were analyzed to determine their essential features.

Illiterate   Unable to read and write well enough to participate in society.

Illness   A person's subjective perception of being unwell.

Imaginary audience   The belief that others are as preoccupied with an adolescent's behavior as he or she is.

Immediate memory   Information retained for up to 10 seconds.

Implicit memory   A memory that a person does not know exists and that is retrieved unconsciously.

Individualized Education Plan (IEP)   A cornerstone of the Individuals with Disabilities Education Act (IDEA); ensures that educational opportunities for students with disabilities are individualized.

Individuation   A process by which a person develops a stronger sense of autonomy.

Induction   Use of explanation and/or rationalizing in an attempt to influence a child's actions.

Infant mental health   An applied field concerned with the social and emotional well-being of infants within their families.

Infantile amnesia   Children's lack of memory for specific events before the age of 3.

Infertility   Inability to achieve pregnancy after one year of sexual intercourse with no contraception.

Information processing   The theory that examines the uptake, selection, coding, and storage of information.

Inhibiting and promoting environments   Contexts assessed in terms of the adequacy of resources for the development of appropriate competencies. Inhibiting environments are contexts with inadequate resources that create conditions that undermine development; promoting environments have adequate resources to promote appropriate developmental competencies.

Instrumental communication   Communication focused on identifying goals and finding solutions.

Intelligence quotient   Mental age divided by chronological age, multiplied by 100.

Intentional means-end behavior   The process by which a child takes several random activities and puts them together to achieve a goal.

Intention-cue detection   Ability to correctly perceive another person's intention; for example, differentiating prosocial, accidental, or hostile acts.

Internalizing problems   Problems of overcontrol, such as anxiety, loneliness, shyness, and/or social withdrawal.

Interrupted career   A regular career interrupted by child-rearing and then reestablished when full-time work is resumed.

Intrauterine growth retardation (IUGR)   Growth slowdown in the prenatal period. Occurs when the fetal weight falls below the 10th percentile for gestational age.

Invisible displacement   In testing for object permanence, moving a toy from one hiding place to another without letting the baby view the process of moving the toy.

Justice perspective Reasoning about moral dilemmas with a focus on the rights of the individual to independently make moral decisions.

Klinefelter's syndrome A condition in which a male is born with an extra X chromosome (XXY).

Lability The rapid shift from one emotion to another within a very brief period of time.

Laissez-faire parenting A parenting style representing two types: permissive indifferent parenting and permissive indulgent parenting. Permissive indifferent parents are uninvolved in their child's life; they are neglectful and unresponsive. Permissive indulgent parents are warm, accepting, and responsive but are undemanding.

Learned helplessness Learning to attribute failures to luck or the difficulty of the task.

Lesch-Nyhan syndrome A disorder that involves a gene on the X chromosome and is characterized by mental retardation, spasticity, and selfmutilation.

Libido According to Freud, the energy that drives all human behavior.

Life course A concept and a perspective for looking at developmental issues that takes into account macro contributions to developmental outcomes.

Life-course-persistent delinquency Delinquency that continues after adolescence into adulthood.

Life expectancy The number of years the average person born in a particular year may expect to live.

Life span The upper limit of years humans can live.

Living will A document that allows a terminally ill person to state that he or she does not want to be kept alive by artificial means.

Logical (natural) consequences A disciplinary strategy, used with young children, that connects logically to the behavior that is being disciplined. For example, if the child is late to the dinner table because of watching TV, the logical consequence is removal of TV privileges.

Loneliness A state of feeling as though one has fewer interpersonal relationships than desired or not obtaining the desired level of personal satisfaction from interpersonal relationships.

Long-term memory Retention of information for days to months.

Love withdrawal The response of withdrawing love when a child's behavior is viewed as inappropriate.

Macrosystems The larger subcultural and cultural contexts in which the microsystem, mesosystem, and exosystem are located.

Malignant tumors Tumors that are not self-contained.

Malpresentation Birth presentation other than head down (i.e., feet first, butt first, shoulder first).

Meconium aspiration Inhalation of fetal waste in the amniotic fluid during delivery. May result in later respiratory problems.

Meiosis The process of cell division that creates the sex cells.

Menarche The first menstruation in pubertal females.

Menopause The cessation of menstrual cycles for a continuous period of time; a woman's ovaries stop functioning and no longer produce the hormones estrogen and progesterone.

Menstrual cycle The series of changes in a nonpregnant female involving the preparation of the endometrium to receive a fertilized ovum; if no fertilization occurs, a portion of the endometrium is shed.

Mental age An intelligence test score that indicates the chronological age at which a child functions cognitively.

Mesosystems The network of personal settings in which we live our lives.

Metacognition Knowledge about knowing. A person's awareness of self as a knower able to use and evaluate strategies.

Metalinguistic awareness The ability to think about language and its properties.

Microsystems Any systems that involve face-to-face or direct contact among the system participants.

Mitosis The cellular process in which a body cell reproduces itself by dividing and producing two new daughter cells.

Mitral valve prolapse A valvular disease of the heart involving the protrusion of one or both cusps of the mitral valve back into the left atrium.

Moderating factors Factors that, when present, weaken the influence of stress.

Monoamines A group of nonacidic neurotransmitters, such as dopamine, norepinephrine, epinephrine, and serotonin.

Mood A prevailing and enduring emotional state.

Moral development The rules of conduct people use in their interactions with others.

Mores Folkways that are considered the right or wrong way of doing things.

Morpheme The smallest unit of meaning in any language system.

Multifactorial disorders Developmental disorders caused by multiple genes.

Multiplex relationship A relationship in which a person has more than one type of exchange with another person.

Munchausen's syndrome by proxy Child abuse in which the caregiver induces symptoms of illness in the child.

Mutation Random events that distort key characteristics in an organism's growth and development.

Myelination The process of coating the nerve cells with myelin, a substance that forms around neurons and acts as insulation, allowing faster and more efficient transmission of nerve impulses.

Myocardial infarction The condition in which insufficient oxygen is directed to the heart's muscle.

Myocarditis An infection or other factor that damages the heart's muscle.

Myth of arrival The myth that someday, after hard work and survived crises, life will be what we always wanted.

Natural (logical) consequences. *See* **logical (natural) consequences**

Natural groups Groups created by naturally occurring events, interpersonal attraction, or the mutual needs of the individuals involved.

Natural helpers Relatives, friends, and neighbors to whom one turns in time of trouble or need.

Negative reinforcement The following of a response with an end to discomfort or with the removal of a negative state of affairs.

Neighboring An individual's emotional, cognitive and social attachment to a neighborhood that makes him or her more likely to participate in neighborhood activities.

Neural-tube defects Birth defects of the brain or spinal cord that include the following: spina bifida, in which one or more vertebrae do not close over the spinal cord—if the cord bulges through the opening the baby has a meningocele; hydrocephalus—excess fluid in the head, resulting in a large head; microcephaly—a much smaller than normal head; anencephaly—absence of all or part of the brain.

Neurons The cells in the nervous system involved in conveying information from one cell to another.

Neurotransmitters Chemicals that are synthesized inside the neuron.

Night terrors A sudden awakening from sleep with intense feelings of panic.

Non-normative events Events or experiences unique to the individual; not the norm, or not predictable.

Normative age-graded influences Predictable experiences that happen universally and are closely tied to age.

Normative history-graded influences Experiences shared by people because they are alive during a particular period.

Norms Expectations and beliefs about appropriate behavior in a group.

Obesity Condition in which body weight is 20% or more above the recommended weight for one's height.

Object permanence The ability to hold an image of an object or person in one's mind.

Obligatory attention Babies' attention to something they find interesting, without being distracted from it.

Occipital lobe Part of brain located below the parietal lobe and involved in the receiving and sending of visual information.

Open adoption Adoption in which the birth mother and sometimes birth father participate in choosing the adoptive family, and often remain in contact with the child after adoption.

Operant conditioning The acquisition of new responses because of their effects on the environment.

Oral rehydration therapy A treatment that prevents dehydration when a child experiences diarrhea.

Organization According to Piaget, a tendency held by all species to systematize their processes into coherent systems.

Osteoporosis The thinning or weakening of bones.

Ovaries Part of the female reproductive system. The ovaries produce the ovum, or egg, and the female hormones estrogen and progesterone.

Overanxious disorder Fears that have no specific focus. Children with this disorder worry that something will go wrong in almost any situation.

Overextension Use of one word to include a larger category. An example is referring to all furry creatures as a dog.

Palliative care Care directed primarily at providing relief to a terminally ill person through symptom management and pain management; also called "comfort care."

Parasympathetic nervous system The branch of the nervous system that counteracts the activities of the sympathetic nervous system and conserves body resources.

Parietal lobe The portion of the brain that is primarily involved in the process of integrating sensory information.

Pattern variables The alternative courses of action in Parson's theory of an action system.

PDP models (Parallel-processing or connectionist models of information processes) Models that assume information processing takes place through interactions of large numbers of simple processing elements called units, each sending excitatory and inhibitory signals to other units.

Peer groups Groups of age mates that are durable and composed of interactions based on an established set of social relationships.

Peptides Chains of amino acids.

Perception The interpretation of information detected by the senses.

Perceptual set Objects perceived as having only their most common or recent functional significance.

Pericardium The thin sac that encloses the heart.

Peripheral nervous system All those nerves that lie outside the brain and spinal cord.

Person-in-environment (PIE) system A system for assessing problems in social functioning, developed by Karls and Wandrei.

Personal fable The adolescent's belief that he or she is indestructible and unique—so much so that no one can understand what it is like to be him or her.

Phenotype The trait expressed by genes in the individual.

Phobias Irrational fears.

Phonemes The most basic identifiable sounds in a language system.

Phonological disorder Difficulty articulating speech sounds.

Phonology The component in language studies that examines the system of sound in languages.

Polyhydramnios Excess amniotic fluid, the presence of which may indicate a problem with the fetus, such as anencephaly.

Posttraumatic stress disorder A psychological disorder that involves an individual feeling as though he or she is reexperiencing or reliving a trauma after it occurred.

Power In a group, a person's ability to obtain control through reward, coercion, expertise, personal characteristics, and legitimacy.

Power-assertive discipline A punitive style of discipline that includes physical punishment, threat of punishment, and/or attempts to control the child's behavior.

Pragmatics The study of the rules that specify how language is used across social contexts.

Prejudice A generalized negative attitude that is directed toward another person's membership in a socially defined group.

Prematurity Birth before the thirty-seventh week of gestation.

Premenstrual Dysphoric Disorder A severe form of PMS that includes sadness and crying, anxiousness, food craving, concentration problems, physical problems, and trouble sleeping.

Premenstrual syndrome (PMS) A set of symptoms some women experience about ten days prior to their menstrual period. The symptoms may include breast tenderness, a bloated feeling, irritability, and negative moods.

Preoperational thought A concept that describes what preschoolers cannot do—they are not capable of operations or mental actions that obey logical rules.

Primary Prevention Seeks to stop a problem or situation from occurring in the first place.

Primary-process thinking Thought based on irrational, illogical, and fantasy-oriented notions.

Proactive aggression Aggressive behavior that is used to achieve specific goals.

Problem-focused coping Strategies that seek to deal directly with the source of stress.

Problems of living Involve the normal difficulties of everyday life, such as losing a job, undergoing a divorce, or fearing rejection.

Problem solving The ability to sort out relevant from irrelevant information and to adopt a strategy or plan for completing the task.

Professional half-life The time it takes for 50% of one's professional knowledge to become invalid or obsolete.

Professional obsolescence The use of information, theories, and technology that are less useful in performing tasks than what is currently available in one's field of practice.

Proliferation The stage in brain development when neurons are produced.

Prolonged labor Labor lasting longer than twenty-four hours for a first-time mother or more than twelve hours for a woman who has previously given birth.

Proteins Any organic compound that has a large combination of amino acids.

Proximodistal Development that progresses from the spine outward to the extremities.

Psychological dimension The systems that contribute to the organization and direction of an individual's mental processes.

Psychological moratorium A gap between childhood security and adult autonomy.

Puberty A period in development that is characterized by maturation of physiological mechanisms, including reproductive capacity and the development of secondary sex characteristics.

Punishment Occurs when a response is followed with pain or an otherwise negative event, or when a response is followed with the removal of a positive reinforcer (response cost).

Purines The category of chemicals that includes adenosine.

Quid pro quo harassment Harassment involving a person in position of power subjecting a person of lower status to unwanted sexual advances.

Quiet sleep The first stages of sleep, characterized by non-rapid eye movement.

Race A large number of people who, for social or geographical reason, have interbred over a long period of time and developed visible physical characteristics and regard themselves and are regarded by others as a biological unit.

Racism Any attitude, action, or institutional structure that subordinates a person because of his or her race.

Rape trauma syndrome A cluster of symptoms experienced by rape victims.

Rapport talk A style of communication that involves discussing similarities and matching experiences.

Reactive aggression An aggressive reaction that is based on anger and includes retaliation.

Readiness Point at which a child's developmental maturity allows him or her to quickly learn a needed skill or ability.

Recent memory The retention of information learned within the last twenty-four hours.

Recessive gene The gene that is not expressed in a trait unless paired with a similar or homozygous gene.

Reciprocal interaction An interaction in which both parties can influence each other. For example, an infant can influence its mother and the mother can influence the infant.

Reductionism Assumes that the whole is the sum of its parts; attempts to understand problems by focusing on smaller and smaller units.

Refractory period The time between one orgasm and the physical capability to achieve another.

Reinforcement Any event that brings about learning or increases the probability that a particular response will occur.

Reminiscence The process of remembering the past and reviewing one's life that may arise when one realizes the inevitability of death.

Remote memory Retention of information occurring several weeks or months in the past.

Reorganization phase The adaptation and adjustment phase a rape victim experiences after a rape.

Repetition A factor in association that assumes that ideas are likely to be associated when they occur together often.

Report talk A style of communication that involves discussing knowledge and displaying skill.

Resiliency The ability to recover from or adjust to problems, adversities, and stress in life.

Reversibility The ability to reverse an action by mentally performing the opposite action.

Rh incompatibility Condition in which the mother has Rh-negative blood and the fetus has Rh-positive blood. The mother makes antibodies that attack the fetal blood cells, resulting in anemia in the fetus and possible fetal death or brain damage.

Rickets A deficiency in either diet or sunshine that can induce permanent damage to the body, such as a flat chest, deformed pelvis, or crooked back.

Rite of passage A ritualized recognition of a person's transition from one life stage to another, such as childhood to adolescence.

Role A pattern of expected behavior that a person acts out in a group.

Role-taking ability The mutual ability to see things from another person's perspective. It involves the reduction of egocentric thought.

Schema An internal cognitive structure that facilitates adaptation.

Schizophrenia A psychological disorder marked by disturbances in thought that spill over to affect perceptual, social, and emotional processes.

School phobia (school refusal) Extreme reluctance to go to school, accompanied by various symptoms of anxiety, such as stomachaches and headaches. May be a fear of school or an expression of separation anxiety.

Secondary prevention Aims to intervene as early as possible in a problem situation, before it becomes severe or persistent.

Secondary-process thinking Thought based on realistic and rational approaches to problem solving.

Secular trend The trend toward earlier maturation compared with previous generations.

Selective optimization and compensation Assumption that successful cognitive aging involves maximizing cognitive strengths while developing compensatory skills to shore up weaknesses.

Self-efficacy Belief in one's own capacity to produce a desired result.

Self-esteem Seeing oneself as a worthwhile person; evaluating oneself positively.

Self-help groups Groups of people who share a particular problem and provide mutual support to one another.

Self-selection An assumption in delinquency theory that individuals tend to select experiences that are consistent with internal traits or dispositions established early in life.

Semantics The area in language studies that deals with meaning.

Senescence In biology, the state or process of aging.

Sensation The process in which receptors detect information that is transmitted to the brain.

Sensitive period The period immediately following birth in which the mother and infant bond. Researchers now believe this postbirth bonding is not as important as once thought.

Separation anxiety Distress displayed by an infant in the absence of the primary caregiver. Usually begins around 8–10 months.

Separation-anxiety disorder Severe anxiety about leaving home or separating from the primary caregivers.

Separation-individuation Developmental process proposed by Margaret Mahler in which the infant grows from having no sense of self as separate from the caregiver to being an autonomous, independent individual.

Sex The biological status of being female or male.

Sex-role stereotypes Categories based on our impressions of what we consider "male" or "female."

Sexual response cycle The three stages that culminate in sexual satisfaction: desire, excitement, and orgasm.

Shaken infant syndrome Infant abuse in which an adult shakes the infant, causing brain damage.

Short-term memory Memory of an event that can be maintained for about 20 to 30 seconds.

Signs Have a valid relationship with the thing for which they stand.

Similarity A factor in associationism that refers to associations being formed because events or ideas that occur close together have features that are similar.

Single-gene disorders Inherited dysfunctions or defects that result from dominant, recessive, or X chromosome–linked genes.

Single representations How preschoolers classify themselves and others: according to age first, gender second, and then by what they can actively do, such as play baseball or climb a tree, and sometimes by what they physically possess.

Slow-to-warm-up child A child who exhibits a sedate, less exuberant orientation to life. These babies are slow to adapt to new situations and many times have negative responses.

Social capital Social connections that form a network of norms, obligations, expectations and trust that occur among people.

Social cognition The level of awareness one has regarding other peoples' thoughts, feelings, and intentions.

Social cognitive monitoring A person's ability to monitor and make sense of his or her social thoughts; a conscious self-awareness.

Social dimension The systems of social relationships that the person interacts with individually or in a group.

Social environment All the expectations, motives, and incentives that place limits on behavior and that are constructed by other people who live in a person's social world.

Social functioning All the factors influencing the performance of roles that enable individuals to achieve a reasonable degree of fulfillment and to function as productive and contributing members of society.

Social-learning theory The view that people can learn by observing events that they do not directly experience or perform.

Social marginality The absence of ties to major social institutions.

Social referencing The process by which an infant looks to others for emotional information about how to respond in an unfamiliar situation or to an unfamiliar person or object.

Social role Role based on a set of rules indicating the expectations or duties to be performed by a member occupying a given position in a social group.

Social skills training A treatment program that assumes problem behaviors can be understood in terms of not having the skills needed to cope with situational demands.

Social support systems Continuing social aggregates that provide individuals with opportunities for feedback about themselves and for validations of their expectations about others, which may offset deficiencies in these communications in larger community contexts.

Socioeconomic status The combination of one's economic status or level of income, social status or level of education, and work status as measured by one's occupation.

Status The ranking of each member's position in a group relative to the other members.

Stepfamily A family whose kinship is determined by remarriage.

Stereotypes Oversimplified or prejudicial beliefs about a target group held by nonmembers of that group.

Stranger anxiety Distress displayed by an infant at the sight of an unfamiliar face. Usually begins around 5–6 months.

Strengths perspective An approach to assessing people by focusing on strengths and capacities rather than identifying only deficits, disabilities, and/or problems.

Stress The condition that occurs when a challenge or a threat in the environment forces a person to adjust or adapt.

Subjective norms Beliefs about what important people or significant others think about an object.

Superego According to Freud, the moral guidance that helps balance the drives associated with the id.

Symbols Words, phrases or written materials that stand for other things or ideas, but do not have a direct relationship with the objects they represent.

Sympathetic nervous system The branch of the nervous system that mobilizes the body for emergencies.

Synaptic cleft The space between any two neurons or between a neuron and another cell.

Syntax The component of language studies that focuses on the rules that govern the way words are combined to form sentences.

System Any set of elements that affect or influence one another.

Systolic pressure A measure of the heart when it is constricting and pumping blood out and through the body.

Task groups Groups that have as their primary purpose to complete the work for which the groups were convened.

Tay-Sachs disease A neurodegenerative disorder that is characterized by progressive mental and physical retardation.

Telegraphic speech The use of only words that are absolutely necessary to convey a message.

Temperament The characteristic pattern by which an infant responds to and interacts with the environment.

Temporal lobe The portion of the brain involved in emotions and human motivation.

Teratogens Substances that cause birth defects and anomalies.

Tertiary prevention Reduction of the complications or negative consequences of a problem situation by preventing handicaps or impairments that are its known consequences.

Testes Part of the male reproductive system. The testes produce sperm and the male hormone testosterone.

Theory of agency. *See* **agency**

Toxemia or eclampsia A serious complication of pregnancy, which can result in maternal death, fetal death, or fetal brain damage. Early stages are referred to as preeclampsia. Symptoms include elevated blood pressure, swelling of hands and face, weight gain, and protein in urine.

Trajectory A specific path or line of development followed by a person to a specific life outcome.

Transient exuberance During infant brain development, the period of rapid growth of dendrites.

Transitional object Something (a blanket, toy, or teddy bear) the infant uses for comfort in the absence of the primary caregiver.

Transitions Short-term state changes that are marked by life events.

Transracial adoption Adoption in which the child is of a different race than the adoptive parents.

Treatment groups Groups that seek to meet members' socioemotional needs.

Trial and error The sequential application of possible solutions to problems.

Tumor Mass of purposeless tissue caused by cell growth.

Turner's syndrome Condition in which a female is born with only one X chromosome (X0).

Turning point A change in direction in the life course; alters the probability of a trajectory toward a specific life destination.

Type A personality Competitive, impatient, and sometimes hostile perfectionists.

Type B personality Relaxed, easygoing, and generally amicable individuals.

Ultrasound A prenatal screening procedure in which high-frequency sound waves are passed through the mother's abdomen to form a picture of the developing fetus.

Uninformative messages Messages that do not clarify the exact meaning being communicated.

Uniplex relationship A relationship in which a person has one type of exchange with a person.

Vaginal bleeding A complication of pregnancy that may be associated with spontaneous abortion or with placental complications.

Values Abstract goals, such as beauty, freedom, or health, that do not have specific objects or reference points.

Verbal control The development of speech through three successive stages: other-external, self-external, and self-internal; the idea that self-verbalizations are related to self-guidance.

Vigilance The capacity of sustaining outward attention over a prolonged period of time.

Wisdom Possession of fundamental pragmatics about life, or good judgment about important but uncertain matters.

REFERENCES

AARP. (2002). *In brief: Servicing the affordable housing needs of older low-income renters: A survey of low-income housing tax credit properties.* Retrieved July 14, 2004, from http://www.aarp.org/research

AARP. (2003a). *In brief: Poverty experience of older persons: A poverty study from a long-term perspective.* Retrieved August 1, 2004, from http://www.aarp.org/research

AARP. (2003b). *Standing ahead of the curve 2003: The AARP working in retirement study.* Washington, DC.

AARP. (2004a). *Portrait of minority elders.* Retrieved July 16, 2004, from http://www.aarp.org/research

AARP. (2004b). *Census 2000 data about grandparents.* Retrieved July 18, 2004, from http://www.aarp.org/slife/grandparents

Abel, E., & Sokol, R. (1987). Incidence of fetal alcohol syndrome and economic impact of FAS-related anomalies. *Drug & Alcohol Dependence, 19,* 51–70.

Abel, R. L. (1982). *The politics of informal justice, vol. 1: The American experience.* New York: Academic Press.

Abramovitch, R., Corter, C., Pepler, D. J., & Stanhope, L. (1986). Sibling and peer interaction: A final follow-up and comparison. *Child Development, 47,* 217–229.

Abuelo, D. N. (1983). Genetic disorders. In J. L. Matson and J. A. Muilick (Eds.), *Handbook of Mental Retardation.* New York: Pergamon Press.

Achenbach, T. M. (1991). *Child behavior checklist.* Burlington: University of Vermont Department of Psychiatry.

Achenbach, T. M., & Edelbrock, C. (1983). *Manual for the child behavior checklist and revised child behavior profile.* Burlington: University of Vermont Department of Psychiatry.

Achenbach, T. M., McConaughy, S. H., & Howell, C. T. (1987). Child/adolescent behavioral and emotional problems: Implications of cross-informant correlations for situational specificity. *Psychological Bulletin, 101,* 213–232.

Achenbach, W. A. & Bengston, V. L. (1994). Re-engaging the disengagement theory of aging: On the history and assessment of theory development in gerontology. *The Gerontologist, 34,* 756–763.

Adams, B. N. (1986). *The family: A sociological interpretation* (4th ed.). San Diego: Harcourt Brace Jovanovich.

Adams, G. R., & Gullotta, T. (1989). *Adolescent life experiences.* Pacific Grove, CA: Brooks/Cole.

Adams, G. R., Abraham, K. G., & Markstrom, C. A. (1987). The relations among identity development, self-consciousness, and self-focusing during middle and late adolescence. *Developmental Psychology, 23,* 292–297.

Adams, K. B. (2004). Changing investment in activities and interests in elders' lives: Theory and measurement. *International Journal of Aging and Human Development, 58*(2), 87–108.

Adams, K. B., & Sanders, S. (2004). Alzheimer's caregiver differences in experience of loss, grief reactions and depressive symptoms across stage of disease. *Dementia, 3*(2), 195–210.

Adams, K. B., Sanders, S., & Auth, E. (2004). Risk and resilience factors of loneliness and depression in residents of independent living retirement communities. *Aging and Mental Health, 8*(6), 465–475.

Adams, M., Blumenfeld, W., Castaneda, R., Hackman, H., Peters, M., & Zuniga, X. (2000). *Readings for diversity and social justice: An anthology on racism, anti-Semitism, sexism, heterosexism, ableism, and classism.* New York: Routledge.

Adams, R. G., Blieszner, R., & de Vries, B. (2000). Definitions of friendship in the third age: Gender and study location effects. *Journal of Aging Studies, 14*(1), 117–133.

Adler, H., Davies, S. P., Bane, F., Reeves, M., & Lewis, M. (1932). *Social Services Review, 6,* 429–451.

Adler, J. (1997, December 15). A matter of faith. *Time,* 49–54.

Adler, N., & Stewart, J. (2004). Self-esteem. Psychosocial working group. John D. and Catherine T. MacArthur Research Network on Socio-economic Status and Health. Retrieved from http://www.macses.ucsf.edu/research/Psychosocial/notebook/selfesteem.html#Bibliography

Adler, S. R., Fosket, J. R., Kagawa-Singer, M., McGraw, S. A., Wong-Kin, E., Gold, E., et al. (2000). Conceptualizing menopause and midlife: Chinese American and Chinese women in the U.S. *Maturitas, 35,* 11–23.

Adler, T. (1989, August). Shy monkeys are born, not made. *APA Monitor,* 5.

Adler, T. (1990, July). Genes and behavior: Old tune in a new key? *APA Monitor,* 8–9.

Adler, T. (1990, December). Melody is the message of infant-directed speech. *APA Monitor,* 9.

Adler, T. (1991, July). Women's expectations are menopause villains. *APA Monitor,* 14.

Administration on Aging. (2004a). *A profile of older Americans* (2003). Washington, DC: Author.

Administration on Aging. (2004b). *Elder abuse.* Retrieved August 3, 2004, from http://www.aoa.gov/eldfam

Ainsworth, M. D. S., Blehar, M., Waters, E., & Wall, S. (1978). *Patterns of attachment.* Hillsdale, NJ: Erlbaum.

Ainsworth, M. D. S., & Eichberg, C. (1992). Effects of infant-mother attachment on mother's unresolved loss of an attachment figure or other traumatic experience. In P. Morris, J. Stevenson-Hinde, & C. Parkes (Eds.), *Attachment across the life cycle* (pp. 160–183). New York: Routledge.

Ajzen, I. (1987). Attitudes, traits, and actions: Dispositional prediction of behavior in personality and social psychology. In L. Berkowitz (Ed.), *Advances in experimental social psychology.* New York: Academic Press.

Akkerman, R., & Ostwald, S. (2004). Reducing anxiety in Alzheimer's disease family caregivers: The effectiveness of a nine-week cognitive-behavioral intervention. *American Journal of Alzheimer's Disease and Other Dementias, 19*(2), 117–123.

Alcoholics Anonymous (2000). *Alcoholics Anonymous.* Alcoholics Anonymous World Services: New York.

Alcoholics Anonymous (2002). *Alcoholics Anonymous: This is how many thousands of men and women recovered from alcoholism.* Alcoholics Anonymous World Services: New York.

Alderman, A. (1997). *The scarred soul: Understanding and ending self-inflicted violence.* New York: Harbinger Press.

Aldwin, C. M., Spiro, A., III, Levenson, M. R., & Cupertino, A. P. (2001). Longitudinal findings from the Normative Aging Study: III. Personality, Individual health trajectories, and morality. *Psychology and Aging, 16,* 450–465.

Alexander, J. F., & Parsons, B. V. (1982). *Functional family therapy.* Pacific Grove, CA: Brooks/Cole.

Alexander, W. M., & McErwin, C. K. (1989). *Schools in the middle: Progress from 1968–1988.* Reston, VA: National Association of Secondary School Principals.

Allen, K. R., & Chin-Sang, V. (1990). A lifetime of work: The context and meanings of leisure for aging black women. *The Gerontologist, 30,* 734–740.

Allen, K., Blieszner, R., & Roberto, K. (2000a). Families in the middle and later years: A review and critique of research in the 1990s. *Journal of Marriage and the Family, 62*(4), 911–927.

Allen, K., Blieszner, R., & Roberto, K. (2000b). Kin upgrading in older families: mixing and postmodern relationships. Paper presented at the 62nd Annual Conference of the National Council on Family Relations, Minneapolis, MN.

Allport, G. W. (1935). Attitudes. In M. Murchison (Ed.), *Handbook of social psychology*. Worcester, MA: Clark University Press.

Als, H., Lawhon, G., Duffy, F., McAnulty, G., Gibes-Grossman, R., & Blickman, J. (1994). Individualized developmental care for the very low birth weight preterm infant: Medical and neurofunctional effects. *JAMA, 272,* 853–858.

Alspaugh, J. W. (1998). Achievement loss associated with the transition to middle school and high school. *Journal of Educational Research, 92,* 20–26.

Altucher, K. A., & Williams, L. B. (2003). Family clocks: Timing parenthood. In P. Moen (Ed.), *It's about time: Couples and careers* (pp. 49–59). Ithaca, NY: Cornell University Press.

Alzheimer's Association. (2003a). *African Americans and Alzheimer's disease: The silent epidemic.* Retrieved October 22, 2003, from http://www.alz.org

Alzheimer's Association. (2003b). *Facts: About genes and Alzheimer's disease.* Chicago, IL: Author.

Alzheimer's Association (2004). *Standard prescriptions for Alzheimer's.* Retrieved July 10, 2004, from http://www.alz.org

Amato, P. R. (1993). Family processes and the competence of adolescents and primary school children. *Journal of Youth and Adolescence, 18,* 39–53.

Amato, P. R. (2000). The consequences of divorce for adults and children. *Journal of Marriage and the Family, 62,* 1269–1287.

Amato, P. R., & Booth, A. (1996). A prospective study of divorce and parent-child relationships. *Journal of Marriage and the Family, 58,* 356–365.

American Academy of Child and Adolescent Psychiatry (2000). *Your child: Emotional, behavioral and cognitive development from birth through preadolescence.* New York: HarperResource.

American Academy of Family Physicians. (2003). *Healthy food choices.* Retrieved May 31, 2004, from http://familydoctor.org

American Academy of Pediatrics. (2000). Diagnosis and evaluation of the child with attention-deficit/hyperactivity disorder (AC0002). *Pediatrics, 105,* 1158–1170.

American Academy of Pediatrics. (2002, August). Responding to children's emotional needs during times of crisis: An important role for pediatricians. Retrieved March 1, 2003, from http://www.aap.org/terrorism

American Academy of Pediatrics, Committee on Adolescence (1999). Adolescent pregnancy—current trends and issues: 1998. *Pediatrics, 103,* 516–520.

American Association of Retired Persons and Administration on Aging. (1994). *A profile of older Americans.* Washington, DC.

American Association of University Women (AAUW) (2001). *Hostile hallways: Bullying, teasing and sexual harassment in school.* Washington, DC: Author.

American Family Physician (2002). Premenstrual Dysphoric Disorder (PMDD). *American Family Physician,* 1–4.

American Psychiatric Association. (2000). *Diagnostic and statistical manual of mental disorders: DSM-IV-TR.*

American Psychiatric Association. (1994). *Diagnostic and statistical manual of mental disorders* (4th ed.). Washington, DC: Author.

Americans for divorce reform (2004). Statistics on adultery. Retrieved November 29, 2004, from http://www.divorcereform.org/stats.html

Ancelet, B. J., Edwards, J. D., & Pitre, G. (1991). *Cajun country.* Jackson: University of Mississippi Press.

Andersen, M. L., & Collins, P. H. (1995). *Race, class and gender: An anthology.* Belmont, CA: Wadsworth.

Andersen, M. L., & Collins, P. H. (2004). *Race, class, and gender: An anthology* (3rd ed.). Belmont, CA: Wadsworth.

Andersen, M. L., & Taylor, H. F. (2003). *Sociology: Understanding a diverse society* (3rd ed.). Belmont, CA: Thomson/Wadsworth.

Anderson, D. R., & Evans, M. K. (2001). Perils and potential of media for toddlers. *Zero to Three, 22*(2), 10–16.

Anderson, M., Kaufman, J., Simon, T. R., Barrios, L., Paulozzi, L., Ryan, G., et al. (2001). School-associated violent deaths in the United States, 1994–1997. *Journal of the American Medical Association, 286,* 1695–1702.

Anderson, R. E., & Carter, I. (1984). *Human behavior in the social environment: A social systems approach* (3rd ed.). New York: Aldine.

Anderson, S. M., & Williams, M. (1985). Cognitive/affective reaction in the improvement of self-esteem: When thoughts and feelings make a difference. *Journal of Personality and Social Psychology, 49,* 1086–1097.

Andreason, N. C. (1984). *The broken brain: The biological revolution in psychiatry.* New York: Harper & Row.

Andreasen, N. C., & Black, D. W. (1991). *Introductory textbook of psychiatry.* Washington, DC: American Psychiatric Press.

Andronico, M. P. (1996). *Men in Groups.* Hyattsville, MD: American Psychological Association.

Anetzberger, G. J. (2000). Caregiving: Primary cause of elder abuse? *Generations, 24*(11), 46–51.

Angelillo, C., Rogoff, B., & Morelli, G. (2002). *Age and kinship of young children's partners in four communities.* Unpublished manuscript.

Annie E. Casey Foundation. (2004). *Children at risk: State trends 1990–2004.* Retrieved November 15, 2004, from http://www.aecf.org/kidscount

Apantaku, L. M. (2000). Breast cancer diagnosis and screening. *American Family Physician, 62,* 596–602.

Apgar, V. (1953). A proposal for a new method of evaluation in the newborn infant. *Current Research in Anesthesia and Analgesia, 32,* 260–267.

Aponte, H. J., & Van Deusen, J. M. (1981). Structural family therapy. In A. S. Gurman & D. P. Kniskern (Eds.), *Handbook of family therapy.* New York: Brunner Mazel.

Appetite suppressant found in brain, researchers say. (1996, January 4). *USA Today.*

Appleby, G. A. (2001a). Dynamics of oppression and discrimination. In G. A. Appleby, E. Colon, & Julia Hamilton (Eds.), *Diversity, oppression, and social functioning: Person in environment assessment and intervention* (pp. 36–52). Needham Heights, MA: Allyn & Bacon.

Appleby, G. A. (2001b). Framework for practice with diverse and oppressed clients. In G. A. Appleby, E. Colon, & J. Hamilton (Eds.), *Diversity, oppression, and social functioning.* Boston: Allyn & Bacon.

Applewhite, S. R. (Ed.). (1988). *Hispanic elderly in transition.* New York: Greenwood Press.

Apter, T. (1995). *Secret paths: Women in the new midlife.* New York: Norton.

Arlington, D. E., & Troll, L. E. (1984). Social change and equality: The roles of women and economics. In G. Baruch & J. Brooks-Gunn (Eds.), *Women in midlife.* New York: Plenum.

Arnett, J. J. (2004). *Emerging adulthood: The winding road from the late teens through the twenties.* New York: Oxford University Press.

Arnett, J. J. (2000, May). Emerging Adulthood: A theory of development from the late teens through the twenties. *American Psychologist, 55,* 469–480.

Aronson, E. (2000). *Nobody left to hate: Teaching compassion after Columbine.* New York: Worth Publishers.

Arrendondo, P. M. (1984). Identity themes for immigrant young adults. *Adolescence, 19,* 977–993.

Ashburn, S. S., Schuster, C. S., Grimm, W. A., & Goff, S. M. (1986). Language development during childhood. In C. Schuster & S. S. Ashburn (Eds.), *The process of human development: A holistic life-span approach* (pp. 257–276). Boston: Little, Brown.

Asher, J. (1987, April). Born to be shy? *Psychology Today,* 56–64.

Asher, S. R., & Dodge, K. A. (1986). Identifying children who are rejected by their peers. *Developmental Psychology, 22,* 444–449.

Asher, S. R., & Renshaw, P. (1981). Children without friends: Social knowledge and social skill training. In S. R. Asher & J. M. Gottman (Eds.), *The development of children's friendships.* New York: Cambridge University Press.

Ashford, J. B. (1994). Child maltreatment interventions: Developments in law, prevention and treatment. *Criminal Justice Review, 19,* 271–285.

Ashford, J. B., & Faith, R. L. (2004). Testing models of justice and trust: A study of mediation in child dependency disputes. *Social Work Research, 28,* 18–27.

Ashford, J. B., Sales, B. D., & Reid, W. H. (2001a). Introduction. In J. B. Ashford, B. D. Sales, & W. H. Reid (Eds.), *Treating adult and juvenile offenders with special needs* (pp. 3–27). Washington, DC: American Psychological Association.

Ashford, J. B., Sales, B. D., & Reid, W. H. (2001b). Political, legal, and professional challenges to treating offenders with special needs. In J. B. Ashford, B. D. Sales, & W. H. Reid (Eds.), *Treating adult and juvenile offenders with special needs* (pp. 31–49). Washington, DC: American Psychological Association.

Ashmore, R. D., & Jussim, L. (1997). Introduction: Toward a second century of the scientific analysis of self and identity. In R. D. Ashmore & L. Jussim (Eds.), *Self and identity: Fundamental issues* (pp. 3–19). New York: Oxford University Press.

Atchley, R. (1976). *The sociology of retirement.* New York: Halsted Press.

Atchley, R. (1989). A continuity theory of normal aging. *The Gerontologist, 29*(2), 183–190.

Atchley, R. (2000). *Social Forces and Aging* (9th ed.). Belmont, CA: Wadsworth.

Atchley, R. C., & Miller, S. J. (1983). Types of elderly couples. In T. H. Brubaker (Ed.), *Family relationships in later life.* Beverly Hills, CA: Sage.

Atkinson, R., Misra, S., Ryan, S., & Turner, J. (2003). Referral paths, patient profiles and treatment adherence of older alcoholic men. *Journal of Substance Abuse Treatment, 25,* 29–35.

Attie, I., & Brooks-Gunn, J. (1989). Development of eating problems in adolescent girls: A longitudinal study. *Developmental Psychology, 25*(1), 70–79.

Atwood, M. (1991). *Cat's eye.* London: Virago.

Austrian, S. G. (2002). *Developmental theories: Through the life cycle.* New York: Columbia University Press.

Avard, D. (1985). Risks and benefits of obstetric epidural analgesia: A review. *Birth: Issues in Perinatal Care and Education, 12,* 215–225.

Avis, N. E., Crawford, S., & Johannes, C. B. (2002). Menopause. In G. M. Wingood & R. J. DeClemente (Eds.), *Handbook of women's sexual and reproductive health* (pp. 367–391). New York: Kluwer.

Azar, B. (1995, May). Avoiding alcohol in real-world settings. *American Psychological Association Monitor,* 20.

Azar, B. (1995, June). Data released from child-care study. *APA Monitor,* 18.

Azar, B. (1997, December). Learning begins even before babes are born, scientists show. *APA Monitor,* 17.

Azar, B. (1998, November). Early diagnosis of autism could help derail its effects. *APA Monitor,* 12, 14.

Bacerra, R. M. (1988). The Mexican American family. In C. H. Mindel, R. W. Habenstein, & R. Wright (Eds.), *Ethnic families in America: Patterns and variations* (3rd ed.). New York: Elsevier.

Backman, L., Small, B., & Wahlin, A. (2001). Aging and memory. In J. Birren & K. Schaie (Eds.), *Handbook of the psychology of aging* (5th ed., pp. 349–377). New York: Academic Press.

Bailey, J. M., Pillard, R. C., Neale, M. C., & Agyei, Y. (1993). Heritable factors influence sexual orientation in women. *Archives of General Psychiatry, 50,* 217–223.

Baillargeon, R. (1987). Object permanence in 3½ and 4½-month-old infants. *Developmental Psychology, 23,* 655–664.

Balaskas, J. (1992). *Active birth: The new approach to giving birth naturally.* Boston: Harvard Common Press.

Baldwin, J. R., & Hecht, M. L. (1995). The layered perspective of cultural (in)tolerance(s). In R. L. Waiseman (Ed.), *Intercultural communication theory.* Thousand Oaks, CA: Sage.

Bales, R. F. (1958). Task roles and social roles in problem-solving groups. In E. E. Maccoby, T. M. Newcomb, & E. L. Hartley (Eds.), *Readings in social psychology.* New York: Holt, Rinehart & Winston.

Ballenger, M. (1983). Reading in the kindergarten: Comment. *Childhood Education, 59,* 187.

Baltes, P. B. & Baltes, M. M. (1990). Psychological perspectives on successful aging: The model of selective optimization with compensation. In P. B. Baltes & M. M. Baltes (Eds.), *Successful aging: Perspectives from the behavioral sciences* (pp. 1–34). New York: Cambridge University Press.

Baltes, P. B., & Staudinger, U. M. (2000). Wisdom: A metaheuristic (pragmatic) to orchestrate mind and virtue toward excellence. *American Psychologist, 55*(1), 122–136.

Bandura, A. (1965). Influence of models' reinforcement contingencies on the acquisition of imitative responses. *Journal of Personality and Social Psychology, 1,* 589–595.

Bandura, A. (1971). *Social learning theory.* Englewood Cliffs, NJ: Prentice Hall.

Bandura, A. (1977). *Social learning.* Englewood Cliffs, NJ: Prentice Hall.

Bandura, A. (1989). Social cognitive theory. In R. Vasta (Ed.), *Annuals of child development vol. 6., theories of child development: Revised formulations and current issues.* Greenwich, CT: JAI Press.

Bandura, A., Ross, D., & Ross, S. (1963). Vicarious reinforcement and imitative learning. *Journal of Abnormal and Social Psychology, 67,* 601–607.

Bank, B. A., Seri, I., Ischiropoulos, H., Merrill, J., Rychik, J., & Ballard, R. A. (1999). Changes in oxygenation with inhaled nitric oxide in severe bronchopulmonary dysplasia. *Pediatrics, 103,* 610–619.

Banton, M. (1994). *Discrimination.* Buckingham, England: Open University Press.

Barash, D. P., & Lipton, J. E. (1985). Sociobiology. In H. Kaplan and B. J. Sadock (Eds.), *Comprehensive textbook of psychiatry* (Vol. 4). Baltimore: Williams & Wilkins.

Barbach. L. G. (2000). *The pause: Positive approaches to perimenopause and menopause.* New York: Plume.

Barkely, R. A. (2000). *Taking charge of ADHD, Revised edition: The complete, authoritative guide for parents.* New York: Guilford Press.

Barkely, R. A. (2003). Does the treatment of ADHD with stimulants contribute to substance abuse? A 13-year prospective study. *Pediatrics, 111,* 97–109.

Barlow, D. H., & Durand, V. M. (2005). *Abnormal psychology: An integrative approach* (4th ed.). Belmont, CA: Wadsworth/Thomson.

Barnes, H., & Parry, J. (2004). Renegotiating identity and relationships: Men and women's adjustments to retirement. *Aging and Society, 24,* 213–233.

Barnes, K. E. (1971). Preschool play norms: A replication. *Developmental Psychology, 4,* 99–103.

Baron, A. (1991). Counseling Chicano college students. In C. Lee and B. Richardson (Eds.), *Multicultural issues in counseling* (pp. 171–184). Alexandria, VA: American Association for Counseling and Development.

Baron, R. A., & Byrne, D. (1984). *Social psychology: Understanding human interaction.* Newton, MA: Allyn & Bacon.

Barranti, C., & Cohen, H. (2000). Lesbian and gay elders: An invisible minority. In R. Schneider, N. Kropf, & A. Kisor (Eds.), *Gerontological social work: Knowledge, service settings, and special populations* (2nd ed., pp. 343–367). Belmont, CA: Brooks/Cole.

Barrett, D. E. (1979). A naturalistic study of sex differences in children's aggression. *Merrill-Palmer Quarterly, 25,* 193–203.

Barry, B. (2001). *Culture and equality.* Cambridge: Polity.

Bartels, A., & Zeki, S. (2004). The neural correlates of maternal and romantic love. *NeuroImage, 21,* 1155–1166.

Barth, R. P. (1996). *Reducing the risk: Building skills to prevent pregnancy STD and HIV* (3rd ed.). Santa Cruz, CA: ETR Associates.

Bartlett, H. (1970). *The common base of social work practice.* Washington, DC: National Association of Social Workers.

Baruch, A. S., & Spaid, W. M. (1989). Gender differences in caregiving: Why do wives report greater burden? *The Gerontologist, 29,* 667–676.

Baruch, G. K., & Barnett, R. C. (1983). Adult daughters' relationships with their mothers. *Journal of Marriage and the Family, 45,* 601–606.

Baruch, G. K., & Brooks-Gunn, J. (1984). The study of women in midlife. In G. Baruch & J. Brooks-Gunn (Eds.), *Women in midlife.* New York: Plenum.

Baruth, L. G., & Manning, M. L. (1991). *Multicultural counseling and psychotherapy.* New York: Merrill.

Bascue, L. O., & Lawrence, R. E. (1977). A study of subjective time and death anxiety in the elderly. *Omega, 8,* 81–90.

Baskett, L. M., & Johnson, S. M. (1982). The young child's interactions with parents versus siblings. *Child Development, 53,* 643–650.

Basow, S. A. (1992). *Gender: Stereotypes and roles.* Pacific Grove, CA: Brooks/Cole.

Bass, E., & Davis, L. (1994). *The courage to heal.* New York: Perennial.

Bassuk, E. L. (1991). Homeless families. *Scientific American, 265,* 66–74.

Bates, E. (1976). *The emergence of symbols.* New York: Academic Press.

Bateson, M. C. (1990). *Composing a life.* New York: Plume.

Baum, E., Jarjoura, D., Polen, A., Faur, D., & Rutecki, G. (2003). Effectiveness of a group exercise program in a long-term care facility: A randomized pilot trial. *Journal of American Medical Directors Associated, 4*(2), 74–80.

Baumeister, D. (1997). The self and society: Changes, problems, and opportunities. In R. D. Ashmore & L. Jussim (Eds.), *Self and identity: Fundamental issues* (pp. 191–217). New York: Oxford University Press.

Baumgartner-Papageorgious, A. (1982). *My daddy might have loved me: Student perceptions of differences between being male and being female.* Denver, CO: Institute for Equality in Education.

Baumrind, D. (1971). Current patterns of parental authority. *Developmental Psychology Monographs, 4* (1, Pt. 2).

Baumrind, D. (1989). Parenting styles and adolescent development. In J. Brooks-Gunn, R. Lerner, & A. C. Petersen (Eds.), *The encyclopedia of adolescence.* New York: Garland.

Baumrind, D. (1991). Effective parenting during the early adolescent transition. In P. A. Cowan & E. M. Heatherington (Eds.), *Advances in family research* (Vol. 2). Hillsdale, NJ: Erlbaum.

Baylor, B. (1977/1978). *The way to start a day.* New York: Macmillan.

Beal, C. R. (1987). Repairing the message: Children's monitoring and revision skills, *Child Development, 58,* 920–928.
Beal, C. R., & Belgrad, S. L. (1990). The development of message evaluation skills in young children. *Child Development, 61,* 705–712.
Beardsley, T. (1995, February). Putting Alzheimer's to the tests. *Scientific American,* 12–13.
Beattie, M. (1987). *Codependent no more.* New York: HarperCollins.
Beck, C. M., Rawlins, R. P., & Williams, S. R. (1988). *Mental health psychiatric nursing: Holistic life cycle approach.* St. Louis, MO: C. V. Mosby.
Beck, D. F., & Jones, M. A. (1973). *Progress on family problems: A nationwide study of clients' and counselors' views on family agency services.* New York: Family Service Association of America.
Becker, G., Beyene, Y., Newsom, E., & Mayen, N. (2003). Creating continuity through mutual assistance: Intergenerational reciprocity in four ethnic groups. *Journal of Gerontology Social Sciences, 58B,* S151–S159.
Beckett, J. O., & Dungee-Anderson, D. (2000). Older persons of color: Asian/Pacific Islander Americans, African Americans, Hispanic Americans, and American Indians. In R. L. Schneider, N. P. Kropf, & A. J. Kisor (Eds.), *Gerontological social work: Knowledge, service settings and special populations* (2nd ed., pp. 257–301). Belmont, CA: Brooks/Cole.
Beers, M. (2000). Age-related changes as a risk factor for medication-related problems. *Generations: Quarterly Journal of the American Society on Aging, 14*(4), 22–27.
Begley, S. (1988, March). All about twins. *Reader's Digest,* 80–85.
Bellah, R. N., Madsen, R., Sullivan, W. M., Swidler, A., & Tipton, S. M. (1996). *Habits of the heart: Individuals and commitment in American life.* Berkeley: University of California Press.
Bellinger, D., & Needleman, H. (1985). Prenatal and early postnatal exposure to lead: Developmental effects, correlates, and implications. *International Journal of Mental Health, 14,* 78–111.
Belsky, J. (1980). Child maltreatment: An ecological integration. *American Psychologist, 35,* 320–335.
Belsky, J. (1981). Early human experience: A family perspective. *Developmental Psychology, 17,* 3–23.
Belsky, J. (1985). Exploring differences in marital change across the transition to parenthood: The role of violated expectations. *Journal of Marriage and the Family, 47,* 1037–1044.
Belsky, J. K. (1990). *The psychology of aging: Theory, research, and interventions* (2nd ed.). Pacific Grove, CA: Brooks/Cole.
Belsky, J., Gilstrap, B., & Rovine, M. (1984). The Pennsylvania infant and family development project: 1. Stability and change in mother-infant and father-infant interaction in a family setting at 1, 3, and 9 months. *Child Development, 55,* 692–705.
Belsky, J., & Rovine, M. (1988). Nonmaternal care in the first year of life and the security of infant-parent attachment. *Child Development, 59,* 157–167.
Bem, D. J. (1967). Self-perception: An alternative interpretation of cognitive dissonance phenomena. *Psychological Review, 74,* 183–200.
Bem, S. L. (1974). The measurement of psychological androgyny. *Journal of Consulting and Clinical Psychology, 42,* 155–162.
Bem, S. L. (1977). On the utility of alternative procedures for assessing psychological androgyny. *Journal of Consulting and Clinical Psychology, 45,* 196–205.
Bem, S. L. (1993). *The lenses of gender: Transforming the debate on sexual inequality.* Binghamton, NY: Vail-Ballou.
Bender, D. A. (2002). *Introduction to nutrition and metabolism.* New York: Taylor and Francis.
Benedict, H. (1979). Early lexical development: Comprehension and production. *Journal of Child Language, 6,* 183–200.
Bengston, V. L. (1985). Diversity and symbolism in grandparental roles. In V. L. Bengston & J. Robertson (Eds.), *Grandparenthood.* Beverly Hills, CA: Sage.
Bengston, V. L., Cuellar, J. B., & Ragan, P. K. (1977). Stratum contrasts and similarities in attitudes toward death. *Journal of Gerontology, 12,* 76–88.
Benjamins, M., Musick, M., Gold, D., & George, L. (2003). Age-related declines in activity level: The relationship between chronic illness and religious activities. *The Journal of Gerontology Social Sciences, 58,* S377–S385.
Benne, K. D., & Sheats, P. (1948). Functional roles of group members. *Journal of Social Issues, 4,* 41–49.
Bennett, D. (2004). Mild cognitive impairment. *Clinics in Geriatric Medicine, 20,* 15–25.
Bensen, P. L. (1997). *All kids our kids: What communities must do to raise caring and responsible children and adolescents.* San Francisco: Jossey-Bass.
Bensen, P. L., & Lerner, R. M. (2003). *Developmental assets and asset building communities: Implications for research, policy, and practice.* New York: Kluwer Academic.
Benson, M. L. (2002). *Crime and the life course: An introduction.* Los Angeles: Roxbury Publishing Company.
Benson, P. L. (1990). *The troubled journey: A portrait of 6th–12th grade youth.* Minneapolis: The Search Institute.
Berck (1992). *No place to be: Voices of homeless children.* Boston: Houghton Mifflin.
Berger, K. (2005). *The Developing Person: Through the life span.* New York: Worth Publishers.
Bergin, D. (1988). Stages of play development. In D. Bergin (Ed.), *Play as a medium for learning and development.* Portsmouth, NH: Heinemann.
Bergquist, W. H., Greenberg, E. M., & Klaum, G. A. (1993). *In our fifties: Voices of men and women reinventing their lives.* San Francisco: Jossey-Bass.
Berk, L. E. (2004). *Development through the lifespan* (3rd ed.). Boston: Allyn & Bacon.
Berke, J. (2004). Demographics of hearing loss. Retrieved November 15, 2004, from http://deafness.about.com
Berkman, B., Maramaldi, P., Breon, E., & Howe, J. (2002). Social work gerontological assessment revisited. *Journal of Gerontological Social Work, 40*(1/2), 1–14.
Berkman, L. F., Berkman, C. S., Kasl, S., Freeman, D. H., Jr., Leo, L., Ostfeld, A. M., Cornoni-Huntley, J., et al. (1986). Depressive symptoms in relation to physical health and functioning in the elderly. *Journal of Epidemiology, 124,* 372–388.
Berko, J. (1958). The child's learning of English morphology. *Word, 14,* 150–177.
Berlyne, D. E. (1960). *Conflict, arousal, and curiosity.* New York: McGraw-Hill.
Bermant, C. (1966). *Diary of an old man.* Holt, Rinehart & Winston.
Bernard, J. (1975). *Women, wives, mothers: Values and options.* Chicago: Aldine.
Bernard, J. (1981). *The female world.* New York: Free Press.
Berndt, T. J. (1979). Developmental changes in conformity to peers and parents. *Developmental Psychology, 15,* 608–616.
Berndt, T. J., & Ladd, G. W. (1989). *Peer relations in child development.* New York: Wiley.
Berrick, J. D., & Gilbert, N. (1991). *With the best of intentions: The child sexual abuse prevention movement.* New York: Guilford Press.
Berrueta-Clement, J., Schweinhart, L., Barnett, W., Epstein, A., & Weikart, D. (1984). *Changed lives: Effects of the Perry Preschool Program on youths through age 19.* Ypsilanti, MI: High/Scope Press.
Berry, P. (1993). Pathological findings in SIDS. *Journal of Clinical Pathology, 45,* 11.
Besharov, D. J. (1985). Right versus rights: The dilemma of child protection. *Public Welfare, 42*(2), 19–27.
Bialystok, E. (1988). Levels of bilingualism and levels of linguistic awareness. *Developmental Psychology, 24,* 560–567.
Bialystok, E. (1999). Cognitive complexity and attentional control in the bilingual mind. *Child Development, 70,* 636–644.
Bialystok, E., Shenfield, T., & Codd, J. (2000). Languages, scripts, and the environment: Factors in developing concepts offprint. *Developmental Psychology, 36,* 66–76.
Biema, D. V. (1996, November 11). Just say life skills: A new school anti-drug program outstrips D.A.R.E. *Time,* 18.
Biesele, M., & Howell, N. (1981). The old people give you life: Aging among !Kung hunter-gatherers. In P. T. Amoss & S. Harrell (Eds.), *Other ways of growing old: Anthropological perspectives.* Stanford, CA: Stanford University Press.
Bigner, J. J., & Jacobsen, R. B. (1989). Parenting behaviors of homosexual and heterosexual fathers. *Journal of homosexuality, 18,* 173–186.
Bilchik, S., Seymour, C., & Kreisher, K. (2001, December). Parents in prison. *Corrections Today,* 108–112.
Birren, J., & Schaie, K. (Eds.) (2001). *Handbook of the psychology of aging* (5th ed.). San Diego: Academic Press.
Bishop, K. K. (2002). Family-Centered Services to Infants and Toddlers with, or at Risk for Disabilities: IDEA, Part C. In R. Constable, S. McDonald, & J. F. Flynn (Eds.), *School social work: Practice, policy and research perspectives* (5th ed). Chicago: Lyceum Press.
Biskupic, J. (2003, February 17). Same-sex couples redefining family law in USA. Retrieved March 19, 2003, from http://www.usatoday.com

Bjorklund, D. F., & Bjorklund, B. R. (1992). *Looking at children: An introduction to child development.* Pacific Grove, CA: Brooks/Cole.

Black, C., Paz, H., and DeBlassie, R. (1991). Counseling the Hispanic Male Adolescent. *Adolescence, 26,* 223–232.

Black, D. (1993). *The social structure of right and .wrong.* San Diego: Academic Press.

Black, D., Gates, G., & Sanders, S. (2000). Demographics of the gay and lesbian population in the United States: Evidence from available systematic data sources. *Demography, 37,* 139–154.

Black, D. J. (1976). *The behavior of law.* New York: Academic Press.

Blaine, B. (2000). *The psychology of diversity: Perceiving and experiencing social difference.* Mountain View, CA: Mayfield.

Blakemore, J. E. O., LaRue, A. A., & Olejnik, A. B. (1979). Sex-appropriate toy preference and the ability to conceptualize toys as sex-role related. *Developmental Psychology, 15,* 339–340.

Blamey, A., Mutrie, N., & Aitchison, T. (1995). Health promotion by encouraged use of stairs. *British Medical Journal, 311,* 289–290.

Blando, J. (2001). Twice hidden: Older gay and lesbian couples, friends, and intimacy. *Generations, 25,* 87–89.

Blanker, M. H., Bosch, J. L., Groeneveld, F. P., Bohnen, A. M., Prins, A., Thomas, S., et al. (2001). Erectile and ejaculatory dysfunction in a community-based sample of men 50 to 78 years old: Prevalence, concern, and relation to sexual activity. *Urology, 57,* 763–768.

Blashfield, R. K. (1984). *The classification of psychopathology: Neo-Kraepelian and quantitative approaches.* New York: Plenum.

Blau, D. M., & Hagy, A. P. (1998). The demand for quality child care. *Journal of Political Economy, 106,* 104.

Blazer, D. (2002a). *Depression in Late Life* (3rd ed.). New York: Springer.

Blazer, D. (2002b). Self-efficacy and depression in late life: A primary prevention proposal. *Aging and Mental Health 6*(4), 315–324.

Blazer, D. (2003). Depression in late life: Review and commentary. *Journal of Gerontology Medical Sciences, 58A*(3), M249–M265.

Blieszner, R. (2001). "She'll be on my heart": Intimacy among friends. *Generations: Quarterly Journal of the American Society on Aging, 25*(2), 48–84.

Block, R. D., & Moore, E. G. (1986). Advantage and disadvantage: A profile of American youth. Hillsdale, NJ: Erlbaum.

Blood, R. O., & Wolfe, D. M. (1960). *Husbands and wives.* New York: Macmillan.

Bloom, L. (1998). Language development: emotional expression. *Pediatrics, 102,* 1272–1277.

Blow, F. C., Brower, K. J., Schulenberg, J. E., Demo-Dananberg, L. M, Young, J. P. & Beresford, T. P. (1992). The Michigan Alcoholism Screening Test—Geriatric Version (MAST-G): A new elderly-specific screening instrument. *Alcoholism: Clinical and Experimental Research, 16,* 372.

Blumstein, P., & Schwartz, P. (1983). *American couples.* New York: Simon & Schuster.

Bly, R. (1992). *Iron John.* New York: HarperCollins.

Boehm, W. W. (1958). The nature of social work. *Social Work, 3,* 10–18.

Boehm, W. W. (1959). *Objectives of the social work curriculum of the future* (Vol. 1). New York: Council of Social Work Education.

Bogard, M. (1991). *Feminist approaches for men in family therapy.* New York: Haworth Press.

Bogatz, G. A., & Ball, S. (1972). *The second year of Sesame Street: A continuing evaluation.* Princeton, NJ: Educational Testing Service.

Bogenschneider, K., Wu, M., Raffaelli, M., & Tsay, J. C. (1998). "Other kids drink, but not my kid": Does parental awareness of adolescent alcohol use protect adolescents from risky consequences? *Journal of Marriage and the Family, 60,* 356–372.

Bohan-Baker, M., & Little, P. (2002). *The transition to kindergarten: A review of current research and promising practices to involve families.* Cambridge, MA: Harvard Family Research Project.

Boney-McCoy, S., & Finkelhor, D. (1995). Psychosocial sequelae of violent victimization in a national youth sample. *Journal of Consulting and Clinical Psychology, 63,* 726–736.

Bonkowski, S., & Yanos, J. (1992). Infant mental health: An expanding field for social work. *Social Work, 37,* 144–148.

Bonnesen, J., & Burgess, E. (2004). Senior moments: The acceptability of an ageist phase. *Journal of Aging Studies, 18,* 123–142.

Bonvillian, J. D., Orlansky, M. D., & Novack, L. L. (1983). Development milestones: Sign language acquisition and motor development. *Child Development, 54,* 1435–1445.

Bookwala, J., & Jacobs, J. (2004). Age, marital processes, and depressed affect. *The Gerontological Society of America, 44*(3), 328–338.

Booth, C. L., Barnard, K. E., Mitchell, S. K., & Spieker, S. J. (1987). Successful intervention with multiproblem mothers: Effects on the mother-infant relationship. *Infant Mental Health Journal, 8,* 288–306.

Booth-Kewley, S., & Friedman, H. S. (1987). Psychological predictors of heart disease: A quantitative review. *Psychological Bulletin, 101,* 343–362.

Bootzin, R. E., & Acocella, J. R. (1988). *Abnormal psychology: Current perspectives.* New York: McGraw-Hill.

Boring, E. G. (1930). A new ambiguous figure. *American Journal of Psychology, 42,* 444.

Bornstein, M., & Sigman, M. (1986). Continuity in mental development from infancy. *Child Development, 57,* 251–274.

Bornstein, R. (1992). Psychosocial development of the older adult. In C. S. Schuster & S. S. Ashburn (Eds.), *The process of human development: A holistic life-span approach* (3rd ed., pp. 831–850). New York: Lippincott.

Bornstein, R., & Schuster, C. S. (1992). Cognitive development during the adult years. In C. S. Schuster & C. Ashburn, *The process of human development.* New York: Lippincott.

Bosma, H. A. (2001). Identity development: Adolescence through adulthood. *Identity, 1,* 95–96.

Bosma, H. A., & Gerlsma, C. (2003). From early attachment relations to the adolescent and adult organization of self. In J. Valsiner & K. Connolly (Eds.), *Handbook of developmental psychology* (pp. 217–237). Thousand Oaks, CA: Sage.

Bosma, H. A., & Kunnen, E. S. (2001). Determinants and mechanisms in ego identity development: A review and synthesis. *Developmental Review, 21,* 39–66.

Boston Women's Health Book Collective (1992). When yogurt was illegal. *Ms., 3,* 38–39.

Botvin, G. J. (2000). *Life skills training: Promoting health and personal development, level I.* New York: Varsity.com

Botvin, G. J., Griffin, K. W., Diaz, T., & Ifill-Williams, M. (2001). Preventing binge drinking during early adolescence: One- and two-year follow-up of a school-based preventive intervention. *Psychology of Addiction, 15,* 360–365.

Botwinick, J. (1984). *Aging and behavior* (3rd ed.). New York: Springer.

Bouchard, T. J., Jr., Lykken, D. T., McGue, M., Segal, N. L., & Tellegen, A. (1990). Sources of human psychological differences: The Minnesota study of twins reared apart. *Science, 250,* 223–228.

Bourne, L. E., Ekstrand, R. R., Dominowski, R. L. (1971). *The psychology of thinking.* Englewood Cliffs, NJ: Prentice Hall.

Bowen, M. (1978). *Family therapy in children practice.* New York: Jason Aronson.

Bower, T. G. R. (1982). *Development in infancy.* San Francisco: Freeman.

Bowlby, J. (1958). The nature of the child's tie to his mother. *International Journal of Psychoanalysis, 39,* 350–373.

Bowlby, J. (1969). *Attachment and loss. vol. 1.: Attachment.* New York: Basic Books.

Bowlby, J. (1980). *Attachment and loss, vol. 3.: Loss, sadness and depression.* New York: Basic Books.

Bowman, L. (2004). New research shows stark differences in teen brains. Retrieved May 11, 2004, from http://www.shns.com

Brabeck, M. (1983). Moral judgment: Theory and research on differences between males and females. *Developmental Review, 3,* 274–291.

Bradley, R. (1987). Providing a stimulating and supportive home environment for young children. *Physical and Occupational Therapy in Pediatrics, 7,* 77–89.

Bradley, R., & Brisby, J. (1990). Assessment of the home environment. In J. Johnson & J. Goldman (Eds.), *Developmental assessment in clinical child psychology* (pp. 219–250). New York: Pergamon Press.

Bradley, R., Caldwell, B., Rock, S., Casey, P., & Nelson, J. (1987). The early development of low-birthweight infants: Relationship to health, family status, family context, family processes and parenting. *International Journal of Behavioral Development, 10,* 301–318.

Bradley, R., Whiteside, L., Mundfrom, D., Casey, P., Kelleher, K., & Pope, S. (1994). Contribution of early intervention and early caregiving experiences to resilience in low-birthweight, premature children living in poverty. *Journal of Clinical Child Psychology, 23,* 425–434.

Bradley, S. J., Oliver, G. D., Chernick, A. B., & Zucker, K. J. (1998). Experiment of nurture: Ablatio penis at 2 months, sex reassignment at 7 months, and psychosocial follow-up in young adulthood. *Pediatrics, 102,* 9–17.

Braginsky, D. D., & Braginsky, B. M. (1975, August). Surplus people: Their lost faith in self and system. *Psychology Today, 9,* 68–72.

Brandl, B. (2000). Power and control: Understanding domestic abuse in later life. *Generations, 24*(11), 39–45.

Bray, J. H. (1999). From marriage to remarriage and beyond: Findings from the Developmental Issues in Stepfamilies research project. In E. M. Heatherington (Ed.), *Coping with divorce, single parenting, and remarriage: A risk and resiliency perspective* (pp. 295–319). Mahwah, NJ: Erlbaum.

Brazelton, T. B. (1973). Neonatal behavioral assessment scale. In *Clinics in Developmental Medicine*, No. 50. Philadelphia: J. B. Lippincott.

Brazelton, T. B. (1992). *Touchpoints: Your child's emotional and behavioral development*. Reading, MA: Addison-Wesley.

Breckman, R., & Adelman, R. (1988). *Strategies for helping victims of elder mistreatment*. Newbury Park, CA: Sage.

Bremmer, J. (1988). *Infancy*. Norwich, UK: Page Bros.

Bremmer, J. N., & van den Bosch, L. (1995). *Between poverty and the pyre: Moments in the history of widowhood*. New York: Routledge.

Brennan, A. (1985). Participation and self-esteem: A test of six alternative explanations. *Adolescence, 20*, 445–466.

Bretherton, I., & Munholland, K. A. (1999). Internal working models in attachment relationships: A construct revisited. In J. Cassidy & P. R. Shaver (Eds.), *Handbook of attachment: Theory, research, and clinical applications* (89–111). New York: Guilford Press.

Bretherton, I., Fritz, J., Zahn-Waxler, C., & Ridgeway, D. (1986). Learning to talk about emotions. *Child Development, 57*, 529–548.

Brewer, W. (1995, June). New cognitive research makes waves. *American Psychological Association Monitor, 17*.

Brice, M. (2003). *Age ain't nothing but a number: Black women explore midlife*. New York: Beacon.

Brieland, D. (1987). History and evolution of social work practice. In A. Minahan (Ed.), *Encyclopedia of social work* (18th ed., pp. 739–754). Silver Spring, MD: National Association of Social Workers.

Briere, J., & Gil, E. (1998). Self-mutilation in clinical and general population samples: Prevalence, correlates, and functions. *American Journal of Orthopsychiatry, 68*, 609–620.

Brill, P., Drimmer, A., Morgan, A., & Gordon, N. (1995). The feasibility of conducting strength and flexibility programs for elderly nursing home residents with dementia. *The Gerontologist, 35*(2), 263–266.

Brim, O. (1975). Macro-structural influences on child development and the need for childhood social indicators. *American Journal of Orthopsychiatry, 45*, 516–524.

Brim, O. G., Jr., & Kagan, J. (1980). Constancy and change: A view of the issues. In O. G. Brim Jr. & J. Kagan (Eds.), *Constancy and change in human development* (pp. 1–25). Cambridge, MA: Harvard University Press.

Brinton, M. C. & Nee, V. (1998). *The new institutionalism*. New York: Russell Sage Foundation.

Brissett-Chapman, S. (1995). Child abuse and neglect: Direct practice. In *Encyclopedia of Social Work* (19th ed.). Washington, DC: NASW Press.

Broberg, A. G., Wessels, H., Lamb, M. E., & Hwang, C. P. (1997). Effects of day care on the development of cognitive abilities in 8-year-olds: A longitudinal study. *Developmental Psychology, 33*, 62–69.

Brock, W. M. (1980). *The effects of day care: A review of the literature* (ERIC Document Ed. 195–348). Los Alamitos, CA: Southwest Regional Laboratory for Educational Research and Development.

Brody, E. M. (1981). "Women in the middle" and family help to older people. *The Gerontologist, 21*, 471–480.

Brody, E. M. (1985). Parent care as a normative family stress. *The Gerontologist, 25*, 19–25.

Brody, G. H. (1998). Sibling relationship quality: Its causes and consequences. *Annual Review of Psychology, 49*, 1–25.

Brody, J. E. (1987, January 21). Guidelines for parents on children's TV viewing. *New York Times*.

Brodzinsky, D. M., & Pinderhughes, E. E. (2002). Parenting and child development in adoptive families. In M. Bornstein (Ed)., *Handbook of Parenting* (2nd ed., Vol. 1, pp. 279–312). Mahwah, NJ: Erlbaum.

Broman, C. (1993). Race differences in marital well-being. *Journal of Marriage and the Family, 55*, 724–732.

Bromberger, J. T., Meyer, P. M., Kravitz, H. M., Sommer, B., Cordal, A., & Powell, L. (2001). Psychologic distress and natural menopause: A multiethnic community study. *American Journal of Public Health, 91*, 1435–1442.

Bromwich, R. (1985, December). Vulnerable infants and risky environments. *Zero to Three*, 7–12.

Bronfenbrenner, U. (1977). Toward an experimental ecology of human development. *American Psychologist, 32*, 513–531.

Bronfenbrenner, U. (1986). Ecology of the family as a context of human development: Research perspectives. *Developmental Psychology, 22*, 723–742.

Bronfenbrenner, U. & Ceci, S. J. (1994). Nature-nurture conceptualized in developmental perspective. A bioecological model. *Psychological Review, 101*, 568–586.

Bronson, W. C. (1985). Developments in behavior with age mates during the second year of life. In M. Lewis & L. A. Rosenblum (Eds.), *The origins of behavior: Friendship and peer relations*. New York: Wiley.

Brooks, C. (2000). Civil rights, liberalism, and the suppression of a Republican political realignment in the United States, 1972 to 1996. *American Sociological Review, 65*, 483–505.

Brooks, D. (2004). *On paradise drive: How we live now (and always have) in the future tense*. New York: Simon & Schuster.

Brooks, G. R. (1998). *A new psychotherapy for traditional men*. San Francisco: Jossey Bass.

Brooks-Gunn, J. (1986). Pubertal processes and girls' psychological adaptation. In R. M. Lerner & T. T. Foch (Eds.), *Biological psychosocial inter-actions in early adolescence: A life-span perspective*. Hillsdale, NJ: Erlbaum.

Brooks-Gunn, J., & Duncan, G. J. (1997). The effects of poverty on children. *The Future of Children, 7*(2), 55–71.

Brooks-Gunn, J., Han, W. J., & Waldgogel, J. (2002). Maternal employment and child cognitive outcomes in the first three years of life: The NICHD study of early child care. *Child Development, 73*, 1052–1072.

Brooks-Gunn, J., & Lewis, M. (1984). The development of early self-recognition. *Developmental Review, 4*, 215–239.

Brooks-Gunn, J., McCormick, M., & Heagarty, L. (1988). Preventing infant mortality and morbidity: Developmental perspectives. *American Journal of Orthopsychiatry, 58*, 288–295.

Brooks-Gunn, J., & Ruble, D. N. (1983). The experience of menarche from a developmental perspective. In J. Brooks-Gunn & A. C. Petersen (Eds.), *Girls at puberty*. New York: Plenum.

Brooks-Gunn, J., & Warren, M. P. (1985). The effects of delayed menarche in different contexts: Dance and nondance students. *Journal of Youth and Adolescence, 14*, 285–300.

Brooks-Gunn, J., & Warren, M. P. (1989, April). *How important are pubertal and social events for different problem behaviors and contexts?* Paper presented at the biennial meeting of the Society for Research in Child Development, Kansas City, MO.

Brothers, L. (1990). The social brain: A project for integrating primate behavior and neurophysiology in a new domain. *Concepts in Neuroscience, 1*, 27–61.

Brotman, S., Ryan, B., & Cormier, R. (2003). The health and social service needs of gay and lesbian elders and their families in Canada. *The Gerontologist, 43*(2), 192–202.

Brower, A. M., & Nurius, P. S. (1993). *Social cognition and individual change*. Newbury Park, CA: Sage.

Brown, B. B. (1990). Peer groups and peer cultures. In S. S. Feldman & G. R. Elliott (Eds.), *At the threshold: The developing adolescent* (pp. 171–196). Cambridge, MA: Harvard University Press.

Brown, B. B., & Mounts, N. (1989, April). *Peer group structures in single versus multi-ethnic high schools*. Paper presented at the biennial meeting of the Society for Research in Child Development, Kansas City, MO.

Brown, C. C. (1976, November). It changed my life. *Psychology Today*, 48–112.

Brown, J. V., Bakeman, R., Coles, C. D., Platzman, K. A., & Lynch, M. E. (2004). Prenatal cocaine exposure: A comparison of 2-year-old children in parental and nonparental care. *Child Development, 75*, 1282–1295.

Brown, L. M., & Gilligan, C. (1992). *Meeting at the crossroads*. New York: Ballantine.

Brown, L. N. (1991). *Groups for growth and change*. New York: Longman.

Brown, M. A., & Woods, N. F. (1986). Sex role orientation, sex typing, occupational traditionalism, and premenstrual symptoms. In V. L. Olesen & N. F. Woods (Eds.), *Culture, society, and menstruation*. Washington, DC: Hemisphere.

Brown, P., & Elliott, R. (1965). Control of aggression in a nursery school class. *Journal of Experimental Child Psychology, 2*, 103–107.

Brown, R. (1958). *Words and things*. Glencoe, IL: Free Press.

Brown, R. (1988). *Group processes: Dynamics within and between groups*. New York: Blackwell.

Brown, R. H. (1994). Reconstructing social theory after the postmodern critique. In H. W. Simons & M. Billig (Eds.), *After postmodernism: Reconstructing ideology critique*. London: Sage.

Browne, A. (1987). *When battered women kill*. New York: Free Press.

Browne, C. V. (1998). *Women, feminism, and aging*. New York: Springer.

Brownell, P., & Wolden, A. (2002). Elder abuse intervention strategies:

Social service or criminal justice? *Journal of Gerontological Social Work, 40*(1/2), 83–100.
Brownlee, S., McGraw, D., & Vest, J. (1997, June 16). The place for vengeance. *U.S. News and World Report,* 25–32.
Brubaker, T. H. (1985). *Later life families.* Newbury Park, CA: Sage.
Bruckner-Gordon, F., Gangi, B. K., & Wallman, G. U. (1988). *Making therapy work: Your guide to choosing, using, and ending therapy.* New York: HarperCollins.
Bryant, S., & Demian. (1990, May/June). When lesbian and gay couples break up. *Partners Newsletter for Gay and Lesbian Couples.*
Budwig, N. (2003). The role of language in human development. In J. Valsiner & K. Connolly (Eds.), *Handbook of developmental psychology* (pp. 217–237). Thousand Oaks, CA: Sage.
Buehler, C. A., Hogan, M. J., Robinson, B. E., & Levy, R. J. (1985). The parental divorce transition: Divorce-related stressors and well-being. *Journal of Divorce, 9,* 61–81.
Buehlman, K. T., Gottman, J. M., & Katz, L. F. (1992). How a couple views their past predicts their future: Predicting divorce from an oral history interview. *Journal of Family Psychology, 5,* 295–318.
Bufe, C. (1987, November). AA: Guilt and God for the gullible. *The Match! An Anarchist Journal.* Excerpted in *Utne Reader* (1988, November/December), 54–55.
Bukowski, W. M. (1998). *The company they keep: Friendships in childhood and adolescence.* New York: Cambridge University Press.
Bullock, B. L., & Rosendahl, P. P. (1988). *Pathophysiology: Adaptations and alterations in function* (2nd ed.). Glenview, IL: Scott, Foresman.
Bullock, L. F., & McFarlane, J. (1989). The birth-weight/battering connection. *American Journal of Nursing, 89,* 1153–1155.
Burdman, G. M. (1986). *Healthful aging.* Englewood Cliffs, NJ: Prentice Hall.
Burgess, A. W., & Holmstromm, L. L. (1985). Rape trauma syndrome and post traumatic stress response. In A. W. Burgess (Ed.), *Rape and sexual assault: A research handbook* (pp. 46–60). New York: Garland.
Burr, J. A., & Mutchler, J. E. (2003). English language skills, ethnic concentration, and household composition: Older Mexican immigrants. *The Journals of Gerontology Series B, 58,* S83–S92.
Burton, L. (1990). Teenage childbearing as an alternative life-course strategy in multigenerational black families. *Human Nature, 2,* 123–143.
Buss, D. M. (1999). *Evolutionary Psychology.* Boston: Allyn & Bacon.
Buss, D. M., & Kenrick, D. T. (1998). Evolutionary social psychology. In D. T. Gilbert, S. T. Kiske, & G. Lindzey (Eds.), *Handbook of Social Psychology* (pp. 982–1026). Boston: McGraw-Hill.
Busse, E. W., & Pfeiffer, E. (1977). *Behavior and adaptation in late life.* Boston: Little, Brown.
Butler, K. (1995, March/April). Caught in the crossfire. *Family Therapy Networker,* 25–29.
Butler, R. M. (1970). *Social functioning framework: An approach to the human behavior and social environment sequence.* New York: Council on Social Work Education.
Butler, R. N. (1963). The life review: An interpretation of reminiscence in the aged. *Psychiatry, 26,* 65–76.
Butler, R. N. (1975). *Why survive? Being old in America.* New York: Harper & Row.
Butler, R. N. (1990). A disease called ageism. *Journal of the American Geriatric Association, 38,* 178–180.
Butler, R. N., Lewis, M., & Sunderland, T. (1991). *Aging and mental health: Positive psychosocial and biomedical approaches* (4th ed.). New York: Macmillan.
Butler, R. N., Lewis, M., & Sunderland, T. (1998). *Aging and mental health* (5th ed.). New York: Macmillan.
Byrne, B. (1998). *The foundation of literacy.* New York: Psychology Press.
Cahill, S., South, K., & Spade, J. (2000). *Outing age: Public policy issues affecting gay, lesbian, bisexual, and transgender elders.* Policy Institute of the National Gay and Lesbian Task Force Foundation. New York.
Cairns, R. B., Cairns, B. D., Neckerman, H. J., Ferguson, L. L., & Gariepy, J. L. (1989). Growth and aggression: Childhood to adolescence. *Developmental Psychology, 25,* 320–330.
Caldwell, B., & Bradley, R. (1984). *Home observation for measurement of the environment.* Little Rock: University of Arkansas Press.
Call, J. D. (1964). Newborn approach behavior and early ego development. *International Journal of Psychoanalysis, 45,* 286.
Calvert, S., & Calvert, P. (1992). *Sociology today.* London: Harvester/Wheatsheaf.
Calvert, S. L., & Jordan, A. B. (2001). Children in the digital age. [Special issue.] *Journal of Applied Developmental Psychology, 22*(1).
Cameron, K., & Richardson, A. (2000). A guide to medication and aging. *Generations: Quarterly Journal of the American Society on Aging, 14*(4), 8–21.
Camp, B. W., Blom, G. E., Herbert, F., & Van Doorninck, W. J. (1977). "Think aloud": A program for developing self-control in young aggressive boys. *Journal of Abnormal Psychology, 5,* 167–169.
Campbell, E. (1985). *The childless marriage: An exploratory study of couples who do not want children.* New York: Tavistock.
Campbell, F. A., & Ramey, C. T. (1994). Effects of early intervention on intellectual and academic achievement: A follow-up study of children from low-income families. *Child Development, 65,* 684–698.
Campbell, J., with Moyers, B. (1988). *The power of myth.* New York: Doubleday.
Campbell, S. B., Cummings, E. M., & Davies, P. T. (2002). *Developmental psychopathology and family process: Treatment, research and clinical implications.* New York: Guilford Press.
Cancer Rates. (1998). U. S. Cancer rates declining. *CNN Interactive,* retrieved March 13, 1998, from http://www.cnn.com/
Canda, E. R. (1989). Religious content in social work education: A comparative approach. *Journal of Social Work Education, 25*(1), 36–45.
Candace (2003): Physical pain of cutting "relieves" mental pain of depression. Retrieved November 11, 2003 from http://www.depressedchild.org/candace.htm
Cantor, M. H. (1979). Neighbors and friends: An overlooked resource in the informal support system. *Research on Aging, 1,* 434–463.
Cantor, M. H. (1983). Strain among caregivers: A study of the experience in the United States. *The Gerontologist, 23,* 597–604.
Cantwell, D. P. (1982). Childhood depression: A review of current research. In B. B. Lahey & A. E. Kazdin (Eds.), *Advances in child clinical psychology.* New York: Plenum.
Caplan, G. (1974). *Support systems and community mental health.* New York: Behavioral Publications.
Caplan, R. (1993). Alcoholism. *Grolier Electronic Encyclopedia.*
Carey, S. (1977). The child as word learner. In M. Halle, J. Bresman, & G. A. Miller (Eds.), *Linguistic theory and psychological reality.* Cambridge, MA: MIT Press.
Carlip, H. (1995). *Girl power: Young women speak out.* New York: Warner Books.
Carnegie Council on Adolescent Development (1989). *Turning points: Preparing youth for the 21st century.* New York: Carnegie Corporation.
Carney, J., Werth, J. L., & Emanuelson, G. (1994). The relationship between attitudes toward persons who are gay and persons with AIDS, and HIV and AIDS knowledge. *Journal of Counseling and Development, 72,* 646–659.
Caroll, D. W. (2004). *Psychology of Language* (4th edition). Belmont, CA: Wadsworth/Thomson.
Carr, D., House, J., Kessler, R., Nesse, R., Sonnega, J., & Wortman, C. (2000). Marital quality and psychological adjustment to widowhood among older adults: A longitudinal analysis. *Journal of Gerontology, 55B*(4), S197–S207.
Carskadon, M. A. (Ed.) (2002). *Adolescent sleep patterns: Biological, social, and psychological influences.* Cambridge, UK: Cambridge University Press.
Carskadon, M. A. (2004). Sleep. Retrieved October 12, 2004, from http://sleepfoundation.org
Carstensen, L. (1992). Social and emotional patterns in adulthood. *Psychology and Aging, 7,* 331–386.
Carstensen, L., Pasupathi, M., & Mayr, U. (2000). Emotional experience in everyday life across the adult life span. *Journal of Personality and Social Psychology, 79,* 644–655.
Carter, B., & McGoldrick, M. (1988). *The changing family life cycle: A framework for family therapy* (2nd ed.). New York: Gardner.
Cartwright, D. (1968). The nature of group cohesiveness. In D. Cartwright & A. Zander (Eds.), *Group dynamics: Research and theory* (3rd ed.). New York: Harper & Row.
Cartwright, D., & Zander, A. (1968). Motivational processes in groups: Introduction. In D. Cartwright & A. Zander (Eds.). *Group dynamics* (3rd ed.). New York: Harper & Row.
Caspi, A., Elder, G. H., & Bem, D. J. (1987). Moving against the world: Life-course patterns of explosive children. *Developmental Psychology, 23,* 308–313.
Cassell, C. (1984). *Swept away: Why women fear their own sexuality.* New York: Simon & Schuster.
Castells, M. (2002). *The power of identity.* Padstow, Cornwall, UK: Blackwell.
Cattanach, L., & Tebes, J. K. (1991). The nature of elder impairment and its impact on family caregivers' health and psychosocial functioning. *The Gerontologist, 31,* 246–255.

Cavanaugh, J. C. (1990). *Adult development and aging*. Belmont, CA: Wadsworth.

Cavanaugh, J. C. (1997). *Adult development and aging* (3rd ed.). Pacific Grove, CA: Brooks/Cole.

Center for Lesbian and Gay Rights (2004). Retrieved November 23, 2004, from www.center4civilrights.org

Centers for Disease Control and Prevention (2001). The global HIV and AIDS epidemic, 2001. *Morbidity and Mortality Weekly Report, 50,* 434–439.

Centers for Disease Control and Prevention (2001). *Healthy aging: Preventing disease and improving quality of life among older Americans.* Atlanta: Department of Health and Human Services.

Centers for Disease Control and Prevention (2004). *Suicide fact sheet.* Retrieved July 12, 2004, from http://www.cdc.gov/ncipc/factsheets/suifacts.htm

Chaikin, A. E., Sigler, E., & Derlega, V. (1974). Non-verbal mediators of teacher expectancy effects. *Journal of Personality and Social Psychology, 30,* 144–149.

Chamberlain, David B. (1994). The sentient prenate: What every parent should know. *Pre- and Perinatal Psychology Journal, 9*(1), 9–31.

Chamberlain, David B. (1998). Prenatal receptivity and intelligence. *Journal of Prenatal and Perinatal Psychology and Health 12*(3 and 4), 95–117.

Chamberlain, P., & Patterson, G. R. (1985). Aggressive behavior in middle childhood. In D. Shaffer, A. A. Ehrhardt, & L. L. Greenhill (Eds.), *The clinical guide to child psychiatry.* New York: Free Press.

Chamberlin, J. (2000). Easing children's psychological distress in the emergency room. *APA Monitor* (June), 40–41.

Chambers, C. (2002). All must have prizes: The liberal case for interference in cultural practices. In P. Kelly (Eds.), *Multiculturalism reconsidered: Culture and equality and its critics* (pp. 151–173). Cambridge, UK: Polity Press.

Chambliss, L. (1994, Fall). Domestic violence—What is the health care provider's responsibility? *Samaritan AirEvac News for Physicians and Managers,* 1–3.

Chandler, M. J., Sokol, B. W., & Wainryb, C. (2000). Beliefs about truth and beliefs about rightness. *Child Development, 71,* 91–97.

Chapkis, W. (1986). *Beauty secrets: Women and the politics of appearance.* Boston: South End Press.

Chapman, J., Siegel, E., & Cross, A. (1990). Home visitors and child health: Analysis of selected programs. *Pediatrics, 85,* 1059–1068.

Charness, N., & Bosman, E. A. (1992). Human factors in aging. In F. I. M. Craik & T. A. Salthouse (Eds.), *The handbook of aging and cognition.* Hillsdale, NJ: Erlbaum.

Chase, S. N., & Clement, P. W. (1985). Effects of self-reinforcement and stimulants on academic performance in children with attention deficit disorder. *Journal of Clinical Child Psychology, 14,* 323–333.

Chase-Lansdale, P. L. (1981). Maternal employment and quality of infant-mother and infant-father attachment (Doctoral dissertation, University of Michigan). *Dissertation Abstracts International, 42,* 2562B.

Chase-Lansdale, P. L., & Owen, M. (1987). Maternal employment in a family context: Effects on infant-mother and infant-father attachments. *Child Development, 58,* 1505–1512.

Chau, A. (2004). *A world on fire: How exporting free market democracy breeds ethnic hatred and global instability.* New York: Anchor Books.

Cheng, T. L., Savageau, J. A., Sattler, A. L., & DeWitt, T. G. (1993). Confidentiality in health care: A survey of knowledge, perceptions, and attitudes among high school students. Journal of the American Medical Association, 269, 1404–1407.

Cherlin, A., & Furstenberg, F. F. (1986). *The new American grandparent.* New York: Basic Books.

Cherry, F., & Deaux, K. (1978). Fear of success versus fear of gender-inappropriate behavior. *Sex Roles, 4,* 97–102.

Chestang, L. (1980). Character development in a hostile environment. In M. Bloom (Ed.), *Life span development.* New York: Macmillan.

Chilman, C. (1979). *Adolescent sexuality in a changing American society: Social and psychological perspectives.* Washington, DC: Public Health Service, National Institutes of Mental Health.

Cho, S. A., Freeman, E. M., & Patterson, S. L. (1982). Adolescents' experience with death: Practice implications. *Social Casework, 63,* 88–94.

Chobanian, A., Bakris, G., Black, H., Cushman, W., & Green, L. (2003). Seventh report of the Joint National Committee on prevention, detection, evaluation, and treatment of high blood pressure. *Hypertension, 42*(6), 1206–1252.

Chow, J., Jaffee, K., & Snowden, L. (2003). Racial/ethnic disparities in mental health use in poverty areas. *American Journal of Public Health, 93,* 792–797.

Christakis, D. A., Zimmerman, F. J., DiGiuseppe, D. L., & McCarty, C. A. (2004). Early television exposure and subsequent attention problems in children. *Pediatrics, 113,* 708–713.

Christensen, A., & Jacobson, N. S. (2000). *Reconcilable differences.* New York: Guilford Press.

Christophersen, E. R., & Mortweet, S. L. (2001). *Treatments that work with children: Empirically supported strategies for managing childhood problems.* Washington, DC: American Psychological Association.

Chu, C. E., Cooke, A., Stephenson, J. B., & Tolmie, P. (1994). Diagnosis in Prader-Willi syndrome. *Archives of Disease in Childhood, 71,* 441–442.

Cicchetti, D., & Schneider-Rosen, K. (1986). An organizational approach to childhood depression. In M. Rutter, C. Izard, & P. B. Read (Eds.), *Depression in young people: Developmental and clinical perspectives.* New York: Guilford Press.

Cicchetti, D., Lynch, M., & Manly, J. T. (1997). *An ecological developmental perspective on the consequences of child maltreatment.* Washington, DC: U.S. Department of Health and Human Services, National Center on Child Abuse and Neglect.

Cicchetti, D., & Wagner, S. (1990). Alternative assessment strategies for the evaluation of infants and toddlers: An organizational perspective. In S. J. Meisels and J. P. Shonkoff (Eds.), *Handbook of early childhood intervention* (pp. 246–277). New York: Cambridge University Press.

Cicirelli, V. G. (1983). Adult children and their elderly parents. In T. Brubaker (Ed.), *Family relationships in later life.* Beverly Hills, CA: Sage.

Cillessen, A. H. N., Bukowski, W. M., & Haselager, G. J. T. (2000). Stability of sociometric categories. In Cillessen, A. H. N., & Bukowski, W. M. (Eds.), *Recent advances in the measurement of acceptance and rejection in the peer system. New Directions for Child and Adolescent Development* (pp. 75–94). San Francisco: Jossey-Bass.

Cintas, H. (1988). Cross-cultural variation in infant motor development. *Physical & Occupational Therapy in Pediatrics, 8,* 1–20.

Clark, K. B., & Clark, M. K. (1939). The development of consciousness of self and emergence of racial identification in Negro preschool children. In R. Wilcox (Ed.), *The psychological consequences of being a black American: A sourcebook of research by black psychologists.* New York: Wiley.

Clark, K., Shute, N., & Kelly, K. (2000). The new midlife. *USNews & World Report, 128,* 70–82.

Clarkberg, M., & Merola, S. S. (2003). Competing clocks: Work and leisure. In P. Moen (Ed.), *It's about time: Couples and careers* (pp. 35–48). Ithaca, NY: Cornell University Press.

Clarke-Stewart, K. A. (1978). And daddy makes three: The father's impact on mother and young child. *Child Development, 49,* 466–478.

Clarke-Stewart, K. A. (1989). Infant day care: Maligned or malignant? *American Psychologist, 44,* 266–273.

Clarke-Stewart, K. A. (1991). A home is not a school: The effects of environments on development. In M. Lewis & S. Feinman (Eds.), *Social influences and socialization in infancy* (pp. 41–61). New York: Plenum.

Clarke-Stewart, K. A., & Fein, G. G. (1983). Early childhood programs. In P. H. Mussen (Ed.), *Handbook of child psychology* (4th ed., Vol. 2). New York: Wiley.

Clasen, D. R., & Brown, B. B. (1987). Understanding peer pressure in middle school. *Middle School Journal, 19,* 21–23.

Cleek, M., & Pearson, T. (1985). Perceived cause of divorce: An analysis of interrelationships. *Journal of Marriage and the Family, 47,* 179–183.

Clinton, T., Greenleaf, I., & Harrison, J. L. (2000). *Attention to detail: A teen's guide to appearance and conduct.* New York: Teen Guide Fund.

Clorfene-Costen, L. (1993, May/June). The environmental link to breast cancer. *Ms.,* 52–56.

Coard, S. I., Nitz, K., & Felice, M. E. (2000). Repeat pregnancy among urban adolescents: Sociodemographic, family, and health factors. *Adolesence, 35,* 193–201.

Coco, A. S. (1999). Primary Dysmenorrhea. *American Family Physician, 60,* 489–496.

Coe, C. L., & Lubach, G. R. (2001). Social context and other psychological influences on the development of immunity. In C. D. Ryff & B. H. Singer (Eds.), *Emotion, social relationships, and health* (pp. 243–261). Oxford, England: Oxford University Press.

Cohen, D. (1983). *Piaget: Critique and reassessment.* London: Croom Helm.

Cohen, D. (1988). Social work and psychotropic drug treatments. *Social Services Review 62*(4), 576–599.

Cohen, G., Yeast, J., & Hu, D. (1994). Epidural analgesia in labor and cesarean delivery for dystocia. *Obstetrical & Gynecological Survey, 49,* 362–369.

Cohen, N. J. (2001). *Language impairment and psychopathology in infants, children and adolescents.* Thousand Oaks, CA: Sage.

Cohen, S. (1982). Arthritis—But what sort? *Geriatrics, 37*, 49–51.

Cohen, S. (2001). Social relationships and susceptibility to common cold. In C. D. Ryff & B. H. Singer (Eds.), *Emotion, social relationships, and health* (pp. 221–233). New York: Oxford University Press.

Cohen, S., & Strauss, M. (1979). Concept acquisition in the human infant. *Child Development, 50*, 767–776.

Coie, J. D., & Dodge, K. A. (1998). Aggression and antisocial behavior. In N. Eisenberg (Ed.), *Handbook of child psychology* (pp. 779–862). New York: Wiley.

Coleman, J. S. (1980). The peer group. In J. Adelson (Ed.), *Handbook of adolescent psychology* (408–431). New York: Wiley.

Coleman, J. S., Campbell, E., Hobson, C., McPartland, J., Mood, A., Weinfield, F., et al. (1966). *Equality of educational opportunity*. Washington, DC: U.S. Government Printing Office.

Coles, R. (1986). *The political life of children*. Boston: Little, Brown.

Coley, R. (2002). *An uneven start*. Princeton, NJ: Educational Testing Service.

Coll, C., & Meyer, E. (1993). The sociocultural context of infant development. In C. Zeaneh (Ed.), *Handbook of infant mental health* (pp. 56–69). New York: Guilford Press.

Colletti, L. (1979). Relationship between pregnancy and birth complications and the later development of learning disabilities. *Journal of Learning Disabilities, 12*, 659–663.

Collins, A. H., & Pancoast, D. L. (1976). *Natural helping networks*. Washington, DC: National Association of Social Workers.

Comas-Diaz, L., & Greene, B. (1994). Overview: An ethnocultural mosaic. In L. Comas-Diaz & B. Greene (Eds.), *Women of color: Integrating ethnic and gender identities in psychotherapy*. New York: Guilford Press.

Combs, M. L., & Slaby, D. A. (1977). Social skills training with children. In B. B. Lahey & A. E. Kazdin (Eds.), *Advances in clinical child psychology*. New York: Plenum.

Comer, J. (1993). *School power* (rev. ed.). New York: Free Press.

Committee on Economic Development. (1987). *Children in need: Investment strategies for the educationally disadvantaged*. Washington, DC: Committee for Economic Development.

Compas, B. F. (1995). Promoting successful coping during adolescence. In W. M. Rutter (Ed.), *Psychological disturbances in young people* (pp. 247–273). New York: Cambridge University Press.

Condon, W. (1975). Speech makes babies move. In R. Lewin (Ed.), *Child alive!* (pp. 75–85). Garden City, NY: Anchor Books.

Condry, J. C. (1989). *The psychology of television*. Hillsdale, NJ: Erlbaum.

Conger, R., Elder, G., Lorenz, F., Conger, K., Simons, R., Whitbeck, L., et al. (1990). Linking economic hardship to marital quality and instability. *Journal of Marriage and the Family, 52*, 643–656.

Connell, S. (1987). Homelessness. In *Encyclopedia of social work* (pp. 789–795). Silver Spring, MD: National Association of Social Workers.

Conner, K. A. (2000). *Continuing to care: Older Americans and their families*. New York: Falmer Press.

Conners, K. (1989). Conners' Teacher Rating Scale—39-item version (*CTRS–39*). North Tonawanda, NY: Multi-Health Systems.

Connidis, I., & McMullin, J. (2002). Sociological ambivalence and family trees: A critical perspective. *Journal of Marriage and the Family, 64*, 558–567.

Connolly, M., & McKenzie, M. (1999). *Effective participatory practice: Family group conferencing in child protection*. New York: Aldine de Gruyter.

Consortium for Longitudinal Studies. (1983). *As the twig is bent*. Hillsdale, NJ: Erlbaum.

Constable, B. (1983). The individualized educational program: Content, process, and the social worker's role. In B. Constable & J. Flynn (Eds.), *School social work: Practice and research perspectives*. Pacific Grove, CA: Brooks/Cole.

Constable, R. (2002). The role of the school social worker: History and theory. In R. Constable, S. McDonald, & J. F. Flynn (Eds.), *School social work: Practice, policy and research perspectives* (5th ed). Chicago: Lyceum Press.

Conterio, K., & Lader, W. (1998). *Body harm*. New York: Hyperion.

Cook, S. W. (1979). Social science and school desegregation: Did we mislead the Supreme Court? *Personality and Social Psychology, 5*, 418–428.

Cooke, T., & Apolloni, T. (1976). Developing positive social-emotional behaviors: A study of training and generalization effects. *Journal of Applied Behavior Analysis, 9*, 65–78.

Cool, L. E. (1987). The effects of social class and ethnicity on the aging process. In P. Silverman (Ed.), *The elderly as modern pioneers* (pp. 211–227). Bloomington: Indiana University Press.

Cooley, C. H. (1902). *Human nature and the social order*. New York: Scribner's.

Cooley, C. H. (1908). A study of the early use of self words by a child. *Psychological Review, 15*, 339–357.

Cooper, C. R., & Grotevant, H. D. (1989, April). *Individuality and connectedness in the family and adolescents' self and relational competence*. Paper presented at the biennial meeting of the Society for Research in Child Development, Kansas City, MO.

Cooper, J. (2004). Dissonance theory: History and progress. In R. A. Wright, J. Greenberg, & S. S. Brehm (Eds.), *Motivational analyses of social behavior* (pp. 19–37). Mahwah, NJ: Erlbaum.

Corah, N., Anthony, E., Painter, P., Stern, J., & Thurston, D. (1965). Effects of perinatal anoxia after seven years. *Psychological Monographs, 79*, 3.

Corcoran, J., Franklin, C., & Bennett, P. (2000). Ecological factors associated with adolescent pregnancy and parenting. *Social Work Research, 24*, 29–39.

Coren, S., & Searleman, A. (1985). Birth stress and self-reported sleep difficulty. *Sleep, 8*, 222–226.

Corner, L., & Bond, J. (2004). Being at risk of dementia: Fears and anxieties of older adults. *Journal of Aging Studies, 18*, 143–155.

Corrigan, P. W., & Penn, D. L. (2001). Introduction: Framing models of Social Cognition in Schizophrenia. In P. W. Corrigan & D. L. Penn (Eds.), *Social Cognition and Schizophrenia* (pp. 3–37). Washington, DC: American Psychological Association.

Costa, P., Metter, E., & McCrae, R. (1994). Personality stability and its contribution to successful aging. *Journal of Geriatric Psychiatry, 27*, 41–59.

Costin, L., Bell, C., & Downs, S. (1991). *Child welfare: Policies and practices*. New York: Longman.

Cote, J. E. (2000). *Arrested adulthood: The changing nature of identity and maturity in the late-modern world*. New York: New York University Press.

Cote, J. E., & Levine, C. (1988). A critical examination of the ego identity status paradigm. *Developmental Review, 8*, 147–184.

Cotterrell, R. (1984). *The sociology of law: An introduction*. London: Butterworths.

Council on Social Work Education. (1990). *Psychopharmacology in social work education*. Alexandria, VA: Author.

Council on Social Work Education. (2001). *Strengthening the impact of social work to improve the quality of life for older adults and their families*. A Project of the Council on Social Work Education/Sage-SW, funded by the John A. Hartford Foundation of New York City.

Courtney, M. E., & Barth, R. P. (1996). Pathways of older adolescents out of foster care: Implications for independent living services. *Social Work, 41*(1), 75–83.

Cowan, C. P., & Cowan, P. A. (2000). Working with couples during stressful transitions. In S. Dreman (Ed.), *The family on the threshold of the 21st century* (pp. 17–47). Mahwah, NJ: Erlbaum.

Cowen, E. L., Pederson, A., Babigan, H., Izzo, L. D., & Trost, M. A. (1973). Long-term follow-up of early detected vulnerable children. *Journal of Consulting and Clinical Psychology, 41*, 438–446.

Coyle, J. T. (2000). Psychotropic drug use in very young children. *Journal of the American Medical Association, 283*, 1156.

Crawford, N. (2002). New ways to stop bullying. *Monitor on Psychology, 33*, p. 64.

Crawford, N. (2003, October). A matter of life and death. *APA Monitor*, 84–85.

Creno, C. (1994, April 19). Bonding before birth: Child's mental health begins at conception, small-but-growing group insists. *The Arizona Republic*, p. E1.

Crnic, K. (1984). Maternal stress and social support: Effects on the mother-infant relationship from birth to eighteen months. *American Journal of Orthopsychiatry, 54*, 224–235.

Crnic, K., & Greenberg, M. (1990). Minor parenting stresses with young children. *Child Development, 61*, 1628–1637.

Crnic, K., & Harris, V. (1990). Normal development in infancy and early childhood. In J. Johnson & J. Goldman (Eds.), *Developmental assessment in clinical child psychology* (pp. 15–33). New York: Pergamon Press.

Crockenberg, S. (1981). Infant irritability, mother responsiveness, and social influences on the security of infant-mother attachment. *Child Development, 52*, 857–865.

Crockenberg, S., Lyons-Ruth, K., & Dickstein, S. (1993). The family contest of infant mental health: II. Infant development in multiple family relationships. In C. Zeanah (Ed.), *Handbook of infant mental health* (pp. 38–55). New York: Guilford Press.

Crohan, S. E., & Antonucci, T. C. (1989). Friends as a source of social support in old age. In R. G. Adams & R. Blieszner (Eds.), *Older adult friendships*. Newbury Park, CA: Sage.

Cronin, M., & Gorman, C. (1991). Should we take away their kids? *Time, 137*(19), 62–63.

Cronin, M., Ludtke, M., & Willwerth, J. (1991). Innocent victims. *Time, 137*(19), 56–60.

Crowther, M., Parker, M., Achenbaum, W., Larimore, W., & Koenig, H. (2002). Rowe and Kahn's model of successful aging revisited: Positive spirituality—the forgotten factor. *The Gerontologist, 42*(5), 613–620.

Csikszentmihalyi, M., & Larson, R. (1984). *Being adolescent*. New York: Basic Books.

Csoti, M. (2003). *School phobia, panic attacks and anxiety in children*. London: Jessica Kingsley.

Cuellar, J. (1980). *Minority elderly Americans: A prototype for area agencies on aging*. San Diego, CA: Allied Home Health Association.

Culbertson, J., & Gyurke, J. (1990). Assessment of cognitive and motor development in infancy and childhood. In J. Johnson & J. Goldman (Eds.), *Developmental assessment in clinical child psychology* (pp. 100–131). New York: Pergamon Press.

Cumming, E., & Henry, W. E. (1961). *Growing old: The process of disengagement*. New York: Basic Books.

Cummings, E. M. (1987). Coping with background anger in early childhood. *Child Development, 58*, 976–984.

Cummins, J., & Swain, M. (1986). *Bilingualism in education: Aspects of theory, research and practice*. London: Taylor & Fry.

Cunningham, A. J., Edmonds, C. V. I., Jenkins, G. P., Pollack, H., Lockwood, G. A., Warr, D. (1998). A randomized controlled trial of the effects of group psychological therapy on survival in women with metastatic breast cancer. *Psycho-Oncology, 7*, 508–517.

Curran, D. D. (1985). *Stress and the healthy family*. Minneapolis, MN: Winston Press.

Cutler, N. (2001). *The NCOA healthy sexuality and vital aging study*. Paper presented at the Gerontological Society of America, Chicago.

Dahl, R., & Lewin, D. S. (2002). Pathways to adolescent health: Sleep regulation and behavior. *Journal of Adolescent Health, 31*, 175–184.

Dalton, J. H., Elias, M. J., Wandersman, A. (2001). *Community psychology: Linking individuals and communities*. Belmont, CA: Wadsworth/Thompson.

Damon, W. (1995, May). Is self-esteem really all that important? *APA Monitor*, 6.

Dan, A., & Bernhard, L. (1989). Menopause and other health issues for midlife. In S. Hunter & M. Sundel (Eds.), *Midlife myths: Issues, findings and practice implications* (pp. 201–217). Newbury Park, CA: Sage.

Dangel, R. F., & Polster, R. A. (1988). *Teaching child management skills*. Elmsford, NY: Pergamon Press.

Daniel, W. A. (1983). Pubertal changes in adolescence. In J. Brooks-Gunn & A. C. Petersen (Eds.), *Girls at puberty*. New York: Plenum.

Daniels, K. (1993). Infertility counselling: The need for a psychosocial perspective. *British Journal of Social Work, 23*, 501–512.

Danziger, K. (1997). The historical formation of selves. In R. D. Ashmore & L. Jussim (Eds.), *Self and identity: Fundamental issues* (pp. 137–159). New York: Oxford University Press.

Danziger, S. K., & Radin, N. (1989, April). *Absent does not equal uninvolved: Predictors of fathering in teen mother families*. Paper presented at the biennial meeting of the Society for Research in Child Development, Kansas City, MO.

Daro, D. (1991). Child sexual abuse prevention: Separating fact from fiction. *Child Abuse & Neglect, 15*, 1–4.

Darwin C. (1859/1958). *The origin of species by means of natural selection or the preservation of favored races in the struggle for life*. New York: New American Library (Mentor Books).

Darwin, C. (1872). *The expression of emotions in man and animals*. New York: Philosophical Library.

Darwin, C. (1899). *Origins of species*. London: John Murray.

Das, J. P. (1984). Intelligence and information integration. In J. Kirby (Ed.), *Theory and research in learning disabilities*. New York: Plenum.

Daugherty, J. (1998). Treatment strategies for premenstrual syndrome. American Family Physician, July 1998. Retrieved September 7, 2004, from http://www.aafp.org/afp/980700ap/daughert.html

Davenport, J. A., & Davenport, III, J. (1995). Rural social work overview. In *Encyclopedia of social work* (19th ed., pp. 2076–2085). Washington, DC: NASW Press.

Davidson, E. (1992). Racial disparity in infant mortality. *New England Journal of Medicine, 327*, 1022–1023.

Davidson, K. (2001). Late life widowhood, selfishness and new partnership choices: A gendered perspective. *Ageing & Society, 21*(3), 297–317.

Davidson, M., & Jamison, P. W. (1983). The clinical social worker and current psychiatric drugs: Some introductory principles. *Clinical Social Work Journal, 71*, 134–150.

Davies, D. (2004). *Child development: A practitioner's guide* (2nd ed.). New York: Guilford Press.

Davies, G. M., & Dalgleish, T. (2002). *Recovered memory: Seeking the middle ground*. New York: John Wiley.

Davis, H., & Rockwood, K. (2004). Conceptualization of mild cognitive impairment: A review. *International Journal of Geriatric Psychiatry, 19*, 313–319.

Davis, I. P., Landsverk, J., Newton, R., & Ganger, W. (1996). Parental visiting and foster care reunification. *Children and Youth Services Review, 18*, 363–382.

Davis, K., Grant, P., & Rowland, D. (1990). Alone and poor: The plight of elderly women. *Generations, 14*, 43–47.

Davis, K. L., Kahn, R. S., Ko, G., & Davidson, M. (1991). Dopamine in schizophrenia: A review and reconceptualization. *American Journal of Psychiatry, 148*, 1474–1486.

Davis, L. (1989). The myths of menopause. In L. Fenson & J. Fenson (Eds.), *Human development 90/91* (pp. 237–241). Guilford, CT: Dushkin Publishing Group.

Dawson, G., & Glaubman, R. (2001). *Life is so good*. New York: Penguin.

de Anda, D. (1984). Bicultural socialization: Factors affecting minority experience. *Social Work, 29*, 172–181.

de Anda, D. (2004). Personal communication. July 15, 2004.

DeAngelis, T. (1995, January). How adoptees fare. *APA Monitor, 23*–24.

DeAngelis, T. (1997b, November). Menopause symptoms vary among ethnic groups. *APA Monitor*, 16–17.

DeAngelis, T. (2001, May). Punishment of innocents: Children of parents behind bars. *Monitor on Psychology*, 56–59.

DeAngelis, T. (2002, February). A new generation of issues for LGBT clients. *Monitor on Psychology, 33*, 42–44.

Deaux, K., Dane, F. C., & Wrightsman, L. S. (1993). *Social psychology in the 90s*. Pacific Grove, CA: Brooks/Cole.

DeCasper, A. J., & Fifer, W. P. (1980). Of human bonding: Newborns prefer their mothers' voices. *Science, 208*, 1174–1176.

DeGangi, G. (2000). *Pediatric disorders of regulation in affect and behavior: A therapist's guide to assessment and treatment*. New York: Academic Press.

DeiCampo, D. S., & DeiCampo, R. L. (2000). *Taking sides: Clashing views on controversial issues in childhood and society* (3rd ed.). Guilford, CT: Dushkin/McGraw-Hill.

Demmo, D. H. (1992). Parent-child relations: Assessing recent changes. *Journal of Marriage and the Family, 54*, 104–117.

Demmo, D. H., & Acock, A. C. (1988). The impact of divorce on children. *Journal of Marriage and the Family, 50*, 619–648.

Demo, D. H., & Cox, M. J. (2000). Families with young children: A review of research in the 1990s. *Journal of Marriage and the Family, 62*, 876–895.

Dempster, F. N. (1981). Memory span: Sources of individual and developmental differences. *Psychological Bulletin, 89*, 63–100.

Denham, S., Salisch, M. V., Olthof, T., Kochanoff, A., & Caverly, S. (2002). Emotional and social development in childhood. In P. K. Smith & C. H. Hart (eds.), *Blackwell handbook of childhood social development* (pp. 307–328). Malden, MA: Blackwell.

Denisoff, R. S., & Wahrman, R. (1979). *An introduction to sociology* (2nd ed.). New York: Macmillan.

Dennis, W. (1960). Causes of retardation among institutional children: Iran. *Journal of Genetic Psychology, 96*, 47–59.

Dennis, W. (1973). *Children of the creche*. East Norwalk, CT: Appleton-Century-Crofts.

Dennis, W., & Dennis, J. (1940). The effect of cradling practices upon the onset of walking in Hopi children. *Journal of Genetic Psychology, 56*, 77–86.

Depner, C. E., & Ingersol-Dayton, B. (1985). Conjugal social support: Patterns in later life. *Journal of Gerontology, 40*, 761–766.

Dettwyler, K. (1989). Styles of infant feeding: Parental/caretaker control of food consumption in young children. *Research Reports, 91*, 696–703.

Devaney, B. L., Ellwod, M. R., & Love, J. M. (1997). Programs that mitigate the effects of poverty on children. *The Future of Children: Children and Poverty, 7*, 88–112.

Devita, V. T., Hellman, S., & Rosenberg, S. A. (1989). *Cancer principles and practice of oncology* (Vol. 1, 3rd ed.). Philadelphia: Lippincott.

DeVitto, J. (1970). *The psychology of speech and language: An introduction to psycholinguistics*. New York: Random House.

Devos, T. & Banaji, M. R. (2003). Implicit self and identity. In M. R. Leary & J. P. Tangney (Eds.), *Handbook of self and identity* (pp. 153–175). New York: Guilford Press.

Diamond, C. & Buskin, S. (2000). Continued risky behavior in HIV-infected youth. *American Journal of Public Health, 90*, 115–117.

Diamond, M. (1993). Homosexuality and bisexuality in different populations. *Archives of Sexual Behavior, 22*, 291–310.

Diamond, M., & Karlen, A. (1980). *Sexual decisions*. Boston: Little, Brown.

Diaz, R. M. (1985). Bilingual cognitive development: Addressing three gaps in recent research. *Child Development, 56,* 1376–1388.

Dick, J. P. R., Guiloff, R. J., Stewart, A., Blackstock, J., Bielawska, C., Paul, E. A., & Marsden, C. D. (1984). Mini-mental status examination in neurological patients. *Journal of Neurology, 47,* 496–499.

Dickerson, L. M., Mazyck, P. J., & Hunter, M. H. (2003). Premenstrual syndrome. *American Family Physician, 67,* 1743–1752.

Diener, C. I., & Dweck, C. S. (1980). An analysis of learned helplessness: II. The processing of success. *Journal of Personality and Social Psychology, 39,* 940–952.

DiMatteo, M. R. (1991). *The psychology of health, illness, and medical care: An individual perspective.* Pacific Grove, CA: Brooks/Cole.

Dinkmeyer, D., & McKay, G. D. (1982). *The parent's handbook: STEP.* Circle Pines, MN: American Guidance Service.

Dinkmeyer, D., & McKay, G. D. (1983). *Systematic training for effective parenting: The parent's guide.* St. Paul, MN: American Guidance Service.

Dinkmeyer, D., Sr., McKay, G. D., Dinkmeyer, D., Jr., & Dinkmeyer, D. (1997). The parent's Handbook: Systematic training for effective parenting. St. Paul, MN: American Guidance Service.

Dion, K., Miller, N., & Magnan, M. (1970). Cohesiveness and social responsibility as determinants of risk taking. *Proceedings of the American Psychological Association, 5,* 335–336.

Dishion, T. J., & Andrews, D. W. (1995). Preventing escalation in problem behaviors with high-risk young adolescents: Immediate and 1-year outcomes. *Journal of Consulting and Clinical Psychology, 63*(4), 538–548.

Dishion, T. J., Kavanagh, K. (2003). *Adolescent problem behavior: An ecological approach to family-centered intervention.* New York: Guilford.

Dishion, T. J., McCord, J., & Poulin, F. (1999). When interventions harm: Peer groups and problem behavior. *American Psychologist, 54,* 755–764.

Dixon, R., & Lerner, R. M. (1999). History and systems in developmental psychology. In M. H. Bornstein & M. E. Lamb (Eds.), *Developmental psychology: An advanced textbook* (4th ed., pp. 3–45). Mahwah, NJ: Erlbaum.

Dlugokinski, E., & Firestone, I. J. (1974). Other centeredness and susceptibility to charitable appeals: Effects of perceived discipline. *Developmental Psychology, 10,* 21–28.

Dodge, K. A. (2000). Developmental psychology. In M. H. Ebert, P. T. Loosen, & B. Nurcombe (Eds.), *Current diagnosis and treatment in psychiatry* (pp. 1–17). New York: Lange Medical Books/McGraw-Hill.

Dodge, K. A., Pettit, G. S., Murphy, R. R., & Buchsbaum, K. (1984). The assessment of intention-cue detection skills in children: Implications for developmental psycho-pathology. *Child Development, 55,* 163–173.

Dodson, J. (1988). Conceptualizations of black families. In H. P. McAdoo (Ed.), *Black families* (pp. 77–90). Beverly Hills, CA: Sage.

Doherty, R. W., Echevarria, J., Estrada, P. E., Goldenberg, C., Hilberg, R. S., Saunders, W. M., et al. (2002). *Research evidence: Five standards for effective pedagogy and student outcomes* [technical report no. G1]. Santa Cruz, CA: University of California, CREDE.

Dohrenwend, B. S. (1978). Social stress and community psychology. *American Journal of Community Psychology, 6,* 1–14.

Dolgin, K. G., & Behrend, D. A. (1984). Children's knowledge about animates and inanimates. *Child Development, 55,* 1646–1650.

Dollinger, S. J., & Gasser, M. (1981). Imitation as social influence. *Journal of Genetic Psychology, 138,* 149–150.

Dornbusch, S. M., Carlsmith, J. M., Bushwall, S. J., Ritter, P. L., Leiderman, H., Hastorf, A. H., et al. (1985). Single parents, extended households, and the control of adolescents. *Child Development, 56,* 326–341.

Dougherty, T. M., & Haith, M. M. (1997). Infant expectations and reaction time as predictors of childhood speed of processing and IQ. *Developmental Psychology, 33,* 146–155.

Dovidio, J. F., Gaertner, S. L., Nier, J. A., Kawakami, K., & Hodson, G. (2004). Contemporary racial bias: When good people do bad things. In A. G. Miller (Ed.), *The social psychology of good and evil* (pp. 141–167). New York: Guilford Press.

Doyle, P. (1995, August 7). Custody fights in adoptions test Indian tribes' power. *Arizona Daily Star,* pp. 1, 8.

Dregni, M. (1989, September/October). Coming out in the age of AIDS. *Utne Reader,* 19–20.

Dreikurs, R. (1964). *Children: The challenge.* New York: Hawthorne Books.

Dreikurs, R. (1993). *A new approach to discipline: Logical consequences.* New York: Plume.

Drews, C. D., Murphy, C. C., Yeargin-Allsopp, M., & Decofle, P. (1996). The relationship between idiopathic mental retardation and maternal smoking during pregnancy. *Pediatrics, 97,* 547–553.

Drucker, J. (2001). *Gay and lesbian families speak out.* New York: Perseus.

Drucker, P. F. (1954). *The practice of management.* New York: Harper & Row.

Dryfoos, J. G. (1990). *Adolescents at risk: Prevalence and prevention.* New York: Oxford University Press.

Dryfoos, J. G. (1994). *Full-service schools.* San Francisco: Jossey-Bass.

Duberstein, P., & Conwell, Y. (2000). Suicide. In S. Whitebourne (Ed.), *Psychopathology in Later Adulthood* (pp. 245–275). New York: Wiley & Sons.

Dubin, M. (1994). Aggravating adolescent years often will hit parents hard. *Arizona Daily Star,* p. 1D.

Dubin, S. (1972). Obsolescence or lifelong education: A choice for the professional. *American Psychologist, 17,* 486–498.

Dubos, R. (1978). Health and creative adaptation. *Human Nature, 1,* 74–82.

Dulcan, M. K. (1986). Comprehensive treatment of children and adolescents with attention deficit disorders: The state of the art. *Clinical Psychology Review, 6,* 539–569.

Dumaret, A. C., Duyme, M., & Tomkiewiez, S. (1997). Foster children: Risk factors and development at a preschool age. *Early Child Development and Care, 134,* 23–42.

Duncan, G., & Brooks-Gunn (2000). Family Poverty, Welfare Reform and Child Development. [Special Issue on "New Directions for Child Development in the Twenty-First Century."] *Child Development, 71*(1), 188–196.

Dunker, K. (1945). On problem solving. *Psychological Monographs, 58*(5, whole no. 270).

Dunn, J. (1991). Sibling influences. In M. Lewis & S. Feinman (Eds.), *Social influences and socialization in infancy* (pp. 97–109). New York: Plenum.

Dunn, J. (2002). Sibling relationships. In P. K. Smith & C. H. Hart (eds.), *Blackwell handbook of childhood social development* (223–237). Malden, MA: Blackwell.

Dunn, J., & Kendrick, C. (1982). *Siblings.* Cambridge, MA: Harvard University Press.

Dunn, J., & Munn, P. (1986). Sibling quarrels and maternal intervention: Individual differences in understanding and aggression. *Journal of Child Psychology and Psychiatry, 27,* 583–597.

Dunst, C., Trivette, C., & Cross, A. (1986). Mediating influences of social support: Personal, family, and child outcomes. *American Journal of Mental Deficiency, 90,* 403–417.

Dura, J. R., Haywood-Niler, E., & Kiecolt-Glaser, J. K. (1990). Spousal caregivers of persons with Alzheimer's and Parkinson's disease dementia: A preliminary comparison. *The Gerontologist, 30,* 332–336.

Durand, M., & Barlow, D. H. (2002). *Essentials of abnormal psychology* (3rd ed.). Belmont, CA: Thomson/Wadsworth.

Durham, W. H. (1991). *Coevolution: Genes, culture, and human diversity.* Stanford, CA: Stanford University Press.

Dusek, J., & Flaherty, J. (1981). The development of the self-concept during the adolescent years. *Monographs of the Society for Research in Child Development, 46* [serial no. 191].

Dutton, D. B., & Levine, S. (1989). Overview, methodological critique, and reformulation. In J. P. Bunker, D. S. Gomby, & B. H. Kehrer (Eds.), *Pathways to health* (pp. 29–69). Menlo Park, CA: Henry J. Kaiser Family Foundation.

Duvall, E. M. (1971). *Family development* (4th ed.). Philadelphia: Lippincott.

Duvall, E. M., & Miller, B. C. (1985). *Marriage and family development* (6th ed.). New York: Harper & Row.

Dweck, C. S. (1986). Motivational processes affecting learning. *American Psychologist, 41,* 1040–1048.

Dweck, C. S. (1999). *Self-theories: Their role in motivation, personality and development.* Philadelphia: Psychology Press.

Dweck, C. S. (2000). *Self theories: Their role in motivation, personality, and development.* New York: Psychological Press.

Dweck, C. S., Davidson, W., Nelson, S., & Enna, B. (1978). Sex differences in learned helplessness: II. The contingencies of evaluative feedback in the classroom, and III. An experimental analysis. *Developmental Psychology, 14,* 268–276.

Dweck, C. S., & Reppucci, N. D. (1973). Learned helplessness and reinforcement responsibility in children. *Journal of Personality and Social Psychology, 31,* 674–685.

Dwyer, K. P. (1995, May). Is self-esteem really all that important? *APA Monitor,* 41–43.

Dziech, B. W., & Weiner, L. (1991). *The lecherous professor: Sexual harassment on campus.* Urbana: University of Illinois Press.

Dziegielewski, S. F., Heymann, C., Green, C., & Gichia, J. E. (2002). Midlife changes: Utilizing a social work perspective. *Journal of Human Behavior in the Social Environment, 6,* 65–86.

Eagly, A. H., & Wood, W. (1991). Explaining sex differences in social behavior: A meta-analytic perspective. *Journal of Sex Research, 36,* 424–435.

Easterbrooks, M. A., & Goldberg, W. A. (1985). Effects of early maternal employment on toddlers, mothers, and fathers. *Developmental Psychology, 21,* 774–783.

Eberstadt, N. (1991). America's infant mortality puzzle. *The Public Interest, 105,* 30–47.

Eccles, J., Barber, B., Jozefowicz, D., Malenchuk, O., & Vida, M. (1999). Self-evaluations of competence, task values, and self-esteem. In N. G. Johnson, M. C. Roberts, & J. Worell (Eds.), *Beyond appearance: A new look at adolescent girls* (53–83). Washington, DC: American Psychological Association.

Eccles, J. S. (1987). Gender roles and achievement patterns: An expectancy value perspective. In J. M. Reinisch, L. A. Roseblum, & S. A. Sanders (Eds.), *Masculinity/femininity*. New York: Oxford University Press.

Eccles, J. S., & Midgley, C. (1989). Stage/environment fit: Developmentally appropriate classrooms for early adolescents. In R. E. Ames & C. Ames (Eds.), *Research on motivation in education* (Vol. 3). New York: Academic Press.

Eckert, P. (1990). Cooperative competition in adolescent "girl talk." *Discourse Processes, 13,* 91–122.

Edelman, M. W. (1987). *Families in peril: An agenda for social change.* New York: Alan Guttmacher Institute.

Edmonds, M. (1990). The health of the Black aged female. In Z. Harel, E. A. McKinney, & M. Williams (Eds.), *Black aged* (pp. 205–220). Newbury Park, CA: Sage.

Edwards, C. (1984). The age group labels and categories of preschool children. *Child Development, 55,* 440–452.

Edwards, C., Johnson, A., Knight, E., Oyemade, U., Cole, O., Westney, O., et al. (1994a). Maternal stress and pregnancy outcomes in a prenatal clinic population. *Journal of Nutrition, 124,* 1006–1022.

Edwards, C., Johnson, A., Knight, E., Oyemade, U., Cole, O., Westney, O., et al. (1994b). Pica in an urban environment (African-American women and their pregnancies). *Journal of Nutrition, 124,* 9545–9554.

Edwards, D., Porter, S., & Stein, G. (1993). A pilot study of postnatal depression following caesarean section using two retrospective self-rating instruments. *Journal of Psychosomatic Research, 38,* 111–117.

Efran, J. & Greene, M. (1999, May/June). Do peers trump parents? Conventional child-rearing theory may be based on wishful thinking. *Psychotherapy Networker*, pp. 57–61.

Egan, S. K., & Perry, D. G. (2001). Gender identity: A multidimensional analysis with implications for psychosocial adjustment. *Developmental Psychology, 37,* 451–463.

Ehrenreich, B. (2001). *Nickeled and dimed: On (not) getting by in America.* New York: Henry Holt & Company.

Einstein, A. (2004). http://rescompstandford.edu/Ðcheshire/Einsteinquotes.html

Eisenberg, N. (Ed.) (1982). *The development of prosocial behavior.* New York: Wiley.

Eisenberg, N., Wentzel, N., & Harris, J. D. (1998). The role of emotion and regulation in empathy-related responding. *School Psychology Review, 27,* 506–522.

Eisendrath, S. J. (1988). The mind and somatic illness: Psychological factors affecting physical illness. In H. H. Goldman (Ed.), *Review of general psychiatry*. East Norwalk, CT: Appleton & Lang.

Ekerdt, D. J., Bossé, R., & Levkoff, S. (1985). Empirical test for phases of retirement: Findings from the Normative Aging Study. *Journal of Gerontology, 40,* 368–374.

Elias, M. (1991). A multilevel action research perspective on stress-related interventions. In M. E. Colten & S. Gore (Eds.), *Adolescent stress*. New York: Aldine de Gruyter.

Eliot, L. (2000). *What's going on in there? How the brain and mind develop in the first five years of life.* New York: Bantam.

Elkind, D. (1976). *Child development and education: A Piagetian perspective.* New York: Oxford University Press.

Elkind, D. (1978). Understanding the young adolescent. *Adolescence, 13,* 127–134.

Elkind, D. (1981). *The hurried child.* Reading, MA: Addison-Wesley.

Elkind, D. (1987). *Miseducation: Preschoolers at risk.* New York: Knopf.

Elkind, D. (2001). *The hurried child: Growing up too fast, too soon.* New York: Perseus.

Elliot, D. S. (1993). Promoting the health of adolescents: New directions for the twenty-first century. In S. Millstein, A. C. Petersen, & E. O. Nightingale (Eds.), *Adolescent health promotion*. New York: Oxford University Press.

Elliott, D. S. (1994). Serious violent offenders: Onset, developmental course and termination. *Criminology, 32*(1), 1–22.

Ellis, S., Rogoff, B., & Cromer, C. C. (1981). Age segregation in children's social interactions. *Developmental Psychology, 17,* 399–407.

Emde, R. (1987). Infant mental health: Clinical dilemmas, the expansion of meaning, and opportunities. In J. Osofsky (Ed.), *Handbook of infant development* (pp. 1297–1320). New York: Wiley.

Emde, R. N., Plomin, R., Robinson, J., Corley, R., DeFries, J., Fulkner, D. W., et al. (1992). Temperament, emotion, and cognition at fourteen months: The MacArthur Longitudinal Twin Study. *Child Development, 63,* 1437–1455.

Emler, N., Renwick, S., & Malone, B. (1983). The relationship between moral reasoning and political orientation. *Journal of Personality and Social Psychology, 45,* 1073–1080.

Emmerich, W. (1959). Parental identification in young children. *Genetic Psychology Monographs, 60,* 257–308.

Emmerich, W. (1966). Continuity and stability in early social development: II. Teacher's ratings. *Child Development, 37,* 17–27.

Enck, R. (1992, July/August). The last few days. *The American Journal of Hospice and Palliative Care,* 11–13.

Englander-Golden, P., Sonleitner, F. J., Whitmore, M. R., & Corbley, G. J. M. (1986). Social and menstrual cycles: Methodological and substantive findings. In V. L. Olesen & N. F. Woods (Eds.), *Culture, society, and menstruation.* Washington, DC: Hemisphere.

Enright, R. D. (2001). *Forgiveness is a choice: A step-by-step process for resolving anger and restoring hope.* Washington, DC: APA Lifebooks.

Enright, R. D., & Fitzgibbons, R. P. (2000). *Helping clients forgive: An empirical guide for resolving anger and restoring hope.* Washington, DC: American Psychological Association.

Entwisle, D. R. (1990). Schools and the adolescent. In S. S. Feldman & G. R. Elliot (Eds.), *At the threshold: The developing adolescent* (pp. 197–224). Cambridge, MA: Harvard University Press.

Ephross, J. (1982). A social work perspective on families with infants who fail to thrive. In P. J. Accardo (Ed.), *Failure to thrive in infancy and early childhood* (pp. 331–347). Baltimore: University Park Press.

Epstein, S. (2005). A queer encounter. In T. L. Steele (Ed.), *Sex, self, and society: The social context of sexuality* (pp. 68–74). Belmont, CA: Thomson/Wadsworth.

Erickson, J. (1996, May 6). Obstetric anesthesia safety called remarkable. *The Arizona Daily Star,* pp. 1B, 4B.

Erikson, E. (1959). *Identity in the life cycle* [monograph 1]. *Psychological Issues, 1,* 1–171.

Erikson, E. H. (1959/1980). *Identity and the Life Cycle.* New York: Norton.

Erikson, E. H. (1963). *Childhood and society* (2nd ed.). New York: Norton.

Erikson, E. H. (1968). *Identity, youth and crisis.* New York: Norton.

Erikson, E. H. (1974). *Dimensions of a new identity.* New York: Norton.

Erikson, E. H., & Erikson, J. M. (1998). *The Life Cycle Completed.* New York: Norton.

Evans, C., & Dion, K. (1991). Group cohesion and performance. *Small Group Research, 22,* 175–186.

Evans, G. W. (2004). The environment of childhood poverty. *American Psychologist, 59,* 77–92.

Ewalt, P. L., & Perkins, L. (1979). The real experience of death among adolescents. *Social Casework, 60,* 547–551.

Eyer, D. (1994). Mother-infant bonding: A scientific fiction. *Human Nature, 5,* 69–94.

Eysenck, H. J. (1989, December). Health's character. *Psychology Today,* 28–32, 34–35.

Fagot, B. (1978). The influence of sex of child on parental reactions to toddler children. *Child Development, 49,* 459–465.

Fagot, B. (1989). The young child's gender schema: Environmental input, internal organization. *Child Development, 60,* 663–672.

Fagot, B. (1991). Observations of parent reactions to sex-stereotyped behaviors: Age and sex effects. *Child Development, 62,* 617–628.

Fagot, B. (1992). Gender labeling, gender stereotyping, and parenting behaviors. *Developmental Psychology, 28,* 225–230.

Fahey, M., & Phillips, S. (1981). The self-concept in middle childhood: Some baseline data. *Child Study Journal, 11,* 155.

Fahlberg, V. (1991). *A child's journey through placement.* Indianapolis, IN: Perspectives Press.

Fain, T. C., & Anderson, D. L. (1987). Sexual harassment: Organizational context and diffuse status. *Sex Roles, 17,* 291–311.

Falk, G. (2001). *Stigma: How we treat outsiders.* Amherst: Prometheus Books.

Farber, H., & Boyette, M. (2001). *Control your child's asthma: A breakthrough program for the treatment and management of childhood asthma.* New York: Henry Holt.

Farmer, T. W., Price, L. N., O'Neal, K. K., Leung, M. C., Goforth, J. B., Cairns, B. D., et al. (2004). Exploring risk in early adolescent African American youth. *American Journal of Community Psychology, 33,* 51–59.

Favazza, A. (1987). *Bodies under siege*. Baltimore, MD: Johns Hopkins University Press.

Fay, R. E., Turner, C. F., Klassen, A. D., & Gagnon, J. H. (1989). Prevalence and patterns of same-gender sexual contact among men. *Science, 243,* 338–348.

FBI (2002). *Hate crime statistics*. Retrieved {December 19 AU: Date retrieved?} from http://www.fbi.gov/

FBI: Racism cause of most hate crime (1993, January 5). *Tempe Daily Tribune,* p. A3.

Feagin, J. R., & Feagin, C. B. (1978). *Institutional racism and sexism*. New York: Prentice Hall.

Fearnley Shapiro, A., Gottman, J. M., & Carrere, S. (2000). The baby and the marriage: Identifying factors that buffer against decline in marital satisfaction after the first baby arrives. *Journal of Family Psychology, 14,* 59–70.

Federal Interagency Forum on Aging-Related Statistics (2000). *Older Americans 2000: Key indicators of well-being*. Hyattsville, MD: Author.

Federal Interagency Forum on Aging-Related Statistics (2004). *Aging statistics online* (www.agingstats.gov).

Feil, N., & Altman, D. G. (2004). Letter to the editor: Validation theory and the myth of the therapeutic lie. *American Journal of Alzheimer's Disease and Other Dementias, 19*(2), 77–78.

Feinberg, J. (2000). Ensuring appropriate, effective, and safe medication use for older people. *Generations: Quarterly Journal of the American Society on Aging, 14*(4), 5–7.

Feinbloom, R. (1993). *Pregnancy, birth and the early months: A complete guide*. Reading, MA: Addison-Wesley.

Feindler, E. L., & Guttman, J. (1994). Cognitive-behavioral anger control training. In C. LeCroy (Ed.), *Handbook of child and adolescent treatment manuals* (pp. 170–199). New York: Lexington Press.

Feingold, B. (1975). *Why your child is hyperactive*. New York: Random House.

Feinman, S. (1991). Bringing babies back into the social world. In M. Lewis & S. Feinman (Eds.), *Social influences and socialization in infancy* (pp. 281–320). New York: Plenum.

Feld, S., & Radin, N. (1982). *Social psychology for social work and the mental health professions*. New York: Columbia University Press.

Feldman, R. A., Caplinger, T. E., & Wodarski, J. S. (1983). *The St. Louis conundrum: The effective treatment of antisocial youth*. Englewood Cliffs, NJ: Prentice Hall.

Fels, A. (2005). *Necessary Dreams: Ambition in women's changing lives*. New York: Bantam Doubleday Dell.

Ferketich, S. L., & Mercer, R. T. (1995). Predictors of role competence for experienced and inexperienced fathers. *Nursing Research, 44*(2), 89–95.

Fernald, A. (1987). Acoustic determinants of infant preference for motherese speech. *Infant Behavior and Development, 10,* 279–293.

Fernald, A. (1991). Prosody and focus in speech to infants and adults. *Developmental Psychology, 27,* 209–221.

Ferrante, J. (1995). *Sociology: A global perspective*. Belmont, CA: Wadsworth.

Ferrante, J. (2003). *Sociology: A global perspective* (5th ed.). Belmont, CA: Thomson/Wadsworth.

Feshbach, S. (1956). The catharsis hypothesis and some consequences of interaction with aggressive and neutral play objects. *Journal of Personality, 24,* 449–461.

Festinger, L. (1950). Informal and social communication. *Psychological Review, 57,* 271–282.

Festinger, L. (1957). *A theory of cognitive dissonance*. Stanford, CA: Stanford University Press.

Field, T. (1978). Interaction behaviors of primary versus secondary caretaker fathers. *Developmental Psychology, 14,* 183–184.

Field, T. (1981). Early development of the preterm offspring of teenage mothers. In K. Scott, T. Field, & E. Robertson (Eds.), *Teenage parents and their offspring* (pp. 145–175). New York: Grune & Stratton.

Field, T. (1983). High-risk infants "have less fun" during early interactions. *Topics in Childhood Special Education, 3,* 77–87.

Field, T., Schanberg, S., Scafidi, F., Bauer, C., Nitza, V., Garcia, R., Nystrom, J., & Kuhn, C. (1986). Tactile/kinesthetic stimulation effects on preterm neonates. *Pediatrics, 77,* 654–658.

Field, T. M., Woodson, R., Greenberg, R., & Cohen, D. (1982). Discrimination and imitation of facial expression by neonates. *Science, 218,* 179–181.

Figel, H. (1960). Mind-body, not a pseudoproblem. In S. Hook (Ed.), *Dimensions of mind: A symposium*. New York: New York University Press.

Fine, G. A. (1980). The natural history of preadolescent male friendship groups. In H. C. Foot, A. J. Chapman, & J. R. Smith (Eds.), *Friendships and childhood relations*. New York: Wiley.

Fingarette, H. (1988). *Heavy drinking: The myth of alcoholism as a disease*. Berkeley: University of California Press.

Fingerman, K. L. (2002). *Mothers and their adult daughters: Mixed emotions, enduring bonds*. New York: Prometheus Books.

Finkelhor, D., & Dziuba-Leatherman, J. (1994). Victimization of children. *American Psychologist, 49,* 173–183.

Finn, J. (1995). Computer-based self-help groups: A new resource to supplement support groups. *Social Work with Groups, 18,* 109–117.

Fischer, J. L., Spann, L., & Crawford, D. W. (1991). Measuring codependency. *Alcoholism Treatment Quarterly, 8,* 87–100.

Fishbein, D., Hyde, C., Coe, B., & Paschall, M. J. (2004). Neurocognitive and physiological prerequisites for prevention of drug abuse. *The journal of primary prevention, 24,* 471–495.

Fishbein, M., & Ajzen, I. (1975). *Belief, attitude, intention and behavior*. Reading, MA: Addison-Wesley.

Fisher, D. E. (2001). The p53 tumor suppressor: Critical regulator of life and death in cancer. *Apoptosis, 6,* 7–15.

Fishman, J. (2000). *Handbook of language and ethnic identity*. New York: Oxford University Press.

Fiske, S. T. (1998). Stereotyping, prejudice, and discrimination. In D. T. Gilbert, S. T. Kiske, & G. Lindzey (Eds.), *Handbook of social psychology* (pp. 357–411). Boston: McGraw-Hill.

Fiske, S. T. (2004). What's in a category? Responsibility, intent, and the avoidability of bias against outgroups. In A. G. Miller (Ed.), *The social psychology of good and evil* (pp. 127–140). New York: Guilford Press.

Fivush, R. (1995). New cognitive research making waves. *APA Monitor,* 53–55.

Fixsen, D. L., Phillips, E. L., Phillips, E. A., & Wolf, M. M. (1976). The teaching family model group home treatment. In W. E. Craighead, A. E. Kazdin, & M. J. Mahoney (Eds.), *Behavior modification*. Boston: Houghton Mifflin.

Flanigan, B. (1992). *Forgiving the unforgivable*. New York: Macmillan.

Flavell, J. H. (1979). Metacognition and cognitive monitoring: A new area of psychological inquiry. *American Psychologist, 34,* 906–911.

Flavell, J. H. (1981). Monitoring social cognitive enterprises: Something else that may develop in the area of social cognition. In J. H. Flavell & L. Ross (Eds.), *Social cognitive development: Frontiers and possible futures*. New York: Cambridge University Press.

Flavell, J. H. (1985). *Cognitive development* (2nd ed.). Englewood Cliffs, NJ: Prentice Hall.

Foddy, M., & Kashima, Y. (2002). Self and identity: When is the conception of the person assumed in the current literature? In Y. Kashima, M. Foddy, & M. J. Platow (Eds.), *Self and identity: Personal, social and symbolic* (pp. 3–25). Hillsdale, NJ: Erlbaum.

Folkman, S., & Lazarus, R. S. (1980). An analysis of coping in a middle aged community sample. *Journal of Health and Social Behavior, 21,* 219–239.

Fonagy, P., Target, M., Cottrell, D., Phillips, J., & Kurtz, Z. (2002). *What works for whom? A critical review of treatments for children and adolescents*. New York: Guilford Press.

Fongruey, L., & Brooks-Gunn, J. (1994). Cumulative familial risks and low-birthweight children's cognitive and behavioral development. *Journal of Clinical Child Psychology, 23,* 360–372.

Fontaine, P., & Toffler, W. (1991). Dorsal penile nerve block for newborn circumcision. *American Family Physician, 43,* 1327–1333.

Forbes, J., & Kelly, M. (Eds.) (1995). *French cultural studies: An introduction*. Oxford: Oxford University Press.

Ford, C. A., Millstein, S. G., Halpern-Felsher, B. L., & Irwin, C. E., Jr. (1997). Influence of physician confidentiality assurances on adolescents' willingness to disclose information and seek future health care: A randomized controlled trial. *Journal of the American Medical Association, 278,* 1029–1034.

Ford, M. E. (1986). A living systems conceptualization of social intelligence: Outcomes, processes, and developmental change. In R. J. Sternberg (Ed.), *Advances in the psychology of human intelligence* (Vol. 3). Hillsdale, NJ: Erlbaum.

Forehand, R. L., & Long, N. (1996). *Parenting the strong-willed child: The clinically proven five-week program for parents of two- to-six-year olds*.

Forehand, R. L., & Long, N. (2002). *Parenting the strong-willed child (revised): The clinically proven five-week program for parents of two- to-six-year olds*. New York: McGraw-Hill.

Foster, R. L., Hunsberger, M. M., & Anderson, J. T. (1989). *Family-centered nursing care of children*. Philadelphia: Saunders.

Fowers, B. J., & Olson, D. H. (1989). ENRICH Marital Inventory: A discriminant validity and cross-validation assessment. *Journal of Marital and Family Therapy, 15,* 65–79.

Fox, J. J., & Bartholomae, S. (2000). Economic stress and families. In P. C. McKenry and S. J. Price. *Families and change: Coping with stressful events and transitions* (2nd ed., pp. 250–278). Thousand Oaks, CA: Sage.

Fox, M. (1995). *The reinvention of work: A new vision of livelihood for our time.* San Francisco: HarperSanFrancisco.

Fozard, J., & Gordon-Salant, S. (2001). Changes in vision and hearing with aging. In J. Birren & K. Schaie (Eds.), *Handbook of the Psychology of Aging* (5th ed., pp. 241–266). New York: Academic Press.

Fraiberg, S. H. (1968). *The magic years: Understanding and handling the problems of early childhood.* London: Methuen.

Fraiberg, S. H. (1980). *Clinical studies in infant mental health.* New York: Basic Books.

Francis, S. (1993). Rape and sexual assault. In B. S. Johnson, *Adaptation and growth: Psychiatric nursing.* Philadelphia: Lippincott.

Frank, A. (1952). *The diary of a young girl.* Garden City, NY: Doubleday.

Frank, D., Silva, M., & Needlman, R. (1993, February). Failure to thrive: Mystery, myth, and method. *Contemporary Pediatrics,* 114–133.

Frankel, M. (1983). Does mother know best? Mothers and fathers interacting with preschool sons and daughters. *Developmental Psychology, 19,* 694–702.

Frankenberg, W., & Dodds, J. (1967). Denver Development Screening Test. *Journal of Pediatrics, 71,* 181–191.

Franklin, C., & Corcoran, J. (1999). Preventing adolescent pregnancy: A review of programs and practices. *Social work in Health Care, 45,* 40–52.

Franks, M., Pierce, L., & Dwyer, J. (2003). Expected parent-care involvement of adult children. *Journal of Applied Gerontology, 22*(1), 104–117.

Frauenhofer, D., Scott, L., Doress, P. B., & Rosenthal-Keese, K. (1987). Relationships in middle and later life. In P. B. Doress, D. L. Siegel, & The Midlife and Older Women Book Project (Eds.), *Ourselves, growing older: Women aging with knowledge and power* (pp. 79–98). New York: Simon & Schuster.

Freedman, D. G., & DeBoer, M. M. (1979). Biological and cultural differences in early child development. *Annual Review of Anthropology, 8,* 579–600.

Freeman, B. J. (1993). The syndrome of autism: Update and guidelines for diagnosis. *Young Children, 6,* 1–11.

Freiberg, P. (1990, November). Outreach helps women at risk for AIDS. *APA Monitor,* 28–29.

Freiberg, P. (1998, February). Prevention studies take a variety of tacks. *APA Monitor,* 33.

French, J., & Raven, B. (1959). The bases of social power. In D. Cartwright (Ed.), *Studies in social power.* Ann Arbor: Institute for Research, University of Michigan.

Freud, A., & Dann, S. (1951). An experiment in group upbringing. *Psychoanalytic Study of the Child, 6,* 127–168.

Fried, L. P., Carlson, M. C., Freedman, M., Frick, K. D., Glass, T. A., Hill, et al. (2004). A social model for health promotion for an aging population: Initial evidence on the Experience Corps model. *Journal of Urban Health, 81*(1), 64–78.

Friedenreich, C. (1995). A review of physical activity and breast cancer. *Epidemiology, 6,* 311–317.

Friedlander, M. L. (1999). Ethnic identity development of internationally adopted children and adolescents: Implications for family therapists. *Journal of Marital and Family Therapy, 25,* 43–60.

Friedman, M., & Rosenman, R. F. (1974). *Type A behavior and your heart.* New York: Knopf.

Friedman, R. C., & Downey, J. I. (1994). Homosexuality. *The New England Journal of Medicine, 331,* 923–930.

Friedrich, L. K., & Stein, A. H. (1973). Aggressive and pro-social television programs and the natural behavior of preschool children. *Monographs of the Society for Research in Child Development, 38*(4), serial no. 151.

Friston, K. J., & Price, C. J. (2001). Generative models, brain function and neuroimaging. *Scandanavian Journal of Psychology, 42,* 167–77.

Frosh, S. (1987). *The politics of psychoanalysis: An introduction to Freudian and post-Freudian theory.* New Haven, CT: Yale University Press.

Fry, P. (2001). The unique contribution of key existential factors to the prediction of psychological well-being of older adults following spousal loss. *The Gerontologist, 41*(1), 69–81.

Fuller-Thomson, E., & Minkler, M. (2001). American grandparents providing extensive child care to their grandchildren. *The Gerontologist, 41,* 201–209.

Furman, W., & Buhrmester, D. (1985a). Children's perceptions of their personal relationships in their social networks. *Developmental Psychology, 21,* 1016–1024.

Furman, W., & Buhrmester, D. (1985b). Children's perceptions of the qualities of sibling relationships. *Child Development, 56,* 448–461.

Furstenberg, F. F., Kennedy, S., McCloyd, V. C., Rumbaut, R. G., & Settersten, Jr., R. A. (2004). *Contexts, 3,* 33–41.

Gabe, T., Lyke, B., & Spar, K. (2001). Child care: The role of the federal government. In B. Ring (Ed.), *The child care disaster in America: Disdain or disgrace?* (pp. 1–24). Huntington, NY: Nova Science Publishing.

Galambos, N. L., & Almeida, D. M. (1992). Does parent-adolescent conflict increase in early adolescence? *Journal of Marriage and the Family, 54,* 737–747.

Galinsky, M., & Schopler, J. (1977). Warning: Groups may be dangerous. *Social Work, 22,* 89–94.

Gallo, J., & Rabins, P. (1999). Depression without sadness: Alternative presentations of depression in late life. *American Family Physician, 60*(3), 820–826.

Gambrill, E. (1997). *Social work practice: A critical thinker's guide.* New York: Oxford University Press.

Ganong, M. D., Hersen, M., Kabacoff, R. I., & Vanhasselt, V. B. (1999). Interpersonal and psychological correlates of marital dissatisfaction in late life: A review. *Clinical Psychology Review, 19,* 359–378.

Ganong, M. D., & Coleman, M. (2004). *Stepfamilies: Development, dynamics, and intervention.* New York: Plenum.

Garbarino, J., & Abramowitz, R. H. (1992a). Sociocultural risk and opportunity. In J. Garbarino, *Children and families in the social environment* (2nd ed.). New York: Aldine de Gruyter.

Garbarino, J., & Abramowitz, R. H. (1992b). The family as a social system. In J. Garbarino, *Children and families in the social environment* (2nd ed.). New York: Aldine de Gruyter.

Garbarino, J., Burston, N., Raber, S., Russel, R., & Crouter, A. (1978). The social maps of children approaching adolescence: Studying the ecology of youth development. *Journal of Youth and Adolescence, 7,* 417–428.

Garbarino, J., Galambos, N. L., Plantz, M. C., & Kostelny, K. (1992). The territory of childhood. In J. Garbarino (Ed.), *Children and families in the social environment* (2nd ed.). New York: Aldine de Gruyter.

Garcia Coll, C., Bearer, E. L., & Lerner, R. M. (2004). *Nature and Nurture: The complex interplay of genetic and environmental influences on human behavior and development.* Mahwah, NJ: Erlbaum.

Garcia Coll, C., Lamberty, G., Jenkins, R., McAdoo, H., Crnic, K., Wasik, B., et al. (1996). An integrative model for the study of developmental competencies in minority children. *Child Development, 67,* 1891–1914.

Garcia-Preto, N. (1994, July/August). On the bridge. *Family Therapy Networker,* 35–37.

Gardner, D. M. (1997, January/February). The 1997 body image survey. *Psychology Today,* 31–84.

Gardner, H. (1980). *Artful scribbles: The significance of children's drawings.* New York: Basic Books.

Garmezy, N., & Rutter, M. (Eds.) (1983). *Stress, coping, and development in children.* New York: McGraw-Hill.

Garmon, L. C., Basinger, K. S., Gregg, V. R., & Gibbs, J. C. (1996). Gender differences in stage and expression of moral judgment. *Merrill-Palmer Quarterly, 42,* 418–437.

Garner, D. M. (1997, January/February). The 1997 body image survey. *Psychology Today,* 31–84.

Garrison, W. T., & McQuiston, S. (1989). *Chronic illness during childhood and adolescence.* Newbury Park, CA: Sage.

Gartner, A., & Riessman, F. (1977). *Self-help in the human services.* San Francisco: Jossey-Bass.

Garvin, C. D., & Seabury, B. A. (1984). *Interpersonal practice in social work.* Englewood Cliffs, NJ: Prentice Hall.

Gaston, M., & Porter, G. K. (2001). *Prime time: The African American women's complete guide to midlife health and wellness.* New York: Ballantine.

Gaylin, W. (1986). *Rediscovering love.* New York: Viking Penguin.

Gelfand, D. E., & Barresi, C. M. (Eds.) (1987). *Ethnic dimensions of aging.* New York: Springer.

Gelles, R. J. (1987). *Family violence.* Newbury Park, CA: Sage.

Gelman, S. A. (2003). *The essential child: Origins of essentialism in everyday.* New York: Oxford University Press.

Gentry, M., Rosenman, L., & Shulman, A. D. (1987). Comparison of the needs and support systems of remarried and nonmarried widows. In H. Lopata (Ed.), *Widows: Vol. II, North America* (pp. 158–170). Durham, NC: Duke University Press.

George, N. (1998). *Hip Hop America.* New York: Penguin Group.

Gerard, M., & Dukette, R. (1954). Techniques for preventing separation

trauma in child placement. *The American Journal of Orthopsychiatry, 24*, 111–127.
Gergen, K. (1991). *The saturated self: Dilemmas of identity in contemporary life*. New York: Basic Books.
Gergen, K. J. (1991, September/October). The saturated family. *Family Therapy Networker*, 27–35.
Gerhart, U., & Brooks, A. (1993). The social work practitioner and antipsychotic drugs. *Social Work, 28*, 454–460.
Germain, C. B. (1991). *Human behavior in the social environment: An ecological view*. New York: Columbia University Press.
Geronimus, A. (1991). Teenage childbearing and social and reproductive disadvantage: The evolution of complex questions and the demise of simple answers. *Family Relations, 40*, 463–471.
Geronimus, A. (1992). Teenage childbearing and social disadvantage: Unprotected discourse. *Family Relations, 41*, 244–248.
Geroski, A. M., & Rodgers, L. A. (1998). Collaborative assessment and treatment of children with enuresis and encopresis. *Professional School Counseling, 2*, 128–135.
Gerstel, N., Reissman, C. K., & Rosenfield, S. (1985). Explaining the symptomatology of separated and divorced women and men: The role of marital conditions and social network. *Social Forces, 64*, 84–101.
Gerth, H. & Mills, C. W. (1953). *Character and social structure: The psychology of social institutions*. New York: Harcourt, Brace.
Gesser, G., Wong, P. T. P., & Reker, G. T. (1987–88). Death attitudes across the life-span: The development and validation of the death attitude profile (DAP). *Omega, 18*, 113–128.
Gfroerer, J., Penne, M., Pemberton, M., & Folsom, R. (2003). Substance abuse treatment need among older adults in 2020: The impact of the baby boom cohort. *Drug and Alcohol Dependence, 69*(2), 127–135.
Giannakoulopoulos, X., Sepulveda, W., Kourtis, P., Glover, V., & Fisk, N. (1994). Fetal plasma cortisol and B-endorphin response to intrauterine needling. *Lancet, 344*, 77–81.
Gibbs, J. T. (1985). City girls: Psychosocial adjustment of urban black adolescent females. *SAGE: A Scholarly Journal of Black Women, 2*, 28–36.
Gibbs, J. T. (1990). Mental health issues of black adolescents: Implications for policy and practice. In A. R. Stiffman & L. E. Davis (Eds.), *Ethnic issues in adolescent mental health*. Newbury Park, CA: Sage.
Gibbs, J. T. (2003). *Children of color: Psychological interventions with culturally diverse youth*. San Francisco: Jossey-Bass.
Gibbs, J. T., & Huang, L. N. (1989). A conceptual framework for assessing and treating minority youth. In J. T. Gibbs & L. N. Huang (Eds.), *Children of color*. San Francisco: Jossey-Bass.
Gibson, E. (1984). Development of knowledge of visual-tactual affordances of substance. *Child Development, 55*, 453–460.
Gibson, P. (2002). Barriers, lessons learned, and helpful hints: Grandmother caregivers talk about service utilization. *Journal of Gerontological Social Work, 39*(4), 55–74.
Giddens, A. (1989). *Sociology*. Cambridge, MA: Polity Press, in association with Basil Blackwell.
Gilbert, D. (2003). *The American class structure: In an age of growing inequality*. Belmont, CA: Wadsworth/Thomson Learning.
Gilbert, D. T., Fiske, S. T., Lindzey, G. (1998). *The handbook of social psychology*. Boston: McGraw-Hill.
Gilbert, K. (1989). Interactive grief and coping in the marital dyad. *Death Studies, 13*, 605–626.
Gilchrist, L. E., Schinke, S. P., & Blythe, B. J. (1985). Preventing unwanted adolescent pregnancy. In L. D. Gilchrist & S. P. Schinke (Eds.), *Preventing social and health problems through life skills training*. Seattle, WA: Center for Social Welfare.
Gilgun, J. F. (1995). We shared something special: The moral discourse of incest perpetrators. *Journal of Marriage and the Family, 57*, 265–281.
Gilligan, C. (1977). In a different voice: Women's conceptions of self and morality. *Harvard Educational Review, 47*, 481–517.
Gilligan, C. (1982). *In a different voice: Psychological theory and women's development*. Cambridge, MA: Harvard University Press.
Gilligan, C. (1985). *Response to critics*. Paper presented at the biennial meeting of the Society for Research in Child Development, Toronto.
Ginsberg, L., Nackerud, L., & Larrison, C. R. (2004). *Human biology for social workers: Development, ecology, genetics, and health*. Boston: Pearson.
Ginsburg, H. P. (1985). Jean Piaget. In H. I. Kaplan & B. J. Sadock (Eds.), *Comprehensive textbook of psychiatry* (Vol. 4, pp. 178–183). Baltimore: Williams & Wilkins.
Girgus, J. (1989, October). Body image in girls pushes rate of depression up. *American Psychological Association Monitor*, 33.
Gish, M. & Spar, K. (2001). Child care issues. In B. Ring (Ed.), *The child care disaster in America: Disdain or disgrace?* (pp. 73–96). Huntington, NY: Nova Science Publishing.

Glass, S. P. (2003). *Not just friends*. New York: The Free Press.
Gleick, E. (1995, February 27). Should this marriage be saved? *Time*, 48–56.
Glenn, N. D., & Weaver, C. N. (1988). The changing relationship of marital status to reported happiness. *Journal of Marriage and the Family, 44*, 317–324.
Glick, P. C. (1984a). American household structure in transition. *Family Planning Perspectives, 16*, 205–211.
Glick, P. C. (1984b). Marriage, divorce, and living arrangements: Prospective changes. *Journal of Family Issues, 5*, 7–26.
Golan, N. (1986). *The perilous bridge*. New York: Free Press.
Gold, M., & Petronio, R. J. (1980). Delinquent behavior in adolescence. In J. Adelson (Ed.), *Handbook of adolescent psychology*. New York: Wiley.
Goldberg, S. (1983). Parent-infant bonding: Another look. *Child Development, 54*, 1355–1382.
Goldenberg, R. (1991). Maternal psychological characteristics and IUGR. *Pre and Perinatal Psychology Journal, 6*, 129–134.
Goldman, L. S., Genel, M., Bezman, R. J., Slanetz, P. (1998). Diagnosis and treatment of attention-deficit/hyperactivity disorder in children and adolescents. Council on Scientific Affairs, American Medical Association. *Journal of the American Medical Association, 279*, 1100–1107.
Goldson, E. (1991). The affective and cognitive sequelae of child maltreatment. *Pediatric Clinics of North America, 38*, 1481–1496.
Goldstein, E. G. (1984). *Ego psychology and social work practice*. New York: Free Press.
Goldstein, R., & Landau, D. (1990). *Fortysomething*. Los Angeles: Tarcher.
Goleman, D. (1997). *Emotional intelligence: Why it can matter more than IQ*. New York: Bantam.
Golombok, S., & Hines, M. (2002). Sex differences in social behavior. In P. K. Smith & C. H. Hart (eds.), *Blackwell handbook of childhood social development* (pp. 265–284). Malden, MA: Blackwell.
Golomobok, S., & Tasker, F. (1996). Do parents influence the sexual orientation of their children? Findings from a longitudinal study of lesbian families. *Developmental Psychology, 32*, 3–11.
Gondolf (1989). *Men who batter: How they stop their abuse*. Paper presented at the second National Conference for Family Violence Researchers, Durham, NH.
Gonsiorek, J. C. (1991). The empirical basis for the demise of the illness model of homosexuality. In J. C. Gonsiorek & J. D. Weinrich (Eds.), *Homosexuality: Research implications for public policy* (pp. 115–137). Newbury Park, CA: Sage.
Goodchilds, J. D., & Zellman, G. L. (1984). Sexual signalling and sexual aggression in adolescent relationships. In N. M. Malamuth & E. D. Donnerstein (Eds.), *Pornography and sexual aggression*. New York: Academic Press.
Goode, E. (1993). Drug abuse. *Grolier Electronic Encyclopedia*.
Goodenough, F. (1931). *Anger in young children*. Minneapolis: University of Minnesota Press.
Goodings, C. (1987). *Bitter-sweet dreams: Girls' and young women's own stories*. London: Virago Press.
Goodrich, C. (1995, February). Fathering in the night. *The Sun*, pp. 12–14.
Goodwin, A. J., & Scott, L. (1987). Sexuality in the second half of life. In P. B. Doress, D. L. Siegel, & The Midlife and Older Women Book Project (Eds.), *Ourselves, growing older: Women aging with knowledge and power* (pp. 79–98). New York: Simon & Schuster.
Goodyear, I. M. (1990). *Life experiences, development, and childhood psychopathology*. New York: Wiley.
Gordon, M. R. (1994, November 6). In poignant public letter, Reagan reveals that he has Alzheimer's. *New York Times*, pp. 1, 47.
Gordon, R. A., Chase-Lansdale, P. L. & Brooks-Gunn, J. (2004). Extended households and the life course of young mothers: Understanding the associations using a sample of mothers with premature babies. *Child Development, 75*, 1013–1038.
Gordon, S., & Gilgun, J. F. (1987). Adolescent sexuality. In V. B. Van Hasselt & M. Hersen (Eds.), *Handbook of adolescent psychology*. New York: Pergamon Press.
Gordon, S., & Snyder, C. W. (1989). *Personal issues in human sexuality: A guidebook for better sexual health*. Boston: Allyn & Bacon.
Gordon, T. (1970). *Parent effectiveness training*. New York: Wyden.
Gordon, T. (2000). *Parent effectiveness training: The proven program for raising responsible children*. New York: Three Rivers Press.
Gorman, C. (1994, November 21). An eye on Alzheimer's. *Time*, p. 89.
Gorski, P. A. (1999). Pregnancy, birth and the first days. In M. D. Levine, W. B. Carey, & A. C. Crocker (Eds.), *Developmental-behavioral pediatrics*, 14–37. Philadelphia: Saunders.

Gotlib, I. H., & McCabe, S. B. (1990). Marriage and psychopathology. In F. D. Fincham & T. N. Bradbury (Eds.), *The psychology of marriage: Basic issues and applications*. New York: Guilford Press.

Gottesman, I. I. (1991). *Schizophrenia genetics: The origins of madness*. New York: Freeman.

Gottfredson, M. R., & Hirschi, T. (1990). *A general theory of crime*. Stanford, CA: Stanford University Press.

Gottfried, T. (2001). *Teen fathers today*. New York: 21st Century.

Gottlieb, S., & Barrett, D. (1986). Effects of unanticipated cesarean section on mothers, infants, and their interaction in the first month of life. *Developmental and Behavioral Pediatrics, 7*, 180–185.

Gottman, J. M. (1994, May/June). Why marriages fail. *Family Therapy Networker*, pp. 41–48.

Gottman, J. M. (1997). *The heart of parenting: Raising an emotionally intelligent child*. New York: Simon & Schuster.

Gottman, J. M. (1998). *Raising an emotionally intelligent child*. New York: Fireside.

Graber, J. A., Petersen, A. C., & Brooks-Gunn, J. (1996). Pubertal processes: Methods, measures, and models. In J. A. Graber, J. Brooks-Gunn, & A. C. Petersen (Eds.), *Transitional domains and context* (pp. 23–54). Mahwah, NJ: Erlbaum.

Graham, S. R. (1992). What does a man want? *American Psychologist, 47*, 837–841.

Graham-Bermann, S. A., & Edleson, J. L. (2001). *Domestic violence in the lives of children: The future of research, intervention, and social policy*. Washington, DC: American Psychological Association.

Gray, A., & Payne, P. (2001). *World health disease*. New York: Open University Press.

Gray-Little, B., & Hafdahl, A. R. (2000). Factors influencing racial comparisons of self-esteem: A quantitative review. *Psychological Bulletin, 126*, 26–54.

Grebb, J. A., Reus, V. I., & Freimer, N. B. (1988). Neurobehavioral chemistry & physiology. In H. H. Goldman (Ed.), *Review of General Psychiatry*. East Norwalk, CT: Appleton & Lang.

Green, J. W. (1995). *Cultural awareness in the human services: A multi-ethnic approach*. Boston: Allyn & Bacon.

Green, J. W. (1999). *Cultural awareness in the human services: A multi-ethnic approach* (3rd ed.). Boston: Allyn & Bacon.

Green, R. G., Beatty, W. W., & Arkin, R. M. (1984). *Human motivation*. Boston: Allyn & Bacon.

Greene, R. R. (1994). *Human behavior theory: A diversity framework*. New York: Aldine de Gruyter.

Greene, R. R. (2000). *Social work with the aged and their families* (2nd ed.). New York: Aldine de Gruyter.

Greenlee, R. T. (2000). Cancer statistics, 2000. *CA: The Cancer Journal for Clinicians, 50*, 24–18.

Greenspan, S., & Greenspan, N. (1985). *First feelings: Milestones in the emotional development of your baby and child*. New York: Viking Press.

Griffith, D. (1988). The effect of prenatal exposure to cocaine on the infant and on early maternal-infant interactions. In I. J. Chasnoff (Ed.), *Drugs, alcohol, pregnancy, and parenting*. Lancaster, UK: Kluwer.

Griffith, D. (1992, September). Prenatal exposure to cocaine and other drugs: Developmental and educational prognoses. *Phi Delta Kappan*, pp. 30–34.

Griggs, S., & Dunn, R. (2004). Hispanic-American students and learning style. ERIC Digest. Retrieved August 3, 2004, from http://www.ericdigests.org/1996-4/hispanic.htm

Grinnell, R. M., Jr., Kyte, N. S., Bostwick G. J., Jr. (1981). Environmental modification. In A. N. Maluccio (Ed.), *Promoting competence in clients: A new/old approach to social work practice*. New York: Free Press.

Grodstein, F., Manson, J. E., Colditz, G. A., Willett, W. C., Speizer, F. E., & Stampfer, M. J. (2000). A prospective, observational study of postmenopausal hormone therapy and primary prevention of cardiovascular disease. *Annals of Internal Medicine, 133*, 933–941.

Gross, M. D., Tofanelli, R. A., Butzirus, S. M., & Snodgrass, E. W. (1987). The effects of diets rich in and free from additives on the behavior of children with hyperkinetic and learning disorders. *Journal of the Academy of Child and Adolescent Psychiatry, 26*, 53–55.

Grossman, D. C., Milligan, C. B., & Deyo, R. A. (1991). Risk factors for suicide attempts among Navajo adolescents. *American Journal of Public Health, 81*, 870–874.

Groth, A. N., & Birnbaum, H. J. (1978). Adult sexual orientation and attraction to underage persons. *Archives of Sexual Behavior, 7*, 175–181.

Grove, D., & Burnaugh, R. (2002). *Invisible men: Finding, engaging and inspiring men in therapy*. Phoenix, AZ: Zeig, Tucker, & Theisen.

Grover, K. J., Russell, C. S., Schumm, W. R., & Paff-Bergen, L. A. (1985). Mate selection processes and marital satisfaction. *Family Relations, 34*, 383–386.

Gruetzner, H. (1988). *Alzheimer's: A caregiver's guide and sourcebook*. New York: Wiley.

Grunwald, L., & Goldberg, J. (1993, July). The amazing minds of infants. *Life*, pp. 46–60.

Grusec, J., & Abramovitch, R. (1982). Imitation of peers and adults in a natural setting: A functional analysis. *Child Development, 53*, 636–642.

Grusec, J., & Lytton, H. (1988). *Social development: History, theory and research*. New York: Springer-Verlag.

Grusec, J. E., Davidov, M., & Lundell, L. (2002). Prosocial and helping behavior. In P. K. Smith & C. H. Hart (eds.), *Blackwell handbook of childhood social development* (pp. 457–474). Malden, MA: Blackwell.

Guernsey, J. (1993). *Abortion: Understanding the controversy*. Minneapolis, MN: Lerner.

Gullotta, T. P., Adams, G. R., & Markstrom, C. A. (2000). *The adolescent experience* (4th ed.). San Diego, CA: Academic Press.

Gump, L. S., Baker, R. C., & Roll, S. (2000). The moral justification scale: Reliability and validity of a new measure of care and justice orientation. *Adolescence, 137*, 67–76.

Gundara, J. S. (1993). Multiculturalism and the British nation-state. In J. Horton (Ed.), *Liberalism, multiculturalism, and toleration*. London: Macmillan Press.

Gunnar, M. (1984). Coping with aversive stimulation in the neonatal period: Quiet sleep and plasma cortisol levels during recovery from circumcision. *Child Development, 56*, 824–834.

Gunter-Hunt, G., Mahoney, J., & Sieger, C. (2002). A comparison of state advance directive documents. *The Gerontologist, 42*(1), 51–60.

Guo, G. (1998). The timing of the influences of cumulative poverty on children's cognitive ability and achievement. *Social Forces, 77*(1), 257–287.

Gurland, B. J., Dean, L. L., Copeland, J., Gurland, R., & Golden, R. (1982). Criteria for the diagnosis of dementia in the community elderly. *The Gerontologist, 22*, 180–186.

Gurland, B. J., Dean, L. L., Cross, P., & Golden, R. (1980). The epidemiology of depression and dementia in the elderly: The use of multiple indicators of these conditions. In J. O. Cole & J. E. Barrett (Eds.), *Psychopathology of the aged*. New York: Raven Press.

Guttuso, T., Jr., Kurlan, R., McDermott, M. P., & Kieburtz, K. (2003). Gabapentin's effects on hot flashes in postmenopausal women: A randomized controlled trial. *Obstetrics and Gynecology, 101*, 337–345.

Haaken, J. (1990). A critical analysis of the co-dependence construct. *Psychiatry, 53*, 396–406.

Haas, R., & Massey, K. (2001). *Eat to win for permanent fat loss: The revolutionary fat-burning diet for peak mental and physical performance and optimum health*. San Francisco: Three Rivers Press.

Hader, S. L., Smith, D. K., Moore, J. S., & Holmberg, S. D. (2001). HIV infection in women in the United States. *Journal of the American Medical Association, 285*, 295–307.

Hagestad, G. (1985). Continuity and connectedness. In V. L. Bengston & J. Robertson (Ed.), *Grandparenthood*. Beverly Hills, CA: Sage.

Hagy, A. P. (1998). The demand for child care quality: An hedonic price theory approach. *Journal of Human Resources, 33*, 683–710.

Hahn, N. (1993). Why children and parents must play while they eat: An interview with T. Berry Brazelton, M.D. *Journal of the American Dietetic Association, 93*, 1385–1387.

Haith, M., & Canfield, R. (1991). Young infants' visual expectations for symmetric and asymmetric stimulus sequences. *Developmental Psychology, 27*, 198–208.

Haley, J. (1990). *Problem-solving therapy*. San Francisco: Jossey-Bass.

Hall, J. A., & Halberstadt, A. G. (1980). Masculinity and femininity in children: Development of the Children's Personal Attributes Questionnaire. *Developmental Psychology, 16*, 270–280.

Halpern, R. (1993). Poverty and infant development. In C. Zeaneh (Ed.), *Handbook of infant mental health* (pp. 73–86). New York: Guilford Press.

Hamark, B., Uddenberg, N., & Forssman, L. (1995). The influence of social class on parity and psychological reactions in women coming for induced abortion. *Acta Obstetricia et Gynecologica Scandinavica, 74*, 302–306.

Hamburg, B. A., & Dixon, S. L. (1992). Adolescent pregnancy and parenthood. In M. K. Rosenheim & M. F. Testa (Eds.), *Early parenthood and coming of age in the 1990s*. New Brunswick, NJ: Rutgers University Press.

Hamdani, R. J. (1974). *Exploratory behavior and vocational development among disadvantaged inner-city adolescents.* Unpublished doctoral dissertation, Columbia University, New York.

Hammer, H., Finkelhor, D., & Sedlak, A. J. (2002). *Runaway/thrownaway children: National estimates and characteristics.* Washington, DC: OJJDP.

Hammond, C. B. (1994). Women's concerns with hormone replacement therapy—Compliance issues. *Fertility & Sterility, 62,* 157–160.

Hann, D. M., Osofsky, J. D., Barnard, K. E., & Leonard, G. (1990). Maternal emotional availability in two risk groups [Special ICIS issue]. *Infant Behavior and Development, 13,* 404.

Hansen, J. F. (1980). *Children's attachment to mother figures and the social development of black infants and young children.* Unpublished manuscript, University of California, Berkeley.

Hanson, H. C. (1962). *Dictionary of ecology.* New York: Philosophical Library.

Hanson, W. (1980, October). The urban Indian woman and her family. *Social Casework,* pp. 476–483.

Harlow, S. D., & Park, M. A. (1996). A longitudinal study of risk factors for the occurrence, duration and severity of menstrual cramps in a cohort of college women. *British Journal of Obstetrics and Gynaecology, 103,* 1134–1142.

Harmon, R. R., & Blieszner, R. (1990). Filial responsibility expectations among adult child–older parent pairs. *Journal of Gerontology: Psychological Sciences, 45,* 110–112.

Harmon-Jones, E. (2004). From cognitive dissonance to the motivational functions of emotions. In R. A. Wright, J. Greenberg, & S. S. Brehm (Eds.), *Motivational analyses of social behavior: Building on Jack Brehm's contributions to psychology,* 39–55.

Harris, B. M., & Franklin, C. (2004). Evidence-based life skills interventions for pregnant adolescents in school settings. In A. R. Roberts & K. R. Yeager (Eds.), *Evidence-based practice manual: Research and outcome measures in health and human services.* New York: Oxford University Press.

Harris, J. R. (1998). *The nurture assumption: Why children turn out the way they do.* New York: Touchstone.

Harris, M. B., & Franklin, C. (in press). *Taking charge: A school-based life skills curriculum for adolescent mothers.* New York: Oxford University Press.

Harris, M. J., & Rosenthal, R. (1985). Mediation of interpersonal expectancy effects: 31 meta-analyses. *Psychological Bulletin, 97,* 363–386.

Harris, S. (2004). *The end of faith: Religion, terror, and the future of reason.* New York: Norton.

Harrison, L., Leeper, J., & Yoon, M. (1991). Preterm infants; physiologic responses to early parent touch. *Western Journal of Nursing Research, 13,* 698–713.

Harrison, L., & Woods, S. (1991, July/August). Early parental touch and preterm infants. *JOGNN,* 299–305.

Harter, S. (1979). *The perceived competence scale.* Denver, CO: University of Denver.

Harter, S. (1982). The perceived competence scale for children. *Child Development, 53,* 87–97.

Harter, S. (1985). *Self-perception profile for children.* Denver, CO: University of Denver.

Harter, S. (1995, May). Is self-esteem really all that important? *APA Monitor,* 44–45.

Harter, S. (1999). *The construction of the self: A developmental perspective.* New York: Guilford.

Hartford, M. E. (1985). Understanding normative growth and development in aging: Working with strengths. *Journal of Gerontological Social Work, 8,* 37–54.

Hartman, A. (1978). Diagrammatic assessment of family relationships. *Social Casework, 59,* 465–476.

Hartman, A., & Laird, J. (1983). *Family-centered social work practice.* New York: Free Press.

Hartman, A., & Laird, J. (1987). Family practice. In A. Minahan (Ed.), *Encyclopedia of social work* (18th ed., Vol. 1, pp. 575–587). Silver Spring, MD: National Association of Social Workers.

Hartney, L. L. (1989, September/October). My mother's keeper. *Family therapy networker,* pp. 38–41.

Hartup, W. W. (1974). Aggression in childhood: Developmental perspectives. *American Psychologist, 29,* 336–341.

Hartup, W. W. (1979). Peer relations and the growth of social competence. In M. W. Kent & J. E. Rolf (Eds.), *Primary prevention of psychopathology: Vol. 3., Social competence in children.* Hanover, NH: University Press of New England.

Hartup, W. W. (1983). Peer relations. In P. H. Mussen (Ed.), *Handbook of child psychology* (4th ed., Vol. 4). New York: Wiley.

Hartup, W. W. (1989). Social relationships and their developmental significance. *American Psychologist, 44,* 120–126.

Hartup, W. W., & Abecassis, M. (2002). Friends and enemies. In P. K. Smith & C. H. Hart (eds.), *Blackwell handbook of childhood social development* (285–306). Malden, MA: Blackwell.

Harwood, D., Hawton, K., Hope, T., & Jacoby, R. (2000). Suicide in older people: Mode of death, demographic factors, and medical contact before death. *International Journal of Geriatric Psychiatry, 15,* 736–743.

Hastorf, A. H., & Isen, A. M. (1992). Social knowledge. In A. H. Hastorf & A. M. Isen (Eds.), *Cognitive Social Psychology.* New York: Elsevier/North Holland.

Hatch, L. R. (1990). Gender and work: At midlife and beyond. *Generations, 14,* 48–51.

Hatch, L., & Bulcroft, K. (2004). Does long-term marriage bring less frequent disagreements? Five explanatory frameworks. *Journal of Family Issues, 25*(4), 465–495.

Hatfield, E., & Walster, G. W. (1985). *A new look at love.* New York: University Press of America.

Haugh, S. S., Hoffman, C. D., & Cowan, G. (1980). The eye of the very young beholder: Sex-typing of infants by young children. *Child Development, 51,* 598–600.

Havighurst, R. (1961). Successful aging. *Gerontologist, 1,* 8–13.

Havighurst, R. J. (1952). *Developmental tasks and education.* New York: David McKay.

Havighurst, R. J. (1972). *Developmental tasks and education* (3rd ed.). New York: David McKay.

Hawkins, J., Pea, R. D., Glick, J., & Scribner, S. (1984). "Merds that laugh don't like mushrooms": Evidence for deductive reasoning by preschoolers. *Developmental Psychology, 20,* 584–594.

Hayden, M. F., & Goldman, J. (1996). Families of adults with mental retardation: Stress levels and need for services. *Social Work, 41,* no. 6, 657–667.

Hayes, N., Stainton, M., & McNeil, D. (1993). Caring for a chronically ill infant: A paradigm case of maternal rehearsal in the neonatal intensive care unit. *Journal of Pediatric Nursing, 8*(6), 355–360.

Hays, J. C., & George, L. K. (2002). The life-course trajectory toward living alone: Racial differences. *Research on Aging, 24*(3), 238–307.

Haywood, K. M. (1986). *Life span motor development.* Champaign, IL: Human Kinetics.

Hazel, J. S., Schumaker, J. B., Sherman, J. A., & Sheldon-Wilder, J. (1981). The development and evaluation of a group skills training program for court-adjudicated youths. In D. Upper and S. M. Ross (Eds.), *Behavioral group therapy, 1981: An annual review.* Champaign, IL: Research Press.

Hazen, C., & Shaver, P. (1987). Romantic love conceptualized as an attachment process. *Journal of Personality and Social Psychology, 52,* 511–524.

Hearn, G. (1979). General systems theory and social work. In F. J. Turner (Ed.), *Social work treatment: Interlocking theoretical approaches* (2nd ed.). New York: Free Press.

Heatherington, E. M. (1987). Family relations six years after divorce. In K. Pasley & M. Ihinger-Tollman (Eds.), *Remarriage and stepparenting today: Current research and theory.* New York: Guilford Press.

Heatherington, E. M. (1988). Parents, children, and siblings: Six years after divorce. In R. A. Hinde & J. Stevenson-Hinde (Eds.), *Relationships within families: Mutual influences* (pp. 311–331). New York: Oxford University Press.

Heatherington, E. M. (1989). Coping with family transitions: Winners, losers, and survivors. *Child Development, 60,* 1–14.

Heatherington, E. M., & Blechman, E. A. (1996). *Stress, coping, and resiliency in children and families.* Mahwah, NJ: Erlbaum.

Heatherington, E. M., Cox, M., & Cox, R. (1979). Play and social interaction in children following divorce. *Journal of Social Issues, 35,* 26–49.

Heatherington, E. M., Cox, M., & Cox, R. (1982). Effects of divorce on parents and children. In M. Lamb (Ed.), *Nontraditional families: Parenting and child development.* Hillsdale, NJ: Erlbaum.

Heatherington, E. M., & Kelly, J. (2002). *For better or worse: Divorce reconsidered.* New York: Norton.

Heatherington, E. M., & Stanley-Hagan, M. (2000). Diversity among stepfamilies. In D. H. Demo, K. R. Allen, & M. A. Fine (Eds.), *Handbook of family diversity.* New York: Oxford University Press.

Heatherington, E. M., & Stanley-Hagan, M. (2002). Parenting in divorced and remarried families. In M. H. Bornstein (Ed.), *Handbook of parenting* (2nd ed., Vol. 3, pp. 287–315), Mahwah, NJ: Erlbaum.

Heaton, T. B. (2002). Factors contributing to increasing marital stability in the United States. *Journal of Family Issues, 23,* 392–409.

Hebert, L., Scherr, P., Bienias, J., Bennett, D., & Evans, D. (2003). Alzheimer disease in the US population: Prevalence estimates using the 2000 census. *Archives of Neurology, 60*, 1119–1122.

Hecht, M. (1993). *African American communication: Ethnic identity and cultural interpretation.* Newbury Park, CA: Sage.

Heilman, J. R. (1995, August 13). The good news about Alzheimer's. *Parade*, 12–13.

Heiney, S., Hasan, L., & Price, K. (1993). Developing and implementing a bereavement program for a children's hospital. *Journal of Pediatric Nursing, 8*, 385–391.

Heise, L. (1989, March/April). The global war against women. *World Watch*, 21.

Helm, H., Hays, J., Flint, E., Koenig, H., & Blazer, D. (2000). Does private religious activity prolong survival? A six year follow-up study of 3,851 older adults. *The Journals of Gerontology Series, A: Biological Sciences and Medical Sciences, 55*, M400–M405.

Henggeler, S. W., Schoenwald, S. K., Rowland, M. D., & Cunningham, P. B. (2002). *Serious emotional disturbance in children and adolescents: Multisystemic therapy.* New York: The Guilford Press.

Hennessy, C. H., & John, R. (1995). The interpretation of burden among Pueblo Indian caregivers. *Journal of Aging Studies, 9*, 215–229.

Hepworth, D. H., & Larsen, J. A. (1989). *Direct social work practice* (3rd ed.). Belmont, CA: Wadsworth.

Hepworth, D. H., & Larsen, J. A. (1993). *Direct social work practice* (4th ed.). Pacific Grove, CA: Brooks/Cole.

Herek, G. M. (1991). Stigma, prejudice, and violence against lesbians and gay men. In J. C. Gonsiorek & J. D. Weinrich (Eds.), *Homosexuality: Research implications for public policy.* Newbury Park, CA: Sage.

Herek, G. M., & Berrill, K. (1990). Violence against lesbians and gay men: Issues for research, practice and policy. *Journal of Interpersonal Violence, 5*, 414–423.

Herman, E. (1988, Summer). The twelve-step program: Cure or cover? *Out/Look: National Lesbian and Gay Quarterly.* Excerpted in *Utne Reader* (1988, November/December), 52–63.

Herrerias, C. T., Perrin, J. M., & Stein, M. T. (2001). The child with ADHD: Using the AAP clinical practice guideline. *American Family Physician, 63*, 1811–1821.

Hersch, P. (1990, July/August). The resounding silence. *Family Therapy Networker*, 18–29.

Hesling, K., & Szklo, K. (1981). Mortality after bereavement. *American Journal of Epidemiology, 144*, 42–52.

Hess, B. B. (1990). Gender and aging: The demographic parameters. *Generations, 14*, 12–15.

Hess, R. O., & Holloway, S. D. (1984). Family and school as educational institutions. In R. D. Parke (Ed.), *Review of child development research: Vol. 7, The family.* Chicago: University of Chicago Press.

Hewitt, M., & Siomone, J. V. (Eds.) (1999). *Ensuring Quality Cancer Care.* Washington, DC: National Academies Press.

High rate of suicide among New York City police (1994, November). *NASW News*, p. 9.

Hilgard, E. R. (1987). *Psychology in America: A historical survey.* San Diego, CA: Harcourt Brace Jovanovich.

Hill, C. R., & Stafford, F. P. (1980). Parental care of children: Time diary estimate of quantity, predictability, and variety. *Journal of Human Relations, 15*, 219–239.

Hill, J. P., & Holmbeck, G. N. (1986). Attachment and autonomy during adolescence. *Annals of Child Development, 3*, 145–189.

Hill, J. P., Holmbeck, G. N., Marlow, L., Green, T. M., & Lynch, M. E. (1985). Pubertal status and parent-child relations in families of 7th grade boys. *Journal of Early Adolescence, 5*, 31–44.

Hinde, R. A., Titmus, G., Easton, D., & Tamplin, A. (1985). Incidence of "friendship" and behavior toward strong associates and nonassociates in preschoolers. *Child Development, 56*, 234–245.

Hinrichsen, G. A. (1990). *Mental health problems and older adults: Choices and challenges.* Santa Barbara, CA: ABC-CLIO.

Hinrichsen, G. A., & Ramirez, M. (1992). Black and white dementia caregivers: A comparison of their adaptation, adjustment, and service utilization. *The Gerontologist, 32*, 375–381.

Ho, M. K. (1987). *Family therapy with ethnic minorities.* Newbury Park, CA: Sage.

Hodgson, L., & Cutler, S. (2003). Looking for signs of Alzheimer's disease. *International Journal of Aging and Human Development, 56*(4), 323–343.

Hoff-Ginsberg, E. (1986). Function and structure in maternal speech: Their relation to the child's development of syntax. *Developmental Psychology, 22*, 155–163.

Hoffman, L. (1987). The effects on children of maternal and paternal employment. In N. Gerstel & H. Gross (Eds.), *Families and work.* Philadelphia: Temple University Press.

Hoffman, L. W. (1989). Effects of maternal employment in two-parent families. *American Psychologist, 44*, 283–293.

Hoffman, M. L. (1970). Moral development. In P. H. Mussen (Ed.), *Carmichael's manual of child psychology* (Vol. 2). New York: Wiley.

Hoffman, S., Mantell, J., Exner, T., & Stein, Z. (2004). The Future of the Female Condom. *International Family Planning Perspectives, 30*, 39–145.

Hogg, M. A. (2003). Social Identity. In M. R. Leary & J. P. Tangney (Eds.) *Handbook of self and identity* (pp. 462–479). New York: Guilford Press.

Hohman, M. (1995). *Self-efficacy and empowerment: A study of women in recovery from alcoholism.* Unpublished doctoral dissertation, School of Social Work, Arizona State University.

Holland, D. (1997). Selves as cultured: As told by an anthropologist who lacks a soul. In R. D. Ashmore, & L. Jussim (Eds.), *Self and identity: Fundamental issues.* New York: Oxford University Press.

Holloway, J. H. (2003). When children aren't ready for kindergarten. *Educational Leadership, 60*, 89–90.

Holm, B. A., Cassidy, S. B., et al. (1993). Prader-Willi syndrome: Consensus diagnostic criteria. *Pediatrics, 2*, 398–402.

Holstein, M., & Minkler, M. (2003). Self, society, and the "new gerontology." *The Gerontologist, 43*(6), 787–796.

Homans, G. C. (1950). *The human group.* New York: Harcourt, Brace & World.

Honzik, M. (1976). Values and limitations of infant tests: An overview. In M. Lewis (Ed.), *Origins of intelligence* (pp. 59–95). New York: Plenum.

Hooyman, N. R. (1994). Diversity and populations at risk: Women. In F. G. Reamer (Ed.), *The foundations of social work knowledge.* New York: Columbia University Press.

Hooyman, N. R., & Lustbader, W. (1986). *Taking care: Supporting older people and their families.* New York: Free Press.

Hooyman, N. R. & Kiyak, H. A. (2002). *Social gerontology: A multidisciplinary approach.* Boston: Allyn & Bacon.

Hopper, K. (2003). *Reckoning with homelessness.* New York: Cornell University Press.

Horenczyk, G., & Munayer, S. (2003). Complex patterns of cultural allegiances: The ethnic identity of Palestinian Christian Arab adolescents in Israel. In P. Weinrich & W. Saunderson (Eds.), *Analyzing identity: Cross-cultural, societal, and clinical contexts.* London: Routledge Taylor & Francis.

Horn, J. L. (1982). The theory of fluid and crystallized intelligence in relation to concepts of cognitive psychology and aging in adulthood. In F. J. M. Craik & S. Trehub (Eds.), *Aging and cognitive processes* (pp. 237–278). New York: Plenum.

Horton, J. (1993). Liberalism, multiculturalism, and tolerance. In J. Horton (Ed.), *Liberalism, multiculturalism, and toleration.* London: Macmillan Press.

Horton, J. (Ed.) (1993). *Liberalism, multiculturalism, and toleration.* London: Macmillan Press.

Horwitz, A. V. (1990). *The logic of social control.* New York: Plenum.

Hothersall, D. (1984). *History of psychology.* Philadelphia: Temple University Press.

Howard, D. V. (1983). *Cognitive psychology: Memory, language, and thought.* New York: Macmillan.

Howard, J. A., & Renfrow, D. G. (2003). Social cognition. In J. Delamater (Ed.), *Handbook of social psychology* (259–281). New York: Kluwer Academic/Plenum Publishers.

Howe, M. (1995, June). New cognitive developments make waves. *APA Monitor.*

Howell, J. C., & Lynch, J. P. (2000). *Youth gangs in schools.* Washington, DC: Office of Juvenile Justice and Delinquency Programs.

Howell, M. C., Allen, M. C., & Doress, P. B. (1987). Dying and death. In P. B. Doress, D. L. Siegel, & The Midlife and Older Women Book Project (Eds.), *Ourselves, growing older: Women aging with knowledge and power* (pp. 392–403). New York: Simon & Schuster.

Hoyenga, K. B., & Hoyenga, K. T. (1988). *Psychobiology: The neuron and behavior.* Pacific Grove, CA: Brooks/Cole.

Huesmann, L. R., Eron, L. D., Lefkowitz, M. M., & Walder, L. O. (1984). Stability of aggression over time and generations. *Developmental Psychology, 6*, 1120–1134.

Huff, C. R. (1993). Gangs in the United States. In A. P. Goldstein & C. R. Huff (Eds.), *The gang intervention handbook* (pp. 3–20). Champaign, IL: Research Press.

Huff, R. G. (2001). *Gangs in America: III.* Thousand Oaks, CA: Sage.

Hughes, C. B., & Page-Lieberman, J. (1989). Totality of bereavement, 25–56-year-old fathers who experienced perinatal loss of infant. *Death Studies, 13*, 537–556.

Hughes, L. (1970). Mother to son. In A. Bontemps and L. Hughes (Eds.), *The poetry of the Negro, 1746–1970*. Garden City, NY: Doubleday.

Hunter, S., & Sundel, M. (Eds.) (1989). *Midlife myths: Issues, findings, and practice implications*. Newbury Park, CA: Sage.

Hunter, S., Sundel, S. S., & Sundel, M. (2002). *Women at midlife: Life experiences and implications for the helping professions*. Washington, DC: NASW Press.

Hurd, L. C. (1999). We're not old! Older women's negotiation of aging and oldness. *Journal of Aging Studies*, 13, 419–439.

Hybels, C., Blazer, D., & Pieper, C. (2001). Toward a threshold for subthreshold depression: An analysis of correlates of depression by severity of symptoms using data from an elderly community sample. *The Gerontologist*, 41(3), 357–365.

Hyde, J. S. (1985). *Half the human experience: The psychology of women* (3rd ed.). Lexington, MA: Heath.

Hyman, P. (1987). Memory lapse and memory loss. In P. B. Doress, D. L. Siegel, & The Midlife and Older Women Book Project (Eds.), *Ourselves, growing older: Women aging with knowledge and power* (pp. 380–391). New York: Simon & Schuster.

Hymel, S., Comfort, C., Schonert-Reichl, K., & McDougall, P. (1996). Academic failure and school dropout: The influence of peers. In K. Wentzel & J. Juvonen (Eds.), *Social motivation: Understanding children's school adjustment* (pp. 313–345). New York: Cambridge University Press.

Hymel, S., Vaillancourt, T., McDougall, P., & Renshaw, P. D. (2002). Peer acceptance and rejection in childhood. In P. K. Smith & C. H. Hart (Eds.), *Blackwell handbook of childhood social development* (265–284). Malden, MA: Blackwell.

Ianniruberto, A., & Tajani, E. (1981). Ultrasonographic study of fetal movements. *Seminars in Perinatology*, 5, 175–181.

Iglowstein, I., et al. (2003). Children and adolescent sleep. *American Family Physician*, 111, 302–307.

Iliffe, S., & Manthorpe, J. (2004). The hazards of early recognition of dementia: A risk assessment. *Aging and Mental Health*, 8(2), 99–105.

Infant Health and Development Program. (1990). Enhancing the outcomes of low-birthweight premature infants. *Journal of the American Medical Association*, 263, 3035–3042.

Ingersoll-Dayton, B., Neal, M. B., & Hammer, L. B. (2001). Aging parents helping adult children: The experience of the sandwiched generation. *Family Relations*, 50, 262–271.

Institute of Medicine (2001). *Crossing the quality chasm: A new health system for the 21st century*. Washington, DC: National Academy of Sciences.

Isaacowitz, D., Vaillant, G., & Seligman, M. (2003). Strengths and satisfaction across the adult lifespan. *International Journal of Aging and Human Development*, 57(2), 181–201.

Isay, B. (1997). *Becoming gay: The journal to self-acceptance*. New York: Owl Books.

Iyengar, S. S., & Brockner, J. (2001). Cultural differences in self and the impact on personal and social influences. In W. Wosinska, R. B. Cialdinia, D. W. Barrett, & J. Reykowski (Eds.), *The practice of social influence in multiple cultures* (pp. 13–32). Mahwah, NJ: Erlbaum.

Izard, C. (Ed.). (1982). *Measuring emotions in infants and children*. London: Cambridge University Press.

Jablonski, N. B., & Chaplin, G. (2002). Skin deep. *Scientific American*, 287(4), 74–81.

Jackson, A. P. (1998). The role of social support in parenting for low-income, single, black mothers. *Social Service Review*, 72, 365–378.

Jackson, A. P. (2003a). The effects of family and neighborhood characteristics on the behavioral and cognitive development of poor black children: A longitudinal study. *American Journal of Community Psychology*, 32, 175–186.

Jackson, A. P. (2003b). Mothers' employment and poor and near poor African-American children's development: A longitudinal study. *Social Services Review*, 77, 93–109.

Jackson, A. P., & Huang, C. C. (1998). Concerns about children's development: Implications for single employed black mothers' well being. *Social Work Research*, 22, 233–240.

Jackson, J. F. (1993). Multiple caregivers among African Americans and infant attachment: The need for an emic approach. *Human Development*, 36, 87–102.

Jackson, P. (1985, April). When the baby isn't perfect. *American Journal of Nursing*, 396–399.

Jacobsen, T., Edelstein, W., & Hoffman, V. (1994). A longitudinal study of the relation between representations of attachment in childhood and cognitive functioning in childhood and adolescence. *Developmental Psychology*, 30, 112–124.

Jacobson, B. (1987). Perinatal origin of adult self-destructive behavior. *Acta Psychiatrica Scandinavica*, 76, 364–371.

Jaffe, M. L. (1991). *Understanding parenting*. Dubuque, IA: Wm. C. Brown.

Jaffee, S., & Hyde, J. S. (2000). Gender differences in moral orientation: A meta-analysis. *Psychological Bulletin*, 126, 703–721.

James, W. (1884). What is emotion? *Mind*, 19, 188–205.

James, W. (1890). *The principles of psychology*. New York: Holt.

Jang, Y., Haley, W., Small, B., & Mortimer, J. (2002). The role of mastery and social resources in the associations between disability and depression in later life. *The Gerontologist*, 42(6), 807–813.

Janis, I. L. (1972). *Victims of groupthink*. Boston: Houghton Mifflin.

Janis, I. L. (1973, January). Groupthink. *Yale Alumni Magazine*, 16–19.

Janis, I. L. (1982). *Groupthink: Psychological studies of policy decisions and fiascoes*. Boston: Houghton Mifflin.

Janis, I. L., & Mann, L. (1977). *Decision making: A psychological analysis of conflict, choice, and commitment*. New York: Free Press.

Jannke, S. (1994). Mandatory drug testing of pregnant women. *Childbirth Instructor*, 4(4), 12–18.

Janosik, E. H. (1986). *Crisis counseling: A contemporary approach*. Boston: Jones & Bartlett.

Janzen, C., & Harris, O. (1986). *Family treatment in social work practice* (2nd ed.). Itasca, IL: Peacock.

Jason, J., & van de Meer, A. (1989). *Parenting your premature baby*. New York: Henry Holt.

Javroff, L. (1996, April 1). Prostate cancer: The battle. *Time*, 58–65.

Jedrychowski, W., & Flak, E. (1996). Confronting the prenatal effects of active and passive tobacco smoking on the birth weight of children. *Central European Journal of Public Health*, 4, 201–205.

Jencks, C. (1985). How much do high school students learn? *Sociology of Education*, 58, 128–135.

Jencks, C. (1995). *Homelessness*. New York: Harvard University Press.

Jenkins, J. (1992). Sibling relationships in disharmonious homes: Potential difficulties and protective effects. In F. Boer & J. Dunn (Eds.), *Children's sibling relationships: Developmental and clinical issues*. Hillsdale, NJ: Erlbaum.

Jennings, K., Wisner, K., Conley, B. (1991). Serving the mental health needs of families with children under three: A comprehensive program. *Infant Mental Health Journal*, 12, 276–290.

Jensen, P. S. (2001). ADHD comorbidity and treatment outcomes in the MTA. *Journal of the American Academy of Child and Adolescent Psychiatry*, 401, 134–136.

Jessor, R. (1987). Problem-behavior theory, psychosocial development, and adolescent problem drinking. *British Journal of Addiction*, 82, 331–342.

Jessor, R. (1992). Risk behavior in adolescence: A psychosocial framework for understanding and action. In D. E. Rogers & E. Ginzburg (Eds.), *Adolescents at risk: Medical and social perspectives* (pp. 19–34). Boulder, CO: Westview Press.

Jessor, R. (1998). *New perspectives on adolescent risk behavior*. New York: Cambridge University Press.

Johnson, B. (2001). A study of sexuality in older adults: A multidimensional framework. Paper presented at the Annual Meeting, *Gerontological Society of America*, Chicago, IL.

Johnson, C. L. (1983). Dyadic family relationships and family supports. *The Gerontologist*, 23, 377–383.

Johnson, C. L., & Barer, B. M. (1990). Families and networks among older inner-city Blacks. *The Gerontologist*, 30, 726–733.

Johnson, C. N., & Wellman, H. M. (1982). Children's developing conceptions of the mind and brain. *Child Development*, 53, 222–234.

Johnson, D. F., Jarenger, E., Randolph, S. J., Cauce, A. M., Ward, J. et al. (2003). *Studying the effects of early child care experience on the development of children of color in the U.S.: Towards more inclusive research agenda*, Child Development, 74(5), 1227–1244.

Johnson, H. C. (1980). *Behavior, psychopathology, and the brain*. New York: Curriculum Concepts.

Johnson, H. C. (1999). *Psyche, synapse and substance: The role of neurobiology in emotions, behavior, cognition, and addiction for non-scientists*. Greenfield, MA: Deerfield Valley Publishing.

Johnson, H. C., Atkins, S. P., Battle, S. F., Hernandez-Arata, L., Hesselbrock, M., Libassi, M. F., et al. (1990, Spring/Summer). Strengthening the "bio" in the biopsychosocial paradigm. *Journal of Social Work Education*, 109–123.

Johnson, J., & Goldman, J. (1990). *Developmental assessment in clinical child psychology*. New York: Pergamon Press.

Johnson, J., Johnson, M., Cunningham, J., Ewing, S., Hatcher, D., & Dannen, C. (1982). *Newborn death: A book for parents experiencing the death of a very small infant*. Omaha, NE: Centering Corporation.

Johnson, J., & Smith, N. (2002). Health and social issues associated with racial, ethnic, and cultural disparities. *Generations, 26*(3). Retrieved June 24, 2004, from www.generationsjournal.org

Johnson, J. H., & Fennell, E. (1983). Aggressive and delinquent behavior in childhood and adolescence. In E. Walker & M. Roberts (Eds.), *Handbook of clinical child psychology*. New York: Wiley.

Johnson, M. H., & Karmiloff-Smith, A. (2004). Neuroscience perspectives on infant development. In Bremner, G., & Slater, A. (Eds.), *Theories of infant development* (pp. 145–173). Carlton, Victoria: Blackwell Publishing.

Johnston, L. D., O'Malley, P. M., & Bachman, J. G. (1988). *Illicit drug use, smoking, and drinking by America's high school students, college students, and young adults, 1975–1987*. Washington, DC: National Institute of Drug Abuse.

Johnston, L. D., O'Malley, P. M., Bachman, J. G., & Schulenberg, J. E. (2003). "Ecstasy use falls for second year in a row, overall teen drug use drops." Ann Arbor: University of Michigan News and Information Services.

Jones, E., & McCurdy, K. (1992). The links between types of maltreatment and demographic characteristics of children. *Child Abuse and Neglect, 16*, 201–215.

Jones, J. (1990, November). APA report puts focus on women, depression, how to treat it. *APA Monitor*, 33.

Jones, J. (1994). Embodied meaning: menopause and the change of life. *Social work in Health Care, 19*, 43–65.

Jones, J. (1997). Representations of menopause and their health care: Implications: A qualitative analysis. *American Journal of Preventive Medicine, 13*, 58–65.

Jones, J. (1999). Hormone Replacement Therapy: Women's decision-making process. *Social Work in Health Care, 28*, 95–111.

Jones, J. (2004). Personal communication.

Jones, S., & Raag, T. (1989). Smile production in infants: The importance of a social recipient for the facial signal. *Child Development, 60*, 811–818.

Jones-Witters, P., & Witters, W. (1986). *Drugs and society: A biological perspective*. Boston: Jones & Bartlett.

Jordan, C., & Franklin, C. (1995). *Clinical assessment for social workers*. Chicago: Lyceum Books.

Josephson Institute of Ethics. (2001). *2000 report card: The ethics of American youth: Violence and substance abuse: Data and commentary*. Marina del Rey, CA: Author.

Kadushin, A., & Kadushin, G. (1997). *The Social Work Interview*. New York: Columbia University Press.

Kaffman, M., & Elizur, E. (1977). Infants who become enuretics: A longitudinal study of 161 kibbutz children. *Monographs of the Society for Research in Child Development, 42*.

Kagan, J. (1978). On emotion and its development: A working paper. In M. Lewis & L. A. Rosenglum (Eds.), *The development of affect*. New York: Plenum.

Kagan, J. (1984a). The idea of emotion in human development. In C. E. Izard, J. Kagan, & R. B. Zajonc (Eds.), *Emotion, cognition, and behavior*. New York: Cambridge University Press.

Kagan, J. (1984b). *The nature of the child*. New York: Basic Books.

Kagan, J., Kearsley, R. B., & Zelazo, P. R. (1978). The effects of infant daycare on psychological development. *Evaluation Quarterly, 1*, 143–158.

Kahn, A. J. & Kamerman, S. B. (1987). *Child care: Facing the hard choices*. Dover, MA: Auburn House.

Kalat, J. W. (1992). *Biological psychology* (4th ed.). Pacific Grove, CA: Brooks/Cole.

Kalat, J. W. (1995). *Biological psychology* (5th ed.). Pacific Grove, CA: Brooks/Cole.

Kalat, J. W. (2001). *Biological psychology* (7th ed.). Belmont, CA: Wadsworth.

Kalat, J. W. (2004). *Biological Psychology* (8th ed.). Belmont, CA: Wadsworth/Thomson Learning.

Kalish, R. A. (1985). *Death, grief, and caring relationships* (2nd ed.). Pacific Grove, CA: Brooks/Cole.

Kalish, R. A., & Reynolds, D. K. (1976). *An overview of death and ethnicity*. Farmingdale, NY: Baywood.

Kalmuss, D., Davidson, A., & Cushman, L. (1992). Parenting expectations, experiences, and adjustment to parenthood: A test of the violated expectations framework. *Journal of Marriage and the Family, 52*, 516–526.

Kalter, N. (1987). Long-term effects of divorce on children: A developmental vulnerability model. *American Journal of Orthopsychiatry, 57*, 587–600.

Kalter, N. (1990). *Growing up with divorce*. New York: Free Press.

Kalter, N., Kloner, A., Schreier, S., & Okla, K. (1989). Predictors of children's post divorce adjustment. *American Journal of Orthopsychiatry, 59*, 605–619.

Kalter, N., & Schreier, S. (1994). Developmental facilitation groups for children of divorce: The elementary school model. In C. W. LeCroy (Ed.), *Handbook of child and adolescent treatment manuals*. New York: Lexington Books.

Kaminer, W. (1992). *I'm dysfunctional, you're dysfunctional*. Reading, MA: Addison-Wesley.

Kaminski, H., Stafl, A., & Aiman, J. (1987). The effect of epidural analgesia on the frequency of instrumental obstetric delivery. *Obstetrics & Gynecology, 69*, 770–773.

Kammerer, N., Mason, T., Connors, M., & Durkee, R. (2001). Transgender health and social service needs in context of HIV risk. In W. Bockting and S. Kirk (Eds.), *Transgender and HIV: Risks, Prevention, and Care* (pp. 39–51). New York: Haworth Press.

Kanfer, F. H., Stifter, E., & Morris, S. J. (1981). Self-control and altruism: Delay of gratification for another. *Child Development, 52*, 674–682.

Kanter, R. M. (1977). Women in organizations: Sex roles, group dynamics, and change strategies. In A. Sergeant (Ed.), *Beyond sex roles*. St. Paul, MN: West.

Kantor, D., & Lehr, W. (1975). *Inside the family*. San Francisco: Jossey-Bass.

Kaplan, P. S. (2004). *Adolescence*. Boston, MA: Houghton Mifflin.

Karls, J. M. & Wandrei, K. E. (1994). *Person-in-environment system: The PIE classification system for social functioning problems*. Washington, DC: NASW Press.

Karnes, B. (1986). *Gone from my sight: The dying experience*.

Kastenbaum, R. (1977). Death and development through the life span. In H. Feifel (Ed.), *New meanings of death* (pp. 18–45). New York: McGraw-Hill.

Kastenbaum, R. (1981). *Death, society and human experience*. St. Louis, MO: C. V. Mosby.

Kastenbaum, R., & Weisman, A. D. (1972). The psychological autopsy as a research procedure in gerontology. In D. P. Kent, R. Kastenbaum, & S. Sherwood (Eds.), *Research planning and action for the elderly: The power and potential of social science* (pp. 214–216). New York: Behavioral Publications.

Kato, T. (2001). Molecular genetics of bipolar disorder. *Neuroscience Research, 40*, 105–113.

Katz, J. N. (2005). The invention of heterosexuality. In T. L. Steele (Ed.), *Sex, self, and society: The social context of sexuality* (pp. 50–61). Belmont, CA: Thomson/Wadsworth.

Katz, M. (1999). *Final report on national standards for culturally and linguistically appropriate services in health care*. U.S. Department of Health and Human Services, Office of Minority Health.

Katz, P., & Zalk, S. (1978). Modification of children's racial attitudes. *Developmental Psychology, 14*, 447–456.

Kauffman, S. E., Silver, P., & Poulin, J. (1997). Gender differences in attitudes toward alcohol, tobacco, and other drugs. *Social Work, 42*(3), 231–241.

Kaufman, A. S., & Kaufman, N. L. (1983). *Kaufman assessment battery for children: Interpretive manual*. Circle Pines, MN: American Guidance Service.

Kaufman, G., & Elder, G. (2002). Revisiting age identity: A research note. *Journal of Aging Studies, 16*, 169–176.

Kaufman, G., & Elder, G. (2003). Grandparenting and age identity. *Journal of Aging Studies, 17*(3), 269–282.

Kaufman, S. (1998). Intensive old age, care, and the problem of death in America. *The Gerontologist, 38*(6), 718.

Kayser-Jones, J. (2002). The experience of dying: An ethnographic nursing home study. *The Gerontologist, 42* (Special Issue 3), 11–19.

Kazdin, A. E. (1987). *Conduct disorders in childhood and adolescence*. Newbury Park, CA: Sage.

Kazdin, A. E. (2000). *Behavior modification in applied settings*. Pacific Grove, CA: Wadsworth.

Kazdin, A. E., & Frame, C. (1983). Aggressive behavior and conduct disorder. In R. J. Morris & T. R. Kratochwill (Eds.), *The practice of child therapy*. New York: Pergamon Press.

Kearney, C. A. (2001). *School refusal behavior in youth: A functional approach to assessment and treatment*. Washington, DC: American Psychological Association.

Keating, D. P. (1980). Thinking processes in adolescence. In J. Adelson (Ed.), *Handbook of adolescent psychology*. New York: Wiley.

Keen, S. (1991). *Fire in the belly: On being a man*. New York: Bantam Books.

Kehoe, M. (1989). *Lesbians over 60 speak for themselves*. New York: Harrington Park Press.

Keith, P. M. (1986). The social context and resources of the unmarried in old age. *International Journal of Aging and Human Development, 23,* 81–96.

Kellner, D. (1990). The postmodern turn: Positions, problems and prospects. In G. Rutger (Ed.), *Frontiers of social theory* (pp. 255–286). New York: Columbia University Press.

Kelly, P. (2002). *Multiculturalism reconsidered: Culture and equality and its critics.* Cambridge, UK: Polity Press.

Kelly, R. K. (1979). *Courtship, marriage, and the family* (3rd ed.). New York: Harcourt Brace Jovanovich.

Kelly, S. (1993). Caregiver stress in grandparents raising grandchildren. *IMAGE: Journal of Nursing Scholarship, 25,* 331–337.

Kemper, S., & Mitzner, T. (2001). Language production and comprehension. In J. Birren & K. Schaie (Eds.), *Handbook of the Psychology of Aging* (5th ed., pp. 378–398). New York: Academic Press.

Kendall, P. C. (2000). *Child & adolescent therapy.* New York: Guilford.

Kendall, P. C., & Braswell, L. (1985). *Cognitive-behavioral therapy for impulsive children.* New York: Guilford Press.

Kendall, P. C., & Treadwell, K. R. H. (1996). Cognitive-behavioral group treatment for socially anxious youth. In E. D. Hibbs & P. Jensen (Eds.), *Psychosocial treatment research of child and adolescent disorders: Empirically based strategies for clinical practice* (pp. 23–41). Washington, DC: American Psychological Association.

Keniston, K. (1971). *Youth and dissent: The rise of a new opposition.* New York: Harcourt Brace Jovanovich.

Kennedy, G. J., Kelman, H. R., Thomas, C., Wisniewski, W., Metz, H., & Bijur, P. E. (1989). Hierarchy of characteristics associated with depressive symptoms in an urban elderly sample. *American Journal of Psychiatry, 146,* 220–225.

Kenrick, D., Ackerman, J., & Ledlow, S. (2003). Evolutionary social psychology: Adaptative predispositions and Human Culture. In J. Delamater (Ed.), *Handbook of social psychology* (pp. 103–122). New York: Kluwer Academic/Plenum Publishers.

Kent, S. (1980). Advances in hypertension research. *Geriatrics,* 103–104.

Kerlikowske, K., Grady, D., Rubin, S., Sandrock, C., & Ernster, V. (1995). Efficacy of screening mammography: A meta-analysis. *Journal of the American Medical Association, 273,* 149–154.

Kiecolt-Glaser, J. K., & Glaser, R. (1988). Behavioral influences on immune function. In T. Field, P. McCabe, & C. Schneiderman (Eds.), *Stress and coping across development.* Hillsdale, NJ: Erlbaum.

Kiefer, C. W. (1988). *The mantle of maturity: A history of ideas about character development.* Albany: State University of New York Press.

Kiesler, S. (1978). *Interpersonal processes in groups and organizations.* Arlington Heights, VA: AHM Publishing.

Kietzman, M. L., Spring, B., & Zubin, J. (1985). Perception, cognition, information processing. In H. I. Kaplan & B. J. Sadock (Eds.), *Comprehensive textbook of psychiatry* (Vol. 4, pp. 157–178). Baltimore: Williams & Wilkins.

Kihlstrom, J. F., Beer, J. S., & Klein, S. B. (2003). Self and identity as memory. In M. R. Leary & J. P. Tangney (Eds.), *The handbook of self and identity* (pp. 68–90). New York: Guilford.

Kilpatrick, D. G., & Ruggiero, K. J. (2004). *Rape in Iowa: One in eight.* Unpublished manuscript.

Kim, J., & Moen, P. (2002). Retirement transitions, gender, and psychological well-being: A life course, ecological model. *The Journals of Gerontology Series B: Psychological Sciences and Social Sciences, 57,* P212–P222.

Kim, S. Y., Hong, G. S., & Rowe, B. R. (2000). The impact of family economic hardship and parental commitment on children's outcomes. *Consumer Interest Annual, 46.* Retrieved June 21, 2004, from http://www.consumerinterests.org

Kimmel, D. C. (1978). Adult development and aging: A gay perspective. *Journal of Social Issues, 34,* 113–130.

Kinsey, A. C., Pomeroy, W. B., & Martin, C. E. (1948). *Sexual behavior in the human male.* Philadelphia: Saunders.

Kinsey, A. C., Pomeroy, W. B., Martin, C. E., & Gebhard, P. H. (1953). *Sexual behavior in the human female.* Philadelphia: Saunders.

Kivett, V. (1996). The saliency of the grandmother-granddaughter relationship: Predictors of association. *Journal of Women and Aging, 8(3/4),* 25–39.

Kivnick, H. Q. (1986). Grandparenthood and a life cycle. *Journal of Geriatric Psychiatry, 19,* 39–55.

Klaus, M., & Kennel, J. (1976). *Maternal-infant bonding: The impact of early separation or loss on family development.* St. Louis, MO: C. V. Mosby.

Klaus, M., Kennel, J., & Klaus, P. (1993). *Mothering the mother: How a doula can help you have a shorter, easier, and healthier birth.* Reading, MA: Addison-Wesley.

Klaus, M., & Klaus, P. (1985). *The amazing newborn.* Reading, MA: Addison-Wesley.

Kleigman, R. (1992). Perpetual poverty: Child health and the underclass. *Pediatrics, 89,* 710–713.

Kline, M., Tschann, J. M., Johnston, J. R., & Wallerstein, J. S. (1989). Children's adjustment in joint and sole physical custody families. *Developmental Psychology, 25,* 430–438.

Klinnert, M., Emde, R., Butterfield, P., & Campos, J. (1986). Social referencing: The infant's use of emotional signals from a friendly adult with mother present. *Developmental Psychology, 22,* 427–432.

Kluckhohn, C. (1949). *Mirror for man: The relation of anthropology to modern life.* New York: Whittlesey House.

Kluger, J. (2003, November 3). Medicating young minds. *Time,* 48–57.

Knight, B. (2004). *Psychotherapy with older adults* (3rd ed.). Thousand Oaks, CA: Sage Publications.

Knight, T., & Ricciardelli, L. (2003). Successful aging: Perception of adults aged between 70 and 101 years. *International Journal of Aging and Human Development, 56(3),* 223–245.

Koegel, P. (1989). Mental illness among the inner-city homeless. *Journal of the California Alliance for the Mentally Ill, 1,* 16–17.

Kohlberg, L. (1969). Stage and sequence: The cognitive-developmental approach to socialization. In D. A. Goslin (Ed.), *Handbook of socialization theory and research.* Chicago: Rand McNally.

Kohn, R., Goldsmith, E., Sedgwick, T., & Markowitz, S. (2004). In-home mental health services for the elderly. *Clinical Gerontologist, 27(1/2),* 71–85.

Konner, M. (1991). *Childhood: A multicultural view.* Boston: Little, Brown.

Kornblum, W. (2002). *Sociology: The central questions* (2nd ed.). Belmont, CA: Wadsworth.

Kornblum, W. (2003). *Sociology in a changing world* (6th ed.). Belmont, CA: Thomson/Wadsworth.

Koss, M. P. (1985). The hidden rape victim: Personality, attitudinal, and situational characteristics. *Psychology of Women Quarterly, 9,* 193–212.

Koss, M. P., Gidycz, C. A., & Wisniewski, N. (1987). The scope of rape: Incidence and prevalence of sexual aggression and victimization in a national sample of higher education students. *Journal of Consulting and Clinical Psychology, 48,* 460–468.

Kotelchuck, M. (1976). The infant's relationship to the father: Experimental evidence. In M. E. Lamb (Ed.), *The role of the father in child development* (pp. 329–344). New York: Wiley.

Kowalski, K. (1985, April). The impact of chronic grief. *American Journal of Nursing,* 398–399.

Kozol, J. (1985). *Illiterate America.* Garden City, NY: Anchor Books.

Kraft-Ebing, R. V. (1933). *Psychopathia sexualis: Antipathic sexual instinct.* Brooklyn, NY: Physicians and Surgeons Book Company.

Kramer, B. (1997). Gain in the caregiving experience: Where are we? What next? *The Gerontologist, 37(2),* 218–232.

Krause, N. (2003). Religious meaning and subjective well-being in late life. *The Journals of Gerontology Series B: Psychological Sciences and Social Sciences, 58,* S160–S170.

Kroger, J. (1999). *Identify development: Adolescence through adulthood.* Thousand Oaks, CA: Sage.

Krown, S. (1974). *Threes and fours go to school.* Englewood Cliffs, NJ: Prentice Hall.

Krugman, R., Bays, J., Chadwick, D., Kanda, M., Levitt, L., & McHugh, M. (1994). Distinguishing SIDS from child abuse fatalities. *Pediatrics, 94,* 124–126.

Kotch, J. B., Browne, D. C., Ringwalt, C. L., Stewart, P. W., Ruina, E., Holt, K., Lowman, B., et al. (1995). Risk of child abuse or neglect in a cohort of low-income children. *Child Abuse and Neglect, 19,* 1115–1130.

Kubey, R., & Csikszentmihalyi, M. (2004). Television addiction is no mere metaphor. *Scientific American Mind, 14,* 48–55.

Kubick-Balicheski, P., Martinez, R., & Walsh, B. (1994, January/February). Coordinating transitions in care for improved perinatal outcomes: The RIMM project. *Discharge Planning Update,* 1–7.

Kübler-Ross, E. (1969). *On death and dying.* New York: Macmillan.

Kuhn, D., Kohlberg, L., Langer, J., & Haan, N. (1977). The development of formal operations in logical and moral judgment. *Genetic Psychology Monographs, 95,* 97–188.

Kukathas, C. (2002). The life of Brian: or Now for Something Completely Difference-Blind. In P. Kelly (Ed.), *Multiculturalism Reconsidered: Culture and equality and its critics* (pp. 184–203). Cambridge: Polity Press.

Kulik, L. (2001). Attitudes toward spousal caregiving in late adulthood: Retirement versus pre-retirement phase. *Journal of Gerontological Social Work, 35(2),* 37.

Kupersmidt, J. B., & Coie, J. D. (1990). Preadolescent peer status, aggression, and school adjustment as predictors of externalizing problems in adolescence. *Child Development, 61*, 1350–1363.

Kupersmidt, J. B., & Dodge, K. A. (2004). *Children's peer relations: From development to intervention*. Washington, DC: American Psychological Association.

Kurdek, L. A. (1999). The nature and predictors of the trajectory of change in marital quality for husbands and wives over the first 10 years of marriage. *Developmental Psychology, 35*, 1283–1296.

Labouvie-Vief, G. (1986). Intelligence and cognition. In J. E. Birren & K. W. Schaie (Eds.), *Handbook on the psychology of aging* (2nd ed.). New York: Van Nostrand Reinhold.

Labouvie-Vief, G. (1994). *Psyche and Eros: Mind and gender in the life course*. New York: Cambridge University Press.

Labouvie-Vief, G. (2003). Dynamic integration: Affect, cognition, and the self in adulthood. *Current Directions in Psychological Science, 12*, 201–206.

Ladd, G. W., Buhs, E. S., & Troop, W. (2002). Children's interpersonal skills and relationships in school settings: Adaptive significance and implications for school-based prevention and intervention programs. In P. K. Smith & C. H. Hart (Eds.), *Blackwell handbook of childhood social development* (pp. 394–415). Malden, MA: Blackwell.

Ladyman, Stephen (2005). Improving postnatal care for every woman. *British Journal of Midwifery, 13*, 68–70.

Lagercrantz, H. (1986). The stress of being born. *Scientific American, 254*, 100–107.

Lahey, B. B. & Waldman, I. D. (2003). Propensity model of the origins of conduct problems during childhood and adolescence. In B. B. Lahey, T. E. Moffitt, & A. Caspi (Eds.), *Causes of conduct disorder and juvenile delinquency* (pp. 76–117). New York: Guilford.

Lalley, J. R., & Keith, H. (1997). Early Head Start: The first two years. *Bulletin of Zero to Three: National Center for Infants, Toddlers, and Families, 18*, 3–8.

Lamb, L. (1994, November/December). Selecting for perfection: Is prenatal screening becoming a kind of eugenics? *Utne Reader*, 26–28.

Lamb, M. E. (1981). The development of father-infant relationships. In M. E. Lamb (Ed.), *The role of the father in child development* (2nd ed.). New York: Wiley.

Lamb, M. E. (1982). *Nontraditional families: Parenting and child development*. Hillsdale, NJ: Erlbaum.

Lamb, M. E., Easterbrooks, M. A., & Holden, G. W. (1980). Reinforcement and punishment among preschoolers: Characteristics, effects, and correlates. *Child Development, 51*, 1230–1236.

Landes, A., Sperry, S., Strauss, M., & Geldmacher, M. (2001). Apathy in Alzheimer's disease. *Journal of American Geriatrics Society, 14*, 1700–1707.

Landy, S., Osofsky, J. D., & Landy, S. (2002). *Pathways to competence: Encouraging health, social and emotional development in young children*. New York: Paul H. Brooks.

Lane, N., & Wallace, D. (2002). *All about osteoarthritis: The definitive resource for arthritis patients and their families*. Oxford, UK: Oxford University Press.

Langer, R. D., & Barrett-Connor, E. (1994). Extended hormone replacement: Who should get it, and for how long? *Geriatrics, 49*, 20–29.

Langlois, J. H. (1986). From the eye of the beholder to behavioral reality: Development of social behaviors and social relations as a function of physical attractiveness. In C. P. Herman, M. P. Zanna, & E. P. Higgins (Eds.), *Physical appearance, stigma, and social behavior: The Ontario Symposium, Vol. 3*. Hillsdale, NJ: Erlbaum.

Langlois, J. H., & Downs, A. C. (1980). Peer relations as a function of physical attractiveness: The eye of the beholder or behavioral reality. *Child Development, 50*, 409–418.

Langlois, J. H., & Stynczynski, L. (1979). The effects of physical attractiveness on the behavioral attributions and peer preferences in acquainted children. *International Journal of Behavioral Development, 2*, 325–341.

Laosa, L. (1981). Maternal behavior: Socio-cultural diversity in modes of family interaction. In R. W. Henderson (Ed.), *Parent-child interaction: Theory, research, and prospects*. New York: Academic Press.

Lapsley, D. K. (1985). Elkind on egocentrism. *Developmental Review, 5*, 227–236.

Lapsley, D. K. (1989). Continuity and discontinuity in adolescent social cognitive development. In R. Montemayer, G. Adams, & T. Gullota (Eds.), *Advances in adolescent research* (Vol. 2). Orlando, FL: Academic Press.

Lapsley, D. K. (1990). Continuity and discontinuity in adolescent social cognitive development. In R. Montemayor, G. Adams, & T. Gullota (Eds.), *From Childhood to adolescence: A transitional period?* Newbury Park, CA: Sage.

Lapsley, D. K. (1996). *Moral Psychology (Developmental Psychology Series)*. New York: Perseus.

Lapsley, D. K., Harwell, M. R., Olson, L. M., Flannery, D., & Quintana, S. M. (1984). Moral judgment, personality, and attitude to authority in early and late adolescence. *Journal of Youth and Adolescence, 13*, 527–542.

Lapsley, D. K., & Power, F. C. (Eds.). (1988). *Self, ego, and identity*. New York: Springer-Verlag.

Lapsley, D. K., & Rice, K. G. (1988). The "new look" at the imaginary audience and personal fable: Toward an integrative model of adolescent ego development. In D. K. Lapsley & F. C. Power (Eds.), *Self, ego, and identity: Integrative approaches*. New York: Springer-Verlag.

Larson, J. H. (1988). The marriage quiz: College students' beliefs in selected myths about marriage. *Family Relations, 37*, 3–11.

Larson, J. H. (2002). *The great marriage tune-up book: A proven program for evaluating and renewing your relationship*. New York: Jossey-Bass.

Lasby, K., Newton, S., Sherrow, T., Stainton, M., & McNeil, D. (1994). Maternal work in the NICU: A case study of an "NICU experienced" mother. *Issues in Comprehensive Pediatric Nursing, 17*, 147–160.

Lawson, W. B. (1986). Racial and ethnic factors in psychiatric research. *Hospital and Community Psychiatry, 37*, 50–53.

Lawton, M. P. (1975). Competence, environmental press, and the adaptation of older people. In P. G. Windley and G. Ernst (Eds.), *Theory development in environment and aging*. Washington, DC: Gerontological Society of America.

Layder, D. (1994). *Understanding social theory*. London: Sage.

Lazarus, R. S. (1991). *Emotion and adaptation*. New York: Oxford University Press.

Lea, S. E. G. (1984). *Instinct, environment, and behaviour*. London: Methuen.

Leahey, T. H. (1987). *A history of psychology: Main currents in psychological thought*. Englewood Cliffs, NJ: Prentice Hall.

Leaper, C., Anderson, K. J., Sanders, P. (1998). Moderators of gender effects on parents' talk to their children: A meta-analysis. *Developmental Psychology, 34*, 3–27.

Leary, M. R. & Tangney, J. P. (2003). The self as an organizing construct in the behavioral and social sciences. In M. R. Leary & J. P. Tangney (Eds.). *The handbook of self and identity* (pp. 3–14). New York: Guilford.

LeBlanc, A. C. (2003). *Random Family: Love, drugs, trouble, and coming of age in the Bronx*. New York: Scribner.

LeCroy, C. W. (1992). Promoting social competence in youth. In K. Corcoran (Ed.), *Structuring change* (pp. 167–180). Chicago: Lyceum Books.

LeCroy, C. W. (1994). Social skills training. In C. W. LeCroy (Ed.), *Handbook of child and adolescent treatment manuals*. New York: Lexington Books.

LeCroy, C. W. (2001). Promoting social competence in youth. In H. E. Briggs & K. Corcoran (Eds.), *Social work practice: Treating common problems*. Chicago: Lyceum Books.

LeCroy, C. W. (2005). Experimental evaluation of "Go Grrrls" preventive intervention for early adolescent girls. *Journal of Primary Prevention, 25*, 457–473.

LeCroy, C. W., Ashford, J. B., Krysik, J., & Milligan, K. B. (1996). Healthy Families Arizona: Evaluation Report. Unpublished manuscript.

LeCroy, C. W., & Daley, J. (2001). *Empowering adolescent girls: Examining the present and building skills for the future with the Go Grrrls program*. New York: W. W. Norton.

LeCroy, C. W., & Milligan, K. B. (1996). Promoting social competence in the schools. In R. Constable, J. Flynn, & S. MacDonald (Eds.), *School social work: Practice and research perspectives* (pp. 376–390). Chicago: Lyceum Books.

Lederman, R. P. (1996). *Psychosocial adaptation in pregnancy* (2nd ed.). New York: Springer.

Lee, C., & Bakk, L. (2001). Later-life transitions into widowhood. *Journal of Gerontological Social Work, 35*(3), 51–63.

Lee, G., DeMaris, A., Bavin, S., & Sullivan, R. (2001). Gender differences in the depressive effect of widowhood in later life. *Journal of Gerontology B: Psychology and Social Sciences, 56*(S56–S61).

Lee, G. R., Seccombe, K., & Shehan, C. L. (1991). Marital status and personal happiness: An analysis of trend data. *Journal of Marriage and the Family, 139*, 839–844.

Lee, S., & Graves, G. (2000). *Your three-and four-year old: As they grow*. New York: Golden Books.

Lefrancois, G. R. (1989). *Of children: An introduction to child development*. Belmont, CA: Wadsworth.

Lehmann, H. E., & Cancro, R. (1985). Schizophrenia: Clinical features. In H. I. Kaplan & B. J. Sadock (Eds.), *New perspectives in schizophrenia*. New York: Macmillan.

Lembau, J. R. (1988). Emotional sequelae of abortion: Implications for clinical practice. *Psychology of Women Quarterly, 12,* 461–472.
Lemeshow, S. (1982). *The handbook of clinical types in mental retardation.* Boston: Allyn & Bacon.
Lemme, B. H. (1995). *Development in adulthood.* Needham Heights, MA: Allyn & Bacon.
Lemme, B. H. (2001). *Development in adulthood.* Needham Heights, MA: Allyn & Bacon.
Lemon, B. W., Bengston, V. L., & Peterson, J. A. (1972). An exploration of the activity theory of aging: Activity types and life satisfactions among in-movers of a retirement community. *Journal of Gerontology, 27,* 511–523.
Leon, I. (1986). Psychodynamics of perinatal loss. *Psychiatry, 49,* 312–322.
Leon, I. (1992). Perinatal loss: choreographing grief on the obstetric unit. *American Journal of Orthopsychiatry, 62*(1), 7–8.
LeProhn, N. S., Wetherbee, K., Lamont, E., Achenbach, T., & Pecora, P. (2001). Assessing Youth Behavior: Using the Child Behavior Checklist in Family and Children's Research. Washington, DC: Child Welfare League of America.
Lerner, R. M. (2002). *Concepts and Theories of Human Development* (3rd ed.). Mahwah, NJ: Erlbaum.
Lerner, R. M., Perkins, D. F., & Jacobson, L. P. (1993). Timing, process, and the diversity of developmental trajectories in human life: A developmental contextual perspective. In. G. Tukewitz & D. A. Devenny (Eds.), *Developmental time and timing.* Hillsdale, NJ: Erlbaum.
Leslie, G. R., Larson, R., & Gorman, B. L. (1973). *Order and change: Introductory sociology.* New York: Oxford University Press.
Lester, B. M. (1992). Infants and their families at risk: Assessment and intervention. *Infant Mental Health Journal, 13*(1), 54–66.
Lev, A. I. (2004a). The complete lesbian & gay parenting guide. New York: The Berkley Publishing Group.
Lev, A. I. (2004b). Transgender emergence: Therapeutic guidelines for working with gender-variant people and their families. Binghamton, NY: Haworth Press.
Levant, R. F. (1990). Men's changing roles. *The Family Psychologist, 6,* 4–6.
Levine, M. D., Carey, W. B., & Crocker, A. C. (1999). *Developmental-behavioral pediatrics.* Philadelphia: Saunders.
Levinson, D. J. (1978). *The seasons of a man's life.* New York: Knopf.
Levinson, D. J. (1985). The life cycle. In H. I. Kaplan & B. J. Sadock (Eds.), *Comprehensive textbook of psychiatry* (Vol. 4). Baltimore: Williams & Wilkins.
Levinson, D. J. (1986). A conception of adult development. *American Psychologist, 41,* 3–13.
Levinson, D. J., Darrow, C. M., Klein, E. G., Levinson, M. H., & Levitt, M. (1986). Social network relationships as sources of maternal support and well-being. *Developmental Psychology, 22,* 310–316.
Lewis, D. W. (2002, February). Headaches in Children and Adolescents. *American Family Physician,* 625–632.
Lewis, K. G. (2000). *With or without a man: Single women taking control of their lives.* New York: Bull Publishing.
Lewis, M. (1987). Social development in infancy and early childhood. In J. Osofsky (Ed.), *Handbook of infant development* (2nd ed., pp. 419–493). New York: Wiley.
Lewis, M. (1990). Social knowledge and social development. *Merril palmer Quarterly, 36,* 93–116.
Lewis, M., & Brooks-Gunn, J. (1979). *Social cognition and the acquisition of self.* New York: Plenum.
Libassi, M. F. (1990). Psychopharmacology in social work education [Contract No. 89MF700390ID]. Washington, DC: National Institute of Mental Health.
Lichtenberger, E. O., Broadbooks, D. Y., & Kaufman, A. S. (2000). *Essentials of cognitive assessment with KAIT and other Kaufman measures.* New York: John Wiley.
Lickey, M. E., & Gordon, B. (1983). *Drugs for mental illness: A revolution in psychiatry.* New York: W. H. Freeman.
Lickona, T. (1983). *Raising good children.* New York: Bantam Books.
Lickona, T. (2004). *Character matters: How to help our children develop good judgment, integrity, and other essential virtues.* New York: Simon & Schuster.
Lieberman, A. (1985). Infant mental health: A model for service delivery. *Journal of Clinical Child Psychology, 14,* 196–201.
Lieberman, A. F. (1977). Preschoolers' competence with a peer: Relations with attachment and peer experience. *Child Development, 48,* 1277–1287.
Lieberman, A. F. (1993). *The emotional life of the toddler.* New York: Free Press.
Limbo, R., & Wheeler, S. (1986). *When a baby dies: A handbook for healing and helping.* LaCrosse, WI: Resolve Through Sharing.
Lindgren, H. C. (1969). *An introduction to social psychology.* New York: Wiley.
Lindsey, K. (1982). *Friends or family.* Boston: Beacon Press.
Linet, M. S., Stewart, W. F., Celentano, D. D., Ziegler, D., & Sprecher, M. (1989). An epidemiological study of headaches among adolescents and young adults. *Journal of the American Medical Association, 261,* 2211–2216.
Lipkin, R. (1995, April 8). Sea worms and plants spur new drugs. *Science News,* 212.
Lippa, R. A. (1994). *Introduction to social psychology.* Pacific Grove, CA: Brooks/Cole.
Lipsitz, J. (1980). *Sexual development in young adolescents.* Invited speech given at the meeting of the American Association for Moral Education, Pittsburgh, PA.
Little, R., & Ervin, C. (1984). *Alcohol problems in women.* New York: Guilford Press.
Littrell, J. (1991). *Understanding and treating alcoholism.* Hillsdale, NJ: Erlbaum.
Litwak, E., & Szelenyi, I. (1969). Primary group structures and their functions: Kin, neighbors, and friends. *American Sociological Review, 34,* 465–481.
Loeber, R., and Farrington, D. P. (2001). *Child delinquents: Development, intervention, and service needs.* Thousand Oaks, CA: Sage Publications.
Loftus, J. (2001). America's liberalization in attitudes toward homosexuality, 1973 to 1998. *American Sociological Review, 66,* 762–782.
Loney, J., & Ordona, T. (1975). Using cerebral stimulants to treat minimal brain dysfunction. *American Journal of Orthopsychiatry, 45,* 564–572.
Long, N., & Forehand, R. (1987). The effects of parental divorce and parental conflict on children: An overview. *Journal of Development and Behavioral Pediatrics, 815,* 292–296.
Long, N., & Forehand, R. L. (2002). *Making divorce easier on your child: 50 effective ways to help children adjust.* New York: McGraw-Hill.
Longino, C. F., & Kart, C. S. (1982). Explicating activity theory: Formal replication. *Journal of Gerontology, 37,* 713–722.
Longres, J. F. (1995). *Human behavior in the social environment.* Itasca, IL: Peacock.
Longres, J. F. (2000). *Human behavior in the social environment.* Belmont, CA: Thomson Brooks/Cole.
Lonner, W. J., Thorndike, R. M., Forbes, N. E., & Ashworth, C. (1985). The influence of television on measured cognitive abilities. A study with native Alaskan children. *Journal of Cross-Cultural Psychology, 16,* 355–380.
Lopata, H. Z., & Barnewolt, D. (1984). The middle years: Changes and variations in social-role commitments. In G. Baruch & J. Brooks-Gunn (Eds.), *Women in midlife.* New York: Plenum.
Lopez, R. I., Kelly, K., & Lopez, R. I. (2003). *The teen health book: A parent's guide to adolescent health and well-being.* New York: W. W. Norton.
Love, J. M., Schochet, P. Z., & Meckstrom, A. (1996). *Are they in any real danger? What research does—and doesn't—tell us about child care quality and children's well being.* Princeton, NJ: Mathematical Policy Research.
Lozoff, B. (1983). Birth and bonding in non-industrial societies. *Developmental Medicine and Child Neurology, 25,* 595–600.
Luborsky, M., & Rubinstein, R. L. (1987). Ethnicity and lifetimes: Self-concepts and situational contexts of ethnic identity in late life. In D. E. Gelfand & C. M. Barresi (Eds.), *Ethnic dimensions of aging.* New York: Springer.
Ludington-Hoe, S. & Golant, S. (1993). *Kangaroo care: The best you can do to help your preterm infant.* New York: Bantam Books.
Ludwig, A. M. (1986). *Principles of clinical psychiatry* (2nd ed.). New York: Free Press.
Luey, H. S., Glass, L., & Elliott, H. (1995). Hard-of-hearing or deaf: Issues of ears, language, culture, and identity. *Social Work, 40,* no. 2, 177–182.
Lukes, S. (1991). *Moral conflict and politics.* Oxford, UK: Clarendon Press.
Lumsden, C. J., & Wilson, E. O. (1981). *Genes, mind, and culture: The coevolutionary process.* Cambridge, MA: Harvard University Press.
Lunneborg, P. (1992). *Abortion: A positive decision.* New York: Bergin & Garvey.
Luria, A. (1961). *The role of speech in the regulation of normal and abnormal behaviors.* New York: Liveright.
Lyman, D. R., & Selman, R. L. (1985). Peer conflict in pair therapy: Clinical and developmental analyses. In M. W. Berkowitz (Ed.), *Peer conflict and psychological growth* (New directions for child development, No. 29). San Francisco: Jossey-Bass.
Lynch, M., Roberts, J., & Gordon, M. (1976). Child abuse: Early warning in the maternity hospital. *Developmental Medicine and Child Neurology, 18,* 759–766.

Lyon, D., & Greenberg, J. (1991). Evidence of codependency in women with an alcoholic parent: Helping out Mr. Wrong. *Journal of Personality and Social Psychology, 61,* 435–439.

Lyons-Ruth, K., Connell, D. B., Grunebaum, H. U., & Botein, S. (1990). Infants at social risk: Maternal depression and family support services as mediators of infant development and security of attachment. *Child Development, 9,* 225–235.

Lyons-Ruth, K., & Zeanah, C. (1993). The family context of infant mental health: I. Affective development in the primary caregiving relationship. In C. Zeanah (Ed.), *Handbook of infant mental health* (pp. 14–37). New York: Guilford Press.

Lyotard, J. F. (1984). *The postmodern critique: A report on knowledge* (G. Bennington and B. Massumi, Trans.). Minneapolis: University of Minnesota Press.

Lytle, L. D., Messing, R. B., Fisher, L., & Phebus, L. (1975). Effects of long-term corn consumption on brain serotonin and the response to electric shock. *Science, 190,* 692–694.

Maalouf, A. (2000). *In the name of identity*. New York: Penguin Books.

Maas, H. (1989). Social responsibility in middle age: Prospects and preconditions. In S. Hunter and M. Sundel (Eds.), *Midlife myths: Issues, findings, and practice implications*. Newbury Park, CA: Sage.

Maccoby, E. E. (1980). *Social development: Psychological growth and the parent-child relationship*. San Diego: Harcourt Brace Jovanovich.

Maccoby, E. E. (1998). *The two sexes: Growing up apart, coming together*. Cambridge, MA: Harvard University Press.

Maccoby, E. E., & Jacklin, C. N. (1974). *The psychology of sex differences*. Palo Alto, CA: Stanford University Press.

Maccoby, E. E., & Martin, J. A. (1983). Socialization in the context of the family: Parent-child interaction. In P. H. Mussen (Ed.), *Handbook of child psychology* (4th ed., Vol. 4). New York: Wiley.

MacDonald, K. (1987). Parent-child physical play with rejected, neglected, and popular boys. *Developmental Psychology, 23,* 705–711.

Mace, N. C., & Rabins, P. V. (1981). The 36-hour day. Baltimore: Johns Hopkins University Press.

Macht, M. W., & Ashford, J. B. (1991). *Introduction to social work and social welfare*. New York: Merrill/Macmillan.

MacIver, D. J., Reuman, D. A., & Main, S. R. (1995). Social structuring of the school: Studying what is, illuminating what could be. *Annual Review of Psychology, 46,* 375–410.

MacReady, N. (2002). New test enhances accuracy of autism screening (Most accurate at 24 months) (The modified checklist for autism in toddlers). *Family Practice News, 32,* 50–51.

Madden, D. (2001). Speed and timing of behavioral processes. In J. Birren & K. Schaie (Eds.), *Handbook of the Psychology of Aging* (5th ed., pp. 288–312). New York: Academic Press.

Madon, S., Jussim, L., Eccles, J. (1997). In search of the powerful self-fulfilling prophecy. *Journal of Personality and Social Psychology, 72,* 791–809.

Madsen, M. C., & Shapira, A. (1970). Cooperative and competitive behavior of urban Afro-American, Anglo-American, Mexican-American, and Mexican village children. *Developmental Psychology, 3,* 16–20.

Magai, C. (2001). Emotions over the life span. In J. Birren & K. Schaie (Eds.), *Handbook of the Psychology of Aging* (5th ed., pp. 399–426). New York: Academic Press.

Magnusson, D., & Stattin, H. (1998). Person-context interaction theories. In W. Damon (Series Ed.) & R. M. Lerner (Vol. Ed.), *Handbook of child psychology: Vol. 1, Theoretical models of human development* (5th ed. pp. 685–759). New York: Wiley.

Mahoney, M. J. (1989). Scientific psychology and radical behaviorism: Important distinctions based in scientism and objectivism. *American Psychologist, 44,* 1372–1377.

Mahoney, M. J. (1991). *Human change processes: The scientific foundations of psychotherapy*. New York: Basic Books.

Mahoney, M. J. (2000). A changing history of efforts to understand and control change: The case of psychotherapy. In C. R. Snyder & R. E. Ingram (Eds.), *Handbook of psychological change: Psychotherapy processes & practice for the 21st century* (pp. 2–12). New York: Wiley & Sons.

Main, M., & Solomon, J. (1986). Discovery of an insecure, disorganized/ disoriented attachment pattern: Procedures, findings, and implications for the classification of behavior. In M. Yogman & T. B. Brazelton (Eds.), *Affective development in infancy* (pp. 95–124). Norwood, NJ: Ablex.

Main, M., & Solomon, J. (1990). Procedures for identifying infants as disorganized/disoriented during the Ainsworth Strange Situation. In M. T. Greenberg, D. Cicchetti, & E. M. Cummings (Eds.), *Attachment in the preschool years* (pp. 121–160). Chicago: University of Chicago Press.

Maluccio, A. N. (1981). *Promoting competence in clients: A new/old approach for social work practice*. New York: Free Press.

Maluccio, A. N., Tracy, E. M., & Pine, B. A. (2002). *Social work practice with families and children*. New York: Columbia University Press.

Manton, K. G., Blazer, D. G., & Woodbury, M. A. (1987). Suicide in middle-age and later life: Sex and race specific life table and cohort analyses. *Journal of Gerontology, 42,* 219–227.

March of Dimes (2002). Multiples: Twins, triplets, and beyond. Retrieved April 10, 2005, from http://www.marchofdimes.com/professionals/ 681_4545.asp

Marcia, J. (1966). Development and validation of ego-identity status. *Journal of Personality and Social Psychology, 3,* 551–558.

Marcia, J. (1987). The identity status approach to the study of ego identity development. In T. Honess & K. Yardley (Eds.), *Self and identity: Perspectives across the lifespan*. London: Routledge & Kegan Paul.

Marcotte, D., Fortin, L., Potvin, P., & Papillon, M. (2002). Gender differences in depression symptoms during adolescence: Role of gender-typed characteristics, self-esteem, body image, stressful life events, and pubertal status. *Journal of Emotional and Behavioral Disorders, 10,* 29–42.

Mare, R. D., & Winship, C. (1988). Ethnic and racial patterns of educational attainment and school enrollment. In G. D. Sandefur & M. Tienda (Eds.), *Divided opportunities* (pp. 173–195). New York: Plenum.

Marin, B. V., Holmes, D. L., Guth, M., & Kovac, P. (1979). The potential of children as eyewitnesses. *Law and Human Behavior, 3,* 295–305.

Markham, L. R. (1984). De dog and de cat: Assisting speakers of Black English as they begin to write. *Young Children, 39,* 15–24.

Markides, K. S. (1990). Risk factors, gender, and health. *Generations, 14,* 17–21.

Markides, K. S., & Mindel, C. H. (1987). *Aging and ethnicity*. Newbury Park, CA: Sage.

Markowitz, L. M. (1991, November/December). After the trauma. *Family Therapy Networker,* 30–37.

Marks, R. (1988, Spring). Coming out. *Out/Look*.

Marksteiner, J., & Schmidt, R. (2004). Treatment strategies in Alzheimer's disease with a focus on early pharmacological interventions. *Drugs and Aging, 21*(7), 415–426.

Markus, H. R., & Kitayama, S. (1991). Cultural variation in self concept. In G. R. Goethals & J. Strauss (Eds.), *Multidisciplinary perspectives on the self*. New York: Springer-Verlag.

Markus, H. R., & Kitayama, S. (1991). Culture and the self: Implications for cognition, emotion, and motivation. *Psychological Review 98,* 224–253.

Marlowe, M. (1985). Low lead exposure and learning disabilities. *Research Communications in Psychology, Psychiatry and Behavior, 10,* 153–169.

Marrale, J. C., Shipman, J. H., & Rhodes, M. L. (1986). What some college students eat. *Nutrition Today, 21*(1), 16–21.

Marschark, M., Lang, H. G., & Albertini, J. A. (2002). *Educating Deaf Students: From Research to Practice*. New York: Oxford University Press.

Marsiglio, W., & Donnelly, D. (1992). Sexual relations in later life: A national study of married persons. *Journal of Gerontology, 46,* 334–338.

Marti, E. (2003). Strengths and weaknesses of cognition over preschool years. In J. Valsiner & K. Connolly (Eds.), *Handbook of Developmental Psychology* (257–275). Thousand Oaks, CA: Sage.

Martin, S. (1995 October). Practitioners may misunderstand black families. *APA Monitor,* 36.

Martin, T. C., & Bumpass, L. L. (1989). Recent trends in marital disruption. *Demography, 26,* 37–51.

Martinez, F. (1996, May). *Can SIDS be prevented?* Presented at the Pediatric Specialty Conference, University Medical Center, Tucson, AZ.

Martinez, R. O., & Dukes, R. L. (1997). The effects of ethnic identify, ethnicity, and gender on adolescent well-being. *Journal of Youth and Adolescence, 26,* 503–516.

Maslow, A. H. (1962). *Toward a psychology of being*. Princeton, NJ: Van Nostrand.

Mason, C. & Elwood, R. (1995). Is there a psychological basis for the couvade and onset of paternal care? *International Journal of Nursing Studies, 32,* 137–148.

Mason, J. (1991). Reducing infant mortality in the United States through Healthy Start. *Public Health Reports, 106,* 479–483.

Masten, A. S. (2001). Ordinary magic: Resilience processes in development. *American Psychologist, 56*(3), 227–238.

Masten, A. S., Best, K. M., & Garmezy, N. (1991). Resilience and development: Contributions from the study of children who overcome adversity. *Development and Psychopathology, 2,* 425–444.

Masten, A. S., & Coatsworth, J. (1998). The development of competence in favorable and unfavorable environments: Lessons from research on successful children. *American Psychologist, 53,* 205–220.

Masters, J. C., & Furman, W. (1981). Popularity, individual friendship selection, and specific peer interaction among children. *Developmental Psychology, 17*, 344–350.

Masters, W. H., & Johnson, V. E. (1966). *Human sexual response*. Boston: Little, Brown.

Matas, L., Arend, R. A., & Stroufe, L. A. (1978). Continuity of adaptation in the second year: The relationship between quality of attachment and later competence. *Child Development, 49*, 547–556.

Matejcek, A., Dytrych, Z., & Schuller, V. (1979). The Prague study of children born from unwanted pregnancies. *International Journal of Mental Health, 7*, 63–74.

Matsakis, A. (2003). *The rape recovery handbook*. San Francisco: New Harbinger.

Matsumoto, D. (2000). *Culture and psychology: People around the world*. Belmont, CA: Wadsworth/Thomson.

Matthews, K. A. (1992). Myths and realities of the menopause. *Psychosomatic Medicine, 54*, 1–9.

Mattson, S. N., & Riley, E. P. (1998). A review of the neurobehavioral deficits in children with fetal alcohol syndrome or prenatal exposure to alcohol. *Alcoholism: Clinical and Experimental Research, 22*, 279–294.

Mawson, A. R., & Jacobs, K. W. (1978). Corn, trypotophan, and homicide. *Journal of Orthomolecular Psychiatry, 7*, 227–230.

Maxmen, J. S. (1986). *Essential psychopathology*. New York: Norton.

Maxmen, J., & Ward, N. (1995). *Essential psychopathology and its treatment*. New York: Norton.

Maxwell, M. (Ed.). (1991). *The sociobiological imagination*. Albany: State University of New York Press.

May, K., & Perrin, S. (1985). Prelude: Pregnancy and birth. In S. M. Hanson & F. W. Boxelt (Eds.), *Dimensions of fatherhood* (pp. 64–91). Beverly Hills, CA: Sage.

Mayes, L. C., & Cohen, D. J. (2003). *The Yale child study guide to understanding your child's health and development from birth to adolescence*. New York: Little, Brown.

Maziade, M. (1987). Influence of gentle birth delivery procedures and other perinatal circumstances on infant temperament: Developmental and social implications. *Annual Progress in Child Psychiatry and Child Development*, 291–295.

Maziade, M., Caron, C., Cote, R., Merette, C., Bernier, H., Laplante, B., et al. (1990). Psychiatric status of adolescents who had extreme temperaments at age 7. *American Journal of Psychiatry, 147*, 1531–1536.

McAdams, D. P. (1997). The case for unity in the (post) modern self: A modest proposal. In R. D. Ashmore & L. Jussin (Eds.), *Self and identity: Fundamental issues* (pp. 46–78). New York: Oxford University Press.

McAdams, D. P., & Bowman, P. J. (2001). Narrating life's turning points: Redemption and contamination. In D. P. McAdams, R. Josselson, & A. Lieblich (Eds.), *Turns in the road: Narrative studies of lives in transition*. Washington, DC: American Psychological Association.

McAdams, D. P., Josselson, R., & Lieblich, A. (Eds.) (2001). *Turns in the road: Narrative studies of lives in transition*. Washington, DC: American Psychological Association.

McAuley, E., Mihalko, S. L., & Bane, S. M. (2000). Self-efficacy determinants and consequences of physical activity. *Exercise and Sport Sciences Review, 28*, 85–88.

McCamman, S., Rues, J., & Cannon S. (1988). Prader-Willi syndrome intervention approaches based on differential phase characteristics. *Topics in Clinical Nutrition, 3*, 1–8.

McCarthy, K. (1990, November). If one spouse is sick, both are affected. *APA Monitor*, 7.

McConachie, H. (1986). *Parents and young mentally handicapped children: A review of research issues*. Brookline, MA: Brookline Books.

McCord, J. (1990). Problem behaviors. In S. Feldman & G. R. Elliott (Eds.), *At the threshold: The developing adolescent*. Cambridge, MA: Harvard University Press.

McCoy, C. R. (1999, June 29). Mom pleads guilty to killing 8 kids: 70-year-old gets house arrest, probation. *The Arizona Republic*, p. A1.

McDavid, J. W., & Harari, H. (1973). Stereotyping in names and popularity in grade school children. *Child Development, 37*, 453–459.

McEntee, M. K. (1995). Deaf and hard-of-hearing clients: Some legal implications. *Social Work, 40*, no. 2, 183–187.

McEwen, B. S., & Wingfield, J. C. (2003). The concept of allostasis in biology and biomedicine. *Hormones and Behavior, 43*, 2–15.

McFarland, P., & Sanders, S. (2003). A pilot study about the needs of older gays and lesbians: What social workers need to know. *Journal of Gerontological Social Work, 40*(3), 67–80.

McGrath, J. E. (1984). *Groups: Interaction and performance*. Englewood Cliffs, NJ: Prentice Hall.

McGregor, D. (1960). *The human side of enterprise*. New York: McGraw-Hill.

McGuire, P. A. (2000, February). New hope for people with schizophrenia. *Monitor on Psychology, 31*, 24–28.

McInnis-Dittrich, K. (2005). *Social work with elders: A biopsychosocial approach to assessment and intervention* (2nd ed.). Boston, MA: Pearson.

McIntosh, H. (1998, November). Autism is likely to be linked to several genes. *APA Monitor*, 13.

McIntosh, P. (1995). White privilege and male privilege: A personal account of coming to see correspondences through work in women's studies. In M. L. Andersen & P. H. Collins (Eds.), *Race, class, and gender: An anthology*. Belmont, CA: Wadsworth.

McKain, W. C. (1972). A new look at older marriages. *The Family Coordinator, 21*, 61–69.

McKee, B. (1974). The psychosocial development of men in early adulthood and the midlife transition. In D. F. Ricks, A. Thomas, & M. Roff (Eds.), *Life history research in psychopathology* (Vol. 3). Minneapolis: University of Minnesota Press.

McLaughlin, B. (1983). Child compliance to parental control techniques. *Developmental Psychology, 19*, 667–673.

McLemore, S. D. (1991). *Racial and ethnic relations in America*. Boston: Allyn & Bacon.

McLoyd, V. C. (1998). Socioeconomic disadvantage and child development. *American Psychologist, 53*, 185–204.

McManus, M. C. (1991). Serving lesbian and gay youth. *Focal Point, 5*, 1–4.

McNeil, D. (1992). Uncertainties, waiting, and possibilities: Experiences of becoming a mother with an infant in the NICU. *Neonatal Network, 11*, 78.

McQuaide, S. (1998) Women at midlife. *Social Work, 43*, 21–31.

McWhirter, J. J., McWhirter, B. T., McWhirter, A. M., & McWhirter, E. H. (1998). *At-risk youth: A comprehensive response*. Pacific Grove, CA: Wadsworth.

Mead, G. H. (1934). *Mind, self and society: From the standpoint of a social behaviorist*. Chicago: University Press.

Meadows, P. (2003). Retirement ages in the UK: A review of the literature. *Employment Relations Research Series, 18*, 50–76.

Mehrabian, A. (1969). Significance of posture and position in the communication of attitude and status relationships. *Psychological Bulletin, 71*, 359–372.

Mehrabian, A. (1972). *Nonverbal communication*. Chicago: Aldine-Atherton.

Meilman, P. W. (1979). Cross-sectional age changes in ego identity status during adolescence. *Developmental Psychology, 15*, 230–231.

Melton, G. B., Petrila, J., Poythress, N. G., & Slobogin, C. (1987). *Psychological evaluations for the courts*. New York: Guilford Press.

Meltzoff, A. N. (2004). The case for developmental cognitive science: Theories of people and things. In G. Bremner & A. Slater (Eds.), *Theories of infant development* (pp. 145–173). Carlton, Victoria, Australia: Blackwell Publishing.

Meltzoff, A., & Borton, R. (1979). Intermodal matching by human neonates. *Nature, 282*, 403–404.

Meltzoff, A., & Moore, M. (1977). Imitation of facial and manual gestures by human neonates. *Science, 198*, 75–78.

Meltzoff, A., & Moore, M. (1983). Newborn infants imitate adult facial gestures. *Child Development, 54*, 702–709.

Menaghan, E. G., & Lieberman, M. A. (1986). Changes in depression following divorce: A panel study. *Journal of Marriage and the Family, 45*, 371–386.

Mercer, J. (1998). *Infant Development: A multidisciplinary introduction*. Pacific Grove, CA: Brooks/Cole.

Meredith, H. V. (1978). Research between 1969 and 1970 on the standing height of young children in different parts of the world. In H. W. Reece & L. P. Lipsitt (Eds.), *Advances in child development and behavior* (Vol. 12). New York: Academic Press.

Meuser, T., & Marwit, S. (2001). A comprehensive stage-sensitive model of grief in dementia caregiving. *The Gerontologist, 41*, 658–670.

Meyers, J. S. (1972). *An orientation to chronic disease and disability*. New York: Macmillan.

Meyers, M. K. (1990). The ABCs of child care in a mixed economy: A comparison of public and private sector alternatives. *Social Services Review, 22*, 117–130.

Meyers, R. (1978, November). A couple that could. *Psychology Today*, 99–108.

Michener, H., DeLamater, J. D., & Myers, D.J. (2004). *Social Psychology*. Belmont, CA: Wadsworth.

Mildred, S., & Hooper, C. R. (1993, July/August). The ancient Apache ceremony of changing woman. *Southwest Passages*, 64.

Miller, A. (2002). *Frequently requested information: Full-day kindergarten*. Champaign, IL: ERIC Clearinghouse on Elementary and Early Childhood Education. Available at http://ceep.crc.uiuc.edu/poptopics/fullday.html

Miller, B. (1992). Adolescent parenthood: Economic issues and social policies. *Journal of Family and Economic Issues, 13,* 467–475.

Miller, B. C. (1976). A multivariate developmental model of marital satisfaction. *Journal of Marriage and the Family, 38,* 643–657.

Miller, B. C., McCoy, J. K., & Olson, T. D. (1986). Dating age and stage as correlates of adolescent sexual attitudes and behavior. *Journal of Adolescent Research, 1,* 361–371.

Miller, C. A. (1992). Biophysical development during late adulthood. In C. S. Schuster & S. S. Ashburn (Eds.), *The process of human development: A holistic life-span approach* (3rd ed., pp. 804–830). Philadelphia: Lippincott.

Miller, G. A. (1956). The magical number, seven, plus or minus two: Some limits on our capacity for processing information. *Psychological Review, 63,* 81–97.

Minkler, M., & Roe, K. (1993). *Grandmothers as caregivers: Raising children of the crack cocaine epidemic.* Newbury Park, CA: Sage.

Minnett, A. M., Vanell, D. L., & Santrock, J. W. (1983). The effects of sibling status on sibling interaction: Influence of birth order, age, spacing, sex of the child, and sex of the sibling. *Child Development, 54,* 1064–1072.

Minuchin, P. P. (1977). *The middle years of childhood.* Pacific Grove, CA: Brooks/Cole.

Minuchin, P. P., and Shapiro, E. K. (1983). The school as a context for social development. In P. H. Mussen (Ed.), *Handbook of child psychology: Vol. 4, Socialization, personality, and social development.* New York: Wiley.

Minuchin, S. (1974). *Families and family therapy.* Cambridge, MA: Harvard University Press.

Mischel, W. (2004). Toward an integrative model for CBT: Encompassing behavior, cognition, affect, and process. *Behavior Therapy, 35,* 185–203.

Mischel, W., & Morf, C. C. (2003). The self as a psycho-social dynamic processing system: A meta-perspective on a century of self in psychology. In M. R. Leary & J. P. Tangney (Eds.), *Handbook of self and identity* (pp. 15–43). New York: Guilford Press.

Mitchell, J. (1993). *Pregnant, substance-using women.* Rockville, MD: U.S. Department of Health and Human Services, Substance Abuse and Mental Health Services Administration.

Mitiguy, J. S. (1990, Fall). Coping with survival. *Headlines: The Brain Injury Magazine,* 2–8.

Mitrushina, M., & Satz, P. (1991). Reliability and validity of the mini-mental status exam in neurologically intact elderly. *Journal of Clinical Psychology, 47,* 537–543.

Moen, P. (Ed.) (2003). *It's about time: Couples and careers.* Ithaca, NY: ILR Press.

Moffitt, T. E. (1996). Adolescent limited and life course persistent antisocial behavior: A developmental taxonomy. *Psychological Review, 100,* 674–701.

Moffitt, T. E. (2003). Life-course persistent and adolescence-limited antisocial behavior: A 10-year research review and a research agenda. In B. B. Lahey, T. E. Moffitt, & A. Caspi (Eds.), *Causes of conduct disorder and juvenile delinquency* (pp. 49–75). New York: Guilford Press.

Moffitt, T. E., Caspi, A., Dickson, N., Silva, P., & Stanton, W. (1996). Childhood-onset versus adolescent-onset antisocial conduct problems in males: Natural history from ages 3 to 18 years. *Developmental Psychopathology, 8,* 399–424.

Mohler-Kuo, M., Dowdall, G. W., Koss, M. P., & Wechsler, H. (2004). Correlates of rape while intoxicated in a National sample of college women. *Journal of Studies of Alcohol, 65,* 37–45.

Molidor, C., Tolman, R., & Kober, J. (2000). Gender and contextual factors in adolescent dating violence. *The Prevention Researcher, 7,* 1–4.

Money, J. (1988). *Gay, straight, and in-between: The sexology of erotic orientation.* New York: Oxford University Press.

Montemayer, R. (1983). Parents and adolescents in conflict: All families some of the time and some families most of the time. *Journal of Early Adolescence, 3,* 83–103.

Moore, J., & Hagedorn, J. (2001). *Female gangs: A focus on research.* Washington, DC: Office of Juvenile Justice and Delinquency Programs.

Morell, C. M. (2003). Empowerment and long-living women: Return to the rejected body. *Journal of Aging Studies, 17,* 69–85.

Morris, R. (1996). The world is a box of crayons. In P. R. Popple & L. Leighninger (Eds.), *Social work, social welfare, and American society* (pp. 645–647). Boston: Allyn & Bacon.

Morrison, R. S., Olson, E., Mertz, K. R., & Meier, D. E. (1995). The inaccessibility of advance directives on transfer from ambulatory to acute care settings. *Journal of the American Medical Association, 274,* 478–482.

Mrazek, P. (1993). Maltreatment and infant development. In C. Zeaneh (Ed.), *Handbook of infant mental health* (pp. 73–86). New York: Guilford Press.

MTA Cooperative Group. (1999). A 14-month randomized clinical trial of treatment strategies for attention-deficit/hyperactivity disorder. *Archives of General Psychiatry, 56,* 1073–1086.

Muehlenhard, C. L., & Linton, M. A. (1987). Date rape and sexual aggression in dating situations: Incidence and risk factors. *Journal of Counseling Psychology, 34,* 186–196.

Mueller, E., & Lucas, F. (1975). A developmental analysis of peer interaction among toddlers. In M. Lewis & L. Rosenglum (Eds.), *Friendship and peer relations.* New York: Wiley-Interscience.

Mueller, E., & Vandell, D. (1979). Infant-infant interaction. In J. D. Osofsy (Ed.), *Handbook of infant development.* New York: Wiley.

Mueller, M., Wilhelm, B., & Elder, G. (2002). Variations in grandparenting. *Research on Aging, 24*(3), 360–388.

Munley, A. (1983). *The hospice alternative.* New York: Basic Books.

Munoz, K. A., Krebs-Smith, S. M., Ballard-Barbash, R., & Cleveland, L. E. (1998). Food intakes of U.S. children and adolescents compared with recommendations. *Pediatrics, 191,* 952–953.

Murray, B. (1999). Via the telephone, group support reaches cancer patients who might otherwise go without it. *APA Monitor.* Retrieved April 25, 2005: http://www.apa.org/monitor/jun99/telephone.html

Murray, S. S., McKinney, E. S., & Gorrie, T. M. (2003). *Foundations of maternal-newborn nursing* (3rd ed.). Philadelphia: Saunders.

Musick, M., Traphagen, K., Koenig, H., & Larson, D. (2000). Spirituality in physical health and aging. *Journal of Adult Development, 7,* 73–86.

Mussen, P. H. (1974). *Child development and personality* (6th ed). New York: Harper & Row.

Mutryn, C. (1993). Psychosocial impact of cesarean section on the family: A literature review. *Social Science and Medicine, 37,* 1271–1282.

Myers, B. (1982). Early intervention using Brazelton training with middle-class mothers and fathers of newborns. *Child Development, 53,* 462–471.

Myers, B., Jarvis, P., & Creasey, G. (1987). Infants' behavior with their mothers and grandmothers. *Infant Behavior and Development, 10,* 245–259.

Myers, D. (2001). *Social Psychology* (7th ed.). Boston: McGraw-Hill.

Nadeau, J., & Barlow, J. (2003). *Sixty million Frenchmen can't be wrong.* Naperville, IL: Sourcebooks.

Naditz, A. (2003, July). Deeply affected: As the nation ages, Alzheimer's will strike more people close to us. *Contemporary Long Term Care,* 20–22.

Nagy, M. H. (1959). The child's view of death. In H. Feifel (Ed.), *The meaning of death* (pp. 79–98). New York: McGraw-Hill.

Najem, G. R., Aslam, S., Davidow, A. L., & Elliot, N. (2004). Youth homicide racial disparities: Gender, years, and cause. *Journal of the National Medical Association, 96,* 558–566.

Nakagawa, M. (1993). Community leaders, police talk, hate crimes. *Asian Week,* p. 12.

Nansel, T. R., Overpeck, M., Pilla, R. S., Ruan, W. J., Simons-Morton, B., & Scheidt, P. (2001). Bullying behaviors among U.S. youth: Prevalence associated with psychosocial adjustment. *Journal of the American Medical Association, 285,* 2094–2100.

Nash, M. (1989). *The cauldron of ethnicity in the modern world.* Chicago: University of Chicago Press.

National Academy on an Aging Society. (1999). *Chronic conditions: A challenge for the 21st century* (Profile No. 1). Washington, DC: Author.

National Academy on an Aging Society. (2000a). *Arthritis: A leading cause of disability in the United States* (Profile No. 5). Washington, DC: Author.

National Academy on an Aging Society. (2000b). *Diabetes: A drain on U.S. resources* (Profile No. 6). Washington, DC: Author.

National Academy on an Aging Society. (2000c). *Hypertension: A common condition for older Americans* (Profile No. 12). Washington, DC: Author.

National Association for the Education of Young Children. (2002). NAEYC position statement on school readiness. Available at http://naeyc.org/resources/position-statements/psredy98.htm

National Association of School Psychologists. (2002). Children and fear of war and terrorism: Tips for parents and teachers. Retrieved March 1, 2003, from http://www.nasponline.org

National Association on HIV over Fifty. *Educational tip sheet: HIV/AIDS and older adults.* Retrieved June 15, 2004, from http://www.hivoverfifty.org/tip.html

National Center for Early Development & Learning. (1997). Quality in child care centers: Early Childhood Research & Policy Briefs. Retrieved December 23, 1997, from www.fpg.unc.edu/ncedl/mcedl.html

National Center for Health Statistics. (2003). *Healthy people 2000 review.* Hyattsville, MD: Public Health Service.

National Center for Infant Mental Health. (2004). Data retrieved October 13, 2004, from www.zerotothree.org

National Center on Child Abuse and Neglect. (1994). *Child maltreatment 1992: Reports from the states to the National Center on Child Abuse and Neglect.* Washington, DC: Government Printing Office.

National Center on Elder Abuse. (2004). The Basics. Retrieved August 3, 2004, from http://www.elderabusecenter.org/default.cfm?p=basics.cfm

National Clearinghouse on Child Abuse and Neglect Information. (2004). *A coordinated response to child abuse and neglect: The foundation for practice.* Retrieved September 9, 2004, from http://nccanch.acf.hhs.gov/pubs/usermanuals/foundation/index.cfm#toc

National Coalition Against Domestic Violence. (2003). *Poll finds domestic violence is women's main concern.* Retrieved September 9, 2004, from http://www.ncadv.org/

National Council for Homelessness. (2003). *Interagency council on homelessness 2003 Annual report.* Retrieved October 25, 2004, from http://www.ssa.gov/homelessness

National Council of La Raza. (February, 2004). *State of Hispanic America 2004: Latino perspectives on the American agenda.* Washington, DC: Author.

National Council on Homelessness. (1999). *Domestic violence and homelessness.* National Council Fact Sheet no. 8 at http://www.national homeless.org/domestic.html

National Governors' Association and National Association of State Budget Officers. (May, 1998). *The fiscal survey of states.* Washington, DC: Author.

National Institute for Literacy. (1998). *Literacy issues in America.* Washington, DC: Author.

National Institute of Child Health and Human Development, Early Child Care Research Network. (1996). Characteristics of infant child care: Factors contributing to positive care giving. *Early Childhood Research Quarterly, 11,* 269–306.

National Institute of Child Health and Human Development, Early Child Care Research Network. (April, 1997). *Mother-child interaction and cognitive outcomes associated with early child care.* Washington, DC: Author.

National Institute of Child Health and Human Development. (2004). NIH News: Labor takes longer for overweight, study finds. Retrieved December 3, 2004, from http://www.nichd.nih.gov/

National Institute of Child Health and Human Development. (2004b). *SIDS: Back to sleep campaign. Babies sleep safest on their backs: Reduce the risk of sudden infant death syndrome (SIDS).* Retrieved December 13, 2004, from www.nichd.nih.gov/sids

National Institute of Environmental Health Sciences. (2004). Asthma and its environmental triggers: Scientists take a practical new look at a familiar illness. Retrieved March 15, 2004, from http://www.niehs.nih.gov/oc/factsheets/asthma.htm

National Institute of Mental Health. (1991). *Caring for people with severe mental disorders: A national plan of research to improve services* (DHHS Publication No. ADM 91-1762). Washington, DC: U.S. Government Printing Office.

National Institute of Mental Health. (2003). *Older adults: Depression and suicide facts.* Retrieved July 12, 2004, from http://www.nimh.nih.gov/publicat/elderlydepsuicide.cfm

National Institute on Aging. (2001). *Portfolio for progress.* Bethesda, MD: Author.

National Institute on Aging. (2002). *AgePage: Sexuality in later life.* Bethesda, MD: Author.

National Institute on Aging. (2004). *Studies suggest people with early AD can still learn.* Retrieved July 2, 2004, from http://www.nia.nih.gov

National Institute on Alcohol and Alcoholism. (2004). *U.S. Census report on alcohol abuse.* Washington, DC: United States Department of Health and Human Services.

National Organization for Women. (1995). *Violence against women in the United States.* Retrieved April 18, 2004, from www.now.org

National Research Council. (1993). *Losing generations: Adolescents in high-risk settings.* Washington, DC: National Academy Press.

National Research Council. (2001). *Educating children with autism.* Washington, DC: National Academy Press.

National Youth Gang Center. (2000). 1998 National Youth Gang Survey. Washington, DC: OJJDP.

Neason, S. (1994). *Prader-Willi syndrome: A handbook for parents.* St. Louis, MO: Prader-Willi Syndrome Association.

Neimark, E. D. (1975). Longitudinal development of formal operational thought. *Genetic Psychology Monographs, 91,* 171–225.

Nelson, E., & Dannefer, D. (1992). Aged heterogeneity: Fact or fiction? The fate of diversity in gerontological research. *The Gerontologist, 32,* 17–23.

Nelson, H. D., Humphrey, L. L., Nygren, P., Teutsch, S. M., & Allan, J. D. (2002). Postmenopausal hormone replacement therapy: Scientific review. *Journal of the American Medical Association, 288,* 872–881.

Nelson, R. E., Gabler, R. E., & Vining, J. W. (1995). *Human geography: People, cultures, and landscapes.* Fort Worth, TX: Harcourt.

Netting, F. E., Kettner, P. M., & McMurtry, S. L. (1993). *Social work macro practice.* White Plains, NY: Longman.

Netting, F. E., Kettner, P. M., & McMurtry, S. L. (2003). *Social work macro practice* (3rd ed.). Boston: Pearson Allyn Bacon.

Neubeck, K. J., & Cazenave, N. A. (2001). *Welfare racism: Playing the race card against America's poor.* New York: Routledge.

Neugarten, B. L. (1968). The awareness of middle age. In B. L. Neugarten (Ed.), *Middle age and aging* (pp. 93–98). Chicago: University of Chicago Press.

Neugarten, B. L. (1969). Continuities and discontinuities of psychological issues into adult life. *Human Development, 12,* 121–130.

Neugarten, B. L. (1974). Age groups in American society and the rise of the young-old. *Annals of the American Academy of Political and Social Science,* 187–198.

Neugarten, B. L. (1986). The aging society. In A. Pifer & D. L. Bronte (Eds.), *Our aging society: Paradox and promise.* New York: Norton.

Neugarten, B. L., & Weinstein, K. (1964). The changing American grandparent. *Journal of Marriage and the Family, 26,* 199–204.

Newberger, E., Barkan, S., Lieberman, E., McCormick, M., Yllo, K., Gary, L., et al. (1992). Abuse of pregnant women and adverse birth outcome: Current knowledge and implications for practice. *Journal of the American Medical Association, 17,* 2370–2372.

Newcomb, M. D., Huba, G. J., & Bentler, P. M. (1986). Determinants of sexual and dating behaviors among adolescents. *Journal of Personality and Social Psychology, 50,* 428–438.

Newman, B. M., & Newman, P. R. (1987). *Development through life: A psychosocial approach* (4th ed.). Pacific Grove, CA: Brooks/Cole.

Newman, B. M., & Newman, P. R. (1991). *Development through life: A psychosocial approach* (5th ed.). Pacific Grove, CA: Brooks/Cole.

Newman, B. M., & Newman, P. R. (1995). *Development through life: A psychosocial approach* (6th ed.). Pacific Grove, CA: Brooks/Cole.

Newman, B. M., & Newman, P. R. (2002). *Development through life: A psychosocial approach* (8th ed). Pacific Grove, CA: Brooks/Cole.

Newman, B. S. (1994). Diversity and populations at risk: Gays and lesbians. In F. G. Reamer (Ed.), *The foundations of social work knowledge.* New York: Columbia University Press.

Newman, L. S. (2001). What is "Social Cognition"? Four Basic Approaches and their implications for research. In P. W. Corrigan and D. L. Penn (Eds.). *Social cognition and schizophrenia.* Washington, DC: American Psychological Association.

Newman, L., & Buka, S. (1991, Spring). Clipped wings: The fullest look yet at how prenatal exposure to drugs, alcohol, and nicotine hobbles children's learning. *American Educator,* 27–42.

Newsweek (1988). December 5, pp. 24, 29.

Nickerson, E. T., & Pitochelli, E. T. (1978). *Learned helplessness and depression in married women: Marriage as a depressing life style for women.* Paper presented at the meeting of the Eastern Psychological Association, Washington, DC.

Nicol, S. E., & Gottesman, I. I. (1983). Clues to the genetics and neurobiology of schizophrenia. *American Scientist, 71,* 398–404.

Nieto, A., Matorras, R., Villar, J., & Serra, M. (1998). Neonatal morbidity associated with disproportionate intrauterine growth retardation at term. *Journal of Obstetrics and Gynecology, 18,* 540–544.

NIH News. (2004). List serve of National Institutes of Health, July.

Nisbet, R. E. (2003). *The geography of thought: How Asians and Westerners think differently . . . and why.* New York: The Free Press.

Niven, C., Wiszniewski, C., & AlRoomi, L. (1993). Attachment (bonding) in mothers of preterm babies. *Journal of Reproductive and Infant Psychology, 11,* 175–185.

Noe, R. A. (1988). Women and mentoring: A review and research agenda. *Academy of Management Review, 13,* 65–78.

Noel, M. (2000). Why geriatrics? *Generations: Quarterly Journal of the American Society on Aging, 23*(4), 83–86.

Nolen-Hoeksema, S. (2003). *Women who think too much: How to break free of overthinking and reclaim your life.* New York: Henry Holt.

Nomas, E. (1992, August 13). All in the family. *The Advocate, 609,* 46–53.

Norton, D., Brown, E. F., Brown, E. G., Francis, E. A., Murase, K., et al. (1978). *The dual perspective: Inclusion of ethnic minority content in the social work curriculum.* New York: Council on Social Work Education.

Nuckolls, K. B., Cassel, J., & Kaplan, B. H. (1972). Psychosocial assets, life crises, and the prognosis of pregnancy. *American Journal of Epidemiology, 95,* 431–441.

Nurcombe, B. (2000). Clinical decision making in psychiatry. In M. H. Ebert, P. T. Loosen, & B. Nurcombe (Eds.), *Current diagnosis and*

Nurcombe, B., & Gallagher, R. M. (1986). *The clinical process in psychiatry: Diagnosis and management planning.* London: Cambridge University Press.

Nurcombe, B., Gwirtsman, H. E., & Ebert, M. H. (2000). Psychiatric interview. In M. H. Ebert, P. T. Loosen, & B. Nurcombe (Eds.), *Current diagnosis and treatment in psychiatry* (pp. 95–114). New York: Lange Medical Books/McGraw-Hill.

Nylund, D. (2002). *Treating Huckleberry Finn: A new narrative approach to working with kids diagnosed ADD/ADHD.* San Francisco: Jossey-Bass.

O'Connell, H., Chin, A., Cunningham, C., & Lawlor, B. (2003). Alcohol use disorders in elderly people—Redefining an age old problem in old age. *British Medical Journal, 327,* 664–667.

Oden, S., & Asher, S. R. (1977). Coaching children in social skills for friendship making. *Child Development, 48,* 495–506.

Offer, D., Ostrov, E., & Howard, K. (1981). *The adolescent: A psychological self-portrait.* New York: Basic Books.

Office of Juvenile Justice and Delinquency programs (2000). *1998 Youth gang survey.* Washington, DC: Author.

Ogbu, J. U. (2003). *Black American students in an affluent suburb: A study of academic disengagement.* Mahwah, NJ: Erlbaum.

O'Hara, M. W., Kohout, F. J., & Wallace, R. B. (1985). Depression among the rural elderly: A study of prevalence and correlates. *The Journal of Nervous and Mental Disease, 173,* 582–589.

Okamoto, S. K., LeCroy, C. W., Dustman, P., Hohmann-Marriott, B., & Kulis, S. (2004). An ecological assessment of drug-related problem situations for American Indian adolescents in the Southwest. *Journal of Social Work Practice in the Addictions, 4,* 47–64.

Okun, B. F. (1984). *Working with adults: Individual, family, and career development.* Pacific Grove, CA: Brooks/Cole.

Olds, D., & Kitzman, H. (1990). Can home visitation improve the health of women and children at environmental risk? *Pediatrics, 86,* 108–116.

Olsen, J. (1980). Social and psychological correlates of pregnancy resolution among adolescent women: A review. *American Journal of Orthopsychiatry, 50,* 432–445.

Olshansky, E. (1992). Redefining the concepts of success and failure in infertility treatment. *NAACOGS Clinic Issues in Perinatal and Women's Health Nursing, 3,* 313–319.

Oltmanns, T. F., & Emery, R. E. (2004). *Abnormal psychology* (4th ed.). Upper Saddle River, NJ: Pearson/Prentice Hall.

Olweus, D. (1977). Aggression and peer acceptance in adolescent boys: Two short-term longitudinal studies of ratings. *Child Development, 48,* 1303–1313.

Olweus, D. (1980). Familial and temperamental determinants of aggressive behavior in adolescent boys: A causal analysis. *Developmental Psychology, 16,* 644–660.

Olweus, D., Limber, S., & Mihalic, S. (1999). *The bullying prevention program: Blueprints for violence prevention.* Boulder, CO: Center for the Study and Prevention of Violence.

Opie, I., & Opie, P. (1987). *The love and language of schoolchildren.* New York: Oxford University Press.

Ornstein, P. (1995, January). New cognitive research making waves. *APA Monitor.*

Orthner, D. (1975). Leisure activity patterns and marital satisfaction over the marital career. *Journal of Marriage and the Family, 37,* 91–102.

Ortiz, L., & Langer, N. (2002). Assessment of spirituality and religion in later life: Acknowledging clients' needs and personal resources. *Journal of Gerontological Social Work, 37*(2), 5–21.

Osofsky, J., Hann, D., & Peebles, C. (1993). Adolescent parenthood: Risks and opportunities for mothers and infants. In C. Zeaneh (Ed.), *Handbook of infant mental health* (pp. 106–119). New York: Guilford Press.

Ostrom, T. (1984). The sovereignty of social cognition. In R. S. Wyer & T. K. Srull (Eds.), *Handbook of social cognition* (Vol. 1, pp. 1–32). Hillsdale, NJ: Erlbaum.

Otto, L. B. (1988). America's youth: A changing profile. *Family Relations, 37,* 385–391.

Ouchi, W. (1981). *Theory Z: How American business can beat the Japanese challenge.* Reading, MA: Addison-Wesley.

Owens, T. J. (2003). Self and identity. In J. Delamater (2003), *Handbook of social psychology* (pp. 205–232). New York: Kluwer Academic/Plenum Publishers.

Oyserman, D., Radin, N., & Benn, R. (1993). Dynamics in a three-generational family: Teens, grandparents, and babies. *Developmental Psychology, 29,* 564–572.

Ozer, E. J., Richards, M. H., & Kliewer, W. (2004). Introduction to the special section on protective factors in the relation between community violence and exposure and adjustment in youth. *Journal of Clinical Child and Adolescent Psychology, 33,* 434–438.

Page, D. S. (1981). *Principles of biological chemistry* (2nd ed.). Boston: Willard Grant Press.

Pahl, J., & Quine, L. (1987). Families with mentally handicapped children. In J. Oxford (Ed.), *Treating the disorder, treating the family* (pp. 39–61). Baltimore: Johns Hopkins University Press.

Pancoast, D. L., & Collins, A. (1987). Natural helping networks. In *Encyclopedia of Social Work* (18th ed., 177–182). Silver Spring, MD: National Association of Social Workers.

Pancoast, D. L., Parker, P., & Froland, C. (1983). *Rediscovering self-help: Its role in social care.* Beverly Hills, CA: Sage.

Papousek, H., & Papousek, M. (1982). Integration into the social world: Survey of research. In P. M. Stratton (Ed.), *Psychobiology of the human newborn* (pp. 367–390). New York: Wiley.

Papousek, H., & Papousek, M. (1987). Intuitive parenting: A dialectic counterpart to the infant's integrative competence. In J. Osofsky (Ed.), *Handbook of infant development* (2nd ed., pp. 669–720). New York: Wiley.

Papousek, H., & Papousek, M. (1992). Beyond emotional bonding: The role of preverbal communication in mental growth and health. *Infant Mental Health Journal, 13,* 43–53.

Papousek, M., Papousek, H., & Bornstein, M. H. (1985). The naturalistic vocal environment of young infants: On the significance of homogeneity and variability in parental speech. In T. Fields & N. Fox (Eds.), *Social perception in infants* (pp. 269–297). Norwood, NJ: Ablex.

Parekh, B. (2002). Barry and the dangers of liberalism. In P. Kelly (Ed.), *Multiculturalism reconsidered: Culture and equality and its critics* (pp. 133–150). Cambridge, UK: Polity Press.

Paris, S. C., & Lindayer, B. K. (1982). The development of cognitive skills during childhood. In B. B. Wolman (Ed.), *Handbook of developmental psychology.* Englewood Cliffs, NJ: Prentice Hall.

Parke, R. D., MacDonald, K., Beital, A., & Bhavangri, N. (1988). The interrelationships among families, fathers, and peers. In R. D. Peters (Ed.), *New approaches to family research.* New York: Brunner/Mazel.

Parke, R. D., & O'Leary, S. (1976). Family interaction in the newborn period: Some findings, some observations and some unresolved issues. In K. Riegel & J. Meacham (Eds.), *The developing individual in a changing world: Vol. 2, Social and environmental issues.* The Hague: Mouton.

Parke, R. D., & Slaby, R. G. (1983). The development of aggression. In P. H. Mussen (Ed.), *Handbook of child psychology* (4th ed., Vol. 4). New York: Wiley.

Parke, R. D., & Tinsley, B. (1987). Family interaction in infancy. In J. Osofsky (Ed.), *Handbook of infant development* (2nd ed., pp. 579–641). New York: Wiley.

Parker, B., McFarlane, J., Soeken, K., Torres, S., & Campbell, D. (1993). Physical and emotional abuse in pregnancy: A comparison of adult and teenage women. *Nursing Research, 42,* 173–177.

Parker, J. G., & Gottman, J. M. (1989). Social and emotional development in a relational context: Friendship interaction from early childhood to adolescence. In T. J. Berndt & G. W. Ladd (Eds.), *Peer relations in child development.* New York: Wiley.

Parrot, A., & Bechhofer, L. (1991). *Acquaintance rape.* New York: Wiley.

Parsons, J. E., Adler, T. F., & Kaczala, C. M. (1982a). Socialization of achievement attitudes and beliefs: Parental influences. *Child Development, 53,* 308–318.

Parsons, J. E., Adler, T. F., & Kaczala, C. M. (1982b). Socialization of achievement attitudes and beliefs: Parental influences. *Child Development, 53,* 322–329.

Parten, M. (1932). Social play among preschool children. *Journal of Abnormal and Social Psychology, 27,* 243–269.

Pasui, K., & McFarland, K. F. (1997). Management of diabetes in pregnancy. *American Family Physician, 55,* 2731–2739.

Patterson, C. J. (2002). Lesbian and gay parenthood. In M. H. Bornstein (Ed.), *Handbook of parenting* (Vol. 3, pp. 317–338). Mahwah, NJ: Erlbaum.

Patterson, G. R. (1982). *A social learning approach to family interventions: Vol. 3, Coercive family process.* Eugene, OR: Castalia.

Patterson, G. R. (1986). Performance models for antisocial boys. *American Psychologist, 41,* 432–444.

Patterson, G. R., DeBarsyshe, B. D., & Ramsey, E. (1989). A developmental perspective on antisocial behavior. *American Psychologist, 44,* 329–335.

Patterson, G. R., Reid, J. B., & Dishion, T. J. (1992). *Antisocial boys.* Eugene, OR: Castalia.

Patterson, J. M., & McCubbin, H. I. (1987). Adolescent coping style and behaviors: Conceptualization and measurement. *Journal of Adolescence, 10,* 163–186.

Patterson, S., Brennan, E., Germain, C., & Memmot, J. (1988). The effectiveness of rural natural helpers. *Social Casework, 69*, 272–279.

Patterson, S. L. (1987). Older rural natural helpers: Gender and site differences in the helping process. *The Gerontologist, 27*, 639–644.

Pattison, E. M. (1978). The living-dying process. In C. A. Garfield (Ed.), *Psychosocial care of the dying patient* (pp. 145–153). New York: McGraw-Hill.

Paulson, R., & Sauer, M. (1991). Counseling the infertile couple: When enough is enough. *Obstetrics and Gynecology, 78*, 462–464.

Pavenstedt, E. (1965). A comparison of the child-rearing environment of upper-lower and very low lower-class families. *American Journal of Orthopsychiatry, 35*, 89–98.

Pawlak, E. J., & Cousins, L. (1999). School social work: Organizational perspectives. In R. Constable, S. McDonald, & J. P. Flynn (Eds.), *School social work: Practice, policy, and research perspectives* (pp. 150–165). Chicago: Lyceum Press.

Peak, T., & Toseland, R. W. (1992). Friends don't really understand: The therapeutic benefit of social group work for caregivers of older persons. In C. W. LeCroy (Ed.), *Case studies in social work practice*. Pacific Grove, CA: Brooks/Cole.

Peak, T., & Toseland, R. W. (1999). Friends don't really understand: The therapeutic benefit of social group work for caregivers of older persons. In C. W. LeCroy (Ed.), *Case studies in social work practice* (2nd ed.). Pacific Grove, CA: Brooks/Cole.

Pearlin, L. I., Mullan, J. T., Semple, S. J., & Skaff, M. M. (1990). Caregiving and the stress process: An overview of concepts and their measures. *The Gerontologist, 30*, 583–594.

Pearson, J. L., Hunter, A. G., Ensminger, M. E., & Kellam, S. G. (1990). Black grandmothers in multigenerational households: Diversity in family structure and parenting involvement in the Woodlawn community. *Child Development, 61*, 434–442.

Pecora, P. J., Whittaker, J. K., & Maluccio, A. N. (1992). *The child welfare challenge: Policy, practice, and research*. New York: Aldine de Gruyter.

Pecora, P., Whittaker, J., Maluccio, A., & Barth, R. (2000). Family foster care. In *The child welfare challenge* (2nd ed., pp. 314–318). New York: Aldine DeGruyter.

Pederson, F., Cain, R., & Zaslow, M. (1982). Variation in infant experience associated with alternative family roles. In L. Laosa & I. Sigel (Eds.), *The family as a learning environment*. New York: Plenum.

Pedro-Carroll, J. L., & Cowen, E. L. (1985). The children of divorce intervention program: An investigation of the efficacy of a school-based prevention program. *Journal of Consulting and Clinical Psychology, 53*, 603–611.

Peek, C. W., Koropeckyj-Cox, T., Zsembik, B. A. & Coward, R. T. (2004). Race comparisons of the household dynamics of older adults. *Research on Aging, 26*(2), 179–201.

Pellegrini, A. D. (2002). Rough-and-tumble play from childhood through adolescence: Development & Possible Functions. In C. H. Hart & P. K. Smith (Eds.), *Blackwell Handbook of Childhood Social Development*. Malden, MA: Blackwell.

Pellegrini, D. S. (1990). Psychosocial risk and protective factors in childhood. *Developmental and Behavioral Pediatrics, 11*, 201–209.

Penfield, W., & Perot, P. (1963). The brain's record of auditory and visual experience. *Brain, 86*, 595–696.

Peng, T. R., Navaie-Waliser, M. & Feldman, P. H. (2003). Social support, home health service use, and outcomes among four racial-ethnic groups. *The Gerontologist, 43*, 503–513.

Pennebaker, J. W., Hendler, C. S., Durrett, M. E., & Richards, P. (1981). Social factors influencing absenteeism due to illness in nursery school children. *Child Development, 52*, 692–700.

Peplau, L. A. (1991). Lesbian and gay relationships. In J. C. Gonsiorek & J. D. Weinrich (Eds.), *Homosexuality: Research implications for public policy*. Newbury Park, CA: Sage.

Peplau, L. A., Bikson, T. K., Rook, K. S., & Goodchilds, J. D. (1982). Being old and living alone. In L. A. Peplau & D. Perlman (Eds.), *Loneliness: A sourcebook of current theory, research, and therapy*. New York: Wiley-Interscience.

Perkins, K., & Tice, C. (1999). Family treatment of older adults who misuse alcohol: A strengths perspective. *Journal of Gerontological Social Work, 31*(3/4), 169–185.

Perrow, C. (1978). The short and glorious history of organizational theory. In J. M. Shafritz & P. H. Whitbeck (Eds.), *Classics of organization theory* (pp. 313–323). Belmont, CA: Wadsworth.

Perzanowski, C. M. C., Perzanowski, M. S., Raymond, A., & Platts-Mills, T. A. (2001). Home intervention in the treatment of asthma among inner-city children. *Journal of Allergy and Clinical Immunology, 108*, 732–737.

Petersen, A. C. (1987, September). Those gangly years. *Psychology Today*, pp. 28–34.

Petersen, A. C., & Crockett, L. J. (1992). Adolescent sexuality, pregnancy, and child rearing: Developmental perspectives. In M. K. Rosenheim & M. F. Testa (Eds.), *Early parenthood and coming of age in the 1990s*. New Brunswick, NJ: Rutgers University Press.

Petersen, A. C., Kennedy, R. E., & Sullivan, P. (1991). Coping with adolescence. In M. E. Colten & S. Gore (Eds.), *Adolescent stress*. New York: Aldine de Gruyter.

Peterson, C., & Seligman, M. E. P. (2004). *Character strengths and virtues: A handbook of classification*. Washington, DC: American Psychological Association.

Peterson, K. (1993). The homeless mentally ill. In B. S. Johnson (Ed.), *Psychiatric–mental health nursing* (3rd ed., pp. 589–601). Philadelphia: Lippincott.

Petri, H. L. (1986). *Motivation: Theory and research* (2nd ed.). Belmont, CA: Wadsworth.

Petri, H. L., & Govern, J. M. (2004). *Motivation: Theory, research, and applications* (5th ed.). Belmont, CA: Wadsworth/Thomson.

Pettit, G. S., Dodge, K. A., & Brown, M. M. (1988). Early family experience, social problem-solving patterns, and children's social competence. *Child Development, 59*, 107–120.

Pfohl, B. (1995, May). Is self-esteem really all that important? *APA Monitor*, 40–42.

Pfrieger, F. W., Barres, B. A. (1997). Synaptic efficacy enhanced by glial cells in vitro. *Science, 277*, 1684–1687.

Phillips, L. (1998). *The girls report: What we know and need to know about growing up female*. New York: National Council on Research for Women.

Piaget, J. (1929). *The child's conception of the world*. New York: Harcourt Brace.

Piaget, J. (1967). *The child's conception of the world*. Totowa, NJ: Littlefield, Adams.

Piaget, J. (1972). Intellectual evolution from adolescence to adulthood. *Human Development, 15*, 1–12.

Piaget, J., & Inhelder, B. (1969). *The psychology of the child*. New York: Basic Books.

Pica, R. (2003). *Your active child: How to boost physical, emotional, and cognitive development through age-appropriate activity*. New York: McGraw-Hill.

Piguet, O., David, A., Grayson, G., Broe, A., Tate, R., Bennett, H., et al. (2002). Normal aging and executive functions in "old-old" community dwellers: Poor performance is not an inevitable outcome. *International Psychogeriatrics, 14*(2), 139–159.

Pinderhughes, E. (1994). Diversity and populations at risk: Ethnic minorities and people of color. In F. G. Reamer (Ed.), *The foundations of social work knowledge*. New York: Columbia University Press.

Pineo, P. (1969). Developmental patterns in marriage. *Family Coordinator, 18*, 135–140.

Pines, M. (1979). Head start in the nursery. *Psychology Today, 13*, 56.

Pines, M. (1979, January). Superkids. *Psychology Today*, 53–63.

Pines, M. (1982, June). It's changing the lives of handicapped kids: Infant stimulation. *Psychology Today*, 48–53.

Pinker, S. (2002). *The blank slate: The modern denial of human nature*. New York: Penguin.

Pinquart, M., & Sorensen, S. (2001). Influences on loneliness in older adults: A meta-analysis. *Basic and Applied Psychology, 23*(4), 245–268.

Pipp, S., Easterbrooks, M. A., & Harmon, R. J. (1992). The relation between attachment and knowledge of self and mother in one-to-three-year-old infants. *Child Development, 62*, 738–750.

Pistrang, N. (1995). The partner relationship in psychological response to breast cancer. *Social Science and Medicine, 40*, 789–797.

Pleck, J. H. (1985). *Working wives/working husbands*. Newbury Park, CA: Sage.

Plomin, R. (1990). *Nature and nurture: An introduction to human behavioral genetics*. Belmont, CA: Wadsworth.

Plomin, R. (1994). Nature, nurture, and social development. *Social Development, 3*(1), 37–53.

Plomin, R., & Daniels, D. (1987). Why are children in the same family so different from each other? *Behavioral and Brain Sciences, 10*, 1–16.

Plomin, R., DeFries, J. C., & McClearn, G. E. (1990). *Behavioral genetics: A primer* (2nd ed.). New York: W. H. Freeman.

Plotnik, R. (2000). Economic security for families with children. In P. J. Pecora, J. K. Whittaker, A. N. Maluccio, & R. P. Barth (Eds.), *The child welfare challenge: Policy, practice, and research* (2nd ed., pp. 95–127). New York: Aldine de Gruyter.

Pollard, K. M., O'Hare, W. P. (1999). America's racial and ethnic minorities. *Population Bulletin, 34*(3), 3–44.

Pomerantz, E. M., & Rudolph, K. D. (2003). What ensues from emotional distress? Implications for competence estimation. *Child Development, 74*(2), 329–345.

Porzelius, L. K. (2002). Overview. In M. Hersen & L. K. Porzelius (Eds.), *Diagnosis, conceptualization, and treatment planning for adults: A step-by-step guide*. Mahwah, NJ: Erlbaum.

Potocky, M. (1996). Refugee children: How are they faring economically as adults? *Social Work, 41*, 4, 364–373.

Potocky-Tripodi, M. (2003). *Best practices for social work with refugees and immigrants*. New York: Columbia University Press.

Poweil, A. G., Farrar, E., & Cohen, D. K. (1985). *The shopping mall high school: Winners and losers in the educational marketplace*. Boston: Houghton Mifflin.

Power, T. G. (1985). Mother- and father-infant play: A developmental analysis. *Child Development, 56*, 1514–1524.

Power, T. G., & Shanks, J. A. (1989). Parents as socializers: Maternal and paternal views. *Journal of Youth and Adolescence, 18*, 203–220.

Pratt, M. W., McLaren, J., & Wickens, G. (1984). Rules as tools: Effective generalization of verbal self regulative communication training by first-grade speakers. *Developmental Psychology, 20*, 893–902.

President's New Freedom Commission on Mental Health (2003). *Achieving the promise: Transforming mental health care in America*. Retrieved December 29, 2004, from www.mentalhealthcommision.gov

Prewitt, V. (2002). Wisdom in the workplace. *Performance Improvement Quarterly, 15*, 64–98.

Price, C. (2000). Women and retirement: Relinquishing professional identity. *Journal of Aging Studies, 14*(1), 81–101.

Pritchard, J., MacDonald, P., & Gant, N. (1985). *Williams obstetrics*. Norwalk, CT: Appleton-Century-Crofts.

Proshansky, H., & Newton, P. (1968). The development of Negro self-identity. In M. Deutsch, A. Jensen, & I. Katz (Eds.), *Race and social class in psychological development*. New York: Henry Holt.

Pulkkinen, L., Caspi, A. (2002). *Paths to successful development: Personality in the life course*. Oxford, UK: Oxford University Press.

Puner, M. (1974). *To the good long life: What we know about growing old*. New York: Universe Books.

Putnam, R. (2001). *Bowling alone: The collapse and revival of American community*. New York: Simon and Schuster.

Quam, J. K. (1983). Older women and informal supports: Impact on prevention. In S. Simson, L. B. Wilson, J. Hermalin, & R. Hess (Eds.), *Aging and prevention: New approaches for preventing health and mental health problems in older adults*. New York: Haworth Press.

Quam, J. K., & Whitford, G. S. (1992). Adaptation and age-related expectations of older gay and lesbian adults. *The Gerontologist, 32*, 367–374.

Quatman, T., & Watson, C. M. (2001). Gender differences in adolescent self-esteem: An exploration of domains. *The Journal of Genetic Psychology, 162*, 93–117.

Quinn, P. (1992). Ethnographic-type techniques in life-span human development courses: Integrating information and developing skills. *Family Relations, 41*, 59–64.

Rabasca, L. (1999). Improving the life for survivors of cancer. *APA Monitor*. Retrieved April 25, 2005: http://www.apa.org/monitor/jun99/survivors.html

Rabasca, L. (1999, November). Knocking down societal barriers for people with disabilities. *APA Monitor*, 1.

Rabasca, L. (2000, March). Listening instead of preaching. *APA Monitor*, 50–52.

Radke-Yarrow, M., Cummings, E. M., Kuczynski, L., & Chapman, N. (1985). Patterns of attachment in two- and three-year-olds in normal families and families with parental depression. *Child Development, 56*, 884–893.

Radke-Yarrow, M., Zahn-Waxler, C., & Chapman, M. (1983). Children's prosocial dispositions and behavior. In P. H. Mussen (Ed.), *Handbook of child psychology* (Vol. 4). New York: Wiley.

Radwin, E. (1993). Literacy and illiteracy. *The new Grolier multimedia encyclopedia* [CD ROM].

Ragozin, A. S., Bashan, R. B., Crnic, K. A., Greenberg, M. T., & Robinson, N. M. (1982). Effects of maternal age on parenting role. *Developmental Psychology, 18*, 627–634.

Raine, A., Brennan, P., & Mednick, S. (1994). Birth complications combined with early maternal rejection at age one year predispose to violent crime at 18 years. *Archives of General Psychiatry, 51*, 984–988.

Ramey, C. T., & Ramey, S. L. (1998a). Early intervention and early experience. *American Psychologist, 53*, 109–120.

Ramey, C. T., & Ramey, S. L. (1998b). Prevention of intellectual disabilities: Early intervention to improve cognitive development. *Preventative Medicine, 27*, 224–232.

Ramirez, M. (1978). A mestizo world view and the psychodynamics of Mexican-American border populations. In S. Ross (Ed.), *Views across the border: The United States and Mexico*. Albuquerque: University of New Mexico Press.

Ramos, S. (1975). *Profile of man and culture in Mexico*. Austin: University of Texas Press.

Rank, M. (2004). *One Nation, Underprivileged: Why American Poverty Affects Us All*. New York: Oxford University Press.

Ransford, H. H., & Palisi, B. J. (1996). Aerobic exercise, subjective health and psychological well-being within age and gender subgroups. *Social Science and Medicine, 42*, 1555–1559.

Rapalje, J., Degelman, D., & Ashburn, S. S. (1986). Psychosocial development during the school-age years. In C. S. Schuster & S. S. Ashburn (Eds.), *The process of human development: A holistic life-span approach*. Boston: Little, Brown.

Rapp, C. A. (1998). *The strengths model*. New York: Oxford University Press.

Rapp, S. R., Espeland, M. A., Shumaker, S. A., Henderson, V. W., Brunner, R. L., & Manson, J. E. (2003). Effect of estrogen plus progestin on global cognitive function in postmenopausal women: The Women's Health Initiative memory study: A randomized controlled trial. *Journal of the American Medical Association, 289*, 2663–2672.

Rauch, J. (1988). *Genetic content for graduate social work education: Human behavior and the social environment*. Washington, DC: Council of Social Work Education.

Ravn, S. H., Rosenberg, J., & Bostofte, E. (1994). Postmenopausal hormone replacement therapy—Clinical implications. *European Journal of Obstetrics, Gynecology, and Reproductive Biology, 53*, 81–93.

Reeder, S., Mastroianni, L., & Martin, L. (1983). *Maternity Nursing* (15th ed.). Philadelphia: Lippincott.

Reedy, M. N., Birren, J. E., & Schaie, K. W. (1981). Age and sex differences in satisfying relationships across the adult life span. *Human Development, 24*, 52–66.

Reiss, I. R. (1980). *Family systems in America* (3rd ed.). New York: Holt, Rinehart & Winston.

Reissland, N. (1988). Neonatal imitation in the first hour of life: Observations in rural Nepal. *Developmental Psychology, 24*, 464–469.

Remafedi, G., Farrow, J. A., & Deisher, R. W. (1991). Risk factors for attempted suicide in gay and bisexual youth. *Pediatrics, 87*, 869–875.

Resnick, C., & Tighe, E. G. (1997, January). The role of multidisciplinary community clinics in managed care systems. *Social Work, 42*, 1, 91–98.

Rest, J. R. (1986). *Moral development: Advances in research and theory*. New York: Praeger.

Retschitzki, J., Bossel-Lagos, M., & Dasen, P. R. (1989). *La recherche interculturelle: Actes du deuxième Colloque de l'ARIC*. Paris: LÐHarmattan.

Revelle, J., Wellman, H. M., & Karabenick, J. D. (1985). Comprehension monitoring in preschool children. *Child Development, 56*, 654–663.

Reynolds, B. C. (1942). *Learning and teaching in the practice of social work*. New York: Farrar & Rinehart.

Reynolds, R. E., & Ortony, A. (1980). Some issues in the measurement of children's comprehension of metaphorical language. *Child Development, 51*, 1110–1119.

Riccio, C. A., Hynd, G. W., Cohen, M. J., & Gonzalez, J. J. (1993). Neurological basis of attention deficit hyperactivity disorder. *Exceptional Children, 60*, 118–124.

Rice, F., Harold, G., & Thapar, A. (2002). The genetic etiology of childhood depression: A review. *Journal of Child Psychology and Psychiatry, 43*, 65–79.

Rich, C. L., Young, D., & Fowler, R. C. (1986). San Diego suicide study. *Archives of General Psychiatry, 43*, 577–582.

Richard, B. A., & Dodge, K. A. (1982). Social maladjustment and problem-solving in school-aged children. *Journal of Consulting and Clinical Psychology, 50*, 226–233.

Richard, J. F., Fonzi, A., Tani, F., Tassi, F., Tomada, G., & Schneider, B. H. (2002). Cooperation and competition. In P. K. Smith & C. H. Hart (Eds.), *Blackwell handbook of childhood social development* (pp. 515–532). Malden, MA: Blackwell.

Richardson, D. K. (1988). The importance of reminiscence and family tradition. In J. Norris (Ed.), *Daughters of the elderly: Building partnerships in caregiving* (pp. 32–36). Bloomington: Indiana University Press.

Richardson, J. G., & Simpson, C. H. (1982). Children, gender, and social structure: An analysis of the contents of letters to Santa Claus. *Child Development, 53*, 429–436.

Richardson, K. (1988). *Understanding psychology*. Philadelphia: Open University Press.

Richardson, K. (2000). *Developmental psychology: How nature and nurture interact.* Mahwah, NJ: Erlbaum.

Richardson, V. (2003). A dual process model of grief counseling: Findings from the changing lives of older couples (CLOC) study. Paper presented at the First National Gerontological Social Work Conference, Atlanta, GA.

Richmond, J. B., Stipek, D. J., & Zigler, E. (1979). A decade of Head Start. In E. Zigler & J. Valentine (Eds.), *Project Head Start: A legacy of the War on Poverty.* New York: Free Press.

Richmond, M. (1917). *Social diagnosis.* New York: Russell Sage Foundation.

Rideout, V. J., Vandewater, E. A., & Wartella, E. A. (2003). *Zero to six: Electronic media in the lives of infants, toddlers, and preschoolers* (Publication no. 3378). Menlo Park, CA: Kaiser Family Foundation.

Ridgeway, C. L. (1983). *The dynamics of small groups.* New York: St. Martin's Press.

Riesen, A. (1947). The development of visual perception in man and chimpanzee. *Science, 106,* 107–108.

Riesen, A., Chow, K., Semmes, J., & Nissen, H. (1951). Chimpanzee vision after four conditions of light deprivation. *American Psychologist, 6,* 282.

Riesenberg, D. (1987). Treating a societal malignancy—Rape. *Journal of American Medical Association, 257,* 899–900.

Riessman, Catherine K. (1990). *Divorce Talk: Women and Men Make Sense of Personal Relationships.* Piscataway, NJ: Rutgers University Press.

Rigby, K. (2002). Bullying in Childhood. In C. H. Hart and P. K. Smith (Eds.), *Blackwell Handbook of Childhood Social Development.* Malden, MA: Blackwell.

Rigsby, L. C., & McDill, E. L. (1975). Value orientations of high school students. In H. R. Strub (Ed.), *The sociology of education: A sourcebook* (pp. 53–75). Pacific Grove, CA: Brooks/Cole.

Rinehart, B. H. (2002). Senior housing: Pathway to service utilization. *Journal of Gerontological Social Work, 39*(3), 57–75.

Ritter, M. (1996, January 2). Genetic missing link to personality found. *The Arizona Daily Star,* pp. 1, 7.

Ritzer, G. (2004). *The McDonaldization of society.* Thousand Oaks, CA: Pine Forge Press.

Rivera, R. R. (1991). Sexual orientation and the law. In J. C. Gonsiorek & J. D. Weinrich (Eds.), *Homosexuality: Research implications for public policy.* Newbury Park, CA: Sage.

Rix, S. (2004). *Update on the older worker: 2003.* Washington, DC: AARP Public Policy Institute.

Roberts, P., & Newton, P. M. (1987). Levinsonian studies of women's adult development. *Psychology and Aging, 2,* 154–163.

Robertson, I. (1977). *Sociology.* New York: Worth.

Robertson, J. F. (1976). Significance of grandparents: Perceptions of young adult grandchildren. *The Gerontologist, 16,* 137–140.

Robertson, M. J., Ropers, R. H., & Boyer, R. (1985). *The homeless of Los Angeles County: An empirical evaluation.* Los Angeles: UCLA School of Public Health.

Robin, A. (1994). Problem-solving training. In C. W. LeCroy (Ed.), *Handbook of child and adolescent training manuals.* New York: Lexington Books.

Robins, E., Dev, D., & Limaye, A. (2001). Sickle cell disease and hereditary spherocytosis: A rate combination of hemolytic anemia presenting as cholelithiasis. *International Pediatrics, 16,* 164–167.

Robinson, B. (1994). Appendix A: Exploring attitudes about age and aging. Retrieved September 5, 2001, from http://ist-socrates.berkeley.edu/Ðaging/ModuleAgeism.html

Robinson, B. E., & Barret, R. L. (1985, December). Teenage fathers. *Psychology Today,* 66–70.

Robinson, J. P. (1977). *How Americans use time: A social-psychological analysis of everyday behavior.* New York: Praeger.

Robinson, N. S. (1995). Evaluating the nature of perceived support and its relation to perceived self-worth in adolescents. *Journal of Research on Adolescence, 5,* 253–280.

Robinson, W. P. (1965). The elaborated code in working-class language. *Language and speech, 8,* 243–252.

Robson, W. L., & Leung, A. K. (1992). The circumcision question. *Postgraduate Medicine, 91,* 237–242, 244.

Roedding, J. (1991). Birth trauma and suicide: A study of the relationship between near-death experiences and later suicidal behavior. *Pre- and Perinatal Psychology Journal, 6,* 145–169.

Roff, M. (1963). Childhood social interaction and young adulthood psychosis. *Journal of Clinical Psychology, 19,* 152–157.

Roff, S. (2001). Suicide and the elderly: Issues for clinical practice. *Journal of Gerontological Social Work, 35*(2), 21–35.

Rogers, R. (1989). Ethnic and birth-weight differences in cause-specific infant mortality. *Demography, 26,* 335–341.

Rogoff, B. (2003). *The Cultural Nature of Human Development.* Oxford, UK: Oxford University Press.

Rokach, A. (2001). Perceived causes of loneliness in adulthood. *Journal of Social and Behavior Personality, 15,* 67–84.

Rokeach, M. (1973). *The nature of human values.* New York: Free Press.

Rollins, B. C. (1989). Marital quality at midlife. In S. Hunter & M. Sundel (Eds.), *Midlife myths: Issues, findings, and practice implications.* Newbury Park, CA: Sage.

Rollins, B. C. & Feldman, H. (1970). Marital satisfaction over the life cycle. *Journal of Marriage and the Family, 32,* 20–28.

Roots of addiction (1989, February 27). *Newsweek,* 37–46.

Rose, S. (1991). Information processing at 1 year: Relation to birth status and developmental outcome during the first 5 years. *Developmental Psychology, 27,* 723–737.

Rose, S. (1992). Infant information processing in relation to six-year cognitive outcomes. *Child Development, 63,* 1126–1141.

Rose, S. A., & Feldman, J. F. (1997). Memory and speed: Their role in the relation of infant processing to later IQ. *Child Development, 68,* 630–641.

Rose, S. A., Feldman, J. F., Futterweit, L. R., & Jankowski, J. J. (1998). Continuity in tactual-visual cross-modal transfer: Infancy to 11 years. *Developmental Psychology, 34,* 435–440.

Rose, S. D. (1989). *Working with adults in groups: A multi-method approach.* San Francisco: Jossey-Bass.

Rose, S. D., & LeCroy, C. W. (2005). Behavioral group therapy with children. In M. Hersen (Ed.), *Encyclopedia of Behavior Modification and Therapy: Volume I.* Thousand Oaks, CA: Sage.

Rosen, R. (1979). Some crucial issues concerning children of divorce. *Journal of Divorce, 3,* 19–26.

Rosenberg, M., & Simmons, R. (1971). *Black and white self-esteem: The urban school child.* Rose Monograph Series. Washington, DC: American Sociological Association.

Rosenberg, S. (1997). Multiplicity of selves. In R. D. Ashmore & L. Jussim (Eds.) *Self and Identity: Fundamental issues* (pp. 23–45). New York: Oxford University Press.

Rosenblatt, A. (1962). The application of role concepts to the intake process. *Social Casework, 43,* 8–14.

Rosenblum, O., Mazet, P., & Benony, H. (1997). Mother and infant affective involvement states and maternal depression. *Infant Mental Health Journal, 18,* 350–363.

Rosenthal, R., & Jacobsen, L. (1968). *Pygmalion in the classroom.* New York: Holt, Rinehart & Winston.

Ross, D., & Whitehead, M. I. (1995). Selecting patients for HRT: Positive indications. *British Journal of Clinical Practice, 49,* 92–94.

Ross, H. (2000). *Closing the gap: A newsletter of the Office of Minority Health.* Washington, DC: U.S. Department of Health and Human Services.

Ross, L., Holliman, D., & Dixon, D. (2003). Resiliency in family caregivers: Implications for social work practice. *Journal of Gerontological Social Work, 40*(3), 81–96.

Roth, L. L., & Atherton, C. R. (1989). *Promoting successful aging.* Chicago: Nelson-Hall.

Rothbart, M. K. & Putnam, S. (2002). Temperament and socialization. In L. Pulkkinen & A. Caspi (Eds.), *Paths to successful development: Personality in the life course.* Oxford, UK: Oxford University Press.

Rothblum, E. D., & Franks, V. (1983). Introduction: Warning! Sex-role stereotypes may be hazardous to your health. In V. Franks & E. D. Rothblum (Eds.), *The stereotyping of women: Its effects on mental health.* New York: Springer.

Rovee-Collier, C., Sullivan, M., Enright, M., Lucas, D., & Fagan, J. (1980). Reactivation of infant memory. *Science, 208,* 1159–1161.

Rowe, J. W. & Kahn, R. L. (1998). *Successful aging.* New York: Pantheon/Random House.

Royce, A. P. (1982). *Ethnic identity: Strategies of diversity.* Bloomington: Indiana University Press.

Rozee, P. D., Bateman, P., & Gilmore, T. (1991). The personal perspective of acquaintance rape: A three-tier approach. In A. Parrot & L. Bechhofer (Eds.), *Acquaintance rape: The hidden crime.* New York: Wiley.

Rubenstein, C. M. & Shaver, P. (1982). The experience of loneliness. In L. A. Peplau & D. Perlman (Eds.), *Loneliness: A sourcebook of current theory, research, and therapy.* New York: Wiley.

Rubin, K. H., Bukowski, W., & Parker, J. G. (1998). Peer interactions, relationships and groups. In N. Eisenberg (Ed.), *Handbook of clinical child psychology vol. 3, Social emotional and personality development* (5th ed., pp. 619–700). New York: Wiley.

Rubin, K. N., Fein, G. G., & Vandenberg, B. (1983). Play. In P. H. Mussen (Ed.), *Handbook of childhood psychology* (4th ed., Vol. 4). New York: Wiley.

Rubin, R. (1970). Cognitive style in pregnancy. *American Journal of Nursing, 70,* 502.

Rukeyser, L., Cooney, J., & Winslow, W. (1988). *Louis Rukeyser's business almanac.* New York: Simon & Schuster.

Ruse, M. (1991). Epistemology. In M. Maxwell (Ed.), *The sociobiology imagination.* Albany: State University of New York Press.

Rushdie, S. (1982, December). The new empire within Britain. *New Society,* 9.

Rushton, J. P. (1980). *Altruism, socialization, and society.* Englewood Cliffs, NJ: Prentice Hall.

Russell, A., & Saebel, J. (1997). Mother-son, mother-daughter, father-son, and father-daughter: Are they distinct relationships? *Developmental Review, 17,* 111–147.

Russell, A., Mize, J., & Bissaker, K. (2002). Parent-child relationships. In P. K. Smith & C. H. Hart (eds.), *Blackwell handbook of childhood social development* (203–222). Malden, MA: Blackwell.

Russell, C. (2002). An explanation of self-harm. Unpublished manuscript.

Russell, J. J. (2000). Topical therapy for acne. *American Family Physician, 61,* 357–366.

Russo, N. (1979). Overview: Sex roles, fertility, and the motherhood mandate. *Psychology of Women Quarterly, 4,* 7–15.

Rutter, M. (1981). *Maternal deprivation reassessed.* Harmondsworth, UK: Penguin Books.

Rutter, M. (1983). School effects on pupil progress: Research findings and policy implications. *Child Development, 54,* 1–29.

Rutter, M. (1985). Resilience in the face of adversity: Protective factors and resilience to psychiatric disorder. *British Journal of Psychiatry, 147,* 598–611.

Rutter, M., Graham, P., Chadwick, F., & Yule, W. (1976). Adolescent turmoil: Fact or fiction? *Journal of Child Psychology and Psychiatry, 17,* 35–56.

Rutter, M., Maughan, B., Mortimore, J., & Ouston, J., with A. Smith (1979). *Fifteen thousand hours: Secondary schools and their effects on children.* Cambridge, MA: Harvard University Press.

Rutter, M., & Rutter, M. (1993). *Developing minds: Challenge and continuity across the life span.* New York: Basic Books.

Ryan, W. (1971). *Blaming the victim.* New York: Vintage Books.

Ryff, C. D., & Singer, B. H. (2001). *Emotion, social relationships, and health.* New York: Oxford University Press.

Ryff, C. D., Singer, B. H., & Seltzer, M. M. (2002). Pathways through challenge: Implications for well-being and health. In L. Pulkkinen & A. Caspi (Eds.), *Paths to successful development* (pp. 302–328). Cambridge, UK: Cambridge University Press.

Ryff, C. D., Singer, B. H., Wing, E., & Love, G. D. (2001). Elective affinities and uninvited agonies: Mapping emotion with significant other onto health. In C. D. Ryff & B. H. Singer (Eds.), *Emotion, social, relationships, and health* (pp. 133–175). New York: Oxford University Press.

Sachs, B., Pietrukowicz, M., & Hall, L. A. (1997). Parenting attitudes and behaviors of low-income single mothers with young children. *Journal of Pediatric Nursing, 12,* 67–73.

Safe Schools (2002). *School violence prevention.* Retrieved August 21, 2004, from http://www.mentalhealth.org/schoolviolence

Sagi, A., Lamb, M. E., Lewkowicz, K. S., Shoham, R., Dvir, R., & Estes, D. (1985). Security of infant-mother, -father, and -metapelet attachments among Kibbutz-reared Israeli children. In I. Bretherton & E. Waters (Eds.), *Growing points of attachment theory and research* (pp. 257–275). Monographs of the Society for Research in Child Development, 50(1–2, Serial No. 209).

Sakamoto, I., & Pitner, R. (in press). Use of critical consciousness in anti-oppressive social work practice: Disentangling power dynamics at personal and structural levels. *British Journal of Social Work.*

Saleebey, D. (1985). In clinical social work practice, is the body politic? *Social Service Review, 59,* 578–592.

Saleebey, D. (1992a). Biology's challenge to social work: Embodying the person-in-environment perspective. *Social Work, 37,* 112–119.

Saleebey, D. (1992b). *The strengths perspective in social work practice.* New York: Longman.

Saleebey, D. (2001). *Human Behavior and Social Environments: A biopsychosocial approach.* New York: Columbia University Press.

Salthouse, T. (2000). Aging and measures of processing speed. *Biological Psychology, 54,* 35–54.

Salthouse, T. A., & Coon, V. E. (1993). Influence of task-specific processing speed on age differences in memory. *Journal of Gerontology, 48,* 244–255.

Sameroff, A. (1993). Models of development and developmental risk. In C. Zeanah (Ed.), *Handbook of infant mental health* (pp. 3–13). New York: Guilford Press.

Sampson, R. J., & Laub, J. H. (1990). Crime and deviance over the life course: The salience of adult social bonds. *American Sociological Review, 55,* 609–627.

Sampson, R. J., & Laub, J. H. (1997). A life course theory of cumulative disadvantage and the stability of delinquency. In T. P. Thornberry (Ed.), *Developmental theories of crime and delinquency* (pp. 133–161). New Brunswick, NJ: Transaction.

Sanchez, S. (1994). Equality of sexes? Give it 1000 years. *USA Today.*

Sanders, S., & McFarland, P. (2002). Perceptions of caregiving roles by sons caring for a parent with Alzheimer's disease. *The Journal of Gerontological Social Work, 37*(2), 61–67.

Sandmaier, M. (1995, July/August). The gift of friendship. *The Family Therapy Networker, 23–34,* 66–68.

Sandstrom, K. L. (1990). Confronting deadly disease: The drama of identity construction among gay men with AIDS. *Journal of Contemporary Ethnography, 19,* 271–294.

Sandstrom, K. L. (1996). Renegotiating sex and intimacy: The sexual self-images, outlooks, and relationships of gay men with HIV/AIDS. *Symbolic Interaction, 19,* 241–262.

Sandstrom, K. L., Martin, D. D., & Fine, G. A. (2003). *Symbols, selves and social reality: A symbolic interactionist approach to social psychology and sociology.* Los Angeles: Roxbury.

Santelli, J. S., Lowry, R., Brener, N. D., & Robin, L. (2000). The association of sexual behaviors with socioeconomic status, family structure, and race/ethnicity among US adolescents. *American Journal of Public Health, 90,* 1582–1588.

Santor, D. A., & Kusumakar, V. (2001). Open trial of interpersonal therapy in adolescents with moderate to severe major depression: Effectiveness of novice IPT therapists. *Journal of the American Academy of Child and Adolescent Psychiatry, 40,* 236–240.

Santrock, J. W. (1986). *Life-span development.* Dubuque, IA: Wm. C. Brown.

Santrock, J. W. (1989). *Life-span development* (3rd ed.). Dubuque, IA: Wm. C. Brown.

Santrock, J. W. (1990). *Adolescence* (4th ed.). Dubuque, IA: Wm. C. Brown.

Santrock, J. W. (1992). *Life-span development* (4th ed.). Dubuque, IA: Wm. C. Brown.

Santrock, J. W. (1995). *Life-span development* (5th ed.). Madison, WI, & Dubuque, IA: Brown & Benchmark.

Santrock, J. W. (2002). *Adolescence* (8th ed.). Boston, MA: McGraw-Hill.

Santrock, J. W. (2003). *Life-span development* (8th ed.). New York: McGraw-Hill.

Santrock, J. W., & Warshak, R. A. (1986). Development, relationships and legal considerations in father custody families. In M. E. Lamb (Ed.), *The father's role: Applied perspectives.* New York: Wiley.

Sarton, M. (1984). *Letters from Maine: New poems.* New York: Norton.

Sattar, S., Petty, F., & Burke, W. (2003). Diagnosis and treatment of alcohol dependence in older alcoholics. *Clinics in Geriatric Medicine, 19,* 749–761.

Sauerman, T. H. (1984). *Read this before coming out to your parents.* Washington, DC: Federation of Parents and Friends of Lesbians and Gays.

Saussure, de, F. (1966). *Course in general linguistics* (W. Baskin, Trans.). New York: McGraw-Hill.

Scanlon, B. (2003). *Recognizing depression in later years.* Retrieved June 24, 2004, from http://healthyplace.healthology.com

Scarf, M. (1992, July/August). The middle of the journey. *Family Therapy Networker,* 51–55.

Scarr, S., & McCartney, K. (1983). How people make their own environments: A theory of genotype-environment effects. *Child Development, 54,* 424–435.

Schachter, F. F. (1981). Toddlers with employed mothers. *Child Development, 52,* 958–964.

Schaefer, E. S., & Burnett, C. K. (1987). Stability and predictability of quality of women's marital relationships and demoralization. *Journal of Personality and Social Psychology, 53,* 1129–1136.

Schaffer, H. R. (1996). *Social Development.* Oxford: Blackwell Publishing.

Schaie, K. W. (1977). Toward a stage theory of adult cognitive development. *Aging and Human Development, 8,* 129–138.

Schaie, K. W. (Ed.) (1983a). *Longitudinal studies of adult psychological development.* New York: Guilford Press.

Schaie, K. W. (1983b). The Seattle longitudinal study: A twenty-one-year exploration of psychometric intelligence in adulthood. In K. W. Schaie (Ed.), *Longitudinal studies of adult psychological development* (pp. 64–135). New York: Guilford Press.

Schaie, K. W. (1987). Intelligence. In G. L. Maddox (Ed.), *The encyclopedia of aging* (pp. 357–358). New York: Springer.

Schaie, K. W. (1994). The course of adult intellectual development. *American Psychologist, 49,* 304–313.

Schaie, K. W. (1996). *Intellectual development in adulthood: The Seattle longitudinal study*. New York: Cambridge University Press.

Schaie, K. W., & Hofer, S. (2001). Longitudinal studies in aging research. In J. Birren & K. Schaie (Eds.), *Handbook of the psychology of aging* (5th ed., pp. 53–77). New York: Academic Press.

Schaie, K. W., & Strother, C. R. (1968). A cross-sequential study of age changes in cognitive behavior. *Psychological Bulletin, 70*, 671–680.

Schaie, K. W., & Willis, S. L. (1986). *Adult development and aging* (2nd ed.). Boston: Little, Brown.

Schaie, K. W., & Willis, S. (2000). A stage theory model of adult cognitive development revisited. In R. Rubinstein, M. Moss, & M. Kleban (Eds.), *The many dimensions of aging: Essays in honor of M. Powell Lawton* (pp. 175–193). New York: Springer.

Schaie, K. W., & Willis, S. (2002). *Adult development and aging* (5th ed.). Upper Saddle River, NJ: Prentice Hall.

Scheiber, B. (1981). *One step at a time*. Washington, DC: U.S. Government Printing Office.

Schein, E. H. (1980). *Organizational psychology*. Englewood Cliffs, NJ: Prentice Hall.

Schilling, R., Gilchrist, L., & Schinke, S. (1984). Coping and social support in families of developmentally disabled children. *Family Relations, 33*, 47–54.

Schinke, S. P., & Gilchrist, L. D. (1983). Coping with contraception: Cognitive and behavioral methods with adolescents. *Cognitive Therapy & Research, 7*, 379–388.

Schinke, S. P., Schilling, R. F., Gilchrist, L. D., Barth, R., Bobo, J. K., Trimble, J. E., et al. (1985). Preventing substance abuse among American Indian youth. *Social Casework, 66*, 213–317.

Schmidt, G., & Weiner, B. (1988). Measuring loneliness in different relationships. *Journal of Personality and Social Psychology, 44*, 1038–1047.

Schneider, B. H. (2000). *Friends and enemies: Peer relations in childhood*. New York: Arnold Publishers.

Schneider, L., Porsteinsson, A., Peskin, E., & Pfeiffer, E. (2003). Choosing treatment for Alzheimer's patients and the caregivers. *Geriatrics: Medicine for Midlife and Beyond, 58*(Supplement 1).

Schneider, R., Kropf, N., & Kisor, A. (2000). *Gerontological social work: Knowledge, service settings, and special populations* (2nd ed.). Belmont, CA: Brooks/Cole.

Schoem, D., Frankel, L., Zuniga, X., & Lewis, E. A. (Eds.) (1993). *Multicultural teaching in the university*. Westport, CT: Praeger.

Schoen, J., & Fischell, A. (1991). Pain in neonatal circumcision. *Clinical Pediatrics, 30*, 429–432.

Schouten, F. (2002). Middle school getting edged to the back. *USA Today*, p. 12D.

Schriver, J. M. (1995). *Human behavior and the social environment: Shifting paradigms in essential knowledge for social work practice*. Boston: Allyn & Bacon.

Schriver, J. M. (2004). *Human behavior and the social environment: Shifting paradigms in essential knowledge for social work practice*. Boston: Pearson.

Schulenberg, J., Wadsworth, K. N., O'Malley, P. M., Bachman, J. G., & Johnston, L. D. (1996). Adolescent risk factors for binge drinking during the transition to young adulthood: Variable- and pattern-centered approaches to change. *Developmental Psychology, 32*, no. 4, 659–674.

Schultz, D. P., & Schultz, S. E. (1999). *A history of modern psychology*. Fort Worth, TX: Harcourt.

Schulz, R., & Martire, L. (2004). Family caregiving of persons with dementia: Prevalence, health effects, and support strategies. *American Journal of Geriatric Psychiatry, 12*(3), 240–248.

Schulz, R., Visintainer, P., & Williamson, G. M. (1990). Psychiatric and physical morbidity effects of caregiving. *Journal of Gerontology, 45*, 181–191.

Schuster, C. S., & Ashburn, S. S. (1986). *The process of human development: A holistic life-span approach* (2nd ed.). Boston: Little, Brown.

Schuster, C. S., & Ashburn, S. S. (1992). *The process of human development: A holistic life-span approach* (3rd ed.). Philadelphia: Lippincott.

Schwartz, S., & Johnson, J. H. (1985). *Psychopathology of childhood*. New York: Pergamon Press.

Schwartzberg, N., Berlinger, K., & Jacob, D. (1995). *Single in a married world: A life cycle framework for working with the unmarried adult*. New York: W. W. Norton.

Schwendinger, R. & Schwendinger, W. (2004). Some characteristics of adolescent subculture. Retrieved August 19, 2004, from http://web.tampabay.rr.com/hschwend/

Schwitalla, A. M. (1930). Proceedings of the National Conference of Social Work (pp. 544–551). Chicago: University of Chicago Press.

Scott, W. R. (2001). *Institutions and organizations*. Thousand Oaks, CA: Sage.

Sears, R. R., Maccoby, E. E., & Leven, H. (1957). *Patterns of childrearing*. New York: Harper & Row.

Sears, W., & Sears, M. (1995). *The discipline book: How to have a better-behaved child from birth to age ten*. New York: Little, Brown.

Seccombe, K. (1991). Assessing the costs and benefits of children: Gender comparisons among child-free husbands and wives. *Journal of Marriage and the Family, 53*, 191–202.

Segal, D., Coolidge, F., & Rosowsky, E. (2000). Personality disorders. In S. Whitebourne (Ed.), *Psychopathology in later adulthood* (pp. 89–115). New York: Wiley & Sons.

Segal, J., & Yahraes, H. (1978). *A child's journey: Forces that shape the lives of our young*. New York: McGraw-Hill.

Segal, J., & Yahraes, H. (1978, November). Bringing up mother. *Psychology Today*, 90–96.

Seidenfeld, M. K., & Rickert, V. I. (2001). Impact of anorexia, bulimia, and obesity on the gynecologic health of adolescents. *American Family Physician, 64*, 445–450.

Seidman, S. (2005). The sexualization of love. In T. L. Steele (Ed.), *Sex, self, and society: The social context of sexuality* (pp. 104–114). Belmont, CA: Thomson/Wadsworth.

Seidman, S. N., & Rieder, R. O. (1994). A review of sexual behavior in the United States. *American Journal of Psychiatry, 151*, 330–341.

Seifer, R., & Dickstein, S. (1993). Parental mental illness and infant development. In C. Zeanah (Ed.), *Handbook of infant mental health* (pp. 120–142). New York: Guilford Press.

Seitz, V., Rosenbaum, L. K., & Apfel, N. H. (1985). Effects of family support intervention: A 10-year follow-up. *Child Development*, 376–391.

Seligman, C. K. (1999). *Life-span development*. Pacific Grove, CA: Brooks/Cole.

Seligman, M. E. P. (1975). *Helplessness: On depression, development, and death*. San Francisco: W. H. Freeman.

Seligman, M. E. P. (1995, May). Is self-esteem really all that important? *APA Monitor*, 6.

Seligman, M. E. P. (2002). *Authentic happiness: Using the new positive psychology to realize your potential for lasting fulfillment*. New York: The Free Press.

Selman, R. L. (1980). *The growth of interpersonal understanding*. New York: Academic Press.

Selman, R. L. (1990). *Making a friend in youth: Developmental theory and pair therapy*. Chicago: University of Chicago Press.

Selman, R. L. (2003). *The promotion of social awareness: Powerful lessons from the partnership of developmental theory and classroom practice*. New York: Russell Sage Foundation.

Selman, R. L., Jaquette, D., & Lavin, D. (1977). Interpersonal awareness in children: Toward an integration of developmental and clinical child psychology. *American Journal of Orthopsychiatry, 47*, 264–274.

Seltzer, J. A., & Bianchi, S. M. (1988). Children's contact with absent parents. *Journal of Marriage and the Family, 50*, 663–677.

Sennett, R. (2003). *Respect: In a world of inequality*. New York: W. W. Norton.

Sepkoski, C. (1992). The effects of maternal epidural anesthesia on neonatal behavior during the first month. *Developmental Medicine and Child Neurology, 34*, 1072–1080.

Seppa, N. (1996, December). When one's parents become neighbors. *APA Monitor*, 34.

Seppa, N. (1997, July). Hard-of-hearing clients often hide their disability. *APA Monitor*, p. 28.

Severino, S. K., Teusink, J. P., Pender, V. B., & Bernstein, A. E. (1986). Overview: The psychology of grandparenthood. *Journal of Geriatric Psychiatry, 19*, 3–17.

Seymour, D. Z. (1974). Black children. Black speech. In F. Rebelsky & L. Dorman (Eds.), *Child development and behavior* (2nd ed.). New York: Knopf.

Shaffer, D. R. (1989). *Developmental psychology: Childhood and adolescence* (2nd ed.). Pacific Grove, CA: Brooks/Cole.

Shaffer, D. R. (1993). *Developmental psychology: Childhood and adolescence* (3rd ed.). Pacific Grove, CA: Brooks/Cole.

Shaffer, D. R. (2002). *Developmental Psychology: Childhood and Adolescence* (6th ed.). Belmont, CA: Wadsworth.

Shaffer, D. R., & Cavanaugh, J. C. (2001). *Developmental psychology with Infotrac: Children and adolescents*. Pacific Grove, CA: Wadsworth.

Shafritz, J. M., & Whitbeck, P. H. (1978). *Classics of organization theory*. Oak Park, IL: Moore.

Shakur, S. (1998). *Monster: Autobiography of an L.A. gang member*. New York: Penguin.

Shanahan, M. J., Elder Jr., G. H. (2002). History, agency, and the life course. In R. A. Dienstbier & L. J. Crockett (Eds.), *Agency, motivation, and the life course* (pp. 145–186). Lincoln: University of Nebraska Press.

Shanas, E., Townsend, P., Wedderburn, D., Friis, H., Milhoj, P., & Stehouwer, B. (1968). *Old people in three industrial societies*. New York: Atherton.

Shantz, C. U. (1983). Social cognition. In P. H. Mussen (Ed.), *Handbook of child psychology* (4th ed., Vol. 3). New York: Wiley.

Shapiro, I. (2002). Democratic justice and multicultural recognition. In P. Kelly (Ed.). *Multiculturalism reconsidered: Culture and equality and its critics* (pp. 174–183). Cambridge, UK: Polity Press.

Shatz, C. J. (1992). The developing brain. *Scientific American, 267*, 60–67.

Shatz, M., & Gelman, R. (1973). The development of communication skills: Modifications in the speech of young children as a function of the listener. *Monographs of the Society for Research in Child Development, 38*(5, Serial No. 52).

Shaw, M. E. (1981). *Group dynamics: The psychology of small group behavior*. New York: McGraw-Hill.

Shea, J. D. C. (1981). Changes in interpersonal distances and categories of play behavior in the early weeks of preschool. *Developmental Psychology, 17*, 417–425.

Sheehan, D., & Schirm, V. (2003). End-of-life care of older adults. *The American Journal of Nursing, 103*(11), 48–59.

Sheehan, G. J., & Martyn, M. (1970). Stuttering and its disappearance. *Journal of Speech and Hearing Research, 13*, 279–289.

Sheehy, G. (1976). *Passages*. New York: Dutton.

Sheehy, G. (1996). *New passages*. New York: Random House.

Sheikh, J. I. & Yesavage, J. A. (1986). Geriatric Depression Scale (GDS): Recent evidence and development of a shorter version. In T. L. Brink (Ed.), *Clinical gerontology: A guide to assessment and intervention* (pp. 165–173). New York: Haworth Press.

Shenk, D., Kuwahara, K., & Zablotsky, D. (2004). Older women's attachments to their home and possessions. *Journal of Aging Studies, 18*, 157–169.

Sherif, M. & Sherif, C. W. (1956). *Groups in harmony and tension*. New York: Harper.

Sherif, M., Harvey, O. J., White, B. J., Hood, W. R., & Sherif, C. W. (1961). *Intergroup conflict and cooperation: The robber's cave experiment*. Norman: Institute of Group Relations, University of Oklahoma.

Sherman, E. (1987). *The meaning of midlife transitions*. Albany: State University of New York.

Shils, E. (1985). Sociology. In A. Juper & J. Kuper (Eds.), *The social science encyclopedia*. London: Routledge and Kegan Paul.

Shipman, G. (1968). The psychodynamics of sex education. *Family Coordinator, 17*, 3–12.

Shoda, Y., Mischel, W., & Peake, P. K. (1990). Predicting adolescent cognitive and self-regulatory competencies from preschool delay of gratification. *Developmental Psychology, 26*, 978–986.

Shoemaker, D. J. (1989). Transfer of children and the importance of grandmothers among the Navajo Indians. *Journal of Cross-Cultural Gerontology, 4*, 1–18.

Shure, M., & Digeronimo, T. F. (1996). *Raising a thinking child: The "I can problem solve" program*. New York: Pocket Books.

Shure, M., & Spivack, G. (1980). Interpersonal problem solving as a mediator of behavioral adjustment in preschool and kindergarten children. *Journal of Applied Developmental Psychology, 1*, 37–52.

Sidel, R. (1990). *On her own: Growing up in the shadow of the American dream*. New York: Viking Penguin.

Siegler, R. S. (1995, January). New cognitive research making waves. *APA Monitor*.

Siegler, R. S. (1998). *Emerging minds: The process of change in children's thinking*. New York: Oxford University Press.

Sigelman, C. K., & Rider, E. A. (2002). *Life-span human development*. Belmont, CA: Wadsworth.

Sigelman, C. K., & Shaffer, D. R. (1991). *Life-span development* (1st ed.). Pacific Grove, CA: Brooks/Cole.

Sigelman, C. K., & Shaffer, D. R. (1995). *Life-span development* (2nd ed.). Pacific Grove, CA: Brooks/Cole.

Sigman, G. S., & Flanery, R. C. (1992). Eating disorders. In D. E. Greydanus & M. C. Wolraich (Eds.), *Behavioral pediatrics*. New York: Springer-Verlag.

Sigman, M. (1991). Continuity in cognitive abilities from infancy to 12 years of age. *Cognitive Development, 6*, 47–57.

Silverman, P. R. (1987a). Mutual aid groups. In *Encyclopedia of social work* (18th ed., pp. 1171–1176). Silver Spring, MD: National Association of Social Workers.

Silverman, P. R. (1987b). Widowhood as the next stage in the life course. In H. Lopata (Ed.), *Widows: Vol. II, North America* (171–190). Durham, NC: Duke University Press.

Silverstein, B., & Krate, R. (1975). *Children of the dark ghetto: A developmental psychology*. New York: Praeger.

Simmons, R. G., & Blyth, D. A. (1987). *Moving into adolescence*. Hawthorne, NY: Aldine.

Simmons, R. G., Rosenberg, F., & Rosenberg, M. (1973). Disturbance in self-image at adolescence. *American Sociological Review, 38*, 553–568.

Simons, M. (1995, September 11). Dutch doctors to tighten rules on mercy killings. *New York Times International*.

Simons, R. (1987). *After the tears*. San Diego, CA: Harcourt Brace Jovanovich.

Singer, D. G., & Singer, J. L. (1987). Practical suggestions for controlling television. *Journal of Early Adolescence, 7*, 365–369.

Singer, L., & Yamashita, T. (1997). A longitudinal study of developmental outcomes of infants with bronchopulmonary dysplasia and very low birth weight. *Pediatrics, 100*, 987–994.

Sizer, T. R. (1983). High school reform: The need for engineering. *Phi Delta Kappan*, 679–683.

Skeels, H. M. (1936). The mental development of children in foster homes. *Pedagogical Seminary and Journal of Genetic Psychology, 49*, 91–106.

Skinner, B. F. (1953). *Science and human behavior*. New York: Macmillan.

Skinner, L. (1979). *Motor development in the preschool years*. Springfield, IL: Charles C Thomas.

Skodak, M. (1939). Children in foster homes: A study of mental development. *University of Iowa Studies in Child Welfare, 16*(1).

Skodak, M., & Skeels, H. (1945). A follow-up study of children in adoptive homes. *Journal of Genetic Psychology, 66*, 21–58.

Skodak, M., & Skeels, H. (1949). A follow-up study of one hundred adopted children. *Journal of Genetic Psychology, 75*, 85–125.

Skolnick, A. (1986). *The psychology of human development*. New York: Harcourt Brace Jovanovich.

Slaby, R. G., & Crowley, C. G. (1977). Modification of cooperation and aggression through teacher attention to children's speech. *Journal of Experimental Child Psychology, 23*, 442–458.

Slaughter-Defoe, D. T. (1995). Revisiting the concept of socialization: Caregiving and teaching in the 90s—A personal perspective. *American Psychologist, 50*, 276–286.

Sleek, S. (1994, November). Therapists, both male and female, fall victim to stereotypes of men. *APA Monitor*, 6–7.

Sleek, S. (1995, December). Battling breast cancer through group therapy. *APA Monitor*, 24.

Sleek, S. (1996, October). Research identifies causes of internal homophobia. *APA Monitor*, 57.

Sleek, S. (1998a, June). After the storm, children play out fears. *APA Monitor*, 12.

Sleek, S. (1998b, August). The basis for aggression may start in the womb. *APA Monitor*, 37.

Sleek, S. (1998c, November). Better parenting may not be enough for some children. *APA Monitor*, 30.

Smart, B. (1993). *Postmodernity: Key ideas*. London: Routledge.

Smeeding, T., & Phillips, K. R. (2002). Cross-national differences in employment and economic sufficiency. *Annals of the American Academy of Political and Social Science, 580*, 103–133.

Smetana, J. G. (1988). Adolescents' and parents' conceptions of parental authority. *Child Development, 59*, 321–335.

Smetana, J. G. (2000). Middle-class African American adolescents' and parents' conceptions of parental authority and parenting practices: A longitudinal investigation. *Child Development, 71*, 1672–1686.

Smetana, J. G., Yau, J., Restrepo, A., & Braeges, J. L. (1991). Conflict and adaptation in adolescence: Adolescent-parent conflict. In M. E. Colten & S. Gore (Eds.), *Adolescent stress* (pp. 43–66). New York: Aldine de Gruyter.

Smilansky, S. (1968). *The effects of sociodramatic play on disadvantaged preschool children*. New York: Wiley.

Smith, C., Perou, R., & Lesesne, C. (2002). Parent education. In M. H. Bornstein (Ed.), *Handbook of parenting* (2nd ed., pp. 233–264). Mahwah, NJ: Erlbaum.

Smith, D. (2001, September). Harassment in the hallways. *APA Monitor*, 38–40.

Smith, M. B. (2002). Self and identity in historical/sociocultural context: Perspectives on selfhood revisited. In Y. Kashima, M. Foddy, & M. J. Platow (Eds.), *Self and identity: Personal, social and symbolic* (pp. 181–206). Mahwah, NJ: Erlbaum.

Smith, P., & Daglish, L. (1977). Sex differences in parent and infant behavior in the home. *Child Development, 48*, 1250–1254.

Smith, P. K., & Connolly, K. J. (1980). *The ecology of preschool behavior*. New York: Cambridge University Press.

Smith, P. K., & Hart, C. H. (2002). The peer group. In P. K. Smith &

C. H. Hart (eds.), *Blackwell handbook of childhood social development* (pp. 263–264). Malden, MA: Blackwell.

Smith, R. (1995, July). The adoption equation, minus race. *NASW News*, 3.

Smith, T. W., & Pope, M. K. (1990). Cynical hostility as a health risk: Current status and future directions. *Journal of Social Behavior and Personality, 5*, 77–88.

Smucker, W. D., & Hedayat, M. (2001). Evaluation and treatment of ADHD. *American Family Physician.* Retrieved May 28, 2004, from http://www.aafp.org/afp/20010901/817.html

Smyth, K., Feinstein, S., & Kacerek, S. (1997). The Alzheimer's Disease Support Center: Information and support for family caregivers through computer mediated communication. In P. Brennan, S. Schneider, & E. Tornquist (Eds.), *Information and networks for community health care.* New York: Springer-Verlag.

Snowden, D. (2001). *Aging with grace: What the nun study teaches us about leading longer, healthier, and more meaningful lives.* New York: Bantum.

Snyder, H., Espiritu, R., Huizinga, H., Loeber, R., Petechuk, D. (2003). Prevalence and development of child delinquency. U.S. Department of Justice Office of Juvenile Justice and Delinquency Prevention Child Delinquency Bulletin Series.

Society for Adolescent Medicine (2004). A position paper of the Society for Adolescent Medicine: Confidential Health Care for Adolescents. Retrieved July 28, 2004, from http://www.adolescenthealth.org/

Solomon, R. C. (1988). *About love: Reinventing romance for modern times.* New York: Simon & Schuster.

Solomon, R. C. (2003). *Not passion's slave: Emotions and choice.* New York: Oxford University Press.

Sommers, C. H. (2000). *The war against boys.* New York: Simon and Schuster.

Son, S., & Kirchner, J. (2000). Depression in Children and Adolescents. *American Family Physician, 62*(10), 2297–2308.

Sonenstein, F., Pleck, J., & Ku, L. (1989). Sexual activity, condom use and AIDS awareness in a national sample of adolescent males. *Family Planning Perspectives, 21*, 152–158.

Southern Poverty Law Center (1994). The intelligence report, August. Atlanta, GA: Southern Poverty Law Center.

Sparrowe, L. (1997). The heart of parenting. *Yoga Journal*, 178–179. Retrieved April 25, 2005: http://natural-connection.com/resource/yoga_journal/the_heart_of_parenting.html

Specht, R., & Craig, G. (1987). *Human development: A social work perspective.* Englewood Cliffs, NJ: Prentice Hall.

Spelke, E. (1985). Perception of unity, persistence, and identity: Thoughts on infants' conception of objects. In J. Mehler & R. Fox (Eds.), *Neonate cognition.* Hillsdale, NJ: Erlbaum.

Spelke, E. (1994). Initial knowledge: Six suggestions. *Cognition, 50*, 431–445.

Spencer, L. J. (1989). *Winning through participation.* Dubuque, IA: Institute of Cultural Affairs.

Spencer, M. B., & Dornbusch, S. M. (1990). Challenges in studying minority youth. In S. Feldman & G. R. Elliott (Eds.), *At the threshold: The developing adolescent.* Cambridge, MA: Harvard University Press.

Spencer, M. B., Dupree, D., Swanson, D. P., & Cunningham, M. (1998). The influence of physical maturation and hassles on African American adolescents' learning behaviors. *Journal of Comparative Family Studies, 27*, 189–200.

Spencer, P. E. (1993). Communication behaviors of infants with hearing loss and their hearing mothers. *Journal of Speech and Hearing Research, 36*, 311–322.

Spiegel, D. (1993). Psychosocial intervention in cancer. *Journal of the National Cancer Institute, 85*, 1198–1202.

Spitz, R. (1945). Hospitalism: An inquiry into the genesis of psychiatric conditions in early childhood. *Psychoanalytic Study of the Child, 1*, 53–74.

Spitz, R. A. (1966). *No and yes: On the genesis of human communication.* New York: International Universities Press.

Spitze, G., & Gallant, M. (2004). "The bitter with the sweet": Older adults' strategies for handling ambivalence in relations with their adult children. *Research on Aging, 26*(4), 387–412.

Sprich-Buckminster, S. (1993). Are perinatal complications relevant to the manifestation of ADD? *Journal of the American Academy of Child and Adolescent Psychiatry, 32*, 1032–1037.

Spurlock, J. (1984). Black women in the middle years. In G. Baruch & J. Brooks-Gunn (Eds.), *Women in midlife* (pp. 67–82). New York: Plenum.

St. Clair, M. (2004). *Object relations and self psychology: An introduction.* Belmont, CA: Thomson/Brooks Cole.

St. James, J. (1987). *Inside baby's head.* Burton, OH: Palamora.

Stacey, N., Deardon, R., Pill, R., & Robinson, D. (1970). *Hospitals, children, and their families: The report of a pilot study.* London: Routledge & Kegan Paul.

Stainton, C., McNeil, D., & Harvey, S. (1992). Maternal tasks of uncertain motherhood. *Maternal-Child Nursing Journal, 20*, 113–123.

Stake, J. E., DeVille, C. J., & Rennell, C. L. (1983). The effects of assertiveness training on the performance self-esteem of adolescent girls. *Journal of Youth and Adolescence, 12*, 435–442.

Staples, R. (1988). The Black American family. In C. H. Mindel, R. W. Habenstein, & R. Wright (Eds.), *Ethnic families in America: Patterns and variations* (3rd ed., pp. 303–324.) New York: Elsevier.

Starbuck, G. H. (2002). *Families in context.* Belmont, CA: Wadsworth/Thomson Learning.

Stark, E. (1989, October). Teen boys get condom sense. *Psychology Today*, 63.

Starr, B. D., & Weiner, M. B. (1982). *The Starr-Weiner report on sex and sexuality in the mature years.* New York: McGraw-Hill.

Staub, E. (1984). Steps toward a comprehensive theory of moral conduct: Goal orientation, social behavior, kindness, and cruelty. In W. M. Kurtines & J. L. Gewirtz (Eds.), *Morality, moral behavior, and moral development.* New York: Wiley.

Staub, E. (2004). Basic human needs, altruism and aggression. In A. G. Miller (Ed.), *The social psychology of good and evil* (pp. 51–84). New York: Guilford Press.

Staudinger, U. M. (1999). Older and wiser? Integrating results on the relationship between age and wisdom-related performance. *International Journal of Behavioral Development, 23*, 641–664.

Staudinger, U. M. & Bluck, S. (2001). A view on midlife development from life span theory. In M. E. Lachman (Ed.), *Handbook of midlife development.* New York: Wiley & Sons.

Steele, T. L. (2005). *Sex, self, and society: The social context of sexuality.* Belmont, CA: Thomson Wadsworth.

Steil, J. M., & Turetsky, B. A. (1987). Is equal better? The relationship between marital equality and psychological symptomatology. In S. Oskamp (Ed.), *Family process and problems: Social psychological aspects.* Newbury Park, CA: Sage.

Stein, N. (1995, June). New cognitive research making waves. *APA Monitor*.

Steinberg, L. (1990). Autonomy, conflict, and harmony in the family relationship. In S. Feldman & G. Elliot (Eds.), *At the threshold: The developing adolescent* (pp. 255–276). Cambridge, MA: Harvard University Press.

Steinberg, L. (1995). *How your child's adolescence triggers your own crisis.* New York: Simon & Schuster.

Steinberg, L. (2001). We know some things: Parent-adolescent relationships in retrospect and prospect. *Journal of Research on Adolescence, 11*, 1–19.

Steinberg, L. (2004). *The ten basic principles of good parenting.* New York: Simon & Schuster.

Steinberg, L., & Silverberg, S. (1986). The vicissitudes of autonomy in early adolescence. *Child Development, 57*, 841–851.

Steiner, R. F., & Pomerantz, S. (1981). *The chemistry of living systems.* New York: Van Nostrand Reinhold.

Stenback, A. (1980). Depression and suicidal behavior in old age. In J. E. Birren & R. B. Sloane (Eds.), *Handbook of mental health and aging.* Englewood Cliffs, NJ: Prentice Hall.

Stepfamily Association of America (2003, May 28). Stepfamily facts. Retrieved November 13, 2004, from http://www.saafamilies.org/faqs/index.htm

Stephens, M. A. P., Kinney, J. M., & Ogrocki, P. K. (1991). Stressors and well-being among caregivers to older adults with dementia: The in-home versus nursing home experience. *The Gerontologist, 31*, 217–223.

Stern, C., Stern, W., & Lamiell, J. T. (1999). *Recollection, testimony, and lying in early childhood.* Washington, DC: American Psychological Association.

Stern, D. (1985). *The interpersonal world of the infant: A view from psychoanalysis and developmental psychology.* New York: Basic Books.

Stern, D. (1990). *Diary of a baby.* New York: Basic Books.

Sternberg, R. J. (1986). A triangular theory of love. *Psychological Review, 93*, 119–135.

Sternberg, R. J. (1988). Triangulating love. In R. J. Sternberg & M. L. Barnes (Eds.), *The psychology of love.* New Haven, CT: Yale University Press.

Sternberg, R. J. (1997). Construct validation of a triangular love scale. *European Journal of Social Psychology, 27*, 313–335.

Sternberg, R. J. (1998). *Cupid's arrow*. New York: Cambridge University Press.

Sternberg, R. J. (2001). Why schools should teach for wisdom: The balance theory of wisdom in educational settings. *Educational Psychologist, 36*, 227–245.

Sternberg, R. J., & Lubart, T. (2001). Wisdom and creativity. In J. Birren & K. Schaie (Eds.), *Handbook of the psychology of aging* (5th ed., pp. 500–522). New York: Academic Press.

Steur, F. B., Applefield, J. M., & Smith, R. (1971). Televised aggression and interpersonal aggression of preschool children. *Journal of Experimental Child Psychology, 11*, 442–447.

Stevens, L. E., & Fiske, S. T. (1995). Motivation and cognition in social life: A social survival perspective. *Social Cognition, 13*, 189–214.

Stevenson, H. (1995, May). Is self-esteem really all that important? *APA Monitor, 9*.

Stevenson, J. C. (1995). *British Journal of Clinical Practice, 49*, 87–90.

Stevenson, L. (1974). *Seven theories of human nature*. New York: Oxford University Press.

Stevenson, L. (1981) *The study of human nature: Readings*. New York: Oxford University Press.

Stewart, R. B. (1983). Sibling Interaction: The role of older child as teacher for the younger. *Merrill-Palmer Quarterly, 29*, 47–68.

Stewart, R. B, Mobley, L. A., Van Tuyl, S. S., & Salvador, M. A. (1987). The firstborn's adjustment to the birth of a sibling: A longitudinal assessment. *Child Development, 58*, 341–355.

Stipp, D. (1995, May 24). Our prehistoric past casts ills in new light, some scientists say. *The Wall Street Journal*, pp. 1, 5.

Stoller, E., & Gibson, R. (2000). *Worlds of difference: Inequality in the aging experience* (3rd ed.). Thousand Oaks, CA: Pine Forest Press.

Stoner, J. A. F. (1961). *A comparison of individual and group decisions involving risk*. Unpublished master's thesis, Massachusetts Institute of Technology, Cambridge.

Stott, D. (1971). The child's hazards in utero. In J. G. Howells (Ed.), *Modern perspectives in international child psychiatry* (pp. 19–60). New York: Brunner/Mazel.

Strahan, D. B. (1983). The emergence of formal operations in adolescence. *Transcendence, 11*, 7–14.

Strauss, M., Gelles, R., & Steinmetz, S. (1980). *Behind closed doors*. New York: Doubleday.

Strauss, M. A., & Gelles, R. J. (1986). Societal change and change in family violence from 1975 to 1985 as revealed in two national surveys. *Journal of Marriage and the Family, 48*, 465–479.

Street, E., & Soldan, J. (1998). A conceptual framework for the psychosocial issues faced by families with genetic condition. *Families, Systems, and Health, 16*, 217–232.

Streissguth, A., LaDue, R., & Randels, S. (1988). *A manual on adolescents and adults with fetal alcohol syndrome with special reference to American Indians*. Rockville, MD: U.S. Department of Health and Human Services.

Stringer, G. M., & Rants-Rodriguez, D. (1987). *So what's it to me?* Renton, WA: King County Rape Relief.

Stroebe, M., & Schut, H. (1999). The dual process model of coping with bereavement: Rationale and description. *Death Studies, 23*, 197–224.

Strong, B., & Devault, C. (2004). *Human sexuality: Diversity in contemporary America*. New York: McGraw-Hill.

Stroufe, L. A., Fox, N. E., and Pancake, V. R. (1983). Attachment and dependency in developmental perspective. *Child Development, 54*, 1615–1627.

Stuart, R. B. (1980). *Helping couples change*. New York: Guilford Press.

Stueve, A., & O'Donnell, L. (1984). The daughter of aging parents. In G. Baruch & J. Brooks-Gunn (Eds.), *Women in midlife*. New York: Plenum.

Substance Abuse and Mental Health Services Administration (2001). *The NHSDA report: Substance use among older adults*. Retrieved June 15, 2004, from http://oas.samhsa.gov/2K1/olderadults/olderadults.cfm

Sumner, W. G. (1906/1960). *Folkways*. New York: New American Library.

Sunderland, T., Lawlor, B. A., Molchan, S. E., & Martinez, R. A. (1988). Depressive symptoms in the elderly: Special concerns. *Psychopharmacology Bulletin, 24*, 567–576.

Suomi, S., & Harlow, H. (1972). Social rehabilitation of isolate-reared monkeys. *Developmental Psychology, 6*, 487–496.

Super, D. E., Kowalski, R., & Gotkin, E. (1967). *Floundering and trial after high school*. Unpublished manuscript, Columbia University, New York.

Suyemoto, K. L., & Kountz, X. (2000). Self-mutilation. *The Prevention Researcher, 7*, 1–4.

Swanson, J. M. (1995). *SNAP-IV Scale*. Child Development Center, UC Irvine.

Swanson, J. M. (2004). *The SWAN Rating scale*. Retrieved May 28, 2004, from www.adhd.net

Swanson, J. M., McBurnett, K., Wigal, T., Pfieffer, E. J., Lerner, M. D., Williams, L., et al. (1993). Effect of stimulant medication on children with attention deficit disorder: A "review of reviews." *Exceptional Children, 60*, 154–162.

Swearer, S. M., & Doll, B. (2001). Bullying in schools: An ecological framework. *Journal of Emotional Abuse, 2*(2/3), 7–23.

Swearer, S. M., Song, S. Y., Cary, P. T., Eagle, J. W., & Mickelson, W. T. (2001). Psychosocial correlates in bullying and victimization: The relationship between depression, anxiety, and bully/victim status. *Journal of Emotional Abuse, 2*(2/3), 95–121.

Symanski, M. (1992). Maternal-infant bonding: Practice issues for the 1990s. *Journal of Nurse-Midwifery, 37*, 67–73.

Takahashi, K. (1986). Examining the strange-situation procedure with Japanese mothers and 12-month-old infants. *Developmental Psychology, 22*(2), 265–270.

Takaki, R. (1993). *A different mirror: A history of multicultural America*. Boston: Little, Brown.

Takamura, J., & Williams, B. (2002). *Informal caregiving: Compassion in action*. Arlington, TX: Arc of the United States.

Takanishi, R. (2004). Leveling the playing field: Supporting immigrant children from birth to eight. *Children of Immigrant Families, 14*, 61–74.

Tannen, D. (1991). *You just don't understand: Women and men in conversation*. New York: Morrow.

Tannen, D. (2001). *I only say this because I love you . . . How the way we talk can make or break family relationships throughout our lives*. New York: Random House.

Task Force on Homelessness and Severe Mental Illness. (1992). *Outcasts on main street* (DHHS Publication No. ADM 92–1904). Rockville, MD: Department of Health and Human Services.

Tavris, C. (1992). *The mismeasure of women*. New York: Simon and Schuster.

Tavris, C., & Wade, C. (1984). *The longest war: Sex differences in perspective*. New York: Harcourt Brace Jovanovich.

Taylor, F. W. (1947). *Scientific management*. New York: Harper & Row.

Taylor, I. (1976). *Introduction to Psycholinguistics*. New York: Holt, Rinehart & Winston.

Teasdale, J. B., & Barnard, P. J. (1993). *Affect, cognition, and change: Re-modeling depressive thought*. East Sussex, England: Erlbaum.

Tedder, J. (1991). Using the Brazelton neonatal assessment scale to facilitate the parent-infant relationship in a primary care setting. *Nurse Practitioner, 16*, 26–36.

Tellegen, A., Lykken, D. T., Bouchard, T. J., Wilcox, K. J., & Rich, S. (1988). Personality similarity in twins reared apart and together. *Journal of Personality and Social Psychology, 54*, 1031–1039.

Terkel, S. (1974). *Working: People talk about what they do all day and how they feel about what they do*. New York: Pantheon Books.

Termine, N. (1988). Infants' responses to their mothers' expressions of joy and sadness. *Developmental Psychology, 24*, 223–229.

The Patient Self-Determination Act of 1990, 4206, 4751 of the *Omnibus Reconciliation Act of 1990*, PL No. 101–508 (November 5, 1990).

The Urban Institute (2000). *A new look at homelessness in America*. Washington, DC: The Urban Institute.

Thiedke, C. C. (2003). Nocturnal enuresis. *American Family Physician, 67*, 1499–1506.

Thoma, S. J. (1986). Estimating gender differences in the comprehension and preference of moral issues. *Developmental Review, 6*, 165–180.

Thoman, E. B. (2001). Sleep-wake states as a context of assessment, as components of assessment and as assessment. In. L. T. Singer & P. S. Zeskind (Eds.), *Biobehavioral assessments of infants* (pp. 423–442). NY: The Guildford Press.

Thomas, A., & Chess, S. (1977). *Temperament and development*. New York: Brunner/Mazel.

Thomas, A., & Chess, S. (1989). Temperament and personality. In G. A. Konnstamm, J. E. Bates, & M. K. Rothbart (Eds.), *Temperament in childhood* (pp. 249–261). New York: Wiley.

Thomas, R. B. (1987). Family adaptation to a child with a chronic illness. In M. H. Rose & R. B. Thomas (Eds.), *Children with chronic conditions: Nursing in a family and community context* (pp. 29–54). Orlando, FL: Grune & Stratton.

Thompson, R. F. (2000). *The brain* (3rd ed.). New York: Worth.

Thornburg, H. D. (1981). Sources of sex education among early adolescents. *Journal of Early Adolescence, 1*, 171–184.

Thorpe, J. A., & Breedlove, G. (1996). Epidural analgesia in labor: An evaluation of risks and benefits. *Birth, 23*, 63–83.

Timasheff, N. S. (1967). *Sociological theory*. New York: Random House.

Timberlake, E. M., Sabatino, C. A., & Hooper, S. N. (1982). School social work practice and P.L. 94-142. In R. T. Constable & J. P. Flynn (Eds.), *School social work: Practice and research perspectives*. Pacific Grove, CA: Brooks/Cole.

Tinsley, B., & Parke, R. (1987). Grandparents as interactive and social support agents for families with young infants. *International Journal of Aging and Human Development, 25*, 259–277.

Tizard, B., & Rees, J. (1974). A comparison of the effects of adoption, restoration to the natural mother, and continued institutionalization on the cognitive development of four-year-old children. *Journal of Child Psychology and Psychiatry and Allied Disciplines, 16*, 61–73.

Tolman, R. M., & Bennett, L. (1992). Group work with men who batter. In C. W. LeCroy (Ed.), *Case studies in social work practice*. Belmont, CA: Wadsworth.

Tomblin, J. B., Spencer, L., Flock, S., Tyler, R., & Gantz, B. (1999). A comparison of language development in children with cochlear implants and children using hearing aids. *Journal of sign language and hearing research, 42*, 497–511.

Tornstam, L. (2000). Transcendence in later life. *Generations, 33*(4), 10–14.

Torrey, E. F. (1988). *Nowhere to go: The tragic odyssey of the homeless mentally ill*. New York: Harper & Row.

Torrey, E. F. (2001). *Surviving schizophrenia: A manual for families, consumers, and providers* (4th ed.). New York: Perennial Currents.

Toseland, R., & Hacker, L. (1982). Self-help groups and professional involvement. *Social Work, 27*, 341–347.

Toseland, R. W., & Rivas, R. F. (1995). *An introduction to group work practice* (2nd ed.). Needham Heights, MA: Allyn & Bacon.

Toseland, R. W., & Rossiter, C. (1989). Group interventions to support caregivers: A review and analysis. *The Gerontologist, 29*, 438–448.

Towle, C. (1945). *Common human needs: An interpretation for staff in public assistance agencies*. Washington, DC: U.S. Government Printing Office.

Towle, C. (1960). A social work approach to courses in growth and behavior. *Social Service Review, 34*, 402–414.

Townsend, A., Miller, B., & Guo, S. (2001). Depressive symptomatology in middle-aged and older married couples: A dyadic analysis. *Journal of Gerontology, 58B*(6), S352–S364.

Troiano, R. P., & Flegal, K. M. (1999). Overweight prevalence among youth in the United States: Why so many different numbers? *International Journal of Obesity and Related Disorders, 23*, 131–136.

Troll, L. E. (1986). *Family issues in current gerontology*. New York: Springer.

Troll, L. E., & Bengtson, V. L. (1982). Intergenerational relations throughout the life span. In B. Wolman (Ed.), *Handbook of developmental psychology* (pp. 890–911). Englewood Cliffs, NJ: Prentice Hall.

Trotter, R. (1987, May). You've come a long way, baby. *Psychology Today*, 34–47.

Trout, M. (1995, October). Infant attachment: Assessment, intervention and developmental impact. Workshop presented by M. Trout, Director of the Infant Parent Institute, Tucson, AZ.

Tsuang, M. T., Bar, J. L., Harley, R. M., & Lyons, M. J. (2001). The Harvard Twin Study of Substance Abuse: What we have learned. *Harvard Review of Psychiatry, 9*, 267–279.

Tucker, R. M. (1980). Is hypertension different in the elderly? *Geriatrics, 35*, 28–32.

Tulman, L., & Fawcett, J. (2003). *Women's health during and after pregnancy: A theory-based study of adaptation to change*. New York: Springer.

Turiel, E. (2000). The development of morality. In W. Damon & N. Eisenberg (2000). *Social, emotional, and personality development, Vol. 3, Handbook of child psychology* (5th ed., pp. 863–932). New York: John Wiley and Sons.

Turner, J. (1972). *Patterns of social organization: A survey of social institutions*. New York: McGraw-Hill.

Turner, J. (1991). *The structure of sociological theory*. Belmont, CA: Wadsworth.

Turner, J. C. (1987). *Rediscovering the social group: A self-categorization theory*. New York: Blackwell.

Turner, L. D., Mille, K. W., & Montgomery, M. B. (2002). *The Gullah people and their African heritage*. Charleston: University of South Carolina Press.

Turner, R. J., & Avison, W. R. (1985). Assessing risk factors for problem parenting: The significance of social support. *Journal of Marriage and the Family*, 881–892.

Twenge, J. M., & Crocker, J. (2002). Race and self-esteem: Meta-analyses comparing Whites, Blacks, Hispanics, Asians, and American Indians. *Psychological Bulletin, 128*, 371–408.

Twente, E. E. (1965). Aging, strength, and creativity. *Social Work, 10*, 105–110.

Twente, E. E. (1970). *Never too old*. San Francisco: Jossey-Bass.

U.S. Bureau of the Census. (1987). *Annual report of fertility rates*. Washington, DC: U.S. Government Printing Office.

U.S. Bureau of the Census. (1989). *Statistical abstract of the United States, 1989*. Washington, DC: U.S. Government Printing Office.

U.S. Bureau of the Census. (1990a). Need for personal assistance with everyday activities. *Current population reports*, Series P-25, No. 19. (Publication No. S/N 803-044-00007-4). Washington, DC: U.S. Government Printing Office.

U.S. Bureau of the Census. (1990b). *Statistical abstract of the United States, 1990*. Washington, DC: U.S. Government Printing Office.

U.S. Bureau of the Census. (1991). *Statistical abstract of the United States: 1991*. Washington, DC: U.S. Government Printing Office.

U.S. Bureau of the Census. (2002). *Statistical abstracts of the United States*. Washington, DC: Author.

U.S. Bureau of the Census. (2002). *Women by the numbers*. Retrieved from http://www.infoplease.com/spot/womencensus1.html

U.S. Bureau of the Census. (2003). *2002 Data Profiles*. Retrieved July 13, 2004, from http://www.census.gov

U.S. Bureau of the Census. (2004). IDB *summary demographic data*. Retrieved October 25, 2004, from http://www.census.gov/ipc/www/idbsum.html

U.S. Bureau of the Census. (2004). *U.S. interim projections by age, sex, race, and Hispanic origin*. Retrieved June 17, 2004, from http://www.census.gov

U.S. Centers for Disease Control. (2001). *STD surveillance*. Retrieved August 13, 2004, from http://www.cdc.gov/std

U.S. Department of Education. (2002). *Digest of education statistics 2001*. Washington, DC: U.S. Government Printing Office.

U.S. Department of Health and Human Services. (2003). *Why are fruits and vegetables important for my health?* Retrieved May 31, 2004, from http://familydoctor.org/

U.S. Department of Justice. (1995). *Women usually victimized by offenders they know*. Bureau of Statistics, available at http://www.usdoj.gov

U.S. Department of Justice. (2002). *Crime in the United States*. Washington, DC: U.S. Government Printing Office.

U.S. General Accounting Office. (1986). *School dropouts: The extent and nature of the problem*. Report to Congressional Requesters.

U.S. Secret Service and U.S. Department of Education. (2002, May). The final report and findings of the safe school initiative: Implications for the prevention of school attacks in the U.S. Retrieved August 17, 2003, from http://www.ed.gov/offices/OSDFS/preventingschoolattacksreport.pdf

U.S. Senate, Special Committee on Aging. (1988). The long-term care challenge. *Developments in aging: 1987* (Vol. 3). Washington, DC: U.S. Government Printing Office.

Underwood, M. K. (2002). Sticks and stones and social exclusion: Aggression among girls and boys. In P. K. Smith & C. H. Hart (eds.), *Blackwell handbook of childhood social development* (533–548). Malden, MA: Blackwell.

Underwood, M. K. (2003). *Social aggression among girls*. New York: Guilford Press.

Utz, R. L. (2003). Assisted living: The philosophical challenges of everyday practice. *The Journal of Applied Gerontology, 22*, 379–404.

Vale, J. R. (1980). *Genes, environment, and behavior: An interactionist approach*. New York: Harper & Row.

Vallant, G. E. (1977). *Adaptation to life*. Boston: Little, Brown.

Valzelli, L. (1980). *An approach to neuroanatomical and neurochemical psychophysiology*. Torino, Italy: C. G. Edizioni Medic. Scientifiche.

Van Den Bergh, N. (1986). Renaming: Vehicle for empowerment. In J. Penfield (Ed.), *Women and language in transition*. Albany: State University of New York Press.

Van Den Bergh, N., & Cooper, L. B. (1987). Feminist social work. In A. Minahan (Ed.), *Encyclopedia of social work*. Silver Spring, MD: NASW Press.

Van Ijzendoorn, M. H., & Kroonenberg, P. M. (1988). Cross-cultural patterns of attachment: A meta-analysis of the strange situation. *Child Development, 59*(1), 147–156.

Van Strien, P., Bouma, A., & Bakker, D. (1987). Birth stress, autoimmune diseases, and handedness. *Journal of Clinical and Experimental Neuropsychology, 9*, 775–780.

Vandenbosche, R. C., & Kirchner, J. T. (1998). Intrauterine growth retardation. *American Family Physician, 58*, 1384–1391.

Vantveer, P. (1994). Diet and breast cancer: Trial and error. *Annals of Medicine, 26*, 453–460.

Vasconcellos, J. (1927). *Indologia: Una interpretación de la cultura ibero-americano*. Barcelona: Agencia Mundial de Liberia.

Veenstra-Vanderweele, J., & Cook, E. H., Jr. (2003). Genetics of childhood disorders: XLVI, Autism, part 5: Genetics of autism. *Journal of the American Academy of Child and Adolescent Psychiatry, 42*, 116–119.

Veevers, J. E. (1980). *Childless by choice*. Toronto: Butterworths.

Verdoux, H. (1993). A comparative study of obstetric history in schizophrenics, bipolar patients and normal subjects. *Schizophrenia Research, 9*, 67–69.

Vernon, I. S. (2001). *Killing us quietly: Native Americans and HIV/AIDS*. Lincoln: University of Nebraska Press.

Vetter, H. J. (1969). *Language behavior and communication: An introduction*. Itasca, IL: F. E. Peacock.

Viney, W. & King, D. B. (2002). *A history of psychology: Ideas and context* (3rd ed.). Pearson: Allyn & Bacon.

Visher, E. B., & Visher, J. S. (1988). Old loyalties, new ties. New York: Brunner/Mazel.

Viviansayles, P. J. (1993, May/June). The politics of breast cancer. *Ms.*, 54–55.

Voda, A. M. (1993). A journey to the center of the cell: Understanding the physiology and endocrinology of menopause. In J. C. Callahan (Ed.), *Menopause: A midlife passage*. Bloomington: Indiana University Press.

Vosler, N. R. & Robertson, J. G. (1998). Non-marital co-parenting: Knowledge-building for practice. *Families in Society, 79*, 149–159.

Vygotsky, L. S. (1962). *Thought and language*. Cambridge, MA: MIT Press.

Wagner, D. A., & Stevenson, H. W. (1982). *Cultural perspectives on child development*. San Francisco: W. H. Freeman.

Wahl, H. W. & Weisman, G. D. (2003). Environmental gerontology at the beginning of the new millennium: Reflections on its historical, empirical, and theoretical development. *The Gerontologist, 43*, 616–627.

Waite, L., & Gallagher, M. (2000). *The case for marriage: Why married people are happier, healthier, and better off financially*. New York: Broadway.

Wald, E. (1989). Family: Stepfamilies. In *Encyclopedia of social work* (pp. 555–561). Silver Spring, MD: National Association of Social Workers.

Walker, L. (1995). Sexism in Kohlberg's moral psychology? In W. M. Kurtines & J. L. Gewirtz (Eds.), *Moral development: An introduction* (pp. 83–107). Boston: Allyn & Bacon.

Walker, L. J. (1989). A longitudinal study of moral reasoning. *Child Development, 60*, 157–166.

Wallerstein, J. S. (1984). Children of divorce: Preliminary report of a ten-year follow-up of young children. *American Journal of Orthopsychiatry, 57*, 199–211.

Wallerstein, J. S. (1988). Children of divorce: Stress and developmental tasks. In N. Garmezy & M. Rutter (Eds.), *Stress, coping, and development in children*. Baltimore: Johns Hopkins University Press.

Wallerstein, J. S. (1995). *The good marriage: How and why love lasts*. Boston: Houghton Mifflin.

Wallerstein, J. S., & Blakeslee, S. (1989). *Second chances*. New York: Ticknor & Fields.

Wallerstein, J. S., & Blakeslee, S. (2003). *What about the kids? Raising your children before, during, and after divorce*. New York: Hyperion.

Wallerstein, J. S., Corbin, S. B., & Lewis, J. M. (1988). Children of divorce: A ten-year study. In E. M. Heatherington & J. Arasteh (Eds.), *Impact of divorce, single-parenting, and step-parenting on children*. Hillsdale, NJ: Erlbaum.

Wallhagen, M., Strawbridge, W., Shema, S., & Kaplan, G. (2004). Impact of self-assessed hearing loss on a spouse: A longitudinal analysis of couples. *Journal of Gerontology: Social Sciences, 59B*(3), S190–S196.

Walsh, D. (2005). West not the best for maternity care. *British Journal of Midwifery, 13*, 87.

Walz, T. (2002). Crones, dirty old men, sexy seniors: Representations of the sexuality of older persons. *Journal of Aging and Identity, 7*(2), 99–112.

Wang, H. Y., & Amato, P. R. (2000). Predictors of divorce adjustment: Stressors, resources, and definitions. *Journal of Marriage and the Family, 62*, 655–668.

Wark, G. R., & Krebs, D. L. (1996). Gender and dilemma differences in real-life moral judgment. *Developmental Psychology, 32*, 220–230.

Warner, J. (2005). *Perfect madness: Motherhood in the age of anxiety*. New York: Riverhead Publishing Co.

Warr, P. (1992). Age and occupational well-being. *Psychology and Aging, 7*, 37–45.

Warren, K. (1985). Alcohol-related birth defects: Current trends in research. *Alcohol Health and Research World, 10*, 4.

Waters, D., & Saunders, J. T. (1996). I gave at the office. *Networker*, 44–50.

Waters, M. (1994). *Modern sociological theory*. London: Sage.

Watson, J. B. (1925). *Behaviorism*. New York: Norton.

Watt, H. M. G. (2000). Measuring attitudinal change in mathematics and English over the first year of junior high school: A multi-dimensional analysis. *The Journal of Experimental Education, 68*, 331–342.

Wattigney, W. A., Srinivasan, S. R., Chen, W., Greenlund, K. J., & Berenson, G. S. (1999). Secular trend of earlier onset of menarche with increasing obesity in black and white girls: The Bogalusa Heart Study. *Ethnic Disease, 9*, 181–191.

Watts, T. (1985). Ethnomethodogy. In R. M. Grinnell (Ed.), *Social work research and evaluation* (pp. 357–369). Itasca, IL: F. E. Peacock.

Waxman, H. M., McCreary, G., Weinrit, R. M., & Carner, E. A. (1985). A comparison of somatic complaints among depressed and non-depressed older persons. *The Gerontologist, 25*, 501–507.

Webb, M. B., & Harden, J. B. (2003). Beyond child protection: The intersection of the child welfare and mental health systems. *Journal of Emotional and Behavioral Disorders, 11*, 49–59.

Webdietician.com (2004). *Geriatric nutrition*. Retrieved July 25, 2004, from www.webdietician.com

Weideger, P. (1976). *Menstruation and menopause*. New York: Knopf.

Weinman, J. (1987). *An outline of psychology as applied medicine*. Bristol, UK: John Wright.

Weinraub, M., Clemens, L. P., Sockloff, A., Ethridge, T., Gracely, E., & Myers, B. (1984). The development of sex-role stereotypes in the third year: Relationships to gender labeling, gender identity, sex-typed toy preferences, and family characteristics. *Child Development, 55*, 1493–1503.

Weinreich, P. (2003). Identity structural analysis. In P. Weinreich & W. Saunderson (Eds.), *Analyzing identity: Cross-cultural, societal and clinical contexts* (pp. 1–76). London: Routledge Taylor & Francis.

Weiss, M. J. & Harris, S. L. (2001). *Reaching out, joining in: Teaching social skills to young children with autism*. New York: Woodbine House.

Weiss, R. S. (1975). *Marital separation*. New York: Basic Books.

Weiten, W. (1992). *Psychology* (2nd ed.). Pacific Grove, CA: Brooks/Cole.

Weiten, W. (1995). *Psychology: Themes and variations*. Pacific Grove, CA: Brooks/Cole.

Weiten, W. (2003). *Psychology: Themes and variations* (6th ed.). Belmont, CA: Wadsworth/Thomson International.

Weiten, W., & Lloyd, M. A. (1994). *Psychology applied to modern life* (4th ed.). Pacific Grove, CA: Brooks/Cole.

Weiten, W., & Lloyd, M. A. (2002). *Psychology applied to modern life: Adjustment in the 21st century* (7th ed.). Pacific Grove, CA: Brooks/Cole.

Weithorn, L. A. (1984). Children's capacities in legal contexts. In N. D. Reppucci, L. A. Weithorn, E. P. Mulvey, & J. Monahan (Eds.), *Children, mental health, and the law*. Beverly Hills, CA: Sage.

Welch, M. J. (2000). *American academy of pediatrics guide to your child's allergies and asthma: Breathing easy and bringing up healthy, active children*. New York: Villard.

Wells, S. J. (1995). Child abuse and neglect overview. In *Encyclopedia of social work* (19th ed.). Washington, DC: NASW Press.

Werner, E. E., & Smith, R. S. (1982). *Vulnerable but invincible: A longitudinal study of resilience and youth*. New York: McGraw-Hill.

Werry, J. S., & Quay, H. C. (1971). The prevalence of behavior symptoms in younger elementary school children. *American Journal of Orthopsychiatry, 41*, 136–143.

West, D. J., & Farrington, D. P. (1973). *Who becomes delinquent?* London: Heinemann.

Westcott, H. L., Davies, G. M., & Bull, R. (2002). *Children's testimony: A handbook of psychological research and forensic practice*. New York: John Wiley.

Westen, D., & Heim, A. K. (2003). Disturbances of self and identity in personality disorders. In M. R. Leary & J. P. Tangney (Eds.), *Handbook of self and identity* (pp. 643–664). New York: Guilford Press.

Westinghouse Learning Corporation. (1969). *The impact of Head Start: An evaluation of the effects of Head Start on children's cognitive and affectional development*. Report to the Office of Economic Opportunity. Washington, DC: Learning House for Federal Scientific and Technical Information.

White, J. L. (1989). *The troubled adolescent*. New York: Pergamon Press.

White, L. K. (1990). Determinants of divorce: A review of research in the eighties. *Journal of Marriage and the Family, 32*, 904–912.

White, R. W. (1959). Motivation reconsidered: The concept of competence. *Psychological Review, 66*, 297–333.

White, R. W. (1966). *Lives in progress* (2nd ed.). New York: Holt, Rinehart & Winston.

Whitfield, C. L. (1991). *Co-dependence: Healing the human condition*. Deerfield Beach, FL: Health Communications.

Whiting, B. B., & Whiting, J. W. M. (1975). *Children of six cultures: A psychocultural analysis*. Cambridge, MA: Harvard University Press.

Whittaker, J. K., & Garbarino, J. (1983). *Social support networks: Informal helping in the human services*. Hawthorne, NY: Aldine.

Whol, T. (1963). Correlation of anxiety and hostility with adrenocortical function. *Journal of the American Medical Association, 183*, 133–144.

Whorf, B. L. (1956). *Language, thought, and reality*. New York: Wiley.

Widmayer, S., & Field, T. (1980). Effects of Brazelton demonstrations on early interactions of preterm infants and their teen-age mothers. *Infant Behavior and Development, 3*, 79–89.

Widom, C. S. (1989). Does violence beget violence? A critical examination of the literature. *American Psychologist, 106*, 3–28.

Wigfield, R. (1994). SIDS: Risk reduction measures. *Early Human Development, 38*, 161–164.

Wilcox, L. S., Kiely, J. L., Melvin, C. L., & Martin, M. C. (1996). Assisted reproductive technologies: Estimates of their contribution to multiple births and newborn hospital days in the United States. *Fertility and Sterility, 65*, 361–366.

William T. Grant Foundation (1988). *The forgotten half: Non-college youth in America*. Washington, DC: Youth and America's future: The William T. Grant Foundation on Work, Family and Citizenship.

Williams, C. L., & Berry, J. W. (1991). Primary prevention of acculturative stress among refugees. *American Psychologist, 46*, 632–641.

Williams, D. R. (2001). Race and health: Trends and policy implications. In J. A. Auerbach & B. K. Krimgold (Eds.), *Income, sociecomomic status and health: Exploring the relationships*. Washington, DC: National Policy Association.

Williams, D. R. (2003a). Explaining the crisis: Why poor men of color have the worst health. *Facts of life, 8*, 2–8.

Williams, D. R. (2003b). The health of men: Structured inequalities and opportunities. *American Journal of Public Health, 93*, 724–731.

Williams, J. B. W., Karls, J. M., & Wandrei, K. (1989). The person-in-environment (PIE) system for describing problems of social functioning. *Hospital and Community Psychiatry, 40*, 1125–1127.

Williams, R. B. (2000). Psychological factors, health, and disease: The impact of aging and the life cycle. In S. B. Manuck, R. Jennings, B. S. Rabin, & A. Baum (Eds.), *Behavior, health and aging* (pp. 135–151). Mahwah, NJ: Erlbaum.

Williams, S. W. & Dilworth-Anderson, P. (2002). Systems of social support in families who care for dependent African American Elders. *The Gerontologist, 42*, 224–236.

Willinger, M., Hoffman, H., & Hartford, R. (1994). Infant sleep position and risk for sudden infant death syndrome: Report of meeting held January 13 and 14, 1994, National Institutes of Health, Bethesda, MD. *Pediatrics, 93*, 814–819.

Willis, D., & Holden, E. (1990). Etiological factors contributing to deviant development. In J. Johnson & J. Goldman (Eds.), *Developmental assessment in clinical child psychology* (pp. 38–57). New York: Pergamon Press.

Willis, S. L. (1989). Adult intelligence. In S. Hunter and M. Sundel (Eds.), *Midlife myths: Issues, findings, and practice implications*. Newbury Park, CA: Sage.

Willis, S. L., & Nesselroade, C. S. (1990). Long-term effects of fluid ability training in old age. *Developmental Psychology, 26*, 905–910.

Willis, S. L., & Schaie, K. W. (1999). Intellectual functioning in midlife. In S. L. Willis & J. D. Reid (Eds.), *Life in the middle* (pp. 105–146). San Diego: Academic Press.

Willis, S. L., Willis, S., & Reid, J. D. (1999). *Life in the middle: Psychological and social development in middle age*. New York: Academic Press.

Wilmoth, J. M. & Chen, P. (2003). Immigrant status, living arrangements, and depressive symptoms among middle-aged and older adults. *Journal of Gerontology Social Sciences, 58B*, S305–S313.

Wilson, E. O. (1975). *Sociobiology: The new synthesis*. Cambridge, MA: Harvard University Press.

Wilson, J. F. (2003). *Biological foundations of human behavior*. Pacific Grove, CA: Brooks/Cole Thomson Learning.

Wilson, K. J. (1987). *Anatomy and physiology in health and illness*. New York: Churchill Livingstone.

Winawer, S., & Shike, M. (1995). *Cancer free: The comprehensive cancer prevention program*. New York: Simon & Schuster.

Wind, R. (2004). U.S. teenage pregnancy rate drops for 10th straight year. New York: Allen Guttmacher Institute.

Wine, J. D., & Smye, M. D. (1981). *Social competence*. New York: Guilford Press.

Winkler, A. E. (1998, April). Earnings of husbands and wives in dual-earner families. *Monthly Labor Review*, 42–48.

Wintgens, A., Lepine, S., Lefebvre, F., Glorieux, J., Gauthier, Y., & Robaey, P. (1998). Attachment, self-esteem, and psychomotor development in extremely premature children at preschool age. *Infant Mental Health Journal, 19*, 394–408.

Wisch, A. F., Mahalik, J. R., Hayes, J. A., & Nutt, E. A. (1995). The impact of gender role conflict and counseling technique on psychological help seeking men. *Sex Roles, 33*, 77–89.

Wise, M. G. (1986). Working with medicated clients: A primer for social workers. *Health and Social Work, 11*, 36–41.

Wise, P. (1992). Infant mortality as a social mirror. *New England Journal of Medicine, 326*, 1558–1559.

Wisensale, S. K. (1992). Toward the 21st century: Family change and public policy. *Family Relations, 41*, 417–422.

Wisniewski, J. J., & Toomey, B. G. (1987). Are social workers homophobic? *Social Work, 32*, 454–464.

Wolf, R. B., & Pillemer, K. A. (1989). *Helping elderly victims*. New York: Columbia University Press.

Wolf, R. S. (2000). The nature and scope of elder abuse. *Generations, 24*(11), 6–12.

Wolff, P. H. (1966). The causes, controls, and organization of behavior in the neonate. *Psychological Issues, 5*, 1–105.

Wolfgang, C. H. (1977). *Helping aggressive and passive preschoolers through play*. Columbus, OH: Merrill.

Wolfson, A. R., & Carskadon, M. A. (1998). Sleep schedules and daytime functioning in adolescents. *Child Development, 69*, 875–887.

Women's Health Initiative (2002). Risks and benefits of estrogen plus progestin in healthy postmenopausal women: Principal results from the Women's Health Initiative randomized control trial. *Journal of the American Medical Association, 288*, 321–333.

Wood, N. (1974). *Many winters*. Santa Fe, NM: William Gannon.

Wood, V., & Robertson, J. F. (1978). Friendship and kinship interaction: Differential effect on the morale of the elderly. *Journal of Marriage and the Family, 40*, 367–375.

Wood, W. (1987). Meta-analytic review of sex differences in group performance. *Psychological Bulletin, 102*, 53–71.

Woodman, N. J., & Lenna, H. R. (1980). *Counseling with gay men and women: A guide for facilitating positive life-styles*. San Francisco: Jossey-Bass.

Woods, N. F., Most, A., & Dery, G. K. (1982). Prevalence of premenstrual symptoms. *American Journal of Public Health, 72*, 1257–1264.

Woodward, K. (1997). *Identity and difference*. London: Sage.

Woodward, K. (2002). *Understanding identity*. London: Arnold.

Worden, J. (2002). *Grief counseling and grief therapy: A handbook for the mental health practitioner* (3rd ed.). New York: Springer.

Worden, W. (1991). *Grief counseling and grief therapy: A handbook for the mental health practitioner*. New York: Springer.

Wright, P. H., & Wright, K. D. (1991). Codependency: Addictive love, adjustive relating, or both? *Contemporary Family Therapy: An International Journal, 13*, 435–454.

Wyer, R. S., & Srull, T. K. (Eds.). (1984). *Handbook of social cognition* (Vol. 1). Hillsdale, NJ: Erlbaum.

Wynn, K. (1992). Addition and subtraction by human infants. *Nature, 358*, 749–750.

Yalom, I. (1985). *The theory and practice of group psychotherapy* (3rd ed.). New York: Basic Books.

Yankelovich, D. (1981). *New rules: Searching for self-fulfillment in a world turned upside down*. New York: Bantam Books.

Yardley, L., & Smith, H. (2002). A prospective study of the relationships between feared consequences of falling and avoidance of activity in community-living older people. *The Gerontologist, 42*(1), 17–23.

Yee, D. (2002). Recognizing diversity, moving toward cultural competence. *Generations, 26*(3), 6–10.

Yeh, C. J., & Drost, C. (2004). Bridging identities among ethnic minority youth in schools. *Eric Digest*. Retrieved July, 29, 2004, from http://www.ericdigests.org/2002-4/youth.html

Yeh, C. J., & Hwang, M. Y. (2000). Interdependence in ethnic identity and self: Implications for theory and practice. *Journal of Counseling and Development, 78*, 420–429.

Yelland, N. (1998). *Gender in early childhood*. New York: Routledge.

Yesavage, J. A., Brink, T. L., Rose, T. L., et al. (1983). Development and validation of a geriatric depression rating scale: A preliminary report. *Journal of Psychiatric Research, 17*, 37–49.

Yogman, M. (1982). Development of the father-infant relationship. In H. Fitzgerald, B. Lester, & M. Uogman (Eds.), *Theory and research in behavioral pediatrics* (pp. 221–279). New York: Plenum.

Yogman, M. W., Cooley, J., & Kindlon, D. (1988). Fathers, infants, and toddlers. In P. Bronstein & C. P. Cowan (Eds.), *Fatherhood today: Men's changing role in the family*. New York: Wiley.

Young, J. E. (1982). Loneliness, depression, and cognitive therapy: Theory and application. In L. A. Peplau & D. Perlman (Eds.), *Loneliness: A sourcebook of current theory, research, and therapy* (375–405). New York: Wiley.

Young, R. F., & Kahana, E. (1989). Specifying caregiver outcomes: Gender and relationship aspects of caregiving strain. *The Gerontologist, 29*, 660–666.

Young, V. H. (1970). Family and childhood in a southern Negro community. *American Anthropologist, 72*(2), 269–288.

Youngstrom, N. (1990, October). Seriously mentally ill need better tracking. *APA Monitor*, 18–19.

Youngstrom, N. (1991, September). Drug exposure in home elicits worst behaviors. *APA Monitor*, 23.

Youngstrom, N. (1991, October). Warning: Teens at risk for AIDS. *APA Monitor*, 38.

Yule, W. (1981). The epidemiology of child psychopathology. In B. Lahey & A. Kazdin (Eds.), *Advances in clinical child psychology* (Vol. 4). New York: Plenum.

Yurgelun-Todd, D. (2004). Teen brains. *Science News*. Retrieved from http://www.sciencenews.org/articles/20040508/bob9.asp

Yussen, S. R. (1977). Characteristics of moral dilemmas written by adolescents. *Developmental Psychology, 13*, 162–163.

Zajonc, R. B. (1980). Feeling and thinking: Preferences need no inferences. *American Psychologist, 35*, 151–175.

Zajonc, R. B. (1984). On the primacy of affect. *American Psychologist, 39*, 117–123.

Zajonc, R. B., & Markus, G. B. (1975). Birth order and intellectual development. *Psychological Review, 82*, 74–88.

Zametkin, A. J., Nordahl, T., Gross, M., King, A. C., Semple, W. E., Rumsey, J., et al. (1990). Cerebral glucose metabolism in adults with hyperactivity of childhood onset. *New England Journal of Medicine, 322*, 1361–1366.

Zane, N., Nagayama-Hall, G. C., Sue, S., Young, K., & Nunez, J. (2004). Research on psychotherapy with culturally diverse populations. In M. J. Lambert (Ed.), *Bergin and Garfield's handbook of psychotherapy and behavior change* (5th ed., pp. 767–804). New York: Wiley.

Zarit, S. (1980). Relatives of the impaired elderly: Correlates of feelings of burden. *Gerontologist, 20*(6), 649–655.

Zarit, S., Femia, E., Watson, J., Rice-Oeschger, L., & Kakos, B. (2004). Memory club: A group intervention for people with early-stage dementia and their care partners. *The Gerontologist, 44*(2), 262–269.

Zastrow, C. & Kirst-Ashman, K. K. (1994). *Understanding human behavior and the social environment* (3rd ed.). Chicago: Nelson-Hall.

Zausmer, E. (1978). Gross motor developmental stimulation. In S. M. Pueschel (Ed.), *Down syndrome: Growing and learning* (pp. 88–105). New York: Andrews, McMeel & Parker.

Zeanah, C. H., Mammen, O. K., & Lieberman, A. F. (1993). Disorders of attachment. In C. H. Zeanah (Ed.), *Handbook of infant mental health* (pp. 249–332). New York: Guilford Press.

Zeanah, C. H., & Emde, R. N. (1994). Attachment disorders in infancy and childhood. In M. Rutter, E. Taylor, & L. Hersou (Eds.), *Child and adolescent psychiatry: Modern approaches* (pp. 490–504). Oxford, UK: Blackwell Scientific.

Zeiss, A., & Kasl-Godley, J. (2001). Sexuality in older relationships. *Generations: Quarterly Journal of the American Society on Aging, 25*(2), 18–26.

Zelazo, R., Zelazo, N., & Kolb, S. (1972). "Walking" in the newborn. *Science, 176*, 314–315.

Zellman, G. L., & Eisen, M. (1984). Factors predicting pregnancy resolution decision satisfaction of unmarried adolescents. *Journal of Genetic Psychology, 145*, 231–234.

Zigler, E. (1973). Project Head Start: Success or failure? *Learning, 1*, 43–47

Zigler, E., & Finn-Stevenson, M. (1992). Applied developmental psychology. In M. E. Lamb & M. Bornstein (Eds.), *Developmental psychology: An advanced textbook* (3rd ed.). Hillsdale, NJ: Erlbaum.

Zigler, E., & Stevenson, M. F. (1993). *Children in a changing world: Development and social issues* (2nd ed.). Pacific Grove, CA: Brooks/Cole.

Zigler, E., Taussig, C., & Black, K. (1992). Early childhood intervention: A promising preventive for juvenile delinquency. *American Psychologist, 47*, 997–1006.

Zigler, E., & Trickett, P. E. (1978). IQ, social competence, and evaluation of early childhood intervention programs. *American Psychologist, 33*, 789–798.

Zigler, E., & Valentine, J. (1979). *Project Head Start: A legacy of the war on poverty*. New York: Free Press.

Zimbardo, P. G. (1987). *Shyness*. New York: Jove.

Zolotow, C. (1968). *My friend John*. New York: Harper & Row.

Zurcher, L. (1977). *The mutable self*. Beverly Hills, CA: Sage.

PHOTO CREDITS

This page constitutes an extension of the copyright page. We have made every effort to trace the ownership of all copyrighted material and to secure permission from copyright holders. In the event of any question arising as to the use of any material, we will be pleased to make the necessary corrections in future printings. Thanks are due to the following authors, publishers, and agents for permission to use the material indicated.

Cover: © Yukimasa Hirota/Photonica

Chapter 1. 1: © José Ortega/The Stock Illustration Source; **23:** © 1995 Council on Social Work Education, Alexandria, VA; **25:** Courtesy of Daniel Brosmer; **34:** Courtesy of Daniel Brosmer; **9 (both):** © José Ashford.

Chapter 2. 41: © Photo courtesy of Jawanda Mast; **55:** © José Ashford; **67:** Bill Branson/National Cancer Institute; **71:** © José Ashford.

Chapter 3. 75: © Steve/Mary Skjold/Index Stock Imagery, Inc.; **79:** Reproduced with permission of Jon Erikson; **82:** © Image Source Limited/Index Stock Imagery, Inc.; **87:** © James Frank/Index Stock Imagery, Inc.; **99:** © Dan Gair Photographic/Index Stock Imagery, Inc.; **101:** © AbleStock/Index Stock Imagery, Inc.

Chapter 4. 114: © Tony Freeman/PhotoEdit; **115:** Courtesy of Carol Germaine's Estate; **127:** © Omni Photo Communications/Index Stock Imagery, Inc.; **137:** © Bill Bachman/Index Stock Imagery, Inc.; **142:** © Aneal Vohra/Index Stock Imagery, Inc.; **148:** © José Ashford; **151:** © Mark Reinstein/Index Stock Imagery, Inc.; **153:** © Lonnie Duka/Index Stock Imagery, Inc.; **156:** © Craig LeCroy; **162:** © Lawrence Migdale/Photo Researchers; **163:** © Elwin Williamson/Index Stock Imagery, Inc.

Chapter 5. 167: © Kevin Radford/Index Stock Imagery, Inc.; **173:** © D.W. Fawcett/Photo Researchers; **175:** © Craig LeCroy; **176:** © Craig LeCroy; **187:** © Rubberball Productions/Index Stock Imagery, Inc.; **189:** © Photo Courtesy of Jawanda Mast.

Chapter 6. 212: © Photo Courtesy of Olga Valenzuela, **215:** © Craig LeCroy; **224:** © Allyson LaBrue; **232:** © Photolibrary.compty.ltd./Index Stock Imagery, Inc., **236:** © Jim McGuire/Index Stock Imagery, Inc., **242:** © Craig LeCroy, **250:** © Craig LeCroy, **262:** © Donald Graham/Index Stock Imagery, Inc.

Chapter 7. 270: © LLC, FogStock/Index Stock Imagery, Inc.; **270:** © LLC, FogStock/Index Stock Imagery, Inc.; **274:** © José B. Ashford; **285:** © Omni Photo Communications/Index Stock Imagery, Inc.; **293:** © Craig LeCroy; **299:** © Henryk T. Kaiser/Index, Stock Imagery, Inc.; **304:** © José Ashford; **306:** © José B. Ashford; **309:** © Michael Newman/PhotoEdit; **315:** © James R. Holland/Stock, Boston.

Chapter 8. 328: © Kindra Clineff/Index Stock Imagery, Inc.; **331:** © Craig LeCroy; **335:** © Tony Freeman/PhotoEdit; **342:** © Robin Sachs/PhotoEdit; **343:** © Jim West; **362:** © Tony Freeman/PhotoEdit; **368:** © Richard Orton/Index Stock Imagery, Inc.; **369:** © Ed Lallo/Index Stock Imagery, Inc.; **376:** © Network Productions/Index Stock Imagery, Inc.

Chapter 9. 386: © Jeff Greenberg/Index Stock Imagery, Inc.; **399:** © José B. Ashford; **408:** © AbleStock/Index Stock Imagery, Inc.; **434:** © ThinkStock LLC/Index Stock Imagery, Inc.; **440:** © Jerry Koontz/Index Stock Imagery, Inc.

Chapter 10. 452: © ElektraVision/Image Source Limited/Index Stock Imagery, Inc.; **468:** © Steve/Mary Skjold/Index Stock Imagery, Inc.; **484:** © Novastock/Index Stock Imagery, Inc.; **489:** © José Carillo/PhotoEdit; **497:** © BSIP Agency/Index Stock Imagery, Inc.

Chapter 11. 507: © Benelux Press/Index Stock Imagery, Inc.; **512:** © Tom Rosenthal/SuperStock; **515:** © Peter Langone/Index Stock Imagery, Inc.; **520:** NCI Clinical Center/Mathews Media Group/National Cancer Institute; **536:** © John Boykin/PhotoEdit; **545:** © Kathryn Betts Adams; **555:** © John Coletti/Index Stock Imagery, Inc.; **558:** © Norman R. Rowan/Stock Boston.

Chapter 12. 568: © Kathryn Betts Adams; **573:** Courtesy of the Baptist General Convention of Texas; **577:** © José B. Ashford; **581:** © Rubberball Productions/Index Stock Imagery, Inc.; **593:** © Omni Photo Communications, Inc./Index Stock Imagery, Inc.; **607:** © Craig LeCroy; **610:** © Allen Russell/Index Stock Imagery, Inc.; **613:** © José B. Ashford.

NAME INDEX

AARP, 580, 608, 609, 610, 611, 612, 613, 614
Abecassis, M., 285, 290, 305, 312, 361, 363
Abel, E., 182
Abramowitz, R. H., 121, 162
Abuelo, D. N., 51, 52, 53
Achenbach, T. M., 350, 351, 408
Achenbaum, W. A., 572, 573
Ackerman, J., 46
Adams, B. N., 473
Adams, G. R., 400, 401, 406
Adams, K. B., 586, 590, 595, 608
Adams, M., 147
Adams, R. G., 608
Adler, J., 486
Adler, N., 398
Adler, S. R., 511
Adler, T. F., 229, 230, 372
Administration on Aging, 570, 577, 612, 615
Agyei, Y., 478
Ainsworth, M. D. S., 234
Aitchison, T., 516
Ajzen, I., 96, 97
Akkerman, R., 595
Albertini, J. A., 341
Alcoholics Anonymous, 535
Alderman, A., 413
Aldwin, C. M., 511
Alexander, J. F., 412
Allan, J. D., 514
Allen, K., 603, 606, 608
Allen-Meares, P., 42
Allport, G. W., 96
Almeida, D. M., 417
AlRoomi, L., 235
Als, H., 198
Alspaugh, J. W., 424
Altman, D. G., 588
Altucher, K. A., 170, 171
Alzheimer's Association, 594
Amato, P. R., 375, 376, 490, 541
American Academy of Child and Adolescent Psychiatry, 291, 294
American Academy of Pediatrics, 282, 351, 352
American Academy of Pediatrics, Committee on Adolescence, 203, 310, 431
American Association of University Women, 436
American Family Physician, 457
American Psychiatric Association, 281, 293, 294, 295, 326, 410

Americans for Divorce Reform, 544
Amsel, E., 16
Ancelet, B. J., 148, 149
Andersen, M. L., 117, 154, 155, 156, 159
Anderson, D. L., 492
Anderson, J. T., 53, 54, 219, 249, 250
Anderson, K. J., 300
Anderson, M., 438
Anderson, R. E., 13, 76, 117
Andreasen, N. C., 58, 88
Andrews, D. A., 77
Andrews, D. W., 413
Andronico, M. P., 555
Anetzberger, G. J., 616
Angelillo, C., 7
Annie Casey Foundation, 314
Apantaku, L. M., 458
Apfel, N. H., 200
Apgar, V., 176
Apolloni, T., 291
Appleby, G. A., 13, 148
Applefield, J. M., 311
Apter, T., 512, 552, 553, 556, 559
Arend, R. A., 235
Arkin, R. M., 71
Arnett, J. J., 454, 509
Aronson, E., 424
Ashburn, S. S., 17, 47, 169, 172, 192, 241, 249, 310, 344, 370, 389
Asher, J., 230
Asher, S. R., 290, 363
Ashford, J. B., 30, 31, 42, 83, 131, 160, 200, 253, 411
Ashmore, R. D., 104
Aslam, S., 438
Atchley, R., 572, 609, 610
Atkinson, R., 599
Attie, I., 391
Atwood, M., 509
Austrian, S. G., 29, 78
Auth, E., 590, 608
Avis, N. E., 511
Avison, W. R., 163
Azar, B., 183, 193, 253, 296, 500

Bachman, J. G., 442
Backman, L., 587
Bailey, J. M., 478
Baillargeon, R., 225
Bakeman, R., 214, 252
Baker, R. C., 405
Bakk, L., 605

Bakker, D., 185
Balaskas, J., 175, 176
Baldwin, J. R., 151
Bales, R. F., 133
Ball, S., 311
Ballard-Barbash, R., 393
Baltes, M. M., 585
Baltes, P. B., 460, 585, 592
Banaji, M. R., 105
Bandura, A., 81, 88, 311
Bank, B. A., 187
Banton, M., 152
Bar, J. L., 534
Barbach, L. G., 511
Barber, B., 423
Barkely, R. A., 294, 351, 358
Barlow, D. H., 6, 78
Barlow, J., 8
Barnard, C., 145
Barnard, K. E., 235
Barnard, P. J., 84
Barnes, H., 604, 610
Barnes, K. E., 306
Barnett, R. C., 545
Barnewolt, D., 554
Barranti, C., 603
Barres, B. A., 60
Barrett, D., 186
Barry, B., 150
Bartels, A., 464
Barth, R. P., 316, 398, 399, 421
Bartholomae, S., 256
Baruch, G. K., 509, 545
Baruth, L. G., 485
Basinger, K. S., 467
Basow, S. A., 151
Bass, E., 538
Bateson, M. C., 553
Baum, E., 576
Baumeister, D., 107
Baumgartner-Papageorgious, A., 159
Baumrind, D., 290, 299, 300
Bavin, S., 605
Baylor, B., 201
Beal, C. R., 340
Bearer, E. L., 6, 14, 21, 22, 30
Beattie, M., 537
Beatty, W. W., 71
Beck, C. M., 50
Becker, G., 613
Beckett, J. O., 17, 612, 613
Beer, J. S., 84, 90, 91, 104
Beers, M., 577, 578
Begley, S., 55, 62
Beital, A., 303

Belgrad, S. L., 340
Bell, C., 249
Bellah, R. N., 141
Bellinger, D., 260
Belsky, J., 121, 200, 246, 247, 252, 480
Belsky, J. K., 124
Bem, D. J., 98
Bem, S. L., 158, 313, 428
Bender, D. A., 274
Benedict, H., 227
Bengston, V. L., 572
Benjamins, M., 592
Benn, R., 248
Benne, K. D., 133
Bennett, D., 592, 593
Bennett, P., 440
Benony, H., 235
Benson, M. L., 30, 31, 32, 36
Benson, P. L., 436, 437
Berck, J., 427
Berenson, G. S., 390
Beresford, T. P., 599
Berger, K., 173, 176, 215, 216, 218
Bergquist, W. H., 550, 556
Berk, L. E., 480, 481, 513, 522, 532, 557
Berke, J., 529
Berkman, B., 596
Berlin, S., 83, 84, 91, 103, 104
Berliner, K., 477
Berlyne, D. E., 306
Berman, P. S., 16
Bernhard, L., 512, 514
Berrick, J. D., 83
Berry, J. W., 374
Berry, P., 220
Beutler, L., 16
Beyene, Y., 613
Bezman, R. J., 354
Bhavangri, N., 303
Bialystok, E., 280, 343
Biema, D. V., 443
Bienias, J., 592
Bigner, J. J., 481
Bilchik, S., 303
Birnbaum, H. J., 478
Bishop, K. K., 370
Bissaker, K., 302
Bjorklund, B. R., 224, 227, 255
Bjorklund, D. F., 224, 227, 255
Black, C., 403
Black, D., 478
Black, D. W., 58, 88
Black, K., 200
Blaine, B., 131

677

Blakeslee, S., 375, 376
Blamey, A., 516
Blando, J., 605
Blanker, M. H., 515
Blau, D. M., 252
Blazer, D., 590, 592, 596
Blechman, E. A., 399
Blehar, M., 234
Blieszner, R., 546, 603, 606, 608
Blissmer, B., 516
Blom, G. E., 340
Bloom, L., 279
Blow, F. C., 599
Bluck, S., 7, 30
Bly, R., 553
Blyth, D. A., 391, 424
Boardman, S. K., 131
Boehm, W. W., 23
Bogard, M., 555
Bogatz, G. A., 311
Bogenschneider, K., 443
Bohan-Baker, M., 308
Bond, J., 587
Bonkowski, S., 242
Bonnesen, J., 587
Bonta, J., 77
Bonvillian, J. D., 341
Bookwala, J., 604
Booth, A., 375
Booth, C. L., 235
Boring, E. G., 86
Bornstein, M., 226
Borton, R., 224, 225
Bosma, H. A., 289, 348, 401
Bossel-Lagos, M., 396
Boston Women's Health Book Collective, 521
Bostwick, G. J., Jr., 117
Botein, S., 163
Botvin, G. J., 364, 421
Bouchard, T. J., Jr., 56
Bouma, A., 185
Bourne, L. E., 88
Bower, G. H., 62
Bowlby, J., 233, 239
Bowman, L., 392
Boyette, M., 275
Bradley, R., 188, 200, 204, 258
Bradley, S. J., 435
Brame, R., 33, 35
Brandl, B., 615, 616
Bray, J. H., 542
Breedlove, G., 176
Bremmer, J. N., 229, 239, 240, 241
Brener, N. D., 440
Brennan, E., 139
Brennan, P., 185
Breon, E., 596
Bretherton, I., 289
Brice, M., 553
Briere, J., 413
Brim, O. G., Jr., 15, 116
Brink, T. L., 597
Brinton, M. C., 147
Brisby, J., 258
Broadbooks, D. Y., 336, 337
Broberg, A. G., 252
Brock, W. M., 252
Brockner, J., 110
Brody, G. H., 304
Brody, J. E., 310
Brodzinsky, D. M., 252
Broman, C., 543
Bromberger, J. T., 512
Bromwich, R., 261

Bronfenbrenner, U., 10, 16, 33, 36, 116, 310
Brooks, A., 42
Brooks, C., 478
Brooks, D., 7
Brooks, G. R., 555
Brooks-Gunn, J., 106, 162, 183, 188, 200, 204, 214, 237, 238, 252, 255, 314, 389, 391, 509
Brothers, L., 102
Brotman, S., 605
Brower, A. M., 102, 103
Brower, K. J., 599
Brown, B. B., 420, 422, 427
Brown, C. C., 358
Brown, J. V., 214, 252
Brown, L. M., 428
Brown, L. N., 130
Brown, M. A., 458
Brown, R., 94, 130
Brown, R. H., 120
Browne, A., 497
Browne, C. V., 614
Brownell, P., 615
Brownlee, S., 528
Bruckner-Gordon, F., 537
Bryant, S., 491
Buck, D., 99
Budwig, N., 280
Buehlman, K. T., 463
Bufe, C., 536
Buhs, E. S., 364
Buka, S., 183, 204
Bukowski, W. M., 290, 419
Bulcroft, K., 604
Bull, R., 339
Bullis, R., 17
Bullock, L. F., 205
Burgess, A. W., 496
Burgess, E., 587
Burke, W., 598, 599
Burnaugh, R., 553, 555
Burr, J. A., 613
Burston, N., 419
Burton, L., 254
Buskin, S., 433
Buss, D. M., 44, 46
Butler, K., 538
Butler, R. N., 574, 587, 589, 591
Butterfield, P., 230
Byrne, B., 279

Cahill, S., 605
Cairns, R. B., 16
Caldwell, B., 258
Call, J. D., 234
Calvert, P., 159
Calvert, S., 159
Cameron, K., 578
Camp, B. W., 340
Campbell, F. A., 257
Campbell, S. B., 292
Campos, J., 230
Cancro, R., 468
Canda, E. R., 17
Candace, 413
Canfield, R., 225
Caplan, G., 29, 136
Caplinger, T. E., 412
Carlip, H., 402, 430, 436
Carnegie Council on Adolescent Development, 424
Carolina Consortium on Human Development, 16
Carr, D., 605
Carroll, D. W., 95

Carskadon, M. A., 394
Carstensen, L., 573, 588, 604
Carter, B., 124, 125
Carter, I., 13, 76, 117
Cartwright, D., 130, 134
Cassel, J., 163
Castells, M., 12, 107, 109, 142
Cavanaugh, J. C., 305, 551, 553
Cazenave, N. A., 154
Ceci, S. J., 10
Center for Lesbian and Gay Rights, 151
Centers for Disease Control and Prevention, 492, 575
Chamberlain, D. B., 192, 193
Chamberlain, P., 412
Chamberlin, J., 408
Chambers, C., 150
Chambliss, L., 205
Chan, R. W., 302
Chandler, M. J., 346
Chapkis, W., 154
Chaplin, G., 44, 45
Chapman, M., 288
Charlesworth, L. W., 29
Chase, S. N., 354
Chase-Lansdale, P. I., 214, 252
Chau, A., 12
Chen, P., 613
Chen, W., 390
Cheng, T. L., 397
Cherlin, A., 548
Chernick, A. B., 435
Chess, S., 10, 230, 231
Chin, A., 599
Chobanian, A., 580
Chow, J., 308
Christakis, D. A., 310
Christensen, A., 463
Christophersen, E. R., 293
Churchman, C. W., 116
Cicchetti, D., 235, 316
Cillessen, A. H. N., 290
Cintas, H., 254
Clark, K., 531
Clark, K. B., 311
Clark, M. K., 311
Clarkberg, M., 171
Clarke-Stewart, K. A., 246, 252
Clasen, D. R., 420
Clausen, J. A., 29, 33, 36
Cleek, M., 490
Clement, P. W., 354
Cleveland, L. E., 393
Clinton, T., 392
Coard, S. I., 440
Coatsworth, J., 408
Cobb, 100
Coco, A. S., 393
Codd, J., 343
Coe, B., 443
Coe, C. L., 67
Cohen, D., 42, 81
Cohen, D. J., 280
Cohen, D. K., 424
Cohen, G., 176
Cohen, H., 603
Cohen, N. J., 342
Cohen, S., 224
Coie, J. D., 285
Coleman, M., 541, 542
Coles, C. D., 214, 252
Coles, R., 401
Coley, R., 307
Coll, C., 253, 254, 255
Colletti, L., 177

Collins, A. H., 139
Collins, P. H., 117, 154, 155, 156, 159
Comas-Diaz, L., 148
Comer, J., 368
Comfort, C., 290
Condon, W., 226
Condry, J. C., 310
Conger, R., 475
Conley, B., 246
Connell, D. B., 163
Conner, K. A., 548
Connidis, I., 606
Connolly, K. J., 287
Connolly, M., 314
Connors, M., 160
Consortium for Longitudinal Studies, 309
Constable, R., 368, 369
Conterio, K., 413
Conwell, Y., 598
Cook, E. H., 296
Cooke, T., 291
Cooley, C. H., 100, 105
Coolidge, F., 596
Cooper, J., 98
Cooper, L. B., 159
Corbley, G. J. M., 457
Corcoran, J., 440
Coren, S., 185
Cormier, R., 605
Corner, L., 587
Corrigan, P. W., 84, 85, 102
Costa, L., 284
Costa, P., 572
Costin, L., 249
Cote, J. E., 400
Cotterell, R., 146
Cottrell, D., 413, 419
Council on Social Work Education, 570
Courtney, M. E., 399
Cousins, L., 424
Cowan, C. P., 480
Cowan, G., 313, 372
Cowan, P. A., 480
Coward, R. T., 613
Cowen, E. L., 363
Cox, M. J., 480
Coyle, J. T., 354
Craig, G., 252
Crawford, N., 374, 494
Crawford, S., 511
Creno, C., 193
Crnic, K., 235, 246, 549
Crockenberg, S., 235, 246, 247, 248
Crocker, J., 400
Crockett, L. J., 432
Cromer, C. C., 361
Cronin, M., 182
Cross, A., 190
Crouter, A., 419
Crowther, M., 573
Csikszentmihalyi, M., 310, 398
Csoti, M., 366
Culbertson, J., 226
Cumming, E., 572
Cummings, E. M., 292
Cunningham, A. J., 520
Cunningham, C., 599
Cunningham, M., 391
Cunningham, P. B., 412
Cupertino, A. P., 511
Curran, D. D., 480
Cutler, N., 578

Name Index

Cutler, S., 587
Cystic Fibrosis Foundation, 51

Daglish, L., 255
Dahl, R., 394
Daley, J., 391, 397, 399, 411, 430, 442, 470
Dalgleish, T., 538
Dalton, J. H., 6, 7
Damon, W., 289
Dan, A., 512, 514
Dane, F. C., 96, 97, 98, 151, 154, 158
Daniels, D., 56
Daniels, K., 482
Dann, S., 305
Dannefer, D., 29, 37
Danziger, K., 107
Danziger, S. K., 440
Daro, D., 206
Darwin C., 44
Dasen, P. R., 396
Daugherty, J., 457
Davidov, M., 288
Davidow, A. L., 438
Davidson, E., 183, 202
Davidson, K., 606
Davidson, M., 468
Davidson, N., 535
Davies, D., 29, 162, 214, 215, 216, 223
Davies, G. M., 339, 538
Davies, P. T., 292
Davis, H., 593
Davis, I. P., 260
Davis, K. L., 468
Davis, L., 513, 538
Dawkins, R., 44
Dawson, G., 573
de Anda, D., 403
DeAngelis, T., 251, 303, 370, 511, 513, 514, 520
Deardon, R., 241
Deaux, K., 96, 97, 98, 151, 154, 158
DeBlassie, R., 403
DeBoer, M. M., 203
DeCasper, A. J., 192
Decofle, P., 183
DeGangi, G., 292
Degelman, D., 370
DeiCampo, D. S., 343
DeiCampo, R. L., 343
DeLamater, J. D., 25, 46, 96, 97, 103, 105, 106, 107
DeMaris, A., 605
Demian, 491
Demo, D. H., 480
Demo-Dananberg, L. M., 599
Denham, S., 281, 282, 302, 346
Denisoff, R. S., 120, 140
DeRoos, Y., 42
Dettwyler, K., 253
Dev, D., 51
Devaney, B. L., 252
Devault, C., 434
DeVille, C. J., 399
DeVito, J., 94
Devos, T., 105
de Vries, B., 608
DeWitt, T. G., 397
Deyo, R. A., 409
Diamond, C., 433
Diaz, R. M., 343
Diaz, T., 421
Dickerson, L. M., 456

Dickstein, S., 246, 247, 248, 260, 261
Digeronimo, T. F., 291
DiGiuseppe, D. L., 310
Dilworth-Anderson, P., 613
DiMatteo, M. R., 58, 69, 70
Dinkmeyer, D., Jr., 358
Dinkmeyer, D., Sr., 358
Dion, K., 134
Dishion, T. J., 31, 412, 413
Dixon, D., 607
Dixon, R. A., 29
Dodds, J. B., 216
Dodge, K. A., 33, 285, 290, 337
Doherty, R. W., 366
Dohrenwend, B. S., 27, 28, 29
Doll, B., 374
Dominelli, 117
Dominowski, R. L., 88
Dornbusch, S. M., 402
Dougherty, T. M., 226
Dovidio, J. F., 154, 155
Dowdall, G. W., 495
Downs, S., 249
Doyle, P., 250
Dreikurs, R., 300
Drews, C. D., 183
Drost, C., 401
Drucker, J., 302
Dryfoos, J. G., 310, 411, 412, 441
Duberstein, P., 598
Dubin, S., 526
Dubos, R., 136
Duffy, K. G., 7, 27, 28, 141
Dukes, R. L., 427
Dukette, R., 240
Dumaret, A. C., 260
Dunbar, 494
Duncan, G. J., 255, 314
Duncker, K., 92
Dungee-Anderson, D., 612, 613
Dunn, J., 248, 304
Dunn, R., 403
Dunst, C., 190
Dupree, D., 391
Durand, M., 78
Durand, V. M., 6
Durkee, R., 160
Dustman, P., 421
Duvall, E. M., 122
Duyme, M., 260
Dweck, C. S., 10, 289, 367, 373
Dwyer, J., 606
Dytrych, Z., 172
Dziech, B. W., 492
Dziegielewski, S. F., 509, 522, 530, 531, 557
Dziuba-Leatherman, J., 373, 438

Eagly, A. H., 135
Easterbrooks, M. A., 235
Eberstadt, N., 178, 202
Ebert, M. H., 87
Eccles, J., 367, 423
Eckert, P., 397
Edelbrock, C., 350
Edelman, M. W., 441
Edelstein, W., 235
Edleson, J. L., 498
Edmunds, M., 219
Edwards, C., 179
Edwards, D., 186
Edwards, J. D., 148, 149
Eells, T. D., 16
Efran, J., 301
Egan, S. K., 370

Ehrenreich, B., 488
Eisenberg, N., 287, 288
Eisendrath, S. J., 13
Ekstrand, R. R., 88
Elder, G., 590, 607
Elder, G. H., Jr., 33, 36
Elias, M. J., 6, 7
Elkind, D., 407
Elliot, N., 438
Elliott, D. S., 32
Elliott, H., 529
Ellis, S., 361
Ellwod, M. R., 252
Elwood, R., 170
Emde, R. N., 230, 232, 235, 241, 242, 246
Emery, R. E., 116
Emler, N., 404
Englander-Golden, P., 457
Enright, R. D., 527
Ephross, J., 242
Epstein, S., 160
Erickson, J., 176
Erikson, E. H., 17, 103, 131, 454, 509, 532, 570
Erikson, J. M., 570
Ervin, C., 183
Espiritu, R., 411
Etzioni, A., 141
Evans, C., 134
Evans, D., 592
Evans, G. W., 122, 162
Exner, T., 493
Eyer, D., 196
Eysenck, H. J., 511

Fagot, B., 255
Fahlberg, V., 260
Fain, T. C., 492
Faith, R. L., 131
Falk, G., 147
Farber, H., 275
Farmer, T. W., 438
Farrar, E., 424
Farrington, D. P., 409, 411
Faur, D., 576
Favazza, A., 413
Fawcett, J., 170
FBI, 150
Feagin, C. B., 152
Feagin, J. R., 152
Federal Interagency Forum on Aging-Related Statistics, 581
Feil, N., 588
Fein, G. G., 307
Feinberg, J., 577
Feinbloom, R., 179
Feindler, E. L., 421
Feinstein, S., 595
Feit, M. D., 4, 29, 42
Feld, S., 97, 98
Feldman, H., 124, 126
Feldman, J. F., 225, 226
Feldman, P. H., 613
Feldman, R. A., 412
Felice, M. E., 440
Fels, A., 253
Femia, E., 595
Fennell, E., 409
Ferketich, S. L., 247
Fernald, A., 229
Ferrante, J., 8, 10, 119, 143, 154, 159
Festinger, L., 97, 134
Field, T. M., 196, 234, 235, 247
Fifer, W. P., 192

Fine, G. A., 105, 110, 148
Fingarette, H., 536
Fingerman, K. L., 557
Finkelhor, D., 373, 426, 438
Finn, J., 138
Fishbein, D., 443
Fishbein, M., 96, 97
Fisher, D. E., 516
Fishman, J., 370
Fiske, S. T., 131, 154, 155
Fitzgibbons, R. P., 527
Flak, E., 183
Flanery, R. C., 393
Flanigan, B., 527
Flavell, J. H., 101, 396, 403
Flegal, K. M., 393
Flint, E., 592
Foddy, M., 103
Folkman, S., 29
Folsom, R., 598
Fonagy, P., 413, 419
Fongruey, L., 188, 200, 204
Forbes, J., 8
Ford, C. A., 397
Forehand, R. L., 287, 358, 375, 376
Forssman, L., 171
Forsyth, D. R., 130, 131
Fortin, L., 430
Foster, R. L., 53, 54, 219, 249, 250
Fowers, B. J., 463
Fowler, J. W., 17
Fox, J. J., 256
Fox, M., 550, 551
Fox, N. E., 235
Fozard, J., 586
Fraiberg, S. H., 241
Frame, C., 340
Frank, A., 391
Frank, D., 241, 242
Frankel, L., 149
Frankenberg, W. K., 216
Franklin, C., 118, 421, 440
Franks, M., 606
Franks, V., 159
Frede, E., 253
Freedman, D. G., 203
Freiberg, P., 492
Freimer, N. B., 61
French, J., 134
Freud, A., 78, 240, 305, 398
Freud, S., 5, 30, 75, 77, 78, 79
Fried, L. P., 609
Friedlander, M. L., 312
Friedman, M., 510
Friedman, S. L., 13, 36
Froland, C., 139
Fry, P., 606
Furino, A., 202
Furstenberg, F. F., 487, 548
Futterweit, L. R., 225, 226

Gabe, T., 252
Gabler, R. E., 10
Gaertner, S. L., 154, 155
Galambos, N. L., 373, 417
Galinsky, M., 132
Gallagher, M., 477, 543
Gallagher, R. M., 14, 91, 110
Gallagher, W., 139
Gallant, M., 606
Gallo, J., 596
Gambrill, E., 411
Ganger, W., 260
Gangi, B. K., 537
Ganong, M. D., 541, 542

Name Index

Garbarino, J., 11, 65, 121, 139, 162, 373, 419
Garcia Coll, C., 6, 14, 21, 22, 29
Garcia-Preto, N., 552
Gardner, D. M., 430
Garmon, L. C., 467
Gartner, A., 138
Gaston, M., 553
Gates, G., 478
Gaylin, W., 76
Gebhard, P. H., 578
Geldmacher, M., 592
Gelles, R., 373
Gelman, S. A., 278, 280, 312
Genel, M., 354
George, L., 592
George, N., 9
Gerard, M., 240
Gergen, K. J., 107, 129
Gerhart, U., 42
Gerlsma, C., 289, 348
Germain, C. B., 116, 136, 137, 138, 139
Geronimus, A., 178
Geroski, A. M., 293
Gerson, M. J., 484, 485
Gerth, H., 14, 24
Gfroerer, J., 598
Giannakoulopoulos, X., 192
Gibbs, J. C., 467
Gibbs, J. T., 427, 488
Gibson, P., 608
Gibson, R., 571, 603
Gichia, J. E., 509, 522, 530, 531, 557
Giddens, A., 143, 146, 153
Gidycz, C. A., 495
Giel, R., 35
Gil, E., 413
Gilbert, D., 141
Gilbert, K., 483
Gilbert, N., 83
Gilchrist, L., 190
Gilgun, J. F., 467
Gilligan, C., 405, 428, 467
Gilstrap, B., 200, 247
Ginsberg, L., 42, 47, 48
Ginsburg, H. P., 82
Glass, L., 529
Glass, S. P., 543
Glaubman, R., 573
Gleick, E., 475, 491
Glenn, N. D., 477
Glick, J., 277
Goff, S. M., 344
Golant, S., 198
Gold, D., 592
Gold, M., 411
Goldberg, S., 196
Goldenberg, R., 183
Goldman, R., 17
Goldman, J., 205, 217, 227, 238, 547
Goldman, L. S., 354
Goldsmith, E., 598
Goldson, E., 204
Goldstein, E. G., 77
Goldstein, H., 57, 59, 60, 70
Goldstein, R., 509, 543
Goleman, D., 338
Golombok, S., 312, 481
Gonsiorek, J. C., 478
Gonzalez-Santin, E., 160, 253
Goode, E., 534
Goodings, C., 418
Gordon, B., 60
Gordon, M., 197

Gordon, R. A., 214
Gordon, T., 358
Gordon-Salant, S., 586
Gorman, B. L., 119
Gorrie, T. M., 169, 170, 172, 173, 215
Gorski, P. A., 169
Gotlib, I. H., 29, 33, 37
Gottesman, I. I., 468, 469
Gottfredson, M. R., 30, 31
Gottfried, T., 440
Gottlieb, S., 186
Gottman, J. M., 281, 290, 338, 463, 475, 476
Govern, J. M., 44, 98, 99, 102
Graber, J. A., 389
Graham, S. R., 554, 555
Graham-Bermann, S. A., 498
Graves, G., 273
Gray, A., 274
Grebb, J. A., 61
Green, C., 509, 522, 530, 531, 557
Green, J. W., 17, 85, 153, 156
Green, R., 301
Green, R. G., 71
Green, T. M., 417
Greenberg, E. M., 550, 556
Greenberg, J., 536
Greenberg, M., 549
Greene, B., 148
Greene, R. R., 156, 571, 591, 606
Greenleaf, I., 392
Greenlee, R. T., 516, 517
Greenlund, K. J., 390
Gregg, V. R., 467
Griffin, K. W., 421
Griffith, D., 204, 248
Griggs, S., 403
Grimm, W. A., 344
Grinnell, R. M., 117
Grodstein, F., 514
Grossman, D. C., 409
Groth, A. N., 478
Grove, D., 553, 555
Grover, K. J., 475
Grunebaum, H. U., 163
Grusec, J. E., 196, 288
Guernsey, J., 171
Gullotta, T., 400, 401, 406
Gump, L. S., 405
Gundara, J. S., 149
Gunter-Hunt, G., 583
Guo, G., 314
Guo, S., 604
Guttman, J., 421
Guttuso, T., 515
Gwirtsman, H. E., 87
Gyurke, J., 226

Haaken, J., 537
Haan, N., 460
Haas, R., 393
Hacker, L., 138
Hader, S. L., 493
Hagan, J., 29
Hagedorn, J., 423
Hagestad, G., 37
Hagy, A. P., 252
Haith, M. M., 225, 226
Halberstadt, A. G., 313
Haley, W., 591
Hall, J. A., 313
Hall, L. A., 255, 257
Halpern, R., 255, 257
Halpern-Felsher, B. L., 397
Hamark, B., 171

Hammer, H., 426
Hammer, L. B., 547
Han, W. J., 214, 252
Hancock, L., 294
Hann, D. M., 235, 262
Hansen, J. F., 237
Hanson, H. C., 115
Harden, J. B., 399
Harley, R. M., 534
Harlow, H., 240
Harlow, S. D., 393
Harmon, R. J., 235
Harmon, R. R., 546
Harold, G., 295
Harris, J. D., 288
Harris, J. R., 301
Harris, M. B., 421
Harris, S., 89, 90
Harris, S. L., 421
Harris, V., 246
Harrison, J. L., 392
Harrison, J., 197, 198
Hart, C. H., 363, 364
Harter, J., 349, 399
Hartford, M. E., 571
Hartford, R., 220
Hartman, A., 117, 122, 603, 623, 624
Hartney, L. L., 546
Hartup, W. W., 285, 290, 305, 312, 361, 363
Harwood, D., 598
Harwood, T., 16
Haselager, G. J. T., 290
Hastorf, A. H., 102
Hatch, L., 604
Haugaard, J., 251, 252
Haugh, S. S., 313, 372
Havighurst, R. J., 468, 532, 572
Hawkins, J., 277
Hawton, K., 598
Hayden, M. F., 547
Hayes, J. A., 555
Hays, J., 592
Heagarty, L., 183, 200
Hearn, G., 116
Heatherington, E. M., 375, 376, 377, 399, 489, 541
Heaton, T. B., 489
Hebert, L., 592
Hecht, M. L., 151
Hedayat, M., 352
Heim, A. K., 110
Heinz, W. R., 36, 37
Heise, L., 496
Heller, K., 27, 139, 142
Helm, H., 592
Henggeler, S. W., 412
Hennessy, C. H., 546
Henry, W. E., 572
Hepworth, D. H., 23
Herbert, F., 340
Herek, G. M., 479
Herman, E., 535, 536
Herrerias, C. T., 294
Hersch, P., 433
Hersen, M., 542
Heymann, C., 509, 522, 530, 531, 557
Hilgard, E. R., 99
Hill, J. P., 417, 419
Hines, M., 312
Hinton, G. E., 84
Hirschi, T., 30, 31
Hodgson, L., 587
Hodson, G., 154, 155

Hofer, S., 586
Hoff-Ginsberg, E., 280
Hoffman, C. D., 313, 372
Hoffman, H., 220
Hoffman, M. L., 357
Hoffman, S., 493
Hoffman, V., 235
Hogg, M. A., 131
Hoggett, P., 139, 140
Hohman, M., 556
Hohmann-Marriott, B., 421
Holden, E., 205, 227, 238
Holland, D., 107
Hollander, J., 102
Holliday, D., 284
Holliman, D., 607
Holloway, J. H., 307
Holmbeck, G. N., 417, 419
Holmberg, S. D., 492
Holmstromm, L. L., 496
Holstein, M., 573
Homans, G. C., 130
Hong, G. S., 308
Honzik, M., 226
Hooper, C. R., 390
Hooyman, N. R., 158, 159, 575, 592, 603, 604, 605, 606, 607, 608, 609, 612, 613
Hope, T., 598
Hopper, K., 558
Horenczyk, G., 109
Horn, J. L., 586
Horowitz, S. V., 131
Horton, J., 149
Horwitz, A. V., 147
Howard, D. V., 89, 90, 92
Howard, J. A., 102
Howard, K., 417
Howe, J., 596
Howe, M., 278
Howell, C. T., 350
Howell, J. C., 422, 423
Hoyenga, K. B., 60
Hoyenga, K. T., 60
Hu, D., 176
Huang, C. C., 252
Huff, R. G., 422
Hughes, C. B., 483
Huizinga, H., 411
Humphrey, L. L., 514
Hunsberger, M. M., 53, 54, 219, 249, 250
Hunter, M. H., 456
Hunter, S., 509, 530, 531, 542, 546, 553, 556
Hutchison, E. D., 29
Hwang, C. P., 252
Hwang, M. Y., 402
Hybels, C., 596
Hyde, C., 443
Hyde, J. S., 405, 429
Hymel, S., 290, 305

Ifill-Williams, M., 421
Iglowstein, I., 394
Iliffe, S., 593
Ingersoll-Dayton, B., 547
Irwin, C. E., 397
Isay, B., 434
Isen, A. M., 102
Iyengar, S. S., 110
Izard, C., 229

Jablonski, N. B., 44, 45
Jacklin, C. N., 313, 372
Jackson, A. P., 214, 246, 252, 255

Name Index

Jackson, J. F., 236, 237
Jackson, P., 189
Jacob, D., 477
Jacobs, J., 604
Jacobsen, R. B., 481
Jacobsen, T., 235
Jacobson, B., 197
Jacobson, L. P., 35, 366
Jacobson, N. S., 463
Jacoby, L. L., 91
Jacoby, R., 598
Jaffee, K., 308
Jaffee, S., 405
James, W., 99, 105, 106
Jang, Y., 591
Janis, I. L., 135
Jankowski, J. J., 225, 226
Jannke, S., 181, 182
Janosik, E. H., 557
Jaquette, D., 347, 348
Jarjoura, D., 576
Jason, J., 188
Javroff, L., 458
Jedrychowski, W., 183
Jencks, C., 558
Jenkins, J., 305
Jennings, K., 246
Jensen, P. S., 294
Jessor, R., 432, 437, 443
Johannes, C. B., 511
John, R., 546
Johnson, 130, 131
Johnson, B., 217, 578
Johnson, D. F., 14, 17, 21
Johnson, H. C., 42
Johnson, J., 205, 217, 227, 238, 580
Johnson, J. H., 409
Johnson, M. H., 217
Johnston, L. D., 442
Jones, E., 204
Jones, J., 512, 513, 530
Jordan, C., 118
Joselson, R., 33
Josephson Institute of Ethics, 438
Jozefowicz, D., 423
Jussim, L., 104, 367

Kabacoff, R. I., 542
Kacerek, S., 595
Kaczala, C. M., 372
Kadushin, A., 278
Kadushin, G., 278
Kagan, J., 15, 215
Kahn, A. J., 252
Kahn, R. L., 573
Kahn, R. S., 468
Kakos, B., 595
Kalat, J. W., 48, 49, 50, 57, 58, 60, 61, 62, 63, 64, 85, 216, 392
Kalter, N., 375
Kamerman, S. B., 252
Kaminer, W., 537
Kammerer, N., 160
Kanter, R. M., 134
Kaplan, B. H., 163
Kaplan, G., 604
Kaplan, P. S., 388, 389, 391, 396, 398, 417, 420, 424, 427, 431, 434, 438, 440, 441
Karls, J. M., 23, 25, 26
Karmiloff-Smith, A., 217
Kashima, Y., 103
Kasl-Godley, J., 578
Kastenbaum, R., 240
Kato, T., 49

Katz, J. N., 160
Katz, L. F., 463
Kauffman, S. E., 534
Kaufman, A. S., 336, 337
Kaufman, G., 590, 607
Kaufman, S., 583
Kavanagh, K., 412
Kawakami, K., 154, 155
Kayser-Jones, J., 583
Kazdin, A. E., 340, 412
Kearney, C. A., 365, 366
Keen, S., 554
Keith, H., 257, 309
Kellner, D., 120
Kelly, J., 375, 377
Kelly, K., 392, 531
Kelly, M., 8
Kelly, P., 150
Kelly, S., 548, 549
Kemper, S., 588
Kendall, P. C., 340
Kennedy, R. E., 388
Kennedy, S., 487
Kennel, J., 175, 197
Kenrick, D., 46
Kenrick-Jones, D. T., 46
Kettner, P. M., 145
Kieburtz, K., 515
Kiefer, C. W., 464
Kiely, J. L., 179, 198
Kiesler, S., 133
Kietzman, M. L., 81, 89
Kihlstrom, J. F., 84, 90, 91, 104
Kilpatrick, D. G., 495
Kim, J., 610
Kim, S. Y., 308
King, D. B., 76
Kinsey, A. C., 578
Kirchner, J. T., 186, 294
Kirst-Ashman, K. K., 17
Kitayama, S., 109, 110
Kivett, V., 607
Kiyak, H. A., 575, 592, 603, 604, 605, 606, 607, 608, 609, 612, 613
Klaum, G. A., 550, 556
Klaus, M., 175, 194, 197
Klaus, P., 175, 194
Kleigman, R., 204
Klein, S. B., 84, 90, 91, 104
Kliewer, W., 438
Klinnert, M., 230
Kluger, J., 469
Knight, B., 589, 596
Knight, T., 573
Ko, G., 468
Kober, J., 438
Koegel, P., 559
Koenig, H., 573, 592
Kohlberg, L., 289, 403, 460
Kohn, R., 598
Konner, M., 330
Kopp, C. B., 117
Kornblum, W., 7, 11, 12
Koropeckyj-Cox, T., 613
Koss, M. P., 495
Kostelny, K., 373
Kotch, J. B., 258
Kotelchuck, M., 237
Kountz, X., 413
Kowalski, K., 189
Kraft-Ebing, R. V., 160
Krakow, J. B., 117
Kramer, B., 595
Krause, N., 592
Krebs, D. L., 467

Krebs-Smith, S. M., 393
Kreisher, K., 303
Kroonenberg, P. M., 236
Krugman, R., 220
Krysik, J., 200
Kubey, R., 310
Kuhn, D., 460
Kukathas, C., 150
Kulis, S., 421
Kunnen, E. S., 401
Kupersmidt, J. B., 337
Kurdek, L. A., 481
Kurlan, R., 515
Kurtz, Z., 413, 419
Kusumakar, V., 421
Kuwahara, K., 611
Kyte, N. S., Jr., 117

Labouvie-Vief, G., 460
Ladd, G. W., 364
Lader, W., 413
LaDue, R., 204, 205
Ladyman, S., 175
Lagercrantz, H., 197
Lahey, B. B., 30
Laird, J., 117, 122, 603
Laking, P. J., 14
Lalley, J. R., 257, 309
Lamb, L., 184
Lamb, M. E., 247, 252, 303
Lamiell, J. T., 339
Lamont, E., 408
Landau, D., 509, 543
Landes, A., 592
Landsverk, J., 260
Landy, S., 291
Lane, N., 580
Lang, H. G., 341
Langer, J., 460
Langer, N., 592
Laosa, L., 302
Lapsley, D. K., 396, 400, 404, 407
Larimore, W., 573
Larrison, C. R., 42, 47, 48
Larsen, J. A., 23
Larson, D., 592
Larson, J. H., 474, 475
Larson, R., 119, 398
Laub, J. H., 36, 37
Lavin, D., 347, 348
Lawlor, B., 599
Lawton, M. P., 611
Lazarus, R. S., 27, 400
Leaper, C., 300
Leary, M. R., 103, 104, 105
Lebassi, 54
LeBlanc, A. C., 122
LeCroy, C. W., 200, 287, 391, 397, 399, 411, 421, 430, 431, 442, 443, 470
Lederman, R. P., 169
Ledlow, S., 46
Lee, C., 605
Lee, G., 605
Lee, G. R., 477
Lee, S., 273
Leeper, J., 197
Lehmann, H. E., 468
Lembau, J. R., 172
Lemeshow, S., 54
Lemme, B. H., 37, 544, 546, 547, 550
Leon, I., 483
Leonard, G., 235
Leonard, L. G., 198,
LeProhn, N. S., 408

Lerner, R. M., 6, 10, 14, 15, 21, 22, 30, 35, 436
Lesesne, C., 358, 360
Leslie, G. R., 119
Lester, B. M., 235
Levanthal, 162
Levav, J., 35
Levenson, M. R., 511
Levine, C., 400
Levine, M., 23, 27, 28, 29
Levinson, D. J., 455, 467, 483, 531, 551
Levitt, M., 246
Lewin, D. S., 394
Lewis, D. W., 393
Lewis, E. A., 149
Lewis, K. G., 477
Lewis, M., 106, 237, 238, 248, 574, 587, 589
Libassi, M. F., 42
Lichtenberger, E. O., 336, 337
Lickey, M. E., 60
Lickona, T., 403, 405, 406
Lieberman, A. F., 232, 235, 236, 242
Lieblich, A., 33
Limaye, A., 51
Limber, S., 374
Lindemann, E., 28
Lindgren, H. C., 97
Lippa, R. A., 6, 102, 151
Lipsitz, J., 441
Little, P., 308
Little, R., 183
Littrell, J., 42, 534
Lloyd, M. A., 94, 136, 486, 495, 533, 537
Loeber, R., 409, 411
Loftus, J., 478
Long, N., 287, 358, 375, 376
Longres, J. F., 161
Lopata, H. Z., 554
Lopez, R. I., 392
Love, G. D., 66, 67
Love, J. M., 252, 253
Lowery, E. H., 140
Lowry, R., 440
Lubach, G. R., 67
Lubart, T., 592
Lucas, F., 248
Ludington-Hoe, S., 198
Ludtke, M., 182
Ludwig, A. M., 85, 87, 89, 93, 101
Luey, H. S., 529
Lukes, S., 149
Lumsden, C. J., 47
Lundell, L., 288
Luria, A., 340
Luborsky, M., 551
Lyke, B., 252
Lynch, J. P., 422, 423
Lynch, M., 197, 316
Lynch, M. E., 214, 252, 417
Lynd, R., 140
Lyon, D., 536
Lyons, M. J., 534
Lyons, P., 4, 29, 42
Lyons-Ruth, K., 163, 238, 246, 247, 248
Lyotard, J. F., 120, 121
Lytton, H., 196

Maalouf, A., 107, 109
Maas, H., 531, 532
Maccoby, E. E., 253, 255, 299, 301, 312, 313, 372, 419

MacDonald, K., 303
Mace, N. C., 547
MacIver, D. J., 366
MacIver, R., 152
MacReady, N., 296
Madden, D., 586
Madon, S., 367
Madsen, M. C., 365
Magai, C., 588
Magnan, M., 134
Magnusson, D., 13, 16
Mahalik, J. R., 555
Mahoney, J., 583
Mahoney, M. J., 7, 30, 31, 35
Main, M., 235
Main, S. R., 366
Malenchuk, O., 423
Malone, B., 404
Maluccio, A. N., 315, 316, 317, 318, 398, 399
Mammen, O. K., 236
Mandler, J. M., 100
Manly, J. T., 316
Mann, 443
Mann, L., 135
Manning, M. L., 485
Mantell, J., 493
Manthorpe, J., 593
Maramaldi, P., 596
Marcia, J., 401
Marcotte, D., 430
Markezich, A., 64
Markowitz, L. M., 496
Markowitz, S., 598
Marksteiner, J., 594
Markus, H. R., 109, 110
Marlow, L., 417
Marlowe, M., 260
Marschark, M., 341
Marti, E., 276, 277, 291, 311
Martin, C. E., 578
Martin, D. D., 105, 110, 148
Martin, J. A., 299, 419
Martin, L., 172, 186
Martin, M. C., 179, 198
Martin, S., 476, 542
Martinez, F., 220
Martinez, R. O., 427
Martire, L., 595, 604
Marwit, S., 595
Maslow, A. H., 532
Mason, C., 170
Mason, J., 202
Mason, T., 160
Massey, K., 393
Masten, A. S., 407, 408
Mastroianni, L., 172, 186
Matas, L., 235
Matejcek, A., 172
Matorras, R., 186
Matsakis, A., 495, 496
Matsumoto, D., 109, 110
Matthews, K. A., 513
Mattson, S. N., 182
Maxmen, J., 60, 61
Maxwell, M., 46
May, K., 170
Mayen, N., 613
Mayes, L. C., 280
Mayr, U., 588
Mazet, P., 235
Maziade, M., 197, 232
Mazyck, P. J., 456
McAdams, D. P., 33, 35, 106
McAuley, E., 516
McCartney, K., 56

McCarty, 310
McClelland, J. L., 84
McCloyd, V. C., 487
McConaughy, S. H., 350
McCord, J., 413, 419
McCormick, M., 183, 200
McCoy, C. R., 259
McCrae, R., 572
McCurdy, K., 204
McDermott, M. P., 515
McDougall, P., 290, 305
McEntee, M. K., 530
McEwen, B. S., 66
McFarland, K. F., 178
McFarland, P., 605, 606
McFarlane, J., 205, 206
McGoldrick, M., 124, 125
McGrath, J. E., 130, 133
McGraw, D., 528
McGregor, D., 145
McInnis-Dittrich, K., 576, 579, 591, 604, 615
McIntosh, H., 295, 296
McIntosh, P., 155
McKay, G. D., 358
McKenzie, M., 314
McKinney, E. S., 169, 170, 172, 173, 215
McLaren, J., 340
McLemore, S. D., 149, 153
McLoyd, V. C., 302, 315
McMullin, J., 606
McMurtry, S. L., 145
McQuaide, S., 509, 557
McWhirter, A. M., 432
McWhirter, B. T., 432
McWhirter, E. H., 432
McWhirter, J. J., 432
Mead, G. H., 105
Meadows, P., 609
Meckstrom, A., 253
Mednick, S., 185
Mehrabian, A., 463
Melton, G. B., 339
Meltzoff, A. N., 222, 224, 225
Melvin, C. L., 179, 198
Memmot, J., 139
Mercer, J., 214
Mercer, R. T., 247
Merola, S. S., 171
Metter, E., 572
Meuser, T., 595
Meyers, J. S., 68, 69, 70
Michener, H., 25, 46, 96, 97, 103, 105, 106, 107
Mihalic, S., 374
Mildred, B., 390
Mille, K. W., 344
Miller, A., 308
Miller, B., 604
Miller, G. A., 89
Miller, N., 134
Milligan, C. B., 409
Milligan, K. B., 200
Mills, C. W., 14, 24
Millstein, S. G., 397
Minkler, M., 573, 608
Minuchin, P. P., 368
Mischel, W., 103, 104, 106, 338
Misra, S., 599
Mitchell, J., 182
Mitchell, S. K., 235
Mitiguy, J. S., 523
Mitzner, T., 588
Mize, J., 302
Moen, P., 29, 610

Moffitt, T. E., 29, 31, 139, 140, 142
Mohler-Kuo, M., 495
Molidor, C., 438
Monat, A., 27
Montemayer, R., 417
Montgomery, M. B., 344
Moore, J., 423
Moore, J. S., 492
Moore, K. L., 174
Moore, M., 225
Morell, C. M., 614
Morelli, G., 7
Morf, C. C., 104, 106
Mortimer, J., 591
Mortweet, S. L., 293
Mounts, N., 427
Mrazek, P., 258
MTA Cooperative Group, 352
Mueller, E., 248
Mueller, M., 607
Mullan, J. T., 595
Munayer, S., 109
Munholland, K. A., 289
Munn, P., 248
Munoz, E., 202
Munoz, K. A., 393
Murphy, C. C., 183
Murray, 261
Murray, B., 520
Murray, S. S., 169, 170, 172, 173, 215
Musick, M., 592
Mutchler, J. E., 613
Mutrie, N., 516
Mutryn, C., 186
Myer, E., 253, 254, 255
Myers, B., 196
Myers, C., 253, 474
Myers, D. J., 25, 46, 96, 97, 103, 105, 106, 107
Myss, C., 17

Nackerud, L., 42, 47, 48
Nadeau, J., 8
Naditz, A., 592, 593
Nagayama-Hall, G. C., 12
Najem, G. R., 438
Nansel, T. R., 373
Nash, J., 62
Nash, M., 156, 157
National Academy on an Aging Society, 580, 581
National Association for the Education of Young Children, 308
National Association of School Psychologists, 282
National Association of Social Workers, 12, 494
National Association of State Budget Officers, 253
National Center for Early Development & Learning, 253
National Center for Education Statistics, 425
National Center for Health Statistics, 202, 433
National Center for Infant Mental Health, 218
National Center for Infants, Toddlers, and Families, 217
National Center on Elder Abuse, 615
National Clearinghouse on Child Abuse and Neglect Information, 316, 317

National Coalition Against Domestic Violence, 497
National Council of La Raza, 151
National Council on Family Relations, 126
National Council on Homelessness, 497
National Governors' Association, 253
National Institute for Literacy, 528
National Institute of Child Health and Human Development Study of Early Child Care, 252, 253
National Institute of Environmental Health Sciences, 274, 275
National Institute of Mental Health, 469, 596, 598
National Institute on Aging, 575, 579, 580, 586, 587, 593, 594
National Institute on Alcohol and Alcoholism, 533
National Organization for Women, 497
National Research Council, 295, 425
National Youth Gang Center, 423
Navaie-Waliser, M., 613
Neal, M. B., 547
Neale, M. C., 478
Nee, V., 147
Needlman, H., 260
Needlman, R., 241, 242
Neimark, E. D., 460
Nelson, H. D., 514
Nelson, R. E., 10
Nesselroade, C. S., 587
Netting, F. E., 145
Neubeck, K. J., 154
Neugarten, B. L., 531
Newberger, E., 205, 206
Newman, B. M., 472, 483, 550
Newman, B. S., 161
Newman, L., 183, 204
Newman, L. S., 90, 102
Newman, P. R., 29, 472, 550, 551, 556, 557, 570
Newsom, E., 613
Newton, P. M., 467
Newton, R., 260
Nickerson, E. T., 486
Nicol, S. E., 469
Nier, J. A., 154, 155
Nieto, A., 186
Nisbet, R. E., 109, 110
Nitz, K., 440
Niven, C., 235
Noe, R. A., 484
Noel, M., 574
Nolen-Hoeksema, S., 470
Novack, L. L., 341
Nuckolls, K. B., 163
Nunez, J., 12
Nurcombe, B., 14, 87, 91, 110
Nurius, P. S., 102, 103
Nutt, E. A., 555
Nygren, P., 514
Nylund, D., 351

O'Connell, H., 599
Oden, S., 363
O'Donnell, L., 546
Offer, D., 417
Office of Juvenile Justice and Delinquency Programs, 422
O'Hare, W. P., 12

Name Index

Okamoto, S. K., 421
Okun, B. F., 78
O'Leary, S., 247
Oliver, G. D., 435
Olsen, J., 172
Olshansky, E., 482
Olson, D. H., 463
Oltmanns, T. F., 116
Olweus, D., 285, 374
O'Malley, P. M., 442
Opie, I., 330
Opie, P., 330
Orlansky, M. D., 341
Ortiz, L., 592
Ortiz, S., 62
Osofsky, J. D., 235, 262, 291
Ostrom, T., 102
Ostrov, E., 417
Ostwald, S., 595
Ouchi, W. G., 145, 146
Owen, M., 252
Owens, T. J., 103, 107
Oyserman, D., 248
Ozer, E. J., 438

Paff-Bergen, L. A., 475
Page, D. S., 59
Page-Lieberman, J., 483
Palisi, B. J., 522
Pancake, V. R., 235
Pancoast, D. L., 139
Papillon, M., 430
Papousek, H., 233
Papousek, M., 233
Park, M. A., 393
Parke, R. D., 247, 303
Parker, J. G., 290
Parker, M., 573
Parker, P., 139
Parry, J., 604, 610
Parsons, B. V., 412
Parsons, J. E., 372
Parten, M., 306
Paschall, M. J., 443
Pasui, K., 178
Pasupathi, M., 588
Paternoster, R., 33
Patterson, C. J., 302, 480
Patterson, G. R., 31, 412
Patterson, S., 139
Paulson, R., 482
Pawlak, E. J., 424
Payne, P., 274
Paz, H., 403
Pea, R. D., 277
Peak, T., 548
Peake, P. K., 338
Pearlin, L. I., 595
Pearson, T., 490
Pecora, P. J., 316, 317, 318, 398, 399, 408
Peebles, C., 262
Peek, C. W., 613
Pelligrini, A. D., 306
Pelzer, D., 319
Pemberton, M., 598
Penfield, W., 90
Peng, T. R., 613
Penn, D. L., 84, 85, 102
Penne, M., 598
Peplau, L. A., 478
Perkins, D., 23, 27, 28, 29
Perkins, D. F., 35
Perkins, K., 599
Perot, P., 90
Perou, R., 358, 360

Perrin, J. M., 294
Perrin, S., 170
Perrow, C., 145
Perry, T., 65, 160, 253
Perry, D. G., 370
Perzanowski, C. M. C., 274
Perzanowski, M. S., 274
Peskin, E., 593, 594
Petechuk, D., 411
Petersen, A. C., 388, 389, 432
Peterson, C., 6
Peterson, D. R., 16
Petr, C. G., 412
Petri, H. L., 44, 98, 99, 102
Petrila, J., 339
Petrinovich, L., 46
Petronio, R. J., 411
Petty, F., 598, 599
Pfeiffer, E., 593, 594
Pfrieger, F. W., 60
Phillips, J., 413, 419
Phillips, K. R., 487
Phillips, L., 397
Piaget, J., 277, 306, 346, 396, 459
Pica, R., 332
Pieper, C., 596
Pierce, L., 606
Pietrukowicz, M., 255, 257
Piguet, O., 586
Pill, R., 241
Pillard, R. C., 478
Pindell, T., 139
Pinderhughes, E. E., 157, 252
Pine, B. A., 315, 318
Pinker, S., 279, 301
Pinquart, M., 590
Pipp, S., 235
Pistrang, N., 517
Pitner, R., 117
Pitochelli, E. T., 486
Pitre, G., 148, 149
Plantz, M. C., 373
Platts-Mills, T. A., 274
Platzman, K. A., 214, 252
Pleck, J. H., 487
Plomin, R., 55, 56
Polen, A., 576
Pollard, K. M., 12
Pomerantz, E. M., 367
Pomerantz, S., 59
Pomeroy, W. B., 578
Pope, K., 435
Porsteinsson, A., 593, 594
Porter, G. K., 553
Porter, S., 186
Porzelius, L. K., 16, 19
Potocky, M., 345
Potocky-Tripodi, M., 427
Potvin, P., 430
Poulin, F., 413
Poulin, J., 534
Powell, A. G., 424
Power, F. C., 400
Poythress, N. G., 339
Pratt, M. W., 340
President's New Freedom Commission on Mental Health, 11
Prewitt, V., 460
Price, C., 610
Price, R., 27, 139, 142
Puri, B. K., 14
Putnam, R., 142
Putnam, S., 10

Quatman, T., 398
Quay, H. C., 352

Rabasca, L., 409
Raber, S., 419
Rabins, P. V., 547, 596
Raboy, B., 302
Radin, N., 97, 98, 248, 440
Radke-Yarrow, M., 288
Radwin, E., 528
Raffaelli, M., 443
Raine, A., 185
Ramey, C. T., 200, 257
Ramey, S. L., 200, 257, 309
Randels, S., 204, 205
Rank, M., 488
Ransford, H. H., 522
Rapalje, J., 370
Rapp, C. A., 161
Rapp, S. R., 514
Rauch, J., 51, 52
Raven, B., 134
Rawlins, R. P., 50
Raymond, A., 274
Reeder, S., 172, 186
Rees, J., 239
Reid, J. B., 30
Reid, J. D., 557
Reid, W. H., 31
Reinharz, S., 27, 139, 142
Reiss, I. R., 122
Renfrow, D. G., 102
Rennell, C. L., 399
Renninger, K. A., 16
Renshaw, P. D., 305
Renwick, S., 404
Resnick, C., 498
Rest, J. R., 404
Retschitzki, J., 396
Reuman, D. A., 366
Reus, V. I., 61
Ricciardelli, L., 573
Rice, F., 295
Rice, K. G., 407
Rice-Oeschger, L., 595
Richard, J. F., 362, 365
Richards, M. H., 438
Richardson, A., 578
Richardson, D. K., 88
Richardson, J. G., 372
Richardson, K., 116
Richardson, V., 590
Richmond, J. B., 309
Rickert, V. I., 393
Rideout, V. J., 310
Rider, E. A., 339, 377, 467
Ridgeway, C. L., 134
Riessman, F., 138
Riger, S., 27, 139, 142
Riley, E. P., 182
Rinehart, B. H., 612
Ritter, M., 56
Ritzer, G., 12
Rivas, R. F., 130, 132, 133, 134, 138
Rix, S., 609
Roberto, K., 603, 606, 608
Roberts, J., 197
Roberts, P., 467
Robertson, I., 153
Robertson, J. G., 247
Robin, A., 440
Robins, E., 51
Robins, L. N., 33
Robinson, D., 241
Robinson, J. P., 487
Robinson, N. S., 399
Rockwood, K., 593
Rodgers, L. A., 293

Roe, K., 608
Roedding, J., 197
Roff, M., 362
Roff, S., 598
Rogers, R., 202
Rogoff, B., 7, 8, 9, 361
Rokach, A., 465
Rokeach, M., 8
Roll, S., 405
Rollins, B. C., 124, 126
Roobeek, A. J. M., 42
Rose, S. A., 225, 226
Rose, S. D., 134, 287
Rose, T. L., 597
Rosenbaum, L. K., 200
Rosenberg, F., 398
Rosenberg, M., 398
Rosenberg, S., 106, 107
Rosenblatt, A., 132
Rosenblum, O., 235
Rosenman, R. F., 510
Rosenthal, R., 366
Rosowsky, E., 596
Ross, D., 81
Ross, L., 607
Ross, S., 81
Rossiter, C., 548
Rothbart, M. K., 10
Rothblum, E. D., 159
Rousseau, M. F., 141
Rovee-Collier, C., 225
Rovine, M., 200, 247, 252
Rowe, B. R., 308
Rowe, J. W., 573
Rowland, M. D., 412
Rubin, K. H., 290
Rubin, K. N., 307
Rubin, R., 169
Rubinstein, R. L., 551
Rudolph, K. D., 367
Ruggiero, K. J., 495
Rumbaut, R. G., 487
Rumelhart, D. E., 84
Rushdie, S., 153
Russel, R., 419
Russell, A., 300, 302
Russell, C. S., 413, 475
Russell, J. J., 393
Rutecki, G., 576
Rutter, M., 33, 62, 240, 408
Ryan, B., 605
Ryan, S., 599
Ryff, C. D., 66, 67, 161, 545

Sachs, B., 255, 257
Saebel, J., 300, 302
Safe Schools, 438
Sagi, A., 236
St. Clair, M., 76, 77, 78
St. James, J., 192
Sakamoto, I., 117
Saleebey, D., 13, 14, 42, 72
Sales, B. D., 30
Salthouse, T., 586
Salzman, 42
Sameroff, A., 246
Sampson, R. J., 36, 37
Sanchez, S., 487
Sanders, P., 300
Sanders, S., 478, 590, 595, 605, 606, 608
Sandmaier, M., 608
Sandstrom, K. L., 105, 110, 148
Santelli, J. S., 440
Santor, D. A., 421

Santrock, J. W., 273, 279, 331, 388, 397, 401, 402, 423, 427, 428, 431, 432, 441, 456, 544
Sattar, S., 598, 599
Sattler, A. L., 397
Sauer, M., 482
Saunders, J. T., 550
Saussure, F. de, 94
Savageau, J. A., 397
Scanlon, B., 596
Scarf, M., 515
Scarr, S., 56
Schaffer, H. R., 104
Schaie, K. W., 525, 526, 576, 585, 586, 587, 592, 596, 604
Scheff, T., 100
Schein, E. H., 131
Scherr, P., 592
Schilling, R., 190
Schinke, S., 190
Schirm, V., 581, 583
Schmidt, R., 594
Schneider, B. H., 419, 420
Schneider, L., 593, 594
Schochet, P. Z., 253
Schoem, D., 149
Schoenwald, S. K., 412
Schonert-Reichl, K., 290
Schopler, J., 132
Schouten, F., 424
Schreier, S., 375
Schriver, J. M., 95, 122, 145
Schulenberg, J. E., 442, 599
Schuller, V., 172
Schultz, D. P., 76
Schultz, S. E., 76
Schulz, R., 595, 604
Schumm, W. R., 475
Schuster, C. S., 17, 47, 169, 172, 192, 241, 249, 310, 344, 389
Schut, H., 590
Schwartzberg, N., 477
Schwendinger, R., 422
Schwendinger, W., 422
Schwitalla, A. M., 42
Scott, W. R., 147
Scribner, S., 277
Searleman, A., 185
Sears, M., 300
Sears, W., 300
Secombe, K., 477
Sedgwick, T., 598
Sedlak, A. J., 426
Segal, D., 596
Seidenfeld, M. K., 393
Seidman, S., 160
Seifer, R., 260, 261
Seitz, V., 200
Seligman, C. K., 289, 367
Seligman, M. E. P., 6, 289, 290, 367, 532
Selman, R. L., 346, 347, 348, 407
Seltzer, M. M., 545
Selye, H., 27
Semple, S. J., 595
Sennett, R., 100
Sepkoski, C., 176
Seppa, N., 425, 529
Serra, M., 186
Settersten, R. A., Jr., 487
Seymour, C., 303
Shaffer, D. R., 51, 52, 78, 106, 117, 127, 215, 216, 227, 229, 230, 255, 301, 305, 343, 372
Shafritz, J. M., 144

Shanahan, M. J., 36
Shapira, A., 365
Shapiro, E. K., 368
Shapiro, I., 150
Shaw, 257
Shaw, M. E., 130
Shea, J. D. C., 290
Sheats, P., 133
Sheehan, D., 581, 583
Sheehy, G., 509
Shehan, C. L., 477
Sheibel, A. B., 62
Shema, S., 604
Shenfield, T., 343
Shenk, D., 611
Sherif, C. W., 130
Sherif, M., 130, 361
Shike, M., 517
Shils, E., 10
Shipman, G., 391
Shoda, Y., 338
Slure, M., 291
Shute, N., 531
Sieger, C., 583
Siegler, R. S., 278
Sigelman, C. K., 51, 52, 78, 117, 127, 339, 377, 467
Sigman, G. S., 393
Sigman, M., 226
Silva, M., 241, 242
Silver, P., 534
Silverberg, S., 419
Silverman, P. R., 136, 137, 139
Simmell, G., 100
Simmons, R. G., 391, 398, 424
Simons, L. G., 31, 36
Simons, R., 489
Simons, R. L., 31, 36
Simpson, C. H., 373
Singer, B. H., 66, 67, 161, 545
Singer, L., 187
Skaff, M. M., 595
Skeels, H. M., 239, 240
Skinner, B. F., 80
Skodak, M., 240
Slanetz, P., 354
Slaughter-Defoe, D. T., 302
Sleek, S., 282, 286, 302, 479, 498, 520, 555
Slobogin, C., 339
Small, B., 587, 591
Smart, B., 120
Smeeding, T., 487
Smetana, J. G., 417, 418
Smith, C., 358, 360
Smith, D. K., 492
Smith, H., 577
Smith, M. B., 107
Smith, N., 580
Smith, P., 255
Smith, P. K., 287, 363, 364
Smith, R., 249, 250, 311
Smucker, W. D., 352
Smyth, K., 595
Snowden, D., 594
Snowden, L., 308
Snyder, H., 411
Society for Adolescent Medicine, 397
Society for Neuroscience, 64
Sokol, B. W., 346
Sokol, R., 182
Soldan, J., 184
Solomon, J., 235
Solomon, R. C., 464
Sommers, C. H., 431

Son, S., 294
Sonleitner, F. J., 457
Sorensen, S., 590
South, K., 605
Southern Poverty Law Center, 150
Sowell, 64
Spade, J., 605
Spar, K., 252
Sparrowe, L., 486
Specht, R., 252
Spelke, E., 225
Spencer, L. J., 136
Spencer, M. B., 391, 402
Spencer, P. E., 227
Sperry, S., 592
Spiegel, D., 520
Spieker, S. J., 235
Spiro, A., III, 511
Spitz, R. A., 239, 291
Spitze, G., 606
Sprich-Buckminster, S., 177
Spring, B., 81, 89
Spurlock, J., 553
Srinivasan, S. R., 390
Srull, T. K., 102
Stacey, N., 241
Stake, J. E., 399
Stanley-Hagan, M., 489, 541
Starbuck, G. H., 122, 170
Staub, E., 131
Staudinger, U. M., 7, 30, 460, 461, 592
Steele, T. L., 160
Steil, J. M., 486
Stein, G., 186
Stein, M. T., 294
Stein, N., 278
Stein, Z., 493
Steinberg, L., 417, 418, 419, 420, 439, 544, 545
Steiner, R. F., 59
Steinmetz, S., 373
Stepfamily Association of America, 124
Stephan, C. W., 131
Stephan, W., 131
Stern, C., 339
Stern, D., 222, 224, 238
Stern, W., 339
Sternberg, R. J., 461, 464, 465, 471, 592
Steur, F. B., 311
Stevens, L. E., 131
Stevenson, H. W., 423
Stevenson, M. F., 177, 218, 226, 227, 240, 241
Stewart, J., 398
Stewart, R. B., 305
Stipek, D. J., 309
Stipp, D., 221
Stoller, E., 571, 603
Stoner, J. A. F., 135
Stoudemire, A., 78
Strauss, M., 224, 373, 592
Strawbridge, W., 604
Street, E., 184
Streissguth, A., 204, 205
Stroebe, M., 590
Strong, B., 434
Stroufe, L. A., 235
Stuart, R. B., 463
Stueve, A., 546
Sue, S., 12
Sullivan, P., 388
Sullivan, R., 605
Sumner, W. G., 146

Sundel, M., 509, 530, 531, 542, 546, 553, 556
Sundel, S. S., 509, 530, 531, 542, 546, 553, 556
Sunderland, T., 574, 587, 589
Suomi, S., 240
Suyemoto, K. L., 413
Swanson, D. P., 391
Swanson, J. M., 352, 353
Swearer, S. M., 373, 374
Swinburne, R., 17
Symanski, M., 196
Symons, D., 44

Tajfel, H., 131
Takahashi, K., 236
Takaki, R., 148, 149
Takamura, J., 546
Takanishi, R., 170
Tangney, J. P., 103, 104, 105
Tannen, D., 461, 462
Target, M., 413, 419
Tasker, F., 481
Taussig, C., 200
Tavris, C., 486, 537
Teasdale, J. B., 84
Tedder, J., 196
Teitelbaum, M. A., 219
Tellegen, A., 56
Terkel, S., 550
Termine, N., 230
Teutsch, S. M., 514
Thapar, A., 295
Thiedke, C. C., 293
Thoman, E. B., 217
Thomas, A., 10, 230, 231
Thomas, R. B., 489
Thompson, R. F., 216
Thorpe, J. A., 176
Tice, C., 599
Tighe, E. G., 498
Timasheff, N. S., 120
Tinsley, B., 247
Tizard, B., 239
Tolman, R., 438
Tomblin, J. B., 342
Tomkiewiez, S., 260
Toomey, B. G., 479
Torestad, B., 13, 16
Tornstam, L., 573
Torrey, E. F., 468, 558
Toseland, R. W., 130, 132, 133, 134, 138, 548
Towle, C., 17
Townsend, A., 604
Tracy, E. M., 315, 318
Traphagen, K., 592
Treadwell, K. R. H., 340
Treasaden, I. H., 14
Trickett, P. E., 309
Trivette, C., 190
Troiano, R. P., 393
Troiden, R., 434
Troop, W., 364
Trotter, R., 229
Trout, M., 239, 240, 241
Tsay, J. C., 443
Tsuang, M. T., 534
Tulman, L., 170
Turetsky, B. A., 486
Turiel, E., 358
Turner, F. J., 131
Turner, J., 118, 599
Turner, J. C., 130
Turner, L. D., 344
Turner, R. J., 163

Twenge, J. M., 400
Tyler, T. R., 131

Uddenberg, N., 171
Underwood, M. K., 285, 288, 411
Unger, D. G., 141
The Urban Institute, 557, 558
U.S. Bureau of the Census, 124, 252, 256, 374, 454, 473, 483, 570, 608, 610
U.S. Centers for Disease Control, 492
U.S. Department of Education, 373, 526
U.S. Department of Health and Human Services, Office of Minority Health, 12
U.S. Department of Justice, 497

Vaillancourt, T., 305
Vale, J. R., 45, 46
Vallant, G. E., 531
Vandell, D., 248
van de Meer, A., 188
Vandenberg, B., 307
Van Den Bergh, N., 159
Vandenbosche, R. C., 186
Vandermassen, G., 10, 44, 47
Vandewater, E. A., 310
Van Doorninck, W. J., 340
Vanhasselt, V. B., 542
Van Ijzendoorn, M. H., 236
Van Strien, J., 185
Veenstra-Vanderweele, J., 296
Verdoux, H., 185
Vernon, I. S., 160
Vest, J., 528
Vetter, H. J., 95
Vida, M., 423
Villar, J., 186
Viney, W., 76
Vining, J. W., 10
Viviansayles, P. J., 518
Voda, A. M., 512
Vosler, N. R., 247
Vygotsky, L. S., 306, 340

Wach, T. D., 13, 36
Wade, C., 486
Wagner, D. A., 423
Wagner, S., 235
Wahl, H. W., 611
Wahlin, A., 587
Wahrman, R., 120, 140
Wainryb, C., 346
Waite, L., 477, 543
Wald, E., 541
Waldgogel, J., 214, 252
Waldman, I. D., 30
Walker, L., 467
Wall, S., 234
Wallace, D., 580
Wallace, L. E., 31, 36
Wallerstein, J. S., 375, 376, 543
Wallhagen, M., 604
Wallman, G. U., 537
Walsh, D., 175
Walz, T., 578
Wandersman, A., 6, 7, 27, 139, 141, 142
Wandrei, K. E., 23, 25, 26
Wang, H. Y., 490
Wapner, 27
Ward, N., 60, 61
Wark, G. R., 467
Warner, D. C., 202
Warren, K., 182
Wartella, E. A., 310
Waters, D., 550
Waters, E., 234
Waters, M., 118, 119, 120, 144
Watson, C. M., 398
Watson, J., 595
Watson, J. B., 79
Watt, H. M. G., 423
Wattigney, W. A., 390
Weaver, C. N., 477
Webb, M. B., 399
Wechsler, H., 495
Weiner, L., 492
Weinman, J., 83
Weinreich, P., 45, 103, 107
Weisman, G. D., 611
Weiss, M. J., 421
Weiss, R. S., 490
Weiten, W., 27, 46, 61, 85, 86, 90, 91, 93, 94, 99, 136, 334, 486, 495, 533, 537
Welch, M. J., 274, 275
Wentzel, N., 288
Werner, J., 253
Werry, J. S., 352
Wessels, H., 252
West, D. J., 409
Westcott, H. L., 339
Westen, D., 110
Westinghouse Learning Corp., 309
Wetherbee, K., 408

Weymann, A., 37
Wheaton, B., 29, 33, 37
Whitbeck, P. H., 144
White, J. L., 413
White, L. K., 475
White, R. W., 102
Whitfield, C. L., 537
Whiting, B. B., 288
Whiting, J. W. M., 288
Whitmore, M. R., 457
Whittaker, J. K., 139, 316, 317, 318, 398, 399
Whorf, B. L., 339
Wickens, G., 340
Widmayer, S., 196
Widom, C. S., 35
Wilcox, L. S., 179, 198
Wilhelm, B., 607
Williams, B., 546
Williams, C. L., 374
Williams, D. R., 458
Williams, J. B. W., 24, 25
Williams, L. B., 170, 171
Williams, S. R., 50
Williams, S. W., 613
William T. Grant Foundation, 487, 488
Willinger, M., 220
Willis, D., 205, 227, 238
Willis, S. L., 525, 526, 557, 576, 585, 586, 587, 592, 596, 604
Willwerth, J., 182
Wilmoth, J. M., 613
Wilson, E. O., 47
Wilson, J. F., 47, 48, 49, 58, 60
Wilson, K. J., 70
Winawer, S., 517
Wind, R., 262
Wing, E., 66, 67
Wingfield, J. C., 66
Winkler, A. E., 170, 171
Wintgens, A., 235
Wisch, A. F., 555
Wisner, K., 246
Wisniewski, J. J., 479
Wisniewski, N., 495
Wisniewski, C., 235
Witherspoon, D., 91
Wodarski, J. S., 4, 29, 42, 412
Wolden, A., 615
Wolf, R. S., 615
Wolff, P. H., 217
Wong, F. Y., 7, 27, 28, 141
Wood, N., 582

Wood, W., 135
Woods, N. F., 458
Woods, S., 198
Woodward, K., 106
Worden, J., 589
Wrightsman, L. S., 96, 97, 98, 151, 154, 158
Wu, M., 443
Wulf, S., 366
Wyer, R. S., 102
Wynn, K., 225

Yalom, I., 134
Yamashita, T., 187
Yankelovich, D., 491
Yanos, J., 242
Yardley, L., 577
Yeargin-Allsopp, M., 183
Yeast, J., 176
Yeh, C. J., 401, 402
Yelland, N., 300
Yersavage, J. A., 597
Yogman, M., 247
Yoon, M., 197
Young, J. E., 466
Young, J. P., 599
Young, K., 12
Young, V. H., 236
Yurgelun-Todd, D., 392
Yussen, S. R., 404

Zablotsky, D., 611
Zahn-Waxler, C., 288
Zajonc, R. B., 99
Zander, A., 130
Zane, N., 12
Zarit, S., 595
Zastrow, C., 17
Zeanah, C. H., 235, 236, 238, 246
Zeiss, A., 578
Zeki, S., 464
Zero to Three Diagnostic Classification Task Force, 217
Ziegler, J. A., 2
Zigler, E., 177, 200, 218, 226, 227, 240, 241, 309
Zimmerman, 310
Zolotow, C., 420
Zsembik, B. A., 613
Zubin, J., 81, 89
Zucker, K. J., 435
Zuniga, X., 149
Zurcher, L., 107

SUBJECT INDEX

Page numbers in italics indicate exhibits.

AA. *See* Alcoholics Anonymous
AAP. *See* American Academy of Pediatrics
AARP, 248, 549, 607
abandonment, fear of, 376. *See also* headings starting with "separation"
abortion, 171–172, 184
abstinence-only programs, 442
abstraction, 93
abuse. *See* child abuse; domestic violence; elder abuse
acceptance of mortality, 531
accommodation, 82, 396
acculturation, 345
acetylcholine, 61
Achenbach Child-Behavior Checklist, 350, *351*
Achievement Place, 412
acne, 393
acquaintance rape, 495
ACTH (adrenocoricotropic hormone), 70–71
acting out, 350
active listening, 358
active sleep, 194, 217
activity theory, 572
acute bronchitis, 70
adaptation, 6, 82
adenosine triphosphate (ATP), 49
ADHD. *See* attention deficit/hyperactivity disorder
Administration on Aging, 609
adolescence, 386–451
   assets for youth, 436–437, *437*
   attitudes and emotions in, 397–400
   biophysical growth and development in, 389–392
   cognitive development and information processing in, 395–396, 418
   communication in, 396–397
   defined, 388
   delinquency in, 30–31, 411–412
   depression in, 408–409, 430–431, 448–450
   developmental changes of, *388*
   drug and alcohol use in, *442*, 442–443
   eating disorders and, 413
   employment in, 438–439
   family and, 417–419
   foster care and, 398–400
   gender issues in, 428–431
   homosexuality in, 433–435
   hormonal changes, 390–392
   immigrants, 427–428
   moral development in, 403–406, *404–405*
   parental relationships, 544–545
   peer groups in, 419–420, 421–422, 427
   pregnancy and birth in (*see* teen pregnancy)
   psychological strengths and hazards in, 407–413
   risk behaviors of, 437–438
   runaways, *426*, 426–427
   school influences in, 423–425
   self-esteem in, 398–401, *401*, 438–439
   sexuality in, 431–436
   social cognition and regulation in, 400–407
   teen parents (*see* teen pregnancy)
adoption
   adolescent parents and, 440
   infants, 248–252
   open, 249
   paternal rights issue, 250–251
   transracial, 249–250, 312
adoption study, 55
adrenal glands, 70
adult day-care programs, 595
adult development, stages of, 454–455, *455*, 525
adulthood. *See* late adulthood; middle adulthood; young adulthood
advance directives for health care, 582–583
affect, 101
African Americans
   adoption and, 249
   AIDS and, 492
   Alzheimer's disease and, 594
   assessment of, 14, 476
   attachment patterns and, 236–237
   breast cancer and, 518
   developmental competencies in minority children, *22*
   dialects of, 344, *485*
   discrimination of (*see* discrimination)
   employment and, 557
   families of, 476
   gangs and, 423
   health disparities and, 458, 521
   homicide rate for teens, 438
   hypertension and, 553, 581
   hysterectomies and, 513
   identity development in, 401–402, 427
   infant mortality and, 202, 220
   late adulthood and, 613
   lead poisoning and, 260
   life expectancy of, 51, 575
   marital satisfaction among, 543
   men's issues and, 555
   parenting styles, 302
   rites of passage for youth, 371
   self-esteem of adolescents, 400
   sexual activity among adolescents, 431
   sickle-cell disease and, 51
age
   at death, 581
   functional age, 571
   of grandparents, 548
   of mother, 178–179
Age Discrimination in Employment Act of 1986, 609
ageism, 614
agency, 118
aggression
   curbing, 286–287
   developmental trajectories for aggressive behavior, *33*
   in early childhood, 285–286
   gender and, 158, *158*
   hormones and, 71
   in middle childhood, 338, 350, 357
   parental discipline and, 357
   parent-training model for, 412
   television and, 286, 310–311
   warning signs in children for, 287
AGIL scheme, 119
AIDS, 479
   adolescent males and prevention, 433
   gay image and, 479
   older adults and, 579
   pregnancy and, 180
   prevention programs, 492–493
   spirituality of women with AIDS, 494
Alcoholics Anonymous (AA), 137–138, 535–536
alcohol-related birth defect (ARBD), 183
alcohol use
   in adolescence, 442–443
   domestic violence and, 498–500
   in late adulthood, 598–599, *599*
   maternal, 182–183
   in middle adulthood, 533–535, 563–566
   in young adulthood, 498–500
   See also fetal alcohol syndrome (FAS)
alertness, 85, 194
allostasis, 66
allostatic load, 67
alpha-fetoprotein blood screening, 183–184
altruism
   in children, 287–288, 346
   genetic altruism, 46
alveoli, 69
Alzheimer's disease, 91, 581, *587*, 592–595
American Academy of Pediatrics (AAP), 202–203, 220, 221, 283
   on TV and preschool children, 310
American Psychiatric Association, 303
American Sign Language (ASL), *341*, 341–342, 463, 529
American Sociology Association, 101
amino acids, 59, 61
amniocentesis, 184
amniotic sac, 173
androcentricity, 158
androgen, 391
androgyny, 313, 428
andropause, 512
anemia, 69, 179, 440
anesthesia and childbirth, 175–176
anger, 282, 476
angina pectoris, 69

687

anhedonia, 596
animism, *284*
anoxia, 185
antidepressants, 354, 469
  See also medications
anxiety, 530–531
anxiety disorders in early childhood, 293–294
Apgar score, 176–177, *177*
aphasia, 91
apraxia. *See* Alzheimer's disease
ARBD. *See* alcohol-related birth defect
ART. *See* assisted reproductive technology
arteriosclerosis, 69
arthritis, 579–580
Asian Health Project, 521
ASL. *See* American Sign Language
Asperger's Disorder, 295
assessment
  of alcoholism, 533
  biopsychosocial, 13
  of childhood behavior, 292–293, 363
  community and organizational, 5
  cultural diversity, 11–13
  current perspective, 13
  developmental perspective, 13
  of fetal alcohol syndrome, *205*
  of home environment, 257–258
  learning, 5
  medical, 4–5
  of mental illness, 469
  of minority infants, 254–255
  multidimensional framework, applying, 17–23
  psychodynamic, 5
  social group, 5
  spiritual dimension, 17–18
  strengths, 5–6
ASSETS, building assets for youth, 436–437, *437*
assimilation, 82, 153, 396
assisted reproductive technology (ART), 179
associationism, 87
asthma, 70, 274–275, 499
astrocytes, 60
ATP (adenosine triphosphate), 49
attachment
  adolescents and, 418–419
  day care and, 252
  infants and, 232–235, *233*, *236*, 239–241
  multicultural considerations, 236–237
attention, 19, 87
attention deficit/hyperactivity disorder (ADHD), 4, 15, 185, 294, 350–352, 381–384
attitude, defined, 96, 97
attitudes and emotions
  in adolescence, 397–400
  in early childhood, 281–288
  in infancy, 229–237
  in late adulthood, 588–590
  in middle adulthood, 530–531
  in middle childhood, 346–348
  nature and function of, 95–101
  pregnancy and, 192–193
  relationship between attitudes and intentional behavior, 97

theories of, 98–101, *100*
  in young adulthood, 464–466
authoritarian parenting style, 299, *300*
authoritative parenting style, 299, *300*, 419
autism, 217, 295–296
autobiographical memory, 90
autonomic nervous system, 58–62, *59*
autosomes, 50
aversive racism, 154–155
avoidant disorder, 294
axons, 60
AZT, 180

babbling, 227
babies. *See* infancy; newborns
Babinski reflex, 194
Back to Sleep Campaign, 221
Bandura's social learning theory, 80–81
basal ganglia, 57–58
basal metabolism rate, 456
battered women. *See* domestic violence
Bayley Scales of Infant Development (BSID), 217, 226
bed-wetting, 293
behavior
  cultural influences, 7–10
  defined, 15
  genetic and environmental effects on, 55–57
  of infants, 234
  of parents, 233
behavioral genetics, 301
behavioral intention, 96
behavioral trait, 301
behaviorism, 79, 104
behavior modification, 359
beliefs, 96
Bem Sex Role Inventory, 428, *429*
benign tumors, 68
bereavement. *See* grief and loss
biculturalism, 402, 552
bilingualism, 95, 280, 342–343
bilirubin, 187–188
binding, 61
Binet, Alfred, 335–336
binge drinking, 442–443
biochemical processes in nervous system, 58–62
biography, 24
biological theories, 44–47
biophysical dimension, 41–74
  in adolescence, 389–395
  applying in multidimensional framework, 17–19
  defined, 14
  in early childhood, 273–276
  in infancy, 215–222
  in late adulthood, 575–585, *576*
  in middle adulthood, 510–524
  in middle childhood, 331–333
  pregnancy and birth, 172–191
  in young adulthood, 456–459
biophysical growth and development, 47–57. *See also* biophysical dimension
biophysical strengths and hazards
  in adolescence, 392–394
  assessment considerations, 19, 66–72
  in early childhood, 274–276

  in infancy, 218–219
  in late adulthood, 579–584
  in middle adulthood, 516–524
  in middle childhood, 332–333
  nutrition (*see* nutrition and diet)
  in pregnancy, birth, and newborns, 177–191
  in young adulthood, 458
  See also specific diseases and illnesses
biopsychosocial framework, 13. *See also* assessment; multidimensional framework
biopsychosocial interaction, 14–16
biracial individuals. *See* race and ethnicity
birth. *See* pregnancy and birth
birth control, 441. *See also* condom use
birth defects, 179, 183–184
  developmental effect of, 188–189
  ethical dilemmas of, 184–185
birthing rooms, 175
bisexual persons, defined, 433
blended family, 124, 541–542, *542*
blindness, 180
blood clotting, 69
  hemophilia, 52
blood, composition of, 69
blood pressure, 68–69
BNAS. *See* Brazelton Neonatal Assessment Scale
body image, 430, *430*
bonding issue, 196
Bowlby's phases of attachment, 233, 235
brain
  anatomy of, 57–58, *57–58*
  congenital conditions and, 189
  effects of injury on family system, 522–523
  stages of development, 62–64, *63*, 216–217, 392, 586
  traumatic brain injury, 65–66
  weight of, *64*
Brazelton Neonatal Assessment Scale (BNAS), 194–195, *195*
breast cancer, 458, 514, 515, 516, 517, 518
breast feeding, 195, 196
breathing problems of newborns, 187
Broca's area, 57, *57*
bronchial asthma, 70
bronchioles, 70
bronchitis, 70
bronchopulmonary dysplasia (BPD), 187
BSID. *See* Bayley Scales of Infant Development
bullying, 373–374
bureaucracy, 143
bureaupathic behavior, 2
B-vitamin folate, 45

Cajuns, 148–149
calcium, 393, 512
canalization, 47
cancer, 67–68, 458, 510, 511, 516–519, *517*

  breast cancer, 458, 514, 515, 516, 517, 518
  coping with, 520–521
  lung cancer, 458
  multifactorial disorders and, 52
  prostate cancer, 517–519
  testicular cancer, 458
capillaries, 70
capital punishment, 527–528
cardiovascular system, *68*
cardiovascular system problems, 68–69
career. *See* work life
caregiving, 233, 536, 546–548, 595, 606, *607*
caregiving career, 547
care perspective, 405
Carnegie Council on Adolescent Development, 424
case conceptualizations, 16–17
categorical self, 106
categorization, 224
cell membrane, 47, *48*
cells
  parts of, 47–48, *48*
  types in nervous system, 60
Center for Research on Education, 366
Centers for Disease Control, 180, 575
central nervous system, 58, *59*, 59–60
cephalocaudal, 216
cerebellum, 58
cerebral palsy, 189, 241
cerebrum, 57
cesarean section, 176, 185–186
child abuse
  checklist, *259*
  in early childhood, 315–317, *316–317*
  effects of, 319
  frequency of, 438
  in infancy, 238–239
  prevention of, 64–65
  reporting and investigating, 317–319
  sexual abuse prevention, 83
Child Behavior Checklist, 350, *351*
child care, 214, 252–253
childhood. *See* adolescence; early childhood; infancy; middle childhood
childlessness, voluntary, 481
child neglect. *See* child abuse
children with disabilities, 488–489
  at birth, 189–190
  infants, 218
  sexual harassment of, 436
child support, 377
cholesterol, 69
Chomsky on transformational generative grammar, 95
chorionic villi, 172
chorionic villus sample (CVS), 184
chromosomes, 48, *49*, 49–50
  disorders, 50, 53–55, 189
chronic bronchitis, 70
chronic health problems, 579–581, *580*
circular influences, 246
circumcision, 202–203
classical conditioning, 80, 88

CLAS standards. *See* Culturally, Linguistically Appropriate Services
cliques, 422
coaching. *See* modeling and coaching strategies
codependency, 536–537
Codependents Anonymous, 537
cognition, 81
cognitive development and information processing
   in adolescence, 395–396, 418
   in early childhood, 276–279
   fetal, 191–192
   in infancy, 222–226
   in late adulthood, 585–587
   in middle adulthood, 525–526, *526*
   in middle childhood, 334–335
   in multidimensional framework, 19–20
   psychological dimension and, 81–93
   in young adulthood, 459–461
cognitive-dissonance theory, 97–98
cognitive-ecological model for direct practice, 103
cohabitation, 473
cohesive groups, 134
cohort effects, 37
cohorts, 510
colic, 220
college students
   alcohol use of, 500
   experiences of, 34–35
color blindness, 52
Columbine killings, 424
commitment, 434, 464
communication
   in adolescence, 396–397
   disorders, 280–281
   in early childhood, 279–281
   fetus and, 192
   gender differences in, 461–463
   in infancy, 226–229
   in late adulthood, 588, 605
   in middle adulthood, 526–530
   in middle childhood, 339–345
   nonverbal, 94, 463
   patterns in groups, 133–134
   psychological dimension, 93–94
   in young adulthood, 461–463
communication agenda, 141
communication patterns, 133–134
communitarian agenda, 141
community, 139–142
   adolescent pregnancy and, 441
   erosion of, 549
   identificational, 141–142
   place as, 139–141
   school relationships, 368–369, 373
community and organizational approaches, 5, 20, 21
companionate love, 465
companionship, meeting needs of, 477
competence, 102
comprehension, 91–92
   deficits in, 91
computer metaphors for brain functioning, 83, *84*
Comte, Auguste, 140

concentration, 87
concrete operations, 395
concrete thinking, 395
condom use, 433, 492, 579
conduct disorder, 4, 409–411, *410*
confidentiality, 397
conflict theories, 119–120, 417–418
conformity in adolescence, 420
congenital heart disease, 68
connectedness, 402
conscience, 77
consciousness, 85
consequences, natural and logical, 360
conservation skills, *334*, 334–335
consummate love, 465
continuity, 88
continuity theory, 572
continuum of care, 611–612
contraception. *See* birth control
controlled reaction, 496
cooing, 226–227
cooperation, 365
coping
   with bereavement, 590
   with illness, 519–521
   with loneliness, 466
   with miscarriage, 482–483
   models of, 27–29
coping skills
   adaptation and, 7
   adolescent use of, 400, 431
   assessment of, 20
   illness behavior and, 72
Cornell Couples and Careers Study, 171
cortex, 216
cortisol, 71
cost of living, 487–488
Council on Social Work Education (CSWE), 11, 12
course, 184
couvade, 170
creolization, 148
cretinism, 333
crime
   adolescent-limited, 30–31
   alcohol and/or drug use associated with, 500
   arrest rates, *31*
   early starters, 30–31
   general theory of, 30
   hazard rate for onset of serious offending, *32*
   late starters, 31
   life-course persistent, 31
crisis
   defined, 28–29
   identity formation and, 400
   infertility, 482
   midlife crisis, 509, 531, 544, 551, 552–553
   parent and caregiver tips for responding to children during, 282–283, *283*
   psychological strengths and hazards, 110
crisis theory, 28
cross-modal transfer, 224–225, *225*
crowds, 422
crying, 226–227
crystallized intelligence, 532, 586
CSWE. *See* Council on Social Work Education

cultural competency, 12
cultural diversity, 11–13, 148–150. *See also* multicultural considerations
cultural influences, 7–10
Culturally, Linguistically Appropriate Services (CLAS standards), 12
culture
   defined, 7, 117
   See also multicultural considerations
cumulative continuity, 30
current perspective, 13
cutting, 413
CVS. *See* chronic villus sample
cynical hostility, 511
cystic fibrosis, 51
cytoplasm, 47

D.A.R.E. *See* Drug Abuse Resistance Education
Darwin, Charles, 44, 98
Darwinism, 44, 46
Das-Luria model of cognitive functioning, 336
date rape, 495
day care
   for adults, 595
   for children (*see* child care)
deafness. *See* hearing impairments
death and dying, 581–584
decision making
   family-group, 314
   group, 135–136
defense reaction of newborns, 203
deinstitutionalization, 558
deletion, 53
delinquency, 411–412
   adolescent-limited, 30–31
   developmental trajectories for aggressive behavior, *33*
   general theory of, 30
   life-course persistent, 31
   predictive factors, *412*
   treatment approaches, 412–413
delirium tremens (DTs), 533
dementia, 91, 586–587, *587*, 592–595
dendrites, 60
denial, 482, 523
Dependent Care Tax Credit, 253
depression
   in adolescence, 408–409, 430–431, 448–450
   in divorce, 490
   in early childhood, 294–295
   gender and, 619–625
   in late adulthood, 596, *597*, 619–625
   maternal (*see* maternal depression)
   menopause and, 512
   in middle childhood, 350
   in young adulthood, 469–470
development, defined, 47
developmental contextualism, 15
developmental delay
   in childhood, 292, 324–326
   early intervention for, 218
   parents with history of, 261
   recognizing, 217–218
developmental flexibility, 7
developmental guidelines
   in adolescence, 444

biophysical dimension, 18, *216*
   in early childhood, 320
   in middle adulthood, *560*
   in middle childhood, *378*
   in young adulthood, *501*
developmental perspective, concept of, 13
developmental psychopathology, 292
developmental waves, 278
diabetes, 71, 579
   gestational diabetes, 178
diabetes mellitus, 71
Diagnostic and Statistical Manual of Mental Disorders, 4th ed. (DSM-IV), 4–5, *410*
diarrhea, 274
diastolic pressure, 69
diet. *See* nutrition and diet
differentiation phase, 64
differentiation theory, 87
difficult child, 231
disabled children. *See* children with disabilities
disadvantaged children. *See* poverty
discipline, 357–358
discrimination, 147–148, 151–153
   awareness of children, 370
   defined, 152
   disabled persons, 530
   gender bias, 151–152, 157–159, 404–405
   non-English-speaking adults, 528–529
disengagement theory, 572
dishabituation, 224
disorganization phase, 495
disoriented states, 85
displaced homemakers, 551
diversification, 6
diversity. *See* cultural diversity
division of labor, 140
divorce, 374–377, *375*, 489–491
   adolescent perspective on, 418
   frequency of, 473, 489
   reasons for, *490*, 490–491
   same-sex couples, 491
DNA, 45, 48, 49, 59
domestic violence, 497–498
   pregnancy and, 205–206
dominant genes, 50
dominant single-gene disorders, 50–51
doula, 175
Down syndrome, 53, 178, 189, 218
dreams, 466–467
dropouts, 425
Drug Abuse Resistance Education (D.A.R.E.), 443
drug testing of pregnant women, 180–182
drug use
   in adolescence, *442*, 442–443
   characterization of drug dependence, 534
   cross-cultural prevention, 364–365
   domestic violence and, 498–500
   maternal, 180–182, *181*, 204, 214
   women and, 534–535

DSM-iV. See *Diagnostic and Statistical Manual of Mental Disorders, 4th ed.*
DTs (delirium tremens), 533
Duchenne muscular dystrophy, 52
durable power of attorney for health care, 582
Durkheim, Emile, 140
dwarfism, 333
dysmenorrhea, 393

early childhood, 270–327
   attitudes and emotions in, 281–288
   biophysical growth and development in, 273–274
   child abuse in, 315–317, *316–317*
   cognitive development and information processing in, 276–279
   communication in, 279–281
   comparison of 1- and 4-year-old children, *272*
   depression in, 294–295
   family and, 298–311
   gender issues in, 300, 312–313
   kindergarten, 307–308, *308*
   peer relationships, 305
   play styles, 303, 306–307, *306–307*
   preschool environment, 307–310
   Project Head Start, 308–310
   psychological strengths and hazards in, 292–298
   social cognition and regulation in, 288–292
   social strengths and hazards in, 313–320
early-pregnancy testing, 173
early starters, 31
easy child, 231
eating disorders, 413
Ebonics, 344
echolalia, 295
ecological systems theory, 115–118, *117*
ecology, defined, 115
ecomap, 117, *118*, 623–624
ecosystems, 116–117
education. See school
educational neglect, 315
Education for All Handicapped Act (PL 94-142), 369
ego, 77
egocentrism, 277, 407
ego-ideal, 77
ego integrity, 532
ego psychology, 78
elder abuse, 615–616
Elderhostel program, 585
elderly persons. See late adulthood
elderspeak, 588
elimination, 293
embryo, 172
emerging adulthood, 454. See also young adulthood
emotional competence, 346
emotional intelligence (EQ), 337–338
emotion-focused coping, 27
emotions
   infant temperament, 230–232
   theories of, 98–101, *100*
   See also attitudes and emotions

empathy, 527
   in children, 287–288
emphysema, 70
employment
   youth employment, 438–439
empty love, 465
enabling behavior, 536–537
encopresis, 293
endocarditis, 68
endocrine glands, 390
endocrine system, *70*
endocrine system problems, 70–71
end-of-life care. See death and dying
enrichment theory, 85
enuresis, 293
environmental context
   infancy, 256–257
   prenatal development, 178–184
environmental gerontology, 611
environmental harassment, 492
environmental paths, 33
enzymes, 59
epigenetic principle, 78
epinephrine, 70
episodic memory, 90
erectile dysfunction, 515, 578, 579
Erikson's theory of psychosocial development, 78–79, *79*
   on adolescence, 400
   on infancy, 214, 215
   on late adulthood, 570
   on middle adulthood, 532
   on middle childhood, 330, 349
   on midlife, 509
   on young adults, 454–455, 464
ERT. See estrogen replacement therapy
essential amino acids, 59
essential hypertension, 69
estrogen, 391, 512, 515
estrogen replacement therapy (ERT), 513, 514–515
ethnicity
   core vs. surface features of, 156–157
   defined, 156
   developmental competencies in minority children, 22
   menopause and, 413–414, *414*
   social consequences of, 156
   See also race and ethnicity
ethnocentrism, 9–10
etiology, 5
evolution, 44–46
evolutionary psychology, 44, 46, 418, 476
executive functioning, 586
exercise
   in late adulthood, 575–577
   in middle adulthood, 516
   in middle childhood, 332
   in young adulthood, 456
existential self, 106
explicit memory, 91
exploitation, 315
expressive communication, 91, 462, 463
expressive language disorder, 280–281
extended family. See family
externalizing problems, 350, 408–409

extinction, 80
extramarital affairs, 543–544

FAE. See fetal alcohol effects
failure, children learning how to handle, 289, 367
failure to thrive, 241–242, 266–268, 317
false memory syndrome (FMS), 538
familiness, 122
family
   adolescence and, 417–419
   adult children and, 544–546
   aging parents and, 546–547
   assessment of, 20
   blended, 124, 541–542, *542*
   changing, 127–128
   defined, 122
   divorce, effect of (see divorce)
   early childhood and, 298–311
   effects of brain injury on, 522–523
   floating, 129
   grandparents (see grandparenthood)
   illness and, 519
   infancy and, 246–248
   late adulthood and, 602–608
   lesbian families, 128–129
   life cycle, 124, *125*
   middle adulthood and, 541–549
   middle childhood and, 357–365
   nontraditional, 302, 473
   parental discipline, 357–358
   parenting styles (see parents)
   parent training, 358–360, *360*, 412
   saturated, 129
   siblings, 248, 303–305
   single-parent, 374, 545
   stepfamilies, 124, 126–127, 374, 541–542, *542*, 545
   systems perspective on, *121*, 121–122
   young adulthood and, 472–483
family intervention, 413
family relocation, 425–426
family structure, 164
FAS. See fetal alcohol syndrome
fathers
   adolescent, 440–441
   infants and, 246–247
   preschoolers and, 302–303
   rights in adoption cases, 250–251
   See also family
fatuous love, 465
fears, 282, 365–366, 530
feedback, 94
feminism, 158–159
fencing reflex, 194
fetal alcohol effects (FAE), 53, 182–183
fetal alcohol syndrome (FAS), 182–183, *183*, 204–205, *205*
fetus, 173–174. See also miscarriage; pregnancy and birth
fictive kin, 603
fine motor skills, 273
fixed income, 610–611
floating family, 129

fluid intelligence, 532, 586
FMS. See False Memory Syndrome
folic acid, 53
folkways, 146
fontanelles, 216
Food and Drug Administration (FDA), 354
forebrain, 57
forgiveness, 527
formal operational thought, 396, *396*, 459–460
formal organizations, 143
formed groups, 130
foster care
   adolescents, 398–400
   infancy, 259–260
"Four Rs," 89
fragile X syndrome, 52, 53–54, *54*
France, 8, 140
Frank, Anne, 391
Freudian stages of psychosocial development, 77, 77–78
friendships, 347–348, *348*, 361, *361*, 420, 608–609
frontal lobe, 57
full-service schools, 310
functional age, 571
functional fixedness, 92
functionalism
   defined, 117
   modern, 118–119
   structural, 118
functional literacy, 528
funnel theory, 30, *30*

gametes, 49
gangs, 100, *422*, 422–423
GAS (general adaptation syndrome), 27
gases, 61
gay
   defined, 433, 477
   See also homosexuality
gay marriage, 122, 478–479, 491
gay men. See homosexuality
gender
   adolescence and, 428–431
   communication skills and, 461–463
   defined, 157
   depression and, 470
   discrimination and, 151–152, 157–159, 404–405
   drug use and, 534–535
   early childhood and, 300, 312–313
   gang membership and, 423
   group interactions and, 134–135
   health disparities and, 458, 521
   homophobia and, 160–161
   infancy and, 255
   late adulthood and, 614
   middle adulthood and, 552–553
   middle childhood and, 331, 370–373
   moral development and, 467
   retirement and, 610
   sex-role stereotypes and, 159–160, 313, 372, 486–487, 555–556
   women's issues, 158, 496, *497*
   workplace and, 483, 556
   young adulthood and, 486–487

gender identity, 370, 372
gender polarization, 158
gene-culture co-evolution, 47
general adaptation syndrome (GAS), 27
General System Theory, 13
general theory of crime and delinquency, 31
generativity, 509
genes, 47
genetic altruism, 46
genetic counseling, 54–55
genetic disorders, 50–52
genetics, 44–47
   alcoholism and, 534
   environmental effects on behavior and, 48–50, 55–57
   mental illness and, 468
genome, 48
genotype, 50
German measles, 179
Germany, 153–154
germinal period, 172
gerotranscendence theory, 574
gestation, 169
   multiple, 179
gestational diabetes, 178
glia cells, 58, 60
goal attainment, 76
goal-directed behavior, 222
gonadotropins, 390
gonorrhea. *See* sexually transmitted diseases (STDs)
goodness of fit, 232, 304
grammar, 95, 344
grandparenthood, 214, 247–248, 548–549, 607–608
gray matter, 62
Great Depression, 35, 36
grief and loss, 283, *284*, 588–590, *589*, 595
gross motor skills, 273
group interventions, 374
group polarization, 135
groups, 130–139, 360–362
   assessment of, 20
   belonging to, 131–132
   classification of, 132
   cohesiveness of, 134
   decision making in, 135–136
   defined, 130, *130*
   ethnic (*see* race and ethnicity)
   formation of, 361–362
   functioning of, 132
   gender and, 134–135
   reminiscence groups in long-term care, 591
   as social subsystems, 130
   status and power in, 134
   support groups, 136–142, 520
   tasks and socioemotional roles of, *133*
   See also peer groups
group socialization theory, 301
group therapy, 413
groupthink, *135*, 135–136
growth, 47–57
   defined, 47
growth spurt, 389
guilt, 413, 495
gynecomastia, 54

HAART. *See* highly active antiretroviral therapy
habitat, 10
habitual tense, 344

habituation, 192, 224
hairlessness in humans, 45
Hall, G. Stanley, 398
happiness, 532–533
harassment. *See* sexual harassment
hate crimes, 150
Hawthorne studies, 145
HCG. *See* human chorionic gonadotrophin
headaches, 393
Head Start. *See* Project Head Start
health care
   access to, 458
   adolescents and, 397
   advance directives for, 582–583
   managed care, 498
   Medicaid and Medicare, 171, 582
   older adults and, 577–578
Health Start, 441
Healthy Families Programs, 200–201
hearing impairments
   communicating with deaf clients, 463, 529–530
   in late adulthood, 604
   in middle adulthood, 529–530
   in newborns, 218
heart defects, congenital, 188
heart disease, 68–69, 510, 512, 579
hemophilia, 52
herpes. *See* sexually transmitted diseases (STDs)
heterosexuality, 160
highly active antiretroviral therapy (HAART), 493
high school
   dropouts, 425
   experiences of, 34
hindbrain, 58
Hispanic/Latino Americans
   discrimination against, 151
   education and, 368
   employment and, 557
   ethnic awareness of children, 370
   families of, 403
   gangs and, 423
   infant mortality and, 202
   late adulthood and, 613
   population of, 148
   racial identity, 403
   sexual activity among adolescents, 431
   young adulthood and, 485
HIV (human immunodeficiency virus), 433. *See also* AIDS; sexually transmitted diseases (STDs)
holism, 116
holophrastic speech, 227–228
HOME Inventory, 257–258, *258*
homelessness
   mental illness and, 558–559
   in society, 557–559
   youth, 427
homophobia, 160–161, 479
homosexuality
   in adolescence, 433–436
   "coming out," 435–436
   continuum of heterosexuality and, 477
   defined, 433
   discrimination against, 151, 160–161

families and, 123–124, 128–129, 302, 477–479, 480–481
gay marriage, 122, 478–479, 491
nonmonogamous relationships and, 544
splitting up of gay couples, 491
hormone replacement therapy. *See* estrogen replacement therapy (ERT)
hormones, 70–71, 390–392, 456–458
hospice care, 582
hostile aggression, 286
hostile parenting, 299–300
hot flashes, 512
housework, 487
housing options for late adulthood, 611
Human Behavior and the Social Environment, dimensions of, 6, 23
human behavior, study of, 6–13
human capital, 161
human chorionic gonadotrophin (HCG), 173
human development, multilevel concept of, 37–38
human immunodeficiency virus (HIV), 433. *See also* AIDS; sexually transmitted diseases (STDs)
human plasticity, 15, 30
human relations school, 145
Huntington's chorea, 50, 184
Hyde amendment, 171
hydrocephalus, 189
hyperactivity, 350–352. *See also* attention deficit/hyperactivity disorder (ADHD)
hyperemesis gravidarum, 177
hyperplasia, 47
hypertension, 69, 553, 579, 580–581
hyperthyroidism, 71
hypertrophic growth, 47
hypervigilance, 87
hypnosis, 90
hypothalamus, 70, 390
hypotheses, selecting interventions based on, 21–23
hypothetical-deductive reasoning, 395
hysterectomies, 513

id, 76
ideal type, 144
identificational community, 141–142
identity achievement, 400
identity assumption, 434
identity confusion, 434
identity development, 103–110, 400–403, *401*, 466–467, 483. *See also* self-concept
identity diffusion, 400
identity foreclosure, 400
identity moratorium, 400
IEP (Individualized Education Program), 369–370
illiteracy, 528
illness
   family-systems perspective on, 519
   infancy, 219–220
   See also specific type of illness

illness behavior, 72
ILO. *See* International Labour Office
imaginary audience, 407
I-messages, 358
immediate memory, 88
immigrants, 427–428, 528–529. *See also* multicultural considerations; refugee children
immunizations, 219, *219*
implicit memory, 90–93
impotence, 578, 579
impoverishment. *See* poverty
incest
   false memory syndrome and, 538
   genetic disorders and, 52
incompatible-response technique, 287
incomplete dominance, 51
incontinence, 512
independence, 466–467
independent conceptualization of self, 109, *109*
Individualized Education Program (IEP), 369–370
Individuals with Disabilities Education Act (PL 101-476), 369
individuation, 402
induction, 357, 358
industry vs. inferiority, 330, 349
infancy, 212–269
   abuse, 238–239
   attachment in, 232–235, *233*, 239–241
   attitudes and emotions in, 229–237
   biophysical growth and development in, 218–219
   brain development, 216
   cognitive development and information processing in, 222–226
   communication in, 226–229, *227*
   day care and, 214
   developmental considerations in, *263*
   environmental context, 256–257
   failure to thrive in (*see* failure to thrive)
   family influences in, 246–248
   foster care, 259–260
   gender issues in, 255
   illness in, 219–220
   immunizations in, 219, *219*
   mental health in, 242–243
   multicultural considerations, 216, 253–255
   playing and, 248
   poverty and, 204
   prevention of accidents and injury, 219
   psychological strengths and hazards in, 239–245
   self-conception and, 106
   SIDS in [*see* sudden infant death syndrome (SIDS)]
   social cognition and regulation in, 237–239, *238*
   social dimension in, 246–263
   temperament, 230–232
infantile amnesia, 278

infant mental health, 217–218
infant mortality, 202, 220, 440
infatuation, 465
infertility, 481–482
informal networks, 142
information processing, 83–89
  in early childhood, 277–278
  in infancy, 223–226
  memory and, 89–90
  in middle childhood, 337
  See also cognitive development and information processing
inhibiting and promoting environments, 21
Institute for Cultural Affairs, 136
institutional discrimination, 152
institutions, 24
instrumental communication, 462
insulin, 71
integrative multidimensional approach, 6
integrity or despair, 570
intelligence, 335–336
  emotional, 337–338
intelligence quotient (IQ), 335.
  See also IQ testing
intentional means-end behavior, 223
intention-cue detection, 337
interdependent conceptualization of self, 109, *109*
interest-oriented communities, 141–142
internalized homophobia, 479
internalizing problems, 350, 408–409
International Labour Office (ILO), 152
interpersonal awareness, *347*, 347–348
interpreters
  for deaf persons, 530
  for non-English-speaking adults, 529
interrupted career, 556
intimacy, 464, 465, 466–467
intrauterine growth retardation (IUGR), 178, 183, 186
invisible displacements, 223
IQ testing
  controversy over, 336–337
  in Head Start, 309
  in infancy, 226
  in middle childhood, 335–336
Iron John, 553
isolation. *See* social isolation
IUGR. *See* intrauterine growth retardation

James-Lange theory of emotions, 99
Japanese identity, 108
Japanese vs. U.S. management approach, 145, *146*
jaundice, 186, 187–188
jobs. *See* employment
judgment. *See* reasoning and judgment
Jung, Carl, 531
justice perspective, 405

Karen people of Thailand and Laos, 9–10
Kaufman Assessment Battery for Children (K-ABC), 336
Kenya, 8–9

ketosis, 535
Khmer refugee children, 374
kindergarten, 307–308, *308*
Kinsey on sexual behavior, 477–478
kin upgrading, 603
Klinefelter's syndrome, 54
Kohlberg's stages of moral reasoning, 403–405, *404*, 467
Kübler-Ross, Elisabeth, 581

lability, 101
labor, *174*, 174–175
laissez-faire parenting style, 299, *300*
La Leche League, 137
Lamaze method, 175
language acquisition and development
  in early childhood, *279*, 279–281
  in multidimensional framework, 19
  nonverbal communication, 94
  speech vs. language, 94
  spoken and written language, 94–95
  See also communication
language-deficit theory, 344
Lanham Act, 214
lanugo, 173
Larmarckism, 44
late adulthood, 568–626
  attitudes and emotions in, 588–590
  biophysical growth and development in, 575–579, *576*
  characteristics by subperiod, *571*
  cognitive deterioration in, 592–595
  cognitive development and information processing in, 585–587
  communication in, 588, 605
  death and dying, 581–584
  depression in, 596, *597*, 619–625
  elder abuse in, 615–616
  family in, 602–608
  friendships in, 608–609
  gender issues and, 614
  grief and loss in, 588–590, *589*, 595
  health problems in, 577–578
  middle-aged adults and aging parents, 546–547
  multicultural considerations in, 570, *571*, 612–614
  parent-child relationships in, 606–607
  psychological dimension in, 585–602
  psychological strengths and hazards in, 591–592
  retirement in, 609–611
  sexuality in, 578–579
  social cognition and regulation in, 590–591
  social strengths and hazards in, 614–619
  suicide in, 598
  widowhood in, 605–606
Latino Americans. *See* Hispanic/Latino Americans
lead poisoning, 260

learned helplessness, 367
learning, 87–88
learning approach, 5
learning theories, 79–80
LeBoyer method of birth, 197
lesbians
  defined, 433
  See also homosexuality
Lesch-Nyhan syndrome, 52
Levinson's stages of adult development, 455, *455*, 531
liberalism, 149
libido, 76
life course, defined, 33
life-course perspective, 29, 33–37, 571
life events, assessment of, 20
life events research, 29
life expectancy, 509, 514, 575
Life Skills Training, 364–365
life span, 575
  perspective, 29–33
limbic system, 57
living will, 582
logical consequences, 360
loneliness, 465–466, *466*, 590
long-term care
  defined, 611
  reminiscence groups and, 591
long-term memory, 89–90, *90*, 586
"looking-glass self," 100, 106
loss, dealing with. *See* grief and loss
love, 464–465
love withdrawal, 357
lumpectomy, 518
lung cancer, 458
lungs, 69

macrophages, 60
macrosystems, 117
male menopause, 512
malignant tumors, 68
malpresentation, 185
managed care, 498
marital conflict, 374–377, *375*
marriage, 472–476
  adjustment to, 474–475
  conflict, 374–377, 475–476
  depression resulting from, 470
  gay marriage, 122, 478–479
  in late adulthood, 604–605
  mental retardation and, 474
  at midlife, 542–543
  phases leading to, 473–474
  quality of relationship, *126*
  selection of partner, 473–474
  See also divorce; family
Marx, Karl, 119–120
masturbation, 313
maternal age, 178–179
maternal alcohol abuse, 182–183
maternal care and support in early childhood, 302
maternal depression
  attachment problems, 235
  cesarean section and, 186
  multiple-gestation births and, 198
maternal drug use, 180–182, *181*, 204, 214
maternal illness, 179–180, 202
maternal nutrition, 179
maternal smoking, 183, 499
maternal stress, 183

MCI. *See* mild cognitive impairment
mean, 336
meconium aspiration, 185
media
  influence on adolescent's behavior, 430
  influence on children's behavior, 81
  influence on middle adulthood, 530
Medicaid and Medicare. *See* health care
medical approach, 4–5
medical power of attorney, 582
medications
  for ADHD, 352
  for AIDS, 493–495
  for Alzheimer's and dementia, 594–595
  for labor and delivery, 175–176
  "off-label" uses of, 354
  older adults and, 577–578
medulla oblongata, 58
meiosis, 49
meiotic errors, 53
melanin, 45
melanocytes, 45
memory, 88–90
  implicit memory, 90–93
  in late adulthood, 586–587, *587*
  in multidimensional framework, 19
  stages of, *90*
  in testimony, 338–339
memory loss, 586–587, *587*
menarche, 390
Mendel, Gregor, 45
meningitis, 220
menopause, 511–513, *513*
men's movement, 553–555
menstrual cycle, 456, 481
menstruation, 389
mental age, 335
mental illness
  client assessment (*see* assessment)
  homelessness and, 558–559
  in late adulthood, 595–596
  parents with, 260–261
  in young adulthood, 468–469
mental retardation
  autism and, 295
  chromosome disorders and, 53–54
  family of adults with, 547
  institutionalization of babies with, 218
  marriage and, 474
  prenatal and neonatal causes, 188, 189 [*see also* intrauterine growth retardation (IUGR)]
  Rh incompatibility and, 180
mentoring, 484
mesosystems, 116
metacognition, 337
metalinguistic awareness, 339, 343
metaphors, 396–397
Michigan Alcohol Screening Test–Geriatric Version, 599, *599*
microcephaly, 189

Subject Index

microglia, 60
microsystems, 116
midbrain, 57–58
middle adulthood, 507–567
　adapting to, 559
　alcohol use in, 533–535, 563–566
　attitudes and emotions in, 530–531
　biophysical growth and development, 510–516
　biophysical strengths and hazards in, 516–524
　cognitive development and information processing in, 525–526, *526*
　communication in, 526–530
　family in, 541–549
　gender issues in, 552–553
　menopause, 511–513, *513*
　midlife as crisis, 509, 531, 544, 551, 552–553
　psychological dimension in, 525–541
　race and ethnicity and, 551–556
　sexuality in, 515–516
　social cognition and regulation in, 531–532
　social strengths and hazards in, 556–559
　work life, 550–551, 556
middle childhood, 328–385
　attitudes and emotions in, 346–348
　biophysical growth and development in, 331–333
　cognitive development and information processing in, 334–335
　communication in, 339–345
　developmental guidelines for, 377, *378*
　family and, 357–365
　gender issues in, 370–373
　peer influences in, 361–363
　play and exercise in, 332
　school influences in, 365–370
　sex roles in, 370, 372
　social cognition and regulation in, 346
　social strengths and hazards in, 373–381
midlife crisis, 509, 531, 544, 551, 552–553
midwives, 175
migraine headaches, 393
mild cognitive impairment (MCI), 593
Million Man March, 555
Mini-Mental Status Exam, 576
miscarriage, 172, 177, 482–483
mitochondria, 49
mitosis, 49, 67
mitral stenosis, 68
mitral valve insufficiency, 68
mitral valve prolapse, 68
modeling and coaching strategies, 287, 291, 364, *364*
moderating factors, 27–28
modernism, 120
modern racism, 154
molestation, 3–4, 315. *See also* sexual abuse
monoamines, 61
mood, 101

mood changes, 398
mood disorders, 292
moral development, 403–407, *404–405*, 467
moral view of human behavior, 6
mores, 146–147
Moro reflex, 194
morphemes, 94
mothers. *See* family; *headings starting with "maternal"*
motor aphasia, 92
motor skills
　in early childhood, 273–274
　in infancy, 216, 216–217
　in middle childhood, 331–332
mourning, 589–590. *See also* grief and loss
movement skills, 332–333
multicultural considerations
　in adolescence, 401–402, 427–428
　assessment of, 21
　attachment, 236–237
　drug abuse prevention, 364–365
　in early childhood, 311–313
　in infancy, 216, 253–255
　IQ testing, 337
　Khmer refugee children, 374
　in late adulthood, 570, *571*, 612–614
　men's issues and, 555
　in middle adulthood, 551–556
　in middle childhood, 365, 370–373
　newborn defense reactions, 203
　in pregnancy and childbirth, 201–203
　prejudice and discrimination, 147–161
　race and social relations, 153–154
　racial and ethnic considerations, 150–151
　refugee children, 344–345
　self and identity, 109–110
　in young adulthood, *485*, 485–487
multidimensional framework, 14–18, *15*, 116
　applying, 17–23
　selecting interventions based on, 22–23
　See also biophysical dimension; psychological dimension; social dimension
Multiethnic Placement Act of 1994, 249
multifactorial disorders, 52–53
multiple gestations, 179, 198
Munchausen's syndrome by proxy, 259
muscle wasting, 575
muscular dystrophy, 52
mutation, 50
mutual aid groups. *See* self-help groups
myelinization, 64, 216
myocardial infarction (heart attack), 69
myocarditis, 68
myth of arrival, 33, 35

Nagele's rule, 174
naming ceremonies, 201–202

narcotics, 534. *See also* drug use
National Alliance for the Mentally Ill (NAMI), 468–469
National Association for Education of Young Children, 308
National Association of Black Social Workers (NABSW), 249
National Association of Social Workers (NASW), 12, 249
National Black Women's Health Project, 521
National Center for Infants, Toddlers, and Families, 217
National Child Abuse and Neglect Data System, 316
National Health and Social Life Survey, 478
National Institute of Alcohol and Alcoholism, 598
National Institute of Child Health and Human Development, 220–221
National Institutes of Aging, 580
Native Americans
　adoption and, 250
　changing woman ceremony, 390
　identity and, 401
　naming ceremonies, 201–202
　newborns and, 203
　sex roles and, 160
　suicide among adolescents and, 409
Native-American Women's Health Education Resource Center, 521
natural consequences, 360
natural groups, 130
natural helpers, 139
naturally occurring retirement communities (NORCs), 611
natural selection, 45
nature-vs.-nurture debate, 301
negative reinforcement, 80, 286
neighborhoods. *See* community
neighboring, 141
neonatal complications, 186–190
neonatal intensive care units (NICUs), 188, 192, 196, 197–198, 208–209
neural-tube defects, 52–53, 183–184, 188–189, 218
neurons, 58, 60, *60*, 62–64, 216
neurotransmitters, *60*, 61
newborns
　assessment of, 187–190
　brain development, 216
　characteristics of, 176
　cultural differences of, 203
　death of, 202, 220
　evaluations of, 176–177
　experience of birth, 197
　NICU experience for, 188, 197–198
　psychological dimension, 191–192
　reflexes of, 194
　social cognition of, 193–196
　states of, 194
　See also infancy; pregnancy and birth; prematurity
new institutionalization, 147

NICUs. *See* neonatal intensive care units
night sweats, 512
night terrors, 282
No Child Left Behind Act of 2001, 366
nocturnal enuresis, 293
nondisjunction, 53
non-normative events, 37
nontraditional families, 302, 473, 480–481
nonverbal communication, 94, 463
NORCs. *See* naturally occurring retirement communities
norepinephrine, 71
normative age-graded influences, 37
normative history-graded influences, 37
normative pillar, 147
norms, group, 132
nucleic acids, 48, 49
nucleus, 48
nursing homes, 612
nutrition and diet
　in adolescence, 392–393
　in late adulthood, 577
　in middle childhood, 333
　in pregnancy, 179

obesity
　in adolescence, 390, 393
　in middle adulthood, 521–522
　in pregnancy, 185
　in young adulthood, 456
object permanence, 222, 225
obligatory attention, 223–224
observational learning, 80
occipital lobe, 57
"off-label" uses of medication, 354
old age. *See* late adulthood
only child's experiences, 363
onset, 184
open adoption, 249
operant conditioning, 80, 88
oppositional defiant disorder, 294
optimism, 532–533
oral rehydration therapy, 274
oral sex, 431
organelles, 47
organizations, 82, 142–147
　bureaucracy, 143
　formal, 143
　management in, 144–145, *146*
　typology of rational action, Weber's, 143–144
organ transplants, 189
orgasm, 515, 579
orientation, 85
osteoarthritis, 579–580
osteoporosis, 512
Our Bodies, Ourselves, 521
outcome, 184
ovaries, 391
overanxious disorder, 294
overextension, 228, 244
overprotectiveness, 519
overregularization, 279
oxytocin, 71

pagophagia, 179
palliative care, 582
palmar grasp reflex, 194
pancreas, 71

Subject Index

parallel-distributed processing (PDP), 84
parallel processor, 84
paraphilia of the pedophilia type, 4
parasympathetic nervous system, 58
parental warmth, 299
parent-effectiveness training (P.E.T.), 358–359
parent-involvement training (P.I.T.), 359
parents
    adult-child relationships with, 544–546, 606–607
    behaviors and attachment, 233
    conflict with adolescents, 417–418, 544–545
    discipline of children, 357–358
    mental illness of, 260–261
    middle-aged adults and aging parents, 546–547
    styles of, 299–302, 419
    training of, 358–360, *360*, 412
    transition to parenthood, 479–480
parietal lobe, 57
passion, 464
Patient Self-Determination Act of 1990, 582
pattern recognition, 89
pattern variables, 118
PDP. *See* Parallel-distributed processing
peer groups
    in adolescence, 399, 419–420, 421–422, 427
    defined, 361
    in early childhood, 305
    in infancy, 248
    in middle childhood, 361–363
    power of, 362–363, 420
    in young adulthood, 484
peer-group therapy, 413
penetration, 315
peptides, 61
perception, 81, 85–87, *86*
perceptual set, 92
pericardium, 68
period effects, 37
period of the fetus, 173
peripheral nervous system, 58, *59*, 60
permanence, 289
permissive parenting, *300*
personae, 531
personal causation, 102
personal-coping groups, 137
personal fable, 407
personality, 76, 510–511, 534
personalization, 290
person-in-environment system (PIE), *15*, 25–27
person memory, 90
pertussis, 219
pervasiveness, 289
phenotype, 50
phenylketonuria (PKU), 189
phobias, 365–366
phonemes, 94
phonological disorder, 281
phonology, 94
physical abuse. *See* child abuse; domestic violence

physical capital, 161
physical changes and psychological consequences, 391–392
physical resilience, 66
Piaget, Jean, 63, 81–83, 85, 222, 277, 396, 459
pica, 179
PIE. *See* person-in-environment system
pituitary gland, 57, 71
PKU (phenylketonuria), 189
PL 99-457 (Part H), Services for Infants and Toddlers with handicapping Conditions, 218
placenta, 174
placenta previa, 177
plasma, 69
plasticity, 15, 30
platelets, 69
play styles
    in early childhood, 303, 306–307, *306*–307
    in infancy, 248
pleasure principle, 76
pluralism. *See* cultural diversity
PMDD. *See* premenstrual dysphoric disorder
PMS. *See* premenstrual syndrome
PMZ. *See* postmenopausal zest
polyhydramnios, 178
positional variables, 21
positive reinforcement, 291
possibilism, 10
postformal thought, development of, 460
postmenopausal zest (PMZ), 512
postmodernism, 120–121, 603
postpartum depression, 196, 247, 261
postpartum early-intervention programs, 200–201
postsynaptic membrane, 61
post-traumatic stress disorder, 282
poverty
    children and, 314
    functions of, 119
    gangs and, 422
    infants and, 204
    in late adulthood, 613
    midlife health issues and, 553
    nutrition and, 333, 577
    public schools and, 367–368
power-assertive discipline, 357
power, in groups, 134
pragmatics, 95
preeclampsia, 177–178
pregnancy and birth, 167–211
    in adolescence (*see* teen pregnancy)
    attitudes and emotions, 169–171, 192–193
    biophysical dimension of, 18, 172–191
    birth defects (*see* birth defects)
    birth process, *174*, 174–175
    bonding issue, 196
    cesarean section, 176, 185–186
    cognitive development and information processing, 191–192
    communication, 192
    complications of, 177–178, 185

    domestic violence and, 205–206
    doula, 175
    drug testing of pregnant women, 180–182
    due date, determining, 174–175
    experience of birth for baby, 197
    fathers and, 170
    fetal development, 173–174
    intervention programs, 200
    Lamaze method, 175
    LeBoyer method of birth, 197
    maternal drug use, 180–182, *181*, 204
    maternal heart rate, 69
    medications for labor and delivery, 175–176
    miscarriage, 172, 177, 482–483
    multicultural considerations, 201–203
    neonatal complications, 186–190
    nutrition and diet, 179
    prematurity, 186–188, 208–210
    prenatal care, 179–185
    prenatal testing, 183–184
    prepared childbirth, 175
    prolonged labor, 185
    sexually transmitted diseases and, 179–180
    social strengths and hazards, 203–206
    in young adulthood, 456
    See also newborns
prejudice
    defined, 151
    See also discrimination
Premarital Personal and Relationship Evaluation (PREPARE), 475
prematurity, 173, 186–188, 208–210, 234–235, 241–242
premenstrual dysphoric disorder (PMDD), 456–457
premenstrual syndrome (PMS), 456, *457*
prenatal care, 179–185
prenatal development
    environmental effects on, 178–184
prenatal drug exposure, 180–182, *181*
prenatal intervention programs, 200
prenatal testing, 183–184
    ethical issues raised by, 184–185
pre-operational stage of cognitive development, 277
PREPARE (Premarital Personal and Relationship Evaluation), 475
preschool age. *See* early childhood
prescribing cascade, 577
President's Freedom Commission, 42
presynaptic terminal, 60
prevention
    accidents and injury in infancy, 219

AIDS, 433, 492–493, 579
    depression over adolescent body image, 430–431
    drug abuse, 364–365, 443, 499, 534–535
    fetal alcohol syndrome, 205
    homelessness, 559
    school dropouts, 425
    types of, 37–38
primary enuresis, 293
primary prevention, 37, 374
primary-process thinking, 76
prisoners, children of, 303
privilege, 155
proactive aggression, 285
problem, defined, 92
problem-focused coping, 27
problems of living, 5
problem solving, 92–93, *93*
    in adolescence, 392, 395
    in childhood, 278, 281, 291
    in middle adulthood, 532
    social skills of, 20
professional half-life, 526
professional obsolescence, 525–526
Project Head Start, 308–310
proliferation, 64
prolonged labor, 185
promoting environment, 21
prostate cancer, 517–519
prostate surgery, 579
proteins, 59
proximodistal, 216
Prozac, 354
psychodynamic approach, 5
psychodynamic theory, 76–78
psychological abuse, 315
psychological dimension, 75–113
    in childbirth and newborns, 191–199
    defined, 14
    in early childhood, 276–298
    in infancy, 222–245
    in late adulthood, 585–602
    in middle adulthood, 525–541
    in middle childhood, 334–356
    in multidimensional framework, 19–20
    in young adulthood, 459–472
    See also attitudes and emotions; cognitive development and information processing; communication; social cognition and regulation
psychological hazards. *See* psychological strengths and hazards
psychological moratorium, 400
psychological strengths and hazards
    in adolescence, 407–413
    assessment of, 20
    in early childhood, 292–298
    in infancy, 239–246
    in late adulthood, 591–592
    in middle adulthood, 532–538
    in middle childhood, 348–354
    pregnancy and childbirth, 196
    scope of, 110
    in young adulthood, 467–470
psychological theories, 76–81
psychology, defined, 16
psychopathology and stress, 28

Subject Index

psychosocial development
  Erikson's theory of, 78–79
  Freud's stages of, 77
puberty, 389, 389–391
punishment, 80
purines, 61

quid pro quo sexual harassment, 492
quiet sleep, 217

race and ethnicity
  biracial individuals, 154
  creolization, 148
  demographic change, 148–150
  everyday social relations, 153–154
  health disparities and, 458
  privilege, forms of, 155
  stereotypes of, 2, 3
  See also discrimination
racial identity, 370
racism, 154–156
radial glia, 60
rape, 495–496
rape trauma syndrome, 495
rapid eye movement (REM) sleep, 194, 217, 282
rapport talk, 462
rational action, typology of, 143–144
RDS. *See* respiratory distress syndrome
reactive aggression, 285
reactivity, 10
readiness, 332
reading, 226
reality principle, 77
reasoning and judgment, 92–93, 395–396, 396
  Kohlberg's stages of moral reasoning, 403–405, 404, 467
  in middle adulthood, 525
  wisdom, 460–461, 592
recent memory, 91
receptors, 61
recessive genes, 50, 51
recessive single-gene disorders, 51–52
recombination, 50
reconciliation, 527
red cells, 69
reductionism, 116
reflexes of newborns, 194
refractory period, 515
Refugee Act of 1980, 345
refugee children, 344–345
Refugee Education Assistance Act of 1980, 345
registration, 89
regulation, 102
  in adolescence, 403–404
  in early childhood, 291–292
  See also social cognition and regulation
Rehabilitation Act of 1973, 530
rehearsal, 89
reinforcement, 80, 88
reintegration, 585
religion, 17, 486
  discrimination against, 149
  in late adulthood, 592
  pregnancy and childbirth, 201, 202

relocation of families, 425–426
reminiscence groups in long-term care, 591
remote memory, 91
reorganization phase, 496
repetition, 88
report talk, 462
resiliency, 314
respiratory distress syndrome (RDS), 187
respiratory synctial virus (RSV), 220
respiratory system, 69
respiratory system problems, 69–70
respite care, 489
response set, 92
reticular system, 58
retirement, 609–611
revenge, 527–528
reversibility, operation of, 335
rheumatoid arthritis, 580
Rh incompatibility, 180
Rhogam, 180
ribonucleic acid (RNA), 49, 59
ribosomes, 49
rickets, 333
rigidity, 92
risk behaviors, 437–438
risky shift, 135
Ritalin, 352, 354
rites of passage, 371, 391
Roe v. Wade (1973), 171
role models, 484
role-playing techniques, 291, 482
role-related achievement potential, 525
roles, group, 132–133
role-taking ability, 346–347
role theory, 24, 25
role transition, 33, 35
romantic love, 465
Rousseau, 141, 292
RSV (respiratory synctial virus), 220
rubella, 179
runaway youth, 426, 426–427
rural unemployment, 256
Ryan White CARE Act, 180

SADD. *See* Students against Drunk Driving
sandwich generation, 545
sarcopenia, 575
satire, 397
saturated family, 129
schema, 82
schizophrenia, 3, 468, 469, 504–505
school
  community relationships, 368–369, 373
  effective design of, 366
  Elderhostel program, 585
  full-service schools, 310
  harassment in, 436
  influences for at-risk children, 367–370, 436–437
  influences in adolescence, 423–425
  influences in middle childhood, 365–370
  interpersonal model of adjustment to, 364

performance, 367
preschool environment, 307–310
teacher expectations, 366–367
violence in, 373–374, 424–425, 438
school dropouts, 425
school phobia, 365–366
scientific management traditions, 144
Seattle Longitudinal Study, 586
secondary enuresis, 293
secondary prevention, 37
secondary-process thinking, 77
secular trend, 390
sedatives, 534. *See also* drug use
selective optimization and compensation, 585
self-concept, 103–110, 104, 348–350, 349, 397, 590–591. *See also* self-esteem
self-efficacy, 81
self-esteem
  in adolescence, 398–401, 401, 438–439
  in childhood, 289, 349
  joblessness and, 557
self-harm, 413
Self Help for Hard of Hearing People (SHHH), 530
self-help groups, 136–139
  functions of, 137–139
  women's health, 521
selfing, 106
self-instructional training, 340–341
self-mutilation, 413
self-perception theory, 98
self-reflection, 105
self-regulation, 10
self-selection, 30
self-system, 101
self-talk, 466
semantic memory, 90
semantics, 94
senescence, 575
senior citizens. *See* late adulthood
sensation, 81, 86
sense of community, 141
sense of well-being, 71–72
sensitive period, 196, 197
sensitization, 434
sensorimotor period of development, 222–223
sensory aphasia, 91
sensory registry, 89
separation after attachment, 240
separation anxiety, 229
separation anxiety disorder, 293–294
separation-individuation, 237
septum, 68
series-completion problems, 93
Services for Infants and Toddlers with Handicapping Conditions, 218
Sesame Street, 311
sex education, 441–442
sexism, 151–152, 157–159
sex play, 313
sex-role stereotypes, 159–160, 313, 372, 428, 429, 486–487
  depression and, 470
  men in therapy and, 555–556

sexual abuse, 3–4, 315, 432, 478, 538. *See also* child abuse; molestation
sexual assault. *See* rape
sexual harassment, 436, 491–492
sexual identity development, 312–313, 433–436
sexuality
  in adolescence, 431–436, 439
  continuum of heterosexuality and homosexuality, 477
  in late adulthood, 578–579
  in middle adulthood, 515–516
sexually transmitted diseases (STDs), 492–495
  pregnancy and, 179–180
  transmission and symptoms, 493
sexual orientation, 161, 433, 477–479, 478. *See also* homosexuality
sexual response cycle, 515
sexual status, 159
shaken infant syndrome, 238
shame, 100–101
shared environment, 56
sharing, 287–288
SHHH (Self Help for Hard of Hearing People), 530
short-term memory, 89, 90, 587
shyness, 100, 230
sibling rivalry, 304
siblings, 248, 303–305, 603
sickle-cell disease, 51
SIDS. *See* sudden infant death syndrome
sign language, 341, 341–342
signs, 5, 94
silent treatment, 357
similarity, 88
single-gene disorders, 50–52
single-parent families, 374, 545
single people, 473, 477
single representations, 289
situation conceptualizations, 16–17
Skinner's learning theory, 80
sleep
  adolescence and, 393–394
  early childhood and, 282, 300
  infants and, 220–221
  menopause and, 512
  newborns and, 194, 217
sleep apnea in infants, 187
slow-to-warm-up child, 231
smoking
  attitudes toward, 458
  costs of, 500
  diseases caused by, 70
  maternal, 183, 499
sociability in early childhood, 290–291
social capital, 161, 314, 487, 549
social-change groups, 137
social cognition and regulation
  in adolescence, 400–407
  in early childhood, 288–292
  in infancy, 237–239
  in late adulthood, 590–591
  in middle adulthood, 531–532
  in middle childhood, 346
  in newborns, 193–196
  psychological dimension of, 101–110
  in young adulthood, 466–467

social cognitive monitoring, 403
social competence, 349, 419, 420, 421
social Darwinism, 46–47
social dimension
    in adolescence, 417–444
    assessment of, 20–21, 114–166
    in childbirth and newborns, 200–207
    defined, 14
    in early childhood, 298–323
    in infancy, 246–265
    in late adulthood, 602–614
    in middle childhood, 357–385
    in young adulthood, 472–506
    See also family; gender; groups; race and ethnicity
social environment, 10–11
social functioning, *15*, 19
    defined, 23–24
social-functioning perspective, 23–29
social hazards. *See* social strengths and hazards
social-identity theory, 131
social impoverishment, 162
social institutions, 146–147
social-interaction theory, 23
social isolation, 363–364, 465–466
social learning theory, 80–81, 88
social referencing, 230, 238
social reinforcement, 280, 359
social responsibility, 532
social role, 23, 346–347
social skills
    assessment of, 20
    training, 420–421, *421*
social strengths and hazards
    in adolescence, 436–443
    assessment of, 21, 161–163
    in early childhood, 313–320
    in infancy, 255–256
    in late adulthood, 614–619
    in middle adulthood, 556–559
    in middle childhood, 373–381
    in pregnancy, childbirth, and newborns, 203–206
    in young adulthood, 487–501
social structure, 23–24
social support groups, 136
social support systems, 136, 262, 377, 480, 614
social system, 116, 119
society, 140
sociobiology, 46–47
sociocultural risk, 162
socioeconomic status, 550
socioemotional roles, *133*
socioemotional selectivity, 573
sociology of emotions, 100
somaticizing, 596
somatic nervous system, 58
Southern Poverty Law Center, 150
spatial ability, 525
speech
    in infancy, 225–228, *227*
    See also bilingualism; communication
speech disorders, 342
speechreading, 529
spina bifida, 53, 184, 188–189
    See also birth defects
spirituality, 17–18, 476, 592
    aging and, 574

women with AIDS and, 494
    work and, 550–551
spontaneous abortion, 177
spouse abuse. *See* domestic violence
standard deviation, 336
Stanford-Binet test, 335–336, *336*
status, 134
STDs. *See* sexually transmitted diseases
stepfamilies, 124, 126–127, 374, 541–542, *542*, 545
Stepfamily Association of America, 124
STEP (Systematic Training for Effective Parenting) program, 359–360
stereotypes
    defined, 151
    race and ethnicity, 151–152
    sex-role, 159–160, 313, 372, 486–487, 555–556
stigmatization, 147
stimulants, 534. *See also* drug use
stimulus-response associationism, 88
stonewalling, 476
stranger anxiety, 229, 294
Strange Situation Procedure, 234
strengths perspective, 5–6
stress
    grandparents raising grandchildren, 549
    illness and, 511, 521
    maternal, 183
    models of, 27–29
    parenthood and, 480
    psychopathology and, *28*
    response to, 27, 458
    sources of, *28*, 374–377, *375*, *458*
stress-resistant adolescents, 408
structural functionalism, 118
structuralist, 82
Students Against Drunk Driving (SADD), 420
Study of Women's Health Across the Nation (SWAN), 413
stuttering, 342
subjective norms, 96
sudden infant death syndrome (SIDS), 183, 217, 220–221, 259
suffering, 584
suicide
    in adolescence, 408–409, 431, 434
    in late adulthood, 598
    of police, 556
    rates by age and gender, *598*
superego, 77
Supplemental Food Program for Women, Infants and Children (WIC), 179, 242, 257
support groups, 136–142, *138*
    for alcoholics, 536
    for cancer patients, 520
    for caregivers, 548
    for parents of children with disabilities, 190
support systems, 21
    in adolescence, 423–427
    for families of adults with mental retardation, 547

in late adulthood, 608–612
    in middle adulthood, 549–551
    in middle childhood, 365–370
    in young adulthood, 483–485
surrogate parenthood, 482
SWAN (Study of Women's Health Across the Nation), 413
SWAN rating scale for ADHD diagnosis, 352, *353*
symbols, 94
sympathetic nervous system, 58
synapses, 61, *61*
synaptic cleft, 60
synaptic excitation, 61
synaptic inhibition, 61
syntax, 94
syphilis. *See* sexually transmitted diseases (STDs)
systematic training for effective parenting (STEP), 359–360
system, defined, 116
systems, categories of, 116–117
systolic pressure, 68–69

tabula rasa, 79
Tannen, Deborah, 461–462
task groups, 132
task-related roles, 133, *133*
Tay-Sachs disease, 52
teacher expectations, 366–367
Technology of Participation, 136
teenagers. *See* adolescence
teen pregnancy, 178, 201, 261–262, 439–441
telegraphic speech, 228
television, 286, 310–311, 549. *See also* media
temperament
    defined, 10
    infant, 230–232, *231*
temporal lobe, 57
teratogens, 180
"terrible twos," 239, 272
tertiary prevention, 37
testes, 390–391
testicular cancer, 458
testify, competence to, 338–339
testing. *See specific type of testing*
testosterone levels, 511, 515
TGG. *See* transformational generative grammar
theory of agency, 118
Theory X and Theory Y, 145
Theory Z, 145
therapy, child, 83, 366
therapy, male, 555–556
therapy, need for, 537–538
think-aloud, 340
thinking. *See* reasoning and judgment
thrownaway youth, *426*, 426–427
thyroid gland, 71
thyroxin, 71
time-out procedure, 287, 359
Title IX of Education Amendments (1972), 436
Title V of Rehabilitation Act (1973), 530
toddlers. *See* early childhood
toilet training, 293
tonic neck reflex, 194
TORCH complex, 179
toxemia, 177
trajectories, 33–34

transformational generative grammar (TGG), 95
transgendered persons
    defined, 433
transient exuberance, 216
transitional object, 229
transitions, 33
    to kindergarten, *308*
    to middle or high school, 424
translocation, 53
transracial adoption, 249–250, 312
traumatic brain injury, 65–66
traumatic events and child development, 64–65, 374
treatment groups, 132
trial and error, 93
triangular theory of love, 464, *465*
trust, 214–215
tumors, 68
Turner's syndrome, 54
turning point, 37
twins, 179
twin study, 55–56, 230, 301, 522
types A and B personalities, 510–511

ultrasound, 183
uncertainty, 184
unemployment, 256, 557. *See also* employment
uninformative messages, 340
unity of consciousness, 107
U.S. Department of Education, 373
U.S. Secret Service, 373
utopian view of human behavior, 6

vaginal bleeding, 177
vaginal dryness, 513, 516, 578
validation therapy, 588, 595
values, 8, 96
variations, 44
vasoprine, 71
verbal control, 340
vernix, 173
Viagra, 515, 530, 578
victimization of children, 438
victims of rape. *See* rape
victims' rights, 528
vigilance, 87
violence
    in adolescence, 438
    alcohol and/or drug use associated with, 500, 533
    in children, *287*
    gang-related, *423*
    hate crimes, 150
    school violence, 373–374, 424–425, 438
    social environment and, 11
    against women, 496, *497*
    See also domestic violence
vitamin D deficiency, 333
voluntary childlessness, 481
volunteerism, 484–485, 609

Watson's learning theory, 79
Weber's typology of rational action, 143–144
Webster v. Reproductive Health Services (1989), 171
Wechsler Intelligence Scale for Children, third edition (WISC-III), 336

TO THE OWNER OF THIS BOOK:

I hope that you have found *Human Behavior in the Social Environment*, Third Edition useful. So that this book can be improved in a future edition, would you take the time to complete this sheet and return it? Thank you.

School and address:_____

Department:_____

Instructor's name:_____

1. What I like most about this book is:_____

_____

_____

2. What I like least about this book is:

_____

_____

3. My general reaction to this book is:

_____

_____

4. The name of the course in which I used this book is:

_____

5. Were all of the chapters of the book assigned for you to read?_____

   If not, which ones weren't?_____

6. In the space below, or on a separate sheet of paper, please write specific suggestions for improving this book and anything else you'd care to share about your experience in using this book.

_____

_____

_____

_____

BUSINESS REPLY MAIL
FIRST-CLASS MAIL   PERMIT NO. 102   MONTEREY CA

POSTAGE WILL BE PAID BY ADDRESSEE

Attn: *Jose Ashford, Craig LeCroy, and Kathy Lortie*
Wadsworth/Thomson Learning
60 Garden Ct Ste 205
Monterey CA 93940-9967

NO POSTAGE NECESSARY IF MAILED IN THE UNITED STATES

OPTIONAL:

Your name: _____   Date: _____

May we quote you, either in promotion for *Human Behavior in the Social Environment*, Third Edition, or in future publishing ventures?

Yes: _____   No: _____

Sincerely yours,

Jose B. Ashford

Craig Winston LeCroy

Kathy L. Lortie

NO POSTAGE NECESSARY IF MAILED IN THE UNITED STATES

BUSINESS REPLY MAIL
FIRST-CLASS MAIL   PERMIT NO. 102   MONTEREY CA

POSTAGE WILL BE PAID BY ADDRESSEE

Attn: *Jose Ashford, Craig LeCroy, and Kathy Lortie*
Wadsworth/Thomson Learning
60 Garden Ct Ste 205
Monterey CA 93940-9967

OPTIONAL:

Your name: _____   Date: _____

May we quote you, either in promotion for *Human Behavior in the Social Environment,* Third Edition, or in future publishing ventures?

Yes: _____   No: _____

Sincerely yours,

Jose B. Ashford

Craig Winston LeCroy

Kathy L. Lortie

TO THE OWNER OF THIS BOOK:

I hope that you have found *Human Behavior in the Social Environment*, Third Edition useful. So that this book can be improved in a future edition, would you take the time to complete this sheet and return it? Thank you.

School and address:_____

Department:_____

Instructor's name:_____

1. What I like most about this book is:_____

2. What I like least about this book is:
   _____

3. My general reaction to this book is:
   _____

4. The name of the course in which I used this book is:
   _____

5. Were all of the chapters of the book assigned for you to read?_____
   If not, which ones weren't?_____

6. In the space below, or on a separate sheet of paper, please write specific suggestions for improving this book and anything else you'd care to share about your experience in using this book.

_____

_____

SUBJECT INDEX 697

Wechsler Preschool and Primary Scale of Intelligence-Revised (WPPSI-R), 336
welfare reform, 488
well-being, 530
Wernicke's area, 57, 64
white cells, 69
WIC. See Supplemental Food Program for Women, Infants and Children
widowhood, 553, 605–606
William T. Grant Foundation, 488
wisdom, 460–461, 592
withdrawal of privileges, 359
women. See gender

Women's Health Initiative, 521
women's issues approach, 158, 496, 497
working mothers, 214, 483
work life
  in middle adulthood, 550–551, 556
  in young adulthood, 483
writing, importance in adolescence, 397
wrongful birth, 184

X chromosome-linked disorders, 52
xeroderm pigmentosum, 45

young adulthood, 452–506
  attitudes and emotions in, 464–466
  biophysical growth and development in, 456–458
  biophysical strengths and hazards in, 458
  cognitive development and information processing in, 459–461
  communication in, 461–463
  depression in, 469–470
  family and, 472–483
  gender roles in, 486–487
  infertility, 481–482
  multicultural considerations in, 485, 485–487
  psychological strengths and hazards in, 467–470
  social cognition and regulation in, 466–467
  social strengths and hazards in, 487–501
  transition to parenthood, 479–480
  voluntary childlessness, 481
  work life, 483

Zero to Three Diagnostic Classification Task Force, 217
zygote, 172